Our Watchword & Song

Our Watchword & Song

THE CENTENNIAL HISTORY OF THE CHURCH OF THE NAZARENE

FLOYD T. CUNNINGHAM, EDITOR
STAN INGERSOL
HAROLD E. RASER
DAVID P. WHITELAW

BEACON HILL PRESS
OF KANSAS CITY

Copyright 2009 by Beacon Hill Press of Kansas City

ISBN 978-0-8341-2444-8

Printed in the
United States of America

Cover Design: Brandon Hill
Interior Design: Sharon Page

All Scripture quotations not otherwise designated are from the King James Version (KJV). The following copyrighted version of the Bible is used by permission:

The New English Bible (NEB). Copyright © by the Delegates of the Oxford University Press and the Syndics of the Cambridge University Press, 1961, 1970.

The *Revised Standard Version* (RSV) of the Bible, copyright 1946, 1952, 1971 by the Division of Christian Education of the National Council of the Churches of Christ in the USA.

Library of Congress Cataloging-in-Publication Data

Ingersol, Stan.
  Our watchword and song : the centennial history of the Church of the Nazarene / Floyd T. Cunningham, editor ; [authors], Stan Ingersol, Harold E. Raser, David P. Whitelaw.
    p. cm.
  Includes bibliographical references.
  ISBN 978-0-8341-2444-8 (pbk.)
  1. Church of the Nazarene—History. I. Cunningham, Floyd Timothy. II. Raser, Harold E., 1947- III. Whitelaw, D. P. (David P.) IV. Title.
  BX8699.N33I54 2009
  287.9'909—dc22

2009015905

CONTENTS

Preface	7
Introduction	9
Part I	15
1. The Wesleyan Heritage	17
2. The Nineteenth-Century Holiness Movement	31
3. Nazarene Beginnings: The Eastern Stream	57
4. Nazarene Beginnings: The Western Stream	79
5. Nazarene Beginnings: The Southern Streams	112
6. Union	139
7. Nazarene Beginnings: Early Accessions	164
Part II	191
Introduction	193
8. The Spirit and the Structure of the Church	195
9. Nazarenes and Society	232
10. Nazarene Responses to Their Mission	245
11. Forging Community	259
12. Shaping the Nazarene Mind	290
13. Shaping the Nazarene Mind: Higher Education	313
14. Adapting to a World in Crisis	326
Part III	343
Introduction	345
15. Administering the Church	347
16. Nazarenes in the Broader World	357
17. The Church Evangelizing	378
18. Behavioral Boundaries	411
19. Worshipping and Discipling in Local Churches	427
20. Discipling Through Christian Education	449
21. Educating Young People at Nazarene Colleges	460
22. The Intellectual Life of the Church	486
Part III Analysis	506
Part IV	509
23. Leaders and Languages	511
24. Crossing Boundaries	525
25. The Church Between Gospel and Culture	549
26. Outreach: Evangelism and Compassion	576

27. Local Churches and Congregations	592
28. The Nazarene Mind	605

Conclusion 619

Appendixes 623
    A. General Superintendents   625
    B. Other General Officers   626

Notes 629

Bibliography 729

PREFACE

This work began as an initiative of the Nazarene Publishing House in 1997. NPH secured Wesley Tracy, former editor of the *Herald of Holiness*, as general editor, and Tracy chose the authors. Bonnie Perry, now director of Beacon Hill Press at NPH, was involved from the initial stages of this book.

Among the authors, Harold Raser has taught Christian history at Nazarene Theological Seminary in Kansas City since 1980. He completed his Ph.D. in history at Pennsylvania State University in 1986. Stan Ingersol has served as the church's archivist since 1985. He earned a doctorate in church history at Duke University in 1989. David Whitelaw, a native of South Africa, where he served as a district superintendent, taught historical theology at Point Loma Nazarene University from 1992 until his retirement. Whitelaw earned a D.Th. at the University of South Africa. Floyd Cunningham has taught Christian history at Asia-Pacific Nazarene Theological Seminary since 1983 and also has served as the school's academic dean and president. In 1984 he received a Ph.D. in history from the Johns Hopkins University, where he studied under Nazarene historian Timothy L. Smith.

The authors met in Kansas City for several sessions over the next few years and shared their understandings of the Nazarene past. They decided to divide the material chronologically. Harold Raser took the early history, extending back to the English Reformation and including the Wesleyan revival, the nineteenth-century Holiness Movement, and the early groups that joined together to become part of the Church of the Nazarene. Stan Ingersol wrote on the years from the time of the unions to the end of the Second World War, and Floyd Cunningham the period from 1945 to 1976. David Whitelaw covered the years from 1976 to the beginning of the twenty-first century. Roughly speaking, these divisions of time corresponded to what the authors considered significant shifts in the church's history. In various meetings together, a consensus of their task as the church's historians and of the church's historical character emerged.

Due to health concerns, in 1999 Wesley Tracy resigned as general editor. From that point, Floyd Cunningham assumed this responsibility. In the final editing of the book, various parts have been moved from one section to another, so it would be difficult now to draw clear distinctions among the authors of the various divisions or even paragraphs of the book.

The work aims to be international, though the authors realize that it falls far short of that goal. Our hope is that many historians from around the world will produce their own stories of the Church of the Nazarene. Our desire is to show the multifaceted character of the Church of the Nazarene through the decades and to picture the church's life in local settings as well as on a denominational level. We hope to give a glimpse of the thoughts and beliefs of laypersons as well as those of theologians. Our conclusion is that overall, intentionally and internationally, the Church of the Nazarene has stayed close to its Wesleyan heritage in structure, practice, and doctrine.

Harold Raser extends his thankfulness to the faculty and students of Nazarene Theological Seminary, Kansas City. Members of the faculty and numerous classes of students in History and Polity of the Church of the Nazarene listened to or read various drafts and pieces of sections of the book. In a variety of formal and informal venues these persons offered valuable suggestions for improving the work and are thus significant collaborators in the final product.

Stan Ingersol is appreciative of his wife's support. Nazarene Archives staff members Meri Janssen, Kara Lyons, Steven Martinez, Karolyn Roberts, Samuel Simoes, and Joel Thornton provided repeated assistance to several of the authors during the research phase. At a later phase, John Bechtold assisted in securing photographs for this book.

A succession of student assistants at Asia-Pacific Nazarene Theological Seminary aided Floyd Cunningham not only in processing multiple drafts of this entire document but also in research assignments. These included Oh Won Keun, who read through various issues of *The Other Sheep, World Mission,* and the *Herald of Holiness;* Charlie Cubalit, who tracked down many annotations; and Dick Eugenio, who waded through microfilms of general board meetings and other documents and also tracked down sources.

David Whitelaw acknowledges with gratitude the $1,000 Summer Scholar 2000 grant from the Wesleyan Center for 21st Century Studies at Point Loma Nazarene University and the use of their facilities and resources during the years 1998 to 2002 (Dr. Maxine E. Walker, director, and staff); also the sabbatical for spring 1999 at Point Loma Nazarene University, which made the completion of the project possible (President Robert Brower and Provost Patrick Allen).

INTRODUCTION

The roots of the Church of the Nazarene run deeply into the soil of Christian history and intertwine with those of Christians everywhere. To describe it in its broadest historical context, the Church of the Nazarene is Christian and Protestant. The church's *Manual* declares that it understands itself to be part of the "one, holy, universal, and apostolic" Church.[1] As such, the Church of the Nazarene seeks to be faithful to the central doctrines and practices that have defined the Christian Church across the centuries and around the world.[2]

An important part of this identification with the history of the Christian Church is the Church of the Nazarene's acceptance of the great early church confessions, beginning with the Apostles' Creed and the Nicene Creed. The Church of the Nazarene embraced these creeds as expressions of its own faith and as cornerstones of its most fundamental identity, embedding the essential ideas of the creeds and even much of their language in its Articles of Faith.

The Church of the Nazarene is also Protestant. Its character has been shaped by the sixteenth-century Reformation, especially the Reformation in England. In the sixteenth century movement to revitalize the Christian Church, Reformers emphasized that salvation is a gift that God gives graciously to those who exercise faith. Human beings cannot earn salvation by their deeds. The Reformers also taught the "priesthood of all believers"—that every Christian believer may approach God directly through Christ and that every Christian may exercise some gift of ministry that will contribute to the body of believers. The Reformers understood that the Bible is the final authority for Christian belief and practice.[3]

At the Church of the Nazarene's core has been the doctrine of Christian perfection as understood and taught by John Wesley and the early Methodists. Individuals and groups of believers from other denominations and religious traditions embraced the Methodist doctrine, or something very much like it, in the nineteenth-century Holiness Movement. Whether one looks at doctrine, patterns of worship and practice, leadership, or the religious background of early members, the predominance of Methodism is unmistakable and has had an enduring influence upon the Church of the Nazarene.

Early Nazarenes deemed the declension of many Methodists away from both the experience and doctrine of holiness as sufficient justification for beginning a new denomination. They saw themselves as returning to the primitive character of Wesleyanism. The Nazarenes' cardinal doctrine was salvation by grace through faith; its distinguishing doctrine, entire sanctification as a cleansing and empowering spiritual event subsequent to conversion. Nazarenes believed their doctrines and preaching to be fully biblical. Their impulse was to go to all the world with the gospel and with the message of holiness. Education was for both laity and clergy. Worship services were lively, with a sense of God's presence. Nazarenes desired out of love to help those in deepest need. Nazarenes remained broad-minded on practices and theological emphases nonessential to holiness.

Nazarenes constructed themselves as a church, balancing emphases upon experience and doctrine, episcopal and congregational polity, evangelism and education, foreign and home missions. In the first years, General Superintendent Phineas Bresee favored building strong, Spirit-filled local congregations. Hiram F. Reynolds represented the church's desire to dutifully participate with other Christians in world evangelism. These emphases represented simultaneous impulses in the church in future decades.

The Church of the Nazarene balanced love and law. The nineteenth-century Holiness Movement mediated between the way of love and accommodation to society, represented by Methodist theologian Phoebe Palmer, and the way of law and rejection of social norms such as the appeasement of slave owners, represented by Free Methodist Church founder B. T. Roberts.[4] Among Nazarenes love, law, and either accommodation to or rejection of society mixed in various forms. Southerners tended to be legalistic but demonstrated love to downfallen women. Bresee championed temperance laws but counted on the Holy Spirit rather than rules to convict persons of their sins. Gradually, Nazarenes preferred respectability and accommodation to the rigors of separation and legalistic holiness.

Another way of conceiving of Nazarene history is to look at generational shifts that accompanied social change. The first generation, those who had doggedly defended holiness during the late nineteenth century, considered Christ, to use H. Richard Niebuhr's classification, as the Transformer of culture.[5] The first generation's orientation was urban. The chief early centers of the church that became Nazarene were in such cities as Brooklyn, Los Angeles, Nashville, and Glasgow. The leaders—including Bresee, Reynolds, A. M. Hills, B. F. Haynes, John T. Benson, and George Sharpe—had come out of established denominations and possessed a sense of custodianship for culture.

Their concerns for society were deep. They built rescue missions and homes for unwed mothers and pushed forward the temperance movement. Though this generation may not have appreciated the extent of their indebtedness to her, the most significant theologian of the first generation was the late Phoebe Palmer. In ministerial preparation, early Nazarenes read Methodists Daniel Steele and John Miley. Church growth in the first generation, which closed with mergers of the last two of the five significant groups that became part of the Church of the Nazarene, the deaths of pioneers such as Bresee, W. C. Wilson, and E. F. Walker, and the end of World War I, was primarily by union with other Holiness groups.

The second generation, by contrast, was rural in orientation. The church won a number of disaffected Methodists in farm states such as Ohio, Indiana, and Illinois, and Nazarene churches expanded in rural areas of India, China, Africa, and other parts of the world. Leaders such as R. T. Williams and J. B. Chapman had not suffered under oppressive situations in older denominations—they had been raised in Holiness schools and camp meetings. The second generation demonstrated holiness by tightening rules. Growth came by aggressive evangelism and revivalism. The dominant theologian was A. M. Hills, who carried over from Charles G. Finney and his own Yale professors a strident anti-Calvinism and emphasis upon free will. This generation saw Christ against culture and withdrew from some of the main currents not only of society but also of evangelical Protestantism.

A third generation rose along with the many changes in post-World War II societies. Congregations in the denomination were drawn toward the suburbs arising around declining urban centers. Leaders such as Hardy C. Powers and Hugh Benner represented a trend toward efficient organization and professionalism. The church grew by such means as house-to-house visitation and built strong Sunday School programs. Nazarene colleges attracted aspiring students and faculty members with respected doctoral degrees. The leading theologian, H. Orton Wiley, reflected nineteenth-century Methodist doctrines and demonstrated the historic integrity of Nazarene beliefs. Certain rules became less important. Nazarenes accommodated themselves to their cultures. For the third generation, at home in the world, Christ was of culture. This generation faded away by about 1976.

The fourth generation witnessed a rapid expansion of the church on its international frontiers. By the end of this era, the Church of the Nazarene was larger outside North America than within it. This was the fruit of the work of generations of missionaries, and reflected, as well, the increasing difficulties of evangelism in the West. Leaders represented the diverse interests of the church. Jerald Johnson articulated its international aspirations, Ray Hurn the multicultural dimensions, and William Greathouse the biblical and Wesleyan roots of Nazarene doctrine. The fourth generation, under the theological influence of Mildred Bangs Wynkoop, returned to John Wesley himself to direct its thoughts. The era saw an emphasis upon compassionate ministries. Nazarenes held Christ and culture in paradox, at home equally in the church and the world and not always recognizing or solving the tensions this involved. New leaders emerged—especially from the growing Spanish-speaking sector of the church. Africa posed ready to overtake North America in Nazarene membership. During the fourth generation, the Nazarene parish indeed became the world.

A way of looking at the church missiologically is that while its central message of holiness remained across the decades, its formulation and evidences varied, representing contextualization processes. The nineteenth-century Holiness Movement differed from Wesley on points of doctrine affected by revivalist measures that brought people into entire sanctification. By the beginning of the twenty-first century the Church of the Nazarene in some places was shedding these revival techniques. Both rules and compassion evidenced holiness from the beginning, but they took different forms in different places over time. Worship practices were much alike among Nazarenes in the beginning eras of the church, but they evidenced great diversity by 2008. Though forms of doing so varied across time and cultures, the essential purpose of making Christlike disciples in the nations united Nazarenes together.

Timothy L. Smith argued that the Church of the Nazarene was born as a church rather than as a sect and developed sectarian-like characteristics later in its history. Though, since there was no state church in America, Smith preferred not to look at *any* religious group as either a "church" or a "sect," the typology developed by Ernst Troeltsch, H. Richard Niebuhr, and others, placed early Nazarenes closer to the "church" than "sect" side. Early Nazarenes' concern for society, believing it could be perfected, and their affirmation of the historic traditions of the church, respect for education, and toleration of diversity all demonstrated churchly characteristics. There was an irony, Smith showed, about the pioneers' church building or denominationalizing leading to the second generation's sectarianism. When members "came out" of the old churches, the Holiness message lost the best means it had of "Christianizing Christianity" and had to concentrate on itself, making sure that it remained revived. As a means of analysis, at different places and times one could see the Church of the Nazarene gravitating between churchly and sectarian characteristics.[6]

The kind of issues that Smith addressed in *Called unto Holiness* reflected those of the times in which it was written, with the church struggling between legalist and more moderate adherents, and still very much North American. Little was on the horizon in 1962 of Pentecostalism. One could not have anticipated the controversies over worship, or the incredible expansion of the church around the world. Leading the broader historical agenda forty years later were issues of gender, ethnicity, and race. Though Smith paid unavoidable attention to the church's women, he could not have anticipated the decline of women in Nazarene leadership roles in the decades following the publication of his book. In *Called unto Holiness*, Smith mentioned little of the church's race relations. The Civil Rights Movement a few years later forced the issue into the open, and historians, including Smith, quickly realized that this was the most important social problem facing the twentieth century.

As historian Arthur M. Schlesinger Jr. observed, "When new urgencies arise in our own times and lives, the historian's spotlight shifts, picking now into the shadows, throwing into sharp relief things that were always there but that earlier historians had carelessly excised from the collective memory."[7] Though one would not accuse Timothy Smith of any sort of carelessness, history indeed requires constant vigilance.[8]

As the business of historians is "the recollection and representation of selected segments of the human past in an intelligible narration based on public data verified by scientific observation,"[9] historical writing by its nature necessitates that historians make choices about what to research and write. Not every record will be uncovered; not everyone's story will be or can be told. Furthermore, the historical narrative must hang together, must be coherent, and must tell a story. As authors, we have striven to be objective, at the same time realizing that we remain not only insiders but loyal to the Church of the Nazarene and appreciative of its traditions. Current perspectives, described above, are analytically useful, but new interpretations inevitably will be developed by others.

PART I

ONE

THE WESLEYAN HERITAGE

Where and when does the story of the Church of the Nazarene begin? The 1923 General Assembly resolved that the 1908 union of the Pentecostal Church of the Nazarene and the Holiness Church of Christ, at Pilot Point, Texas, be considered the birth date of the church. Assembly delegates understood that this event signified what the Church of the Nazarene was and hoped to be. At Pilot Point, using the language of the time, various "streams of the 'water of life'" flowed together in "glorious confluence," and diverse individuals "united as one people" in Christ.[1] Pilot Point delegates came from cities and small towns. Some were rich; many were poor. As members of small independent Holiness groups, they differed on some specific points of doctrine and practice. Most once had been Methodists, Congregationalists, Presbyterians, Friends (Quakers), or Baptists. They came from Eastern, Western, and Southern parts of the United States and had established missions in India, Japan, and the Cape Verde Islands. They transcended their differences and united in order to more clearly proclaim and faithfully demonstrate Christian holiness.[2]

The 1923 General Assembly delegates believed that Pilot Point spoke well of a church with a clear sense of calling and mission, a church that challenged people of diverse backgrounds and experience to respond to the call and to embrace the mission of proclaiming biblical holiness throughout the world. By 1923 the Church of the Nazarene reported over 51,000 members spanning the United States, Canada, the British Isles, India, the Cape Verde Islands, Guatemala, Cuba, Mexico, and Swaziland. In choosing Pilot Point and 1908 as the symbolic beginning of the Church of the Nazarene, the members of the 1923 General Assembly did not intend to say that the historical roots of the church went no deeper than the dusty soil of early twentieth-century Texas. Many of that assembly had helped to build the various independent Holiness groups that came to form the Nazarenes. New Englander A. B. Riggs, Texan C. B. Jernigan, Scotsman George Sharpe, and Californian E. A. Girvin (all members of the Committee for the Correction of the Historical Statement in 1923) knew firsthand the many important events of the Holiness Movement that had taken place decades prior to 1908.[3]

WESLEYANISM

An appropriate starting point for the history of the Church of the Nazarene is *not* Pilot Point, Texas, in 1908, in spite of its significance, but the eighteenth-century revival in which John and Charles Wesley played significant parts. Nazarenes have always understood that they are direct spiritual and theological heirs of the Wesleys.

John Wesley (1703-91) and his brother Charles (1707-88) rose to prominence during a tumultuous time in British history. During the eighteenth century, Great Britain gained economic and military control over many parts of the globe and laid the foundations for the British Empire. Great Britain also experienced the early effects of an industrial revolution, which changed the country's economy and its people's ways of life. Large factories arose across the countryside. Thousands dug in mines for the coal needed to fuel the machines. Changes in manufacturing, together with other social factors, led people to move from ancestral homes to take advantage of economic opportunities. Abandoning old villages, workers created new population centers. The Church of England struggled to maintain its hold on people's lives.[4]

The Church of England had been established under King Henry VIII (reigned 1509-47). Henry sought an annulment for his marriage to Catherine of Aragon, daughter of King Ferdinand and Queen Isabella of Aragon and Castile, for her not bearing Henry the son he desired. Henry and Catherine's daughter, Mary, was raised in a Spanish Catholic convent. In order to pressure Rome to grant Henry's divorce, in 1529 the English Parliament criticized the abuses of church courts, the immorality of the clergy, and the vast extent of monastic lands and other church holdings. Thomas More (1478-1535), Henry's highly esteemed chancellor, resigned in 1532 rather than give sanction to Henry's moves against the Roman Church. In 1532 Henry obtained the Submission of the Clergy, committing clergy to enact no church laws without the monarch's prior approval and to submit all existing church laws for the king's review. In 1533 Parliament forbid appeals to Rome for court decisions involving the church and its clergy. Finally, after Archbishop Thomas Wolsey was unable to persuade Rome to grant the annulment, contrary to the church Henry divorced Catherine and wed Anne Boleyn. She bore him a daughter, Elizabeth. Thomas Cranmer (1489-1556) replaced Wolsey as archbishop of Canterbury. Ordained in 1523, Cranmer himself had married secretly in 1532. In 1534 Parliament passed the Supremacy Act that made the monarch the only supreme head of the Church of England. Parliament's Act of Succession explicitly took away the possibility of Mary, a Roman Catholic, inheriting the throne. Thomas More refused to sign the Act of Succession, was imprisoned, and in 1535 beheaded for high treason. The following year, Henry had Anne beheaded on charges of adultery and wed Jane Seymour. She bore Henry a son, Edward. Meanwhile, Henry disbanded the monasteries and sold monastic land to local gentry. Still, though England formally had broken with Rome, except for allowing priests to marry it retained the theology and practices of the Roman Catholic Church.[5]

Gradually, England opened itself to Reformation theology. William Tyndale (1494-1536) had already argued and written on justification by faith and the authority of the Bible. He had criticized church leaders, who drove him out of England. Archbishop Cranmer, a Reformation figure very different from Luther or Calvin, decreed in 1539 that the once suppressed English translation of the Bible undertaken by Tyndale be used in churches and circulated as widely as possible among the people. At the same time, Cranmer played a crucial role in modifying and disseminating Reformation theology by compiling, editing, and writing significant portions of *The Book of Common Prayer*. But the first version of *The Book of Common Prayer* was too Roman for the increasing number of English clergy influenced by the continental reformation.

Upon Henry's death in 1547 and the ascension to the throne of Henry's ten-year-old son, Edward (who reigned from 1547 to 1553), Protestant ideas gained wider circulation. Church leaders, led by Cranmer, undertook a reform of the liturgy and, in 1549, published a revised *Book of Common Prayer*. The church intended *The Book of Common Prayer* to be "grounded upon the Holy Scriptures" and "agreeable to the order of the primitive church," while "designed to be unifying to the realm" and "intended for the edification of the people." A further revised *Book of Common Prayer*, published in 1552, represented a middle way, or *via media*, and withstood various challenges that it was either too Roman or too Protestant. The 1559 Act of Uniformity imposed this *Book of Common Prayer* upon all English churches.[6]

During the century and a half between Henry VIII and the Wesleys, the English church was a theological battleground where various forces fought to determine the church's shape and substance. Large elements wanted the church in England to retain as many elements of its Roman heritage as possible. Some secretly longed for reunion with the Roman church. Under the disruptive rule of Mary (1553-58) Protestants were persecuted, imprisoned, and killed. Those who held steadfast to their faith came to know what it meant truly to be Protestant. Upon Mary's death, these Christians wanted a more thorough reformation that would align the church with the Reformed churches in continental Europe. Radicals sought a return to primitive Christianity.[7]

Queen Elizabeth I (who ruled from 1558 to 1603) managed this conflict by a truce among the various parties. The Elizabethan Settlement reaffirmed the monarch as the supreme head of the Church of England and *The Book of Common Prayer* as the standard for worship. Doctrinally written *Homilies* explicated the Articles of Religion and preserved English theology's defense of both free grace and free will. The intention of the settlement was to steer a middle course between Roman Catholicism (without the authority of the pope) and the sort of Protestantism that John Calvin had introduced in Geneva, Switzerland, and that was gaining influence through John Knox in Scotland. The thirty-nine Articles of Religion could be broadly interpreted.[8]

This settlement did not satisfy all English Christians. Roman Catholic-leaning high churchmen wanted no concessions to the Reformation. The radical Protestants, on the other hand, wanted to purify the English church of every last vestige of Romanism. They became known as Puritans. Both parties worked to reach their goals, even if this meant imprisonment or other punishment.

After Elizabeth, the Roman Catholic-sympathizing Stuart monarchs silenced the most vocal Protestants and dealt harshly with anyone who challenged the provisions of the settlement. Some Puritans immigrated to Holland and from there in the 1600s to North America. Puritans who remained in England sided with the political opponents of the Stuart King Charles I during the English Civil War of the 1640s. When Oliver Cromwell defeated the king, Puritans found themselves in control of both government and church. During the period of the Commonwealth or Protectorate (1653-60), when England had no king or queen, Puritans tried to make the Church of England into a Reformed church. When the monarchy returned to the Stuarts in 1660, however, the middle way was restored, and the Puritans were suppressed once again.

In 1688, Parliament forced the abdication of the Roman Catholic-leaning James II and invited his staunchly Protestant daughter Mary and son-in-law William to accept the throne. The following year Parliament passed the Act of Toleration (1689). Those Puritans who chose to remain outside the Church of England became Dissenters with legal protections. They organized their own congregations and worshipped according to their convictions. This ended the Puritan crusade to dominate the Church of England. Differing among themselves on such issues as church government and baptism, Puritans divided into groups of Congregationalists, Presbyterians, and Baptists. Both of John and Charles Wesley's grandfathers were dissenting Puritan ministers.[9]

When John Wesley and his brother Charles were born early in the eighteenth century, the Church of England had been through nearly two centuries of turmoil and conflict. The British people desired peace and stability, not upheaval and disorder. Nevertheless, there were forces at work that guaranteed that the eighteenth century would be anything but placid. The intellectual movement known as the Enlightenment called for a thorough rethinking of fundamental ideas about the world and humanity's place in it by appealing to reason. Through philosophers such as Thomas Hobbes (1588-1679), John Locke (1632-1704), and David Hume (1711-76), the Enlightenment offered a way out of endless disputes about religious doctrines by favoring reason and scientific investigation over revelation and faith. Enlightenment thinkers made important inroads in the universities. Their logic and methods influenced preaching, including that of clergymen such as John Wesley, who, like many British Christians, reacted strongly against the Enlightenment's ideas about religion.[10]

Pietism, a religious movement arising on the European continent, challenged the supremacy of reason and emphasized religious experience. Pietism sought to turn Lutheran and Reformed churches preoccupied with doctrinal precision, ritual, and organization to a greater concern for personal faith. Pietists urged Christians to devote themselves to living according to the example of Christ and to spiritual disciplines: Bible reading, prayer, and meeting together with other Christians in small groups for mutual support and accountability. Pietists believed that since the Reformation, the European Protestant churches had forgotten the matter of simple, godly living. Pietists called the churches to what they believed to be the churches' fundamental mission: to represent Christ in the world through humble, loving service that faithfully reflected the character of Jesus. The Spirit of Christ, Pietists believed, dwelt in the faithful believer's heart. Pietists from the European continent, such as the Moravians, began settling in England and America in the early 1700s. Some Puritans, as well, became more interested in cultivating good Christians than in establishing correct doctrine or maintaining certain forms of worship or organization.[11]

With *The Book of Common Prayer* uniting them, Calvinists and Arminians, Rationalists and Pietists abided, however uncomfortably, together in the Church of England. The High Church Anglicans who treasured the liturgical Catholic heritage coexisted with Low Church Anglicans preferring simpler forms of worship. Both parents of John and Charles Wesley had left the dissenting Puritan movement in which they had been raised and turned to the Church of England.

Seventeenth-century theologians such as Henry Hammond and Peter Heylyn identified a coherent center for all Anglicans in the early years of the Christian church, especially those preceding the Council of Nicaea, A.D. 325. Here, they believed, Christian thinking was not yet divided by the cultural, geographic, political, and even linguistic differences (Latin in the West, Greek in the East) that affected the church in later centuries. As compared to post-Nicene theologians, including Augustine, these Anglicans believed that early theologians such as Irenaeus and Chrysostom had a greater understanding of Christian faith. This led to a rich and flourishing scholarship in Patristics (from the Latin for "father").[12]

Though John and Charles Wesley's two grandfathers had been Puritan ministers, their parents, Samuel and Susanna (Annesley) Wesley, were loyal members of the Church of England, a church that promoted fidelity to the monarch, order, and harmony. Samuel Wesley affiliated with the Society for the Propagation of Christian Knowledge, a voluntary association of small groups within the Church of England.[13]

CHRONOLOGY OF JOHN WESLEY'S LIFE

DATE	EVENT
Nov. 11, 1689	Marriage of Samuel Wesley (d. 1735) and Susanna Annesley (d. 1742)
June 17, 1703	John Wesley born in Epworth, Lincolnshire
Dec. 18, 1707	Charles Wesley born
1720	Entered Christ Church College
1724	Graduated from Lincoln College, Oxford University
1725	Ordained as a deacon; first sermon
1726	Elected a Fellow of Lincoln College, Oxford University
1727	Received M.A. from Oxford University
1727-29	Curate at Wroote
1728	Ordained as a priest in the Church of England

1729	Returned to Oxford
1735	Left for Georgia as a missionary
1737	Returned to England
May 24, 1738	Aldersgate experience
1739	Preached in open at Bristol by the invitation of George Whitefield
1742	Began appointing lay preachers
1743	Announced general principles of the Methodist society
1744	First Methodist Conference held in London
1747	First travel to Ireland
1751	Married Mary Vazeille
	Visited Scotland for the first time
1757	John Fletcher joined the Methodists
1766	Published *A Plain Account of Christian Perfection*
1769	Appointed the first missionaries for America
Sept. 30, 1770	Death of George Whitefield; gave funeral sermon
1770	Calvinist controversies intensified
1771	Francis Asbury sent to America
1777	City Road Chapel erected
1778	First publication of *Arminian Magazine*
1784	With James Creighton and Thomas Coke ordained Richard Whatcoat and Thomas Vesey for ministry in America, and designated Coke and Francis Asbury as cosuperintendents
Mar. 29, 1788	Charles Wesley died
Oct. 24, 1790	End of John Wesley's Journal
Feb. 29, 1791	Last sermon—at Leatherhead
Mar. 2, 1791	Death of John Wesley
Mar. 9, 1791	Burial at City Road London Chapel

John Wesley responded to the various currents of his time by formulating his theology, as did other Anglican theologians, upon a quadrilateral of Scripture, reason, tradition, and experience. Of the four, Scripture always had priority. In this respect, Wesley was consistent with Protestant principles. Wesley interpreted and applied Scripture in light of reason, tradition, and experience. His understanding of Scripture arose from a kind of conversation between the text of Scripture, the tradition of the church, the God-given reason of human beings, and experience. By tradition Wesley primarily meant the thinking and practice of the church of the early fathers, especially the Greek ante-Nicene fathers, but, more broadly as well, the accumulated heritage of the whole church through the ages (which Wesley believed was most perfectly seen in the Church of England). By experience Wesley meant the collective testimony of earnest Christians who reflected on practical aspects of their lives as believers. Experience for Wesley was not simply subjective feeling; it was a *corporate* reality based on careful examination of the fruits of Christian life. Reason emphasized the plain meaning of Scripture and prompted the use of contemporary forms of philosophical inquiry. Reason provided a means of expressing sound theology. These four sources of authority guided Wesley as he navigated among the competing currents of English Christianity and shaped his responses to various ideas and practices.[14]

With George Whitefield, Jonathan Edwards, and his brother Charles, John Wesley provided leadership in evangelicalism, a broad-based British and American movement that sought the renewal of Christianity. Some evangelicals, such as Whitefield and the Wesleys, were members of the Church of England. Others were scattered among the various dissenting sects. Evangelicals believed that British Christianity neglected central matters of faith and that this had resulted in churches careful about worship forms but lacking in spiritual vitality. They believed that too much preaching focused on inconsequential theological issues or encouraged a form of moral do-goodism that was not really rooted in Christ and the Christian gospel. In their efforts to bring renewal, evangelicals emphasized: the Atonement, a focus on Christ's redeeming work on the Cross as the center of theological reflection; conversion, the new birth as necessary for making true Christians; the centrality of the Bible as the final religious authority; and activism, an energetic devotion to religious duties that included both evangelism and social involvement. Evangelicals desired preaching that highlighted both essential Bible doctrines and practical Christian living. Evangelicals found ways to present the gospel to large numbers of people who, because of the many changes occurring in society, the church no longer influenced. They helped church members to establish and cultivate a personal knowledge of God through Christ and to daily live lives of obedience and service to God. This involved, as it did for Pietists, believers meeting in small groups. German Pietists, including the Moravians, with whom Wesley was well acquainted, called these *collegia pietatis*, schools of piety. Small groups promoted both corporate and individual study of the Bible, regular private and common prayer, and consistent works of service. All of this was to supplement, not replace, regular participation in the life of one's church.[15]

John Wesley's spiritual pilgrimage occurred within the Anglican Church. As he entered into a life of active ministry, and began tutoring at Oxford University in 1726, his great passion was to help people personally experience divine grace and to aid them in developing truly Christian character. Wesley believed that authentic "scriptural Christianity" (a favorite Wesley term) required a definite personal, transforming experience of God's grace in a believer's life, the new birth, as well as an ongoing awareness of grace at work in one's life.

As the Evangelical Awakening developed and expanded through much of the eighteenth century both in the British Isles and North America, revivals appeared suddenly and lasted for short periods of time but had explosive effects on the churches and society. Through newspapers, letters, and, especially, the cross-Atlantic evangelism of George Whitefield, the movement remained tied together. In the midst of the British awakening John Wesley created the Methodist Connection, a network of societies and small groups of believers. Methodist societies soon were scattered throughout the British Isles. Wesley's organization of his Methodist societies, and his and Charles's constant travels to care for these societies, was one very important part of the evangelical movement in the British Isles.[16]

John and Charles Wesley's theological orientation was Arminian rather than Calvinist or Reformed. Jonathan Edwards and George Whitefield were theological disciples of John Calvin (1509-64) and his various interpreters. The Wesleys followed a different theological school with deep roots in medieval and Anglican theology that had much in common with the Dutch theologian Jacob (or James) Arminius (1560-1609). A pastor, and later theology professor at the University of Leiden, Arminius early in his life was an ardent disciple of Calvin. Arminius studied under Theodore Beza, Calvin's successor as leader of the Reformation at Geneva. However, Arminius became dissatisfied with Calvinism, coming to believe that it distorted important teachings of the Bible.

Arminius especially opposed the Calvinist doctrines of predestination and unconditional election. The Bible convinced Arminius that God's election to salvation extended to all who believe in Christ and who persevere in faith and obedience. Election is conditioned on the response of the believer. Arminius taught that saving grace is not irresistible, as the Calvinists said. Due to God's enabling grace, men and women possessed the ability to freely choose Christ, but because grace is chosen, it may be resisted. Believers

James Arminius

might fall from grace. This contradicted the Calvinist doctrines of the perseverance of the saints and eternal security.[17]

Arminius attracted disciples who, after his death, promoted his ideas in the Reformed Church in Holland. However, in a time when doctrinal controversy had serious political and social implications, Dutch clerics formally denounced his ideas at the Synod of Dort in 1619 and forcibly suppressed his followers thereafter.

Independently of Arminius, in the sixteenth and seventeenth centuries, Anglican theologians such as Richard Hooker and Lancelot Andrews arrived at what later would be called Arminian ideas regarding the universal benefits of the Atonement and the gracious provision of free will. These Anglican theologians had derived their ideas from nominalism, a medieval Catholic philosophy, and their ideas were expressed in the *Homilies* that every Anglican priest read.[18]

Arminian ideas influenced the debate that took place in England over the shape of the church after it was freed from papal authority. As in Holland, Arminianism had political implications. Church leaders who opposed the Puritan attempt to dominate the English church and defended the monarchy adopted some form of Arminian theology. Most Puritans were Calvinists, while the most zealous defenders of the middle way were Arminians. The kind of Arminianism embraced by theologians such as John Tillotson became little more than rationalism. Anti-Calvinist defenders of the middle way and their ideas bordered on moralism and diminished the importance of divine grace and revelation. This so-called Arminianism became compatible with Enlightenment Deism.[19]

John Wesley, however, confounded the usual categories. Scripture, as interpreted in conversation with reason, tradition, and experience, convinced Wesley that an Arminian understanding of the divine-human relationship was truer than the Calvinist one. Wesley was also indebted to the Anglican theologians who had arrived at Arminian ideas independently of Arminius. His first reading of Arminius was through other theologians who embedded Arminius's writings in their own. Once Wesley had thoroughly read Arminius, late in life, he fully realized the affinities between his theology and that of the Dutch Reformer.[20]

Wesley parted company with Calvinists on the matter of assurance, which placed election to salvation in the realm of the unknowable decrees of a sovereign God. Strictly speaking, for Calvinists there could be no definite assurance, for God's decrees remained veiled. Calvinist theologians wrestled often with this issue and suggested various tests by which the elect might establish degrees of their assurance of salvation. However, these tests could never provide certainty; they were always conditioned by the fact that God's will in predestining persons to salvation was ultimately known *only* to God.[21]

Wesley emphasized the response of human beings to God. Wesley believed, like Calvinists, that human salvation was utterly dependent upon divine grace and the initiative of God. However, unlike Calvinists, Wesley believed that saving grace was preceded by prevenient or enabling grace, which God made available to *every* person, not certain predestined ones. Prevenient grace, a concept found in Arminius and in elements of the Catholic heritage retained in the Church of England, restored a measure of moral freedom to sinful human beings, enabling them to freely and responsibly embrace or reject God's offer of salvation.[22]

Wesley concluded that human beings could have immediate and direct assurance of their salvation. Salvation involved establishing and maintaining a relationship between a loving, holy God and a responsible believer. Wesley believed that the state of such a relationship could hardly be a matter of uncertainty. A believer could not remain insensible to the presence of divine grace or the work of God's Holy Spirit in his or her life. Wesley placed great emphasis upon Rom. 8:16: "The Spirit itself beareth witness with our spirit, that we are the children of God." The believer could know God in an increasingly deeper way, and, as a result, could take on more and more of the character and nature of Christ.[23]

The Holy Spirit enabled holiness. Christian perfection became *the* distinguishing mark of the Wesleyan movement. British evangelicals as a whole became convinced that genuine Christianity involved a personal, transforming experience of divine grace. Such an experience resulted in believers developing Christian virtues. Wesley differed with others over the means of acquiring these virtues, and the extent to which a Christian might actually come to reflect the character of God.[24]

Wesley shared Protestants' regard for divinely initiated grace, and fully understood that salvation depended alone upon grace, and not human effort. Wesley read Scripture through the eyes of the early fathers of the Church that had been preserved in Anglicanism, and embraced an optimism of grace. The purpose of salvation was to restore to humanity the image of God. Only divine grace could enact such a "renewal of our souls after the image of God."[25] If God intended to bring about the total spiritual transformation of every person, Wesley believed, then divine grace could do its renewing work here and now. Human sinfulness could yield to the power of grace. Christian believers could live lives of complete love to God and neighbor. Wesley believed that the Bible, interpreted in light of reason, Christian tradition, and experience, both demanded of and promised to believers such present holiness, or Christian perfection.[26]

Largely through the testimonies of his followers, Wesley became convinced that sanctification, the process of being renewed in the image of God, could be complete here and now. Though Wesley did not believe that Christians ever reached a state at which they were beyond temptation or the possibility of falling from grace, there was a decisive point in the process wherein grace enabled believers to devote all of themselves to God. Divine love could fill believers' hearts and could expel everything opposed to God's love. Wesley called this entire or full sanctification.[27]

Finally, Wesley's reading of Scripture sparked in him a great passion for poor and disadvantaged members of society. Convinced that wholehearted love to God must be expressed through compassionate service to one's neighbor, Wesley developed a burden for the weakest and most vulnerable, those without power and influence, those slipping beyond the influence of the churches in eighteenth-century England. Wesley went to them with the gospel. This meant more than preaching. Wesley and his Methodists sought to embody the gospel by responding to the whole range of human need. Methodists visited and served as advocates for those in prison, collected and gave money and clothing to poor persons, nursed the sick, taught hygiene to those who lived in squalor, started schools for the illiterate, and fought to end British trade in African slaves.[28]

Through all of this Wesley had become convinced that the doctrine of Christian perfection, with all that it entailed, was "the grand depositum which God has lodged with the people called Methodists."[29] Even though the concept of Christian perfection became a source of misunderstanding and controversy in Wesley's own time, he faithfully defended it to the end of his life.

JOHN FLETCHER

The man whom Wesley hoped would succeed him as the overseer of British Methodists was John Fletcher (1729-85). Fletcher, who was born in Switzerland, immigrated to England in 1750. He

John Fletcher

soon joined Wesley and the Methodist movement. He became an Anglican priest, ordained in 1757, and served from 1760 to 1785 as rector of the Church of England parish in Mandelay.[30]

Fletcher's *Checks to Antinomianism* (1775) was a handy manual for explaining how Methodists differed from Calvinists. One chapter of the *Checks* was devoted to explaining the Wesleyan understanding of Christian perfection. Though Fletcher's teaching on Christian perfection was in most ways identical to John Wesley's, Fletcher identified entire sanctification with Pentecost. Fletcher understood that the biblical writer Luke used the terms "baptism of the Holy Spirit" or "filled with the Holy Spirit" loosely. Sometimes the terms referred to the occasion of new birth, which was the way both Calvinists and John Wesley interpreted Luke, and at other times in relation to subsequent outpourings of the Holy Spirit. Fletcher taught that when the disciples of Jesus were filled or baptized with the Holy Spirit at Pentecost, they were entirely sanctified. Fletcher was, apparently, the first in Methodist circles to make this identification. Wesley seemed to make clear to Fletcher that he did not agree with this interpretation. However, neither man considered the matter worth public dispute.[31]

Wesley urged believers to seek an experience of sanctifying grace that was available now, and in an instant.[32] At the same time, he considered such an experience to be part of a larger process of transformation of being remade in the image of God that took place over a whole lifetime of Christian devotion. Fletcher's linking of sanctification to the imagery and events of Pentecost highlighted the instantaneous aspect.[33]

Another distinctive feature of Fletcher's holiness teaching was that whereas Wesley hesitated to appeal to his own experience, Fletcher did not. Wesley appealed to the experience of Christian believers taken as a whole as a resource for understanding the activity of God and the witness of Scripture. However, he never appealed to his own individual experience as authoritative. In fact, Wesley was so reticent to appeal to his own individual experience that it is difficult to find any testimony to the blessing of full sanctification. On the other hand, Fletcher related that he had been entirely sanctified four or five times but had lost the blessing by failing to testify to it. As a result, he believed that testifying to the blessing in clear and definite terms was an obligation of every entirely sanctified believer.[34]

A third difference in Fletcher's teaching was that God worked dispensationally. The first dispensation was that of God the Father, under whom the Law was given. The second dispensation was that of the Son, who inaugurated the atonement of sins for all, and justification. The third dispensation was that of the Holy Spirit, which commenced at Pentecost and birthed the Church. This Spirit gifted human beings with both the witness, or inward assurance of their salvation, and sanctification. These three dispensations were both historical and personal. Every Christian believer underwent a spiritual journey from law to grace, and through grace to the abiding presence of the Holy Spirit.[35]

CONCLUSION

The roots of the Church of the Nazarene run deep into the soil of Christian history. The Church of the Nazarene professes to be a branch of the universal and apostolic church. At the same time, Nazarenes believe that as spiritual heirs of John Wesley, they have a special calling. This Wesleyan identity is one of the strongest elements in Nazarene self-understanding. Nazarenes claim fidelity to John Wesley's core convictions, including the universal benefits of the Atonement, prevenient grace (which enables free will), and Christian holiness.

TWO

The Nineteenth-Century Holiness Movement

The Church of the Nazarene represents a combination of British and American evangelicalism. The eighteenth century contributed the movement's theology and much of its structure. Later revivals employed methods appropriate to nineteenth-century British and American people. These revivals led to the beginning of several Holiness groups that united to form the Church of the Nazarene.

THE RELIGIOUS SOIL OF AMERICA

Early in the seventeenth century, Protestants from England, Holland, Germany, and several other European countries began immigrating to North America. Some of these settlers adhered to the state churches; others belonged to various dissenting groups forming across Europe in the wake of the Protestant Reformation. These religious bodies soon acquired an American identity.[1]

Geographic space in itself facilitated change within each group. The Europeans soon clashed with native peoples (the so-called Indians). Space allowed the early settlers to find, if they wanted it, a degree of independence. New England Puritans imposed religious conformity to stamp out dissent, and banished Baptists such as Roger Williams, who simply found another wilderness in which to settle. An eighteenth-century French immigrant to North America observed: "Zeal in Europe is confined; here it evaporates in the great distance it has to travel; there it is a grain of powder enclosed, here it burns away in the open air, and consumes without effect."[2] With sufficient space for all, the various groups of Europeans gradually learned degrees of toleration. New conceptions arose in the spirit of religious freedom and diversity.[3]

The churches adapted to an environment that lacked the social structures and conventions that Europeans left behind. At the outset, there was no government; there were no laws, no roads, and no schools—nothing except what the settlers created for themselves. Establishing Christianity and churches in such a void required innovation, creativity, and flexibility, as the immigrants soon discovered. Such a spirit became a permanent part of American religious life.

Religious pluralism shaped Christianity in America. The immigrants from Europe had lived under governments that penalized dissent. Both Puritans and traditional Anglicans expected that a similar form of church and state relations would exist in the New World. Yet, though New England Puritans established and enforced religious uniformity, this never gained widespread support. A remarkably rich diversity of churches and religious bodies thrived in British America. Christians with different beliefs and practices intermingled with each other to a degree unknown anywhere else in the world. While New Englanders moved from religious consensus toward diversity, the other British colonies—the Middle colonies, the Chesapeake colonies, the Southern colonies, and even the Caribbean colonies—moved from fragmentation toward community.[4]

When the United States was founded after America's War for Independence, or Revolutionary War (1776-83), the new nation abandoned the practice of many centuries: there was no established church. Citizens were free to practice religion as they chose. The First Amendment to the United States Constitution explicitly forbade such establishment: "Congress shall make no law respecting an establishment of religion, or prohibiting the free exercise thereof." All religious bodies would have the same legal rights and privileges. Citizens were free to worship (or not to worship) according to their conscience.[5]

Persuasion alone confined the power of the churches. Without a national church, and with freedom for all religious groups to exist, America created a kind of religious marketplace. Every variety of Christianity, and other religions as well, were available to the religious consumer. Numbers preoccupied them. Religious groups invented a host of methodologies to attract people and skillfully attracted new members. American churches and other religious organizations relied on voluntarism and survived by maintaining the commitment and support of their members. When members no longer voluntarily supported a church with their time and money, that church died. Pastors became promoters.[6]

These forces, and others, transformed the transplanted churches and religious bodies of Europe into new kinds of religious organizations. They were neither churches (in the European sense of an established or national church) nor sects, yet resembled both. They were *denominations,* branches of the universal church, called or denominated by a particular name, existing alongside and tolerating other denominations. The American churches sometimes worked together for common causes while maintaining their own distinctiveness. Spirited competition among denominations remained.[7]

A final characteristic of American religious life was its democratic impulse. Americans in the Revolutionary era and beyond rejected authoritarian patterns of organization and leadership. For some, even the idea of a professional clergy was a problem. Ordinary people accessed leaders and affected decisions. Ordinary people could interpret the Bible and competently decide doctrinal matters.[8]

The democratic impulse resulted in many churches being organized on congregational bases. Even though local congregations belonged to and supported regional or national associations, they were virtually autonomous and self-sufficient. Both the Congregationalist and Baptist churches followed this kind of organization. But even denominations with hierarchal structures, such as the Roman Catholics and the Episcopalians, were much more congregationally governed than in other settings.[9]

METHODIST DEVELOPMENT IN AMERICA

In the mid-1760s immigrant Irish lay preachers Robert Strawbridge in Maryland and Phillip Embury in New York started the first Methodist societies in North America. Wesley himself had little knowledge of these societies until about 1768, when he received a letter from Thomas Taylor, a member of a Methodist society in New York, requesting preachers. Wesley responded by sending Richard Boardman and Joseph Pilmore. When they arrived in America in 1769, they found a Methodist movement already well underway and growing under the ministry of lay preachers.[10]

From its founding until 1784, as in England itself, American Methodism formally remained a society within the Church of England. However, the Church of England never had enough ordained ministers, and until after the Revolutionary War, no resident bishops in North America. Over time the relationship between the Methodist movement and Anglicanism became strained. In America only one Anglican minister, Devereux Jarratt, in Virginia, actively supported revival. During the American Revolution, patriots criticized the Anglican Church for its loyalty to the king of England. Many Anglican ministers returned to England or moved to the Canadian colonies. This left Methodists, as well as other Anglicans, without ordained ministers to conduct public worship and administer the sacraments. In Maryland local Methodist Robert Strawbridge took over these responsibilities. This reflected the democratic impulse in American Christianity but caused sharp controversy.[11]

From England, John Wesley followed the progress of the American Revolution, which he vigorously opposed. In 1784, after the Americans gained independence, and following years of deliberation on the issue of separation, Wesley, with two other Anglican ministers, James Creighton and Thomas Coke, ordained Richard Whatcoat and Thomas Vasey as ministers and set apart Coke and Francis Asbury as cosuperintendents for the Methodist churches in North America. Though Methodists in England still remained part of the Church of England, American Methodists, Wesley saw, would have to make it on their own. Coke arrived from England with a letter to the Americans, a liturgy for Sunday worship, and twenty-four Articles of Religion that Wesley had abridged from the thirty-nine Articles of Religion of the Church of England. Wesley hoped that the Articles of Religion and the liturgy would provide a common bond between British and American Methodists. Wesley also recognized of the Americans that "they are now at full liberty simply to follow the Scriptures and the Primitive Church. And we judge it best that they should stand fast in that liberty wherewith God has so strangely made them free."[12]

Just before Christmas in 1784, American Methodist lay preachers met together in a Methodist chapel in Baltimore, Maryland. Thomas Coke (1747-1814) and Francis Asbury (1745-1816) presided. Asbury was the only one of the preachers whom Wesley had sent to America prior to the Revolutionary War to have stayed during the whole conflict. He remained the dominant force in American Methodism until his death in 1816.[13]

This conference of preachers organized the Methodist societies into a church. It chose the name Methodist Episcopal Church (the Episcopal part indicating an intention to remain within the historic Anglican tradition). Coke ordained Asbury and twelve other preachers. But Asbury refused to accept Wesley's appointment of him to the position of superintendent unless so elected by his fellow preachers. He was, unanimously. Asbury was ordained by Coke a deacon one day, an elder the next, and superintendent the third.[14]

Francis Asbury

Wesley realized that American Methodists would move further from his control. He hoped the Americans would remain in fellowship with British

Methodists. Wesley did not have to convince American Methodists that they should act freely; they fully intended to. Though retaining the twenty-four Articles of Religion, the American Methodists found Wesley's liturgy too formal.[15]

In spite of the fact that they arrived late on the American religious scene, Methodists quickly made their mark. When the Methodist Episcopal Church was formed in 1784, Methodist societies had about 15,000 members. By Wesley's death in 1791 the church had surpassed the number of Methodists in the British Isles. By 1800 there were nearly 65,000 American Methodists, and by 1833 the number of Methodists had swelled to 600,000.[16]

Much of the credit for Methodist growth goes to Francis Asbury. Aggressively evangelistic, Asbury promoted the concept of a traveling ministry of circuit riders. Like Wesley, Asbury believed that itinerant ministers were much more effective in spreading both the gospel and the Methodist societies than ministers who stayed in one place. Often on horseback, these traveling Methodist ministers became a common sight throughout America. "When the new homesteader drove his stakes into the ground," it was said, "the echo was heard somewhere by a Methodist preacher."[17] The circuit riders, usually single men, formed a monastic-like order within Methodism. They were remarkably successful in making converts and extending the church.[18]

REVIVALS AND CAMP MEETINGS

Revivals and camp meetings became defining parts of American Methodism. A series of powerful religious awakenings swept across America in the eighteenth and nineteenth centuries. Spiritual outpourings occurred through the instrumentality of Jonathan Edwards, Gilbert Tennent, George Whitefield, and others during the middle 1700s, and waves reverberated for decades.[19]

The first camp meetings began in frontier Kentucky around 1800, though the Scots had held outdoor religious gatherings in Scotland and some parts of America throughout the 1700s. Early camp meetings reached a largely unchurched population scattered over a thinly settled country. They were social events as well as religious gatherings and generated tremendous excitement. For frontier settlers who lived miles from their closest neighbors, the camp meetings broke the isolation and monotony of their lives.[20]

Though a few denominations were wary of it, revivalism, with its protracted meetings and camp meetings, spread throughout America. Rigid Calvinists, including Old School Presbyterians such as Princeton theologian Charles Hodge, disliked both revivalism's methods and its message, which invited not just the elect but all to salvation. Liberals disliked revivalism's emphasis upon religious affections rather than reason. Nineteenth-century Congregationalist pastor Horace Bushnell (1802-76) criticized revivalism's excessive individualism; its emphasis upon sudden, dramatic experiences over steady growth in grace; and its tendency to undervalue the accumulated wisdom of Christian tradition and to overvalue the new and the novel. Experience threatened to become an independent source of authority, challenging Scripture as well as reason and tradition. Meanwhile, the *Book of Mormon*, which relied on the extraordinary experiences of its founder, Joseph Smith Jr., supplanted the Bible for the Church of Jesus Christ of Latter Day Saints, begun in the 1830s.[21]

The American churches quickly recognized the value of revivalist methodology. If churches could generate revivals at will, they would control powerful means of making converts and of recruiting church members in the highly competitive system of American denominationalism. Revivals and awakenings might also be useful tools for spreading Christian influence throughout American society. Evangelist Charles G. Finney (1792-1875) in 1835 in his *Lectures on Revivals of Religion* outlined the basic principles of revivalism as he had discovered and practiced them during his years as a traveling evangelist. He believed that revivals rested on divine spiritual laws that were just as definite and dependable as any observable laws of nature. "A revival is not a miracle," Finney declared, "it consists entirely in the right exercise of the powers of nature. It is a purely philosophical [i.e., scientific] result of the right use of the constituted means . . . as much so as any effect produced by the application of means."[22]

Charles Finney

Revivalism, as practiced by Finney and many others, had several components. One of these was the protracted meeting, a series of evangelistic preaching services held over an extended period of time. A protracted meeting could last for several days, weeks, or even, in some cases, months. The purpose of the protracted meeting was to call sinners to repentance and Christian believers to renewed devotion to God. Either a full-time professional evangelist (such as Finney) or a nearby pastor conducted protracted meetings. Skilled preachers roused the emotions of hearers and prompted response. Music, prayer, Bible reading—revivalists intended everything to prepare persons in the congregation to respond. The climax of each service was the invitation to kneel at the mourner's or "anxious" bench to seek God's grace. This "altar call" gave people an immediate opportunity to respond to the evangelist's sermon, to be born again, to give up some harmful habit, or to rededicate their lives to God and to the church.

Originally intended to be special times in the life of churches, revival meetings exerted a much wider influence. They set a pattern for every worship service. Pastors modeled sermons after successful revivalists. Evangelism became a central focus of American Protestant worship, and evangelistic pastors became the norm in many Protestant pulpits.

Methodists embraced and honed the new methodology. Itinerant Methodists organized revivals and camp meetings throughout the country. Methodist churches in towns and cities held frequent protracted meetings. Fervent evangelistic preaching and the informal, emotionally charged worship of revival services were among the reasons that, by 1850, Methodism had become the largest Protestant body in America, with over 1.2 million members. The Methodists had more churches than any other denomination in twenty of the thirty-one existing states. One-fourth of all church members in the country were members of Methodist churches.[23]

CONCERN ABOUT CHRISTIAN PERFECTION

Though largely obsessed with evangelism and expansion, early American Methodism had shown the same zeal for Christian perfection as British Methodism under Wesley's leadership. Methodists maintained class meetings and bands. These encouraged spiritual renewal and vitality through helping individuals to earnestly pursue holiness. By the middle of the nineteenth century, however, organizational machinery controlled an expanding network of institutions, ranging from publishing interests, to colleges and fledgling seminaries, to missionary work in several parts of the world. Growth brought social responsibility and respectability, but not every Methodist was happy with the direction of change. How could such an expanding body maintain the purpose for which Methodism had begun?

A tendency distressing to some Methodists in both America and the British Isles was the increasing neglect of Wesley's doctrine of Christian perfection. Hard evidence for such neglect is difficult to come by, but it is clear that many Methodists in the early nineteenth century were convinced that Christian perfection no longer held the central place that it once had.[24]

Since Wesley had declared Christian perfection to be the "grand depositum" given to the Methodists for the benefit of the whole Christian church, this was a critical issue. Believing in, clearly teaching, and living out the grace of perfect love was what most distinguished Methodists from other groups of

Christians. To neglect Christian perfection was to turn away from that which the founder of Methodism declared to be its very essence.[25]

In addition, Christian perfection was central to a larger cluster of ideas and doctrines that made Methodism stand out among denominations. Wesley's theological system informed people that divine grace was freely available to *all*. Sinners could choose whether to respond to God's offer of salvation, and those who accepted saving grace could possess assurance of their reconciled relationship with God. This relationship required a life of constant watchfulness and careful cultivation of spiritual disciplines, for saving grace also could be lost. So the loosened thread of Christian perfection threatened to unravel the whole fabric of Wesleyan theology. Within fifty years of the founding of the Methodist Episcopal Church, concerned Methodists such as Timothy Merritt, Nathan Bangs, and Phoebe Palmer called for a renewed emphasis on Christian perfection.[26]

THE HOLINESS REVIVAL

Through Methodism and the revivalism it helped generate, the Holiness message reached people in other denominations. These included Presbyterians and Congregationalists. Both churches stood in the tradition of John Calvin and embraced the Westminster Confession, which had been drawn up by English Puritans and Scottish Presbyterians in 1646. Revivalism undercut Calvinist doctrines of election, predestination, limited atonement, and irresistible grace. Highly philosophical and speculative doctrines that separated various theological heirs of Jonathan Edwards perplexed rather than satisfied laypersons. Democratic impulses and optimism toward continued social progress also impacted Presbyterians and Congregationalists. Theologians restated traditional Calvinist theology in ways that fitted society. Nathaniel William Taylor (1786-1858), a Congregational minister and theologian, revised the traditional Calvinist concept of total depravity. He moved the emphasis in the doctrine of salvation from divine sovereignty and irresistible grace to human moral responsibility before God, and human choice. Taylor highlighted the obligation as well as moral ability of humans to reject sin and obey God. Christian experience beyond justification interested Taylorites, who questioned Calvinist ways of understanding the perseverance of the elect. Many Congregationalists and Presbyterians, including those such as Lyman Beecher who were promoting revivals, hailed Taylor's moves. Taylor opened Congregationalists and Presbyterians to ideas that once many would have rejected. His Calvinist opponents charged him with Arminianism.[27]

Taylor's theology increased interest in perfection outside Methodism, as did the exuberant optimism of the early nineteenth century. The boundaries of the United States were expanding, population was increasing, and entrepreneurs generated wealth at unprecedented levels. Revivals reinvigorated churches. Thousands confessed faith in Christ. Church membership dramatically increased. Zealous Christians planted hundreds of new churches.

Revivals inspired social reform. Motivated partly by Taylor's new theology, with its emphasis on moral responsibility before God, revivalists urged the newly converted and the spiritually awakened to pour their energies into reforming and perfecting society. The optimistic spirit of the times convinced them that Christians could succeed, with God's blessing, through hard work and proper organization. The result was a massive effort to purge sin and injustice from society. Thousands joined voluntary organizations that addressed illiteracy, abuse of alcohol, poverty, and similar problems. Other associations tackled more controversial issues such as slavery, women's rights, and even world peace.[28]

> Evangelists such as Finney reminded Christians that they had the responsibility before God to bring justice, morality, and compassion to their society:
>> The great business of the church is to reform the world—to put away every kind of sin. . . . The very profession of Christianity implies the profession and virtually an oath to do all that can be done for the universal reformation of the world. The Christian Church was designed to make aggressive movements in every direction—to lift up her voice and put forth her energies in high and low places—to reform individuals, communities, and governments, and never rest until the Kingdom and the greatness of the Kingdom under the whole heaven shall be given to the saints of the Most High God—until every form of iniquity shall be driven from the earth.[29]

Optimism could also be seen in thoughts about the end times and the second coming of Christ. Most Christians of the era believed that the millennium was very near. The revivals and the zeal for evangelism and social reform that they inspired, many believed, were the means that God was using to bring the millennium to earth. Churches and Christian organizations would soon bring the world to Christ and introduce Christian principles into every area of life. This would result in a thousand years of peace and righteousness, *after* which Christ would return to execute final judgment. This view came to be known as *post*millennialism, since Christ was not expected to return until the end of the millennium.³⁰

Nineteenth-century interest in social reform and postmillennial eschatology implied a belief in the perfectibility of societies as well as individuals. The setting was right for widespread acceptance of theological doctrines that promised perfection. Interest in Christian perfection rose across the denominational spectrum at the same time that Methodism was growing at phenomenal rates. People began to seriously examine Methodism's "peculiarity."³¹

OBERLIN PERFECTIONISM

Charles G. Finney became a major spokesman for the doctrine of Christian perfection outside Methodism. He began his ministry as a Presbyterian. Finney embraced Christian perfection after leaving full-time revivalism and settling at Oberlin College, a small Christian college in Ohio, where he served as professor of theology. In 1835, the same year that he published his famous *Lectures on Revivals of Religion,* Finney's columns in the *Oberlin Evangelist* made clear his growing interest in Christian perfection.³²

At Oberlin Finney worked closely with Asa Mahan (1799-1889), the school's president. The two men had much in common. Both were Presbyterians influenced by the theology of Nathaniel Taylor, both were ardent revivalists, both zealously advocated social reform, and both had explored ideas of Christian perfection even before they arrived at Oberlin. Collaborating, they became more definite and clear in their teaching. In late 1836 and early 1837 they entered together into several months of intense study and reflection, emerging as convinced teachers of Christian perfection. Recalling this time, Finney later wrote: "I gave myself earnestly to search the Scriptures, and to read whatever came to hand upon the subject, until my mind was satisfied that an altogether higher and more stable form of Christian life was attainable, and was the privilege of all Christians." He continued, "I was satisfied that the doctrine of sanctification in this life, and *entire* sanctification in the sense that it was the privilege of Christians to live without known sin, was a doctrine taught in the Bible, and that abundant means were provided for the securing of that attainment."³³

Many influences converged to bring about the conversion of Finney and Mahan to the doctrine of Christian perfection. The most crucial was the Methodist literature they studied, which included John Wesley's *A Plain Account of Christian Perfection* and John Fletcher's *Last Check to Antinomianism* (often identified as the *Treatise on Christian Perfection*). Finney and Mahan also steeped themselves in popularly written spiritual autobiographies of Methodist saints such as Hester Ann Rogers and William Carvosso, the very same works read by Methodists such as Phoebe Palmer. Like these Methodists, Finney and Mahan taught that God called believers toward Christian perfection and that divine grace was sufficient to all believers to enable them to fulfill God's expectation. Through the power of the sanctifying Holy Spirit, Christians could live lives governed by a perfect intention to please God and to do good to humankind.[34]

Not all welcomed the perfectionist teaching. To the most rigid, Christian perfection was pure heresy. Because of Finney's support for Nathaniel Taylor's theology, his "new methods" revivalism, and his abolitionism, among other convictions, Presbyterian criticisms intensified. Even the more tolerant Congregationalists opposed Oberlin's doctrines. Yet Oberlin theology spread.[35]

By the eve of the American Civil War, Finney, Mahan, and others had inspired a significant Holiness awakening among many Protestant churches. This paralleled the Holiness revival that was building momentum in the Methodist Church. These two streams converged to produce a powerful spiritual impulse that energized both revival and reform.[36]

PHOEBE PALMER

Phoebe Palmer (1807-74) left a large imprint upon the Holiness Movement. She was born in New York City, the daughter of prominent Methodist lay leaders. Her father, Henry Worrall, was a businessman. Phoebe and her eight brothers and sisters grew up surrounded by Methodist leaders and absorbed much of the spirit of early Methodism. In 1826 Phoebe Worrall married a young physician, Walter C. Palmer, who also had been raised in the Methodist Church. At one time he had considered entering the ministry but chose medicine instead. The couple became energetic lay leaders.[37]

At about the time she married Walter Palmer, Phoebe began seeking Christian perfection, a pursuit that lasted eleven years. This quest coincided with the growing anxiety among some Methodists regarding Christian perfection. In 1832, near the midpoint of her personal struggle, Methodist bishops exhorted General Conference delegates: "Why . . . have we so few living witnesses that 'the blood of Jesus Christ cleanseth from all sin?'" "Among primitive Methodists," the bishops continued, "the experience of this high attainment in religion may justly be said to have been common; now, a profession of it is rarely to be met with among us. Is it not time for us . . . to return to first principles?" "Only let all who have been born of the Spirit," the bishops admonished, "seek, with the same ardor, to be made perfect in love as they sought for the pardon of their sins."[38]

In this same year the editor of the *Christian Advocate and Journal*, the church's official paper, urged ministers and laypeople to organize special meetings for the promotion of holiness. In response, the congregation to which Phoebe and Walter Palmer belonged, the Allen Street Methodist Episcopal Church, held a four-day protracted meeting for this purpose. This sparked a revival that continued for two years and spilled over into nearby congregations.[39]

In this atmosphere Phoebe Palmer finally experienced, in 1837, entire sanctification. From this time until her death in 1874 Christian perfection was her dominating passion. Palmer sympathized with those Methodists who believed that their rapidly growing, increasingly wealthy and changing church was in danger of losing its distinctive character. God, Palmer became convinced, was calling her to play a leading role in the effort to keep this Wesleyan distinctive at the center of Methodism. It meant that she would have to move beyond her circle of home and family and take on public responsibilities, something most women in her day did not do. Palmer overcame her misgivings. For over three decades, she crisscrossed the United States and Canada and traveled to Great Britain, speaking and teaching in churches, camp meetings, colleges, seminaries, and public auditoriums. She was one of the most widely recognized revivalists in the world during this heyday of Protestant revivalism.[40]

Phoebe Palmer

Palmer also promoted holiness through writing. Beginning in 1843 with *The Way of Holiness*, she published nearly twenty books. A male reviewer of *The Way of Holiness* suggested that Palmer's time would have been better spent in "washing her dishes, than in writing."[41] In response, Palmer's *Promise of the Father* provided powerful biblical and theological rationale in support of women who sensed a divine call to ministry. Her books went through multiple editions. Some were published in several languages. She also edited an influential journal, *The Guide to Holiness*, from 1864 to 1874.[42]

Phoebe Palmer for nearly thirty-five years conducted weekly a meeting for nurturing Christian holiness—the Tuesday Meeting for the Promotion of Holiness. Persons from various Protestant denominations attended the Tuesday Meetings. Laypeople and clergy, women and men filled the Palmers' parlor every week. Crowds of several hundred sometimes overflowed the premises to hear testimonies of changed lives and sanctifying grace. Some visitors to the Tuesday Meetings organized similar meetings when they returned to their homes. In time, hundreds of such gatherings were taking place across North America and other parts of the world.[43]

This was not all. Believing like John Wesley that perfect love would necessarily flow out to neighbors in need, Palmer invested time and energy in ministries of compassion. She considered Wesley's concern for the poor "the glory of Methodism" in its founding days, and she worked to keep it central for Methodists in the nineteenth century. Palmer regularly visited prisons. She served for many years as secretary of the Female Assistance Society, a group of volunteers who aided poor needing medical attention. She was a founder of the Five Points Mission, an ambitious work in the heart of one of New York's most destitute neighborhoods. The mission, in 1850, educated children, housed and clothed a number of poor families, and distributed food. The Five Points House of Industry, with which the mission was connected, employed over five hundred people. Phoebe Palmer carried a special burden for orphans, a vulnerable group in mid-nineteenth-century society, and throughout her life supported a Home for the Friendless. Through her influence and connections children who ended up there found permanent homes. On at least one occasion (she was forty-five years old at the time) Palmer took an orphaned infant into her home, intending to raise him as her own. In the end this did not work out since she was traveling almost continually, but the Palmers kept in touch with the child and helped support him until he reached adulthood.[44]

Through these various ministries, Palmer emerged as the chief spokesperson for the movement to keep Christian perfection at the center of Methodism. Methodists intensified their efforts to preach, talk, write about, and experience sanctifying grace. *The Guide to Christian Perfection* circulated the testimonies of persons professing to be perfected in love. Meetings for the promotion of holiness sprang up. Pastors and camp meeting evangelists called upon Christians to offer themselves to God's perfecting grace. "The Gospel of Christian holiness thus became a chief strain in the melody of mid-century Methodism,"[45] observes Timothy Smith. Through her far-flung work, Palmer's teachings on Christian holiness surfaced in Baptist, Presbyterian, and Congregationalist circles, as well as in other denominations.

The Holiness Movement was taking organizational shape by the time of her death in 1874. Palmer's ministry encouraged women to listen carefully for a divine call and to respond when they heard it. Her concern for social needs moved scores of women and men. The ideas and images she employed for thinking and speaking about holiness became the standard vocabulary for many Christians.[46]

Palmer the Theologian

There can be little doubt that the Holiness revival of the nineteenth century, and the teaching of Phoebe Palmer in particular, drew from several sources. Palmer's vision of Christian life was rooted in John Wesley's concept of Christian perfection. She had read many of Wesley's writings. Her understanding was also influenced by John Fletcher and Hester Ann Rogers, mediators of Wesley. She followed Fletcher's interpretation of Pentecost as the time and place wherein the disciples were entirely sanctified. Fletcher's testimony to sanctifying grace circulated in *An Account of the Experiences of Hester Ann Rogers,* a book that Methodists in both Britain and the United States read widely. Wife of an English Methodist preacher, Rogers (1756-94) was a personal friend of both Fletcher and Wesley. Palmer read Rogers's book, sprinkled references to Rogers throughout her writings, and understood holiness through Rogers's experiences. For example, one of the distinctive emphases of Palmer's teaching on holiness was the necessity of frequent, definite testimony to the blessing of entire sanctification. This grew out of Rogers's account of Fletcher's views.[47]

Revivalism also influenced Palmer's theology and the nineteenth-century Holiness Movement generally. Employing all the usual revivalist methods (and creating a few new ones herself), Palmer urged believers to respond immediately to Holiness preaching. Just as revivalists invited seekers to receive God's justifying, pardoning grace now, Palmer invited seekers to experience God's sanctifying grace *now*. When, following Palmer, other Holiness preachers presented entire sanctification in protracted or camp meetings, they emphasized immediacy. This heightened the instantaneous dimension of sanctification. With powerful urgency preachers exclaimed that God would grant the instantaneous second blessing *now*. Exuberant preachers portrayed the immediate blessing as bestowing all the benefits of Christlike character in a moment. One late century evangelist declared that an entirely sanctified Christian would be "as perfect a man or woman as it is possible for [them] to be. [Entire sanctification] will cause a person to lay aside every filthy and useless habit; it will cleanse his [or her] lips of all foul speech; it will lead him [or her] to discontinue the use of all bywords and exaggerated forms of expression; in short, it does away with all that is hurtful to the soul, body or influence . . . it is opposed to everything that would not be proper in the Lord Jesus Christ."[48] This emphasis, derived from Palmer, drowned out the idea that entire sanctification was "constantly both *preceded* and *followed* by a gradual work" of grace.⁴⁹ It reduced sanctification as a transforming process, of which *entire* sanctification was one critical part, to entire sanctification *only* as an attainable-now instantaneous blessing.

The mind that shaped Palmer and the mid-nineteenth-century revival could be described as both pragmatic and impatient. Pragmatism, threading American culture, determined the value of an idea or action according to its practical effects. What worked in practice must be true.⁵⁰ Palmer sought short and simple paths to holiness. In *The Way of Holiness* she made clear her impatience with the strain and struggle displayed among seekers after perfect love. Raising the question as to "whether there is not a *shorter way* of getting into this way of holiness than some of our [Methodist] brethren apprehend," she answered it with a firm "Yes . . . THERE IS A SHORTER WAY! O! I am sure this long waiting and struggling with the powers of darkness is not necessary. There is a shorter way."⁵¹ Definite steps would lead believers to Christian perfection. Palmer put these steps into a formula that she taught through her preaching and writing. First, God's requirement of and provision for holiness is plainly revealed throughout the Bible. God expects believers to acknowledge this and to respond by seeking holiness. Second, entire consecration is the key to holiness. What enables Christians to receive perfect love is their entire devotion to God, which occurs in the act of consecration. Third, seekers must exercise faith, which fastens on to the promise that sanctifying grace will be given to those who are sincere. Fourth, the seeker is obliged to testify. Faith must be expressed through a clear, definite testimony that the blessing of full sanctification has been received. To Palmer, these steps were clearly outlined in the Bible. They also emerged from her own personal spiritual pilgrimage. Seekers who followed these four simple steps could be certain of receiving the blessing of perfect love just as soon as all the steps were carefully and sincerely completed. "The act, on your part, must *necessarily induce* the promised result on the part of God," she wrote.⁵²

Palmer and others theologizing amid the nineteenth-century Holiness revival often neglected John Wesley's theological method (the so-called quadrilateral). Wesley depended upon the community of believers to interpret and verify doctrine. Wesley derived doctrine from Scripture, as interpreted by reason, guided and informed by the wisdom of the Church through the ages, and tested by Christian's experience.⁵³ In contrast, revivalism constructed doctrine in an intensely individualist sense. Revivalists understood experience as a momentary, highly charged emotional state rather than as believers' perception of the activity of divine grace over a period of time. The emphasis upon experience flowed out of revivalism and the discontent of Methodists with the seemingly lifeless creedalism of the Reformed tradition. "A man may freely assent to every statement of the most rigid creed—yes, to every statement in the Bible," wrote F. H. Newhall in 1880 (and echoed by Nazarene J. B. Chapman forty-five years later in the middle of the battle between modernism and fundamentalism), "and yet not have a trace of the faith that saves the soul."[54] In Methodism this emphasis on experience strained the careful balance Wesley had maintained among the various sources of his theology. By the early twentieth century the emphasis on experience led some Methodists toward modernism, which had little use for either Scripture or tradition as sources of theology. At the same time, historian Grant Wacker shows, the emphasis on experience led others toward Pentecostalism, which highly valued dreams, visions, and personal revelations.[55]

CIVIL WAR AND THE POSTWAR HOLINESS CRUSADE

Methodism underwent a series of schisms in the early and mid-nineteenth century. African-American Methodists formed the African Methodist Episcopal Church (1816) and the African Methodist Episcopal Church, Zion (1821). The Methodist Protestants broke over the issue of episcopal control in 1830. The Wesleyan Methodists split in 1843 because the church refused to take a direct stand against slavery. Methodism divided along sectional lines with Southern Methodists creating the Methodist Episcopal Church, South, in 1845. The Free Methodist Church formed in 1860 when the resulting northern Methodist Episcopal Church tolerated slavery among its border-state members. The Free Methodists also criticized other ways that the church accommodated itself too easily to culture. Free Methodism included, among its Articles of Faith, a clear doctrine of entire sanctification, the first denomination to do so. These Methodist schisms, and those that divided the Baptist and Presbyterian denominations, foreshadowed the political division of the United States. With churches themselves divided, Christians offered little moral guidance for the country. The American Civil War (1861-65) mocked the invitation to perfect love and suppressed the fervor of the Holiness awakening.[56]

During the war the churches provided religious justifications for the political and military objectives of either side. The churches sponsored organizations that eased the loneliness and discomfort of young soldiers away from home, and provided army chaplains. Revivals even took place around army campfires. But the bloodshed and suffering silenced the once robust calls to holiness and social reform. Those who had proclaimed that perfect love would lead to spiritual vitality in the churches and righteousness in the nation, and even the arrival of the millennium, pondered what had gone wrong. Phoebe Palmer and Charles Finney spent considerable time preaching in Great Britain during the war years, but their absence in America was deeply felt. The *Guide to Christian Perfection,* which had helped launch the Holiness Movement and to spearhead its early expansion, nearly went out of business for lack of subscribers. Excitement about Christian holiness waned. After four years of vicious fighting the Civil War came to an end, and Americans, exhausted and seriously weakened by the war, began to reconstruct their lives and churches. Christians whose lives had been transformed by the message of holiness longed to see the power of the prewar revival restored. The war had battered the dream of a millennium of righteousness, justice, and peace, but had not destroyed it.[57]

THE NATIONAL CAMP MEETING ASSOCIATION FOR THE PROMOTION OF HOLINESS

Just a year after the end of the war, a casual conversation between John Wood, a Methodist minister, and Harriet Drake, a wealthy Methodist layperson, led to a plan to restore new life to the Holiness Movement. They lamented that many Methodist camp meetings no longer gave special attention to the "doctrine and distinctive experience of entire sanctification,"[58] and concluded that Methodists needed camp meetings especially devoted to the promotion of Christian holiness. Drake volunteered to contribute half the cost of a Holiness camp meeting, should one be held. The need for rejuvenation of the Holiness Movement, as well as Drake's generosity, led a group of Methodist ministers and laypeople that met in June 1867 to organize such a camp meeting at Vineland, New Jersey, the very next month. Vineland was a well-known Methodist community.

Announcements were quickly printed and distributed to churches and published in religious papers and magazines. Reflecting the breadth of the Holiness Movement before the Civil War, and seeking to revive the movement's interdenominational impact, the camp meeting was open to "all, irrespective of denominational ties, interested in the subject of the 'higher Christian life.'" "The *special* objects of this meeting," the announcement read, "will be to offer united and continued prayer for the revival of the work of holiness in the Church" and to "help any who would enter into this rest of faith and love." The organizers aimed to "strengthen the hands of those who feel themselves comparatively isolated in their profession of holiness."[59]

Even though quickly planned and hastily advertised, several thousand attended the camp meeting at Vineland. They evidenced great interest in and yearning for Christian perfection. Special camp meetings, organizers began to think, might be divinely blessed means of promoting holiness. The organizers formed the National Camp Meeting Association for the Promotion of Holiness. John S. Inskip, a Methodist minister who had professed entire sanctification under the ministry of Phoebe Palmer, became president.[60]

John Inskip

This changed the course of the Holiness Movement in the years following 1867. At first, the National Camp Meeting Association organized just one general Holiness camp meeting each summer, in the eastern United States. These quickly became so large, and interest in them so widespread, that the association sponsored additional camp meetings. These Holiness camp meetings were typical of the time except for their emphasis on Christian perfection. Campgrounds provided space for tents and other temporary shelters, and an outdoor site for worship. At established locations in mountains or hills, by the sea, or in picturesque rural areas (but within reach of existing transportation systems) those attending the meetings erected cottages or cabins, and large tabernacles for religious services. The camp meetings became small villages of religious retreat. A few, such as Martha's Vineyard and Ocean Grove, developed into popular resorts. Highly organized and tightly scheduled, little of the unstructured spontaneity of the early frontier camp meetings remained. A typical camp schedule was something like the following: "The bell rang at five in the morning for the benefit of the sleepy. Half-past five a prayer meeting was held in the pavilion; after breakfast, at eight o'clock, prayer and experience meeting; half past two preaching from the stand; after tea, a six o'clock prayer meeting; and then the closing public service at seven o'clock. At ten the bell rang for all to retire."[61]

The efforts of the National Camp Meeting Association for the Promotion of Holiness reignited interest in the doctrine and experience of Christian perfection. The association's national camp meetings drew tens of thousands of participants. Some saw this as a sign that the millennium might be near. Declared one minister attending the third national Holiness camp meeting, held at Round Lake, New York, in 1869, "This meeting has rolled the world a hundred years toward the millennium! We are coming into Isaiah's holy visions."[62]

In addition to sponsoring camp meetings, the National Camp Meeting Association, under the National Publishing Association for the Promotion of Holiness name, issued *The Christian Standard and Home Journal*. Inskip edited the paper. In 1870, the Association started a second paper, *The Advocate of Christian Holiness*. Eventually the two papers merged, renamed *The Christian Witness*. The association's publishing arm also issued books and inexpensive Holiness literature.[63]

Inskip led the expansion of the association. He pastored the Green Street Methodist Church in New York City until 1869, when he began ministry at Eutaw Street Methodist Church in Baltimore. In 1871 he left this pastorate and became a full-time evangelist, devoting himself to the National Camp Meeting Association. The association purchased a 4,000-seat tent and other equipment, which allowed Inskip and a group of workers he recruited to take Holiness camp meetings around the country. The association tried to gain the approval of church leaders in the areas where it held meetings. The national camp meetings became more truly national. Following the completion of the transcontinental railroad, in 1871 Inskip and his workers traveled from the East Coast of the United States to the West Coast and back, covering some 20,000 miles and conducting over six hundred services. In one year three national camp meetings were held in California. By 1875 the association had introduced its meetings to Canada.[64]

At first committed to reviving the Holiness Movement in the United States, and to strengthening America's churches, the National Camp Meeting Association became keenly aware of the opportunity and need that existed for Holiness teaching in other countries. In 1880 an international Holiness crusade took association workers to Great Britain, India, and Australia. The international tour evidenced the national association's expanding global vision. The Student Volunteer Movement for Foreign Missions, an interdenominational organization of college students formed in 1876, aimed for "the evangelization of the world in this generation." This group and others like it, as well as a number of denominational missionary societies, sent hundreds of missionaries abroad. Methodists joined in the rapidly growing mission effort, but Methodist missionary candidates with Holiness leanings sensed themselves blocked from appointment. Some found acceptance with the missions established by William Taylor, a Methodist missionary bishop active in India and Africa, with strong ties to the Holiness Movement. Those who supported the National Camp Meeting Association and its expanding activities decided that the association also coordinate the sending and supporting of missionaries committed to Christian perfection. In 1910 they formed the

Missionary Society of the National Association for the Promotion of Holiness, later renamed the National Holiness Missionary Society, and later still the World Gospel Mission.[65]

Meanwhile, in 1875 an interdenominational group of Holiness leaders around Boston, led by Charles Cullis, commissioned and even ordained Lucy Drake (later the wife of William Osborn, a well-known Holiness leader in the Methodist Church) for missionary work. Cullis, an Episcopal physician and lay evangelist, had been swept into the Holiness Movement during the 1857-58 revival and emphasized divine healing. With the support of this group, and Cullis in particular, Drake set out for India. She settled in Washim, Maharashtra, a rural area in the center of India, as the place for her ministry. As she understood it, the place had not yet been touched by the gospel. After studying the Marathi language in Bombay, Drake reached Washim in 1877. She witnessed to various poor women. Though Drake stayed only one year, before she left she was joined by other missionaries sponsored by Cullis. One, Laura Wheeler, remained in Washim for more than twenty years. National Camp Meeting Association workers, including Amanda Smith, renowned African-American Holiness evangelist, visited Washim in 1880. In 1884 Wheeler married William Moore, another missionary sent out by Cullis. Laura Wheeler Moore was instrumental in beginning a boarding school and orphanage in Washim and itinerated within a forty-mile radius. She and her husband remained with the mission after it transferred to the Methodist Episcopal Church in 1895. Missionaries serving for a number of years in Washim under the Methodist board included V. G. and Celia Ferries McMurry, both of whom transferred to the Methodist Church from the Holiness-minded Free Methodists. This same Washim area, possessing a long history in the Holiness Movement, even predating the founding of the groups that formed the Church of the Nazarene in America, became part of the Church of the Nazarene in 1935.[66]

Not all Holiness leaders, however, accepted Cullis's emphasis upon divine healing. In the 1880s, when A. B. Simpson promoted the idea that the atonement of Christ provided healing by faith, William MacDonald, one of the most prominent leaders of the National Holiness Association, was his severest critic. Similarly, when, in the 1890s, some evangelists connected to the National Camp Meeting Association began promoting premillennialism Holiness leaders such as Charles J. Fowler warned them that such emphases would sidetrack attention from holiness. Methodist leaders such as *Christian Advocate* Editor James M. Buckley considered millennialism a "foraging ground of fanatics, lunatics, and all kinds of eccentrics."[67] Theologian Milton

S. Terry believed "chiliasm" inculcated a misleading and harmful method of interpreting Scriptures by pressing literal meanings on prophetical passages. Such doctrines damaged piety by instilling unrest.[68] So the association of holiness with premillennialism would add only further disrepute to entire sanctification. Besides that, Fowler and other Holiness leaders remained postmillennialists. The 1897 meeting of the National Holiness Association stated, in a series of resolutions:

> WHEREAS, The holiness movement of the times is having associated with it, more or less, the questions of bodily healing, and the doctrine of our Lord's second coming in its relation to the millennium, . . . RESOLVED, That this annual meeting of the National Association of the promotion of holiness continues to recognize that our mission is to spread scriptural holiness over these lands, as it has been from the beginning. RESOLVED, That whatever value these other questions may have in themselves they are not comparable to the question involved in our mission, as we have ever and instantly and earnestly and publicly declared.[69]

The National Holiness Association remained conservative at a time when, on the fringes of the movement, people with other agendas were pulling away. The Church of the Nazarene inherited the same focus as the National Holiness Association—upon its central mission to proclaim holiness.[70]

While national camp meetings remained popular, other Holiness associations emerged. The Western Holiness Association of Illinois (organized in 1872), the Southwestern Holiness Association (representing parts of Missouri and Kansas and organized in 1879), and the Southern California and Arizona Holiness Association (1880) were regional. Others, such as the South Providence Holiness Association in Rhode Island (organized in 1886), were local. The local and regional associations brought Holiness camp meetings and well-known evangelists connected with the National Camp Meeting Association to their localities. Even among Methodists, Christians who professed to be entirely sanctified or perfected in love were a minority. These Holiness associations provided fellowship with like-minded Christians for those who found little support in their local congregations and from their pastors for their profession of perfect love. Though predominantly Methodist in membership, all such Holiness associations were interdenominational.[71]

THE CHURCH QUESTION

Prior to the Civil War, the Holiness Movement had had no organizational structure. Hopes for holiness rested in revivals within existing denominations. The National Association gave an organizational arm to the movement that it had never had before. The local and regional Holiness associations gave the movement immediate visibility. As well as organizing camp meetings and revivals, local associations opened training schools and sponsored Holiness publications, orphanages, rescue homes for unmarried pregnant women, and urban missions. In the tradition of Phoebe Palmer, and John Wesley before her, Holiness people sought out orphans, prisoners, the unemployed, prostitutes, and other oppressed and powerless people in order to offer them a gospel of both physical aid and spiritual transformation. Holiness Christians gave perfect love practical expression.[72]

This occurred during a tumultuous time. Cities were growing at an unprecedented rate. Overcrowding, unemployment, poverty, and crime were increasing, overwhelming the American churches. A few urban congregations found creative ways to meet the daunting needs around them. Others, however, abandoned demographically changing areas and relocated to more stable and generally more affluent neighborhoods. Holiness associations in the cities recognized the need and opportunity created by these conditions and moved into the void left by the retreating congregations of major denominations. The local and regional Holiness associations connected once downcast people with the Holiness Movement and made the Holiness Movement more truly a movement of the people. Holiness associations provided both a source of identity and a means of service. The associations drew new converts and sanctified believers committed to the doctrine and to the tangible expression of perfect love in urban missions. Few intended the Holiness groups to be churches, but their local activities, which sometimes included public worship, together with their connection to the National Camp Meeting Association, gave them the appearance of being churches in the making. They presented a challenge to existing denominations.[73]

Since Methodists comprised the largest number of constituents of Holiness associations, Methodist leaders reacted strongly to the spread of "organized holiness." The *Christian Advocate and Journal*, the official voice of Northern Methodism, concluded in an editorial in 1875 that the National Camp Meeting Association was "an irresponsible agency, the outcome of which will be another and mischievous *secession.*"[74] Daniel Whedon, editor of the respected *Methodist Quarterly Review*, charged in 1878 that, "The holiness association, the holiness periodical, the holiness prayer-meeting, the holiness preacher, are all modern novelties. They are not Wesleyan. We believe that a living Wesley would never admit them into the Methodist system."[75] Another Methodist leader, W. D. Kirkland, editor of the *Southern Christian Advocate*, declared: "No self-constituted and irresponsible 'association' with its many objectionable features, must be allowed to stand forth before the world as the only, or even as the chief, exponent of holiness."[76]

The concern about the divisive potential of the Holiness groups was not unfounded. Occasional camp meetings did not satisfy the desire of Holiness people for places where they could freely testify to and sing about their entire devotion to God and love for their neighbors. A philosophy of "come-outism" emerged in the late 1870s in some of the Holiness associations. Separatists held that Christians committed to the doctrine and experience of Christian perfection ought to come out from the denominations of which they were members and form independent Holiness churches.

Some come-outers held to a view of the Church derived from the restoration movement, which owed much to the spirit of the sixteenth-century Anabaptists. The restoration movement birthed groups such as the Disciples of Christ, Christian Churches, Churches of Christ, and Churches of God. Among its central beliefs was that sectarianism (what restorationists considered the system of denominations) was a violation of God's will for the unity of the Church, and thus sin. Church membership rolls deceived people into believing that they were saved. All the American denominations were guilty of this sin before God. His will, restorationists believed, was for true believers to come out from the fallen sects of the denominational system and join together in one unified, pure fellowship made up only of those born again, the restored Church of Jesus Christ, true believers. The pattern for this restored Church was the New Testament. This provided a sufficient guide, in restorationists' eyes, for belief, practice, and organization. Nothing else was needed. Restorationists declared that they required and honored "no creed but the Bible."[77]

Restoration ideas about the Church suited the growing concern in the Holiness Movement about the spiritual condition of the denominations, especially Methodism. Asbury Lowrey, a Holiness leader, noted within Methodism the expansion of "ecclesiastical machinery"; the increased wealth, respectability, and popularity of the church; the neglect of Holiness literature; the abandonment of class meetings, prayer meetings, family prayer, and the like; tolerance by the church of respectable vices such as dancing, attending the theater, and even consuming alcohol; and the admission to the church of large numbers of unconverted members.[78] Similarly, George Hughes complained that Methodism was being "inundated with formality and worldliness" and was no longer capable of being a true New Testament Church, a "holy church, 'without spot or blemish, or any such thing.'"[79] If this were so, then a new church was needed to proclaim and live out the full gospel that

God had entrusted to the Methodists. The heart of this New Testament gospel, Holiness people believed, was full sanctification.[80]

Come-outer Holiness people wedded the restoration concept of the one New Testament Church to the doctrine of Christian holiness. They agreed with restoration thinking that denominations were apostate because they were made of unbelievers and divided the church of Christ. There can only be *one* true church, they argued. Believers needed to come out of the sects and join together in one true Church. For Holiness restorationists this true New Testament Church would be a *Holiness* church, a church composed only of true believers, clearly teaching Christian perfection, as well as freed from the sin of sectarian disunion.

Holiness Restorationism gained a significant following. Its most influential spokesperson was Daniel S. Warner (1842-1925). Warner absorbed restoration ideas while pastoring in the Churches of God of North America, a small restoration group of German background. When he embraced Holiness teaching after attending a Holiness camp meeting about 1877, he adapted restoration theology to it. His Holiness ideas did not fit well with the leaders of the Churches of God of North America, who expelled Warner. In 1881 Warner founded the Church of God Restoration Movement (eventually headquartered at Anderson, Indiana).[81]

Some come-outers acted because they believed that they could no longer be faithful to the doctrine of Christian perfection and to their experience of sanctifying grace while remaining part of their denominations. Just as Wesley's followers had grown discontent worshipping in the Church of England, these believers felt themselves to be a marginalized remnant within Methodism and other churches.

Indeed, Holiness believers reported that pastors opposed, belittled, and silenced their witness to perfect love. A subscriber to the New York Methodist *Christian Advocate,* for example, described an incident in which, "A minister of the Methodist Episcopal Church was so enraged against holiness that he sent for a policeman to take out of his church a member who would testify that the blood of Jesus Christ cleanses from all sin."[82] Another Methodist complained of a presiding elder who had "taken pains to crush out all definite testimony on the subject of holiness" on his district.[83]

On a more theological level, a series of late nineteenth-century Methodist theologians—including Southern Methodist J. M. Boland, in *The Problem of Methodism* (1888), and Northern Methodist James Mudge, in *Growth in Holiness Toward Perfection, or Progressive Sanctification* (1895)—consciously discarded John Wesley and argued that entire sanctification was a gradual process and could not be attained in a moment. A generation of Methodist preachers gave up preaching the doctrine, feeling that "Christian perfection is not in its proper terms a workable doctrine." At the same time that this same generation gave up its emphasis upon attaining entire sanctification in a moment, it also gave up an emphasis upon conversion. Influenced by Horace Bushnell, Methodists believed that "gentler" means could bring about Christian nurture. By the early twentieth century Methodist conservatives were battling to maintain room within the Methodist Course of Study and publications for a theology and practice of the new birth.[84]

By the final years of the nineteenth century, both Holiness advocates and those who opposed organized holiness could see things moving toward a culmination. Whereas once Methodism appeared quite hospitable to the Holiness Movement's desire to promote Christian perfection, by the 1890s that was not true. Methodist leaders resented the growing number of organizations, meetings, and publications devoted to holiness. The 1894 General Conference of the Methodist Episcopal Church, South, complained that "there has sprung up among us a party with holiness as its watchword; they have holiness associations, holiness preachers, holiness evangelists, and holiness property." The delegates continued, "We do not question the sincerity and zeal of these brethren; we desire the Church to profit from their earnest preaching and godly example; but we deplore their teaching and methods in so far as they claim a monopoly of the experience, practice and advocacy of holiness, and separate themselves from the body of ministers and disciples."[85] The church question had to be faced. Would Holiness people remain loyal members of their denominations and submit to denominational authority? Or, would they leave in order to form independent churches?[86]

Even though restorationism suited Holiness come-outism, it was not attractive to most Holiness believers. John Inskip, John Wood, Charles Fowler, and other loyal Methodist leaders of the National Camp Meeting Association for the Promotion of Holiness strongly opposed come-outism and suppressed discussion of separation in Holiness conventions. They linked separation to undue emphases upon the Second Coming and divine healing. Association leaders perceived a cycle: the more talk of separation, the more bishops would suppress holiness, and the more the bishops suppressed holiness, the more sentiment toward separation. The bishops desired order. Association leaders urged believers in entire sanctification to submit, to remain in their denominations and to work within them to promote Holiness teaching and spiritual vitality. Leaders intended for the national association and the local and regional Holiness organizations to leaven and supplement, not duplicate or replace, the existing churches. They vigorously denied that the network of Holiness associations and ministries was, or should become, bases for independent Holiness churches.[87]

Nonetheless, by the time of the last national Holiness convention, held in Chicago in 1901, at least a dozen separate independent groups of churches with entire sanctification as their distinguishing doctrine had been formed. At the local level of the Holiness Movement, in the growing number of small bands, missions, and Holiness associations, support for come-outism grew. Having begun with the formation of D. S. Warner's Church of God in 1881, a significant exodus of Holiness believers from the churches was taking place. Motivated either by the restoration idea, or, more commonly, by frustration from struggling against unsympathetic, or even hostile denominational leaders, more and more Holiness believers concluded that God intended the Holiness Movement to have its primary home outside the existing denominations.[88] Yet at Pilot Point, Texas, in 1908 "graying divines," as Timothy L. Smith noted, "cherished still the dream of an interdenominational crusade for a national Pentecost."[89] Though coming together to organize a Holiness church, Nazarenes still prayed for revival within existing denominations and their country as a whole.

THREE

Nazarene Beginnings: The Eastern Stream

The Church of the Nazarene had its beginnings in persons and events that rose directly out of the nineteenth-century Holiness Movement. Nazarene identity has been marked by several strands of Christian faith and practice and by wider historical and geographical contexts. Yet, at its heart is the doctrine of Christian perfection as understood and taught among Methodists. Whether one looks at doctrine, patterns of worship and practice, leadership, or the religious background of early Holiness church members, the predominance of Methodism is unmistakable. The first, small independent Holiness groups shared common roots in the Holiness Movement and organized in response to local events and needs. Almost all of the members of these churches had come out of existing denominations and were the fruit in some way of the vigorous evangelism undertaken by the National Camp Meeting Association. By 1900 there were dozens of independent Holiness churches or groups. Among these was the Association of Pentecostal Churches of America.[1]

THE ASSOCIATION OF PENTECOSTAL CHURCHES OF AMERICA

Several northeastern United States groups coalesced to produce the Association of Pentecostal Churches of America. Chronologically, the first Holiness body that would later become part of the Church of the Nazarene appeared in this part of the country. The Association of Pentecostal Churches of America formed from William Howard Hoople's work in New York and the Central Evangelical Holiness Association in New England. This part of the United States was Phoebe Palmer's base of activity, the birthplace of the National Camp Meeting Association, the site of the earliest national Holiness camp meetings, and the center of Holiness publishing.

The mother church of the Church of the Nazarene in the East was the People's Evangelical Church, which was organized July 21, 1887. The founders of the People's Evangelical Church were members of St. Paul Methodist Episcopal Church in Providence, Rhode Island. That congregation of about 240 members, like many Methodist churches, experienced stress and conflict during the closing decades of the nineteenth century. Cities such as Providence faced a massive influx of immigrants from Southern and Eastern Europe, most of them Roman Catholic. In such a setting, inner convictions mattered much to those holding on to traditional Protestant truths. In 1881 during the time of Pastor T. J. Everett the church underwent a powerful Holiness revival under evangelist Lizzie Boyd. The pastor and his wife were the first to seek entire sanctification. Others included layman Fred Hillery, a class leader. Camp meeting-like scenes were repeated at the church, including persons lying prostrate under the power of the Holy Spirit. Following the revival, laypersons maintained, in Phoebe Palmer fashion, Tuesday testimony meetings. Boyd came for a second series of Holiness meetings in 1883.[2]

Not all members of St. Paul responded positively to the revival. The Ladies Aid Society, for instance, opposed it. They preferred a socially respectable and theologically broad Methodism. This group found allies in the two pastoral successors to Everett, C. H. Ewer and E. D. Hall, who did not possess any enthusiasm for either the doctrine of entire sanctification or the Holiness Movement. Instead of an attitude of polite indifference, they actively opposed Holiness people in the congregation. This ignited conflict, polarized the church, and drove a sharp wedge between Holiness advocates and those committed to less partisan forms of Methodism.[3]

Fred Hillery was instrumental in organizing the South Providence Holiness Association on May 12, 1886, and became the organization's president. Just as John Wesley had avoided holding Methodist society meetings at the same time as Church of England services, the association avoided scheduling meetings at the same hour as the Methodist church. Nonetheless, Pastor Hall removed Hillery as a class leader, stating that "the means of saving souls in the Methodist Episcopal Church is by method."[4] Hall refused to allow class members to attend association meetings.

Later in 1886, a fire swept the Methodist church and devastated its Sunday School classrooms. Seizing the moment, the Holiness association began its own Sunday School with ninety-five members in January 1887. For this, the pastor brought Hillery to church trial. Hillery was officially expelled from the Methodist Episcopal Church on March 15, 1887. This action led other members to withdraw from the church. On July 21, 1887, they organized the People's Evangelical Church with fifty-one charter members, all in sympathy with and, said the official history, many enjoying the experience of entire sanctification. As the schismatics saw the situation, Methodist polity itself was culpable for opposition to the experience and profession of entire sanctification. Methodist leaders had become so preoccupied with maintaining the letter of the *Discipline* that the spiritual life of the church was slipping away.⁵

In 1888 Hillery founded and became the editor of the *Beulah Items* (the *Beulah Christian* after 1892), which became an influential Holiness paper. In 1889 Hillery was ordained in a service conducted by thirteen independent New England Holiness ministers. The church maintained the class meetings characteristic of early Methodism, and five standing committees: Sunday School, Sick and Destitute, Care of the Church, Finance, and Baptism. Hillery remained as pastor of the People's Evangelical Church until 1904.⁶

Fred Hillery

Similar independent Holiness congregations arose across New England. In 1890 these congregations, including the People's Evangelical Church, formed the Central Evangelical Holiness Association. The purpose of the CEHA was "to promote scriptural holiness by united counsel and action, and give strength and encouragement to all those who from loyalty to this divinely inspired truth [of entire sanctification] are without the privileges of real Christian fellowship."⁷ Each of the CEHA congregations had its own *Manual* or *Discipline*. Their statements on the doctrine of holiness were similar. The People's Evangelical Church in Providence, for instance, understood entire sanctification to be an act of the Holy Spirit whereby all thoughts, words, and actions were "governed by pure love."⁸ Among the other congregations was one in Lynn, Massachusetts, established in 1888 and led by Baptist evangelist C. Howard Davis. This congregation's purpose, explicitly stated in its *Manual*, was "the up-building of its members in holiness, the entire sanctification of believers, the conversion of sinners." This, the church believed, was to be obtained by "preaching and teaching the whole word of God," and by "the use of such means and agencies as shall best secure these results."⁹ In 1890 the Lynn church planted a daughter church in Malden, Massachusetts, pastored by Anna Hanscome until her death in 1896. The Malden church, in turn, sent D. J. McDonald as a missionary to India.¹⁰

Methodist leaders responded quickly to this small step toward independence. If Holiness believers sought fellowship, they might find it in the General Holiness League, which National Holiness Association leader William McDonald started in 1891. The league included some non-Methodists such as George Morse, a Baptist, and such Methodists as J. N. Short, H. N. Brown, and H. F. Reynolds. The latter ministers saw the league as an alternative to leaving the Methodist Church. But the following year the New England Conference of the Methodist Episcopal Church warned that Methodist ministers must not hold meetings in the parishes of other Methodist ministers without first obtaining their permission—a measure like that taken by Anglican bishops against John Wesley in England more than a century before. These measures added to the sense of persecution felt by those pursuing Christian perfection.[11]

Hiram F. Reynolds (1854-1938) was a link between the Central Evangelical Holiness Association and the Association of Pentecostal Churches of America. Reynolds was born in 1854 near Chicago. After his father's death when he was six, Reynolds was raised on farms in Illinois by strict and at times abusive foster parents. As a teenager, Reynolds enjoyed gambling, dancing, liquor, and tobacco. At age twenty he moved to Chicago to live with a brother. In December 1874 Reynolds moved to Vermont, where his now remarried mother was living. Reynolds lived with and worked on the farm of the Stiles family. The Stileses were leading members of the Landgrove Methodist Church. The family's testimonies and his experiences with them ushered Reynolds to his conversion in 1875 and into the Methodist Church in 1876.

Reynolds soon felt called to ministry. Briefly, in 1878, he attended the Congregationalist Seminary in Manchester, Vermont. He also attended the Montpelier Methodist Seminary. Then he joined the Methodist Conference as a local pastor. His first appointment was to the Bondville, Vermont, church in 1879. The same year he married Stella Byerd. A daughter was born the following year. In 1880, while pastoring in Bondville, Reynolds suffered what he termed a nervous breakdown and briefly left the pastorate to work in a sawmill. Soon thereafter he attended the North Clarefield Methodist Camp Meeting. Under the influence of A. B. Riggs (a Methodist minister who later found his way into the Church of the Nazarene), Reynolds professed to be both healed and sanctified. He began preaching holiness. He accepted the challenge of starting a church in Plymouth Notch, Vermont (where future President of the United States Calvin Coolidge attended the Sunday School). The bishop transferred Reynolds to the Bernard and East Barnard Circuit, a comfortable position but where there was great opposition to Holiness preaching. The bishop transferred Reynolds to the Topshen Circuit, a hard circuit, but where Reynolds held many successful revivals and camp meetings, including a Holiness convention with Quaker evangelist Seth Rees.

Reynolds was ordained a deacon in 1884. He handled Chelsea and West Chelsea, a circuit warm toward holiness. In 1886 Bishop John F. Hurst ordained Reynolds an elder. Meanwhile, Reynolds held successful revivals, camp meetings, and Holiness conventions, and almost as soon as he was ordained applied for a "supernumerary" relation to the conference that would allow him to do full-time evangelistic work. The bishop, instead, offered to make him a presiding elder. Reynolds refused this appointment but agreed to accept the pastorate of the Underhill church, which, he knew, had Holiness sympathies.

In 1892 the Methodist Conference granted Reynolds supernumerary status and he entered full-time evangelism. Along with O. J. Copeland, a Methodist layman residing in Montpelier, Reynolds helped to organize the Vermont Holiness Association, which affiliated with the National Holiness Association. Copeland secured tents in which to hold revivals. Reynolds's evangelistic itinerary took him to New Brunswick and Nova Scotia, Canada, as well as many parts of New England. Holiness papers such as the *Christian Witness*, published in Boston, carried news of various small Holiness groups springing up across the country, and Reynolds's travels as an evangelist allowed him to become acquainted with Holiness leaders throughout the Northeast, including William McDonald, C. J. Fowler, and H. N. Brown, and a small group of churches centered around Brooklyn, New York, known as the Association of Pentecostal Churches of America.[12]

William Howard Hoople (1868-1922) was the young leader of these churches. Hoople was born in Herkimer, New York, the son of a successful leather merchant. Hoople experienced entire sanctification at the historic John Street Methodist Church in Manhattan in the early 1890s. Hoople became acquainted with Charles BeVier, the choir director of a Methodist church in Brooklyn, who was holding a Holiness meeting in his home in Brooklyn while also being in charge of a Methodist mission on Bushwick Avenue. In January 1894 Hoople and BeVier opened a mission on Schenectady Avenue next to a brothel. A congregation grew, and the small group constructed a building on Utica Avenue later that year. In 1895, two additional congregations began under Hoople's and BeVier's leadership. John Norberry pastored the church on Bedford Avenue in east Brooklyn.[13]

William Hoople

In December 1895, representatives from these three congregations, somehow envisioning a national organization, formed the Association of Pentecostal Churches of America (APCA) for the purpose of "supporting a faithful ministry among us, for relief of the poor, and for the spread of the gospel over the earth." The language and image of the baptism with the Holy Spirit, and its implications for world missions, greatly influenced the founders. While still a group of urban missions centered in Brooklyn, leaders reflected concern for the wider world. They expressed their global concerns in an early (1895) mission statement: "We will cheerfully contribute of our earthly means as God has prospered us, for the support of a faithful ministry among us, for the relief of the poor, and for the spread of the Gospel over the earth."[14] The association formed a Missionary Committee in December 1895, with three pastors and three laypersons, and a women's missionary auxiliary.

A camp meeting the following year in Cliftondale, New York, led to another organized congregation, and Reynolds, after a deep struggle between allegiance to the doctrine of entire sanctification and to the Methodist church that increasingly opposed the doctrine, and seeing the fervor of these folk, decided to leave the Methodist Episcopal Church and join this small band of Holiness advocates. Reynolds moved to Brooklyn, where his friend O. J. Copeland had already moved and had opened a granite business. Reynolds, again following Copeland, joined the Utica Avenue Church of the Association of Pentecostal Churches of America. Reynolds brought solid credentials as a pastor and Holiness evangelist, and contacts with the New England Holiness movement.

In November 1896 representatives of the Central Evangelical Holiness Association met with Hoople in Brooklyn and together approved a plan of union. Like other organizations of the era, the CEHA sought greater "organization, efficiency and power."[15] The group decided that "Association of Pentecostal Churches of America" well represented their aspirations, so accepted that as the name of the new denomination. The union between the Pentecostal Association with the Central Evangelical Holiness Association, as Reynolds described it, came about "for the purpose of increased efficiency in the advancement of the Redeemer's kingdom, by the spread of scriptural holiness in home and foreign fields."[16] The reason for the union of the CEHA and the APCA was because leaders "saw they could increase efficiency in the spread of Scriptural holiness in the home and foreign fields." Though a few of the New England churches refused to go along with the union, and stayed out, in 1897 fifteen CEHA congregations joined the Pentecostal Association.[17] The *Beulah Christian* became the official publication of the united group.[18]

Leaders developed a constitution that guaranteed independence to the local churches, stating: "We believe each church to be complete in itself; that Christ is the Head of each and the Head of all; that the Scriptures are its sole statute book; that in the choice of its officers, in the admission and dismission of the members, and in the administration of all its affairs, each church is independent of the authority of other churches."[19] Ordination to ministry rested in the hands of a "presbytery" and consisted of three or more regularly ordained ministers laying hands on the one being ordained. The stipulation was that the minister being ordained be in the present and clear experience of entire sanctification. Though members of the association held congregational principles, they also recognized the "duty" of the association itself "from time to time, to suggest to the churches such measures as may be judged wise and proper to promote the interests of the Messiah's kingdom and the spread of Scriptural holiness throughout the world."[20] Local manuals, which varied from congregation to congregation, expressed global visions. At the same time, leaders knew that it was necessary for the advancement in other places for there to be solid home congregations. Both in the homeland and abroad the association aimed at people and places neglected by others.[21]

The April 1897 assembly of the Association of Pentecostal Churches of America voted to send a group of missionaries under the leadership of M. D. Wood to India. Wood had already served one term in India and had joined the association at what seemed to be a providential time. To supervise this venture, the association elected a twelve-member Missionary Committee, with William Hoople as chairman. The Missionary Committee desired to send Wood with a team of sanctified workers to India. The assembly put Reynolds in charge of raising the necessary funds. In October that year the committee appointed Reynolds as Home and Foreign Missionary secretary. Reynolds held three-day missionary rallies and other conventions and campaigns in association churches to raise money to send missionaries abroad. He wrote a regular missionary column for the *Beulah Christian*. From that time until the merger with the Church of the Nazarene the APCA Missionary Committee received and disbursed $33,000 for foreign missions.[22]

In 1899 the Woman's Foreign Missionary Society of the Pentecostal Churches of America was formed. There were still only twenty churches in the association. Like the separate organization of women in the Methodist Church and other denominations, women in the association initially sponsored their own missionaries, such as Julia Gibson in India. Largely, however, led by Susan N. Fitkin, a former Quaker, the women cooperated with the association's Missionary Committee.

From the beginning of the Holiness Movement in the northeast, from Phoebe Palmer onward, women played a large role. Early association evangelists and pastors included Anna Hanscome, Martha Curry, Henrietta Moke, Lura Horton, and Ada Reid, in addition to Fitkin. A few of these women—including Hanscome in 1892, Curry in 1902, and Fitkin in 1907—became ordained ministers.[23]

Susan Norris Fitkin (1870-1951) represented not only the number of Quakers who eventually found their way into the Church of the Nazarene but also the number of Canadian immigrants. Norris was born in Quebec of Quaker parents. Her mother was active in the Womans Christian Temperance Union. Susan Norris was converted in 1890 and soon began to think about foreign missions. She offered herself to the China Inland Mission. The society refused her because of her health (she had suffered from typhoid). Instead, Norris began holding young people's meetings in churches near her home. She was a delegate to the Christian Endeavor Society Convention in New York City in 1892. The Christian Endeavor Society was an interdenominational youth ministry popular at the time. At this conference she heard J. W. Malone, an evangelical Quaker, speak, and she decided to attend the institute he headed in Cleveland, Ohio. Among her classmates were fellow Canadian Mary Emily Soul and Soul's future husband Edgar Ellyson, both of whom were Quakers who later found prominent positions in the Church of the Nazarene. Continuing to sense a call to preach, Norris became assistant pastor in a small church in Northern Michigan in 1893. After conducting revivals among Quakers in Vermont, one church invited her to remain as pastor. A "recorded" or official minister among the Friends, in about 1895 she attended a Holiness convention in a Methodist church and experienced entire sanctification. The following year she met Abram Fitkin, a seventeen-year-old evangelist, and they began holding revivals together. Marriage and four children followed. Reports of their revivals reached the *Christian Witness* and other Holiness papers. In late 1896 the Fitkins organized an independent congregation in Hopewell Junction, New York, and then guided the church into the Association of Pentecostal Churches of America. The Fitkins occasionally settled for brief pastorates. Fitkin retained her lively interest in missions. If she could not go herself, she would support others. Beginning in 1898, Stella Reynolds and Susan Fitkin organized a series of congregation-based societies among the association churches. This led to the organization of the women's auxiliary of the association's Foreign Missionary Society. Fitkin promoted missions in conventions and rallies.

In 1903 Abram Fitkin left evangelism to pursue a career in public finance and utilities. He became very successful in this but left churchgoing to his wife. Susan Fitkin remained active in the John Wesley Church in Brooklyn. As Abram Fitkin accumulated immense wealth, he gave generously to the church, and Susan Fitkin was able to use some of that wealth for missions.[24]

By 1907 the APCA missionary society had grown to four hundred members. In spite of Fitkin's urging, the 1907 General Assembly that united the APCA with the Church of the Nazarene did not organize a national society. Eight years later, the 1915 General Assembly authorized leaders of the movement to create a constitution and elect officers. The stated purposes of the organization were to promote the missions within the church through advocacy, education, and fund-raising.[25]

Reynolds likewise zealously supported missions. He inspired people with his seemingly boundless energy, enthusiasm for world evangelism, and organizational acumen. The missions policies developed under him did not come, at least explicitly, from contemporary theories of mission; but Reynolds clearly imbibed the missions spirit of his age. Like missions executives of larger agencies, Reynolds managed not only missionaries on the field but also public relations at home. Reynolds possessed the kind of optimism characterized by the Student Volunteer Movement that with sufficient planning and hard work Christians could evangelize the world within a generation.[26]

Reynolds was a pragmatist. The paradigm Reynolds molded for the church emphasized world evangelism, Christian responsibility, and organization. He appreciated the need for efficiency, procedures, and frugality. A Holiness church to him was one endeavoring by the power of the Spirit to do its part for the evangelization of the world. In doing so, Reynolds in effect emphasized the "cardinal" doctrine of the church, justification by faith, rather than its "distinguishing" doctrine of entire sanctification. Reynolds strongly believed in financial stability, organizational systems, and hierarchical methods of control over both missionaries and mission fields.[27]

Reynolds's salary was derived primarily from his evangelism. The jobs of foreign and home missions were divided in 1903, with C. H. Davis assuming responsibility for home missions and Reynolds retaining foreign missions oversight. In 1905 Reynolds's title became missionary secretary and superintendent of Foreign Missions. This was a full-time job, with a promised salary of $1,000 per year, but Reynolds always gave sacrificially to missions.[28]

THE GROWTH OF THE ASSOCIATION OF PENTECOSTAL CHURCHES OF AMERICA

A few independent Holiness congregations in New England decided to affiliate with the Evangelical Association, a German-American denomination that had been entirely swept up in the Holiness Movement. John N. Short (1841-1922) left the Methodist Church after being transferred, so he believed, for his Holiness advocacy from a strong church in Lowell, Massachusetts, to a struggling one in Beverly. Short had graduated from Boston University's School of Theology and had been ordained in 1873. While holding a series of pastorates, Short became active in Holiness revivalism, becoming vice president of the well-known Douglas Camp Meeting. Once deciding to leave the Methodist Church, Short looked for an alternative denomination for himself and his followers. He joined the Evangelical Association in 1894 and formed an Evangelical Association congregation in Cambridge.[29]

The Evangelical Association was started by Jacob Albright, a Methodist exhorter, who preached to German-speaking people in Pennsylvania in the 1790s. (In 1946 this group united with the similar United Brethren in Christ to form the Evangelical United Brethren, which, in turn, united with the Methodist Church in 1968 to form the United Methodist Church.) The Evangelical Association had a clear statement on Christian perfection in its *Discipline:* "Experience has moreover taught that, ordinarily, this state of Christian perfection is attained gradually, by an upright course of life in following the Lamb; however, during this gradation, this work is perfected in the soul, sooner or later, by a sudden and powerful influence of grace and outpouring of the Divine Spirit."[30] However, after a few years, Short (and others like him) wearied of control by German-American bishops. In 1903 Short decided to join the Association of Pentecostal Churches of America. He formed another congregation in Cambridge.[31]

The association grew by enfolding independent congregations and planting others in the northeastern United States and Canada. The congregations that made up the APCA continued to have their own *Manual* or *Discipline*, though often copied from each other. These congregations reflected the teachings of Holiness people not only in regard to entire sanctification but also in regard to other doctrines. The People's Evangelical Church, for instance, maintained a statement on the Scriptures that reflected the Anglican and Methodist tradition rather than the budding fundamentalism that was beginning to be heard across the country. "We believe that the Holy Bible, containing the Scriptures of the Old and New Testaments, is the revelation of divine truth, and the record of God's will, from whence we derive all correct knowledge of religious truth and duty; and that it is the only sufficient rule of a Christian's faith and practice." The 1897 Constitution of the APCA stated simply that the Holy Scriptures were "His inspired Word, and the only rule of faith and practice." The Lincoln Place, Pennsylvania, Pentecostal Church stated at bit more in 1904: "We believe in the Holy Scripture as God's inspired Word and the only rule of faith and practice," words similar to the Church of England's Articles of Religion. However, the Lincoln Place Church went on to reason: "If moved by the Holy Ghost to speak, then what they said must be without any admixture of error. All things profitable and necessary are contained in the Scriptures." The church affirmed: "They are also a perfect treasure of heavenly instruction and comfort, and the supreme standard by which all human conduct, creeds and opinions be tried." As explicit as this statement was, it fell short of what fundamentalists later would affirm about the "inerrancy" of the Scripture.[32]

On the Second Coming, the People's Evangelical Church said simply that it would come at the end of the world. Other nonessential matters related to baptism. The People's Evangelical Church left its mode up to the candidate. The People's Evangelical Church did not list rules of behavior in its *Manual*. However, the Beulah Pentecostal Church in Hopewell Junction, New York, maintained very clear and strict rules. Members were not to express opinions opposed to or subversive of the church's Confession of Faith. They were to conduct family prayers and attend to other "means of grace." They were not to devote any part of the Sabbath to what is unnecessary or worldly pleasure. They must contribute to the church. The church would not support itself by church suppers and the like; it would rely on tithes. Members must not sell or use intoxicating drinks. However, the Hopewell Junction church explicitly did *not* teach that anyone who used tobacco could not be a child of God, only that tobacco hindered "growth in grace," and certainly no one, the church believed, could be entirely sanctified until he or she first gave up the "foul weed." So convinced of this was the church that anyone claiming to be sanctified who still used tobacco could be disciplined. On the matter of apparel, the Hopewell Junction church considered jewelry and costly and gaudy apparel "after the manner of the world," and understood that no one who dressed in this way could be a "conservator of Christianity."[33]

Though small, the APCA manifested concerns for society as a whole. By its very existence the APCA expressed a degree of discontent with the social order. In 1900 E. E. Angell expressed his displeasure with the current war in the Philippines. God required the "march of civilization," but never with the sword.[34] In 1901 the association's annual meeting sent a letter to President William

McKinley protesting prostitution being licensed by American forces occupying the Philippines.[35] Standing resolutions placed the association on the side of prohibition. Association missionaries and deaconesses undertook educational, medical, and other compassionate work. Because of the New England setting out of which they came, and because it was common among Holiness people in the nineteenth century to establish both schools and rescue missions, it seemed a natural part of the association's responsibility in India.[36]

The growth of the Association of Pentecostal Churches in Canada should not be surprising. Phoebe Palmer had preached in Canada as early as 1853 and ministered there regularly for the rest of her life. Other Holiness Movement evangelists routinely itinerated in Canada among Methodist and other churches. As in the United States, Holiness advocates ran afoul of their denominations and formed Holiness missions, out of which came independent associations of churches. One of the first independent Holiness groups to emerge in Canada was the Reformed Baptist Alliance, formed at Woodstock, New Brunswick, in November 1888. This group grew quite rapidly and within seven years had twenty-two churches with 540 members.[37] The Reformed Baptist Alliance became the main refuge for Holiness people in Atlantic Canada. Some of its members became Nazarenes and encouraged the union of the two churches, but the Reformed Baptist Alliance remained independent until it united with the Wesleyan Methodist Church in 1966.[38]

Nonetheless, one of the earliest Nazarene congregations in Canada was the product of a Holiness revival sponsored by the Reformed Baptist Alliance. The revival, at Oxford, Nova Scotia, in 1902, was conducted by L. J. King, a former Roman Catholic priest-turned-holiness-Baptist. Though most of the people who experienced entire sanctification in the Oxford revival were Methodists, the local Methodist church did not favor Holiness revivalism, and the newly sanctified folks sought a distinctly Holiness church. As one put it, "Our fellow members were unsympathetic to our testimonies of entire sanctification, to the extent that we no longer felt at home in the Methodist Church."[39] Unwilling, however, to accept the Baptist traditions of the Reformed Baptist Alliance, they contacted Hiram F. Reynolds of the Association of Pentecostal Churches of America. Reynolds had preached in the Maritime Provinces frequently during his years as an evangelist, and in 1902 he was once again preaching in the area for the APCA. Reynolds agreed to organize a congregation at Oxford and also another at Springhill, Nova Scotia. Later, congregations were formed in Yarmouth, Nova Scotia, and St. John, New Brunswick. Eventually these churches became part of the New England District of the Church of the Nazarene. Out of these Maritime churches came persons who pioneered the Church of the Nazarene elsewhere in Canada.⁴⁰

While expanding north into Canada, the Association of Pentecostal Churches of America also moved further south into the Middle Atlantic region of the United States. A substantial congregation was formed in Washington, D.C., out of Holiness work among the poor started by two Quaker sisters, Phoebe Hall and Sarah Hall, in 1888. By 1900 many involved in this independent work desired a regular church home and invited William Hoople to organize a congregation of the APCA. Thirty-two members of the Hall mission became charter members. Hoople persuaded C. Howard Davis to move from Lynn, Massachusetts, to pastor the church. After a couple of years Davis was succeeded by another New Englander, H. B. Hosley. By 1910 this congregation had 261 members.⁴¹

The Association of Pentecostal Churches also expanded westward. A strong independent congregation in Pittsburgh, pastored by John H. Norris, joined the APCA with 163 members in 1899. This church organized new congregations in neighboring cities and towns. These provided the foundation for the Pittsburgh District of the Church of the Nazarene when it was formed in 1907. Even further west two small APCA congregations were established at Findlay, Ohio, and Hazelton (northeast of Waterloo), Iowa.⁴²

The association demonstrated its churchliness not only by retaining a lasting interest in missions but by also engaging in compassionate ministries. At home, deaconesses worked in impoverished urban areas. Yet it was not duty springing out of a sense of noblesse oblige that motivated Holiness people, many of whom were on common economic ground with those they sought to help. Abroad, education and forms of social work were legitimate components of the church's task. Holiness people never decided fully whether educational, medical, and other such enterprises were ends in themselves, as expressions of hearts made perfect in love, or means of evangelism. Reynolds seemed not to mull over the issue. Duty as much as love motivated social activities. Reynolds sanctioned literacy training, elementary schools, clinics, flood relief projects, and other such enterprises in India, where he considered these to be needed. Simply, these were the church's duty under God as part of a nation destined, so he thought, to redeem the world.⁴³

Though aiming not to impinge upon congregational rights, the Missionary Committee of the association defined its duties very broadly. It took action on ordinations and the transfer of ministerial credentials from other denominations. Once the Missionary Committee had approved a person for ordination, the ordained members of the committee laid hands on the one being ordained. The committee also maintained contacts with other Holiness bodies. As early as 1899 the committee invited any interested party to send delegates with the object "to promote Scriptural Holiness at home and in foreign mission fields," and with the belief that "the work can be more effectively done by uniting in one body the distinctive Holiness Churches Associations and Bands in this country."[44] In 1905 the Missionary Committee specifically invited both the Church of the Nazarene of Los Angeles and the Pentecostal Mission of Nashville to send representatives to its next annual meeting.[45]

PENTECOSTAL COLLEGIATE INSTITUTE

The Association of Pentecostal Churches of America quickly became concerned not only with missions but also with education and in 1899 established a Committee on Education, with J. H. Norris, pastor of the Pittsburgh church, as chairman. The committee voted to establish both a Course of Study for Ministers, much like that of the Methodist Church, and a school. The leaders expected the school to reflect the unique ethos of the Holiness denomination.[46]

The Pentecostal Collegiate Institute and Bible Training School opened in 1900 in a rented resort hotel in Saratoga Springs, New York, and moved into a permanent building, a vacant hotel, for its second year of operation. The president of the school was Lyman C. Pettit, a graduate of Syracuse University and pastor of the Grace Pentecostal Church in Saratoga Springs. This congregation had been established in 1896 and had been known as the Congregational Methodist Church before joining the association in 1899. Pettit was one of the main advocates for starting the Pentecostal Collegiate Institute. The school began with fifty-one students in 1900, and the following year over one hundred enrolled, including children of Reynolds and other preachers of the association. The school included elementary, high school, and preparatory departments, the latter for educating ministers. Unlike Bible colleges of the time, which, as historian Virginia Brereton describes, considered liberal arts in the curriculum an "unwanted extravagance," the PCI catalog listed courses in Latin, Greek, modern languages, art, music, and oratory. The future seemed bright.[47]

Typical of Christian colleges of the era (and not unlike John Wesley's structure at the Kingswood School that he established), PCI aimed to develop Christian character through tight regulations. "We rise at 6:30," reported one student, "have breakfast from 7:00-8:00 tidying our rooms, and have private devotions from 8:00 to 8:30. We go to chapel from 8:30-9:00, then have classes until 12:00. Dinner is from 12:30-1:00. When we have studied from

1:00 to 3:30, we have recreation period until 5:00, then private devotions to 5:30. After supper at 6:00, we have chapel until 7:45, study until 9:00, have private devotions 9:00 to 9:30, and then lights out at 10 o'clock." Other rules regulated "mixed assemblages" and prohibited any "gentleman and lady" to "ride, or walk out together; nor may any lady receive calls from any gentleman, without permission."[48]

President Pettit and the Education Committee of the Association of Pentecostal Churches became embroiled in a battle over the school's finances and other matters. Pettit himself (rather than the association), held the deed to the school's property and had contracted debts without the knowledge of the committee. After an investigation, the Education Committee decided to dismiss Pettit and to disown the school. Pettit withdrew from the association and continued to run the school on his own for a couple more years. Eventually, however, he disposed of the property. Later he became a minister in the Presbyterian Church.[49]

The Education Committee of the Association of Pentecostal Churches hurriedly purchased property with buildings in North Scituate, Rhode Island, about ten miles west of Providence, and managed to open a school there in the fall of 1903 that they again called Pentecostal Collegiate Institute. By the time the association purchased the property the buildings, which dated to the 1830s, had been vacant for many years. The association rehabilitated the facilities, appointed an administration and a small faculty, and recruited a student body.[50]

After a series of principals, the school achieved some stability under the leadership of the appropriately named Ernest Angell, who became both principal of the school and moderator of the association in 1906. Angell had previously pastored the association church in Saratoga Springs and the John Wesley Church in Brooklyn. Before experiencing entire sanctification in 1901, Angell, a graduate of Wesleyan Theological College in Montreal, had pastored Congregationalist churches in Vermont. He served at PCI until 1913. Pentecostal Collegiate Institute, which changed its name to Eastern Nazarene College in 1918, remained on the Rhode Island campus until 1919, when it moved to Quincy, Massachusetts.[51]

MISSION IN INDIA

Reynolds and the Missionary Committee members were new at the missions task. M. D. Wood, on the other hand, whom the association appointed to lead its missionary force in India, had not only experience in India with the Christian and Missionary Alliance but also preparation at the missionary training school of the Christian and Missionary Alliance in Nyack, New York. Wood had gone to India under the Missionary Alliance, arriving in Bombay in 1892. He studied Marathi for two years and was stationed in Buldana, Berar—east of Bombay. About sixty other Alliance missionaries were stationed in the vicinity. Wood's wife died in October 1895.[52]

M. D. Wood

Wood returned on furlough to the United States the following year and attended the Holiness camp meeting in Douglas, Massachusetts. Here he met people affiliated with the recently organized Association of Pentecostal Churches of America. Wood became a member of Hoople's Utica Avenue Tabernacle in Brooklyn and married Anna Matlack, a nurse, and a member of an association church in Pennsylvania.[53]

In addition to Wood and his wife, the association appointed Lillian Sprague and two others (who did not stay long with the Association after reaching India) as missionaries. On December 11, 1897, the same day that the missionary party set sail for India, the APCA Missionary Committee issued a policy statement that tied the missionaries closely to the sending body. "No step of any importance" was to be undertaken without the prior approval of the Missionary Committee. Missionaries were *not* to act unilaterally on major issues. All money would be channeled through the association's treasurer and not be sent directly to the field. There was to be one station, the permanent headquarters of the mission, which must be approved by the Missionary Committee in America and not moved without its consent. Property must be held in ways consistent with the laws of the host country, but any books, papers, and other material articles belonged to the association. Missionary officers included the superintendent, assistant superintendent, secretary, treasurer, business manager, and medical missionary. The duty of the medical missionary was "to use every practical means to care for the physical needs of those with whom she may be brought in contact." Missionaries were to master the language.[54]

After a stop in England, the band arrived in Bombay in January 1898. The group settled in Igatpuri, Berar, eighty-five miles inland from Bombay, where both the CMA and the Methodists were already at work. The renowned holiness Methodist Bishop William Taylor had organized a Methodist society in Igatpuri in 1873.[55]

The missions philosophies that Wood brought with him into the association were indebted to the CMA and to the faith missions concepts of J. Hudson Taylor, both of which emphasized the leadership of the Holy Spirit and the importance of prayer and faith. Alliance missionaries emphasized purely evangelistic work, yet sponsored industrial work, orphanages, and ministerial education. As he had been accustomed, and as many Protestant groups were doing in these years of intense famine in India, Wood immediately began to take in orphans. The purpose was twofold: not only would they be saved from almost certain starvation, but they might be raised by missionaries as Christians. Wood informed the Missionary Committee of his action, but the committee feared the excessive financial burden the orphans might create for the struggling churches at home and chastised Wood sharply. Nevertheless, since Wood had already acted, the Missionary Committee agreed to sponsor the orphans. It solicited pledges for the orphans through the *Beulah Christian*.[56]

Wood chafed under any constraints and pled with Reynolds for more freedom and trust. Wood addressed Reynolds as "my very dear little brother" (Reynolds was older by thirteen years) and reminded the missionary committee of its own inexperience. Wood did not inform the Missionary Committee before deciding upon various issues, including even the mode of baptism (sprinkling), which, according to the association, should be left up to the candidate. On the matter of ordination, however, Wood refrained from ordaining a worker, his converted Marathi teacher, upon receiving Reynolds's negative response—negative because the candidate for ordination was not yet entirely sanctified. In September 1899, without giving any warning to the Missionary Committee, Wood moved the mission, including the orphans, further inland, to Buldana. The Missionary Alliance, Wood knew very well, maintained a strong work in Buldana. For the next several years, as the association established itself, there were strained relationships between the two missions. Wood desired for the mission to be self-supporting, which meant, to Wood, that the mission find indigenous ways of supporting itself. The reason for his establishing a farm in Buldana was not only so that the orphans might raise cows and grow crops for their own sake but also so that the mission might sell the excess butter, milk, and produce for its own support. A medical clinic begun by Anna Wood was self-supporting from its inception. The Missionary Committee encouraged Wood in these directions.[57]

Social ministries continued. The hesitancy of Reynolds and the committee to undertake orphanage work was financial, not philosophical, for the association soon rallied behind support for the children. Inevitably, as needs presented themselves, the missionaries took up primary school education and famine relief. There was no suggestion from Reynolds that the mission should desist from institutional concerns in order to devote itself exclusively to preaching and evangelism. Both Wood and Reynolds, despite their differences, agreed that compassionate works were their Christian duty. There was not, at least not yet, a breakdown in the Holiness Movement's consensus that both social concern and evangelistic preaching accompanied perfect love. Out of both love and duty the mission in India clothed the naked, fed the hungry, visited the sick, and supported the weak.[58]

In 1903 M. D. Wood, Anna Wood, and Lillian Sprague furloughed to the United States. They returned to India with a new group of missionaries in 1904. The group included Leighton Tracy, Ella Perry, her daughter Gertrude (who soon married Leighton Tracy), Nellie Barnes, Julia Gibson, Priscilla Hitchens, and three others who soon left the mission. Reynolds now demanded that Wood submit detailed weekly reports. Wood's reports contained conflicting accounts about the idiosyncratic actions of the newer missionaries, on the one hand, and descriptions of a revival in their midst on the other. One missionary, according to Wood, was "full of the devil," another was "living in sin," and a third was "full of herself." But Wood was optimistic that the revival was straightening them out. In news regarding the revival Wood stated his conviction that Christians needed to be filled with the Holy Spirit *after* they were cleansed. Was Wood teaching a third work of grace? Pandita Ramabai's mission near Bombay, and the Christian and Missionary Alliance area in Gudjerat were among the places where a revival involving "baptism with fire" broke out in 1905 and where, by December 1906, unknown tongues were being spoken.[59]

This movement conflicted with the accepted Holiness Movement teaching that linked the baptism of the Holy Spirit with cleansing from inbred sin. Pentecostalism was appearing on the fringes of the Holiness Movement in different places at this time and was one factor that hastened the denominational organization of Holiness groups. Perhaps Reynolds feared fanaticism on the mission field as well as insubordination. At the same time, Reynolds, who was well acquainted with the new missionaries and respected their maturity, suspected that Wood may not have been in a position to criticize them. Reynolds asked Tracy, a twenty-two-year-old Canadian who had been a student at the Pentecostal Collegiate Institute, to send him additional reports about what was going on.

The Missionary Committee soon decided to reorganize the missionaries in India, to force Wood to share leadership under a three-person executive committee made up of Wood, Sprague, and Tracy. Soon, however, Reynolds designated himself superintendent of the field while, of course, remaining in America. These actions proved to be the breaking point for Wood. In a letter to the Missionary Committee, Wood, Anna Wood, and Sprague, who remained loyal to Wood, voiced their frustrations and put forward several demands, including allowing contributors to send money directly to them without having to go through the association's treasurer, freedom to expand the work as God would lead, and autonomy. Actually, Wood had already circumvented the committee in financial appeals.[60]

When Wood had been sent out in 1897 the association was only a loose band of independent Holiness congregations. But much had changed in eight years. The denominational and hierarchical character of the association had been strengthened. Its leaders, themselves strong-willed pastors of local congregations, had been forced to deal with Lyman Pettit, the independent first principal of the Pentecostal Collegiate Institute. Reynolds had been actively involved in reorganizing PCI and could easily draw parallels to the situation in India. Because of the crises at PCI and India, the association pulled away from a Congregationalist or Baptist polity. Like Pettit, Wood believed that the Holy Spirit should control the work, not a committee. After all, Wood said, missionaries were not the "servants of men," but servants of God and the "government shall be upon His shoulders." Wood reminded Reynolds, "God called us here and not you."[61] But Reynolds was resolute. He saw the need for both superintendency and accountability; and independence to this former Methodist was as dangerous as anarchy.[62]

When Wood, Anna Wood, and Lillian Sprague pressed their demands, the association committee accepted their resignations and instructed Wood to turn over administration of the mission to Tracy. Rather than doing so, in February 1906 Wood and the two women, along with younger missionary Nellie Barnes, abruptly left the mission in the middle of the night along with the orphans (whom they left in the care of the Methodist station in Washim).[63]

Meanwhile, in order to prevent misunderstanding within the association, the committee published large parts of the correspondence between Wood and the committee in the *Beulah Christian*. Members of the association would see, hoped leaders, that a well-superintended organization would best contribute to the spread of holiness around the world.[64]

Through the leadership of Leighton Tracy and others the church eventually regained its reputation. Tracy based the purpose and direction of the mission on loyalty to the home church. Tracy stayed with the association—gladly, as he said, putting himself under the authority of holy men and women.[65]

Leighton and Gertrude Tracy remained in Buldana. Ella Perry, a practical nurse, carried on medical work on the field until her own death by cholera in 1919. Priscilla Hitchens worked in Igatpuri, to which the association had returned in 1906, and Julia Gibson labored for the most part alone in Chikhli. Seeing the plight of women around her, Gibson found herself praying for India's "blighted childhood, enslaved wifehood, sorrowing widowhood and weakened manhood."66

MISSION IN CAPE VERDE

The APCA undertook one other missionary enterprise during these years of its history. A young Cape Verdean, John Diaz (1873-1964), began work in the Cape Verde Islands. Diaz had come to America in 1889, at the age of sixteen, and had settled first in New Bedford, Massachusetts, and then in Providence, Rhode Island. There he joined the People's Evangelical Church and experienced entire sanctification. Soon after this Diaz began to evangelize Cape Verdeans in New England. By 1900 he had decided to return to the Cape Verde Islands to carry the gospel there. The People's Church promised its support. In February 1901 he and some companions sailed for his home island of Brava, one of the smaller islands located in the far south of the island chain, and nearly inaccessible.67

John Diaz

Though receiving funds to help with his work, for the next thirty-four years John Diaz ministered in the Cape Verde Islands without ever receiving a visitor from the Association of Pentecostal Churches of America, or (after 1907) the Church of the Nazarene. Reynolds tried twice to visit Cape Verde but was unsuccessful. Diaz organized congregations, founded and operated a school, and preached the message of Christian holiness. He and converts suffered immense persecution. His work established a firm foundation for the Church of the Nazarene that flourished and eventually helped to establish Portuguese-speaking Nazarene congregations around the world, including Portugal itself.68

Even though the People's Evangelical Church had guaranteed the support of Diaz, the "faith missions" idea never stood a chance under Reynolds's leadership. The pull was in the opposite direction, away from unbridled independence and congregationalism and toward superintendency. Reynolds doubted claims to the leadership or guidance of the Holy Spirit on some project unless they were backed up with the planning and finances necessary to get the job done. To him, the Spirit worked through structure.[69]

TOWARD WIDER ASSOCIATION

Several factors led the APCA away from strict congregationalism and toward both more superintendency and wider association. By 1905 Reynolds was not only foreign missions secretary but also the general agent for the Pentecostal Collegiate Institute. Though his public jobs entailed fundraising and promotion, behind the scenes Reynolds also advised missionaries and strategized for the church both at home and abroad. The association had standing committees for foreign missions, home missions, and education. Projects demanded support and required organized and systematic giving on the part of the member churches. Association churches saw the necessity of pooling their resources for the sake of establishing new churches. Reynolds faced problems created by leaders desirous to go their own ways apart from the wisdom and counsel of the church. Association members were discontent with independence and congenial toward union with other Holiness bodies. The dealings with Wood in India and with Pettit at the Pentecostal Collegiate Institute convinced not only Reynolds but others in the association of the necessity of greater superintendency. Ex-Methodist leaders such as Reynolds, H. N. Brown, and J. N. Short were accustomed to superintendency, and others, as well, now saw the wisdom of it. These were factors pulling the association in the direction of Methodist polity and union with other Holiness bodies.[70]

More broadly, at the turn of the century, and the decade that preceded it, the United States was undergoing significant cultural shifts. Northeastern cities faced deep social changes that stirred religious responses. In rural areas, secession from the denominations was not yet necessary. But in the cities, Christians adopted different lifestyles. Immigration and urbanization were among the factors that, as historian Kevin Christiano notes, increased religious diversity, demanded both an "adjustment of religious group boundaries" and greater organization, and curtailed independency among Protestants. The Association of Pentecostal Churches of America, in the few years of its development, evidenced this very search for order and stability.[71]

The various Holiness journals that crisscrossed the mails contained news of Holiness groups like the association springing up all over the United States and the United Kingdom. No wonder, then, that the association received a warm letter from J. O. McClurkan, whose Pentecostal Mission centered around Nashville, and who was as equally committed as the association not only to holiness but also to both urban and foreign missions. Another letter from Phineas F. Bresee, whose expanding Church of the Nazarene, like the association, ministered in the "neglected places," invited the association to send observers to his church's annual meeting in Los Angeles. The appearance of Bresee's assistant, C. W. Ruth, at the June 27, 1906, meeting of the association's Missionary Committee made the invitation personal, and the committee appointed three veteran pastors—J. N. Short, A. B. Riggs, and H. N. Brown—to make the long journey across the United States. A union with the Nazarenes, if it were to take place, the committee believed, would "materially help our missionary work."[72]

CONCLUSION

Those churches in the eastern part of the United States that became part of the Church of the Nazarene represented, as Timothy Smith points out, a clergy-centered orientation. The association represented well-established churches rather than simply a string of urban missions. In worship and belief, the association exhibited "churchly" characteristics, strong in means of grace and liberal education, with hymnals, Sunday Schools, and auxiliaries that included home and foreign missions. They sought to preserve a heritage that encouraged both camp meetings and relief for the poor, both emanating out of their insistence upon sanctifying grace.[73]

FOUR

Nazarene Beginnings: The Western Stream

The band of Holiness believers in Los Angeles, California, that met together for the first time on October 6, 1895, contributed the name by which the present-day church is identified. The group centered around one remarkable person, Phineas Franklin Bresee (1838-1915). Though Bresee did not organize the Church of the Nazarene in Los Angeles single-handedly, he dominated its early history. The Southern California beginnings of the Church of the Nazarene mark the denomination as broadly representative of American Christianity.[1]

PHINEAS F. BRESEE

Phineas Bresee was born in a log cabin near the town of Franklin in Delaware County, on the boundary with Otsego County in the Catskill Mountains of southern New York state. His parents, Phineas Phillips and Susan Brown Bresee, raised Phineas, an older sister, and a younger brother (who died when Bresee was about three years old) in a devout Methodist home.[2]

Methodist circuit riders entered the Catskill area shortly after the American Revolution, accompanying the first European-American settlers into that part of New York. The first Methodist class meeting was officially organized in a local schoolhouse in Bartlett Hollow in 1823, just fifteen years before Bresee was born. This territory was typical of frontier Methodism, with itinerant preachers, numerous preaching points, outdoor meetings, fervent sermons, and exuberant revivalist worship. New York was home to many abolitionist groups. The Wesleyan Methodist Connection, a group of Methodist churches, left the Methodist Episcopal Church in 1843 to protest its refusal to unconditionally condemn slavery and embrace abolitionism.[3]

Bresee early developed an interest in the colorful Methodist preachers he heard. Even before Bresee's conversion, he believed that God was calling him to ministry. As an adult Bresee remembered: "I always felt called to preach from the time I was born, or began to know anything."[4] Though Bresee delayed following the divine call, he never wavered from this direction for his life.

Bresee's growing-up years were typical for a boy in this region at the time. He worked on the family farm and attended grammar school, when he could, through the age of twelve. He spent part of two years at the Delaware Literary Institute in Franklin, where he was introduced to broad areas of learning. This was the extent of his formal education, but Bresee remained throughout his life a student of literature and history. When his father sold the family farm and bought an interest in a small general store as Bresee entered his teenage years, Phineas went to work there.[5]

In February 1856 a protracted meeting, typical of revivalist Methodism and much of American Protestantism at the time, was held on the circuit where Bresee's parents lived. During the revival one of the preachers, James W. Smith, paid an afternoon visit to the store where Bresee worked. Smith, Bresee remembered, "spoke a few words to him about his soul," and this caused Bresee to fall "under conviction." He attended the revival meeting that very night in order to "seek salvation" and responded to the altar invitation at its close, but was not converted until a couple of days later. At a Sunday morning Methodist class meeting, as Bresee later recalled, he "realized that the peace of God came into my soul."[6]

Almost immediately Bresee took up the call to ministry. He held prayer meetings in the community and talked to his neighbors about spiritual matters. But when it came to preaching to a congregation of strangers, which Smith arranged for him to do, the "very bashful and modest" Bresee failed to show up. Still, Smith secured for him an exhorter's license (the first step in Methodism in recognizing a person's call to ministry), which, Bresee reported, "I proceeded not to use."[7]

A year after his conversion, Bresee mustered enough courage to preach to a small congregation in a schoolhouse. According to Bresee's own recollection, he preached all the spiritual truth he knew, but the sermon lasted only twenty minutes. Bresee "wondered what in the world a fellow would ever preach about" in a second sermon, "for I had everything [I knew] in that" first one. This was only a few weeks before the Bresee family left the area, having decided, in the summer of 1857, to move westward to Iowa.[8]

BRESEE IN IOWA

The Bresee family became part of a vast migration of settlers to the rolling plains of Iowa (granted statehood in 1846) that was swelling the state's population from less than 200,000 in 1850 to almost 700,000 by 1860. While the new settlers pouring into Iowa represented many different denominations and religious traditions, Methodism, as in most frontier areas, moved in quickly and aggressively, and flourished. When the Bresees arrived, Methodism was the largest denomination in the state. It continued to grow rapidly. With a great need for Methodist preachers, the local presiding elder soon drafted young Bresee to help as a "junior preacher" on the Marengo Circuit. Bresee was assigned a "four weeks' circuit," meaning that it took the preacher four weeks to visit all of its preaching points. The circuit covered several hundred square miles, and its preaching points included schoolhouses, farmhouses, and log cabins. When the preachers arrived for services, the settlers living in the area "would come with their oxen, wagons, horses, guns, babies and older children, and people would gather from far and near."[9] Then the circuit riders would preach the Word, call sinners to repentance, urge Christians to greater devotion, and, every three months at festive quarterly meetings, administer the sacraments of baptism and the Lord's Supper. The traveling preachers offered whatever pastoral care was possible, but much of the responsibility for the preaching points remained with faithful laypersons. Meanwhile, Bresee studied theology and other subjects of the Methodist Course of Study under the direction of a mentor, an older, more experienced minister. That prepared him for eventual ordination and full membership in the Iowa Annual Conference.[10]

In addition to their regular responsibilities Methodist circuit riders conducted periodic revival meetings among their people. Bresee's mentor assigned him this major task. As circuit evangelist, Bresee held numerous revival meetings during 1857 and 1858. He developed skill as an evangelist and became convinced at the very outset of his ministerial career that the health of the church necessitated frequent revivals.[11]

In the fall of 1858, the bishop appointed Bresee, just short of his twentieth birthday, to the Pella Circuit. In this area, a much larger population of non-English-speaking Dutch Calvinists and a sizable group of Baptists reduced the Methodists to a small, scattered minority. Bresee did not have great success here in enlarging the Methodist presence, although he considered his two years on the Pella Circuit to be blessed by God and marked by revival among Methodist believers.[12]

SLAVERY AND TEMPERANCE

Bresee's next assignment was to the Grinnell Circuit, which had five or six preaching points. This assignment, too, was difficult. However, here Phineas enjoyed the support of a companion, having returned to New York just prior to the 1860 Iowa Annual Conference to marry Maria E. Hibbard.[13]

While at Grinnell, Bresee actively supported the abolition of slavery. The Bresee family's move to Iowa had coincided with the Dred Scott Decision in which the U.S. Supreme Court had ruled that slaves were not citizens and did not have the legal rights or protections of citizens. This court action had further polarized and divided a country already on the brink of disorder. The issue of slavery and national union rapidly heated to explosive proportions.[14]

The young state of Iowa, a free state, prohibited slavery, but it shared some two hundred miles of common border on its south with Missouri, a slave state. Iowa was also neighbor to Kansas Territory, a soon-to-be-state that experienced conflict and violence between antislavery and proslavery settlers. Further, the Methodist Church itself had been fractured by the conflict, dividing into separate Northern and Southern General Conferences in 1844. The Northern Church operated in Iowa, while the Southern Church dominated just across the border in Missouri.[15]

Rev. and Mrs. P. F. Bresee

One of the preaching points on the Grinnell Circuit was made up mainly of settlers from the South. Elsewhere as well, Bresee confronted members who supported the rebellion of Southern states from the Union. Bresee, faithful to what he understood the gospel to say about human equality and love for neighbor, angered his Southern-sympathizing parishioners by preaching what they considered abolition doctrine.[16] Further, it is likely that this was also the place, mentioned by E. A. Girvin (though not identified), where Bresee "made a practice of draping his pulpit with the American flag," bringing the wrath of Southerners down upon him.[17]

Bresee asked to be released from the Grinnell Circuit after one difficult year but found himself appointed in 1861 to an even more difficult assignment, the Galesburg Circuit. He developed an "awful determination to win and succeed in accomplishing something" on this "hard scrabble" circuit. Conducting revivals across the circuit, Bresee received 140 people into church membership.[18]

Bresee developed a passion for temperance. Bresee became a member of the temperance committee of the Iowa Annual Conference in 1860, the same year that he was ordained a deacon in the Methodist Episcopal Church, a step toward ordination as elder. This committee recommended that each minister preach at least one temperance sermon per year to every church on his circuit, that Methodists vote only for political candidates who supported prohibition, and that sellers of alcoholic beverages be condemned the same as manufacturers. Bresee vigorously promoted the temperance cause for the rest of his life, and the Church of the Nazarene bore Bresee's imprint in its sustained opposition to alcohol.[19]

Many Christians during the nineteenth century and the early decades of the twentieth century took up this cause. The temperance crusade was an effort to regulate the production, sale, and consumption of alcohol. The conviction that the abuse of alcohol was at the root of many social problems plaguing American society motivated the temperance campaigners. Alcohol-induced evils, reformers believed, included poverty, various kinds of crime, sexual immorality (including the steady growth of prostitution), and domestic violence. The crusade inspired Thomas Welch in 1869 to develop a process for making and distributing pure unfermented grape juice for Communion services so that Christians would no longer have to ingest alcohol during the sacrament of the Lord's Supper. This marked the founding of the Welch's Grape Juice Company.[20] The prohibition crusade also produced organizations such as the Women's Christian Temperance Union (founded 1874) and the Anti-Saloon League of America (founded 1895). It eventually led to the adoption of the Eighteenth Amendment to the U.S. Constitution (1920), which banned the manufacture, transportation, and sale of beverage alcohol in the United States until the Twenty-First Amendment to the Constitution in 1933 overturned this action and handed over the regulation of alcohol to individual states.[21]

Bresee's work on the Galesburg Circuit brought him notice throughout Iowa Methodism. When appointments were made for 1862, the twenty-three-year-old Bresee found himself assigned to Des Moines, a city congregation with a permanent building and a parsonage, though struggling under a heavy financial burden. One of the members of this church was the Iowa secretary of state.[22]

During Bresee's stay at Des Moines (1862-64) the congregation saw measurable improvement in nearly every area. The church wished to retain him for a third year, but the bishop appointed him instead as a presiding elder—superintendent over a group of churches and preachers on the Winterset District in western Iowa. Bresee was only twenty-five years old, an uncommonly young age for this level of responsibility. The work involved almost continuous traveling by horse and carriage over prairie expanse. Bresee used these long hours to his advantage, however (as had John Wesley as he traveled throughout the British Isles), by reading a small library of books, acquiring a kind of college education while on the move. This reading significantly deepened Bresee's knowledge of the world and sharpened his skill as a theologian and preacher.[23]

During his two years as presiding elder Bresee pushed revivals. Converted in a revival, apprenticed for ministry by conducting revivals, and using revivals to good advantage as a pastor, Bresee was unconditionally committed to revivalism, seeing it as vital to Christianity. He held protracted meetings wherever he pastored, but he considered a "constant tide of salvation" or an "ongoing state of revival" even better. As presiding elder he conducted revival campaigns and, as had early nineteenth-century Methodists, made district conferences occasions for revival. Bresee carefully planned meetings, even to the point of choosing hymns to sing and preparing a corps of lay altar workers. Of his demanding years as presiding elder, Bresee observed: "I had a big load of carnality on hand always" which "had taken the form of anger, and pride, and worldly ambition." He also reported that he struggled with doubt about some fundamental doctrines of Christian faith. Apparently he was encountering some of the intellectual skepticism of the age for the first time, and he was unable to answer sufficiently the questions that were being put to him by parishioners or by the popular literature he may have been reading. Bresee asked to be relieved of the superintendency after two years.[24]

Bresee rose to a place of prominence and prestige in the Methodist Episcopal Church. Following his tenure as presiding elder, Bresee served as pastor of Methodist churches in Chariton (1866-68) and Des Moines (1868-70), the same congregation he had left four years before. During his second appointment to Des Moines Bresee sent an account of the entire sanctification of one of his parishioners to *The Guide to Holiness*, edited by Phoebe Palmer. He pastored Council Bluffs (1870-73), which, at the time, was "on the extreme western frontier of civilization" and a major center of Mormonism. During this tenure at Council Bluffs he served as editor for a time of the *Inland Christian Advocate*, a regional Methodist publication. In 1872 he was elected a delegate to the General Conference in Brooklyn, New York. Possibly the youngest delegate there, he played an important role in throwing the support of the Iowa delegation behind Gilbert Haven, an outspoken champion of racial equality (and friendly to the Holiness Movement). Bresee then moved on to Red Oak (1873-76). When in 1876, Bresee turned down a second appointment as presiding elder, the bishop assigned him to Clarinda, a church of considerable wealth and influence. Among the members were successful professionals, community leaders, and a member of the United States Congress. Bresee then pastored at Creston (1879-81) and returned a second time to Council Bluffs (1881-83).[25]

SANCTIFICATION, EDUCATION, AND SPECULATION

About Phineas Bresee during these Iowa years, three things stand out as significant for the history of the Church of the Nazarene: his religious struggle while at Chariton, his involvement with the Methodist college at Indianola, Iowa, and his business ventures.

Bresee went to Chariton in 1866 after having struggled through difficult assignments. He was exhausted in body and spirit. He was steadily climbing the ladder of ecclesiastical success and working extraordinarily hard to make things go. The Chariton congregation, although the most affluent and prestigious church in town, was worldly and contentious. Bresee said that about a quarter of the congregation was always angry with him for something, "but not the same quarter, as they took turns."[26]

All of these things converged in the early months of Bresee's pastorate at Chariton to provoke a personal crisis. Bresee himself served as the evangelist during a protracted meeting during his first winter at the church (a typical Bresee practice). On a bleak, snowy night, with the temperature 20 degrees Fahrenheit below zero, the crowd was small, but Bresee preached fervently and urged seekers to the altar. No one responded, even though Bresee moved among the congregation, personally inviting people to pray (another typical Bresee practice). Then, suddenly, Bresee recalled, "in some way it seemed to me that this was *my time*, and I threw myself down across the altar and began to pray for myself."[27] In response, he experienced what Bresee called, in later years, his "baptism with the Holy Ghost." He admitted, however, that at the time he did not know what it was that he needed, sought for, or received, other than that "the Lord gave him more grace, liberty, and blessing in every way."[28]

By this time the Holiness Movement was moving decisively into its organizational stage. Was the experience at Chariton Phineas Bresee's entire sanctification, the spiritual blessing subsequent to justification that Bresee so fervently advocated and promoted during the last thirty years of his life? Bresee himself thought so, in retrospect, and E. A. Girvin called it this in his biography of Bresee published in 1916, the year after Bresee died. However, from 1866 until he left Iowa in 1883, there was very little emphasis in Bresee's preaching on Christian perfection, and Bresee testified upon relocating to California in 1883: "I was not in the clear enjoyment of the blessing [of entire sanctification]."[29]

When Bresee moved to Chariton, he was appointed to chair a committee to study the educational needs of the Des Moines Annual Conference. Methodists were supporting several schools. The conference had established a school at Indianola, just south of Des Moines, in 1860. The committee recommended that the school in Indianola develop as a liberal arts college. It became Simpson Centenary College (known today simply as Simpson College), in honor of Methodist Bishop Matthew Simpson (1811-84) and the centennial anniversary of American Methodism, celebrated in 1866. Bresee was elected to the reorganized school's first board of trustees, and he served on this body for the next sixteen years. He played a major role in the development of the school, helping to place it on a sound financial footing by buying and then auctioning off at a profit lots adjacent to the college's campus. (Bresee employed this method many years later at the Nazarene University in California.) At the end of his service to the school, the college conferred on Bresee the honorary doctor of divinity. Bresee's involvement with Simpson Centenary College planted in him an interest in and respect for Christian higher education that would later have implications for the Church of the Nazarene.[30]

Bresee also served during this same time as a conference visitor or representative to Garrett Biblical Institute in Evanston, Illinois, which educated persons for Methodist ministry. Bresee was quite positive in his evaluation of the school.[31]

Another development was Bresee's involvement in several business ventures. This murky part of Bresee's life revolved around his friendship with Joseph Knotts, a Methodist minister who at one time had been Bresee's presiding elder. Knotts had retired from ministry in midlife for health reasons and thereafter supported himself through various speculative business enterprises, such as silver mines. Bresee became involved with Knotts's ventures during his tenure at Red Oak (1873-76). Apparently, Bresee became not only a major investor in but a major recruiter of other investors, many of them Methodists. Silver mines were a popular, and highly risky, investment interest of the time. Knotts and Bresee promoted silver mines in Mexico. Exactly what happened is not certain, except that the business ultimately failed and that those who had invested lost their investments. Bresee remembered this as largely due to an accident (an explosion and flood), but there is evidence that Knotts, the mastermind of these projects, may have been guilty of fraud, and that the mines may never have existed.[32]

The major role that Bresee played in Knotts's failed companies was the chief reason that Bresee left Iowa in 1883 and moved to California. Bresee acknowledged: "I felt some degree of embarrassment at the thought of remaining in a country where I was supposed to be wealthy, when, in fact, I was very poor. Hence, I deemed it best to take a transfer to some distant Conference."[33] Furthermore, Bresee found it impossible to mingle with people, fellow ministers and laypeople (including members of his own congregation), who had lost their savings in schemes for which he was partly responsible.

At the same time, failed mining investments cured Bresee of any undue fascination with business or wealth. As he climbed the ladder of ecclesiastical success in Iowa he had cultivated friendships with businessmen in his congregations. The mining failure cleared his mind. "I formed the firm conviction, at that time," Bresee stated, "that I would never more attempt to make money, but would give the remainder of my life, whatever it might be, to the direct preaching of the Word of God."[34]

THE MOVE TO CALIFORNIA

Faced with an uncomfortable, perhaps impossible, future in Iowa, Phineas Bresee considered two possible destinations: San Antonio, Texas, and Los Angeles, California. Some Methodists he knew in San Antonio urged him to become their pastor. Bresee was wary of this, however, because the Southern Methodist Church dominated in Texas, and there was prejudice against Northerners. Bresee had not forgotten the difficulties with Southern sympathizers on the Grinnell Circuit.[35]

Joseph Knotts recommended Southern California. Knotts had visited there and was much impressed. Knotts paid the Bresee family's expenses so that they could move there. Bresee also knew a few recently relocated Iowans in Southern California, including H. C. Sigler, a prominent banker-turned-real estate-developer who arranged for the Methodist presiding elder in Los Angeles to receive Bresee into the Southern California Conference. In August 1883 Bresee and his extended family, which by this time included his parents, wife, six of his seven children (one remained in Iowa to attend college), and nephew, set out for Los Angeles on the Union Pacific Railroad.[36]

The Bresees had little idea of what they would find. Southern California in 1883 was undergoing swift and dramatic transition. For centuries a small, fairly isolated Spanish pueblo surrounded by sprawling cattle ranches, Los Angeles was just beginning to make its way into "Anglo" consciousness. Los Angeles was the center of a new rush for sun, land, health, and wealth. Railroads fueled this. The Southern Pacific had arrived first, in 1876, linking Los Angeles with San Francisco to the north, and to the eastern parts of the United States. The Atchison, Topeka, and Santa Fe Railroad completed its line in 1885, cutting across the deserts of the Southwest. The railroads worked hard to sell this unfamiliar part of the continent to the rest of America. Railroad publicity agents blitzed the rest of the country with word and picture images of Southern California as a sun-drenched, mountain-ringed, ocean-side paradise. This place of empty expanses, temperate climate, clean air, and impressive scenery was an ideal place to visit, to live, and to make one's fortune. Historian Kevin Starr notes: "The railroads brought new varieties of Americans to the Southland: the homesteader, the urban immigrant, the health seeker, the tourist."[37]

The publicists did their job well. The 1880s, when the Bresees arrived, was a decade of explosive growth. By 1890 Southern California as a whole had 130,000 residents, many of them, like the Bresees, new arrivals from the Midwest. Los Angeles grew by nearly 500 percent, from 11,000 people in 1880 to 50,000 in 1890. The once Spanish pueblo was quickly becoming a bustling urban center, while the ranches surrounding it were giving way to new towns and neighborhoods.[38]

This was the frontier, but vastly different from the kind of territory that Bresee had faced in Iowa. On the stark Iowan frontier the Methodist circuit rider rode miles between settlements. In Southern California, by contrast, there were cultural roots already existing in the Spanish and indigenous ("Indian") cultures. Adding to this, migrating settlers created a new society. The speed and intensity of the new settlement, together with the physical distance of Southern California from the rest of the United States, made this area a wide-open and dynamic place. California attracted people seeking the new, the better, the untried, and perhaps even the seemingly impossible.[39]

BRESEE'S MINISTRY IN SOUTHERN CALIFORNIA METHODISM

Even though Los Angeles was strange and unfamiliar territory, Bresee found himself welcomed by Methodists. A. M. Hough, who had been one of Bresee's pastors many years before in New York, pastored the University Methodist Episcopal Church on the campus of the University of Southern California, a school begun by Methodists in 1880. The Annual Conference, which took place the second week he was in town, tasked Bresee with many responsibilities. The conference named him an examiner for the Course of Study, a visitor (trustee) to the University of Southern California, and pastor of one of the city's strongest churches, the oldest and largest Methodist church in the area, the Fort Street Methodist Episcopal Church, also known as First Church.[40]

The scandal of the mining investments did not follow Bresee, or, if it did, the Methodist community in Southern California did not hold it against him. He assumed a place of respect and influence among fellow ministers. Bresee spent three years at Fort Street Church. The congregation included a sizable group of Holiness people who gave clear and definite testimony to the blessing of entire sanctification. They promoted the National Holiness

Association, as the National Camp Meeting Association for the Promotion of Holiness was by then known, and Holiness meetings. One member, Leslie F. Gay (1845-1930), hosted a weekly Holiness meeting in his home patterned on Phoebe Palmer's Tuesday Meeting for the Promotion of Holiness. At last, Phineas Bresee had encountered the organized Holiness Movement.[41]

In 1886 Bresee was appointed to the First Methodist Church in Pasadena. At that time, Pasadena, established in 1873 by migrants from Indiana, was a small but growing town on what had previously been Spanish ranch land, about ten miles northeast of Los Angeles. Starr notes that the settlers of Pasadena "made a vigorous effort to preserve the values of bourgeois life through churches, schools, libraries, and associations for music and debate."[42] Bresee was successful in Pasadena. Finding a church of just over one hundred members, he took it to a membership of more than one thousand. Part of the dramatic increase of this congregation was due to the rapid growth of Pasadena itself, which was in the midst of an intense land boom when Bresee arrived. The sanctuary of the church became so crowded with worshippers that they built a large board tabernacle (like those that could be found at some camp meeting grounds at the time and like Bresee would build later for the Nazarenes) seating two thousand next door to the church. Bresee added evening street corner meetings to reach transient construction workers who were in town building houses in rapidly rising neighborhoods.

Before Bresee left the church in 1890, however, the congregation had declined to under six hundred. Financial difficulties, and perhaps some class conflict, plagued the congregation. Bresee's aggressive leadership of temperance forces in Pasadena stirred opposition in the business community. This distressed some wealthy and influential people in Bresee's congregation. The church lost members due to an exodus of people from Pasadena after its early boom collapsed. The church had overextended its resources in the building of a new sanctuary, and conflict arose over the crude tabernacle built adjacent to the large, attractive new sanctuary, which was to have been a showpiece of a socially and economically respectable Methodism. The board tabernacle harkened back to an earlier, rural and rustic era of Methodism, when Methodists were poor outsiders. The tabernacle would not appeal to the sort of person that Pasadena First wanted to attract. Although Bresee himself did not refer publicly to this controversy, the records of the official church board preserve the story.[43]

A further continuity with Bresee's earlier ministry was his leadership in the prohibition cause in Southern California. By the time Bresee moved to Pasadena, that small city had already voted to be "dry"—that is, to enforce a complete prohibition against selling and buying alcoholic beverages within the city. It banned alcohol in restaurants, hotels, and other public places. However, the city was having difficulty enforcing this law, and the distillers, brewers, and would-be saloon owners contested through the court system the vote for prohibition. The California State Supreme Court upheld the city's right to enforce prohibition. But the judicial process took several years, and during these years there was intense conflict over the issue. Bresee led the fight to keep Pasadena dry and to keep the antiprohibition forces at bay. He supported a boycott against businesses that refused to enforce the city's law, as well as businessmen who would not openly support the prohibition cause. As a result his opponents sometimes disrupted his worship services and attacked him in the public press. On one occasion a group of antiprohibition demonstrators burned Bresee in effigy.[44]

Bresee in Southern California remained, as he had been in Iowa, a popular figure among his peers. He was regularly elected at the Annual Conference to places of leadership and responsibility, capped in 1891 by his election on the first ballot as a delegate to the 1892 General Conference. At the same Annual Conference he was appointed presiding elder of the Los Angeles District.

Bresee exhibited his same passion for revivals in Southern California as in Iowa. He scheduled revival meetings in every congregation he pastored, sometimes serving as his own evangelist and sometimes inviting noted guest preachers. When he became presiding elder he spent three of his first six months conducting revival meetings in various churches across the district. The stirrings of revival were essential to a healthy Christianity.[45]

BRESEE AND ORGANIZED HOLINESS

The spiritual vitality of the Holiness-minded laypersons in his congregations impressed Bresee. They in turn embraced and supported Bresee, although, initially, they knew that he was, at this point, not in full sympathy with them. Bresee later recalled that "they seemed to appreciate whatever efforts I could and did make in assisting them in the work of holiness" while "they doubtless prayed much for me," noting that "they did not pray at me, and they stood close by me, and sustained me in every way throughout my ministry."[46]

During the second year of his ministry at First Church (1885), Bresee had William MacDonald, president of the National Holiness Association, and George D. Watson, also a prominent Holiness evangelist, conduct a three-week revival. The most remarkable result according to Bresee's recollection was upon Bresee himself. He became aware of his own deep spiritual needs. "This realization grew more and more intense," Bresee reported, "until my heart cry began to go out to God for the mighty grace that was adequate to all my needs."[47]

Bresee experienced an unusual event. Bresee remembered:

> I had been for some time in almost constant prayer, and crying to God for something that would meet my needs, not clearly realizing what they were, or how they could be met. I sat alone in the parsonage, in the cool of the evening, in the front parlor near the door. The door being opened, I looked up into the azure in earnest prayer, while the shades of evening gathered about. As I waited and waited, and continued in prayer, looking up, it seemed to me as if from the azure there came a meteor, an indescribable ball of condensed light, descending rapidly toward me. As I gazed upon it, it was soon within a few score feet, when I seemed to hear a voice saying, as my face was upturned towards it: "Swallow it; swallow it," and in an instant it fell upon my lips and face. I attempted to obey the injunction. It seemed to me, however, that I swallowed only a little of it although it felt like fire on my lips, and the burning sensation did not leave them for several days. While all of this of itself would be nothing, there came with it into my heart and being, a transformed condition of life and blessing and unction and glory, which I had never known before. I felt that my need was supplied.

Though Bresee said very little about this experience, he believed that there came into his ministry "a new element of spiritual life and power." People were both converted and brought into the blessing of "full salvation." During the last year of his ministry at First Church there was almost constant revival. What was significant for Bresee was his sense of new spiritual resources, with visible results in his ministry.[48]

Bresee himself never referred to this as his entire sanctification and explicitly identified his experience in Chariton, Iowa, seventeen years before, as his "baptism with the Holy Ghost."[49] Yet Bresee also stated that when he first arrived in Southern California he was not "in the experience," and that, if he had been, he might "have swept the whole of [Southern California] Methodism into holiness." So Bresee's testimony to entire sanctification is almost as perplexing as the lack of such in the writings of John Wesley.[50]

These turning points were part of a larger story, the arrival of organized holiness in Southern California. Hardin Wallace, a Methodist minister from Illinois who had become a full-time itinerating Holiness evangelist in the early 1870s, organized the Southern California and Arizona Holiness Association in July 1880. Just prior to his work in California he had organized a Holiness association in Texas. In January 1881 Wallace held meetings in Fort Street

Methodist Episcopal Church, where Phineas Bresee became pastor two years later. Beginning as bands whose purpose was to promote Holiness revivalism and provide fellowship for Holiness believers from various denominations, the Southern California and Arizona Holiness Association soon became a hub for come-outism. Several influential leaders of the association—especially James Washburn and Josephine Washburn, James Swing, and B. A. Washburn—advocated ideas about the Church similar to those of D. S. Warner and other restorationist Holiness leaders in the Midwest. They taught that a pure New Testament Church, the true church, was made up of only entirely sanctified believers. Beginning in 1882, bands connected with the association incorporated themselves as independent Holiness churches, and the association soon reorganized itself as the Holiness Church of California.[51]

When Phineas Bresee arrived in Los Angeles in 1883 Hardin Wallace's work was well underway. During Bresee's first Methodist Annual Conference in California, delegates addressed the matter of unauthorized evangelists. The conference adopted a resolution that "no member of this Conference shall employ any evangelist or any person doing the work of an evangelist on his charge, unless such evangelist or person shall have an annual written certification of character and fitness for evangelistic work from the Presiding Elder ... and the consent of the majority of the official members of such charge."[52] The Methodist Church's restrictions on itinerants reflected its desire for boundaries and order. (Had the Church of England and the established churches in early American history been successful in preventing itineration, there would have been no Wesleyan or Methodist movement.)[53] The same conference approved disciplinary action that stripped Hardin Wallace and B. A. Washburn of their Methodist ministerial credentials.[54]

Several months after this Bresee's ministerial colleagues chose him to preach at a district conference. He preached on Christian perfection, but, obviously aimed at Wallace, Washburn, and other Holiness come-outers, condemned using the doctrine as an instrument of schism. "Full sanctification," said Bresee, was not "an end" in itself, but a condition that allowed the "graces of the Spirit" to more fully "live and grow in us." Testimony to full sanctification should be made humbly and prudently, *not* "always and everywhere." The most effective and appropriate testimony to holiness is not words at all, Bresee admonished, but a *life* that exhibited the gracious transformation of character. That was the truest expression of holiness. Bresee further declared that when "the name and profession of holiness have been made the scape-goat for attempts to create schism in the Church of God—when it has been made a pretense for slandering the ministers of religion, and slighting the means of grace—when in the name of holiness men are urged to forsake the mother that bore them and turn their back on the churches that have carried them in their arms—when this is done until the community is almost sickened at the very name [of holiness] itself, good men bow their heads in sorrow."[55]

The convention responded to Bresee's sermon by adopting a resolution affirming that "it is the duty of all Christians to be holy in heart and life," and "it has been and is the especial mission of our church to spread 'scriptural holiness' over all lands." The convention formed a committee that included Bresee to correspond with the National Holiness Association "with a view to the establishment of a branch association" in Southern California. This was an attempt to curtail come-outism by endorsing and supporting a denominationally loyal form of the Holiness Movement.[56]

Bresee's appointment to a committee charged with cultivating ties with the National Holiness Association was an important factor in his willingness to receive NHA evangelists MacDonald and Watson into his own pulpit a year later. Still, Bresee did not yet embrace the organized Holiness Movement. Bresee stated: "At that time I did not preach the second work of grace very definitely. I preached it, but did not give it such emphasis as called out opposition, or as led so many people into the experience as otherwise would probably have been the case." He also noted that "during my pastorate in the First church, my ministry was in the transition state."[57] Bresee was trying to determine his place.

In his Pasadena pastorate, from 1886 to 1890, Bresee finally cast his lot with the increasingly vocal, visible, and controversial Holiness advocates in the Methodist Episcopal Church. William MacDonald, among the early organizers of the National Camp Meeting Association, and J. A. Wood, author of the widely published *Perfect Love* and *Purity and Maturity*, held meetings for Bresee. At his own special services, Bresee promoted holiness and made full salvation an emphatic part of his regular preaching and pastoral teaching. Some of his congregation objected to this. Girvin stated simply, "At the end of the fourth year [of Bresee's pastorate], opposition of some strength had developed against the preaching and work of holiness, and a few of the members, who were influential because of their wealth and standing, opposed Dr. Bresee, and objected to his return to the charge, because of his favorable attitude toward holiness."[58] The Methodist Episcopal Church had extended the maximum term for pastors to stay in one congregation from three to five years, and Bresee's presiding elder and bishop wanted to appoint Bresee for a fifth year, but he declined. "He felt that he could not work advantageously in a church where some of the members were antagonistic to the gospel that he preached."[59]

Rather than stay in Pasadena for another year, Bresee agreed to go to the Asbury Methodist Church in Los Angeles. This church was struggling and some of its members thought that Bresee was just the person to help them through a number of difficult issues. Soon after his appointment he organized a Holiness campaign with MacDonald and Wood. The famous black evangelist Amanda Berry Smith (1837-1915) also preached for Bresee during this time. According to Bresee's own recollection, the result was that nearly all the members of the church board "came into the experience of sanctification." There was a "great tide of victory" throughout the congregation. Bresee spent nine weeks of his tenure at Asbury away from Los Angeles preaching in National Holiness Association revivals.[60]

After barely a year at Asbury Church Bresee expected to return as pastor, but instead Bishop Willard Mallalieu, a friend to holiness, appointed Bresee presiding elder of the Los Angeles District. Not wanting to simply mark time as an ecclesiastical administrator, and more and more impressed with his obligation to lead Christians into the blessing of full sanctification, Bresee seized the opportunity as presiding elder, as Mallalieu hoped he would, to push the work of holiness among all the churches on the Los Angeles District. Bresee, assisted by Holiness preachers, conducted evangelistic meetings and conferences on entire sanctification. According to Bresee, these meetings profoundly affected many churches. However, not surprisingly, they also stirred opposition.[61]

Presiding at the 1892 Annual Conference was Bishop John H. Vincent, an outspoken critic of organized holiness. Vincent was a leading advocate of the modern, respectable Methodism that was emerging in the late nineteenth century. He headed the Chautauqua movement, which replaced traditional camp meetings with adult education, popular lectures, and family recreation. Vincent fraternized with American presidents and other people of power and influence. He did not consider the passionate, evangelistic promotion of Christian perfection as advocated by Bresee and his National Holiness Association colleagues to be desirable in a denomination honored among churches and society. Vincent did not reappoint Bresee as presiding elder (a decision with which Bresee declared he was in complete accord). Instead, Vincent appointed Bresee pastor of Simpson Church in Los Angeles.[62]

Bresee had met with some members of this church prior to the Annual Conference. They had asked Bresee to become their pastor, should the bishop approve. Simpson Church, heavily in debt, was on the verge of financial collapse. The recently built sanctuary seated twenty-five hundred people, but the congregation consisted of only a few hundred. Apparently misled about the size of Simpson's debt, Bresee discovered a dire situation. A severe economic depression sweeping the country threw people out of work, inspiring strikes and labor unrest, causing people to lose their homes and savings and forcing many to move in order to find work. Within a few months after becoming pastor, a discouraged Bresee recommended that the church close and the congregation merge with another, or that the church relocate to a more affluent part of town where it would have a better chance to survive (an interesting suggestion in light of Bresee's later commitment to minister to the poor). Bresee had supporters in the congregation, including a prominent Los Angeles judge and businessman, R. M. Widney, and his family; a well-known attorney, W. S. Knott, and his wife, Lucy (who would become one of the first persons ordained in the Church of the Nazarene), and Bresee's own son, Phineas W. Bresee, who was by this time a successful merchant. Yet Bresee attributed his difficulties at Simpson to the fact that there "were very few in the church who were willing to accept the deeper things of God, and such consecration and faith as were required to enable them to enter into the glory and power of the Pentecost."[63]

After just a year at Simpson, Bresee was appointed pastor of the Boyle Heights Church just east of downtown Los Angeles. Boyle Heights, like Simpson, had financial and other problems. However, Bresee was able to work through these and his year as pastor (1893-94) ended with statistical increases in every area of congregational life and a strong sense of spiritual victory among the members.[64]

PENIEL MISSION

Bresee's year at Boyle Heights, though not the most noteworthy of his career, was a critical turning point. During this year Bresee conversed with Theodore P. and Manie Payne Ferguson, who operated a nondenominational Holiness mission in downtown Los Angeles. Theodore Ferguson was a graduate of Oberlin College, where perfectionist teachings were still influential when he attended in the 1870s. Moving to California in 1879, Ferguson, a Presbyterian, experienced entire sanctification in a camp meeting held by the Holiness bands associated with Hardin Wallace and others.[65]

The Fergusons saw people in Los Angeles "sleeping on floors, in railroad cars, and many more comical places." Manie Ferguson later recalled, "Ordinary accommodations bore no proportion to the influx of people that crowded everywhere."[66] Burdened for these new urban masses, and aware that the established churches did not have the resources to minister adequately to them, the Fergusons rented quarters and began the Los Angeles Mission, a small work that offered evangelistic services every night (starting with street-corner meetings to attract a crowd), a simple meal, and inexpensive accommodations. The mission occupied temporary quarters.

During much of his career in the Methodist Episcopal Church, Bresee had pastored large, flourishing, affluent churches. He fellowshipped comfortably with wealthy parishioners. There is little hint before 1894 that this was distasteful to him or that he considered wealth and power a danger to the Church. After the business failure in Iowa Bresee had decided that he "would never more attempt to make money" but would focus all his energy on the "direct preaching of the Word of God."[67] He applied this precept only to himself, not to other Christians, even other ministers. Bresee had passionately opposed slavery too; but preference for the poor was not a major mark of his ministry prior to 1894. Bresee simply said in remarks to E. A. Girvin that "it had been my long cherished desire to have a place in the heart of the city, which could be made a center of holy fire, and where the gospel could be preached to the poor. In the early part of this year (1894), such an opportunity presented itself."[68]

P. F. Bresee

In 1894 the Los Angeles Mission, now called Peniel Mission, moved into permanent quarters, a new three-story building named Peniel Hall. "Peniel" or "Penuel," commonly used in the Holiness Movement, was taken from Gen. 32:30-31, where Jacob wrestled all night with a divine being and named the place "Peniel," "the face of God." Many Holiness people thought of Jacob's encounter with God as a fitting image for receiving the blessing of entire sanctification—a "second" encounter with God. (Jacob's first encounter was at Bethel, recounted in Gen. 28). The building was paid for by a wealthy Englishman, George B. Studd, whose interest in sanctification had been stimulated by D. L. Moody, the Higher Life conferences that took place in Keswick, England, and the Holiness conferences at Star Hall, Manchester. The Peniel Mission housed a thousand-seat auditorium as well as ample space for many other church enterprises. Bringing Phineas F. Bresee, perhaps the best-known Holiness preacher in Southern California, into the leadership of the mission seemed a masterful idea.[69]

Another prominent Methodist active in the mission was Joseph Widney, a brother of Judge R. M. Widney, one of Bresee's parishioners at Simpson

Church. Joseph Widney was a physician, businessman, and educator. Widney was one of the principal founders of the University of Southern California's medical school. He served for a time as president of the university while Bresee served on the school's board of trustees. While serving as president of USC, Widney agreed to be one of the preachers at Peniel Hall and to organize a medical training program for Christian workers. Widney recently had been licensed to preach in the Methodist Episcopal Church and was pursuing ordination.[70]

In early 1894, only a few months into his pastorate at Boyle Heights, Bresee joined the staff of Peniel Mission as editor of its paper, the *Peniel Herald*. Bresee believed that it would be simple for his bishop to assign him to Peniel Hall rather than to a regular Methodist congregation. He made such a request to his Annual Conference in 1894. Yet, his request for a special "supernumerary" relationship to minister in a non-Methodist organization was nearly unprecedented and proved controversial. The conference denied the request. Bresee stated the situation succinctly: "The action of the Conference placed me in a position where I could not remain one of its members and go on with the work for which I had arranged, without transgressing the law of the church. So, after a night of prayer and thought, I told my Presiding Elder that he might ask for me a location. This he did, and it was granted without apparent reluctance. . . I was now out of the Conference."[71]

The "location" to which Bresee referred was Methodist language for an ordained minister no longer holding regular ministerial assignments within the church. Such a minister still held ministerial credentials but no longer had membership in an Annual Conference. He was considered on retired or inactive status. This was a huge blow to one who had served in Methodist ministry for nearly forty years. "I had been a member of an annual Conference from the time of my boyhood, having united with the Iowa Annual Conference when I was 18 years of age," Bresee recalled. "I scarcely knew any other home relationship in the church than the annual conference, and when I laid it down that day, it seemed to me that I had laid down everything pertaining to the church which I had so loved and labored for."[72]

Bresee's unceremonious expulsion occurred less than a year after he formed his relationship with the Peniel Mission. The Fergusons and their main financial supporter, G. B. Studd, made the major decisions, leaving Bresee out of important deliberations. While Bresee was in the eastern United States in the summer of 1895, preaching in camp meetings sponsored by the National Holiness Association, the Fergusons informed him that they no longer needed him on the mission staff. Bresee was fired.[73]

Hints here and there help to define what separated Bresee not only from the Fergusons but from other elements in the broader Holiness Movement. Bresee simply said about the episode, "I prefer to draw a veil."[74] Neither Theodore Ferguson, influenced by Oberlin, nor Studd, introduced to sanctification teaching by D. L. Moody, spoke of holiness in the same terms as Methodists such as Bresee. They differed as to whether sin was "cleansed" from believers' hearts by the baptism with the Holy Spirit.

Another source of conflict may have developed around divine healing. Various views of healing swirled through the Holiness Movement, including the teaching among some that resorting to professional medical help revealed a lack of faith in God to heal the body. A. B. Simpson, like T. P. Ferguson, a former Presbyterian, held special meetings at Peniel Mission and forcefully advocated "faith healing." Bresee considered divine healing to be a side issue. The first Nazarene *Manual*s did not mention divine healing. J. P. Widney taught medical skills to young workers at Peniel Mission. Any deprecation of physicians and medicine, explicit or implied, would certainly undermine this.[75]

Another cause of conflict was the desire of the Fergusons that the Peniel Mission broaden its scope to include foreign as well as urban missions. By late 1895 the Fergusons had opened branches of the Peniel Mission in Alaska and the Marianas Islands. To Bresee this was a distraction from Peniel's purpose and an unnecessary diversion of its resources. He hoped that the mission would be a center of fire for holiness, a place to reach impoverished urban people with the gospel of full salvation.

Related to this was the matter of whether the Peniel Mission would continue to be nondenominational, supported by contributors and volunteers who were members of the various denominations, or whether Peniel Mission would attract its own parishioners and assume the role of a congregation for those who had no other church. Within just a few months of his joining the mission, Bresee published in the *Peniel Herald*, which he edited, a Declaration of Principles, a statement of faith that persons connected with the mission would be expected to endorse. Bresee remarked that the mission must care for "those that are being gathered in, who have no church home and work." The editor of the *California Christian Advocate*, the official voice of the Methodist Episcopal Church in the state, charged that Bresee was setting up a new church. This called forth ghosts of painful schisms in Methodism and focused attention on the divisive potential of holiness.[76]

Finally, there was the matter of worship. From his earliest days as a Methodist minister, Bresee had advocated fervent, revivalistic, free styles of worship that included spontaneous shouts of praise, testimonies, and lively hymn singing. Like both Jonathan Edwards and John Wesley, Bresee did not deny that emotional expressions might authentically express the divine presence.[77] The Fergusons, however, preferred formality. Manie Payne Ferguson wrote poetry and hymns, and one of her best-known was "Blessed Quietness," which was published about the time the split with Bresee occurred. She penned: "Blessed quietness! Holy quietness! / What assurance in my soul!" "Bringing life and health and gladness: / and we just obey and rest," and "What a peaceful habitation! / What a quiet resting place." Some referred to the Fergusons and their associates as the "Blessed Quietness crowd." (Her hymn had an enduring place in Nazarene hymnals nonetheless.)[78]

THE CHURCH OF THE NAZARENE

The fundamental fact for Phineas Bresee in the fall of 1895 was that, at age fifty-seven, he suddenly had no place to minister. He had effectively resigned from Methodist ministry and now had been dismissed from Peniel Mission. Persons who had formed attachments to Bresee during his years of Methodist ministry in Los Angeles, and who embraced Bresee's advocacy of Christian perfection, rallied. Bresee's well-placed friends, including J. P. Widney, attorney W. S. Knott and Lucy Knott, Bresee's former parishioners, came forward, as did Bresee's own businessman son, Paul Bresee. This strong nucleus of supporters persuaded Bresee to organize a congregation and to become their pastor.

The group rented space in Red Men's Hall (owned by the Society of Red Men, a men's fraternal organization), a small building only a block from the spacious Peniel Mission. Bresee immediately secured the services of evangelist J. A. Wood, who had worked closely with him in the past. The group announced its first meeting in local newspapers:

Permit us to inform you that Rev. P. F. Bresee, D.D., will preach next Sabbath, October 6th, at 11:00 a.m., in the hall at 317 South Main Street, Los Angeles, Cal., instead of at Peniel Hall as heretofore. There will be a special holiness meeting in the same place at 3 p.m., conducted by Rev. J. A. Wood, D.D. Rev. J. P. Widney, L.L.D. will preach at 7:30 p.m. We are also very glad to be able to announce to you that Drs. Widney and Bresee have arranged to associate themselves, together with such Christian people as may desire to join with them to carry on Christian work, especially evangelistic and city mission work, and the spreading of the doctrine and experience of Christian holiness.[79]

The presence of Wood on this first Sunday lent credibility. The *Los Angeles Times* reported on these services the next morning under the headings "New

Denomination" that "Drs. Bresee and Widney will found a new church." Girvin recorded in his diary less than two weeks after this first meeting: "The Doctor has been driven to it, and regards it as the will of the Lord that he should do this."[80] Whether or not Bresee intended to lead Peniel Mission away from nondenominationalism when he affiliated with it in 1894, by October 1895 he had established an independent church.

On October 20, 1895, Bresee's followers officially organized themselves into the "Church of the Nazarene." By the time the roll of charter members closed a few days later, it contained over one hundred names.[81] These first Nazarenes knew why they had come together. They professed a definite sense of divine calling. They intended to be a church, not a mission or association. They were committed to the doctrine of entire sanctification as a second definite work of divine grace. And, finally, they believed that they had a special mission to the urban poor. The congregation elected Phineas Bresee and J. P. Widney as copastors and cosuperintendents of the new church.

The official minutes recorded the earliest steps toward organization: "Feeling clearly called of God to the carrying on of His work in the conversion of sinners, the sanctification of believers and the building up in holiness of those who may be committed to our care we associate ourselves together as a church of God under the name of the Church of the Nazarene." The congregation affirmed that "the field of labor to which we feel especially called is in the neglected quarters of the cities and wherever also may be found waste places and souls seeking pardon and cleansing from sin." The means of carrying out this ministry would include "city missions, evangelistic services, house-to-house visitation, caring for the poor, comforting the dying." The minutes also included seven simple articles of faith, declaring belief

1. In one God, the Father, Son and Holy Ghost.
2. In the inspiration of the Holy Scriptures as found in the Old and New Testaments, and that they contain all truth necessary to faith and practice.
3. That man is born with a fallen nature, and is thus by nature inclined to evil and that continually.
4. In the sure loss of the finally impenitent.
5. That the atonement through Christ is universal, and whosoever hears the word of the Lord and repents and believes on the Lord Jesus Christ is saved from the condemnation and dominion of sin. That a soul is entirely sanctified subsequent to justification through faith in the Lord Jesus Christ.

6. That the Spirit of God bears witness in the human heart to justification by faith and to the further work of entire sanctification of believers.
7. In the resurrection of the dead and the life everlasting.[82]

The name these first Nazarenes chose for themselves was significant. Unlike the Wesleyan Methodists and Free Methodists, the name did not readily identify the group as Methodist in background. Unlike several other new groups, they did not adopt a name with "holiness" in it. Although they acknowledged organizing themselves together as "a church of God," they chose not to call themselves Church of God or Church of Christ, names popular in Holiness circles. Unlike the New Englanders, neither did they use the term "Pentecostal." Instead, they called themselves "the Church of the Nazarene," meaning, "the Church that follows or belongs to Jesus, who was called 'the Nazarene.'"

During the 1890s a few Protestant pastors with sympathies for the social gospel criticized the middle-class formalities of their denominations and identified the struggles of their toiling, working-class members with Jesus the Carpenter. "The church has lost its way," a song published in 1894 complained: "she follows not the path of old; and the cross has lost its sway. They follow not the laws of Christ, that lowly Nazarene; the Bible on the shelf is laid; and gold is king supreme."[83] In ways similar to the social gospeler Washington Gladden, Bresee and Widney envisioned preaching to middle-class persons who could effect social change for the working-class and urban poor.[84]

On the morning of the church's official organization Widney preached from Matt. 4:19, Jesus' call to Peter and Andrew to "follow me." The central mission of the new church, Widney told the congregation, was to respond to this same call, to live life with Jesus and to live it like Jesus. Everything else was secondary. Christianity was not primarily a creed, he told those gathered, nor was it essentially an institution or a ritual. It was, rather, a life of obedience to Jesus. The New Testament accounts of Jesus' life revealed one who mingled with outcasts—prostitutes, tax collectors, beggars, and the physically disabled, and who brought good news of God's grace and forgiveness to such forgotten people. The New Testament depicted a Jesus who was mocked and reviled by people with power and influence because of His close identification with lowly and powerless people. Even the town where He was brought up, Nazareth, was a source of scorn: "Can there any good thing come out of Nazareth?" (John 1:46).[85] Thus, according to Widney, the most fitting name for a Christian church, a gathering of followers of Christ, was the "Church of the Nazarene," a name that symbolized "the toiling, lowly mission of Christ" and the mission of Christ's followers. Those who sought to truly follow Jesus of Nazareth, Jesus "the Nazarene," gave themselves to the outcasts and neglected persons of this world, and might find themselves similarly scorned and reviled as Nazarenes.[86]

The first piece of literature these Nazarenes printed was a small flyer advertising their meetings. It identified the Church of the Nazarene as

a simple, primitive church, a church of the people and for the people. It has no new doctrines, only the old, old Bible truths. It seeks to discard all superfluous forms and ecclesiasticism and go back to the plain simple words of Christ. It is not a mission, but a church with a mission. It is a banding together of hearts that have found the peace of God, and which now in their gladness, go out to carry the message of the unsearchable riches of the gospel of Christ to other suffering, discouraged, sin-sick souls. Its mission is to everyone upon whom the battle of life has been sore, and to every heart that hungers for cleansing from sin. Come.

The flyer also carried the note: "We endeavor to supply medical attendance for those who are unable to provide it for themselves."[87]

EARLY DEVELOPMENT AND EXPANSION OF THE CHURCH OF THE NAZARENE

Within a month after the first service at Red Men's Hall, the growing congregation required a larger meeting place. On Thanksgiving Day 1895 the Nazarenes moved to a larger building, where they stayed until the early spring of 1896. A decision by the owner of the building to renovate forced them to move again.

After much prayer and discussion, the congregation decided to lease property and erect a temporary building. They found and leased a lot and purchased boards and shingles for the building. Members of the congregation did much of the work. This well-remembered Glory Barn was "a board structure with sides and roof, but in the mild climate of Southern California, it was sufficiently comfortable."[88] At first able to seat about four hundred, it was later enlarged. The congregation worshipped there for the next seven years, and the odd building itself became a sort of tourist attraction in Los Angeles. One eastern tourist, finally getting a look at the celebrated Nazarene Glory Barn, stood gazing at it for a long time, then asked his bus driver, "Is that all?" Other visitors told their friends about Nazarene worship: "You never saw anything like it. The people sang and shouted and stood up and said they were sanctified, and it was the greatest thing you ever saw."[89]

A stream of nationally known Holiness evangelists passed through the board tabernacle, connecting the Los Angeles congregation to the larger Holiness Movement. Evangelists such as Henry Clay Morrison, Bud Robinson, C. W. Ruth, and Seth C. Rees spread news of the Nazarenes everywhere they went. In January 1898 the new church started *The Nazarene* (in 1900 changed to *The Nazarene Messenger*) to systematically publicize its work. At first Bresee and Widney edited the paper, assisted by several associate editors.

In January 1897 Bresee held meetings in Berkeley, California, at the invitation of E. A. Girvin. A Methodist, Girvin discovered the Nazarenes during his many trips to Los Angeles to do business on behalf of the California Supreme Court as a stenographer. Bresee organized a congregation in Berkeley with Girvin as pastor, the second congregation to bear the name Church of the Nazarene. Three months later Bresee organized a third Church of the Nazarene in Oakland, California. During the summer and fall he formed new congregations in the Elysian Heights section of Los Angeles (east of downtown) and in South Pasadena. By the spring of 1898, the Church of the Nazarene in California had thus grown to five congregations. Bresee and Widney called a council of the churches, which laid the groundwork for a "delegated meeting" six months later.

The October 1898 Assembly, held at the board tabernacle, ratified a *Manual* for the whole church. The *Manual* provided a simple, clear form of organization and committed the church to a brief statement of beliefs and essential practices. Organization was pragmatic: "It has not been thought wise to encumber the Church with unnecessary machinery, but to leave to the future such legislation as the growth and development of the work may demand. We deem primitive simplicity in church government the most desirable, and this is what we have sought."[90]

Unlike the Methodist Church (which had derived the practice from the Church of England), the Church of the Nazarene chose not to ordain ministers as deacons as a step toward being ordained as elders. Each local congregation was to elect a church board consisting of stewards and trustees, and a Sunday School superintendent to work together with the pastor. Significantly, the *Manual* included among its general rules the statement, "We recognize the equal right of both men and women to all offices of the Church, including the ministry."[91] The church's forthright acceptance of women as ministers came in the middle of lively debates in the Methodist Episcopal Church over seating women as delegates in its General Conferences.[92]

Similar to the responsibilities the Methodist Church gave to bishops, the *Manual* gave to the general superintendents powers to organize new congregations and to appoint pastors. The *Manual* provided for an annual assembly of both pastors and lay delegates to enact legislation and elect the general superintendents. When the church began in 1895 Bresee and Widney had been elected general superintendents for life. However, by 1898 there was uneasiness about this, and delegates decided to shorten the term of office to one year and to vote on the superintendents annually. The assembly asked both Bresee and Widney to resign and to stand again for election. Both then resigned as general superintendents *and* as copastors of the Los Angeles congregation. Rather than submit to reelection as general superintendent, Widney resigned from the Church of the Nazarene. Historian Carl Bangs contends that Widney was becoming uncomfortable with several developments in the new church, including the free expression of emotion in worship, an emphasis on definite, dramatic religious experiences, and, possibly, the control of finances. Widney returned to the Methodist Church, which recognized his Nazarene ordination, and established a mission that he called the Nazarene Methodist Episcopal Church. However, within a few years Widney left Methodism and organized a less traditional independent congregation, "Beth-El, a Chapel and Manse of the Church of the All-Father." Always an energetic entrepreneur, during the rest of his long life (he lived to the age of ninety-seven) Widney engaged in an astonishing variety of religious, philanthropic, civic, and political enterprises. After Widney's withdrawal from the Church of the Nazarene, Bresee was reelected as general superintendent (for a one-year term), as well as pastor of Los Angeles First Church.[93]

The second General Assembly convened in the board tabernacle on October 16, 1899. Thirty-three delegates attended, eleven ministers and twenty-two laypeople. This assembly heard reports from the Board of Directors of the Nazarene Publishing Company, from new congregations, including the Mateo Street Mission (cofounded and pastored by Lucy P. Knott), and churches in both Cucamonga and Redlands (northeast of Los Angeles), as well as from the churches in Elysian Heights, South Pasadena, Oakland, and Berkeley.[94]

In addition, leaders described a lively youth ministry involving Company E for young women and the Brotherhood of Saint Stephen for young men. Both organizations had been formed to meet the spiritual and social needs of young people and to give them a place of significant ministry in the church. On occasion they held street meetings in Los Angeles like this one:

> One Tuesday evening . . . [the Brotherhood of Saint Stephen] held their regular weekly service at the Plaza, and had great victory. A sister who was with them, sang a song in Spanish, and a Mexican, who had been converted the previous Sabbath, gave a clear testimony of the power of God to save. Then Brother Shaw, standing in the open air, and in the heart of the . . . Mexican business section of the city, earnestly urged seekers to come to the fountain of Jesus' blood. While he was exhorting,

a bright young man . . . knelt on the ground, and the Lord's children knelt around him and engaged in fervent prayer. He soon wept his way to Calvary, and with shining face told the people what God had done for his soul, at the same time exhorting them to do as he had done.[95]

On a typical occasion in which over one thousand Nazarenes, young and old, participated, "Boating, bathing and a good picnic did good service to the outer man, while a genuine Nazarene service refreshed the spirits of all."[96] At other times young people enjoyed fellowship (always with a spiritual objective!) at Los Angeles area beaches.[97]

Subsequent annual assemblies, with Bresee presiding, followed until the union with the Association of Pentecostal Churches of America in 1907. Delegates discussed matters of importance to the growing denomination and, when needed, crafted and adopted legislation.[98]

Timothy L. Smith provides a good summary of the characteristics of the early Nazarenes before the mergers of 1907 and 1908. First, they possessed a democratic church government. The local church board was powerful. But board members took no pledges to raise money, nor did they directly solicit or collect tithes. All was to be voluntary. The church kept no records of individuals' gifts. Deaconesses undertook work among the poor. The church recognized the right of women not only to preach the gospel but also to be ordained.[99]

Second, the Church of the Nazarene preached holiness to the poor. By their example as well as their words the Nazarenes protested fine, expensive church buildings. Rather, everything should say "welcome" to the poor." Still reacting to the practice of paid pew rentals, Bresee's philosophy was that the poorest of the poor were entitled to a front seat at the Church of the Nazarene.

Third, discipline depended more upon the work of the Holy Spirit than either written rules or church punishments. The few specified rules included ones admonishing members not to profane the Lord's Day by unnecessary labor or business. They must not use intoxicating liquors or buy or sell the same for profit. They must not be dishonest in any sort of business transaction. And, finally, the *Manual* admonished Nazarenes to avoid the indulgence of pride in dress or living. Bresee and his pastors informally admonished members against membership in secret societies and the use of tobacco. They avoided becoming too explicit on women's dress. Bresee's aim, Smith concludes, "was not to make well-to-do people dress poorly, but to inspire them to love and service. Both rich and poor, he believed, must learn to worship and work and pray together in the joyous unity which Pentecost could bring."[100] Bresee urged broadness of spirit. He warned against emphasizing nonessentials and against imposing standards on others.

Fourth, Bresee's church kept doctrinal beliefs to a minimal core. Perfect love was the one doctrine around which all could unite.[101]

Fifth, worship was joyously free. Bresee sought to "bring the glory down" in worship services. The church held Sunday School picnics at the beach. Members visited neighbors and the sick and shut-in on Sunday afternoons. In their new church, completed in 1906, they cooked Sunday dinners in the church basement especially for the needy. Other activities included the old Methodist custom of love feasts, undertaken around Christmastime. Nazarenes sang the latest popular hymns and gospel songs, accompanied by a musical band. They clapped their hands while singing. Bresee perfected a conversational style of pulpit delivery. He spoke as if he were talking personally to each one. Bresee's personal attributes, greeting each one when he or she came into the church, and escorting the most poorly dressed ones to their seats, set the tone of service. Bresee remained in the front of the sanctuary after each service in case someone might have a spiritual need.

EXPANSION BEYOND CALIFORNIA

As large a field as California was for Holiness evangelism, the Church of the Nazarene reached beyond. The first Nazarene congregation outside of California was organized by a zealous young itinerant minister, William Allison, at Schiller, Texas (near San Antonio), in November 1901. A natural move for the church was into the Pacific Northwest, where the first Nazarene congregation was formed at Spokane, Washington, in 1902. The Washington State Holiness Association had begun the John 3:16 Mission in Spokane under the leadership of Elsie Wallace in 1899. The directors of the mission invited C. W. Ruth, Bresee's assistant pastor at the time, to hold evangelistic meetings in January 1902. By the end of the week Ruth had convinced the group to form a Church of the Nazarene. Fifty charter members joined, and Bresee appointed Elsie Wallace as pastor. The same year, Bresee visited Spokane and ordained Wallace a minister in the Church of the Nazarene, the first woman Bresee ordained.[102]

In the summer of 1902 Bresee preached at a Washington State Holiness Association camp meeting, where he met Robert Pierce, a young evangelist who led a Society of Friends (Quakers) in Boise, Idaho, that was committed to holiness. Pierce agreed to bring this group into the Church of the Nazarene. Bresee noted, "It is something of a transition from Quakerism to the ways of the Church of the Nazarene, but, having the Spirit, they soon catch the step and rhythm."[103] Soon after, Nazarene congregations were formed at Garfield (near Spokane), North Yakima, Seattle, and Walla Walla, Washington, and Portland, Oregon, as well as several other places in the Northwest.[104]

Bresee followed Methodist precedent in then organizing the churches into a district placed under the care of superintendents. In December 1904, Bresee created the Northwest District, which included all of Washington, Oregon, Montana, and Idaho. He appointed H. D. Brown, a former Methodist presiding elder and pastor of the Nazarene congregation in Seattle as the first Nazarene district superintendent.[105]

In the summer of 1905, on his way back to Los Angeles from conducting the first District Assembly of the Northwest District, Bresee visited the churches in the San Francisco Bay area and while there organized them into the San Francisco District. Bresee appointed P. G. Linaweaver, associate pastor at Berkeley, as district superintendent.

Even further, prepared by the work of Holiness evangelists, some of whom by this time had joined the Church of the Nazarene, and by accounts in Holiness papers, small Nazarene congregations appeared in other areas. In 1903, for instance, a congregation of fifty-two in Maples Mill, Illinois (near Peoria), joined. In Omaha, Nebraska, the First Pentecostal Mission Church became a Nazarene congregation. Soon after, Nazarene churches began in Minneapolis and Chicago, to be joined later by churches in Hammond and Indianapolis, Indiana; St. Louis; and Des Moines, among other places. In September 1905 Bresee met with an assembly of these Midwestern churches and formed the Central District. He appointed I. G. Martin, a well-known evangelist, as district superintendent.

Finally, in September 1907 Bresee established the Southern California District of the Church of the Nazarene. Bresee himself had been acting as a district superintendent over this region of the church, but by 1907 it was clear that it needed its own superintendent. C. V. LaFontaine, Bresee's assistant pastor, was elected district superintendent. By 1907, before mergers with other Holiness groups, the Church of the Nazarene was a denomination national in scope.[106]

MISSIONS

Bresee was convinced that the *special* calling of the Church of the Nazarene was *first* to plant "centers of holy flame" in the great cities of America. These would spread outward to engulf the entire country. In the resulting holy conflagration the great churches of America would be purged and empowered to more effectively take the gospel to the world. The mission of the Church of the Nazarene was thus to "Christianize Christianity" in America. The result of this would be a great worldwide spiritual awakening. Bresee held that "our first great mission field is this country [the United States] ... No mission work at this time is so essential for the redemption of this world from sin, as the preaching and establishing of holiness in America ... Whatever else we may be able to do, we *must* possess this land, both for its own sake, as well as for the conditions of service to every land."[107]

The statement on Foreign Missions placed in the 1898 Nazarene *Manual* declared the church to be "in hearty sympathy with the cause of missions" and realized that Christ required Christians "to go out into all the world and preach the Gospel to every creature." It also said, *"In so far as the Lord permits us,* we will go out as Christ's ambassadors among the multitudes who sit in the regions of darkness and death, *or not being able to go ourselves, will help to send others."* It commended the work of various missionary organizations, Bible translation endeavors, and the importance of praying for missionaries. The church envisioned only a limited role for itself in the direct sending of missionaries abroad.[108]

Nazarene missions started at home. Work among Spanish-speaking residents of Los Angeles began in 1904 under the leadership of Mae McReynolds (1854-1932). McReynolds had migrated to California from Minnesota in 1883. Her husband was a railroad agent. They were among the first members of the Church of the Nazarene. Determined to preach to the Mexicans, Mae McReynolds learned Spanish. In her first year of ministry, one hundred were converted. Bresee ordained her in 1906 and appointed her as pastor of the First Nazarene Mexican Church, Los Angeles. She was seated among the district superintendents in General Assemblies. Later, she edited the Spanish edition of the *Herald of Holiness.* She pastored Spanish-speaking churches nearly until the time of her death.[109]

Soon enough, Bresee's congregation in Los Angeles agreed to sponsor a girls' school and orphanage in Calcutta. The work came to the attention of Bresee through Emma Eaton, wife of E. G. Eaton, an Oregon fruit farmer who was also a minister in the Evangelical Church. They were not members of Bresee's church but had acquaintances in it. Since the 1890s Emma Eaton had been hearing of and praying for the work Sukhoda Banarjee. After trying other ministries, in 1905 Banarjee started a refuge for young widows in Calcutta. The Eatons were already helping to finance the work, when, in 1906, Banarjee traveled in the United States in order to further raise funds. With her was a young Indian preacher, her son-in-law, Promotha B. Biswas. Through Eaton's friends at the Church of the Nazarene, Banarjee was invited to speak one Sunday evening. After an impassioned plea, a "hallelujah march" brought in a good offering and the church's Mission Board agreed to carry a large amount of the financial responsibility for the work, its first commitment to an overseas mission. In fact, Bresee officially appointed Banarjee, Biswas, Eaton, and her husband as missionaries. Along with V. J. Jacques, a wholesaler and Nazarene layperson who initially supported himself, they were soon on their way to Calcutta. Although Bresee and leaders of the California wing of the church had given less thought to missionary philosophy and policy than their Eastern brothers and sisters, at this stage they considered local workers to be their best prospects for leadership positions. Banarjee seemed ideally suited to spearhead the church's work with the assistance of lay American missionaries.[110]

Banarjee's work was renamed the "Hallelujah Village." The mission took in girls whose husbands had either divorced them or had died. Many had been married when they were still children to much older men, and their fate in Indian society was dismal. They normally were relegated to begging or to serving their in-laws for the rest of their lives. Such accounts stirred the compassion of Bresee and the Nazarenes, who had given women in their own midst the right to preach and to be ordained. The plight of women in India was well known to American Protestants. It was a frequent object of concern among missions in India. It was not unusual, then, that the church support an Indian woman's ministry, especially one that targeted women and girls, in an urban location.[111]

Bresee and others in the Los Angeles congregation were not overly concerned with denominational labels. Bresee was still trying to tie together the various strands of the Holiness Movement in the United States. None of the leaders who were sent to India, with the possible exception of Jacques, had much familiarity with Bresee's church. It was unlikely that Banarjee understood the nuances of entire sanctification. That was not the priority. Rather, the church in Los Angeles delighted in ministry to the urban poor as a demonstration of perfect love. Its original mission had been "to preach holiness to the poor." Presented with such a case overseas, the Nazarenes could not turn down Banarjee's pleas for help.[112]

NAZARENE HIGHER EDUCATION

For several years a group of Holiness-minded women prayed and looked for opportunities to start a Bible school in Los Angeles. They formed the Bible College Prayer Circle. By 1901, this group became convinced that the growing Church of the Nazarene was the best hope for such a school. The members of the circle joined the Church of the Nazarene and began to press their concerns upon Bresee. He was not enthusiastic, but his associate, C. W. Ruth, was, and pled the group's case before Bresee.[113]

Bresee was doubtful regarding the Bible college philosophy the group supported. He had been deeply involved with higher education in Iowa (at Simpson College) and with the University of Southern California in Los Angeles and was convinced that liberal arts education was superior to the narrow focus of a Bible school. However, he realized that the Church of the Nazarene did not have the resources at this point to support a four-year college.[114]

Gradually Bresee embraced the Bible college proposal as the only timely option. A Board of Trustees was elected, property purchased, and a small faculty gathered. In September 1902 Pacific Bible College opened with Bresee as president and Ruth as vice-president. Forty-one students enrolled. The college operated for eight years at San Pedro and 28th Streets in Los Angeles. By 1905, however, enrollment had climbed to sixty-one students, more than the facilities could accommodate. This inspired talk of moving the school and also of broadening the school's mission to include a college preparatory academy and liberal arts curriculum.

In 1906 a wealthy layperson, Jackson Deets, a charter member of the Ontario, California, Nazarene congregation, donated $30,000 to purchase land for a new college campus. This seemed to be the providential answer to the need for more space and for a liberal arts institution. Available property was located in Hollywood, and some Nazarene families quickly purchased adjacent lots there, believing that this would become a Nazarene community. In acknowledgment of Deets's gift and in the belief that the church would soon be operating a four-year college on the new campus, Pacific Bible College was renamed Nazarene University and Deets Pacific Bible College. However, a complicated situation developed over the next several years involving finances. Some withdrew from the denomination. In the end, the Hollywood property was sold (nothing having been built there).[115]

The church purchased an altogether new property in Pasadena, in the foothills of the Sierra Madre mountains. Bresee knew the area well. The school, renamed simply Nazarene University, moved to the campus in 1910. Deets Pacific Bible College remained as one department. A second department was a college of liberal arts and a third department was the preparatory academy (high school). Nazarene University (later renamed Pasadena University, then Pasadena College) would serve the Church of the Nazarene on this campus until 1973 when it relocated to San Diego.[116]

CONCLUSION

While building up the college, Nazarene worship never lacked emotional power. Inviting parishioners into the experience of entire sanctification, Bresee preached: "Only the heart that is melted with the most intense love, that is heated with divine fire in the furnace of the most holy affection, is in condition to be a channel of the holiest and fullest love to men [and women]."[117] Yet, even in spiritual expression, Nazarenes retained order. When Leslie Gay, in Bresee's congregation, would anticipate the climax of a message, and begin to shout "amen" or "hallelujah" before the point had been made clear, Bresee admonished him, "Not yet, Brother Gay, not yet, until I have made this teaching clear." Then, after a few minutes, after he had finished expounding the text, and God's Spirit had come, Bresee allowed, "Now, Brother Gay, you may shout." The walls of the church would reverberate with the people's great audible affirmation of truth.[118]

FIVE

Nazarene Beginnings: The Southern Streams

The Holiness revival within American Methodism and other denominations prior to the middle of the nineteenth century was largely confined to the Northern states. In a period of history when a host of urgent political, economic, and social issues (the greatest of which was slavery) were driving a sharp wedge between Northern and Southern states, the Holiness revival was mainly a phenomenon of the rapidly industrializing North. Some vocal supporters of the Holiness revival before the Civil War were also ardent abolitionists. The revival of 1857-58, sometimes called the Prayer Meeting Revival, the Laymen's Revival, or the Businessmen's Revival, historian Kathryn Long says, "appeared most visibly in the North, where systems of communication and commerce were more highly developed than in the South and the population more densely concentrated in cities and towns."[1]

The Northern Methodists organized the National Camp Meeting Association for the Promotion of Holiness, causing suspicion toward the Holiness Movement among some Southerners. Perhaps these Northerners intended to usurp Southern religious organizations just as did other "carpetbaggers" who grabbed positions of political and economic power in the defeated Southern states after the Civil War.[2]

During its first five years, the National Camp Meeting Association limited its camp meetings to Northern and Western states. In 1872, however, the association held one of its five national Holiness camp meetings that summer in Knoxville, Tennessee (where Northern Methodism had considerable support). The meeting was reasonably successful, and the NCMAPH returned to Knoxville again in 1873. Numerous local and regional Holiness associations began to form in the Southern United States and to launch Holiness periodicals. As independent Holiness evangelists itinerated throughout the South, organized holiness in this part of the country caught up with similar developments elsewhere. Some Holiness workers were affiliated with major denominations, some with small Holiness associations or missions, and many supported themselves through freewill offerings and sympathetic individuals.[3]

THE NEW TESTAMENT CHURCH OF CHRIST

A young married couple, Robert Lee Harris and Mary Lee (Wasson) Harris, were part of this growing contingent of evangelists and Christian workers spreading the message of Christian perfection across the South by the final decade of the nineteenth century. Robert Lee Harris, a native of Mississippi, the son of a distiller, described himself as "drunkard from childhood." Converted at age fourteen, he was called to preach. But he backslid. Spending his teen years in Texas, he abused alcohol, gambled, and indulged in other vices while working as a cowboy and drifting lawlessly from place to place. After reclamation as a Christian, with almost no formal education (he claimed he attended school only two weeks), he learned to read by reading the Bible, and he memorized hundreds of verses. With no particular church background, Harris preached on street corners, in vacant lots, and wherever he could find a hearing, sometimes sleeping in the woods for lack of better shelter. He struggled spiritually, he claimed, sensed his need for a clean heart, and finally found the blessing for which he was searching. Eventually, he joined the Free Methodist Church, the Northern denomination highly critical of Methodism's flirtation with affluence, class-consciousness, and theological liberalism. Free Methodists energetically promoted the Wesleyan doctrine of Christian perfection. The church had only a few congregations in the South or Southwest. That Harris embraced this Northern group in the post-Civil War South suggests that Harris had a nonconformist character. Harris became a minister in the Texas Conference of the church. Not gifted for pastoral work, Harris excelled as an evangelist, drawing hundreds of people to his meetings.[4]

Robert Lee Harris

Inspired by publicity about Christian missions in Liberia, the African colony established by American abolitionists in 1822 for freed slaves, Robert Harris asked the Free Methodist Church to appoint him as a missionary to Africa. He solicited financial support for this work. Like some others within Free Methodism, Harris advocated that independent ministries run on faith principles. That is, ministry should be undertaken simply at the Spirit's leading. Harris opposed the tendency of denominations to overemphasize order and organization. It was wrong, he said, to think that missionaries needed formal education. There should be immediate results if the Holy Spirit is relied upon, he said. With the backing of like-minded Free Methodists, Harris set off for Africa with a small party of workers in 1885.[5]

Harris's success in Africa was mixed. Though able as a traveling preacher, Harris was a poor organizer and overseer. Some of his coworkers suffered health problems and returned to the United States. One died of a tropical disease. There were interpersonal disputes. After three years, Harris became convinced, God released him from his call to Africa.[6]

In the United States once again by 1888, Harris evangelized in the Free Methodists' Texas Conference. However, his independency made him restless, and after a year he withdrew from the Free Methodist Church and joined the Methodist Episcopal Church, South.

Within the much larger MEC, South, Harris found an expanded field. He traveled about the South with a minimum of denominational supervision, operated very much by his own rules, and organized converts, not all of whom were Methodists, into what he called Calvary Holiness Bands. These were small groups similar to early Methodist class meetings or bands. They had no formal connection to any denomination. Harris created the bands to help converts mature spiritually and to help them experience and cultivate the blessing of entire sanctification. These bands became a source of friction between Harris and leaders of the MEC, South.

Several times during these years Harris held revivals in and around Moulton, Alabama. One of the reasons for his attachment to Moulton was a young woman he met during his first meeting there, Mary Lee Wasson. Mary Wasson was about twenty years old and in the midst of spiritual struggles when she heard Harris preach. Converted in a Methodist revival at age fifteen, she developed an intense interest in foreign missions and other Christian ministries. She believed herself called to be a missionary, and even wondered if God might be leading her to be a preacher, although such was unheard of in the American South. Rigid hierarchical relations prevailed between sexes, races, and classes. Women had their place in the home, not in roles of public leadership or authority. When Wasson shared her calling with others, they rebuffed her. When she told her mother of her desire to be a missionary, she remembered, her mother replied, "Child, hush; don't think of such a thing, for I had rather see you in your grave any day." When a brother-in-law heard that she was considering preaching, he warned her that if she did, his children would never again call her "Aunt." Another part of Wasson's struggle with her calling was her own sense of personal inadequacy. She felt that she was "only a country girl, timid, with practically no educational advantages, she had never gone to school except in the two and three months country schools—had never been out of the county in which she was born until she was twenty-five years old—had never seen a railroad train until she was past twenty years of age." Surely she must be mistaken about her call![7]

In this condition Wasson heard clear, definite preaching about entire sanctification from the Texas Cowboy Evangelist Robert Lee Harris. As she recalled, Harris was the "first holiness preacher" that "came into that part of the country. It caused great excitement, and people far and near went to hear him."[8] However, many considered Holiness preaching a novelty and fanaticism. She was hesitant about getting "mixed up with that holiness business."[9] Nevertheless, Harris's preaching called upon her to abandon herself completely to God. She yielded and experienced a profound release accompanied by peace and joy: "It was simply wonderful—for days she seemed to walk on air, and Jesus was the most real thing on earth to her."[10]

For several years Wasson kept in touch with Harris while he traveled and preached in the United States and Africa. Periodically he would return to Lawrence County, Alabama. In 1891 they married.[11] Mary found marriage both liberating *and* constraining: liberating in the sense that she could now claim her call to preach by becoming Robert's ministry partner and coevangelist, constraining because Mary considered Robert the much superior preacher and tended to "hide" her own calling in his much larger, bolder shadow. "She would sing, pray, do personal work and hold prayer meetings, but left the preaching to him."[12]

The partnership worked well. The Harrises traveled throughout Alabama, Tennessee, Mississippi, and Texas under the auspices of the Methodist Episcopal Church, South. But they mostly worked independently. Their Calvary Holiness Bands functioned as congregations. *The Trumpet*, a small paper, linked the bands together and publicized the Harrises' evangelistic work.

The Harrises became critical of trends within the MEC, South. With other Holiness advocates, they were troubled by the church's perceived departure from the old paths of Methodism. The church no longer emphasized simplicity of lifestyle, plain and unadorned dress, and avoidance of popular vices such as dancing, card playing, and using tobacco. The Harrises also embraced ideas about the Church held by the restorationist wing of the Holiness Movement.[13]

Efforts within the Methodist Episcopal Church, South, to regulate the activities of freewheeling evangelists such as themselves distressed the Harrises. This became an issue in 1893 when the couple held meetings in Fulton, Kentucky, where the local MEC, South, congregation was bitterly divided over holiness. The local pastor asked that the Harrises not conduct the meetings. Ignoring this, the Harrises went ahead in a shed next to the church, holding a Sunday morning service when the congregation was conducting its own Sunday School and morning worship! This sparked new conflict within the congregation and throughout the town. Methodist periodicals in Memphis and Nashville published complaints against the Harrises. An editor charged Robert Harris with being a "fomenter of discord and schism" and warned him that "everybody must learn that there is law in the Methodist Church, and submit to it."[14]

Their Calvary Holiness Bands already dotted the landscape in an area from Memphis northeast to the Kentucky line that seemed especially receptive. The Harrises held their first meeting in Milan, Tennessee, in the summer of 1893 in response to a request from Donie Mitchum, the wife of Robert Mitchum, a prominent merchant and civic leader. Donie Mitchum was a Southern Methodist who had been entirely sanctified in a revival in 1879. The Harrises held services "day and night." Their ministry galvanized the town. Overflow crowds filled their tent. But significant opposition also surfaced. A local Baptist pastor lambasted the Harrises in a Sunday morning sermon titled "The Mistakes of Modern Holiness." This led to a two-day public debate in which Robert Harris defended Holiness and a well-known Baptist author invited in for the occasion attacked it. The debate drew hundreds, including many reporters, but seemed to change few minds one way or the other. One result, in addition to many conversions and professions of entire sanctification, was the friendship that developed between the Harrises and the Mitchums, in whose home the Harrises stayed in between revivals.[15]

A similar friendship was forged between the Harrises and Edwin and Elliott (commonly known as "E. J.") Sheeks. Edwin Sheeks, like Robert Mitchum, was a businessman. The Harrises and Sheekses became acquainted when the Harrises held a revival in Bells, Tennessee (between Milan and Memphis), soon after the Milan revival, in the summer of 1893. The Sheekses home in Memphis became a stopping-over place for the Harrises during their evangelistic travels. E. J. Sheeks, together with Mary Harris and Donie Mitchum, became a prominent minister and leader in the new church.

By the autumn of 1893 Robert Harris had developed tuberculosis and was finding it difficult to travel and preach. He and Mary lived with the Sheekses in Memphis while Robert tried to recuperate. The Harrises kept the Calvary Holiness Bands alive and connected through *The Trumpet*. Mary Harris and E. J. Sheeks set the type for each issue of the paper in the Sheekses' basement.

By January 1894 Robert Harris was strong enough to participate with several other preachers in revival services at the Cumberland Presbyterian Church in Milan. While there the Harrises were offered a free lot on which to build a house if they would settle in Milan. In the spring the Harrises moved in with the Mitchums, intending to build their own house as well as to conduct another revival campaign in Milan that summer. At about the same time Edwin and E. J. Sheeks purchased a half-interest in Robert Mitchum's business and also moved to Milan.

In early May the Harrises began their second revival in Milan. At the very outset of this revival they announced that they were withdrawing from the Methodist Church. Still weakened by tuberculosis, Harris shared preaching responsibilities during the meetings with Emma Woodcock, Susie Sherman, and Grace B. George, workers from the Vanguard Mission in St. Louis. (Mary Harris still would not preach.) This group was associated with the Missionary Bands of the World, which had been organized by former Free Methodists and others within the Holiness Movement who advocated independent faith ministries like one that Robert Harris had earlier attempted in Liberia. They held restorationist ideas about strict New Testament patterns for church order, belief, and practice. The bands advocated the full equality of women with men in ministry and many leaders of the bands were women.[16]

The three women from St. Louis not only helped to launch the revival that would result in the founding of the New Testament Church of Christ but also provided a model of female ministry that left a permanent mark on that church. From its first moments, strong women ministers shaped and led the New Testament Church of Christ.

During the first week in July, in the revival tent in Milan, Robert and Mary Harris, having severed their Methodist ties and having embraced a narrow theology of what a true church should look like, organized their own church. As Mary Harris described it, "God was opening the Scriptures to [Robert Harris] and showing him His plan for a Bible church, which of course would be a holiness church."[17] The initial membership list included slightly more than a dozen persons (half of whom were the Harrises, the Mitchums, and the Sheekses). They chose to call themselves simply the Church of Christ. In typical restorationist fashion the new church declared Scripture alone to be its rule or discipline. It affirmed the principle of congregational sovereignty, with individual congregations given the right to call their own pastors and teachers, send missionaries, and admit and expel members according to their own standards of discipline. Soon the name would be lengthened to the New

Testament Church of Christ, apparently to distinguish it from the many other restorationist groups using the name Church of Christ.

The new church restricted membership to the converted, who would give evidence of their relationship with God through holy living. The New Testament Church of Christ affirmed the doctrine of entire sanctification as a definite work of grace subsequent to justification. It forbade members to belong to any secular organization or association on the grounds that this would violate the biblical injunction that Christians "be . . . not unequally yoked together with unbelievers" (2 Cor. 6:14). The church explicitly gave women the same right as men to preach and teach. It expected members to dress plainly and simply and forbade "costly or gaudy apparel." Members abstained from tobacco, intoxicating beverages, and drugs such as morphine and opium. The church urged members to give themselves to works of charity, especially "the relief of the poor." Somewhat uniquely, the new Church of Christ also affirmed that the only valid biblical method of baptism was by pouring. Robert Harris reasoned that water baptism was a "likeness of the baptism of the Holy Ghost" in the Book of Acts. Since the Holy Spirit was "poured out" upon the disciples on the Day of Pentecost, so, too, should water be "poured out" upon believers when they were baptized into the fellowship of the church.[18]

The newly organized church worshipped under a tent. Robert Harris's tuberculosis worsened that summer and he became bedridden. Still, he carried on ministry as people visited his sickroom in the Mitchum's house for counseling, to be baptized, or even to be ordained as ministers in the new church.[19]

Mary Harris Assumes Leadership

Robert Harris's failing health thrust before Mary Harris once again the issue of her call to preach. Partnering with Robert in evangelistic ministry for three years, Mary had let him preach and fulfilled her calling through other forms of ministry. However, with Robert dying, and the new Church of Christ only barely organized, Mary could no longer hide. She had to decide whether to embrace her call and take Robert's place or shrink back and perhaps let the new church die along with her husband. She pled with God to heal her husband and persuaded herself that God would do it. However, Robert himself believed "that his work was done" and encouraged his wife to realize that God did not intend to heal him. Mary Harris persisted. She bargained with God, telling God that if Robert were healed, she would preach. But God seemed to say, "Whether or not I heal your husband, will you do what I want you to do?" This triggered what Mary called "the most bloody battle of all her life." In the end she was able to say, "Yes, Lord, whether my husband lives or dies, I will obey Thee."[20]

On November 26, 1894, Robert Lee Harris died in the Mitchums' home. A large crowd gathered for the funeral, which was held in the Milan opera house, where the Church of Christ worshiped until it was able to build its own sanctuary. It was conducted by the Cumberland Presbyterian pastor with whom Robert had developed a close friendship. Harris was buried in the Mitchum family plot. Had the New Testament Church of Christ been buried there with him?

The answer was not long in coming. Mary Harris, together with Donie Mitchum and E. J. Sheeks, supported by Robert Mitchum and Edwin Sheeks, took charge of the infant church and devoted themselves not only to saving the small Milan congregation but also to extending the Church of Christ into new territory. Mary Harris became the chief preacher for the Milan congregation.

In January 1895, less than two months after Robert Harris's death, Mary Harris and Donie Mitchum visited the Calvary Holiness Band at Cottage Grove, Tennessee, not far from Milan, one of the small Holiness societies that the Harrises had established during their evangelistic travels. Here the women organized about twenty members of the band into the second congregation of the New Testament Church of Christ. At about this same time Edwin and E. J. Sheeks sold their interest in Robert Mitchum's business and moved back to Memphis. Though this weakened the Milan congregation, the Sheekses cultivated the area in and around Memphis for the fledgling New Testament Church of Christ. In the spring of 1895 Mary Harris visited the Sheekses in Memphis. She and E. J. Sheeks conducted home meetings, preached to prisoners in the Memphis jail, and held services in a rescue home for unwed mothers. At the rescue home, Mary Harris related, "One dear girl got saved and sanctified and later got a call to India and made as fine a missionary as was ever on the foreign field."[21]

Shortly after Mary Harris returned from Memphis to Milan, she received an invitation to participate in a revival over the border in Kentucky (probably in Fulton, Kentucky). Harris experienced a freedom and joy in preaching that allowed her to embrace her calling once and for all and to "take authority," as she put it, as a preacher of the gospel for the rest of her life. In the third person, Harris recounted, "She went out in the afternoon to service—the tent was filled with people and her heart cry was for liberty. She got on the large platform, took her text and began to speak, and God turned her loose—

absolutely broke every fetter—it was heaven to her. It was the first time in her life that she could turn the pulpit loose—she ran from one end of the large platform to the other and shouted and praised God and preached with the Holy Ghost sent down from above. Saints shouted," she recalled, "and sinners got under conviction. It was a permanent loosing from that day, and she has never been bound again. Although of a shrinking, backward disposition, she has never seen a crowd since that day large enough to make her knees tremble, and she has preached to thousands. Our God is great!"[22]

At this revival Harris also formed an evangelistic partnership with Fannie McDowell Hunter that would continue for many years and contribute to the growth and expansion of the New Testament Church of Christ. Hunter was a Southern Methodist whose grandfather had been a pioneer Methodist circuit rider and missionary to Native Americans. Hunter, like Harris, had been widowed after less than three years of marriage; just like Robert Harris, her husband, W. W. Hunter, had died of tuberculosis. Fannie Hunter was musically gifted and an accomplished preacher. Together these two young widows traveled hundreds of miles preaching holiness and organizing congregations of the New Testament Church of Christ.[23]

Rules for Holy Living

Mary Harris and Fannie Hunter's first extended evangelistic tour took them to Arkansas. They preached in churches, camp meetings, and the state prison. Harris preached with confidence. However, a serious issue surfaced during a camp meeting at Beebe, Arkansas, over the matter of the external evidence of entire sanctification, especially as expressed in women's clothing. This was not a new issue for the Holiness Movement. John Wesley had addressed the matter of attire with his Methodists in the eighteenth century, calling for both women and men to dress plainly and modestly. Wesley had urged Methodists to avoid "costly apparel" and to use the money they might have spent on "excessive adornment" to help the poor and needy.[24] Leaders of the American Holiness revival, such as Phoebe Palmer, echoed Wesley and added their own specific advice. Palmer, for example, taught that "the wearing of gold, when the object is mere adornment is wrong." She continued, "And how unseemly in the eye of God, angels, and men, that a hallowed temple, which, through the Spirit, has been made a habitation for God, should be adorned as though it were set apart as a heathen temple for the God of this world, with gold and pearls and costly array."[25]

The post-Civil War Holiness Movement intensified the concern with externals. Those identifying with the National Camp Meeting Association for the Promotion of Holiness and its various agencies, and the independent Holiness churches that arose in the 1880s, gave new urgency to the question of what it was that outwardly distinguished Holiness believers from those Christians who were neither fully sanctified nor actively seeking the blessing. The theological answer was perfect love. The *practical* answer to the question, however, was framed in terms of appearance and behavior, centering on what believers did *not* do or places to which they did *not* go in contrast to the unsanctified or even the unconverted. Cataloguing these forbidden or worldly behaviors was an undertaking certain to cause discord, conflict, and division. However, this did not stop believers from trying.[26]

This emphasis on externals was not unique to Holiness churches. Southern Baptists, for instance, had specific codes of behavior expected of members, even if frequently violated. In many churches, North and South, tolerance on such issues often accompanied theological liberalism.[27]

Yet some Christians were stricter than others. Robert Harris had emphasized the external evidences of holiness. The Free Methodist Church, which had shaped his thinking, held to standards of dress and behavior so strict that many persons in the Holiness Movement were hesitant to work very closely with them.[28] Harris preached regularly about externals and called Christians to abandon worldly practices and behaviors. Under this kind of intense preaching, Mary had been entirely sanctified. Robert Harris's preaching about "pride and worldly dress" struck at her vanity as a young, attractive single woman. In response, desiring to give herself fully to God, Mary "hunted up the plainest dress she could find," did not "powder her face," and "never curled her hair" again. After the Harrises married, they promoted these mores wherever they preached. The New Testament Church of Christ embodied their views. The importance of externals characterized Mary's preaching after Robert's death.[29]

Some who attended a camp meeting at Beebe, Arkansas, in the spring of 1895, where Harris was the speaker, represented a somewhat less legalistic stream and were put off by Harris's rigid views. A camp meeting leader took her aside at one point and suggested that she tone down her condemnations of "holiness professors" who were "wearing gold, feathers, and flowers, and worldly dress in general." This forced Harris to reexamine her beliefs. Had she been preaching the truth, or had she not? Should she alter her message, or should she continue to preach what she, and Robert Harris before her, had always preached? She pored through her Bible for guidance, and at one point went off into the woods to seek the mind of God in prayer.[30]

In the end, Harris became more convinced than ever that her views were sound and biblical. She refused to change her mind. Harris returned to the camp meeting pulpit for her next sermon and preached even more pointedly that God required earnest Christians seeking after holiness to give up the world, including its standards of fashion. "God forbade His children to wear ornaments" of any kind, she warned. At the end of the sermon she gave an "altar call." According to Harris's own account: "The message was a nail in a sure place . . . the people rushed to the altar—knelt down solidly all over the space in front of the altar and down all the aisles. The scene beggared all description—such praying and crying, and stripping themselves of their ornaments. One young lady, a school teacher and a fine character . . . took off a gold ring from her finger and also her gold class pin, and arose shouting the praises of God."[31]

This response, to Harris, vindicated her decision to press the matter of externals. This kind of preaching characterized her ministry throughout the rest of her life. More importantly, Harris's views profoundly marked the New Testament Church of Christ to which she gave leadership. The New Testament Church of Christ emphasized holiness as separation from sin and worldliness and carried this outlook into its associations with other Holiness churches, including the merger with the Pentecostal Church of the Nazarene in 1908. Harris and former New Testament Church of Christ members in the South and Southwest, bringing their firm rules-oriented ethic with them, made sure that the Church of the Nazarene did not overlook the importance of standards for holy living.[32]

Growth and Expansion of the New Testament Church of Christ

By the time Harris returned to Milan in the summer of 1895, she was so weak that some thought she, too, might have contracted tuberculosis. However, after some rest, she regained her strength and returned to traveling and conducting revivals. In December 1895 she was invited by Harris's family to spend Christmas with them in Texas. This trip became an unexpected occasion for extending the New Testament Church of Christ into Texas.

While visiting with her in-laws, Harris received an invitation from W. H. Pack, an independent Holiness evangelist, to join him in meetings in the small prairie settlement of Swedonia, Texas. The town, on the plains west of Abilene, was populated mainly by Swedish, Norwegian, and German immigrants. Pack had been in Milan shortly before Robert Harris's death and liked what he saw of the New Testament Church of Christ. He hoped that

Harris's coming to Swedonia might result in the establishment of a similar congregation there. Harris preached for a week on "God's plan for a church, and laid down His rules and regulations in His Word,"[33] and then organized a New Testament Church of Christ with thirty-one charter members.

Following the week at Swedonia, Harris held meetings at a schoolhouse six miles away, and after just a few services she organized the Mount Zion New Testament Church of Christ. From there, she accepted an offer to preach in the courthouse at Roby, Texas. At the end of another week she organized the third New Testament Church of Christ in Texas with twenty-nine members. Then, assisted by Annie Johnson, she held meetings at nearby Eskota, Texas, where the local Methodist pastor was convicted under Harris's preaching of his tobacco habit. He was entirely sanctified and became a minister in the New Testament Church of Christ.[34]

Harris returned to Milan in early 1896 more certain than ever of her calling to preach holiness and organize New Testament Churches of Christ. An effective method emerged using Harris and the two other founding mothers of the New Testament Church of Christ, Donie Mitchum and E. J. Sheeks. Harris divided her time between Milan and West Texas, with occasional stopovers in Arkansas. Mitchum concentrated on western Tennessee, holding revivals in neighboring communities, meeting with scattered Holiness bands, and, where possible, organizing new congregations. Her husband assisted her as his business interests permitted. E. J. Sheeks traveled to areas of Tennessee, Missouri, and Arkansas and started new congregations, which she pastored several at a time, developing a circuit like the frontier Methodists. Through all this time of energetic expansion, the Milan congregation served as the mother church and center of the expanding church. Holiness preachers and workers united with the Milan congregation, even if their work generally kept them elsewhere. In March of 1896 the Milan congregation moved into its own permanent building.[35]

HOLINESS IN TEXAS AND THE SOUTHWEST

When in 1895, Mary Harris "set in order" the first congregation of the New Testament Church of Christ in Texas in Swedonia, the American Southwest, including Texas, New Mexico, Arizona, and Oklahoma (still designated "Indian Territory"), had become a center for Holiness evangelism, both organized and otherwise. By the end of the nineteenth century the Free Methodist Church had thirty congregations in Texas. The Holiness Church Association, one of the earliest come-outer groups to form within the Holiness Movement, also had work in Texas. It had begun in California, where, in

1883 two of its founders, Hardin Wallace and B. A. Washburn, had had their Methodist minister's credentials revoked. Dennis Rogers and George Teel founded the Holiness Church Association in Texas in 1886. The Holiness Church Association, like the New Testament Church of Christ, held restorationist views on the nature of the Church and advocated congregational autonomy and minimal central organization. Both the Free Methodist Church and the Holiness Church Association had the disadvantage of disallowing musical instruments.[36]

In addition to the Free Methodists and the Holiness Church Association, the northern Methodist Episcopal Church took members, clergy, and even property away from the MEC, South. Giving credence to the fears of Southerners that the Holiness Movement was a ploy of Northern Methodism to gain power and influence in the South, the Northern Methodists targeted Holiness people in the MEC, South, for special attention. Willard Mallalieu, a friend to holiness, was the sometime Northern Methodist bishop in jurisdiction in Texas. When the MEC, South, harassed the Holiness people in its ranks, the Northern Methodist Church offered them a place of refuge (which was ironic, since in the north the MEC was often hostile to Holiness advocates). When the Holiness revival moved into the South in the 1870s, it found ministers and evangelists within the Methodist Episcopal Church, South, ready to acknowledge entire sanctification as an authentic part of the Wesleyan-Methodist heritage and to propagate the doctrine through the publications and official agencies of the denomination.[37]

A bit less organized than the Free Methodists or the two MEC bodies, or even the Holiness Church Association, were various regional Holiness associations. The first, the Texas Holiness Association, formed in 1878 in the wake of a revival in the area between Dallas, Corsicana, and Waco. The purpose of the association was identical to that of the National Camp Meeting Association for the Promotion of Holiness, to sponsor Holiness camp meetings. This was the only function of the Texas Holiness Association during its ten years of existence. The camp meetings conducted by the Texas Holiness Association drew support from Southern Methodists and Free Methodists, and some Baptists, Cumberland Presbyterians, and members of other denominations. Various other interdenominational Holiness associations came and went in Texas during the 1870s and 1880s.[38]

In addition, dozens of evangelists not accountable to any church or organization traversed Texas promoting holiness. Some were native Texans and others were outsiders. Often they traveled in teams called bands and developed followings. The Hudson Band (including "Mother" Hudson, her sons Bob and

Bluford, Oscar and Nettie Hudson, and "Stammering John" Friar), the Cluck-Farmer Band (C. C. Cluck and I. D. Farmer, with Cass and Flora Walker), the DeJernett-Jernigan Band (E. C. DeJernett, along with C. B. Jernigan and his wife, Johnny Jernigan), and many others promoted a continuous tide of Holiness revivalism across Texas and the surrounding region.[39]

These Holiness evangelists and bands were not always appreciated. Like the eighteenth-century revival in England, Holiness preaching challenged both the order of established churches and popular folkways. The Northwest Texas Holiness Association in 1883 declared plainly that its aim was to bring revival within the MEC, South. Holiness people's claims of entire sanctification rankled and irritated their peers. It sounded like spiritual pride and met with violent opposition. On one occasion in 1886 when two Holiness workers were holding meetings just north of Dallas "a mob of about thirty masked men, armed with shotguns, came at night to take these preachers out and whip them." However, C. B. Jernigan related, a local man who had just been converted in the meeting "went out into the road when he heard of their coming, and all alone met this mob and passed among them, for they were his neighbors." He shamed them for "coming armed to take two unarmed holiness preachers." When the mob saw that they were recognized, "they slipped off in the dark and disappeared, to be seen no more."[40] The Texas Methodists mounted another direct attack on holiness at its 1893 Conference. After Holiness advocates left or, like Bud Robinson in 1899, had their credentials pulled, the holiness controversy among Texas Methodists faded.[41]

The various Holiness evangelists and bands left scattered Holiness believers across the Southwest. However, they provided few means for these small groups of Christians to be nurtured or brought into fellowship with other Holiness believers. Few found their way into the Free Methodist Church or the Holiness Church Association.

Efforts to Unite The Holiness People of Texas

The Holiness Movement in Texas was severely fragmented. This made it vulnerable to false teaching, fanaticism, and shallow spirituality. In 1898 a group of Holiness leaders led by E. C. DeJernett and C. B. Jernigan launched an ambitious attempt to bring the scattered Holiness people in Texas together in a single organization. A "general convention of all Holiness people" met in Terrell, Texas (east of Dallas), in August of that year in connection with a camp meeting conducted there by nationally known Holiness preachers Henry Clay Morrison and Reuben "Bud" Robinson. Not all members of this convention thought it best for Holiness people to organize another Holi-

Texas Holiness Association

ness denomination. Some urged the Holiness people in Texas to unite en masse with one of the existing denominations, such as the Free Methodists. No general consensus could be reached. Just as John Wesley had urged the Methodists to stay within the Church of England, the convention ended by urging Holiness people to remain where they were and to bear witness to their experience of sanctifying grace by all possible means. The convention encouraged those who had been pushed out of an existing denomination, or who had fellowship only with some loosely organized band or association, to find and to join an acceptable church.[42]

Since this convention failed to bring the Holiness people of Texas any closer to unity, DeJernett called for another general convention of Holiness people for November 1899 at Greenville, Texas (northeast of Dallas). The year before, DeJernett had been expelled from the MEC, South. Greenville was two miles from Peniel, where a new Holiness school, Texas Holiness University, had opened two months before. Those who attended this second convention again debated what the Holiness people of Texas should do. One vocal member of the group, Rev. J. W. Lively, who had been expelled from the MEC, South, but who was now a presiding elder in the northern MEC, strongly urged all Holiness preachers and laypeople to join this denomination and to make use of its extensive resources to promote Christian holiness. In a passionate speech he declared, "Come home . . . to your mother. Methodism is the mother of holiness."[43] Most of those who attended the convention, however, remained unconvinced by this plea. Once again unable to reach a consensus, this gathering also adjourned without taking any action.

Frustrated with two glaring failures to bring the Holiness people of Texas and the Southwest closer together, C. B. Jernigan, a licensed preacher in the MEC, South, and an associate of DeJernett, invited a select group together in his home the night the second convention adjourned. This group met again the next month and formed the Texas Holiness Association (not to be confused with the earlier Texas Holiness Association, which already had disbanded) and planned for another general convention in the spring. Dennis Rogers, a leader of the Holiness Church Association, was present at the December meeting. A convention the next spring was held at the Holiness Church Association campground, and members of the Holiness Church Association agreed to join the Texas Holiness Association. Leaders convened another meeting in November 1900 to draw up a constitution and statement of doctrine, and this document was ratified by delegates meeting at Pilot Point. This came shortly after the General Holiness Assembly held in Chicago in early May 1901, which Jernigan and other Southerners attended.[44]

The statement of doctrine of the Texas Holiness Association began with the Apostles' Creed. This was a check to the fanaticism and false teaching that had sometimes arisen in the fragmented Holiness Movement in Texas. Second, the association drew up a long, nuanced statement on holiness:

> We believe in holiness, or entire sanctification; that it is a second definite work of grace in the heart, whereby we are thoroughly cleansed from all sin; that only those who are justified and walking in the favor of God can receive this grace; that it is not absolute perfection—that belongs to God alone. It does not make man infallible. It is perfect love—the pure love of God filling a pure heart. This love is capable of increase.
>
> It prepares for more rapid growth in grace. It may be lost, and we need to continually watch and pray. It is received by faith, after consecration. It is accomplished by the baptism of Jesus Christ foretold by John the Baptist. It is loving the Lord our God with all the heart, soul, mind, and strength, and our neighbor as ourself (Matt. 22:27-30). It was this which the disciples received in the upper room at Jerusalem on the Day of Pentecost . . . Our preachers are to definitely preach it and urge it upon all believers—it is the privilege and duty of all believers to seek and obtain it.[45]

The statement is significant in that it reflected a very strong core of Wesleyan teaching. Much of it echoes the substance and even the language of John Wesley's *Plain Account of Christian Perfection*. That is, entire sanctification is subsequent to justification, is not absolute perfection, is perfect love, is capable of increase, and may be lost. The distinctive teachings of Phoebe Palmer and the nineteenth-century Holiness Movement were also evident in phrases such as: "we receive it in faith *after consecration*"; "it is accomplished by the baptism . . . foretold by John the Baptist"; and "it was this which the disciples received . . . on the Day of Pentecost."

Despite the desires of some of its founders, including Jernigan, the association did not make provisions for ordaining ministers, which would have clearly identified it as a church. Rather, the association claimed only the power to "license" or "recommend" preachers, evangelists, and other Christian workers.

Another significant stand of the association applied holiness to the most deplorable social situation facing the nation, race. Lynching, in particular, was a rampant practice in the turn-of-the-century South. In 1907 association members issued this statement: "With humiliation we confess that we and our fathers, of the white race, of this country, have not done near as much as we might have done toward the well-being and advancement of the colored race and are willing to take our part of the blame for the unneighborly and unbrotherly feeling which has sprung up and seems to be growing every day." They went on to say that they must take the initiative in "correcting the wrong and effecting a reconciliation, and if we have the spirit of Christ, to accomplish this, we will be willing even to yield up some of our rights and preferences, to suffer wrong rather than do wrong." They admonished white employers to supply Christian literature to African-American workers and even to worship with them. Evangelists should take opportunities to preach to both whites and African-Americans and to attend their worship services, association members advised. White preachers should speak out both publicly and privately about crimes committed against African-Americans and advocate speedy trials whenever they are accused. At the same time, Holiness people should denounce mob violence. For the time and place, at the height of "Jim Crow" segregation in the American South, the affirmations of the Holiness Association of Texas were remarkably enlightened and bold.[46]

The Texas Holiness Association and Peniel

With the adoption of a constitution and statement of doctrine, the Texas Holiness Association represented a clear alternative for Holiness people in Texas. The association made its headquarters at Peniel. Together with Texas Holiness University, the campground, an orphanage, and the *Texas Holiness Advocate* (later renamed the *Pentecostal Advocate*), which became the semiofficial voice of the association, Peniel became a thriving center for Holiness leaders. In addition, the association helped to support the Berachah Rescue Home for "fallen girls" at Arlington, Texas. It also supported the work of several foreign missionaries, notably, later, Harmon Schmelzenbach in Africa.[47]

The school at Peniel became noteworthy among Holiness people throughout the country. DeJernett invited A. M. Hills, a Congregationalist minister then teaching at Asbury College in Wilmore, Kentucky, to become first president of the proposed school. Hills immediately sought the advice of one of his Asbury students, Will Huff, who was already an outstanding evangelist. The two prayed about it together on their knees. When Hills felt God leading him toward Texas Holiness University, Huff followed him there. When Hills first arrived in Greenville (to become president of a thirty-seven-acre cow pasture, as he later remembered it), "Bud" Robinson was speaking at a camp meeting then going on. Hills, a scholarly graduate of two fine universities and author of several widely circulating books, heard this former cowboy preach, "sitting on the ground in the straw and looking up into his Spirit-illuminated face and weeping," as he put it, "as I heard him tell the story of his sinful early life and his conversion and entrance into the ministry . . . How humble I felt . . . as utterly outranked . . . by this saint of God."[48]

Holiness people all over Texas and the Southwest sent their young people to THU. Holiness evangelists promoted the school as they traveled. Typical was Seth C. Rees, known across much of the country, who widely boosted the school after he held a revival there in 1902. Rees exhorted parents to "stop at once and take your children out of the Christless schools and send them to this holiness university."[49] By 1906, when Hills resigned as president, Texas Holiness University occupied several permanent buildings and had a student body of nearly 350.[50]

The school advertised itself as a university, which demonstrated its intention to provide its students a broad liberal arts education. It introduced students to literature, history, and philosophy. The school also offered practical training in such fields as bookkeeping, business administration, and music, together with instruction in the Bible and methods of Christian work.[51]

The Peniel community became a little Holiness enclave separated from the evil influences of outside society. Some parents not only sent their children to Texas Holiness University but also moved to Peniel in order to be closer to the school and to raise their children in a safe Christian environment. Evangelist Bud Robinson was one of these. He moved his family to Peniel in 1900. For the rest of his life Robinson was a staunch supporter of Christian higher education. The beloved evangelist often used his own money to help needy students to attend a Christian college.[52] Civic life in Peniel was organized on a Christian basis. A town constitution adopted in 1903 professed to make holiness the foundation of a local government "where the impelling force should be love and not fear," and where all would "live together in brotherly love and mutual helpfulness." All persons eighteen years of age or older who were "willing to be governed by the law of Christian love and service," and who subscribed to the constitution, could be citizens. A monthly mass meeting of all citizens, resembling the town meetings of the Puritan settlements in early America, debated and adopted all important laws. The penalty for breaking the law was to be "the expressed disapprobation of the community."[53]

Yet the Texas Holiness Association could not serve the needs of the Holiness people in Texas and the Southwest. Though more inclusive than any earlier association, and supporting a variety of vital ministries, it was still a voluntary, interdenominational association with no authority over the churches and individuals who were members. It left its members scattered in the churches where they were, or in no church at all.

The Independent Holiness Church

From the beginning of the efforts to unite the Holiness people of Texas, C. B. Jernigan (1863-1929) was one of the most outspoken advocates for creating a church rather than another loose association. In each Holiness convention he pushed strongly for an organization to gather the fragmented pieces. At first, more conservative leaders prevailed. But Jernigan realized that believers with no access to the sacraments and little Christian fellowship, and coming from a variety of denominational backgrounds, easily fell prey to false teaching. For instance, though Jernigan gave clear accounts of divine healing, like those leading the National Holiness Association he disavowed ministers preaching more on healing than holiness and criticized those who discounted medicine and medical treatment.[54]

Jernigan, once a licensed preacher in the MEC, South, joined the International Apostolic Holiness Union (a forerunner of the Pilgrim Holiness Church). Based in Cincinnati, Ohio, and led by Martin Knapp, the league had almost no work in Texas. Jernigan was ordained by this group, as was Johnny Jernigan, his wife. One of the leaders of the league was Seth C. Rees, who had preached in Texas and shared Jernigan's dream of a national Holiness denomination, which, they hoped, would emerge from the league.[55]

In June 1901, just one month after the final constitution and statement of belief of the Texas Holiness Association had been ratified, Jernigan organized a group of converts at Van Alstyne, Texas (south of Sherman), where he had just held a revival, into an independent church. Jernigan agreed to become their pastor. They chose the name Independent Holiness Church to distinguish themselves from either the league, which, said Jernigan, "did not seem to satisfy the demands of the South," and the Holiness Church Association with which Dennis Rogers and others were connected. Jernigan recalled that "not a man in the whole number of charter members was a land owner. All poor renters, but God was with them." He also noted that in order to pay for the printing of the first church *Manual*, one of the members, "a very poor man, living on a rented farm, volunteered to sell a load of wheat out of his granary that he was keeping for his own family flour."[56]

Jernigan gave half of his time to pastoring this congregation and half to evangelistic work. From this time on, wherever he held meetings, if there was interest, he organized a congregation of the Independent Holiness Church.

Some of the members of the Texas Holiness Association supported Jernigan's move and saw it as a legitimate expression of the association's desire to more effectively organize holiness. Others, however, considered it a further fragmentation of Holiness people into independent, competing sects. Henry Clay Morrison, Asbury College president and a nationally known Holiness evangelist who often held meetings in Texas, considered Jernigan's action arrogant. Morrison had been expelled from and then reinstated as a minister in the Methodist Episcopal Church, South, and encouraged Holiness people to remain within it. Preaching in a revival service at Texas Holiness University in 1902, with Jernigan sitting in the congregation, Morrison lashed out at him and his new church. Morrison, in a folksy, but pointed manner told the congregation: "An unknown wood chopper had gotten him a jack knife and corn stalk and sat down under the shadow of a haystack and whittled him out a church to suit himself, and now was trying to herd the whole holiness movement into it.... When we need a new church we will call a great convention and we will find us a Moses, and when he starts down the road there will be a dust in the desert."[57]

Undeterred by Morrison's rebuke, Jernigan continued organizing congregations of the Independent Holiness Church. By February 1903 there were enough congregations to call for a council of leaders, the first of several. This council elected Jernigan as president of the Independent Holiness Church and James Blaine Chapman as secretary. At the time, Chapman (1884-1947) was an eighteen-year-old Holiness preacher and student at Texas Holiness University. Chapman had been one of the first to join Jernigan's new church and was a zealous advocate for organizing and uniting the Holiness people of the Southwest. Chapman even chose this first council of the Independent Holiness Church as the place for his wedding to Maude Frederick. Jernigan conducted the ceremony. The next morning after the wedding the young couple traveled to Bee, Indian Territory, where Chapman helped conduct a revival. Chapman organized congregations for the Independent Holiness Church in eastern Texas as well as in Oklahoma and Louisiana and, along with Jernigan, encouraged greater church union. "I joined the Independent Holiness Church," said Chapman, "and since then I have let the church do the joining."[58] He went on to become one of the most influential leaders in the Church of the Nazarene.[59]

At the end of 1903 the second council of the Independent Holiness Church convened, this time in Greenville, near Peniel and the headquarters of the Texas Holiness Association. Jernigan thought some union with the Holiness league might yet transpire, and he invited Rees to attend with that in mind. But Rees did not attend. Other townspeople who were critical of Jernigan's work reportedly snubbed and ignored the sixty or so delegates from the twelve congregations of the Independent Holiness Church. Jernigan boarded half of them in his own home and fed them from his own table. The third (and as it turned out, last) council of the Independent Holiness Church met in October 1904. By then there were twenty-seven congregations.[60]

The church established a sort of headquarters in the small town of Pilot Point, northeast of Denton. Several ministries converged there. The first was an orphanage that had been established by the Hudson Band of Holiness workers about 1900. A second Pilot Point ministry was the Rest Cottage for unmarried pregnant girls established in 1903 by J. P. Roberts, a member of a band of Holiness preachers known as the "Roberts Boys," and his wife, Minnie Lindberg Roberts. After hearing a sermon by evangelist Seth Rees, the Robertses felt called to this type of work. Rees was a chief advocate in the Holiness Movement of efforts to fight prostitution and to take up the plight of unwed mothers. While staying in Pilot Point, Roberts had a vision of ten girls, kneeling outside his door, "begging him to help them out of their old life of sin, and give them another chance in life." When Roberts shared his vision in a public service the next day, over $3,000 was almost immediately collected (a *huge* sum of money for generally poor Holiness people in that day) to purchase property for a haven for unwed mothers. The Rest Cottage soon opened. In its first fifteen years it provided shelter and medical care for 750 young women. The Pilot Point Rest Cottage eventually became part of the Church of the Nazarene and was operated by the denomination until 1971.[61]

Another enterprise at Pilot Point was a church paper. Founded in 1904, and at first called *Highways and Hedges*, the paper linked the congregations of the new denomination and promoted the work of the orphanage and the Rest Cottage. The paper was later renamed *The Holiness Evangel* and later still merged with *The Pentecostal Advocate*, the voice of the Texas Holiness Association. In 1911 *The Pentecostal Advocate* merged with other regional papers to create the *Herald of Holiness*, the official paper of the Church of the Nazarene.

The Independent Holiness Church sought wider fellowship and organization. Talks with a group of Holiness Baptists about possible merger failed because Jernigan could not agree on this group's insistence upon baptism by immersion. The third council of the Independent Holiness Church elected delegates to attend the council of the New Testament Church of Christ scheduled to meet the next month at Rising Star, Texas (southeast of Abilene). The purpose was to pursue the possible union of the two churches.[62]

THE NEW TESTAMENT CHURCH OF CHRIST IN TEXAS

By this time the Tennessee-based New Testament Church of Christ was solidly planted in Texas. With its restorationist doctrine of the Church, which emphasized strict congregational autonomy, and its demanding rules of conduct, the church was not particularly eager to join in movements for Holiness unity unless others embraced the same understanding of the church and the holy life. New Testament Church of Christ leaders did cooperate in evangelistic efforts with other Holiness folks, and congregations supported ministries of compassion and other work of the wider Holiness Movement, but they were only interested in union on their own terms.

Though Mary Lee Harris, the driving force behind the church's expansion in Texas, returned periodically to Milan, Tennessee, she spent more and more time in Texas. She evangelized with Annie Johnson and later with Trena Platt, a musician. During these years, Harris recalled, "many young people were called into the work . . . and the churches planted at this time are among the best in the movement."[63] However, these years were not without difficulty. The issue of women preachers came up repeatedly. Sometimes lurid stories were circulated about Mary Lee Harris and Trena Platt—that they had abandoned their husbands and families, had robbed the U.S. mail, and had at one time operated houses of prostitution! Usually, though, stories like these only raised the level of curiosity and drew larger crowds to their services.[64]

Harris attracted and developed a core of capable leaders. Some independent Holiness people in Texas joined the New Testament Church of Christ. Among these was J. A. Murphree of Waco, Texas, who operated both a rescue mission and a missionary training school and published a Holiness paper, *The Evangelist*. In 1898 Murphree joined the mother church at Milan, Tennessee, and his paper became the semiofficial voice of the New Testament Church of Christ for a time. Murphree moved his training school to Buffalo Gap, Texas, where Harris had organized a congregation in 1899. This became the center of the church in Texas. A Bible school operated at Buffalo Gap until 1910. Murphree's young associate, William E. Fisher, quickly became an influential leader. Another of the Texas independents who joined in 1897 was J. T. Upchurch, the founder of the Berachah Rescue Home in Arlington, Texas. Holiness people throughout the Southwest, including members of the Texas Holiness Association at Peniel, supported this work.[65]

Changes in the New Testament Church of Christ

In Tennessee, Arkansas, Missouri, Georgia, Alabama, and Mississippi similar expansion occurred. As in Texas, the church made converts through aggressive evangelism and attracted independent Holiness people looking for a church home. In 1899 the mother church at Milan held a series of meetings to discuss modes of baptism acceptable to the church, how pastors of local congregations were to be called and supported, the biblical view of divorce, and the ordination of women. After three days of intense debate and "much prayer and fasting" as to whether believers who had been baptized by immersion rather than by pouring (the only mode of baptism practiced in the New Testament Church of Christ) could be members of one of their congregations, the council decided that they could. Regarding ordaining women, though much of the church's expansion had been spearheaded by a core of gifted women ministers, the prominence of women among its leadership disturbed some of the newer members of the church, who began to raise questions about this. After consulting scripture and praying for divine guidance, the church declared the ordination of women scriptural and right. To underscore its decision, the church held an ordination service in which its cofounder, Mary Lee Harris, was ordained together with E. J. Sheeks.

In 1900 the Milan congregation invited representatives from all the other congregations of the New Testament Church of Christ to attend its annual meeting so that there could be a wider discussion of important issues. A number of congregations sent representatives. This council agreed that its decisions were not binding on other congregations but also decided that every congregation of the church should be represented in future annual meetings and that these meetings should be held in different locations. Thus, the New Testament Church of Christ began to take a few significant steps toward organizational structure.[66]

In August 1900 Mary Lee Harris married one of her Texas converts, Henry Clay (H. C.) Cagle, in the big tent at Buffalo Gap while a New Testament Church of Christ-sponsored camp meeting was being held there. A thousand people reportedly attended the wedding. Shortly after, Henry Cagle went to Peniel to attend Texas Holiness University and Mary went back on the evangelistic trail with her associate Trena Platt. Mary Cagle also agreed to preach at least once a month at the Buffalo Gap Church. Later, for many years the Cagles evangelized across Texas, New Mexico, Arizona, California, and other parts of the United States. On several occasions they settled down for a short time and pastored congregations. During one notable interlude, in 1919, Henry Cagle served as superintendent of the New Mexico District of the Church of the Nazarene, with Mary Cagle serving as district evangelist.⁶⁷

By 1901 the New Testament Church of Christ in Texas had in many ways taken on a life of its own. Separated by vast expanses from the church's birthplace, those in the Texas wing established close connections among themselves. Mary Cagle suggested that

H. C. Cagle and Mary Lee Harris Cagle

each Texas congregation send at least two representatives to the camp meeting at Buffalo Gap in the summer of 1901 for the purpose of consultation and counsel regarding the work of the churches. This led toward a separate Western council.

The following year, at Christmastime, a convention at Buffalo Gap received reports from churches and preachers, ordered a statement of doctrinal points, and conducted other church business. The members of the next annual council, which met in November 1903, numbered fourteen ministers, five of whom were women. They adopted and printed a *Constitution of the Council of the Churches of Christ in Texas,* which set forth numerous organizational principles and overturned one of the founding tenets of the church, that members could not belong to any other organization, religious or secular. They declared that church members *could* belong to other organizations, except for secret societies and labor unions, which the council explicitly banned. This freed New Testament Church of Christ members to join Holiness associations among other interdenominational Christian organizations. The council also, in a move toward a less restorationist stance, urged its congregations to use Sunday School literature produced by the Free Methodists. In addition, it pledged to support Texas Holiness University, which it called "the grand center of holiness education" in the state of Texas. This meeting of the Western council of the New Testament Church of Christ would be its last. Leaders, including those in the East, entered into conversation with Jernigan and the Independent Holiness Church to discuss union. Jernigan's zeal for a national Holiness church and the New Testament Church of Christ's moves toward greater order converged. Union was the logical next step in gathering together the Holiness people of Texas and beyond.⁶⁸

THE 1904 UNION AT RISING STAR

Representatives of both the New Testament Church of Christ and the Independent Holiness Church met at Rising Star, Texas (southeast of Abilene), in November 1904. Each group had already discussed the union within its own ranks, so came prepared to work through any remaining issues and to go ahead with union. Present also were representatives from several other small Holiness groups that were interested in this meeting's implications for the Holiness Movement in the South.

Rising Star Union

The major issue concerned baptism. The New Testament Church of Christ had struggled with this already. Founded with an exclusive commitment to pouring as the only scriptural mode of baptism, it had recently decided to allow persons immersed or sprinkled to be members of the church. The Independent Holiness Church, however, allowed even believers who had not been baptized at all to become members. Mary Cagle and others were adamant that they could not be part of a church that did not require baptism of all members. Baptism was one of Christ's clearest commandments. After some heated debate, the gathering agreed to require baptism of all members but to leave the mode of baptism up to individuals or congregations: "We believe that water baptism may be administered in any manner to satisfy the individual conscience of the candidate; by any person called by God to preach the gospel and recommended to this work, by the congregation to which he or she belongs. Matt. 28:18-29. And under circumstances of necessity, a single disciple may administer water baptism. Acts 9:10-18. Persons applying for membership, who have previously received water baptism, may be accepted into the congregation."[69] These were remarkable concessions for the New Testament Church of Christ, which had emerged in a setting where strictures on baptism by pouring had been in place since the founding of the church. Now, for the cause of holiness, modes of baptism were among the nonessentials.

The convention appointed a committee to draw up a manual and statement of doctrine to serve as a basis for union. This committee chose the name that the church would bear, combining elements from the uniting groups, the Holiness Church of Christ. They agreed upon a doctrinal statement, typical of all Holiness organizations, that emphasized the possibility and necessity of deliverance from sin through sanctifying grace, and the call to live a holy life animated by divine love filling believers' hearts. Rules prohibited liquor and tobacco; secret societies and lodges; wearing gold, pearls, and other "costly or gaudy" apparel; worldly amusements, including dances, theatres, circuses, horse races, baseball games, parties, and gambling; and encouraged giving "for the support of the gospel and the relief of the poor," and prayer and fasting. As for organization, the manual provided that each congregation would have the right to call and ordain its own ministers, to send missionaries, and to otherwise carry on its own local work. This preserved the strong bias toward congregational autonomy in both of the uniting bodies.[70]

At the same time, the manual also endorsed consultation and counsel among representatives of local congregations. The church established three annual councils, one for West Texas, one for East Texas (east of Fort Worth, plus Oklahoma), and one for all of the areas formerly represented by the eastern council of the New Testament Church of Christ. In addition, the convention created a new layer of organization, a general council to be made up of delegates from the three annual councils. The first of these general councils of the Holiness Church of Christ met at Texarkana, Arkansas, in the fall of 1905.[71]

Thus, one of the narrowest Holiness groups in Texas and Tennessee had made an unlikely marriage with a group seeking the union of all Holiness people everywhere in one inclusive Holiness church. This pairing would have profound consequences for the Church of the Nazarene.

MISSIONS AND THE SEARCH FOR ORDER

The inadequacy of "faith" alone to finance foreign missionaries in the Holiness Church of Christ was a factor that led this group toward union with the Church of the Nazarene in 1908. The Holiness Church of Christ, and its forerunners, energetically sent out missionaries—primarily to Mexico, Central America, and the Caribbean, places that had historic interests and ties to the South. Two representing the HCC worked in Japan.

Unlike either the Association of Pentecostal Churches in the Northeast or the Church of the Nazarene in California, the HCC subscribed to the "faith mission" principles circulating among evangelical groups enamored over the success of J. Hudson Taylor's China Inland Mission. The right of any congregation to send out missionaries was stated explicitly in HCC council proceedings and governing documents. Members guarded and cherished this privilege as part of the congregationalist principles dear in these years of exodus from denominations. There was something exciting to local laypeople in rural Southern towns linking their faith directly to missionaries around the globe. Young people from their churches who expressed a missionary call sailed abroad with prayers and promises of support from their congregations. But the small bands sending them out were themselves struggling financially. They supported not only too numerous pastors and evangelists but also Bible schools, rescue missions for unwed mothers, and an orphanage.[72]

Until 1905 there were no means of systematically promoting, financing, or supervising missionary work in the HCC. Then, realizing the disservice this did to the missionaries themselves as well as to local churches, leaders set up provisions for the licensing and commissioning of missionaries, and centralized missions giving. While they reaffirmed their commitment to the right of local congregations to send money for missions directly to the field, and not necessarily through the organization's general treasurer, leaders sensed, by 1906, the need for a missions secretary. After sending observers to the union of the Association of Pentecostal Churches of America with the Church of the Nazarene in 1907, Holiness Church of Christ leaders strengthened the role of the Committee on Missions to select, send, and support missionaries. S. M. Stafford, superintendent of the work in Mexico, recommended to the Eastern Council that all money for missions pass through the church's Committee on Missions, that all persons claiming a call to the mission field be carefully examined by the same committee, and that, if accepted, missionary candidates be both appointed and ordained by the committee. Though the HCC did not act upon these before its merger with the Pentecostal Church of the Nazarene at Pilot Point, Texas, in October 1908, the recommendations demonstrated the changed sentiment of the church toward the organization and leadership of its missions program.[73]

SIX

Union

By the first decade of the twentieth century many supporters of holiness remained in major denominations, witnessing to Christian perfection where they were. They joined Holiness associations, subscribed to Holiness journals, attended Holiness camp meetings, and pressed the cause of full sanctification. Their loyalty to their denominations and aversion to schism held them back from joining the independent Holiness churches springing up.

Others called believers into fellowship with what they considered the restored New Testament church. These first come-outers, who had been active since about 1880, included those who joined the Church of God (Anderson, Indiana) and the Church of God (Holiness). They invited all Holiness believers to come out of denominations and unite with congregations that patterned themselves on the apostolic church. All other churches, even supposedly Holiness churches, were apostate sects, infected with the spirit of worldly competition and self-glorification. The only way for fully sanctified Christians to please God, according to the restorationists, was to unite in Scripture-based, locally autonomous bodies of believers.

Those supporters of organized holiness who preferred more traditional patterns of church order found themselves in the Wesleyan Church, the Free Methodist Church, or the Church of the Nazarene. Some of those who joined such groups had been put out or expelled from their churches. These persons joined Holiness churches as a last resort, having nowhere else to go. Other come-outers had voluntarily left their denominations in order to witness to holiness without constraints. Then, of course, there were the many churchless, those who had embraced holiness through the ministry of evangelists or rescue workers. These had no experience of the Church other than the fellowship of Holiness people.

By the opening years of the twentieth century North American Holiness churches and organizations that would come together to form the core of today's Church of the Nazarene were flourishing. Each of these Holiness churches sought effective means of organization. They had left behind denominations with well-established policies, regulations, and structures of authority, churches with financial, educational, and other resources. They started over with none of these, but Holiness pioneers from New England to Southern California and from Canada to Texas quickly created alternatives for what they had left behind. Holiness bodies busily carried on aggressive evangelization and ordered congregational life. They conducted works of mercy, created and sustained educational institutions, published Holiness literature, and publicized their work through regional papers. In addition, these groups expanded beyond the United States and Canada and conducted ministries in several parts of the world.

Those who came out sensed their own divine vocation. They were pragmatic in their view of the Church. William Howard Hoople voiced the typical outlook when he explained why he was organizing a chain of Holiness missions in Brooklyn. After noting growing opposition to the teaching of holiness in the established denominations, he said simply, "We thought the most sensible thing for us to do was to walk alone with the Triune God."[1] Similarly, Phineas F. Bresee, when answering the question, "Why have a Church of the Nazarene?" replied, "The answer is plain. Simply because it is needed."[2] Bresee declared that "God led us forth or we would never have dared to undertake a work so colossal."[3] Leaving well-organized churches behind, the founders tried the methods with which they were familiar, and sometimes erred. On practical grounds the groups influenced by restorationist views, such as the New Testament Church of Christ, modified their system. Similar church patterns emerged when those who prized congregational autonomy, such as the Association of Pentecostal Churches of America and the Holiness Church of Christ, added elements of central organization to their system when responsible coordination of ministry and missions demanded it.

THE UNION MOVEMENT

By the opening years of the twentieth century the regional Holiness churches were growing in size and expanding geographically. Not only did the Holiness churches resemble each other in purpose and methods, as they expanded their work and supported missionaries in other parts of the globe they crossed each other's boundaries. The California-based Church of the Nazarene had churches in Illinois, Texas, and Calcutta. The East-coast based Association of Pentecostal Churches of America had churches in Ohio, Iowa, and Buldana. There were congregations of the Tennessee-based Holiness Church of Christ in Kansas and Colorado as well as Tennessee, Arkansas,

Texas, and Igatpuri, India. Clearly, there was wisdom in these churches uniting to carry on the work as one body.

The Holiness Movement always had been international and interdenominational. Preachers and teachers of holiness declared the blessing to be the privilege of all Christians. A separate, distinctive Holiness church was not their original or primary goal. Rather, it was to ignite a revival that would sweep through and purify Protestantism. A powerful undercurrent of Holiness ecumenism carried the several regional groups toward each other and made it possible for them to "restore the bonds of nationwide fellowship, cherished in their memories and now challenging to their hopes."[4]

Still, not all Holiness people were in favor of such union. D. S. Warner, John P. Brooks, and other restorationists saw the expansion of the regional bodies as simply another form of sectarianism, to which they themselves offered the only alternatives. Others endorsed the regional churches, but opposed any union of them. They feared that a national Holiness denomination would acquire the elements of ecclesiasticism and "churchianity" that Holiness people had rejected in the denominations out of which they had come. Independent Holiness churches were fine, but better they remain small and pure than that they unite and fall into the temptations of the older, larger denominations. Many other Holiness people stayed with Methodist and other churches.[5]

THE UNIFIERS

Against this backdrop several persons emerged with a clear vision of the possibilities and advantages of uniting the various Holiness churches. Those who played vital roles in creating the Church of the Nazarene included Phineas F. Bresee, Hiram F. Reynolds, C. W. Ruth, and C. B. Jernigan.

Of the four, Bresee generally has been remembered by Nazarenes as the chief unifier of the denomination. Bresee possessed a lively vision of a national Holiness church. "We are a small, detached force," he told Nazarenes in 1901, "called by God for special and most important work," which "work *for the time* may be comparatively local, but your flashing blades have been seen throughout the land, and if faithful the light of your spears will reach the ends of the earth."[6]

Well-known from his days in Methodism, and as the founder of the Church of the Nazarene in Los Angeles, Bresee traveled as a Holiness camp meeting speaker and, increasingly, on behalf of the Church of the Nazarene. Using to good advantage leadership skills developed as a Methodist minister of large congregations, presiding elder, and trustee of educational institutions, Bresee

> The demand for such a work of organized holiness with broad, generous, brotherly impulses, with love toward all, yet with courageous fidelity to this great Pauline-Wesley doctrine and experience [of full sanctification]—at once free from narrow sectarianism and from fanaticism; liberal as to nonessentials, tenacious for all that is absolutely necessary to holiness—is so great, on the part of the sanctified people both in the pew and pulpit, that there is widespread conviction that the Church of the Nazarene has "come to the kingdom for such a time as this."[7]

Phineas F. Bresee

established personal friendships with Holiness leaders. He possessed a passion for organizing well. Bresee believed that "order and method are a necessity" in the Church. The "early church did all things in an orderly way," he insisted. "The conquering work of Jesus Christ is not to be done in a haphazard, slipshod way." Bresee wanted to see the forces of holiness unified and efficiently organized, the better to further "the conquering work of Jesus Christ."[8]

A passion for unifying Holiness people also defined C. B. Jernigan's ministry. From his earliest days as part of the DeJernett-Jernigan Band of Holiness evangelists in Texas, Jernigan promoted fellowship among the scattered Holiness believers of the Southwest. He had been one of the driving forces behind the founding of the Texas Holiness Association in 1900, hoping that it would be the start of a "real church" for Holiness people in Texas and the Southwest and beyond. After it became clear that the association would not serve that purpose, Jernigan established the Independent Holiness Church.

C. B. Jernigan

Just a few years later he helped bring about the merger of the Independent Holiness Church and the New Testament Church of Christ, the latter group substantially influenced by the restorationist wing of the Holiness Movement and not previously much interested in union with other churches. Following this merger (1904), Jernigan remained on the lookout for opportunities for union with other Holiness groups.

Hiram F. Reynolds, like Bresee a former Methodist pastor, also had excellent administrative skills and an enthusiasm for efficient organization. He understood that Holiness churches could carry on their mission much more efficiently and effectively if they united rather than remained separated. One of his first acts after joining the Association of Pentecostal Churches of America in Brooklyn in 1895 was to push for union with the Central Evangelical Holiness Association in New England. Following that union in 1896-97, Reynolds became one of the main shapers of the new church. Reynolds recognized the weaknesses inherent in congregationalism. As home and foreign missionary secretary, and school promoter, Reynolds demonstrated the value of careful oversight of the church's ministries. He drew the congregations of the association closer together around their common desires for missions and education. This was a difficult task. The APCA had strong, independent-minded leaders, one of them being Hoople, the founder, who resented any compromise of congregational autonomy. The problems on the mission field in India and at the school in Saratoga Springs strengthened Reynolds's hand. These crises helped to tilt the APCA toward more central organization and openness to union with other churches, which might help to control independence and both stabilize and preserve the achievements of the association.[9]

H. F. Reynolds

Of the Nazarene unifiers, C. W. Ruth (1865-1941) is perhaps the one most often forgotten. Ruth constantly sought new challenges. Born in Bucks County, Pennsylvania, Ruth's parents were members of the German holiness sect, the Evangelical Association. With barely any education, and apprenticed to a printer in Indianapolis, Indiana, Ruth was converted in a camp meeting in 1882. Within a short time, he experienced "something in my heart that hindered me," as he put it, "and even defeated me."[10] Within a year after his conversion, he sought entire sanctification. In 1884, he felt himself called to ministry and resigned from the printer's shop and entered evangelism. In his first twenty years of evangelism, he reckoned that more than 30,000 people had bowed at altars in response to his preaching.

Ruth began his ministry in the Holiness Christian Church, which four times elected him a presiding elder. In 1897 he assisted Martin Knapp and Seth Rees in the formation of the International Holiness Union and Prayer League, which he served as treasurer. He much preferred holding camp meetings to being tied down with pastoral or administrative work, however.

Among his revivals was one held for Phineas Bresee in 1901 at Los Angeles First Church of the Nazarene. Afterward, Bresee persuaded him to become his assistant (later changed to "associate") pastor and, as well, "assistant general superintendent." The arrangement lasted only eighteen months, 1901 to 1903, during which the church gave Ruth several months to continue evangelistic work. Bresee gave Ruth authority to organize new congregations, as he did, for instance, in Spokane, Washington. Ruth also served as vice president of Deets Pacific Bible College. In addition, Ruth wrote for the *Nazarene Messenger*. Ruth quickly became convinced that the Church of the Nazarene was the ideal Holiness church, with strengths and resources not held by other Holiness churches. Ruth's travels made him keenly aware of the needs of Holiness people for a larger fellowship, for less overlap in the many ministries they carried on, and for a greater unity and common direction of effort. If there were to be a great union of Holiness people (and Ruth hoped for this), the Church of the Nazarene was the church most suited to accomplish it. From 1901 on Ruth publicized and zealously promoted the Church of the Nazarene everywhere he went in his far-flung travels.[11]

C. W. Ruth

After the merger of the Church of the Nazarene with the Association of Pentecostal Churches of America in 1907 and the further merger with the Holiness Church of Christ in 1908, both of which he helped to engineer, Ruth returned to full-time evangelism. He and Bud Robinson, who became a Nazarene in 1908, were among the half-dozen best-known, most popular, and most widely traveled Holiness evangelists of their time. Ruth maintained a network of personal contacts within the Holiness Movement matched by few. Ruth held no leadership role in the Church of the Nazarene and gave much of his time to interdenominational Holiness organizations such as the National Holiness Missionary Association, which he served as president from 1925 to 1941, and Asbury College, upon whose board of trustees he served, all the while remaining a loyal and devoted Nazarene.[12]

THE EAST-WEST UNION

An important part of the union between the Church of the Nazarene and the Association of Pentecostal Churches of America was the migration of Eastern Holiness people to Southern California. C. W. Griffin, one of the charter members of the APCA congregation at South Portland, Maine, moved to Los Angeles in 1904 and joined the Church of the Nazarene. He regularly kept Bresee abreast of developments in the East and reported on the Nazarenes to family and friends in the APCA. Another New Englander, John W. Goodwin (1869-1945), moved to Southern California in 1905. Goodwin had been expelled from the Christian Advent Church after attending Holiness camp meetings, and then professing and preaching holiness. He joined Bresee's church and became pastor of the Nazarene congregation in Pasadena. Goodwin also helped direct Bresee's attention to the East. Goodwin wrote in the *Nazarene Messenger* in 1905, soon after his arrival in California, that "in many ways the Nazarene work is like the Pentecostal [APCA] work in the East, and it may have been providential that these two great movements should have been started, one on the Eastern and the other on the Western coast; moreover, it may be in the Divine order that these two movements for organized holiness unite their forces somewhere in the Middle West in the near future."[13] Goodwin was expressing his own opinion, but his suggestion was soon acted upon.

In early 1906 the Missionary Committee of the APCA invited Phineas Bresee to the annual meeting of the association in April. Bresee was not able to attend but, in reply, encouraged further contacts. That summer C. W. Ruth held a revival in the John Wesley Church in Brooklyn and participated in the Grandview Park Holiness camp meeting near Haverhill, Massachusetts, where the Missionary Committee of the APCA was meeting. Ruth openly discussed the possibility of union between East and West with the pastor of the John Wesley Church, E. E. Angell, and with the Missionary Committee. The committee minutes record that "Bro. Ruth appeared before the Committee and presented the thought of uniting the Nazarene Church and the Association of Pentecostal Churches of America. While he was not able to present the matter in an official capacity, yet he expressed the wish that a Committee be appointed to meet the General Assembly of the Church of the Nazarenes [sic] and felt confident that it would materialize in a blessed union."[14]

Easterners Go West

The Missionary Committee voted to send a delegation of three to the Nazarene General Assembly and to pay their expenses out of the missionary treasury, "inasmuch as such a union if culminated would materially help our missionary work."[15] The three delegates were J. N. Short, H. N. Brown, and A. B. Riggs, all former Methodists.

The delegation left on September 14 for the Nazarene assembly that would not convene until October 3. They planned their trip purposely to have time to preach in Nazarene churches along the way. They held meetings in Chicago; Spokane and Seattle; Portland, Oregon; and San Francisco and Oakland, California, before reaching Los Angeles. In each place they quickly won the trust and affection of the Nazarenes.

John Short

Albert Riggs

Henry Brown

As the APCA delegation was on its way to Los Angeles, Phineas Bresee told readers of the *Nazarene Messenger* that

> the coming from New England of the representatives of the Pentecostal Churches, who have wrought so successfully for the last decade—more especially in the East—with outstretched hands to the Church of the Nazarene, whose field has been more especially in the West, certainly marks an epoch of possibility. It may be that a central line of fire may be drawn from Maine to Southern California, with which might coalesce other such organizations as have formed providential life for this work, and who would multiply their power by unity with those of like faith and purpose.[16]

Bresee, with his own roots in New York, was dreaming greatly as the General Assembly, and the APCA delegates whom Bresee referred to as the

"Three Wise men from the East," drew near. Bresee, Ruth, and W. C. Wilson, Nazarene pastor at Upland, California, formed a committee to meet with the Easterners. In several sessions the six men discussed the various issues involved in their possible union. Ignoring possible hindrances to the union, the committee claimed that the Church of the Nazarene and the APCA were "at one" in doctrine, basis of church membership, general superintendency, and, of course, the "all embracing purpose to spread scriptural holiness over the land." The committee based its understanding of the substantial unity of the two churches upon the provisions of the Nazarene *Manual* of 1905. The union of the two could and should proceed without serious obstruction. The committee acknowledged only that there could be a problem with the "basis of ownership of property" but thought that this could be resolved easily by making unspecified "adjustments."[17]

The Nazarene General Assembly received the report of the committee on union and passed a resolution stating that "for the purpose of more effectively carrying on the work of God on the earth and hastening the triumph of the Redeemer's kingdom," it favored uniting the Church of the Nazarene and the Association of Pentecostal Churches of America "into one organic Church." The assembly resolved that as soon as the APCA had approved the union through its own organizational procedures, the officers of both churches would issue a joint call for an assembly of the two churches to perfect and complete the merger.[18]

The Debate Over Organization

The "three Wise Men" headed home, eager to sell the union to their colleagues there. The APCA leaders planned to discuss the union with the congregations during the winter in preparation for the annual meeting of the APCA in Brooklyn in April 1907. However, Brown, Riggs, and Short quickly ran into criticism. The issues of congregational autonomy, the power of superintendents, and the manner in which congregations held property, which had seemed minor points in Los Angeles, proved to be matters of great concern to some. APCA leaders were wary of either excessive episcopal control or unregulated congregational autonomy. Though the trend was toward a more centralized organization, and though through Reynolds's responsibilities with the missionary and education committees he exercised de facto superintendency, still, the APCA had been founded as an *association* of independent congregations. From its beginning the APCA had prized and protected the sovereignty and autonomy of every local church.

Bresee argued that the congregational form of church government allowed too many opportunities for individual congregations to sabotage and undermine the work of the whole body. "There can be no great, aggressive movement, where-in all are united, and new churches are founded, through their united effort, missions and schools established, without a fair degree of consolidation, and a condition of things that would make impossible the secession . . . of any part of the body," he wrote. "Men of judgment will not put their time and money and themselves into the building up of institutions that a whiff of wind may blow down."[19] Later, sensing the strength of the opposition in the East, Bresee modified his views and affirmed the "largest liberty" for individual congregations so long as they used this for "righteousness." Still, he also held that the whole body should have power to prevent an individual church from "going wrong." No church should "have the right to go off on lines of fanaticism, or higher criticism, or any other evil way, if it can be prevented," he declared.[20]

A week after Bresee's pointed attack upon congregationalism, William Howard Hoople wrote in the *Beulah Christian:* "Now this effort is being made to *force* our Association *into* a union which *necessitates an entire change in form of government* . . . and the line of argument that some are taking in trying to make it appear that we are like the government of the Church of the Nazarene is not honorable and is unworthy of Holiness." Hoople continued: "With some of us our present form of government is a matter of principle." Should the Church of the Nazarene "consent to the Congregational form of government," he said, he could place "heart and soul in favor of the union." On the other hand, Hoople warned, "if it is to be the connectional Episcopal form there is one person in the Association who will be left out of the Union—the writer."[21] The APCA was, and always had been, a voluntary association of independent congregations and this was fundamentally different from the model of organization embraced by the Nazarenes in the West.

Westerners Go East

A lively debate went on all winter between spokespersons for the APCA and the Church of the Nazarene. The annual meeting of the APCA in Brooklyn in April 1907 made union its chief order of business. Bresee, C. W. Ruth, H. D. Brown, and E. A. Girvin represented the Church of the Nazarene at this meeting. They met with an APCA committee that included Hoople, H. B. Hosley, John Norris, J. N. Short, John Norberry, J. C. Bearse, and A. B. Riggs to prepare a workable basis of union.

The committee reached a consensus on most matters. After two days it presented a basis of union to the APCA annual meeting. Though still not addressing many details, the two churches agreed upon "the doctrines considered essential to salvation," which they specified as the doctrine of justification by faith, and "entire sanctification subsequent to justification also by faith." They further agreed "on the necessity of a superintendency" to foster and care for churches already established and to organize and encourage the organizing of churches everywhere. This was a victory for the faction in the East that desired centralized organization, and a setback for those committed to unmodified congregationalism. At the same time, to mollify the strict congregationalists and to allay their fears of episcopal tyranny: "We agree that authority given to superintendents shall not interfere with the independent action of the fully organized church." That is, the power of superintendents would be strictly limited. Local congregations would retain the right to call their own pastor, to elect their own delegates to assemblies, to manage their own finances, and to control "all other things pertaining to their local life and work."

On the much-contested issue of church property, the committee reached a significant compromise. In the Church of the Nazarene church property was held "in trust" by the whole body. The Nazarene *Manual* stipulated that the property of a congregation withdrawing from the denomination, or ceasing to function as a congregation of the Church of the Nazarene, could not be "diverted to other purposes." Rather, it would "pass to the control of the General Assembly for the use of the Church at large, as the General Assembly shall direct." In the APCA, on the other hand, each congregation held title to its own property and could dispose of it in any way it chose. Bresee and other Nazarene leaders viewed the APCA system as fostering weakness and instability, while some Easterners considered the Nazarene system as little more than a confiscation of resources that individual congregations had sacrificed dearly to attain. The compromise held that "any Church of the Pentecostal Association going into this organization who may feel it imperative with them to continue to hold their property in like manner as at present shall be at liberty to do so." However, any APCA churches *not* taking advantage of this proviso, as well as any *new* congregations formed after the merger was complete, would be subject to the Nazarene policy. The basis of union also stated that "the further details for completing the union" would be "left to the first assembly of the united body," which would meet in Chicago the following October.[22]

The committee's work was unanimously and enthusiastically ratified by the APCA delegates, "amidst tears and laughter and shouts and every other possible manifestation of holy joy." Some present had given up a great deal in order to reach this point, perhaps no one more than Hoople. When Hoople stood to address the meeting, he confirmed that he had had to "gulp a good deal down in order to make the union possible." But he believed that he and others had submerged secondary matters in the interest of the most important one, a "combined attack on the powers of hell and darkness."[23] Girvin, among the Nazarene representatives, exulted that this marked "the beginning of the era of organic unity among the various branches of organized holiness in the United States. Christ's prayer [for the unity of His followers] was being answered, and God was pleased." The name chosen for the new church was "the Pentecostal Church of the Nazarene."[24]

Between April and October leaders gave more thought to amending the Nazarene *Manual*, which had been designated the "working basis" of the merger. Meanwhile, even such champions of denominational loyalty as C. J. Fowler, president of the National Holiness Association, and Henry Clay Morrison, leader of the Interdenominational Holiness Union, both Methodists, praised the merger for giving strength to the Holiness Movement, making its work "more efficient and aggressive." Fowler declared that the union "should rejoice the hearts of all lovers of holiness."[25]

1907 Chicago General Assembly

In October delegates from East and West set off toward Chicago, most traveling by train. The place of meeting eased the travel of delegates from both sections of the country, as well as "fraternal delegates" from other churches and Holiness organizations. Chicago marked the coming together of East and West. The California delegates carried tracts printed for the occasion by the Nazarene Publishing House. As they passed through train stations on their way to Chicago they threw these "to the winds," in hopes that they would be "picked up by the people and read with interest." Each leaflet announced that it had been dropped "by the California delegation, consisting of a car-load of happy Nazarenes, who bear witness to the fact that Jesus Christ is 'Able to save unto the uttermost all that come unto God by Him.'"[26]

Eastern delegations began from Boston and New York. They filled their hours on the train singing, praying, and testifying. One New York delegate reported, "God gave us the hearts of the train men and we had salvation of the Pentecostal type from start until the finish of our journey. We sang, shouted, and prayed in the Holy Ghost, and had a miniature camp-meeting. Hallelujah!" When some other passengers in the car attempted to play cards, they were sent off to the smoking car by the conductor, protesting as they went that the conductor had "let those sanctified cranks sing, shout, jump and do as they liked" ever since the trip started. However, "the cards had to go while the saints of God shouted the victory."[27]

The assembly, meeting at Chicago First Church of the Nazarene, spent much time in worship and celebration. The pastors and laypeople from East and West cemented their union with shared experiences of Pentecostal glory and a sense of the greatness of their undertaking. Nearly one thousand worshippers filled Chicago First Church at the opening service. One delegate reported that the meeting eclipsed any he had ever witnessed for its expressions of "holy joy and triumph." As delegates and onlookers "took one another by the hand, so "filled were they with holy joy, that for many minutes it was impossible to restrain it." The "waving of nearly 1,000 handkerchiefs, and the repetition of chorus after chorus, was a scene the better of which we do not expect to witness this side of the pearly gates."[28]

All was not celebration and glory, however. Fifteen committees consisting of nearly 250 delegates met in numerous sessions to deal with evangelism, education, Sunday Schools, young people's societies, publications, temperance, and a host of other concerns, including the power of superintendents and the rights of local congregations. Hoople was having second thoughts on what had been worked out in Brooklyn. Hoople and H. B. Hosley briefly considered keeping the Brooklyn congregations and several other APCA churches out of the final union. In the end, the framework of organization adopted by the assembly was almost identical to that set forth in the Nazarene *Manual* of 1905.

The assembly proceeded to elect two general superintendents. Bresee was elected first, by acclamation, followed by Hiram F. Reynolds. Though Reynolds had superintended a lot of work in the East, his election was by no means inevitable. Unlike the Church of the Nazarene, the Association of Pentecostal Churches of America did not have one key founder. Instead, it had a number of strong leaders, any one of whom might serve well as general superintendent. Hoople, though twenty years younger than Bresee, was an obvious candidate, as was John H. Norris, then serving as the APCA moderator and pastor of a strong church in Pittsburgh. Fred Hillery, editor of the *Beulah Christian* and pastor of the oldest congregation in the association, was another possibility. The assembly did not discuss the necessity of electing one Westerner and one Easterner. In a sense Bresee himself, with his background in New York and Iowa, represented the church's geographic range. Nearly half of those on the first ballot for the second general superintendent were Westerners, the name appearing most frequently being that of T. H. Agnew, superintendent of the Central District of the Church of the Nazarene.[29]

C. W. Ruth was another strong choice. Ruth and Reynolds were nearly tied through three ballots. By the final ballot, Reynolds had only twenty votes more than Ruth. The assembly bestowed on Ruth a kind of consolation prize in the form of a resolution: "Whereas our dear brother, Rev. C. W. Ruth, has helped to bring about the union of the Association of Pentecostal Churches of America with the Church of the Nazarene ... we extend to him our hearty commendation expressing to him our love, appreciation and thanks for his services rendered."[30] Reynolds would serve in the general superintendency for twenty-five years.

The union of the Association of Pentecostal Churches of America and the Church of the Nazarene was now official. The now-designated "Pentecostal Church of the Nazarene," standing in place of the two former denominations, stretched from the Atlantic to the Pacific, from Canada to Cape Verde, to Calcutta. Its ninety-nine congregations and membership of just over six thousand marked meager beginnings. Girvin voiced the belief of many when he declared (inspired by Isa. 41:18), "This Assembly was not gathering blessings from the skies for the day, but to open ever flowing rivers of love and salvation to the ends of the earth, and as long as time endures."[31]

THE NORTH-SOUTH UNION

Before the Chicago Assembly, C. W. Ruth corresponded with the General Council of the Holiness Church of Christ, inviting them to send delegates and to join the union. C. B. Jernigan pushed for it. Seven fraternal delegates—Jernigan; J. P. Roberts, from the Rest Cottage at Pilot Point; J. D. Scott, an evangelist, rescue worker, and missionary; Joseph Speakes, a prominent pastor from the Eastern Council of the church; S. M. Stafford, a missionary to Mexico; E. J. Sheeks, the Harris's friend from early days in Tennessee; and T. J. Shingler, a layman who had just brought an independent congregation in Donalsonville, Georgia, into the Holiness Church of Christ—represented the HCC at the Chicago General Assembly. These Southerners participated in various legislative committees and raised their own concerns. They observed whether or not these Nazarenes worshipped with the same holy freedom as they. Although Nazarenes envisioned their mission being to the poor, they themselves maintained moderate social positions.[32] Southern observers to the Chicago Assembly wondered whether truly holy people could dress as stylishly as the Nazarenes. The Southerners had given up even wedding rings in order to simplify their lives and give more of their meager earnings to missions. But to the Southerners' surprise, these urban people prayed and testified as mightily as themselves to holiness of heart. J. D. Scott was "happily disappointed" that the Nazarenes and "Pentecostalers" could shout as loudly as Holiness folk in Texas. The HCC delegates were well satisfied.³³

> Jernigan told the readers of the *Holiness Evangel:*
> The spiritual power [of the Chicago Assembly] was the greatest of any convention I ever attended. There was liberty in it clear through, and not a dry song, prayer or sermon throughout the entire session. They came from the Pacific slope and the Atlantic coast, and if I had shut my eyes I would have declared that I was in an old-fashioned Texas holiness camp meeting where the fire was falling . . . The Mason and Dixon line . . . was obliterated and we all melted together like pieces of lead in a red-hot ladle.³⁴

As for organization, the Southerners seemed comfortable with the system being worked out by the APCA and the Nazarenes. Like the APCA delegates, the representatives of the HCC were ready for tighter organization and greater oversight of both missions and individual congregations.³⁵

Other important concerns were doctrinal and ethical. Though the Southerners had no quarrel with the Nazarene *Manual* on justification, entire sanctification, and the like, they objected to the omission of any specific doctrinal statements on the second coming of Christ and divine healing. These were major issues in the South, not only within the HCC but, as well, in other Holiness groups. Jernigan let it be known before the Chicago Assembly that though he was for "real union," this could only exist where all are "really one in doctrine." For him this meant that "Post and Pre-Millennialism will not mix, tobacco chewers and clean men would not unite." Further, he declared, "We cannot afford to get tangled up with Godless secret societies in a Holiness Church."³⁶

The Southerners' premillennialism reflected the shift taking place among evangelicals. The optimistic postmillennial eschatology that Christ's kingdom was coming on earth predominated among nineteenth-century Christians. However, late nineteenth-century prophecy conventions popularized premillennialism, which held that Christ would come back soon to rescue Christian believers from a world sliding into an abyss of wickedness. Many in the Holiness Movement still held to the older, more optimistic view. Increasingly, others embraced the new view. Premillennialism was especially persuasive to Southerners. They had experienced defeat in the Civil War and had struggled through the period of reconstruction. The South still suffered economic weakness. Such Southern Methodists as W. B. Godbey and Henry C. Morrison adopted strong premillennial positions.[37]

The Nazarene *Manual* had no article of faith on the Second Coming, though a statement on "Destiny" affirmed belief in resurrection, judgment, and everlasting rewards and punishments. But this statement did not mention Christ's return in connection with these.[38] Bresee affirmed that Christ would come again "according to His promise," but he believed that "there are some thoughts of His coming and attitudes toward it which hinder Christian experience and the ministries of salvation," a position like that of the National Holiness Association. "It is not our special business to be watching for His coming," Bresee declared.[39] But the Holiness Church of Christ representatives wanted more specificity.

Again reflecting the position of the National Holiness Association, the Nazarene *Manual* made no reference to divine healing. A few on the fringes of the Holiness Movement taught that the full atonement of Christ provided perfect healing for the body as well as for the soul. Sickness and infirmity, just like sin, they said, were contrary to the will of God and may be eradicated from the body through a prayer of faith. Resorting to medical treatment revealed a lack of complete reliance upon God's willingness and power to perfectly heal, and thus was evidence of sin in the heart. Traditional Holiness leaders avoided the doctrine of healing because of the extreme forms it sometimes took. They considered it a troublesome side issue that could unnecessarily divide Holiness people. The champions of divine healing, however, held it to be a practice of the New Testament. Seeing the Holiness Movement as a renewal of the experience and life of New Testament Christianity, they argued that one should expect primitive spiritual gifts such as healing to be manifested in Holiness churches.[40]

Holiness Church of Christ delegates wished for the church to take more definite stand on worldly adornment and the use of tobacco. Regardless of the tobacco farms plentiful in the South, A. M. Hills, while president of Texas Holiness University, wrote a book on *The Tobacco Vice*. Already, in that day and age, Hills linked the "poison of nicotine" to cancer as well as to other diseases. Tobacco debilitated self-control in many areas of life, including sexual restraint. To Hills, tobacco use was anything but an "innocent" habit. The Southerners even for a time maintained a Nicotine Hospital in Greenville, Texas. "God's idea of manhood cannot be realized by one who is defiled and degraded by tobacco."[41]

In response, the 1907 General Assembly added two statements to the Nazarene *Manual*, one on the second coming of Christ and one on divine healing. The Second Coming statement explicitly affirmed belief in the return of Christ but stopped short of endorsing premillennialism or any other particular theory. "We do not," its final paragraph read, "regard the numerous theories gathering around this Bible Doctrine as essential to salvation, and so we concede full liberty of belief among members of the Pentecostal Church of the Nazarene."[42] The statement on divine healing urged moderation: "The harmony and unity of holiness people is absolutely essential, and while we recognize that God heals with and without means, we hold that no one has the right to take such an extreme position as it may result in the death of any person without medical attention."[43]

On the matter of "externals" the Nazarenes again bent a bit. Under the heading "Church Membership and General Rules" the Nazarenes already had pledged that they would avoid "the indulgence of pride in dress or behavior; the laying up for themselves treasures on earth." At the urging of the HCC delegates this was reworded: church members would avoid "the indulgence of pride in dress or behavior. We urge our people to dress with the Christian simplicity that becometh holiness. 'Whose adorning let it not be that outward adorning of plaiting of hair, and of wearing of gold, or of putting on of apparel' (I Peter 3:3). Nor should they lay up for themselves treasures on earth."[44]

In addition, the Nazarenes strengthened their statement on "Secret Societies." The existing statement read, "We advise our people to abstain from membership in worldly, secret, oath-bound lodges and fraternities, inasmuch as the obligation of some and the spirit of others are contrary to the devotement and spiritual life of the salvation of Jesus Christ." The new statement was more binding, as well as broader in its condemnation of secret societies: "We *insist* that our people abstain from membership in, or fellowship with, worldly, secret, or other oath-bound lodges and fraternities, inasmuch as the spirit and tendency of these societies are contrary to the principles of our holy religion."[45] However, the statement was kept in the section of the *Manual* headed "Special Advices," rather than moved to "Church Membership and General Rules" as suggested by the HCC delegates. The "advice" on tobacco use remained where it was, among the "Special Advices," contrary to the desire of the Southerners. Nonetheless, as Jernigan returned to Texas he wrote to *Holiness Evangel* readers, "They gave us all that we asked for." He included the full text of the new doctrinal statements on the second coming and divine healing and the stronger special advices on adornment and secret societies.[46]

The attention by the Chicago Assembly to the Southern delegation's requests led many to believe that union with the Holiness Church of Christ was certain and that a further assembly to ratify the action might not be necessary. The assembly provided for the addition of HCC members to the General Missionary Board that had been elected by the assembly and authorized General Superintendents Bresee and Reynolds to appoint a third general superintendent from among the Southerners.[47]

From Chicago to Pilot Point

Like the Association of Pentecostal Churches of America, the Holiness Church of Christ operated with a largely congregational form of organization. Individual churches would need to discuss and act on the matter of union. The HCC visitors to Chicago returned to their churches to push the merger. The various congregations of the Eastern Council gave almost immediate approval for the union and put the *Manual* of the Pentecostal Church of the Nazarene into effect without delay. The Texas wing, with some of the strongest leaders, including Mary Cagle, was more difficult to convince. This group vigorously debated the union. They wanted still stronger statements on divine healing and tobacco in the *Manual*. A few other issues surfaced. The Texans heard reports that some of the Nazarene sisters at Chicago had worn "too many frills and feathers," related in their minds to worldly adornment. The Texans wanted the use of a ring in the marriage ritual stricken from the *Manual*. Nonetheless, the Pentecostal Church of the Nazarene talked of holding its General Assembly to coincide with the next General Council of the Holiness Church of Christ, scheduled for October 1908 at Pilot Point, with the expectation that there the union between the two churches would be completed.[48]

Nazarene leaders had a different interpretation of the Chicago compromises than had Jernigan. For example, Robert Pierce wrote in the *Nazarene Messenger* that the assembly had intentionally kept the advices on tobacco and secret societies out of the General Rules in order to leave them "for the individual conscience to settle under the light of the Word and the Holy Spirit." Pierce claimed that the assembly had proved that "holiness people can come together and organize on the basis of gospel essentials, and with perfect love grant freedom and liberty in those things which do not pertain to or hinder the salvation of the soul."[49]

In the months leading to the assembly both sides argued for their positions. The Southerners wanted rules, the Pentecostal Nazarenes "liberty in non-essentials." Just prior to the October assembly, J. N. Short published an "Open Letter" in the *Nazarene Messenger*, in which he warned of trying to make the *Manual* "a textbook to explain the Bible." The simpler the better, Short asserted. Wise and holy people did not always see eye to eye on every issue. "Not being infallible in judgment," he wrote, "we cannot legislate to make every man see in all particulars certain interpretations of faith which we may accept." Furthermore, "Having our Bible," we do not need "a Manual to be a supplement or to explain it."[50] One would have expected a restorationist, but not a former Methodist, to have had such sentiments.

The Peniel Addition

In the months between the Chicago and Pilot Point assemblies the Church of the Nazarene gained an important addition. In January 1908 C. W. Ruth held a revival at Texas Holiness University in Peniel, Texas. Ruth discussed with the school's president, Edgar P. Ellyson (1869-1954), the developments that were bringing Holiness people together. Ellyson, a Ohio-born holiness Quaker, was very interested. He had been trying to move the Texas Holiness Association allied with the school toward denominationalism. Ellyson also had improved relations between the Peniel community and the Holiness Church of Christ congregations in the area. Ellyson invited Bresee to preach at Texas Holiness University in April.[51]

At the same time that Ruth was at Peniel, the most famous Peniel resident, Bud Robinson, was conducting a revival at Chicago First Church of the Nazarene. Following that, Robinson preached in Nazarene churches in Seattle and Portland before going on to a Southern California Holiness Convention held at Bresee's church in Los Angeles.[52]

Bresee visited Peniel on his way east to hold district assemblies. After preaching in the college chapel, on April 7, 1908, Bresee invited any who so desired to immediately unite with the Pentecostal Church of the Nazarene. One hundred and three people, including President Ellyson and the entire faculty, came forward. In just a few minutes Bresee organized a Pentecostal Church of the Nazarene. Members proceeded to choose a church board and to call Mary Emily Ellyson (1869-1943), wife of Edgar Ellyson, as their pastor.[53]

Was Bresee's action an impulse of the moment or planned in advance? Likely such a move had been discussed by Ellyson and Ruth the previous January and arranged by Bresee and Bud Robinson during Robinson's visit to Los Angeles in March. Whatever the case, Bresee then went from Peniel to Pilot Point, the stronghold of the Holiness Church of Christ, where he visited the Bible institute and the Rest Cottage and preached several nights at the Pilot Point church, which J. B. Chapman pastored. Only then did Bresee officially announce that the next General Assembly of the Pentecostal Church of the Nazarene would convene at Pilot Point in October. The Nazarenes were carefully courting the Southerners to bring the HCC into the union. These personal contacts were crucial in a time when many Southern and rural people distrusted remote, controlling social forces.[54]

THE HOLINESS CHRISTIAN CHURCH

The addition of a large part of the Peniel community to the Pentecostal Church of the Nazarene was not the only accession preceding the 1908 General Assembly. Another was a conference of the Holiness Christian Church. C. W. Ruth came from this group. With deep roots among German-speaking immigrants in eastern Pennsylvania, those associated with the church in its earliest days came from Pietist and Anabaptist backgrounds and included Mennonites, Amish, River Brethren, and Brethren in Christ, as well as Methodist forms of this tradition.

In 1882 a nondenominational association called the Heavenly Recruits formed to spread the doctrine of full sanctification and identified itself with John Wesley and the American Holiness Movement. It wrapped its commitment to preaching holiness securely within essential elements of the German Brethren tradition. For example, Heavenly Recruit Association beliefs and practices included baptism only of adult believers and only by immersion, foot washing as a mandatory ordinance of the church, prayer veiling for women, plain dress for all believers, beards for men, and the rejection of musical instruments. Under the leadership of Jonas Trumbauer, and others, the Heavenly Recruits expanded. By the mid-1880s there were several Heavenly Recruit missions in the eastern and midwestern United States, including two in Indiana that had been planted by Ruth.[55]

The association held annual conferences of representatives from the various congregations. In 1892 it established a paper, the *Crown of Glory*. In 1894 dissension surfaced among the Heavenly Recruits involving several legal issues connected with the incorporation of the group and the use of the "Heavenly Recruits" name. The majority of members voted to reorganize under the name Holiness Christian Association and elected C. W. Ruth as presiding elder. In October 1896 the group voted to establish two separate conferences, the Pennsylvania Conference and the Indiana Conference. At the annual conference the following March, held in Reading, Pennsylvania, the group changed its name to "The Holiness Christian Church." At the same conference Jonas Trumbauer's son, Horace, was both ordained and elected as editor of the *Crown of Glory*. The younger Trumbauer excelled in this work and became the primary leader of the church's Pennsylvania Conference.[56]

From the mid-1880s to the late-1890s C. W. Ruth, while a member of the Heavenly Recruits and Holiness Christian Church, and even while serving this group as its presiding elder, traveled widely, preaching wherever the

Holiness Movement had a presence. In 1901 he became Bresee's assistant and joined the Church of the Nazarene.[57]

In 1907 Horace Trumbauer attended the Chicago assembly that united the Association of Pentecostal Churches of America and the Church of the Nazarene. Trumbauer presented an enthusiastic report of the assembly to the Pennsylvania Conference, which by this time had split from the General Conference of the Holiness Christian Church. Trumbauer recommended union. In March 1908 the Pennsylvania Conference of the Holiness Christian Church, made up of fifteen congregations, voted for the union. In September 1908, just prior to the Pilot Point General Assembly, Hiram F. Reynolds, representing the Nazarenes, met with leaders of the Pennsylvania Conference to officially complete the union. The churches were organized as the Philadelphia District of the Pentecostal Church of the Nazarene, and Reynolds appointed Horace Trumbauer as district superintendent. The stronger western conferences of the Holiness Christian Church merged in 1919 with the International Apostolic Holiness Church, which subsequently became part of the Pilgrim Holiness Church.[58]

One missionary who came into the Church of the Nazarene from the Holiness Christian Church was Etta Innis. The Holiness Christian Church's Indiana Conference had sent her as a missionary to South Africa in 1907. In 1910 she joined Harmon and Lula Schmelzenbach and the Church of the Nazarene in South Africa and soon made her way with them to Swaziland.[59]

THE PILOT POINT ASSEMBLY, 1908

The Second General Assembly of the Pentecostal Church of the Nazarene thus convened in Pilot Point, Texas, on October 8, 1908. Jernigan, writing in the *Holiness Evangel,* announced: "You are requested to be present at the marriage of the Pentecostal Church of the Nazarene and the Holiness Church of Christ, which is to take place at Pilot Point, Texas, October 8-14 where the union of these two Holiness churches will be fully consummated in joint assembly. Men and angels will be made to rejoice at this marriage. The Father, Son and Holy Ghost will bestow their blessings upon this union."[60]

The assembly met under a large tent that held one thousand people, pitched beside the Rest Cottage. Wagons and horses surrounded the camp. An amused Eastern delegate wrote back to the *Beulah Christian,* "About forty or fifty carriages were seen standing at some of the services. Men on horseback, and 'prairie schooners' were in evidence."[61] Important issues remained. The Southerners wanted rules. The Westerners and Northerners wanted liberty. At one point the debate became so frustrating that H. D. Brown, from the northwest, suggested that if the union could take place only at the cost of adding rules, the Nazarenes should pull out of the union and let the Southerners go. Brown repeated the speech several times until he finally fell to pleading, "Mr. Chairman, let them go! Let 'em go! Let 'em go!" Phineas Bresee, who was presiding, responded each time, "Brethren, we shall not let them go; they are our own folks."[62]

In the end, the only significant adjustments were to elaborate the *Manual*'s General Rule on modesty and simplicity to include explicit scriptural references to women's dress from 1 Tim. 2:9-10 and 1 Pet. 3:8. Also, the delegates modified the advice on tobacco to forbid selling as well as using tobacco and rephrased the statement on divine healing to make it more positive and affirming. The Nazarenes also agreed to remove the exchange of rings from the marriage ritual in the *Manual*. These actions satisfied the Southerners and sealed the union of the Pentecostal Church of the Nazarene and the Holiness Church of Christ.[63]

When it became clear that union was certain, the assembly erupted. "An aged brother from South Texas rose and said, 'This morning is the first time I ever hugged a Yankee.' He and Brother Hoople immediately clasped each other in their arms amid great shoutings. Amen, forever!"[64] Phineas Bresee put the motion for union to a vote, and it passed unanimously.

> Regarding the scene at Pilot Point, Jonnie Hill Jernigan, C. B. Jernigan's daughter, recalled many years later,
>> When it was announced that the vote for union was unanimous, the assembly could not contain its exuberant joy. The Mason-Dixon Line and the ugly scars of the Civil War were forgotten and the chasm between the North and South was bridged forever! The delighted delegates waved their handkerchiefs in the air as tears of joy flowed down their cheeks. Loud shouts of "Hallelujah," "Praise the Lord," "Glory to His Name," rent the air. Shaking of hands, hugs, and slaps on the back led to a grand "Hallelujah March" around the outside of the huge tent. Just how many times the Nazarenes marched round the tent no one will ever know. But their faces were aglow with joy and determination to "encircle the globe with salvation with Holiness Unto the Lord."[65]

Once the excitement subsided, important business remained. They would continue to use the name Pentecostal Church of the Nazarene. "Pentecostal" was synonymous with "holiness," in their minds, and there was no difference whatsoever between "Church of Christ" and "Church of the Nazarene." The assembly elected three general superintendents. On the first ballot, Bresee received 159 votes and Reynolds 92 votes, and so were declared reelected. William Howard Hoople and Edgar P. Ellyson both received 67 votes on the first ballot. Ellyson went on to receive 97 votes on the second ballot and was declared elected. Given the many strong leaders in the Holiness Church of Christ, this was a somewhat surprising choice. The Holiness Church of Christ delegates were so divided in their support among their various leaders that no one of them gained enough votes for election. Yet Ellyson was a Midwesterner, and until just a few months before, he had been a member of neither of the uniting churches. The assembly elected an eighteen-member General Missionary Board with six representatives each from North, West, and South. The assembly also drew the boundaries for eighteen districts across the country. Some of the district superintendents chosen were the most ardent advocates of congregationalism. These included William Howard Hoople, New York; H. B. Hosley, Washington, D.C.; and J. D. Scott, Dallas.[66]

The newly elected general superintendents declared that "our first great mission field is this country," and they set a goal of having one thousand churches in one thousand central cities in the next five years. At the time of the union, only eight churches had more than 150 members: Los Angeles First Church (1,150); Chicago First Church (600); Pittsburgh (240); Pilot Point, Texas (183); Lowell, Massachusetts (180); Washington, D.C. (180); John Wesley Church, Brooklyn (163); and Harrington, Delaware (160).[67]

REFLECTIONS ON PILOT POINT

The events at Pilot Point loomed large in Nazarene memory ever after. In 1923 the Nazarene General Assembly designated the Pilot Point General Assembly of 1908 as the official date of the "wedding" that established the family called the Church of the Nazarene. To the delegates of 1923, many of whom had been present at Pilot Point, the events of 1908 seemed the most fitting historical marker of what the Church of the Nazarene was and what it hoped to become, a body uniting Holiness people.

Pilot Point brought together distinct elements of the Holiness Movement. In some ways these clashed, but in the end, like in all good marriages, they became complementary, adding their own strengths to the union. Pilot Point was a coming together of three different regions of the United States, the West, the North, and the South. Observers noted the bridging of the deep divide between North and South that occurred at Pilot Point. The Northern and Southern Methodists would not reunite until 1939, the Northern and Southern Presbyterians until 1983. The Baptists remain divided. Creating a national denomination across these regional lines was an audacious undertaking. Through purposeful actions to prevent sectionalism undertaken by the general superintendents, it succeeded.

The union signified the triumph of theology and experience over regionalism. Yet even holiness could not eradicate the prejudice some carried. Other events in history, especially the Spanish-American War, had brought North and South together, but at the expense of African-Americans. The Northerners gave up their early championing of a republic that would lift up Blacks and keep down white Southerners. In some respects, the Church of the Nazarene reflected this exclusion of African-Americans for the sake of bringing in the Southerners.[68]

The union represented a coming together of urban and rural white cultures. The Pentecostal Association had its major churches around sprawling urban areas such as Boston, Brooklyn, Washington, D.C., and Pittsburgh. The Western wing likewise was predominantly urban, with centers in Los Angeles, Chicago, San Francisco, Seattle, and St. Louis. The Holiness Church of Christ congregations, on the other hand, were in places like Swedonia, Buffalo Gap, Rising Sun, and Pilot Point, Texas, and Milan, Tennessee. The Eastern and Western Nazarenes had joined the internal migration of white people from farms to cities. Members of the Holiness Church of Christ remained country and small-town folk.[69]

The Pilot Point General Assembly was also a coming together of two ethical traditions within the Holiness Movement. Wesleyan and Holiness people always wrestled with what it meant to live a holy life in the world. One strand emphasized purity, cleansing from sin, and separation from worldliness. A favorite Bible passage was 2 Cor. 6:17: "Wherefore come out from among them, and be ye separate, saith the Lord, and touch not the unclean thing; and I will receive you." The other ethical tradition emphasized perfect love. The heart cleansed of sin and filled with divine love would follow impulses of that love in all the concrete arenas of life. A favorite Bible passage was Rom. 13:10: "Love worketh no ill to his neighbour: therefore love is the fulfilling of the law." While neither of the ethical traditions was a stranger to any part of the Holiness Movement, the *tendency* was for the purity tradition to be stronger in the South and the "love is the fulfilling of the law" tradition to be the stronger in the West and North. This was at the heart of the debate at Pilot Point over externals.[70]

What was it that brought these two different groups together in union and made it possible for them to submerge their differences? Their common commitment to Wesley's doctrine and to the experience of entire sanctification, and a shared passion to spread the Holiness message across the nation and the world outweighed differences. Those at Pilot Point believed the union rested on firm bases. Jernigan had stated it in advance of the assembly in the "wedding invitation" he published in the *Holiness Evangel:* "Men and angels will be made to rejoice at this marriage. The Father, Son and Holy Ghost will bestow their blessings upon this union."[71]

SEVEN

Nazarene Beginnings: Early Accessions

Once the three main churches—the Association of Pentecostal Churches of America, the Church of the Nazarene, and the Holiness Church of Christ—had united at Pilot Point, Bresee, Ruth and others continued to pursue possible union with other groups. Few responded.

The 1911 General Assembly in Nashville witnessed hopes of union with the Reformed Baptists of the Maritime Provinces in Canada and the Louisiana Conference of the Methodist Protestant Church, as well as the Pentecostal Church of Scotland. Most assuredly, the delegates assumed, there would be union with their hosts, the Pentecostal Mission. The Reformed Baptists remained cordial but did not unite with the Nazarenes. Roy T. Williams gave a report for a joint commission, formed the previous year, that had been meeting with the Louisiana Conference of the Methodist Protestant Church. The Louisiana Conference had the distinction of being the only conference in the Methodist Protestant Church to ordain women. The president of that conference, T. C. Leckie, spoke to the Nazarene assembly and proposed a Basis for Union. The Assembly failed to ratify the proposal. Nonetheless, soon after the 1911 General Assembly, J. E. Gaar, who previously had been president of the Louisiana Conference for four years, and the conference evangelist for two years, joined the Church of the Nazarene. Gaar later pastored Nazarene churches in Peniel and Hamlin, Texas; Olivet, Illinois; and Des Moines, Iowa.[1]

Successful unions occurred, nonetheless, over the next decade with the Pentecostal Church of Scotland, which brought an international dimension to the key constituent core of the early Church of the Nazarene; with the Pentecostal Mission, a group centered around Nashville, with extensive missions abroad; and with the Laymen's Holiness Association of the American Dakotas.

THE PENTECOSTAL MISSION

As organized holiness made inroads into the South, it encountered both resistance and receptivity. One pocket of resistance was the Central Tennessee Conference of the Methodist Episcopal Church, South, which encompassed Nashville, the denomination's headquarters. As the home of church officials, the church's publishing house, and Vanderbilt University, which represented Southern Methodism's highest cultural aspirations, Nashville wielded great influence. In 1885 well-known Methodist evangelist Sam P. Jones held widely noted revivals in Nashville, but as Southerners considered the Holiness Movement an extension of *Northern* Methodism, they were wary of Holiness partisans.[2]

In 1894, when Robert Lee and Mary Lee Harris were founding the New Testament Church of Christ halfway across the state in Milan, Tennessee, Benjamin Franklin Haynes (1851-1923), pastor of McKendree Methodist (South) Church, the headquarters church in Nashville, professed entire sanctification. He served as presiding elder of the East Nashville District for a year, 1889-90, and also edited the *Tennessee Methodist*, the official paper of the Central Tennessee Conference. Haynes led his conference's delegation to the 1894 General Conference, where he spoke often in debate. Haynes distanced himself from other Southern Methodists, however, by ardently embracing prohibition, which many Southerners at the time considered another attempt by Northerners to regulate Southern culture.[3] Haynes began to promote second blessing full salvation in the paper. Denominational leaders strongly opposed this, and, after two years of spirited controversy, the conference disowned the paper. Haynes responded by pointing out the "phenomenal inconsistency of a Methodist conference repudiating its conference organ, because it teaches a Methodist doctrine." Haynes continued publishing the paper as a private venture under the name *Zion's Outlook*. In 1900 Haynes sold the paper to a fellow partisan in the Holiness campaign, the rising Nashville evangelist J. O. McClurkan. Haynes became an active supporter of McClurkan's Pentecostal Mission while retaining his credentials in the Methodist Church. After several demotions to small churches, where he was sent as discipline for his insubordinate ways, Haynes left Tennessee.[4]

James O. McClurkan (1861-1914), the Holiness evangelist who bought Haynes's paper, was a native Tennessean, born in the town of Erin, about sixty miles northwest of Nashville, in 1861. McClurkan's father was a Cumberland Presbyterian minister, and three of McClurkan's brothers were also ministers in the church. While other Presbyterians subscribed to the classical Calvinism of the Westminster Confession, Cumberland Presbyterians had broken away from the larger body of Presbyterians in the early years of the nineteenth century, endorsing revivalism and camp meetings, and embracing Arminian theology.[5]

James O. McClurkan

McClurkan pastored Cumberland Presbyterian churches in Texas for two years and in California for seven years. His last pastorate in California was in San Jose, where McClurkan engaged in a vigorous ministry of house-to-house visitation and personal evangelism, with special efforts to reach children and young people, in order to restart a once vibrant church. He built it into the largest Cumberland Presbyterian congregation on the West Coast, with over three hundred members.[6]

San Jose was pivotal in McClurkan's ministry. In 1895, the same year that Phineas F. Bresee and J. P. Widney organized the Church of the Nazarene 350 miles to the south in Los Angeles, Beverly Carradine, a well-known Southern Methodist Holiness evangelist, held a series of meetings at the Methodist Church in San Jose. At the invitation of friends, McClurkan and his young family attended these meetings. Carradine's preaching stirred a spiritual hunger within McClurkan, and before the meetings ended McClurkan sought and professed the second blessing. This changed the direction of his life. Soon after her husband, Martha Frances Rye McClurkan also experienced entire sanctification.[7]

McClurkan shared his spiritual discovery with his congregation, preached sanctification, and led many of his parishioners into the experience. However, McClurkan's work as a Holiness preacher in San Jose did not last long. Even before the Carradine meetings McClurkan had negotiated a year's leave from his church to travel with his family to Tennessee to visit relatives. He planned to return to the church in San Jose.

On the way from California to Tennessee, McClurkan held evangelistic meetings. These multiplied to the point that McClurkan could barely accommodate them. What he had planned as a one-year sabbatical in Tennessee turned into a two-year itinerant campaign. The McClurkans did not reach Tennessee until 1897 and never returned to San Jose.

When the family arrived, a revival was in progress at McClurkan's boyhood church and he was invited to preach. Aware that his allegiance to the doctrine of sanctification might not sit well with these Cumberland Presbyterians, he hesitated. He told the pastor, his brother-in-law J. J. Rye, "I am preaching a doctrine that is not popular in many churches, and it might hurt you with your membership. I want you to think about it." Rye replied, "Are you preaching the Bible?" "Yes, I am preaching the Bible as I understand it," McClurkan (according to his daughter) assured him. "Well, then, go right ahead," said Rye, "I am not afraid of the Bible." McClurkan preached on "The Fullness of the Blessing," and Rye was "himself gloriously sanctified in his own meeting" and became "a mighty witness to the truth of holiness."[8]

Shortly after, McClurkan's only son, Emmett, became critically ill. Doctors advised the McClurkans to take him to Nashville for treatment. McClurkan there kept up his evangelistic preaching and became a leading voice for the Holiness Movement. Holiness Methodists such as B. F. Haynes welcomed him. Not being a Methodist, McClurkan was not under the threat of discipline by the MEC, South. He unified Holiness advocates in Nashville and Central Tennessee, attracting a substantial group of followers and associates, Methodist and non-Methodist. McClurkan believed that his efforts in Nashville were divinely ordained. Said his daughter: "He saw Nashville, with its favorable location, its transportation facilities, its educational structure, as a center strategic to the dissemination of scriptural holiness throughout the South."[9] McClurkan decided to stay in Nashville and to cultivate the work to which he believed God had led him.

His first step was to appoint six of his followers as a committee to help him decide how to proceed. This group, which included Arthur S. Ransom, E. H. Welburn, John T. Benson, Ed W. Thomas, F. M. Atchison, and Robert Jackson, rented the Nashville Conservatory of Music throughout the winter of 1897-98 to serve as a temporary place for revival meetings and other gatherings. These never conflicted with the regular services of the various churches to which McClurkan's followers belonged. Rather, these meetings were either evangelistic or something on the order of Methodist class meetings, providing caring support and accountability for those seeking to walk in the way of scriptural holiness.[10]

In the spring, members of the Tulip Street Methodist Episcopal Church gave McClurkan the use of that congregation's old building, free of charge. Tulip Street Methodist Episcopal Church was a historic landmark in Nashville, built during the Civil War but locked up and abandoned when its congregation moved to a larger, more ornate facility several blocks away. McClurkan's group scrubbed and cleaned the old facility and occupied the building for the next five years.[11]

McClurkan's advisory committee met eight times between May 14 and June 8, 1898, and ambitiously planned to consolidate and expand the Holiness Movement in central Tennessee, beginning with a series of tent revival meetings in the summer at the Tulip Street Church. The committee purchased three revival tents. The committee elected McClurkan as the superintendent of this yet-to-be-named Holiness association. Clearly, McClurkan and his committee were looking beyond Nashville. This would be their base, but there were many Holiness believers scattered throughout central Tennessee who needed focus to accompany their fervor for holiness.[12]

In July 1898 McClurkan and his group hosted a convention at the Tulip Street Church. According to the minutes of that meeting, "The Convention was held . . . for the purpose of organizing the Holiness people of Middle Tennessee into some kind of band for the promotion of God's work." However, the minutes added tersely, "No new denomination contemplated."[13] The convention adopted a name by which the associated Holiness folk would be known, The Pentecostal Alliance. The convention planned to draw together various prayer bands, mission groups, and other circles of Holiness believers into a Pentecostal Alliance. The convention elected an executive committee, composed of four ordained elders (Cumberland Presbyterians J. O. McClurkan and J. J. Rye; one Southern Presbyterian, B. Helm; and one Southern Methodist, B. F. Haynes) and three laypersons (J. T. Benson, John Radcliff, and Arthur S. Ransom) to oversee the new work. The convention drew together articles of faith and organizational procedures for the alliance, and ordered one thousand copies of these to be printed. The convention provided for issuing credentials to preachers, missionaries, and other Christian workers in the name of the Pentecostal Alliance, and for ordaining preachers. Ordination came in Presbyterian fashion, upon the recommendation of the executive committee through the hands of the ordained elders on the committee. McClurkan, as well as serving as superintendent of the alliance, continued as pastor of the group of Holiness believers at Tulip Street Church. Services remained on Sunday afternoons and evenings, and Thursday nights, so as not to conflict with other churches.[14]

The name Pentecostal Alliance was notable for two reasons. "Pentecostal," as used by holiness people, was synonymous with holiness. Holiness people associated entire sanctification with the outpouring of the Holy Spirit upon the disciples on the Day of Pentecost as described in Acts chapter 2 in the New Testament. Entire sanctification was a personal Pentecost when a believer received the full baptism with the Holy Spirit, who purified their hearts by faith (see Acts 15:9). Adherents regarded the Holiness Movement as a renewal of Pentecost, a "latter day" empowerment of the church for greater ministry in the world. Before the rise of the modern Pentecostal movement in the first decade of the twentieth century, "Pentecostal" did not carry the connotations that it would later acquire associating Pentecost with speaking in tongues and other spiritual gifts. The 1908 Pentecostal Mission explicitly condemned tongues.[15]

A few of McClurkan's associates did become leaders in the burgeoning tongues-speaking Pentecostal movement. N. J. Holmes, a former Southern Presbyterian, presided over both the Tabernacle Pentecostal Church and the Holmes Bible College near Greenville, South Carolina, founded in 1898. Until 1907 Holmes attended the annual meetings of McClurkan's Pentecostal Mission. He left the Pentecostal Mission after he experienced speaking in tongues. In 1910 Holmes's Tabernacle Church affiliated with the Pentecostal Holiness Church. Holmes himself did not join the Pentecostal Holiness Church, preferring his college to remain interdenominational. Among other one-time McClurkan associates, Henry G. Rodgers and Mack M. Pinson helped to found the Assemblies of God.[16]

"Alliance" came directly from a movement launched eleven years earlier by prominent Presbyterian minister Albert Benjamin Simpson. Leaving a Presbyterian pastorate in 1881 to give himself to the poor in New York City, Simpson founded the Christian Alliance in 1887. He envisioned this as an interdenominational fellowship of Christians cooperating in various forms of ministry while remaining members of established denominations. At the same time, Simpson established the Evangelical Missionary Alliance to promote and support foreign missions. In 1897 these two groups merged into the Christian and Missionary Alliance (CMA). Intended as an interdenominational fellowship to carry out and support various ministries neglected by existing denominations, the CMA evolved into a typical denomination.[17]

Simpson combined an unusual and eclectic mix of ideas, doctrines, and practices. From the Holiness Movement he absorbed the doctrine of holiness, or "the Christ life," as he sometimes called it. This became central to his teaching and to the organizations that he founded. However, Reformed rather than Wesleyan and Methodist theology influenced his ways of articulating full sanctification. After Simpson himself experienced healing, he developed intense interest in miraculous divine healing. He also stressed the soon return of Christ. The evangelization of the world needed to be finished immediately because Christ might return at any time. These strands of thought came together in Simpson's teaching of what he called the fourfold gospel: Christ is Savior, Sanctifier, Healer, and Soon-coming King.[18]

Each of these emphases of Simpson could be found in the teaching of McClurkan and the Pentecostal Alliance. For the first three years of its existence, the Pentecostal Alliance *was* the Christian and Missionary Alliance in central Tennessee. The Pentecostal Alliance pledged to send its foreign missionary candidates to the CMA Training Institute at Nyack, New York, and to channel its missionary giving through the CMA headquarters there.[19]

About one hundred delegates and supporters attended a second convention of the Pentecostal Alliance held in November 1899 at the Tulip Street Church. One of the main speakers was Henry Wilson of New York, an Episcopalian minister representing the CMA. One service, led by Wilson, was given to praying for the sick. The convention issued credentials to eleven lay evangelists and raised $2,000 for foreign missions, a large sum at the time for so small a group.[20]

A notation in the minutes of the 1899 convention refers to the presence of G. A. Goings, one of the lay evangelists credentialed by the convention, and his wife, who were "colored." Other African-Americans among McClurkan's associates included Allie Green, an evangelist in Springfield, Tennessee, and J. T. Brown in Nashville. This indicated that though "Jim Crow" laws segregated Blacks and whites elsewhere, the Pentecostal Alliance allowed African-Americans in their midst. McClurkan was convinced, in fact, that such racial fellowship was a necessary evidence of full sanctification. The Holiness Movement, he believed, could eradicate both the race problem and hostility between North and South. "Thank God that holiness is the great resolvent of this problem," he wrote. "The sanctified heart is absolutely cleansed of all war or race prejudice. Holiness deepens and sweetens and broadens the nature until every man of all and every section and nationality and color and condition is loved as a brother. There is no North, no South, no Jew, no Greek, no Barbarian to the sanctified."[21]

The Pentecostal Alliance expanded in many directions. A sizable congregation filled the Tulip Street Church. In the summer of 1900 Pentecostal Alliance members organized a camp meeting in Lebanon, Tennessee (east of Nashville). There hundreds of people were converted and professed entire sanctification. Local newspapers compared the event to the great Tennessee and Kentucky frontier revivals at the beginning of the nineteenth century. The alliance erected a tabernacle in Lebanon, which soon became the heart of a permanent Holiness campground.[22]

Also in 1900 the Pentecostal Alliance purchased the financially troubled *Zion's Outlook* from B. F. Haynes. The paper was barely sustainable, and Haynes had gone deeply into debt trying to keep it alive. McClurkan saw the paper, which he urged the alliance to buy, as a means of organizing the Holiness people of central Tennessee. Renamed *The Living Water* in 1903, the weekly publication became an effective means "through which [McClurkan's] voice and teachings were amplified a hundred times over," an instrument, McClurkan's daughter remarked, which McClurkan "considered did more good than any single means he was able to employ."[23]

The Pentecostal Alliance made several other thrusts. Outgrowing its quarters at the Tulip Street Church, the alliance moved to the Old Hynes School, Nashville's first grammar school (built in 1862, during the Civil War). The alliance occupied this three-story building by the time its Third Annual Convention in November 1900. At that convention, attended by delegates from ten states, from Mississippi to New York and from South Carolina to Texas, the alliance launched a foreign missionary program, sending W. A. Farmer to China under the auspices of the CMA.[24]

The Pentecostal Alliance's weekly meetings at the Old Hynes School for the first time included a Sunday School and Sunday morning worship services. The alliance abandoned the original practice of avoiding conflict with established churches and now encouraged Holiness believers to make the Pentecostal Alliance their church home.[25]

In 1901, the Pentecostal Alliance voted to change its name to The Pentecostal Mission, Incorporated, and to place all of its operations under a committee of twenty-five members, subdivided into a Home Mission Committee and a Foreign Missionary Bureau. The Pentecostal Mission drew back from further association with the Christian and Missionary Alliance and discontinued urging prospective missionaries to attend Nyack and encouraging local churches to send money for missions to the CMA treasurer.[26]

Another development was the adoption of formal statements of essential beliefs and purpose. "Our Mission is to seek the salvation of the lost; the sanctification of believers; the deepening of the spiritual life; the dissemination of Scriptural knowledge of the Lord." The list of doctrines committed members to "the verbal inspiration of the Bible." This reflected concerns about the nature and authority of the Bible being raised by the nascent fundamentalist movement and reflected the same position as Simpson and the CMA. Though others within the Holiness Movement shared this belief, few considered it worth making explicit in doctrinal statements. The Articles of Faith of the Church of the Nazarene, for example, stated simply, "We believe in the inspiration of the Holy Scriptures as found in the Old and New Testaments, and that they contain all truth necessary to faith and practice."[27] The Pentecostal Mission's adoption of a specific view of biblical inspiration set it apart from others within the Holiness Movement who affirmed the authority of the Bible in the traditional Anglican sense. Membership in the Pentecostal

Mission was based on agreement with these doctrines, together with evidence of Christian character.[28]

> A statement in the Pentecostal Mission's doctrinal statement affirmed:
>
>
> **Pentecostal Mission**
>
> Repentance, regeneration, justification by faith in Christ, sanctification for the believer, obtainable in this life, through faith in the blood of Jesus Christ and the personal indwelling of the Holy Ghost; the healing of the bodies of believers by Jesus Christ in answer to the prayer of faith; the pre-millennial coming of our Lord and Savior Jesus Christ to reign on earth as King; the obligation of the great commission resting on every believer, "Go ye into all the world and preach the Gospel to every creature."[29]

In spite of the institutional separation, the Pentecostal Mission's doctrinal statement continued to reflect the fourfold gospel of Simpson and the CMA. Christ's imminent, premillennial return made world evangelization urgent. McClurkan's "Eleventh Hour" convictions, also borrowed from the CMA, posited that history was nearing its completion and that at "midnight," which was almost here, Christ would return. Time for the evangelization of the world was very short and workers must be deployed as rapidly as possible. This, again, reflected the mission's alignment with one particular stream of thought within the Holiness Movement and within Protestantism more generally. For some Protestants, views of eschatology indicated one's general theological orthodoxy. And, for these, increasingly, holding to the premillennial return of Christ was the only possible position.[30]

Having cut ties with the CMA and its Missionary Training Institute in Nyack, New York, McClurkan and his Mission began their own school to prepare missionaries and other Christian workers. McClurkan recruited a small student body and faculty, and the Pentecostal Literary and Bible Training School opened in the Hynes School building in the fall of 1901. McClurkan served as president and dean and as instructor in subjects ranging from the Bible to astronomy. The school originally provided only very basic instruction in "literary" subjects, with the majority of instruction focused on the Bible and methods of Christian work. The primary objective was for each student "to learn how skillfully to bring souls to Christ."[31] By 1905 the Pentecostal Mission had outgrown the Hynes School building, and the school and mission moved to a larger facility.

> McClurkan's daughter stated clearly the purpose of the school in Nashville:
> The Holiness Movement . . . thrust into its ranks a body of choice men and women eager to enter its ministry as preachers, missionaries, and evangelists. Many of these men and women were poor and had been denied by force of circumstances the benefits of formal education. All of them, regardless of their backgrounds, needed special training to equip them for the responsibility at hand. Father was alert to the dangers threatening the cause of holiness if its leadership were given over into untrained hands, and he was quick to sense the basic need of education and training for those who were to preach and teach its doctrine.[32]

By this time McClurkan had become convinced that the school had a broader purpose than simply producing Christian workers as quickly as possible. Unlike other Bible schools that remained devoted exclusively to practical religious training, Trevecca grew into a four-year program leading to a bachelor's degree. McClurkan renamed the school Trevecca College for Christian Workers. McClurkan borrowed the name Trevecca from the school established in Wales in the eighteenth century that provided education to young men wanting to enter the Methodist ministry but who were too poor to have access to universities. Sponsored by Lady Selina Huntington, the school refused to take sides in the quarrel between Calvinistic Methodists such as George Whitefield and Arminian Methodists led by John Wesley. McClurkan found Trevecca a fitting name for his own school.[33]

McClurkan strongly opposed the ordination of women, though early photographs of the student body of the Pentecostal Literary and Bible Training School in Nashville indicate that half or more of the students were women. Clearly McClurkan and the mission believed that God called women to important roles of ministry within the Church and that they needed the same sort of preparation for their ministry as men. The Pentecostal Mission believed that women could be preachers, teachers, and evangelists. They directed missions in various localities and frequently superintended circuits of missions. Women should not, however, be *ordained* for ruling positions, McClurkan believed; this was the teaching of Scripture. This view set the Pentecostal Mission apart from the rest of the groups that were coalescing in the Church of the Nazarene.

There was little question, debate, or argument on the ordination of women in the Association of Pentecostal Churches of America, the Church of the Nazarene, and the various groups that formed the Holiness Church of Christ. McClurkan's Pentecostal Mission was an exception, and it was among the strongest factors holding the Pentecostal Mission back from union with the Church of the Nazarene. Letters back and forth between McClurkan and Bresee expressed their differences of opinion. Neither of them was willing to compromise on this matter for the sake of union. For Bresee, the ordination of women was essential to the gospel of Jesus Christ, while McClurkan could not reconcile the ordination of women with traditional church practices or what he considered the clear teaching of Scripture. Bresee's point of view represented a long-held view among some sectors of Methodism, represented by Phoebe Palmer and the Holiness Movement, and was consistent with the "higher law" principles that had overturned traditional biblical justifications for slavery.[34]

Other enterprises flourished. In 1902 the mission established the Pentecostal Mission Publishing Company to print and distribute Holiness literature. This grew out of McClurkan's practice of carrying a basket of tracts, pamphlets, and gospel songbooks through the streets of Nashville as he went from place to place and visited people in their homes. The publishing company survived the Pentecostal Mission's union with the Church of the Nazarene as an independent entity and eventually became the John T. Benson Publishing Company, which specialized in Christian music.[35]

The Pentecostal Mission aggressively pressed missions work both at home and abroad. By 1903 there were twenty-six Pentecostal Missions in Tennessee and others in Georgia and South Carolina.[36]

After W. A. Farmer, other foreign missionaries followed. When the Pentecostal Mission severed relations with the CMA, some of its missionaries, already scattered around the world, continued under the CMA board. In 1901 the Pentecostal Mission sent out six missionaries: two to China, one to the Sudan, one to the Congo, and two to India. In 1902 it sent out seven more missionaries, six to Cuba and one to India. The Pentecostal Mission sent Rev. and Mrs. J. T. Butler and Emma Goodwin and Rev. C. G. Anderson and Mrs. Daisy Anderson to Guatemala. Rev. and Mrs. Richard Anderson of South Carolina joined them in 1904 and served more than forty years in the country. Coban became the center of the work. Rev. and Mrs. J. L. Boaz and Leona Gardner opened the work in Cuba in 1902. Between 1900, when its first missionary went out, and 1915, when it united with the Church of the Nazarene, the Pentecostal Mission overextended itself, sending out nearly fifty missionaries to various parts of the world.[37]

News of the merger of the Church of the Nazarene and the Association of Pentecostal Churches of America circulated throughout the Holiness Movement. In January 1907, ten months before the Chicago Assembly, McClurkan wrote Phineas Bresee: "We have longed to see a movement of sufficient breadth and Spiritual force to embrace the Pentecostal [i.e., holiness] people of the different temperaments and denominational bias." The leaders of the Pentecostal Mission had "been looking around for other kindred spirits with whom we might affiliate in such an organization." McClurkan declared, "The Church of the Nazarene comes nearer our ideal than any other which we know." As McClurkan continued corresponding with Bresee, however, critical issues arose. The Pentecostal Mission's foreign work was extensive, with missionaries serving in Japan, China, India, Persia, the Sudan, Cuba, and Guatemala. Would these be supported? McClurkan wondered. Also, doctrinal breadth mattered to McClurkan. "The vast majority of our people are Arminian in their views," he assured Bresee, but the Pentecostal Mission tried to steer away from the "extreme statements" of either Arminianism or Calvinism. "Our candid judgment is that the holiness movement as a body would be strengthened by a little more emphasis being put upon Grace," McClurkan told Bresee. "In our zeal to arouse a worldly church we have stressed works to such an extent that the Grace side has been neglected." At the same time, McClurkan acknowledged that the Pentecostal Mission had come to a "parting of the ways" and that it needed either to join some better-organized Holiness body or form one of its own. "Independence is exposed to too many dangers," he confessed to Bresee.[38]

Bresee responded to McClurkan after the successful Brooklyn annual council of the Association of Pentecostal Churches and on the eve of the Chicago Assembly. "No one can tell how glad I would be for you and your people to come in, and for us all . . . to join hands, and by our united faith and multiplied power stretch our hands to fill the earth with full salvation."

Bresee explained to McClurkan his philosophy of union: "A doctrinal basis of necessary belief should be very simple and embrace what is essential to holiness. All not essential to holiness should be relegated to personal liberty." Bresee also told McClurkan that the Nazarenes and the Pentecostal Association Churches would be uniting on the organizational basis of the Nazarene *Manual*, except for some "slight modifications to meet the notions of some extreme Congregationalists" in the APCA. As for "undenominational work," Bresee thought that "much no doubt can be done for a little, but it must pass away soon." Those who "seek wide and lasting results must organize and by staying together build strongly for Him who has called us." Bresee also mentioned to McClurkan that other Holiness churches in the South were considering becoming a part of the union. Bresee and the Nazarenes were urging them to come along. McClurkan was well aware of the Holiness Church of Christ, which often lent support to the missionaries sent out by the Pentecostal Mission.[39]

Like Bresee, McClurkan saw the necessity of establishing strong Holiness congregations at home in order to push the work of "the Full Gospel to the uttermost parts of the earth."[40] Like the Association of Pentecostal Churches in the Northeast, and Bresee's work in California and Calcutta, the Pentecostal Mission was urban in orientation. However, McClurkan was not as hesitant as Bresee to send out missionaries. Like the Holiness Church of Christ, the Pentecostal Mission sent out missionaries on faith. Yet the executive committee of the Pentecostal Mission spent many long hours over problems with missionaries. It forged policies as time went on and problems arose—much as the Association of Pentecostal Churches had done. Sometimes several local churches pledged support for a certain missionary. Each missionary before going out confessed "a personal trust in God for financial support."[41] But one of the chief reasons for the Pentecostal Mission's merger with the Church of the Nazarene was that its missions program needed a firmer financial base.[42]

The Holiness groups and various sectors of society in the same period moved toward stricter order in the first decade of the century. In the Pentecostal Mission leaders attempted to gain more centralized control over both home and foreign missions projects. Taking organizational steps like the other groups that became part of the Church of the Nazarene, the Pentecostal Mission eventually guaranteed its missionaries a monthly income ($25.00), which it solicited through *The Living Water*. Persons of various denominations supported Pentecostal Mission missionaries. In time, the Missions Committee thought it wise to interview and commission prospective missionaries rather than to leave this to local churches. The Pentecostal Mission Convention established policies and guidelines that stated, first, that, regardless of the missionary's source of income, each was responsible in conduct, doctrine, and work to the mission's executive committee. Policy directed missionaries to plant churches along "New Testament" lines. It gave ordained missionaries the right collectively to ordain local workers.[43]

Merger talks stalled. The Pentecostal Mission sent a delegation to the Pilot Point General Assembly in October 1908. The issues separating the Pentecostal Mission from the Church of the Nazarene related to premillennialism, the ordination of women, and the fate of the Pentecostal Mission missionaries. The Pentecostal Mission wanted the Church of the Nazarene to take a strictly premillennial stand on Christ's second coming, and it wanted the church to prohibit women from being ordained. Bresee and other Nazarenes had already indicated their unwillingness to prescribe premillennialism, and they were not about to compromise on ordaining women, a biblical precept dear to each of the previously uniting groups. McClurkan wondered whether union would offer anything to the mission's foreign work. According to one observer, "It was the frightening picture of failing in their avowed responsibilities to their missionaries" that kept them at that time away from union, since they feared the Nazarenes would not support them all. In 1908 the Pentecostal Mission was far ahead of the already united Church of the Nazarene in both the size of its missions budget and the number of missionaries it was supporting. By 1911, however, when the Nazarenes held their General Assembly in Nashville, the new denomination had already doubled what the Pentecostal Mission was doing in both regards.[44]

The next years were ones of financial crisis in the Pentecostal Mission. The mission barely maintained its commitments to its missionaries. When McClurkan died in 1914, the remaining leaders, led by John T. Benson, again approached the Nazarenes. Leaders won assurances from the Nazarenes that Pentecostal Mission missionaries would remain in India, Cuba, and Guatemala. They decided to support union—although each local mission would decide whether or not to join the Church of the Nazarene.[45]

The merger of J. O. McClurkan's Pentecostal Mission with the Church of the Nazarene in 1915 strengthened the church's work around the world, and especially in Latin America. The Boazes went back to the United States in 1905, returning to Cuba from 1914 to 1917. Gardner carried on alone, often supporting herself by teaching school, until 1927. In 1915, upon the mergers with the Church of the Nazarene, the Butlers in Guatemala decided to join another mission, while the Andersons in Guatemala and Gardner in Cuba agreed to become Nazarenes.⁴⁶

Though McClurkan and the Pentecostal Mission fit squarely within the Wesleyan-Holiness movement, his Cumberland Presbyterian background and early association with Simpson and the Christian and Missionary Alliance marked his uniqueness among founders. One of the disputes that led Cumberland Presbyterians to separate from the larger body of Presbyterians was over the authority of the Westminster Confession. Despite various religious awakenings in frontier areas such as Tennessee and Kentucky, where Presbyterians cooperated in camp meetings with Methodists and others, strict Calvinists wanted to impose adherence to the Westminster Confession upon Presbyterians. Revivals themselves challenged Calvinist doctrines of election and implied Arminian understandings of free grace: salvation was offered to every person and all were invited to receive grace. By the early 1900s Presbyterian revivalists such as E. F. Walker had their own understanding of how loosely binding the Westminster Confession must be. Though never a classical Calvinist, McClurkan emphasized means of grace both in the receiving and in the maintaining of the experience of sanctification.⁴⁷

Timothy L. Smith, writing in 1962, referred to "the memories old timers have of the doctrinal controversies between [McClurkan] and other Wesleyans," and to the misunderstandings that still circulated in the Church of the Nazarene.⁴⁸ In fact those who believed McClurkan too Calvinistic in his emphasis upon grace simply had not read John Wesley deeply enough. Nineteenth-century Methodists such as Phoebe Palmer and theologian John Miley had placed consecration and free will in a context outside grace, but Wesley never did. McClurkan, Smith observed, was "Wesleyan through and through, despite his friendship and respect for many who clung to a more 'Calvinistic' view of [Christian holiness]." More than he knew, in emphasizing grace McClurkan was more Wesleyan than many Methodist and Holiness theologians of his time.⁴⁹

THE PENTECOSTAL CHURCH OF SCOTLAND AND NAZARENE BEGINNINGS IN THE BRITISH ISLES

The Church of the Nazarene in the British Isles today represents the confluence of various strong Holiness groups that emerged in the late nineteenth and twentieth centuries. Much united the Holiness Movement in Great Britain and the United States. Ever since George Whitefield, British and American preachers had crisscrossed the Atlantic Ocean. Robert Strawbridge,

Francis Asbury, and Hester Rogers brought Wesley's teachings to America. Evangelicalism, both in its Calvinistic and Arminian varieties, was created in the course of this dynamic interchange of both doctrines and styles of evangelism. Charles Finney, James Caughey, Phoebe Palmer, Asa Mahan, and a host of other Holiness preachers traversed the ocean on behalf of second blessing holiness. As a result, one could find little difference between the preaching of British Holiness leaders such as William Arthur, Samuel Chadwick, W. D. Drysdale, and Oswald Chambers, and their American counterparts. Great Britain and America shared a common Holiness language and literature.[50]

By the early twentieth century, British scholar Alex Deasley observed, "Seasoned churchmen at opposite ends of the United States and in Great Britain had reached the same conclusion," that only distinct organizations would "guarantee the continuance of their mission."[51] George Sharpe, who spent several years of his early ministry in the United States, where he pastored Methodist churches in New York State, embraced the doctrine of entire sanctification through the preaching of National Holiness Association evangelists. But he found, upon returning to his home country of Scotland, that a number of people in Scotland and England taught and believed the doctrine just as he.

For instance, the Holiness Movement had come to Manchester, England, largely through the promotion of Francis W. Crossley (1839-97), a wealthy rubber products and gasoline engines manufacturer. He began a chapel in his factory and helped the poor and needy in Manchester, whom he found living in a "smoke-laden, grimy atmosphere." A city journal reported at Crossley's death that he felt it the "duty of the rich to care for and identify themselves with the submerged class."[52] His views resonated with those of William Booth, the founder of The Salvation Army, and Crossley developed a warm friendship with Booth. Crossley renovated Star Hall, an old music hall, for the poor. It included dining rooms, bathrooms, and residences for workers as well as a large auditorium for worship. Crossley became known as the "St. Francis of Ancoats," the section of Manchester where Star Hall was located,[53] and Star Hall became a "center of a movement for a higher and more consistent standard of Christian living,"[54] as the *Manchester Guardian* saw it. Though affiliated in some ways with the "higher life" movement, Crossley was more radical than Keswick teachings in his understanding of the grace of God to cleanse from all sin. The editor of the *Liverpool Daily Post* was astute enough to note that "the theology taught at Star Hall was almost identical with that of John Wesley," "luminous with the perfection of obedience which it strove to offer to the commands of Jesus Christ."[55]

The Manchester Conventions and Star Hall proved rallying centers for a number of British persons committed to nondenominational holiness and missions to the poor. William McDonald, among other National Holiness Association leaders, spoke at the conferences. George Grubb, speaking at the Manchester Convention in 1892, told of two English lords walking along a London street. Suddenly one of the Lords crossed the street to shake hands with and to converse with an old crossing-sweeper. The other Lord complained, why talk to that dirty old man. The first Lord explained, he has royal blood and I am nearer in relation to him than to you—we are related by blood. With such sentiments, holiness provided a powerful critique of British social structures. Several other congregations or missions, most in the Manchester area, formally affiliated with Star Hall. A. M. Hills spent several years in Manchester preaching at Star Hall: 1908-9, 1910-11, and 1913-15. He wrote and published an attack on Keswick theology at Star Hall. Hills preached widely among various British Holiness groups, including George Sharpe's in Scotland. *The Way of Holiness*, published by Star Hall, included articles by Hills, C. W. Ruth, Bud Robinson, and nearly every other prominent American Holiness writer.[56]

Crossley's funeral services were conducted by J. Rendel Harris, a Quaker scholar who won important academic appointments on both sides of the Atlantic and participated in the Holiness Movement mounting in Manchester in the last years of the nineteenth century. At the 1891 Manchester Conference, Harris took the Pentecostal model to imply that there was something good in Christians coming together to wait for the baptism with the Holy Spirit. In the same conference, he demonstrated the differences between the Manchester and Keswick understandings of holiness. Rendel Harris's wife lamented any kind of sanctification that "leaves the root right in the soil of our hearts to spring up continually into new manifestations of envy or wrath or hatred or jealousy."[57]

Another center of the British Holiness Movement, founded by Reader Harris, was Speke Hall in London. Harris had spent a few years in Bolivia as an engineer and had considered himself an agnostic. He was born again in 1883. He served at the Moody Mission in South London and started services in Battersea. In 1885, he opened Speke Hall. Harris professed to be baptized with the Spirit of God in 1889. In 1891 he began the Pentecostal League of Prayer. The Pentecostal League of Prayer provided many leaders for the British Holiness Movement.[58]

David Thomas, a follower of Harris, embraced holiness during the 1891 conference in Manchester, and Speke Hall nurtured his faith. Thomas founded the International Holiness Mission. This mission sponsored John Thomas, David Thomas's brother, in Korea, who served under the Oriental Missionary Society, and David Jones in South Africa. The International Holiness Mission published *The Holiness Mission Journal,* which contained frequent articles from Nazarene and future Nazarene leaders such as Bud Robinson. The IHM built a strong work in South Africa among the Shangaan and Basuto tribes. The IHM purchased five hundred acres in Cottondale as the center for this work.[59]

British Holiness leaders in Manchester and London became interested in George Sharpe's founding of the Pentecostal Church of Scotland in Glasgow. Sharpe (1865-1948) was a miner's son, born near Craigneuk, Lanarkshire, Scotland, and brought up in the Church of Scotland. Sharpe was converted in 1882 and soon sensed a call to preach. But rather than act upon this conviction, Sharpe immigrated to the United States in 1886 with an invitation to train as an industrial manager. By the time Sharpe arrived, the offer had fallen through.

Sharpe joined the Methodist Episcopal Church in Cortland, New York, and renewed his calling to preach. He started college studies and became a minister. Sharpe was ordained in 1893. He was pastoring the Methodist Church in Chateaugay, New York, about 1899 when Holiness evangelist L. Milton Williams held a series of revival services. Shortly after his wife, Sharpe embraced the experience of entire sanctification, praying: "O Lord, I give Thee all. My spirit, soul and body, my time, my talents, my friends, all I have and all I ever will have, all I know and all I ever will know, to be anything and to go anywhere for Thee. Amen." God sanctified him, Sharpe believed, and "the Holy Ghost came and filled the cleansed temple."[60] Sharpe was not naive. He knew that his espousal of second blessing holiness would put him into conflict with Methodist leaders. Sharpe also championed temperance. He held revivals with L. M. Williams and E. F. Walker, who, in the next several years, became Nazarenes, and who, after Sharpe established a ministry in Scotland, preached for him there. Like other Holiness preachers, Sharpe emphasized plain dress and rejected the suppressionist doctrines of Keswick.[61]

Sharpe returned to Scotland for vacation in 1901 and was called upon to pastor the Congregational church in Ardrossan. He stayed. In 1905 he accepted a call to the Parkhead Congregational Church in Glasgow. Soon, however, members objected to Sharpe's teaching on holiness. In 1906, after a visit of his friend L. M. Williams, Sharpe decided to form a separate congregation. Eighty sympathetic members from the Congregational church joined him. In October 1906 Sharpe formed the Parkhead Pentecostal Church. Soon he organized similar congregations in Paisley and Uddington. He launched a Bible college, and, finally, in 1909, formed the Pentecostal Church of Scotland. Through various Holiness publications as well as through his evangelist friends, Sharpe was well acquainted with the bodies that had come to form the Church of the Nazarene. Like many of them, Sharpe's work began in a strategic urban center. In polity, the Pentecostal Church of Scotland was patterned after the Nazarene *Manual*.[62]

Remarkably, Sharpe allowed women to preach and be ordained. Like the Holiness groups in the United States, the Pentecostal Church of Scotland entered the decision to ordain women in full consciousness of its implications. "We endorse the action of other Holiness Churches and put ourselves on record," Sharpe wrote in 1909, "that the privileges granted young men for gaining a place amongst us in the ministry shall at all times be extended to women in the Gospel who know that they have a call from God and who in the judgment of the Church have been specially chosen by the Holy Spirit to the ministry."[63] In 1911 Jane Sharpe, George Sharpe's wife, became, likely, the first woman in Scotland so ordained. Olive Winchester, formerly a teacher at the Pentecostal Collegiate Institute of the Association of Pentecostal Churches of America, taught at Sharpe's Parkhead Holiness Bible College from 1909 to 1913 and served as president of the church's missionary society while pursuing advanced studies in divinity at the University of Glasgow. The Pentecostal Church of Scotland ordained her in 1912, the same year that she received the bachelor of divinity degree from the University of Glasgow, the first woman to achieve that distinction.[64]

Movements toward union with other Holiness groups in the British Isles were not entirely in the hands of Sharpe. Star Hall leaders, led by Crossley's daughter, Ella, called for an assembly of British Holiness churches and missions in May 1909. She saw the necessity of permanent organization to "unite and preserve." The conference of Holiness people was held at Sharpe's Parkhead Church in Glasgow. The conference opened with a service of "sermon and sacrament." The third session was a "Full Salvation Meeting" conducted by Ella Crossley and Miss Hatch of Manchester.[65]

Ella Crossley's leadership of the Holiness Movement centered in Manchester indicates that here, too, women were prominent proponents of entire sanctification. In *Holiness Teaching* Ella Crossley admonished contemporary Methodists to "go back to the Bible, and preach the old truths and seek the old fire!"[66] She rooted her understanding of holiness in John Wesley and advised preachers to stress instantaneous holiness by faith, which, she was convinced, would enable persons to enter into a second, definite work of grace. She used baptism with the Holy Spirit language to emphasize the second blessing aspect of the grace of entire sanctification. Sin is twofold, she said, and so is grace. At the same time, like Wesley, Crossley differentiated between sins and infirmities.[67]

Perhaps in response to the 1909 Conference, organized by Star Hall leaders, the Pentecostal Church of Scotland (PCS) articulated its own mission "as a Church" to "propagate the doctrine of Scripture and to advance the course of Holiness. The Pentecostal Church of Scotland we believe is to carry the Message of Full Salvation through the Baptism of the Holy Ghost and to conserve the work of Holiness that it may spread over the Land."[68] This language, which, again, included "baptism of the Holy Ghost" terminology, clearly reflected that of the Holiness Movement on both sides of the Atlantic. It also reflected the desire of the PCS to be more than a mission or an assembly of independent congregations. It aspired, as did the North American Holiness bodies emerging at the same time, to churchliness. Like the bodies in North America, the PCS understood that the Holiness message was best propagated through separate organization. The PCS sought to multiply Holiness churches, to unite Holiness people, and to put a "true brand" on those who had received the grace of entire sanctification. The weakness of the British Holiness Movement, Sharpe perceived, lay in its fragmentariness. Holiness leagues, missions, associations, and societies were not sufficient. Just as Phineas Bresee believed, Holiness people needed a church.[69]

The 1914 Annual Assembly of the Pentecostal Church of Scotland demonstrated the continued attention to social issues among Holiness groups in the British Isles. The April assembly passed a resolution against the liquor traffic and commended legislation shortening work hours.[70]

By this time, Sharpe had begun active talks with leaders of the Church of the Nazarene regarding affiliation. Nazarene General Superintendent E. F. Walker, whose Presbyterian background and exegetical style of preaching commended itself to the Scots, attended the PCS Assembly in 1914. A "Special Committee of the Proposed Union" gathered information that would enable the PCS churches to fairly consider union.

General Superintendent Hiram F. Reynolds was not entirely sure that the Church of the Nazarene was in a position to assimilate the Pentecostal Church of Scotland. But Olive Winchester urged union, and Reynolds respected her advice. He agreed to visit Scotland to see whether union could be effected. Reynolds's visit to several churches under Sharpe was helpful. Reynolds reported that "the proper arrangements were made, which practically effects the union of the Pentecostal Churches of Scotland and England with the Pentecostal Church of the Nazarene." Reynolds's impression was that the people he found on his trip were "real Pentecostal Nazarene people and have the experience for which we stand."[71] Reynolds appointed Sharpe provisional district superintendent, with his leadership to take effect on January 1, 1915. Reynolds's only hesitancy was about giving missions money to places already Christian and where English was spoken. In 1915, the Church of the Nazarene brought in the Pentecostal Mission and was now responsible for supporting many of its missionaries. Would the British group be another strain upon the church's budget? Nonetheless, Reynolds, in the trip to Scotland, agreed that the General Missionary Board could underwrite a major part of the district superintendent's salary. Reynolds encouraged the British to raise money for foreign missions.[72]

The General Assembly of the Church of the Nazarene, meeting in Kansas City in October 1915, voted to approve the union. At that time, the PCS included eight churches, 665 members (350 in the Parkhead Church), and a Sunday School enrollment of 841. The Nazarene General Assembly recommended that the British Isles be formed into a district with George Sharpe as superintendent, tasked to organize new churches. The assembly agreed to a $1,000 a year budget to help support the nascent Nazarene work in the British Isles. On November 5, 1915, the Seventh Annual Assembly of the PCS, held at the Parkhead, Glasgow, Church, and chaired by Sharpe, dealt with the question of affiliation and voted unanimously for union.[73]

It is likely that this affiliation with the Church of the Nazarene disappointed certain British Holiness people, including those leading Star Hall. Before 1915, Star Hall's publication, *The Way of Holiness*, had frequently carried articles written by Sharpe and American Nazarenes. It had reported on the growth of the PCS from its founding. But *The Way of Holiness* did not even mention the PCS's affiliation with the Church of the Nazarene and, afterward, ignored Sharpe's church in the pages of *The Way of Holiness*, which continued to carry notices of other Holiness missions in Glasgow, such as those being sponsored by the Primitive Methodists. Though there might have been a variety of reasons for this, it seemed as though leaders at Star Hall preferred a British Holiness denomination rather than an American Holiness church to be the center of the Holiness Movement in the British Isles. Meanwhile, Star Hall supported many of the missionaries being sent out by the International Holiness Mission and such groups as the Oriental Missionary Society. Star Hall affiliated with The Salvation Army in 1918. However, in the same year, Star Hall started the Manchester Tabernacle, which later affiliated with the International Holiness Mission. Pastors included H. E. Jessop, J. H. Farmer, and Maynard James, all of whom were at one time or another

Nazarenes. The congregation itself became Nazarene when the International Holiness Mission joined the Church of the Nazarene in 1952.[74]

George Sharpe pastored the Parkhead Church from 1906 to 1921. As a preacher, his sermons were the "product of reason and imagination, ability and passion, education and consecration, natural gifts and the Spirit's fullness, and blood, sweat, and tears," observed George Frame, a young colleague of Sharpe. His sermons contained careful logic and exegetical rationality to support his contentions that entire sanctification represented a second blessing experience for the people of God. Sharpe served as district superintendent from 1915 to 1924 and from 1928 to 1932. He served as missionary superintendent for Africa and India from 1923 to 1925. He became pastor, again, of the Parkhead congregation, serving from 1932 to 1938.[75]

THE LAYMEN'S HOLINESS ASSOCIATION

In the 1920s, many Midwestern Methodists became disillusioned with the liberal trends of their denomination. Some of these embraced holiness and a few found their way into the Church of the Nazarene. Those who became Nazarene in the 1920s were committed not only to holiness but often to premillennialism, the inerrancy of Scripture, creationism, and issues of concern to fundamentalists in other denominations. The Laymen's Holiness Association, centered in the Dakotas, typified this trend and illustrated the fundamentalist influences rising in the Church of the Nazarene. These rural Methodists felt alienated from urban culture. They observed a heightened sense of tragedy following the First World War and associated modernism with German historical criticism and philosophy in general. They feared further upheaval from Bolshevism, atheism, and world revolution. Their piety and pessimism outweighed social concern. Fear colored the whole sphere of sociological change. Many Holiness people, like other Americans, became caught up in the view that there was some plot working against the basic premises and morals of Christianity. The sources of these fears were foreignism, biblical criticism, modernism, Darwinism, Christian Scientism, evolutionism, atheism, and Communism.[76]

James G. Morrison (1871-1939), who led members of the Laymen's Holiness Association into the Church of the Nazarene, was born in Iowa. After financial reverses, his family moved to the Dakota Territory in 1873 and soon began worshipping in a Methodist Church. Morrison attended the university at Vermillion (later named the University of South Dakota), married, and prepared himself for pastoral ministry. He read J. A. Wood's holiness classic *Perfect Love*. Morrison began preaching about the necessity of a second blessing even before he entered into the experience himself. "Several of my hearers," Morrison wrote, "were under conviction for the blessing before I had received it myself." He continued, "I consecrated all. I abandoned everything to Jesus my Lord and Master." Finally, Morrison "reached the place where the great God dared to release His burning baptism upon my heart," he wrote. "Like a great spiritual light it slowly rose above the horizon of my soul. It shined and burned and melted away all the feverish, gunpowdery, carnal, disposition that I had. It filled my heart and my life. It cleansed and sanctified my soul. The Holy Ghost had come!" Morrison exclaimed.[77]

J. G. Morrison

Morrison was ordained as a deacon by Bishop Isaac Joyce in 1895 and as an elder by Bishop John F. Hurst in 1897. Morrison pastored in Litchfield, Minnesota, from 1895 to 1898, and at the Franklin Avenue Methodist Church in Minneapolis from 1898 to 1901. His wife died during this time. While pastoring next in Fergus Falls, Minnesota, he remarried. He wrote of these days, "When I left each pastorate for a new one there remained a devoted band of sanctified people at each place. These bands later became churches when the Nazarene movement came our way."[78]

While pastoring in Jamestown, South Dakota, from 1904 to 1911 Morrison found a like-minded soul and strong advocate of holiness in his district superintendent, S. A. Danford. In his years as Methodist superintendent (or "presiding elder," as the term was prior to 1908) on the Fargo District (1904-9) and Bismarck District (1909-15), Danford drew many toward holiness. Though not known as a good administrator, Danford was a "magnetic personality, organizer of ability, a flaming evangelist."[79] With the help of laypersons, in 1905 Danford and Morrison established the Jamestown Camp Meeting. Morrison's own influence grew as editor of the *North Dakota Methodist* beginning in 1908.

The Holiness Movement produced a recognizable split in the Methodist Church in the Dakotas. To those who remained loyal to the Methodist Church, it seemed the "second blessing" supporters placed lesser value on Sunday Schools and youth groups known as Epworth Leagues, and more value on emotionally laden special meetings. The Holiness faction accused the others of coldness, lack of spirituality, and modernism. The differences between the two factions grew with each Annual Conference.

A camp meeting association, rather than the Methodist Church, owned the property of the Jamestown camp. They called recognized Holiness evangelists to lead the camp meetings. While many Methodists returned to their home churches from the camp meetings to "do great work for the Lord," others, pastors found, were "cantankerous divisionists with whom neither God nor man could work constructively"![80] Methodist Bishop William Quayle became concerned that the Holiness Movement was dividing the church. In 1915 Quayle secured the transfer of Danford to Eugene, Oregon. Rather than appoint Morrison to succeed him as superintendent of the Bismarck District, as the Holiness faction desired, he appointed Morrison to the Larimore Circuit. Morrison transferred to Sebring, Florida, in 1916, but the next year his friends in the Dakotas persuaded him to return. They elected him president of the Jamestown Camp Meeting and superintendent and field evangelist of the newly formed Laymen's Holiness Association (LHA). Morrison also edited its paper, *The Holiness Layman*.

In January 1921, the special speaker at an LHA gathering in Jamestown was Nazarene General Superintendent John W. Goodwin. Though Goodwin's approach was low-key, many laypersons decided to join the Church of the Nazarene at that time. Meanwhile, a Church of the Nazarene had begun in Minneapolis. Morrison preached a revival in this church in 1922. At the close of the revival, the church's pastor, E. E. Wordsworth, took Morrison in as a member.

Quickly, the general superintendents seized the opportunity and appointed Morrison as district superintendent of an area that encompassed Minnesota and North and South Dakota. He served in this capacity until 1926, using his contacts in the Laymen's Holiness Association to begin Nazarene churches. As a Methodist historian later observed, by this time revivals and Holiness interest in the Methodist Church in the Dakotas had petered out, leaving the Methodists to "get on with the business for which the church was founded."[81] By 1940 the Church of the Nazarene numbered thirty-two churches in the Dakotas and 1,127 members—nearly all of them former Methodists.

A premillennialist eschatology filled a large place in Morrison's evangelistic ministry. In a fundamentalist way, also, Morrison reflected the era's mood by linking the German aggressions of the Great War to the teachings of evolution and modernism. Yet like other Nazarene preachers and leaders, entire sanctification remained preeminent in Morrison's concerns. His theology of holiness reflected the common understandings of the era—with all of its affirmations and qualifications. Regeneration began a "marvelous development" in Christian life and bestowed power, a graciously given ability, to refrain from sin. One may grow *in* but not *into* holiness. It came through a baptism with the Holy Spirit. One secured a testimony to entire sanctification by inward assurances and by studying the promises of Scripture and prayer. Yet even the holiest were guilty of unconscious offenses each day. Not until heaven was there deliverance from "infirmities." There was a "human side" to entire sanctification. The experience did not bring perfect conduct. These were "trespasses," said Morrison, not sin, and were consistent with the holy life. To maintain entire sanctification, one must maintain full consecration.[82]

In 1926 the Northwest Nazarene College Board of Trustees elected Morrison president. He served for only one year. H. F. Reynolds persuaded him to come to Kansas City to assist him in the running of the Foreign Missions department. After one year assisting Reynolds, Morrison became executive secretary of Foreign Missions. He served from 1927 to 1936. (For two years, 1932 to 1934, he also served as general treasurer.) Morrison took the opportunity to visit Nazarene churches in Trinidad, South Africa, Argentina, Mexico, and Scotland. The 1936 General Assembly delegates on the fifth ballot elected the sixty-five-year-old Morrison general superintendent. He died in office three years later.[83]

CONCLUSION

Holiness folk disagreed on matters pertaining to ecclesiology, sacraments, eschatology, and behavior. Though they even explained Christian holiness somewhat differently, all agreed that God provided, and Scripture witnessed to, the possibility of Christian believers living truly holy lives. Consistent victory over sin and a Christlike character that was dominated by love to God and to one's neighbor reflected such holiness. Entire sanctification was a gracious gift of God that Christian believers could receive subsequent to their initial conversion. Those in the Holiness Movement referred to the subsequent or "second" work of grace by a variety of names: entire sanctification, full sanctification, the baptism with the Holy Ghost, circumcision of the heart, being wholly sanctified or perfected in love, among other terms. They had similar ideas about the subsequent work of grace, the conditions necessary for receiving this grace, and the evidences manifest in a believer who indeed had been fully sanctified.

Phoebe Palmer, the mother of the nineteenth-century Holiness Movement, blended, as historian Melvin Dieter says, "the American mind, prevailing revivalism, and Wesleyan perfectionism."[84] Palmer's formulation of Christian holiness informed and influenced the American and British Holiness Movement for a century. She refined John Wesley's teachings in ways she thought suitable for her time and place. Others associated with the Holiness Movement did likewise in the early twentieth century. Nonetheless, among the groups that became part of the Church of the Nazarene, loyalty to Wesley's theology of entire sanctification was conscious and sure. What drew together those who became Nazarene was a commitment to an essential doctrinal and experiential core.

PART II

Introduction

The young Nazarene church had already emerged by 1915 as the primary ingathering denomination of the Wesleyan-Holiness revival. By the end of that year the church embraced previously separate and independent denominations: the Association of Pentecostal Churches of America, the Church of the Nazarene, the Holiness Church of Christ, the Pentecostal Church of Scotland, and the Pentecostal Mission. The church also had absorbed the Holiness Christian Church's Pennsylvania Conference, many leaders and members of the Louisiana Conference of the Methodist Protestant Church, and so many members of the Holiness Association of Texas that it had no further reason to be and disbanded. The Laymen's Holiness Association in the Dakotas yielded similar accessions in the 1920s. The next round of accessions did not occur until after the Second World War, and unlike those between 1907 and 1915, they were not mergers between partners of similar strength.

Denominations formed through merger must establish a common life, and while united around the doctrine of holiness, the Nazarene parent bodies differed in their modes of organization and governance, membership standards, and emphases. The Church of the Nazarene embraced people with strongly differing regional and national outlooks. In its first quarter century, one of its central tasks was to establish the common priorities that would unite Nazarenes into one body, to achieve, as Timothy Smith described it, the "inner reality of union."[1]

Nazarenes took various steps to accomplish this. With the 1911 General Assembly's decision that established the Nazarene Publishing House in Kansas City, Missouri, the new denominational paper, the *Herald of Holiness*, replaced the regional papers. Colleges inherited from the parent bodies maintained regionalism, but general superintendents moved college administrators from one place to another. Some schools consolidated. A shared philosophy of higher education guided surviving ones. The church's colleges stamped upon youth denominational values and identity. The church's theology developed at the hands of theologians associated with the colleges. Missions and youth auxiliaries also unified the church. Each development strengthened the inner sinews of connectionalism binding the Nazarenes into one people.

The church's sense of mission to the world become one of its highest priorities. This reflected the influence of H. F. Reynolds, whose executive skills and sheer passion for missions rallied the people. Reynolds dreamed of significant Nazarene participation in world evangelization, but did not labor alone. Though the role of women in the church's ordained ministry rose and then fell, laywomen and clergywomen from across the church formed the Woman's Missionary Society. The high priority given to cross-cultural missions by 1925 established a fundamental tone within denominational life. A purpose beyond local concerns shaped who Nazarenes were and what they would become. The success of early missions laid the necessary foundations for decisions taken a half-century later when the 1976 General Assembly embraced the concept of "internationalization." The church would enter the twenty-first century as one undivided and global body.

The early priority that the General Board of Foreign Missions assumed in the church's life highlighted another concern. Between 1911 and 1919 the General Assemblies created a series of boards to carry out specific ministries. The General Orphanage Board, the General Board of Home Missions, the General Board of Social Welfare, and the General Board of Church Extension were among these. Each had its own set of directors and raised its own funds. But how would the church manage competition between these boards, as each sought the funding needed to fulfill its task? The need to shape priorities and allocate funds impartially brought these boards into one cohesive whole in 1923 with the creation of the General Board, with authority to shape one General Budget for financing all ministries mandated by the General Assembly. Financial crises prompted three successive General Assemblies (1923, 1928, and 1932) to take legislative action bringing all of the essential aspects of the church under the General Board's authority. The basic structure of Nazarene social ministry changed, leaving scant evidence by 1940 that the church had earlier demonstrated a sense of obligation and compassion toward orphans and unwed mothers.

In the period inclusive of two world wars, amid harsh economic, political, and social realities, Nazarenes examined and affirmed the foundations of their common life. World War I, racial barriers, the Great Depression, and, finally, World War II, shaped a secular reality marred by streaks of brutality and other reminders of humanity's fallen estate. But Nazarenes strove to shape another reality—a reality of the spirit manifested in both individuals and in life together.

EIGHT

The Spirit and the Structure of the Church

The newly created Pentecostal Church of the Nazarene wrestled with the circumstances of its origins. Regionalism shaped its initial character. In regional associations leaders had enjoyed freedom. The united church developed its own identity as a national, even international, body by establishing a common agenda with national and international rather than simply regional leaders.

The general superintendents and other national leaders held the most important keys to the process that moved the church toward a common identity. H. F. Reynolds, R. T. Williams, and J. B. Chapman contributed significantly, as did B. F. Haynes, H. Orton Wiley, and Susan Fitkin. District leaders, college presidents, pastors, and key laity did so as well.

The erection of an appropriate structure was central to shaping a Nazarene identity. Through Bresee's influence, the church undertook a democratic form of Methodism. While Nazarenes organized their common life in ways that reflected their own sense of mission, their church resembled other denominations in the Wesleyan tradition, especially older churches whose founders had likewise dissented from Episcopal Methodism: Methodist Protestants, Wesleyan Methodists, and Free Methodists.[1] The Nazarenes' quadrennial General Assembly, *Manual,* yearly district assemblies, and annual meetings of congregations, reflected Methodism's pattern. So did the three tiers of assemblies, with congregations electing district assembly delegates, district assemblies electing General Assembly delegates, and General Assembly decisions binding, in turn, the whole denomination. The deed restrictions on local property made the district, not the congregation, the de facto owner, and this was another Methodist influence that, Bresee insisted, Nazarenes must embed in their structure. Each feature underscored his intention that this church was to be *connectional,* with all its parts interdependent.

Two other fundamental Methodist assumptions were at work in Bresee's thinking. One was the conviction that Nazarenes were not the whole Church of God but merely one expression of the Church Universal. Bresee's first

Manual stated this, as did the united church's *Manual* in every subsequent edition. The church's founders understood that the Bible revealed no specific design for church government. Therefore, provided that no practices directly contradicted Scripture, the appropriate forms of church governance could be shaped by common consent. In this equation, *mission* shaped *structure*. Though the same assumption gave British Methodism a structure *without* bishops and American Methodism a structure *with* bishops, the essence of Methodist governance was not a particular type of episcopacy, nor episcopacy itself. Rather, Methodists perceived the need for superintendency and the connectional nature between the levels of governance. Nazarenes embraced these concepts in the 1907 Basis of Union.

The relationship among the three levels of governance—congregation, district, and general—did not change. But one issue remained unsettled: how to structure the church to best care for the general interests. Until 1932, one General Assembly after another tinkered with the organization of the general interests before all the elements came together. After that date, the church made no major revisions for nearly a half-century.

THE GENERAL SUPERINTENDENCY

The Chicago and Pilot Point assemblies in 1907 and 1908 brought together congregationally oriented churches in the East and South with superintendency-oriented churches in the West. But the assemblies did not erase all doubts among those who questioned superintendency. All agreed that the general superintendent in the Nazarene system would not be as strong as the office of bishop in Methodism. Bresee's adoption of the term "general superintendent" harkened back to two precedents. John Wesley had appointed Thomas Coke and Francis Asbury as "general superintendents" (rather than bishops) of the Methodist societies in America. Over the next century, dissident Methodists objected from time to time to the degree of authority concentrated in the office of bishop, particularly the bishop's ability to appoint pastors. The Wesleyan Methodists simply relied on district superintendents and rejected general executives altogether until the mid-twentieth century. Free Methodists, on the other hand, democratized the concept of episcopacy and, until 1907, when they replaced the term "general superintendent" with "bishop," revived Wesley's original term for the office. Bresee's adoption of the term "general superintendent" harkened, then, to Wesley's original wording and Free Methodist practice.[2]

Bresee modeled a grace-filled style of superintendency that reassured many, though not all. W. C. Wilson, a Bresee confidant, doubted that others could bear the office with Bresee's dignity. The general superintendents were not paid salaries. They raised their incomes elsewhere. Near his own death, Bresee admonished the church to provide a salary that would allow the general superintendents to be full-time.[3]

Hiram F. Reynolds became the senior general superintendent upon Bresee's death in 1915. Reynolds was 61, and his influence on Nazarene life, already considerable, emerged more forcefully. Reynolds traveled far more than any of his early colleagues. He shared Bresee's understanding of limited superintendency within a democratic system and bore its weight similarly. Nazarenes knew Reynolds for his passion for foreign missions and for his zeal for organizational efficiency, though not particularly for his preaching. Headquarters employees remembered his cheerfulness. One gushed that when Reynolds visited, it was as "though a sunbeam had suddenly brightened a dark room or a spring breeze had floated through an open window."[4]

Reynolds's ability to communicate his vision and inspire others to share it testified to his dogged determination and persuasive powers during his years of greatest effectiveness. The prioritizing of Nazarene life around world evangelization touched all aspects of the church. It defined the role of the General Board and necessitated a General Budget as the primary means through which Nazarenes carried out their collective ministry. It inspired the creation of the Woman's Missionary Society, which soon organized general, district, and local chapters, with societies in most Nazarene congregations, including those being established outside North America. While Bresee fashioned the church's early mechanisms of governance and championed its distinguishing doctrine of holiness, Reynolds laid the foundations that resulted in the Church of the Nazarene entering the twenty-first century as a global denomination.[5]

Reynolds's colleagues on the Board of General Superintendents brought different backgrounds and strengths. Besides Bresee (1907-15), Reynolds served with Edgar P. Ellyson (1908-11), Edward F. Walker (1911-18), William C. Wilson (1915), John Goodwin (1916-40), Roy T. Williams (1916-45), and James B. Chapman (1928-46).

Edgar P. Ellyson (1869-1954) was a man in early

E. P. Ellyson with Minnie Staples and Japanese students at Pasadena College

midlife and full of vigor. He regarded himself as an educator, not an administrator. Born in Damascus, Ohio, he spent one year studying at the Cleveland Bible Institute. In 1893 he married M. Emily Soul of Quebec, Canada. They were ordained in the Friends Church and served three years as pastors and one year as evangelists. In about 1897 they founded the Christian Worker's Training School in Marshalltown, Iowa, and Edgar Ellyson served there as president until called to the same position at Texas Holiness University in 1906. Under Ellyson's presidency, which he retained during his years as general superintendent, enrollment at THU reached 400. Emily Ellyson served as head of the Bible and theology department and pastored the college church. Ellyson served a single term as general superintendent. He declined reelection in 1911 and became president of the Nazarene school in Pasadena.

Edward F. Walker (1852-1918) was born in Ohio and moved when he was eleven to California, where he learned to become a printer. He was converted as a young man through Methodist influences. Preachers and evangelists, including J. S. Inskip, William McDonald, and Maggie Newton Van Cott nurtured Walker's call to ministry. Walker attended the University of the Pacific and held several Methodist charges. Bishop Matthew Simpson ordained him a deacon. But Walker became a Presbyterian before his ordination as a Methodist elder. He pastored Presbyterian and Congregational churches in the San Francisco area, and then in Nevada, before entering the Presbyterian seminary in Pittsburgh, Pennsylvania. He subsequently pastored Presbyterian churches in Pennsylvania, Ohio, Indiana, Kansas, and Colorado. He made Greenfield, Indiana, his base for full-time evangelistic ministry, which he launched in 1891. By 1895 Walker was one of the National Holiness Association's leading evangelists. After a complaint from another part of the country, in 1898 the presbytery of Indianapolis reprimanded him for his Holiness preaching. It reinstated him to good standing later that same year after he preached to the full presbytery. Walker had a prominent role at the General Holiness Assembly in Chicago in 1901. In 1903 he spoke at the Annual Meeting of the Pentecostal Mission in Nashville. As a preacher, Walker addressed the great theological themes of the Bible. He preached exegetically in an era when topical sermons prevailed. He was witty, well-read, and knowledgeable of New Testament Greek. Like Bresee, Walker quoted various poets, authors, preachers, and scholars.[6]

Walker was serving as moderator of the Indianapolis Presbytery before moving with his family, after the 1908 Pilot Point Assembly, to California to pastor Pasadena First Church of the Nazarene. Walker later served as associate pastor under Bresee at Los Angeles First Church. Walker's stature within the wider Holiness Movement made him a natural candidate to succeed E. P. Ellyson in 1911. In an address to the General Assembly two days before his election, Walker extolled the virtues of the Church of the Nazarene as a model of democracy. His critics would find those words ironic.[7]

In 1912, a year after his election, Walker met with disgruntled members of the Washington, D.C., congregation. Because of some disagreements, Pastor H. B. Hosley had forced these members to leave the church. For this, the former members wanted Hosley disciplined. They called for the general superintendents to intervene. Walker reviewed their grievances. Hosley, a former Quaker, was wary of superintendents. To him, Walker's interference was intolerable. An investigation committee, chaired by William Howard Hoople, a champion of local church autonomy, exonerated Hosley of any wrongdoing. Hosley decided to leave the denomination anyway. His congregation, having been a part of the Association of Pentecostal Churches of America, had retained the title to its property and so withdrew from the Church of the Nazarene with it buildings and property intact.[8]

The 1915 General Assembly, the first to be held in Kansas City, proved just how uncertain the politics of general superintendency could be. Many believed that Bresee, Reynolds, and Walker needed a fourth colleague. Once the assembly convened, it became obvious to the delegates that Bresee was dying. The assembly honored him in a touching ceremony that included testimonials from representatives of each original parent body of the church. Despite W. C. Wilson's reservations about the office, associates in the West favored him should a fourth general superintendent be elected. Bresee urged the election of four general superintendents, stating in various ways that Reynolds was the only one of the present trio capable of discharging his responsibilities. Slighted by such remarks, Walker addressed the General Assembly to resign as general superintendent and from the church's ministry and membership. A committee met with him and reassured him of the General Assembly's continued support. He rescinded his resignations the following day.[9]

This was only the beginning. C. E. Cornell, pastor of Los Angeles First Church, made remarks during public debate that delegates from Texas thought belittled their ability to follow parliamentary procedures. This fueled growing sentiment among the Southern delegates that a fourth general superintendent, if elected, should come from outside California, where Bresee and Walker lived. As a result, former general superintendent Ellyson, then serving at Olivet College in Illinois, was elected on the ninth ballot. Ellyson was not present, and when he arrived by train three days later, he spoke briefly with Walker, who had played a role in terminating Ellyson's presidency at

Nazarene University in Pasadena in 1913. Ellyson addressed the assembly and declined his election. Voting began again, and W. C. Wilson was elected general superintendent two ballots later.[10]

Despite the strange dynamics, Wilson's election was widely considered beneficial. As a native Kentuckian, Wilson (1866-1915) represented the South. Like Ellyson, he was in midlife. He had been active in the Holiness Movement in both the Upper South and the West. In California he pastored at Upland, Long Beach, and Pasadena First before following J. W. Goodwin in 1911 as superintendent of the Southern California District. Like Goodwin, Wilson worked closely with Bresee, and in autumn 1914, when Bresee was too ill to conduct the district assemblies assigned to him, Wilson presided in his stead, a clear sign of Bresee's favor. Attentive to the sentiments of the Southern delegates, Wilson quickly let it be known that he would move to Nashville so that one general superintendent would reside in the South. He seemed the picture of health and vigor, and the church expected him to fill the office for many years. The church expected Bresee's death, which occurred in November. But Wilson's demise from an acute and excruciating infection on December 19, 1915, just five weeks after Bresee's death, shocked the church.[11]

The *Manual* provided for the district superintendents to elect new general superintendents when vacancies occurred between general assemblies. With Walker's health precarious, and only Reynolds able to fill the office with vigor, Reynolds and Walker determined that both Bresee's and Wilson's vacancies should be filled. By mail ballots, in January 1916 the district superintendents elected John Goodwin and R. T. Williams as general superintendents. The decision to fill two vacancies proved correct. Walker died before his term ended. Reynolds, Goodwin, and Williams formed the Board of General Superintendents for the decade spanning 1918 to 1928.

John W. Goodwin (1869-1945) tended to move behind the scenes. A native of Maine, he was converted in a Free Will Baptist Church in Dover, New Hampshire, in 1887, through the influence his grandparents. After marrying Bertha Billings in 1888, Goodwin joined the Advent Christian Church, to which she belonged. Advent Christians, like Seventh-Day Adventists, arose from the millenarian movement of the 1840s led by William Miller. Advent Christians did not share the doctrines of Anna White that shaped Seventh-Day Adventists but were an evangelical denomination, congregational in government. Advent Christians required members to affirm Christ's premillennial second coming. They believed in the annihilation rather than the eternal punishment of unrepentant sinners, and in the theory of "soul sleep," that "the dead in Christ" have no consciousness until the general resurrection of the dead. After supplying pulpits for a year, in 1893 Goodwin was ordained in the Advent Christian Church. He served congregations in Massachusetts and Rhode Island, during which time he joined other Protestants in the prohibition movement.

The New England Holiness Movement soon drew him as well. While pastoring in Haverhill, Massachusetts, from 1895 to 1899, a core group of laypersons prayed for his entire sanctification. Both H. C. Morrison and C. J. Fowler preached in his church, and Goodwin participated in Holiness camp meetings and revivals in churches of various denominations. He gradually accepted Methodism's primary doctrines and rejected his own denomination's doctrines of conditional immortality and soul sleep. He retained the Adventists' premillennialism.

For health reasons, Goodwin and his family spent a year, 1900-1901, in California, pastoring a small Christian Advent church. During this time, Goodwin became acquainted with Phineas Bresee. Returning to New England, Goodwin completed a correspondence course in theology offered by Taylor University, a Holiness college in Indiana, and read the major works of Methodist theologians William Pope and John Miley. Goodwin pastored a strong Advent Christian church in Springfield, Massachusetts, where he promoted Holiness revivals and camp meetings.[12]

Goodwin was ready for a decisive break. In 1905, Goodwin moved his family to the West Coast in order to unite with the Church of the Nazarene. Immediately, Bresee appointed him to the church in Pasadena. After two years there, Goodwin pioneered churches in Whittier and San Diego. In 1908 he was elected district superintendent. Observing Goodwin's dedication and capacity for common sense, Bresee incorporated Goodwin into his inner circle, a group that included C. W. Ruth, E. A. Girvin, A. O. Hendricks, C. J. Kinne, C. V. LaFontaine, H. Orton Wiley, Fred Epperson, and W. C. Wilson. In 1911 Goodwin resigned as district superintendent in order to assist the Nazarene college full-time in fund-raising. He saved the school from collapse during a grave financial crisis in its early years. After two years, Goodwin returned to the pastorate and served in Pomona and, again, in San Diego. He conducted a healing service at the 1915 General Assembly in which a great number presented themselves for prayer, and "among them many testified by victorious shouts that they had found that which they sought."[13] That service was Goodwin's defining moment. Among Nazarenes, he represented something close to A. B. Simpson's fourfold gospel that prominently included divine healing and premillennialism alongside the doctrines of justification and sanctification.[14]

Goodwin was forty-seven years old when elected in 1916 to succeed Bresee on the Board of General Superintendents. Goodwin wrote several books dealing with spirituality and holiness. Like other general superintendents he helped tie the denomination together by advising district and college boards to consider electing leaders from different parts of the country. Goodwin served until 1940, retiring at age seventy-one.[15]

R. T. Williams (1883-1946), though fifteen years younger, overshadowed Goodwin. Williams shared the Methodist background of other early leaders. His church was the M.E. Church, South. Williams was born in Milam, Texas, in 1883 and raised thirty miles east, in Many, Louisiana. His conversion occurred at the kneeling rail of the New Hope Methodist, South, Church. He attended Texas Holiness University, where he was known as austere and aloof but also as a natural orator who intentionally desired to improve his speaking abilities. Williams finished a bachelor of arts in 1904 and a bachelor of divinity also at THU in 1906. Williams became active in the Holiness Association of Texas during these years. After graduation, still only in his twenties, Williams became president of Bell City College, an aspiring Holiness school in Louisiana. For some period of time, perhaps a year, he studied at the University of Chicago. While in Chicago, he worshipped at First Church of the Nazarene.

In 1908 Williams joined the faculty of Texas Holiness University. As part of the colony of Holiness people that included E. C. DeJernett, Bud Robinson, and the Ellysons, Williams was among those joining the Nazarene congregation organized at Peniel by Bresee in the spring of 1908. He was ordained by Reynolds at Pilot Point during the General Assembly. In 1911 Williams succeeded Ellyson as president of THU. He served until 1913, when he became a full-time evangelist. Given the opportunity to address the 1915 General Assembly, his deep, rich voice and bearing impressed delegates.

He was only thirty-two when elected general superintendent. Williams was a meticulous and tenacious administrator, traits that the church put to use during financial crises in the 1920s and 1930s. For a year, February 1917 to April 1918, Williams pastored Nashville First Church. This was Williams's only experience in the pastoral ministry, and this was after he had been elected general superintendent. In the same way that H. F. Reynolds was known for his advocacy of missions, Williams was known for his advocacy of youth. Until moving to Kansas City in 1934, Williams made his home in Texas. He owned a cotton farm in Denton County, Texas, a wheat farm in

Miller County, Missouri, and, for ten years, a twenty-acre orange grove in Florida. His close friend I. C. Mathis, superintendent of the Dallas District from 1936 to 1949, wrote of Williams that "when that crowd of people called Nazarenes want help and advice, when they really need a leader, there is one man above all others that they go to."[16]

> Williams attended to his public image as general superintendent. Preaching was still a powerful means by which early leaders extended their influence over the denomination, and Williams was perhaps best known for his preaching. Nazarene preachers for a generation widely imitated Williams. A. S. London, his contemporary, said of Williams, "[He was of] sturdy physique, portly, manly, and commanding in the pulpit. He was handsome, and [a] winsome type of public speaker. His diction was clear, his voice easy, and his pulpit manners forceful. He was a master as a pulpiteer. He was always neatly dressed. He stood erect and was a worthy example of a gospel preacher." His countenance itself, as he stood behind the pulpit, James McGraw observed, "gave the impression of strong and virile leadership" and "inspired confidence in the minds of his listeners." At first, as THU President A. M. Hills had taught him, Williams wrote out full sermon manuscripts. This detailed preparation, J. B. Chapman later observed, helped "develop a certain accuracy" and discipline in Williams's sermon preparation, as it had for his mentor. Because of this, Williams "preached well rather than excessively" and "gave the impression of having something important to say rather than having very much to say." Unlike many Nazarene evangelists of his day, Williams never "walked the platform." He moved very little while preaching. The superintendent did not rely on the theatrics of some other preachers. His mode of delivery was less animated, more direct, and more forceful.[17] There was deliberateness and clarity in his preaching. As he began to speak more extemporaneously, his sermons always had a "firstly," "secondly," and "thirdly." Admirers spoke of his black hair and piercing, penetrating eyes, "expressive of pathos and sympathy." He overcame any Southern accent he may have had. He possessed a rich, baritone voice and used the intonations of "elevated conversation." Many of his illustrations came from his own life's experience. Any person could understand him, and he made listeners "feel they were listening to a man who loved them, understood them, and knew the solution to their problems."[18]

James B. Chapman (1884-1947), born in Illinois, had moved with his family to the Indian Territory (Oklahoma) in 1899. He quickly became associated with C. B. Jernigan and the Independent Holiness Church. He began preaching and was both ordained and married before age twenty. At the time of the Pilot Point merger with the Church of the Nazarene, Chapman had just transferred from his leadership of the Texas-Oklahoma Council of the Holiness Church of Christ to the pastorate of the college church of Arkansas Holiness College. Upon graduating from the same college in 1910, Chapman became its president. After a year, he left to continue his studies at Texas Holiness University. He was superintendent of the Southeast District of the Church of the Nazarene for a year, then returned, in 1912, to Texas Holiness University as professor and dean. This was followed by his presidency of the school from 1913 to 1918, during which time the school changed its name to Peniel University and then, losing some of its pretensions, to Peniel College. Chapman pastored the Nazarene church in Bethany, Oklahoma, from 1918 to 1919, and then was a full-time evangelist for two years before moving to Kansas City to assist Haynes in editing the *Herald of Holiness*. In 1922 Chapman succeeded Haynes as general editor of the *Herald of Holiness*. He became widely known throughout the denomination not only as an editor but as a camp meeting preacher and author.[19]

THE SETH REES CONTROVERSY

In 1917 tensions long simmering in Southern California became a full-blown crisis. At the center was Seth C. Rees (1854–1933), a Quaker evangelist who had become a Nazarene upon accepting the pastorate of University Church of the Nazarene in Pasadena in 1912. Raised in Indiana, Rees experienced conversion in 1873. His emphatic evangelistic style led to his nickname "Earth-Quaker." He adhered to a branch that departed from Quaker tradition by conforming to popular evangelical beliefs and practices. He was, for instance, baptized by immersion, though Quakers traditionally did not baptize. While pastor of a Friends church in Providence, Rhode Island, Rees became active in New England's Holiness camps. Rees established a chain of Rest Cottages, maternity homes for unwed women, which stretched from New England to California. (Those located in Kansas City and Pilot Point, Texas, later forged Nazarene affiliations.) In 1897, he joined Martin Wells Knapp in founding the International Holiness Union and Prayer League. Nondenominational at first, it evolved into a church. Knapp founded God's Bible School in Cincinnati and published *The Revivalist* (later *God's Revivalist*) in conjunction with the league. Expecting the Independent Holiness

Church in Texas to unite with the league, Rees, as league president, ordained C. B. and Johnny Hill Jernigan in 1902. The Jernigans, in turn, ordained J. B. Chapman the following year. Rees broke with the league in 1905 after a dispute with Knapp's widow.[20]

The Pasadena University Church to which Rees was called in 1912 attracted Holiness people who migrated to the West Coast. Located on Nazarene University's campus, and sharing its facilities, the church offered Rees influence over faculty and students. Rees aspired to leadership but did not fit easily on a district shaped in Bresee's image. Bresee and Rees held to different principles about the church's nature and governance. Quakers had a mystical understanding of the church and bred individuals who disdained ecclesiasticism. Some Quakers such as E. P. and Emily Ellyson, and Susan Norris Fitkin, adjusted to the Church of the Nazarene's system of governance. Others, such as H. B. Hosley and Seth Rees, did not. Rees had neither the experience nor the temperament for a connectional system, even one as democratized as the Church of the Nazarene. He disdained many church processes, criticized Bresee's methods, and clashed with Bresee's circle.[21]

One conflict concerned procedures when bad behavior was alleged against ministers or laypersons. F. R. Matthews, a Nazarene evangelist and book salesman, was arrested and jailed for publicly beating his sons. Rees ordered his name stricken from University Church's membership roll. But Matthews insisted that a son had lied to authorities and demanded that his name be restored, or that a church trial determine his status. Rees, like H. B. Hosley, believed that pastors should have authority to remove church members. The next district assembly voted to seat Matthews as a clergy delegate, and heard his case. The assembly exonerated him. The 1915 General Assembly upheld this decision. Rees fumed and still refused to reinstate Matthews.[22]

A similar case involved Fred Epperson, a Bresee protégé, who served as district secretary from 1910 to 1915 and as the General Assembly secretary in 1911. Rees accused him of improperly associating with a young woman in her late teens whose mother attended University Church. Epperson, who was married, took the young woman on a hunting trip. They were in the company of others except for the ride to the hunting lodge. The girl insisted there was no misconduct.[23]

The rumors evoked painful memories of an earlier incident. C. V. LaFontaine, Bresee's cousin, became associate pastor at Los Angeles First Church in 1903. In 1905 he fell asleep on a streetcar returning from Long Beach, and his head rested on the shoulder of a married woman who was a member of First Church. The Nazarene *Manual* distinguished between "imprudent" and "immoral" behavior. "Imprudent" conduct would not necessarily trigger dismissal. Bresee considered LaFontaine's conduct foolish but neither immoral nor fatal to his ministry. But a vocal faction within First Church demanded LaFontaine's resignation. He resigned but soon became pastor of another Nazarene church. Fifty members of First Church, including a few board members, withdrew and formed an independent church. They then sought for this church to be received into the Southern California District. Bresee felt betrayed, but in 1910 District Superintendent Goodwin allowed the church to unite with the district.[24]

The rumors about Epperson roused these anxieties. Bresee dealt with Epperson, as he had LaFontaine, according to the *Manual*. But Rees whispered that Bresee "covered up sin."[25]

Other practices riled Rees. He attacked honorary doctorates as vanities. (Bresee had received an honorary doctorate from Simpson College in Iowa and had been called "Dr. Bresee" ever since.) At district assemblies, Bresee followed the practice of Methodist bishops and made committee appointments from a list prepared by the district superintendent. Rees branded the practice "ecclesiasticism" and Bresee's methods "a steamroller." District Superintendent Wilson responded that those who "hollered" about "steamrollers" were usually adept at such methods themselves. There was another clash over the Hillcrest maternity home that Rees had established with district support. After two years of operation, C. E. Cornell and John Goodwin persuaded the district assembly to drop Hillcrest as a district ministry.[26]

And there was conflict over worship. Nazarenes were well-rooted in revival traditions. Bresee quieted emotional demonstrations during the sermon, believing that it was never time for "the glory" to come until the sermon was preached and the point made. "Glory" was a response to the preached gospel, not its substitute. Rees considered worship "dead" if people were not demonstrating vocally and physically. Rees communicated this attitude to impressionable students at Nazarene University.[27]

District Superintendent Wilson conferred with Bresee several times about how best to manage Rees. District leaders concluded that Rees recklessly tarnished others' reputations in a crusade to purify and control the district. In the last years of his life, Bresee witnessed the rise of parties vying for leadership in the very district in which the Church of the Nazarene's Western wing had begun.[28]

When a revival began at Nazarene University in January 1914, all regarded it as a genuine work of God. H. Orton Wiley, who had been the college president for only a few months, encouraged the revival and relied on Rees's help.

A. J. Ramsey, dean of the theology department, warmly supported the revival. Students testified in classes, which turned into prayer meetings. The chapel became a gathering place at any hour of the day. Rees implored each student to confess sins and make restitution as if Jesus Christ would return that day. But concerns arose. A. O. Hendricks, pastor of Pasadena First Church, and C. E. Cornell, pastor of Los Angeles First, heard of emotional excesses and questioned the manner in which Rees sought to keep the students in a state of perpetual fervor. Rees, in turn, discounted other Nazarene churches as spiritually dead. The university's trustees worried about whether Rees was exerting influence over the inexperienced Wiley. A sizable contingent of students looked to Rees for leadership and sat in judgment of pastors, laypeople, and faculty who expressed concerns about the revival's ongoing tempo.[29]

Wilson wearied of being district superintendent. In 1915 he supported the successful bid of Howard Eckel to be his successor. The membership of Los Angeles First Church declined to 983, while the University Church in Pasadena reported 437 members. Within six months, Bresee and Wilson were dead, and Goodwin, elected general superintendent in January, traveled on behalf of general interests. The district had lost its three most seasoned leaders.[30]

The pastor at Whittier, California, Howard Eckel was a Pennsylvanian and former Methodist. He had affiliated with the Association of Pentecostal Churches of America in 1902 and afterward pastored in Haverhill, Massachusetts. After the 1908 Pilot Point merger Eckel served as district superintendent in Kentucky.

Tensions on the district escalated. A. J. Ramsey, head of the theology department, was a graduate of Union Theological Seminary in Virginia and had been pushed out of the Baptist church after experiencing a "second work of grace." Besides teaching, Ramsey wrote for and edited the Nazarene Sunday School curriculum. But critics stated that Ramsey rejected the idea that human depravity was "total" and that he did not believe that entire sanctification "eradicated" the sin nature. Wiley delivered a series of chapel lectures designed to address these issues. At one point, Ramsey stood and publicly challenged Wiley. Rees and his contingent of students took up the battle cry, claiming that Ramsey and the college no longer stood for holiness. A committee appointed to examine Ramsey concluded that his theology was

A. J. Ramsey

sound. In April, the trustees gave Ramsey a strong vote of confidence and called upon outside forces to stop stirring up trouble. They also donated three lots off-campus for University Church to build its own church—a measure intended to disentangle the two institutions. Wiley's alliance with Rees undermined his position. Upon the motion of Judge William S. Knott, the chair, the trustees authorized a search committee to secure a new president. Aware that he was on his way out, Wiley resigned the day after commencement. So did Ramsey. The controversy had disillusioned him with the Nazarenes.[31]

Those opposed to Rees continued the offensive. Two pastors filed nine formal charges against Rees for character assassination and for fomenting discord. The trial took place in May at Los Angeles First Church, with a jury of five elders appointed by the District Advisory Committee. Los Angeles and Pasadena newspapers, which Rees courted, sensationalized it. For several days jurors read depositions and heard witnesses. The majority voted to convict Rees, but the *Manual* required a unanimous verdict. Acquitted, Rees returned to Pasadena, leading hundreds of supporters in a triumphant parade.[32]

When the fall term began, the trustees appointed Professor Fallis as acting president. A. M. Hills replaced Ramsey in the theology department. Yet students complained that neither Hills nor Fallis was a "true Holiness man." In February, when Fallis was speaking in chapel, a student arose and began shouting that students did not want professors who did "not believe in holiness." When Fallis challenged him to prove that he spoke on behalf of others, the student turned and walked out. Fourteen students followed immediately, and then others, until thirty-six had left, about half the student body. Four teachers also left. Nearly all attended Rees's church. On February 23, Rees wrote John Goodwin, denying advance knowledge of the walkout but defending the student leader as "one of our hottest young men" and calling those who left with him "thirty-six of the most spiritual students." Nellie Goodlander, a music teacher who walked out, told the local press that "lectures from the [chapel] platform and in the classrooms attack vital prayer." Another declared that "the school has lost all its religion." A local paper characterized the factions as "those who desire the old way of intense religious demonstration" and those who are "inclined to be more conservative in their form of worship."[33]

The college trustees had donated land for University Church to erect a building, but the congregation had taken no action. Now the trustees ordered the congregation to vacate the campus by March 1—just two weeks away. The church's members hastily erected a tabernacle on the donated property and prepared to transfer from the campus on the first Sunday of March.[34]

Rumors flew. Rees heard that a group was collecting evidence to file new charges against him and that "Dr. Hills was editing it." Eckel heard that University Church had deeded its property to a member of the congregation in violation of the *Manual*'s "trust clause" and concluded that this stratagem was designed to place the property beyond the district's reach.[35]

Eckel concluded that radical steps had to be taken. He consulted General Superintendent Walker, who agreed to support him. On February 25, Eckel appeared at University Church as the congregation met for its final Sunday morning service on campus and read a prepared statement. He said that the congregation had exhibited a rebellious attitude and sown discord in the college and on the district. He cited the *Manual* paragraph giving superintendents authority to disorganize churches. Then he stunned everyone by pronouncing that University Church, the young denomination's third largest congregation, was now officially disorganized. He pledged that he would issue letters of transfer for members wishing to unite with other congregations. Then Eckel walked out, leaving behind an angry, hurt, and bewildered people.

The news spread quickly throughout the denomination. Did Eckel have authority to do this? The 1915 *Manual* declared, "When it seems clear to a District or General Superintendent that a local Church organization should no longer continue as such, it may be disorganized by the action and formal pronouncement of either Superintendent." The wording did not specify the circumstances, though few believed that the General Assembly had envisioned the disorganization of strong churches. The Basis of Union had stated that superintendents could not interfere in the operations of a fully organized church. When loyal Nazarenes questioned Eckel's authority, Walker also issued a formal announcement of dissolution, further alienating Rees and his band.[36]

Rees circulated an open letter predicting a denominational split if the other general superintendents did not reverse Eckel's action immediately. Others echoed the sentiment. From Los Angeles, E. G. Anderson wired Reynolds on March 6, insisting on immediate action to reverse Eckel's decree: "I believe unless some definite action is taken to reinstate University Church we will have a split." Wiley wired Reynolds, asking if the other general superintendents could overrule Walker and Eckel. On the East Coast, William Howard Hoople and H. B. Hosley (who had already left the Church of the Nazarene) were furious. Hoople wished to do away with district and general superintendents alike. Eckel had forced into the open the tension between connectional and congregational principles.[37]

The denomination did not split. What held it together? First, Eckel and Walker maintained the support of most Southern California Nazarenes.

A district meeting convened at Los Angeles First Church two weeks after Eckel's action. For nearly three hours, Eckel and Walker spoke from their hearts about the tensions that had troubled the district for years. They answered questions. They admitted that dissolution was an extreme measure but insisted that the future promised more conflict and the college's potential collapse without an extreme remedy. Cornell, Hendricks, and other pastors pledged to stand with them. E. G. Anderson reversed his position after attending the meeting. Again wiring Reynolds, he now advised that the general superintendents "hold steady and do nothing" because "the course taken was the only remedy." Others counseled the same. Hendricks wrote that he had been in the Nazarene movement for eighteen years, and that the general superintendents needed to "stand by Dr. Walker and Rev. Eckel at this time." "If you do not," he warned Reynolds, "there will be nothing but ruin ahead for us." "The spirit of disloyalty, insubordination and general lawlessness has been rampant," Hendricks continued, "and I have been surprised that we have averted a crisis as long as we have." Yet "what a sad spectacle for men and angels to look at," Hendricks lamented. Eckel wrote Reynolds that he had the support of all the large churches on the district except San Diego, where the pastor, Harry Hays, was a former Quaker and close friend of Rees.[38]

Bud Robinson echoed the sentiments of others across the church: the general superintendents as a group "have been as Mum as Clams," and "we are under an Iron clad Ecleasical [sic] Machine." Reynolds sympathized, acknowledging Robinson's distress, but he emphasized that the general superintendents had to work patiently and collect evidence from both sides of the controversy, or it would inflame the situation. Reynolds added too humbly: "I am only one of the General Superintendents and the least among them all."[39]

Reynolds decided upon a slow, deliberate approach. He sought information and opinions. He contacted those who had served on the *Manual* revision committee at the previous General Assembly, inquiring about the *Manual* provision for disorganizing churches. Most of them replied that the intention was for closing small, struggling churches. But R. B. Mitchum and William E. Fisher, who had been affiliated with the Holiness Church of Christ, which had placed very high value on local churches, told Reynolds that the provision could be used to protect the denomination's wider interests.[40]

On March 31, Reynolds called the other general superintendents to a joint meeting set for April 4 and 5. Meanwhile, Los Angeles First Church's board unanimously adopted resolutions approving Eckel's course. So did the board at Pasadena First Church. Judge Knott wired Reynolds that the Immanuel Church, led by his wife, Lucy Knott, backed Eckel. Then Walker wrote, stating that he would not join the general superintendents' summit. He reasoned that Eckel's action was reviewable only by the district assembly and that his own action was reviewable only by the General Assembly: "The General Assembly alone has authority to 'review and revise' acts of the General Supts. It has not given that authority to others; and assuredly not to the superintendents themselves." University Church, he wrote, "is out of existence and can be restored only by the action of the General Assembly at its discretion." But, Wiley asked Reynolds, "is it right to injure four hundred people because [district leaders] *think* that one man is wrong?"[41]

Reynolds, Williams, and Goodwin met in Kansas City's Victoria Hotel to review assembled materials. Two days later they issued their interpretation of the *Manual*: the only grounds for disorganizing a church were when it was too weak to continue or when it "has become hopelessly unorthodox or immoral in its practices and positively refused to be corrected." They stated that a church could appeal a decision to the district assembly and that it "has a right to continue its organization until final settlement of the appeal." They sent Walker a copy and published their statement in the *Herald of Holiness*. Walker responded. He did not recognize his colleagues' authority to review his actions and disagreed with their interpretation of the *Manual*. Still, he was willing to "make any correction possible that would tend 'to heal' the division throughout the church." To that end, his open letter, also published in the *Herald*, addressed the University Church members: if they formally appealed his decision and gave "proper pledges of good faith and expression of fealty to the denomination," he would "effect a stay of all proceedings in the case until it is finally disposed of by the General Assembly."[42]

Rees's response was the third factor that held the denomination together. Though Reynolds, Goodwin, and Williams had clearly stated the right to appeal, and Walker had offered to allow such an appeal, none was filed. Perhaps Rees thought it would not change the outcome, or perhaps he was just tired of the conflict. Historian Timothy Smith observed that Rees had become convinced that he should head a new movement. In any case, Rees and his followers went their own way. The Pentecost Pilgrim Church (later shortened to Pilgrim Church) was organized on May 26, and a church paper, *The Pilgrim*, debuted under the editorship of Seth Rees's son, Paul Rees. Pilgrim Bible College opened in October with the assistance of John Matthews, Kansas City First Church's former pastor, whose blast at the Nazarenes was titled *Rise and Fall of the Nazarene Movement*. C. A. McConnell also assisted, and G. Arnold Hodgin joined the Pilgrims in January. Harry Hays was expelled from the Church of the Nazarene for dissension and took many San Diego

First Church people with him into the Pilgrim Church. Wilmot C. Stone, president of Bresee College in Kansas, joined by students Francisco and Nettie Soltero, later Pilgrim missionaries, joined the Pilgrims. The issue divided families. Bud Robinson stayed with the Nazarenes, but Miss Sallie, his wife, joined the Pilgrim Church.[43]

The split might have widened in the Northwest were it not for H. O. Wiley. Nazarenes in Idaho, whose ranks included many former Quakers, and where Harry Hays had been district superintendent before going to San Diego, admired Rees. Wiley had accepted the presidency of the Holiness college in Nampa upon resigning from Nazarene University with the conditions that he be granted one year to study at the Pacific School of Religion in Berkeley. The Pasadena College faculty members and many of the students who had walked out of Nazarene University headed for Nampa after learning that Wiley, their ally, would head the institution. Wiley assumed full-time duties in the summer of 1917. He learned that the local leaders had called John Matthews and Seth Rees to preach at the annual camp meeting. Wiley suddenly was in the middle. Reynolds and Northwest District superintendent J. T. Little wrote searching letters questioning Wiley's loyalty. But Wiley's mind was settled. He felt that University Church had been grievously wronged but that Rees had erred by starting the Pilgrim movement and not appealing the decision of Eckel and Walker. Loyal not only to the memory of Bresee, who once admonished him to "stand by the college" in Pasadena, Wiley also admired the general superintendents for rebuffing Walker. He considered the "radical congregationalism" of the Pilgrims wrong in principle and thought a new denomination "neither right nor expedient." When Rees and Matthews arrived for the camp meeting, Wiley made it very clear that he would exert his influence and energies to keep the college inside the Church of the Nazarene. Wiley happily reported later that they preached only the gospel and avoided church politics.[44]

Yet familiar patterns recurred at the college in Nampa. "Hot" Pilgrim students regarded others as "dead." Demonstrative students picked up the kneeling rail and marched it around the sanctuary on their shoulders. Some threw chairs, claiming they needed to do so to "get the victory." Student Charles Howard asked wryly: why not break up the piano, "pay a larger bill, and get a larger victory?" Professor Fred Shields offered pointed advice on corporate prayer that the Pilgrim contingent heard as an attempt to "cool" them off. When Wiley made it clear that Shields had his confidence, in January the Pilgrim-leaning faculty and students left the school. Wiley was relieved, commenting: "They expected me to swing this school and district for the

Pilgrims and I gave them very plainly to understand that I wouldn't.... They then dropped me flat, and this seems to be the spirit of the thing,—do as I say or you are backslidden." He wrote Ada Bresee: "They consigned us to the 'compromisers' and the 'cooled off crowd' and went where they could have 'liberty' and be free from 'ecclesiastical bondage.'. . . They fell into a critical habit and developed an unteachable spirit."[45]

In 1922, Rees led 457 Pilgrims, 325 of them members of Pasadena's Pilgrim Temple, into the International Holiness Church, then numbering over 15,000. He thus reunited with the group he had cofounded with Martin Wells Knapp a quarter-century before. They adopted the Pilgrim Holiness Church name. In 1926 Rees was elected one of its three general superintendents. He was its sole general superintendent when he died in 1933. In 1968 the Pilgrim Holiness Church united with the Wesleyan Methodist Church to form the Wesleyan Church.[46]

In 1918, Howard Eckel was reelected district superintendent on the first ballot. He stepped down from that role in 1920. Later he was pastor of Miami First Church and Florida District Superintendent. Walker died in 1918. He was serving as president of Nazarene University at the time. Hendricks and Cornell officiated at his funeral, assisted by Eckel and C. J. Kinne. Of the tributes that appeared in the *Herald of Holiness*, the most glowing ones were written by Californians. The 1919 General Assembly specified the requirements for disorganizing a church, requiring a district superintendent's recommendation and approval by the full Board of General Superintendents. John Matthews returned to the Nazarenes in 1920 and publicly apologized for earlier condemning them.[47]

Persistent questions remained. The Basis of Union stated that superintendency was "a necessity" in the Church of the Nazarene, but E. F. Walker himself posed a question in the wake of the Rees ordeal: Should the office of general superintendent be abolished? Would district superintendents alone not be sufficient? Howard Eckel had proven that district superintendents could act firmly. J. B. Chapman responded that church unity lay in doctrine and "a compact organization conditioned upon our Superintendency." He noted that "officers may make mistakes and abuse their power. Like other men, they may even commit personal sins as well as official blunders." But they are elected periodically, so "no permanent abuse or mistake of any office in our church is possible."[48]

GENERAL OVERSIGHT

Hiram F. Reynolds did not enter this discussion, but the conception and scope of *general* superintendency evolved through the impact of his personality and actions. As both general superintendent and general missionary secretary, he urged Nazarenes to rally behind the cause of missions at each district and general gathering he attended. In December 1913 he embarked on a world tour, leaving San Francisco with ten missionaries headed for assignments in Japan, China, and India. He wanted to be better informed when corresponding with missionaries and national leaders. He spent one month in Japan, where he visited the work in Kyoto, contacted mission leaders of other denominations, and surveyed cities where no Nazarene work yet existed. He spent the next month in China, where he settled in new missionaries Peter and Anna Kiehn and Glennie Sims. His visit to India was more difficult. In Calcutta a disheartening situation required him to remain there for nearly three months. He dismissed several missionaries and national workers, received other resignations, and reorganized the mission staff. Resuming the world tour, in July he reached Swaziland, where he examined the work of Harmon Schmelzenbach. He was unable to meet with John Diaz when he passed through the Cape Verde Islands, but he reached the United Kingdom and visited George Sharpe and the Pentecostal Church of Scotland, encouraging the merger with the Nazarenes that occurred the following year. The world tour added depth to Reynolds's perceptions and was a boon for missions promotion. Reynolds sent news of his trip to *The Other Sheep* and *Herald of Holiness*, and he published *World-Wide Missions* (1915), illustrated with his own photographs. The tour established an important principle: general superintendents were to engage the whole work, including missions and churches outside North America. The experience convinced Reynolds that the church's highest officials could not simply rely on reports from the field. He set the example, visiting Cuba and Central America in 1916 and returning to Japan and China in 1919. In 1921 he returned to the British Isles, South Africa, and India, and visited the Middle East, where there were churches and missions in Syria and Palestine. Reynolds made his third trip to Japan and China in 1922, presiding at the Japan District's first assembly, at which Rev. J. I. Nagamatsu was appointed superintendent.[49]

Partly to compensate for the reticence of Reynolds's colleagues to travel abroad, the 1923 General Assembly created an office of missionary superintendent, what a later generation would call "regional director." George Sharpe of Scotland supervised missions in Africa, J. E. Bates in Asia, and J. D. Scott, who had a good understanding of Spanish-American culture as well as the

Spanish language, Central and South America. The missionaries in Peru had called upon the church to appoint a superintendent such as Scott, but his appointment led to the demotion of V. G. Santin in Mexico from superintendent to secretary-treasurer of the Mexico District. On rare occasions, missionary superintendents facilitated ordinations. For instance, Scott delivered the ordination certificate of Augie Holland from her home district in Tennessee and ordained her in Peru in October 1924.[50] However, when calls for retrenchment came, these missionary superintendents were thought more expendable than missionaries active in the field. The church abolished the position, effective January 1, 1926. Reynolds opposed this move but found himself, as he wrote Scott, part of a church in which democracy ruled.[51]

In 1927 Reynolds visited the Caribbean and organized the Trinidad and Barbados Districts. Since no colleague seemed willing to, he planned another world tour. Convinced that the 73-year-old man would die on such a trip, Williams and Goodwin opposed this. Reynolds relented only after the 1928 General Board specifically asked that General Superintendents Williams and Goodwin visit the mission fields in Japan, China, India, Palestine, and Africa. While Reynolds had been an eager world traveler, his colleagues had not ventured outside of the United States. Said Williams, "For fifteen years I had found excuses for not going abroad and had exhausted my fund of excuses." Though neither Williams nor Goodwin enjoyed their trip, Williams admitted that he could now see the "viewpoint of the missionary."[52] Reynolds had made his point: the general superintendency was neither local nor regional in character; it was international.[53]

J. B. Chapman became Reynolds's ardent disciple on this point. Elected general superintendent in 1928, Chapman made his first international trip in 1931, ordaining two men and two women as elders in Argentina and returning to tell colleagues that "proper superintendency" was necessary for the growing work in Latin America. The Latin American fields had passed from "the pioneering period to that of organization. And from now on we must work directly and constantly for the organization, education and establishment of a self-directing and self-supporting district in each of our Latin American fields." He insisted: "The indefinite continuation of North American paternalism in the Church of the Nazarene in these lands is neither necessary nor wise." How did he propose to address this? "We must provide superintendence. In order to do this properly it will be necessary for a General Superintendent to visit each field once every quadrennium at least. And it will also be necessary to send out as missionaries men of District Superintendent type." Based on his personal observations, Chapman urged the creation of Bible schools, the development of a ministerial course of study in Spanish, and Spanish-language publications.[54]

GENERAL AUTHORITY

The general superintendents of the church exerted authority by virtue of office itself more than by a defined job description. Bresee stressed the importance of maintaining "the unity of our Superintendency . . . that whatever number be elected, they always act as one man." That had not happened in the Rees controversy, and in its aftermath H. O. Wiley asserted that "it will be necessary to so adjust matters concerning the Gen. Supts. that they will collectively rule instead of making each one supreme in a certain district."[55] But to "rule," the superintendents had to prove their spiritual and pastoral right to do so. They held evangelistic meetings in local churches and preached in district camp meetings. The general superintendents resolved disputes among pastors and laypersons, between pastors and district superintendents, and between congregations and district leaders. The credibility of the general superintendents depended on their judgment and counsel in ordinary matters.[56]

Their spiritual authority was visible in their power to ordain persons for ministry. In their years as a Board of General Superintendents, Reynolds, Goodwin, and Williams maintained a formal litany for each ordination service. The ordination service began with the missionary hymn, "We'll Girdle the Globe," expressing the church's expansive aims: "We'll girdle the globe with salvation, / with holiness unto the Lord; / and light shall illumine each nation, / the light from the lamp of his word." Following a prayer, the congregation sang "The Refiner's Fire," which referred to Charles Wesley's hymn "Jesus, Thine All-Victorious Live." "Refining fire, go through my heart," went one stanza of the hymn, "illuminate my soul; / scatter thy life through every part, / and sanctify the whole." The service included scripture readings and responsive readings with these themes: (I) God calls, or chooses, His ministers; (II) God makes, or qualifies His ministers; (III) If God chooses and qualifies His ministry, then He should have the right to say what they shall preach; (IV) If so, then God has a right to their being persons of good character. The attention that the church gave to this formal liturgy, amid a great deal of otherwise informality, indicated the high place it gave to ordained ministers and the authority that remained in the ordination charge, given only to the general superintendents.[57]

LEADERSHIP CRISES IN JAPAN

While the Rees controversy faded from memory, it had lasting repercussions in Japan. The church's leading missionaries, Minnie Staples and William Eckel, represented the two opposing factions in Southern California, with sharply different views of church structure. The story illustrates that the balance between Spirit and structure had to be worked out in each place the church maintained a witness.[58]

The Church of the Nazarene's work in Japan predated the Pilot Point Assembly. The Holiness Church of Christ had two missionaries in Japan in 1905, Lillian Poole and Lulu Williams. After 1908, with several Japanese students studying at Pasadena College, and with a thriving mission to Japanese in Los Angeles, the Southern California wing of the church, and Bresee himself, took special interest in Japan. In 1912 Bresee ordained J. I. Nagamatsu, one of the Japanese students who had graduated from the college, and in early 1913 Nagamatsu returned to Japan. He established a lively work among children in Fukuchiyama, in the mountains northwest of Kyoto. With Bresee's blessing, Cora Snider went for a short term in 1912 and stayed in Japan to assist Nagamatsu and to superintend the work.

In early 1914, Reynolds arrived with a party of four missionaries, including Lillian Poole and Lulu Williams for their second terms, and Rev. and Mrs. L. H. Humphrey, to relieve Snider. The arrival of Hitoshi Kitagawa and Minnie Staples a year later, and Nobumi Isayama and William Eckel a year after that, greatly altered the composition of the mission force in Japan.

Minnie Staples with her husband and unidentified child

Staples, born in Tyler, Texas, in 1880, never finished grammar school. She was active as an evangelist for five years in the Friends Church before joining the Church of the Nazarene at Upland, California, in 1906, when W. C. Wilson was pastor. By that time she had married a widower, Isaac B. Staples, seventeen years her senior, a birthright Quaker and telegrapher for the Santa Fe Railroad. During their years in Upland, Minnie Staples became burdened for the Japanese migrant farm workers. Desiring to preach to them, she secured Hiroshi Kitagawa as her translator and tutor in Japanese. In January 1910, Kitagawa was converted. Staples and Kitagawa began a Japanese church in Upland but soon both moved to the Los Angeles area—he to study at the Nazarene college and she to take charge of the Nazarene mission to

Japanese. With the support of her friends in California, who included Leslie Gay, Seth Rees, and W. C. Wilson, the foreign missions board could scarcely refuse her application for missionary service. Isaac Staples felt it was his duty to follow her, but everyone knew *she* was "the missionary."[59]

Kitagawa returned to his own people. Born in Kumamoto, on Kyushu island in southern Japan, in 1888, he was a son of Russian Orthodox parents, a tradition far outside of the dominant Shintoism, but which proved a stepping-stone toward Protestantism. Kitagawa went to America at age eighteen to seek his fortune. For a while he tended pigs, sheep, and cattle, and translated for Japanese sharecroppers. He suffered under anti-Japanese discrimination, which hardened his attitudes against his bosses, their religion, and America. After his conversion, Kitagawa entered Pasadena College, where he finished both his high school and a bachelor's degree in religion. While studying he became friends with both Nagamatsu, a fellow student at Pasadena College, and Nobumi Isayama, who was converted at the Japanese mission. Before leaving with the Stapleses for Japan Kitagawa raised support for Nazarene missions by touring churches with Reynolds, who ordained him at the Chicago District Assembly in 1914.

Hiroshi Kitagawa and family

The church at Kumamoto, which Kitagawa and Staples organized within a few months after their arrival in Japan (the first organized Nazarene church in the country), included his brother Shiro Kitagawa, who became a minister. Members of the church in Kumamoto included professionals and college students. Soon Kitagawa began a Bible school. A well-prepared clergy, as Kitagawa saw it, was necessary to reach the higher classes.[60]

Staples devoted her energies to revivalism. Her skills and enthusiasm for evangelism complemented the more pastoral Kitagawa. At the same time, her evangelistic and church-planting efforts far outdid any of the male missionaries. In her many revivals and tent meetings, she demanded that converts forsake their Shinto idols. She required that converts undergo a period of probation to make sure they had really changed before she would either baptize them or receive them into church membership. In spite of these requirements, within two years she had baptized 130 persons. One early convert was a Japanese Anglican minister who attended her Bible classes and came to profess entire sanctification. While his wife busied herself with revivals,

I. B. Staples drove the car for her and helped to pitch the tent under which she preached. He also tended to the financial records of the mission.[61]

In spite of all of the successes that her ministry showed, almost immediately after the Eckels' arrival, Staples and Eckel became embroiled in quarrels that affected the Nazarene mission in Japan for decades. Eckel, born in 1892, the son of Howard Eckel, attended both Olivet College in Illinois and Pasadena College. Bresee ordained him in 1912. After Staples's departure for Japan, Howard Eckel, as district superintendent, appointed his son to lead the Japanese mission in Los Angeles.

Staples, a member of the Pasadena University Church, remained loyal to Rees. Both enjoyed freedom of expression in worship. Neither liked episcopal control. On a trip to California for an operation in 1917, soon after the University Church split, Staples spoke at Pilgrim Tabernacle. She joined Rees in criticizing the actions of both Eckel and Walker. Throughout her ministry in Japan Staples circumvented general church leadership. She instilled the same feelings in Kitagawa, although the sources of Kitagawa's attitudes toward American control were personal and nationalistic as well as based on loyalties to her. Eckel, on the other hand, imbibed his father's Methodist heritage of respect for superintendency.[62]

For more than 40 years, Eckel worked side-by-side with Nobumi Isayama, ten years his senior. In 1898 Isayama found his way across the Pacific to the United States and stayed for seventeen years. He became a Christian in 1913 after attending some English classes at the Japanese Nazarene mission in Los Angeles. Staples was instrumental in his conversion. When she and Kitagawa left for Japan Isayama welcomed Eckel and served as his Japanese language teacher. For a time he lived in the mission hall with the Eckel family. Isayama returned to Japan in 1915 only with the intention of finding a wife. But L. H. Humphrey persuaded him to stay in order to become the key national worker for the Kyoto area, even though Isayama was neither ordained nor prepared for ministry. Isayama thus was there to greet the Eckel family when they arrived in February 1916. At first, Eckel and Isayama concentrated upon the city of Kure. Eckel was determined from the beginning not only to learn Japanese but to think and act Japanese. He was respectful toward the culture and its customs.[63]

Following missions policy, both Nagamatsu and Kitagawa, as ordained ministers, were entitled to full participation in the administration and direction of the district. Each of the four mission stations that were operating at this time—Fukuchiyama, Kumamoto, Kyoto, and Kure—functioned quite autonomously. After the Humphreys left in 1915, there was no mission superintendent. In March 1917, Reynolds appointed Eckel to preside over a district assembly planned for later that year. In Eckel, then only twenty-five years old, and with only one year on the field, Reynolds had a person (like Leighton Tracy in India) in whom to trust. Reynolds planned to be present at the next assembly, but World War I prevented the scheduled trip.[64]

Eckel held an assembly in July 1918, but Staples refused to attend it. Both Nagamatsu and Kitagawa participated in the assembly and voiced their opinions on various matters along with the missionaries, as equal partners. But dissension brewed on the status of Japanese workers. The assembly established and set budgets and stationed both missionaries and Japanese workers. Lulu Williams and several other missionaries strongly opposed including Kitagawa and Nagamatsu. The participants elected Paul Thatcher, then stationed at Omuta, rather than Eckel, as district superintendent. However, since the assembly deepened rather than solved problems, Reynolds placed each station under his own direct control and refused to accept the election of Thatcher.[65]

In May 1919 Reynolds himself convened a district assembly. Before coming he had asked Nagamatsu to translate the *Manual* into Japanese, an indication both that Reynolds was eager for more national involvement and that he saw the *Manual* as an internationally binding church constitution. Reynolds listened to the arguments of several missionaries against the participation of the Japanese leaders in the assembly. They told Reynolds plainly that either the Japanese leaders must be treated as subordinates, or they themselves would leave. Reynolds acted in the same way as he had with the Woodses and Lillian Sprague in India some years before. He accepted their resignations. To Reynolds there were two issues necessitating this: the missionaries would not accept the Japanese ministers as having equal rights and privileges with themselves, and they had expressed contempt toward the policy of the church.[66]

Before departing, Reynolds moved Eckel from Kure to Kyoto and ordained Isayama, thus making him also a member of the council. He appointed Eckel as "acting" district superintendent but saw the necessity of keeping Eckel and Staples from infringing upon one another. Reynolds met separately with the Stapleses. Unlike his actions with the other missionaries, Reynolds did not move against Staples. Reynolds knew of the deep support that they had in the Southern California District. He could not deny Minnie Staples's effectiveness. Reynolds appointed her district evangelist and Isaac Staples district treasurer. Nagamatsu remained in Fukuchiyama.[67]

Nagamatsu praised Reynolds for saving the work in Japan as a result of these actions, and through letters the Japanese pastor advanced in the esteem of both Reynolds and E. G. Anderson, who served as both general treasurer and Foreign Missions secretary. Reynolds took a bold and yet strategic move on his next visit to Japan in the fall of 1922. He appointed Nagamatsu as district superintendent. By this action Reynolds reaffirmed his commitment to the advancement as quickly as possible of national leaders and mission fields to regular district status. Japan was in some ways experimental. Its leadership was ahead of others in educational and other attainments. Only Mexico had a local leader, V. G. Santin, serving as superintendent at this time, of any Nazarene district outside of North America and the British Isles. Reynolds genuinely desired the indigenization of the work and possessed confidence in Nagamatsu, but his appointment was a way of solving the conflicts between Eckel and Staples without alienating either one of them or their constituents in America.[68]

Nagamatsu received funds directly from individuals and local churches in America as well as from the general church. Funds to the Fukuchiyama station supported children enrolled in his church's kindergarten, and several Sunday Schools. For one often republished photograph he rounded up scores of children who were not actually attending the school. Isaac Staples, in charge of the district finances, found some discrepancies in Nagamatsu's reporting. With remorse, Nagamatsu sent E. G. Anderson notice of his resignation from the superintendency. "Alas! I confess you I have betrayed your confidence on [sic] me. . . . I was entirely fell in the Devil's trap. I am very sorry that I sinned against God, against Christ and lost your confidence on the money sake." He continued: "I pray you would not distrust my countrymen because of me. My heart is broken because I have contaminated the Glory of God." Nagamatsu stated his plans to repay the church.[69]

Reynolds appointed Kitagawa as superintendent in Nagamatsu's stead. As Nagamatsu had hoped it would not be, Reynolds's faith in Japanese leadership was not shattered by the failings of one man. Kitagawa moved from Kumamoto to Kyoto in 1922, since Reynolds wanted to keep the headquarters of the work in Kyoto. Kitagawa relocated the Bible school there also.

In the mid-1920s, ill will toward Minnie Staples on matters relating to her independent ways of raising support circulated in Southern California. Against Staples was J. E. Bates, then the missionary superintendent for the "Orient." Until being appointed to this office Bates had served as district superintendent in Southern California. Staples brought, Bates thought, embarrassment to the church. Bates wrote to the general superintendents that

Asians would not accept a woman, especially one so outspoken as Staples—even though she had demonstrated for over a decade successful evangelistic ministry in Japan. Criticisms, coupled with financial problems in the general church in the mid-1920s, clouded her return to Japan after a furlough in the United States. Reynolds himself initially opposed her return.[70]

Staples circulated reports that the church could not return her because it had invested and lost money in business deals with L. Milton Williams, a well-known evangelist. Also, there were charges that she had, without permission from the Foreign Missions department, raised money both in and out of the denomination in order to return to Japan on a "faith" or independent basis. Some accused her of affiliation with the Pentecostal (tongues) movement. An investigating committee included Reynolds, Bates, and Leslie Gay. On the first point, if Staples had made such statements about the church's investments they were at least partly true. The committee laid the second and third charges to rest as groundless. The exoneration did little good. Reynolds and other members of the Foreign Missions department still decided that the church was in such financial difficulties that it could not return her. The decision was made also in light of the maturity of the church in Japan, which Reynolds felt did not require missionaries.[71]

Reynolds was less prone to place women in positions of leadership than Bresee had been. Bresee appointed Emma Eaton and Sukhoda Banarjee to head the work in Calcutta. He had sent Cora Snider to superintendent the work in Japan. Mae McReynolds superintended ministries to Spanish-speaking people in the United States. Reynolds, on the other hand, pled for more men to answer the call to missionary service. He told some Nazarenes gathered in Nampa in 1917, "There are mighty few men who seem to think [missions] is a big job. What is the matter with our men folks anyway?" To this, one in the congregation wondered why, if missions were a man's job, "the women have to do it." Reynolds wondered the same. "Why don't we have more men to help in this? Why don't more men go as missionaries. They are so few, and mostly girls and women."[72] Yet Reynolds's preferences for Eckel rested more upon church loyalty than upon gender.

Staples lacked such loyalty for a diverse set of reasons: her Quaker heritage, her personal relation with ousted leaders such as Seth Rees, her finding an untraditional sphere, outside of the home, in which to use her gifts and talents. Her refusal to be bossed by men led her to empathize, though perhaps too condescendingly, with Japanese people. This sense of identity with them was part of her success as a missionary. She stood with them against impersonal forces in Kansas City.[73]

Staples had influential supporters. E. G. Anderson justified her return to Japan on "faith" on grounds that any district in the denomination, including the Japan District, had the right to call for an evangelist. As district superintendent, Kitagawa had made such a call, so Staples really needed no permission from the Foreign Missions department in order to accept the position. Leslie Gay, whom Minnie Staples addressed as "Father" Gay, was still an influential and revered figure. Gay warned the Foreign Missions department that Staples *would* return to Japan whether or not it was under the official auspices of the church. He secured money from his own pocket, from pledges among members of Los Angeles First Church, and from other supporters, for her passage to Japan and for her needs on the field. Thus circumventing normal channels, and much to Reynolds's annoyance, Staples returned to Japan in late 1925. She and her husband resided in a modest apartment fixed for them adjacent to the Honmachi Church in Kyoto, pastored by Kitagawa.[74]

Meanwhile, Anderson decided that if the department did not have enough money for the Stapleses' official reappointment, it did not have enough for the Eckels either. In 1925 Anderson sent Eckel a letter of recall and then cut off his salary. Even while he knew that Staples was on her way, Anderson stated that it was the plan of the board to have *no* missionaries in Japan. Eckel rallied his own supporters in America and found a job teaching in a government school in order to remain in Japan with his family.[75]

Japanese leaders were eager to gain independence from control by Kansas City. As their country was becoming more nationalistic, so were their aspirations for the Nazarene church in Japan. In truth, Reynolds and others had not thought through what self-support would mean in relation to self-governance by the time the Japanese Nazarenes were calling for independence. They saw self-support as setting themselves as a Nazarene national church separate from Kansas City. The Japanese petitioned the General Board in 1928 to establish the Japan District as a regular district. The Japanese believed that they were ready. The board referred the matter to J. G. Morrison, foreign missions secretary. The Foreign Missions department then recommended that Japan be listed along with other fully organized districts in North America and the British Isles. The Japanese waited for general superintendents to ordain their ministers. That remained the emblem of their Nazarene identity, and Japanese nationalism strained even that tie.[76]

FINANCIAL CRISES AND THE RISE OF THE GENERAL BOARD

The rise of the General Board reflected connectional principles and was closely related to the need for a unified General Budget. The search for sound methods of funding the church's general interests had distinct stages. Lack of coordination, competition between ministries, and continual appeals for money characterized the first stage (1907-23). The next period was characterized by the search for a centralized system (1923-32). After that, there was a four-decade long period of stability and the gradual adoption by the churches of the nearly sacred ethic of "10 percent giving."

Nazarenes lacked general and districts budgets in their first sixteen years. Nearly every General Assembly created new general offices, and each office appealed for funds through the *Herald of Holiness* and directly to local churches. This was true of the General Board of Foreign Missions, the General Board of Home Missions, and the Boards of Education, Church Extension, Publication, Orphanages, and others. Each board had its own directors who met regularly, adding travel and meeting expenses to funds needed to run the ministries.

Union, church growth, and economic prosperity led the Nazarenes to dramatic increases in giving to missions in the years immediately after the First World War. Giving through the general headquarters in 1908 totaled only $12,000, reached over $22,000 in 1911, and more than doubled this by 1916. Giving remained strong during the war, and the church sent out new missionaries. By 1919 the total for missions was an astounding $122,500. At the 1919 General Assembly Reynolds challenged the church to raise $1 million for missions between the 1919 and 1923 General Assemblies. The church almost reached this goal, raising $857,615 over the next five years. The church sent out thirty-seven new missionaries in 1920 alone. Giving peaked in 1921, when about 45,000 Nazarene members contributed a total of $203,000 to world missions.[77]

The Church of the Nazarene sent out missionaries based on anticipations of continued increases, which, it turned out, could not be sustained. The economic hardships of the American Midwest during the 1920s and, later, the Depression, led to severe financial reverses. At the same time, the church developed other priorities. Districts planted dozens of new churches, most in rural areas. Members sacrificed to keep open the church's colleges, which, they believed, protected their children from the world and kept them in the faith.

E. G. Anderson served the church in important capacities during these years. From 1910 to 1915 he was treasurer of the General Board of Foreign Missions. After four years as business manager of Illinois Holiness University, in 1919 he returned to Kansas City to serve again as treasurer of the General Board of Foreign Missions. In 1921 Anderson became the church's general treasurer as well. And in 1923 he became general secretary of Foreign Missions, replacing Reynolds.[78]

Anderson soon realized that the funding system did not operate well. Churches sent money to ministries of their choosing and ignored others. World missions received the largest share of giving. The system failed to provide steady income for general superintendents, who derived financial support from other work. Bresee had drawn his primary salary as pastor of Los Angeles First Church. Reynolds drew a salary as Foreign Missions secretary. Ellyson and Walker were college presidents while serving as general superintendents. Goodwin and Williams supplemented their salaries by holding revivals. Editor B. F. Haynes considered the situation "a great reproach to us as a church."[79]

Church leaders knew by the time of the 1919 General Assembly that the system was inadequate. The first attempt at reform was through a plan called "Correlated Boards," in which the various boards met at the same time and same location. This allowed communication among members of different boards and allowed the general superintendents greater involvement. This plan, only a slight improvement, did not address the most pressing needs. Pastors complained of unceasing fund-raising appeals. So, too, did district superintendents such as Allie Irick in Texas, who reminded Reynolds and Goodwin that "the various drives from time to time, while good and of vital importance, have worked hardships on our general and regular method and system of financing. . . . This MUST be remedied in some way or other."[80]

During the 1920s Anderson, as both general treasurer and treasurer of Foreign Missions, issued repeated calls for funds. A deficit that had stood at $10,000 in June 1921 had risen to $50,000 by August and to $90,000 by December that same year, he reported to readers of *The Other Sheep*. The church needed the money immediately in order to avoid "calamity" and retrenchment. B. F. Haynes urged Nazarenes to borrow money from their banks, or from friends, to meet the immediate need. Somehow, because of emergency giving, the church closed its fiscal year without any deficit. However, the Foreign Missions Board informed Nazarenes that though they had forestalled the necessity of calling missionaries home, they would not be sending out missionaries in the following year.[81]

In 1923 the financial situation again threatened retrenchment, and rumors circulated that leaders had unwisely invested money. Anderson replied defensively, stating that the financial condition of the United States was not conducive for giving and that people had not fulfilled the pledges they had made. The Foreign Missions Board reduced the living allowances for missionaries, delayed sending furloughing missionaries back to their fields, and otherwise reduced the budget. Missionary lines were thin and growing thinner, Anderson warned. He urged the Foreign Missions Board to consolidate missions in certain countries and abandon stations that were in nonstrategic locations. The Foreign Missions Board adopted Anderson's recommendations and ruled that no more missionaries be sent out, except under extraordinary circumstances. While Reynolds recognized the necessity of finding a more systematic way of budgeting, he urged the Foreign Missions Board to raise $21,000 to meet immediate needs. Due much to his passion and influence, the church did not call missionaries home.[82]

Under this duress, E. A. Girvin, as chairman of the Commission on *Manual* Revision, and E. G. Anderson, played key roles in conceptualizing a new General Board. As a result of their recommendations, the 1923 General Assembly consolidated most of the church's boards, making them departments of a new entity, the General Board. Beginning that year, a single board of directors oversaw most of the church's general ministries. The step relieved pastors and churches by sharply reducing the number of financial appeals and brought deliberation and coordination to the process of disbursing general funds. Fundraising appeals after 1923 supported the whole of the General Board's ministries rather than its individual parts. The 1923 General Assembly authorized two new full-time officers: the general church secretary and the general treasurer. The Office of General Church Secretary combined two existing part-time offices, general assembly secretary and general statistical secretary, and to these added the responsibilities of arranging and hosting the General Board's annual meetings and serving as the church's chief legal and corporate officer. E. J. Fleming was elected to fill the office. E. G. Anderson was elected the church's first general treasurer. J. B. Chapman hailed the new General Board as "the greatest single work of the General Assembly" and believed that it would avoid duplication and friction among the general interests.[83]

However, giving remained low. In the first year after the General Assembly the General Board cut expenses by $100,000. Yet leaders felt that they must not fail the Great Commission. The church sent out twenty new missionaries "by faith," believing that Nazarenes would support them. Because of this expansion, in late 1925 Anderson again cautioned that retrenchment was necessary. He had in mind closing the work in Peru, Argentina, and Eastern India. Anderson wrote to Carlos Miller in Argentina that the work would close. Miller offered to reduce his salary, but it was not enough. Miller could remain in the country, Anderson wrote Miller in October 1925, but the Church of the Nazarene would not be responsible for his support. Miller joined the Christian and Missionary Alliance Church (under which he had worked earlier) in order to stay in Argentina. As a result of Anderson's dire warnings, between December 1925 and January 1926 the church raised $100,000, and so kept other missionaries on the field. But some of this money came in the form of short interest-bearing loans to the church, not outright gifts.[84]

Nazarene laypersons must have been confused. Church leaders issued dire warnings, people gave, and the church averted retrenchment—time and again. The consolidated system of budgeting did not seem to make a difference. And, still, rumors flew regarding how Kansas City handled finances. By 1925 the truth of some of the rumors that had been circulating for a few years, about the church's unwise investments, could no longer be hidden.

Anderson sought ways to increase the church's resources. In November 1921, Anderson had invested $50,000 of the church's money in 2,064 acres of North Dakota real estate valued at $150 per acre but selling at half that price. The church signed an agreement with evangelist L. Milton Williams, who brokered the investment. Williams personally paid $35,000 cash and took out a $70,000 loan for the remaining selling price. The church agreed to pay Williams $105,000 the following year. Almost immediately land prices fell drastically. Nineteen twenty-two proved to be a year, Williams reported, of "unkept pledges and broken promises." No money was available to farm the land. Williams turned over the deeds to Anderson in return for property that Anderson personally owned in Pasadena, California, valued at $12,000, and Anderson cancelled the contract with Williams. Anderson proceeded to sell parcels of the land in North Dakota in order to pay the remaining money owed to Williams. By 1925 1,600 acres had been sold. The 1925 General Board meeting passed resolutions censuring Williams, but Williams, unable to work as an evangelist because of the damage to his reputation due to this affair, threatened to sue the church.[85]

A Special Committee of the General Board, which included Reynolds, F. M. Messenger, the chairman of the General Board, and L. D. Peavey met with Williams, Anderson, and General Secretary Fleming in Chicago in July 1925. It recommended that the censures of the earlier General Board meeting against Williams be dropped, and exonerated Williams of all wrong. The church deeded back to Williams the remaining 464 acres in North Dakota still owned by the church.[86]

Nazarenes blamed Anderson, and, what hurt most, concluded that all the while that Anderson had made repeated calls for money, and spread dire warnings of retrenchment, he had mishandled their offerings. Frequently, Anderson had mixed personal with church money. With money drawn on his own account he had advanced money to missionaries and repaid Nazarenes who had made interest-bearing loans to the church. Rather than receiving back their investments, with interest, some Nazarenes held personal promissory notes from Anderson.[87]

Anderson resigned as general treasurer, effective January 1, 1926. He promised to repay the church nearly $50,000. In his stead, the church appointed Mervel Lunn, a layperson and accountant who had been serving as manager of the publishing house since 1922. Lunn accepted the position with the provision that full publicity be given to the financial situation. Anderson published a public apology for his mistakes in the February 10, 1926, issue of the *Herald of Holiness*. The 1926 General Board called upon the church to establish a strong tithing program and a method by which the General Budget could come directly from the local churches to the general treasurer, rather than by personal checks and solicitations. Lunn brought professionalism to the position, and the trust of the denomination toward its financial leaders returned.[88]

It was obvious that Anderson's tenure as Foreign Missions secretary also must terminate. Reynolds resumed the position until the 1928 General Assembly and the church's respect for and confidence in the missions department returned. Reynolds made the difficult decision to recall 29 missionaries and cut the operating expenses of the department by one-third. The Woman's Missionary Society stepped in to provide funds for some national workers. In 1927 J. G. Morrison resigned from the presidency of Northwest Nazarene College to assist Reynolds as Foreign Missions field secretary.[89]

The budget situation improved. The system provided a steady, somewhat predictable stream of income, and after 1926 the church did not resort to bank loans to help it through shortfalls. But daunting problems remained. General Superintendent R. T. Williams raised pledges for missions at the 1928 General Assembly amounting to $109,000. In the quadrennial address of the general superintendents, Williams noted that "the problem of financing the church has always been and will ever be a very difficult one." He continued, "The budget is instrumental in systematizing funds, but it is not an agency for the accumulation of money. It requires flesh and blood, living personality, to get money to supply the needs of the church. We must have propaganda, education, inspiration and agitation, in order to do the work to which we have been divinely called." A General Board committee reported that "our church as a whole is beginning to appreciate the advantages of forecasting their requirements a year in advance and then applying ourselves to the task of underwriting it through our district assemblies, which, in turn, distribute it among the individual churches. This has proven to be a vast improvement over the old system of frenzied appeals and great drives for money." A new special rule was added to the *Manual*, urging the weekly collection of funds and, "wherever possible and practicable, [that] the pastor's salary be paid regularly every week." It emphasized tithes and offerings as "the scriptural method of gathering money for the support of the Church" and called on churches to "adopt and practice the budget plan," so that "wherever possible the general and the district apportionments be paid monthly."[90]

In 1928 Morrison became the church's first full-time general secretary of Foreign Missions. Rather than lamenting the lack of funds, as Anderson had done repeatedly, Morrison wrote to Nazarenes through *The Other Sheep* of the many revivals and spiritual victories on the fields. Giving increased.

Just when the church began experiencing some financial stability came the Depression. In 1930 Morrison issued a plea to each of the countries in which the Church of the Nazarene had work, asking for their greater financial contribution to the work of the church. The success of the church on mission fields, wrote Morrison, had "so drawn upon the resources of our people as to embarrass us," so that "unless we can have help from many of our good people who have found Christ, we may become more heavily loaded than we can carry." He urged the Nazarenes around the world to begin by tithing and paying their own pastors' salaries. This savings alone would enable the church to expand to other countries where there was opportunity and need. Nazarenes around the world responded sacrificially to Morrison's appeal.[91]

Districts and local churches, with many members unemployed, found the church's levying a General Budget upon them difficult to bear and compared it to taxation. But, general leaders admonished, this was the only path forward for the church if it really wanted to advance the gospel in the world. Nazarenes undertook a whole month of "self-denial" in November 1931.[92]

The 1932 General Assembly took further action on budget allocations. A paragraph that remained in subsequent *Manual*s read: "When the total amount of the general budget has been fixed for the next fiscal year by the General Board, the General Board and the Board of General Superintendents are authorized and empowered to apportion the general budget to the several Assembly Districts on a basis of equity to both the district and the general interests affected." A "basis of equity" was important. Some districts were comparatively affluent, while others teetered on the brink of poverty. Per capita income in the southern United States was only a fraction of the national per capita. The General Board and the Board of General Superintendents apportioned the budget to the districts; the districts, in turn, allocated it to the individual churches. The assembly added paragraphs regarding the general and district budgets to the "Duties of the Pastor." The 1932 General Assembly made clear one other matter, that "storehouse tithing" meant "placing the tithe in that church to which the member belongs," for "the local church is the only storehouse properly recognizable in a scriptural sense. Therefore, to widen the scope of the definition but weakens its import and value." That is, Nazarenes were not to submit their tithes to headquarters, colleges, or other organizations, but to their local churches.

There was another issue. The quadrennial address stated frankly that the Woman's Foreign Missionary Society, "one of the outstanding departments of the Church, has raised its money exclusively for one interest of the General Budget, which partially destroys the complete budget unity," adding that "we must have a General Budget with all departments of the church participating fully and freely and each one supporting all the items of the budget." In response, the General Assembly directed that "all general funds raised by each department of each local church, including the Woman's Foreign Missionary Society, after its fixed items of relief and retirement and general contingent have been excepted, shall be paid into the General Budget until the General Budget apportionment of the local church be paid in full for the year."[93]

After 1932, budget processes ceased to be matters of significant General Assembly attention until the 1970s. Various assemblies attempted to add or delete entities funded by the General Budget, but these were largely defeated. One exception was Ministerial Relief. Originally designated as a local interest, it moved through the budget to become "a district interest" in 1933, and then a general interest in 1941.[94]

CONCLUSION

The Church of the Nazarene refined its connectional ties throughout this era. In 1946, his last year of life, Chapman inducted G. B. Williamson, successor to R. T. Williams, into the office of general superintendent. In the induction address, Chapman enunciated his mature views on superintendency. He noted that *superintendency* and *connectionalism* were intertwined. The Church of the Nazarene, "is a federation, not a confederation." The distinction was that "the Church of the Nazarene is composed of ministers and members, not of churches and districts," so "superintendency is of the whole church and all of the members of the church, and not simply of some subdivisions or sections." The general superintendents were "superintendents of the whole church, and not of some special area or section of the church. And the district superintendents are in reality assistant general superintendents, and not superintendents of independent units.... This conception is basic in our system."[95]

As always, Chapman chose his words very carefully. When he stated that the church was a *federation*, not a *confederation*, he drew an analogy from early American history. After the War of Independence, the thirteen colonies became thirteen sovereign states. They cooperated for several years under a weak form of government, the Articles of Confederation, without ceding their sovereignty. This proved impractical, and a new federal government was established under the constitution. This time, the states ceded much of their authority to it. And here was Chapman's point: Nazarene districts and churches were units, but not independent ones, and so the Church of the Nazarene was not a confederation of independent entities. Instead, it was a federation in which churches and districts were units within a connectional system. That was why district superintendents assisted the general superintendents in the supervision of "the whole church." *This* was the conception that Chapman insisted was "basic in our system."

NINE
NAZARENES AND SOCIETY

Many of those persons who joined the various groups that became part of the Church of the Nazarene had, as members of larger denominations, taken keen interest in social issues. Both John Wesley and the nineteenth-century Holiness Movement had taken a holistic concern for the material as well as the spiritual welfare of human beings. The era between 1915 and 1945 saw a reversal in those trends. Modernism, which embraced the social gospel, and fundamentalism, which rejected it, polarized American Protestantism and this carried over into various parts of the world. The reversal of a sense of guardianship for society among Nazarenes accompanied the period in which the church was forging its own identity, and increased its sectarian-like tendencies.

SOCIAL CONCERNS

During the nineteenth and early twentieth centuries the temperance movement in America and Great Britain brought churches into politics. Through this issue churches perceived that they must reform society and not just save sinners. The prohibition movement was an urban as much as a rural cause, and Pasadena, California, and Nashville were among its centers.[1]

That temperance was more than a matter of personal piety was evidenced by Bresee's 1899 *Manual:* "Total abstinence from all intoxicants is the Christian rule for the individual, and the total prohibition of the traffic is the duty of the civil government. It cannot be licensed without sin, and voters in a republic are responsible for the acts of the government." The regular temperance column in Bresee's *Nazarene Messenger* was called "Civic Righteousness." Bresee intended for the Church of the Nazarene to be actively involved in this social issue.[2]

The church's stand against drink was evidenced at the First General Assembly in Chicago in 1907, which viewed the "saloon," in particular, as "the rallying station for criminals, causing the expenditure of enormous sums to support our police, courts and criminal institutions and fill our poor houses and insane asylums."[3] The 1911 General Assembly appointed a delegation of ten, headed by H. B. Hosley, pastor in Washington, D.C., to represent the Church of the Nazarene at the next national convention of the Anti-Saloon League.[4]

Phineas Bresee was not the only Nazarene leader for whom prohibition, next to holiness, was the chief reason for the church's being. Benjamin Franklin Haynes, the church's first editor of the *Herald of Holiness,* had a long history of temperance advocacy. In 1909 Haynes, then pastoring a Methodist Church in Nashville, accused liquor interests of bringing a train car load of "beautiful fallen women" into Nashville to influence members of the Tennessee state legislature to vote against prohibition.[5] After joining the Church of the Nazarene, Haynes looked at the broader social issues. For the evil that institutions perpetrated, its constituents must accept responsibility. Where moral wrong existed, and multitudes suffered, there must be moral blame. Haynes wrote: "Sin is sin in one, or a thousand acting in a corporate capacity, and each must answer before God personally for the corporate sin. This is a truth needing to be burned into the intelligence and conscience of multitudes in this high day of finance and corporate greed." He went on to call the "divorcement of politics from all moral and religious influence" a "dire calamity."[6]

Among Nazarene members in Southern California, Lucy Wilhoit bragged of her companionship with Carrie A. Nation in smashing saloons in the early days of temperance activism. Wilhoit remained active in the Women's Christian Temperance Union after she joined the Church of the Nazarene in 1908 and was ordained in 1922. In 1935, at age 80, she was made a deputy sheriff of San Bernadino County.[7] Similarly, George Hammond, one of the early leaders of the New Testament Church of Christ (ordained by Mary Lee Harris and E. J. Sheeks in 1899), combined evangelistic and temperance work throughout his ministry. He served as pastor of several important Nazarene churches, including Kansas City First Church, and Albuquerque, New Mexico, First Church.[8]

Naturally the passage in January 1919 of the Eighteenth Amendment to the United States Constitution, which prohibited the "manufacture, sale, or transportation of intoxicating liquors within, the importation thereof into, or the exportation thereof from the United States and all territory subject thereof," pleased Nazarenes. The 1919 General Assembly applauded this as a "great moral triumph" that encouraged the church to press the battle against other forms of social evil such as gambling, Sabbath desecration, tobacco, and immodest dress. At the same time the church feared "any effort made by the present administration of our government, or the expression of any sentiment, which would again open the saloons of this nation." The delegates went so far as to place themselves on record that in their desire to shun even the appearance of evil they would not imbibe "the use of soft drinks that would embarrass our good name."[9]

On mission fields as well, Nazarenes likewise stood for total abstinence. As part of a revival campaign Pastor Abel Escobar in Guatemala, in 1926, held three public lectures on temperance.[10]

Nazarenes also supported the Eighteenth Amendment's "twin," the Nineteenth Amendment to the United States Constitution giving women the right to vote. The principle of "neither male nor female" (Gal. 3:28) had finally a place in law, said J. B. Chapman.[11] Nazarenes likewise favored the so-called Christian Amendment to the Constitution that would declare the United States a Christian country.[12]

Outside of the United States, missionaries avoided politics but could not avoid the associations others made between their evangelistic endeavors and foreign policy. For instance, the bitterness of Mexicans toward Americans made it difficult to reach them with the gospel, complained S. D. Athans (who then reported ninety seekers at an altar during a revival in El Paso, Texas) in 1916. Upon news of the reelection of Woodrow Wilson, in many places the anti-American feelings lessened. Argentineans looked more favorably upon Americans once World War I was over.[13]

The church soon saw that prohibition and the right of women to vote had failed to bring social perfection. Some thought the United States on the brink of anarchism. The possible repeal of prohibition became a lively political issue. The 1928 General Assembly went on record to oppose any presidential candidate who did not openly commit himself to support the Eighteenth Amendment. In that election, Alfred Smith, a "wet" Democrat opposed "dry" Republican Herbert Hoover. The Nazarenes commended the Republican Party in 1932 for standing firmly opposed to the repeal of the Eighteenth Amendment.[14] In the 1930s, nonetheless, the political landscape was quite wide, even for Nazarenes. A professor at Northwest Nazarene College (albeit soon dismissed) supported Socialist Upton Sinclair's bid for office in California. At about the same time, NNC President Russell V. DeLong courted and was courted by conservative state Republicans. DeLong invited William Borah, the long-time Republican U.S. Senator from Idaho, and other politicians to address the student body. However, in 1936 DeLong accused Borah of being too complimentary of the "godless" Russian state.[15]

COMPASSIONATE MINISTRIES

Compassionate ministries remained a response to the material needs of the world. Nazarenes maintained several orphanages, maternity homes, and urban rescue missions until the 1920s. Johnny Hill Jernigan established the Nazarene Home for unwed mothers in Bethany when her family moved there in 1908. Evangelists Oscar and Nettie Hudson operated an orphanage from their home in Lamasco, Texas. Later they transferred the children to the Peniel Orphanage, which they supported through their revival work. J. F. Spruce cared for orphans in north Texas for several years. In Seattle, H. D. Brown helped establish an orphanage and a maternity home. Santos Elizondo established an orphanage in Juarez, Mexico, soon after she began home mission work there. Nazarene orphanages were located in India and Swaziland. The General Board of Social Welfare and the General Orphanage Board advocated for these types of ministries.[16]

The newly begun *Herald of Holiness* in its Easter 1913 issue described the rescue mission work at that time within the church. The cover featured a picture of Jesus before the woman who was about to be stoned for adultery (John 8:7-11). For Editor Haynes there was "no phase of Christian endeavour more absolutely in harmony with the very heart throb of our Saviour than the work of rescuing these fallen, friendless, unpitied ones." God loves the sinner with "mother-love." This love, Haynes said, was the primary motivation for rescue work. Seth Rees gave several reasons for engaging in such work, beginning with the basic fact that "the uplifting of the fallen is the true genius of our holy Christianity." "White slave" traffic (forced prostitution) was enormous. Other "apostate" churches, said Rees, were neglecting the task, preferring their own "church entertainments, card parties, and the social dance." Rees related that he himself had founded and superintended ten rescue homes "without earthly backing." Robert Pierce of Los Angeles believed that the Church of the Nazarene was uniquely able to undertake rescue work because of its "deep spiritual life and bright, joyous methods." He continued, "Let there be a deeper bond of sympathy between the church and the rescue mission, and the financial question will take care of itself." Another article, by Lou Miller, pleaded for rescue workers especially trained for such ministries. The beginnings of rescue work around Arlington, Texas, Johnny Hill Jernigan related, was the result of simple and sincere compassion toward "fallen girls" whom society shunned. She noted that it was necessary to change a girl's environment to bring her to Christ. "The churches," she wrote, "will not take her case." F. M. Lehman depicted in further detail the "traffic in girls." He mentioned that the problem could not be left to politicians and policemen. J. Stuart Martin described the double standard of morals in a society that degraded the fallen women yet sanctioned the men with whom they were involved. Jennie Hodgen told the story of one prostitute rescued in a mission who became a preacher's wife. J. T. Upchurch argued that it was "absolutely necessary" to have homes for the redemption of fallen girls. "If a woman is to be redeemed, she must be *redeemed* from all those things which helped to wreck her." Rescue homes should be convenient to major cities, he said, while the main brunt of the work should be done by women. Homes listed at the end of the issue included: Berachah Home, Texarkana, Texas; Hope Cottage, Swampscott, Massachusetts; Rest Cottage, Kansas City; Rest Cottage, Pilot Point; Refuge Home, Hutchinson, Kansas; The Nazarene Home, Oklahoma City; Rest Cottage, Oakland, California; Chicago Rest Cottage; and Rescue Home, Pasadena, California.[17]

Such ministries testified to the humanitarian impulse that denominational founders associated with the call to holy living. General Superintendent Goodwin wrote in 1920: "Pure religion always has and always will have its two sides, purity and service. To neglect service in the welfare of others is to demonstrate a lack of purity. Holiness people should be preeminent in social service. This is what chiefly characterized the Early Church—their untiring service to bless their fellowmen and care for their widows and fatherless children." In its first decade, the *Herald of Holiness* devoted several special issues to orphanages or rescue homes.[18]

The tides that ebbed and flowed in Nazarene life shaped the context of social ministry. In 1923 only a handful of the social ministries founded in the previous twenty years still existed. The denominational *Yearbook* identified only four at that time: the Peniel Orphans Home, the Bethany Training Home in Memphis, and the Rest Cottages in Kansas City and Pilot Point. Bethany Training Home was gone by 1925, and the Nazarene Orphan's Home in Peniel, Texas, was the only one of these to become a general institution of the church. Established in 1901 at Pilot Point, Texas, it was an offshoot of the Oklahoma Orphanage in Oklahoma City operated by Mattie Mallory. It moved to Peniel in 1902, becoming an official institution of the Holiness Association of Texas. When the association dissolved in 1910, the Nazarene districts in Texas began supporting it. The 1919 General Assembly adopted it as a general ministry, but the reform-minded 1923 General Assembly reversed course, abolishing the General Orphanage Board and urging that the orphanage's assets be transferred "to the Districts of the Southern Educational District." The orphanage survived with district support only until 1928.[19]

The second generation leaders of the church were not, for the most part, ones who wedded social compassion with the mission of the Church of the Nazarene. Leaders such as Roy T. Williams and James B. Chapman, convinced premillennialists, possessed little optimism toward reform in society. Before all things, Nazarenes were to evangelize. The secretary of Home Missions, N. B. Herrell, stated in 1923: "Our vision, passion and heart cry should be 'Give us souls! Give us souls!' For this purpose we exist, and when we fail in this we have no right to continue as a church."[20] The reversal in social concerns also occurred because Midwestern Methodists who joined the Church of the Nazarene criticized modernism and social gospel trends in their former church. Authors Basil Miller and U. E. Harding contrasted the fundamentalists' approach to the modernists': "One holds up the Word of God, and the other offers a bowl of soup." By 1928 the general superintendents warned that social ministries in the church such as maintaining orphanages should be done on a "very conservative basis and continued in a limited way."[21] The role of the church was spiritual. Revivals would "save the world from sin and spiritual darkness," as General Superintendent Williams put it in 1933.[22] D. Shelby Corlett, then managing editor of the *Herald of Holiness*, lamented this, saying in 1935 that "we have done nothing for society as a whole" and that Nazarenes were more obsessed with avoiding evil than doing good.[23]

A "great reversal" of social concern was underway. The compassionate impulse that had given rise to orphanages, rescue missions, and homes for unwed mothers did not die, however. Medical ministries arose as a component of cross-cultural missions and preserved a continuous thread of social ministry from the era of the founders to the present. It was the church's primary type of social ministry until Nazarene Compassionate Ministries emerged in the 1980s with a wider agenda. Nazarene missions had medical components from their beginning. "Field work" performed by nurses was preeminent at first, but clinics and dispensaries soon appeared. These were followed by hospitals and schools of nursing in China, Swaziland, India, and, later, Papua New Guinea.

The Samaritan Hospital and School of Nursing in Nampa, Idaho, represented this impulse in North America. Thomas E. Mangum's interest in medical missions was stimulated partly by his sister, Myrtle, a missionary in India. Encouraged by H. Orton Wiley, Mangum built a hospital in Nampa adjacent to Northwest Nazarene College. In 1920 the hospital opened in a house adapted to Mangum's purposes. Its twin purposes were to care for missionaries on furlough and train nurses for overseas ministry. The first class of nurses graduated in 1931. By 1933, a fifty-bed hospital building was completed. The Samaritan Hospital and School of Nursing trained a number of nurses who later were assigned by the Department of Foreign Missions.[24]

The Fitkin and Hynd names were similarly linked to the Nazarene hospital in Swaziland. Harmon Schmelzenbach had wanted medical work in Africa at the beginning, but the General Missionary Board allocated its resources to evangelism. Why did a gospel preacher like Harmon Schmelzenbach see medical ministry as an asset to the church's presence in Africa? The motivations that Nazarene medical personnel articulated were not fundamentally different from those driving other types of Christian social ministry: there was a need, and duty compelled action. Nurse Lillian Cole expressed such sentiment in 1916: "We must have a hospital as soon as possible, properly furnished to supply the needs of these poor people, and we must have a doctor for this field as soon as someone can be secured. We have very many sad cases." The editor of *Other Sheep* stressed the compassionate impulse:

> Some may question the wisdom of investing money in a hospital in Africa, arguing that, with our limited means, it would be advisable to invest our funds in workers who devote their entire time to preaching and evangelizing. Seemingly they forget that one of the great agencies employed by our Master while on earth was through ministering to their physical needs ... [we] should use every agency that can be used to reach those who live in great darkness; not only spiritual darkness, but in great darkness concerning the care of the body, which is the temple of the Holy Ghost.[25]

At the same time, on mission fields such as Africa, medical approaches to illness directly conflicted with worldviews that attributed illness to evil spirits and magic.

Funds were not forthcoming until 1919. The death of ten-year-old Raleigh Fitkin in 1914 began, as Susan Fitkin's biographer expressed it, "a longing in his parents' heart to do something tangible" in his memory. And it was indeed tangible: a hospital in Swaziland, later over $1 million given to build and endow a children's wing at Yale University hospital, and $500,000 to establish Raleigh Fitkin-Paul Morgan Memorial Hospital in Asbury, New Jersey.[26]

The first hospital that the Fitkins financed in Swaziland, and completed in 1920, was small, located at Pigg's Peak, where there were other missionary interests. Construction was completed in 1920. It had 18 beds under the direction of Lillian Cole. Physician Charles West arrived in 1921, but British authorities rejected his American medical credentials. (The missions board moved him to China in 1925.) The Swazi hospital faced another problem: it was located in a low population area. The missionaries urged a larger hospital in a more populous area and received the support of George Sharpe, missionary superintendent in Africa during these years. In 1925 the Swazi government donated a tract of land for a hospital at Bremersdorp (now Manzini), situated on a major road leading from the Swazi capital. The Fitkins, with Ada Bresee, were again the primary donors to the project. Sharpe's son-in-law, Scottish surgeon David Hynd, supervised the building of the new hospital. Hynd taught himself basic construction methods. The hospital was completed and dedicated in 1927. With Raleigh Fitkin Memorial Hospital as its hub, other Nazarene interests relocated to Bremersdorp, the effective headquarters of the Nazarene mission in Africa for many years.[27]

The hospital's subsequent history was interwoven with Hynd's determined personality. A training program for nurses began in 1928. During Hynd's long tenure, the hospital added "a children's ward, maternity ward, male and female medical and surgical wards, X-ray equipment, and a modern sanitary system." Elizabeth Cole, assigned to the hospital in 1935 and later to field nursing, developed a ministry to lepers. Through her efforts and Hynd's, the government established the Mbuluzi Leper Hospital forty miles from Manzini, which RFM Hospital operated as an extension of its work.[28]

David Hynd

C. J. Kinne simply referred to Christian medical work as "following the Great Physician." Bresee Memorial Hospital in China was his personal vision. As the founding manager of the Nazarene Publishing House, Kinne knew the obstacles associated with establishing a new institution. As early as 1913, he wanted to see a credible medical work in China. Missionary Peter Kiehn later recalled that Kinne spent several years in self-education about medical missions before broaching the subject with the General Missionary Board. After leaving the publishing house, Kinne spent two years in California as district missionary evangelist, preaching and organizing classes to study missions. This provided his base constituency when he founded the Nazarene Medical Missionary Union in 1921. Among its stated aims: to establish hospitals "under the direction of the General Missionary Board."

Kinne visited China in 1923. He examined hospitals operated by other denominations and settled on Daming, center of the Nazarene work in northern China, as the best location for a Nazarene hospital. After returning to America to secure funds, Kinne went back to China in 1924, serving as on-site construction supervisor. Local wars hindered progress, and financial problems arose. The hospital's main part was completed by 1925 and opened in October with 100 beds, but further construction ground to a halt. Kinne's wife, who had remained in California, died in his absence. Determined to complete the job, Kinne returned to America and raised more funds. In 1927 he married Sue Bresee, daughter of the late general superintendent, who accompanied him to China the following year. Meanwhile, Mary Pannell had initiated a training program for Chinese nurses. Kinne resumed the role of construction supervisor and was pastor of the missionary force congregated in Damingfu. The hospital was completed and equipped when Kinne left China in 1930. Bresee Memorial Hospital was the only hospital in a city of some 14,000 residents, and it was estimated that its constituency was as great as 2 million people. In this setting, dedicated physicians worked with Chinese doctors and nurses. In the late 1930s, missionary accountant Catherine Flagler estimated that one-third of General Budget funds spent on China supported medical work there. In 1935 J. B. Chapman visited the hospital in China, and was impressed with both Dr. Henry Wesche, a National Holiness Association missionary who was giving part-time service to the Nazarene hospital, and Dr. Feng Lan-xin, who was proving to be a "true Christian and a good surgeon, and a tireless worker."[29] Other doctors—both Chinese and missionary—followed for brief periods. Hester Hayne worked at the hospital as a nurse from 1921 to 1926, and following her evacuation in 1926 and furlough, she finished an M.D. degree at the University of Kansas. Returning to China in 1934, she continued studies at the Peking Union Medical Center and served at Bresee Hospital from 1936 to 1941. In the meantime, Wesche as well had become full-time with the Nazarene mission. The war with Japan forced Bresee Memorial Hospital to close in 1941. The ascendancy of Mao's Red Army prevented its reopening.[30]

Hospitals and clinics arose elsewhere around the world. In Guatemala, for instance, the Nazarene hospital in Coban began in 1926 under a nurse, Bessie Branstine, who had gone to Guatemala at her own expense. She and her work was accepted and placed under the Church of the Nazarene in 1930. But in 1932, when, after returning from a furlough, Branstine married a native Guatemalan, the church disowned her and her work. An infirmary, nonetheless, continued under various other nurses.[31]

Amid economic downturns, Nazarenes constructed Reynolds Hospital in Basim, India, in the 1930s. The hospital ministered to Muslims as well as Hindus and Christians. Dr. Orpha Speicher almost single-handedly built the hospital and pressed the work forward. The hospital, which served only women until 1952, proved to be a highly visible form of the church's witness. In the public defense of the work, missionaries emphasized to leaders and to the North American constituency its evangelistic role. Speicher repeatedly emphasized that the hospital provided an opportunity for witnessing to people who otherwise would not approach Christians.³²

The church added other hospitals in the post-World War II era. The International Holiness Mission, a British denomination, had a hospital in Acornhoek, South Africa, which became a Nazarene institution when the IHM merged with the Church of the Nazarene in 1952. In 1958 the Nazarene World Missionary Society raised funds to build a hospital in Kudjip, Papua New Guinea as its fiftieth anniversary project.³³

MORAL BOUNDARIES

In Nazarene minds, clear ethical distinctions were part of the means by which modern, immoral trends could be halted. The perceived breakdown of morality in civil society after the First World War was among the factors leading to Nazarenes' tightening their rules. The mergers with the Southern groups, the Holiness Church of Christ and the Pentecostal Mission, increased the sense that holiness needed to be tightly structured around rules. Southern evangelicals in particular had erected clear boundaries of behavior. The General Rules included avoiding taking advantage in buying and selling, and indulging in pride in dress. Nazarenes were to avoid songs, literature, and entertainment not to the glory of God, the theater and the ballroom along with lotteries and other games of chance. Many evangelists and preachers interpreted the general statement on "pride of dress" to prohibit women's makeup and jewelry, including, in many places, especially in the South and Midwest, a wedding ring. Nazarene proscriptions on such matters as circus attendance represented strictness even for Southerners. The Kansas District in 1925 considered "worldly conformity" immodest dress, bobbed hair, "false complexions," "public bathing," obscene pictures, unholy amusements, and cigarette smoking.³⁴

Evangelists who preached against jewelry collected rings, necklaces, and bracelets from those spiritually convicted. Sometimes penitent ones surrendered their jewelry right at the kneeling rails. Evangelists sent these objects to Kansas City so that the church could sell the jewelry and use the proceeds to keep missionaries on the field. That is, at their best, preachers and evangelists did not encourage plainness for the sake of plainness, but as a disciplined lifestyle that fit the sacrifices of Christ. In times of both financial and moral crisis, as people perished without Christ, no one could afford to live beyond his or her needs. Instead, Nazarenes were to devote themselves to doing good, and to spend time in family devotions. In close-knit ways they fed the hungry, clothed the naked, and pressed the claims of the gospel upon the unsaved. Through such commitments Nazarenes linked themselves to a common cause and forged a communal identity and distinguished themselves from the world.[35]

The Nazarene *Manual* affirmed that divorce was only to be permitted on the "scriptural ground" of adultery. If this was not the basis, and Nazarenes were to remarry, they would be living in adultery and would not be worthy of membership. Only adultery justified the innocent party in remarrying. If a woman married a man who had been divorced for other than adultery, she would be living in adultery herself. W. M. Tidwell, prominent pastor of the First Church of the Nazarene in Chattanooga, Tennessee, and a former associate of J. O. McClurkan, underwent a divorce in which his wife left him. He remained single for a number of years before marrying Eva Cook Sutherland who, herself, had experienced the "agony of an unfaithful companion." The church permitted their remarriage because both Tidwell and Sutherland, as the church saw it, had been the innocent victims. Tidwell remained a revered preacher, known for his strict preaching about behavior and obedience to rules.[36]

Nazarene farmers in Kentucky during the Depression wondered whether it was permissible for them to raise tobacco. The *Manual* had declared that Nazarenes must not "traffic" in tobacco, but what about growing it? The opinion of General Superintendent Chapman was lenient on this. At the same time, Nazarenes accused First Church of the Nazarene in Nashville as being too liberal for tolerating tobacco use among its members.[37]

The 1928 General Assembly, meeting in Columbus, Ohio, added a statement to the Appendix to the *Manual* that Nazarenes were to avoid "promiscuous bathing places." While some Nazarenes abhorred "mixed bathing" (which meant men and women swimming together), the church did not look upon this issue uniformly. West Coast Nazarenes, for instance, even Los Angeles First Church, long held church outings at the beach.[38]

Sociologically, the adherence to strict rules marked Nazarenes as "outsiders." They would have gloried in this designation during these second generation years. Furthermore, as Timothy Smith astutely points out, the increased attention to rules in the second generation arose from fears of declension from the first generation. The danger was that adherence to rules might substitute for religious experience.[39]

NAZARENES AND EVANGELICALS

Nazarenes participated in the founding of the National Association of Evangelicals during the Second World War, even though it took decades for the church to join the organization. Among those signing a call for a unified front of evangelicals, General Superintendent Emeritus J. W. Goodwin and Foreign and Home Missions Secretary C. Warren Jones did so as individuals rather than on behalf of the denomination. Various evangelical leaders met in St. Louis in April 1942. Their goal was to establish an organization that would counteract the liberal influences of the National Council of Christian Churches and establish an organization that would be doctrinally broad enough to include "all groups which have remained faithful to the great doctrines of the Church," but narrow enough to "exclude those who have rejected the authority of God's Holy Word."[40] Stephen Paine and Leslie Marston, leaders of the Wesleyan Methodist Church and the Free Methodist Church, respectively, were among the primary movers in the meeting. Paine warned against the "intrusion of doctrinal criteria not really essential to the evangelical position."[41] But the perception remained that the NAE was "top-heavy with Calvinism."[42] Among the 150 delegates to the St. Louis Conference, only about 22 represented Holiness denominations.

A Constitutional Convention of the NAE met in Chicago in 1943. At this meeting, D. Shelby Corlett, editor of the *Herald of Holiness*, represented the Church of the Nazarene. Corlett was elected one of twenty-five on the NAE's Board of Administration. Leslie Marston was elected first vice president of the Executive Committee. The Statement of Faith of the National Association of Evangelicals affirmed the Bible as "the inspired, the only infallible, authoritative Word of God." It also affirmed "the present ministry of the Holy Spirit by whose indwelling the Christian is enabled to live a godly life." The constitution did not require adherence to premillennialism and did not stipulate the Bible's "verbal" inerrancy. In short, there was little in the organization's doctrinal position with which the Nazarenes could object. However, the NAE included Pentecostal denominations, and there was such animosity between Nazarenes and Pentecostals that it seemed impossible to cooperate with them even at this level. Only in 1984 did the Church of the Nazarene join the National Association of Evangelicals.[43]

Pentecostals remained estranged cousins of Nazarenes. When she was being discredited by critics, one of the charges laid upon missionary to Japan Minnie Staples was that she had attended prayer meetings with Pentecostals. C. E. Roberts, whose family had been active in the founding of the Rest Cottage at Pilot Point, and wife, Mae Roberts, left the Church of the Nazarene over this issue. When they desired to return, they had to defend themselves by saying that they had never spoken in tongues. They believed that speaking in tongues was one of the gifts of the Spirit, the Robertses said, but not the evidence of the baptism with the Holy Spirit. But even this moderate stand distanced themselves too greatly from accepted Nazarene understandings. The boundaries of Nazarene identity were already drawn.[44]

TEN

NAZARENE RESPONSES TO THEIR MISSION

The Church of the Nazarene was slow to develop a strategy for evangelizing the world. Instead, it built upon preexisting work and entered open doors. From the beginning Nazarene leaders understood that they would contribute with others to world evangelism. Unlike some other Holiness missions organizations, the Church of the Nazarene cooperated with other missions and sought comity arrangements where these existed.

A WORLD PERSPECTIVE

Hiram F. Reynolds shaped the philosophy and practice of world missions in the Church of the Nazarene. He established mission policy in key fields and set patterns for decisive leadership. On his worldwide missionary tour in 1913, Reynolds drafted a policy, similar to the policy the Association of Pentecostal Church's Missionary Committee had drawn up for India sixteen years before, specifically to govern the work of the Church of the Nazarene in Japan. The policy placed the work under the *Manual*. The policy asserted the "manifestations of the Holy Spirit are practically the same in all countries." The primary role of the missionaries was to "get souls saved and sanctified, and trained for the work of the Kingdom of God on earth." At the same time entire sanctification was to be "kept to the front." Methods of evangelism were to be virtually the same as in North America: visiting house-to-house, organizing Bible classes, establishing Sunday Schools, opening preaching stations, and distributing literature. Local churches should assume as much of the support of the work as possible. A local church reaching self-support could call for and retain a pastor as provided in the *Manual*. When the district as a whole achieved self-support and (unclearly defined) measures of self-government, "all missionary control [would] be relinquished except such superintendency as is provided in the *Manual*." The work would be both responsible to and a part of the General Assembly, and accountable to the general superintendents it elected. Until the district achieved self-support, policy gave the appointed missionary district superintendent a firm position of authority over the national church. Though the policy gave missionaries front-line roles in the beginning, their stay was temporary.[1]

The policy mentioned no important institutional aspects of the work. At the time other Protestants were working in Japan's slums and were active in combating prostitution and other social evils. India required medical and primary school work. But in Japan, the church's response was different. Maintaining a large force of missionaries was neither necessary nor expedient.[2]

Reynolds's next stop was China. Reynolds had seized upon an opportunity for the denomination in a young couple, Peter Kiehn and Anna Schmidt Kiehn, both of whom were former missionaries to China. Peter Kiehn had been raised Mennonite and was a member of a Holiness congregation in Hutchinson, Kansas, that became Nazarene in 1908. Kiehn had attended the Holiness Bible school in Hutchinson before first sailing to China in 1906 at the age of twenty-one. He worked in Shandong Province under the Mennonite Missionary Society. Like Peter Kiehn, Anna Schmidt had been raised a Mennonite. She arrived in China in 1906 and also worked in Shandong province. She and Kiehn were married in China in 1908. They helped establish a station in cooperation with the South Chili Gospel Mission. They furloughed in 1912 and united with the Church of the Nazarene while attending college in Bethany, Oklahoma. Kiehn was ordained by Reynolds in 1913. Both Peter and Anna Kiehn were eager to return to China as Nazarene missionaries.[3]

Meanwhile, Reynolds learned through C. W. Ruth that there was a good possibility of the fledgling National Holiness Association work in China affiliating with the Nazarenes. However, Ruth warned that a premature departure for China by Kiehn might cause negotiations between the Church of the Nazarene and the NHA to fail. Nevertheless, Reynolds took Kiehn and his wife, along with Glennie Sims, on his trip as the officially appointed Nazarene workers to China. Reynolds's eagerness for the Church of the Nazarene to enter China was fueled by the opportunities that awaited Christianity under China's new Republican government. Reynolds, the Kiehns, and Sims made their way to the NHA headquarters in Nankwantao. The NHA work impressed Reynolds. Amiable and frank talks ensued between Reynolds and the NHA missionaries. In a letter that soon followed to the General Missionary Board of the Church of the Nazarene, the NHA missionaries expressed their desire to give their converts the privileges of a church home. They understood that the National Holiness Association did not plan to take denominational form and found it acceptable for the NHA mission in China to be taken over by the newly organized Nazarene church and governed according to its *Manual*. They presented themselves as candidates for missionary appointment. Their only stipulation was that the Nazarenes assume full financial responsibility by November 1916.

While waiting for the matter to be decided, the NHA gave one half of the area assigned to it by a Protestant Council to the Church of the Nazarene. This partition would become unnecessary if and when union took place. The Kiehns took a station in the area apportioned to the Nazarenes, at Chaocheng, in Shandong province. NHA missionaries had regularly itinerated there and recently had begun Sunday worship services in the city.[4]

Before going on his way to India (to meet a host of crises in Calcutta), Reynolds, along with Peter and Anna Kiehn and Glennie Sims, established a policy statement particularly for China. In contrast to the one drawn for Japan a few weeks earlier, the China policy encouraged institutional work. The primary impetus remained evangelism, which was to be accomplished through touring from village to village, visiting house-to-house, opening new stations and preaching at fairs and markets. In addition, China necessitated medical work, literature (translating and selling Holiness books), schools, and even industrial training. The missionaries must encourage Chinese Christians to tithe. That Reynolds and the church in general had not thought through the ultimate goals of church government was clear in one statement Reynolds made: that China would eventually have its own general as well as district superintendents, along with evangelists and college presidents.[5]

Reynolds was optimistic about the union with the NHA. But the Pentecostal Mission, headquartered in Nashville, united with the Church of the Nazarene in 1915, and its extensive missions lay upon the church's heavy financial obligations. World War I created global uncertainties. Accessioning the NHA work was too great an undertaking for the young denomination.[6]

Reynolds's next stop was Calcutta. Like Japan, East India informally had been under the jurisdiction of Bresee until this time. Reynolds found the mission at a dismal ebb. Emma Eaton, whom Bresee had commissioned in 1906 to cosuperintend with Sukhoda Banarjee the work in Eastern India, had had a recent operation. Her husband had suffered a sunstroke. But that was hardly the worst. Banarjee was making allegations that her relations with a missionary, who had recently returned to California, were romantic and that the missionary had promised to marry her. Reynolds decided that Banarjee must leave the mission. Reynolds prepared a document for Banarjee to sign, consisting of her resignation, her severance of all relations with Hope School and Hallelujah Village, and a pledge not to interfere with the mission. Reynolds remained in Calcutta for more than a month, during which time Eaton resigned as superintendent and her husband as treasurer. Hulda Grebe remained to work in the school and her sister, Leoda, to head the dispensary, but they were inexperienced and did not know the local language, Bengali. Before Reynolds left, Leighton S. Tracy arrived from Central India to take over the Calcutta station. Ten Indian workers and 120 boys and girls remained. The situation reinforced to Reynolds the necessity of strong administrative oversight and strict accountability.[7]

Reynolds proceeded from Eastern to Central India, where he led missionaries through the forming of a policy for their field. Much related to themselves. All missionaries should receive the same salary (a response to the previous merger of Nazarene with Holiness Church of Christ missionaries). Missionaries must not engage in secular business. Terms would be fixed—six years for the first term, seven for the next. All would have a six-week annual rest period. No missionary would be appointed for life. The first year of missionary service should be devoted fully to language study. The inability either to use the language or to adjust to the culture would be grounds for a missionary's recall. Missionaries were to be engaged in touring villages, in visiting house-to-house, in preaching in fairs and bazaars, and in both establishing and maintaining mission stations. They were to care for the Christians, also, through Bible classes, Sunday Schools, and general pastoral work. The missionaries recognized that "the primary object of our work is spiritual, i.e., the salvation of sinners, the sanctification of believers and building them up in the holy faith. Such auxiliary works as orphanages, schools, industrial and medical works, translation, publication and other usual branches of missionary effort may be opened whenever they can serve our primary object." The policy put the mission's social ministries in the context of more "spiritual" endeavors. The church's primary concern was the salvation of individuals.[8]

The policy set three stages of district development. At the first stage, missionaries and any ordained Indian elders, along with delegates from self-supporting Indian churches, would compose the district assembly. Though there were not yet any Indian elders or self-supporting Indian churches, the thought was of cooperation between missionaries and Indians. When Indian members of the assembly outnumbered missionaries, a second stage became possible. Missionaries then would form a mission council apart from the district assembly. At that time the assembly would deal with questions directly related to the self-supporting Indian churches, and the missionaries in their council would control only money coming to the mission from abroad. The council would also be in charge of assigning missionaries to stations around the field. The third stage of development would be a self-supporting district. At that stage, the district assembly would station missionaries as well as national workers; employ, supervise, and dismiss Indian workers; examine both missionaries and Indian workers in the course of study for ministers; audit mission accounts; elect a District Executive Board; and nominate a district superintendent to the general missionary board. Missionaries intended these formulations to promote self-support and measures of self-government. Self-support was the critical prerequisite for regular district status. In the meantime the policy allowed missionaries to control every detail of the work.[9]

The three policies drawn up by Reynolds for Japan, China, and India agreed in basic principles. Missionary presence served to prepare the church for self-support and, with it, measures of self-government. Since churches would remain tied together by the *Manual*, the goal was not the establishment of autonomous national bodies. This differentiated Nazarene missions from those of most other denominations.

Though Reynolds had planned to visit Palestine on this trip, he made a brief return trip to Calcutta to see if everything that he had tried to establish under Tracy was proceeding smoothly. He then sailed directly from Calcutta to South Africa—a twenty-seven day trip—and then immediately to Swaziland. Here missionaries Harmon and Lula Schmelzenbach and Etta Innis had been eagerly expecting him for some time, but Reynolds stayed for only nine days.

Reynolds had hoped to stop in the Cape Verde Islands on his return across the Atlantic, but the war prevented him from doing so, and he was detained getting across the Atlantic. His way took him, nonetheless, through Liverpool, England, and Glasgow, Scotland, where he saw George Sharpe. At this time, the Pentecostal Church of Scotland, led by Sharpe, had not yet decided to join the Church of the Nazarene.

The Church of the Nazarene agreed to abide by comity arrangements (by which denominations agreed to remain within mutually agreed upon geographic boundaries) in China, India, and Swaziland. Reynolds directed that missionaries work harmoniously with churches already in the area. The presupposition behind Reynolds's agreeing to abide by comity was that the "second blessing," the denomination's distinctive doctrine, was *not* essential for salvation. If he had believed that entire sanctification was necessary for salvation, he would have advocated evangelizing Presbyterians, Baptists, or Methodists who did not claim the experience. Some in the Holiness Movement, indeed, held to an aberration of Wesley's doctrine of holiness, and suggested that the Bible verse "holiness, without which no [one] shall see the

Lord" (Heb. 12:14) restricted salvation to those who had experienced entire sanctification in this life. However, this was not the position of John Wesley or the model the Church of the Nazarene followed. Reynolds's willingness to cooperate reflected a more churchly than sectarian tendency. In Peru, later, the Church of the Nazarene divided work with the Free Church of Scotland, which gave to the Nazarenes a large section of area inhabited by "forest Indians." This Aguarunaland became a place of ministry for Roger Winans and later Nazarene missionaries.[10]

This did not mean that Nazarenes considered other churches sufficient. There were limits to denominational charity. Carlos Miller, missionary to Argentina, found Methodism in that country to have "forsaken its moorings," and the Baptists "holding up the Savior as far as they go," but confessing their own need for a deeper work.[11]

STRATEGIES FOR GROWTH IN THE INTERWAR YEARS

In the years following the First World War, increased pessimism about social morality and the rise of premillennialism accompanied the church's sense of urgency to evangelize the world. In part because of fundamentalist "leavening," premillennialism eclipsed postmillennialism. This intensified the sense of necessity to evangelize the world quickly. Even Reynolds, whose nineteenth-century Methodist roots predisposed him toward postmillennialism, used the rhetoric of premillennialism to prod church members to work as energetically as they could and to give as much as they could for the redemption of the world. "What if there is a gracious and world-wide revival within the next few years, and then the rapture? Don't we want the biggest possible part in the first that we may be found in the second? With all these solemn responsibilities upon us, and the Lord's coming imminent, how can we hoard up money?" Duty demanded the pursuit of lost souls who would perish forever unless the gospel reached them in time.[12]

In the 1920s the mission policy became global rather than field-based. It affirmed that "the primary object of our work is spiritual, namely, the salvation of sinners, the sanctification of believers and building them up in the holy faith." Yet the policy also affirmed that orphanages, schools, industrial and medical work, translation and publication all were legitimate in certain fields insofar as they served the primary, evangelistic objective. As well as this cardinal mission, the church's policy also voiced its distinguishing mission to keep the doctrine and experience of entire sanctification "to the front."[13]

The successive policies all maintained that the "work and manifestations of the Holy Spirit are practically the same in all countries." Reynolds's ministry in various countries seemed to confirm this. He never mentioned adapting or contextualizing the message for his audiences. Yet, under his preaching, people around the world testified to a "second blessing" and gave up various vices. That was sufficient enough evidence for him that revival methods as well as the Holiness message were universally applicable.[14]

Other Nazarene missionaries and preachers testified to the same. On a mission trip to Barbados, Susan Fitkin heard J. I. Hill preach on the "two baptisms." Fifty persons raised their hand desiring the "second" baptism with the Holy Spirit. There was not enough room for them to kneel at the rail. "I suggested they might rise and we could then all pray that God would sanctify them wholly. This was done," Fitkin recounted, "and what a Pentecost we had!"[15]

The church did not rush quickly into new areas of the world. This reflected Reynolds's careful rejection of the "faith missions" philosophy, and understanding that other denominations were effectively working throughout the world. Further, it reflected financial realities. The 1928 General Board directed that "we do not enter any new mission fields but attempt to conserve the work that we now have."[16] After his world trip in 1928 to 1929, R. T. Williams came to the same conclusion, that the church must concentrate on certain fields, not all, that it should be where it could be most "felt," and that it should go to the more accessible countries.[17] In 1931 General Superintendent J. B. Chapman noted, in support, that there were ten million people in areas where the Church of the Nazarene already worked who still had not accepted the gospel. As a result of this policy the church lost early opportunities to open work in Egypt and the Philippines. The church had to let wait a host of missionary applicants "longing, desiring to be sent, alleging that God has undoubtedly called them to the mission field."[18] In 1938 K. J. Jaroszewicz, president of the Union of Churches of Christ in Poland and other Slavic countries, representing 25,000 members and three hundred churches, approached General Superintendent John Goodwin at the Pittsburgh District Assembly about the possibility of affiliation with the church. Jaroszewicz desired financial help from the church. The general superintendents felt that the Church of the Nazarene could not help without diminishing its already existing work, and nothing came of Jaroszewicz's proposal.[19]

WORLD LEADERS

Both Bresee and Reynolds favored using as key leaders persons from the countries in which the Church of the Nazarene desired to work. In several cases, potential leaders arrived on the doorstep of the Church of the Nazarene in America. These included three men who pioneered the work in Japan, J. I. Nagamatsu, Hiroshi Kitagawa, and Nobumi Isayama. Another was Samuel Krikorian, an Armenian. His grandfather, Krikore Harootunian, was a minister affiliated with the American Board of Commissioners for Foreign Missions (the mission board of the Congregational Church), and the first native Protestant minister to be ordained in Central Turkey. His aunt, Rebecca Krikorian, who attended the American Girl's College in Constantinople (under the American Board), traveled to the United States in 1895, partly sponsored by the Women's Christian Temperance Union, shortly before the massacres of Armenians in Turkey. She worked energetically to raise support for Armenian people. Nazarene churches on the West Coast gave her opportunities to make appeals. Meanwhile, in 1909, Samuel Krikorian immigrated to America. While studying at a Church of the Brethren school in Granthem, Pennsylvania, he professed entire sanctification. His aunt suggested that he finish his education at Pasadena College. Krikorian decided to join the Church of the Nazarene after his graduation there in 1917, and he was ordained the year following.

The Great War changed the political landscape of the Near East. Krikorian and his aunt felt impressed to open work in Jerusalem, where many Armenians had fled, and which the British now occupied, rather than to return to Turkey. Over the next three years, they raised money for a mission in Jerusalem as a platform from which to evangelize Muslims. The Nazarene Board of Foreign Missions, with Reynolds's enthusiastic recommendation, agreed to take up this mission. Krikorian arrived in Syria in August 1921 and proceeded to Jerusalem. Krikorian began ministering to Armenian refugees, most of whom were members of the ancient Gregorian Christian Church. Worship services began at Christmastime. Missionaries Alvin and Naomi Kauffman joined Krikorian in 1922. They began work among Armenian refugees in both Haifa and Jaffa the following year.

The missionaries organized Jerusalem First Church of the Nazarene with twenty-one members, all Armenians, in April 1924 (a month after Samuel Krikorian had married Hranoush, an Armenian refugee). The church rented a hall inside the walls of the old city. Later in 1924, through donations, the mission purchased land outside the city walls near the YMCA. By 1928 there were 75 members, and the Nazarene Sunday School, reputed to be the largest in Palestine, attracted two hundred pupils. In the 1930s the Church of the Nazarene was the largest evangelical church serving the Armenian community and operated a day school with about sixty students.[20]

Political conflicts upset the work in Palestine. Jewish immigration caused much social upheaval with the local Arab population, with Armenians caught in between. The Krikorians carried on during the Second World War, but as soon as the war ended, new strife began. Nearly all of the Armenians in Jerusalem fled to other cities in Palestine and Jordan.[21]

Another national worker in the Near East was Milhem A. Thahabeyah, a Syrian of Roman Catholic background. He immigrated to America in 1911 and settled in Fort Wayne, Indiana. In 1915, after his conversion, Thahabeyah joined the Church of the Nazarene in Pioneer, Ohio, and soon professed a call to preach. He briefly attended God's Bible School in Cincinnati and then planted a Nazarene church in Montgomery, Michigan. He completed his studies at Olivet College and was ordained in 1920. E. G. Anderson encouraged him to open the work of the Church of the Nazarene in Syria. In November 1920, at age twenty-seven, he sailed for Syria. Thahabeyah opened a school in a family home in the town of Bludan. Reynolds visited Bludan in 1922 and organized the church there. Thahabeyah began a second church in Zahlah. Many of the converts were from the Greek Orthodox Church. Thahabeyah remained a Nazarene missionary in Syria until his retirement in 1955.[22]

Meanwhile, the indigenization of the work in Mexico came about because of political necessity as much as missiological strategy. The Holiness Church of Christ had established a mission in Chiapas, in southern Mexico, beginning in 1903. Missionary Carlos Miller opened the work in Mexico City a few years later. But because of government restrictions all missionaries were forced out of Mexico by 1912, leaving the church in the hands of Vicente G. Santin (1870-1948). For decades Santin shaped the Church of the Nazarene in Mexico. His father, a preacher in the Methodist Church, died when he was young. Santin himself became a preacher in the Methodist Church at age eighteen. At the same time, he attended medical school and became a medical doctor. He left the pastorate. Hearing Nazarene missionary preaching, Santin sensed his need for a second work of grace and testified to his being sanctified in May 1907. He soon joined the Nazarene ministry, becoming pastor of Mexico City First Church, which was organized in December 1908. The Church of the Nazarene in Mexico experienced harassment under local officials. Law prohibited people from gathering to worship in houses. Santin maintained his medical practice. During the year 1918, Santin reported, he preached 159 times, had 350 seekers, received 23 members, and treated 2,553 patients.[23]

In 1919, Santin was appointed district superintendent—aside from Sharpe in Scotland, the first national leader in such a position. Santin continued to pastor Mexico City First Church and, in 1922, opened the Seminario Nazareno de Mexico. The general church encouraged Santin's desire that the seminary in Mexico City remain the focal point of ministerial education. To students taking the three-year course he was "a strict man, wise in counsel, fervent in prayer, and above all, helpful to the end."[24] Out of the school came significant church leaders. During the difficult financial times of the 1920s and 1930s, Santin supplemented his income by affiliating with a university faculty. The Mexican church gave liberally to an "Easter Sacrifice Offering" in 1930. Later the same year it volunteered for a 10 percent reduction in salary stipends being sent from Kansas City to Mexican pastors. Upon Santin's retirement as district superintendent, his son Alfredo became district superintendent. The elder Santin remained pastor of Mexico City First Church.[25]

The Church of the Nazarene in Guatemala also grew strong on the basis of significant national leaders. J. B. Chapman ordained five Guatemalans upon his visit to the Nazarene field there in 1931. One of them, Javier de la Cruz, had been a drunkard and was saved through the efforts of his common-law wife, Magdalena, who had heard the gospel from missionary Annie Anderson. The couple married and, amid persecution, began conducting worship services in their home in Tactic. A breakthrough with neighbors began when the couple's eight-year-old son died. The de la Cruzes' hopefulness witnessed to their belief in the resurrection. Soon many in the town became Protestants, and the de la Cruzes pastored them.[26]

Effective workers emerged in Africa as well. Josef Mkwanazi had already become a Christian through the efforts of Scandinavian Alliance missionary Mallie Moe before linking himself to Harmon Schmelzenbach, who was working near Mkwanazi's home in Endingeni, Swaziland. One observer remarked that Mkwanazi and Schmelzenbach "recognized a bond of spiritual kinship which developed into a beautiful friendship that deepened with the passing of years," with the "two making a perfect team in holy zeal for the highest interests of the mission."[27] Mkwanazi capably served for years as the district evangelist on the Swaziland field.[28]

Other early workers in Swaziland included Samuel Dhlamini, who became evangelist over the Peniel District, as it was called. Zakeu Dhlamini started as a helper in the home of an English magistrate before entering the Nazarene church's Evangelists' Training School. While pastoring the church in Stegi, he prayed for revival. Breakthroughs came only after his death due to blackwater fever in 1931. Another leader, Lillian Bhembe, attended the Nazarene Girls' School run by Louise Robinson. After finishing her course at the school she passed government examinations and became a teacher herself at the same school, and also a preacher. Alice Kumalo similarly attended the Girls' School. While she served as a cook for the mission workers, she also was the assistant preacher at the Schmelzenbach Memorial Station. Another bright story among the women who were converted through the mission in Swaziland, Kelina Shongwe was impressed with the medical facilities of the Nazarene hospital in Bremersdorp (now Manzini), and became one of the first three to graduate from the hospital's nurses' training school. She served the hospital as a nurse.[29]

In Portuguese East Africa (Mozambique) Daniel Mketi became a Christian while working in the gold mines near Johannesburg. When his contract was finished, he returned to his people and witnessed to his family and people in Gazaland, and began a church. When missionaries C. S. and Pearl Jenkins met Mketi, they introduced him to an understanding of holiness and drew him into the Church of the Nazarene. Mketi became an evangelist. By the mid-1930s he was overseeing twenty stations. Similarly, John Mazivila worked in the mines in South Africa. When he returned to his home place near Manjacaze in 1924, he found Nazarene missionaries already at work, and became a Christian. A few months later he professed entire sanctification, began to testify boldly to his neighbors, and sensed a call to preach. With Mketi, Mazivila became one of the mission's two overseers, also supervising twenty mission stations. Another early worker in Mozambique was Ana Matusi. She became a Christian through the Girls' School run by Pearl Jenkins, and she felt herself called to preach—though this, for a Mozambique woman, was contrary to custom and culture. The confirmation of her call came when, through her preaching, many were converted. She married Zakaria Matusi, and the two ministered among mine workers in South Africa.[30]

Nazarenes could cite many instances around the world where revivals were taking place. In Cape Verde, John Diaz, whom the APCA had sent back to Cape Verde to work among his own people, worked patiently in the town of Brava. In the early years he faced the active persecution not only of the Roman Catholic Church but also of his own extended family. Once he was beaten nearly to death and converts were imprisoned. But when Diaz built cordial relations with a priest, relations with the people improved. By 1921 Diaz had made about 100 converts, opened a school, and built a church seating about four hundred persons. The Brava mayor and even some Roman Catholic priests began attending Diaz's church.[31]

In 1932, Jose Freire, a Protestant Portuguese evangelist, held revivals on the Cape Verdean island of St. Vincent that led to a Nazarene church being established there. The church was led for many years by a layperson, Augusto

Miranda, a government secretary. Also in 1932, Charles S. Jenkins, a Nazarene missionary returning to Mozambique who could speak Portuguese, stopped in Cape Verde on his way to Africa and for eight weeks held revivals that led many new converts into the church. Diaz himself was an extraordinary evangelist. The church could hardly keep pace with the thousands converted through his ministry. By 1934 about one in every one hundred residents in Brava was a Nazarene. The general church sent missionaries to help fuel the revival fire that was taking place in Cape Verde. These included Everette and Garnet Howard, who were greeted by a town parade when they arrived in 1936. Within a few months Diaz left Cape Verde and settled in California. The Howards, who remained as missionaries in Cape Verde until 1951, witnessed remarkable conversions and testified to miracles occurring through their ministry. The Church of the Nazarene built a high profile in Cape Verde with the construction of the Templo Nazareno in Praia, the capital city, and the Templo Nazareno in Mindelo. The church in Mindelo was on property donated by the city's mayor, and sat two thousand.[32]

The key to the success of the church around the world was the development of strong local leaders. Even if missionaries seemed slow to actually turn over authority to local leaders, they saw their purpose, as William Esselsytn, missionary to South Africa put it, "to help to build and train a corps of native workers who shall be able to carry on God's work in this land and to help prepare and publish holiness literature in the native languages."[33]

INTERNATIONAL DEVELOPMENT

The church's policies likewise affirmed the goal of establishing churches and districts with strong local leaders: "We must guard against the danger of keeping the native congregation in baby clothes too long. This will hinder the Holy Spirit in His freedom of operation among the people." Yet the same 1923 policy stated that it would be an error to release "our parental control over them before they are able to stand alone." Church leaders worried over "doctrinal confusion, and a low standard of experience" in the mission churches. These shortcomings would lead the church to be ashamed to call its progeny "Nazarene."[34] Leaders felt that if the Church of the Nazarene were to err it would be better for it to err in keeping missionaries in control too long rather than in releasing them too quickly, before local leaders were adequately prepared. In order for the districts in mission fields to reach maturity, the policy charged missionaries with the task of raising up converts who would be not only saved and sanctified but also prepared for leadership.

This required Bible schools, and missionaries established these in nearly every country the Church of the Nazarene entered.³⁵

Policy (still influenced by Reynolds) clarified the relationship between the mission council and the district assembly. However, the goals of the church remained unchanged: "to secure the conversion to Jesus Christ our Lord of the people of foreign lands, lead them into heart holiness as a definite work of grace, and establish them in local church membership, on each foreign mission field."³⁶ Policies described three stages for districts: a mission council-controlled district; a "missionary district" under national leadership; and a regular district. A "regular" district was entitled to proportional representation at the General Assembly, based on membership. Successive policies linked measures of self-government to self-support and maintained the vision of an international church. The policy set few criteria as to when a work might reach "missionary district" status. Missionaries proved slow in recommending their organization. Church leaders such as Chapman, after he became general superintendent, often prodded in this direction.

In January 1936, the General Board officially granted the Japan District regular status while at the same time, and without the prior consent of the Japan District, it created a second, "missionary" district to the northeast, centered in Tokyo. Morrison appointed William Eckel and Nobumi Isayama to lead the work in Tokyo. There was but one church in Tokyo, having begun in 1933 through contacts made by one of Isayama's former church members. There was another independent church pastored by a graduate of Pasadena College, which affiliated with the Nazarenes when the district began. According to the General Board action, the Western or Kwansai District would be the regular district, with all the rights and privileges of any of the North American and British Isles districts subject to the *Manual* and the General Assembly. Insofar as Morrison was concerned, after May 1, 1936, the church no longer considered the Kwansai District a "mission field."³⁷

Nobumi Isayama

Though Nazarene leaders could not foresee all of the implications of this, by the 1930s policy-makers such as Reynolds, Chapman, and Morrison envisioned a church made up of self-supporting districts located around the world that one day would need no missionary supervision and that would have equal rights, privileges, and responsibilities with any North American or British Isles district. Leaders did not aim toward the development of autonomous national churches, but a federation of districts. They did not plan for indefinite missionary control. Without a great deal of thought about where this would lead, without consciously copying any other denomination's model of church government, and without much theological reflection, the Church of the Nazarene became an international body.[38]

As old fields developed in the 1930s and the world situation darkened, leaders gave increased attention to the evangelistic purpose of the Church of the Nazarene in the world. Many Nazarene writers of the era echoed A. M. Hills in seeing Pentecost as the link between the distinguishing doctrine of entire sanctification and the cardinal mandate of evangelism. Pentecost, Nazarenes understood, gave the Early Church in the first century and gave the present church now its power to witness and impelled it to go into the world with the gospel. J. Glenn Gould, a pastor and theologian associated with the Eastern wing of the church, wrote that the Holy Spirit gave power both to cast out demons and to translate the gospel into many languages and bestowed on believers power to witness boldly to the unconverted. He advised the church to concentrate on evangelism. "The Nazarene work is an evangelistic movement," Gould wrote, "our genius lies along this line. To this end were we called forth." Nazarenes, he warned, must avoid allowing church buildings, schools, colleges, hospitals, or orphanages, at home or abroad, to become ends in themselves. "Evangelism," Gould said, "has been the church's central objective. God grant it may never change."[39] Gould's comments were in part a reaction to the interdenominational Laymen's Report, *Re-Thinking Missions*. Gould devised his thoughts within an evangelical culture uneasy with anything that seemed like a "social" gospel. He wanted Nazarene missionaries to be convinced of the complete lostness of people apart from faith in Christ. Gould's position fell within the Reynolds paradigm that emphasized evangelism and cooperation with others seeking the conversion of souls. The common mission, requiring common sacrifices, united Nazarenes together around the world.[40]

ELEVEN
Forging Community

Holiness revivalism in the nineteenth century had already formed a wide community based on entire sanctification as a second blessing and shared ethical and behavioral norms. Holiness people participated in common forms of worship. They sang the same songs. They heard the same preachers. They read the same articles whether in regional or national publications. Anyone studying these publications would recognize the common theology, the common names, and the common moral concerns. The first-generation community was largely Methodist in background. The church during its second generation was still primarily made up of white persons of northern European ancestry. With few exceptions in North America and the British Isles, there were few persons of color. Yet common ethnicity played much less a role in the identity of the denomination than theology. Forms of communication and worship, including publishing interests and music, bound the people together.

DISTRICT LIFE

Two events formed the nucleus of early district life: the assembly and the camp meeting. These two annual events were quite different in the early twentieth century than they were at its end. Both were events at which connectionalism was experienced. The district assembly was one of the primary centers of the church's internal political culture, while the district camp meeting was a distinct expression of the revival culture at the heart of early Nazarene life and experience.

The early district assemblies were business meetings, but they were also much more. They were times of worship, combined with the social experience of the extended church family. The assembly typically lasted for one week, drawing together pastors, their families, and key laity from the various churches. The presiding general superintendent was not only present but also available to the pastors, many of whom came to know the general superintendents personally, strengthening the bonds between pastors and local churches with the general church. Much assembly work was done by committees, such as those on the "State of the Work," prohibition, rescue work, publications, "foreign" missions, home missions, and deaconesses.

Among the early district home missions of the Church of the Nazarene were efforts to minister to minorities. The Southern California District, for instance, organized missions among Chinese, Japanese, and Mexicans. In some cases, the church organized itself into ethnic rather than purely geographic zones to meet the needs of minorities. At the 1911 General Assembly A. O. Hendricks spoke on behalf of Carl Erickson, the superintendent of the Scandinavian District of the Northwest. At the same assembly, Mae McReynolds, who had been instrumental in beginning the First Mexican Church of the Nazarene in Los Angeles in 1906, reported along with the other district superintendents for the string of Spanish missions she oversaw in the Southwest. In 1921 McReynolds began a Spanish-language paper, *Heraldo de Santidad*.[1]

Based on language, the church put Spanish-speaking churches on a separate district under the foreign missions rather than the home missions department. From 1926 to 1945 Edward Y. Davis superintended the Southwest Mexican District that included Spanish-speaking churches in California, Arizona, New Mexico, Texas, and Northern Mexico along the Rio Grande River. E. Y. Davis and Martha Davis had become Nazarene in 1917. Previously, E. Y. Davis had served the Methodist Church (South) as an educator and school head in Cuba. Among the churches on the Nazarene Southwest Mexico District was the Ruiz Street Mission in San Antonio, Texas. This began through the concerns of Anglo laypersons for the Spanish-speaking people of the city. Enrique Rosales, an insurance company executive, joined the mission church in 1933. Subsequently, Rosales began work on the Mexican side of the border in the area of Monterrey and became a key leader.[2]

Santos Elizondo maintained a church and orphanage on the Mexican side of the border near El Paso. The Mexican government was ready to close the orphanage. The Mexican law said that "no man shall have an orphanage in connection with the church." But, as Santos Elizondo was a woman, and not a man, the government allowed her to continue operating it! On the Texas side of the border she ministered to Mexicans, most of them widows and children, waiting for deportation back to Mexico. The Church of the Nazarene, under her ministry, became known as the church that cared for widows and orphans.[3]

District superintendents bore the primary responsibility for overseeing the planting of new churches. Few better exemplified the pioneer spirit than C. B. Jernigan, who in 1908 became superintendent of the Oklahoma-Kansas District with only five churches. He set out to build a district and did so courageously and innovatively. While his wife remained in ministry at the orphanage and rescue home in Peniel, Texas, he itinerated with a revival tent. He also carried a camera and operated a mobile photograph studio—taking pictures of families on remote farms—during the day. This not only provided him an income but also opened doors for evangelism. He conducted revival services at night. If conditions were favorable, he organized a new church at the end of the revival and appointed a pastor. Jernigan was so successful at church planting that Kansas became a separate district after one year and the Oklahoma District, where he remained, was divided into two districts in 1913. While ministering in Oklahoma, Jernigan initiated work among the Ponca people, an Indian tribe that had been displaced from the north central region of the United States.

Jernigan found difficulty adjusting to the New York District, which elected him district superintendent in 1924. Jernigan was just visiting the New York District Assembly in 1924 when he was given floor privileges. (One must wonder whether H. F. Reynolds, who was presiding that year over the assembly, and who knew that the district would be electing a new superintendent, had maneuvered this.) Jernigan was elected district superintendent on the twenty-second ballot, but declined. Then he reconsidered overnight (perhaps, again, in consultation with Reynolds) and agreed to accept the superintendency. Over the next year, Jernigan started five new churches on the district. He bragged of organizing African-American churches, believing that as a Southerner he had more understanding and empathy for Blacks. A great challenge for the church, as Jernigan saw it, was in reaching the number of foreign-born persons in the population on the district. Whether for such advocacy or, more likely, the cultural strains between the Yorkers and their Texan superintendent, one supply pastor refused him entrance to his church and padlocked the church door. Jernigan removed the padlock and went ahead with the services. The people, Jernigan reported, "endured my enthusiastic ways and methods." But Jernigan was voted out as district superintendent by a large majority the following year.[4]

The district superintendents often relied on evangelists for help. In 1925, Agnes Diffee and Eupha Beasley held a revival in Batesville, Arkansas, that gathered a strong group. District Superintendent John Oliver soon came and organized them into a congregation. Maria Stewart was called as the first pastor and the church "flourished under her leadership." The Western Oklahoma District asked evangelist A. L. Cargill of Bethany to devote part of a year to assisting in home missions by conducting a series of tent revivals across the district. At Center City, Cargill held a campaign beginning in mid-April 1932 and organized a church shortly after the meetings closed in early May. He proceeded to Stillwater and did the same, organizing a church with fifteen members on June 12. The Stillwater flock called Joseph Pitts as their pastor in August. The national and local economy necessitated frugal ways, so the congregation purchased a used building from the Church of God in January. It reported sixty-five members one year later.[5] Many Nazarene congregations across North America started in similar ways.

WOMEN, SPIRIT, AND STRUCTURE

The order of deaconess was an avenue of lay ministry. Many churches had one or more deaconesses. The modern order of deaconess originated in mid-nineteenth-century European Protestantism and had been incorporated by the Methodist Episcopal Church well before the century's end. Shortly before learning of his ouster from the Peniel Mission, Bresee was in Chicago visiting a famous training center for deaconesses operated by Methodist laywoman Lucy Rider Meyers. The first deaconess in the Los Angeles wing of the Nazarene movement was Arabella Widney, sister of J. P. Widney, whose status as a Methodist deaconess was recognized by Los Angeles First Church. Other deaconesses were soon authorized. While ministers were *ordained*, deaconesses were *consecrated*. The difference in wording emphasized the lay character of their ministry. The *Manual* required a deaconess to work under a pastor's supervision and in harmony with the church's local program. The Church of the Nazarene continued consecrating new deaconesses through 1985, when their order was superseded by a new order of ordained deacon open to men and women alike.

A deaconess's particular ministry was determined by her interests and abilities, the desires of the congregation to which she was accountable, and community needs. The flavor of deaconess ministry was captured in reports filed in the early *Herald of Holiness*. Mrs. M. E. Gasaway reported: "I am still in Plantersville, Miss., and so far in 1919 I have prayed in 125 homes, held three meetings, helped forty souls to get saved, reclaimed, or sanctified, and held two street meetings, preached six times, and have the victory just now." In New England, Elsie Rideout wrote that her work of the previous year "proved that a deaconess' duties are manifold—calling on the sick and dying, sympathizing with so many in their sorrow and bereavements, sharing their burdens, and so fulfilling the command of Christ." In Beverly, Massachusetts, deaconess Pearl Jenkins met physical and spiritual needs during an epidemic that swept her community. Mrs. E. J. Lord devoted much time to organizing support for a Bible school in Hutchinson, Kansas, that later became Bresee College. In Oklahoma, Nellie Barrett ministered to local jail prisoners, adding: "No service is too small for a deaconess to do. Each week I find time to visit the sick, the aged, the poor, and the stranger." Anna McPhee of Detroit was consecrated as a deaconess in August 1928. Her pastor noted that hers "was a life of service for others. Pursuing her calling, she visited hospitals, jails, infirmaries, and homes of shut-ins and needy ones. Thousands of tracts, Scripture portions and copies of *Herald of Holiness* were distributed; clothing, food and medicine were administered until she was held in the hearts of the people as was Dorcas of old."[6] Some early deaconesses went abroad as missionaries. Others, like Miriam Auxier, carried the greater share of the local visitation program and occasionally preached in a worship service. The church paid Auxier a modest salary, but she also drew income from working at a facility for homeless boys.[7]

The decline of the Nazarene deaconess movement was apparent by the late 1920s and paralleled the order's decline within American Protestantism generally. Los Angeles First Church had six deaconesses on staff in 1916, at a time when there was practically one deaconess for every Nazarene congregation and deaconesses composed over a fourth of the total Nazarene ministry. Twenty years later, there was only one deaconess for every six churches, and they comprised only 10 percent of the denomination's ministers.

While the deaconess movement declined, the number of women active in their local missionary societies dramatically increased. The creation of a missions auxiliary for women helped bind the Pentecostal Nazarenes into one people. The network of laywomen and clergywomen who formed the missionary societies played an important role in promoting missions and raising it to a denominational priority. By 1930 a majority of Nazarene congregations had local missionary societies, and these included societies in Asia, Africa, Latin America, and the Middle East, as well as North America and Great Britain.

The rise of the Woman's Missionary Society is significant from the standpoint of both mission history and the story of women and religion. Only single women had careers in late nineteenth-century and early twentieth-century America; married women did not. But a growing number of married middle-class women gained a degree of leisure time due to the increased availability of canned foods, manufactured clothing, and labor-saving devices. They filled some of this time by forming voluntary societies. Some societies were literary and cultural. But, as historian Anne Firor Scott notes, many women were convinced "that if their families needed them less, the Lord had work for them to do."[8] Women's voluntary societies expanded in nearly all Protestant denominations. In the case of the Nazarenes, though, the rise of the Woman's Missionary Society was a partnership between laywomen and clergywomen. This is exemplified in the leadership roles assumed by Rev. Susan Norris Fitkin of Brooklyn, New York, who became the most visible female leader in the Church of the Nazarene for a generation, and Ada Glidden Bresee, Phineas Bresee's daughter-in-law, and an active lay woman on the Southern California District. Fitkin's independent wealth, derived from her husband's career, allowed her to work independently of men if she so chose. On mission trips abroad, she paid the way for herself and her companions, who usually included Emma Word, the society's secretary-treasurer. Fitkin and her husband, who no longer attended church, contributed thousands of dollars for various projects through the New York District of which she remained an elder.[9]

The proliferation of local missionary chapters met resistance from some clergy, who viewed the local society and its female leaders as threats to their own leadership within the congregation. This attitude slowly changed. The societies proved beneficial to the church program. Women sought affinity with one another, and the missionary movement in the Church of the Nazarene grew in strength with each passing year. Pastors recognized the increasing number of women who joined and participated in the societies. In 1920 only a little more than 8 percent of Nazarenes belonged to a woman's missionary society. By 1930, a majority of Nazarene congregations had a local chapter, and nearly 27 percent of Nazarenes belonged to one. Until 1932, funds raised by the mission societies were channeled directly into missions and nothing else. After that time the church used a portion of the money for general and administrative purposes, such as supporting the salaries of general superintendents and denominational officers. By 1935, 85 percent of congregations had a society and 32 percent of all Nazarenes were members of a local chapter.[10]

Local missionary societies developed in other countries. In 1935, the Japanese chapters sent money for the Nazarene work in Palestine and also raised money to help the ethnic Korean work in Japan itself. The WMS president noted that the Japanese chapters held monthly and quarterly meetings. She noted that "our women in all our stations are faithful in evangelistic work and street meetings and cottage prayer meetings." In India, the WMS at Buldana organized in December 1933 with 17 charter members. In China, there were 32 societies and 703 members by 1935. The Chinese societies studied the Nazarene work in other countries, and Katherine Wiese, a missionary, served as district president. When Ida Vieg, a missionary who had taught elderly women to read, was unable to return to China because of the church's financial difficulties, the Chinese WMS took up a collection for her return. The societies in Peru were led by district president Lucille Taylor, a missionary. In the city of Jaen, Nazarene men joined the women in a Prayer and Fasting League, whose offerings helped to purchase a truck for district evangelism. Four other societies in Peru applied their money to evangelization among the Aguaruna population. Kanema Hynd was the district president in Africa, where the 173 local societies and 29 junior societies in 1935 were divided into four zones or districts, with a total membership of 1,344. She described sacrifices of the African women: "So many of the WMS members have no money, and no way of raising any, so they bring chickens or food as their dues. The evangelist and his wife have to buy these if they want to hand in the money. We are glad to do this, but the difficulty is getting them here, since some of the outstations are forty miles or more away, and they have to walk to get here." In spite of these hindrances, she reported, "the WMS last year paid $857 in dues."

The participation of women in the WMS sometimes shifted their perspectives. In Bludan, Syria, M. A. Thahabeyah wrote: "Our women see themselves now in a different world. They never felt so responsible for others before, neither for their own souls. But now they feel their responsibility, not only for their own salvation but 'For Others' as well." He noted that those women, who were poor, sold some of their few eggs "and gladly gave that money in the Missionary Society." There were monthly meetings, with an offering taken at each meeting. The Mexico District reported twelve societies and 208 members in 1935 under the leadership of Rebeca L. de Santin, who remarked: "the women seemed surprised to see *a woman* taking any leading part in the church. They had come from a branch of Protestants who do not allow women to preach."[11]

Women were crucial in other ways to the growth and development of the Church of the Nazarene. Whether at home or abroad, they were able to identify with marginalized persons. In Swaziland, India, and other countries, Nazarenes began grade schools and boarding schools for girls as quickly as for boys. "Apart from Christ," wrote Margaret Stewart regarding her work among girls in India, "not one of them has, or can have, her God-given rights. The Indian nation can never rise above the standards of its womanhood. The function of our school is to mold and fashion our girls in His blessed likeness during their plastic years. Eventually they will fill important places in our ranks as Christian teachers, preachers' wives and real home-makers."[12] Even though Stewart limited her vision of women in India to what was within the bounds of domesticity, for her the education of girls was a labor of liberation.

Agnes White Diffee

Agnes White Diffee pastored the large Little Rock First Church from 1931 to 1949. Diffee studied at Arkansas Holiness College, Peniel College, and at Oklahoma State Teachers College and was ordained in 1919. She taught school for eight years, while serving as an evangelist. After serving as a full-time evangelist and, for two years, as the pastor of the Amity, Arkansas, church, she became assistant pastor of Little Rock First and senior pastor in 1931. Under her, the radio ministry of Little Rock First Church set trends in the 1930s and 1940s. Church attendance grew from 300 to 1,100, becoming the sixth largest in the denomination. Diffee was by far the highest paid pastor on the Arkansas District. After resigning from Little Rock First in 1949, Diffee pastored at Pine Bluff, Arkansas, for nine years, and seven more years at the Little Rock Westwood Church. She retired in 1967, at the age of eighty.[13]

Women found themselves given many opportunities on mission fields. Mary Cooper (1898-1995), for instance, pastored in Michigan for six years after her graduation from Olivet College before going to Africa. She was paid just a few dollars a week. Though acknowledging that God supplied all of her needs, she still had no money at times for rent or coal. Once, during Cooper's struggles, her church called a male evangelist and, following the revival, paid him $118.50. In spite of her own deprivations, Cooper led the congregation through the purchase of a church building. The Nazarene Foreign Missions Board required her to raise $500 for her first year's support before sending her. Having done that, the Decatur Church promised her support for the remaining six years of her first term. Within a few months, in December 1928, she was on her way to Portuguese East Africa (Mozambique). This was to be her place of ministry for the next forty-two years. She served as a superintendent and planted 181 churches. Obviously, her work was not conditioned by "women's work for women," the missions policy adage of other denominations. Cooper was attuned to the potentials of women and the plight of girls. In one case, an eleven-year-old girl's parents both had died and she was being raised by a demon-worshipping, heathen uncle. Cooper talked with the man, and as a result the girl was allowed to follow her own conscience and become a Christian. Cooper mentored Bible women. One effective disciple was Matita, who in turn explained the way of salvation to elderly women. One year Cooper collected $100 among poor women for evangelism. Listening to her local coworkers, she devised a campaign targeting preliterate girls and women. She used the Frank Laubach method, "each one, teach one," and literacy spread throughout the district of Mintlawa. Some of the then literate females went on to Bible school or nurses' training.[14]

EVANGELIZING

Though the general church maintained a small budget for planting churches within North America, the responsibility for evangelizing fell to the districts. Limited general funds were given to weaker districts, some to district superintendents' salaries on these districts, and some for money to buy revival tents.[15]

In many places mass evangelism made successful appeals to people. People attended Sunday evening evangelistic services and special revivals. Even during times of world crisis, retrenchment, and financial constraints, dozens of Nazarene evangelists crisscrossed the denomination, sharing similar ideas about salvation, holiness, and moral behavior among Nazarenes, both urban and rural. Around the world, Nazarenes evangelized similarly. Revivalists and pastors called seekers forward to the kneeling rail—the "altar"—and there and then invited them to repent and receive Christ as Savior or to seek the baptism of the Holy Spirit for cleansing from sin. People confessed, wept, promised to give up vices, felt blessed and revived, and stood to testify. With little awareness that their methods were historically laden, missionaries reached people in many different cultures by these means. Whether for novelty sake or otherwise, altar calls led men and women with no acquaintance with the methods of nineteenth-century revivalism into experiences of saving and sanctifying grace.

In North America, the premier evangelist was Reuben Robinson (1860-1942), "Uncle Bud" to generations of Nazarenes. He was born in Tennessee, one among thirteen children, and his father died when he was twelve. Possessing a noticeable speech impediment, Robinson stuttered and lisped. He received a third grade education. His mother moved the family to Texas in 1876. Robinson became a cowboy and engaged in various vices. While attending a camp meeting in Bluff Springs in 1880, Robinson was saved. Not having any idea of the various denominations, he was baptized by pouring and joined the Methodist Episcopal Church, South, simply because that was the denomination of the preacher at the camp meeting. His conversion gave him a desire for education, and he learned to read and write. Soon he confessed a call to preach. A Methodist steward told him that he "stuttered so bad and had so little sense" that he "would bring reproach on the church and do more harm than good."[16] But an old local preacher encouraged him and told him to apply for a license at the next Methodist quarterly conference. A presiding elder examined him. Robinson recalled, "I answered nary a question he asked me. He asked me about the laws of the Church and the rules of discipline and I had never seen a discipline or studied one in my life, did not know what they were for. I stuttered so bad I could not tell him my name or what I wanted to do." In spite of these limitations, the quarterly conference gave him a license to exhort. By the next quarterly conference, recalled Robinson, "I had held twenty-seven prayer meetings, I had tried to preach fifty times, I had prayed in ninety-five homes and had about sixty people converted. When I got to the Quarterly Conference and was called on for my report I got up and tried to read it and couldn't—I broke down and commenced to cry and I got to shouting." The presiding elder read Robinson's report for him and advised him to "keep on."[17] In his first year of preaching three hundred were converted.

But Robinson sensed his need for a "better religion." He often lost his temper, especially, it seemed, when dealing with stubborn farm plow mules. He heard W. B. Godbey, a Holiness preacher popular in the South, speak on entire sanctification, and Robinson began to seek this grace and even to preach about it. Unlike some others who went through a crisis of entire sanctification shortly after their conversion, Robinson struggled for years before finally finding, ten years after his conversion, the blessing—in a corn field: "Anger boiled up, and God skimmed it off, and pride boiled up, and God skimmed it off, and envy boiled up, and God skimmed it off, until it seemed to me that my heart was perfectly empty. I said, 'Lord there won't be anything left of me.' God seemed to say, 'there will not be much left, but what little there is will be clean.'"[18] He immediately saw his preaching become more effective. In 1890 he traveled 17,000 miles and saw five thousand persons converted or sanctified under his ministry.[19]

Bud Robinson

In 1891 Robinson began studying in the high school department of Southwestern University in Georgetown, Texas. He received his diploma eight months later. Robinson then began preaching for The Salvation Army. But he faced a choice between staying with The Salvation Army and marriage. In 1893 he decided to marry and rejoined the Methodist Episcopal Church, South. A Holiness faction, however, was upsetting the Southern Methodist leaders. After the 1894 General Conference, paragraph 120 of the

Southern Methodist *Discipline* required evangelists to secure the permission of local pastors before preaching in their area. Like Robert Lee Harris at the same time, chaffing under the same rule, Robinson found himself on the margins, shunned by pastors and feeling persecuted by presiding elders. In 1894 Robinson decided to join the Northern Methodists, who were, in his part of Texas, open to Holiness preaching.

Until this time, Robinson suffered epileptic seizures. He experienced a dramatic healing from these seizures in 1896. From 1898 to 1900 the Northern Methodists assigned Robinson to a circuit near Fort Worth. In 1900 Robinson moved to the Holiness community centered around Texas Holiness University. He built the largest house in the town and took in students as borders. He wrote frequent articles for Henry C. Morrison's *Pentecostal Herald*. His evangelism reached a national scope. Robinson teamed with other evangelists, including, for several years, Will Huff. Robinson's unique expressions, amazing recall (he memorized a third of the Bible), and homespun stories made him famous among Holiness people nationwide. His revivals brought him into contact with the Church of the Nazarene in Los Angeles. When Phineas Bresee visited Peniel in April 1908 and invited all who would to join the Church of the Nazarene, Robinson was among those who did.[20]

In 1912 the Robinsons moved to Pasadena. They continued a ministry to students. Throughout his ministry, Robinson promoted education and encouraged young people to attend Nazarene colleges. He often worked with Nazarene college presidents to raise funds for the schools. Robinson received hundreds of calls to preach in revivals and camp meetings. For a year, 1916-17, he teamed with L. Milton Williams and several other workers in a national campaign, carrying a tent from place to place.

After an automobile accident in San Francisco in 1919, Robinson's career mellowed. His messages took on new depth, with a vision of the "beautiful city." In coast-to-coast meetings Robinson averaged 17,000 miles of travel and preached about five hundred times each year. He spoke in seventy-two denominations. Though Robinson's evangelism was unique, it set a standard and model for evangelism among Nazarenes. He interlaced quotations from the Bible with story narratives of himself and common life experiences. Humility and genuineness characterized him. His folksy and picturesque language and humor had people laughing one minute and crying the next. "A sanctified man has a shining face," Robinson wrote,

> an easy conscience, and a light heart, and is as bold as a lion, as patient as an ox, as swift as an eagle, as wise as a serpent, as harmless as a dove, as gentle as a lamb, and as sweet as honey. If you were to slap his jaws you

would get honey all over your hand, and as you walked away you would feel something sticky on your hand. Lick it off and get under conviction, and come back to see what ailed him, and find out it was perfect love."[21] Even the Duke University School of Religion had him preach. Robinson told the stories he usually did in revivals—of his poverty-stricken early life, conversion, call to ministry, and sanctification. One of the divinity students asked a professor what he thought of Robinson. The professor responded, "Really, I have no criticism to make of 'Uncle Bud.' That old man is one of God's prophets."[22]

Robinson made himself available to Nazarene district superintendents, helping them in district tours and revivals as a means of planting churches. In 1923 he took on a ministry of promoting the *Herald of Holiness,* and over the years secured 53,000 subscriptions for the magazine. He himself contributed "Good Samaritan Chats," signed "Uncle Buddie," on a regular basis. He once told the *Herald* editor, "You know I am not very good at this punctuation business, so here are a lot of periods, commas, etc. [and he included a considerable number in a line across the page]. Just sort these in wherever they belong."[23] Many of these "Chats" related to his experiences in camp meetings and revivals (inside and outside of the Church of the Nazarene), and other encouraging reports. By 1926 he reckoned that he had seen more than eighty thousand at "mourners' benches" through his ministry. He kept a rapid pace of evangelism even during the Depression. He scheduled his meetings three years in advance. In 1934 he visited Palestine and wrote a small book about his experiences. In later years he was often paid $100 per service, a considerable sum for the times, but gave most of it away. His wife died in 1940, when Robinson was eighty, but he preached throughout the year.[24]

Revivalists and missionaries attempted the same form of evangelism as Robinson. Revivals were a distinctive part of congregational life. Each church had at least one, and many had two revivals a year. Occasionally another pastor was called to conduct these, but usually full-time evangelists held the meetings, with each revival campaign typically lasting for two weeks. In November 1925, Jarrette and Dell Aycock conducted a revival meeting in Henryetta, Oklahoma, where they had previously been pastors. They reported 123 new converts by its conclusion, with 23 of these ready to join the local church. Three hundred and sixty-two children were present for a special service that Dell Aycock held for them on a Sunday afternoon. That same year, a pastor in Livermore Falls, Maine, reported: "We feel that the prayers for a revival to reach throughout the New England District has fallen upon our church." As a result, "nearly all of our children and young people have been converted,"

> Everyone who met Bud Robinson seemed to have a story about him. Lewis T. Corlett, president of Northwest Nazarene College at the time of Robinson's death in 1942, remembered:
>
>> Two things impressed me greatly about "Uncle Bud." It was my privilege to travel with him in the campaign for "Bud Robinson Hall." He had the flu while on the road and it was my privilege to sleep with him several nights in caring for him. One night I woke up and heard him very quietly praying and calling the names of a number of leaders and missionaries asking God to bless them. He finished by saying, "Thank you, Jesus," and dropped off to sleep again.
>>
>> The other matter which impressed me was his living in the consciousness of heaven at all times. While on the same trip, not feeling well, often for the evening meal he would make a broth with bouillon cubes. One evening in West Texas we were entertained at the Smith home. When we sat down to eat there was a large plate of pork-back-bone in front of Uncle Bud and a round plate of corn bread at his right. I noticed the bouillon cubes go into his pocket and he partook heartily of back-bone and corn-bread. After a little I mentioned to him that he forgot the cubes and laughingly he answered, "I only have to stand before the Lord once and I figured there was no better way than to be full of corn-bread and back-bone." He helped me to live with a greater consciousness of God in my life.[25]

including a six-year-old boy who tarried at the altar and twenty probationary members were received.[26]

Evangelists used all means possible to save some. In Latin America, missionaries as early as the mid-1910s were using lanterns and slide presentations for evangelism. Missionary Richard S. Anderson owned slide sets on the Parable of the Sower, Talents, Ten Virgins, Prodigal Son, Blind Man Healed, and the Good Samaritan, and was looking for other slide sets. A local Guatemalan congregation of seventy-five fed one hundred prisoners and soldiers at Christmastime and Anderson exhorted them. Missionaries in Guatemala used the kneeling rail as an altar, where, as in other places around the world, one would find seekers crying and "praying through." In 1936, in a typical event, Anderson shared preaching with Native American evangelist Santiago Chon in a revival at Chamelio, near Coban. In the course of the eight-day meeting, fifteen were saved and other backsliders reclaimed. Several testified to sanctification. Six couples, five of them Native American, joined the local church.²⁷

In places where Roman Catholicism was strong, Nazarenes often faced opposition from officials and took their evangelistic methods to streets and homes. In aggressively evangelistic services during Holy Week in Mexico City, pioneer V. G. Santin saw the Holy Spirit come powerfully upon the people. "Many came spontaneously to the altar seeking counsel and pardon," Santin reported to H. F. Reynolds in 1916, "manifesting desires to follow a new life and to follow Jesus resolutely without giving importance to that which it costs to walk in this new way."²⁸ Along the U.S.A./Mexican border a converted Roman Catholic priest preached alongside missionary S. D. Athans, admonishing the people to "come out of the Roman Babylon and turn to God."²⁹

In Swaziland for the dedication of the Raleigh Fitkin Memorial Hospital in 1927, Susan N. Fitkin participated in a camp meeting. The services were held in a tabernacle made of cornstalks and grass seating six hundred and held up by heavy poles. Fitkin sensed, "God's presence and power were manifest." As elsewhere in the world, seekers bowed at kneeling rails, "praying, groaning, and weeping," and "God came and brought peace and blessing." On another occasion, on the same trip, Swazi Christian workers gave "clear second-blessing testimonies" and, Fitkin was pleased, "got blessed just as we do."³⁰

For many years, the Nazarene practice in Swaziland was for the last day of a camp meeting to be set aside for the dedication of babies and the examination of candidates for membership. Those desiring membership first had to prove themselves worthy during two years of probation. On the last day of camp meeting, missionaries and district leaders interrogated prospective members further, for hours, about their Christian walk. Could they testify to their conversion? Had they been tithing? Had they been a member of a missionary society? Had they fasted and prayed? Had they won other souls to Christ? Had they lived at peace with members of their family? If the committee was satisfied, these persons were baptized on this last day of camp meeting and accepted as members of the Church of the Nazarene.³¹

In Mozambique some years later, Mary Cooper borrowed a tent from Methodists and set up revival services with Mufundisi Siweya as evangelist. A chief attended the services. Forty-five came forward as seekers during an altar call, with the congregation singing "Softly and Tenderly." The song might as easily have been heard in altar calls in the Pontiac, Michigan, church that Cooper had pastored before going to Africa.³²

Minnie Staples and Hiroshi Kitagawa were responsible for almost all of the church growth of the Church of the Nazarene in Japan during the 1920s and early 1930s, frequently using tent revivals. Staples held eighty-nine tent revival crusades from 1925 to 1937. Seekers testified to becoming born again, believers to being entirely sanctified. Restitution followed. Some claimed visions. Staples also initiated an ongoing evangelistic work to lepers living near Kumamoto. Her tent meetings and gospel hymns were pure revivalism, but somehow it produced converts. Pastors watched over and guided the new converts' lifestyles. Then, in 1937, as part of the Japanese government's increased control over religion and all areas of public and private life, the government placed restrictions on the holding of tent meetings. Revivals could still be held in churches, but the use of tents had been Staples's main means of evangelism. She resigned her commission as district evangelist and returned with her ailing husband to California late in 1937. In sending her off Kitagawa remarked that only God knew what the Stapleses had meant to the work in his country. "Sister Staples is needed in evangelistic work and [as a] mother to our workers."[33]

PUBLISHING

The union of regional publishing companies was a critical step toward achieving "the inner reality of union." Separate publishing companies in Providence, Rhode Island; Pilot Point, Texas; and Los Angeles continued operating after the Second General Assembly. The latter published Sunday School curricula, and each continued publishing its own regional paper. All three papers were considered "official organs" of the church. Editors urged readers to subscribe to other papers outside their region; each carried some national news, including notes from the general superintendents. But the papers, which had played a crucial role in shaping the identities of the regional churches, now threatened to perpetuate these identities at the expense of the united church.

For a short time, the general superintendents were willing to use the regional papers to achieve denominational goals. Shortly after the Pilot Point assembly, they asked the publishing company in Pilot Point to discontinue the *Holiness Evangel* and give way to its rival at Peniel—the *Pentecostal Advocate* published by the Holiness Association of Texas. This was difficult for C. B. Jernigan, J. D. Scott, and others who had founded and supported the *Holiness Evangel*. From his new outpost as superintendent of the Oklahoma-Kansas District, Jernigan argued his case to H. F. Reynolds, insisting that Nazarenes in the Southwest had no desire to exchange their denominational paper for a nondenominational one. The *Holiness Evangel* had been founded *for* denominationalism. Why dilute the Nazarene message? And yet Jernigan ended his plea on a note of submission, stating that he and others would do what was asked if the general superintendents were convinced that the paper's closing was an absolute necessity. For their part, Bresee and Reynolds were heeding the advice of E. P. Ellyson and others at Peniel, who were persuaded that this move would attract new members to the church. The Evangel Publishing Company (and the *Holiness Evangel*) continued for one more year. In 1909 its stockholders gave in to general church leaders. J. D. Scott, Dennis Rogers, and others, though, shipped the printing press at Pilot Point to Chiapas, Mexico, where they were founding a Nazarene mission.[34]

In 1911, the Third General Assembly authorized a central publishing house, a single denomination-wide paper, and a Committee on Publications to oversee these. The creation of a central publishing house and paper symbolized and carried forward the union of regional churches that had begun four years earlier. The committee recommended that the new publishing company be located in Kansas City. This decision proved momentous. It initiated the relationship between the Church of the Nazarene and metropolitan Kansas City. Located on the western edge of the border state of Missouri, Kansas City was predominantly "Southern" in spirit, but part of a bi-state metropolitan community adjacent to the "Northern" state of Kansas. The Nazarene headquarters grew up around the publishing house. C. J. Kinne of Los Angeles and B. F. Haynes of Nashville were key members of the Committee on Publications that made these recommendations. Another member was A. S. Cochrane, formerly a Methodist minister, who was pastor of the small Nazarene congregation in Kansas City, which, with this decision, was suddenly poised to grow beyond its expectations. The nineteenth-century cattle drives from Texas to Kansas had spurred the growth of the Kansas City stockyards because of the city's central location in the national railroad system. For the same reasons, from Kansas City the church's weekly paper could be delivered throughout the United States.[35]

Later that year, the *Nazarene Messenger* and the *Pentecostal Advocate* ceased publication. Their publishing companies yielded their assets to the church. In Texas, however, the *Pentecostal Messenger,* the paper of the Pilot Point Rest Cottage, expanded its pages and its coverage and sought an enlarged role among Nazarenes in the Southwest. It, too, found it hard to go against the denominational flow and after several years again narrowed its focus to the interests of the Rest Cottage Association. In New England the stockholders of the Beulah Christian Publishing Company characterized the central publishing house as risky and refused to join the united action. They sought but failed to receive recognition of the *Beulah Christian* as an official paper. The *Beulah Christian* carried on without official church endorsement under the editorship of F. A. Hillery until 1915.

Three seasoned editors and publishers were elected to key positions in the central publishing enterprise. Each understood the importance of the press in fostering connectional bonds. C. J. Kinne was elected manager of the publishing house. B. F. Haynes of Nashville was elected general editor of the *Herald of Holiness*. Charles A. McConnell of Peniel was appointed the *Herald*'s office editor.

Kinne was born in Iowa in 1869 and became a Methodist preacher around 1890. Five years later he united with Bresee's Nazarene movement on the West Coast. He became business manager of the Nazarene Messenger Company and assistant editor of the *Nazarene Messenger*. He oversaw production of the weekly paper, books, and curriculum materials. In Kansas City, he organized the new company, purchased equipment under the restraints of limited finances, and launched the publishing house. Years later, McConnell reflected on those early days and dubbed Kinne "the Columbus of our publishing interests." McConnell continued, "[Kinne] knew that if the recently merged streams of holiness thought and experience from the West, the East, and the South should ever become a denomination, one in ideas as well as in ideals, it would be such through the literature of a common publishing house. . . . It is not a figure of speech to say that he put his life into the foundation of the Publishing House." The publishing house occupied a single house on Troost Avenue. McConnell described that first year: "That was the spring of the deep snow. How cold it was in that old residence building, with its two floors, attic, and basement. Down in that dark basement were finally installed a cylinder press, a job press, a second-hand linotype machine, two imposing stones [or composing tables], and a small cabinet of type." In 1915 an adjacent building was added to the plant.[36]

Like his father, McConnell, a layman, had been the owner, editor, and publisher of Midwestern newspapers. His journalism led him into politics, and he served in the first South Dakota legislature, where he helped write the state's prohibition law and measures affecting education and family homesteads. Up to that point he was a "free thinker" without church or religious creed. When his father moved to Texas for health reasons, McConnell abandoned his political career and moved there to keep the family intact. He was converted through his wife's influence and two years later testified to the experience of entire sanctification. Urged by Holiness Association of Texas leaders, McConnell moved to Peniel and helped publish and edit the *Pentecostal Advocate*. In Kansas City, his passion for missions and his position within the publishing house led him to found *The Other Sheep*, a monthly magazine published on behalf of Nazarene missions, which McConnell edited from 1913 to 1918. Both the *Herald of Holiness* and *The Other Sheep* pushed the cause of the Church of the Nazarene around the world and provided information for Nazarenes in ways that editors intended would both inspire and quicken their response as well as their inspiration.[37]

Benjamin Franklin Haynes's election as general editor gave an important platform to a noteworthy figure in Tennessee Southern Methodism. Haynes was both flamboyant and inflammatory in style. He had edited the *Tennessee Methodist*, which served as an official paper of the Tennessee Conference. In 1896, however, the conference disowned the *Tennessee Methodist* when Haynes began propagating prohibitionist, premillennialist, and perfectionist viewpoints. Haynes continued publication of the paper under different names until 1900, when he sold it to the Pentecostal Mission. Meanwhile, under the Methodists, Haynes was systematically demoted to increasingly obscure parishes. He became president of Martin Female College in Pulaski, Tennessee, in 1902, and served as president of Asbury College in Wilmore, Kentucky, from 1905 to 1908. After other ventures, he taught for a year at Texas Holiness University, where, in 1911, he joined the Church of the Nazarene. He attended the 1911 General Assembly, where he was placed on the Publications Committee, which elected him editor.[38]

The first issue of the *Herald* appeared on April 17, 1912. Quickly the importance of this publication serving connectional interests became obvious. Haynes kept the paper broad in scope and provided a forum for diverse voices to be heard in the church. His own enthusiasms never dominated the *Herald*'s agenda. One early feature was "The Open Parliament," which ran for several pages and carried short articles and opinion pieces by pastors and leaders on issues ranging from theology and personal discipleship to the Ku Klux Klan and war and peace. For instance, in the second month of the *Herald*'s publication, C. E. Cornell, prominent pastor of Los Angeles First Church, openly opposed the reelection of Republican William Howard Taft as president. Taft, Cornell said, was friendly toward both Mormonism and Catholicism, and was "in no sense fit to lead Christian America toward loftier ideals of morality and honor."[39] The better options were either Theodore Roosevelt, running that year as a Progressive, or the Democrat Woodrow Wilson.

In the months leading up to general assemblies, Haynes used the *Herald* to spark lively discussion of the issues that delegates would face when the assemblies convened. He believed that the whole church should be brought into the discussion of pressing issues and the delegates exposed to the various viewpoints before they gathered. In his editorials, Haynes underscored the church's Methodist roots. Each weekly issue contained sixteen large pages, including news, feature articles, and commentary from over a dozen pastors and other leaders.

Fiercely concerned with what he considered the disintegration of the world around him, Haynes's writing reflected the fears that forced its way upon the church. He feared that the activities of labor would lead to Bolshevism. The wave of crime, caused by foreigners, lax laws, and automobiles, unnerved faith in social advancement, Haynes said. Disobedience to the Prohibition Amendment indicated that the country was "on the verge of anarchy," not social utopianism. Big money interests, gamblers, and "back-alley negroes" assisted the decline. Yet such racism did not alter Haynes's firm stand against the Ku Klux Klan. Democracy without God would fail. So the nation must return to the "fundamentals." Fearing that the United States might become militaristic, Haynes urged its government to expend less for war preparation and encouraged disarmament. Like the general public mood of the period after World War I, Haynes advocated the United States' withdrawal from world politics. At the same time, Haynes encouraged the missionary expansion of the church. The "engulfing peril of the present age," and the spiritual nature of humankind falling far behind its material progress, would only find its solution in Christ. The church would affect society most through an ethical-living ministry and laity. In relation to domestic concerns, Haynes was shocked by the rapidly changing styles and standards of morality in the "jazz age." He published a series of articles by W. E. Shepherd titled "Fads, Fakes, Freaks, Frauds, and Fools," which demonstrated the church's association of the new morality with modernist theology. Haynes remained the paper's senior editor until 1922 and contributed to the paper until his death in 1924.[40]

The business side of the Nazarene Publishing House proved difficult. Kinne poured himself into its work until he grew mentally and emotionally exhausted. In 1915 he resigned and returned to California. He was succeeded by Jack F. Sanders, who had been converted in Spokane, Washington, through the ministry of Elsie and DeLance Wallace. Sanders had managed the business affairs of the college in Pasadena and had established the Fifth Street Mission in Los Angeles. The pressing issue he faced in Kansas City was the large debt that the publishing house already had incurred. In the autumn of 1916, just a few months after his election as general superintendent, R. T. Williams proposed a church-wide campaign to eliminate the publishing house debt completely. The campaign was a success, but finances continued to plague the publishing house. Sanders resigned in 1919. DeLance Wallace succeeded him and served until 1922. By then, another financial campaign was needed to "save" the publishing house. John Goodwin, for one, believed that the mechanical side of the operation was "the cause of nearly, if not all our difficulties." He thought it might be wise to eliminate it and take outside bids for printing and binding. Ultimately the mechanical department was retained. By the 1923 General Assembly the debt and accrued interest had been fully paid.

By this time Mervel S. Lunn was the manager. This became his life's work. The son of Danish immigrants, Mervel Lunn grew up in Racine, Wisconsin. In his teens, he took a job with the J. I. Case Threshing Machine company as a traveling representative and in 1912 was assigned to Kansas City. There he came into contact with the Church of the Nazarene. In 1913 he became a bookkeeper at the publishing house. He met his wife in the subscription department. Lunn's rise to manager was paved by constant study to improve his skills. As part of a reorganization in 1923, a number of employees were released, and Lunn was forced to personally manage various departments of the operation served previously by departmental managers. That was not all. Beginning in 1926, for nineteen years, he served simultaneously as the church's general treasurer. For sixteen years he was also executive secretary of the Minister's Benevolent Fund. Lunn worked patiently to stabilize the Nazarene Publishing House and was known for careful business methods, economy, and personal integrity. He brought professionalism and stability to the church in key areas. Lunn remained at this post until 1960, when he was succeeded by his son, M. A. "Bud" Lunn.[41]

Haynes was joined in the editorship in 1921 by James B. Chapman. Unlike Haynes, Chapman had not come out of an established denomination but had been nurtured and educated in the Holiness Movement. Compared to Haynes, Chapman lacked a thorough sense of custodianship for society. Under Chapman the *Herald* reflected the sectarian interests of the time, a way of holiness separate from the world. Chapman's language kept the Holiness message in a kind of theological ghetto. The *Herald of Holiness* became less of means of propagating holiness and more a means of defining it and forging denominational identity.[42]

Yet Chapman brought skill, wit, and wisdom to his task. Known for his common sense, he was dubbed "the Socrates of the Nazarene movement." Chapman was a lifelong learner. Early in life he had married a schoolteacher, who pushed him to improve his writing and speaking skills. His teaching at Peniel for several years established his knowledge of theology. Chapman believed that education was imperative. By the mid-1920s, he was agitating for the church to establish a graduate theological seminary. For several decades he and H. Orton Wiley made up the core of the church's General Board (later Department) of Education. Chapman urged someone to write a denominational history and finally did so himself, publishing *A History of the Church of the Nazarene* in 1926. Chapman used the *Herald*'s editorial columns to advocate repeatedly for the merger of the various Holiness churches—Nazarenes, Pilgrim Holiness, Free Methodists, Wesleyan Methodists, and Church of God (Holiness)—demonstrating that the founding ideals of Pilot Point still burned inside him.

Through the Question and Answer feature Chapman began in the *Herald of Holiness*, he made its pages accessible to common Nazarenes. Chapman advised on such matters as divorce and birth control. "Be fruitful and multiply," he admonished Nazarenes. Have at least four children. One Nazarene who had just had his thirteenth child moved up to a "higher class" in Chapman's estimation. Between 1921 and 1925 the number of *Herald of Holiness* subscribers climbed from eight thousand to twenty-five thousand.[43]

Chapman pushed for a monthly magazine of theological and homiletic value for ministers, and he became founding editor of the *Preacher's Magazine*, which appeared in 1926, full of sage advice. H. Orton Wiley and others gained a regular platform to address pastors on theological topics. Chapman edited the *Preacher's Magazine* until his death in 1947.

Chapman was elected general superintendent in 1928. The same General Assembly elected H. Orton Wiley as editor of the *Herald*. Initially Wiley resigned from his second presidency of Pasadena to serve as general editor. But after two years in Kansas City he moved back to California to embark on his third term as president of Pasadena College while still serving as general editor of the *Herald of Holiness*.

At the time of his election, Wiley had been researching and writing a systematic theology for the church for nearly a decade. He brought to his editorship a keen appreciation for theology. He balanced the "progressive" and instantaneous elements in sanctification, noting that early Methodists had done the same. Methodists, however, said Wiley, now emphasized the progressive nature of sanctifying grace to the exclusion of its instantaneous aspects. The Holiness Movement, on the other hand, had committed the opposite error, falsely pitting instantaneousness against progressive sanctification. For Wiley, the ability to understand and articulate the balance between progressive and entire sanctification, and the way in which each reinforced the other, was absolutely vital. Wiley disliked theological confusion. Many issues, including social and ethical issues, went untouched.[44]

Wiley stepped down as editor in 1936 and was succeeded by D. Shelby Corlett (1894-1979), managing editor under both Chapman and Wiley and an active leader in the Nazarene Young People's Society. Born in Pennsylvania and reared a Methodist, Corlett and his family joined the Church of the Nazarene in 1910. He attended Arkansas Holiness College for two years before transferring to Pasadena College in 1917. After serving in World War I, he became pastor of the Nazarene church in Upland, California. From 1923 to 1936, while continuing to pastor in Yakima, Washington, and Dallas, Texas, Corlett served as executive secretary of the Nazarene Young People's Society. Moving to Kansas City in 1928, Corlett divided his time between NYPS and the Home Missions and Church Extension department, which he served as executive secretary. He also edited the *Young People's Journal.* Corlett was general editor until 1948 and also succeeded Chapman as editor of the *Preacher's Magazine.*[45]

SUNDAY SCHOOL LITERATURE

Nazarenes appreciated Sunday Schools and recognized early "the need of Sunday School literature in which the teaching is in harmony with the doctrine of sanctification."[46] The denomination's parent bodies solved their need for curriculum in different ways. The Texas Council of the New Testament Church of Christ advised its congregations to purchase materials from the Free Methodists. Nazarenes on the West Coast used curriculum published in Louisville, Kentucky, by the Pentecostal Publishing Company. Known as the "Pentecostal Sunday School Literature" line, it was designed for intermediate and senior students and was edited by H. C. Morrison and John Paul, Methodists connected to Asbury College. In 1907 the Nazarene Publishing Company purchased this line from its previous owners and began publishing it in Los Angeles. For several years the effort marketed beyond Nazarene circles. Isaiah Reid and C. E. Cornell, two of the Holiness Movement's well-known and able writers, became editors in 1908.

Like other American Protestant churches, Nazarene curriculum followed the International Sunday School Outlines (later known as the Uniform Lesson Series). This meant that on any given Sunday morning, Nazarene Sunday School classes studied the same Bible passages as Episcopal, Presbyterian, and Methodist churches. In 1911, the *Pentecostal Bible Quarterly* for students was supplemented with *The Pentecostal Bible Teacher* for instructors. General Superintendent Walker served as general editor of the quarterly and teacher's guides from 1911 until his death in 1918, except for 1915, when A. J. Ramsey stepped in. Walker wrote extended Bible expositions for the teacher's guide. After Walker's death, others took turns as general editor, including Kinne. Meanwhile, Sunday School literature publication moved to Kansas City. Kinne stated that two intentions were foremost: "clear teaching of the Bible doctrine concerning sin and salvation, including entire sanctification," and the "aim to encourage individual thought on the part of the student."[47] Leading Nazarenes wrote columns in *The Pentecostal Bible Teacher*, including Bresee, Emily Ellyson, John Short, B. F. Haynes, and C. E. Cornell. For years, each Sunday's Bible passages were printed side-by-side in two translations—the King James and the American Standard versions. By 1923, over 1,100 Nazarene churches had local Sunday Schools.[48]

The 1923 General Assembly created the Department of Church Schools, electing former general superintendent Ellyson as its head. As his primary assistant, Ellyson selected his wife, Emily Ellyson, who had taught with him in the religion departments of several Nazarene colleges. Ellyson added theological specialists S. S. White and Olive Winchester to his editorial team. Ellyson used insights from psychology and contemporary educational theory. He headed the Department of Church Schools until 1938.[49]

CONGREGATIONAL LIFE

The early Nazarenes participated in a distinct religious subculture that was shared with Free Methodists, Wesleyan Methodists, Pilgrim Holiness, and the camp meeting wing of the Methodist Church. Its ambience was inherited from two basic sources: classic Methodism and the Wesleyan-Holiness revival of the nineteenth century. This culture was enshrined in district and congregational life and expressed and perpetuated in the church's system of higher education. And it was exported from North America to Nazarene communities elsewhere in the world, where it fused with local elements but remained discernible.

J. B. Chapman observed that the earliest Nazarene congregations in the United States had a cosmopolitan membership, since the church was an heir to a Holiness Movement of interdenominational scope. But his observation went further. He noted, too, that "more Nazarenes are of Methodist extraction than of any other one denomination" and that "from the standpoint of doctrine and purpose, the Church of the Nazarene is Methodistic." Mallalieu Wilson, also present at the beginning, sharpened the observation, noting that early Pasadena First Church, like many others, contained "strong dependable members" who were "for the most part holiness people who had been Methodists. There were many others who were good people, but who were from such widely varying religious and cultural backgrounds that building them into a united loyal group demanded pastoral diplomacy and statesmanship of a high order." Among the non-Methodists he noted some who "had already changed denominations several times and were restless at being tied down in any burdensome program. They liked to go where the shouting and singing were free and hilarious, but didn't like the drudgery of teaching Sunday school or paying the bills."[50]

While a few congregations were organized independently and then joined the Nazarenes, the great majority of new churches were organized deliberately through systematic district and mission planning. Thus, they came into existence as local concrete expressions of the connectional ideal. This was obvious in world areas where new churches resulted from the concerted efforts of personnel working under the General Board of Foreign Missions. But it was equally the case in North America, where the Boards (later Departments) of Home Missions and Church Extension provided resources to district superintendents and pastors in starting new churches. (The Board of Church Extension primarily managed a loan fund to assist new congregations. Eventually it was merged with the Department of Home Missions.)

The fully organized congregation typically had a Sunday School department, a Nazarene Young People's Society, a Woman's Missionary Society, a board of trustees, and a board of stewards. The church in Elmira, New York, for instance, had all these within eighteen months of its founding. Other departments existed according to local tastes. In 1924, Pasadena First Church also had a junior church, a Children's Missionary Society, a Men's Brotherhood, a Hospital Worker's circle, and a Jail Worker's circle.[51]

Nazarenes generally preferred a free and easy worship style, but some pastors placed boundaries on vocal expressions. If enthusiasts shouted too much or spoke too long, pastors knew how to "cut them off" by "singing them down."[52] The Nazarenes were no louder than the Methodist camp meetings had been, but the campgrounds were in rural areas; the Nazarenes brought camp meeting worship into sanctuaries located in urban neighborhoods, and there are many instances where their neighbors complained about the noise generated by their music and enthusiastic worship. The 1928 General Assembly placed boundaries around certain expressions that had arisen in Pentecostalism, passing a resolution against hand-clapping and foot-stomping in church.

The early Church of the Nazarene had numerous clergywomen and clergy couples. The Jernigans, Iricks, Cagles, Wallaces, Davises, and Wines were among other clergy couples for whom the "working" wife's labors as an evangelist or pastor stabilized the income of the district superintendent's family. William E. Fisher, one of the church's founders in Texas, and the pioneer superintendent of the Abilene District, which included most of Texas and all of New Mexico, was supported so haphazardly by the freewill offerings of the district's churches that Annie May Fisher, his wife, who was pastor of a small church in west Texas, not only earned the family's meager livelihood through her ministry but gave a portion of that to defray her husband's travel on behalf of the district. After struggling with the same lack of financial support during several terms as superintendent of the San Antonio District, Fisher told the district assembly that he would not accept reelection as its superintendent. They reelected him anyway. He refused the election and became a Methodist the following year.[53] The clergy couples who served as pastors typically divided the worship services between them, as Charles and Mary Hopkins did in Hartford, Connecticut. Each preached on Sundays, but they alternated weekly between the morning and evening services. They were remembered as "spiritual, loving, and caring" and their ministry as "a season of interest in young people and children." In Shreveport, Louisiana, pastors C. V. and Bessie Dillingham divided the preaching responsibilities differently: he usually preached a doctrinal or discipleship sermon on Sunday mornings, while she usually preached an evangelistic sermon on Sunday nights.[54]

Bresee was the preeminent model for Nazarene preachers at the beginning. Dignified but dynamic, he was noted for the strong spiritual content of his sermons and a dynamic presentation of the gospel. Isaiah, his favorite Bible book, was a frequent source for sermon texts. His preaching was instrumental in Los Angeles First Church's emergence as the denomination's largest congregation, and his powerful sermon at the opening of the Second General Assembly at Pilot Point was still remembered decades later by those in attendance. He sometimes used dramatic devices. Preaching once on Ps. 23, he invited two young men from the congregation to join him on the platform, dubbed them "goodness" and "mercy," and bid them follow behind while he walked back and forth across the platform preaching on verse 6: "Surely goodness and mercy shall follow me all the days of my life." Bresee's sermon manuscripts had complete outlines with numerous "lead in" sentences. A. M. Hills approached preaching differently and fully wrote out sermons. He also insisted that his students do the same. Hills believed that preparing a full-length sermon manuscript taught the preacher orderly thinking and created a logical progression of ideas that the congregation could follow. R. T. Williams followed the Hills method for over a decade before he felt free to enter the pulpit with something less substantial, but by then he had gained mastery of the basics upon which Hills insisted. Bud Robinson, raised in Tennessee and Texas, offered a third approach. His preaching was Southern, folksy, and affective. Nazarenes heard him preach mainly in church revivals, camp meetings, and public auditoriums, and they appreciated his humor, storytelling, and poetic imagination. A product of the well-developed oral culture of the American South, Robinson adeptly created vivid word pictures and frequently used matters of everyday life to draw spiritual analogies.

Most Nazarene churches took Holy Communion on a quarterly basis. The roots of this schedule lay in frontier Methodism, where many newer circuit riding preachers were not yet ordained ministers. Following John Wesley's Church of England, the Methodist Episcopal Church insisted that the Lord's Supper be presided over by ordained clergy. To solve the problem posed by the number of unordained ministers that were deployed, the Methodists instituted the Quarterly Conference, which was under the direction of the district's presiding elder (district superintendent). Here the Lord's Supper was offered by ordained ministers. The quarterly schedule was intended as a minimum, not a maximum, but the *Discipline's* quarterly requirement became the standard that Nazarenes inherited from their Methodist forbears and likewise wrote into their *Manual*. The power of habit could be strong. Rev. A. B. Anderson offered monthly Communion when he came to the church at Hartford, Connecticut, but after a year the church board voted to go to a quarterly schedule.[55]

The typical church had two worship services on Sunday and a midweek service, but there were variations. In 1916, the Sunday services at Los Angeles First Church began with an 11:00 A.M. worship service, followed by the People's Meeting for Praise and Testimony at 3:00 P.M., the Young People's service at 6:00 P.M., and an evangelistic service at 7:30 P.M. The church also had a weekly Tuesday Holiness Meeting at 2:30 P.M., instituted earlier under Bresee's ministry in imitation of Phoebe Palmer's Tuesday Meeting for the Promotion of Holiness. By 1928, the Tuesday meeting had been changed into a Bible study, and there were three prayer meetings scheduled: Tuesday, Wednesday, and Friday evenings. By 1930, the Bible study and the Tuesday prayer meeting had disappeared from the schedule.[56]

The midweek service had many of the characteristics of a small group. In 1925, the pastor in Oxford, Nova Scotia, remarked that "Wednesdays are special prayer and feast days, when we have two circles of prayer where the real work for God and holiness is wrought."[57]

Churches and pastors alike were often innovative. One pastor solicited the businessmen of his city to raise money for musical instruments for the church orchestra. The Henryetta, Oklahoma, church began mailing newsletters in 1942 so that rural members, unable to attend regularly due to war-time gasoline rationing, could remain abreast of congregational developments.[58] Urban churches were almost always located near a streetcar line. One congregational historian noted that the Woman's Missionary Society spurred growth within the local church during the 1930s and early 1940s, while the Sunday School became the engine of growth in the late 1940s and 1950s.[59]

One area of innovation was radio, whose growing impact was evident by 1934, when the church's publishing house issued *Christian Certitudes and Other Radio Sermons*—representative sermons from eleven Nazarene preachers, including J. B. Chapman, R. T. Williams, and two who joined them as general superintendents in 1940, H. V. Miller and Orval J. Nease. There were at least thirty local Nazarene broadcasts on the air by 1935. Little Rock First Church's was the most extensive, with a daily one-hour broadcast beginning at 10:00 A.M., an expanded two-hour broadcast on Sunday morning, and over two hours on Sunday evening. The Sunday broadcasts included the morning and evening services in their entirety. Their popularity made Pastor Agnes Diffee the best-known Nazarene in Arkansas, where Nazarenes were known offhandedly as "Sister Diffee's church." The pastor in Lexington, Kentucky, broadcast the "Bible School of the Air" on Saturday morning. Detroit First Church had a one-hour Sunday morning broadcast and a Sunday night music program. The Malden, Massachusetts, congregation had a thirty-minute Good Cheer Service on Friday afternoons and "The Nazarene Hour" on Sunday mornings. The Chicago Council of Nazarene Churches had a joint radio ministry supervised by J. T. Myers, pastor of the area's Austin Church of the Nazarene. They offered a daily program at 7:00 A.M. and a Sunday service at 11:00 A.M. Raymond Browning spoke on "The Nazarene Hour" on Sunday afternoons in Columbus, Ohio, while Denver First Church sponsored Pastor Melza Brown's early Sunday morning broadcast. These local broadcasts prepared the way for the "Showers of Blessing" radio program, launched ten years later by the Nazarene Radio Commission.[60]

Music and a common hymnody were forces shaping the Nazarenes as a people. The church drew upon three music traditions. Traditional hymnody was one of these. The music of the Wesleys, Isaac Watts, and other great English and German hymnists was always part of Nazarene life. Charles Wesley, particularly, left a large and important body of hymns that enshrined the heart of Wesleyan theology, including the themes of God's mercy, freedom from sin, the joys of salvation, and the blessings of the sanctified life. One Nazarene songbook, *Waves of Glory* published in Los Angeles in 1905 and edited by Methodists J. M. Harris and William Kirkpatrick, contained forty Charles Wesley hymns and another eighty-four "standard hymns."[61] This tradition particularly affected Nazarene music and worship in British Commonwealth countries, who often sang different tunes than the Americans to Wesley's hymns. Nazarenes also inherited the songs of the camp meeting tradition—a richly symbolic music characterized by an emphasis on "Beulah Land" and "Canaan" as symbols for entering into entire sanctification, and the Christian as a pilgrim in this world. The third strain was the new, upbeat gospel music that grew popular through the great urban evangelistic crusades of D. L. Moody and his music leader, Ira Sankey. Gospel music was conversion-oriented and emphasized the atoning blood of Jesus and new relationship with God. Fanny Crosby wrote many songs in this genre. Phineas Bresee journeyed with others into the new gospel music. Bresee loved spirited singing but could not carry a tune, so he kept beat with his hands. William Howard Hoople, on the other hand, used his melodious voice to raise the spirits of his congregations. He later put it to good use in France as a YMCA entertainer for American troops stationed there in World War I. Camp meeting and gospel music entered Nazarene sanctuaries and competed with hymns for a place in the people's hearts. The Nazarenes fused these music elements together. While the camp meeting and crusade songs originated in North America and Great Britain, many were translated into Spanish and other languages and used around the world. "Called unto Holiness," written by Methodist Lelia Morris in 1900, was sung by Nazarenes nearly everywhere and became something of the church's unofficial theme song. All three elements could be combined in the same songbook, as they were in *Pentecostal Praises*, edited by C. E. Cornell, Nellie Liscomb, and C. J. Kinne and published in Los Angeles by the Nazarene Publishing Company; I. G. Martin's *Pentecostal Songs of the Nazarene*, published originally in 1902 by the Christian Witness Company but reissued as a Nazarene imprint; and *Waves of Glory*, edited by Methodists J. M. Harris and William Kirkpatrick. After the merger of churches, its title lived on in the united church's first hymnal, *Waves of Glory No. 2*.[62]

Nazarenes produced their own popular songwriters. Arthur Ingler and Haldor Lillenas headed the list. An Easterner, Ingler became an evangelist at the age of nineteen. Later he served as pastor of Nazarene churches in New England and in the Pacific Northwest. He composed numerous songs and edited songbooks with titles such as *Burning Bush Songs, Canaan Melodies,* and *Songs of the Blood Washed*. Some Nazarene songwriters were noted for only one or two particular songs—C. B. Widmeyer for "Come and Dine" (1907) and "In the New Jerusalem" (1911), F. M. Lehman for "The Love of God" (1917), and Rhea Miller, wife of general superintendent H. V. Miller, for "I'd Rather Have Jesus" (1922).

The music company most closely tied to the Church of the Nazarene bears the "Lillenas" name. Haldor Lillenas was born on a Norwegian island south of Bergen. His family immigrated to America when he was two and moved during his childhood from the Dakotas to Oregon, and then to Minnesota. At age twenty-one, Lillenas returned to Astoria, Oregon, where he worked in a box factory. He came into contact with the Peniel Mission there and experienced conversion in 1906. He soon joined the Nazarenes and moved to Pasadena to attend Nazarene University. He met Bertha Wilson, daughter of W. C. Wilson, in one of the college's traveling music groups. Her contralto and his tenor complemented one another. They married in 1910. Both preached, sang, and composed. Their careers alternated between copastorates and periods of full-time evangelism, but whatever their field of service, they shared the preaching and music responsibilities during their ministry. Their first assignment was to lead the Peniel Mission in Sacramento. Both were ordained by H. F. Reynolds in 1912. They subsequently copastored churches in California, Texas, and Illinois and served as pastors of Indianapolis First Church from 1923 to 1926. The membership grew from 150 to 250 during their time. Bertha Lillenas's brother wrote that during this pastorate, "as Haldor gave increasing attention to music, Bertha took more of the preaching responsibility."[63]

Haldor and Bertha Lillenas

Haldor Lillenas dreamed of owning his own music publishing company, and in 1926 they resigned from their pastorate. Bertha conducted revivals. Haldor assisted when he could, but he focused his energies on launching a Christian music business. The Lillenas Publishing Company's success depended on his talent and enterprise, but it also succeeded because of his unique marriage. Married American women rarely worked in professional life at that time, but Nazarene clergywomen were exceptions, and Bertha Lillenas was a key element in her husband's ability to fulfill his dream. Her financial contributions were the buffer as the Lillenas Publishing Company made its way through difficult early years. In 1930, the Nazarene Publishing House in Kansas City wanted to improve its music program with a proven leader and offered to buy the Lillenas Publishing Company as a subsidiary and retain Haldor Lillenas as its manager. Lillenas accepted the offer and the Lillenases moved to Kansas City. They continued working on music and often traveled, promoting the product of the music company that still bore their name. Around 1940, they moved to "Melody Lane," a stone house in central Missouri near the Lake of the Ozarks. Haldor Lillenas used the train to visit the publishing house one day a week for meetings but composed and edited at his home office.[64]

John T. Benson was another great Nazarene music publisher. A native of Nashville, Benson came from a long line of Methodists and attended the Mimms School for Boys and Vanderbilt University before entering his father's general merchandise business. He loved singing and had a fine baritone voice. Both he and his wife directed revival music and led public services. Benson united with J. O. McClurkan and became the most influential layperson and businessman behind both the Pentecostal Mission and Trevecca College. In 1902 Benson founded the Pentecostal Mission Publishing Company to publish McClurkan's paper and other religious literature. After the Pentecostal Mission united with the Nazarenes, the company was renamed the John T. Benson Publishing Company. It became Benson's own vehicle for publishing gospel songbooks and literature. To support that goal, an auxiliary, Benson Printing Company, accepted contract work and grew into one of the South's largest printing firms. His sons joined him in the business. A devoted trustee and benefactor of Trevecca College, Benson served as chairman of the board and as president (1925-26) during a time of institutional crisis. He served on various church boards, including the General Board of Foreign Mission, the Nazarene Publishing House Board, and the General Board. Benson (and his son after him) led the music at Nashville First Church for many years.[65]

Another influential Nazarene musician was James D. Vaughn, a pivotal influence on the development of Southern gospel music. Like Benson, he had a Methodist background and was a staunch prohibitionist. He began his career as a public school teacher and principal, but he had a side business: teaching shape-note gospel singing, which was his real passion. When he was nearly forty, he left his school career and established the James D. Vaughn Music Company in Lawrenceburg, Tennessee. Says historian James Goff, Vaughn "revolutionize[d] the gospel music business in the South." Vaughn experimented with a variety of methods for stimulating interest and sales. The Vaughn School of Music, launched in 1911, offered a course lasting several weeks. The Vaughn Quartet promoted his publications through appearances at churches and conventions and proved so popular that by the late 1920s as many as sixteen Vaughn quartets, all using that name, toured simultaneously. The slates of the Vaughn Radio Quartet and the Vaughn Trio were regularly published with those of other evangelists in the *Herald of Holiness*, but their influence reached far across denominational lines. Vaughn published a monthly magazine, the *Musical Visitor*, established radio station WOAN in Lawrenceburg in 1923, and had his own record label—Vaughn Phonograph Records. He soon averaged sales of 200,000 songbooks per year. The methods he pioneered were imitated by others and directly influenced the rising gospel music industry. Vaughn was active in local affairs, serving on the school board, the city council, and as mayor. He owned and edited the county paper for nearly twenty years. He was probably the most prominent man in his county when he united with the Nazarenes in the mid-1920s. His influence also brought the famous singing Speer Family into the denomination. Vaughn faithfully supported his local church, known today as Vaughn Memorial Church of the Nazarene. The local papers estimated that seven thousand people attended his funeral in 1941.[66]

CONCLUSION

Gospel music, Sunday School literature, revivalists and revival methods, the *Herald of Holiness*, the Woman's Missionary Society, and the Nazarene Young People's Society were among the lively factors holding Nazarenes joyously together. While the doctrine of entire sanctification provided a common worldview, the inner dynamics of the movement flowed from laypersons and leaders who together built a unique Nazarene ethos.

TWELVE

Shaping the Nazarene Mind

The Church of the Nazarene's Articles of Faith grounded the church in the Anglican-Methodist tradition. The articles distinguished the Church of the Nazarene from the Church of God and other Holiness groups coming out of noncreedal and restorationist heritages. Since Wesleyan-Holiness theology was part of a long process, it is not surprising that this tradition continued to develop during the twentieth century, a context that included various shades of liberalism, the social gospel, neoorthodoxy, and fundamentalism. A discourse between two extremes, modernism and fundamentalism, shaped the outward contour of early twentieth-century Christian thought. The creedal nature of the Church of the Nazarene protected it from both.[1]

The roots of modern doubt rested in the eighteenth-century writings of agnostic philosopher David Hume and the French social critic Voltaire, who both exemplified a skeptical tradition of Enlightenment rationalism. The nineteenth-century science formed different questions. Fossils embedded in the layered rock formations seemed compelling evidence of an ancient earth. Yet Scriptures recorded an earth only a few thousand years old. Uniformitarianism became the prevailing theory in geology. It held that the earth's physical features resulted from geological forces shaping and reshaping the landscape over millions of years. The vast time-scale of the new geology paved the way for Charles Darwin's theories of the evolution of species through natural selection. As new theories emerged in the fields of geology and biology, science and religion, some concluded, were at war. T. H. Huxley, Robert Ingersoll, and other agnostics attacked Christian beliefs. To persons with religious doubt, the appeal of the sciences lay in their ability to support a new understanding of human origins and behavior apart from reference to the divine. The new social sciences—sociology, anthropology, and psychology—also shaped the modern worldview. Logical positivism insisted that only matters verified by scientific observation and testing should be affirmed. This way of thinking became embedded in many university departments. And yet many people believed that none of the new sciences, nor all of them taken together, were inherently hostile to Christian faith. Christians from a wide variety of faith perspectives, including evangelical Protestants, participated in their development.[2]

The Christian response to modern doubt and the new scientific age took various forms. Harvard botanist Louis Agassiz strongly attacked Darwin's theories. His colleague, Asa Gray, however, a soundly orthodox Calvinist, emerged as Darwin's first great champion in America. Gray regarded the grim struggle for dominance painted by natural selection's emphasis on the "survival of the fittest" to be fully compatible with Christianity's pessimistic assessment of fallen human nature. By 1920 a large sector of European and American Protestants accepted uniformitarian geology and evolutionary biology while maintaining allegiance to spiritual disciplines and the Christian faith. Many found ways to reconcile historic Christianity and modern science. Only thoroughgoing modernists rethought religion entirely from the standpoint of scientific methods and drifted to more radical conclusions.[3]

J. P. Widney, who proposed the "Church of the Nazarene" name in 1895 but left the church three years later to rejoin the Methodists, was among those who drifted away from Christian orthodoxy. Early twentieth-century anthropology and his own musings led him to reject the Trinity, original sin, and atonement through Christ. In Widney's understanding of human evolutionary progress, Aryans were the most highly developed race, Anglo-Saxons the most advanced Aryans, and the civilization of Southern California (his home) the most enlightened sector of Anglo-Saxon culture! Widney believed that he was being "scientific." But the project was poorly timed. It coincided with the rise of National Socialism in Germany. A decade later the world was in no mood to entertain notions of Aryan superiority. Still, Widney retained to the end of his long life a devout belief in a personal God whom he could know through prayer. A strong spiritual vision reminiscent of the Unitarian Transcendentalism of Ralph Waldo Emerson and Henry David Thoreau guided him.[4]

In Great Britain John Hutton Hynd also embarked on a radical religious path. A Scot who pastored the Nazarene congregation in Morley, England, Hynd informed his district assembly of his growing difficulty "with the literal statements of Christian Truth" expressed in the Nazarene *Manual.* He was given a year to reconcile his convictions with the Articles of Faith but could not and resigned in 1925. He united with Felix Adler's Ethical Culture Union, an association of rationalists who rejected classical theism but acknowledged a debt to the moral values and traditions of Western philosophy and religion. Its local societies were much like church congregations. Hynd was active in the London society before moving to America, where he led the St. Louis Ethical Culture Society (1933-50) and was president of the American Humanist Association (1947-48). Thirty years later Charles Templeton, whose ministry began with the Nazarenes in Canada, embarked on a similar journey into skepticism despite his early partnership with Billy Graham and his own renown as an evangelist.[5]

On the other extreme, fundamentalists reacted negatively to the new age. Though they shared with modernists a commitment to empirical methods, fundamentalists girded themselves for battle against atheists, agnostics, evolutionists, and modernists. Fundamentalists' view of Scripture stressed biblical inerrancy. Virtually all Protestants had asserted the Bible's *authority*, but stress on its *inerrancy* (or absence of historical and scientific error) grew out of Reformed theology. Since the time of John Calvin, Reformed theology had made formal logic central to its theological method. In the mid-1800s, however, theologians at Princeton Seminary argued for the Bible's "inerrancy" out of the need they perceived to limit reason and defend the Scripture's integrity. Having asserted inerrancy, they defended every statement in Scripture on the grounds that a single error would falsify the whole. J. Gresham Machen's *Christianity and Liberalism* reflected the thesis that Christianity and modernist theology were separate religions.[6]

Fundamentalism drew its passion less from old school Calvinism than from the spread of dispensationalism. A form of premillennialism, dispensationalism anticipated Christ's soon coming. Dispensationalists stressed the world's irredeemable corruption and charged that the Christian Church at large was "apostate" and "ruined." The viewpoint originated with John Nelson Darby, one of the founders of the British Plymouth Brethren. In the latter nineteenth century D. L. Moody and a circle of associates popularized these millennial views through various Bible and prophecy conferences. Dispensationalism spread more widely in the twentieth century through Bible institutes; the popularity of the *Scofield Reference Bible* (1909), an annotated edition of the Scriptures; and the emergence of Pentecostalism.[7]

Dispensationalism's assessment of human progress ran directly counter to the optimism of earlier evangelicals, including Jonathan Edwards and Charles G. Finney. Postmillennialists took heart from numerous religious awakenings, the antislavery crusade, and the Protestant missionary enterprise. They saw the world as increasingly under the sway of Jesus Christ and His reign. Dispensationalism's pessimistic assessment of widespread social and spiritual ruin gave passion to fundamentalism's reaction against science and social change.[8]

Where did the Church of the Nazarene stand in these theological controversies? In the years between the world wars, Nazarenes clearly sympathized with fundamentalism against skepticism, biblical criticism, Darwinism, and liberal Protestantism. Nazarenes regarded modernism as an unwelcome accommodation of the Christian faith. Like various evangelical denominations, the Church of the Nazarene went through a fundamentalist phase. But to what extent would fundamentalism alter the Church of the Nazarene's self-understanding? Would the church's identity remain intact? Or would that identity be swallowed up by affinity with a newer and larger twentieth-century movement whose spirit and purposes were different from those that gave rise to the Church of the Nazarene and to the Holiness Movement from which it sprang?

THE CHURCH'S THEOLOGICAL IDENTITY

The Holiness Movement had cut a broad swath across the North American and British religious landscape, and the early Church of the Nazarene gathered people of diverse religious backgrounds. Congregationalists, Baptists, Quakers, Presbyterians, and even Episcopalians joined the new church. But former Methodists comprised the core of early Nazarene congregations, and the church's most basic assumptions about governance and polity reflected Methodist traditions: the General Assembly, the *Manual*, the general and district superintendency, and even the deed restrictions on church property. The church's General Rules retained much of John Wesley's original structure and wording. Methodism was most evident in the church's formal statements of doctrine—the Articles of Faith and the Agreed Statement of Belief—the heart of John Wesley's theology.

At the same time, Nazarene founders regarded their Methodist "mother" as having lost her way and, like the earlier Wesleyan and Free Methodists, saw themselves as truer heirs to John Wesley. Leaders who entered the Church of the Nazarene from non-Methodist backgrounds perceived the church's relationship to Methodism in this way. A. M. Hills, a former Congregationalist, for instance, said that he had "long felt that the Church of the Nazarene is the fairest flower that has ever bloomed in the Methodist garden, the most promising ecclesiastical daughter the prolific Mother Methodism has ever given to the world. If we studiously cultivate our great parent's virtues and prayerfully avoid her mistakes, no human mind can grasp and foretell what the future may have in store for us. Think from what a holy ancestry we have sprung!" He continued, "We Nazarenes are lineal descendants of Methodism, and God will expect us to live accordingly."[9]

The Church of the Nazarene was positioned theologically as a "believers' church" as well. Nazarenes viewed themselves as called into existence through the Holy Spirit to restore New Testament practices and doctrines. They emphasized a regenerate membership. Nazarenes required neither baptism nor catechism but a declaration of saving faith as the basis for church membership. The church used a simple pattern of worship, stressed Bible study and charitable works, and disciplined moral offenders. In many ways Nazarenes resembled Anabaptists, Puritans, the Church of the Brethren, early Congregationalists, Disciples of Christ, Baptists, and others who originated with the conviction that the religious establishment had accommodated to secular power and society and thereby lost its spiritual vitality. Nazarenes were moderate in their expression of the believers' church idea. The New Testament Church of Christ was the only parent body that was "antidenominational" in origin. It abandoned its restorationist claims within a few years. Unlike more radical expressions of the believers' church, members of the New Testament Church of Christ avoided the notion that they had restored some scriptural mode of church structure and governance.

A churchly way of life was essential to early Nazarene self-understanding from the very beginning—a fact so evident to Timothy L. Smith that he contrasted the first generation to the sectarian shield that second generation Nazarenes soon erected. Smith argued that the church's trajectory reversed the direction taken by most religious groups. If, as H. Richard Niebuhr suggested, new religious groups began as sects and evolved into denominations, Nazarenes, Smith contended, began as a denomination and devolved into a sect as it grew increasingly inward. More perhaps than Smith realized, presuppositions common to believers' churches shaped this sectarian-like way of life.[10]

THEOLOGICAL ORIENTATION OF MINISTERS

Ministers transmitted the church's Wesleyan identity. The Course of Study that ministers were required to complete before ordination nurtured Wesleyan doctrines. Candidates for ordination around the world read the same books, stipulated in the *Manual*, in biblical, systematic, and practical theology.[11]

Systematic theology shaped most how ministers thought and preached. Methodist writers dominated the required reading during the Church of the Nazarene's first three decades. John Miley's *Systematic Theology* (1892) was on the Course of Study from 1911 until 1932. Thomas Ralston's *Elements of Divinity* (1847, with subsequent editions), the first American Methodist systematic theology, was added to the Course of Study in 1919 and listed as an alternate to Miley's text until 1932, when Ralston's text replaced Miley's. The addition of *Elements of Divinity* to the Course of Study was important, for, in spite of its indebtedness to Scottish common-sense philosophy, it was more traditionally Wesleyan in spirit than Miley's *Systematic Theology*. The first substantial systematic theology written by a Nazarene was A. M. Hill's *Fundamental Christian Theology* (1931), added to the Course of Study in 1932 but listed second, as an alternate to Ralston. In 1940 the first volume of H. Orton Wiley's 3-volume *Christian Theology* appeared, replacing all other systematic theologies on the Course of Study. Until 1940, then, two Methodist theologians provided Nazarene ministers with their first comprehensive introduction to Christian theology.

John Wesley's life and writings also influenced early Nazarene ministers. Like their Methodist counterparts, ministerial candidates in the Church of the Nazarene were required to read a Wesley biography. At first this was W. H. Fitchett's *Wesley and His Century*. Later (1928-44) it was John Telford's *Life of John Wesley*. A small collection of Wesley's sermons was also published by the Nazarene Publishing House and was required reading from 1915 until 1932. The collection included "Scripture Way of Salvation," "Sin in Believers," "Repentance in Believers," "Perfection," "Charity," "Patience," "Temptation," "Friendship with the World," "The Cure of Evil Speaking," and "Christian Fellowship."[12] J. A. Wood's *Christian Perfection, As Taught by John Wesley*, a lengthy compilation of Wesley's writings from many sources, was required reading from 1919 to 1932. In short, Nazarene ministers going through the Course of Study had to read a Wesley biography, a selection of his sermons, and a compilation of his statements on Christian holiness. Chapman, for one, insisted in 1946: "Every preacher of full salvation should make John Wesley and his works a fundamental study."[13]

Other Methodist influences in ministerial education included the works of E. M. Bounds on prayer and William Arthur on the doctrine of the Holy Spirit. Bishop John F. Hurst's *Short History of the Christian Church* appeared from 1923 through 1944. The Course of Study included books by Bishop Randolph S. Foster, *Christian Purity;* William McDonald, *Life of Rev. John Inskip;* Asbury Lowry, *Possibilities of Grace;* Bishop Matthew Simpson, *Lectures on Preaching;* Daniel Steele, *The Gospel of the Comforter;* Samuel Chadwick, *The Way to Pentecost;* and Jesse T. Peck, *The Central Idea of Christianity*, among others. Some of these writers were deeply involved in the nineteenth-century holiness revival, while others were not. Their collective influence underscored the Church of the Nazarene's intention to draw consciously on the theological and spiritual resources of Methodism during its first decades.[14]

THEOLOGICAL DEVELOPMENT

Nazarene writers gradually added their own work to this body of literature. E. P. Ellyson's *Theological Compend* (1908) contained brief summaries of biblical passages on selected doctrines of the faith. His Quaker background shaped the book, which contained sections not generally included in doctrinal treatises ("Doctrine of Prayer" and "Doctrine of Testimony"). The book lacked references to theological development since the biblical period. There was the barest doctrine of the church and no mention of many standard Wesleyan themes. Ellyson based the book on classroom lectures that he developed at the Christian Worker's Training School, the nondenominational Holiness school in Marshalltown, Iowa, which he had founded. Ellyson's theology evolved, and a much-revised edition, published in 1932 as *Doctrinal Studies*, was more substantial, with a stronger ecclesiology and a chapter on the sacraments, which the earlier work did not even mention.[15]

The dominant Nazarene theologians were A. M. Hills and H. Orton Wiley. The agenda of nineteenth-century Methodist theology, centered upon the Wesleyan-Arminian struggle with Calvinism, shaped the theologies of both. Each approached the theological task from a different angle, however, which reflected different eras, backgrounds, and experiences. Individualism and self-reliance tinged the theology of Hills. Wiley rooted his theology more broadly and was more closely Wesleyan.

Aaron Merritt Hills (1848-1935), a native of southern Michigan, was raised in the Congregational Church. Hills's prosperous uncle, A. M. Chesbrough, however, supported institutions of the Free Methodist Church. Hills's immediate family identified with Charles Finney's blend of revivalism and social reform, especially after their move to Mount Vernon, Ohio, where their pastor was an Oberlin College graduate. Hills himself attended Oberlin when Finney was an aged but unbowed presence. Hills graduated in 1870 and immediately entered the Divinity School of Yale University. There the "New School" theology, forged by National Taylor and taught, in Hills's day by Noah Porter, Samuel Harris, Timothy Dwight the Younger, and historian George Fisher, represented a very modified Calvinism. Both Oberlin and Yale represented schools of thought reacting strongly and consciously against rigid forms of Calvinism. Hills finished his bachelor of divinity in 1873. He then entered the Congregational Church's ministry and held pastorates that included Ravenna, Ohio, 1874-84, where he grew acutely conscious of his theological differences with some of the other ministers on the conference, who included Washington Gladden, one of the chief voices for the social gospel.

Hills pastored in Allegheny, Pennsylvania (near Pittsburgh), 1884-90, where he became an outspoken foe of the Masonic lodge. This period of Hills's life was one of growing estrangement between him and other ministers in the Congregational Church.[16]

Hills pastored the Olivet College Congregational Church in Michigan from 1890 to 1891, before becoming state evangelist for the Congregational Home Missionary Society, 1891-93. He took a small home missions church in Springfield, Missouri, 1893-94, and then entered full-time evangelism in 1894. Residing in Oberlin, by 1895, he experienced entire sanctification. He became a registered evangelist with the National Holiness Association and was a sought-after revivalist. Hills conducted meetings in Congregationalist and Methodist churches alike. An early publication, *Holiness and Power for the Church and Ministry* (1898), filled with testimonies of sanctifying grace, became a popular book. After a year teaching at Asbury College, 1898-99, Hills became founding president of Texas Holiness University, where he stayed until 1906. He was president of Central Holiness University in Oskaloosa, Iowa, 1906-8, before returning at age sixty to full-time evangelism. He made his first trip to Great Britain, 1908-9. From 1909 to 1910 he was president of Illinois Holiness University, precursor to Olivet Nazarene College. He returned to Great Britain in 1911 and again in 1913, teaching both times at Star Hall, a Holiness mission in Manchester. He ended his career at Pasadena College, where he taught theology and pastoral ministry subjects from 1915 until his retirement at age eighty-three in 1931. Along the way, he wrote dozens of books, including biographies of Charles Finney, temperance reformer Mary Woodbridge, Martin Knapp, and Phineas Bresee; treatises against tobacco use and lodges; and studies in doctrine, particularly the doctrine of holiness. A major work was *Homiletics and Pastoral Theology*, published in 1929. His two-volume magnum opus was *Fundamental Christian Theology*, published in 1931. The work was a systematic compilation and editing of articles and chapters that Hills had written over the previous decades. A one-volume abridgement followed a year later.[17]

A. M. Hills

The system of thought that Hills presented in *Fundamental Christian Theology* showed the influence that revivalism, with its emphasis on human decision and responsibility, exerted upon Wesleyan thinking. In the nineteenth century and beyond, the spirit of enterprise, achievement, and assumed moral innocence was often at odds with older Christian concepts.

Nineteenth-century theology developed in a context of a diminishing sense of sin and an expanding confidence in human potential. Understanding himself to have become a type of Methodist in uniting with the Church of the Nazarene, Hills intended to write a Wesleyan theology. Many basic views in *Fundamental Christian Theology* came from Wesley, though little from contemporary Methodists. Church historian Paul Bassett identifies free will as the organizing principle of Hills's theology. The priority Hills gave to human freedom limited his conception of divine grace. Hills, like his teachers at Oberlin and Yale, found repugnant the Calvinist understandings of predestination and election, which limited human beings' ability to choose salvation. But Hills rejected one of the most basic concepts in traditional Wesleyan theology, prevenient grace, the idea that grace is given to all persons prior to salvation and prepares them to receive saving grace. Hills rejected it entirely, quoting Charles Finney on the point at great length. Hills characterized the doctrine of "gracious ability" as "inconsistent with the true doctrines of Methodism," thus viewing prevenient grace as an internal contradiction in classical Wesleyan theology. Wesley viewed free will as an endowment of the Holy Spirit given freely to all, while Hills (following Finney and his Yale professors) viewed free will as a natural ability. This shift, once it was made, affected the basic definition of faith. The emphasis in Hills's doctrine of grace shifted from Wesley's idea of faith as God's gift to the view that faith is essentially "a voluntary and responsible action of the will." Faith, in other words, is an offering to God, not God's gift. Compared to Wesley, Hills enlarged the role of human freedom and diminished the scope of divine activity in the work of salvation. The very same shifts away from Wesley's understanding of free grace toward free will were taking place within Methodist theology.[18]

H. Orton Wiley (1877-1961) brought a different outlook to his work and emerged as the most influential Nazarene theologian of the twentieth century. Wiley was born in Marquette, Nebraska, but grew up primarily in northern California. Wiley's faith was nurtured by the United Brethren in Christ, a German-American form of Methodism. He received a teaching diploma from the Oregon State Normal School in 1898 and proceeded to earn a pharmacy degree. He moved to Berkeley, California, in 1901 and entered the United Brethren ministry the following year. He served two pastoral charges before joining the Church of the Nazarene in Berkeley in 1905 through E. A. Girvin's influence. Wiley's student, theologian Carl Bangs, remarked, "In Wiley's experience, the United Brethren Church of his youth had been a Wesleyan church; but while it had esteemed entire sanctification, it had not insisted upon it. For Wiley, the Church of the Nazarene was the last and best hope of Wesleyanism."[19] Wiley continued studies at the University of the Pacific, where he earned a bachelor of arts in 1910. In the same year he earned a bachelor of sacred theology from Pacific Theological Seminary. He earned a master of sacred theology degree in 1917 at the same school, renamed Pacific School of Religion, and a doctor of sacred theology degree there in 1929.

In subsequent years Wiley made a distinct mark on Nazarene higher education, influencing denomination-wide educational policy and proving a capable college administrator. Wiley succeeded E. P. Ellyson as president of the Pasadena College in 1913. He was Pasadena College's president at three different times, president of Northwest Nazarene College for ten years, and editor of the *Herald of Holiness* for eight. In 1919, when Wiley was forty-two, the General Assembly commissioned him to write a systematic theology for the church. Largely because of administrative responsibilities, the first volume did not appear until twenty-one years later. But he exerted a strong theological influence during that intervening time, conveyed through the pulpit, classroom, the *Herald of Holiness*, and the *Preacher's Magazine*. He was on the *Manual* editing committee from 1919 to 1932. His theological influence proved pivotal in general assemblies that discussed the Articles of Faith.[20]

H. Orton Wiley

Personalism, developed by Boston University philosopher Bordon Parker Bowne, influenced Wiley much. Boston University, a Methodist school, was the primary center of personalism, but a West Coast school of personalism developed under Wiley's teacher John Wright Buckham. Personalism was indebted to Immanuel Kant and held that personality was the ultimate principle in the universe. A form of personalism that remained consciously accountable to the Wesleyan tradition made its home in the Holiness Movement. Theologian Thomas Langford views Wiley's statement that "truth in its ultimate nature is personal" as his fundamental principle. Wiley developed his theology looking backward to Wesley and forward to personalism. A variety of Nazarene preachers, philosophers, and theologians followed after him.[21]

In spite of the personalist influences, Wiley, said Carl Bangs, was committed to "a classical Wesleyanism." For Wiley, Bangs wrote, "the Nazarenes were not to be a sect, cut off from Christendom. Wiley poured a whole stream of history into his perception of his church. He was at heart a Methodist in the style of Wesley, and that meant that Anglicanism was his heritage as well."

Bangs recalled that in Wiley's classes he would refer to "the creed," and by this "often he meant the 39 Articles of the English Reformation. [His students] were to know them, study them." The Church of the Nazarene was, for Wiley, said Bangs, "to be an heir of the whole catholic tradition that had come alive in the Wesleyan revival of biblical faith."[22] Whether the topic was grace, election, baptism, or holiness, the Anglican-Methodist orientation underlay Wiley's thinking. His difference with Hills reflected another way of appropriating and using the theology of the Protestant Reformers and, behind them, the theologies of the Eastern and Western churches. Hills read Protestant theology as an ongoing debate between Calvin and his critics. Hills's doctrine of free will registered in the strongest possible way his antagonism to Calvinism's emphasis on predestination. On the one hand, Wiley spoke of grace as being "preeminent" in its relation to the human will, and of prevenient grace being unconditionally bestowed on all persons as a benefit of the Atonement. On the other hand, much like A. M. Hills, Wiley spoke of Adam's fall not destroying the will's moral power to choose good.[23] Wiley's commitment to prevenient grace, though not fully developed, allowed him to reject predestination as well, but in a way that more clearly affirmed the priority of faith as God's gift. Behind this disagreement lurked differences concerning the doctrine of the church, the nature of theology, and theology's sources: would these be narrow or broad? Wiley read Christian history as a complex story with many heroes and appreciated Methodism's Anglican roots. This opened the way for Wiley and those who followed to appropriate the early church fathers and the best of the catholic tradition while anchoring theology in the Protestant priority of salvation by grace alone. Phineas Bresee had insisted that the Church of the Nazarene had a mission to "Christianize Christianity." Wiley's personal appropriation of Bresee's vision for the church lay, said Bangs, in the fact that he "would not settle for a narrow sectarianism [but] accepted the task of being a church *dogmaticus* in the broad stream of Christian history."[24]

Olive Winchester (1879-1947) was another theologian of distinction in the Church of the Nazarene's first half-century. She was one of the best-educated women of her time. In 1902 she earned a bachelor's degree from Radcliffe College, the women's college associated with Harvard University. Her instructor in Semitic languages regarded her as "a student of exceptional ability." She taught at the Pentecostal Collegiate Institute

Olive Winchester

of the Association of Pentecostal Churches of America from 1902 to 1908. Then she went to Scotland, where in 1912 she became the first woman to graduate from the divinity school of the University of Glasgow. She taught for George Sharpe's fledgling college, and she was ordained for ministry by the Pentecostal Church of Scotland. She returned to America to head the theology department at Pentecostal Collegiate Institute while serving as vice principal. In 1916 she moved to Berkeley, California, to study for a master of sacred theology degree at Pacific School of Theology. Wiley, her fellow student, invited her to teach at Northwest Nazarene College, where he was headed the following year.

As academic dean and vice president at NNC, Winchester played an integral role in organizing the college's scholarly life and fostering respect for academic standards. She taught Greek, Hebrew, biblical literature, and sociology. Winchester also grew interested in education in local churches and developed and taught a series of courses in religious education. She contributed frequent articles to church papers and curriculum resources. Traveling back and forth from Nampa to New Jersey for study at Drew Theological Seminary, she earned a doctor of theology degree, focusing on biblical literature, in 1925. In 1935 Wiley persuaded Winchester to follow him to Pasadena College, where Winchester became professor of biblical literature and languages and dean of the Graduate School of Religion.[25]

In 1935, while Wiley was still editor of the *Herald of Holiness*, Winchester published a series of articles on the theology of John Wesley. Winchester published three books, including studies of Moses, the prophets, and the life of Jesus. Winchester championed an amillennialist interpretation of Christ's second coming at a time when premillennialism was gaining nearly universal appeal among Nazarenes. She was conservative in her application of the biblical criticism she had learned at Glasgow and Drew. *Crisis Experiences in the Greek New Testament*, published after her death by former students, stood in the linguistic-exegetical tradition. Like Daniel Steele, a nineteenth-century Methodist theologian who had taught at Boston University, Winchester defended the doctrine of entire sanctification by a careful study of the New Testament writers' use of the Greek aorist tense.[26]

SHIFTS IN POPULAR THEOLOGY

Nazarenes tolerated a wide variety of different views pertaining to baptism and Christ's second coming at the time of the church unions. They deemed these differences unessential and subordinated such emphases to the primary importance of salvation and holy living. But some distinct shifts occurred in popular theology between the two world wars. The growing theological liberalism within the Methodist Church and the surging numbers of Baptists changed the nature of evangelicalism. Though still maligned, Pentecostals also became a perceptible force. These shifts affected Nazarenes and generated intellectual distance between popular thinking and academic theologians, who viewed themselves as guardians of the church's identity.

One area where popular theology shifted concerned baptism. Among early Nazarenes were former Quakers and members of The Salvation Army, who practiced no sacraments. The church's three major parent bodies independently had come to the view that the mode of baptism should be the choice of the one being baptized, and the *Manual* allowed both infant baptism and believer's baptism. This open stance prevented union with other Wesleyan-Holiness churches that rejected the practice of infant baptism. Early Nazarenes not only tolerated diverse baptismal views but actually expected them and allowed freedom of conscience. Mary Lee Cagle's experience underscores this. She was convinced in her early ministry that *pouring* was the only scriptural mode of baptism. The downward flow of pouring water visibly symbolized the promised outpouring of the Holy Spirit upon individual believers and the church. Later she saw wisdom in allowing individuals to be baptized by any mode dictated by their conscience. This broadening of her mind led to an amazing scene in New Mexico, where she and her husband performed a community baptismal service in a remote town with no organized churches and few visiting clergy. She later described: "It was one time they baptized every way under the sun—by every mode possible. They dipped—they plunged—they poured—they sprinkled and they baptized babies. It was a time of rejoicing; and the shouts of the redeemed echoed and re-echoed through the hills."[27]

Through the 1920s the church widely baptized infants. Parents had sought out Phineas Bresee at district assemblies to baptize their infant children. Several districts incorporated a service of infant baptism into the agenda of each annual district assembly, taking advantage of the presiding general superintendent to conduct the baptisms. This typically occurred immediately before the ordination service, displaying remarkable symbolism since the general superintendent, as the episcopal officer, represented not only the Church of the Nazarene but in a larger sense the Church Universal. For instance, at the 1924 assembly of the Eastern Oklahoma District, "at 2 o'clock Dr. Reynolds baptized six babies, which occasion was a blessing to all. After this a great ordination service followed." Similarly, at the 1927 San Antonio District Assembly, "Dr. Reynolds called for all who wished to bring their children for baptism and seven were presented." Even in the 1930s General Superintendents R. T. Williams, J. B. Chapman, and John W. Goodwin rendered similar service.²⁸

There was a discernible movement toward a more uniform baptismal practice within Nazarene life, however, in a way that intensified the denomination's pull toward the believers' church tradition. Infant baptisms grew less common, though the practice never disappeared. In 1936 a service for infant dedication was added to the ritual section of the *Manual* as an alternative to infant baptism. The districts that once scheduled infant baptism services in their assembly schedules abandoned the practice. By the mid-twentieth century, infant dedications were common and infant baptisms rare among Nazarenes.²⁹

Another important shift in baptismal practice came in the growing popularity of immersion. Questions about baptism were put frequently to the editors of the *Herald of Holiness* and became opportunities for the editors to instruct the church. Editor Chapman personally favored immersion but accepted the adequacy of the other modes. He defended infant baptism and the church's embrace of plural baptismal theologies as acceptable and commendable. Chapman counseled ministers to baptize by modes they might not prefer rather than make people wait for a minister in wholehearted agreement with their parishioners' mode of choice. He did *not* defend the membership of unbaptized Christians in the Church of the Nazarene, however, and insisted: "It is expected that people who unite with the Church of the Nazarene shall have *some* water by *some* mode."³⁰ Yet the *Manual* itself did not directly connect baptism with church membership. Theologian S. S. White declared that he had been baptized "as a baby in my mother's arm" and had "never doubted the validity of this baptism," but he recommended to ministers at mid-century to "see to it that there was a baptistery" in Nazarene churches so that immersions could be conducted with no inconvenience to those intending to be baptized by that mode. The inconvenience related to either finding a suitable creek or river, or borrowing a nearby Baptist church for the occasion. The emphasis on immersion was a distinctive idea of the Baptists and the closely related Disciples of Christ/Churches of Christ tradition, both particularly strong influences in the American South and border states. At the same time, as Nazarenes expanded to predominantly Roman Catholic countries, missionaries urged converts, many of whom had been baptized as infants, to be rebaptized by immersion.³¹

Popular views on Christ's second coming also changed between 1910 and 1950. God's Bible School in Cincinnati, Ohio, and Asbury College in Wilmore, Kentucky, emerged as premillennialist centers within the Wesleyan-Holiness movement. Their leaders, Martin Wells Knapp and Henry C. Morrison, were keenly premillennial, as were Seth Rees and C. W. Ruth, cofounders with Knapp of the International Holiness Union and Prayer League. After Knapp's death, and the departures of Ruth and Rees in 1901 and 1905, the league developed under George Kulp's leadership into the primary parent body of the Pilgrim Holiness Church, in which the doctrine of Christ's premillennial coming was a formal article of faith. God's Bible School influenced the conservative Holiness Movement and particularly Nazarenes in the Midwest. Rees, a New Englander, and Ruth, a Pennsylvanian, were among the many bringing premillennial perspectives into the Church of the Nazarene.[32]

H. C. Morrison, W. B. Godbey, L. L. Pickett, J. O. McClurkan, and B. F. Haynes were among the Holiness leaders in the South who combined premillennial views with Holiness teachings. McClurkan viewed the Holiness Movement's place in history in a particular context—as one strand within a larger worldwide revival destined to reap a harvest of souls in the "Eleventh Hour" before Christ's return to put an end to human history. McClurkan was influenced by A. B. Simpson, the Christian and Missionary Alliance founder and a major propagator of Plymouth Brethren dispensationalism. Pickett and Godbey spread their views throughout the Southern Holiness camp meetings, where they were popular speakers. Godbey's knowledge of the Greek New Testament cast an aura of authority over his insistence upon Christ's premillennial second coming. Pickett used public debates to spread his beliefs. Haynes accepted premillennialism in the early 1890s, a few months after he became active in the Holiness Movement. Haynes devoted a chapter of his autobiography to his "three Bibles," a term for the three interpretive lenses that shaped his understanding of the scriptural message. The "Methodist Bible," known since his childhood, understood the biblical witness to emphasize human sinfulness, conversion, and turning from sin, and the witness of the Holy Spirit to forgiveness. His "second Bible," superimposed on the first, was the knowledge that the doctrine of perfect love was a central component of the biblical message. His "third Bible" was the "glorious dispensational truth" of Christ's premillennial second coming.[33]

World War I widened the acceptance of premillennialism. The war was particularly brutal, and its scope was large, involving nations whose colonial empires spanned the globe. The conflict's global nature spurred apocalyptic speculation. C. B. Jernigan and E. E. Angell were among the Nazarene leaders emphasizing the Second Coming either during the war or in its aftermath. Jernigan wrote two books on prophecy between 1918 and 1920. Angell was long associated with Eastern Nazarene College and New England, where, as reflected in the *Beulah Christian*, Methodist theologian Daniel Steele's solid

Holiness credentials and firm commitment to postmillenialism held sway for many years. Originally Angell accused premillennialism of being "hatched by Jesuits—picked up by Darby." He believed that the theory of a tribulation period after the Rapture undermined Holiness teaching by giving people a second chance. However, World War I led him to reassess his eschatology, and Angell embraced premillennial views. Other Nazarene authors in the 1920s identified the Antichrist with Italian dictator Benito Mussolini. The spread of premillennialism throughout the Church of the Nazarene heightened the sense of alienation from the modern world and hastened retreat from both ecumenical and social endeavors. Boundaries between Christian culture and culture-at-large were distinct and clearly demarcated. This attitude had direct implications for Christian ethics, both individual and social, and for the role that the church envisioned for its institutions of higher education as bastions against modernism.[34]

The spread of dispensational premillennialism was a factor in the fundamentalist crusade. The primary Nazarene theologians resisted dispensational theology. Teachers of Nazarene theology were honor-bound to stress that the Church of the Nazarene took no stand on behalf of one millennial theory or another. Wiley deflected questions regarding his personal convictions about eschatology, and *Christian Theology* dispassionately surveyed the various viewpoints. Assessments of Wiley's eschatology differed.

Hills, on the other hand, deflected nothing. He remained an ardent postmillennialist and staunch critic of dispensational premillennialism. That outspokenness played a role in his leaving the presidency of two Holiness colleges. At Pasadena College Hills frequently voiced opposition to premillennialism, greatly annoying some faculty members and students. At one point President A. O. Hendricks sternly warned the venerable professor Hills to tone down his rhetoric or lose his position. When an early draft of his *Fundamental Christian Theology* circulated, Hills was advised that it would need to say something positive about premillennialism before it could be used as a Nazarene text. The theology was not published by the Church of the Nazarene, its postmillennialism being among the factors. When the book finally appeared, published by C. J. Kinne, it included a section by Chapman setting forth a positive argument for premillennialism, alongside Hills's defense of postmillennialism.

Meanwhile, Olive Winchester, as an amillennialist, interpreted the Book of Revelation as a coded record of events that had occurred in the New Testament era, perhaps during Nero's reign, not predictions of the future. There was neither time, place, nor reason for a literal millennium on earth, from the amillennialist perspective, as Christ would judge the living and the dead and initiate a new heaven and new earth at the time of His second coming. "Millennium" was a figure of speech for an eternity of time. The editors of the *Herald of Holiness* consistently steered a neutral course when they dealt with millennial theology. Haynes and Chapman indicated which particular view they favored but always fairly stated the various views and upheld the principle that plural views should be expected within the church on these issues. In this way they mediated between different opinions and, increasingly, between the academic voice and the popular voice within the Church of the Nazarene.[35]

FUNDAMENTALISM'S CHALLENGE TO NAZARENE IDENTITY

Nazarene theologians shared several common objectives with fundamentalists in their opposition to theological modernism, but ultimately the church's theological moorings prevented Nazarenes and other conservative Wesleyans from surrendering to fundamentalism. The pessimism of premillennialism, particularly after World War I, reinforced strains of antimodernism within the church. The church viewed evolution with great suspicion. In 1921 Chapman reassured Nazarenes that "we do not have an evolutionist on the teaching force of the schools of our church." Though the schools might use textbooks that discuss evolution (since Nazarene students needed to be aware of current scientific issues), not a single graduate of a Nazarene school, Chapman believed, questioned the "biblical account of creation, or of any other historical account of the Bible."[36] A. M. Hills, Chapman's teacher, had a long history of opposing organic, though not geological evolution. Hills held to the idea of an ancient earth. Olive Winchester, who had a standing series in *The Young People's Journal,* turned her attention to science and religion in 1931. She opposed both "the higher critics" and organic evolution as "subversive of the Christian viewpoint." But she rejected the idea that the seven days of creation in Genesis were solar days. They were, she believed, indeterminate, perhaps vast, periods of time. She affirmed "the planetesimal theory" of cosmic evolution as "a feasible explanation of the development of the solar system, if admission is made that these elementary forms of matter were created" through a process in which God was the first cause. Earth's features, likewise, she saw as formed through secondary causes. But she totally discounted the evolution of species and regarded this evolutionary hypothesis as a threat to orthodoxy. She quoted the Scottish theologian James Orr: "It is not only a particular theory of the origin of sin that is put in question by the evolutionary conception: the very idea of sin, in the Christian sense, is essentially altered. Sin is no longer the voluntary defection of a creature who had the power to remain sinless. The very possibility of sinless development is excluded. Sin becomes a natural necessity of [humanity's] ascent."[37] Yet J. W. Goodwin, after his retirement as general superintendent, remarked to his classes at Pasadena College in the early 1940s that "the Bible does not profess to be a treatise on Science." Like Winchester, Goodwin was open to a creation "day" being defined figuratively. Wiley similarly believed in an ancient earth and saw numerous parallels between the Genesis account of creation and the discoveries of modern science.[38]

Biblical inspiration was not the issue in understanding creation. A. M. Hills posed a series of specific tests to young ministers on the authority of the Bible, including: "Do you believe in [the Bible's] account of creation? . . . The Psalms as largely the work of David? Do you believe in one Isaiah or many?"[39] Yet, Hills distanced himself from fundamentalists by his sharp attacks on the Scofield Reference Bible. A friend had noted that the Scofield Bible had "gained a large circulation, and is used extensively," "both by preachers and people." Hills fumed over this, since the work was "saturated and soaked and dripping with Calvinism and opposition to holiness."[40]

Chapman, who disagreed with Hills on millennial doctrines, also warned Nazarenes against using the Scofield Bible because it imposed Calvinist interpretations on Scripture and promoted suppression rather than cleansing of sin. While it was true that no one would ever be saved by "question marks," and that when preachers preached it must be with "thus saith the Lord," at the same time the church must not confuse the preservation of right doctrine with the revival of vital Christianity.[41] The victories of fundamentalist "orthodoxy" did not assure a revival of the vital religion. Even orthodoxy may be "dead." What men and women needed, Chapman said, was conversion to Jesus Christ. What cured doubts about the Bible were not rationalistic arguments (for that, after all, was the root of the modernist problem) but a "worldwide revival." Heresy must be differentiated from apostasy. One was the error of the head; the other the error of the heart. Like Wesley, Nazarenes emphasized experience over rational assent. That no successful revival had ever been conducted by modernists indicated sufficiently that human beings could not be saved by denying the virgin birth, and the deity and Lordship of Christ. But the final guard against heresy, said Chapman, was possession of the Holy Spirit, who brought both purity and power. To exhibit a life of holiness was the primary calling for Nazarenes. The majority of fundamentalists, Chapman warned, denied the possibility of freedom from all sin. They omitted the most fundamental of all fundamentals, holiness. Were Nazarenes "fundamentalists"? Chapman declared that the use of "fundamentalism" required special discrimination. When asked whether one is a fundamentalist, one must determine whether it is used as a common or proper noun. Chapman was intent on preventing Reformed theology from taking root in the church through fundamentalism's impact on laypersons. Fundamentalists were Calvinists, Chapman warned Nazarenes. They wove their basic theology of eternal security and predestination into their attacks on modernism. The leading fundamentalist intellectual, J. Gresham Machen, and his Presbyterian colleagues skewered Wesleyan-Arminian theology as adeptly as they did modernist ideas. Though sometimes claiming, "we are all fundamentalists," Nazarenes like Chapman realized that in crucial ways they were not.[42]

Other Nazarenes likewise perceived a danger in the church identifying too closely with fundamentalism. W. R. Cain found fundamentalist speakers "brainy" but ventured that 95 percent belonged to secret societies. "We believe in Bible Fundamentalism," Cain concluded, "but not the mutilated sort."[43] C. E. Cornell searched for a third alternative. Whether a whale really swallowed Jonah or whether Paul wrote Hebrews was not the gospel; it did not satisfy spiritual needs. Such questions diverted the church from important social issues, Cornell wrote in 1926, including labor conditions and ethnic relations. "Let the hair-splitting controversy cease." The "essentialist" movement that Harold Paul Sloan was launching among conservative Methodists apparently attracted Cornell. Similarly, S. S. White reminded Nazarenes that the Holiness Movement did not arise out of a protest to modernism. The issues over which fundamentalists fought were not the issues over which the Church of the Nazarene had come into existence. The main emphasis of the Holiness people was their "personal contact with God through Christ." White would begin with this, Christian experience, rather than with doctrinal affirmations, in discussing faith with modernists. Without Christian experience, fundamentalism remained harsh and legalistic.[44]

Popular fundamentalism was at a point of crisis when Nazarenes gathered in Columbus, Ohio, for the 1928 General Assembly. Since the Scopes Trial, when Tennessee's law prohibiting the teaching of evolution in the state's public schools was challenged in the courts and upheld, fundamentalists had lost ground in public opinion. R. T. Williams noted, nonetheless, in the quadrennial address that Nazarenes were not divided by recent events. "We have absolute solidarity in doctrine," and "what one Nazarene believes as to fundamentals and essentials, every Nazarene in the world believes the same thing." Yet in the theological climate of the day, delegates to the 1928 General Assembly were in a mood to carry out an extensive reform of the

Manual. One of the changes proposed for the Articles of Faith included the addition of the word "inerrancy" to the article on Scripture. The defense of an "inerrant Bible" was now commonplace in the literature of fundamentalism. It popularly meant that the Bible was without error in all matters, including those of history and science. The way in which the Nazarene General Assembly handled the issue testified to Wiley's influence and ability to ensure that the church retained as nearly as possible a theological identity consistent with the Anglican-Methodist orientation he believed proper for a Wesleyan-Holiness church. "Of the Sufficiency of the Holy Scriptures for Salvation," the Article of Faith on Scripture in both the Thirty-nine Articles of the Church of England and the Twenty-Five Articles of Methodism read: "The Holy Scriptures contain all things necessary to salvation; so that whatsoever is not read therein, nor may be proved thereby, is not to be required of any man that it should be believed as an article of faith, or be thought requisite or necessary to salvation." The revised article on Scripture adopted by the Nazarenes in 1928 stated: "We believe in the plenary inspiration of the Holy Scriptures by which we understand the sixty-six books of the Old and New Testaments, given by divine inspiration, inerrantly revealing the will of God concerning us in all things necessary to our salvation; so that whatever is not contained therein is not to be enjoined as an article of faith." The term "plenary" rather than "verbal," commented John W. Goodwin some years later, was sufficiently strong. It meant that "full and complete inspiration extended to all the subjects dealt with." But while avoiding fundamentalism's more extreme emphasis, like the Articles of Faith in Anglicanism and Methodism, the revised article on Scripture in the Nazarene *Manual* in fact centered the church's faith in Scripture as a reliable guide and trustworthy witness to salvation. What was "inerrant" was the Bible's pathway toward salvation.[45]

Wiley was nine years into researching and writing his systematic theology at this juncture. Wiley wrote articles to blunt fundamentalism's influence, but his most sustained argument was made when the first volume of *Christian Theology* appeared in 1940. In a discussion of authority in theological matters, Wiley discussed "three unworthy Monarchs" that had "scepters falsely thrust into their hands" at different points in church history. These false authorities included tradition and reason, but he identified the third as the Bible itself. There was a danger, he noted, when appeals to the Bible lapsed into a "bibliolatry" that elevated the written word of Scripture to a place of supremacy over the Living Word of Christ. Wiley was writing explicitly about the second period in Protestant theology, often dubbed "the Scholastic period," which followed the Reformation and was marked by theological rigidity, the drawing of clear lines between contending Lutheran and Reformed theologies, and denunciations of those outside the bounds of one's own "orthodoxy." In contrast, Wiley emphasized the subordination of the written word to the Personal Word, which is Christ, noting that "the original source of the Christian knowledge of God must ever be, the Lord Jesus Christ." As historian Paul Bassett notes, Wiley's discerning readers understood that the Protestant Scholasticism's era, and the "false Monarch" of bibliolatry that characterized it, paralleled the current fundamentalist era. The Nazarene church was positioned theologically to participate in the broader evangelical renaissance that would follow World War II.[46]

THE BOUNDARIES

For many Nazarenes, the pull was toward fundamentalism. Others, however, found the church's theological commitments already too narrow. As more and more Nazarene scholars attended master's and doctoral programs in leading universities, often Methodist, they widened Nazarenes' understanding of faith. The nuances between Hills and Wiley on free will and free grace went unnoticed as Nazarene scholars embraced personalism. As long as certain landmarks remained, Nazarene leaders and laity could tolerate a degree of diversity. Theologians' testimonies to experiences of saving and sanctifying grace, and their ability to preach evangelistically in revivals and camp meetings, went a long way to assure the church that its schools were safe. If scholars could defend their beliefs in nonconfrontational ways and affirm second blessing holiness, they stood a good chance of a hearing, whatever their opinions on other theological issues.

When Charles H. Wiman applied for missionary service in 1935, before finalizing his appointment, the Foreign Missions department faced concerns over articles that he had published while working in the Sunday School department. Wiman had served for two years as a missionary to Japan in the early 1920s. In the 1930s he had taken an editing position at Nazarene headquarters, working under E. P. Ellyson. One article that Wiman reprinted in 1934 in the *Bible School Journal,* published for Nazarene Sunday School teachers, suggested that children did not need to come to a conversion experience to be saved—they could simply grow up as Christians. Wiman said to an investigating committee in May 1935 that he now regretted having reprinted the article. Yet, when questioned about it, Wiman did not regret another article, "Sunday School and Evangelism," that he himself had written in 1931. In this article Wiman said that Sunday Schools prepared the way for revivals, and that revivals would not "stem the tide" of sin unless followed up by religious training (or what a later generation would call discipleship). "The evangelist who ridicules religious education," Wiman affirmed to the committee, "is murdering his strongest ally. The teacher who would belittle evangelism is tying the hands of his most effective harvester." In 1935 Wiman had written another article on "Forgiveness," in which he said that a sanctified person may come to God for forgiveness. Did he believe a sanctified person sinned? Wiman replied that it depended on one's definition of sin. In the way in which Nazarenes defined sin, no, he told the committee, a sanctified person does not voluntarily transgress known laws. But even sanctified persons needed forgiveness from God for the unintentional ways they fell short of being like Christ. Wiman's responses satisfied the committee, which found him "very worthy and acceptable," and recommended that he be appointed a missionary. Wiman soon found himself with his wife, Maud, on their way to Peru, where he became district superintendent and served until 1943.[47]

Suspicions about the orthodoxy of R. E. Gilmore, a star theologian, educator, and evangelist in the church, who had taken the leadership of Northwest Nazarene College in 1932, turned out otherwise. Gilmore, born in Arkansas, had graduated from Arkansas Holiness College and had enrolled at Peniel College before transferring to Oklahoma University, where he finished a bachelor's degree and a master of arts in philosophy. He began a doctoral program at the University of Chicago, known for its modernism, and by 1929 had finished the coursework. All the while, Nazarene leaders knew him as a forceful revivalist. After Gilmore (at age thirty) became president of Northwest Nazarene College, gradually students and others sensed that some liberal drift underlay his teachings, especially as related to entire sanctification. Indeed, Gilmore himself came to realize within his tenure at NNC that he could no longer hold to this essential tenet of the church. At commencement at NNC in 1935 General Superintendent Chapman asked Gilmore about his understanding of the church's distinguishing doctrine. Upon hearing Gilmore's doubts, Chapman advised him to resign. Though Gilmore had many detractors among the NNC constituency, others appreciated his sincerity and desired him to remain as head of the school. Chapman himself changed his mind about the necessity of Gilmore's departure. But Gilmore felt it was not right for him to remain. As he himself put it, he could not affirm his vows to the church while retaining his own private interpretation of this doctrine. He left, he wrote R. T. Williams, with no bitterness. The Church of the Nazarene had provided him opportunities to preach in its largest churches. But because of his admittedly "liberal" views, he had increasingly realized that "temperamentally and otherwise I do not fit."[48] He was sad that he had disappointed friends. Leaving NNC, Gilmore resumed his doctoral studies, this time at Boston University, and pastored a Congregationalist church in Massachusetts. Gilmore wrote his successor at NNC, R. V. DeLong, who had just finished his own doctorate at the same school, "This is like heaven to me."[49] Though DeLong advised Gilmore that neither theologian Albert C. Knudson nor philosopher Edgar Brightman had "the message for this age," Gilmore heartily embraced their personalism. Indeed Gilmore later expounded personalism "with all the evangelistic fervor of one who had come after stormy seas into a safe harbor and who longed to bring others to the same anchorage." Gilmore joined the Methodist Church. From 1953 to 1968 he taught theology at Wesley Theological Seminary in Washington, D.C. There students and faculty alike considered him a "traditionalist."[50]

While there might have been disagreements over the issues of prevenient grace among the church's leading theologians, and misunderstandings about where the church stood on issues such as premillennialism, the verbal inerrancy of the Bible, and baptism, no one could mistake what the church taught and preached about entire sanctification. More than any other doctrine, this doctrine set the boundaries for what was and who were Nazarene.

THIRTEEN

Shaping the Nazarene Mind: Higher Education

The period between the wars witnessed growth, stability, and struggle among Nazarene schools and colleges. The colleges met the needs of the inward-looking church. A primary aim was to have a ministry deeply committed to the premises of second blessing holiness. Another aim was to provide a place for the conversion, nurture, and growth of Nazarene young people. For parents, the schools were havens safe from the immoralities of society. A warm, revival spirit pervaded the campuses. Teachers held personal concerns for the students and sacrificed much for the sake of the church. At the same time, the church's colleges aspired to higher levels and committed themselves to a liberal arts core. Teachers shared the knowledge they had learned in secular universities and in other denominations' colleges. They brought current knowledge and a passion for inquiry that, as long as the teachers professed entire sanctification and integrated their faith with their learning, exhibited, for such a young denomination, remarkable breadth.[1]

From very early days the schools sought to win the approval of society. They aimed to maintain standards that would befit the colleges of the day. The schools advertised on the basis of the university degrees and the number of M.A. holders (a doctoral degree was scarce) among their faculty members. The qualifications imposed by secular standards upon education were just, wrote J. B. Chapman in 1920, two years after he had left the presidency of Peniel College to enter full-time evangelism. A faculty made up of novices was insufficient. The schools needed adequate laboratories and libraries. "A smattering of objectors to the 'scientific mind' among the promoters of a school insures its final failure." Chapman admonished that bachelor's degrees granted by Nazarene schools must be truly earned, or else there was a violation of educational ethics.[2]

LIBERAL ARTS COLLEGES

Bethany-Peniel College

Bethany-Peniel College was the product of six schools that by 1940 had merged to become one. The oldest of these, the school that began in Greenville, Texas, in 1899, and which was known as Texas Holiness University until 1914, represented Holiness people affiliated with the Texas Holiness Association. The school's presidents included A. M. Hills, the founder, who remained until 1906. E. P. Ellyson served as president from 1906 to 1911, during the time of the college church's affiliation with the Church of the Nazarene in 1908, and through his tenure as general superintendent. R. T. Williams was president from 1911 to 1913, and J. B. Chapman from 1913 to 1918. Chapman was the one who determined that the "university" ascription far outshone the school's attainments, and under him, the name was changed to Peniel College. It merged in 1920 with Oklahoma Holiness College and moved to Bethany.

The Holiness Church of Christ ran two schools. One was the Bible Training School that began in Waco, Texas, in 1899, before moving to Buffalo Gap, Texas, the following year. The other was the Bible Training School that began at Pilot Point, Texas, in 1905. In 1910, these two schools merged and moved to Hamlin, Texas, where it was known as Central Nazarene University. This school, in turn, merged in 1929 with the school at Bethany.

Arkansas Holiness College began in Old Cove, Arkansas, in 1900, and moved to Vilonia, Arkansas, in 1906. Its early leaders were Free Methodists, who complained that Nazarenes had hijacked the school. It merged with the school at Bethany in 1931.[3]

The school in Hutchinson, Kansas, began in 1905 and was known as Kansas Holiness College. It became Nazarene in 1911 and was renamed Bresee College. Its last two presidents were S. T. Ludwig, who served from 1927 to 1936, and Harold Reed, who served from 1936 until the merger with Bethany-Peniel in 1940.

Beulah Heights College began in Oklahoma City in 1906 with Mattie Mallory as head and moved to Bethany, Oklahoma, in 1909. From then until the Peniel College merger it was known as Oklahoma Holiness College. Lela McConnell, a historian, compared the town of Bethany's founding to that of the Puritans in New England. There were few differences in the motives and purposes, McConnell said. In both cases, the goal was a pure and holy community of the elect or, in the case of Bethany, the entirely sanctified. Among the laws that could be legislated and enforced in Bethany were strict "blue laws" that kept shops from opening on Sunday. But whereas the New Englanders could legislate against wearing gold, silver, or silk laces, Bethany's founders could only preach against such things and refer people to the Nazarene *Manual*. After the 1920 merger and amid other accessions the school was known for thirty-five years as Bethany-Peniel College. A. K. Bracken served as president from 1920 to 1928 and from 1930 to 1942, S. S. White served from 1928 to 1930, S. T. Ludwig served from 1942 to 1944, and O. J. Finch from 1944 to 1947. The school changed its name to Bethany Nazarene College in 1955 and to Southern Nazarene University in 1985.[4]

Bethany—Bresee Hall

Eastern Nazarene College

Eastern Nazarene College was the name chosen in 1918 by patrons of Pentecostal Collegiate Institute, still located in North Scituate, Rhode Island. The name reflected the school's aspirations. J. E. L. Moore served as president of the school from 1917 to 1919, during the transition period. Moore was a Southerner. He previously had served as president of Central Nazarene University, in Hamlin, Texas. General Superintendent Goodwin was behind Moore's coming to ENC, as the general superintendents continued the process of forging a national church by appointing people such as Moore from one part of the church to another. Moore (and later administrators) emphasized the academic rather than industrial departments of the school. Moore sold the school's broom factory. The enrollment declined during the Great War, partly because of the influenza epidemic. The school was deeply in debt. Goodwin himself raised $50,000 for the school in a one-month campaign in 1918. In 1919 ENC moved to the Wollaston area of Quincy, Massachusetts.[5]

The move to Wollaston signaled the desire of the eastern Nazarenes to move in the direction of liberal arts education. When Moore left ENC in 1919 to become president of Olivet, Goodwin suggested and the Board of Trustees approved the election of Fred J. Shields, then serving as registrar at Northwest Nazarene College, as president. Goodwin traveled with Shields on the move East and stopped at Taylor University in Indiana to persuade Bertha Munro (1887-1983) to return to the school. Munro had taught at PCI from 1910 to 1916 and had left because of her feeling that the constituents were not fully committed to the idea of building a strongly academic school that could justly call itself a college. One of the reasons for the transfer of the school from Rhode Island to Quincy was to assert the desire of the school to develop as an academic institution. The proximity of Quincy to Boston allowed professors to more easily pursue higher academic degrees. Electric cars (later, a subway system) ran between Quincy and Boston. The location provided a suburban setting and access to libraries, art, music, and culture.[6]

When the school opened in Wollaston, the 1919 catalog asserted that its mission was to "educate young men and women mentally and spiritually, in order that they shall be capable of intelligently spreading Scriptural Holiness, as ministers, Christian workers; also as business and professional men, and as cultured men and women of God in any of the ordinary walks of life." The school was to be more than a place for the training of pastors, and leaders saw no contradiction between pursing holiness and the highest standards of education.[7]

Bertha Munro

Bertha Munro strengthened the commitment of not only ENC but the Church of the Nazarene as a whole to liberal arts education. She and her family, who had been Baptists, joined the Association of Pentecostal Churches congregation in Cliftondale, Massachusetts, in 1898. She earned a bachelor's degree at Boston University in 1907 and a master of arts in English literature at Radcliffe College in 1916. Her area of expertise was the Puritan writers John Milton and John Bunyan. In the 1920s she pursued doctoral work at Harvard University, studying literature with Irving Babbitt. Under her influence, many ministerial students studied English literature and later interlaced their sermons with literary allusions.[8]

Because ENC still was not chartered to offer bachelor's degrees, its first degrees were granted, because of Shields's contacts there, through Northwest Nazarene College. Among ENC's first graduates, Alice Spangenberg successfully went through an M.A. program in English at Boston University, and this paved the way for others.[9]

Bertha Munro and Floyd Nease, who served as president of ENC from 1923 until his sudden death in 1930, were instrumental in working through the processes of securing, in 1930, the charter that allowed ENC to grant bachelor's degrees in its own right. The school then worked toward accreditation under the New England Association of Colleges and Secondary Schools, one of the most demanding of such bodies in the country. In the meantime, ENC professors pursued advanced degrees. In various fields, many studied at Boston University. Adding to ENC's academic depth, James H. Shrader, who had earned a Ph.D. in chemistry at Johns Hopkins University, joined the faculty in 1939. Shrader edited the *Journal of Milk Technology* and published *Food Control: Its Public Health Aspect*. In 1943 ENC earned accreditation.[10]

Meanwhile, ENC had experienced significant financial crises. In late 1932 and again in 1934 general superintendents worked with the region's district superintendents and school leaders to prevent bank foreclosure. They sought money for the school through contributions from local congregations. Faculty and their families received food rations in the school's dining hall as partial payment of their salaries. Cash payments were based solely on family needs. Even when the school had regained financial stability, ENC professors earned less than Nazarene college faculty members living in less affluent parts of the country.[11]

Pasadena College

The school that Phineas Bresee had established in Los Angeles moved to its new site in Pasadena in 1910 and was renamed Nazarene University. H. Orton Wiley served as dean of the College of Liberal Arts, W. W. Danner as dean of Pacific Bible College, and Cora Snider (later a missionary to Japan) as principal of the high school level academy. Enrollment rose dramatically, from 113 in 1910-11 to 429 in the 1914-15 school year. In 1911 E. P. Ellyson turned down another term as general superintendent and came as president, with his wife, M. Emily Ellyson, as dean of the Bible college. Ellyson served just two years. Wiley succeeded him, serving, in this first of three terms, from 1913 to 1916. A. J. Ramsay came as dean of the Bible college in 1913. Wiley resigned amid many difficulties to become president of Northwest Nazarene College and took some students with him. Between the two assignments, Wiley studied at the Pacific School of Religion.[12]

General Superintendent E. F. Walker stepped in as president for a year, 1917-18, followed by A. O. Hendricks from 1918 to 1923. Hendricks had pastored the Pasadena First Church from 1913 to 1918 and pastored Los Angeles First Church from 1918 to 1920. In 1918, the school was reincorporated in order to avoid bankruptcy and was renamed Pasadena University. By 1922, the school had achieved solvency, but only after Hendricks had refused any salary as president for more than four years, borrowed money personally to keep the school open, and secured $10,000 and a note for $60,000 more from his brother N. O. Hendricks in Canada to save the school. C. B. Widmeyer, dean of the Bible college, became president in 1923 and served three years. Under Widmeyer, the name of the school was changed once more, in 1924, to Pasadena College.[13]

In 1926, H. Orton Wiley, after finishing, to the day, his ten-year contract with NNC, returned to the presidency of Pasadena. He resigned in 1929, however, after being elected editor of the *Herald of Holiness*. Orval J. Nease, who had been Wiley's associate, became president next, serving from 1929 to 1933. Nease had graduated from Pasadena in 1916, had earned an M.A. at Boston University, and had done further graduate studies at Ohio State University. When Nease returned to a pastorate in 1933, Wiley again assumed the presidency, which he retained until his retirement in 1949.

By 1933 Pasadena had mounted a debt of $100,000. Under a "Let's Do Something" campaign led by A. E. Sanner, the Southern California district superintendent, the debt was liquidated in 1943. In the same year, Pasadena won accreditation. In 1944 Pasadena College, which had already been offering bachelor of theology and master of arts in religion degrees, launched a Graduate School of Religion. This may have been an attempt to forestall or even derail the beginnings of Nazarene Theological Seminary, a brainchild of J. B. Chapman. Olive Winchester, whom Wiley persuaded to come from Nampa to Pasadena in 1935, served as dean of the School of Religion until her death in 1947 and was followed by Orval J. Nease, who served until his reelection as general superintendent in 1948.[14]

Northwest Nazarene College

Northwest Nazarene College

Northwest Nazarene College during the years between the wars was strengthened by the same team, the leadership of H. Orton Wiley from 1916 to 1926, and Olive Winchester, who served as vice president from 1922 to 1935 and academic dean from 1923 to 1935. J. G. Morrison served as president for a year, 1926-27. Russell V. DeLong served two terms as president, from 1927 to 1932 and from 1935 to 1942. R. E. Gilmore was president from 1932 to 1935. Enrollment rose at NNC, nearly doubling from its

1927-28 enrollment of 105 to 209 in 1931-32, but then dipping to 169 the following year. Enrollment rose, however, to 292 by 1938.[15]

Though located in the prairies, NNC was known as a missionary-sending school. The school attracted students from various countries, maintained an enthusiastic student missionary band, and sent graduates around the world. A Scandinavian Society functioned in the early 1930s (long before the Church of the Nazarene began work in a Scandinavian country). Leslie Fitzlan, son of long-serving missionary to India, A. D. Fitzlan, led the Foreign Missions Band in 1935-36. During that year each Tuesday was Missionary Day, when chapels were devoted to missions and the noon hour was spent in prayer and fasting. Students raised $150 to support three students at the Guatemala Bible School for one year, and another $50 toward the purchase of a printing press there. NNC's nearby Nazarene Missionary Sanitarium and Institute, which included a School of Nursing, trained prospective missionary nurses and cared for furloughing missionaries.[16]

During Gilmore's days, the constituency feared the rise of modernism at NNC, coming no less than from the president himself. A critical district superintendents' report in March 1935 lamented the lack of emphasis on the cardinal doctrines of the Church of the Nazarene in chapel. There was no freedom of the Spirit. They were concerned that Gilmore had introduced a program of athletics that was out of harmony with 1923 and subsequent General Assembly statements. When DeLong returned to the presidency, J. G. Morrison admonished him: "Please, please, please don't compromise with that liberal, modernistic spirit that has crept in there since you left."[17]

Nevertheless, under DeLong, NNC became a bit less conservative than other schools on some issues. While still frowned upon by many Holiness people, female students and faculty alike wore their hair in the latest "bobbed" style. While other Nazarene colleges were prohibiting it, NNC allowed athletics and sports competition. "Ideals of physical fitness must have their place," President DeLong said in 1930.[18] Intercollegiate sports began in 1934 with a basketball team. Four of the five on the squad were ministerial students, all known for their high ideals and loyalty to the church and to the school. "All voiced their opinion that athletics must never lessen their devotion to God," remarked one teacher who knew of the controversy on this issue in other quarters of the church. But some constituents in the NNC educational region opposed intercollegiate sports. From 1940 to 1964 the Nazarene *Manual*'s appendix declared that intercollegiate sports was out of keeping with Nazarene standards. The *Manual* only allowed intramural athletics. But NNC and other colleges contravened this statement.[19]

DeLong's decisions along such lines, and his forceful leadership style, were controversial. The son of a New England Nazarene pastor and a graduate of Eastern Nazarene College, DeLong finished his master of arts in philosophy of religion at Boston University at age twenty-five and began teaching the same year, 1926, at NNC. When J. G. Morrison left NNC after serving only a year as president, the Board of Trustees elected the youthful DeLong to succeed him. After serving as president for five years, DeLong desired to finish his doctoral degree. In 1935 DeLong finished his Ph.D. at Boston University, where he studied under the noted Methodist philosopher Edgar S. Brightman. When Gilmore left, NNC trustees brought DeLong back as president. DeLong was noted for his preaching, characterized by fierce yet reasoned attacks upon modernism. John Riley characterized him as an "unusual blend of dynamic, effective revivalist and scholarly, argumentative philosopher."[20] He proved that education, even under liberal Methodists, need not weaken faith. His rhetoric reached common Nazarenes. He was in demand as a revival and camp meeting speaker and led city-wide evangelistic campaigns. DeLong became friends with William Borah, the long-serving Republican senator from Idaho, and Idaho state Republicans unsuccessfully urged DeLong to run for the United States Senate.[21]

Under DeLong, NNC became the first Nazarene college to gain accreditation. The process began in 1930 with accreditation by the Northwest Association of Schools and Colleges as a two-year junior college, and ended with full accreditation as a four-year college on April 7, 1937.[22]

Periodically, all Nazarene schools experienced great revivals. In NNC, one came in late 1931. After an evangelistic service, students began an all-night prayer meeting. As they prayed fervently for fellow students they deemed unsaved, many of whom had gone to their dormitory rooms for the night, small groups of students were dispatched to rouse them and bring them back in. Those who were saved testified to the experience immediately. Some knelt to be sanctified. At another session in the dining hall, students sang choruses led by a music professor, raised their hands in praise, and shouted hallelujah. They forgot about their food. Any who were unsaved either knelt right there and then in the dining hall or exited. Student waitresses, instead of serving food, "went around the room shouting or crying." A senior sought sanctification over his plate and, receiving the blessing, stood on his chair, hands up, and issued a loud acclamation of victory. Another student strode around the dining hall with a chair over his shoulder, shouting at the top of his voice. Some walked around waving plates and spoons. Yet, for all of this, said a student reporter, there was no "fanaticism." One hundred four students were saved or sanctified in this revival. "Hardened sinners cried out for mercy," said one eyewitness, "back-sliders were brought back into the fold, and believers completed their consecration with victory."[23]

In 1932 the Depression had a deep impact on NNC, as on other Nazarene colleges. Most of the NNC faculty moved into the student dormitories and received board and room from the school instead of their cash pay. All made do without sugar, meat, shortening, and eggs. Sagebrush was their only fuel. Faculty members remaining off campus received five dollars a month. During second semester 1932-33 the classes operated on a six-day week in order to finish a month earlier. Matters improved during the following school year. The faculty received fifty percent of their allotted salary. By the 1934-35 school year, the faculty had moved out of the dormitories.[24]

NNC had strong connections with Eastern Nazarene College. Many of its professors, including Olive Winchester and Russell DeLong, had either taught there or had graduated from ENC. After DeLong returned to NNC for his second term, he brought R. Wayne Gardner, the president of ENC from 1930 to 1936, as his vice-president, registrar, and professor of mathematics. E. E. Angell, longtime stalwart of ENC, went to NNC as professor of theology and biblical literature in 1939.[25]

Olivet College

In October 1912 the Chicago District Assembly, with Phineas Bresee presiding, accepted, adopted, and endorsed Illinois Holiness University as a Nazarene institution. The school had been offered as a gift to the Church of the Nazarene by its sixteen trustees, all of whom were Nazarene. Leadership of the school, however, remained a problem. From 1912 to 1926 seven persons (including E. F. Walker from 1914 to 1915 and E. P. Ellyson from 1915 to 1917) served as presidents of the school.

Longer-serving presidents brought needed stability. T. W. Willingham, who had been pastor of the nearby church in Danville, Illinois, served as president from 1926 to 1938 and A. L. Parrott from 1938 to 1945. In 1939 a fire destroyed the administration building, which included classrooms and the library. Of the $100,000 damage, insurance covered only $25,000. The board faced the decision of whether to rebuild or to relocate the school and decided to sell the property at Olivet, Illinois, and move to Bourbonnais, Illinois. The board purchased a Roman Catholic college, consisting of forty acres and five buildings, for $200,000, with the $25,000 from the insurance as the down payment. It kept the Olivet name, becoming Olivet Nazarene College. Within five years, under Parrott's leadership, the debt was liquidated.[26]

Trevecca College

Trevecca College, the school in Nashville begun under J. O. McClurkan, became the regional college of the Church of the Nazarene in the southeastern part of the United States. Another school begun in Donaldsonville, Georgia, by T. J. Shingler, attempted to make itself Nazarene. Donaldsonville was the site of a Holiness Church of Christ congregation begun by Leona Shingler in 1902. In 1912 T. J. Shingler, a wealthy landowner and evangelist, built a primary school, high school, and Bible school on forty acres of property that he set aside for this purpose. In 1917 he persuaded Edgar P. Ellyson to become president of the fledgling school and turned over the property to the Georgia District of the Church of the Nazarene. The district changed the name of the school to Southeastern Nazarene College. But just a few months later, in October 1917, Trevecca officially came under the auspices of the Church of the Nazarene. Almost immediately, consolidation talks began. The school in Donaldsonville closed in December 1918, and Ellyson moved to Nashville to become dean of its Christian Workers' School.[27]

For much of the period between the wars, Trevecca was led by C. E. Hardy. Trained as a medical doctor, Hardy led the school in three terms, 1915 to 1919, 1921 to 1925, and 1928 to 1936. From 1926 to 1928 Hardy pastored Los Angeles First Church of the Nazarene. Hardy was a typical country doctor, not so suited to the city.

Though the Depression affected each of the Nazarene colleges, the school most seriously affected was Trevecca. When the Depression began, the school was conducting classes on its campus at Gallatin Road in Nashville, where McClurkan had founded the school. As finances tightened, the school could not afford to pay the faculty. While many accepted the idea of routinely turning over their paychecks to the school, some faculty members objected and took the school to court. In 1931 these debts and others forced the school into receivership. Some leaders, including the local District Superintendent S. W. Strickland, and H. H. Wise, the pastor of Nashville First Church, opposed the idea of relocating. But Hardy saw no other way. The Gallatin Road property, including all furnishings and equipment, and even the library books, was sold at bank auction for $25,000.

Hardy decided to move to a campus at Whites Creek owned by Northern Baptists. The Baptists had established the school at Whites Creek for African-Americans. Hardy, with only $6,000 cash, believed that he would be able to secure enough bonds to purchase the Whites Creek property, which was suitable, Hardy felt, for an income-generating dairy farm. The cows arrived. In September 1932 Trevecca's Board of Trustees reincorporated the school under the Southeastern Educational Board. In the midst of such pressures, Trevecca tightened its theological boundaries. In 1932, Hardy pushed through a stipulation that the school would hire only premillennialists. Finances still prevented the faculty from being paid. Professors lived in student dormitories and ate meals with students. Those who had money purchased food for others. Some students trapped birds to eat. The college community steadily consumed biscuits until one sponsor donated a "car load" of pork and beans. It lasted for a few weeks. Yet, amid all this, the college raised $48.61 to send to the Birchards, Nazarene missionaries in Guatemala, and took an offering to support two orphans in India.

But after two years at Whites Creek, the school still had not been able to pay the Baptists, and so had not received the title to the property and was forced to vacate. Trevecca was not only penniless but homeless. Nashville First Church took the orphaned school in for a year, 1934-35, during which time the school managed to purchase twelve acres of property on Murfreesboro Road. Doing so, the school obtained a new charter under the name Trevecca Nazarene College.

Hardy sought relief from the presidency. For a year, he allowed A. B. Mackey, a layperson with a master's degree in education from George Peabody College, to be acting president. Mackey assumed full leadership of the school in 1937 and led Trevecca until 1963.[28]

Schools Outside of the United States

Outside of the United States, the Church of the Nazarene established Bible schools and colleges to prepare ministers. Unlike within the United States, these schools did not rapidly move toward the liberal arts or the education of young people; they remained focused on preparing pastors. Missionaries were insufficient for the evangelization of the countries in which the Church of the Nazarene was working, and the church depended on local ministers to reach their own people, so ministerial education was the priority. Bible schools, said C. Warren Jones in 1940, gave the Church of the Nazarene "a native ministry that will reach the needy millions with the gospel," and should become, more and more, a factor in evangelism. With more members, the districts could more quickly become self-supporting, was the logic. However, with limited course offerings and small student bodies, the schools remained dependent on missions funding. By 1940 the Church of the Nazarene was supporting twelve Bible schools. In some places, including Swaziland, India, and China, the church also maintained other schools ranging from elementary to high school levels, and nurses' training schools.[29]

Both missionaries and national leaders perceived the educational system as vital to church development. In India, Nazarenes maintained a boys' boarding school with British government standards in the grade school and also taught trades such as carpentry and weaving. In one year nine Hindu boys attending the school became Christians. In the minds of the Nazarene workers this fact justified the school as an "agency for evangelism."[30] Meanwhile, all recognized that the continued development of the church depended upon "qualified, indoctrinated, [and] spiritual Indian leaders," educated in the church's own Bible Training School. The boarding school was a step in the development of Christian leaders.[31]

Women missionaries often spearheaded education, including ministerial training, on mission fields. Sarah Cox, for instance, was the first director of the Nazarene Bible School in Guatemala, and in Mozambique generations of ministers were educated under long-serving missionary Mary Cooper.[32]

Revivals like the one at the Bible Training School in Daming, China, affirmed both the spiritual character of the educational work and the capabilities of the students. The school was led by Francis C. Sutherland, a Canadian educated at Montreal Theological College (M.A. and licentiate in sacred theology). He had worked with the Student Volunteer Movement before venturing as a Nazarene missionary to China in 1920. The school began in 1923 with a two-year course. Thirty students of varying educational backgrounds enrolled. Students paid their own way. Nevertheless, there were always more applicants for admission than the school was able to care for.[33]

When revival came upon the mission compound in 1926, Sutherland dismissed the school sessions and Chinese teachers and students scattered to their hometowns. In this way the revival spread throughout the Nazarene field. This was a very different student activity than what had transpired some time earlier, when the same Bible school students had taken to the streets of Daming making speeches against foreigners.[34]

The Chinese government prevented the school from continuing for several years. During the interim years missionaries sent the most promising pastors elsewhere, such as to the National Holiness Association school in Tianjin, for their education. After several years away, Sutherland returned in 1936 to resume charge of the school. In the political turmoil, the missionaries focused on the education of leaders. They knew their own days in China were short. The structured and regimented life of the students, along with the tuition they paid (which made the school self-supporting) neither dampened the spiritual ardor of the students nor hindered numbers from applying. Many were turned away for lack of space on the compound. One hundred thirty were enrolled in the late 1930s. Among the teachers was Hsu Kwei-pin, who was made vice-president in 1939. He and other teachers emphasized evangelism. The school regularly sent bands of students into the field to evangelize. Zealous Chinese students such as Chang Chin and missionaries such as John Pattee were involved in village evangelism. Pattee trained a succession of students at the Bible school in preaching and soul winning by traveling with them from town to town. The evangelistic teams attracted crowds of five hundred or six hundred at village fairs and market days. One group of students sent into Daming County in 1939, for instance, included sixty-eight workers who visited 133 villages and preached to over twenty-two thousand people. A class of forty graduated in 1940, and another smaller one in 1941. These graduates carried the church forward over the next decades of persecution and trial.[35]

CONCLUSION

Wherever in the world it happened, whether in Nampa or Daming, the union of evangelism and education delighted Nazarenes. Revivals erupting on campuses proved that education did not lessen spiritual fervor. Whether as evangelists, teachers, or chemists, graduates returned to local churches with spiritual fire and loyalty to the Church of the Nazarene.

FOURTEEN

Adapting to a World in Crisis

While many had hoped that the First World War would be a war that would end all wars, the world faced many social and moral changes, financial crisis, militarism, and totalitarianism. Nazarenes remained grounded in biblical foundations as had been laid for them by the nineteenth-century Holiness Movement and built sturdy shelters to protect them and their children from stormy conditions. At the same time, Nazarenes reached out to others, far and near. They found many of their neighbors equally unsure of the social conditions and looking for eternal truths, and Nazarenes took their message of holiness to far areas of the world.

FINANCIAL PRESSURES

The church had already faced significant financial problems before the Depression. The Depression quickened the necessity of placing the financial resources of the church on a wider basis. The Depression hit churches, pastors, missions, and missionaries hard and made life difficult for evangelists and retired ministers, who, unlike local pastors or missionaries, had no base of support to which to turn.[1]

Missionaries coped with repeated cuts in salaries and allocations. The church began paying missionaries in silver rather than gold currency, which in China meant a fifty percent reduction in their allotment. In South Africa, missionary William Esselstyn leased a farm so that Bible school students could grow their own food. Missionaries on the field who were due furloughs had to remain on the field because the church lacked the funds to return them home. The church likewise was unable to send back missionaries who were on furlough. Several were forced into early retirement.[2]

Yet a few Nazarenes with information about the headquarters' leaders wondered why the church's general leaders were collecting their full salaries while the church was retrenching in other areas. Facing the criticism, in January 1932 seven key leaders issued a statement declaring that they would double their tithes and make frequent offerings until the financial crisis was over.³

To forestall further retrenchment, the general superintendents, in 1932, recruited a "reserve army" of ten thousand Nazarenes willing to give one dollar whenever the generals called for it, promising not to issue such a call more than five times per year. In some cases, local districts raised money for the support of certain missionaries, enabling them to either stay on or return to their fields. As they had the previous year, the general superintendents called for a month of "self-denial" in November 1932.⁴

In the winter of 1933, just after the inauguration of Franklin Roosevelt as president of the United States, General Superintendent Williams, then preaching in a revival in Los Angeles First Church, professed to being awakened one night and impressed to order the general treasurer of the church to immediately withdraw in cash all the money that the church, including the publishing house, had in its bank in Kansas City. M. Lunn obeyed. Five minutes after he made a $10,000 withdrawal, Roosevelt declared a "bank holiday" of undetermined length. The $10,000 enabled the church to carry on the foreign missions work and other programs.⁵

During the Depression, Foreign Missions Secretary J. G. Morrison and the general superintendents issued constant calls for money for the church's missions program. The church took special Easter Offerings. The Easter Recovery Offering in 1934 raised $40,000 to keep missionaries on the field. Members gave to a Special Thanksgiving Offering that same November. Through sacrificial giving, and the restriction of appropriations, the church managed to continue its missions. Morrison's call for churches abroad to take responsibility for their own pastors also took a positive effect.⁶

Rather than focusing further on financial restraints, at the January 1935 meeting of the district superintendents eighty-one-year-old H. F. Reynolds, now general superintendent emeritus, issued an impassioned plea for worldwide revival. As a result, the church launched its first Crusade for Souls campaign and called upon the church to "give herself unstintingly to a special effort to promote an intensive revival in an endeavor to reach the vast unchurched masses."⁷ The 1935 Easter Offering was taken for that purpose. Local churches held prayer days, rallies, and evangelistic campaigns, and reports of revival from around the world soon arrived.⁸

Another factor allowing the church to keep its missions program afloat during these years was the increased membership base. Church membership rose from 88,762 in 1930, the beginning of the Depression, to 180,014 by 1940. By 1936 giving had begun to rebound, and the trend continued. General Budget receipts raised by the missionary society rose from $253,927 in 1936-37 to $322,673 in 1939-40.[9]

Yet the Nazarene Mutual Benefit Association, which had been set up in 1919 as an insurance program, was nearly bankrupt in 1938. The history of this association went back to a plan initiated by the Michigan District in the 1910s. The 1919 General Assembly arranged for the transfer of Michigan's Mutual Aid Societies to the general church to be put under the direction of General Secretary E. J. Fleming. At the same time, the church established a Board of Ministerial Relief and, over it, a General Board of Mutual Benefit. Not all Nazarenes believed in such measures, and thought that the pastors should rely by faith upon God rather than upon financial planning. In response, F. M. Messenger, who served as president of the General Board of Mutual Benefit, asked, "Which is better, to stand by with folded hands and say to the widows and orphans, 'Be ye warmed and filled,' while with dry eyes and sanctimonious looks behold their unalleviated distress, or make our church responsible for some kind of corporate action whereby these distresses may be relieved?"[10] The idea of the Mutual Benefit Board was to rely on contributions. Each active minister and deaconess was to contribute one dollar per year for the plan, and each church was to contribute ten cents per member. But even this modest scheme never took hold. By 1922 there were many more requests for funds than were available.[11]

The 1923 General Assembly that produced one General Board to take the place of the several that had been functioning did not leave clear directions for the development of ministerial aid, and the next meeting of the General Board only set up a study committee. A 1928 plan to enlist at least five hundred in a Ministers' Contributory Reserve Pension Plan never got underway before the Depression hit.

Nonetheless, the Mutual Benefit Association was recognized and approved under the state laws of Arkansas and Nevada as well as Missouri and, by the time of the Depression, enrolled five thousand persons, most of them pastors. Between 1931 and 1932 the association cut its meager benefits to pastors by 80 percent. Nazarene Publishing House agreed to contribute 35 percent of its net income to the fund. By the time of the 1936 General Assembly, the pension plan was being supported solely by gifts, gratuities, grants, and NPH profits. Williams and Chapman moved to dissociate the company from the church and succeeded in doing so in 1939. Fleming, however, felt responsible to the members. He resigned after twenty years as general secretary to stay as the head of the organization, which was reincorporated as the Christian Mutual Benevolent Association. In 1940 the General Assembly initiated the Nazarene Ministers' Benevolent Fund to take the place of its old pension plan. The NMBF was not to be a pension plan, exactly. Rather, the church agreed to raise funds for ministers through the General Budget and other means. Almost immediately local churches began to contribute to this fund, and the plan was underway by the beginning of the war. The social security system, initiated by President Franklin Roosevelt, did not extend to ministers until 1954.[12]

Around the world, veteran Nazarene pastors, lacking pension plans, often toiled on long past retirement age.

THE CHURCH IN A WORLD AT WAR

By virtue of its perfectionism, the Church of the Nazarene initially remained ambivalent toward the First World War. The report of the 1915 General Assembly's State of the Church Committee, chaired by Howard Eckel, placed the Church of the Nazarene on record as "entirely opposed to war, especially as a means of settling international disputes."[13] However, when the United States did finally enter the war, the New York District Assembly assured President Woodrow Wilson of its loyalty, prayers, and support. The assembly wanted to correct reports in the Associated Press that the Church of the Nazarene was a pacifist church. Hoople, pastor of the John Wesley Church in Brooklyn, the largest church on the district with 265 members, joined a YMCA team that accompanied American troops to France. Quickly, the premillennialist faction in the church saw war as inevitable and as a sign of the end of the times before Christ would come.[14]

After the war, Nazarenes, like other Americans, supported a worldwide reduction in armaments and through the 1930s sought the isolation of the United States from world affairs. By the 1940 General Assembly, however, the world was already at war. The Committee on State of the Church and Public Morals supported a statement that "while thus committed to the cause of peace the Church of the Nazarene recognizes that the supreme allegiance of the Christian is due to God and, therefore, it does not endeavor to bind the conscience of its members relative to participation in military service in case of war; although it does believe that the individual Christian as a citizen is bound to give service to his own nation in all ways that are compatible with the Christian faith and the Christian way of life." As a result, Nazarenes anticipated that some of its members would have "conscientious objection to certain forms of military service," and so, in anticipation of a draft system into military service, the church claimed "for conscientious objectors within its membership the same exemptions and considerations regarding military service as is accorded members of recognized noncombatant religious organizations." As a result, the assembly instructed the church's general secretary to establish a registry for members who supplied evidence that they are truly conscientious objectors to war. Within nine months, seven hundred Nazarenes had registered themselves with the general secretary as conscientious objectors.[15]

The same General Assembly passed a protest against anti-Semitism, which was rising not only in Germany but also in the United States, even among fringes of the fundamentalist movement. "Whereas God 'hath made of one blood all nations of men for to dwell on all the face of the earth' it is surely unscriptural and un-Christian to permit racial prejudice to be promoted in the world without a most rigorous protest from the Church." The delegates pledged the Church of the Nazarene to raise "its voice in protest against the wave of Anti-Semitism which is becoming so widespread in this nation" and to "work for the triumph of good will toward all races, religious faiths and minority groups, to do our utmost to preserve our priceless national heritage of religious liberty to all." Delegates called upon Nazarenes to "join with other Christians in exposing the unchristian character of this Anti-Semitic propaganda, its nature and its sources."[16]

Regarding the church, General Superintendents Goodwin, Williams, and Chapman, addressing the 1940 General Assembly, had reason for optimism. The church's membership had doubled in the previous decade. The leaders believed that the success of the church was due to adhering to its fundamental mission to gain souls, rather than raising peripheral issues. "To glorify God and save souls is the passion of the church. To this end must every law be passed and every plan formulated."[17] The general superintendents believed that people were looking for what the Church of the Nazarene offered, "a religion that combines head and heart, reason and emotion,"[18] a "middle-of-the-road" church that was neither too liberal nor too narrow-minded.[19] Yet they perceived the danger of professionalism, of substituting creeds and programs for the presence and power of the Holy Spirit, and of institutionalism and "over-organization." They expressed their own fears of episcopal control. They also feared legalism, which gave "more attention to law than to human beings." Legalism was "law without love," they said, and would "draw us away from grace."[20]

War came sooner to Nazarenes in Great Britain than to Nazarenes in the United States. Hoping to provide a positive witness, the British Isles District bought two mobile canteens to help distribute food after air raids and to help the "homeless, the hungry and the needy." George Sharpe wrote to General Superintendent Williams that "the people are facing the future with hearts of oak and determined to see the end of Nazism." In September 1941 British Isles District Superintendent George Frame expressed sympathy for the war effort and described Nazarenes as remaining "steadfast in their belief in victory." He hoped that the United States would soon join with the British against Germany. He planned, on his trip to the United States for the 1942 General Board meeting, to speak in churches on behalf of the war effort. However, church officials discouraged Frame from attending, not only because of the danger involved in the travel but because, even at this late date, they feared the effect of his British "propaganda." Nonetheless, in general, Holiness people in Great Britain remained inclined toward pacifism. The prevailing opinion before and throughout the war seemed to be that Christians would not engage in military service but, at the same time, would be tolerant of those whose consciences allowed them to enlist.[21]

In the United States, the vast majority of eligible Nazarenes joined the armed forces as combatants. When war came, one young man asked advice from General Superintendent Williams as to whether he could or should fight if called to arms. He had been trying to live as a "Bible Christian" and, as such, to love his enemy, and he felt often that he could with "all ease." If he were in a spot to kill his enemy, he asked Williams, could he do so and remain innocent in heart? Could he retain a clear conscience? He wrestled with this. "When I see what our nation is facing, I think every man should take up arms," the young man wrote, "even to take lives. I don't know whether I have conscientious scruple to justify or not—just what do you think?"[22] (We do not have Williams's response.) When Congress passed the Selective Service Act and National Defense program in 1942, the church appointed E. E. Grosse, pastor of the Washington, D.C., Church of the Nazarene, to represent the denomination on the National Service Board. Though seven hundred registered as conscientious objectors in 1940, when the war actually broke out, only twenty Nazarenes chose this course. General church leaders distanced themselves from responsibility for these.[23] When war began, college presidents wrote letters to local draft boards certifying the standing of students preparing for ministry. Some Nazarene ministerial students nonetheless dropped out of college to enlist. Northwest Nazarene College President R. V. DeLong believed that this was a mistake. They should complete their education so that they could be used, if necessary, in the highest forms of service.[24]

As to how the Church of the Nazarene should respond to the Second World War, J. B. Chapman labeled the church's mission "predominantly evangelistic." "We believe," Chapman affirmed in 1943, "we can make our best contribution to world peace and every other reform and world good by preaching old-time, personal salvation and praying down a heaven-sent revival upon our churches and upon the world." At the same time, he believed that the pacifist stance was mixed up with a "social program or with communistic philosophies." Every Nazarene, Chapman was sure, "will have to do the best he can in the light of those evil days to 'render unto God the things that are God's and unto Caesar the things that are Caesar's.'"25

John L. Peters

By April 1943 an estimated ten thousand American Nazarene men and women were serving in the armed forces, and a year later the number had reached twenty-five thousand. The Church of the Nazarene proudly noted that its Nazarene Young People's Society President, John L. Peters, was among the more than forty Nazarenes who joined the military chaplaincy.26

As the war continued, the government required permits for conventions and even camp meetings and placed restrictions on tires and gasoline. District and general superintendents as well as pastors faced limitations on their travel. Though district assemblies expressed to the government their concern about this, since it was "essential to our morale and existence," as the 1942 San Antonio District expressed it, leaders also encouraged Nazarenes to buy war bonds. Assembly delegates pledged themselves to "give hearty cooperation to the efforts of our government in carrying on for freedom in this critical hour of our history."27

THE CHURCH AND WAR IN ASIA

The expansion of the Japanese Empire by force brought hardships for Nazarenes in this part of the world. As in other countries, Nazarenes in Japan were unaccustomed to taking political stands, but in general, Japanese Nazarenes supported their country's invasion of China and its war effort.28

In July 1937, war between China and Japan began full-scale in northern China. Hiroshi Kitagawa, in an editorial in *The Heavenly Way*, soon affirmed: "We pray for our imperial army, for its perpetual victory. We also pray that Japan may pursue our mission in the Orient. We pray that Asian people may be saved from darkness and anti-religious power, and serve God in peace, receiving the favor of the emperor. Our prayer is 'Thy Kingdom come, thy will be done on earth as it is in heaven.'"29 Within a few months the Japanese army took control of the area that was the center of Nazarene work in China in the southern part of Hebei Province.

In Japan itself, during the late 1930s the government drafted several Nazarene pastors to serve on the front lines. One pastor sent back this testimony: "Even in muddy trenches God's grace is in my heart, and between battles my soul communes with God and I seek after spiritual blessings found in his Word."[30] Other pastors were forced into factories or other work. This prevented much being carried on in local congregations, but in a way the war reminded Japanese Nazarenes of their responsibilities. "We are Christians but at the same time we are Japanese," went an article in *The Heavenly Way* in 1937. "When the peace is achieved, we Japanese Christians intend to lead and guide the Asian peoples and cooperate with them. Any Japanese who does not love Japan cannot be a true Christian."[31] A Nazarene pastor, K. Kaku, began church services among Japanese soldiers while recuperating from his own injuries in Tianjin, China. He returned there to pastor after the army discharged him. The church in Tianjin became fully self-supporting and reached out to Chinese. This encouraged Kitagawa to take an offering for the entire Nazarene church in China. Sunday School children as well as other members contributed sacrificially. Afterward, in 1939, Hiroshi and Shiro Kitagawa traveled to China to personally present the money and to meet the Chinese Nazarenes. Later, upon learning that Japanese bombs had destroyed the Chaocheng Nazarene church in China, Japanese Nazarenes took an offering for its rebuilding. Such acts evidenced both a sense of Japanese responsibility for the repercussions of the war in China and a willingness to assume leadership for mission work in Eastern Asia.[32]

Shiro Kitagawa himself became eager to go as a missionary. The East Asia Christian Mission, a Japanese mission organization, sent him to Soochow, near Shanghai, in mid-1939. Hiroshi Kitagawa explained the missionary call of his brother and the other Japanese Nazarenes: "We are yet weak but we must have a missionary spirit and we felt that we must begin missionary work while we are yet weak. Japanese preachers can help solving problems between Chinese and Japanese officers, besides preaching to them both this wonderful gospel of salvation."[33]

The social and political situation heightened the sense of urgency in preaching the gospel in Japan. Missionary William Eckel himself interpreted Japan's rise to world power apocalyptically: "Yes, out of the very armies of the Kings of the east, the Church of the Nazarene of the Orient is to gather that number to hasten the coming of the Lord!"[34] The Korean work was especially heartening.

Already, Koreans who were staying in Japan were responsible for beginning the Church of the Nazarene in Korea. The country had been under Japanese political control since 1895 and had been formally accessioned by the Japanese in 1910. For that reason, Nazarene work in Korea was under the Japan District. Before entering Korea itself, the Nazarenes already had two established Korean congregations in Japan, one at Osaka and the other at Kyoto. They consisted of Koreans conscripted for work in Japan. Chang Sung Oak pastored the Osaka church. Chang worked for the police as a Korean language translator. He studied at the Oriental Missionary Society's Holiness Bible School in Tokyo. In 1932 Chang returned to Korea with the support of the Japan District. He proceeded to Pyongyang, where Christianity was strong, and planted a Nazarene church there. In 1936 Chang was joined by Cho Jung Hwan, who had pastored the Korean Nazarene Church in Kyoto before city officials forced its closing. Cho began a church in Heijo, in the northern part of Pyongyang. Two hundred attended the Christmas 1937 service there. Like many Korean pastors, Cho conducted daily 5 A.M. prayer meetings. When the General Board divided the Japan District in early 1936, it placed Korea on the Eastern Japan (Kwansai) District, under William Eckel and Nobumi Isayama.[35]

In 1938 Isayama visited Korea. An independent "Gospel" church in Youngchun, Seoul, which had been started by a Japanese pastor, and which had about forty members, approached Isayama about becoming Nazarene. Isayama agreed to take it in. In October 1938 the congregation was organized as the third Nazarene church in Korea. Though the Japanese ordered both of the Nazarene churches in Pyongyang to close, they continued secretly, led by lay leaders. Chang Sung Oak pastored the Seoul congregation until June 1941, when his refusal to obey Japanese demands for him to bow toward the emperor's shrine forced him to leave the church and turn to farming.[36]

In Japan itself, Japanese police watched Eckel at every corner and read his mail. "The strain," confessed Eckel, "has been hard."[37] Of pressing concern to the Japanese church was a question as to whether a Nazarene might bow before a state shrine, a sign of loyalty. To the government this was a civil rather than religious function. Common people, however, associated the shrine with the Shinto religion. In a letter to missionary secretary C. Warren Jones, Eckel asked, "Could we as Christians go there and take off our hat and bow because we are told to do so, but in our heart we resent it and have no spirit of worship and yet be a Christian?"[38] Japanese Nazarenes followed social dictates and bowed. They assured themselves that bowing was only out of respect, but it was an action for which the Japanese Nazarenes later repented.[39]

Restrictions on religious freedom increased. Jones appointed Isayama as district superintendent in March 1940, and the districts reunited. Kitagawa, Isayama, and Eckel attended the 1940 General Assembly. Jones and the general superintendents realized that the political tension might very soon rend the church in Japan apart from America. They placed authority upon the shoulders of Kitagawa and Isayama for whatever accommodations might be necessary in the future.[40]

Immediately upon returning to Japan after the General Assembly, Isayama and Kitagawa found that the religious situation had changed. The government now demanded that various denominations combine into blocks within the Christian Church of Japan. Each block needed at least five thousand members and fifty churches. This was more than the Church of the Nazarene had, and the Free Methodists were in the same predicament. Even before the arrival from the United States of Kitagawa and Isayama, Free Methodist Bishop Tsuchiyama, a Pasadena College graduate, had consulted with Nazarene pastors and had made preliminary plans toward union. Nazarenes agreed on the necessity of uniting with the Free Methodists. At a union assembly in April 1941 the Church of the Nazarene in Japan joined the Free Methodists and two other small Holiness groups, the Scandinavian Missionary Alliance and the World Missionary Society, to form the Nihon Seika Kirisuto Kyodan (Japan Holiness Church of Christ). Free Methodist Bishop Tsuchiyama became the leader, and he ordained thirty ministers, nine of whom were Nazarenes. Isayama was in charge of the Nazarene segment and continued to strengthen the churches in Tokyo. He also maintained contact with the Korean and Chinese work. Though under dire circumstances, the Church of the Nazarene in Japan was in the hands of well-prepared, strong-willed, and forceful leaders. In one of his last letters before the outbreak of war Isayama wrote: "Whatever may be the developments in the future, [the missionaries] have laid the foundation, and it is my prayer that we may be enabled to build thereon a superstructure that will stand the test of fire."[41] In November 1942 the block system was abolished in favor of a unified church order. Both Tsuchiyama and Isayama served on the Executive Council of the Nihon Kirisuto Kyodan, the Christian Church of Japan.[42]

During the war members scattered. Pastors subsisted along with others on sweet potatoes or pumpkins. Kitagawa's family bartered clothing for food. Remarkably, Isayama's church in Tokyo escaped harm from a fire that destroyed nearby buildings. After a bombing raid, the military used it as a temporary hospital, and the church floor became stained with blood. The church in Hiroshima was left standing after the nuclear attack there, but the pastor, Kikuo Nagase, soon succumbed to the bomb's radiation.[43]

Meanwhile, one Japanese man, Shiro Kano, wrestled differently with the issues of war. He attended Eastern Nazarene College in the late 1930s and had become a favorite among the school's students, teachers, and administrators. He preached in various churches. In 1940, after Kano's graduation from ENC, General Superintendent Chapman ordained him. Kano continued studies in philosophy of religion at Boston University. Chapman viewed Kano as a potential leader for Japan and offered to finance his doctoral work. However, Kano was incarcerated soon after Pearl Harbor. He was given the choice of translating communiqués for the U.S. government or repatriation. His American friends urged him to stay. But Kano knew that returning to Japan was the only way in which he might effectively minister to his own people after the war. He chose repatriation. After he reached Japan, he found that it was impossible for him to preach. About September 1943 he joined the Japanese navy as a translator and set out for the South Seas. Although escaping one bombing, aboard a second ship he did not, and Kano died in the area of the Solomon Islands in January 1944.[44]

Nazarene chaplains with the U.S. armed services were the first to make contact with the church in Japan after the war. After a long search through the rubble of Tokyo, Joseph S. Pitts and Orval J. Nease Jr. finally found Isayama. Mrs. Isayama had the young men take off their muddy boots before entering her home. Only with reluctance did Pitts comply with this request and to the customary bowing that accompanied his greetings toward Isayama. But Pitts brought much-needed food and arranged for Isayama's employment as a translator. In Kyoto, after difficulty, Nazarene Clifton Mayhew found Kitagawa's church. Soon food, clothing, and other supplies came to Kitagawa's family and neighbors through this and subsequent contacts with Nazarenes serving in the military.[45]

In China, there was great urgency toward the church's self-support and self-government during the 1930s. The sharp decline in giving for missions during the Depression limited the general church's expenditures overseas. For either political or economic reasons missionaries might at any time be forced out of China, and missionaries wanted the Chinese church's own leaders to be ready.[46]

The war years began early in China. In 1931, the same year that Japan invaded Manchuria, the Chinese chose eight pastors to compose a District Board, one step toward greater self-government. Among the pastors on the board was Hsu Kwei-pin, the only Chinese elder, having been ordained in

1929 by General Superintendents Roy T. Williams and John Goodwin. Formerly affiliated with both the Presbyterian Church and the South Chili Gospel Mission, Hsu pastored Nazarene churches in Chaocheng and Daming, where he also served as a teacher in the Bible school.[47]

There was still no officially organized district assembly in China, and in 1933 the Chinese asked for a say in mission council proceedings. Though they were grateful for the money given from America for the Chinese church, the leaders stated in 1935: "We do not hope to receive such help financially, also we hope that the time will come when we will not need people of other countries to preach for us. We sincerely hope that we can be free, that is self-supporting and propagating ... that we may help the poor and needy in our land."[48]

Hsu Kwei-pin

When General Superintendent Chapman arrived in China in October 1935, he reminded both the missionaries and the Chinese leaders that the aim of the church was to develop "self-directing and self-supporting" churches. Problems commonly arose, Chapman told them, when the indigenous church clamored for self-direction before it achieved self-support. He assured the Chinese that the missionaries would stay only as long as necessary, meaning, until the churches were able financially to carry on for themselves. "And just as we hope that the indigenous church may become self-directing and self-supporting, the mission must remain so itself, and when this is impossible or unnecessary, the mission should be definitely withdrawn and the field left to the indigenous church." Chapman also told the missionaries and Chinese workers, "There is the strongest bond in the world that binds us together, and that is our love for the Lord Jesus Christ. This bond is stronger than blood or race or language ... and it is sufficient to make us one in both purpose and effort. We want to spread his Kingdom everywhere because of our love for him."[49]

The sound of artillery punctuated evangelistic services in China when the Japanese moved to conquer northern China in 1937. This followed episodes with Chinese bandits, and a time of famine, flooding, and even earthquake. When the Japanese invaded, missionaries hung a large American flag prominently in the center of the mission compound. As the Japanese still did not want to widen the war, this temporarily protected the missionaries, and the compound served as a refuge for the Chinese. In 1938 Japanese ground troops reached Daming. By this time, most missionaries had evacuated. The

Japanese allowed missionaries to return to the field in 1939. The missionaries, themselves deeply disturbed by the Japanese and empathetic to the plight of the Chinese, sensed that the Chinese people were now open to the gospel more than ever. While Chinese students at the Bible school studied all the more fervently, evangelistic bands spread the message of salvation under the eyes of the Japanese occupation forces.[50]

In early 1941 missionaries placed Hsu Kwei-pin in charge of the Bible school and designated him to become "chairman" of the district should they leave. They had faith in Hsu. As Katherine Wiese later described it, her husband, Harry Wiese, the mission director, and Hsu "worked together like one man; they loved each other and had faith in the other. Truly Hsu was co-Superintendent as Brother Wiese always consulted him on Chinese problems. . . . These two men had worked together constantly for nearly eleven years. Sometimes Hsu was head sometimes Brother Wiese but I don't believe either thought of who was boss. They were workers together and loved each other like David and Jonathan."[51]

When the missionaries evacuated North China, after Pearl Harbor, there were 130 enrolled in the Bible school, with a Chinese faculty of eight; 134 workers, including the medical staff, Bible women, and seventy-five pastors; fifty-four organized churches; 2,120 full and 3,412 probationary members; and eight elementary schools enrolling 260 students. The Chinese church was contributing well to its overall expenses.[52]

The Japanese incarcerated the Nazarene missionaries on the field: Leon and Emma Osborn, John Pattee, Arthur Moses, who had recently arrived to help administer the hospital, and Mary Scott, who also had but recently come to China. When the Japanese took over the mission compound, they also jailed Hsu and other Chinese leaders. While interred, missionaries deeded the Bible school to the Chinese and handed over a complete record of all other property held by the church, including the hospital. Osborn, then serving as superintendent, authorized the Chinese church to irregularly ordain several Chinese pastors, including Yu Wan-ch'ien and Ma Hsueh-wen.[53] Chinese leaders met and planned the next annual meeting. As if to prove to the missionaries that the church would go on without them, by the time the interred missionaries left the country the Chinese had already built four new churches. The Japanese repatriated all except Mary Scott, who expressed her preference to stay in China. She remained imprisoned throughout the war.[54]

The hardships of the church during the war with Japan only increased the number of preaching points, and churches assumed full support for their pastors. Hsu Kwei-pin continued the Bible school until 1942 or 1943, and workers were added to those who had graduated previously. The situation, as John Pattee observed, "by one stroke made the Chinese church entirely independent and self-supporting."⁵⁵ The achievement of self-support, self-government, and self-propagation came not at the end of the slow processes of missions strategy and planning, but because of social and political realities. There were no further contacts with the field until the end of the war. When the Japanese evacuated at the close of the war, the Communist army of Mao Ze-dong quickly moved in. Nevertheless Wiese and Pattee returned to Beijing in 1946 and conversed with some Chinese workers, who advised them that it was best not to attempt to visit the Daming area. From that point onward, until the late 1980s, little was known of how the Chinese Nazarenes had fared under Communism.⁵⁶

PREPARING FOR THE POSTWAR WORLD

The general superintendents led the church toward rapid expansion of the missionary effort once the war was over. R. T. Williams was said to have noted during the war that "we did not send enough missionaries to convert the Japanese and now we must send soldiers to destroy them."⁵⁷ The church did not want to repeat that mistake.

Money matched the mood. In a 1942 United Stewardship Council study, the Church of the Nazarene ranked first in per capita giving among the nineteen denominations surveyed. Nazarene members contributed $35.97 per capita, compared with the Reformed Church, which ranked second, with $26.63. Though the Methodist Church raised $89.7 million dollars for all purposes—twice the amount of the second-placed Southern Baptists—this represented only $13.67 per Methodist. While in membership the Church of the Nazarene placed seventeenth among the groups studied, in the total raised for all purposes it ranked eleventh.⁵⁸

Giving to the church's General Budget nearly doubled between 1940 and 1943, from $286,122 in 1940 to $513,083 in 1943. Missions Secretary C. Warren Jones advised General Superintendent H. V. Miller in May 1943 that the church had $261,000 on hand for foreign missions and $24,000 for home missions. Miller's response was to put as many missionaries on the field as soon as possible. Of the $566,739 designated for missions in 1943-44, the church disbursed only $386,949. A sizable "war chest" was mounting, waiting for peace.⁵⁹

The Church of the Nazarene sent out forty-one missionaries between 1940 and 1944—nine more than it had sent out in the previous quadrennium—to safe regions of the world, such as South America, India, and Africa.

The church was ready to push a "new offensive," Jones exclaimed at the 1944 General Assembly. He hoped to raise $1 million in 1944 "to help evangelize the heathen and build the kingdom."[60] Jones drew up an ambitious strategy to spend $1 million a year in each of the next four years beginning in 1945. His budget earmarked $500,000 for China and Tibet alone, and $50,000 for each new country the church might enter.[61]

J. B. Chapman lent his support to these efforts. In his "Nazarene Manifesto," issued in 1944, he declared: "We should not hesitate another day in adopting a million dollar budget for world evangelism." He called for missionary recruits of the "highest caliber" to join the effort.

> It is time now for a great world crusade, and if we are worthy to be classed as the progeny of Wesley who claimed the world for his parish, we must lead that crusade and not permit its forward moving chariots to push us from behind. A million dollars for missions and five hundred new missionary recruits. The figures are not extravagant, and the need is more than pressing. I know not what others may do, but as for me I am ready for the biggest, fullest push for God and souls that a people of our number and ability ever undertook in the history of the world.[62]

LEADERSHIP CRISES

While the world was shaken by the threats of totalitarianism, the Church of the Nazarene in the 1940s underwent its own leadership crises. General Superintendent J. G. Morrison died in 1939, and J. W. Goodwin retired in 1940. Along with H. V. Miller, the General Assembly elected Orval J. Nease to the general superintendency in 1940. Within a little more than a year, Nease's son, who had a minister's license, faced an issue of severe moral failing. Rather than seeing that his son face the normal procedures of church discipline, Nease helped to secure a position at a church for his son on another district, without making known to the local district superintendent all of the details or issues involved in the transfer. Only when the son was about to be installed as pastor of a church in Little Rock, Arkansas, did it become known that Nease had stepped in on behalf of his son in what seemed to be a misuse of his authority as a general superintendent and had circumvented the *Manual*. Nease, slated to preside over the next Arkansas District Assembly, asked R. T. Williams to do so instead. In March 1942 Nease wrote Williams: "I live with this situation day and night. Any suggestion or help you can give me for the sake of the church, my boy and my ministry I will forever appreciate," and implored, "I do need a brother and a friend right now."[63] Nease also sought counsel from D. Shelby Corlett, a friend as well as editor of the *Herald of Holiness.* Corlett warned Nease that "in your anxiousness to save your boy and yourself that unconsciously you have left the impression that you do not sense the seriousness of the whole matter."⁶⁴

The issue reverberated throughout the church, with rumors and innuendos circulating rampantly. The four general superintendents met in April 1942. Nease's three colleagues, Williams, Chapman, and Miller, demanded that Nease's son resign from his pastorate but absolved Nease the father from blame. Yet district leaders called for Nease's resignation, and some district superintendents advised Williams, Chapman, and Miller that they would not accept Nease on their districts or allow him to preside over their district assemblies. In July 1942, Williams, Chapman, and Miller expressed their desire to Nease that he resign. They pressed for his resignation to be tendered at their next meeting in January 1943. Though Nease seemed to agree at the time, he consulted with friends in California, where he lived, and reconsidered. He decided that he should not resign and informed his general superintendent colleagues of this in March 1943. In April the three general superintendents decided to assign to themselves all of Nease's district assemblies and official duties.⁶⁵

Nease wrote to his colleagues in May 1944: "I am sincere when I tell you that as much as I have appreciated the office I would have sought release long since if I could have felt that by such a withdrawal under pressure it would not have been an acknowledgement of that of which I am not guilty." Rather, it would have brought ruin to his ministry, Nease felt. He sought a "Christian way" to satisfy the "existing confusion" rather than to allow unrest to persist. He said that his name should not be considered for reelection at the coming General Assembly. "I place the future of my leadership and my ministry in your hands."⁶⁶

The clouds were dark over the 1944 General Assembly, meeting in Minneapolis in the middle of a war. While the war raged, the general superintendents admonished the church, Nazarenes must keep their own hearts pure, clean, and straight—and pray for victory as well as peace.⁶⁷

Predictably, Williams, Chapman, and Miller easily garnered the two-thirds vote needed for their reelections. But Nease received less than 40 percent of the vote on the first ballot. Nease lost votes on the second and third ballots. Finally, Nease stood to address the assembly: "The Church of the Nazarene, of which I am a part, can make it without me," he said, "but I cannot make it without the Church of the Nazarene."⁶⁸ He withdrew himself from consideration. The delegates breathed easier and elected Hardy C. Powers, the Iowa District Superintendent, on the eighth ballot. As Nease himself later saw it, "I treated the matter as a family rather than a public affair."⁶⁹

The crisis demanded that the general superintendents function more as a board. In addition, in order to avoid a repeat of the situation over the previous few years, the 1944 General Assembly delegates resolved that: "The office of any General Superintendent may be declared vacant, for cause, by the unanimous vote of the remaining members of the Board of General Superintendents, supported by a majority vote of all the District Superintendents."[70] Williams predicted to those beside him on the platform that at the next General Assembly Nease would be reelected and that the church would be healed. But neither Williams nor Chapman, beloved elders of the church, would live to see this.[71]

Even after the Nease affair, the general superintendents found it difficult to forge united stands. Chapman spoke at the 1944 Leadership Conference in support of the founding of a graduate theological seminary. This infuriated Williams, since the issue had not first been discussed among the general superintendents. Chapman had caught Williams "off guard" by having a presentation regarding the seminary ready. Because it had been presented by a general superintendent, it was taken as an official move. Certainly the general superintendents should be able to speak out on minor issues, but not on such major ones, Williams counseled Chapman.[72]

Williams suffered a stroke in late 1945. Among his last statements to his fellow general superintendents, Williams admonished them to be "conservative in our expansion efforts to send out new missionaries" and to know, first, that each is fully qualified. In March 1946 Williams died. Williams had served as general superintendent for thirty years.[73]

Upon Williams's death, the remaining general superintendents, in accordance with the *Manual*, called for an election by the district superintendents to replace him. They elected G. B. Williamson, who had been president of ENC from 1936 to 1944 and pastor of Kansas City First Church since 1944.

Then, unexpectedly, Chapman died in July 1947. Like Williams, he was only sixty-three at the age of death. The proximity of the death of these long-serving general superintendents marked the end of an era for the Church of the Nazarene. They exemplified the maintenance of sectarian values, norms, and rules as well as the distinguishing doctrine of holiness.[74]

PART III

Introduction

A third generation of Nazarenes entered leadership after the Second World War. Over the next three decades, these leaders expanded and broadened the church, separated Nazarene ethics from shifting social norms, strengthened the church's schools and commitments to liberal arts, and proclaimed holiness to the age.

The Second World War produced political and social changes that affected the Church of the Nazarene. As a condition for American entry into the war, Franklin Roosevelt won assurances that the British would soon dismantle their far-reaching empire.[1] Within two years after the war, India, the most populous of British colonies, became independent. Shortly after, China, which had received more Protestant missionaries before the war than any other country, became Communist and shut the doors to Western influences, including those of the church. In Asia and Africa, newly independent governments added further uncertainty.

Christians saw opportunity in postwar uncertainty. Around the world, Christianity grew rapidly. In particular, the influence of American Protestantism reached its zenith.[2]

Many denominations undertook extensive church reconstruction projects in devastated countries where they had worked before the war. By the 1960s, however, some of these denominations were sending far fewer missionaries than they had earlier in the century. As a matter of policy, they emphasized that missions should decrease so that local churches could flourish and local leaders take charge. The change in missions strategy also reflected the growing uncertainty that the gospel needed to be proclaimed and accepted in order for men and women to be saved.[3]

But evangelicals such as Nazarenes remained anxious about the millions that they believed were perishing without the gospel. Evangelical organizations burst out of the wartime with tremendous energy and sufficient resources to send hundreds of missionaries abroad. They poured millions of dollars into world evangelization. The spread of Communism contributed to the sense of urgency.[4]

The tumultuous 1960s did nothing to hinder the worldwide spread of evangelical Christianity. But Protestants were divided on social issues. Some called for an end to racial segregation in places such as South Africa and the American South, and some protested America's war in Vietnam. Others, however, associated the peace movement with free love, drugs, and hippies, supported American policies in Vietnam, and opposed integration.[5]

The Church of the Nazarene emerged from its sectarian tendencies. In administration the church became much like other United States-based denominations. Like their Methodist forbears, Nazarenes were great organizers. Leaders were conservative and stable. They evidenced a corporate mentality and passion for efficiency not unlike their secular counterparts.

Early Nazarenes had centered Holiness work in Boston, Brooklyn, Los Angeles, Calcutta, Tokyo, Glasgow, and Nashville. Their successors had tended to be rural. The church shifted attention from Tokyo to Kyoto and from Calcutta to Buldana and, in America, from the cities to the Midwestern farm belt. In the postwar era, however, many Nazarenes moved to burgeoning suburbs and accommodated themselves to suburban culture.[6]

American Nazarenes acquired the washing machines, station wagons, and other material things that went along with rising affluence. When married, they could afford wedding rings. They bought televisions. Like their neighbors, suburban women started going to beauty parlors. These trends troubled some Nazarenes. In the mid-1950s a few who were very strict about women's dress, jewelry, entertainment (including the television), and other issues of behavior began to leave the Church of the Nazarene. Their departure had the effect of moving Nazarenes a bit closer to the social and religious center. True, there were still issues such as smoking tobacco, drinking alcohol, and attending movies that still marked Nazarenes as a "peculiar" people. But perhaps they were a little less peculiar in relation to society than the previous generation.[7]

Intellectually, too, the postwar church increasingly identified itself with the center of the Christian faith. H. Orton Wiley's systematic theology planted the church's Wesleyanism in historic creeds and councils.

Increasingly, Nazarenes stressed their commonalities rather than their disagreements with the broader church and the societies in which they lived. They were committed to the same mission as other evangelicals, to evangelize the world. At the same time, Nazarenes continued their "distinguishing mission" to proclaim and to evidence holiness and to transmit the doctrine and experience around the world.

FIFTEEN

Administering the Church

The Nazarene leaders who emerged in the postwar era maintained a course close to that of their predecessors. They, too, chose a middle way for the church between extremes, between legalism and freedom, between evangelism and education, between spirit and structure. As the church grew, so did its administrative structure. Leaders retained tight control on many aspects of the church.

The leadership transitions in the 1940s were similar to those that occurred in the 1910s. Nease's failure to be reelected to the general superintendency in 1944 was followed two years later by the death of R. T. Williams and, in 1947, by the death of James B. Chapman. "No task confronts us requiring more painstaking effort than the passing on to another generation the same ideals and vision and full passion that moved our fathers," said the remaining general superintendents in their 1948 quadrennial address.[1] But later in 1948, H. V. Miller, then the senior general superintendent, died in office; and Nease himself died in 1950, two years after his reelection as General Superintendent.

Other leadership transitions occurred at headquarters. In 1945, Albert Harper, with a doctorate in psychology, became head of Church Schools. In 1946, John Stockton, a banker, became general treasurer. In 1948 the church added Roy Smee as full-time secretary of Home Missions, Evangelism, and Church Extension; S. S. White, a well-educated theologian, took over from D. Shelby Corlett as editor of the *Herald of Holiness;* Remiss Rehfeldt, a young and energetic district superintendent, replaced C. Warren Jones in Foreign Missions; and Louise Robinson Chapman, a former missionary, succeeded Susan Fitkin as president of the Nazarene Foreign Missionary Society. In 1950 Mary Scott, former missionary to China, replaced Emma Word as general secretary of the missionary society. Each of these new leaders reflected increased professionalization at top church levels.[2]

The same was true of the men the church chose as general superintendents. Each had proven himself a worthy administrator and a loyal churchman. Hardy C. Powers, elected in 1944 to succeed Orval J. Nease, served until 1968. Prior to this, Powers had served for fourteen years in Iowa—first as pastor of the church in Council Bluffs and, after 1936, as superintendent of the Iowa District. Iowa was one of the strictest areas of the church on matters of dress and behavior. Powers remained sensitive to the concerns of this element of the church after becoming general superintendent. He argued that the church and its leaders must act in ways that did not harm the consciences of any. After his election as general superintendent, Powers continued to live in Des Moines for two years and then moved to Dallas. Though lacking the charisma of Williams or Chapman, Powers had his own style. He liked to arrive late at preaching engagements and entered from the rear of the church, shaking hands with the people as he made his way to the platform.[3]

According to one of his colleagues, for Powers "the church did not possess a mission, she was the mission." That is to say, for Powers and others like him, the expansion and international development of the church itself was the goal. This was a shift in thinking. An earlier generation had conceived of the Church of the Nazarene as the means to promote holiness in Christendom. Leaders such as Powers attended to the church itself. Its own programs were of primary importance.[4]

Gideon B. Williamson, elected to succeed R. T. Williams in 1946, had pastored churches in Farmington, Iowa; Chicago; Cleveland, Ohio; and Kansas City. Reflecting his urban pastorates and work in the East, Williamson was less strict than his colleagues on matters of behavior. More than they, he often voiced his own opinions publicly. He represented the progressive forces in the church on many matters. At the same time, in bearing, he was "every inch a bishop" in the estimation of one successor.[5]

When J. B. Chapman died, the general superintendents decided to wait for the 1948 General Assembly to elect a replacement. The same assembly expanded the number of general superintendents to five. Delegates returned Orval Nease to the superintendency and elected Samuel Young to the fifth position on the Board of General Superintendents.

A native of Scotland, Young and his family had been members of the Sharpe's Pentecostal Church of Scotland in Glasgow before immigrating to the United States in 1916. Young was serving as president of Eastern Nazarene College when he was elected general superintendent. He had pastored in Ohio and Portland, Maine; had served as superintendent of the New England District from 1934 to 1940; and had pastored the Wollaston Church at ENC from 1940 to 1945—at the same time serving as ENC's professor of theology and religion department head. Young was known for his theological perspective, financial expertise, and wit.[6]

The general superintendents called for an election by the district superintendents when H. V. Miller died a few months after the 1948 Assembly. The district superintendents elected one of their own, D. I. Vanderpool. He had been superintendent of the Northwest District since 1937. Prior to that, Vanderpool had pastored some of the denomination's leading churches, including Denver First Church; Bresee Avenue Church in Pasadena, California; and the Walla Walla, Washington, congregation. Vanderpool continued living in Walla Walla after his election as general superintendent and later moved to San Jose, California. People were fond of Vanderpool's common-man appeal. His stories were often drawn from his rural Missouri upbringing.[7]

After his reelection in 1948, Nease had an eventful tour of Asian fields in late 1948 and early 1949. But he overtaxed himself physically. When he died in 1950, Powers wanted to call upon the district superintendents to elect his successor. But the other general superintendents preferred to wait until the next General Assembly, and they prevailed.[8]

The 1952 General Assembly elected Hugh C. Benner, president of Nazarene Theological Seminary since its founding in 1945, to fill Nease's position. Prior to this, Benner had taught history and music at both Pasadena and ENC, had pastored a home missions church in Santa Monica, California, and had pastored the Spokane First and Kansas City First churches. Benner was a pianist and church musician.[9]

Powers, Williamson, Young, Vanderpool, and Benner made a strong board. The average age of the general superintendents rose from fifty-six in 1946 to sixty-five in 1968. Three of the five had been school administrators, and the other two had been district superintendents. Each possessed both powerful preaching skills and a managerial and professional style. The general superintendents served as go-betweens for pastors wanting to transfer from one district to another and counseled pastors in financial matters. Still accessible to local churches, the general superintendents were sounding boards for laity. Constantly, district superintendents, missionaries, and pastors requested money from them. The general superintendents gave advice on building projects and property. In addition to conducting district assemblies, they preached in camp meetings. Believing that problems often worked themselves out, the general superintendents often practiced "administration by delay." When they did act, they did so autocratically. Though they might disagree with each other within their boardroom, once a decision was made, each should stand by it and defend it. They were to speak to the church with one voice.[10]

The general superintendents intimidated pastors. Philosophically, S. W. Strickland, who had come into the Church of the Nazarene out of McClurkan's

Pentecostal Mission, saw and feared the loss of congregational autonomy and the founders' balance between congregationalism and episcopacy.[11] At the local level, the general superintendents "were deeply loved," wrote Jerald Johnson. "But it could probably be added that by many they were lovingly feared."[12]

Though this leadership style represented the triumph of organization, it did not come without perils. In 1952, amid the denominational push to reach more souls for Christ, Edward Lawlor, then superintendent of the Canada West District and an active evangelist, wondered "if we have not transferred our dependence from the divine power of Pentecost to the human power of organization."[13] During the fiftieth anniversary year C. William Fisher, one of the church's most prominent evangelists, worried that holiness might easily become "identified with organization and policy and administration." If it were to become so, the Holiness message's "throb" would be "softened" and its mission "contained." Whatever organization did the "containing" ceased to be the "primary channel through which God moves humanity to holy living."[14]

Meanwhile, the district superintendents became less involved in evangelizing and planting of churches and increasingly involved in the administration of churches and pastors. The likes of A. E. Sanner in Southern California and E. O. Chalfant in Illinois were passing away. Chalfant, whom W. T. Purkiser called "eccentric," was raised in Indiana and had United Brethren background. After graduating from Huntington College, Chalfant began holding revivals with John T. Hatfield and other senior Holiness evangelists. In 1908, while Chalfant was studying at Kingswood College, he heard H. F. Reynolds speaking about organized holiness, but it was not until 1916 that Chalfant joined the Church of the Nazarene. Soon thereafter, leaving many years of evangelism, Chalfant became pastor of the Muncie, Indiana, First Church of the Nazarene. He continued citywide campaigns with Holiness evangelists, including Bud Robinson, and soon other Nazarene churches began in and around Muncie. In 1919 Chalfant went to Indianapolis to pastor the Westside Church. Once more, Chalfant initiated citywide evangelistic campaigns. In 1922 he was elected superintendent of the Chicago Central District. He became a stalwart friend of Olivet Nazarene College and in 1926 was instrumental in raising funds to keep the college open. The district grew so under Chalfant's leadership that it was divided three times—in 1936, when Wisconsin became a separate district; in 1943, when southern Illinois separated to form its own district; and again in 1948 when the denomination formed the Northwestern Illinois District. Nazarene membership in this part of the country rose from twenty-two hundred in 1922 to fourteen thousand in 1950.[15]

While Chalfant led the growth of the church in Illinois, Charles A. Gibson oversaw the church's expansion in Ohio. Born in Indiana, Gibson came to the Church of the Nazarene from a Holiness Christian Church background in 1913. He served as an evangelist and pastor, including three years at the Boise, Idaho, church, before being elected superintendent of the Northern California District in 1920. He became superintendent of the Ohio District, which included the western two-thirds of the state, in 1925. Like Chalfant, Gibson closely related himself to Olivet Nazarene College. While district superintendent, he evangelized and held home mission campaigns. New churches began in emptied storefront buildings. He served in Ohio until transferring to Michigan as superintendent in 1943 and to Wisconsin in 1945. He retired in 1957.[16]

Sanner had been a member of the same Church of God (Holiness) as G. B. Williamson and D. I. Vanderpool. After graduating from McGee Holiness College in Missouri, Sanner became an evangelist. After preaching a revival in Yuma, Colorado, he agreed to have the Nazarene district superintendent organize the work as a Church of the Nazarene and himself appointed as pastor. In 1917 the Colorado District, which consisted of eight churches, elected Sanner superintendent. In 1923 Sanner was elected superintendent of the Idaho-Oregon District. Leaving the superintendency for a time, Sanner pastored the Alhambra, California, church from 1930 to 1933, when the Southern California District elected him superintendent. He developed the slogan, "Let's Do Something." Often he stepped into the life of Pasadena College at critical moments to raise support and finances. When the district was divided in 1950, Sanner remained for two years as superintendent of the Los Angeles District before agreeing to supervise Casa Robles, the home for retired missionaries, in Temple City, California, where he remained until his retirement in 1966.

During his thirty-one years as superintendent, Sanner organized one hundred churches—sixty-three of them in Southern California. These churches often began with the vision and assistance of existing Nazarene churches. Sanner found and secured loans to purchase property. In Southern California, Sanner established two Japanese churches, one in Los Angeles (1935) and the other in Pasadena (1940). He opened African-American churches in Pasadena (1941) and in Los Angeles (1951). He also reestablished a Chinese church in Los Angeles (1950). Among other churches that began under Sanner's superintendency, in 1947, for example, after receiving permission from Sanner, evangelist Art Atkins conducted tent revivals in West Long Beach. The church began with seventy-three charter members. The Oxnard church, which began the following year, met in a Masonic Temple and then in a community center, before finishing its own building in 1951. The New Life church in Pismo Beach was originally a nondenominational congregation that sought affiliation with the Church of the Nazarene. Sanner not only secured seasoned pastors for the churches on his districts but also felt a keen responsibility for the nurture and care of young men and women entering ministry.[17]

In the earlier part of the postwar period, many district superintendents had served for various times as evangelists and brought revival methods to church planting. For instance, Edward Oney had started out with the Pilgrim Holiness Church and had served in Japan with the Oriental Missionary Society before becoming an evangelist. He was serving as pastor in West Chester, Pennsylvania, when elected as district superintendent for the West Virginia District, where he served from 1940 to 1959. Jarrette Aycock and his wife, Dell Aycock, were well-known evangelists before Jarrette Aycock was elected superintendent of the Kansas City District in 1943. He served until 1961. Ray Hance also had served as an evangelist in early years before settling into a series of strong pastorates. He served as district superintendent of the Northwest Oklahoma District from 1946 to 1948 and the Kansas District from 1948 to 1975.[18]

Often those deemed successful district superintendents were selected for positions in headquarters or elected to lead Nazarene higher education institutions. D. I. Vanderpool moved directly from the superintendency of the Northwest District, where he had served since 1938, to the general superintendency in 1949. Roy F. Smee served as a successful superintendent of the Northern California District from 1931 to 1948, when he became executive secretary of Home Missions and Evangelism, serving until his retirement in 1964. Similarly, V. H. Lewis from the Houston District, Edward Lawlor from the Canada West District, and first Orville Jenkins and then Ray Hurn from the West Texas District brought their expertise in evangelism to the general headquarters. John L. Knight led the Florida District from 1946 to 1968 before moving to Kansas City.[19]

Certain districts were known for being more conservative than others on matters of dress and behavior. Among the church's most conservative leaders, Elbert Dodd served as district superintendent in Louisiana, 1938-56; Glenn Griffith in Idaho-Oregon, 1937-45; and Remiss Rehfeldt, Iowa, 1944-48. Gene Phillips led the Indianapolis District from 1944 to 1948 and the Iowa District from 1948 to 1971. Equally conservative, A. A. E. Berg led the Australia District from 1950 to 1979.

At the same time, the district superintendents, as active boosters of the Nazarene colleges on their zone, were prime candidates for the presidency of these institutions. Roy Cantrell was serving as superintendent of the Minnesota District when elected president of Bethany in 1946, and W. Shelburne Brown as district superintendent of the Los Angeles District before becoming president of Pasadena College in 1963. Brown's successor as district superintendent, L. Guy Nees, went to the presidency of Mount Vernon and then became director of the World Mission Division. After twenty successful years as superintendent on the Northwest Oklahoma and Chicago districts, Mark Moore became president of Trevecca. L. S. Oliver, a well-liked camp meeting speaker as well as district superintendent in Illinois, became president of Nazarene Bible College in Colorado Springs. Kenneth Pearsall served as district superintendent in Upstate New York and New England before becoming president of Northwest Nazarene College in 1973. His successor on the New England District, Donald Irwin, after serving two years as district superintendent, was elected president of Eastern Nazarene College. After five years, Irwin returned to the superintendency, this time in Arkansas. Other times, as well, college presidents became district superintendents. T. W. Willingham served Olivet from 1926 to 1938 and later became district superintendent in Missouri. George Frame served as head of the Hurlet College from 1945 to 1954 before settling into eighteen years of superintendency in the British Isles.[20]

Meanwhile, every local church treasurer for a generation made checks out to "John Stockton, general treasurer." Stockton warned leaders when cash resources ran low and kept the denomination running in the "black." Stockton represented headquarters in matters related to its location. He was a member of the South Central Business Association of Kansas City and a member of the city's Chamber of Commerce during the tumultuous years of racial integration and the exodus of white residents to neighborhoods in the southern part of the city. He retired in 1970.[21]

M. Lunn

Sound business methods were evident at Nazarene Publishing House. Between 1912 and 1952 the Publishing House had generated $21.74 million in gross income. That amount was matched between the two quadrennia from 1952 and 1960. In 1960 M. Lunn handed leadership of NPH to his son, "Bud" Lunn, who had been assistant manager since 1946. Under Bud Lunn's leadership, NPH sales rose from $2.5 million in 1960 to $7.5 million in 1974.

Bud Lunn

NPH heavily subsidized the church's publications, including the *Herald of Holiness* and the *Preacher's Magazine*.[22]

The 1956 General Assembly set up a commission to study the office of the general superintendency. As a result of the commission's recommendation, the 1960 General Assembly added a sixth general superintendent. Delegates elected V. H. Lewis, who had served as Evangelism secretary since 1956. For nine years before that Lewis had been superintendent of the Houston District. George Coulter replaced Vanderpool when the latter retired at age seventy-three in 1964. (This was the first time since Goodwin in 1940 that a general superintendent had retired; all since then had died in office!) Born in Northern Ireland, Coulter was then serving as secretary of Foreign Missions. Coulter had been superintendent of the Northern California District from 1948 to 1960. The district had grown well under him. Lewis's and Coulter's elections indicated a pattern of electing headquarters executives to the superintendency.[23]

The years between 1968 and 1976 represented a transitional period of leadership. Because the 1964 General Assembly had decided that general superintendents could not stand for reelection after passing their sixty-eighth birthday, Powers, Williamson, and Benner were forced to retire in 1968, and Samuel Young in 1972. To replace them, the church chose Edward Lawlor, Orville Jenkins, and Eugene Stowe in 1968, and Charles Strickland in 1972. Lawlor had served as executive secretary of the Department of Evangelism since 1960. Lawlor was born in England and was a convert from Roman Catholicism. He had served a succession of pastorates before being elected district superintendent of Western Canada in 1946. Like Lewis, Coulter, and Lawlor, Jenkins had been a headquarters executive, directing the Department of Home Missions since 1964. Prior to that he had been a district superintendent in Texas. Eugene Stowe, only forty-six when elected, represented a shift to a younger generation. He had served two years as president of Nazarene Theological Seminary. Prior to that, he had been pastor of the Nampa College Church for ten years and district superintendent on the Central California District from 1962 to 1966. He also had served as president of the Nazarene Young People's Society from 1956 to 1960.[24]

For one quadrennium, 1968 to 1972, three of the six general superintendents were men born outside the United States: Young in Scotland, Coulter

> **GUIDELINES FOR GENERAL SUPERINTENDENTS**
>
> As a means of inducting new general superintendents into the ethos of the Board, the general superintendents issued a set of "Guidelines for General Superintendents" sometime in the mid-1960s:[25]
>
> He is not to exaggerate his private opinions . . .
>
> It is of fundamental importance that personal relationship among the Board members shall be cordial and communication shall be candid and without tension. No General Superintendent should take the liberty either in private or in public to embarrass a colleague or to antagonize him by the undue emphasis upon personal differences. . . .
>
> The norm shall be to be present on time and stay until adjournment of the session. . . .
>
> When such action has been taken, each General Superintendent should be bound upon his honor to support the action of the corporate body. . . .
>
> The relationship [to departments of the General Board and permanent commissions] is on an advisory basis. Dictatorial or arbitrary pronouncements are not expected.
>
> [On mission fields] where differences exist between missionaries or between the missionaries and the nationals, the General Superintendent should take the position of a conciliator. . . . [and] should show due respect for his predecessor and seek as much as possible to carry out the plans he has made. . . .
>
> [At district assemblies] a presiding General Superintendent should feel that his first concern shall be to give a spiritual tone to the assembly. He should feel responsible for being a fair moderator. . . .
>
> An hour for the ordination service should be chosen with a view to making the occasion as impressive and meaningful as possible to the candidates, the ministers and the members of the assembly. . . .
>
> [Finally], he should put forth every effort to be an effective soul winner and to build up the members of the Body of Christ in the Holy Faith.

in Ireland, and Edward Lawlor in England. Charles Strickland's election in 1972 added to the international perspective of the church. Prior to his election as founding president of Nazarene Bible College in 1965, Strickland had

The Board of General Superintendents around 1970

served for seventeen years as a missionary in South Africa.[26]

These elections as well as retirements necessitated shifts in other executive positions. John L. Knight, superintendent of the Florida District, became executive secretary of the Department of Evangelism in 1968; while Raymond Hurn, superintendent of the West Texas District, followed Jenkins in Home Missions. William Greathouse, president of Trevecca since 1963, succeeded Stowe as president of Nazarene Theological Seminary—serving until his own election to the general superintendency in 1976. Hurn and Greathouse represented new interests in the church that characterized the next generation. Hurn actively promoted urban and ethnic ministries. Greathouse represented the church's renewed interest in John Wesley.

Marking the increased importance of central control in the church, the headquarters payroll rose from $500,000 in 1961 to $1.9 million in 1974. In 1975, Lawlor, who himself had worked in Kansas City offices since 1960, warned that "an overstaffed headquarters can become a drag on the assignment that is ours." He worried that the headquarters staff was losing its sense of service to the denomination and was just "ecclesiastically busy." On the other hand, Lawlor also recognized that the church must be "conducted on business principles."[27]

CONCLUSION

In 1975 Albert Harper stepped down as editor of Sunday School Publications. In the same year, W. T. Purkiser retired as editor of the *Herald of Holiness* and Mary Scott retired as general secretary of the Nazarene World Missionary Society. By 1976 the leadership of the church had been passed to another generation.

The postwar years ushered in a set of leaders committed to organized efficiency. Though they attempted to prove that the denomination would not fail its fallen stalwarts, the new leaders realized that they were living in an age that called for businesslike ways of reaching into the world with the unchanging gospel.

SIXTEEN
NAZARENES IN THE BROADER WORLD

The nineteenth-century Holiness Movement engaged in social reforms. After the First World War, Nazarenes, like most evangelicals, turned inward. After the Second World War, Nazarenes remained aloof. They believed that society fostered a "virtual paganism,"[1] and they feared "atheistic" communism.[2]

NAZARENES AND COMMUNISM

The cold war shaped Nazarene ideas of the world. After the "fall" of China to Communists in 1947, Nazarenes expected that the same could happen elsewhere. Nazarenes in South Africa worried that the native people were "gullible" and that their country was the "perfect seed bed for Communist propaganda."[3]

In China itself, after World War II Nazarene missionaries could not return to minister in their old area. Harry Wiese and John Pattee were certain, though mistaken, that the nationalist government would soon defeat the Communists. Acting upon the suggestion of China's National Christian Council, they began work in southern Jiangxi Province in August 1947. Mandarin, the dialect the missionaries had learned in the North, was spoken in the area. The mission quickly established a compound and Bible school. Hsu Kwei-pin and Yu Wan-ch'ien from the old field fled south and found the Nazarene work. Hsu taught in the Bible school. Yu became pastor of the church in Kanhsien and easily persuaded Christians in the city to become Nazarene. Unlike the North, where most of the converts were poor farmers, members in the Southern field were involved in businesses and professions.[4]

The missionaries soon realized that the Communists would take over the entire country and, just as they had in the north before the war with Japan, concentrated upon creating a self-supporting church with indigenous leaders. When General Superintendent Orval Nease toured eastern Asia in

1948 and visited Jiangxi, he was impressed with the Chinese leaders and the solid beginnings of the work. He recognized the earlier, irregular ordinations of Yu and Ma Hsueh-wen, and ordained Chi Yuew-han, who had worked with Peter Kiehn and John Pattee before the war. After twenty-one months of work, all of the missionaries left. There were three churches and seventy members, plus two hundred probationers in the South. The Bible school continued under Hsu for at least one year. However, by the mid-1950s, Hsu was living in a woodshed and, afterward, was forced to live in a mud hut. He died in the mid-1970s.

How did the Nazarenes who remained in North China deal with the political situation? Most of their church buildings either had been destroyed during the war or taken over by the government. They had no outside support. Their senior leaders had scattered. Some of the younger pastors had been killed. Yet the church thrived. Young Bible school graduates situated themselves in each of the counties and major towns. They evangelized and itinerated. Churches met in homes.

During the Cultural Revolution, which began in 1966, all churches closed and Christians faced persecution. Beginning in 1979, the government allowed churches to reopen. Workers in the old Nazarene field registered churches with the government. As long as they did not talk or preach politically, they could preach as they always had. Preachers preached holiness. The workers and lay members were thoroughly aware of their Nazarene heritage.

But these churches were unknown to Nazarenes outside of China during this time. During the Korean War the church sensed the urgency of evangelizing the world, training national leaders, and supporting anti-Communist efforts. Though "great areas of the world are now open to the gospel," General Superintendent Benner warned in 1954, "any or all of these may be closed at an early date." Wrote Remiss Rehfeldt: "Let us prove to God and a dying world that our God is greater than all the forces of evil that communism can unleash." Converted Communists could be found among Nazarene pastors in the Philippines, Mexico, and other countries.[5]

The threat of Communism seemed close at hand as the Church of the Nazarene met for its 1960 General Assembly. The "Commission on Communism," which reported to the assembly, declared that the "Church of the Nazarene is unalterably opposed to godless Communism and its atheistic oppression around the world." To counteract it, the church needed to reaffirm certain "cardinal principles" of the Christian faith, the commission advised, including the "supremacy of God in human history," the dignity and worth of every individual, and the impossibility of redemption through economic or political means. Love was to be the basis for human relations.[6]

In the same year, Cuba became Communist and expelled missionaries. Nazarenes, who had reopened the work in Cuba in 1945, had not yet organized a district. John Hall, the last missionary to leave, appointed Hildo Morejon, an early convert and a lay pastor, to head an executive committee. Some of the members and pastors who were most convinced that the church and Communism could not coexist fled to the United States. Like fellow Nazarenes in China, those who remained found ways of being Christian within a Communist society.

Fidel Castro's government in Cuba took over the ten-acre compound that had served as the Nazarene Bible School but gave the church a larger property west of Havana. Classes continued for a time. However, the government confiscated church property, harassed worshippers, infiltrated congregations, and imprisoned pastors. After 1964, Nazarenes and other Protestants sent money to Cuba through Cuba's Council of Evangelical Churches. Beginning in 1967 Cuban Nazarenes held an assembly every two years. In 1969 some Mexican Nazarenes visited and preached. Morejon traveled to Peru and Costa Rica in 1975. Gradually, some of the harsher measures against the churches lessened.[7]

Because anti-Communism was associated with godlessness and atheism, Nazarenes were prone to identify God's work in the world with American interests. To R. V. DeLong, "Americanism" was the only "practical, workable method by which men of all races, of all colors, of all nationalities may live peaceably and happily." To bring such peace, DeLong advocated military as well as economic, moral, and spiritual preparedness. "Half-committed Americans," DeLong warned, "will never triumph over fully-committed Communists."[8]

Any other ways of responding to the world crisis caught the church off guard. In 1953, during the Korean conflict, someone asked Mary Li, a Chinese Nazarene pastor ministering in northern California, "What business have Chinese troops in Korea?" Her response was, "What are you Americans doing there?" The next year she voluntarily returned to Shanghai.[9]

"Perfect love," said Carl Bangs, demanded a concern for the social and economic as well as the spiritual needs of others. He argued against any identification of God's agenda with "Americanism." Holiness, Bangs stressed, repudiated class interest as well as self-interest.[10]

NAZARENES, POVERTY, AND POLITICS

Missionaries, who often were from lower middle-class families, found themselves faced with social inequities. Considered wealthy in the places where they served, some missionaries accepted their elevated status; others' consciences wrestled with the poverty surrounding them. Yet their presence in these countries depended on national governments. One young missionary in Nicaragua graphically described the country's poverty in a letter to her parents. When the letter was published in a local newspaper, it reached Nicaraguan officials, and the missionary and her husband were forced to leave the country immediately.[11]

The threat of Communism provided arguments for a "practical Christianity" that addressed the social effects of sin. In addition to its older medical missions, postwar Nazarenes sponsored relief efforts in Taiwan, medical missions in Papua New Guinea, and primary schools in Haiti. Nazarenes had a great influence upon Swaziland through their elementary schools, Teacher Training School, hospital, Nurses' Training School, and Leper Colony as well as churches. Swazi leaders, including the long-reigning King Sobhuza II, welcomed the church's involvement. Though Sobhuza had too many wives

---

Missionary James E. Kratz Sr., a newly arrived missionary in Brazil, submitted this annual report in October 1961:[12]

In a society in which there is some marked class distinction I find myself in a psychological and ethical conflict. Although we do have work among the lower middle class people, it makes sense in a fledgling industrial nation that we endeavor to reach the middle and upper class, especially in as much as our program is geared to rely upon the financial resources of this group. I know that in a society with class distinctions the type of people we attract will determine the class of folk we reach in the future.

And yet, over this very thing, I have been in abject misery. I find within my heart disturbing emotions. At the mere suggestion that we should especially try to "impress" certain types of people, I have a fierce rebellion within myself . . . along with a deep-seated sense of unworthiness. . . . if there must be any effort to "impress" anyone, I must go to my own kind, the poor, the unlovely, the not-so-promising.

to consider becoming a Christian, Nazarenes prayed for him and, sometimes, with him.

David Hynd, a British subject, was an influential figure in Swaziland. He served on various national boards, including the Advisory Board for Native Education, and was instrumental in forming the High Commission Territories Nursing Council in 1948. He became the first president of the Swaziland Medical Association in 1957. When the nation was preparing for independence in the early 1960s, Hynd advocated equal political privileges for Blacks and criticized the apartheid system in South Africa. In 1962 Hynd attended negotiations between the Swazi National Council and the European Advisory Council in London. Because of his increasing involvement in the emerging nation, Hynd retired from missionary service. He continued to live in Swaziland and was a key speaker at independence celebrations in 1968.[13]

Many Swazi leaders in the newly independent nation had been educated in Nazarene schools. Some princes studied in Nazarene colleges in the United States. S. T. M. Sukati, a Nazarene, served as Swaziland's ambassador to the United States. Ephraim Dlamini, a General Board member, was Swaziland's minister of education from 1972 to 1977, secretary for Public Service from 1977 to 1979, and, later, cabinet secretary.[14]

In Mexico, meanwhile, the government did not allow churches to own property. According to the 1917 Constitution, church buildings and parsonages belonged to the state. Yet only in 1966 did Nazarenes begin to transfer property to the government. On each "nationalized" church, "federal property" was posted, a permit to operate was framed and visible, and a national flag waved.[15]

It became important in Mexico for the Nazarene church to speak to government officials with one voice. In 1966 Nazarene leaders formed a "Board of Administration" composed of each district superintendent and all of the members of each of the District Advisory Boards. The Board of Administration oversaw the nationalization of churches, maintained a roster of pastors, approved major programs and projects, and resolved legal problems. It elected a chairman from among the district superintendents. This organization, though not described in the Manual, provided a model for other countries with similar needs.[16]

In Mozambique, civil war threatened churches in the 1970s. In June 1975, at the beginning of the civil conflict, two Nazarene missionaries, Armond Doll and Hugh Friberg, were arrested on suspicion of being agents of the CIA. The intervention of both the U.S. State Department and the

United Nations won Friberg's release after eight months and Doll's after a year. Meanwhile, the mission station at Tavane had become an army base.[17]

In other places, Nazarenes served in national governments. In Canada, Alex B. Patterson pastored for seventeen years before being elected to Parliament in 1953. He was reelected in 1965, 1972, and 1974. During a year out of office, 1964-65, he traveled as an evangelist.[18] Similarly, in Guatemala, Elizardo Urizar Leal, a Nazarene educator, served in the senate from 1974 to 1978.[19]

Most American Nazarenes in the 1950s were comfortable with President Dwight Eisenhower's conservativism. During Eisenhower's administration, "under God" was inserted in the "Pledge to Allegiance" to the American flag, and "In God We Trust" became the national motto.[20]

John F. Kennedy's Roman Catholicism was a political issue in the 1960 presidential election. A month before the election, which pitted Kennedy against Richard Nixon, Orville Jenkins, pastor of Kansas City First Church, preached that Roman Catholicism was "a vast ecclesiastical institution which extends to the whole world and presides monolithically and dictatorially over the religious life of more than 200 million adherents." In contrast, Jenkins said, Protestants believed in the separation of church from state and opposed using taxes for parochial schools. Jenkins told how B. Edgar Johnson, the Nazarene pastor in Whittier, California, had called upon Nixon's ill father, how Nixon himself had invited the Nazarene pastor into the house, and how Nixon had knelt in prayer with Johnson. The message to the Kansas City congregation was clear enough.[21] With the consent of the general superintendents, the general secretary issued a statement less than two weeks before the 1960 election that it was "high time Protestants were alerted to the seriousness of the world aims of the Vatican instead of being lulled to sleep by the tranquilizers dispersed from Rome."[22]

Trends in the United States in the 1960s inclined Nazarenes toward politically conservative positions. Samuel Young said he knew of no "leftist" tendencies in the hierarchy of the church. In fact, he said in 1961, leaders lean "very far toward the right."[23] Young Republican clubs drew about twice as many members as Young Democrat clubs on Nazarene campuses in the 1960s. At the 1972 General Assembly in Miami, one general leader assured an assistant to Richard Nixon that Nazarene young people were consistently behind the president. Politically liberal sons and daughters of Nazarenes were prone to leave the denomination.[24]

During the Nixon administration, Richard Schubert, an ENC and Yale Law School graduate, served in the Labor Department, first as solicitor and then, from 1973 to 1975, as undersecretary. Schubert was a high-ranking official in the Bethlehem Steel Corporation both before and after his stint at the Labor Department. Later, he became president of the American Red Cross.²⁵

American Nazarene support for military involvement in Vietnam built upon anti-Communist sentiments. "We do not live in an ideal world," said W. T. Purkiser in 1964, in which "all disputes between men and nations would be settled by peaceful and rational means."²⁶ Instead, said West Texas District Superintendent Lyle Eckley in 1970, "We see the endeavors of Communism throughout the land to capture attentions of youth of our generation—promoting an ideology which would tear down the Church and fundamentals for which our government has stood."²⁷ The *Herald of Holiness* printed the names of Nazarene soldiers killed in Vietnam. *Conquest* published letters from Nazarene servicemen who were not much older than the teenagers who read the magazine.²⁸

Nazarenes had little sympathy for antiwar demonstrations. "It is distressing and disgusting," said C. William Fisher on the denomination's "Showers of Blessing" radio program, "to see a generation that never built anything tear down everything others have built up." "They ridicule," Fisher went on, "freedoms they never fought for, try to destroy a country they are unwilling to defend, and cry for a peace they are too soft to make and too lazy to keep."²⁹ Nazarenes sensed that there was something wrong with persons who rebelled rather than with the society against which they were rebelling. Conversion to Christ was the best means of overcoming "radicalism."³⁰

Yet, just as was done during the previous wars, the general secretary maintained a roster of "conscientious objectors." A few Nazarenes, including some in Great Britain with backgrounds in the Calvary Holiness Church, which had remained pacifist during the Second World War, opposed the war in Vietnam.³¹

On the theological front, Mildred Bangs Wynkoop described John Wesley a "Christian Revolutionary" and called Wesleyanism "sanctified revolution." True Wesleyanism, for her, represented involvement in social issues. She warned the church in these turbulent years that "to cut off our contact with the world to preserve our purity is to corrupt our own purity, for purity does not consist in what we preserve but in the outflow of the love shed abroad in our hearts by the Holy Spirit."³²

NAZARENES AND RACE

The social involvement that Wynkoop had in mind was not evident in the church's response to race, the greatest social issue facing churches in America, South Africa, and other places. While the church found it much easier to send missionaries to Africa than to reach out to African-American neighbors, the growing number of African-American migrants to Northern and border cities such as Kansas City presented a challenge to the church. Previous opportunities to accession African-American Holiness churches interested in joining the Church of the Nazarene had gone unheeded.[33]

J. B. Chapman urged the 1944 General Assembly to authorize the general superintendents to find a means of reaching African-Americans. Later that year the church organized a "Colored District" (much like the Methodist Church's "Central" jurisdiction). At the time, Nazarene African-American pastors and churches could be numbered on one hand. The general superintendents hoped that local district superintendents would organize African-American churches, which then would be placed under the Colored District. Certain district superintendents, including E. O. Chalfant in Chicago and O. J. Finch in New York, were eager to plant African-American churches. But not all district superintendents were. In 1949 James Oliver, a white pastor in Arkansas, pled heedlessly with his district to begin work among African-Americans.[34]

One of the church's needed priorities became educating African-American leaders. In 1948 the church began Nazarene Bible Institute in Institute, West Virginia. The West Virginia district superintendent, Edward Oney, a former missionary to Japan, was cooperative. The Nazarene church in Institute had begun six years earlier among teachers at West Virginia State College, a school for African-Americans. General Superintendent Powers secured E. E. Hale, a white evangelist, to head the school. Hale had been a district superintendent in New Mexico in the 1920s and pastor of Indianapolis First Church from 1934 to 1939 and Kansas City First Church from 1939 to 1941. During World War II Hale oversaw African-American chaplains and often preached to Negro troops.[35]

Hale set up a two-year certificate program. He served as president of the school until 1954, when R. W. Cunningham, an African-American, became acting president. Cunningham had become a Nazarene under the ministry of G. B. Williamson in Cleveland, Ohio. Cunningham had earned a bachelor of theology degree at Cleveland Bible Institute and had taken additional classes at both Nyack College and the Winona Lake School of Theology. He was pastoring an integrated Wesleyan Methodist congregation in Zanesville, Ohio, when Warren Rogers, a Nazarene African-American evangelist, introduced him to Hale, who, in turn, persuaded Cunningham to rejoin the Church of the Nazarene and teach at the school. In 1949, Cunningham became pastor of the local congregation in Institute and a teacher in the school. Joining him on the faculty was Clarence Bowman, who had a theology degree from Gordon College. Bowman served as dean of men and treasurer and pastored a church in Charleston, West Virginia. Cunningham became president (no longer acting president) in 1958.[36]

In 1951 there were 150 African-American members in the nine churches that comprised the Colored District. These were located in Oakland, Chicago, Indianapolis, New Orleans, Detroit, Brookhaven (Mississippi), Oklahoma City, San Antonio, and Institute. By 1953 this had risen to sixteen congregations, but in 1959 there were still only 218 African-American Nazarene members on the segregated district.[37]

R. W. Cunningham

The first African-American leaders of the Church of the Nazarene in the South either transferred from other denominations or had been pastors of independent churches. For instance, Boyd Proctor brought an independent congregation in Richmond, Virginia, into the church, and "Elder" D. A. Murray had worked in Mississippi with Bishop C. P. Jones, the founder of the Church of Christ (Holiness).[38]

In Louisiana, M. M. Snyder organized the New Orleans Central Church of the Nazarene in an abandoned saloon in October 1943 and, in 1946, began work in the same city among "wealthy colored oil people." This became the First Colored Church of New Orleans. (The name was later changed to First Negro, and then to Bethel Church of the Nazarene.) Snyder found it difficult to get along with Elbert Dodd, the local district superintendent, who sometimes conducted revivals among African-Americans and believed that he knew "Southern Negroes." Dodd confided to General Superintendent Vanderpool, "You have to handle them with a stick like a mule."[39]

African-American pastors working in Mississippi found similar racism. A congregation in Meridian, Mississippi, led by C. S. Goodwill, joined the Church of the Nazarene in 1950. But because of disagreements with J. D. Saxon, the local district superintendent, Goodwill left the Nazarene fold that same year. Nonetheless, the Meridian Fitkin Memorial Church, as it was called, became one of the strongest African-American churches in the denomination.[40]

Because of the problems with Southern district superintendents, the church dissolved the Colored District in 1953 and formed the Gulf Central District with its own district superintendent, Leon Chambers, a white minister. African-American churches in the South became part of this district, while those elsewhere were integrated into surrounding districts.[41]

In 1958 Warren Rogers became superintendent of the Gulf Central District. Rogers had joined the Nazarene church in Kenmore, New York (near Buffalo), in 1940 while ministering with an evangelistic team. In 1949 he became pastor of a Nazarene church in Oakland, California. The Home Missions Board of the Northern California District had begun this African-American congregation by purchasing the building of a white congregation that had relocated. Later Rogers pastored the Jubilee Church of the Nazarene in Detroit.[42]

As district superintendent, when Rogers traveled in the South, he often could not find eating, lodging, or restroom facilities. On one occasion, Ku Klux Klan members accosted Rogers and the Florida district superintendent he was with when they arrived at a white church, where they were to hold a meeting with local pastors interested in starting work among African-Americans. The white pastors were so afraid for Rogers's life that after the meeting they escorted him, two cars ahead and two cars behind, until he was forty miles outside the city.[43]

Rogers served as district superintendent until the Gulf Central District closed in 1969. Under him, the district grew from twelve to thirty-seven churches. Rogers also helped other district superintendents plant African-American churches on their districts and recommended pastors for them. When the Gulf Central District closed, the African-American churches became part of their surrounding districts. Initially, various superintendents did little to assimilate these churches.[44]

Meanwhile, Nazarene Training Institute faced difficulties. Many of its students were from nearby churches. Leaders realized that the school would be more attractive if it offered a college degree rather than merely the three-year certificate in theology that satisfied Nazarene ordination requirements. Cunningham was rebuffed when he sought affiliation with Trevecca Nazarene College in order to upgrade the program. Nevertheless, the institute educated nearly all of the pastors who served on the Gulf Central District.[45]

The 1964 General Assembly decided to establish a Nazarene Bible college in the United States. Cunningham hoped that the school at Institute would become this Bible college. In 1965, with his Board of Trustees' approval, he issued a catalog changing the name of the school to Nazarene Training College. At Cunningham's insistence, in 1968 the Board of Trustees removed all mention of "colored" from the school's bylaws.[46]

These bids failed. The 1968 General Assembly directed the Home Missions Department to consider merging the school in West Virginia with the newly begun Nazarene Bible College in Colorado Springs. The department decided that it had no other choice. In 1970 Clarence Bowman joined the faculty of NBC and moved to Colorado Springs. Cunningham remained at Institute to pastor. In 1972 he accepted a position at Mount Vernon Nazarene College.[47]

Although the closing of the school was traumatic for African-American leaders, by now there were some opportunities and scholarships available for African-Americans to study in Nazarene liberal arts colleges. In 1974, twenty-five African-American students were enrolled in Colorado Springs and one hundred in other Nazarene liberal arts schools, including thirteen at Trevecca. By the 1976-77 school year 562 African-Americans were included among the 11,175 enrolled in Nazarene colleges.[48]

President A. B. Mackey had opposed integration at Trevecca. "We must love the Negro as ourselves," Mackey said, but "the only true integration is a result of perfect love operating in human relationships." Trevecca's Board of Trustees realized that the "question of integration is at our door" but did not advocate opening the door to African-Americans.[49] Nonetheless, Trevecca students, with the assistance of the College Hill Church, had helped organize an African-American "Community" church in 1955. Similarly, later Trevecca students helped establish the Rogers Chapel Church, an integrated congregation in Nashville.[50]

Mackey retired in 1963. The first Black student was Winston Best, a Nazarene from Barbados, who entered Trevecca in 1964. This was "sort of getting in the back door, for he is not an American," Alpin Bowes commented, but it was "a victory and will lead to the same possibility for others." In 1965, after the United States government decreed that no federal funds would be granted to schools that remain segregated, trustees gave permission for President William Greathouse to assure the government that Trevecca would abide by federal statutes.[51]

In the early 1970s African-American students at Trevecca organized an Afro-American Society "to maintain a black cultural identity and create understanding between blacks and whites."[52] African-Americans played on the school's basketball team. Only in 1974 did Trevecca include African-Americans on one of its traveling singing groups. Even then, some churches on its educational zone would not allow African-American students on evangelistic teams in their worship services and would not entertain or lodge them if they arrived in town.[53]

The Race Question in Local Churches

Local congregations faced growing African-American populations in their communities. When faced with change, they could choose to integrate, sell and move to another location, or find a way to turn over their buildings to African-American Nazarenes.

Thousands of African-Americans from the South migrated to Kansas City, where they formed a "city within a city." Kansas Citians were supposed to have had a "genuine liking" for Negroes, but only as long as they stayed in their "proper place."[54] Kansas City residents denied service to African-Americans in hotels, theaters, and restaurants. The only places downtown where African-Americans could eat were stand-up counters in drugstores. There were few restrooms. There were clauses in contracts that stipulated that property "shall not be conveyed to, owned, used, nor occupied by Negroes as owners or tenants." In 1940, over 90 percent of Kansas City's African-Americans lived in an area of the city bounded, from north to south, by Independence and 27th streets.

The Nazarene headquarters, publishing house, and seminary were located between 27th and 30th Streets. After the Second World War, offices were severely overcrowded. The 1948 General Board authorized a Commission on Location of General Interests. The commission, which included John Stockton, M. Lunn, Hugh Benner, T. W. Willingham, and District Superintendents E. O. Chalfant, D. I. Vanderpool, and V. H. Lewis, looked into the relocation of all Nazarene interests. The commission reported to the 1948 General Assembly that the streets around the headquarters were becoming unsafe and said: "We are realistically facing the fact that a strong Negro population in a community develops problems and situations that are not conducive to the best interests of work such as ours, and for which we are not justified in taking responsibility."[55]

Acting on the report, the General Assembly decided in favor of relocation and appointed a commission. The commission canvassed various parts of Kansas City and decided upon a twenty-one-acre parcel of land about four and a half miles south of the church's current location, at the junction of The Paseo, a major north-south artery, and 63rd Street. The property was purchased for $89,500. By this time, the seminary had raised money for relocation, and ten acres were designated for seminary use. The publishing house and the General Board were to share the remaining costs.[56]

However, Lunn, the publishing house manager, expected urban redevelopment in the inner city and opportunities to buy adjacent property cheaply, so, though the publishing house contributed money for the purchase of the new property, it remained where it was on Troost Avenue.[57]

The seminary raised additional funds through a concerted building campaign beginning in 1950 and was able to break ground in the spring of 1952. Meanwhile, a special denomination-wide relocation offering was taken, and the church sold its building at 30th and Troost. The three-story headquarters building facing The Paseo was completed in December 1954.[58]

While the church was relocating, Kansas City itself underwent significant race problems. African-American delegates to the General Assemblies held in Kansas City in 1952, 1956, and 1960 found it impossible to find hotel rooms. Warren Rogers found accommodations for them only by renting rooms in private homes. Yet the 1956 General Assembly, in still-segregated Kansas City, condemned racial discrimination as incompatible with Scripture and with God as Creator, and contrary to "the experience and doctrine of pure love."[59]

In 1952 Kansas City closed swimming pools in Swope Park, a few miles from the relocated Nazarene headquarters, rather than allow them to be integrated. After losing its case in federal courts, the city reopened the pools in 1954. In 1955 the federal government forced the city to desegregate its school system. At the same time, it pressured the city to enforce "fair housing." African-Americans began moving south of the 27th Street barrier. But not until 1968—when Kansas City was hit by rioting, looting, and violence after the assassination of Martin Luther King Jr.—did the city pass laws that prohibited discrimination in the buying and selling of property.[60]

This was the setting in which Nazarene leaders lived and worked daily. It was not until 1961 that an African-American church began in Kansas City. The veteran district superintendent Jarrette Aycock declared that he had been praying for a "colored" church in the city for nineteen years.[61]

Those who worshipped at Kansas City First Church faced the issues that many Nazarene congregations around the country were encountering. For twenty years the church had been located on 24th and Troost. As more African-Americans moved to Kansas City during the Depression, this part of the city changed. In 1936 the congregation moved to a former Presbyterian Church at 41st and Harrison. In 1955, after African-Americans began buying property south of the old 27th Street dividing line, the church decided to move. It bought property and, taking their Presbyterian pipe organ with them, constructed a church close to the relocated headquarters and seminary, on Meyer Boulevard, near 63rd Street.[62]

By the early 1970s, 63rd Street was on the edge of an expanding African-American community. For a time, like some other urban congregations, First

Church bused African-American children to Sunday School classes. But the children were unruly. Cars were stolen or broken into on the church's parking lot. Members feared attending Sunday evening and Wednesday prayer services. The roof leaked. In 1977 the congregation sold the church. It worshipped for three years in the seminary chapel and then moved to property it purchased on 118th Street.[63]

Some Nazarenes, including many at First Church, were open to integrated churches. In the 1940s, for instance, several African-Americans attended First Church of the Nazarene in Hutchinson, Kansas. "It would seem to me that a church congregation should pretty well reflect its surrounding neighborhood," one pastor commented. "If a church wishes to remain in a given location that is in the process of changing, it should also be in the process of integrating." In 1968 the Kankakee, Illinois, Central Church divided, with one part of the congregation staying in its old location in order to be a truly "neighborhood" church. "Since the gospel is for all mankind," said one leader who remained, "it is our mission to endeavor to reach as many as possible. The race barrier is down at the church. We welcome anyone of any race or any social standing."[64]

Elsewhere in the Midwest, Joe Edwards, the African-American pastor of the Providence Church of the Nazarene in Oklahoma City, worked for civil rights. In 1969 he and members of his congregation supported a sanitation workers' strike. Since most of the sanitation workers were African-Americans, it was, to Edwards, a race issue. While Episcopalians and Catholics helped feed the striking workers, Nazarenes were having a Holiness convention at Bethany. Edwards lamented, "Who do you think sinners are going to believe loves them?" The Providence Church sponsored a city housing project and organized a Good Samaritan Home for needy children. Edwards pastored the church for forty years, until his death in 1995.[65]

Transferring Nazarene buildings and property to African-American congregations worked in a few places. Because of St. Louis's changing racial composition, its First Church merged twice with two other white congregations before 1958, when the Missouri District made it financially possible for the congregation to hand over its building to an African-American Nazarene congregation and relocate elsewhere. Similar strategies worked in Etterick, Virginia, and Port Arthur, Texas. In the cases of Grace Church in Kansas City, Parkway Church in Lubbock, Texas, and Springfield Gardens, New York, the churches lost most of their white members. Those who remained integrated with African-Americans and other ethnic minorities.[66]

In the South, a few white churches and laypersons took interest in establishing African-American churches. In the mid-1950s, A. L. Webb, a businessman, helped organize an African-American church in Calvert, Alabama. At about the same time, E. E. Weatherby angered neighbors when he started an African-American congregation in an abandoned Nazarene church in Concord, North Carolina. In Orlando, Florida, Earl Gorman, a white businessman, helped organize the Gorman Memorial Church, which, under Pastor Archie Williams, became one of the region's strongest African-American Nazarene congregations. The Bethel Church in Gainesville, Georgia, began when white members of the city's First Church called upon Warren Rogers to hold a revival. Similarly, the Lockwood Chapel Church in Houston began as an outreach of the Spring Branch Church in the same city.[67]

Inside the sanctuary of Bethel Church of the Nazarene, Gainesville, Georgia

After his conversion in 1969, Paul Holderfield, a white fireman in North Little Rock, Arkansas, became active in a club for African-American youth. He wanted to invite some of the boys to his local Nazarene church, but it became clear that they would not be welcome. So Holderfield, with the support of the local district superintendent, launched another Nazarene church, appropriately called the Friendly Church of the Nazarene. This integrated church began a number of compassionate ministries.[68]

Meanwhile, Charles Johnson, pastor of the Fitkin Memorial Church in Meridian, Mississippi, became active in the Civil Rights Movement in his city during the 1960s. A graduate of the Bible Institute in West Virginia, Johnson began his ministry under the segregated Gulf District led by Warren Rogers. In 1964, after attending the General Assembly, and soon after the deaths of three African-Americans, likely killed by Klansmen, near his city, Johnson organized the Meridian Action Committee. Initiated as a union of domestic helpers working for extremely low wages, it sought to provide jobs for African-Americans. In 1964 Johnson helped organize Freedom Summer to register and educate voters. Then Johnson created the Opportunities Industrialization Center, which received federal funding, to train young African-Americans. He served on city and state-wide commissions addressing race issues. He became involved in the Council of Federated Organizations, a Mississippi-wide organization. In the administration of Jimmy Carter, he served on the President's Council of Human Resources. All the while, he was a popular camp meeting speaker. Amid the difficulties and trials of the Church of the Nazarene in its relations to the African-American population, Black pastors such as Charles Johnson chose to remain within the Church of the Nazarene. Trevecca Nazarene University, the last Nazarene college to be integrated, conferred upon him an honorary doctor of divinity.[69]

In the East, the predominantly Caribbean congregations in New York City thrived. The Utica Avenue Church, the mother church of Hoople's original Association of Pentecostal Churches of America, had formed a daughter church among Barbadians in Brooklyn—the Beulah Church of the Nazarene. It was the home church of Carlotta Graham, a pioneer Nazarene missionary in the West Indies. By 1944 the white members of the Utica Avenue Church had died or moved, so the Beulah congregation purchased the old church building. Under Levi Franklin, a native of Barbados who led the congregation from 1925 to 1960, and Randolph Holder, a Guyanese who served from 1960 until 1981, the Beulah congregation planted five other churches in Brooklyn.[70]

The Miller Memorial Church in Brooklyn was pastored for several decades by William Greene, a Barbados native. In 1957, he was followed by Clarence Jacobs, a Jamaican who had studied at Olivet Nazarene College and had pastored in Indianapolis. Under Jacobs's ministry the Miller Church emphasized care for the neighborhood and opened Spiritual Clinics that offered counseling. Miller Memorial and Beulah were the strongest congregations on the New York District. With the assistance of professors from ENC, the West Indian congregations in Brooklyn trained their own pastors.[71]

In the West, Bethel Church began in Pasadena in the early 1950s after students at the college visited homes in an African-American section of the city. San Diego First Church sponsored an African-American church in the southeastern part of the city. District auxiliaries established a predominantly African-American congregation in Fresno. The Los Angeles Grace Church, near Watts, once an "all white church in an all white community," decided to remain in the city when the neighborhood changed. In helping to persuade the congregation to stay, A. Roy Smith stressed Phineas Bresee's vision for ministry to the urban poor. The church started programs that reached into the community and ministered to people following the Watts riots in 1965.[72]

Prejudice in the Heart

Holiness did not necessarily remove prejudice. Nazarenes unthinkingly reflected the prejudices in which they were raised. Phineas Bresee, when he conveyed the deed of his house to Pasadena College in 1911, did so with the proviso that only Caucasians would live in it. Susan N. Fitkin, when visiting Africa in the 1920s, called Swazi Nazarene preachers "boy evangelists."[73]

In 1953 Clarence Barrows, a public school teacher in Canton, Ohio, began a "Caravan" club for African-American children and asked district leaders if they could attend the summer boys and girls camp. They would not be welcome, district leaders told him. "Could it be that our public schools are so much better than our holiness churches?" Barrows complained in a letter to Nazarene headquarters. The response was for Barrows to accept the reality that Ohio Nazarenes "would not permit their children to go to camp and swim in the same water and participate in the various activities of the camp life if the colored children were permitted to attend."[74]

In 1964 F. O. Parr, a professor of sociology at Olivet who had been reared in the South, surveyed attitudes toward race and integration on the Olivet zone. He found that three-fourths of Nazarenes on the zone felt that they could worship in integrated churches. The others, however, felt that when African-Americans moved into a community, white residents were justified in selling their property and leaving. One remembered, "We had a Negro family come to our church. We didn't mistreat them, but we didn't go out of our way to have them come back."[75] A pastor did not mind having Negroes attend, but he had a "southern element" in his church. "If the Negro families started coming, I am afraid my people would go to other churches or quit altogether." Anyway, African-Americans wanted their own churches, the pastor felt. A Nazarene pastor linked integration to other political movements and advised:

> Fight it as long as possible (integration), then move if possible. The Negro is different than ours. This has not been forced on us by them. It has come by political force (needed votes) and the Socialistic and Communistic element has pushed it to divide our thinking and living which they envy and hate. I love the Negro as a Negro, have preached to them several times and changed pulpits with their preachers but I do not care to live with them or see our young people pulled to their level.[76]

Even comparative liberals feared that integrated churches would lead to biracial dating and marriages.[77]

Parr believed that "hate goes out when Perfect Love comes in" but admitted that "fears and other emotions remain." One pastor acknowledged that "prejudice is deep" and that religion cannot "wipe out the lines that have been set by our society."[78] Nazarenes were so busy winning individuals, Parr lamented, that they overlooked "group wickedness." "We southern holiness folk," Parr confessed, "have absorbed this from our culture apparently without any question as to its rightness."[79]

For many, indeed, the only adequate way to address racial issues was to remove the "prejudice in our hearts." Nazarenes distrusted social intervention. Legislation would accomplish nothing unless the heart was changed. Inward reform must precede social reform. But the Los Angeles District in 1964 pushed Nazarenes to reach beyond this norm. L. Guy Nees, then pastor of Los Angeles First Church, perceived civil rights to be the "burning issue of our times" and urged Holiness churches not to remain silent. Phineas Bresee's prohibition crusade and commitment to the poor indicated to Nees that the church had fought for social reforms and must now fight against injustice.[80]

> In 1964, Los Angeles District Assembly delegates adopted the following resolution:
>
>> In view of the rapidly increasing Negro population in southern California, the colored people are moving into communities which have been heretofore all white. We urge that our people prepare their thinking that mixed communities are inevitable and that they exercise what means they can to make this adjustment as easy as possible for themselves and for the people of the community in which they live.
>>
>> Believing that Christians value all persons as equal in God's sight, we urge that Nazarenes be committed to racial justice and love in all areas of our social life, so that we may help speed the day when no citizen of this country, because of the color of his skin, will be denied the freedom of choice in such matters as where he wants to live, the school or university he chooses to attend, the restaurant in which he wants to eat, the hotel in which he prefers to sleep, the church in which he desires to worship, or to be denied any other freedom which is generally provided for citizens of this great country.[81]

The 1968 General Assembly, meeting two months after the assassination of Martin Luther King Jr., passed a statement that all individuals "regardless of race, color or creed should have equality before law, including the right to vote, equal access to educational opportunities, to all public facilities, and to the opportunity, according to one's ability, to earn a living free from any job or economic discrimination."[82] The same assembly decided to phase out the Gulf Central District and place African-American Nazarene churches under local districts and superintendents. (Methodists dismantled their segregated Central Jurisdiction the same year.) Church leaders instituted a "Black Council" of African-American leaders to guide the church on race issues. The council later was superseded by an Interracial Advisory Committee.[83]

In 1973 there were only two thousand members in fifty-eight predominantly African-American churches. Thirty-seven of these congregations were inside the boundaries of the old Gulf Central District; five were on the New York District. Yet over 350 other congregations had at least some African-Americans attending.[84]

But observers saw little indication that the Church of the Nazarene wanted integration. Michael Haynes, an African-American Baptist preacher, included Eastern Nazarene College among the New England Christian colleges that needed to "get some black faces on their faculties and staffs, and get more black students" and "provide full and partial scholarships for needy black young marginal Christian men and women." Cheryl Sanders, a Church of God (Anderson) scholar and pastor, included the Church of the Nazarene among the "basically lily-white, middle class, holiness groups reflecting the sin and shame of Racist America."[85]

Racism in South Africa

In South Africa, Nazarenes accepted the government's policy of apartheid or "separate development." The government placed restrictions on the "intermingling" of different races. Like missionaries elsewhere, the ones working in South Africa were forbidden by Nazarene policy from taking part in or expressing themselves "concerning the politics of the country in which they were laboring." Since the South African government had been "helpful and considerate" toward Nazarene efforts by allotting sites for churches and granting permits for missionaries to live in Bantu areas, the church cooperated with official restrictions. They abided by regulations that prevented whites from "lodging" with "Bantu" people, entertaining them in their homes without a government permit, conversing with them for long periods of time in public places, having any physical contact beyond shaking hands, and interfering in Bantu courtship and marriage arrangements. Following these guidelines, Nazarene missionaries refrained from either eating meals in African homes or inviting Africans to meals in theirs. When attending African churches, missionaries sat separately.[86] Privately, some Nazarene missionaries feared that Communism lay behind the antigovernment actions of African Blacks such as Nelson Mandela.[87]

At the same time, at least a few Nazarenes sensed the gulf between the racism and the highest ideals of the church. Though, David Hynd observed, the church had sometimes been more of a hindrance than a help to race relations, when white farmers were saved and sanctified race relations between them and the "natives" became revolutionized. Hynd reported to General Superintendent Powers: "I feel very much that the message of holiness has a great part to play in solving some of these problems in the personal realm. We have had many proofs of it in even Afrikaans people who have been sanctified and whose whole attitude to the native has been automatically changed when the Holy Spirit has come in all His fullness."[88]

Even if such victories could be counted on the personal level, society demanded that the Church of the Nazarene in South Africa build a system of segregated districts and Bible colleges. There were geographically overlapping and separate districts for "Coloureds," East Indians, and Europeans in addition to the ones made up of Bantu Africans. The European District, pioneered by Charles Strickland in 1948, was under the Home Missions department and included members with both English and Afrikaner (Dutch) ancestry. Strickland considered it a triumph that these two groups remained together in one district. The South Africa Nazarene Bible College for these "Europeans" opened in 1954.[89]

In Great Britain, meanwhile, a 1960 article written by Maynard James and published in *The Flame*, which James edited, justified the apartheid system, suggesting that holiness was compatible with racial segregation. James had visited South Africa and had become convinced that though there were injustices, the country must be careful of casting off lawful restraint in a time when a "world-wide conspiracy" was sweeping the world. James was satisfied with the Nazarene policy of noninterference.[90] Alex Deasley wrote an opposing article, and David Tarrant, then pastoring in Port Glasgow, likewise argued that "the thought of depriving a fellow human being of any of the freedom or privilege which is regarded as the right of every citizen of an enlightened society, merely on the ground of his race, is utterly repugnant."[91]

Upon his election as general superintendent in 1972, Strickland answered a reporter's inquiry about the Church of the Nazarene's stance toward apartheid. "The fundamental thrust of the Church is bringing persons to the Lord," Strickland said. "Although we may not go along with a country's politics, we do not preach against them. The societies and churches in South Africa that have protested apartheid have been closed down. If we were to do so, our work there would be over."[92] Even so, Strickland and other Nazarene missionaries found ways to build personal relations with those from other races.[93]

CONCLUSION

Unlike the century preceding, when evangelicals had been in the forefront of the antislavery cause, and unlike decades before, when they had fought for prohibition, there was little attempt among Holiness and evangelical churches during this time period to change society except through personal transformation. While Nazarenes attempted to reach out to African-Americans, the church's actions barely kept up with society as a whole. Morality was privatized. Social systems went unchallenged. Nazarenes evangelized Black people in America and Africa without addressing larger issues.[94]

SEVENTEEN
THE CHURCH EVANGELIZING

The Church of the Nazarene at midcentury pushed its boundaries through evangelism and missions. Evangelism was central to the church. Entire sanctification, Nazarenes believed, empowered them to be witnesses for Christ in the world and enabled them to give sacrificially and compassionately. In truth as well as aim, the world increasingly became the parish of Nazarene ministry. Evangelizing the world remained an imbedded priority among the church's top leaders as well as among its laypersons.

THE CHURCH'S MISSION

Following World War II, Nazarenes were eager to evangelize the world. In 1945, Foreign Missions Secretary Jones was waiting for peace in order to send out a backlog of eager missionary recruits. During the years of global conflict the church amassed its own financial war chest for missions expansion. Giving to missions reached a $500,000 by 1943-44, and $1 million by 1946-47. With the money for missions stockpiled during the war, the church rapidly expanded its missionary force. Leaders were as optimistic and as organized as Hiram Reynolds had been in an earlier era. Like him, postwar leaders believed that what was required for world outreach were the Holy Spirit's power, efficient organization, and financial resources. After decades of constant pleading for money to keep missionaries on their fields, in the immediate postwar years the church could not spend quickly enough. Leaders prepared to seize the moment the postwar world offered. The missions force jumped from 78 missionaries in 1944 to 200 by 1948, 300 by 1952, and 400 by 1960. In 1976 there were 549 Nazarene missionaries.[1]

Like other evangelicals, Nazarenes took Matt. 28:23-28 as their "Great Commission." A firm belief in the eternal "lostness" of people apart from faith in Christ coupled with the desire to obey Christ pushed missions forward.[2] As the missions policy put it, in going to a lost world the primary objective was spiritual: the salvation of sinners, the sanctification of believers, and the establishment of the church in "the most holy faith as taught in the

Word of God." The church must not only "effect the salvation of people in foreign lands by presenting Christ as their Savior" but also "lead them into heart holiness as a second definite work of grace and to establish them in holy living." The means of accomplishing this goal was by organizing "Christians into churches and training them to the point of establishing an indigenous church." This "training" required Bible schools and colleges for ministers and, in some places, primary and secondary schools. Nazarenes believed that "the work and manifestations of the Holy Spirit" were "practically the same in all countries." The church made little room for cultural differences.[3]

As the church approached its fiftieth anniversary in 1958, Nazarenes gauged whether the church had been faithful to its original purpose and mission. The year started with watch night services in which Nazarenes prayed for a lost world and confessed their own spiritual needs. In October, about 4,500 Nazarenes trekked to Pilot Point, Texas, where various speakers, including witnesses to the 1908 gathering, invoked the spirit of the pioneers. The salvation of souls was the church's "objective," said General Superintendent Powers, while "scriptural holiness" was the "theme song" or "distinguishing doctrine" of the church's founders.[4] God had given Nazarenes a "particular mission—the spread of the message of full salvation, scriptural holiness as a second definite work of divine grace, over the earth." The church dare not become just another denomination, General Superintendent Benner warned, lest it stagnate like the rest.[5]

Other ministries served the goal of evangelism. "Our policy is not primarily one of education," wrote C. Warren Jones in 1955, "but the salvation of the heathen," and evangelism "must always stand above education in im-

---

In 1958 the church erected a bronze marker at Pilot Point. The marker read:[6] "Phineas F. Bresee, in many respects the founder and moving spirit of the new organization, expressed the vision of them all in this confession: 'We are debtors to every man to give him the gospel in the same measure as we have received it.' Today some 350,000 people call themselves Nazarenes, and their missionary enterprise reaches into 40 world areas."

portance." Though the church believed in "social uplift," Jones went on, these goals "must come second to preaching for personal Christian experience." In regards to health programs, said Jones, "we are for medical missions, but only as a means to an end, and that end must be the salvation of the lost."[7] In writings intended to encourage laypeople to give to missions, doctors and others stressed the evangelistic impact of medical missions.[8]

Missionary Bronell Greer, who went to India in 1944 and served there for forty-six years, believed that institutions were strangling the true mission and were unsustainable by the local church. The Great Commission of the church was not to heal the sick or to reform society, he protested in 1969, but to preach the gospel. "All divinely ordained work of the church has its importance," Greer agreed, "but not all God given vocations are equally important. Evangelism holds the highest priority."[9]

At the Conferencia Centroamericana de Pastores in 1969, Ernesto Bello affirmed that the church's fundamental mission was evangelism. He warned it to stay out of politics. At the same time, he recognized that the majority of the church was poor. The Word of God must be given to them through good works, he said.[10]

Yet the Communist takeover of China demonstrated the importance of preparing local leaders. To bear fruit, the church's roots must be deep. W. C. Esselstyn emphasized that in the African context if all the church's money and effort were in evangelism, there would be shallow faith and commitment.[11] Similarly, after looking at the church in India, G. B. Williamson suggested, "Those who have engaged in evangelism and have neglected to conduct a program of education have discovered that it was all but impossible to accomplish abiding results."[12] The "primary purpose" of the church was "redemptive," and in carrying out this commission there was a large place for adequately preparing leaders, healing the sick, feeding the hungry, and giving water to the thirsty. "The points of ethics emphasized by the preachers of the social gospel have been included all along in the teaching of holiness," Williamson wrote in 1953.[13] Williamson suggested that training in cleanliness, hygiene, sanitation, literacy, and vocational arts validly accompanied the gospel. Unless basic needs were met, Williamson saw, converts would be tempted to revert to old ways of life. Williamson's views represented a more holistic model of missions than Jones's. Williamson believed that "we must export not only the gospel of God's love and grace, but also Christian civilization must be made to cover the earth as waters cover the sea."[14]

David Hynd, longtime missionary and medical doctor, believed that hospitals testified to the "regenerating power of the gospel with its spirit of divine compassion." Medical work was not simply a means of making converts. Though Hynd could report many examples of conversions taking place at the hospital in Manzini, compassionate ministries, to him, were in themselves the "most effective interpretation of the Christ-like Spirit."[15]

Both Williamson and Hynd would have been comfortable with examples of the "Bresee paradigm" (practical holiness) evident in Haiti, Swaziland, and Papua New Guinea, and with renewed attention to American cities. Quoting Bresee, General Secretary S. T. Ludwig wrote in 1952 that the mission of the church was to establish "a thousand centers of holy flame."[16] Also reflecting Bresee's thought, Alpin Bowes of the Home Missions department wrote that "perhaps the Church of the Nazarene, in the white-hot intensity of holiness evangelism, has the responsibility, not only to the lost, but to act as leaven among the denominations, proclaiming God's call to his people to be holy and zealous of good works."[17]

Whether the church saw compassionate ministries as a civilizing work, an evangelistic tool, or an expression of perfect love, the church maintained its hospitals in India and Swaziland and undertook responsibility for the International Holiness Mission's hospital in South Africa. It began a new hospital in Papua New Guinea and feeding programs and clinics in Haiti.

A 1973 survey of missionary vocations indicated that 30 percent of the church's 527 missionaries were directly involved in evangelism and church planting, 26 percent in education, and 17 percent in health. Others were involved in a variety of other ministries, including homemaking. Women comprised 60 percent of Nazarene missionaries.[18]

REACHING OUT THROUGH EVANGELISM

In spite of increased membership, declining growth rates worried leaders. In an urgent address in January 1946, J. B. Chapman called for a denomination-wide Crusade for Souls that would "awaken the dormant forces of our people, young and old" and "re-emphasize old-time moral and spiritual conditions." Already, in Chapman's mind, the founders' "passion for souls" was being lost or diluted.[19] A year later Nazarene evangelists met in Kansas City for a Conference on Evangelism that focused on the theme "All Out for Souls." A committee on evangelism, meeting in September 1947, chaired by G. B. Williamson, was unanimous that the church needed to awaken to the possibilities of having an "informed laity on fire" and affirmed that what the church needed was both technique and the Holy Spirit. The 1948 General Assembly launched the evangelistic campaign that Chapman had urged. The crusade included both "home" and "foreign" fields. The uncertain postwar times added urgency to the call. The following years in Nazarene history were marked by intentional and zealous evangelism.[20]

In response to the 1948 call for a Crusade for Souls, churches launched evangelistic campaigns. Churches used visitation as a means of evangelizing. Selling products door-to-door was common in suburban America in the 1940s and 1950s. Elmer Kauffman, a successful trainer of door-to-door Fuller Brush salesmen, coauthored, with Albert Harper, *First Steps in Visitation Evangelism*. The book instructed laypersons to go house to house in teams of two, knocking on doors to find "needy neighbors." "Do you know of a boy or girl in this block or neighborhood who does not attend Sunday School?" the teams were to ask. The purpose was not really to find out about local children, Kauffman and Harper admitted, but to gauge the religious commitment of the persons to whom the question was addressed. There was rarely a "discourteous" reply. Those who made calls might pray, leave a card or tract, and ask if the residents would like a pastor to visit. If the team were invited into the home, they were to compliment something about the furnishings, avoid religious arguments, and make friends. Unlike later visitation strategies, this approach relied on getting people to church to be "saved." Offer to milk a man's cows if he would come to the Nazarene revival meetings, *First Steps* suggested.[21] Nazarenes in the Philippines and in other countries attempted similar means of visitation evangelism. Visitation found persons who felt themselves to be alone in an increasingly impersonal society or members of churches that had forgotten them. Nazarenes surrounded them with "friendship, fellowship, and love."[22]

Leaders extended the Crusade for Souls into the next quadrennium (1952-56). Nazarenes started 1,177 new churches in the United States between 1946 and 1956 and added 86,000 members. Average Sunday School attendance grew from 369,726 in 1946 to 611,319 in 1956, though this was the fruit of the postwar baby boom as much as the Crusade for Souls. Per capita giving rose from $82 in 1946 to $130 in 1956.[23]

Growth was so rapid that some feared that the new Nazarenes would "dilute" the church. District superintendents warned pastors not to accept into membership those who were not fully separated from the world. Nazarene leaders felt that the church's strict rules, rather than being obstacles to growth, represented the kinds of moral boundaries for which modern men and women were searching.[24]

Revivals remained a primary means of reaching communities, converting children and young people in the church, keeping believers from backsliding and guiding them into entire sanctification, and renewing the commitment of all. Revivals, like other aspects of the church, were well organized. Techniques for a successful revival went from prerevival publicity and prayer to postrevival "shepherding."[25] A revival at the church in Basim, India, in 1947 found Hindus, Muslims, and Christians kneeling together around the altar. In the Philippines, revival services, camp meetings, and the annual District Assembly were conducted under large canvas tents.[26]

Scores of Nazarene evangelists crisscrossed the United States and traveled to other countries. C. Hastings Smith, the "poet of the Ozarks," combined humor and drama with evangelism. Paul Martin preached positive, self-effacing, and often humorous messages to young people while encouraging them to seek holiness. "Warmth, wit, enthusiasm, imagination, sensitivity, [and] faith" filled his voice. Martin possessed an intuitive rapport with his audiences and an ability to communicate by speaking simply and directly to the heart and mind of his hearers.[27] Albert Lown, who had been a member of the International Holiness Mission before its merger with the Church of the Nazarene, wore his clerical collar even in American revivals and camp meetings. He preached richly illustrated, deductive sermons. College professors such as Mel-Thomas Rothwell and Reuben Welch, and seminary professors, including James McGraw, W. T. Purkiser, Richard Taylor, Mendell Taylor, and William Greathouse, spoke with great impact in revivals and camp meetings. Their unction convinced the church that the schools were not veering away from the evangelistic center of the church.[28]

Paul Martin

Many Nazarene evangelists were women. In her forty-year career in Mozambique, Mary Cooper's primary work was evangelism. She traveled thousands of miles and at one time superintended a district of ninety churches. C. Helen Mooshian, an Armenian immigrant saved in Lawrence, Massachusetts, graduated from ENC and pastored home missions in Western Canada and the Western United States before entering evangelism in 1945. Preaching for other conservative Holiness groups as well as the Church of the Nazarene, by 1970 she had reached 180 countries. Nettie Miller and Lelia Dell Miller were sister evangelists from Georgia who traveled widely around the denomination. Estelle Crutcher, born in India to British missionaries, pastored in New Jersey, New York, and Ohio but was best remembered as an evangelist in the 1950s and 1960s. A contemporary, Doris McDowell, had worked in fashion design in Southern California and had raised a family before entering twenty-five productive years of evangelism in 1951. She spoke at Nazarene colleges, often about the proprieties of courtship, and several times toured British Isles churches. Later, she pioneered a church in California and pastored the English-speaking congregation in Manzini, Swaziland.[29]

Juliet Ndzimandze, the daughter of the first Swazi Nazarene pastor, became an evangelist after teaching for twenty years at the Nazarene Bible School in Siteki. She had been the first full-time Swazi teacher at the school. In 1966, she became the first Swazi woman to be ordained. From 1966 to 1969 she was president of the district NYPS. That led her into full-time evangelism in 1970. She preached throughout Swaziland and in other African countries. In 1978 she became evangelist to the Nazarene schools in Swaziland, and in 1984 she was appointed evangelist for the whole continent of Africa.[30]

The Department of Home Missions and Evangelism strategized for continued growth. S. T. Ludwig served simultaneously as general secretary and executive secretary of the Department of Home Missions and Evangelism from 1944 to 1948. In 1948 the General Board appointed Roy F. Smee to head the Home Missions and Evangelism Department. Smee, a successful superintendent of the Northern California District from 1931 to 1948, stressed church planting. In 1949, the Church Extension office, earlier under the general treasurer, was brought under Home Missions. Smee secured Alpin Bowes to serve as office manager. Bowes, who served at Home Missions until 1969, became involved in a number of areas, from church architecture to ministries to African-Americans.[31]

The division of labor between the Home and Foreign Mission departments reflected ethnic rather than geographic distinctions. The Home Missions Department oversaw work among African-Americans, Chinese Americans, and Spanish-speaking Americans. The department was responsible for work in Alaska (which began in 1938 and was organized as a district in 1951), Australia (1948), Bermuda (1961), Denmark (1959), Hawaii (1946), Italy (1948), the Netherlands (1967), New Zealand (1952), the Panama Canal Zone (1953), Samoa (1960), European South Africa (1948), and West Germany (1958).

Work among Native Americans was transferred from Home Missions to Foreign Missions in 1944. Supposedly, those groups or countries under Home Missions were headed for self-support more rapidly than those put under Foreign Missions. The Home Missions work was more directly under the control of the general superintendents, and that sometimes determined which countries went under Home Missions. Sometimes English was a factor. At one point General Superintendent Powers, who oversaw Home Missions work for several quadrennia, foresaw the evangelization of the continent of Europe through the British Isles.[32]

In order to finance new churches, in 1955 Smee established a General Church Loan Fund. The department periodically raised the amount that a local church could borrow and, as well, the amount of interest charged to local churches. From 1947 to 1970 the General Church Loan Fund distributed $8.45 million to 726 churches on seventy-six districts.[33]

The general superintendents were worried over the slowdown in church planting, in spite of Smee's efforts. During the 1959-60 church year Nazarenes in the United States planted only forty-four churches. The general superintendents chose "Evangelism First" as the theme for the 1960-64 quadrennium.[34]

In 1956 Evangelism became a separate department. V. H. Lewis, who had served as an evangelist, pastor, and district superintendent, became its director. Lewis stressed that visitation should do more than invite neighbors to church—it should lead them to Christ. He set up a bureau of "moving Nazarenes" so that pastors could alert one another when a Nazarene family moved to another locality. Lewis, elected general superintendent in 1960, was succeeded by Edward Lawlor, who served eight years before himself being elected a general superintendent. The Evangelism Department then came under John L. Knight, who had been the district superintendent in Florida.[35]

Smee remained in charge of Home Missions until retiring in 1964. His successor was Orville Jenkins, who served until his election as a general superintendent in 1968. Raymond Hurn replaced Jenkins in Home Missions. Hurn became interested in establishing ethnic minority churches in U.S. cities. The church, Hurn wrote, must not crawl into its "own little enclave, polish the saints, refuse contact with outsiders, maintain personal piety, and totally miss the real mission of Christ in the world."[36] Hurn and Paul Orjala, professor of missions at Nazarene Theological Seminary, embraced the "homogenous unit principle" of church planting taught by Fuller School of Missions professor Donald McGavran. They believed that the church should target one ethnic and social group when planting a church.[37]

In 1976 the Home Missions and World Missions departments redrew their boundaries. The American Indian and Latin Districts were transferred to the Home Missions department and (much to the ire of British Nazarenes) all the non-North American districts were transferred to World Mission.[38]

NEW WAYS OF REACHING OUT

Nazarenes always looked for effective methods of sharing the gospel. Like other evangelicals, Nazarenes used technology to advance the gospel. Some Nazarene congregations had their own radio programs. In the 1930s and 1940s Agnes Diffee had made the Church of the Nazarene known in Arkansas and surrounding states through her broadcasts from Little Rock First Church.[39] In 1945, the church established a Nazarene Radio League with T. W. Willingham as executive secretary. After several special broadcasts, "Showers of Blessing" began. R. V. DeLong became its regular preacher. By 1960 "Showers of Blessing" was carried on more than four hundred stations around the world, including Australia, Barbados, Haiti, Jamaica, Korea, Nicaragua, the Philippines, Puerto Rico, South Africa, Taiwan, and Trinidad. As a leading churchman, college administrator, evangelist, seminary professor, and preacher, Russell V. DeLong was one of the most influential Nazarene preachers of his generation. His sermons demonstrated cadence and rhythm and appealed to the "common man," but they also evidenced DeLong's philosophical personalism. DeLong spoke on the program until 1968. His successor was evangelist C. William Fisher.[40]

Paralleling "Showers of Blessing" was the Spanish-language "La Hora Nazarena," which began production in 1953. H. T. Reza served as its preacher from 1953 to 1974. The program was produced in Kansas City until 1981, when it was transferred to Costa Rica. Eventually it aired on more than seven hundred radio stations in Mexico, Central and South America, and the United States.[41]

Various other countries had their own broadcasts. In India, the church began occasional radio programs in 1952 and, in 1960, secured time on the Far East Broadcasting Company. The Nazarene program was produced at the Basim compound, used the Marathi language, and aired six times a week. Bronell Greer, Samuel Bhujbal, S. T. Gaikwad, Padu Meshramkar, and others taped fifteen-minute segments. The program included a Bible correspondence course under the direction of M. V. Ingle that enrolled thousands.[42] In Cape Verde Nazarenes broadcast "Messengers of Light" and, by the early 1970s, "A Hora Nazarena," produced by Jorge Barros. It was used in various Portuguese-speaking countries around the world.[43]

Local congregations found other creative ways to reach out. By the 1960s it became less possible in America to go door to door. The days of getting non-Christians to attend revival services were waning. So the church found alternatives. Nazarenes began production of a few television specials that were aimed especially at young people. "Shade-tree evangelism" was successful in a few urban and suburban areas. A church organized a team and found a shade tree four or five blocks from the church under which to hold programs for children. Teachers got to know each child by name and, through them, reached into the neighborhood.[44]

Copying successful Sunday Schools in other denominations, in the late 1960s and 1970s various Nazarene churches bought old school buses and lay "bus pastors" loaded them with children each Sunday to take to church. This increased Sunday School attendance and provided a way into otherwise unreached homes.

Problems developed, however. Maintaining and insuring the old buses was expensive. Many of the pupils being bused were from underprivileged homes and were, in the eyes of some church members, undisciplined. They tested Nazarene love to people outside their own social boundaries. Patience wore thin.[45]

Long Beach First Church was among the churches that reached into its community through an array of programs. It sponsored small-group Bible studies for both singles and married couples; evangelistic Bible studies for those still not "born again"; "Fascinating Womanhood," a ten-week course for women; a musical ensemble; and a crafts class. For youth, the church had board games, table tennis, volleyball, film showings, coffeehouses, a "Fifth Quarter" program after high school basketball games, and a Jesus rock group. For children there were preschool and kindergarten classes, after-school clubs, and a summer karate class. The church arranged with local schools for children to be let out of classes forty minutes early once each week for religious instruction.[46]

On the other side of the United States, the Church of the Nazarene in New Milford, New Jersey, reached disenchanted youth. In 1969 Pastor Paul Moore started a coffeehouse in the church basement. He brought in rock groups, including one led by Charlie Rizzo, a "Christ-centered hippie,"[47] and formed the Maranatha Band. Soon the church was packed. The CBS television network produced a thirty-minute segment on the church, "Lamp unto My Feet."[48] By 1970 the coffeehouse was reaching five hundred people each week. About 40 percent were Jewish, and another 40 percent Roman Catholic. There was an "uninhibited, loose and joyful" atmosphere of continual revival.[49] Young people on drugs were converted. Much like other Jesus People movements, there were emphases upon the second coming of Christ, the literal interpretation of the Bible, and bold witnessing. About half of the New Milford church members, including board members, privately spoke in tongues. But Moore did not allow tongues, with or without an "interpretation," in worship services. By 1971 about four thousand young people had found Christ through the church's ministry. During the 1972 General Assembly, the church's Maranatha Band played on the beaches of Miami.⁵⁰

Such ministries were a bit too "worldly" for some Nazarenes just outgrowing their hesitancies about having kitchens in the church. Said one embittered Nazarene of the young people at New Milford, "It is mockery to envision the Holy Spirit standing among that crowd."⁵¹

EVANGELIZING CITIES AND ETHNIC COMMUNITIES

Milford was a special case. In the postwar era, the Church of the Nazarene in America remained a predominantly white, middle-class denomination, dominated by its suburban churches. Nonetheless, the church knew that it could not very well proclaim perfect love without reaching out to those who were socially marginalized.

The church had had ministries to ethnic minorities since its founding. Los Angeles First started a Chinese Sunday School in 1927. It helped establish a Chinese church, which was organized in 1952. Most of its members were Cantonese-speaking. Harry Wiese, former missionary to China, superintended the Chinese work on the West Coast. By the early 1960s Nazarenes had Chinese churches in San Diego, Los Angeles, and San Francisco.⁵²

In the early 1950s the San Francisco church was led by Mary Li. She had come from China in 1947 to work with Youth for Christ. Joining the Church of the Nazarene in 1948, she earned an M.A. in religion at Pasadena College in 1950 and was ordained in 1952. She returned to China in November 1954. Settling in Shanghai, she taught Bible, English, and music for seven years in the only Protestant theological seminary that was open in China during this time. Not until a letter from Li reached then World Mission Secretary Jerald Johnson in 1979 did the Church of the Nazarene resume contact with her.⁵³

Work among Native Americans had an early history. In 1944 there were thirteen Native American churches—six in Oklahoma and seven others scattered in New Mexico, Arizona, California, Montana, and New York. The first North American Indian District Assembly was conducted in 1945. The district extended from California to Oklahoma. The churches in Oklahoma included Comanches, Cheyennes, Arapahos, and Poncas; in New Mexico, Navajos, Pueblos, and Apaches; in Arizona, Navajos, Cocopahs, Dieguinos, Quechans, Pimas, Marocopas, Mojaves, Hopis, Papagos, and Lagunas; and, in California, Mojaves and Quechans. The general superintendents appointed Dowie Swarth, who had been district superintendent in Arizona, as superintendent of the new district. A Bible school, which began at the sixth grade and went through high school, began in 1948 at Lindrith, New Mexico. It moved near Albuquerque in 1954. Swarth served until 1957 and was replaced by G. H. Pearson. In 1975, the district elected Julian Gunn, a Mojave, as superintendent. At that time there were sixteen hundred members.[54]

The church increased its efforts toward Mexican and other Spanish-speaking immigrants in the southwestern part of the United States. In 1942 the Southwest Mexican District, which included churches on both sides of the Mexican border from California to Texas, was divided into Western and Central Latin American districts. In 1945 the churches on the Mexican side of the Texas border were separated into a district led by Enrique Rosales. The Western Latin American District continued to include churches in northwestern Mexico until 1972, when it was divided to create a separate district in Northwestern Mexico.[55]

Nazarenes established an Eastern Latin American District in 1958. Spanish-speaking churches were located in New York, Connecticut, and New Jersey. Many of the members were of Puerto Rican descent. Work among Cuban refugees—some already Nazarenes—began in Miami, Florida, in 1961 under John Hall, a former missionary in Cuba. The Spanish-speaking pastors in the United States held their first national conference in June 1975.[56]

The church began work in Hawaii in 1946. What developed there was a kind of microcosm of the multiethnic mix to which the church aspired. By the 1960s it included ministries to Japanese, Samoan, Filipino, Chinese, and white ethnic groups. Pastors of these congregations reflected the same diversity.[57]

STRUCTURES FOR REACHING OUT

Nazarenes sought to maximize the work of the Spirit through sane and efficient organization. The segment of the church most responsible for promoting the church's missions outside North America was the missionary society. Susan Fitkin remained as president until 1948. In her last years she moved from Brooklyn to Oakland, California. Fitkin continued to give out of her own independent wealth as she saw need. Emma Word, the society's secretary-treasurer, who was also treasurer of the Foreign Missions department, lived in Kansas City and controlled the day-to-day operations of the society. Word corresponded with missionaries, sent them advice and money, and traveled with Fitkin on world tours.[58]

In 1948 Louise Robinson Chapman succeeded Fitkin. Under her, in 1952, the society was enlarged so as to include men. The name of the organization was changed from the Woman's Foreign Missionary Society to the Nazarene Foreign Missionary Society.[59]

Louise Robinson Chapman, a tireless and effective missions promoter, was in constant demand as a speaker. She had served in Swaziland from 1920 to 1940. During World War II she spoke often in missions conventions. In 1942, she married J. B. Chapman, whose first wife had died in 1940. Unlike Fitkin, Robinson Chapman lived in Kansas City and became involved in the Society's day-to-day operations. She had personal influence upon the general superintendents and a loyal following among laypersons. This allowed her to pursue projects with or without permission from the Foreign Mission department.[60]

Louise Robinson Chapman

Working closely with Louise Robinson Chapman in the missionary society was Mary Scott, who replaced Emma Word in 1950 and served as general secretary until 1975. Scott had served briefly in China before the war and remained interred by the Japanese until 1945. From 1947 to 1949 Scott worked in Kiangsi Province. Like Louise Robinson Chapman, Scott often spoke in missionary rallies. Both were ordained ministers.

Under Scott, the missionary society continued to offer local churches creative ideas for presenting information regarding the global church and its needs. Led by the women of the church, churches normally held monthly missionary society meetings on Sunday evenings. They might tell stories from *The Other Sheep*, prepare food from the country under discussion, and show slides or have mock interviews with a "missionary."[61]

Following Robinson Chapman's retirement in 1964, the society's presidents became less directly involved in the running of the society, leaving more in the hands of Scott. At the same time, the society and its leaders had less capacity to influence missions decisions and served more purely as a fund-raising and promotional auxiliary. The society raised the denomination's General Budget, which paid administrators' salaries as well as provided funds that kept the missions program of the church expanding.[62]

Another important figure in the society was Helen Temple, who edited the society's promotional magazine from 1952 to 1984 and authored dozens of missionary reading books that captured the spirit of Nazarene missions around the world.[63]

In 1964 the society changed its name once more, this time removing the word "foreign," which now seemed both pejorative and out of step with internationalization. The church had no "foreigners." The society was now the Nazarene World Missionary Society.⁶⁴ For similar reasons, in 1975 the society changed the title of its missions publication from *The Other Sheep* to *World Mission*. There were no "other" sheep, just one big flock in the Church of the Nazarene. Every Nazarene, no matter where he or she lived, was part of the church's one mission to the world.⁶⁵

Mary Scott

The 1972 NWMS Convention elected its first man, Paul Gamertsfelder, to its General Council and launched the Men-in-Mission Crusade. Mission was no longer the domain of women. Men found that the church needed particular work skills as well as financial resources. The first Witness Crusade took place in Panama in January 1974. So dramatic were the results that quickly other churches were sending teams to countries around the world. In 1975 the World Mission Division appointed a coordinator for what was now called Work and Witness. Laypersons took back to local churches from trips understanding of and enthusiasm for missions. Churches involved in Work and Witness team projects maintained and increased their General Budget giving while contributing to various mission field projects.⁶⁶

NONDENOMINATIONAL STRUCTURES

Not all of the channels through which Nazarenes reached into the world were denominational. Several nondenominational missions had strong Nazarene ties. Many Nazarenes across the years served, for instance, with the Oriental Missionary Society.⁶⁷

E. G. and Emma Eaton had returned to India in 1920, but not under the Church of the Nazarene. Emma Eaton, a proficient fund-raiser, formed the Heart of India Mission Band. In 1931 the Eatons formed the India Gospel League, which distributed Christian literature by mail throughout India. Its headquarters moved from India to Pasadena in 1946.⁶⁸

Robert Hammond, a Nazarene minister, founded the Voice of China (later, Voice of Asia), a radio broadcast and missions organization also based in Pasadena. Before World War II Hammond had been a missionary to Hong

Kong under the South China Peniel Holiness Mission. After forming his own mission, Hammond solicited funds for clothing to be shipped to Taiwan. His agency sent Michael and Elizabeth Varro, former Nazarene missionaries in South China, to Taiwan.[69]

Another California-based agency was World-Wide Missions, led by Basil Miller. Established in 1950, the organization was "devoted to carrying the Gospel to the ends of the earth through national preachers, evangelists, doctors, nurses, teachers and other workers" (rather than through missionaries).[70] It began by lending support to thirty-five churches in Nigeria and by the mid-1960s was supporting one thousand local workers in seventy countries. Despite Miller's preference for helping local leaders, World-Wide Missions also sponsored "faith" missionaries responsible for raising their own support. One World-Wide mission that appealed to Nazarenes was the Twin Wells project among Navajos in New Mexico. Because World-Wide Missions established procedures for ordaining ministers, Nazarene leaders accused Miller of starting his own denomination.[71]

INTERNATIONALIZING THE CHURCH

In the postwar era the Church of the Nazarene accessioned independent groups and Holiness missions, entered new fields, and strengthened existing work. Foreign Missions directors C. Warren Jones and Remiss Rehfeldt oversaw rapid postwar missions expansion. Their successors from 1960 to 1980, George Coulter, E. S. Phillips, and Jerald Johnson, pushed toward internationalization.

Coulter, who had emigrated from Northern Ireland to Canada, instructed missionaries to make the development of self-supporting churches the priority, while Phillips, who led the missions department from 1964 until his death in 1973, encouraged local leadership and solicited advice from church leaders outside North America. That the age of colonialism was over shaped the new face of missions, Phillips realized. The role of the missionaries must change from church planters and evangelists to advisers.[72]

At the Central American Pastors' Conference in 1969, Federico Guillermo, district superintendent in Guatemala, stated that though the missionaries had been amiable, altruistic, generous, and longsuffering, they were still outsiders, speaking with a "foreign accent." He called them "imperialists" and "Yankees" who were not able to comprehend Central Americans. Nationalism and Latino pride longed for Central American leadership and for those reasons as well as economic and political ones, missionaries needed to transfer leadership to Central Americans.[73]

These sentiments came at a time of heightened racial conflict and soul-searching in the United States. A Missionary Study Commission in 1972 recognized "the clamor of men of every race and culture and of differing systems of government and of different stages of development to be heard and to have a voice in the determination of their own destiny." The commission recognized "that the gospel has too often been thought of as a white man's religion," and urged that more non-North Americans be appointed to missionary service and that districts be granted increased autonomy.[74]

In response, at the 1972 General Assembly Phillips met with leaders from churches outside of North America in order to listen to their perspectives, facilitate better relationships between them and missionaries, and take steps that might enable the church to become truly international. Phillips believed that the church was at a turning point. It would have to decide whether to allow its missions to become autonomous national churches, to create a federation of national churches, or to continue being an international church with an administrative and theological connection maintained through its *Manual*, General Assembly, General Board, and general superintendents—a structure in which each self-supporting district had equal rights, privileges, and responsibilities.[75]

The 1972 General Assembly established four levels of districts based on self-support, self-government, and growth. A pioneer district was organized when the church was just entering a new area. At the national-mission district level there were measures of growth and self-support and a local district superintendent. The intent was for missionaries to step aside from leadership early in a district's development. At the next, mission district level, there was to be 50 percent self-support and an elected national district superintendent. At these stages the duties of the Mission Council were separated from those of the local superintendent. However, the Mission Council president served on the District Advisory Board and the district superintendent presented budget needs to the Mission Council. The District Advisory Board and the Executive Committee of the Mission Council jointly approved how money from Kansas City was apportioned. General Board funds used for building projects and institutions remained under the Mission Council. Both the district superintendent and the Mission Council president submitted regular reports to the Department of World Missions. A district achieved regular status when it became fully self-supporting and there were at least one thousand members. The number of delegates to the General Assembly depended on the level.[76]

When districts were evaluated by these criteria, the World Mission Division identified thirty-two pioneer districts, twenty-nine national-mission districts, and five mission districts. Only one district, the Northeast Guatemala District, received regular district status. Missionaries in Guatemala had intentionally prepared the church for self-support. A careful policy that led to self-reliance had been implemented in the 1930s. But not until 1963, in part due to "internal strife" among missionaries, was a Guatemalan, Federico Guillermo, appointed district superintendent. Local leaders like Guillermo appeared around the world with increasing regularity. There were only fifteen national district superintendents in 1970, but the number had risen to seventy-five by 1980.[77]

Because it was spoken by so many Nazarenes, Spanish became the second language of the church. The 1944 General Assembly established a Spanish department to develop Holiness material for all of the Spanish-speaking parts of the church. This eliminated duplication of effort, smoothed production processes, relieved the burden to produce Spanish material in every country, and, in effect, brought unity among Spanish-speaking Nazarenes. The Spanish department was located in Kansas City, where it had access to the Nazarene Publishing House. Under the direction of H. T. Reza, it published *El Heraldo de Santidad,* the Spanish version (and not simply a translation) of the *Herald of Holiness,* Spanish Sunday School material, *Mana Ministerial* (a preachers' magazine), Christian Service Training books, a hymnal *(Lluvias de Bendicion),* a magazine for teenagers, and various books for the ministerial course of study. Major translation projects included Adam Clarke's *Commentary* and the *Beacon Bible Commentary* series. It produced materials and sponsored workshops covering every facet of church life.[78]

H. T. Reza

Reza increased the church's sensitivity to its non-North American members and promoted the use of local workers rather than missionaries. Local leaders could live more cheaply and could adjust more easily, knew the language, and could communicate the gospel to their people in ways missionaries never could. They did not bring customs and aspects of culture that might be confused with the gospel.[79] Among those who Reza brought to Kansas City to work with him in the Spanish department were Sergio Franco of Mexico and Ismael Amaya of Argentina.[80]

Honorato T. Reza (1913-2000) entered a Nazarene primary school in Telolapan, Mexico, in 1919. He was converted in 1923 and sanctified under V. G. Santin some years later. He studied at the Nazarene seminary in Mexico City and pastored for two years in Oaxaca, Mexico.

In 1937 Reza entered Pasadena College, where he lived with General Superintendent Goodwin and his family. Basil Miller tutored him in English. Reza earned A.B. and Th.B. degrees at Pasadena and in 1938 returned to Mexico to teach in the seminary. He organized Mexico City Third Church of the Nazarene. In 1939 he married a granddaughter of Santin. Reza was ordained the same year. He earned an M.A. at the National University. In 1942 Pasadena College persuaded him to head its Spanish department for pastors' training. At the same time he pastored the Mexican Church of the Nazarene in Santa Monica. He developed a talent for translating English hymns into Spanish.

In 1946 the Spanish department was phased out at Pasadena. Reza became director of the Spanish department in the Department of Foreign Missions and moved to Kansas City. His role involved a number of duties and titles and was broader than any of them signified. He was editor of *El Heraldo de Santidad* and translated such books as H. Orton Wiley and Paul Culbertson's *Introduction to Theology*. As the speaker on La Hora Nazarena, Reza became, literally, the voice of the Church of the Nazarene throughout Latin America. Under his editorship, by the 1970s the Church of the Nazarene was the second largest publisher of Spanish Protestant materials in the world. His oversight expanded to include Portuguese publications. This led, in 1976, to the reorganization of the Spanish department into the International Publications Board, which Reza headed until 1982. Among his other tasks, he served for twelve years on the book committee of the publishing house and was a part-time lecturer in missions at Nazarene Theological Seminary. Reza helped to reestablish the Nazarene Seminary in Mexico City and served as its president from 1980 to 1987.[81]

Reza translated Spanish correspondence to headquarters, served as an unofficial adviser to general superintendents on issues related to Latin America, explained policy to local leaders, and influenced mission theory. He traveled with general superintendents to district assemblies. In the 1970s he reestablished contact with Nazarenes in Cuba. If Reza were a generation younger, Jerald Johnson said, he would have been elected a general superintendent.[82]

Adequate missionary training in the Church of the Nazarene was slow to develop. Missions courses at Nazarene Theological Seminary were taught by missionaries on furlough and by resident professors who had scholarly interests in missions and who had traveled abroad but who had no experience as missionaries and little awareness of missiological theory. With the addition of Paul Orjala to the faculty in 1964, NTS strengthened its ability to prepare missionaries. Orjala had been a successful, pioneering missionary to Haiti. He also soon completed a Ph.D. at the Kennedy School of Missions at Hartford Seminary Foundation. Donald Owens, who had served as a missionary in Korea and who had earned a Ph.D. in cultural anthropology, joined the faculty in 1974.[83]

OPENING NEW FIELDS

The work in Australia was indebted to contacts made between a Nazarene serviceman and a local pastor. Ted Hollingsworth was recuperating in Australia in 1944 while en route from New Guinea to the United States. During his seven weeks in Brisbane, Hollingsworth met Albert Berg, an army officer with Plymouth Brethren background. Berg already had read books on holiness and was seeking the experience. Finally, he testified to entire sanctification. Correspondence began between Berg and the general superintendents. In January 1945 the General Board asked Berg to represent the Church of the Nazarene in Australia. The church appointed E. E. Zachary as missionary to Australia. However, because of visa restrictions, Zachary was only able to stay for short periods. Berg became the district superintendent. He persuaded several other pastors of different backgrounds to join the church. Berg remained district superintendent until his death in 1979.[84]

The idea of opening work in Papua New Guinea began with Berg, who shared his vision with Hardy C. Powers. In 1955 the church sent Sidney and Wanda Knox to Kudjip, in the Wahgi Valley, to an unevangelized area in the PNG highlands. They cleared space for an airfield. Both education and medical care were needed. Knox promised government officials that the Church of the Nazarene would erect a hospital.[85]

Sidney Knox died of cancer in 1958. His death excited Nazarenes' attention to the heroism of missions. Wanda Knox reinforced this sense of sacrifice when she returned to the field in 1960 with her two young children. The church also was impressed when, in 1965, Dudley Powers, a medical doctor and son of the general superintendent, began missionary service in PNG.[86]

As they had in India, Nazarenes established a boarding school for boys so that they could be separated from their animistic environment. With the

PNG government's encouragement, the church developed village primary schools between Kudjip and Mount Hagen. Samuel Young agreed with the strategy: "Our church must start at the bottom of the people's needs: schools, medical help, evangelism. Schools are a must. We must get these folk young and rear our own Christian workers."[87] The government subsidized and set standards for the schools and their teachers. This kept the cost to the mission very low.[88]

Once the church had persons who had graduated from the sixth grade, in 1962, they began a Bible school. Since students raised their own food, the Bible school, too, was of minimal cost to the mission. It graduated its first students in 1966.[89]

The government pressured the Church of the Nazarene to keep its commitment regarding medical work. There were one hundred thousand people in the area without a hospital. In March 1967 the Nazarene Hospital at Kudjip was dedicated. Patients who had the ability paid for medical treatments. The government provided subsidies for medicine and equipment. This kept low the cost of the hospital to the church. Providing medical care and education won the trust of the Papuans. Missionary Bruce Blowers noted, "Compassion is the force that breaks the barriers, revealing the love of God."[90]

Just as in India and Swaziland, there were occasional strains between missionaries involved in institutional work and those involved in evangelism. Those stationed at the hospital felt overwhelmed by the needs. Those involved in the schools pleaded for more teachers. Wallace White, as mission director, balanced the needs of the mission and calmed nerves. "We are all about the Master's business," he assured Samuel Young in 1966, "and I don't think any of us are going to be hard-headed enough to be a hindrance to that."[91] The church broke with comity arrangements in 1967 when it entered a Koban tribal area covered by Anglicans.[92]

Nazarenes from Cape Verde translated materials and helped to open work in other Portuguese-speaking countries. Jose Oliveira was among the first missionaries to Brazil in 1958. Joaquin Lima, another Cape Verdean, became district superintendent of the South East Brazil District in 1975. Francisco Reis worked in Mozambique. In 1973 a Cape Verdean, Jose Delgado, was instrumental in planting the church, finally, in Portugal itself and became pastor of the church in Lisbon.[93]

Acacio Pereira was a Portuguese Roman Catholic priest serving in Mozambique when he was converted in 1966 through the efforts of Manuel Dias, who pastored in Maputo. Dias had written a booklet, *Why I Believe*, addressed to Roman Catholics. After his conversion, Pereira studied for two years at the

Nazarene school in Cape Verde and then returned to Mozambique, where he pastored in Matola and Maputo. He was able to establish better relations between Roman Catholics and Nazarenes in the country. In 1975, when the civil war began in Mozambique, Pereira returned to Portugal, where he pastored near Lisbon. Later he edited and translated Nazarene materials and served in the Portuguese publications department in Kansas City.[94]

Brazil became a major part of the church's work in South America. The church followed many Nazarene Cape Verdeans who had immigrated there. Brazil became a golden anniversary project for the church. Earl and Gladys Mosteller, who had served in Cape Verde since 1946, transferred to Brazil in 1958 and were soon joined by young missionaries Charles and Roma Gates. Campinas, sixty miles from São Paulo, became the hub.[95]

Samoa was a case of the church's running into difficulties with the local leader responsible for bringing the denomination into the country. Chief Robert S. Manuma, a wealthy businessman, retired U.S. Navy officer, and deacon in the London Missionary Society, had become acquainted with the Church of the Nazarene in Hawaii. He asked the Church of the Nazarene to supply a pastor for an independent church he had established in Pago Pago. D. I. Vanderpool, the general superintendent, spent four days with him in American Samoa in 1959. In 1960 the church appointed Jarrell and Berniece Garsee as missionaries. Manuma considered Garsee too young and meddlesome and soon stopped attending the church. Later he joined the Baha'i World Faith. Hopes were dashed that the Samoan work quickly would be self-supporting. The Nazarene church grew better in Western Samoa, which it entered in 1964.[96]

STRENGTHENING OLD FIELDS

The church in South Korea had begun under the Japan District before World War II. After the war, Chung Nam Soo (also known as Robert Chung), persuaded Nazarene leaders to appoint him as a Nazarene missionary to his own people. As a young man, Chung Nam Soo had associated with anti-Japanese nationalist leaders. He fled with one of them to Europe. Eventually Chung reached the United States. He was educated at Asbury College and entered ministry in the Methodist Church. In 1926, at the urging of missionary E. Stanley Jones, he returned to Korea. Chung became an active and prominent evangelist in the Korean Holiness Church. After discussions with C. Warren Jones after World War II, the general superintendents agreed to appoint Chung Nam Soo a Nazarene missionary.[97]

Chung Nam Soo quickly persuaded a group of pastors to become Nazarene. In October 1948, Orval Nease, on an extended trip to Asia, met with Chung Nam Soo and these pastors, as well as Chang Sung Oak and Seung Hak Su, Nazarene pastors who had been working in Korea since the 1930s. Nease organized a Native Missionary Council with Chung Nam Soo as chairman. Nease assured the council that the church would not send American missionaries. The Korean War intervened. Chung Nam Soo fled to the United States, where he spoke frequently and raised funds, and then returned to Korea in late 1952. He found it difficult to build on what remained, however. Chung Nam Soo realized that the development of the work required training pastors. He requested Kansas City to send a missionary.[98]

Chung Nam Soo

Donald and Adeline Owens arrived in May 1954. Within a year Owens had started a Bible Training School, registered church property, said goodbye to Chung Nam Soo, who unexpectedly returned to the United States, and saw revival penetrate the church. Owens prepared the churches for a district assembly, at which Park Ki Suh, who had been ordained by Nease in 1948, was elected district superintendent. The quick organization of a district kept missionaries in the background. By 1960 there were 1,968 members, fourteen ordained ministers, and thirty churches.[99]

During the 1960s the Bible Training School played a key role in leadership development, as did Bible conferences and training institutes held each winter and summer. Concerted evangelistic efforts coupled with self-support measures. Congregations grew. By 1970 there were 6,155 members, fifty-eight ordained ministers, and seventy churches.[100]

The church's witness in Swaziland remained close to its schools and hospital. From 1935 until retiring in 1972 Elizabeth Cole devoted her life to working among lepers. When one visitor observing Cole cleaning the wounds of a leper exclaimed, "I would not do that for a million dollars!" Cole responded, "I would not either—not for a million dollars, but I would for Christ." Dorothy Cook supervised the Nurses' Training College. At the same time, for most of her forty years in Swaziland Ruth Matchett, a nurse, operated a clinic and cared for sick and abandoned children in her own home.[101]

In a celebrated case, noted Chicago surgeon and General Board member Howard Hamlin volunteered for missionary service and joined the Nazarene hospital staff in Swaziland in 1963. He was immediately put in charge of the hospital and began reorganizing it. "All activity within the organization must funnel upward through all necessary echelons."[102] Hamlin's administration did not go over well with the longer serving staff. In 1969 Hamlin was transferred to the hospital in Acornhoek. While the Hamlins were on furlough in 1973, the missionaries on the field voted (as it was then the custom for missionaries to vote on colleagues) that they not return. "It was the darkest hour I ever lived," Hamlin admitted.[103] Nevertheless, Hamlin remained a sought-after speaker in Nazarene churches and camp meetings, and he continued to champion the cause of medical missions.[104]

As the costs for running the hospitals rose, by the 1970s, the Nazarene hospital in Manzini was surviving through money from German and Dutch foundations as well as the Swaziland government.[105]

While the church put a great deal of effort into its medical and educational work in Swaziland, the church actually grew faster in neighboring Mozambique, where the church sent fewer missionaries, emphasized ministerial training, and relied on local leaders. Lorraine Schultz served as principal of the Tavane Bible Training School, which opened in 1954, for twenty-two years. Noah Mainga, a Swazi, taught at the Bible Training School from 1958 to 1976. Benjamin Langa became the first Mozambique district superintendent in 1964. He had attended the Bible school in Swaziland for a year and then the school in Tavane. He taught in Bible school, pastored several churches in Gaza, and was ordained in 1958. Langa, according to Oscar Stockwell, was able to "bring harmony in the midst of division" and successfully promoted tithing.[106]

In India, the church's oldest field outside North America, an increase in the number of public schools lessened the need for Nazarene schools. But young Indians moved to Mumbai and other cities, and membership stagnated. Nazarenes confined themselves to the old comity arrangements in rural Maharashtra until 1962, when Luther Manmothe opened work in Aurangabad. Reynolds Memorial Hospital in Washim remained important, but the Indian government forced the church to indigenize its hospital and restricted the number of missionaries. In 1967 D. M. Kharat became principal of the Bible Training School, and in 1976 Dr. Kamalakar Meshramkar took over for Orpha Speicher as superintendent of the hospital. When Kharat became superintendent of the Eastern Maharashtra District in 1972, Padu Meshramkar, who had been educated at Nazarene Theological Seminary in Kansas City, became the Bible school director.[107]

Missionary control was also an issue in Peru, where the Church of the Nazarene was one of the largest Protestant denominations in the country.

As early as the 1940s Peruvian Nazarenes pressed missionaries to relinquish some of their control. When they were slow to do so, a schism, called the National Church of the Nazarene, drew away a few congregations and pastors. The Church of the Nazarene did not have a Peruvian district superintendent until Esperidion Julca was appointed in 1967. The district was geographically divided in 1974, and in 1976, the North District became one of the first in the denomination to receive regular district status.[108]

In Peru's Upper Amazon region, growth continued among the Aguaruna tribes. Elvin and Jane Douglass and, later, Larry and Addie Garman, who arrived in 1965, dispensed medicine, evangelized, and developed schools, including, eventually, the Aguaruna Bible School.[109]

In Guatemala, Nazarenes maintained strong work among Kekchi, Pokomchi, Rabinal-Achi, and Maya-Mopan peoples. William and Betty Sedat translated the Bible into Kekchi. William Sedat began working on this task in 1936 under the American Bible Society. He attended Summer Institutes of Linguistics, and during the Second World War, Pasadena College. In 1945 the Sedats became Nazarene missionaries. In 1954 the Sedats, along with Guillermo Dannemann Paau, who also was instrumental in the translation work, began a Nazarene Bible school for Kekchis. In 1961, when the Kekchi New Testament translation was published, it was the language of 250,000 people. Following this, the Sedats began working with the Pokomchi language and people. The first eight books of the New Testament were completed in Pokomchi by 1969. William Sedat died while on furlough in 1971, but Betty Sedat returned to Guatemala and resumed work on the translation. By the time of her retirement in 1982 the Pokomchi New Testament had been completed.[110]

Although the Church of the Nazarene was a denomination made up of districts, national identities emerged more strongly in the postwar era, and missionaries yielded control to local leaders. Bible colleges provided venues for preparing leaders. Even if the polity of the Church of the Nazarene had no place for national assemblies, preachers' conferences and the like increased a sense of national unity and identity and provided places for an interchange of ideas, including those proposing specific evangelism programs.[111]

ACCESSIONS

In several countries the Church of the Nazarene started work through national leaders who were interested in finding denominational support for work that they had already begun. The Nazarene work in Puerto Rico, for instance, began in 1944 through contacts with Juan Lebron Valazquez. The church named Lebron superintendent of the work, sent him money, and promised him that it would not send missionaries. In addition, Lebron was District Treasurer and Pastor of San Juan First Church. He began a radio ministry. Lebron had friends among government and church officials on the island. Lyle Prescott, stationed in Cuba, made occasional visits. However, it became evident that the work had problems. Without the church's knowledge or permission, Lebron had incorporated both the church in Puerto Rico and, separately, the San Juan First church under his own name. In 1952 the missions department sent Harold Hampton to establish a Bible school and to serve as district treasurer. This generated opposition from Lebron, who abruptly left the church. The Church of the Nazarene filed a lawsuit (settled out of court) in order to retain property it had purchased.

The Bible Institute opened in Puerto Rico in 1954 and continued for seventeen years. After it closed in 1971, ministerial candidates went to the Nazarene Bible College in San Antonio. In 1976 Benjamin Roman, a Puerto Rican, became district superintendent and the remaining missionaries left.[112]

A similar situation occurred in Haiti. Carlos Egen contacted C. W. Jones about uniting his two churches, thirteen preaching points, and about two hundred members with the Church of the Nazarene. General Superintendent Powers visited the island in 1947 and recommended that the church accept Egen's work. In 1950 the church sent Paul and Mary Orjala to open a Bible school. Disagreements developed and Egen left.[113]

Orjala began work in Port-au-Prince, the capital city, rather than in the rural provinces. He wanted to establish a church that would be both true to holiness and "distinctively Haitian." The church combated remnants of African religions. Orjala believed that Haitian religious patterns represented African cultural traditions combined with folk Roman Catholicism.[114] Meanwhile, Haitian Christians witnessed to neighbors and emphasized their separation from the world. They loved the church. Strong Haitian leaders emerged. Worship styles blended with the culture. The expiration of a concordat between the government and the Roman Catholic Church in 1960 hastened conversions by allowing more freedom to Protestants. From 1950 to 1960 membership in Haiti rose from 734 to 6,153. In 1969 the country was divided into two districts, each with a Haitian district superintendent—Massillon Pierre in the North and Florentin Alvarez in the South. By 1970 the membership had topped 20,000, which made it the most successful mission field in the church. Membership reached 31,500 in 1980, 58,600 in 1990, and 83,000 in 2000.[115]

The work of Church of the Nazarene in Haiti was like its work earlier in the century in India and China. The church established day schools, provided medical work, and cared for social and economic as well as spiritual needs. The Bible school was decentralized in 1972, when the church moved to more Pastoral Extension Training programs. However, the church soon returned to a campus program. The Bible school was reopened under the leadership of Jeanine van Beek in 1975.[116]

Another case of the church's beginning through a local leader was Italy. Nazarene work began through Alfredo del Rosso, who, after leaving Roman Catholicism, had studied in a Waldensian school and had become a Baptist. Del Rosso established four independent churches before World War II. As the war ended, he began preaching to both Italians and invading soldiers. Among those soldiers were two Nazarenes, who explained to him the church's doctrines. Del Rosso said he had been preaching holiness for years. He attended the 1948 General Assembly. In the same year his four congregations became Nazarene. In 1952 Earl and Thelma Morgan arrived as missionaries.[117]

Meanwhile, in the United States, the Hephzibah Faith Missionary Association headquartered in Tabor, Iowa, united with the Church of the Nazarene in 1949. This association had begun in 1893 under the leadership of George Weavers. A Baptist born in England, Weavers established Churches of Christ, sometimes called Holiness Churches of Christ, in Iowa, Missouri, and Nebraska. Many members had Brethren backgrounds. Like other Holiness groups, Hephzibah was strict on rules. For decades, the association did not allow its men to wear neckties. Hephzibah women refrained "from trying to make [themselves] attractive." Yet women were allowed to preach.[118]

A missionary training school opened in Tabor in 1893. Hephzibah helped sponsor missionaries who went out under the United Missionary Church, the Oriental Missionary Society, the International Holiness Mission, and other groups. Hephzibah members supported these missionaries by collectively farming a one hundred-acre tract called "sacred ground" near Tabor and donating the proceeds.

Nazarene evangelists often held camp meetings with the Hephzibah association. By 1949 the association's pioneers had died and Bible school enrollment was low. Younger leaders, including Roy Adams and Paul Worcester, both sons of Hephzibah founders, turned to the Church of the Nazarene. In September 1949, Gene Phillips, the Iowa district superintendent, received the Tabor congregation into the Church of the Nazarene. The following year the association turned over 150 acres of Iowa land and the remaining school buildings in Tabor to the Church of the Nazarene.[119]

Occasionally other Holiness groups around the world affiliated with the Church of the Nazarene. An independent Holiness mission that Boyd and Neva Skinner had established in Chile in 1952 became the foundation of the Nazarene work in that country. In 1962 the Skinners became Nazarene missionaries.[120]

The Church of the Nazarene saw significant accessions in Great Britain, and, as a consequence, in Africa. In 1949 Speke Hall Mission in London decided to unite with the Church of the Nazarene. The congregation had begun in 1885 (two years before the People's Evangelical Church of Providence, Rhode Island) through special meetings conducted by Reader Harris, a lawyer who became an active booster of the Holiness Movement in Great Britain. In 1891 Harris brought into affiliation several Holiness missions along with the Speke Hall Mission to constitute the Pentecostal League. Supporters stayed members of other churches while attending these missions, which numbered 150 by the turn of the century. Though Harris had been determined to keep the league nondenominational, the Speke Hall Mission became the Clapham Junction Church of the Nazarene.[121]

David Thomas, businessman and colleague of Harris in the work of the league, broke with Harris in 1906 over whether the league, in remaining nondenominational, best served new believers and whether it "nourished them with Holiness teaching and training to serve."[122] Thomas, like Bresee and others who left established denominations, believed that holiness could best be propagated outside existing churches and so established the Holiness Mission. The center of the work was in Sydney Hall in Battersea, London. The Holiness Mission became the International Holiness Mission in 1914 after a Holiness work in South Africa, begun by Welsh missionary David B. Jones in 1908, affiliated with the mission. The work in South Africa grew considerably faster than the work in Great Britain itself.[123]

The International Holiness Mission united with the Church of the Nazarene in 1952. Like the merger of the Pentecostal Mission with the Church of the Nazarene in 1915, the main reason for the IHM union was missions. The IHM's nine hundred members and twenty-seven congregations in England and Wales attempted to support thirty-two missionaries, the Ethel Lucas Memorial Hospital at Acornhoek, and a Bible college and clinic at Rehobeth, South Africa. In spite of great sacrifices, the IHM's members could not sustain all of these efforts. David Jones died in 1950. After that IHM leaders created an Investigation Committee to explore union with the Church of the Nazarene. The joint committee expressed their "united and supreme desire that the outcome of the Committee's explorations should be for the furtherance of the truth and testimony of holiness in Great Britain and overseas."[124] J. B. Maclagan, who previously had been a Nazarene, by then headed the IHM and led the way toward merger. General Superintendent Powers presided over the union assembly in England. He also established two districts in the British Isles. George Frame became superintendent over the North District and Maclagan over the South.[125]

Meanwhile, Nazarene and IHM leaders in Africa agreed that union was "highly desirable, as it would help to expedite the evangelization of the heathen, and promote the propagation of Scriptural Holiness among the African people, which is our God-appointed mission."[126] They desired to continue their distinctive ministries under the Church of the Nazarene. Hardy Powers and Remiss Rehfeldt conducted a second merger ceremony in Arthurseat, South Africa. The IHM had over eighteen hundred members in Africa.[127]

Though Nazarenes attempted to maintain the Ethel Lucas Memorial Hospital in South Africa as well as the Raleigh Fitkin Memorial Hospital in Manzini, Swaziland, this proved impossible. Each lacked doctors and nurses. By the early 1970s all of the support for the Acornhoek hospital came from the South African government, and officials pressed the church to turn over the hospital to the nation. The hospital was nationalized in 1975.[128]

Another British Isles accession came in 1955. The Calvary Holiness Church had split from the IHM in 1934. Certain IHM pastors, led by Maynard James and Jack Ford, deemed the IHM leaders too conservative in their approach to evangelism. Ford and James evangelized by "trekking," holding tent revivals. Early centers included Salford, Oldham, Queensbury, and Bradford. Maynard James was elected president-for-life of the CHC in 1939. James also edited the *Flame,* which circulated widely among Holiness people in the British Isles. Under his editorship, the *Flame* proved controversial, as James's interpretations of Scripture identified the Antichrist, promoted Anglo-Israeli Zionism (but missed comment on the German invasion of Poland), and in later years saw papal influences in the founding of the European common market. The CHC retained the IHM's interest in missions. Norman Grubb, of the Worldwide Evangelization Crusade, served as missionary secretary. The CHC supported a mission in Pakistan and two missionaries, Samuel and Gwladys Heap, in Colombia. In 1947 the CHC began Beech Lawn Bible College in Stalybridge, England, with James as principal.[129]

James's attitudes toward tongues-speaking proved controversial. At a revival service in which James was preaching, a man broke out in a "torrent of unknown words" accompanied by other "unseemly behavior" such as clutching at his hair and casting away some of his clothing. The man later confessed that he had been dabbling in spiritism and was powerless over strange powers. "I am convinced," James wrote, "that very much of what passes as the working of the Holy Spirit in the form of ecstatic utterance is psychic or purely human." James never accepted that tongues-speaking was an infallible sign of being filled with the Holy Spirit. It did not connect to deep spirituality or discernment. It was not for all Christians. The only "infallible" evidence of the baptism with the Holy Spirit was love and to "exalt" tongues "to a paramount importance as an offset to the complete lack of the gift in the great denominations, or to make it almost a fetish or spiritual idol, is to grieve the blessed Holy Spirit and cause unnecessary division and contention among the saints." A drift toward Pentecostalism in the CHC worried James. Yet, James became convinced, tongues were truly scriptural. It would be "puerile and blasphemous" to assume that all tongues-speaking was of Satan.[130]

CHC leaders, James included, wanted holiness, not spiritual gifts, to be central. The CHC had not grown much after the war. Leaders observed the union of the Nazarenes with their parent body, the IHM, both carefully and favorably. Merger talks, however, were difficult. CHC pastors administered the Lord's Supper each Sunday. Elements of fundamentalism could be seen in the CHC's practice of baptizing only believers, by immersion, and in its strictly premillennial ways of interpreting the Bible. They emphasized divine healing. While CHC leaders did not speak in tongues or believe that speaking in tongues was evidence of the baptism with the Holy Spirit, they still understood that there was a "genuine gift of 'tongues' in operation today."[131]

The Nazarene general superintendents, who were aware of the issue of tongues in relation to the CHC, gave authority to the British Advisory Council to negotiate the basis of union. George Frame, the Nazarene district superintendent, felt sure that CHC members who held different views on tongues than Nazarenes would not be troubled or bothered in the Church of the Nazarene. A carefully worded statement on tongues passed the union assembly, over which Samuel Young presided in June 1955: "We understand that in welcoming us into the Church of the Nazarene the authorities give us freedom to hold these convictions although they may not express the official Nazarene attitudes."[132] The Church of the Nazarene added twenty-four churches and three hundred members. Beech Lawn College merged with the Hurlet Nazarene College in Glasgow, and the school reopened in Manchester as British Isles Nazarene College.[133]

Among the congregations that came into the Church of the Nazarene with the Calvary Holiness Church merger was one in Ashton-under-Lyne, which had been established in 1874—making it, probably, the oldest congregation in the denomination with a continuous history. The Old Cross Mission, as it had been known, was in the Manchester area. A succession of Holiness evangelists, including Thomas Cook, Amanda Smith, Reader Harris, C. J. Fowler, A. M. Hills, George Sharpe, and David Thomas all preached at the mission. It affiliated with Star Hall in 1912. When Star Hall affiliated with The Salvation Army in October 1918, likewise did the Old Cross Mission. Within a short time, however, it returned to its independent status. After affiliating with the Emmanuel Bible College and adopting its doctrinal statement, the congregation in 1939 joined the Calvary Holiness Church. When, then, the Calvary Holiness Church joined the Church of the Nazarene in 1955, so did the Old Cross Mission.[134]

Another small group that came into the Church of the Nazarene during these years was the Ontario, Canada-based Gospel Workers Association. The GWA had begun in 1900 under Frank Goff and, at the time of the union, was led by Albert Mills. Samuel Young presided over a union assembly in June 1958. The church added five congregations, 162 members, and camp meeting grounds in Clarksburg.[135]

REACHING OUT TO OTHER CHRISTIANS

What kept further unions with larger Holiness bodies from occurring in these decades was not theology, but the church structures that the Nazarenes and other denominations built. Each group had its own leaders, its own colleges, and its own denominational ethos. The Church of the Nazarene maintained a policy of "kindly cooperation without affiliation" with fellow Holiness people in the National Holiness Association.[136] Beginning in 1957 various Holiness denominations began joint church school publication ventures. A Federation of Holiness Churches convention was held in Chicago in late 1966, with representatives from eleven denominations affiliated with the National Holiness Association. The denominations included the Church of Christ in Christian Union, the Evangelical Methodist Church, the Brethren in Christ, the Free Methodists, the Pilgrim Holiness Church, and the Wesleyan Methodist Church. Free Methodist Myron Boyd led Federation talks. Cooperative work could mean a more effective outreach, Boyd said, to African-Americans, Native Americans, and other minorities. T. E. Martin, a prominent Nazarene pastor, urged stronger alliance among Holiness bodies. Boyd hoped even the Evangelical United Brethren might federate with these Holiness groups, but it was already in dialogue with the Methodist Church and united with the latter in 1968. In the same year the Wesleyan Methodist and Pilgrim Holiness churches merged to form the Wesleyan Church. Only in 1969 did the Church of the Nazarene as a body join the National Holiness Association.[137]

On family and personal levels, Holiness people and preachers often crisscrossed denominations. On mission fields Holiness missionaries often held revivals and other meetings for each other. In the Philippines, Guyana, and Peru, Nazarenes built upon what Pilgrim Holiness workers had laid.[138]

In Latin America ecumenical councils represented all Protestant interests, and Nazarenes joined. Elsewhere, Nazarenes avoided councils dominated by denominations associated with the World Council of Churches. Andres Valenzuela, the Nazarene district superintendent, became prominent in the Philippine Council of Evangelical Churches when it was formed in 1967 to balance the WCC-oriented National Council of Churches in the Philippines.[139]

North American Nazarenes were at best ambivalent and, at the extremes, paranoid toward the World Council of Churches (WCC). As Nazarenes understood it, the goal of the WCC was to create one church. If this were to happen, J. Kenneth Grider wrote in 1954: "Essential doctrines would be compromised. Dogmas would be diluted. Convictions would be exchanged for convenience. A broad tolerance would be agreed upon. The result would approach a mutual vacuity of belief. Such union would strike the deathblow to Biblical, aggressive, impassioned Christianity."[140] The WCC became associated with socialism and armed struggles for political and economic liberation.[141]

Nevertheless, leaders of several denominational departments had contacts with the WCC-affiliated National Council of Churches of Christ in the USA (NCCC). The Nazarene Evangelism department director corresponded with his NCCC counterpart so that Nazarenes could be part of a summer chaplain program in the National Parks. The Education department was a member of the NCCC's Council for Protestant Colleges and Universities. The Nazarene director of Communications was on the Board of Managers of the NCCC's Broadcasting and Film Commission. The church cooperated with the NCCC's United Stewardship Council and with its Christian Education Division. Albert Harper, editor of Church Schools for the Church of the Nazarene, was a prominent member of the Uniform Lesson Series committee affiliated with the Christian Education Division of the NCCC.[142]

At first the general superintendents defended the church's participation with the NCCC agencies. They noted that since its inception the Church of the Nazarene always had cooperated with the International Council of Religious Education, which became the NCCC's Department of Christian Education in 1950.[143] Harper defended the Uniform Lesson Series and Nazarene participation on the committee that produced the lessons. It provided, he said, an opportunity for the Wesleyan Holiness message to influence other denominations, and Harper believed that the lessons magnified the Bible "magnificently."[144]

But these affiliations with the NCCC troubled a few vocal Nazarenes, especially those who listened regularly to fundamentalist radio preachers. They brought their complaints to the attention of the General Assembly in 1968. The General Assembly established a commission, with its members appointed by the general superintendents, to study the church's relation to the NCCC. But commission members themselves were uncertain as to whether their role was to sever ties with the NCCC or only to advise in this regard.[145]

H. T. Reza vigorously defended ties to the WCC. In countries outside of the United States, Reza knew, contacts with the WCC had proven helpful. The only legal way to get financial assistance to Nazarene pastors in Cuba was through the WCC. If the church were forced to end this, Cuban pastors would suffer. If severing relations with the WCC meant ending ties with national councils that were affiliated with it, this would hinder efforts to legitimate the church in various countries. Divisions in American Protestantism, Reza argued, should not affect Nazarene churches in other parts of the world. These matters ought not to be decided by a General Assembly dominated by those who had only American issues in mind, Reza argued. He proposed "that we allow our own Nazarenes in Latin America to decide for themselves as heretofore concerning their affiliation to local councils based on the advantage they may enjoy from such affiliation."[146]

Such arguments had little effect upon the commission. It recommended that all departments, commissions, and committees of the General Board immediately sever all ties to the NCCC. It directed the NCCC divisions to cease listing the Church of the Nazarene as an affiliate. The commission recommended that the Church Schools department sever ties to the Education department of the NCCC within twelve months. But in a concession to Harper, it allowed Church Schools to use the Uniform Lessons for the time being, while exploring other options. It recommended that no changes be made in the Spanish department's relations to the WCC but also that this should be reviewed periodically by the World Mission department. The General Board approved these recommendations at its 1970 meeting. The 1972 General Assembly voted for the church to sever all NCCC connections.[147]

CONCLUSION

By all kinds of means, Nazarenes conveyed their understanding of holiness to the world. The Nazarene "kinship" expanded greatly during the postwar years. Though their rhetoric often separated evangelism from compassion, their actions did not. They began with their neighbors and extended their concern to other ethnic groups and to people far around the world. By intention as well as almost instinctually Nazarenes were led toward the lower strata of society. The sense of community within the church in a time when community structures were elsewhere breaking down attracted many. Their distinctive Holiness language, when learned, was a means of establishing and retaining a sense of being a distinct people. Nazarenes felt themselves to be part of a dynamic and growing movement with a God-called mission and message to the world.

EIGHTEEN

Behavioral Boundaries

Postwar social changes forced Nazarenes to reexamine some of their moral codes. In the 1950s and 1960s, a minority faction decried any adjustments to old standards and rules. Some left the church, and leaders who remained navigated a middle course.

Nazarenes believed that their rules represented the common consensus of Christians before the churches had succumbed to worldliness, and that they were applications of biblical principles. For some, what it meant to be a Nazarene was to follow certain strict rules. The General Rules of the church prohibited: taking the name of God in vain; profaning the Lord's Day; using or "trafficking" in intoxicating liquors and tobacco; quarreling; being dishonest; indulging in pride in dress or behavior; and being entertained in ways that did not glorify God. Interpretations of these rules differed—particularly on the matters of dress and entertainment. Because of changes in social behavior, the 1976 General Assembly added an eighth prohibition, sexual immorality.[1]

During the sectarian period, Holiness people had become less concerned for society as a whole. They united around no great social causes similar to slavery or prohibition in the post-World War II era. Personal morality and living in harmony with the expectations of other church members were of great importance. The congregation was the principal source of fellowship for many Nazarenes. Behaving according to their church's codes assured acceptance and a sense of belonging.

The postwar generation leading the church in the 1940s defended rules and standards. Leaders feared the same breakdown in morality that had affected society in the 1920s. They also feared declension away from the faith entrusted to them. Keeping the rules demonstrated both aversion to worldly norms and loyalty to the collective conscience of the church.[2]

At the same time, postwar leaders recognized that true righteousness could not be "legislated." General Superintendents Miller, Powers, and Williamson told the 1948 General Assembly that love, not law, was the central evidence of holiness. Nazarenes too easily could follow the rules of the church and be critical, severe, and faultfinding. Instead, they should act charitably toward those who disagreed with them. Echoing Phineas Bresee, the general superintendents told the church that it must have both inflexibility on "essentials" and flexibility on "nonessentials."³

Among the "essentials," the church remained vigilant on tobacco smoking. By the 1940s, long before it became a national concern, the church cited studies showing that tobacco was addictive, that nicotine was poison, that smoking irritated the mouth, nose, and throat, and that it caused heart disease. Just like sin itself, smoking was "enslaving." But Nazarenes were optimistic that grace could liberate from this bondage.⁴

Movies, Nazarenes believed, weakened moral standards. They "advertised sin," aroused emotions, and led to sexual promiscuity. Movies were too filled with violence. They "hardened hearts." Movies wasted Christians' money and led them away from spiritual pursuits, including church attendance and prayer. Nazarenes asked themselves: "Which of us would like to be caught on our Lord's return patronizing a theater where we had just contributed to the box-office support of some oft-divorced, careless-living Hollywood character cavorting his way through a worldly production in which drinking, smoking, dancing, and gambling are presented as being sophisticated, intelligent, and desirable activities?"⁵

There were local variations on how strictly the rules on drinking, smoking, and watching movies were maintained. But these were not prohibitions over which Nazarenes voiced much disagreement in the 1940s, 1950s, and 1960s.⁶

On the other hand, real controversy arose when postwar Nazarenes began to dress more like the rest of society and to buy luxuries that their hardworking parents had not been able to afford. Depression-era Nazarenes had lived frugally. In spite of their own dire needs, they had given sacrificially to keep their pastors' families fed and clothed, Holiness colleges open, and missionaries on the field. Not wearing jewelry and the like was not only a matter of self-denial but also a matter of stewardship. Even if one could afford otherwise, Nazarenes should live in "Christian simplicity" and ask: "Are all of the financial needs of my church cared for? Can my pastor and his family afford to dress as well as I? Have I been generous with missions?"⁷

The prosperous postwar generation found that good things could be accomplished without the same level of sacrifice. No longer did Nazarenes have to choose between paying the pastor and buying a new suit or dress, or between giving to the college and buying a new car. There was enough for God's causes as well as a television and a wedding ring.⁸

One postwar trend, upsetting to some, related to sports. The 1940 General Assembly had placed in the appendix to the *Manual* a statement against any but intramural sports. Succeeding General Assemblies retained the statement. But the colleges, following NNC, participated in basketball and other competitions—usually playing against other small, Christian colleges. Conservatives, including Glenn Griffith, while he was a district superintendent on the NNC zone, complained about sports at the college.[9]

In the mid-1950s, Pasadena College attracted Jim Bond on the basis of its basketball program (which Bethany, nearer his hometown in Texas, did not offer). Bond made the all-American team. Later he turned down an offer to join the Minneapolis Lakers because it would have required him to play on Sunday. Bond's resolve took away some misgivings that sports loosened standards.[10]

Jim Bond

Bowing to trends in the colleges, the 1964 General Assembly changed the *Manual* statement to indicate that the schools "shall be bound by such regulations regarding intercollegiate activities as the General Department of Education shall decide." The Education department, in turn, left the matter to each school's president and Board of Trustees. Except at Trevecca, which kept away from sports longer than the other schools, Nazarene presidents reported positively regarding the contributions of intercollegiate sports to their colleges. In 1968 basketball star Jim Bond was elected president of the Nazarene Young People's Society.[11]

Conservative Nazarenes were careful about honoring the Lord's house. The 1940 General Assembly went on record "as being opposed to the use of any part of our church buildings for recreational and entertainment purposes." The statement stayed in the Appendix of the *Manual* until 1968. William Tidwell, the much-respected pastor of Chattanooga First Church, believed that congregations lost their burden for souls when they installed church kitchens and "substituted the beef roast" for "the Holy Ghost."[12]

The way women looked also greatly concerned conservatives. They warned women not to appear either "loose" or "manly" by "bobbing" their hair. First Corinthians 11:15 admonished, "if a woman [has] long hair, it is a glory to her: for her hair is given her for a covering." "Bobbed" hair represented a woman's lack of submission to God and her husband. They complained about "painted" and "bejeweled" women teaching children's Sunday School classes. Women, conservatives warned, had to be careful not to tempt men. They should not waste money wearing makeup and going to beauty parlors. "Do our Nazarene women really feel it necessary to conform to the rest of the world in dress, in adornment, in the painted and over-painted countenance?" one asked. "Or do they really seek that inward adornment which is of great worth in the sight of our Lord and part of that progression unto true holiness?"[13] Even Albert Harper, who people criticized for picturing women with short hair in Sunday School publications, thought that "finger rings, bracelets, necklaces, ankle chains, and earrings are out of place among devout people of God." There was a general consensus, Harper believed, that Nazarene women should not use "rouge, lipstick, nail painting and eyebrow penciling." Any woman looking like this would feel "conspicuous," Harper was sure, in a Church of the Nazarene.[14]

By the 1940s some Nazarene women were wearing wedding rings, which extreme conservatives considered a form of jewelry. General Superintendent Miller in 1948 wrote to a concerned woman in Indianapolis that the Church of the Nazarene held no position on the wedding ring and believed that it was acceptable for those whose consciences were clear about it. Miller was sure that no pastor would refuse church membership to a person who wore a wedding ring. But others took literally both 1 Tim. 2:9, which instructed women to "adorn themselves in modest apparel, with shamefacedness and sobriety; not with broided hair, or gold, or pearls, or costly array." Conservatives complained that rings were being used in marriage ceremonies while no ring was mentioned in the *Manual*'s wedding ritual.[15]

Though General Superintendent Powers would not ordain a man unless his wife removed her wedding ring, and not ordain a woman if she wore a wedding ring, his colleague G. B. Williamson ordained qualified married women as ministers regardless of whether or not they wore a wedding ring,

G. B. Williamson

and men whether or not their wives wore wedding rings. A simple wedding ring, to Williamson, was simply a symbol of marriage vows. In some parts of the world, he noted, it was immoral for a married woman not to wear a wedding ring. Since the Church of the Nazarene was international, "what is necessary in one place as a sign of moral integrity cannot be considered worldly anywhere." The wedding ring should not be made an issue, Williamson warned, and "no church or district has the right to discriminate against persons who choose to use the accepted symbol of marriage." Williamson accused the extreme conservatives of "Phariseeism." Williamson's public statements displeased the other general superintendents. They assured concerned pastors that he was not speaking for the Board of General Superintendents, but only for himself.[16]

With or without the general superintendents, the church moved toward a centrist position on wedding rings. Stalwart district superintendents such as E. O. Chalfant and L. T. Wells supported compromise, not extremism. S. S. White, through the *Herald*, accused those who rejected marriage bands of being proud of their own plainness.[17]

There were problems on these issues outside the United States. Joseph Pitts, the first Nazarene missionary to the Philippines, was afraid that Holiness people were losing their distinctiveness and accommodating to the world. Whatever the American church might do or become, he was determined that the Nazarene church in the Philippines would remain pure. He directed women converts not to wear jewelry (including wedding rings), not to wear makeup, and not to cut their hair. He persuaded newly appointed women missionaries not to cut their hair and to take off their wedding rings. But how long could he keep the Philippine church outside the movement of the general church away from such practices?[18]

Another matter of great debate in the 1950s was whether it was moral for Holiness people to own televisions. William Tidwell called television a "Satanic miracle."[19] To Tidwell and those like him, consistency with the church's stand against movies meant that it must also reject television. Nazarenes must not invite Hollywood into their very living rooms! By 1952, when the General Assembly hotly debated the television issue, about one-third of all American homes had televisions. The 1952 assembly inserted a statement in the Appendix warning "that the most rigid safeguards be observed to keep homes from becoming secularized and worldly." It criticized the "sensuous appeal" of many TV programs but refused to ban the television from Nazarene homes.[20]

Glenn Griffith, who had served as superintendent of the Idaho-Oregon and Colorado Districts before entering full-time evangelism in 1951, believed that that the church had severely compromised with the world in its decision to allow televisions. The television was the most major of many complaints that Griffith had concerning a church he thought had grown "cold, anemic and formal."[21]

In November 1955, after a Holiness campaign in Caldwell, Idaho, Griffith organized the Bible Missionary Union. It won additional followers, including William Tidwell, after the 1956 General Assembly again failed to ban televisions. "I am not for the unscriptural, apostate innovations that are flooding the church," wrote Tidwell upon joining the schismatics.[22] In Louisiana the Nazarenes lost twenty-six ministers and seven hundred members to the Bible Missionary Union. The district closed fourteen churches as a result. Among those who joined were Elbert Dodd, the Louisiana district superintendent, and Spencer Johnson, a prominent pastor on the district. W. L. King, a Pennsylvania pastor who broadcasted the "Voice of the Nazarene" over a Pittsburgh radio station and published a periodical by the same name, also joined. At its 1956 General Conference the new denomination became the Bible Missionary Church.[23]

Shortly after the 1956 Assembly, Griffith circulated "Nineteen Reasons Why I Am Leaving the Church of the Nazarene." The church was not preaching the "law," he said, which was necessary to convict people of sin and lead them to repentance. Education seemed more important than being "baptized with the Holy Ghost and with fire." Nazarenes had shifted their emphasis away from being loyal to God toward being loyal to the church. Griffith and others believed that they were following old Nazarene ways. Why the changes in the standards? Even if society changed, what made it wrong in one generation to wear a wedding ring and "bob" one's hair, and permissible in the next? Did God's Word or the demands of holiness change?[24]

Stalwart A. O. Hendricks challenged Griffith's views about what practices really represented the old Nazarene way. Hendricks widely circulated a response to Griffith's "Nineteen Reasons." Hendricks indicated, among other things, that Maria Bresee had worn a wedding ring her entire married life, and that, as her pastor, he had buried her with it. The wedding ring was not an "ornament," Hendricks said; it was sanctioned in the Bible. Regarding education, "Please pardon me," Hendricks wrote, "but there is no premium on ignorance. Some so-called preachers are too lazy to secure a proper education for the ministry. They prefer to rant and snort and throw songbooks around, and call that Holy Ghost fire. Please excuse me. I secured my preparation for the ministry the hard way." Hendricks asked Griffith to remember: "Anybody can tear down. It takes a real Christian to build the kingdom of God."[25]

The Bible Missionary Church represented not only the conservative extreme of the Holiness Movement but also a fundamentalist influence. The church stipulated that "the one hope of the world is the premillennial coming of Jesus" and specifically asked incoming members, "Do you believe in the premillennial coming of Jesus?" The church also was narrower than the Church of the Nazarene on baptism, stipulating that baptism was for believers only. Ordination came through ordained ministers, not a general superintendent. The

Bible Missionary Church established its headquarters in Duncan, Oklahoma, started a Bible Missionary Institute in Rock Island, Illinois, and developed missions work in Guyana, Barbados, India, New Guinea, and Japan.[26]

But questions over divorce soon divided the Bible Missionary Church. Dodd was willing to receive persons who had divorced on the scriptural grounds of adultery into both membership and ministry, as was Tidwell, himself divorced. But Griffith was not. In 1959 Griffith formed the Wesleyan Holiness Association of Churches. The next year King withdrew from the BMC in order to form the Nazarene Baptist Church. Soon, however, King found himself embroiled in a libel case for inflammatory comments he made on his radio program about the Knights of Columbus.[27]

With the general superintendents' backing, in 1956 the General Board appointed Robert and Mathilda McCroskey to the Philippines, knowing that "Tillie" McCroskey had short hair and that neither she nor her husband were disposed to her removing her wedding ring. This signaled that the general superintendents were ready to confront legalism in the Philippines. When Pitts learned of the McCroskeys' appointment, he reminded the generals that one of the crucial tests for new missionaries was their willingness to adjust to the field and that Kansas City knew full well the standards in the Philippines.

When the McCroskeys arrived and refused to obey Pitts, he assigned them to Manila, where, he believed, they would have the least influence on the predominantly rural church. At the 1957 District Assembly, with the McCroskeys sitting right before him in the congregation, Pitts declared: "We regret to speak about worldliness coming into our mission work.... We regret that a double standard now exists in our mission work: one for the nationals in our Bible School and churches and another among the missionaries."[28]

Learning of the conflict, the general superintendents called Pitts to Kansas City. Before leaving the Philippines, Pitts organized the Filipino Nazarene Ministers Association, made up of most of the pastors. After arriving in Kansas City, heated discussions ensued with the general superintendents, who were willing to appoint Pitts elsewhere, so as not to make a martyr of him, but Pitts countered that the Lord himself had called him to the Philippines. He rallied lay supporters in Louisiana, where his brother pastored, and in Wilmore, Kentucky, and sent money directly to the Filipino pastors.[29]

Many of the Filipino pastors remained loyal to Pitts. They sensed no particular bonds to the general church. Most Filipino women in the rural areas where the Church of the Nazarene was strongest did not cut their hair anyway. It was not a moral issue, just a social custom. A wedding ring was not common either. Women might wear many rings, none with special significance, or none at all. Pitts's standards on makeup made little difference in rural barrios. More importantly, thought the Filipino pastors, how could it be morally wrong one Sunday for women to cut their hair and permissible the next? How could pastors who had preached strongly on these issues face their congregations without shame and tell them they had been wrong? Was the Bible changeable? Nationalism also was evident in Epifania Encarnacion's letter to Kansas City: "We only want worldliness banned and a little voice in the running of the mission field, because we feel we know our people and our country."[30]

Marciano Encarnacion, who had begun the first Church of the Nazarene in the Philippines in 1946, hoped that Hugh Benner would listen to the Filipino side when Benner came to the Philippines to preside over the 1958 District Assembly. Encarnacion thought that the denomination had been hasty in making decisions that affected them. Kansas City administrators could not possibly understand Filipino customs, Encarnacion believed. Benner handled the situation badly. He felt no sympathy for legalists and believed that it was better for the mission to make a decisive break with Pitts. Benner refused to meet with Filipino leaders to discuss the issues. This wounded Encarnacion and caused him and others to walk out of the assembly and out of the Church of the Nazarene.

With financial help from Holiness people from several denominations, Pitts returned to the Philippines the same year. He incorporated the Holiness Church of the Nazarene with himself as chairman and Marciano Encarnacion as vice-chairman. In some places Pitts began local congregations near Nazarene churches. He initiated legal cases in order to gain property that he had helped to secure for the Bible college near Baguio.[31]

In other places, some missionaries, including Earl and Mabel Hunter, who served in Guatemala and Bolivia, left Nazarene service over the denomination's perceived worldliness. The Hunters joined Basil Miller's World-Wide Missions and went to Nigeria. They sent appeals for travel, equipment, and support to Nazarene friends. Under Hunter, the World-Wide Missions work in Nigeria grew to 400 churches and was incorporated as the Gospel Preaching Church of Nigeria. Later, however, the Hunters returned to the Nazarene church.[32]

The departure of some outspoken conservatives allowed Nazarenes to relax a bit. Women's wedding rings and short hair no longer were issues. After the Griffith split, G. B. Williamson wrote in the *Herald*, so that all Nazarenes could see it, that though it was "the duty of the church to raise high standards of morality," to defend legalism was "to isolate the church and force upon it the loss of contact with the world it is designed to redeem." Legalism, he said, became "a deadly wound" that produced a "decadent, ingrown, pharisaical sect."[33] The general superintendents no longer worried about the "extremists" who, said H. C. Benner at the fiftieth anniversary of the church, made God's people look "eccentric and queer."[34]

More and more, leaders placed rules in the broader contexts of holiness. W. Shelburne Brown began a book about the church's rules with the statement that there was a "middle ground between the libertarian and the legalist." The rules, wrote Brown, were never intended to "regiment" members but to "warn them of some of the enemies to the truly spiritual life." Similarly, missionary Lyle Prescott saw the tragedy of someone keeping the rules while abusing family members: "The man who harangues a woman over her jewelry, then turns to slap his little daughter fiercely for a slight interruption—what has he accomplished? Who will believe in his religion?"[35]

If the children of good Nazarene homes were to be convinced of holiness and incorporate it into their ethos, parents and church leaders would need to prove their holiness by their love, not by harsh criticisms or lists of taboos, wrote Oscar Finch, superintendent of the Colorado District, to D. I. Vanderpool.[36] Likewise, A. J. Smith, a former missionary to China and one-time district superintendent in Canada, argued that a slavish following of rules gave people a false sense of assurance about their salvation. "You may not go to the show, but you have fits of anger, that shows you are unsaved no matter what you profess. You don't go to the ball games, but you slander your neighbor and speak evil of others. You do not drink, smoke or chew etc., but you have idols in your heart, which shows God is not first in your life. You do not curse, but you are mean and ugly to wife, husband or children. You do not use 'make up' but you make up for it by being proud over your plain clothes. . . . You do not gamble, but you talk mean about your pastor behind his back."[37]

"External standards are not obliterated," Mildred Wynkoop wrote in 1958, "but love, driven inward, safeguards the vast areas of decision which cannot be covered by laws." She reminded the church that it was "possible to perfectly obey the law and yet be carnal, materialistic, wooden, hard, loveless."[38]

When the church spoke of "holiness" it was not talking about not smoking, drinking, dancing, or attending movies, wrote Ponder Gilliland in 1960 as he was finishing his term as executive secretary of the Nazarene Young People's Society. "Worldliness," Gilliland believed, was any "attitude, action, or method of the world" that was "un-Christlike." On a variety of issues, Gilliland said, people should be left to their own opinions and not criticize or force their behavior on others. As a pastor, Gilliland aimed to free his people from their "bondage" to legalism.[39] Similarly, John May reminded Nazarenes in 1960 that sanctification was a level of Christian living in which persons were not easily offended, did not try to manipulate people or events to their own advantage, did not gossip, slander, or use cutting words. "The sanctified will be hard on themselves and easy on others. They will not be quick to comment on the failure of others." They would not become "judges and criticizers."[40]

However, the Bible Missionary Church and its offshoots had not attracted all of the Nazarenes concerned about loosened rules and standards in the church. The extreme conservatives who remained in the church were uncomfortable with sentiments like Gilliland's. In particular, Remiss Rehfeldt, the church's Foreign Missions secretary, lamented the direction the church was taking. Rehfeldt had served as superintendent of the Iowa District from 1945 to 1948 before replacing C. W. Jones as secretary of Foreign Missions.[41]

On April 3, 1957, Rehfeldt and several others drove from Kansas City through the rain for a night of prayer "for the preservation of Holiness evangelism for which our church fathers lived and died" at the small, nearly abandoned, Enon Church of the Nazarene in Excelsior Springs, Missouri.

Remiss Rehfeldt

They agreed "to stand for and promote Holiness with standards; a strong evangelistic emphasis; and a crusade of believing, intercessory prayer." The group circulated a "Historic Enon Covenant" that called upon Nazarenes to pray for the moral recovery of the church. In mimeographed tracts the group charged that the church was losing its way. A cadre of like-minded men and women across the denomination agreed. Fearing another schism, the general superintendents wanted to do nothing that would force Rehfeldt's resignation or victimize him in people's eyes.[42]

When the General Assembly met in 1960 Rehfeldt polled third for the new, sixth general superintendent position. (Evangelism Secretary V. H. Lewis was elected.) Rehfeldt resigned as Foreign Missions secretary. In their parting words to Rehfeldt the general superintendents declared that Rehfeldt's service had "been of incalculable and enduring value." They hoped for him "a future of ever increasing effectiveness and blessing."[43] Behind the scenes, they were happy to see him go. Rehfeldt entered full-time evangelism. After three years, the Indianapolis District, one of the strictest in the denomination in matters of dress and behavior, elected him superintendent.[44]

The general superintendents had stalled, but they did not stop the schism that they feared. In July 1967 Rehfeldt resigned as district superintendent. He and others, including disaffected conservatives from the Pilgrim Holiness and Wesleyan Methodist churches, formed the Church of the Bible Covenant. The First General Convention of the denomination, held August 10-13, 1967, in Cleveland, Indiana, elected Rehfeldt and Marvin Powers, a nephew of General Superintendent Hardy Powers, as general presiding officers. In the Philippines, Joseph Pitts turned over the Holiness Church of the Nazarene to the Church of the Bible Covenant.[45]

What had been unwritten taboos among Nazarenes were made explicit in the Church of the Bible Covenant. It prohibited church kitchens, recreational halls, "immodest apparel, worldly fashions, and jewelry." Members could not use a ring in the marriage ceremony, have a television, engage in either mixed swimming or intercollegiate sports, or attend professional sports games. Neither were members to attend skating rinks, carnivals, or bowling alleys. The Sabbath was to be kept holy by avoiding unnecessary shopping, joy riding, and secular reading. Churches could not use drama, have award-giving contests, or show movies or slides. Ministers were to strictly enforce these rules.[46]

The Bible Covenant Church established the Covenant Foundation College in Greenfield, Indiana. It used Nazarene publications for its Course of Study for ministers. But the church was in decline by the 1980s. By that time Rehfeldt himself was attending the Ozark Chapel Church of the Nazarene in Kissee Mills, Missouri. In 1990 Marvin Powers rejoined the Church of the Nazarene.[47]

The schisms indicated tension among different subgroups within the denomination, which experienced and responded differently to the challenges of secular society. While some such as Griffith and Rehfeldt attempted to resist the processes of secularization altogether, other Nazarenes found ways of partially accommodating to the pressures of society. Even more so now than after the Griffith schism, Nazarenes forgot their worries about the length of a woman's hair, wedding rings or jewelry, cosmetics, television, and the like. By 1968 Nazarenes fit into society so easily that a newspaper reporter at the General Assembly that year found "folk-singing teenagers" and "mini-skirted co-eds."[48]

Younger Nazarenes, influenced by the '60s generation, stressed that there was "freedom and joy in the life of holiness" and that holiness did not place a person "under the servitude of a legalistic system!"[49] The "legalist" was bound by the law and was not free, wrote Albert Gamble. "Legalism says, 'We must hold the standards.' Love says, 'We must give all we have and are,' and ever seeks to increase and improve the gift. Legalism sees the broken law; love sees the broken heart of God and is brokenhearted for the lawbreaker."[50] In a book on church membership, Jerry McCant stressed that Nazarenes were not legalists. "Spirit-filled Christians should not need the legislation of standards," he wrote. He assured prospective Nazarenes that Holiness people behaved and dressed normally.[51]

At Trevecca, where the men's basketball team played in long pants until 1968 and women's teams wore split skirts until 1973,[52] theologian H. Ray Dunning reminded Nazarenes that keeping the rules should never be confused with spiritual maturity, since external criteria were not a guide to inward spiritual realities. Dunning advocated returning to "advices" as Bresee intended, rather than maintaining "rules" in the Nazarene *Manual*. Almost all of the present rules, Dunning observed, were "historically conditioned." In many cases, they were nothing more than "Southern mores sanctified by proof-text support." Most of the people who were questioning the rules were not being rebellious, said Dunning. Rather, they were "sincerely perplexed" in their search to see how particular modes of conduct enabled one to "project the life of holiness in this generation."[53]

While there were those such as Gilliland and Dunning who were speaking out against legalism, other Nazarenes worried that the pendulum was swinging too far away from rules. Richard Taylor commented in 1968: "We have been told so many times in recent years that 'worldliness' does not consist of what one wears or where one goes, but in the attitude of hearts, that our people might conclude that what one wears or where one goes is inconsequential to one's state of grace." "Herein is the thin wedge of ethical relativism."[54] One could still hear, in 1969, Ross Price urging Nazarenes to avoid "shopping, ironing, housecleaning, shoe polishing, car washing, beginning long journeys, unnecessary labor, hunting, fishing, branding cattle or harvesting the crops, spraying the fields or planting them on the Lord's Day."[55] Those who had opposed women's short hair in the 1950s opposed men's long hair in the 1960s. To conservatives both seemed a conspiracy to "break down the manliness of American men."[56] As late as 1970 the youth magazine *Conquest* got angry subscription cancellations for picturing women in slacks. Districts outside the United States often remained conservative. The Coloured and Indian District in South Africa remained perturbed by short skirts and sleeveless and low-neck dresses. Nazarenes in Brazil still had hesitancies about wedding rings in the early 1970s.[57]

The general superintendents, too, became worried that the church was losing the "spirit of sacrifice and self-denial" that had characterized the church's formative years. Society, it seemed to Edward Lawlor in 1972, was "destroying our moral fiber," and televisions were weakening standards of decency in Nazarene homes.[58] Similarly, V. H. Lewis wished that the church could inject the rules with "new vigor and meaning to our people" and worried about shifts away from modesty and simplicity and about Nazarenes attending movies. Even pastors and their spouses, Lewis feared, had gotten away from the "old fashioned standards."[59]

True, in the midst of a suburban mentality in which "like-mindedness reverberated upon itself"[60] Nazarenes took more and more of their behavioral cues from their neighbors and peers, and fewer from church authorities. The 1972 General Assembly, meeting in sunny Miami surrounded by beaches, modified the 1928 resolution (found until then in the *Manual*'s Appendix) that prohibited Nazarenes from going to "promiscuous public bathing places." Now Nazarenes were cautioned simply to "exercise Christian judgment" and "modesty"[61] and, undoubtedly, left the assembly halls relieved to be able to swim in the beckoning waters with less conflicted consciences.

The 1972 General Assembly changed the Special Rules to permit divorced persons "at such a time as they have given evidence of their regeneration and an awareness of their understanding of the sanctity of marriage" to become members. Some had been attending Nazarene churches for decades, but because of a past divorce on "unbiblical grounds" they had been barred from membership. Even though the church still recognized only adultery as grounds for divorce, it acknowledged that many had fallen short of the "divine ideal." If persons had, before their conversion, been divorced outside the scriptural grounds of adultery and remarried, they could now become members of the Church of the Nazarene.[62]

Meanwhile, African and Papua New Guinean Nazarenes had other problems regarding marriage. In its early years, the church in Swaziland had come to certain conclusions about wives involved in a plural marriage. If converted, the first wife could become a full member of the church. Second and subsequent wives could be members but could not hold church offices. This was intended to show the church's disapproval of polygamy while encouraging a woman who could not free herself from her husband to follow the Lord. By 1960, however, there was a feeling that Swazis were not as ignorant as they once had been about polygamy. There seemed now no excuse for women who had been raised in Nazarene churches and educated in Nazarene schools to freely enter into polygamous marriages. The sentiment among African leaders was that allowing these women to take the Lord's Supper was too large a concession.[63]

Regarding polygamous men, the church granted them "permanent" probationary membership. In all of the church's years in Africa, only once had a converted polygamist given up all his wives. After all, the polygamists had been legally married and the Church of the Nazarene stood against divorce! To demand divorce would create social havoc for the divorced women and their children. So the church had never encouraged converted polygamists to give up their wives. Yet allowing these men only probationary membership prevented them from both baptism and communion.[64]

The situation was similar in Papua New Guinea, but the church handled it differently. The early missionaries looked upon the situation as analogous to the Old Testament. If the church stipulated that a person must divorce his second or third wife before becoming a Christian, it would be requiring something that the Bible did not. Like the missionaries in Africa, it was clear to missionaries in PNG that because polygamy was legal, it did not constitute adultery. In PNG, marriage had little to do with love, companionship, or even friendship. It was a transaction within or between tribes, a means of securing a worker and a producer of children. Polygamy was not committed out of lust but out of economic and social necessity. So those in polygamous marriages (either men or women) could join the Church of the Nazarene and enjoy all of its means of grace. Not that the church sanctioned polygamy. No Nazarene minister could perform a polygamous marriage ceremony, and no Nazarene could enter into a polygamous marriage.

In 1965 general leaders advised the PNG Nazarenes that allowing those in polygamous marriages to join the church must stop. In response, the PNG church separated baptism from membership. Unlike the church in Africa, the church in PNG continued to baptize polygamists but now barred them from church membership. That is, requirements for being a member were higher than those for being a Christian. In the 1970s, 20 percent of PNG Nazarenes were still practicing polygamy.[65]

After the 1972 General Assembly changed the rule on divorced persons becoming Nazarenes, PNG leaders appealed to the general superintendents to reconsider their position on polygamy. Why not give membership to Christian men who had taken second wives prior to their conversions? "The church should be redemptive in its approach to a fallen and unenlightened society." Polygamy, in the eyes of PNG Nazarene leaders, was "irrevocable but not unforgivable." As in Africa, it was impossible to demand separation from second or subsequent wives. It would have constituted a requirement to divorce them and would have produced social chaos.[66]

> Based on the situations in Africa and PNG, on December 9, 1975, the general superintendents issued a formal "Statement on Polygamy" to be included in Missionary Policy:[67]
>
> Where it seems imperative for us to accommodate a local group due to an overriding long-standing tradition, . . . a probationary membership program may be applied so long as the following principles are understood:
>
> 1) Probationers shall always be considered temporary, except in the case of a polygamist, whose probationary relationship shall be considered permanent unless he is able to work out a marriage relationship which is compatible with . . . monogamy.
>
> 2) Every effort shall be put forth to get him to work out a monogamist relationship, understanding that the first wife he married, who is still living, shall be considered the only wife entitled to his monogamist relationship.
>
> 3) The wives of a polygamist relationship shall be treated in the same manner as a polygamist husband as far as the church membership is concerned.

LIFE AND BEHAVIOR IN A CHANGING WORLD

As if to check itself, the same 1972 assembly that loosened the statements on divorce and swimming also established a Commission on Holiness Ethics. As a result of the commission's report, important changes were made in the 1976 *Manual*. Until 1976, the church had specified that one "profaned" the Lord's Day not only by "unnecessary" labor and "holiday diversions" but also by the "patronizing or reading of secular papers." The latter was dropped. The General Rules, in prohibiting any "habits and practices known to be destructive of physical and mental well-being" now were broad enough to include misused drugs; and specific mention of liquor and tobacco was transferred to the more easily amended Special Rules. Previously, the statement on dress and behavior had quoted, without elaboration, 1 Tim. 2:9-10 and 1 Pet. 3:3-4. The 1976 statement used only the words "simplicity and modesty." Until 1976 the General Rules had prohibited the theater, the ballroom, the circus, lotteries and other games of chance. Mention of these was replaced by a more simple statement, that Nazarenes should avoid music, literature, and entertainment that displeased God. The paragraphs on "Growth in Grace" that had been part of the Special Rules were incorporated into the Article of Faith on Entire Sanctification: "We believe that the grace of entire sanctification includes the impulse to grow in grace. However, this impulse must be consciously nurtured and careful attention given to the requisites and processes of spiritual development and improvement in Christlikeness of character and personality. Without such purposeful endeavor one's witness may be impaired and the grace itself frustrated and ultimately lost."[68] More explicit statements were found in the Special Rules. In order to allow Nazarenes to see that beneath rules were principles that needed to be internalized, the 1976 Manual provided a rationale for each Special Rule. In sum, the church allowed both more biblical guidance and freedom of conscience than it had ever before.[69]

Some rejoiced that the church was outgrowing its legalism; others feared that the church was losing its distinctiveness. Was it succumbing to the tendencies toward accommodation that had plagued the Methodist church a century before? By society's standards, Nazarenes were still conservative. The residents of Miami during the 1972 General Assembly still found the Nazarenes a bit quaint. They neither went to nightclubs nor left big tips. But "some of the ice cream parlors around town [were] doing a whopping business."[70]

NINETEEN

Worshipping and Discipling in Local Churches

The life and heart of the church was in the local congregations. Wherever they were located, Nazarene congregations sought ways to find and save the "lost," bring children to repentance, usher believers into the experience of entire sanctification, and minister to the faithful.

PASTORS AND CONGREGATIONS

Pastors encouraged members to follow the guidelines of the church, attend Sunday School and worship services, tithe, and witness to their neighbors. Pastors enforced *Manual* rules and might expel members for using tobacco as quickly as for committing adultery. In Africa, a convert was on "probationary" status for two years.[1] Nazarenes did not apologize for these high expectations: "The church does not invite people to mediocrity but to be their best selves," was the philosophy.[2]

Pastors knew very well that their high expectations were not always fulfilled. Often it was those who had grown up in the church who chafed most at making the same self-denying commitments that their parents and grandparents had made. They did less evangelistic calling, one evangelist complained, yet sat up "far into the night playing Rook or canasta, or watching some comic program on the television," and neglected the basic habits of spiritual life.[3] In pastors' and evangelists' eyes, these adults needed revival. If a Nazarene grew "cold" or, even worse, "backslid," pastors did their best to "shepherd" the soul back into the life of the church.[4]

On the other hand, parishioners had high expectations for their pastors. People expected pastors to conform to levels of propriety exceeding their own. In small town societies, they did not like to be embarrassed by pastors' behavior. Parishioners in Jasper, Alabama, complained to the general superintendent about some hapless pastor who caused them embarrassment. Their pastor coached ball games, "yelling and acting so crazy in public," one described, and demonstrating a "poor spirit." Their pastor needed greater dignity in dress. As well, he overindulged in watching television.[5]

Commitment to the mission of the church spurred Nazarenes to give. Per member, North American Nazarenes were at or near the top of Protestants in giving. In 1950 the per capita giving of Nazarenes ($145) was significantly higher than the Southern Baptists ($40) and Methodists ($37), and outdistanced the Lutherans ($69), Episcopalians ($59), and Presbyterians ($55). In 1975 Nazarenes members were averaging $187, whereas the United Methodists were giving $63 per member.[6] The gap between Nazarenes and members of other denominations may have been because Nazarenes more tightly controlled membership. In addition, parents trained their children to tithe. "Everyone old enough to be saved is old enough to tithe," Nazarenes taught.[7] Although there were efforts to boost tithing, neither pastors nor board members directly solicited funds from members. Giving was confidential, between members and God, except that, because of tax exemptions for charitable giving, the church treasurer or money counters kept records of who had given and how much. Actually, one way or another, pastors seemed to know who was tithing and who was not. The *Manual* stated that only tithers were eligible for election to the church board. Members did not give with the expectation that God would reward them monetarily for it. Giving, Nazarenes believed, should not be a bargain with God. Rather, giving was motivated by love to God.[8]

Giving sustained the church around the world, while pastors' salaries and retirement benefits remained low. The 1948 General Assembly established a Commission on Ministerial Benevolence. But after the United States government allowed ministers to enroll in Social Security, the 1956 General Assembly substituted Social Security benefits for the church's own pension plan.[9]

PASTORAL CARE

Nazarene pastors counseled laypersons on a variety of personal issues. A previous generation attributed emotional and psychological problems to spiritual causes. Increasingly, pastors realized that not every problem could be solved by justification and sanctification. NTS Professor Louis A. Reed wrote that "it is very possible that a person can be a good Christian and yet have mental disorders."[10] This was a significant admission. There was a growing consensus that "saved and sanctified" Nazarenes might undergo periods of emotional depression and even spiritual doubt. Though there should be a sincere motivation to do the will of God, sanctified Christians should not expect to be in constant states of joy and happiness.[11]

Theologians attributed problems to physiological and psychological infirmities, not remaining sin. Modern society itself, commented Lewis Corlett in 1952 (the same year he became president of NTS), produced depression and nervous collapses. His brother, D. Shelby Corlett, the former editor of the *Herald of Holiness*, had faced such problems. "The answer," Lewis Corlett wrote, "lies in the physical and mental rather than in the spiritual."[12] The stressful dislocations of society, as Cecil Paul later observed, produced "deeply troubled and disorganized personalities."[13]

No longer, as some once did, did Nazarenes consider counseling the liberals' alternative to the kneeling rail. James Hamilton, who taught pastoral counseling at Nazarene Theological Seminary, hoped that pastors and laypersons would be able to work through problems "without feeling that it is a denial of the faith of the layman, an admission of ineffectiveness of the minister, or an insult to the theological tradition of both."[14] Hamilton saw the counseling session as a place where laypersons' theological understandings of God could be helped. Damaging understandings of God and self were as much the result of theological instruction as personal development.[15] Released from the concept that every malady was attributable to personal or original sin, Nazarene preaching became need-centered. Not every sermon ended in an altar call because not every spiritual, much less psychological, problem was solvable that way. In the 1960s and beyond, Nazarene laypersons became more open about depression and other emotional difficulties.[16]

The heightened understanding that not all problems were spiritual also meant that the church could take a more sympathetic look at pastors and their families and the emotional stress that they experienced. The church realized that even pastors and their spouses underwent depression and marital conflict. By the 1970s the conception of ministers as ones who needed to separate themselves from deep, caring interrelationships with laypersons weakened. Pastors freely admitted their own humanness. Ministers and their wives became more apt to receive as well as to give care to others.[17]

WOMEN IN MINISTRY

Usually there were more women than men in local churches. They did much of the visitation, local church evangelism, and teaching. They controlled the missionary society. Women always had ministered as ordained elders in the Church of the Nazarene—a privilege that they did not have in other denominations.[18]

Women served with particular freedom on mission fields. Women such as Fairy Chism and Della Boggs in Swaziland; Orpha Speicher, Mary Anderson, Jean Darling, and Carolyn Myatt in India; Lillian Pattee, Frances Vine, Flora Wilson, and Norma Armstrong in the Philippines; Wanda Knox and Evelyn Ramsey in Papua New Guinea; Ruth Saxon in Trinidad; Eunice Bryant in El Salvador; Eugenia Coats, Neva Lane, and Betty Sedat in Guatemala; and Jeanine van Beek in Haiti and at European Nazarene Bible College served as schoolteachers and college directors, church planters, evangelists, translators, and hospital administrators.[19]

True, in many countries, such as India, local women had fewer prerogatives than missionary women. The first Japanese woman ordained (in 1959) was the widow of a pastor killed by the effects of the atomic blast on Hiroshima. In other countries, including the Philippines, women were more readily accepted as pastors. In Trinidad, Carlotta Graham pastored the Tunapuna Church for thirty-eight years before retiring in 1965.[20]

In Argentina, Lucia Garcia de Costa (1903-84) pioneered and pastored several churches. Her father was a skeptic, and her mother a devout Roman Catholic. At age twelve, Garcia joined the Catholics' Daughters of Mary and took a teacher's course in college with the intention of becoming a Roman Catholic missionary to Indians. Then newly arrived Nazarene missionaries to Argentina, Carlos and Leona Miller, rented a house from her family. Under their ministry, she was converted in 1919 at age sixteen and was rebaptized by sprinkling. She was among the first seven members of the Church of the Nazarene in Argentina. She faced persecution from her family but continued toward her teacher's certificate. The Nazarenes opened an elementary school in 1923 with Garcia as director and, at the same time, opened a Bible school with Garcia as a student. In 1924 she was among the first to receive a preacher's license. The church in Argentina faced several difficulties, among them financial problems that forced the Millers, with whom Garcia had worked closely, to transfer to the Christian and Missionary Alliance and then to another field. Nonetheless, in 1927 Garcia finished a Christian Workers course, received a district license, and was assigned a church.

Lucia Garcia de Costa and Natalio Costa

In 1931 Garcia was among the first group of Nazarenes in Argentina to be ordained (by J. B. Chapman). She edited the district paper and taught in the Bible Training School. After learning English, she translated holiness literature, including Hannah Whitall Smith's *The Christian's Secret to a Happy Life* and J. O. McClurkan's *Wholly Sanctified*. In 1935 she married Natalio Costa, an Italian immigrant and former Presbyterian who was attending her church. After their marriage he felt called to preach. They copastored the church in Merlo until 1947. They enjoyed pastoring in rural locations. But upon the recommendation of General Superintendent Powers, they transferred to a church in Buenos Aires. In 1950 she finished a doctorate in classical languages at the University of Buenos Aires. She continued to teach (Hebrew and Greek among other subjects) at the Bible school. In 1953, however, she left the school to pioneer for the Church of the Nazarene in the northwestern area of Argentina. She organized a church in Tucuman in 1954. While planting churches, she and her husband also served as colporteurs for the Argentina Bible Society. They remained in northwestern Argentina until 1958 and then transferred to western Argentina. She pastored in Mendoza from 1958 to 1966 and started Bible school classes there. In 1966 they returned to Buenos Aires so that Garcia could resume teaching at the Bible college. She taught until 1981. At the same time she and her husband planted a church in Monte Grande, which they served until 1972, and then another in San Antonio de Padua, which they served until 1982.[21]

Meanwhile, though the percentage of women Nazarene pastors in North America declined from 12 percent in 1925 to 6 percent in 1945, the half-decade 1950-55 saw the largest increase of any similar period in the number of women ministers (ordained or district licensed) in North America. The 875 women ministers in 1955 represented 12 percent of the total number of ministers in the church. Of these, 17 women were evangelists and 234 were pastors. Geographically, most women pastors during this time were located in a belt extending from West Virginia through Ohio, Indiana, Illinois, Arkansas, Oklahoma, and Texas. Though these areas were conservative on rules and women's dress, local churches more easily welcomed women ministers.[22] Among these, Emma Irick's church in Lufkin, Texas, regularly led its district in Sunday School attendance. After retiring from the Lufkin church in 1959, Irick maintained an active evangelistic ministry until 1978, when she was ninety.[23] Sadie Hall pastored thirteen years in Marietta, Ohio. Before joining the Church of the Nazarene in Ohio in 1937, at the age of sixty, she had been a Free Methodist evangelist. Hall never drove a car. She walked from house to house doing visitation and personal evangelism. When she began pastoring in Marietta, the church had twelve members and was badly in debt. When she retired, the church had one hundred members and no debt.[24]

Often women were partners in ministry with their husbands. Maud Widmeyer, married to C. B. Widmeyer, pastored and taught in various colleges. She was an editor and wrote Sunday School lesson material for the publishing house for twenty-one years. In retirement she and her husband taught on several mission fields.[25] Similarly, though not ordained, Audrey Williamson, who had earned a master's degree in speech from Northwestern University before her marriage to G. B. Williamson, widely used her skills as a public speaker. She recited long passages of Scripture. She also improved the preaching skills of pastors as a personal coach and teacher and, after retirement, while teaching at Nazarene Bible College in Colorado Springs.[26]

At the same time, by the 1950s and 1960s, pastors' wives were apt to be less active than they once were in preaching and more confined to certain other spheres. Churches hired pastors more readily if their wives could play the piano and teach Sunday School. Churches expected pastors' wives to visit members with their husbands, be gracious hosts and good cooks, keep the pastor well-groomed, and manage households on their husbands' meager paychecks. Few worked outside the home. An "outside income," according to one pastor's wife, too easily resulted in "misunderstanding and difficulty within congregations."[27]

Nazarenes increasingly emphasized a domestic and less public role for women. To an extent, this was a reaction to the feminist movement sweeping in the United States. In 1975 there were only eighty-two women pastors (2 percent of the total number of pastors) and forty-five women serving as evangelists in North America. Women had made up 43 percent of the denomination's evangelists in 1908 and 23 percent in 1945 but only 9 percent in 1975.[28]

LOCAL CONGREGATIONS

What a church could afford influenced architecture. The nicer church buildings—including those with pipe organs—were likely to have been purchased from other denominations. For instance, on the Chicago Central District in 1954, Danville First worshipped in a building it had bought from the Methodists in 1921, the Douglas Park Church in the same city in a formerly Cumberland Presbyterian Church it had purchased in 1946, and the Waukegan Church in a formerly Lutheran church also procured in 1946. The district also had purchased a Presbyterian church building in Evanston. On the other hand, the newly organized Orlan Park Church had been renting a former dance hall and in 1954 was worshipping in a former tavern. Otherwise, Nazarene churches were simple and functional. They followed Nazarene priorities. For instance, since Nazarenes did not consider baptism necessary for a person's salvation, or require it for membership, a baptistery was not crucial.[29]

Preaching was central in Nazarene worship, so the pulpit was in the middle of the platform, high enough for visibility, but not so as to separate preacher from people. During the 1960s and 1970s some pastors experimented with informal styles of preaching and reduced the size of the pulpit. A few did away with it altogether.[30]

But the kneeling rail or altar stayed. Although it was a place where worshippers might receive the Lord's Supper, as Methodists did, it was primarily a place where people confessed their sins and were converted, prayed for cleansing and were sanctified, and made other spiritual decisions. The altar needed to be low enough for children, since they were subjects for conversion. Kneeling beside them might be women giving up "gaudy jewelry" or men "reeking with tobacco smoke and liquor." Nazarenes were not to mind; the altar was where repentant sinners ought to be. The altar had to be sturdy enough so that a 200-pounder, in agonized attempts to pray through, could not dislodge it. The altar had to be wide enough so that "altar workers" could lay out their big Bibles on it while they pointed seekers to Scripture. Tissues were kept close for "those wonderful tears" that accompanied tender hearts.[31] By the 1960s some churches were having "open" or "family" altars during pastoral prayers, but some feared that this might confuse the use of the kneeling rail as primarily a place for finding spiritual victory.[32]

Adequate space for Sunday School classes was important. Often previously in church basements, the Sunday School moved upstairs, either to surround two sides of the sanctuary or, in larger churches, to separate educational wings.[33]

Most Nazarenes worshipped in small churches. In 1960, 20 percent of Nazarenes in the United States worshipped in churches with fewer than fifty members and only 2 percent in churches with more than three hundred members. Half of these churches were in medium-sized towns and suburbs; one-fourth were in rural areas or in towns with fewer than ten thousand people; and one-fourth were in cities of more than fifty thousand. Demographics alone closed many rural Nazarene churches. By 1972, the average size of Nazarene churches was somewhat larger: only 14 percent worshipped in churches with fewer than fifty members and 15 percent in churches with more than three hundred members.[34]

Pastors of smaller churches looked to pastors of larger churches as models. For many years, Bethany, Oklahoma, First Church was the denominational leader in Sunday School attendance and membership. Its pastors included C. B. Strang (1940-49), E. S. Phillips (1950-64), M. Harold Daniels (1964-70), and Ponder Gilliland (1970-85). The church grew from 890 members in 1941

Ponder Gilliland

to 1,868 in 1970. A new semicircular auditorium finished in 1969 accommodated 3,000 people in theater-style seats. The sanctuary included twelve stained-glass windows, a bell tower, a pipe organ, and a 210-foot altar rail. Gilliland removed the pulpit in order to more comfortably "share" the message.[35]

On the West Coast, a trend-setting congregation was the Portland, Oregon, First Church. Pastor Leslie Parrott relied on sound business management, sensible planning, and needs-oriented preaching. He advised fellow pastors to create a welcoming, spiritual atmosphere. People had to be treated as consumers, Parrott said. To attract them

> Ponder Gilliland was a model of the professional minister. He had attended graduate schools of business and conducted his own management seminars. After serving as superintendent of the San Antonio District, Gilliland was executive secretary of the Nazarene Young People's Society from 1956 to 1960. He became pastor of Long Beach First Church in 1962 and initiated a variety of innovative ministries. Under his ministry Bethany First Church grew to thirty-two hundred members.[36]

pastors needed to "promote" the church. People no longer went to church out of duty or obligation. Special events, dynamic speakers, and lively singing attracted people. Posters, newspaper advertisements, and letters brought new people in. Once they were inside the church's doors, Parrott advised, there should be designated greeters to welcome them. Church members should immediately contact first-time visitors. Pastors needed to make sure, Parrott said, that their churches did not appear run-down or second-rate. Churches might consider remodeling or even relocating in order to attract worshippers. In short, Parrott wrote, in addition to prayer and dependency upon the Holy Spirit there was much that a pastor could do to build a church.[37]

In Southern California, Pasadena First, under Pastor Earl Lee, flourished even after Pasadena College moved to San Diego in 1973. Lee had served two terms in India in the 1950s and then had pastored Nampa, Idaho, First. His sermons on the "Cycle of Victorious Living" reflected a realistic and less triumphal way of looking at Christian life.[38]

The "suburban captivity" of the North American Nazarene church became quite evident between 1950 and 1970, when several venerable congregations moved from downtown sites. In 1951 Los Angeles First Church, under M. Kimber Moulton, moved from 25th and Magnolia, where it had been located only since 1939, to South Juanita Avenue. There were still 700 members in the early 1960s, but by 1970 the church's membership had declined to 548 and its average Sunday School attendance to 289.[39]

Chicago First had begun as a storefront in 1904. Averaging 700 members, in 1905 it had built a brick building at 64th and Eggleston. In 1953, under the leadership of Pastor C. B. Strang and Building Chairman Howard Hamlin, Chicago First Church moved from 64th to 83rd Street. At its new site, the church began the Highland Christian School. But membership declined. In 1974, under Pastor Robert Cerrato, the church sold its property to an African-American Baptist congregation and moved twenty-five miles west to suburban Lemont, Illinois. More than thirty years later, the nearly all-white First Church agreed to take over responsibility to rehabilitate an abandoned church in the Austin section of Chicago, a predominantly African-American neighborhood—and thus returned to the city it had left.[40]

Elsewhere, on the Washington District, in 1953 Washington First Church moved from Seventh Street, where it had been since 1921, to Sixteenth, in the affluent northwestern section of the city. At about the same time, Baltimore First moved to a colonial-style building on Woodbridge Avenue. However, fifteen years later the church found itself in the middle of a racially changing neighborhood. It relocated to a farm field in Ellicott City, west of Baltimore. Meanwhile, Washington First determined to remain in its location.[41] Historic Nashville First Church remained in the center of the city and continued ministries to urban dwellers. By the early 1970s these ministries included Christian day-care and counseling centers.[42]

In New Bedford, Massachusetts, the Portuguese (later "International") Church ministered to Cape Verdeans. Manuel Chavier, a graduate of Gordon College and Eastern Nazarene College, became pastor of the church in 1949 and served it for over fifty years. As well as being active on district and camp meeting boards, Chavier was a well-known civic leader—active in the local Kiwanis Club, Legal Aid Society, Red Cross, Boys Club, and other organizations.[43]

Larger churches hired associate pastors. In 1950, at Bethany First, Bennett Dudney became one of the denomination's first full-time ministers of Christian education. The CE director's task was to develop lay leaders, serve as a planning and resource person for various church departments, and, in general, to support the pastor.[44] As their numbers grew, associates sensed themselves to have a unique calling and ministry. They formed the Association of Nazarene Directors of Christian Education in 1960. This marked another step in the professionalization of Nazarene ministers. The association published a Newsletter as a forum for exchanging ideas.[45]

The Church of the Nazarene ordained 348 persons in North America in 1951. Despite the denomination's growth, it ordained only 164 in 1966. Leaders worried that not enough Nazarene young people were preparing for ministry. One reason, leaders feared, was that churches paid low salaries. One-third of Nazarene pastors or their spouses had jobs outside the church and home. Only the fact that the number of Nazarene churches was not rapidly increasing (and decreased, for the first time, in 1969) allowed there to be more ministers than churches.[46]

NAZARENE WORSHIP

During the 1950s and 1960s many Nazarenes distanced themselves from the emotionally charged worship services that had characterized the church in earlier years. Third generation Nazarenes did not want to be confused with Pentecostals. Outside of camp meetings, loud "amens" and "hallelujahs" embarrassed many. Church bulletins, once considered too confining to the Holy Spirit, now were commonplace. By comparison to earlier years, in the eyes of some, worship in the Church of the Nazarene was in danger of becoming "lifeless, fireless, frigid ritual, unrelated to the problems and needs of the people."[47] In 1968, Reeford Chaney, superintendent of the Alabama District, admonished his churches to keep the worship "services 'old-fashioned,' Spirit-anointed meetings, where sinners will be convicted, believers made hungry for holiness, and the saints edified and challenged."[48]

Though the sermon remained the center of Nazarene worship, by the 1950s typical Sunday morning sermons were as short as twenty-five minutes. Nazarene preachers aimed at the "ordinary" man and woman "with ordinary education and ordinary opportunities and the usual twentieth-century thought concepts. We must make the truth transparently clear," theologian Richard Taylor admonished, and not speak "over the heads of the people."[49] Leslie Parrott agreed. A sermon was a "verbal expression" of a pastor's "continuing love and concern for the people."[50] Typically, Nazarene preachers organized sermons in deductive, three-point outlines, alliterated, if the pastor were particularly creative. The pastor might open with a humorous story that would catch the listener's interest and might close with a heartrending illustration that would bring the point home. By the 1960s, pastors avoided some of the Holiness clichés that did not seem to communicate to the "younger generation." They jettisoned words that had become only "sectarian eccentricities." Along with Ponder Gilliland, some turned to "sharing" rather than "preaching." But only a few advocated a style of worship that reflected a "coffee-house, folk-rock combination, with religious lyrics."[51]

Though most sermons remained topical, increasingly pastors desired to ground preaching truly in biblical exposition. If the sermon was not exegetically sound, William McCumber warned a gathering of Southern preachers in 1962, "you are not preaching holiness, even though you wear a black necktie, yell at the top of your lungs, wave the *Manual* in your right hand, and quote J. B. Chapman!"[52]

Sunday morning worship in Nazarene churches typically began with a prelude, followed by a hymn (or possibly two), a responsive reading from the hymnal, pastoral prayer, the choir, announcements and welcome, the offering and offertory, a special song (usually a solo), the sermon, and a closing hymn. Nazarenes were likely to sing "All Hail the Power of Jesus' Name," "Holy, Holy, Holy," "Praise Him! Praise Him!" "Come Thou Fount," "Guide Me, O Thou Great Jehovah," "Lead On, O King Eternal," Luther's "A Mighty Fortress Is Our God," and Wesley's "Arise, My Soul, Arise" and "Love Divine." Three good closing hymns were "More Love to Thee," "Trust and Obey," or "Satisfied."[53]

In the 1960s larger churches introduced children's church, which was conducted concurrently with the adult worship services. Children's church, leaders thought, allowed parents to enter more meaningfully into worship, developed leadership abilities in children, enabled their participation in a worship service they could understand, met the needs of children at their own level, and won them to Christ.[54]

Nazarenes took Communion quarterly. C. B. Strang, senior pastor at Bethany First and then Chicago First, used Communion times to reawaken memory of the life and passion of Jesus Christ. Strang gained a consciousness of the sacraments while serving in England and worshipping in the Methodist Church during World War II. He carefully scripted the liturgy and trained stewards and musicians to appreciate the order of service. Strang was atypical in his attention to the sacraments. As in most Nazarene churches, the pastor simply added the sacrament to the end of a worship service. The moments for kneeling to receive the elements, or having them passed through the pews in Presbyterian fashion, were short.[55]

Though similar, worship reflected cultural patterns. For instance, in public prayer, German Nazarenes always stood, folded their hands, and looked heavenward. Nazarenes used traditional German hymns and closed with the song "So Nimm denn meine Haende" ("So Take Then, Lord, My Hands").[56] Similarly, Nazarenes in Great Britain had difficulty accepting choruses with tunes that savored "too much of the world." For David Tarrant, choruses were offensive and, too often, ungrammatical. Nonetheless, Tarrant made use of choice choruses in the evening services of the Port Glasgow church he pastored in the early 1960s.[57]

The worship services in Korea were more structured and formal than in American Nazarene churches and were more like the Presbyterian type of services common among Koreans. By the 1960s the Nazarene church in Korea had moved away from revivalist practices such as the "altar call." It used a hymnal common to all Korean Protestants. Since every Korean had the same Bible translation, responsive readings could be taken directly from the Scripture. As was customary in Korea, Nazarene pastors read the names of contributors after the offering, which was typically taken after the sermon.[58]

In Haiti, Paul Orjala and early leaders encouraged indigenous styles of music. Nazarenes composed evangelical words for old Haitian folk tunes. Worship services were long. They included enactments of Bible stories, skits, music "throbbing with African rhythms," and accompanied by clapping. Early morning prayer meetings and evening worship services went on every day of the week.[59]

In Swaziland, on the other hand, converts rejected reminders of their pagan past. In fact, observers felt that there was too little African music used in the Nazarene churches in Swaziland.[60]

In Italy, and in other predominantly Roman Catholic countries, Nazarenes refrained from baptizing infants. They rebaptized those who had been baptized as infants in Roman Catholic churches, and who had converted as adults. In these same countries, leaders either were ashamed of or hid the fact that the Nazarene *Manual* provided a ritual for infant baptism. In Italy, missionary Roy Fuller, working on a translation of the *Manual*, sought to delete the section that mentioned infant baptism. Missionary Secretary E. S. Phillips told him that to do so would be "tampering" and refused the request.[61]

SUNDAY EVENING AND WEDNESDAY EVENING SERVICES

Sunday evening and Wednesday evening services were less attended than Sunday morning services but remained lively centers of spiritual warmth for the faithful who attended. They provided people a greater sense of spiritual intimacy not only with God but also with each other. Many Nazarenes believed that the spiritual barometer of their churches could be found in the

Sunday night services. Sunday mornings were directed "upward." Sunday evenings were directed "outward." They aimed at evangelism.[62]

Songs of testimony, assurance, and heaven set the mood: "Glorious Freedom," "Pentecostal Power," "He Brought Me Out of the Deep Miry Clay," "He Abides," "The Comforter Has Come," and "When We All Get to Heaven." John T. Benson Jr., who led the music at Nashville First Church, kept "Victory in Jesus" alive in the 1940s and 1950s. Churches used gospel choruses in Sunday evening services. The people—especially teenagers—appreciated the "singability" of lively choruses such as "I've Discovered the Way of Gladness," by Floyd Hawkins, and "Everybody Ought to Know," and the sense of intimacy with God provided through songs such as "Jesus Is the Sweetest Name I Know" and "Spirit of the Living God, Fall Fresh on Me." Special music included young people's choirs, trios, duets, and solos. If the soloists got off key, Hugh Benner advised, they could be drowned out by increasing the volume of the accompaniment![63] Typically, they ended with an altar call as the congregation sang "Just as I Am" or "I Surrender All."

Increasingly, however, Sunday evening services were more "inward"-directed. They focused on strengthening members. By the 1970s those attending Sunday evenings were the loyal core, not the "lost." Sunday evenings provided time for testimonies. They allowed people to face personal problems. Evening services still often ended with hymns of commitment or invitation and prayer around the altar.[64]

The content of Wednesday evening prayer meetings varied. In the 1940s and 1950s many were Sunday-evening-like services with hymns and choruses, a sermon, and time for personal testimonies and prayer requests, followed by "seasons" of prayer kneeling at the altar.[65]

NAZARENE MUSIC

Nazarenes prided themselves on the fervency of their singing. During these years, the "amazing uniformity" of Nazarene music was a force, along with the doctrine of holiness, the *Manual*, and the rules, that kept the denomination together. Rightly handled, Nazarenes felt: "A song service led of the Spirit, flexible in the Spirit, with discernment of the Spirit, with a singable tempo should bring new vigor, enthusiasm, excitement, blessing, and emotion to the soul."[66] But only a few thought that "the louder you sing and the more rhythm you have, the more spiritual you are."[67]

A common hymnal was essential to the sense of knowing what it meant to be Nazarene. The 1915 General Assembly commissioned an official hymnal. Haldor Lillenas solicited the advice of five hundred pastors, evangelists, and church leaders before publishing *Glorious Gospel Hymns* in 1931. *Glorious Gospel Hymns* contained 94 hymns by Lillenas himself, 50 by Lelia Morris, the holiness Methodist writer, 29 by the Wesleys, 24 by Isaac Watts, and 20 by Fanny Crosby.

With each successive hymnal the church shifted slowly away from nineteenth-century Holiness hymns and the compositions of Haldor Lillenas. *Praise and Worship*, published in 1952, eliminated 332 hymns that had been in *Glorious Gospel Hymns* and added 126 new titles. Many of those eliminated were "standard" hymns based on the progressive development of a theme or a text, in the style of Charles Wesley or Isaac Watts. Many of those substituted were "gospel" hymns with refrains and choruses and with a single thought. There were only 35 hymns by Lillenas remaining in *Praise and Worship*, 25 by Morris, 12 by the Wesleys, 13 by Watts, and 22 by Crosby. Non-Nazarene congregations also purchased the hymnal. It sold 1.5 million copies—about three times the number of Nazarene members.[68]

Plans for a new "distinctly North American" hymnal began in 1969. Floyd Hawkins chaired the steering committee. *Worship in Song*, published in 1972, lowered the keys to many hymns and increased the number of responsive readings. Lillenas's contributions were reduced to 22, Morris's to 11. The number of Wesley hymns rose to 18. It included 13 hymns by Watts and 21 by Crosby. *Worship in Song*, Fred Mund observed, evidenced the move of the Church of the Nazarene away from sectarianism and toward greater affinity with the wider Christian movement.[69]

Certain songs appeared in each of the first three major Nazarene hymnals. Wesley's "O for a Heart to Praise My God," "Arise, My Soul, Arise," "Jesus, Lover of My Soul," "Jesus, Thine All Victorious Love," "Love Divine," and "Forever Here My Rest Shall Be" were sung by Nazarenes of each generation. Lelia Morris's "Holiness unto the Lord" remained the church's unofficial anthem, sung at every district assembly. The church joined with evangelicals everywhere in singing Fanny Crosby's "Blessed Assurance" and gospel hymns such as "Such Love" and, later, "The Old Rugged Cross."[70]

The church published several other hymnbooks. These included *Lluvias De Bendicion* (1947), published for the Spanish-speaking church; *Rejoice and Sing* (1958), intended for junior high through college-age young people; and the *Wesley Hymnbook* (1963), which was a reprint of one published in England, with a foreword by the Wesley scholar Franz Hildebrandt but with tunes unfamiliar to North Americans.[71]

Lillenas Publishing Company was a highly successful venture. Sales rose from $122,000 in 1946 to over $1.5 million twenty-five years later. Following Haldor Lillenas's retirement, Robert Stringfellow, a businessman rather than a musician, administered the company. Floyd Hawkins, a songwriter and student of hymnology, served as the music editor after 1957.[72]

Very large churches hired full-time music directors. In some large churches, the music director often was also the youth director. In smaller churches the pastor or a layperson with or without formal music training led the singing. In large churches directors encouraged as large a choir and as many choirs as possible. Choirs were a means of involving people in the church's life. Family and friends came to church if they knew someone who was participating.[73]

The 1960 General Assembly formed a commission to study the status and trends of Nazarene music. The commission found that 80 percent of the churches relied on the Nazarene hymnal for preludes, offertories, choir selections, and special music as well as hymns. For almost two-thirds of the churches, according to the survey, the accompaniment was only an upright piano. The piano was played with gospel ruffles and flourishes, sometimes by gifted if untrained musicians who could "improvise, transpose, and in many cases play by ear."[74] Other churches had a Hammond organ. Only 3 percent of the churches (many of the ones that had purchased their building from other denominations) had pipe organs. A few churches had bands or orchestras.[75]

Some church leaders feared that the church's music, like its worship, was becoming too formal. General Superintendent Benner, who wrote the chorus "Not My Will, but Thine," warned college music departments not to educate students in classical music without also preparing them to be helpful to local congregations.[76]

However, Paul Willwerth, a music professor at ENC, defended the colleges. "Our Music Departments can compromise only so much," Willwerth believed, "for to go beyond that point means a sacrifice of personal and professional integrity." If the music departments concentrated solely on gospel music, it would mean that a music graduate would not be educated "for the highest level of service to society in his chosen profession," always the goal of Nazarene liberal arts education.[77] By the 1970s, perhaps because of greater expectations, medium-sized churches were getting rid of their old uprights and purchasing grand pianos, and Hammond organs were less acceptable in local churches. "Regretfully," remarked James Miller, "Hammond instruments never seem to wear out."[78]

PENTECOSTALISM

One of the most divisive issues in the Church of the Nazarene in the 1960s and 1970s was speaking in tongues. The church had rejected Pentecostalism from its surfacing at Azusa Street in April 1906, not far from Bresee's Church of the Nazarene. Bresee concluded that those experiencing the gift of tongues were "more or less people whose experience is unsatisfactory, who have never been sanctified wholly, or have lost the precious work out of their hearts, who will run after the hope of exceptional or marvelous things, to their own further undoing," and concluded that "people who have the precious, satisfactory experience of Christ revealed in the heart by the Holy Spirit, do not hanker after strange fire, nor run after every suppositional gift, nor are they blown about by every wind of doctrine."[79]

One of Bresee's members, Clara Lum, joined the Pentecostals' Apostolic Faith Mission, but Nazarenes who joined the Pentecostal movement tended to be few. Certain Pentecostal denominations—such as the Church of God (Cleveland, Tennessee), and the Pentecostal Holiness Church—were more influenced by the Wesleyan-Holiness movement than others. There was little influence of the Holiness Movement upon the largest Pentecostal denomination, the Assemblies of God.[80]

The issue arose again in the 1920s. J. B. Chapman, then editor of the *Herald of Holiness,* advised Nazarenes neither to cooperate with nor to go on tangents opposing those who speak in tongues. Nazarenes gained nothing by "fighting." The best antidote is a positive message. In relation to any "heterodox movement," the church must simply preach "something better."[81] Another Nazarene observer, B. F. Neely, understood that Pentecostals taught a "third" work of grace and, on that basis, considered the tongues movement a "dangerous heresy." The reports of tongues did not convince Neely that what had taken place in the New Testament Book of Acts was the same as that which was transpiring in his own day. Similarly, Pascal Belew, another Nazarene writer of the times, did not find the origins of modern tongues-speaking in the Spirit of God. Rather, he identified tongues-speaking with frenzy and did not see any connection between it and the proclamation of the gospel.[82]

The same attitudes toward Pentecostalism continued in the postwar period. Pentecostals, Nazarenes believed, mistakenly taught that everyone would receive the gift of tongues. Pentecostals made speaking in tongues, rather than heart cleansing, the sign of the baptism with the Holy Spirit. They suggested that one who spoke in tongues had a sort of superior spirituality. Tongues-speaking disconnected human minds in the very moments when people ought to have been "listening most intently" for what God had to say to them, remarked Timothy Smith.[83] Holiness people (not to be outdone in their pursuit of spiritual things) sought the "more excellent" gift of love and the fruits of the Spirit. In traditional Nazarene theology, the authentic experience of Pentecost was the cleansing and empowering work of the Holy Spirit. One common Nazarene response to Pentecostals was that the authentic New Testament gift was a known language used to communicate the gospel. When Paul said, "I speak in tongues more than you all" (1 Cor. 14:18, RSV), he meant that he spoke Hebrew, Greek, Latin, and probably Aramaic, and communicated the gospel in all of these languages. At Pentecost, wrote John May in 1952, there was "no gibberish, hysteria, hissing, or unintelligibility."[84] W. T. Purkiser, Richard S. Taylor, Timothy L. Smith, and other respected Nazarene scholars likewise believed that the authentic gift of tongues was what happened at Pentecost, the gift of a known language for the purpose of intelligibly communicating the gospel. The situation at Corinth was that of a congregation in which many different languages were spoken. The problem was that someone would stand and testify in a language that others did not understand. An interpreter was needed. Purkiser hypothesized that 1 Cor. 12 referred to the valid gift of languages and 1 Cor. 14 to the counterfeit gift of ecstatic utterance.[85]

There were exceptions to these interpretations. Ralph Earle and Norman Oke believed that the Bible was not clear enough about what was happening at Corinth to indicate whether they were real languages being spoken or ecstatic utterances. Albert Harper got into trouble with the Nazarene constituency and the general superintendents for positing in an adult Sunday School lesson in 1963 that the tongues that occurred at Corinth were different from the tongues at Pentecost. Whereas what happened at Pentecost was speaking in a known language for the purpose of communicating the gospel, what occurred at Corinth were ecstatic utterances, Harper conjectured.[86]

Other Nazarene scholars, including Donald Metz, who taught at Bethany before helping to found MidAmerica Nazarene College, and Harvey Blaney, who taught at Eastern Nazarene College, substantially agreed with Harper's understanding that what took place in the Book of Acts and what took place in Corinth were different. While the Book of Acts described speaking in a foreign language, what Paul described as taking place in Corinth was an ecstatic utterance. Metz considered the Corinthian practice a carryover from the converts' heathenism. The genuine gift of tongues, said Metz, was what occurred at Pentecost.[87] Similarly, Blaney believed that the Corinthians spoke in some sort of ecstatic language but that the genuine gift of tongues was a language used to communicate the gospel. Paul was tolerant of the kind of tongues-speaking practiced in the Corinthian church, said Blaney, just as he was tolerant of slavery. But it was "an expression of undeveloped Christian spirituality."[88]

Contrary to these positions, both T. W. Willingham and Richard Howard posited that there was a genuine gift of "unknown" tongues that expressed mysteries, and not a foreign language. Howard understood, like Metz and Blaney, that what Luke described in the Book of Acts and what Paul described in his letter to the Corinthians were different phenomena. Howard, though, believed that Paul's writings to the Corinthian church showed that he allowed for a genuine gift of tongues as an ecstatic utterance. Paul placed many restrictions on the gift of tongues, and in Howard's estimation, the Corinthians were to practice the gift more in their private devotions than in public worship. Howard also argued that the gift had always caused divisions within the church, from Paul's time to his own.[89]

Some Nazarenes who spoke in tongues wanted the church to change its position. From their standpoint, the Church of the Nazarene was losing its original fire while Pentecostalism was blazing. In 1971 a student editor at Bethany published an account of his own speaking in tongues—boldly professing that he was both Pentecostal and Nazarene! He warned the church's elders not to "dictate to the Holy Spirit how He may or may not minister to our spirits."[90] Likewise, Wilbur Jackson, pastor of the Filicity City, Ohio, Church of the Nazarene, received "a fluid prayer language" and began, he said, "a new relationship with the Father." When he related his experience to his district superintendent, he was forced out of the denomination within twenty-four hours. He began an independent church. Other Nazarene pastors who spoke in unknown tongues were quickly ushered out of the church.[91]

The issue affected the church in various places around the world, perhaps none more than in Brazil. In the early 1970s there were nineteen organized Nazarene churches in the country. Tongues-speaking was occasionally heard in four Nazarene churches. About half of the Brazilian Nazarene pastors privately spoke in tongues. These had been taken into the Church of the Nazarene from Pentecostal denominations. Several were eligible for ordination. The issue was whether the Church of the Nazarene would ordain pastors who spoke in tongues.

Earl Mosteller, the church's pioneer missionary to Brazil and Mission Council chairman, gathered the opinions of the other missionaries as to whether he should nominate these pastors for ordination. Three missionaries did not see tongues as a barrier to ordination. Don Stamps, one of the missionaries, revealed to Mosteller that he himself spoke in tongues. Mosteller wrote to Kansas City for guidance. General Superintendent V. H. Lewis replied firmly: "We will not ordain any tongues-speaking candidates or men who believe in speaking in tongues whether they have gone through what they claim is that experience or not, and this I am sure would hold in any area of the church."[92]

Mosteller was willing to accept Lewis's ruling. The other missionaries were divided. Most believed that Mosteller had not handled the problem well. At the next opportunity they voted him out as council chairman. (The church soon appointed him to open the work in Portugal.) Some reacted strongly against Lewis's response. They believed that the position of the Brazilian pastors was not greatly different from that of Harper and Metz. General Superintendent Emeritus G. B. Williamson was called into service and visited the field. He advised the missionaries to go along with the general church or leave their assignments.

Lewis felt that the matter required his personal presence. He went to Brazil in November 1971. Lewis kept to his uncompromising position. No persons could become or should remain Nazarene ministers if they spoke in tongues or believed that unknown tongues were a sign of the baptism with the Holy Spirit. Lewis required the Brazilian pastors, if they would be ordained, to promise not to speak in tongues either publicly or privately and to renounce unknown tongues as an authentic spiritual gift. He also required Nazarene missionaries to accept and defend his interpretation of tongues.[93]

Jim Bond, Roger Maze, and Don Stamps left missionary service in the Church of the Nazarene over this issue. Bond had given up his position as NYPS president and his pastorate at Nampa College Church to become a missionary. Though not many reasons for the decision to leave Brazil were known at the time, Bond's resignation reverberated throughout the denomination. Stamps soon joined the Assemblies of God mission in Brazil.[94]

The tongues issue created controversy at the 1972 General Assembly. Each delegate received a packet of materials advocating that the Church of the Nazarene change its stand and allow tongues. Warren Black, a former accountant at the Nazarene Publishing House and a member at Kansas City First Church before he received the gift of tongues, was partly behind this push. Black hoped that a charismatic revival would awaken and renew the church. "Immersion in the Holy Spirit" was something more than sanctification, he said, and praying in tongues, to him, brought "new spiritual power."[95]

General Superintendent Emeritus Hugh C. Benner referred to this in his address to the assembly. He called the attempt to get the church to change its position on tongues a "highly organized and strongly financed operation."

What could the church do? "Have something better—an old-fashioned, second-blessing holiness that brings the fullness of the Spirit with joy and freedom and blessing." His advice to those advocating speaking in tongues was for them to find another denomination and "not to be unethical enough to try to infiltrate or confuse or proselyte our people."[96] In response, the 1972 General Assembly resolved that: "Any practice and/or propagation of speaking in tongues, either as the evidence of the baptism with the Holy Spirit or neo-Pentecostal ecstatic prayer language shall be interpreted as inveighing against the doctrines and usages of the Church of the Nazarene."[97] Not giving up, Black helped organize the Wesleyan Holiness Charismatic Fellowship, headquartered in Athens, Georgia, as a means of maintaining pressure upon the Church of the Nazarene and other Holiness churches to open themselves to tongues-speaking.[98]

In an attempt to solve the continued problem within the church, the general superintendents issued strongly worded statements in their Quadrennial Address to the 1976 General Assembly and, in October 1976, in the *Herald of Holiness*. Tongues, they said, was an "aberration" of the Holiness doctrine of the baptism with the Holy Spirit. The general superintendents urged pastors to preach entire sanctification with doctrinal precision as a means of guarding against tongues.[99]

In its October 15, 1976, issue, the *Herald of Holiness* published the following statement of the general superintendents:

It is our considered judgment and ruling that any practice and/or propagation of speaking in tongues either as the evidence of the baptism with the Holy Spirit or as a neo-pentecostal ecstatic prayer language shall be interpreted as inveighing against the doctrines and usages of the Church of the Nazarene.

. . .

From the beginning we have believed that the authentic gifts of the spirit belong to the Church. While it is God's will that every believer should be baptized and empowered with the Holy Spirit, it is not God's promise that every believer should receive any particular gift. On the contrary, the gifts are distributed by the Holy Spirit to the various believers according to the Spirit's sovereign will (I Corinthians 12:11).

The gift of tongues is related to the miraculous gift of many languages on the Day of Pentecost. On that great day

> the Church was enabled to cross language barriers. The people present were astonished because each one heard the gospel being preached in his own native dialect (Acts 2:6, 8). This special miracle was an expression of God's desire to reach every man everywhere through the spoken and written word. Language is the vehicle of God's truth.
>
> We believe that the biblical material supports one authentic gift—a language given to communicate the gospel and not an unknown babble of sounds. It is our understanding that in I Corinthians 12; 13; 14, Paul was seeking to prevent the abuse of the authentic gift and condemning that which was spurious and of the flesh. We believe that the religious exercise called "tongues" which is not a means of communicating truth is a false gift and a dangerous substitute. We do not believe in a so-called prayer language.
>
> We have concluded that what is being practiced and promoted today is not the true scriptural gift and is therefore not to be condoned by our church.
>
> . . . Therefore, we counsel that people practicing "tongues speaking" or promoting it in any way should be encouraged and advised to seek membership elsewhere unless they are willing to discontinue their practice and their advocacy.
>
> Furthermore, we believe that our people should not participate in services or meetings which encourage the practice of speaking in tongues or schedule in our churches speakers or singers who are known to be active in the so-called charismatic movement.
>
> In taking this stand, we do not wish to reflect on the sincerity or integrity of those who differ with us on these matters. We recognize as fellow members of His universal body all who are in Christ and extend to them the right hand of Christian fellowship. . . .
>
> BOARD OF GENERAL SUPERINTENDENTS

The general superintendents' interpretation of tongues expressed the thinking of Nazarene scholars such as Purkiser and Smith and found support among many pastors and laypeople. Others, however, including a contingent of students at Nazarene Theological Seminary, doubted the wisdom of the general superintendents using their ecclesiastical position to speak authoritatively on what was a matter of biblical interpretation.[100]

To Maynard James, the former president of the Calvary Holiness Church, which merged with the Church of the Nazarene in 1955, the general superintendents' statements in 1976 seemed both "unscriptural" and "divisive." James criticized Pentecostals for believing that everyone who was filled with the Holy Spirit spoke in tongues and believed that love was the "infallible evidence" of a pure heart. Gifts, James said, could never satisfy deep human longings. Nevertheless, like Richard Howard, James believed that there was a genuine gift of tongues among Pentecostals. The church dare not prohibit it. James liked the Christian and Missionary Alliance philosophy, "seek not, forbid not."[101]

The rise of Pentecostalism in the world set clearer boundaries around the Church of the Nazarene. Nazarenes contrasted their own concern with "purity" and the "fruits" of the Holy Spirit with the Pentecostals' search for "power" and emphasis upon the "gifts" of the Holy Spirit. When early Nazarenes spoke of "power," it was in relation to the boldness to witness and evangelize. Tongues-speaking disturbed the Nazarene sense of order and discipline.

CONCLUSION

Local congregations fostered a sense of "kinship" and community for people. In the postwar era, crises drew people toward religious communities. Membership in a local congregation linked Nazarenes not only to the intimate lives of fellow worshippers that they saw weekly but also to tens of thousands of other people around the world. Through giving and prayer in local churches, lives became intertwined. There were enough similarities in music and worship as well as theology and ethos among Nazarenes that a member would have felt at home anywhere even if he or she could not understand the local language being used in a Nazarene church service.

Pastors sought to meet the needs of their people through lively, Spirit-filled worship services and admonishments toward holy living. Nazarene lay members assisted in the work of education and evangelism. They gave generously toward missions. Together, pastors and laypeople reached out to neighbors and friends and nurtured an atmosphere of spiritual welcome and warmth. They drew members away from a sometimes cold and impersonal world and into a tightly knit community. In addition to providing an inwardly satisfying sense of belongingness, the Church of the Nazarene also provided members a sense that they belonged to an enterprise that was global and expanding.

TWENTY

DISCIPLING THROUGH CHRISTIAN EDUCATION

"Everybody ought to go to Sunday School," the church sang. Sunday Schools expanded to meet the needs of the postwar generation. The general church upgraded its curriculum and materials. The Sunday School, however, was only one component of the discipling of believers of all ages in local churches.

MINISTRIES TO CHILDREN

To instill values in their own children and to reach into communities, churches improved Sunday School facilities and found innovative ways of teaching children. Parents wanted to see their children "saved" as early as possible. Children represented a ready "harvest field" of souls for the pastor and the church to win. Children could be "saved" when they reached the "age of accountability," when they felt guilty for personal sins that they had freely committed.[1] As children reached this "age of accountability," the church paid close attention to means through which they might receive Christ and internalize the church's ethics. Parents did not take it for granted that their children would grow up in faith, but worked to win them. Sunday School and other children's programs were aimed less toward catechism or indoctrination than toward the child's experience of "new birth." If children were saved, parents knew, they could escape the evils of the world. Clear directions early in life would lead to greater usefulness in the Kingdom and to success in life. At whatever age a child could testify to being born again, with minimal regard to doctrinal understanding, he or she was eligible for church membership.[2]

The Cradle Roll was a home ministry and evangelistic tool that reached young mothers and families. Churches went on "baby hunts" to contact as many new mothers as they could. Sometimes churches formed "mothers clubs." In some cases, the Cradle Roll program became a ministry to parents on the verge of marital separation.[3]

Nazarene Sunday School attendance swelled from 200,000 in 1944 to 376,000 in 1954, and to 458,000 in 1958. During these years there were three persons attending Sunday School for every two church members. The church used Sunday School attendance rather than worship attendance or membership to gauge growth. Studies showed, unsurprisingly, that 95 percent of the members had attended Sunday School prior to joining the church.[4]

The churches employed all kinds of methods to build their Sunday Schools. They conducted contests and awards to bring in new Sunday School members. Competitions might divide the church into two groups pitting the pastor's group against the Sunday School superintendent's, or two Sunday School classes, or two churches of similar size might compete against each other. Activities might include a "family month," a "mother of the month," rally days in which a king and queen would be crowned depending on who had brought the most people, and "fill a pew" contests, as well as awards of silver dollars, bubble gum, ice cream, or goldfish. One pastor reported thirty-five people converted as the direct result of a Sunday School contest. Yet Sunday School evangelist Lyle Potter, author of many creative Sunday School ideas, warned that, "We defeat the whole purpose of a contest when so much time is spent in explaining, tabulating points, counting the people, and giving awards that there is not sufficient time for presenting the gospel message in each class."[5]

Sunday Schools declined in the 1960s. The Sunday School had grown 49 percent from 1938 to 1948, and 50 percent from 1948 to 1958, but only 8 percent from 1958 to 1968. Nonetheless, numerical attendance increased until 1976, when it peaked at 463,000 in North America. By then the ratio of members to Sunday School attenders has dropped to one church member for every person attending Sunday School. Attempting to maintain attendance, some churches followed other evangelicals and bused in children. Others conducted backyard Bible clubs for children, learning centers, and children's crusades. Teachers used puppets and creative multimedia presentations.[6]

YOUTH MINISTRIES

The church expected much of its youth. Parents hoped that their children could make life commitments to God and the church during adolescence. Pastors encouraged teens, like adults, to attend church, to tithe, to yearn to know what God had for them to do in life, and to realize that God needed loyal disciples in all professions.[7]

The message to Nazarene young people in the 1950s and 1960s was that they should expect other teens to ridicule them for behaving and dressing differently. Indeed, Nazarene youth felt out of place among their school peers. The church expected teens to share their testimonies with classmates, invite them to church, and win them to Christ. Nazarene teens rang doorbells with other church members in door-to-door evangelism. "Contrary to popular belief," confessed a teen, "I'm not as normal as some folks seem to think I am. You see, I'm a Christian and that, according to all my friends, seems to make me a bit different at times."[8] Leaders told Nazarene teens not to seek popularity but, rather, to limit themselves to church activities. Pastors advised young people to date persons with the same ideals, standards, and interests. Couples were supposed to date where they might enjoy "wholesome" fun. Advice became quite explicit in the 1960s, when pastors and parents cautioned teens to delay sex until after marriage. District camps provided friendships beyond the small bands of teens that clung together in local churches.[9]

The Nazarene Young People's Society (later Nazarene Youth International) provided the structure for youth ministries and activities. NYPS undertook missions projects—raising, for instance, $50,000 for Bible schools in South Africa and Australia during the 1952 to 1956 quadrennium. Youth in India raised money to start a church in Jamaica.[10] Paul Skiles, a lay leader who served as general secretary of the NYPS from 1960 to 1974, brought new energy and creativity to the position and appealed to a younger generation. He generated relevant and active youth programs throughout the turbulent 1960s and 1970s. He balanced intimate and institutional styles. His tools of communication were a baseball pitcher's glove and a musician's trombone.[11]

Paul Skiles playing trombone

Paul Skiles was the first layperson elected NYPS general secretary. Before this, he was minister of youth and music at the Bakersfield, Eureka, and Santa Ana churches on the Northern California District. He was thirty-three when he arrived in Kansas City. Skiles identified naturally with the church's young people, and the NYPS became more person- than program-centered. Skiles communicated in ways modern youth could understand. Philosophically, Skiles was committed to offering the highest quality materials that the church could produce and engaging youth in the total mission of the church.

From 1974 to 1994 Skiles served as director of Media and Communications for the Church of the Nazarene.[12]

Witnessing to unbelievers remained an important part of being a Nazarene young person in the 1960s. Immediate Personal Action for Christ Teams (IMPACT) involved teens singing contemporary songs and witnessing in their own or other communities. Some went to other countries. IMPACT teams were reminded to be polite, to express what the Bible, not their church, said, to be alert for openings in conversations with nonbelievers, to make sure that they themselves were living above reproach, yet to be "natural"![13]

Whether through IMPACT or not, teens' testimonies in the 1960s became less rehearsed, less repetitive of trite phrases. Youth aimed to say something relevant and meaningful to their peers. "Wow!" one teen reported to Paul Skiles in 1971, "things are really happening around here. About eight people from our teen group have really gotten excited about Christ. Every Sunday afternoon we go out witnessing. Last Sunday two guys accepted Christ and today two girls accepted Christ."[14]

Skiles initiated the Student Mission Corps and, in 1963, as a joint project of NYPS and the Foreign Missions department, Nazarene Evangelistic Ambassador teams. Participants met young people in other countries whose homes were much poorer but whose spiritual experience often was much richer than their own. NEA led some toward missionary service. It provided, for others, an alternative to antiwar and other protest movements.[15]

Teens were impressed when Jim Bond resigned as NYPS president, as well as pastor of College Church in Nampa, Idaho, in order to become a missionary to Brazil. Before going, in 1970, Bond held Youth and Missions rallies around the country.[16]

Large-scale Youth Institutes, which began in 1958, modeled current trends in youth ministries such as drama and skits. They knit together teen leaders from throughout the United States and, eventually, the world. In 1965, 215 attended an all-European NYPS gathering in Innsbruck, Austria. Hundreds more attended the International Institute that met in Estes Park, Colorado, in 1970. The NYPS aimed to enlarge the "operational vision" of the church. In order to "be consistent with the church's official and unofficial efforts toward internationalization" the 1974 World Youth Conference met in Switzerland. In organizing multinational conferences, the NYPS became the first church auxiliary to demonstrate the international shape of the church.[17]

In the 1960s and 1970s, in response to crises in society, local churches refocused their ministries for teens. The Pasadena Bresee Avenue church, for instance, held a Teen Hour during the Wednesday evening prayer meetings, and, once a month, Teen Hour Plus as a venue for inviting unsaved, non-church friends. It included prayer, testimonies, singing, and Bible study. The church sponsored dinners for teens on Sunday afternoons, a teen choir, and teen retreats, including one to a Native American reservation.[18]

Congregations located near secular colleges and universities reached out through Bresee Fellowships. These targeted Nazarene students attending non-Nazarene schools. Nearby churches developed programs to keep students involved. Bresee Fellowships operated in a score of places. The church in Stillwater, Oklahoma, saw opportunities to "give guidance, support, reinforcement, [and] inspiration" to students of various denominations attending the University of Oklahoma, and local Nazarenes developed an integrated "center" that included recreation facilities. Unlike typical Nazarene churches (according to one comment) the center's pastor "dressed in style."[19]

With student unrest everywhere, the Nazarene church held a Campus Ministry Conference in July 1969. Soon after, the growing Campus Ministries work was taken out of the education department and put under Paul Miller in the youth department. Campus ministries (no longer called Bresee Fellowships) grew. There was an Agrupacion de Universitianos Nazarenos in Rio Piedras, Puerto Rico, for instance, for those attending schools in the San Juan area. In Edmonton, Alberta, Canada, a campus ministry developed for students at the University of Alberta. Pastor Don Posterski encouraged young people to call him "Pastor Don" and to drop by the church for a "rap session" and coffee. He encouraged them to align their Christian faith with "rational respectability and intellectual integrity."[20]

One high profile youth worker was Ann Kiemel. Raised in a Nazarene parsonage in Hawaii, Kiemel taught junior high school students after graduating from NNC. She became minster of youth at Long Beach First Church in 1970. Soon Kiemel was ministering to more than five hundred teenagers in the church and local high schools. At the time, Kiemel noted, big-church youth ministries aimed at keeping teenagers busy. Kiemel's approach was different. "I think we communicate ourselves more than we ever communicate an idea," she reminded other youth directors. "You bring teenagers in and you surround them with love and that's all they want. That's all they need." Kiemel likewise encouraged young people to love each other and to love those outside their own groups.[21] After two years at Long Beach, Leslie Parrott, then president of ENC, invited Kiemel to become dean of women. Only twenty-six, she did not project the traditional image of a dean of women. Soon Kiemel was speaking widely outside the Church of the Nazarene and writing books that circulated far beyond Nazarene borders.[22]

The following indicates Ann Kiemel's approach and the kind of stories she related whenever she spoke.

There's a boy in my youth room whose name is John. He's 16 years old and I mean he walks around like this all the time, just like this! His back is hunched, his head is down. One day John didn't come. I mean you even say "Hi" to John and he just kinda shakes. It's just like he's so insecure and inferior, he doesn't want you to even speak to him. He's scared to death. And one day John wasn't there. I said to the kids, "I want us to experiment. What would happen if we really loved John?" That's all I said. The next time John came in, I mean we put him right in the middle of the circle. Everybody prayed for John. Everyone was around John. It wasn't just the first Sunday. They'd called him in the middle of the week, and after about a month one of my kids said, "Boy, Ann, you know I mean it's pretty hard to love John. You call him on the phone, 'Hi, John, this is Allen, how are ya?' Ummmmm, alright.' 'Well, John, how did your day go at school?' 'Ummmmm, okay.'" They said, "How can you carry on a conversation with John, he can't even talk!" I said, "We're gonna keep loving him." We surrounded him with love. We loved him. We prayed for him. The kids wrote him notes. He never responded until about three months later. And the first time he smiled, we nearly fell off our chairs and everyone noticed, John smiled. And a couple of weeks later, he laughed out loud. I mean my kids said, you know, John was sitting over here and they were all, "Psst . . ." You know, they didn't want John to see but they were trying to get my attention. Had I noticed, he had actually laughed out loud! That was so exciting! And today, John prays out loud all the time and he laughs quite frequently and a few weeks ago his mother called me. His mother said, "Ann," (he does not come from a church home at all) "we were up in the mountains camping not too long ago, and one day John burst into tears and sobbed and sobbed and sobbed." She said, "I haven't seen John cry since he was five and I kept saying, 'John, what's wrong? What's the matter?' 'I'm such a failure! I'm such a failure!'" She said that's all he could come out with. And she said, "For five hours that's all he could do was just sob and cry and I finally said, 'I know what it is, John, it's that church you go to over there. They're not treating you right, are they?'" And she said he just immediately said "No! That's my only hope. Ann and the kids love me over there!" And she said "from that moment on we've seen a difference in John."[23]

The message that Kiemel and youth leaders like her projected centered upon personal love and acceptance in a time of social turmoil. Few articles in Nazarene teen literature commented upon the political events of the 1960s and 1970s. Leaders had the impression that they could not address divisive issues in Nazarene publications.[24]

MINISTRIES FOR ADULTS

The Christian Service Training (CST) program prepared laypeople who desired to become better church workers. Begun by the 1940 General Assembly, CST represented an enlargement of the earlier Leadership Training program. R. R. Hodges headed CST until 1948, Norman Oke from 1948 to 1955, Kenneth Rice from 1955 to 1959, Bennett Dudney from 1959 to 1971, and Earl Wolf from 1972 to 1982. The director's position became full-time in 1964, the same year the church created a multidepartmental commission to oversee CST. The commission approved courses for all areas of leadership education in the church and selected book projects and authors.[25]

Thousands of Nazarenes learned how to be better personal evangelists, Sunday School teachers, board members, and ushers through this material. CST courses were taught in local churches, in training schools, and at institutes or camps. First Series courses required three hundred minutes of class time. Second Series texts were more difficult and required six hundred minutes. For courses taught in local settings, pastors approved teachers. Kansas City maintained records of credits earned. The only costs were for the textbooks, which were available from Nazarene Publishing House. Through home study a Sunday School teacher in a small rural church could study the books, mail in assignments, and receive back helpful comments from some of the church's leading scholars, such as Richard S. Taylor, who served as graders. CST granted 6,648 credits in 1940, 16,106 in 1948, and 110,000 in 1965. A full Spanish language CST program was available in 1972. It included such pertinent works as *Errores Fundamentales del Romanismo* by Gutierrez Marin.[26]

The Department of Church Schools created in 1973 the Senior Adult Ministries (SAM). Previously, senior adult ministries had been under the home department, with the assumption that seniors were shut-in and homebound! A senior adult program first developed at Bethany First Church under Sam Stearman. SAM encouraged and enabled senior adults to remain active in local church programs and prepared them to lead Bible studies. In September 1973 the church began Nazarene International Retreats of Golden Agers (NIROGA). The first one, held in Glorieta, New Mexico, drew 457 senior adults.[27]

DENOMINATIONAL OVERSIGHT OF CHRISTIAN EDUCATION

For nearly thirty years Albert Harper was responsible for the church's Sunday School curriculum. Under him, Sunday School attendance doubled and enrollment tripled.[28]

Albert F. Harper

Albert Harper grew up in southern Idaho and was converted as a child. He was educated at NNC and earned a Ph.D. in philosophy and educational psychology at the University of Washington. He came to the Kansas City office after teaching at NNC from 1929 to 1935. While serving as NNC's academic dean from 1935 to 1941, the school achieved accreditation. He taught at ENC during the war. In 1944 he published *The Story of Ourselves*, a book that based Christian education upon developmental and educational psychology. His appointment to Church Schools in 1946 signified the professionalism of key church positions.[29]

Harper's first priority was developing age-related or graded materials for all levels. By 1948 such materials took the place of uniform lessons. Junior high lessons began in 1952, lessons for primary pupils in 1957, and lessons for juniors in 1958. To make the literature appealing, two-color printing of story papers was introduced in 1951 and magnetic "Nu-Vu" teaching aids (to take the place of flannel boards) in 1954. Harper wanted teachers to understand their pupils from the standpoint of their psychological and cognitive development. A series of "better teaching" books and teacher training filmstrips produced under Harper aimed in this direction.[30]

On a college level, in 1955 the church began publication of the Exploring series. Beginning with *Exploring the Old Testament* and *Exploring the New Testament*, the books represented a conservative Wesleyan approach. Sunday School teachers, laypersons enrolled in CST subjects, college students, and those in the Course of Study for ministers used these books. More ambitiously, the Publishing House launched the Beacon Bible Commentary. Its authors included leading scholars from several Holiness denominations.[31]

In 1959 the Pilgrim Holiness Church joined with Nazarenes to produce kindergarten and Vacation Bible School materials. Eventually the Wesleyan Methodists, the Churches of Christ in Christian Union, and the Evangelical Methodist Church cooperated, and other groups, including the Evangelical Friends and the Free Methodists, joined in specific projects. Harper encouraged this. The coordinating committee chose the name Aldersgate for these joint publications. Nazarene Publishing House printed the materials. Free Methodists were instrumental in producing the Aldersgate Biblical Series, a book-by-book Bible study, and Wesleyan Methodists the Aldersgate Doctrinal Series, 13 weeks of lessons on entire sanctification. "Such cooperative projects," Harper hoped, drew "holiness people closer to each other" and even offered "some eventual possibilities of church union."[32]

While Harper remained executive editor of the Church Schools department, Kenneth Rice joined the staff in 1961 as executive secretary. Rice, who earned a doctor of religious education degree at Southwestern Baptist Theological Seminary, saw his role as chief "cheerleader" for Sunday Schools. He traveled widely. His 1964 book *How Sunday Schools Grow* advocated enlisting and training more workers, starting more classes, providing more space, finding more prospects, and doing more visitation. When the department was reorganized in 1976, Rice became director of Adult Ministries.[33]

Harper received all kinds of criticism. Various persons disliked pictures of women with short hair in Sunday School material, Sunday School writers who referred to any translation except the King James, and the church's participation in the Uniform Lesson Series Committee, which was regulated by the Christian Education Department of the National Council of Churches of Christ in the USA. The NCCC, some feared, promoted communism and racial integration. Harper defended the church's relationship with the Uniform Lesson Committee. Harper served on the committee's steering committee and was its chairman from 1955 to 1958. As such, Harper believed that he was able to infuse Wesleyan theological points of view and keep the lessons acceptable to evangelicals. But the 1972 General Assembly voted to sever ties with the Uniform Lessons Committee. Since the lessons were planned years in advance, this allowed for a gradual withdrawal.[34]

Other forces exerted pressure on the curriculum. In the 1970s the general superintendents directed that lessons at all levels relate to evangelism. One lesson each quarter gave Sunday School teachers the opportunity to lead pupils toward repentance and conversion. At the junior high level, seventy thousand "Life Can Have Meaning" tracts were distributed with Sunday School materials. Among senior high students there was a month-long salvation unit. Adults, meanwhile, studied *New Testament Evangelism Today*, written by Wesley Tracy.[35]

While the church provided rich Sunday School materials for the North American church, only Spanish-speaking Nazarene churches had comparable resources in their own languages. Material coming from North America was not suited to other cultures, even those using English. Despite many translation efforts, many Nazarenes had little that was either useful or affordable.[36]

By the 1970s, Nazarene Sunday School publications were competing fiercely with other evangelical presses. In order to appeal to their children, local churches wanted materials that approached the quality of the public schools. The trend of local congregations away from Nazarene Sunday School material signified their tolerance of broad evangelical positions.[37]

It took some time for Nazarene publications to catch up to the market by the time this lesson was learned. Eventually, Church Schools launched new curricula, introduced more audiovisual resources, and made publications more attractive. Harper hired a new group of curriculum editors: J. Melton Wienecke for Vacation Bible School materials, Jeanette Wienecke for nursery, J. Paul Turner for senior high, Wesley Tracy for youth and young adults, and John B. Nielson for adults. In 1971 the Dialog Elective Series began for adult classes that wanted issue-oriented material. PROBE materials for young adult classes began in 1974. Unlike the regular adult quarterlies, which "begged to be lectured," these materials aimed to produce discussion. The changes were not enough to satisfy denominational leaders, who felt that Harper was not up to the job of thoroughly revising publications. In 1974 Harper left the department and took a full-time teaching position at Nazarene Theological Seminary.[38]

The general superintendents chose Donald Metz to replace Harper. Metz had a doctor of religious education degree from Southwestern Baptist Theological Seminary and a Ph.D. from the University of Oklahoma. He had been a key leader shaping MidAmerica Nazarene College. As director, Metz reexamined the Church Schools Department's philosophy, curriculum, objectives, and format. For him, Christian education had to be both "God-centered" and "life-related," and employ educational styles suited to the learner. Metz conducted forums for local pastors to vent their complaints about Sunday School materials. They wanted, he found, more attractive material, lessons related to life, teaching aids, student involvement, and in-depth Bible studies. The pastors suggested that publications stop using the King James Version exclusively. Some wished for materials for bus ministries and inner-city children.[39]

Metz came to the office realizing that the church was planning further reorganization. The office of executive editor was abolished in 1976 to make way for an executive coordinator of the Division of Christian Life and Sunday School Ministries. Metz returned to MidAmerica.[40]

CONCLUSION

Christian education was a crucial means of teaching the Bible, doctrines, and Christian behavior. It led children and young people to faith. It equipped laypeople for greater effectiveness in ministry. The church remained committed to seeking vital Christian experience and leadership among all ages but struggled to maintain the high standards of excellence and relevance that local churches demanded.

TWENTY-ONE

EDUCATING YOUNG PEOPLE AT NAZARENE COLLEGES

Nazarene higher education remained close to its liberal arts and evangelical moorings. At the same time, during the postwar era, Nazarene schools elevated standards, hired well-qualified and committed faculty members, and increased the number of academic disciplines. Among its various ministries, Nazarenes could be proud of their colleges.

PHILOSOPHY OF NAZARENE HIGHER EDUCATION

The 1948 General Assembly appointed a commission to formulate a philosophy to guide Nazarene higher education in the postwar era. Bertha Munro, ENC's academic dean, was chiefly responsible for the statement that the commission finally agreed upon.[1] The commission affirmed that Nazarene teachers should introduce students to the best scholarship in their fields. Faculty members (even those in religion departments) should seek neither to indoctrinate students nor to force God's will upon them.

The Commission on Education presented a report that was adopted by the General Board in June 1952:[2]

Our educational philosophy is based on the creed of the church, . . . [and] is concerned with two areas: (1) the personal development of the individual, intellectual, moral and spiritual, and (2) the social directive of Christian service.

Confident that all truth is one and self-consistent and will ultimately be so demonstrated, but certain that Absolute Truth is revealed in the Holy Scriptures and in Christian experience, this philosophy surveys all fields of knowledge but avowedly finds its center in Christ's teachings and His redemptive work for man.

It therefore . . . concerns itself with enabling young people to organize their total thinking in relation to the cross of Christ and to live in the light of all its implications. . . . The educational objective of our college is to be recognized as a fusion of holy character and sound education. . . .

Our <u>social</u> objective relates to the all-embracing purpose of the Church of the Nazarene, to advance the whole cause of Christ in the world. The church is committed to the proposition that the message of holiness, with its emphasis on the second crisis, is indispensable and that its witness can best be maintained in the present age through the organized effort of a distinctively holiness denomination. Therefore, the educational institutions are expected to provide their denomination with a ministry which shall be orthodox in belief, sound in Christian experience, trustworthy in example, wise in counsel, and efficient in practice; and with a laity who shall be intelligent and clear-thinking, loyal to the sacred mission of a holiness church, devoted and earnest—ministry and laity adjusted in a working unit, with a vision of world needs and a warmth of love for Christ and His kingdom. . . .

The educational institutions are thus to assume responsibility for the adequate preparation of youth for <u>life</u> and <u>service</u>. While their distinctive province is intellectual development, they are to hold themselves responsible also for <u>spiritual growth</u> and <u>ethical training</u>. . . .

The duty of the Christian teacher is to have found his own Christian integration, then to be able and willing to explain how he arrived and lead the way for others. . . .

Finally, the Nazarene educational institutions will fulfill their purpose and accomplish their unique objectives primarily by maintaining a sane, positive religious and spiritual atmosphere and emphasis. The administration and staff must carry on a continuous program of self-evaluation and self-improvement in the light of the above stated philosophy, objectives, and methods in order to maintain a current spiritual dynamic on the campus which will challenge each succeeding generation to the privileges, possibilities, and responsibilities of Christian service.

> **THE COMMISSION ON EDUCATION**
> L. T. Corlett, Chairman   Mack Anderson
> H. W. Reed, Secretary   Edward Lawlor
> S. T. Ludwig   Paul Garrett
> Bertha Munro   A. E. Sanner
> R. V. DeLong

The philosophy allowed Nazarenes to freely explore social and natural sciences. Nazarene colleges were remarkably similar in affirming the liberal arts. The colleges pursued and maintained accreditation. An increasing number of teachers earned doctorates. At the same time, before the bell rang (so to speak), teachers expressed their own convictions. They aimed not to leave students in doubt. College campuses were laboratories for the "verification of the principles," Nazarenes taught.[3] Teachers and administrators attempted to model holiness. Their own sacrifices, they hoped, would motivate graduates to live selflessly.[4]

General leaders embraced the liberal arts philosophy. At the inauguration of John Riley at NNC in 1952, for instance, G. B. Williamson insisted that the church not take any "shortcuts" in education, because doing so resulted in "a dwarfed intellect" and "a narrow, straightened, unsympathetic soul."[5] Similarly, Hugh Benner reminded Nazarenes that the church was "committed to a strong educational emphasis" and to colleges where one could find both "hot hearts and trained minds."[6]

At the same time, leaders emphasized the schools' mission to and place in the church. In 1959 Benner admonished colleges to keep the percentage of Nazarene students high, not to hire too many non-Nazarene professors or to tolerate teachers who violated Nazarene standards, not to yield to "worldliness" in students' dress and behavior, and not to produce preachers who knew more about theologians Niebuhr, Barth, or Tillich than the Word of God. The colleges must not, V. H. Lewis warned some years later, return students to their home churches cast "adrift with scorn for the church that can show them how to live, to rear their children in the faith, and meet their destiny before God."[7]

TRENDS IN LIBERAL ARTS COLLEGES

As postwar enrollments rose, the colleges remained sensitive to the churches they served. Parents expected the sons and daughters they sent to Nazarene schools to be strengthened in their values and commitments. The colleges risked misunderstanding if they adjusted behavioral codes on campuses to suit changing times, yet they sought to prepare students for the world as well as for the church. Veterans, many of them married, took advantage of U.S. government-funded education grants. This created housing shortages and other problems. Schools could not expect the veterans to live by the same curfew rules that governed teenagers. Meanwhile, the colleges became less dominated by ministerial students and religion professors. Instead, education programs flourished. Almost one-half of the students at Northwest in 1972, for instance, were enrolled in teacher education programs. The colleges drew to their education faculty persons with long experience in public education.[8]

Nazarenes supported their colleges well. A 1952 study found that, per member, only Lutherans gave proportionately more to their denominational schools than Nazarenes.[9] Throughout the postwar period, 75 percent of college budgets came from tuition. From local churches, giving for Nazarene colleges in North America jumped from $1.84 per member in 1950 to $2.94 in 1964, to $17.06 in 1976. Per member, Nazarenes on MidAmerica's zone gave the most and those on the Trevecca zone the least. Total income from local churches increased from $261,000 in 1950 to $7,861,000 in 1978. In 1947 one-fifth of Nazarene colleges' total income had come from local churches; by 1978 it was only one-eighth. This was because by 1978 the colleges were receiving substantial grants from the United States federal government. By the mid-1970s college presidents believed that the schools could not survive without federal support.[10]

The leadership of the colleges was remarkably stable in the postwar years. A. B. Mackey served as president of Trevecca from 1936 to 1963. He was followed by William Greathouse, who served from 1963 to 1968, and then by Mark Moore. Roy Cantrell served as president of Bethany from 1947 to 1972; Edward S. Mann at ENC, 1948 to 1970; Harold W. Reed, Olivet, 1949 to 1975; and John Riley, NNC, 1952 to 1973. Leadership was less stable at Pasadena. W. T. Purkiser replaced H. Orton Wiley in 1949 and served until 1957; R. V. DeLong, served from 1957 to 1960; Oscar Finch, 1960 to 1964; and W. Shelburne Brown, 1964 to 1978. Each of the college presidents had the responsibility of balancing intellectual and spiritual life. They had to do what was right for the academic integrity of the school and keep accrediting agencies satisfied while keeping the broader Nazarene community happy.[11]

The colleges remained a sphere where women continued to influence the church. Among the many, Bertha Munro helped to shape the church's philosophy of education. Thelma Culver, who earned an Ed.D. at the University of Colorado in 1947, served as academic dean at NNC from 1946 to

1970 and headed the school's education department. Maude Stuneck, with a Ph.D. from the University of Chicago, taught in the religion department at Trevecca from 1949 to 1964. Mildred Bangs Wynkoop served as president of Japan Nazarene Theological Seminary, taught at Trevecca from 1966 to 1976, and finished her career teaching at Nazarene Theological Seminary.

Other later trends on Nazarene colleges indicated that, because of accreditation standards as well as several General Assembly directives, more laypersons were serving as college trustees. In order to attract students, during the 1960s Bethany offered a political science major; Bethany and Olivet, criminal justice; Olivet, earth and space science; Trevecca, majors in library science and health sciences; ENC and NNC, social work; NNC, engineering; Point Loma, speech pathology. Nazarene professors affiliated with scholars and professional organizations in their disciplines. Their salaries lagged far behind colleagues in other schools, but were rising. Library holdings in Nazarene colleges grew markedly. In 1978 the two largest libraries were Point Loma, which had 164,000 volumes, and Trevecca, which had 145,000.[12]

Revivals continued on Nazarene colleges. The revival at Asbury College and Theological Seminary in 1969-70 spilled over into Bethany, Olivet, and Trevecca. Testimonies of students indicated that they were finding the faith of their parents, but not necessarily in the same way. The Jesus People movement loosened formality. Students with long hair, beards, and beads carried thick, well-worn Bibles to chapel and class.[13]

The Nazarene Student Leadership Conference, made up of student body leaders from the colleges, began in 1964. Later in the same decade, many student leaders were sympathetic toward protests and demonstrations that took place on secular campuses. The NSLC sharply criticized the Nazarene "establishment" and reevaluated accepted procedures and policies on Nazarene campuses. Clearly, Nazarene schools were stepping out of their sectarian isolation. Nazarenes, in the estimation of Randall Spindle, had entered the "mainstream of American higher education."[14]

Trevecca

Trevecca reflected its constituency. Under A. B. Mackey the earlier non-denominational character of the school was replaced by loyalty to the Church of the Nazarene. Having seen the bankruptcy and financial difficulties that Trevecca went through during the Depression, Mackey feared debt, would not borrow money, and always moved cautiously. Mackey suffered a Board of Trustees that meddled into the management of the school. All this meant few infrastructure projects under his administration. In the 1950s Mackey prohibited faculty members from owning televisions. He prevented racial integration. He was proud, when he left office, that all faculty members were Nazarene and that half were ordained ministers.[15]

Accreditation was Trevecca's greatest woe. By 1950, both Peabody College and the University of Tennessee accepted Trevecca graduates into its master's programs with full standing, a good sign. In 1955, the Tennessee Department of Education granted full approval to Trevecca's teacher education program. Yet the Southern Association of Colleges delayed accreditation. One factor was financial. The association required a $300,000 endowment. Mackey argued that the stable income that the college received from local churches was equivalent to an endowment, but the association was not persuaded. Another factor that delayed accreditation was that too few faculty members had earned doctorates. Also, the association disliked the school's denominational focus. To address this latter issue, in 1962 the trustees approved a statement on academic freedom. At that time, only six faculty members had doctoral degrees.[16]

Having been a teacher at the school and head of its religion department before becoming president, William Greathouse administered the school less paternalistically and more collegially than Mackey. Greathouse's family had been Methodist before trying out a new church in Jackson, Tennessee, the Church of the Nazarene. Greathouse attended Bethany-Peniel College in Oklahoma for a year, then returned to his home state and graduated from Lambuth College in 1941. He earned a bachelor of theology degree from Trevecca and then enrolled in the Divinity School of Vanderbilt University. He finished a master's degree in theology in 1948. By that time, he was teaching at Trevecca while pastoring the Nazarene church in Clarksville, Tennessee. He became dean of Trevecca's School of Religion in 1955. Greathouse resumed studies toward a doctorate in theology. He became pastor of Nashville First Church, however, in 1958. In 1963 he was elected president of Trevecca College. As president, Greathouse added H. Ray Dunning (1964) and Mildred Wynkoop (1966) to a theology faculty that already included John A. Knight, who had earned a Ph.D. at Vanderbilt.

Greathouse understood the urgency of accreditation. It was, he told the trustees, the "badge of academic legitimacy" that would bring Trevecca out of its "perpetual mediocrity." The fall after Greathouse became president an accrediting team visited the school. It criticized Trevecca's preference for producing good Nazarenes rather than for preparing world leaders. This prevented, in the team's estimation, "a lively liberal arts atmosphere."[17] In response, Greathouse hired new teachers and sought intentionally to build a place conducive to creative thinking. He replaced top Trevecca administrators, expanded the library, and improved facilities. In Greathouse's five years as president enrollment rose from three hundred to eight hundred and the school began to accept African-American students. This enabled Trevecca to receive more than $1 million in 1967 from the U.S. government for science and physical education buildings.[18]

The unaccomplished accreditation task was left in the hands of the next president, Mark Moore, who previously had been superintendent of the Central Chicago District. An Accrediting Committee in 1968 issued another negative assessment based mostly on Trevecca's finances. As a result of the report, Trevecca lost about one hundred students, which further worsened its situation. Undeterred, Moore initiated a new style of team leadership and improved relations with the association. Finances improved. Finally, the association granted accreditation in December 1969 and a ten-year accreditation extension in 1973. During these years, under Moore, Trevecca established a Division for Extramural Studies for adult education, launched an East Campus in Nashville, and built a large Health Care Center.[19]

Bethany

At Bethany (Bethany-Peniel until 1955) Roy Cantrell (1904-97) strengthened the faculty and curriculum, wrestled with a conservative constituency, and saw the school through financial crisis. Bethany's business program, spurred by the increasing real estate and oil-made wealth of Nazarenes in the area, became an important part of the school. Like other colleges, Bethany benefited from federal grants.[20]

The school's Board of Trustees sanctioned intercollegiate sports in 1964 and soon allowed women to wear slacks, which (administrators argued) were more modest than the short, tight skirts then in fashion. The school's leaders believed, as Loren P. Gresham and L. Paul Gresham later put it, that "the attempt to enforce all the rules of a past generation would have been both ludicrous and impossible."[21] American colleges could no longer play the in loco parentis role that they had in previous decades. Neither the students nor society would have tolerated it. Nevertheless, some constituents criticized the school for loosening its behavioral standards. A few associated relaxed rules with decreased spirituality. When MidAmerica Nazarene College opened in 1966, these conservatives were presented an alternative.[22]

From the perspective of Bethany, the church miscalculated the effect that the opening of another Nazarene college in nearby Kansas would have upon the school. In the fall of 1968 Bethany's enrollment stood at 1,809. It dipped to 1,580 for the spring semester, fell to 1,548 in the fall of 1969, and to 1,450 the following spring. This represented a 20 percent, $500,000, decline in tuition revenues. By 1971, the school was $600,000 in debt. During a spring revival that year, students themselves raised $100,000 for the school. Nonetheless, Cantrell was forced to dismiss twenty faculty members and seven administrators. Misunderstandings developed as to why certain people were fired and others retained. Cantrell saw the retrenchment through and retired in 1972.[23]

At this difficult stage, Stephen Nease, who had been president at Mount Vernon Nazarene College, became president. He served for four stabilizing years. In years when students in secular universities protested against authority and took over campuses, Nease expected Bethany's to understand that they were part of a school that had certain policies and standards and that they must not subvert the mission of the school.[24]

Eastern Nazarene College

President Edward Mann (1908-2005) served as ENC's president from 1949 to 1970. Mann was a layman and mathematician who had been associated with the school since 1928. In the mid-1950s, he attempted to implement a budget system for the school whereby each local church would support the college with a certain percentage of its giving. There was little enthusiasm for the idea on the region. But Mann's plan won the endorsement of the church as a whole at the 1964 General Assembly.[25]

As Bertha Munro anticipated and encouraged, faculty members pursued advanced degrees in various disciplines, frequently at Boston University. Munro retired as dean in 1957 but continued to teach until 1969. Even afterward, she wielded influence over decisions at the college.[26]

ENC faced an unexpectedly difficult reaccreditation in 1955. The accreditation team advised the school to begin a counseling program, to consolidate its departments, and to require the Scholastic Aptitude Test for applicants. As a result of changes in each of these regards, the school won reaccreditation in 1958. ENC changed its bachelor of theology to an M.A. in religion in 1964.[27]

Mann expected faculty members to be in accord with the mission, purposes, and ideals of the school. For him, "academic freedom" was freedom to do research unhindered by the school, not freedom to challenge the institution itself.[28] It was difficult, then, for him to accept the developments of the late 1960s. Antiestablishment protests at ENC reached a climax during the 1968-69 school year. Antiwar sentiments spilled over into demands for more student participation in the school's governance. Unauthorized newspapers edited by students appeared. Mann met with students, instituted student forums, tolerated radical views against the war in Vietnam, and appointed students to various committees. But Mann angered students when he removed Donald Brickley as dean of students after Brickley had seemed to appease student demands too easily. In March 1969 students walked out of a chapel in which General Superintendent Eugene Stowe was the speaker. To the students, Stowe represented authoritarianism.[29]

At the same time, ENC faced declining enrollment and financial problems resulting from the beginning of Mount Vernon. In 1970 Mann resigned as president and became general secretary of the Department of Education and Ministry, which he remained until 1979. Leslie Parrott moved from his pastorate in Portland, Oregon, to serve as president of ENC from 1970 to 1975. Just as he had been as a pastor, Parrott as president was a master communicator and promoter. He left to accept the presidency of Olivet and was followed at ENC by Donald Irwin, the New England district superintendent.[30]

A Long Range Study Commission that began its work in 1975 explored the possibility of moving the school out of Quincy. The costs of staying in the Boston area were high, the school had little room for expansion, and Quincy was not near the center of the educational zone. Some who disliked the urban surroundings were sending their sons and daughters to Mount Vernon. In 1977 the school's trustees voted to relocate. Administrators looked at possible sites in rural Pennsylvania. Upon hearing this, city and state officials met with the college's leaders to persuade the school to remain in Quincy. Many alumni likewise opposed the move. Meanwhile, sites in Pennsylvania did not work out, and the Wollaston campus did not attract potential buyers. By the time of the 1978 commencement, the trustees issued a statement indicating their decision to drop the plan to relocate, and to make improvements on the existing campus.[31]

Olivet Nazarene College

At Olivet, Harold Reed (1909-92) exemplified a professional approach to leadership. Reed, who had earned a doctorate at the University of Southern California in 1943, accepted the presidency of Olivet on the condition that the trustees not interfere in the management of the school. Reed found Olivet $500,000 in debt. To handle it, he persuaded districts to pay their education offerings in advance and secured personal loans.[32]

Olivet sought accreditation from the North Central Association of Colleges and Secondary Schools. It had been accredited by the Illinois State Department of Public Instruction since 1939 and recognized by the University of Illinois as a "Class A" four-year liberal arts college since 1943. But the association turned down accreditation in 1951. In response, Olivet discontinued its Bible school for non-high-school graduates. Willis Snowbarger

(1921-2008), with a fresh Ph.D. in history from the University of California, Berkeley, replaced C. S. McClain as academic dean in 1953. But over concern for the faculty's academic qualifications, the weak library, the curriculum, student services, and finances, the association again denied accreditation in 1955. Reed and Snowbarger aggressively addressed each of these issues. Accreditation was granted in 1956.[33]

Reed wanted to develop a university. Enrollment rose from 871 to over 2,000 in 1975, making Olivet the largest Nazarene college. The number of faculty members with doctorates at Olivet rose from one in 1942, to six in 1952, to twenty-five in 1972. Though Olivet lost one-third of its territory to MidAmerica and Mount Vernon Nazarene Colleges, its income rose from $500,000 in 1949 to $4 million in 1975. The initiation of a nursing program, and master's degrees in religion (1965) and education (1973) were part of the plan to create a university. Olivet took advantage of government grants to construct the Reed Hall of Science, which facilitated geology and astronomy courses. The school also expanded on one hundred fifty adjacent acres that Reed purchased early in his tenure.[34]

However, Snowbarger and some other faculty members worried that expansion diminished academic excellence. When it became evident in 1969 that the Board of Trustees favored Reed's vision for Olivet's future, several faculty members resigned. It took time to rebuild. A 1975 study indicated that administrators, faculty members, students, and alumni all perceived Olivet as academically weak. Reed retired and Leslie Parrott became president the same year.[35]

Northwest Nazarene College

Issues that arose at Northwest Nazarene College reflected denominational concerns about higher education, and the pressures that general church leaders as well as constituents put upon the schools. General Superintendent Vanderpool, who once had been superintendent of the Northwest District, frankly told President John E. Riley (1909-2001) in 1957 that he was "bothered about what seems to be a lack of rugged emphasis on the doctrines and standards of our church in our colleges; also, the lack of precept and example in proper dress and behavior—the wearing of jewelry and make-up."[36] Later he chastened Riley for allowing an advertisement from a local jewelry dealer to appear in an issue of the student paper, the *Nazarene Crusader*. Vanderpool was hearing that NNC was placing little emphasis on Christian experience. These kinds of reports, Vanderpool told Riley, did little to inspire local churches to contribute to the school. He encouraged Riley to "maintain a rugged 'middle-of-the-road' Nazarene program."[37]

Like other Nazarene college presidents, Riley accepted responsibility for maintaining and building spirituality in Nazarene colleges. He admitted that there were fewer revivals on campus than in previous eras and less clarity regarding entire sanctification as a second work of grace. Students had weaker commitments. The "creeping paralysis of materialism" complicated lifestyles. But, Riley said, all of these were symptoms and signs of the denomination as a whole, and its local churches, not just the college. The church, Riley admonished, could not expect the schools to reverse inevitable trends.[38]

During the late 1960s, NNC also faced student unrest. In response to the times, Riley opened decision-making processes to students. He allowed a degree of "hippy" attire. But he could not tolerate it when students' desires for greater freedom from authority took the form, one time, of dancing in the dining hall. Riley suspended six students involved. He also had problems with the *Crusader*, which criticized the administration and made comments Riley considered to be vulgar and obscene. As early as 1965, NNC heard speakers address the Vietnam crisis. Pacifist and antiwar speakers, including Idaho Senator Frank Church, a Democrat, spoke at the college. Church received an honorary doctorate from NNC in 1970.[39]

Meanwhile, NNC strengthened its academic program. Gilbert Ford, who had earned a Ph.D. in physics at Harvard, and who had been involved in nuclear research, joined the faculty in 1950 and became academic dean when Thelma Culver retired in 1970. Ford headed an outstanding science program. Taking advantage of government loans and grants, Northwest constructed a science hall, a library, and other buildings.[40]

Pasadena/Point Loma

In both church and society, loyalty was an important value in the 1950s. At Pasadena, W. T. Purkiser made difficult decisions about faculty members who seemed disloyal to the church's historic positions. Purkiser agreed with the Nazarene philosophy of education that teachers should not indoctrinate in the sense of saying, "These are our doctrines, you accept them or else." Yet, Purkiser believed, they should be able to say, "This is what I believe, and here are the reasons why."[41] It

Pasadena

was difficult for him when religion professors posed too many unanswered questions to students' faith. Ultimately, Purkiser affirmed, the school must "stand for the Divine inspiration, credibility, authority and self-efficiency of the Holy Bible."[42] In 1957, in the midst of troubles over dismissing a religion professor who questioned the Virgin Birth, Purkiser accepted a position at NTS. Pasadena's trustees elected Russell V. DeLong to succeed him.

DeLong dreamed big regarding the college. He launched an "All Out Campaign" to raise $1.5 million to buy additional land and erect new science and fine arts buildings. Administratively, DeLong downgraded the academic dean and dean of students and appointed two new vice presidencies: R. T. Williams Jr., as vice president for public relations, and Kenneth Armstrong, as vice president for planning, expansion, and financial development.[43]

Tense relations grew between administrators and faculty members. DeLong tried to build an "acquiescent subculture," as historian Ronald Kirkemo put it. Professors disliked DeLong's "denominational parochialism" and desire to control the intellectual life of the campus. A visit of the Western College Association revealed this discontent and gave the school only a three-year reaccreditation.[44]

At each annual Board of Trustees meeting DeLong resigned and requested a new five-year contract. He believed that he needed repeated support from the board for his ambitious plans. DeLong resigned as usual in 1960. This time the board accepted his resignation. DeLong was "shocked" and "amazed." He returned to full-time evangelism.[45]

The board chose Oscar J. Finch (district superintendent in Colorado) to replace DeLong. Like his predecessor, Finch believed "the church must restrain the intellectual dynamics of the college."[46] This attitude dulled faculty morale. Finch also failed to channel various gifts to the school through the business manager. Concerned, the board accepted Finch's resignation in 1964.[47]

W. Shelburne Brown, district superintendent in Los Angeles since 1952, was then elected president. He assembled his own team and presented a process- rather than personality-centered administrative approach. Brown projected, in Kirkemo's words, "a cosmopolitan and urbane image" and added a more "human face to holiness."[48]

New faculty members, including Frank Carver and Reuben Welch, deepened the sense that holiness must be based on solid exegesis and related to human needs. Carver became chairman of the religion department in 1968, and Welch college chaplain the same year. E. E. Zachary, the conservative superintendent of the Northern California District, complained about Reuben Welch's approach to holiness. Others, including Southern California District Superintendent Nicholas Hull, worried over the college's seeming lack of denominational loyalty. Ross Price, who had been teaching theology at Pasadena for twenty years, felt that H. Orton Wiley's legacy was being lost. He left Pasadena in 1969. Art professor James Dobson worried over the school's loss of spiritual fervor. Soon he transferred to MidAmerica Nazarene College.[49]

A Day of Reflection on the Vietnam War in November 1969 provided information, opened dialogue, and motivated prayer. Work for Peace buttons appeared. Students donated money to send food to Vietnam and read letters from former Pasadena students who served in the war.[50]

There was little room for expansion of the college in Pasadena. Ethnic minorities inhabited the neighborhoods surrounding the campus. In 1973 the college purchased the ocean-side site of United States International University and moved to the Point Loma section of San Diego.[51]

NEW NAZARENE COLLEGES

After the Second World War leaders looked for ways to expand the church's educational system. In 1946 Kletzing College, in Oskaloosa, Iowa (called Central Holiness College from 1906 to 1924 and John Fletcher College from 1924 to 1936) barely escaped becoming another Nazarene liberal arts college. In a period of transition, G. B. Williamson, an alumnus, was elected chairman of the board. He secured Roy Cantrell, then district superintendent in Minnesota, as president. However, the Iowa Supreme Court ruled that the Nazarene takeover of Kletzing violated the nondenominational stipulations of the school's charter. The court required that Nazarenes relinquish leadership of the school.[52]

The Education Commission appointed in 1948 suggested that Nazarene schools not seek large enrollments. Both students and faculty members, the commission felt, needed to be in "frequent contact with the spirit and doctrinal emphasis" of the church.[53] The commission also recommended creating a North Central Education zone and beginning a junior college in this area to serve as a "feeder" school for both Bethany and Olivet. If not Kletzing, the school in rural Tabor, Iowa, associated with the Hepzibah Faith Association, which had recently joined the church, seemed a likely site. However, Nazarene leaders soon realized that the school in Tabor would require too much work to become a viable college, and they dropped the plan.[54]

At the same time, many Nazarenes, including some district superintendents, believed that the church was not preparing enough pastors—especially for its rural churches. The number of ministerial students in Nazarene colleges was declining. But delegates to the 1956 General Assembly defeated a motion to establish a Bible college in North America.[55]

The 1960 General Assembly empowered a commission to study Nazarene education and ministerial preparation in North America. The commission, led by Leslie Parrott, reviewed the history of education in the church and sent questionnaires to various stakeholders. Its report, presented to the 1964 General Assembly, projected rising enrollments because of the postwar baby boom. Like the 1948 Commission, Parrott's report argued that there was a maximum optimal enrollment for a liberal arts college. The report recommended establishing two junior colleges and suggested Muncie, Indiana, and Dayton, Ohio, as possible sites. The commission also recommended that local churches give the equivalent of 5 percent of all money raised for local interests to their regional college. In addition to its financial benefit, this assured that the colleges would remain accountable to their constituents and loyal to the church.[56]

A more controversial recommendation of the commission was that a Bible college in North America not be established. Many district superintendents, the commission found, "believed that advanced degrees were not essential for effective pastoral ministry." Only 56 percent of the district superintendents themselves had graduated from college. To put it favorably, this indicated the district superintendents' "native ability and inner-dynamic." If there were a choice between a Bible college and a Bible college program operated through the existing colleges, the commission found, more district superintendents preferred a Bible college. Ministers and laypersons were more ambivalent about a Bible college. Those who stated a preference strongly favored a Bible college. But only 19 percent of students then enrolled in the Course of Study indicated that they would transfer to a Nazarene Bible College if one existed. Taking this into account, the commission's fourth recommendation followed, that Bible certificate programs be offered through the existing colleges and that the church strengthen campus-based correspondence courses for ministerial preparation.[57]

In response to the commission, the 1964 General Assembly authorized two new educational zones. The East Central zone included all of West Virginia and Ohio, where Nazarenes were heavily concentrated, and eastern Kentucky. It took away districts from the Eastern, Trevecca, and Olivet educational zones. The new North Central zone consisted of Iowa, Missouri, Kansas, Nebraska, Minnesota, North Dakota, and South Dakota. It took away districts from the Northwest, Olivet, and Bethany zones.

The assembly also approved the 5 percent plan and authorized the revitalization of Bible certificate and correspondence programs for noncollege ministerial students. It also authorized the employment of a full-time executive secretary for the Department of Education.

The assembly hotly debated the issue of a Bible college. Many felt that a Bible college would detract from the ministries of the liberal arts colleges. But South Carolina District Superintendent Otto Stucki moved to amend the commission's report on this key point in order to establish a Bible college. Unexpectedly, from the assembly floor, General Superintendent Williamson spoke passionately in favor of it. The church, Williamson argued, desperately needed pastors for its many small rural churches. Williamson believed that a Bible college would prepare those who, because of their stage in life, could not afford a four-year liberal arts degree. Williamson's actions angered fellow general superintendents, who had resolved collectively to oppose a Bible college. Powers, who had sought to avoid this sort of division among the general superintendents, personally rebuked Williamson. Stung, Williamson offered to resign.[58] The assembly voted by a close margin, 345 to 306, to establish a Bible college. The assembly then elected a Board of Trustees for the school.[59]

Meanwhile, independently, Nazarenes in Detroit established another college. Kenneth Armstrong, former assistant to R. V. DeLong at Pasadena College, was pastor of the affluent Detroit First Church. In 1969 Armstrong spearheaded the formation of the John Wesley Educational and Development Foundation, which, as he envisioned it, would establish John Wesley colleges or centers on secular campuses. These centers would offer credited religion courses while ensuring that Christian students enjoyed fellowship and nurture. Detroit First Church mortgaged its property to raise $285,000 for the foundation.[60]

At the same time, nearby Owosso College became available. Owosso had been a Pilgrim Holiness college. The Pilgrim Holiness Church united with the Wesleyan Methodist Church in 1968. The merged denomination decided to close Owosso College. In exchange for $7,500 and assumption of the school's debts, Owosso's Trustees transferred the school's charter to the John Wesley Foundation. Armstrong became chairman of the school's Board of Trustees. He persuaded his old mentor DeLong to become president. The school claimed $4.4 million in assets.[61]

Nazarene leaders at Olivet were furious. General Superintendents were outraged. Lawlor warned Armstrong that his action violated "our concept of the mission and purpose of the local church" and was "illegal." The *Manual* gave clear procedures about and prohibitions concerning both the use of local church funds and the establishment of colleges. Under criticism, Armstrong resigned from Detroit First in 1970. But he continued his involvement in the college and became president when DeLong retired in 1972. By 1980 the school was defunct.[62]

MidAmerica Nazarene College

Various cities, including Wichita, Topeka, and Council Bluffs, were under consideration as sites for the North Central zone college. Paul Cunningham, pastor in Olathe, Kansas, alerted local businessmen to the possibility of locating the school in their community. Olathe businessmen offered eighty acres. The search committee, chaired by General Treasurer John Stockton, decided on Olathe.[63]

From the beginning, MidAmerica Nazarene College possessed a clear mission. R. Curtis Smith, the first president, had served in public relations at Bethany since 1952. Donald Metz (1916-2008), the first academic dean, had taught in Bethany's religion department. Both men, as Metz himself said, were "frankly conservative in theological persuasion and spiritual dynamics."[64] They sought to establish a school that would take conservative positions on both behavioral and theological issues. Smith thought of MidAmerica as the church's "last bastion of orthodoxy."[65]

The college served "middle America." It connected pride of religious commitment to unabashed fervor for the American dream. MidAmerica reveled in patriotic symbolism. Its rectangular, colonial-style brick buildings rose starkly from the flat Kansas cornfields. The school's first emblem had a church building on the left side, the Statue of Liberty on the right, and the Bible in the middle. The school inaugurated the American Heritage Banquet tradition in 1967. It was a response to a practical need—fund-raising for buildings—but it also represented a symbolic reaction against the revolt of youth in the 1960s. Some saw the initiative as "irrational jingoism or as a mindless flag-waving technique" but the administration saw this as a positive "love and loyalty of country."[66] While students elsewhere were protesting the war in Vietnam, MidAmerica's leaders sponsored lectures, artists, and awards that promoted respect for law, individual freedom, spiritual values, and loyalty to the "American heritage."[67]

While "hippies" might trouble other schools, Smith was proud that there were no "freaks" at MidAmerica, no sit-ins or walkouts. Students were in their rooms by 10 p.m. and in chapel twice a week. They could not play cards (except Rook). Women could not wear miniskirts or pants. Men could not wear jeans, have beards or long hair, or "disdain" soap. Nazarene parents could confidently send their children to such a school. Yet, Metz carefully stated

MidAmerica

that the school did not appeal to rightist groups for finances. Like other Christian colleges, MidAmerica accepted government grants and student aid.[68]

In 1972 Kansas granted accreditation to MidAmerica's teacher education program. Two years later, the North Central Association of Colleges granted full accreditation. It praised the school's clear institutional purpose but lamented the "homogeneity" of MidAmerica's faculty and students. By 1975, more than nine hundred were enrolled at MidAmerica, making it the largest private college in Kansas. Under Paul Cunningham, the Olathe College Church became one of the denomination's largest and leading congregations.[69]

Mount Vernon Nazarene College

There was no strident conservative agenda at Mount Vernon. In 1966 the trustees elected Stephen Nease, the public relations officer at ENC, to become the school's founding president. Various communities near Columbus, Ohio, offered themselves as a location for the new school. The town of Mount Vernon raised $212,000 to buy land for the school and offered the Nazarenes 209 acres of corn and wheat fields. The school opened in October 1968 as a two-year college.[70]

Stephen Nease, the son of Floyd Nease, who had been president of ENC in the 1920s, was strongly influenced by the educational philosophy of Bertha Munro. The stated purpose of the new school reflected her ideas. Mount Vernon sought to "create a community of scholars concerned with mastery of the techniques of learning, understanding of our cultural heritage, and application of intellectual processes to contemporary problems of individuals and society," with the "conviction that the highest type of scholarship is motivated by the Christian search for Truth."[71] Nease warned that no one mistakenly equate "Christian commitment with inferior academic goals," since "the highest type of scholarship is motivated by the Christian search for truth."[72] The first academic dean was Lloyd Taylor, a chemist strongly devoted to liberal arts. He devised a curriculum that enabled associate of arts graduates to transfer smoothly to degree programs at ENC, Olivet, and Trevecca.[73]

Mount Vernon granted its first associate of arts degrees in 1970. Two years later it began a baccalaureate program. Transfers remained common, however, until Mount Vernon was accredited. Enrollment dropped from 532 in 1972 to 439 in 1974. This, at a time when faculty members were being added to the college in order for it to be accredited, caused financial strain. But Nazarenes on the zone gave sacrificially. After Mount Vernon earned accreditation in March 1974, enrollment increased. By then Mount Vernon was comparable to the other Nazarene colleges in finances and enrollment as well as accreditation status.[74]

MINISTERIAL PREPARATION

Ministerial schools were common in almost every area around the world. The church saw it as imperative to have a well-prepared ministry. In the United States the church established two schools devoted to ministerial education, Nazarene Theological Seminary, a graduate-level school in Kansas City, and Nazarene Bible College in Colorado Springs.

Nazarene Theological Seminary

Leaders such as J. B. Chapman had been issuing appeals for a seminary since the 1920s. Chapman understood the need of pastors for seminary education. He feared the influences of other traditions upon Nazarene doctrines. The 1936 General Assembly gave its approval for the general superintendents and General Board to pursue the idea. But the 1940 General Assembly, after cautious words from R. T. Williams, tabled a motion that would have led to the establishment of the school. By the 1940s several Nazarene colleges were offering bachelor of theology degrees. Pasadena was offering a master of arts in religion. If trends continued, the church would have six graduate schools of religion. This, Chapman feared, would lead to theological fragmentation.[75]

At the 1943 District Superintendents Conference, R. V. DeLong, then serving as district superintendent in Northwestern Indiana, proposed a seminary. J. B. Chapman raised the issue even more strongly with the district superintendents when they met the following year. The district superintendents presented the general superintendents with a resolution to establish the school. The General Board ratified their proposal. As a result, the general superintendents formed a Seminary Commission, chaired by DeLong, to report to the 1944 General Assembly. The primary purpose of a seminary, according to the commission, was to "conserve, maintain, advocate and promulgate the great Bible doctrine of 'Entire Sanctification' as a second distinct work of divine grace wrought in the heart of the believer subsequent to regeneration."[76] The 1944 Assembly voted in favor of establishing the seminary and elected a

Russell V. DeLong

Board of Trustees. The trustees elected H. C. Benner, then pastor of Kansas City First Church, as president of the school.⁷⁷

Benner drew together a faculty made up of several of the denomination's leading scholars, all of whom were loyal churchmen. DeLong, who yearned to be president, served instead as academic dean and taught both philosophy of religion and evangelism courses. L. A. Reed, who had pastored some of the denomination's leading churches, including Kansas City First, Pasadena First, and Chicago First, became professor of preaching and pastoral ministry. Mendell Taylor, who had a doctorate in history from Oklahoma University, became professor of church history. S. S. White, with a Ph.D. in philosophy from the University of Chicago, became professor of theology. Ralph Earle became professor of New Testament. He had received his doctor of theology degree from Gordon Divinity School. Earle became one of the most well-known Nazarene scholars in wider evangelical circles.⁷⁸

Upon Benner's election as general superintendent in 1952, the general superintendents nominated DeLong as president. The trustees, however, rejected DeLong. They unanimously approved a second nominee, Lewis T. Corlett, president of NNC. Soon after becoming president, Corlett accepted DeLong's resignation. Mendell Taylor, who had been serving as registrar, became academic dean.⁷⁹

Corlett proceeded toward accreditation. Benner, fearing that the school would lose its distinctive character if it sought outsiders' standards, had not favored this. As general superintendent, Benner hindered Corlett's moves in this direction.⁸⁰

In its first years the seminary faced suspicions from district superintendents that it was producing cerebral and liberal scholars unable and unwilling to handle home missions or plant churches. However, a 1952 survey of the first 205 graduates of NTS found that 146 (71 percent) were pastoring churches and half of these churches had fewer than fifty members. An additional 36 NTS graduates were serving as missionaries, evangelists, teachers, or chaplains. The seminary received further criticisms in the 1960s, when, it seemed, too many graduates were joining other denominations.⁸¹

William Greathouse followed Eugene Stowe, who served only two years as president after succeeding Corlett in 1966. In an effort to improve the academic quality of NTS, Greathouse appointed Willard Taylor academic dean, initiated a self-study, and proceeded aggressively toward accreditation. As he had at Trevecca, Greathouse built a collegial working atmosphere. Enrollment rose significantly as the baby boom generation entered seminary.[82]

Nazarene Bible College (Colorado Springs, Colorado)

Nazarene Bible College provided, in Randall Spindle's words, a "symbolic antithesis" to Nazarene Theological Seminary. NTS represented the church's intellectual strain; NBC its Pietist side.[83]

The Board of Trustees elected at the 1964 General Assembly selected Colorado Springs, Colorado, as the site for the school and chose Charles Strickland as president. Strickland had pioneered the European District in South Africa and had established a Bible college there. Nazarene Bible College in Colorado Springs opened in 1967. Two years later Nazarene Training College in West Virginia merged with the school.[84]

In 1970 NBC began granting associate in arts degrees that required three years to complete. The general superintendents refused to allow the school to offer bachelor of theology degrees, fearing that this would conflict with college religion departments. Furthermore, in 1973 the general superintendents ordered NBC not to enroll anyone under age twenty-two, believing that these students should be in the liberal arts schools. Exception was made for African-American students.[85]

When Strickland was elected general superintendent in 1972, trustees elected L. S. Oliver, the superintendent of the Illinois District, to succeed him. Beulah Oliver, his wife, served as general president of the Nazarene World Missionary Society.[86]

EDUCATION OUTSIDE OF NORTH AMERICA

The church established Bible rather than liberal arts colleges outside North America. The curricula in these Bible colleges included liberal arts subjects, since these were required for ordination under the *Manual*. But the schools focused on students mastering the Bible and emphasized the practical arts of ministry. Everywhere, the church wanted pastors loyal to the denomination and zealous for the doctrine of holiness. Theological education, in H. T. Reza's mind, was a "prescription for permanence," since, he believed, the future success of the church depended upon the ministerial training provided its young people.[87]

Exceptions to the general trend of having Bible schools outside of the United States were the nurses' schools in India and Swaziland, Japan Christian Junior College, and Nazarene Teacher Training College in Swaziland. By 1962 the latter school had trained five hundred fifty teachers in its two-year course. It had a deep impact on education throughout the small country.[88]

In Japan the Bible college, which had been closed during World War II, reopened in 1951. William Eckel served as president, with veteran leaders Hiroshi Kitagawa and Nobumi Isayama among the teachers. They held on to the hope that a Nazarene liberal arts college could be established in Japan. The church took a step in that direction when, after a visit to Japan in 1959, General Superintendent Benner authorized the purchase of a junior college in Chiba, outside Tokyo. The church reconfigured the school to include two departments, English and religion. The Japanese government approved graduates of the English program to teach at the junior high school level. Harrison Davis, who began a long career in Japan in 1950, articulated the ideals: "We feel that the preparation of Christian teachers as well as ministers is basic in the evangelization of cultured and education-conscious Japan."[89]

Mildred Bangs Wynkoop

Mildred Bangs Wynkoop agreed with these ideals and reorganized theological education in Japan during the five years that she and her husband served with the Church of the Nazarene in the country. "God" had little meaning to Japanese, Wynkoop found, and "sin" was a foreign concept. The emphasis upon conformity to social mores disinclined the Japanese toward Christianity and kept them tied to Shintoism. To break through, she wrote in 1963, the "evangelistic arm" of the church had to be supported by "educational muscles and bones."[90] When Wynkoop went on furlough in 1966, thinking that she and her husband would return to Japan, the missions department could not even find a one-year replacement for her. The church, it seemed to her, was not committed to advanced theological education on mission fields. It seemed futile. Instead of returning to Japan, she accepted the invitation to teach theology and missions at Trevecca.[91]

In Canada, the Nazarene college, like other schools around the world, offered a solid core of liberal arts. But its purpose was to educate Christian workers. The school, first located in Red Deer, Alberta, was established in 1928. However, Canadians in the Maritime Provinces remained on the Eastern Nazarene

College zone. Many Canadians in the West studied at NNC. The temptation was for graduates to stay in the States. Increasingly, Canadians talked about having an accredited university-level school. They petitioned the 1960 General Assembly to establish Canada as a separate educational zone.[92]

The resolution passed. The next year the college moved from Red Deer to Fort Garry, near Winnipeg, Manitoba. Now more centrally located, the college unified Canadian Nazarenes. In 1964 the Canadian government empowered the school to grant degrees. The school began offering bachelors in theology, sacred music, sacred literature, and Christian education. President Arnold Airhart made overtures to the University of Manitoba for affiliation. The university stipulated that the school increase the number of faculty members with doctorates. But it was difficult to attract such professors. The size of the school made it impossible to compete with salaries offered by United States colleges. But eventually the school met the university's requirements for affiliation.[93]

Minister-training schools began in almost every country the church entered. While most of these were intended for only one country, there were several in which students from various countries came together to study. While finances were one important factor for the establishment of multinational schools (it was cheaper to maintain one school than several), they also reflected the missiological aims of the church—not to establish autonomous national churches, but mutually strong, supportive, and responsible districts.

An example of a multinational school was the Nazarene training college in Trinidad, which opened in 1949. Although most students were from Trinidad, an East Indian from British Guiana was the first to enroll. Barbados began sending students to the school in 1953. In 1957 the General Board officially made the school a regional college. George Coulter approved a multinational board in 1961, with each of the English-speaking districts in the region electing trustees. Because of British Commonwealth ties, the school affiliated with Canadian Nazarene College to grant bachelor of theology degrees. The name of the school was changed to Caribbean Nazarene Theological College in 1974. At that time there were forty students, half from Guyana, twelve from Trinidad, and others from Saint Croix, Barbados, Antigua, Jamaica, and Tobago. Ruth Saxon taught at the school for forty years, much of the time serving as academic dean.[94]

The Nazarene Bible School in Lebanon was also multinational. It served as the center for the education of Nazarene pastors in the Middle East from the time it opened in 1954 under the leadership of Donald Reed until it closed in 1969. During these years, the administration strengthened admission requirements to include a high school diploma, proficiency in English (the language of instruction), and the willingness to abide by Nazarene standards. The two main factions in the student body, Arab and Armenian, reflected the ethnic backgrounds of most Middle Eastern Nazarenes. In 1967 the school enrolled twelve students: five from Lebanon, five from Jordan, and one each from Syria and Germany. It was looking toward the possibility of establishing a bachelor of theology program. However, not all of the students were Nazarene, and some used the school to gain visas to the United States. This, and the low number of students, caused the church to close the school.[95]

A more successful multinational school was European Nazarene Bible College. Fearing difficulties with the Roman Catholic Church, Nazarenes had not established a Bible college in Italy and thought, instead, of establishing a school in Switzerland. Meanwhile, Nazarene work expanded to West Germany, Denmark, and the Netherlands. Oscar Finch, visiting Europe and the Middle East in the early 1960s, recommended that the church open an "international school for the continent of Europe," rather than separate national schools. He advocated English as the medium of instruction and Switzerland as the site.[96]

Though British Isles Nazarenes wondered why their college could not serve all Europe, church leaders were persuaded. G. B. Williamson appointed John B. Nielson, a New England pastor, as rector. In January 1966 classes began in Büsingen, West Germany (a German enclave within Switzerland), with twelve students from six countries (Finland, Sweden, Denmark, Holland, Germany, Italy, Pakistan, and the United States). Nielson quickly grasped that the purpose and character of the school reflected the internationalization goals of the church. Diverse cultures were "bridged by a common rallying cause," a common language, English, and holiness. English conveyed ideas of holiness that, Nielson believed, were confused by the influence of Roman Catholicism upon other European languages. "Christ came to tear down walls," Nielson said, and ENBC was to be a place where cultures blended and a "third culture," a Christ-culture, took root. Students would return to their own nations with transformed outlooks.[97] Nielson served until 1969, was followed for a year by Richard Taylor, and then by William Prince, pastor of Minneapolis First Church, who served from 1970 to 1976.[98]

Church leaders looked to the possibilities of a Spanish language college. In 1947 the Spanish Nazarene Bible and Mission Training Institute opened in San Antonio. It replaced both Pasadena College's Spanish Department and the seminary in Mexico City and drew students from Mexico, Puerto Rico, and Spanish districts in the United States. Its first president, Hilario

Pena, served only two years. He was followed by Edward Wyman and, in 1955, by William Vaughters. In 1963 the name of the school was changed to the Spanish American Nazarene Seminary. It offered a four-year bachelor of sacred theology program. Like other Nazarene Bible colleges around the world, the school included a strong core of liberal arts subjects, including English, Spanish literature, philosophy, sociology, psychology, and science as well as Bible, church history, theology, and pastoral ministry. Even though three Mexicans served on the school's Board of Directors, the school failed to attract many students from "south of the border." Mexican leaders, including C. E. Morales, looked forward to the time when a school for training pastors could be reestablished in Mexico itself.[99]

In 1970, a multinational school, also speaking Spanish, the Seminario Nazareno de las Americas, opened in Costa Rica. Church leaders began thinking about one school for Central America in the mid-1960s, to replace the schools in Guatemala and Nicaragua and to serve El Salvador and Panama as well. There were cultural similarities among these countries as well as a common language. Having one school rather than four made financial sense. Planners aimed for the school "to serve our young people in the level they require to become preachers of the gospel in the Spanish language and to serve the expanding urban areas,"[100] and to provide "adequate ministerial training within each cultural context to help ministers meet needs of their own societies."[101] W. Howard Conrad, who had been serving at the Nazarene Bible School in Peru, became director. The church closed the Spanish Bible school in Coban, Guatemala, and turned over that campus to training Kekchi and other tribal people.[102]

The school in Costa Rica derived its income from local districts as well as from the World Mission Division and student fees. It had a predominantly Hispanic faculty that included Eduardo Aparicio of Bolivia, Jacinto Ordonez of Guatemala, Daniel Monerro of Costa Rica, and Suzanna Terrones of Peru. The school accepted those who had not graduated from high school and offered college level courses for those who had. At first, few enrolled at the college level.[103]

In Africa, Nazarenes long had talked of a baccalaureate-level theological college in Swaziland. More progress was made in South Africa, where the Lulu Schmelzenbach Memorial Nazarene Bible College, located in Acornhoek, opened in 1963. Instruction was in English, Zulu, and Pedi, with the fourth year entirely in English. By 1969 the school was offering a bachelor of theology degree validated by Canadian Nazarene College. Ted Esselstyn became rector in 1970. In the same year, E. S. Phillips organized a committee for higher theological education in the Church of the Nazarene in Africa in order to coordinate ministerial education on the continent.[104]

The school in Australia included both Australia and New Zealand and, in addition, for a time, served Samoa. Located in Thornleigh, Sydney, the school opened in March 1953 with Richard Taylor as director. Though Taylor had earned a doctor of theology at Boston University, he also had been an evangelist and centered the school on practical education. The school, offering a three-year diploma and a Christian worker's certificate, accepted those who had not graduated from high school. Students came from countries as far as Holland, India, and Indonesia. Adding to the cultural mix, it included students preparing to pastor Greek congregations in Australia and to become missionaries in Papua New Guinea. Taylor served until 1960.[105]

Richard S. Taylor

In the 1960s various problems affected the school. Tongues became a divisive issue. The school's enrollment remained low—often fewer than ten. Samoan students sometimes outnumbered students from all of the other countries. Discipline problems arose. Australia's district superintendent, A. A. E. Berg, believed that the school was not contributing enough to the winning of converts or to the planting of churches. He appointed pastors who had not been trained at the school. Efforts by the school's directors to initiate a Th.B. program were defeated by the board of trustees. In 1974 the school closed in order to transfer the campus from Sydney to Brisbane and reopened there in 1976.[106]

CONCLUSION

Liberal arts philosophy underlay the educational patterns of the church in North America. But in other parts of the world the church raised up Bible colleges to serve its needs. Why did the church not move in the direction of establishing liberal arts colleges outside the United States, where such schools served the church so well? Postwar leaders were eager to evangelize the world as quickly as possible. The harvest was ripe. The cold war tension contributed to expectations about Christ's soon return. There was no time. Furthermore, though it was important to them to educate their own children in Holiness colleges, Nazarenes saw little need to direct their financial resources to establish colleges for young people abroad. Missionary giving was for evangelism, and all institutions justified their existence in terms of how many souls they won to Christ.

While the North American schools emphasized content, schools elsewhere, with their concentration on training ministers, emphasized Bible competency and spiritual fervor. The liberal arts core in the church's ministerial Course of Study transmitted the values of western civilization. In Bible colleges there were few culturally specific courses. During this period, the church assumed that the Holiness message, the most important aspect of the church's message, and ministerial skills were alike across cultures—and needed little contextualization. In both the Bible and the liberal arts colleges, character was built through the nonformal curriculum of chapel services, revivals, and faculty mentors. Since holiness was not merely a doctrine to be taught but a life to be lived, the modeling of Christian life was crucial in every form of Christian education that served the Church of the Nazarene.

TWENTY-TWO

The Intellectual Life of the Church

Though holiness was an experience to Nazarenes, ideas as well as behavior and worship mattered much. Nazarenes knew that they were "holiness," and neither "eternal security" people nor "modernists." They chided Calvinists for teaching that persons could be saved regardless of how they lived, and fundamentalists for neglecting the most fundamental biblical truth, holiness. From 1946 to 1976 Nazarene theologians positioned Holiness theology in the historic traditions of the faith and interacted with issues outside of the movement.[1]

THEOLOGY IN THE SERVICE OF THE CHURCH

H. Orton Wiley's three-volume *Christian Theology*, published in the 1940s, provided a broad theological context in which to locate sanctification. In good Wesleyan fashion, Wiley grounded Christian doctrines upon the Bible, reason, experience, and tradition. He cited ancient councils and creeds and classic theologians of Roman Catholic and Protestant faith. For Wiley, "a doctrine was not to be determined or understood until one knew what the whole church had said about it."[2] However, Wiley was not influenced by the renaissance in Wesley studies that began after he was at work on his systematic theology. Wiley cited nineteenth-century Methodist theologians, especially John Miley, more than Wesley himself. The German philosopher Immanuel Kant influenced many strands of nineteenth-century thought, including Wiley's theology. What Max Otto said of America's taking the great epistemologies of Europe and turning them into guidelines for ethical living can be seen in Wiley's theology. Broadly speaking, nonetheless, Wiley enabled the church to emerge from its theological provincialism.[3]

Stephen S. White (1890-1971) had a great deal of influence upon the church's theology in the postwar years, though not as lasting an influence as Wiley. White was born in Texas and had a Methodist background before attending Peniel College. In 1908, when the Peniel congregation chose to do so, White joined the Church of the Nazarene. He earned a bachelor of divinity at Drew Theological Seminary in 1914, where he studied under Olin A. Curtis; an M.A. at Brown University; and a Ph.D. in philosophy at the University of Chicago in 1938. By 1945, when he joined the founding faculty of Nazarene Theological Seminary, White had taught at Pentecostal Collegiate Institute, Olivet, Trevecca, Bethany-Peniel, and ENC. In 1948 he also became editor of the *Herald of Holiness*.

White's focus was more sectarian than Wiley's, more limited to the doctrine of holiness. White saw himself as a defender of entire sanctification as valid "scripturally, rationally, and experientially."[4] For much of his career, like A. M. Hills, White taught the freedom of the human will apart from grace. In the 1950s, however, after reading Harald Lindström's study of Wesley's doctrine of sanctification, and Wesley's own writings, White modified his views. White afterward understood that indeed free will had been lost by Adam's fall. As a result, "man could not exercise his free moral agency and turn to God." Only "through the grace which comes to all men by the death of Jesus Christ, which was to say, like Wesley, prevenient grace, this power of free choice was restored."[5] After retirement in 1960 from both NTS and the *Herald*, White taught at Olivet.

S. S. White

Until chastened by Wesleyan studies, Personalism pervaded Nazarene theology and educational philosophy. Unlike contemporary neoorthodox theologians who stressed the infinite and qualitative difference between God and humanity, Personalists emphasized human free will and the continuity between human nature and grace. Both Wiley and White were Personalists. They affirmed the likeness of God to humanity based on personhood and free will.[6]

Nazarenes found Methodist schools such as Boston University and the University of Southern California, where Personalism dominated, conducive places to study. Personalism attracted Holiness theologians raised in the legalism of the age because it, too, leaning on the teachings of Immanuel Kant, stressed moral duty. Boston graduates included Russell V. DeLong, Earl Barrett (who taught at Olivet), Mel-Thomas Rothwell (who taught at Bethany), Harvey J. S. Blaney, Alvin Kauffman, and Wilbur Mullen (who all taught at

Eastern), and Delbert Gish and Richard Taylor (who taught at NTS). Most studied under philosopher Edgar S. Brightman, who viewed God's power as self-limited and God's nature as in the process of perfection. Nazarenes receiving advanced degrees at the University of Southern California included Harold Reed, John Cotner, and Otto Hahn (who taught at Olivet), Oscar Reed (who taught at Bethany), and W. T. Purkiser and Ross Price (who taught at Pasadena).[7]

Like their colleagues in other departments, Nazarene theologians introduced religion majors to current trends in their discipline. They challenged their students to think through their faith. Professors presented various sides of a theological issue. They believed that students would hold to their convictions "more assuredly" if they were "in constant dialogue with critical scholarship."[8] However, this strategy created confusion and stress in some students, and local pastors often complained to college presidents about what was being said in religion classes.[9]

Although this scenario was common to one degree or another in all Nazarene colleges, Pasadena College suffered severely over theological issues in the 1950s. Like many influenced by neoorthodoxy, Professor Warren B. Martin, who had finished a Ph.D. at Boston, held that the Virgin Birth was not historically necessary in order for one to believe in Christ. Martin's teachings greatly concerned Pasadena's president, W. T. Purkiser, as well as Ross Price, the school's theology professor, and H. Orton Wiley, who urged Purkiser to fire Martin. Some local pastors threatened to withdraw their financial support of the college if Martin continued to teach at Pasadena. Martin responded that he was only raising issues with students for debate. His supporters included Estes Harvey, the chairman of the Department of Philosophy and Religion, and George Taylorson, pastor of the Bresee Avenue Church in Pasadena, where many students and faculty members attended. Before the close of the 1957 school year, Purkiser fired Martin. This angered many students and faculty members, who saw the issue as one of academic freedom.[10]

In addition to Martin, the church lost other scholars as well as pastors and potential leaders in the 1950s and 1960s. At Bethany, Professor J. Prescott Johnson, who introduced students to nineteenth-century Danish philosopher Søren Kierkegaard and existentialism, sensed that the church inhibited the honest pursuit of truth. Finally, said Johnson, "I could no longer breathe the atmosphere of mere dogma."[11] He left Bethany in 1956. Gary Hart, one of Johnson's students, went from Bethany to Yale to continue his study of philosophy. Soon Hart left the Church of the Nazarene. Hart believed that the Church of the Nazarene needed to reform its "established creeds," which, he felt, were "resistant to new ideas and regenerating reform."[12] During the 1960 presidential election, Hart switched from philosophy to law. Eventually Hart became a United States senator.

Scholars who remained in the church risked criticism whenever they strayed too far from conservative positions. In the mid-1950s, Olivet President Harold Reed attempted to impose a fundamentalist test regarding the inspiration of the Bible upon Olivet faculty members. Carl Bangs, a Wiley protégé, who was completing his Ph.D. in historical theology at the University of Chicago and teaching at Olivet at the time, objected. In 1961 Bangs joined the faculty of St. Paul's School of Theology, a Methodist seminary located in Kansas City. This gave Bangs, who wrote a major historical theology of James Arminius, the opportunity to teach at the graduate level. Though Bangs soon joined the Methodist Church, he presented papers in Nazarene conferences and eventually produced a major biography of Phineas Bresee.[13]

THE DOCTRINE OF HOLINESS

The center of theological concern remained holiness. During the period from 1946 to 1976 Nazarenes became more sensitive to the human element of holiness and emphasized growth in grace following the "second crisis." Theologians tried to balance between claiming too much or too little for the experience.[14]

Emphasizing the human element and growth in holiness, some theologians reacted against the language of eradication. This term indicated the complete cleansing of original sin through entire sanctification and had helped Holiness people retain a distinct identity among Protestants. Other evangelicals used the term "suppression" rather than "eradication" to describe how sin was dealt with in a Christian's life.[15] Neither the Bible nor John Wesley had used the term "eradication," H. Orton Wiley realized, but both the Bible and Wesley described the destruction, cleansing, purging, and crucifying of sin. These biblical terms implied (in Wiley's and others' minds) as much as if not more than the "eradicating" of original sin. "Eradication" was a misleading metaphor, Wiley warned, since it suggested that sin was a "'thing,' a material entity that occupies spatial relations in the soul." Rather, said Wiley, using the same metaphor as Wesley, original sin was like a disease that affected every aspect of a human being.[16] S. S. White, on the other hand, insisted on "eradication." White tied eradication to the baptism with the Holy Spirit so as to emphasize the crisis and "second blessing" aspect of holiness. White argued that a person could not "grow into" either justification or entire sanctification, since each was a gift of God. Neither could holiness be attained by human effort, and "growth in grace is absolutely impotent so far as getting us into these states of grace."[17]

Though, like his mentor, S. S. White, defending "eradication," J. Kenneth Grider (1921-2006) also presented a tempering strain. Grider turned Nazarene theology away from Personalism's human-centeredness and emphasis upon reason and experience, toward revelation and God-centeredness. Personalism, said Grider, attached itself to Platonism and denied original sin. Grider grew up in extreme poverty in a Roman Catholic home in the Missouri Ozark Mountains and was converted in a Nazarene church. He made his way to Olivet Nazarene College, where he studied under White, and then to NTS, where he was among the seminary's first graduates. He proceeded to Drew University to study under Methodism's neoorthodox theologian Edwin Lewis. Grider finished his Ph.D. at Glasgow University. He taught at NTS from 1953 to 1991, influencing a generation of Nazarene pastors and theologians.[18]

Grider carefully distinguished between humanity and carnality. Like Wesley's *Plain Account of Christian Perfection*, Grider's description of the difference between humanity and carnality explained why there were still failures and weaknesses in Christian life following entire sanctification. When carnality is cleansed, Grider said, it saves human beings from whatever detriments they had received from Adam, but not from acquired traits or personality characteristics. If a person was race prejudiced, for instance, it was because of social conditioning, not carnality. Prejudice could be removed as the person grew in Christian grace and perfect love. This was not to be construed an excuse for sinning. Every Christian was given grace sufficient to overcome temptation.[19]

J. Kenneth Grider

Grider celebrated the world and nature as a channel of grace and bearer of the holy. He emphasized the role of the sacraments and the visible church in mediating salvation to men and women. At the same time, Grider believed that Platonism had crept into Christian theology in the form of mysticism and ideas about the "immortality" of the soul. Grider drew the church toward "biblical realism." He used neoorthodox insights on sin and grace to interpret Wesleyan theology. Grider's recovery of grace rather than free will as central to Wesleyan theology lent a truer understanding of Wesley's theology than many of Grider's fellow theologians in the 1950s. With Methodist historian

George Croft Cell, Grider emphasized the prevenient grace context of Wesley's understanding of free will, and Wesley's closeness to John Calvin on the doctrine of original sin.[20]

Yet Grider disagreed with Wesley on certain points. Like Phoebe Palmer and most others in the Holiness Movement, Grider saw good in testifying boldly to entire sanctification. Grider also believed that Holiness theology had been strengthened by accepting, as Wesley had not, Pentecost as the disciples' "second blessing" and the baptism with the Holy Spirit as effecting entire sanctification.[21]

New Testament scholar Richard Howard convinced Grider and others that the traditional Holiness interpretation of "old man" (Rom. 6:6; Eph. 4:22), identifying it with original sin, erred. A. M. Hills, S. S. White, and a host of other Holiness theologians had made this identification. Howard demonstrated that "old man" was related to the former, unregenerated way of life, rather than with carnality. Howard's *Newness of Life* underscored the necessity of starting with Scripture in determining doctrine. He contrasted Paul's Hebraic or "Semitic" perspective to Platonism. The Bible, Howard pointed out, stressed the unity and wholeness of human nature.[22]

Another significant theological voice was Richard S. Taylor (1912-2006). Through his popular writings and sought-after preaching, Taylor had a wide impact upon ideas of holiness. Taylor taught theology and missions at NTS following his return in 1960 from Australia. He also edited *The Preachers Magazine*. Taylor used traditional language to describe original sin and entire sanctification. Unlike Grider, Taylor remained a Personalist. Personhood was the "metaphysical" base common to both God and humanity. Out of personhood flowed human beings' understanding of "right conduct" and "goodness in character." Human holiness was acquired, God's essential or inherent. Human holiness was capable of error, God's was not. Only in that God's holiness was associated with His glory and majesty was there a qualitative difference between God's and humanity's holiness.[23]

Like other postwar theologians, Taylor understood that holiness did not solve all personal problems. There was still a "battle" with sin after entire sanctification. Taylor dared address the area of life upon which American Nazarenes needed the most discipline, eating too much. Like human appetites for food, even the sex "instinct" was not automatically controlled by the Holy Spirit. The sanctified person would be bothered by "yearnings." It was part of being human. These thoughts became "sin" only when there was "consent of the will." Too often, Taylor admitted, Holiness people had not been able to face their sins because they believed that they were in a sanctified state and could not sin. The goal of Christian life following entire sanctification was "the disciplining and maturing of our whole being into the habits and thought patterns of full Christian character." Taylor reacted against preaching that implied that sanctification made "victory automatic, with no further discipline or watchfulness necessary."[24] Continued victory necessitated spiritual discipline, including Bible reading, prayer, and fasting.[25]

Though Taylor emphasized discipline and right-willingness as means of retaining sanctification, he criticized trends in Holiness theology that implied that sin was only a matter of "wrong willing." Taylor understood "inherited depravity" to be "contra-volitional," an innate inability to act as one knew one should. Only direct, supernatural action by the Holy Spirit could cleanse and keep cleansed this tendency. Holiness was not merely a matter of getting into right relationship; it was a matter of a deep, inward purification.[26]

THE REDISCOVERY OF WESLEY IN NAZARENE THEOLOGY

Many longed for theological renewal in the church. "We have tended to develop a sort of 'institutional holiness,' theoretical and abstract, static and somewhat rigid," W. T. Purkiser admitted in 1969. "It is precisely structured, but lifeless and sterile and lacking in warmth and personal realism." Purkiser continued, "We have come to suffer somewhat from 'hardening of the categories.'" Part of the problem, as he saw it, was the tendency to reduce the "sanctifying Lordship of the Spirit to a 'thing' to be sought, found, kept, or, perhaps, sadly, lost." On the contrary, what people should be talking about was the "warm, living, personal relationship with Christ into which the Holy Spirit brings."[27]

Purkiser was not the person to develop a fresh approach in Nazarene theology, but the church found in its rediscovery of John Wesley new sources of theological life. Slowly, the renaissance in Wesley studies that began among Methodist and other scholars in the 1930s reached the Church of the Nazarene.[28] Nazarenes had never lost sight of Wesley as a theological mentor and guide regarding entire sanctification. But, like Methodists, Nazarenes revered Wesley more for his "life and labors" and organizational skills than for his theology.[29] In the 1950s Nazarene Publishing House distributed *Wesley and Sanctification: A Study in the Doctrine of Salvation,* written in 1946 by Harald Lindström, a Swedish Lutheran theologian. Lindström agreed with the Nazarene view that Wesley taught a crisis experience of sanctification subsequent to regeneration. In 1964 NPH published *John Wesley's Concept of Perfection,* by Leo Cox, a Wesleyan Methodist theologian. Like Lindström,

Cox demonstrated the essential fidelity of Holiness theology to Wesley. Both Lindström and Cox helped Nazarenes to more deeply appreciate Wesley's other doctrines, particularly prevenient grace, and to place sanctification within Wesley's understanding of the process of salvation. Fueling the interest in Wesley, NPH, in cooperation with Zondervan, reprinted the 14-volume Thomas Jackson edition of the *Works of John Wesley*.³⁰

Wesley's theology became a passion to William Greathouse and other leading theologians. The "Trevecca connection," consisting of H. Ray Dunning, John A. Knight, and Mildred Bangs Wynkoop, as well as Greathouse, emphasized Christlikeness, perfect love, which came by grace, not by works of righteousness, and the moment-by-moment impartation of the Spirit of Christ within the sanctified life. The teachings of John Wesley, to these scholars, rang true to both the Bible and experience. Greathouse, like Purkiser, believed that Nazarenes were in danger of substituting "institutional holiness" for the indwelling Spirit. Nazarene "folk theology," Greathouse feared, emphasized free will outside of the context of free grace, and became, thus, "outright legalism."³¹

Greathouse

In 1968 Greathouse was elected president of Nazarene Theological Seminary. Though many thought he would be elected general superintendent in 1972, others were happy for him to remain at NTS for another quadrennium. He brought both Wynkoop and Rob L. Staples, a scholar of the theology of John Wesley, to the faculty. The following General Assembly elected him general superintendent, and he served until 1989. During his time as general superintendent, he promoted the theological work of his protégé H. Ray Dunning and saw into publication by NPH Dunning's *Grace, Faith, and Holiness* (1988). After retirement, Greathouse remained a productive preacher and scholar, publishing major works on both holiness and Romans.³²

> William Greathouse's inaugural address as president of Nazarene Theological Seminary in 1968 evidenced the denomination's turn to Wesley for theological guidance:³³
>> [W]e may say that the Nazarene stance is catholic (as opposed to sectarian), conservative (as opposed to fundamentalist), and evangelical (as opposed to Pelagian). . . .

Man has fallen away from God . . . [and] has neither inclination nor power of himself to return to God; left to himself, his only freedom is the freedom to sin. . . . [But,] in Wesley's words, the "grace or love of God, whence cometh our salvation, is FREE IN ALL, and FREE FOR ALL."

This concept of universal prevenient grace, as opposed to irresistible grace for the elect, is a distinctive Wesleyan-Arminian contribution to theology. . . .

Our cardinal doctrine is not Christian perfection, but redemption through Christ. . . . [W]ithin the framework of evangelical Protestant faith we declare that our distinguishing tenet is entire sanctification. . . .

[W]e do not do this in such a way as to place ourselves outside the mainstream of Christian tradition. Our position is not sectarian. In common with historic Christian faith we believe that sanctification is the . . . total process of moral and spiritual renewal which begins at the moment of conversion and continues to glorification. . . .

[T]he fully sanctified man feels deeply his imperfections and lapses from the perfect law of love and maintains a penitent and open spirit which saves him from Pharisaism. He never forgets that he is justified, not by works, but by grace, and thus leans wholly upon the Lord. . . . [H]e knows that the perfect love which is God's gift to him through the Spirit is a "moment-by-moment" impartation of God's life to his soul. . . .

We devoutly believe that God has entrusted to the Church of the Nazarene "the grand depositum" of this New Testament teaching of heart holiness. If we cease to "groan after" this perfection in Christ, if we fail to make this emphasis the focus of salvation truth in our preaching, if we do not pay the full price for Pentecost in our individual experience and in the life of the church, we will forfeit our Nazarene birthright and our very reason to exist. Most tragic of all, we will fail God, who commissioned us to "spread scriptural holiness over these lands." . . .

[W]hen the holiness revival was at its zenith during the nineteenth century, it had a genuine social concern, for it imbued men and women with Christ-like compassion . . . for real people everywhere and in all kinds of circumstances . . . and particularly for the poor. . . . And when we are truly sanctified and made perfect in love by the infilling of the Spirit of Christ, we too become like persons. It is the nurture and intensification of compassion which is perhaps our most pressing need.

Breaking down sectarian language walls, returning to biblical understandings, and reconstructing Holiness theology were very much concerns of Greathouse's colleague Mildred Bangs Wynkoop (1906-97). Wynkoop was a student of H. Orton Wiley. She followed him from Northwest Nazarene College to Pasadena College, where she earned an A.B. in 1931 and a bachelor of theology in 1934. She helped Wiley with early drafts of his *Christian Theology*. Following graduation, she and her husband served as pastors and evangelists. During the 1940s Wynkoop was a popular young peoples' convention speaker. She then pursued advanced degrees that culminated in 1955 with a doctor of theology from Northern Baptist Theological Seminary.

Wynkoop taught theology at Western Evangelical Theological Seminary in Portland, Oregon, from 1955 to 1960 and then spent a year teaching in Korea, Taiwan, Hong Kong, and Japan with the Oriental Missionary Society (OMS). In 1961 the Church of the Nazarene asked her to redevelop its theological education program in Japan. She was dean of the junior college from 1961 to 1963 and president of the seminary from 1963 to 1966. Wynkoop taught missions and theology at Trevecca from 1966 to 1976. Especially after the publication of *A Theology of Love* in 1972, she became a sought-after lecturer. She was president of the Wesleyan Theological Society in 1973. Wynkoop finished her career as theologian in residence at NTS from 1976 to 1980.[34]

Wynkoop railed against "hollow" holiness orthodoxy. Like Grider, she rejected Platonism, but Wynkoop found recourse not in "realism" but in "relationalism." Wynkoop retained Personalism's view that personality and freedom in God and human beings corresponded and allowed communion. Her years in Japan—a society that highly valued smooth interpersonal relations—confirmed her relational emphases. "Substantival" terms, in contrast, Wynkoop believed, obscured the biblical meaning of holiness. Often in Christian history, original sin had become associated with human flesh. "Original sin," she said, obscured personal moral responsibility. "Original sin" signified a "thing" to be "eradicated" rather than a broken relationship between God and human beings. Wesley, Wynkoop believed, employed biblical ways of thinking. He stressed that human beings were accountable for their own personal sins, not "original sin." True Wesleyanism was like Christian existentialism in its call for radical moral responsibility.[35]

Wynkoop

The goal of "relational" theology was to "support a thoroughgoing moral involvement in all 'stages in the Christian way,' as over against any suggestion of 'magic' or subrational or deterministic concept." Her view that relational theology affirmed "that God's initiative is prior to any response on man's part" kept her close, she believed, to John Wesley's understanding of prevenient grace. Holiness, said Wynkoop, must be tested outside of the cozy altar settings in which many spiritual decisions were made. Holiness had to be lived out in the "idiom" of life. Perfect love, she said, not the "eradication of original sin," was the "essential inner character of holiness." Holiness could not exist apart from love.[36]

Sanctification, to her, was an ongoing, ethical, and personal relationship between God and human beings that restored the image of God and led toward Christlikeness. By demanding and enabling moral decisions and obedience at every juncture in Christian life, sanctification restored true humanity. Sanctification brought "perfect integrity" and "moral integration." It was never a "state." Rather, sanctification was a "way," a "life."[37]

Wynkoop was afraid that both the biblical message and the vital experience of holiness were hidden by overly emphasizing two crises. The sometimes harsh and critical spirits among those who testified to two crises produced a "credibility gap." The goal should never be the "second experience" itself, Wynkoop warned, but Christlikeness and perfect love. She criticized Holiness preachers who had misconstrued biblical texts, including those relating to Pentecost and the baptism with the Holy Spirit, in order to justify sanctification's "secondness."

She did not reject secondness, however. She based it upon the necessity of making moral decisions, upon human development, and upon the distinction between justification and sanctification. Entire sanctification represented a qualitative step, a deliberate, voluntary, and often difficult point at which the depths of self-centeredness became apparent. Not something that was grown into, entire sanctification required conscious decision.[38]

Wynkoop's language and methodology were markedly different from her contemporaries. Even Grider, who became a critic, recognized that Holiness theologians had "tended to rigidify the open and dynamic theology of Mr. Wesley" and commended the "genius" that was at work in Wynkoop's *Theology of Love*.[39]

But Grider, Richard Taylor, Donald Metz, and others believed that Wynkoop "slighted" grace, tended toward Pelagianism in denying inborn sin and in limiting sin to wrong willing, and reduced sanctification to consecration. Her view of original sin, they pointed out, departed from both John Wesley and H. Orton Wiley.[40]

Yet the influence of Wynkoop upon the theology of the church was great. In two widely read books, *In His Likeness* and *The Holiness Pilgrimage*, John A. Knight emphasized that holiness both initiated and encompassed a "divinely stimulated movement or process of grace and obedience" that extended "from conversion to the final goal of glorification."[41] Without growth toward Christlikeness holiness degenerated into "static perfectionism, esoteric quietism, or even dangerous antinomianism."[42] "Christ-likeness is holiness, and increasing Christ-likeness is increasing holiness."[43]

Rob Staples, who joined the faculty of Bethany in 1963 and taught there until moving to NTS in 1976, found similarities among Wesley, Alfred North Whitehead, and Martin Buber. Whitehead emphasized process and freedom. Buber, a Jewish philosopher, used relational categories to describe God and human beings. Staples was optimistic that Wesleyan theology was the "best-equipped of all theological traditions both to creatively appropriate from and to constructively offer correctives to, the central insights of modern man." He motivated students to expand the "frontiers" of Wesleyan theology.[44]

Like Wynkoop, Staples believed that Nazarenes who emphasized the "circumstance" of entire sanctification often neglected the "substance" of holiness. Like her, Staples believed that the Bible was very clear that the "what" of holiness was love and that it was silent on the "how" and "when" of holiness. Staples accused the Holiness Movement of using "unsound exegesis, faulty logic, and inappropriate analogy" in its attempt to "prove" two works of grace. Instead, Staples grounded the twofoldness of sanctification upon the growth of identity and the necessity of commitment in Christian life.[45]

This generation of theologians engaged contemporary theologians more than their teachers had. Wiley was steeped in ancient theology to a degree unmatched in the Holiness Movement but was unaware of or silent on many twentieth-century developments. Wiley's language was that of nineteenth-century Methodism and the Holiness Movement. Although Grider defended traditional language, he compared and contrasted Wesleyan teachings with the shades of difference between the neoorthodox theologies of Karl Barth and Emil Brunner, for instance. Courses in contemporary theology dotted the curricula of the denomination's religion departments. To a degree, the church emerged from a stage in which Nazarenes read and responded only to each other.

Sometimes exasperating older members listening for traditional language, Nazarene preachers found new ways to communicate Holiness doctrine and experience. Pastors such as Ponder Gilliland rediscovered Wesley along with religion professors. Pastors showed patience for human weaknesses remaining in the lives of their members. They emphasized that sin was manifest in selfishness, not simply broken rules, and that holiness entailed love and Christlikeness, not simply spiritual crises. Pastors showed less concern for getting members to the altar another time and greater concern for their spiritual growth. Holiness, they preached, could not be thought of or lived out apart from others. Reuben Welch, chaplain at Pasadena and a well-liked speaker on other Nazarene campuses, emphasized: "We really do need each other. God made us this way. The quality of life within this fellowship of those who share the life of Jesus is to be one of openness and confession and honesty before him."[46]

THE BAPTISM WITH THE HOLY SPIRIT CONTROVERSY

One theological issue debated in the 1970s was whether "baptism with the Holy Spirit" and "Pentecost" imagery in the New Testament really referred to entire sanctification. John Wesley himself had not related Pentecost or the baptism with the Holy Spirit with entire sanctification. But the association had a long history in the Holiness Movement. The Nazarene Articles of Faith stated that original sin continued in the life of regenerate Christians until "eradicated by the baptism with the Holy Spirit," and entire sanctification was "wrought by the baptism with the Holy Spirit."[47] Wiley understood that the "baptism with the Holy Spirit" cleansed Adamic depravity, filled the believer with life in Christ, and brought full devotion to God.[48]

But Pentecostalism and the charismatic movement also emphasized the work of the Holy Spirit and associated Pentecost and the baptism with (or "of") the Holy Spirit with tongues-speaking. Nazarene scholars began reexamining the biblical basis for attaching the baptism with the Holy Spirit and Pentecost to entire sanctification. Wynkoop, Staples, and Dunning suggested that the nineteenth-century Holiness Movement had shifted away from Wesley's emphasis upon Christ and the Atonement as the basis for sanctification. Pentecostals, they pointed out, had followed Holiness writers in making normative or prescriptive for all Christians the portions of Acts that dealt with Pentecost and the baptism with the Holy Spirit. Wynkoop, Staples, and Dunning embraced a more traditionally Calvinist understanding and exegesis and related Pentecost and the baptism with the Holy Spirit to conversion, not (or not exclusively) to the "second" crisis. Staples hoped that his teaching might be "a catalyst in helping the Church to reaffirm the multiple traditions in her heritage and thus preserve the breathing room built into her doctrinal statements." In order to maintain fidelity to the Articles of Faith, as well as to what they believed the Bible taught, Staples, New Testament scholar Alex Deasley, and others embraced positions somewhat like that of John Fletcher, that the baptism with the Holy Spirit understood biblically could refer to regeneration, entire sanctification, or other in-fillings.[49]

Stalwarts believed that in all New Testament descriptions of the baptism with the Holy Spirit the subjects previously had been regenerated. The baptism with the Holy Spirit was their second crisis experience and brought them both purity of heart and power to witness. The pre-Pentecost lives of the apostles, full of inner conflicts, demonstrated their need for Spirit baptism. By appeals to Scripture, the Holiness Movement tradition, and the Articles of Faith, Grider in particular resolutely defended this interpretation.[50]

THE BIBLE AMONG NAZARENES

Postwar Nazarenes maintained distinctly Wesleyan ways of looking at the inspiration and authority of Scripture. Scholars longed for a translation of the Bible that would reflect the best ancient texts. However, as in the previous era, fundamentalist ideas about the Bible and the revered Authorized, "King James" Version influenced laypersons and many pastors and evangelists.[51]

At first, the publication of the *Revised Standard Version* excited scholars. Olive Winchester and, after her death, Roy Swim, who taught New Testament Greek at Nazarene Theological Seminary, served on the RSV's Advisory Board. Ralph Earle praised the RSV New Testament when it appeared in 1946. The biggest problem he found was that it used "consecrate" rather than "sanctify" in John 17. Earle, Swim, and other Holiness scholars complained to the RSV translators about this; and when the complete Old and New Testament RSV Bible was published, it used "sanctify" rather than "consecrate"—a significant concession to Wesleyans. In 1951 S. S. White stated that he would "not want to be without" the RSV. He hoped that the version would "find a place in every home." It made the Bible accessible to the average English-speaking person, White believed.[52]

White did not realize how controversial the RSV would be. Most of the translators were members of denominations that belonged to the National Council of Christian Churches. Conservatives linked the NCCC to the "one world church" movement and, by implication, to Communism. In addition, RSV translators of Isa. 7:16 had removed the word "virgin" (as it had appeared in the KJV) and had used instead "maiden." To conservatives this indicated

> The general superintendents published the following in the February 4, 1953, issue of the *Herald of Holiness:*[53]
>
> A Statement
>
> . . . We acknowledge the value of sound scholarship to help us understand God's revelation, but we find no reason for accepting the theological emphases and pronouncement of liberal scholars. The doctrinal bias of translators is often manifested in any given translation. The theological views of those who have done the work on the *Revised Standard Version* are not concealed. There is some evidence of a tendency to weaken certain fundamental and historic Christian doctrines. . . .
>
> In light of the total situation, we find no justification for replacing the King James Version with the *Revised Standard Version,* or any other modern translation. We urge our ministers and people of the English-speaking world to continue the use of the King James Version for preaching, teaching, and public worship.
>
> Board of General Superintendents

the translators' bias against the virgin birth of Christ. In 1953 the GSs issued a directive urging Nazarenes to retain the KJV.[54]

The general superintendents told Albert Harper not to use the RSV in Church School publications. However, even though conservatives objected, Harper allowed writers to cite newer translations whenever they were helpful. In 1970 Harper suggested to the general superintendents (three new ones had been elected in 1968) that they reevaluate the church's stand regarding the RSV, but they decided not to change the church's position.[55]

The general superintendents' stand disappointed the church's scholars. In "Gleanings from the Greek," a column published regularly in the denomination's *Preacher's Magazine,* Ralph Earle repeatedly demonstrated the limitations of the KJV. "If we are honestly concerned that people should know the truth of God's saving Word," Earle said, addressing himself to conservatives who opposed any version but the KJV, "we shall seek to give them a translation that says clearly in today's language what the inspired Greek and Hebrew originals actually say. This is what has been attempted in recent translations."[56] Earle also described how Calvinist prejudices had skewed the KJV translation and showed how much the meaning of English words (such as "Comforter") had changed in the 350 years since the KJV's publication. He explained that John Wesley himself had recognized the limitations of the KJV and had made his own translation.[57]

Eventually Earle realized that the RSV would never be accepted by evangelicals. That was one reason, in 1965, that he and other evangelical scholars undertook a fresh translation—to be known as the *New International Version.* Earle served as chairman of the NIV Committee on Bible Translation. "My greatest desire," Earle wrote to General Superintendent Lewis, was "to help communicate the inspired Word of God accurately and adequately to the people of our day." He sensed a calling to make the Word of God "more clearly known" to "this strategic generation."[58]

Ralph Earle

Like the denomination's theologians, Earle held a Wesleyan understanding of biblical inspiration. From Methodists and from its deeper roots in the Church of England, Nazarenes understood full or "plenary" inspiration (the word used in the Nazarene Articles of Faith) to pertain to the Scriptures as a whole. The Bible was "infallible" in what it was intended to convey: truth concerning God and salvation. The *Manual* statement that the Bible was "the infallible Word of God, the authoritative Rule of Faith and Practice in the Church" stated it well, Nazarene theologians agreed. With Wiley, they criticized the fundamentalists' "mechanical" view of Scripture, which excluded the role of human rationality and the social and historical context of the authors. As W. T. Purkiser put it, the Nazarene Article on Scripture saved the church from "bondage to a fundamentalistic literalism which affirms the dictation of each word of the original autographs, and which sometimes seems to extend the same sanctity to a certain English version."[59] Nazarenes stressed that the Holy Spirit needed to work in the hearts of the Bible's hearers in order for its words to convey the message of salvation.[60]

The Nazarene view of the Bible baffled fundamentalists such as Harold Lindsell, who made "verbal inerrancy" central to his understanding of what it meant to be evangelical. He conjectured that early Nazarenes, because of the "low estate of their educational and theological background," must originally have accepted biblical inerrancy![61]

Yet there were some Nazarenes who believed that the church should narrow its *Manual* statement on the Holy Scriptures. Harold Reed suggested that the church specify that "plenary" inspiration meant the Bible's "infallible, complete, permanent, supreme, and final authority for all saving knowledge, faith, obedience, and practice." To him, the Bible was "trustworthy" when it spoke on "history, science, ethics, [and] geography, as well as theology."[62]

Similarly, Olivet Professor Earl Barrett understood that the infallibility of the Bible extended to science and history—and not just faith and practice.⁶³

Given their understanding of the Bible, Nazarene scholars generally distanced themselves from fundamentalists by not taking a militantly premillennial stand on the Second Coming. In the midst of great evangelical interest in the topic, Ralph Earle emphasized that biblical prophecy related more to preaching than to predicting. He interpreted the Book of Revelation as containing descriptions of what was happening at the time of its writing in the Roman Empire. But he did not deny the possibility that there were contemporary fulfillments of biblical prophecy.⁶⁴

On the popular level, most Nazarenes were premillennialists. In the 1970s Sunday School classes discussed *The Late Great Planet Earth* and with its author found signs of the soon coming of Christ in the deterioration of society and in international political events. Israel was especially significant, as it seemed a key element of biblical prophecy. Some Nazarenes were "pretribulationists," believing that Christ would come to "rapture" or take into heaven those believers who had died, and those still living, before the Tribulation.⁶⁵ Other Nazarenes were "post-tribulationists," understanding that believers would endure the rule of the "Antichrist" on earth before Christ's return, resurrection of the dead, final judgment, and reign on earth.⁶⁶

In distinction to popular speculations on the Second Coming and other doctrines, Nazarene scholars were comfortable with the "biblical theology" movement. It stressed that the Bible was primarily "salvation history" and understood God's self-disclosure as historically conditioned. The culmination of biblical theology among Nazarenes was *God, Man, and Salvation*, coauthored by W. T. Purkiser, Richard Taylor, and Willard Taylor, published in 1977.⁶⁷

THE BIBLE AND SCIENCE

The church's views of Scripture and its liberal arts philosophy of education influenced how members interacted with science. Biblical scholars insisted that Genesis was a religious document not intended to be taken cosmologically or scientifically. The "days" of creation need not be twenty-four-hour periods. The poetic "creation hymn" answered who God was, not how or when He created the universe, said H. Orton Wiley.⁶⁸ The section on creation in *Exploring Our Christian Faith* (1960), the denomination's foundational theology textbook, concluded that "the author of Genesis made no effort to give a metaphysically precise account of the beginning and structure of the universe" and that it was "unreasonable to expect that the creation record should be scientifically complete since the purpose of the account is obviously religious." Any effort to read science into the Genesis account, the authors believed, was "a misguided apologetic that does injustice to both Genesis and science."[69]

At the 1967 Education Conference Bethany Professor Mel-Thomas Rothwell encouraged theologians and scientists to join efforts in the pursuit of truth. Their spheres were different: science explained *what* is; religion explained *why*. But "science," said Rothwell, was "not the work of the devil." On the contrary, it could become "the handmaiden of the Lord." Waving "the Bible in the face of every piece of evidence and every argument" supporting evolution did no one good, Rothwell explained. Science served humanity and did a better job than theology in uncovering human origins. The theologian's task, Rothwell believed, was to construct a system of thought broad enough to include data from the empirical sciences. The theologian could "accept the valid empirical discoveries of science without any fear" and could "maintain his faith in the eternal Word of God, the Bible, without any apology." "In fact," Rothwell continued, "if he denies either he will not only be helplessly isolated and quite lonely, but he will at the same time truckle to doubtful entrenched interests and become a servant of their well-known prejudices and blind provincialism."[70]

In presenting the theories of astronomers and geologists on the age of the universe, Nazarene science professors felt that they were in tune with the liberal arts philosophy of the denomination and in harmony with their colleagues in the religion departments. College presidents and deans encouraged science departments. They wanted graduates fully up-to-date and competent in any major they chose, including biology, and boasted to constituents when graduates were accepted into advanced programs in medicine and the sciences. As Nazarenes pursued careers in science, they became persuaded that there was no conspiracy among scientists to attack the biblical account of creation, just attempts to understand evidence. Nazarene scientists encouraged the church's publications to fairly present current science. Robert Lawrence, one of the church's leading scientists and educators, hoped that the church could work out Wesleyan ways of correlating science, particularly evolution, and theology. Lawrence championed the liberal arts philosophy of education set down by Nazarenes, which provided a Thomistic-like pursuit of Truth along two paths, reason and revelation.

When questions regarding creation or the age of the earth were asked of Nazarene professors, they answered carefully and so dispassionately that students understood that the professors saw no essential disjunction between their personal faith and evolution. In 1971, a speaker representing the antievolution Institute for Creation Research created such division among

Pasadena students on the issue that the science faculty avoided talking about evolution for several years. Postwar religion departments created more controversy for administrators than the science departments. Nazarenes were less concerned with the theory of evolution than they were with maintaining Holiness "standards." Belief or disbelief in evolution was not one of the essentials over which the church began, and it did not become one of the essentials among Nazarenes during this period.[71]

NAZARENE SELF-IDENTITY

In preparation for the fiftieth anniversary celebration of the Church of the Nazarene in 1958, the Board of General Superintendents appointed a Church History Commission. It met in May 1955 and asked Timothy L. Smith to gather material for the project. At the time, Smith was teaching at Eastern Nazarene College and was in the process of publishing *Revivalism and Social Reform,* based on his Harvard Ph.D. dissertation, in which he described pre-Civil War evangelicals as being in the forefront of attempts to both end slavery and uplift the urban poor. There being yet no denominational archives, Smith traveled around the denomination gathering material and interviewing elderly church pioneers.

Timothy Smith

The commission gave Smith a great degree of freedom to publish what he discovered, in spite of the fact that some of the incidents (such as the rift at Pasadena College between Seth Rees and Howard Eckel) were unflattering to all concerned. Even at the level of history, postwar Nazarenes seemed willing to accept both a scholar's objectivity and their own humanity.[72]

In the resulting work, *Called unto Holiness,* Smith found that, contrary to H. Richard Niebuhr's understanding that all denominations began as sects, the Church of the Nazarene had begun with strong "churchly" tendencies. It moved not from being a sect to a church but, rather, from "churchliness" to sectarianism. Smith's overall purpose was to show that in the context of denominationalism "church" and "sect" were misleading typologies. Furthermore, Smith refused to look upon early Nazarenes as plain rural frontier people. If they represented a rural mind-set as they moved into cities, they were not much different from thousands of others migrating to urban areas.

Writing in a time when schisms over rules were occurring in the church, Smith demonstrated that the urban Eastern and West Coast pioneers had had less concern with laws than those who came out of the Holiness Church of Christ. The second generation had departed from the wisdom and balance of the first.[73]

Timothy Smith was an exception, as he won an appointment to the history department of Johns Hopkins University in 1968. The Church of the Nazarene produced few other scholars known outside of its own boundaries. Nazarene schools kept professors busy with heavy teaching loads and administrative assignments. Scholars who in other settings might be doing research were instead giving spiritual counsel to young students. The priorities were modeling Christ and deepening students' faith. Ordained professors held revivals and preached in camp meetings. Instead of working on articles for scholarly journals, they wrote devotional material and Christian Service Training books for laity. Scholarship served the church. The Wesleyan impulse toward experiential piety and moral responsibility kept education wedded to evangelism.

Part III Analysis

With their roots in nineteenth-century revivals and crusades against both slavery and alcohol, the first generation of Holiness people believed that Christ could transform culture. Just as God worked in them individually to cleanse sin, Holiness people believed, God could so work through their compassion to morally renew society. The next generation of Holiness people was less optimistic. Christ stood against culture. They did not have the same sense of obligation to society. They saw prohibition fail. Holiness became for most an individual matter related to strict behavior codes, not social transformation. Society seemed far beyond any ability to be redeemed. Christ, they expected, would come and take His saints away. In the meantime, second generation Nazarenes had their own denominational shelter. They withdrew from the world. For them, Christ stood against almost everything they saw in culture.[1]

The third generation reflected determination that Christ be Lord of society. According to one observer, J. B. Chapman's 1946 appeal for a Crusade for Souls was "the defining moment when the church was turned redemptively outward to world-wide evangelization rather than inward to judgmental legalism."[2] Through the leaders who replaced Chapman, the church expanded its outreach, found creative ways of evangelizing, and strengthened its educational system. Like their forebears, Nazarenes in the postwar period believed that there was sanctifying grace beyond regeneration that purified, empowered, and led to Christlikeness; yet they also moved away from their sectarian mode.[3]

Emergence from sectarianism was not easy. Many feared accommodation. When Nazarenes celebrated the fiftieth anniversary of their union, leaders wondered whether the church had maintained its "particular" mission to spread holiness "as a second definite work of divine grace, over all the earth." The Church of the Nazarene did not have to be like other Protestant denominations, said General Superintendent Benner; it need not lose its purpose and suffer spiritual decline.[4]

Attempting to decrease the possibility of declension, the general superintendents instituted a managerial and centralized system of governance. Gone were charismatic administrators such as Hiram Reynolds, R. T. Williams, and J. B. Chapman, who could inspire, rally, and sway the church. Postwar general superintendents, by their own design, worked together and for the church both collegially and professionally, and on most matters became indistinguishable from each other.

Largely, doctrine, experience, and behavior remained essential factors identifying what it meant to be a Nazarene. Commitments to the Bible, to the Wesleyan understanding of redemption, to "second blessing holiness," and to education served as benchmarks of unity. Doctrines were relevant because they defined experience. District Superintendent Morris Chalfant feared that the third generation would believe the truth of holiness but fail to experience it: "It is not enough to be sound in our thinking—we must be right in our feelings and living. It is possible to be orthodox in the head and heterodox in the heart. When this condition results, the holy heritage is already lost."[5] Yet experience too often became "routinized." Unless Holiness theology was revitalized, theologians feared, both the doctrine and the experience would be lost.

Though maintaining their theological moorings, Nazarenes behaved less and less like outsiders in society. With its increasingly suburban orientation, the denomination lost some of its resistance to the behavior of the dominant society. The church outgrew its desire to build tightly controlled religious communities where members followed rules out of loyalty, duty, or fear. "Atheistic Communism" pushed Nazarenes toward a larger consensus. Nazarenes were willing to do their part alongside others to win the world for Christ and to turn back Communism. The church heard only occasional voices of dissent to the linkage of its mission with American values and foreign policy. Like their neighbors, Nazarenes made more money than ever before. Though there was less need to give as sacrificially as their parents during the Depression, they used their wealth to support church colleges and scores of missionaries as well as local churches.

Local congregations nurtured faith. Pastors trusted somewhat more than their predecessors the inward rule of the Holy Spirit and cultivated Christ's "law of love." Especially after the Bible Missionary Church and the Church of the Bible Covenant secessions, pastors lessened their roles as keepers and guardians of rules. They preached, instead, that holiness was a "harmonizing" and humanizing experience. Increasingly, Nazarene pastors had some training in counseling or, at least, knew enough to refer cases to other professionals. Sermons were more crafted and exegetically based—and less crisis-driven and emotional. Larger churches had staff members with specific training in religious education. Sunday morning music and worship was more intentional and dignified than previously. Pastors recognized the professional nature of their calling and work.[6]

The church's schools were attuned to the best scholarship and contemporary studies. Nazarenes were proud of teachers who had won advanced degrees from leading universities, and bragged when students went on to the best graduate schools. The church's college leaders believed that they were preparing students not only for the church but also for the world.

During the 1960s, however, there was a breakdown in the political and social consensus. Unlike the previous two decades, in this time of great social upheaval, Nazarenes had a difficult time discerning God's work. While some denominations turned to the left, Nazarenes, though aware of economic and racial divisions, identified with those attempting to preserve values. Nazarenes of this era still believed that God worked primarily in individuals, not societies. In all, however, post-World War II Nazarenes were more genuinely aware than the previous generation had been of their neighbors and, perhaps, of themselves.

PART IV

TWENTY-THREE

LEADERS AND LANGUAGES

Pilot Point, the place of union in 1908, was only a few miles away from Dallas, where the 1976 General Assembly met. Pilot Point symbolized something significant in Nazarene history: the ability through grace to overcome class and culture conflict through the cleansing blood of Christ. The church intentionally ministered to the poor and broken. A vision of worldwide ministry energized early Nazarenes. They regarded education a basic component of the denomination. Entire sanctification was central and distinguishing. Pilot Point provided a reference marker for the unifying and ongoing direction of Nazarene missions, a "unity in holiness" that transcended gender, class, race, and nationality.[1]

SACRED GATHERINGS

In 1908 there were 10,034 Nazarenes in 228 churches, representing East, West, and South, with nineteen missionaries. In 1976, the church reported 168,252 new Nazarenes since the previous General Assembly, 6,736 congregations, and a total world membership of 586,532.[2] The church drew together not simply the three streams of East, West, and South, but sixty nations. In late 1991, the Church of the Nazarene reached 1 million members around the world. Forty-three percent of Nazarenes in 1991 lived outside the United States. In 1997, when the church met again in Texas—this time in San Antonio—there were 308,824 new Nazarenes and a world membership of 1,216,657 in 116 world areas and 340 districts served by missionaries originating from twenty-nine different countries. There were 12,134 Nazarene congregations around the globe in 1997, including at least one church in 73 out of 111 cities worldwide with at least 2 million people. By 2000 the church's membership had reached 1.39 million worshipping in 12,578 local churches. The church's membership outside of the United States had doubled in the previous ten years and now made up 53 percent of the total world membership of the denomination. Among the 636,564 Nazarene members in the United States in 2000, about 80 percent attended Sunday morning worship services, and about 33 percent attended Sunday evening services.

At the 1977 General Board eight of the forty-four members represented areas outside the United States, and in 2005, twenty-two out of forty-six General Board members resided outside of North America. In 2007, on the eve of the church's centennial, there were over 1.7 million Nazarenes around the world in 151 countries. By this time, 62 percent of the membership of the church resided outside North America. More than 20 percent of all Nazarenes resided in Africa, and more than 20 percent of Nazarenes spoke Spanish as their first language.[3]

"Cyclic rites," like General Assemblies, sustain for the journey through periodic recounting and renewal of the group's life.[4] In Nazarene life, general, regional, and district assemblies seemed like sacred places and times that shaped and renewed denominational life. With John Wesley, Nazarenes believed that such conferences strengthened witness, inspired faith, and energized the church. Looking back at events in a specific past, Nazarenes took heart and found direction for the future. The Nazarene World Youth Congress that met in Fiesch, Switzerland, in 1974, for instance, signaled the church's growing desire to reach beyond national and cultural walls. In 1976, the nineteenth General Assembly wrestled with the denomination's structure. Should districts outside North America and Great Britain be broken off and formed into national churches, as earlier Protestant denominations had done, or should the Nazarene people remain one? The Nazarene Compassionate Ministries Conference in 1985 was another significant watershed conference that placed "compassionate ministries back on the church's agenda." It represented "an unmistakable groundswell of support for rediscovering social ministries in Christ's name."[5]

As the church expanded, there remained a question implicit in denominational gatherings, was there still a distinctive "language" by which Nazarenes from around the world would recognize and identify with each other as belonging to a global family? Internationalization, which represented the primary development of the church in the years after 1976, embraced optimism that a common language unified the church's vision of gospel and church, mission and world. Integrated vision brought identity, organizational strength, numerical growth, and inner strength.[6]

Literally, of course, the church spoke German, Russian, Spanish, Portuguese, Mandarin, Korean, and Arabic. In such languages and many others the church uttered its distinctive words: "heart holiness," "holiness evangelism," and "entire sanctification." That Nazarenes translated and reminted distinctive phrases was not simply a matter of communication but a question of internalizing the ethos, the distinctive character, spirit, and attitudes of a community. Embodying holiness in structures and strategies while learning new theological terms, practicing new worship styles, and obeying Christ remained the church's goal. Nazarenes yearned to be both a global as well as a Spirit-led communion. A century after Pilot Point the challenge was no longer the establishment of a denomination but the development of structures that organized holiness on a global scale. How could Nazarenes create means and ways of connecting with each other? Could denominational loyalty survive at both the congregational and global level?[7]

General Assemblies reflected Nazarene aspirations. First-time General Assembly delegates wondered who the new general superintendents would be and what kind of international church they were constructing.[8] The international character was evident at Dallas in 1976. The gathering resembled a great global corporation assembled for business as much as an international family of believers gathering for celebration. On the first day of the General Assembly, Cho Moon Kyung, superintendent of the Korea District, led in prayer. Retiring General Superintendent Edward Lawlor, a Canadian born in England, brought the Communion message. "The dominant note of our message and mission," Lawlor reminded the assembly, "has been a call to holiness of life, character, and conduct by the people called Nazarenes. We have built a worldwide church, and it is my prayer that we will make a solemn and sacred obligation during this General Assembly to keep ours an international church founded upon the immovability and impregnability of scriptural holiness."[9] In the afternoon Sylvia Peters from Guyana and Hans Mehltreter from West Germany sang and missionary Hugh Friberg (released recently from prison in Mozambique) spoke of his experiences. The Peru North and Guatemala Northeast districts received special recognition for achieving regular district status.

Typical Nazarene delegates would probably not have thought of themselves as stakeholders in a global company. The celebration of Communion undercut that image. The church in which Nazarenes moved and interacted shaped who they were, how they lived, and who they were to become. The goal remained that of becoming an international family, centered in Christ, which was learning together what it meant to be a people seeking holiness in communion with each other.[10]

THE LANGUAGE OF HOLY EXCITEMENT

Nazarenes inherited revivalist, "holy excitement" language from the nineteenth-century Holiness Movement. Nazarenes spoke it in camp meetings and revivals, in testimonies, and around the altars of prayer. A dynamic tension continued between the eager spontaneity of the Spirit and more formal worship, or between "being moved by the Spirit" and prepared order. Nazarene worship services, said Maurice Griggs Sr., longstanding member of Nashville First, "had an intensity about them!"[11] Whenever Nazarenes gathered for "business," whether at General Assemblies, regional, district, or local gatherings, they worshipped and celebrated the presence of God. For instance, in 1995 reports of a revival at Eastern Nazarene College brought unexpected results at the following Philadelphia District Assembly. "It was the most unusual assembly I have seen in the 30 years I have been in the district," said Jack Thorne, assistant to the district superintendent. Presiders suspended normal pastoral reporting for three hours to allow for sharing and spontaneous prayer.[12]

"Holy excitement" translated into denominational and doctrinal loyalty. The place for holy presence was in a dynamic and growing church. Essential was the conviction, firmly rooted in Nazarene historical consciousness, that inward devotion and personal experience were quickly starved if not vitally connected in a living fellowship of organized believers. In 1997, *Herald of Holiness* editor Wesley Tracy suggested that church-centered loyalty was to be preferred to "independent church fever." Such movements, he gently criticized, while not "bad or even negative," do not or cannot stress "entire sanctification as a second definite work of grace in which inner sin is cleansed." So, Tracy urged, let us not be ashamed to sing, "I've got the Nazarene enthusiasm down in my heart."[13]

THE LANGUAGE OF SACRED SYMBOL AND STORY

Nazarenes had left churches because they questioned the integrity of both speech and structures, and a hundred years later, Nazarenes wanted to remain sure that their practices reflected the joy, integrity, grace, and truth embodied in practice. *Visual* and *visional* language enabled Nazarenes to convey their theology and ethos. Preachers, evangelists, and missionaries told stories derived from a sense that God was with them. Tracy used picture language to make his point that sanctification was both a "moment" and a "journey." "Christ taught by symbols," so "why should not we also draw from all things the blessings of light, comfort and instruction?" The grass, the flower, the tree, the sparrow, the social customs of life, the earth, and the sky, all were invested with "some great religious truth."[14] One sees visual language as well in Paul Orjala's sentiment that: "When God wants to send a message, he wraps it in a person and sends that person." Preaching the gospel meant "living the language of God."¹⁵ Harmon Schmelzenbach, grandson of the pioneer Nazarene missionary to Swaziland, spoke the language of symbol and story. After he preached at Olivet Nazarene University in 1992, a professor of Old Testament commented, "We have just heard and seen a first hand example of how the dramatic accounts of the activity of Yahweh, God of Israel, were communicated."¹⁶ All the elements of saga, symbol, drama, and enactment were present. Richard Zanner's stories from Africa throbbed with this same quality of vivid storytelling, where prose and poetry combined with descriptions, interpretations, and implications.¹⁷

The Media and Communication Division remained in tune with contemporary sounds and sights. Publications International, which had started as Spanish Publications, kept pace with the church's expansion and became World Mission Literature in 1996. By 1997, the number of languages used in radio and publications had grown to seventy-five. There were 423 Spanish titles in print, 118 in Portuguese, 47 in French, and 16 in intercultural English (English as a second language).¹⁸

The 1997 General Assembly merged the *Herald of Holiness* with *World Mission* magazine to form *Holiness Today* and renamed the General Budget the World Evangelism Fund. Both actions signified the aspiration that the church be global in nature, that it existed in one world and did not distinguish between those in or outside of North America. Before the General Assembly Nazarene Youth International delegates had elected Dierdre Brower as general secretary. She pastored on the British Isles South District.¹⁹

One accentuation of "seeing" in Nazarene circles was the JESUS Film Project, announced by the Department of World Mission in 1998. Its object was the screening of the *JESUS* film to millions of people in the decade ahead. Even in the West, a shift had taken place from predominantly *verbal* to *visual* styles of communication. Local churches used various media in worship.²⁰

THE LANGUAGE OF ORGANIZED HOLINESS

The Protestant heritage, the Holiness Movement, and the founders of the Church of the Nazarene possessed confident assurance in biblical faith and proclamation. From their Methodist forebears Nazarenes inherited a strong devotion to church membership and discipline, rational order, and efficiency. Nazarenes implemented their vision through effective organization. As Nazarenes saw it, the energies released by obedience to the Spirit required firm yet flexible structures to propagate and preserve and organize holiness.²¹

For their sense of certainty about salvation, Nazarenes preferred the Wesleyan language of assurance, mediated through faith in Christ, to the Calvinist language of "security." Nazarenes found assurance from each other through outward conversation as well as the whisperings of the Spirit. Nazarenes had always prayed and counseled around kneeling rails. Now churches expanded their vestibules and served coffee and doughnuts in Sunday School classes to encourage meaningful talk that testified to God's grace. When it came to entire sanctification, however, many Nazarenes wanted doctrinal precision and clarity, not ambiguity or diversity.[22]

The Division of World Mission (dropping the "s" from "Missions" in 1980) communicated the core values of the church in the world. World Mission directors in this period—Jerald D. Johnson (1973-80), L. Guy Nees (1980-86), Robert H. Scott (1986-94), and Louis E. Bustle (1994-)—clarified and translated the church's goals and purposes into mission policy.

To his positions as World Mission director and general superintendent, Jerald Johnson brought an ability to speak German and cross-cultural leadership skills learned on the frontlines of missionary service in Europe. Born in Curtis, Nebraska, in 1916, Jerald Johnson graduated from Northwest Nazarene College in 1949 and served pastorates in Coeur d'Alene, Idaho, and Eugene, Oregon. Johnson and his family pioneered the Church of the Nazarene in West Germany in 1958, and he became the first district superintendent of the Middle and Northwest European Districts. Returning to the United States, Johnson pastored in San Jose, California (1969-70), and Nampa, Idaho, College Church (1970-73). He became director of the World Mission Division in 1973 and served until 1980, when he was elected general superintendent. Johnson authored several books, including *We Live in Germany* (1960); *Exploring Denmark* (1962); *Land of Our Adoption* (1965); *New Strategies for Missions* (1975); *The International Experience* (1982); *Hardy C. Powers: Bridge Builder* (1985); and *D. I. Vanderpool: His Stories and Anecdotes* (1985); and coauthored *Strickland Safari* with Carol Zurcher (1993). He retired in 1997.[23]

Jerald Johnson

Following many of the policies and philosophies initiated by E. S. Phillips, Johnson believed it necessary to move beyond a "they-us" mentality to inclusiveness, where the church is "one in the Spirit."[24] To signal this, in 1980

Johnson appointed Richard Zanner, his coworker in Germany, director of the Africa Region.

Nees was serving as president of Mount Vernon Nazarene College when chosen to lead the division. Prior to this, he had pastored in Idaho and British Columbia and, from 1947 to 1949, had served as president of Canadian Nazarene College (then in Red Deer, Alberta). He continued pastoral ministry in Toronto, Ontario; Kankakee, Illinois (College Church); and Los Angeles First Church, which he served from 1957 to 1964. Nees was superintendent of the Los Angeles District from 1964 to 1975, when he became president of Mount Vernon. The church entered thirteen new countries under Nees's leadership. At the time of his departure, 30 percent of Nazarenes lived in world mission areas. He implemented a system of regional offices and directors stationed around the world, which in effect added another administrative tier. He emphasized both theological education and compassionate ministries.[25]

Scott had been serving as superintendent of the Southern California District since 1975 when the General Board chose him to head the division. He had served on the World Mission department of the General Board. Under his leadership, the church's presence grew from 85 to 109 countries.[26]

In Bustle the General Board chose a missionary to lead the World Mission Division. Bustle had served in the Virgin Islands, had pioneered the church in the Dominican Republic, had served a year in Peru, and had been South America Regional director since 1983. In each of his assignments the church had grown markedly.[27]

The division placed increased authority in regional directors. At the same time the church recognized the strategic importance of local pastors. General church leaders became less well known at the local level, even in the United States, and district superintendents confronted the disconcerting question, "Who are you? What brings you here?" when new Nazarenes encountered them in local churches.[28]

Regional accents sounded with greater frequency and force in assemblies and leadership gatherings. The number of non-North American delegates to the General Assemblies doubled from 264 in Dallas in 1976 to 536 in San Antonio in 1997, a significant shift. Though Nazarenes spoke hundreds of languages, Spanish remained the "second language" in San Antonio, where Christian Sarmiento, Bruno Radi, and Mario Zani augmented the aging voice of Honorato Reza. Over 20 percent of the General Assembly delegates in 1997 were Spanish-speaking.[29]

Such changes presented new challenges to leaders to communicate cross-culturally. How was a leader from a predominantly English-speaking context to interact with a leader from the Korean church? How was a German superintendent to understand leaders from Cape Verde or South Africa? Several of the leaders of the period were equipped to bridge cultures and nurture a global family. Charles H. Strickland, elected general superintendent in 1972, could speak Afrikaans (South African Dutch), Jerald Johnson, elected in 1980, could speak German.

The Methodist churches often elected scholars as bishops. In the Church of the Nazarene the pattern was rarer. But in William Greathouse, elected in 1976, and John A. Knight, elected in 1985, the church indeed chose as general superintendents churchmen-theologians of its highest rank. Greathouse spoke the language of a lifelong student of John Wesley and the Bible, specializing in Romans. In his view the church's mission should always be tested by this theological center. "My acknowledged presuppositions are those of John Wesley," Greathouse wrote, "who saw his Anglican faith and practice as a 'middle way' between Reformation and Catholic understandings of salvation and holiness." Publications by Greathouse included: *The Fullness of the Spirit, From the Apostles to Wesley, Introduction to Wesleyan Theology* (coauthored with H. Ray Dunning), and *Exploring Christian Holiness*, Volume 2 (with Paul Bassett). After retirement, Greathouse wrote *Wholeness in Christ: Toward a Biblical Theology of Holiness*. Greathouse's call was to a renewal in biblical holiness and Wesleyan theology, and for "Nazarenes to seek to continue as a dynamic spiritual movement" where the "Secret of Holy Living" was simply learning to permit "Christ to live His holy life in you."[30]

John A. Knight was elected general superintendent at Anaheim in 1985 alongside Raymond Hurn, who represented the evangelistic side of the church as certainly as Knight represented its educational interests. Knight's father, John L. Knight, served the church as pastor, district superintendent, and director of evangelism. The younger Knight pastored on the Tennessee District for ten years and taught at Trevecca while earning a Ph.D. in theology at Vanderbilt University, doing his dissertation on the theology of Wesley's protégé John Fletcher. Later Knight taught at Bethany and Mount Vernon and served as president of Mount Vernon from 1972 to 1975. In January 1975, he was elected editor of the *Herald of Holiness*, this lasted only until August 1976, when Knight was elected president of Bethany, where he was serving when elected general superintendent.

Like Greathouse, Knight was a scholar called upon by the church to high administrative tasks. Knight found in Fletcher helpful guidance for the holiness "pilgrimage." Knight stressed that "the Church of the Nazarene is a connectional church, and that in a time when the structures of society were changing, Nazarenes could cope with change in the power of the Spirit, evaluate change, and employ change, without becoming either reactionary or undiscriminating." Knight asked, "Are we as leaders articulating fundamental Christian teachings—particularly those surrounding holiness and our distinctive doctrine of entire sanctification? Our call as ministers is to depict and dramatize—in ways that are relevant and attractive—the possibilities of holy living in Christ through the indwelling Holy Spirit." Knight authored several books, including *The Holiness Pilgrimage: Developing a Life-Style That Reflects Christ* (1973), *In His Likeness* (1976), and *Bridge to Our Tomorrows: A Millennial Address to the Church of the Nazarene*.[31]

The 1989 General Assembly elected two college presidents, both with cross-cultural ministry experience, William Prince and Donald Owens, general superintendents.[32]

Owens was born in Missouri in 1926 and graduated from Bethany-Peniel College in 1952. He pastored churches in Nebraska and Oklahoma (1952-54 and 1968-69), served as missionary to Korea (1954-66 and 1971-72), taught missiology at Bethany Nazarene College (1966-74) and then at Nazarene Theological Seminary (1974-81). He completed a Ph.D. in cultural anthropology at the University of Oklahoma in 1975. In 1976 he was chosen to begin a graduate level seminary in Asia. In 1981 Owens became director of the Asia Region and moved to the Philippines. Asia-Pacific Nazarene Theological Seminary began in 1983. In 1985 he was chosen president of MidAmerica Nazarene College, where he served until his election as general superintendent.[33] Owens chaired the Commission on Internationalization from 1985 to 1989. Owens authored *Challenge in Korea* (1957), *The Church Behind the Bamboo Curtain: The Story of the Church Inside Red China* (1973), *Revival Fires in Korea* (1977), and *Sing, Ye Islands* (1979). He retired in 1997.[34]

Donald Owens

William Prince, elected alongside Owens, also had the cross-cultural experience that many perceived was needed for the job. After graduating from Bethany-Peniel College and Nazarene Theological Seminary, Prince pastored churches in California and Minneapolis. In 1970 he was called upon to lead European Nazarene Bible College. After six years, Prince returned to the United States to pastor in Dayton, Ohio. He served as superintendent of the Pittsburgh District and then, in 1980, became president of Mount Vernon

Nazarene College. He had been elected president of Southern Nazarene University in 1989 when the General Assembly elected him general superintendent. Prince retired in 2001.[35]

In 1993 the General Assembly chose pastors of two larges churches as general superintendents, Paul Cunningham and James Diehl. Many interpreted the election of these prominent pastors as a sign of increasing support and concern for the role and importance of the local pastor and the local church. Diehl was senior pastor of Denver First Church of the Nazarene when elected. Prior to this, he had been superintendent of the Colorado District (1985-89) and of the Nebraska District (1979-85). He had also served as assistant to the president at MidAmerica. Paul G. Cunningham said, when elected, "I think [what has happened here] is recognition of the fact that the local church is where the action is—that's where lives are being changed." He had served as pastor of Olathe College Church for twenty-nine years (1964-93), ever since graduating from Nazarene Theological Seminary, and had seen it grow from a small group to over two thousand in membership. He had been a longtime member of the General Board of the denomination.[36]

The 1997 Assembly elected Jim Bond and Jerry D. Porter general superintendents. Porter was forty-seven years old and had served as the superintendent of the Washington District since 1992. The son of missionaries William Porter and Juanita Porter, he grew up in Puerto Rico speaking Spanish along with English. With Louis Bustle, Jerry Porter helped to start the church's work in the Dominican Republic. He became rector of the Seminary of the Americas in San Jose, Costa Rica, in 1979. He expanded the extension education program of the school so that it reached an enrollment of three thousand. Porter was director of the Mexico/Central America Region from 1986 to 1992. After his election as general superintendent, Porter affirmed his desire to "fan the flame of multicultural enthusiastic evangelism. I wish this assignment to be a bridge, not just to the new century, but across the distance that separates generations." He continued in Spanish, "I am a bridge between the North American church and the rest of the world." "We are a great united family around the world."[37]

Jim Bond, sixty-one when elected, had served as president of Point Loma Nazarene College since 1983. He earned a B.A. from Pasadena College, a master of divinity from Nazarene Theological Seminary in Kansas City, and a doctor of ministry from Fuller Theological Seminary. After his missionary assignment in Brazil, Bond served as chaplain and professor of theology at Nazarene Bible College and as assistant to the president for institutional development at Point Loma. To the Board of General Superintendents, Bond brought not only a California West Coast voice but also a deep interest in Nazarene education. In various contexts, Bond distinguished between the Wesleyan tradition of the Church of the Nazarene and fundamentalist views prevailing in much of American evangelicalism.[38]

Bond's concern was that Nazarenes were losing their distinctive voice in a choir of blended parts. The "people's church" language offered commonality with other denominations. The characteristics of evangelicals that Nazarenes shared included participation, pragmatism, competition, and personal discipline. Some Nazarenes embraced liturgy, and others the worship style of Pentecostals. The distinctive songs of Wesley and the nineteenth-century Holiness Movement declined. The managerial *Manual*-ese of churchly order, which carried the undertones and overtones of corporate institutional language, united Nazarenes, but the idioms of an older generation were lost on a younger generation that focused on "believability." Many Nazarenes understood their faith in terms of a heightened apocalyptic religious and conservative political language used as well by partisan fundamentalists.[39]

The diversity and dissonance of languages and accents were being interwoven into a new tapestry. "Whatever form the Church of the Nazarene takes in the twenty-first century," Wesley Tracy commented in 1996, "I would hope that the church will be enriched by cultural diversity, united in essentials, gracious in celebrating our oneness in Christ and mission, and fearless enough to trust the global church to the Lordship of Christ."[40]

Holy excitement walked in partnership with organized holiness, and both learned to tell their stories in the poetic language of symbol and vision, as well as in the hard grammar of clarity and certainty. Language was the "palette" from which Nazarenes colored their lives and culture in this new global family identity.

In 1999, General Superintendent William Prince, along with Regional Director Brent Cobb, China Ministries Field Director James Williams, and Floyd Cunningham attended a worship church in China. The Chinese preacher had attended the Nazarene Bible School about sixty years earlier. The Chinese translator, an evangelical Christian, had a difficult time making sense of the preacher's message. Jim Williams, however, captured it entirely: the preacher was using the Nazarene language, speaking of heart holiness, the baptism with the Holy Spirit, the second blessing, and entire sanctification.

In 2001, Talmadge Johnson and Jesse Middendorf were elected general superintendents to replace the retiring John A. Knight and William Prince. From 1994 until his election, Johnson had been serving as director of Sunday School Ministries at headquarters. Previous to this, he had been a district superintendent, serving the Mississippi District (1975-80) and the Tennessee District (1980-94). He had been a full-time evangelist (1958-61), had pastored in Oklahoma (1961-75), and had been general president of the Nazarene Young People's Society (1972-76). Because of the mandatory retirement clause in the *Manual*, not allowing the reelection of a general superintendent who had reached the age of sixty-eight by the time of the General Assembly, Johnson served only one term.[41]

Middendorf's election continued the trend of selecting general superintendents from among the church's leading pastors. He had been superintendent of the Northwest Oklahoma District from 1985 to 1991 but had been pastoring the Kansas City First Church for ten years prior to his election as general superintendent. About a decade prior to Middendorf's pastoring Kansas City First Church, the congregation had moved from Nazarene Theological Seminary, where it had been worshipping several years, to its new location in an affluent area on the south side of the city. After worshipping for several more years in a "sanctinasium" (a combination sanctuary and gymnasium), the church completed a sanctuary. The church conducted separate traditional, liturgical, and contemporary worship services. Middendorf earned a doctor of ministry degree from Nazarene Theological Seminary during these years of pastoring Kansas City First and published *The Church Rituals Handbook* as a supplement to the *Manual*'s rites.

At the turn of the century, the church revisited its core values. Even if the language was not the same in every place, and in each generation, there seemed to be an enduring character and ethos relative to the Church of the Nazarene that centered in its sense of calling to a unique mission.

The two general superintendents elected in 2005 represented both the international thrust of the church and the crucial leadership importance of pastors. Nina Gunter, the first woman elected general superintendent, had served as general director of Nazarene Missions International since 1986. During her tenure, annual local church giving to missions doubled from about $30 million to more than $60 million. Prior to her assuming the leadership of the NMI, she had served with her husband as copastors of churches in Tennessee, Missouri, and South Carolina, and she had been president of the South Carolina NMI for fifteen years. Her husband, D. Moody Gunter, was superintendent of the South Carolina District and became general treasurer when Nina Gunter was selected to lead the NMI. She graduated from Trevecca and had a master's degree in education.[42]

J. K. Warrick, also elected general superintendent in 2005, had been pastoring the Olathe, Kansas, College Church for twelve years. Prior to this, he had pastored the Indianapolis Westside Church for eleven years. In that urban setting, he was active in establishing Shepherd Community, a compassionate ministry.[43]

In December 2006 the general superintendents, after much discussion and deliberation, moved to revise the church's mission statement to succinctly represent its core values: "To make Christlike disciples in the nations." The statement embodied the church's Christian, holiness, and missional values. As Jerry Porter explained, "The essence of holiness is Christlikeness." Middendorf added, "We're also moving from a 'sending' to a 'sent' church. The re-

---

The church's core values were articulated in a booklet widely circulated by the general superintendents.

I. We Are a Christian People

As members of the Church Universal, we join with all true believers in proclaiming the Lordship of Jesus Christ and in embracing the historic Trinitarian creedal statement of Christian faith. We value our Wesleyan-Holiness heritage and believe it to be a way of understanding the faith that is true to Scripture, reason, tradition, and experience.

II. We Are a Holiness People

God, who is holy, calls us to a life of holiness. We believe that the Holy Spirit seeks to do in us a second work of grace, called by various terms including "entire sanctification" and "baptism with the Holy Spirit"—cleansing us from all sin; renewing us in the image of God; empowering us to love God with our whole heart, soul, mind, and strength, and our neighbors as ourselves; and producing in us the character of Christ. Holiness in the life of believers is most clearly understood as Christlikeness.

III. We Are a Missional People

We are a "sent people," responding to the call of Christ and empowered by the Holy Spirit to go into all the world, witnessing to the Lordship of Christ and participating with God in the building of the Church and the extension of His kingdom (2 Corinthians 6:1). Our mission *(a)* begins in worship, *(b)* ministers to the world in evangelism and compassion, *(c)* encourages believers toward Christian maturity through discipleship, and *(d)* prepares women and men for Christian service through Christian higher education.

sponsibility is to be a witness, helping make Christlike disciples, in whatever nation we happen to be."⁴⁴

International leaders moved significantly to the forefront in the Church of the Nazarene in the early years of the twenty-first century. The 2005 General Assembly nearly elected someone from outside North America as general superintendent. Aguiar Valvassoura, pastor of the Campinas Central Church of the Nazarene in Brazil, the largest Nazarene church in the world, was on his way toward election when he withdrew from consideration in order to continue his ministries. He and his church were in the process of beginning a Nazarene university in the city. Valvassoura also served as superintendent of the Southeast Paulista District. He began pastoring the Campinas church in 1980 and by 2005 it had 6,159 members and had started twenty-four daughter churches.

The church's regional directors included several non-North Americans by this time. In the church's earlier years, George Sharpe, the British Isles district superintendent, from Scotland, had served as missionary superintendent for Africa. Under the system of regional directors revived by L. Guy Nees, Thomas W. Schofield, superintendent of the British Isles South District from 1967, became regional director for Europe and the Middle East in 1984. Richard Zanner, a German, was regional director in Africa until 2000. When Louis Bustle was elected to lead the World Mission department, his successor as regional director for South America was his colleague and associate Bruno Radi. Mario Zani, an Argentinean, served as regional director over Mexico and Central America from 1993 to 1999. Christian Sarmiento, a Colombian, served as director over the Mexico and Central America Region from 1999 to 2005, and then, upon Bruno Radi's sudden death, over South America. Gustavo Crocker, a leader from Guatemala, was selected to lead the Eurasia Region in 2004. By 2008 the regional directors included also Carlos Saenz, a native of Panama, serving the Mexico and Central America Region, and Eugenio Duarte, from the Cape Verde Islands, the Africa Region.⁴⁵

TWENTY-FOUR

Crossing Boundaries

Nazarenes spent more time crossing borders than drawing boundaries. Expansion beyond frontiers was the spirit that moved the church. The impact of becoming an international church was clearly being felt. With unprecedented expansion and growth came the pressing need for structures that were both flexible and strong.[1]

CROSSING NATIONAL BOUNDARIES

The Nazarenes' twenty-first-century mission was grounded in powerful religious legacies stemming from Europe and England as well as from North America. Anglican, Puritan, Methodist, and Holiness roots provided successive models and undercurrents in the Nazarene story. Like Anglicans, Nazarenes respected tradition, history, and authority. Like Puritans Nazarenes sought congregational order and communal discipline shaped by Scripture. Like early Methodists and contemporary evangelicals, Nazarenes wanted reasonable enthusiasm and worship infused by vital and living faith. Like their Holiness Movement forbears and Pentecostal contemporaries, Nazarenes wanted malleable church structures able to be moved by the Spirit.[2]

As a people called to holiness, Nazarenes could not remain comfortable within Western parochialism. Nazarenes moved beyond the assumption that what happened in the West was normative for the making and telling of the gospel story. The church explored ways of organizing itself as a global family. Internationalization signified consciousness of a world made up of many national identities, and hope that ethnocentrism could be transcended while respecting cultures and celebrating diversity. The success of missions fueled this hope.[3]

E. S. Phillips, as executive secretary for World Missions, recommended in his 1972 quadrennial report: "The administrative bodies of the church must be internationalized. That portion of the church which lives overseas, about one out of five, and which is growing at a rate twice that of the church in

North America, must be given full voice in the councils of the church." He advocated a "clear doctrinal position, which can be worked out across diverse cultural settings" and "flexibility in both administration and programming to meet rapid changes in the world." The gospel needed to be *contextualized* and the programs of the church internationalized. Phillips pointedly stated: "Care must be constantly exercised these next 28 years to extricate the gospel we preach from Western or Americanized or Europeanized cultural or social patterns. If racism and nationalism are issues, as indeed they are, it will be of critical importance to 'universalize' the content of the message and the style of its presentation."[4] In January 1975 professor of missions Paul Orjala spoke of two organizational options for the church: "separate, autonomous national churches in each country with a loose world fellowship" or a "world fellowship of districts which are bound together by structural ties for the purpose of achieving a common goal to evangelize the world for Christ and holiness." His conviction was that even before 1908 those who became Nazarenes had possessed an international "scope and spirit" that lent itself to the second option. Now this "scope and spirit" had to be translated into "structure."[5]

Recognizing the need to sort through these issues, in 1976 the Board of General Superintendents took various actions. In 1976 it recommended, and the General Assembly approved, the appointment of a Commission on Internationalization. It was "to function for the coming quinquennium for the purpose of studying means by which the next stage of internationalization might be implemented." The same assembly created three Intercontinental Zones: Euro-Africa (Europe, the Middle-East, and Africa); Oceania-Asia (the South Pacific and Asia, including China); and Hispanic America (Mexico, Central America, the Caribbean, and South America). In January 1978 fifty-two leaders from thirty-five countries assembled in Kansas City for the first international district superintendents' conference. Many of these leaders had been involved prior to this in youth congresses and institutes. The district superintendents traveled together by bus to the Mid-Quadrennial Evangelism Conference in Oklahoma City.[6]

Nazarene Youth International (as the NYPS was renamed in 1976) contributed greatly to internationalization. In 1978 twenty-five hundred young people from sixty-eight nations converged on Estes Park, Colorado, for the sixth Nazarene World Youth Conference. This resulted from denominational response to the sociocultural revolution in North America in those years that produced a generation of young people suspicious of institutions and vibrant with a new wave of idealism. Paul Skiles aimed to channel the energies of youth into the mission of the church. Through Youth in Mission, enthusiastic and committed young leaders became directly engaged in world mission. In equipping youth to be "global Christians" Nazarene youth leaders aimed to see them become "followers of Jesus Christ who have a passion for God and His mission in the world and are actively seeking ways in which to become involved in that mission."[7]

The 1980 General Assembly articulated more specifically the process toward internationalization. The general secretary reported that during "the past four years we have functioned for the first time with a world-wide data base" and that this "reflected the larger concept of internationalization of the Church."[8] Delegates expressed a strong commitment to be a global church and at the same time to maintain "nonnegotiable core values, and, at the center of these values, entire sanctification." The assembly offered a "nonsymmetrical structure" for the global church. Delegates agreed on the importance of flexibility and adaptability. The church established a new level of leadership to accommodate these needs. The General Assembly "resolved that a new chapter in church government be entered between district and general government to describe the purpose and functions of regions in the Church of the Nazarene organization," approved the term "region" rather than "zone," and divided the three "zones" into six "regions": Africa; Asia and the Orient; Europe and the Middle East; Mexico, Central America, and the Caribbean; South America; and the South Pacific. This was perceived as a major step in restructuring the denomination, with attendant debates over whether the relationship between international regions would result in the "federalization" of the church. The 1980 General Assembly also appointed a second Commission on Internationalization.[9]

In 1982 Jerald Johnson published *The International Experience*, which summarized his aspirations for the church. Johnson claimed that "the word internationalization should be understood as no more than a contemporary application of the principles of the Great Commission." He continued, "Accepting each other as equals in the Church of the Nazarene is as critical to the continued development of the Church, today, as it was to the early Christians in Jerusalem." He concluded, "Brotherhood equal and worldwide is a unique quality of the holiness message we preach."[10]

Voices from outside North America reflected upon the church's goals. Richard Zanner advised the church to study and address real cultural, philosophical, and psychological differences among Nazarenes, as well as their socioeconomic and political contexts. Representation, finances, structure, program, and "cultural-based ethics" would have to be worked out, without tying "money" to "authority," Zanner advised.[11] David Tarrant, district superintendent of the British Isles North District, suggested that it was "the North American church, not the church around the world," that needed to be internationalized. The church needed to resist being seen as or becoming "an American based multinational corporation."[12]

The sense of the church as a global body was evident locally. As the regions organized, regional gatherings were reminiscent of the energy and enthusiasm of earlier general assemblies. Africa Regional Director Zanner wanted even small churches to recognize their place in these "big picture" events. "A tree does not only consist of a trunk and large branches; a tree has small twigs with leaves, buds and blossoms," Zanner believed. "All are a part, and all contribute for it to be a healthy tree."[13] Brazilian Nazarenes were proud of being "part of something beyond the national boundaries as part of fulfilling the Great Commission." It was, noticed one missionary, common in Brazil to see on church letterheads or painted on church vans: "The Church of the Nazarene, functioning in 136 countries." The smallest congregations were "aware and proud to be a part of an international body."[14]

Recommendations from the Commission on Internationalization to the 1985 General Assembly included one that regional directors (where possible) be appointed from the regions in which they were born. The commission asserted that the "further development of regional identities and relationships [was] imperative. This concept may well be one of the most contributive factors toward the bonding of all areas of the church in a truly international body." The commission endorsed the concept of "the General Assembly as the final legislative authority of the church," but provided for "cultural adaptations of local, district, and regional church government procedures." The commission hoped that "true internationalization [would] provide a proper balance between fiscal privilege and responsibility."[15]

The 1985 General Assembly led further in the direction of strengthening the privileges and responsibilities of districts. By the time of General Assembly twenty districts had achieved "regular" district status. Delegates redefined the stages of district development: Phase 1 (Pioneer), Phase 2 (National Mission), Phase 3 (Mission), and Phase 4 (Regular). The assembly approved regional councils and conferences, and national administrative boards, when necessary, "to administer the business and to be "the established authority of the Church of the Nazarene."[16]

The Commission on Internationalization that met between 1985 and 1989 concluded that the local church is and would remain the fundamental unit of the denomination and that, in polity, democracy was to characterize Nazarene church government at all levels. The commission advised the

Church of the Nazarene to remain a denomination of districts (not nations). Regional structures were only to "contribute to better communication and understanding between districts and the general church." Regional offices were to guide, facilitate, and coordinate. The church's goal should be to "provide general church servicing and supervision to all districts without distinction." Whenever possible, the commission concluded, district and regional boundaries should follow geographic rather than ethnic or racial lines. Because regions were multicultural, the commission urged subregions for better administration.[17] The 1989 General Assembly stated three bases or principles for internationalization: (1) shared mission; (2) national identity; and (3) indigenization. Yet the church was unsure about moving in the direction of regional governments. Some opposed the solidification of a new tier of leadership. Already, regional directors were perceived by some to have as much or more authority within their regions as general superintendents. The 1989 General Assembly reduced the number of district categories from four to three: Phase 1—Pioneer Area/District; Phase 2—Mission District; Phase 3—Regular District. At the same time it disavowed a "commonwealth" or "federalization" of the church in favor of the concept of a "global family." Facing the breakup of apartheid in South Africa, the General Assembly affirmed: "no district shall be constituted on the basis of ethnicity, but rather on the basis of geography." It approved a U.S.A. National Board and continued the Internationalization Commission under the name "Commission on the International Church." The assembly established the International Board of Education, which subsumed the Department of Education and the World Mission Committee on Theological Education (WOMEC).[18]

Delegates approved a new Article of Faith on "The Church." For several years, Nazarenes had attempted to arrive at a clearer understanding of the church that might guide them on issues of structure. The article that found its way into the Nazarene *Manual* defined the church as "the community that confesses Jesus Christ as Lord, the covenant people of God made new in Christ, the Body of Christ called together by the Holy Spirit through the Word." The church was "a historical reality, which organizes itself in culturally conditioned forms; exists both as local congregations and as a universal body; sets apart persons called by God for specific ministries."[19] Thus, while the General Assembly recognized the importance of the local church (and elected two pastors as general superintendents), it also recognized that the church was more than this.[20]

The Commission on the International Church that met between 1989 and 1993 faced a difficult task. A 1989 Gallup survey posed the question of internationalization to American Nazarene clergy, laity, and district superintendents. The laity overwhelmingly supported the idea that "everyone should be treated equally everywhere" in the church. From an organizational and structural point of view, however, the survey found, Nazarenes frequently understood "internationalization" as something done by the American church to make it easier for non-American cultures to function within the denominational structure. At the leadership level, where there was greater concern over finances and control, there were more reservations about the practical possibility of building "one church around the world." The survey concluded: "If there is one issue on which district superintendents, pastors, and the laity are most apart it is internationalization."[21] The commission focused on the concept of mission and reaffirmed that rather than a federated group of national churches, the Church of the Nazarene was an international church. The commission believed that Nazarenes should find ways to preserve the "family" feeling of interrelated connectedness. The church should emphasize mission more than structures and recognize that structures should fit local necessities. It recommended that the church "disavow structures and conclusions that are built and based on a perception of the world as symmetrical." Rather than a "symmetrical cone," the church should embrace the "kaleidoscope of colors, cultures, geography, languages, [and] history" that made up the church. Therefore the commission did "not attempt to construct an architecture of internationalization with rigid criteria or patterns or structures."[22]

In 1993 the *Manual* defined the role of the regional director "to work in harmony with the policies and practices of the Church of the Nazarene giving leadership to the districts, churches, and institutions of said region in fulfillment of the mission, strategies, and program of the church." Each regional director was "administratively accountable to the World Mission Division, and the General Board, and in jurisdictional matters, accountable to the Board of General Superintendents."[23] The regional directors distributed World Mission funds and presided over district assemblies in the absence of a general superintendent.

In 1994 Jerald Johnson reminded the church that its structure had to bend with new growth. The traps of comparison or condescension between "haves" and "have-nots" were to be avoided. "For all time an exclusive, cultural religion would have to be rejected." Equal participation and representation by all Nazarenes everywhere was the goal. "One thing is certain," Johnson believed, "the Church of the Nazarene is not destined to smallness identified by bigotry and self-centeredness." Inclusiveness and adaptability were primary values.[24] The mission and objectives of the church, Johnson said, were "to respond to the great Commission of Christ 'to go and make disciples of all nations.' Our key objective is to advance God's kingdom by the preservation and propagation of Christian holiness as set forth in Scripture."[25]

In 1997 the church redefined "region" and identified fifteen world regions. These included the eight educational zones in the United States and the one in Canada as "regions." In the regions outside North America field directors served under regional directors.

In 1976 the total amount raised for all purposes by the denomination was $51.4 million, and in 1997 it had increased tenfold to $586.9 million, yet 92 percent of this was raised by North American Nazarenes. The challenge was how to balance local, district, regional, and international needs. About 90 percent of the World Evangelism Fund ($37 million in 1999) was provided by the North American church, and of this, fewer than five hundred local churches were responsible for 50 percent of the money raised. "This reminds me of the elephant in the room syndrome," thought Russell Bredholt. The elephant "doesn't need too much attention, but it should not be ignored either."[26] Leaders needed savvy as well as sensitivity to strengthen the bonds that united the church. They faced the challenge of leading a rapidly expanding community and finding institutional processes that embodied historic values.[27]

The words "internationalization" and "globalization" gained currency in quite close sequence. Mario Zani, in 1999, in his induction as professor of missions at NTS, clarified their meanings and rooted them in the biblical concept of *koinonia,* the fellowship "that transcended any differences, assignments, or titles." *Koinonia* spoke not of agendas and strategies so much as interacting with cultures different from one's own, through joy and frustration, through sounds and signs and working together, until "goodwill communication" was established.[28] By "globalization," Zani continued, "is meant that process by which we become sensitized and responsive to the multicultural, multi-lingual, multi-ethnic, and multi-national world of which we are a part. The process begins with one's own context but has worldwide implications. That process is vitally important for all of us who care deeply about the effective communication of the Gospel and about fulfilling the Great Commission."[29] Internationalization implied strategies and agreed administrative policies often managed with restrictions rather than with openness, Zani observed. "International" implicitly recognized the importance of national units. Zani approved the word "globalization" as more spontaneous and more candid, with "less predetermined structural commissions or legislation for implementation." Though the Church of the Nazarene was international from its conception, Zani said, it was not truly global.[30]

GENDER BOUNDARIES

The Church of the Nazarene always opened all of its ministries to women as well as men. In this Nazarenes differed from the broader evangelical subculture and surprised new members coming from fundamentalist backgrounds. However, in practice there was a decline in the numbers of active women pastors in the Church of the Nazarene. In 1975 women made up only 2 percent of Nazarene pastors, and this slipped to 1.7 percent in 1995. Among all credentialed clergy, women comprised 6.2 percent in 1975 and 6.7 percent in 1995.[31]

General Superintendent Greathouse, among others, lamented this situation. "It reflects," he noted, "the influx of teachings and theologies which are in basic disagreement with our historic biblical position." Greathouse appealed for young women graduates from Nazarene colleges to find places to serve the Lord in the church. He argued that "a woman who is filled with the Spirit and otherwise prepared to preach is fully entitled to a Christian pulpit." If Nazarenes in the beginning were "revolutionaries who made all clergy and lay offices open to women," by the end of the century this pathway required, Greathouse observed, pioneering all over again.[32]

Melvin Shrout advocated "the return of the deaconess" as a pathway to the recovery of partnership in ministry for women. Historically deaconesses engaged in compassionate ministries. In 1983, 113 consecrated deaconesses were on assembly rolls church-wide. Instead, the 1985 General Assembly widened the ministry to include "deacons," both men and women.[33]

The Nazarene World Missionary Society, in spite of its having allowed men to join, remained a preserve for women in the denomination—the only general church organization in which women had a significant voice. Wanda Knox served as general secretary of the NWMS following the retirement of Mary Scott in 1975. Knox had, with her husband, pioneered the Nazarene work in Papua New Guinea, and she had returned to the country after his death. Phyllis Hartley Brown Perkins followed Knox in 1980. Perkins had served as a missionary to Japan in the 1960s. Perkins resigned in 1985 to teach at Nazarene Bible College, where she became academic dean. The church then chose Nina Gunter to be general director (as the position was now called). In 2001, the NWMS, following the lead of the Young People's Society, changed its name to Nazarene Missions International.[34]

While the missionary society provided a warm enclave for women, leadership opportunities elsewhere waned. Jane Brewington, an elder in the Church of the Nazarene, came to the 1993 General Assembly to plead that "women who love the church and the Lord Jesus Christ" be given permission "to help." Her experience was that any woman who questioned male authority in the church was labeled as having "an attitude." There was a "glass ceiling," she said, "suffocating godly women called to ministry." Clearly women were not trusted in leadership beyond the level of associates to men, Brewington believed, in spite of being acknowledged as "equally called."[35] Floyd Disney concurred. He appealed to Nazarenes to discard "an unwritten rule against calling women pastors and evangelists." On some districts the Advisory Boards remained an "ecclesiastical 'old boys' club."[36] "Why should the church accept only the women with extra-ordinary abilities?" Rebecca Laird wondered. "Men professing a call who have mediocre abilities have a right to be called by churches or accepted as theological educators, but a woman has to be extra-ordinary?"[37] Similarly, Nazarene Theological Seminary President Gordon Wetmore was troubled that though women who attended NTS came with the clear call of God "to be pastors, evangelists, chaplains, missionaries" and take "other specific leadership roles" and often achieved top results in seminary classes, they were "not placed as pastors in our local congregations." Some transferred to other denominations.[38]

In response, 103 Nazarenes attended the first International Conference for Wesleyan/Holiness Clergywomen in April 1994. "If instead of assigning our women preachers only to tiny churches already under a death sentence, we would set their spiritual vitality loose in the mainstream of the faith community, we just might see a significant renewal of the movement," commented one denominational executive. Nina Gunter declared that the call to women came "not from the church, the bishop, the moderator, the district superintendent, but from God."[39]

While the 1998 Multicultural Ministries Conference focused on racial reconciliation, Kim Lundell, a Korean woman pastor, urged the assembly to embrace the Church of the Nazarene's early history by giving women an equal place in ministry. "Women know how to nourish, feed, and give birth to babies." The same principles, she said, "can be applied spiritually to ministry."[40]

Janine Metcalf agreed. "District superintendents, pastors, and laity need tools to educate the church about our century-old polity of mutuality in ministry. I am seeing signs of progress, but I continue to pray and keep our leaders' feet to the fire." Though women "continue to receive glowing endorsements from our general superintendents and a growing number of division leaders," Metcalf detailed the hidden resistance in high and low places to women, unless they were willing to fill secondary roles. Metcalf had been a young TV news reporter in the 1970s when she responded to the gospel under the ministry of Pastor Earl Lee and Hazel Crutcher Lee at Pasadena First Church of the Nazarene.[41]

Women found it easier to enter other ministries. Rebecca Laird Christiansen, as a freelance writer and editor, chronicled the story of the first generation of Nazarene ordained women. Several women taught religion in North American Nazarene colleges at the turn of the century. Diane LeClerc pastored in Maine, earned a Ph.D. at Drew, and taught historical theology and preaching at NNU. She was president of the Wesleyan Theological Society 2007-8.[42]

In contrast to the rather dismal prospects for women in the United States, in places such as the Caribbean, Mozambique, Swaziland, Kenya, the Philippines, Haiti, and Switzerland women were prominent in ministry and leadership. The Nazarene Church in Korea ordained its first woman, Song Jung-mahn, in 1994, and other countries were making further strides.[43]

Rosa Lee

In 1990 Rosa Lee was appointed superintendent of the Leeward/Virgin Islands District, thus becoming the first woman district superintendent in the church since Elsie Wallace seventy years before. General Superintendent Donald Owens made the appointment. Lee had become pastor of the Beacon Light Church of the Nazarene in Antigua, Leeward Islands, following her husband's death in 1979. Formerly members of the Pilgrim Holiness Church, the Lees had planted this church and had brought it into affiliation with the Church of the Nazarene. Made up of nine churches and six hundred members, the district, under her leadership, became self-supporting and grew to nearly twelve hundred members. She refused to allow churches needing repair to wait until Work and Witness teams arrived. Several churches started compassionate ministries. Lee retired in 1999.[44]

As pastor of the Central Church in Maputo, Mozambique, from 1991, Bessie Tshambe emphasized outreach and evangelism. Membership grew to fifteen hundred, with Sunday morning attendance topping twenty-five hundred, and the church planted five daughter churches. Similarly, Lucinda Tamayo pastored a church of several hundred in Taytay, Rizal, on the outskirts of Metro Manila, Philippines.[45]

Key women served Nazarene schools abroad. Jeanine van Beek served as president of the Nazarene School in Haiti and then became rector of the European Nazarene Bible College. She was followed at ENBC (renamed

European Nazarene College) by Dr. Corlis McGee. Leah Marangu, a Kenyan who had earned a Ph.D. at Iowa State University, was influential in the founding of Africa Nazarene University and served as vice-chancellor. In the Philippines, Dr. Julie Macainan Detalo served as president of Visayan Nazarene Bible College from 1987.[46]

In South America, Ruth Arce, Susanna Garcia, and Nelda Aurora Calvo de Saez each served as a district superintendent. Arce attended the Wesleyan Institute in Medellin, Colombia, and because a pastor in the Wesleyan Church. In 1984 she shifted to the Church of the Nazarene and continued her studies at the Nazarene school in Quito, Ecuador, completing bachelor's and master's degrees. In several places in her ministry, she preached in prisons. In 1999 she became an extension education coordinator for the South-Central Colombia District and also taught at the school in Quito. After a few years, she became district superintendent for the South Colombia District. In Argentina, Nelda Aurora Calvo de Saez was a secular school teacher before being entirely sanctified in 1979. Gradually she felt a call to ministry. In 1990 she graduated from a theology course at the Nazarene seminary in Pilar, Argentina. She then taught among the Tobas Indians. In 1993 she was ordained. She continued studies in Ecuador and earned a master's degree in missions. Eventually, she earned a doctor of ministry degree. By this time, she was working in extension education in Panama. In 2000 she became superintendent of the Central District, during which time she planted two churches among the Kuna Indians. In 2006 she became superintendent of the West Buenos Aires District. Also in Argentina, Susanna Garcia, while herself a new convert, with her husband, at the urging of Bruno Radi, planted a church in Ceibas. She also went to the Nazarene seminary in Argentina and was ordained in 1999. In 2006 she became a district superintendent.

With the election of Josie Owens as district superintendent of the New England District in 2004, of Corlis McGee as president of ENC in 2005, and of Nina Gunter as general superintendent in 2005, Nazarenes placed women in key leadership roles in North America. Owens had pastored the Second Church of the Nazarene in Dorchester, Massachusetts, prior to her election and earned a doctorate in education at Boston University.[47]

In 2007, Asian women also assumed top leadership positions in India and Japan—two countries where women in ministry were rare. In March, Motoko Matsuda was elected district superintendent in Japan. She had pastored the Church of the Nazarene in Hiroshima for fifteen years. Kim Singson became district superintendent of the Northeast India District in May of the same year. She and her husband, who had died in 2001, had planted thirty-eight churches.⁴⁸

CROSSING BOUNDARIES IN AFRICA

Richard Zanner served from 1980 to 2000 as director of the Africa Region. Zanner, born in Germany, immigrated to South Africa in 1953. He married a Nazarene and enrolled in the Bible college. When Zanner visited Germany, Jerald Johnson persuaded him to stay and pastor. For nine years Zanner pastored the Frankfurt Church of the Nazarene. In 1969 he was appointed superintendent of the Middle-Europe District. Returning to Africa, under Zanner's leadership of the region, Nazarene membership in Africa grew from 29,553 in 1980 to 216,934 in 2000.⁴⁹

Richard Zanner

The nations on the Africa Region when it was established included Cape Verde, Malawi, Mozambique, Namibia, Nigeria, South Africa, Swaziland, Zambia, and Zimbabwe. In the 1980s the church entered five additional African nations: Botswana (1984), Kenya (1985), Côte d'Ivoire (1987), Senegal (1988), and Uganda (1988).⁵⁰

In 1984 the Africa Nazarene Theological College of Southern Africa was established through a merger of three ethnically segregated campuses from Florida, Siteki, and Port Elizabeth, with the new campus being in the Muldersdrift area on the West Rand, in Gauteng.⁵¹

The church made significant moves in Nigeria. In 1988, sixty-five hundred members of a Nigerian group that had registered themselves as the Church of the Nazarene in 1964 officially joined the denomination. This group probably had roots in the World-Wide Missions agency of Basil Miller, which employed former Nazarene missionaries. The merger represented the largest of one group with the Church of the Nazarene since Pilot Point. The Nigerian church was led by Jeremiah Ekaidem, who became superintendent of the South East Nigeria District. In 2000, Nazarene membership in Nigeria numbered eighty-four hundred.⁵²

During the 1990s the church entered eighteen African nations: the Democratic Republic of the Congo (1990), Ghana (1990), Liberia (1990), Rwanda (1990), Tanzania (1990), Angola (1992), Ethiopia (1992), Eritrea (1993), Lesotho (1993), Madagascar (1993), Burkina Faso (1997), Congo

(1997), Sao Tome (1997), Benin (1998), Togo (1998), Burundi (1999), Cameroon (1999), and Gabon (1999).⁵³

The "key objective of the Church of the Nazarene on the African Region," read the region's 1993 Mission Statement, was to "minister on the basis of God's Word to the spiritual needs of every individual within the African region, irrespective of religious, ethnical, social, political, or economical origins. Physical and material needs were to be kept in perspective at all times since the Bible clearly directs its message to the whole person, body, mind, and spirit."⁵⁴ Long-serving missionary (and the son of missionaries to Africa) Ted Esselstyn noted the shift from discipling new converts before membership to discipling converts after membership. This was how, in Esselstyn's estimation, the Africans had reaped such "harvest" in the last two decades of the twentieth century. Esselstyn asked whether general conferences of the church should not deal with important regional concerns such as witchcraft, demons, and polygamy. Reflecting upon the church's slowness to respond to segregation, he also wondered when and how the church should get involved in sociopolitical public issues. In Rwanda more than forty Nazarene pastors had been killed.⁵⁵

After the turn of the century, the Church of the Nazarene entered Equatorial Guinea, Reunion, Guinea-Bissau, Sudan, and Sierra Leone.

CROSSING BOUNDARIES IN THE ASIA-PACIFIC REGION

The 1980 General Assembly established the Asia and South Pacific regions. In 1981 Donald Owens, then teaching at NTS in Kansas City, became regional director of the Asia Region. It included India, Taiwan, Hong Kong, Japan, Korea, and the Philippines. Regional conferences began with one held in Seoul, Korea, in April 1983. At the time there were 599 churches and 54,253 members on the region. The South Pacific Region included Australia, New Zealand, Papua New Guinea, Samoa, and Indonesia. It was led by Darrell Teare, who also, from 1979 to 1994, served as superintendent of the Hawaii District.

The church entered Myanmar (Burma) in 1983 through the efforts of Robin Seia, a Burmese. Seia had become a Nazarene while attending Fuller Theological Seminary in Pasadena, California, through contacts with retired Nazarene missionaries at Casa Robles, including Louise Robinson Chapman and John Pattee. The Burmese government did not allow missionaries, but Seia was able to register the church. The district, organized in 1985, had grown to fourteen hundred members and fifteen churches by 2000.

In 1985, when George Rench replaced Owens, the South Pacific Region merged with the Asia Region, and India became part of the newly designated Eurasia Region. Rench had begun his missionary career in Taiwan in 1959 and had pioneered the work of the church in Indonesia in 1971. Under Rench's regional leadership the church entered Thailand (1989), Cambodia (1992), and the Solomon Islands (1992). Liuga Faumui, a Nazarene layman from Samoa who served with the United Nations, helped the church begin ministries in several countries.[56]

It seemed unlikely that the Church of the Nazarene would have been able to enter Thailand, which controlled the number of missionaries allowed to work in the country. Samuel Yangmi, who had graduated from MidAmerica Nazarene College in 1984, was working in northern Thailand with the Asia Christian Mission, which had "slots" it was not using of which Yangmi hoped the Church of the Nazarene could avail. With the approval of the Japanese church, sale from Nazarene property in Japan went to finance the opening of the work in Thailand. Rench selected Mike McCarty, with whom he had served in Indonesia, to begin the work in Thailand. McCarty centered upon Bangkok, but the church grew more quickly among the tribal people in the north. Yangmi, an American citizen who had been born in Southern China, joined the Nazarene mission in 1993 and led the thriving MaeTang Tribal Children's Home in the north. It ministered primarily to tribal Lahu children. In 1993 Rev. and Mrs. Park Hae-rim of Korea were appointed regional missionaries to Thailand, and later, when the Parks transferred to China ministries, the church appointed Tomo and Ceny Hirahara (he from Japan and she from the Philippines) to Thailand.[57]

The trend was moving away from dependency upon North American missionaries. Andrew Moime, an entrepreneurial Papua New Guinean pastor, pioneered the church's work in the Solomon Islands.

Rench died in 1993. He was succeeded by A. Brent Cobb, who had served ten years in Korea in the 1970s and, following that, had pastored on the West Coast. Under Cobb, the church entered "creative access" countries in the region and several Pacific island states, including Fiji and Palau in 1995, and Chuuk, Pohnpei, Saipan, Tonga, and Vanuatu all in 2000. The work in Chuuk began through the invitation of the governor of the island, who had become a Nazarene while studying in California. The first missionaries were Rex Ray and Perlita dela Peret, from the Philippines, who previously had served in Guam. Workers from both Papua New Guinea and Indonesia helped the church open work in the new country of East Timor in 2001.[58]

On August 13, 1996, a group of five Nazarenes (General Superintendent Owens, Regional Director Brent Cobb, New Delhi District Superintendent Vijah Singh, Gary Morsch, and Bob Helstrom) made an official visit to the Democratic People's Republic of Korea (North Korea). Singh, who had studied in South Korea and could speak Korean, had visited the country four months earlier to see that a grain shipment for thousands of flood victims, coordinated by Nazarene Compassionate Ministries, had reached the proper destination. A follow-up shipment of medicine sent jointly by NCM and Heart to Heart opened doors for Nazarenes to visit. The church prayed that North Korea's isolation policy would be abandoned and that Christianity and the Church of the Nazarene would be able to enter the country openly.[59]

CROSSING BOUNDARIES IN CANADA

Canada established its unique identity during these years. Between 1976 and 2000 the church in Canada grew from 8,083 to 12,200 members.

One of the most important markers for the Church of the Nazarene in Canada included the expansion of the Canadian National Board to reflect lay and pastoral voices and ideas. An executive board had been established by an act of the House of Commons in 1946 and was composed of the Canadian district superintendents. In 1976 one layperson from each district was added, and Robert Rimington of Calgary, Alberta, became the first "administrator" of the board. In 1989, additional laypersons and pastors from each district were added to the board.[60]

The national board initiated several self-studies and reports. These reflected an alignment of purpose and method among the five Canadian districts. Canadian Nazarenes, scattered across an immense continent, joined the Evangelical Fellowship of Canada in 1986, in order "to participate more formally in the evangelical life of Canada." It joined the Canadian Foodgrains Bank in 1988 "in order to have a cooperative means of meeting world-wide hunger need." Church policy was brought formally into line with Canadian law that regulated the transfer of funds to "foreign bodies." Canada opted to form its own pension plan for pastors and withdrew from the general church plan. A Long Range Planning Commission examined the health, effectiveness, and structure of the church. The Commission on the Ministry and the Commission on the Laity together with Cross Country Consultations outlined the roles of clergy and laity in the church in the twenty-first century. The Canadian churches maintained a "strong sense of theological conviction," and All-Canada Conferences as well kept the church united. The church constitution, changed in 1990-91, renamed the executive board the national board and the administrator the national director. The national board developed ministry guidelines that reflected Canadian viewpoints.[61]

"Target Toronto," 1989-91, was the response of the national board in Canada to the denominational Thrust to the Cities. The plan was conceived on the Canada Central District. Marjorie Osborne, lay member of the Canada Central District Advisory Board, directed the effort, which resulted in twenty-eight church plants, several compassion evangelism centers, and a family counseling program. The Wesley Christian Academy/Some Place Special Day Care institution was founded with Marjorie Serio as principal.[62]

In 1995, under President Riley Coulter, Canadian Nazarene College moved from Winnipeg, Manitoba, to Calgary, Alberta. One of the consequences was that it received recognition by the Province of Alberta as an approved private college with the ability to grant certain arts and sciences degrees. In 2003, the school united with the Alliance University College of the Christian and Missionary Alliance, forming Ambrose University.[63]

CROSSING BOUNDARIES IN THE CARIBBEAN

In 1982 James Hudson, who had served as missionary in Guatemala from 1952 to 1974 and then as a staff member in the World Mission Division, became the first area coordinator, serving the Asia, Latin America, and Caribbean zones. In 1982 Hudson established the Mexico, Central America, and Caribbean Region, with headquarters in Guatemala. In 1985, when this region was divided, Hudson became the first regional director for the Caribbean and established its headquarters in Miami. The Caribbean Region consisted of Antigua, the Bahamas, Barbados, Belize, Cuba, Dominica, the Dominican Republic, Grenada, Guyana, Haiti, Jamaica, Martinique, Puerto Rico, Saint Kitts-Nevis, Saint Lucia, Saint Vincent, Suriname, Trinidad and Tobago, and the Virgin Islands. The church entered Guadeloupe in 1986 and French Guiana in 1988.[64]

Following Hudson's retirement in 1993, Juan Vazquez Pla served as the interim regional director. The Quadrennial Report in 1993 indicated that the Caribbean Region had grown from 622 to 729 churches, with an increase in membership from 76,872 to 87,876. John Smee, who had served as a missionary to Jamaica in the 1970s and several years in key positions at the World Mission Division in Kansas City, was appointed Caribbean Region mission director in 1994. The church entered the islands of Saint Martin in 1994 and Aruba in 2000. By 2000, the region had grown to 119,000 members and 896 churches.[65]

Haitian Nazarenes continued to lead in membership, evangelism, and church planting. Regional educational institutions included Caribbean Nazarene Theological College in Trinidad, Instituto Biblica Nazareno in Cuba, Seminaire Theologique Nazareen d'Haiti, and Seminario Nazareno Dominicano in the Dominican Republic.[66]

CROSSING BOUNDARIES IN EURASIA

The Church of the Nazarene entered France in 1977, Switzerland in 1978, and Spain in 1981. L. Guy Nees served as both World Mission director and regional director for the Europe and Middle East Region from 1980 until 1982. In 1983 Thomas Schofield, district superintendent in the British Isles, was appointed regional director. Under Schofield, the Church of the Nazarene entered the Azores (1984), Cyprus (1985), Egypt (1985), and Ireland (1987). The work in Egypt began when pastors with small house churches in Cairo, Alexandria, the Suez, and elsewhere affiliated with the Church of the Nazarene. The Eurasia Region, as it was reconstituted in 1985, included not only Europe, including the British Isles, but North Africa, the Middle East, and South Asia (then including only India). The first Eurasia Regional Conference after the restructuring of the region in 1985 occurred at Fiesch in the Swiss Alps with about 230 people from nineteen districts. Between 1988 and 1992 the Eurasia Region grew from 288 to 574 churches and from 13,516 to 56,002 members.[67] Schofield served until his retirement in 1989 and was replaced by R. Franklin Cook. Cook's appointment coincided with the fall of the Berlin Wall, which immediately opened the possibilities to expand in new world areas, including the former East Germany and those countries formerly making up the Soviet Union. In 1989 Hermann Gschwandtner, a German pastor, became coordinator for Eastern Europe. He had started contacts with Christians in Eastern Europe, including East Germany and Hungary, even before the fall of the Berlin Wall. At the same time, Nicolaj Sawatsky, a German/Russian graduate of European Nazarene Bible College, became coordinator for Russian Radio and Literature. In rapid succession the church entered Romania, Russia, Ukraine, Albania, Bulgaria, Hungary, Kazakhstan, Croatia, Poland, Macedonia, Armenia, Greece, the Madeira Islands, Slovenia, and Moldova.

The church's official entry into Romania in 1992 followed a visit of German Nazarenes determined to take humanitarian aid to the country. They initiated "Rom-Aid," a holistic approach to ministry in the country. Eastern Nazarene College offered courses in Romanian culture. ENC students, under the direction of Professor Dorothy Tarrant, visited and studied in Romania and, at the same time, engaged in compassionate service. In 2000, there were seventy-three Nazarene members in Romania.[68]

Gschwandtner and Sawatsky registered the Church of the Nazarene in Russia. In 1992, Chuck and Carla Sundberg arrived in Moscow as missionaries. Nazarene Compassionate Ministries accompanied the church. Various evangelism teams assisted the Sundbergs as they reached out, especially, to youth, and by the end of the year, a church had begun. In 2000, there were five Nazarene churches and 146 members in Russia.[69]

In addition to these European countries, the church began work in Bangladesh, Pakistan, Nepal, Sri Lanka, Turkey, Jordan, Lebanon, Syria, and Iraq.

Once breaking out of the old Maharashtra area where the church had begun work in India by comity arrangements, the Church of the Nazarene expanded across the subcontinent. The Tamil Nadu District, the first district in the south, began in 1981, and the Karnataka-Andhra Pradesh District, also in the south, a year later. Both of these were under the leadership of veteran missionary Bronell Greer and grew with the help of the South India Biblical Seminary, which the denomination supported cooperatively with other Holiness churches.[70]

The church in India expanded most dramatically, however, under the leadership of Vijai Singh. Singh had worked as an evangelist with the Methodists in India from 1969 to 1975, when he went to South Korea for further studies. While Singh was studying for a master of theology degree in a Presbyterian Seminary in Korea, Nazarene missionary Brent Cobb persuaded him to join the Church of the Nazarene. Singh returned to India in 1983 and began working with John and Doris Anderson, the Nazarene missionaries stationed in New Delhi, and the four churches then making up the New Delhi District. By the end of the year he had started a Korean church in India. Soon Singh lured various independent Indian churches, pastors, and evangelists, all interested in the doctrine of holiness, into the Church of the Nazarene. Singh became district superintendent in 1985 and expanded the church's reach across north India. By 1990 the district had seventeen thousand members and was the largest district in the denomination. In the previous year, forty-six churches had been organized and seven thousand new Nazarenes accepted into membership. In 2000, there were 51,500 Nazarene members throughout India.[71]

The church did not or could not station missionaries in several South Asian countries. When the denomination entered Bangladesh it actually was reentering an area that it had left in the 1930s when it had closed its field in eastern India. In what was now Bangladesh, it found some who still remembered the Church of the Nazarene. These included Samed Choudhury, who had been ordained by General Superintendents Goodwin and Williams in 1930. The Church of the Nazarene in Bangladesh included many compassionate ministries. Sukamal Biswas served as the district superintendent. There were fourteen hundred Nazarene members in Bangladesh in 2000.[72]

The church began in Pakistan by building upon an existing evangelical work of several congregations and five hundred members centered in Lahore, and upon Nazarene compassionate ministries.[73]

The church opened work in Sri Lanka after C. S. Dhas, superintendent of the Eastern Tamil Nadu District in India, gathered some Christians from warring Sinhale and Tamil ethnic groups together in *JESUS* film teams. That the team could work together was as much a testimony to the gospel as the film itself.[74]

On the other side of the region, new faculty members Kent Brower, Tom Noble, and Herbert McGonigle pushed the Nazarene school in Great Britain into the forefront of theological education. The school's motto remained: "Scholarship on Fire." The first bachelor of divinity candidates graduated in 1982. During 1989-90 the school took final steps toward formal membership as an Associated Institution of the Council for Academic Awards. In 1990 the college changed its name from British Isles Nazarene College to Nazarene Theological College. The school took a significant step on July 27, 1992, when affiliation with the University of Manchester was approved by both institutions. An increase in enrolment from 35 in 1976 to 230 in 2001 gave indication of the strides made in the strength of the institution. By the latter year, NTC was offering B.A., M.A., master of philosophy, and Ph.D. programs in affiliation with the University of Manchester.[75]

The region established a European Educational Council under Cook and Regional Education Coordinator John Haines. European Nazarene Bible College in Büsingen, Switzerland, responded to the collapse of the Berlin Wall by establishing various extension centers. Corlis McGee became rector in 1998. Nazarene Bible College in India decentralized and with a roster of dozens of faculty members taught courses across the continent.[76]

CROSSING BOUNDARIES IN MEXICO AND CENTRAL AMERICA

James Hudson served Mexico and Central America as well as the Caribbean Region as director from 1985 to 1989. Jerry Porter served as MAC regional director from 1989 to 1993. Mario Zani, an Argentinean, succeeded him, serving until 1999. He was followed by Christian Sarmiento, the first convert of the Church of the Nazarene in Colombia. Sarmiento had served as a missionary to Bolivia, as director of theological education in the South America Region, and in the Caribbean regional office. The countries on the region included Costa Rica, El Salvador, Guatemala, Honduras, Mexico, Nicaragua, and Panama.[77]

In 1993 the seminary in Costa Rica, which served Spanish-speaking students from three regions, was granted university status and began graduate programs. However, in 1995 the school's Board of Trustees decided to decentralize the graduate program, and the name of the school reverted to its previous one, Seminario Nazareno de las Americas.[78]

Other educational providers on the region included Escuela Biblica Nazarena de la Huasteca, Mexico; Instituto Biblico Nazareno, Guatemala; Instituto Biblico Nazareno del Noroeste, Baja California, Mexico; Instituto Biblico Nazareno del Sureste, Mexico; Seminario Nazareno Mexicano, Mexico; and Seminario Teologico Nazareno de Guatemala. Many developed extension education for ministers. From 1994 to 1997 lay leadership training and Impacto evangelism reaped gains in the number of churches, which grew from 641 to 977 and, in members, from 59,104 to 77,982.[79]

CROSSING BOUNDARIES IN SOUTH AMERICA

Louie Bustle, who had pioneered the work of the Church of the Nazarene in the Dominican Republic in 1975, became South America regional director in 1985. The first regional council was held in 1987 in Campinas, Brazil. In 1993 the region reported a quadrennial increase in membership from 49,150 to 80,408, and in number of churches from 692 to 1,232. By 2000, membership on the region reached 141,000, worshipping in 1,775 churches. The countries in the region included Argentina, Bolivia, Brazil, Chile, Colombia, Ecuador, Paraguay, Peru, Uruguay, and Venezuela.[80]

Venezuela was the last remaining Spanish-speaking country in America for the church to enter. In 1982, in anticipation of the denomination's seventy-fifth anniversary, the Missionary Society had a goal of $200,000 to begin the church in Venezuela. "La Hora Nazarena," which had been broadcast into the country, prepared the way. L. Guy Nees chose William and Juanita Porter, veteran missionaries to Puerto Rico, to start the work. By 1985, the church had given nearly $600,000 for the work in Venezuela.[81]

In 1993, when Bustle was chosen World Mission director, Bruno Radi (Radziszewski), his protégé, became regional director. Radi, an Argentinean born in Italy, had been a pastor, evangelist, field director, and coordinator

Bruno Radi

of evangelism. Radi continued with the "each one reach one" campaign that he and Bustle had devised. At the South America Regional Evangelism Conference in 1995 Radi reported that the region had planted more than twelve hundred churches during the previous twelve years. South American churches used the "each one win one, each one train one, each one plant one" strategy for evangelism and church growth. Membership in Brazil rose 60 percent between 1993 and 1997. Extension education for clergy blossomed. In the late 1990s the JESUS Film Project augmented church planting.[82]

CROSSING EDUCATIONAL FRONTIERS

One of the church's strongest global links was its system of education. In 1970 Edward S. Mann, the former president of Eastern Nazarene College, became general secretary for the Department of Education. He served until his retirement in 1979. In 1972 the General Assembly expanded the duties of the department to include the Course of Study for ministers. NTS Professor Richard S. Taylor worked with Mann to develop and monitor ministerial studies. From 1979 to 1987 Mark R. Moore, former president of Trevecca, served as executive secretary. The name of the department changed from Department of Education and Ministry to Department of Education Services. In 1985 the care for the ministers' Course of Study transferred to the Department of Evangelism. From 1987 to 1989 Willis Snowbarger, who had served in a similar position from 1965 to 1970, returned as acting secretary for Education Services.[83]

Meanwhile, unconnected with the Department of Education, in the mid-1970s Jerald Johnson called into being the World Mission Education Committee (WOMEC). WOMEC's goal was to "upgrade and standardize" the educational program in the World Mission areas of the church. It supervised the educational work in the world regions under World Mission. At the time, there were thirty-eight ministerial educational institutions: eleven in Africa, ten in Asia and the South Pacific, six in South America, five in Mexico and Central America, three in the Caribbean, and two in Eurasia. Of these, eighteen used English as the language of instruction and twelve used Spanish. WOMEC introduced two manuals for the orientation and operation of seminaries and Bible colleges: the *Basic Accreditation Manual* and *A Guide to Self-Evaluation*.[84]

In 1985 the General Board set up an Education Commission to "engage in in-depth study of the total educational needs of the church and assess the ability of the present educational institutions to meet these needs."[85] The Education Commission agreed that "education in the Church of the Nazarene, rooted in the biblical and theological commitments of the Wesleyan and Holiness movements and accountable to the stated mission of the denomination, aims to guide those who look to it in accepting, in nurturing, and in expressing in service to church and world consistent and coherent Christian understandings of social and individual life."[86]

The 1989 General Assembly, on the basis of the Education Commission Report, created the International Board of Education (IBOE) to replace and succeed WOMEC as well as the denomination's Department of Education Services. The purpose of the IBOE, as the commission saw it, was "to function as the general church advocate for educational institutions in the Church of the Nazarene worldwide." The commission proposed that the administrator of the board be called the commissioner of education. The General Assembly charged the IBOE office with providing "such support services as consulting, advising, recommending, coordinating, and accrediting in the areas of curriculum, improvement of instruction, professional development, administrative procedures, personnel needs and placement, legal advice, financial counseling, theological reflection, policy formulation, mission clarification, and strategic planning."[87] The IBOE was to advise and support all Nazarene baccalaureate- and graduate-level institutions worldwide. Board members were to include six elected members (at least four of whom were to have had cross-cultural perspective and experience as educators), and four by virtue of their offices—the two education representatives on the General Board, the World Mission Division director, and the commissioner of education.

In 1989 Stephen W. Nease left the presidency of Eastern Nazarene College to become the IBOE's first commissioner. By 1993 IBOE was serving thirty-six undergraduate- and graduate-level institutions throughout the international church. The IBOE produced *Guidelines for Recognition of Undergraduate and Graduate Level Institutions of the Church of the Nazarene*. Nease served until 1994.[88]

In the same year, Jerry Lambert, the president of Nazarene Bible College in Colorado Springs, was elected education commissioner. Lambert had overseen the expansion of extension centers while serving NBC. Prior to his work at NBC, Lambert had pastored and had served as the Pittsburgh district superintendent from 1980 to 1984.[89]

Lambert greatly expanded the profile of the IBOE. In 1997, the IBOE sponsored a Global Education Conference. In the same year a Resource Institute for International Education was launched through cooperative effort among Nazarene Theological Seminary, the World Mission Division, and the Church Growth Division. It linked together the "people resources" of the by then fifty-nine educational institutions of the Church of the Nazarene. The institute envisioned five components: registering qualified persons; bringing educators together in conferences; licensing educational programs; designing workshops to develop new curriculum; and accessing educational consultants to build new mission education programs.[90]

Finances for many schools outside North America came through the World Evangelism Fund (General Budget). These schools remained under the supervision of the World Mission Division. In regional budgetary matters, regional directors were forced to balance educational interests with evangelism and other concerns. The World Mission Division created the position of world education coordinator to serve the schools and assure that academic credibility accompanied the fulfillment of World Mission objectives. LeRoy Stults served in this position and was followed by Robert Woodruff. The role of the regional education coordinator grew in importance, especially after the IBOE initiated a mission review process for each school.[91]

Increasingly, the International Board of Education became the general church's advocate for educational institutions worldwide. In 1999 Lambert outlined the primary goals of the IBOE in developing "A Global Strategy for Theological Education." IBOE's task was to appropriately guide and endorse the establishment and status of educational institutions. It advised each school to seek both government recognition and accreditation. IBOE's vision remained to develop a worldwide system of quality education that prepared leaders to carry out the mission of the church in the twenty-first century. Lambert retired in 2008 and was replaced by LeBron Fairbanks, who had recently retired as president of Mount Vernon.[92]

CONCLUSION

Complexity in structures and diversity in cultures multiplied enormously after Pilot Point. The symbol was enduring, however, that Nazarenes' call to holiness and pursuit of perfection must be embodied in a global body yearning to transcend personal and group loyalties. The Nazarene story expanded beyond its American roots, where a vision and program for world mission existed from the beginning, to a global communion with an international consciousness. Latin America reminded the world that the story of Jesus resonated powerfully among the poor, and showed the way for holiness to move into societies departing from the rituals of centuries-old Catholicism. Tribalism had been the bane of Africa for centuries, but the boon for Nazarene heritage was the gift of the heritage of African community in the global tapestry. The Asia-Pacific Region introduced a teeming field of world religions for Christianity to encounter. Eurasia had open doors eastward.

By tradition the General Assembly was the great gathering place for the Nazarene family. As time and distance from the point of Nazarene beginnings increased, it became more and more imperative to find ways to "return home" to the family. Whenever they did so, Nazarenes found themselves crossing boundaries. To them this was what it meant to be in mission, to be "pilgrims on the way" transversing tribal and national borders. The church created means for this outward journey.

Crossing frontiers created new congregations, new districts, and new regions. The gospel ideal was "global communion." The church was attuned to contemporary socioeconomic currents that others termed "globalization." Leaders concluded that globalization was to be embraced and managed, not rejected. Globalization changed the structure of society. The challenge, wrote Franklin Cook, was to "recognize our connectedness and to respond together as a global church in the third millennium." Leaders affirmed that globalization was a process of sharing characterized by reciprocity, mutuality, and identification with all people groups. Leaders wanted globalization to provide universal access to Nazarene structures worldwide. This understanding, Cook believed, brought together "both the mission motivation and energy necessary to create holiness systems internationally."[93] A church crossing boundaries in mission found itself between the gospel it embodied and the cultures it sought to engage.

TWENTY-FIVE

THE CHURCH BETWEEN GOSPEL AND CULTURE

Like the marks on the two posts and the lintel of the doorways in Moses's Egypt, daubed with lamb's blood according to the Exodus account (12:7), early Nazarene churches boldly proclaimed "The Blood of Jesus Cleanses from All Sin." Sanctuaries' stained-glass windows and Sunday School classrooms displayed a shepherd Jesus with the words, "Come unto Me." The Church of the Nazarene had been named for the despised and rejected One from Nazareth, who walked in Galilee among the poor and the disenfranchised. In the interwar years Nazarenes were known as a "peculiar people" and rejoiced in that peculiarity. After World War II the church's witness to the world expanded. Toward the twenty-first century, like other evangelical churches, Nazarene congregations sought "seeker acceptance" and relevancy and guarded against being "too different." Examining the "multiple sets of worldviews and value orientations" of Nazarenes, sociologist and Pastor Ron Benefiel identified trends that affected Nazarene identity. He noted that the loss of a sectarian "shield" made the church more vulnerable to competing sociopolitical, religious, and theological values functioning in other groups and in society as a whole.[1]

The Church of the Nazarene came into being at the close of the nineteenth century because it sought a churchly order of holy living that would "Christianize Christianity and reform the nation," as Bresee said. Its self-understanding as a people with a global mission, as Reynolds emphasized, remained compelling. The Church of the Nazarene, after one century of world mission enterprise, possessed a global identity and a world-encompassing structure. The process of internationalization inevitably begged the question, "What is the Church?" Was it the local congregation, or the global body? Or some combination of both?[2]

Changes in society were so rapid and profound in the latter half of the century that churches faced considerable challenges in determining how to respond. Between 1976 and 2000 the Church of the Nazarene, in various ways, clarified its mission in the world. The church emphasized distinctive ethical principles (embodied in habits and practices leading toward Christlikeness) rather than cultural norms and rules. The church faced the choice of whether it would adopt a *conservative* (preserving) or a *liberal* (progressive) stance toward the cultures in which it existed, or whether it would rediscover a *radical* (renewing, reforming, and transforming) Christian identity. The church's witness to the world was not something separate from its own embodied existence in that world. The church attended to its internal well-being because that was its witness in the world. The late century church restructured itself, reformulated its ethics in relation to society, and reconsidered its core values.[3]

As the church expanded internationally, and as local church programs grew more complex, headquarters came under pressure. The 1972 General Assembly ordered a Commission on Church Program, Organization, and Structure to study the needs of the local congregation, local, district, and general church organization, and the function of the departments and commissions of the General Board and church auxiliaries. The commission's initial answer to the question "What is the Church?" was simply, "The *primary* church is the *local* church." "The local church is seen as the primary unit of the church. The district and general church exist to assist the local church in its ministry, and to extend the areas of service of each congregation to its broadest perimeters." The general church existed to enable the local church to fulfill its task.[4]

Acting upon the commission's report, the 1976 General Assembly created the Division of Christian Life, which combined Church Schools, Youth Ministry, and Christian Education. The purpose was to reduce duplication and increase unity at the local level, while improving efficiency at the general level. The report revealed that the "present general church organization" existed in the form of "quite autonomous units which often function independently" and at times "appear to operate without due regard to the work of the other departments or agencies."[5]

In 1980 the General Board requested the general superintendents to study the "Functions, Relationships, and Structure of the General Board." The general superintendents presented their report to the 1980 General Assembly, which created a Commission on General Board Organization. The commission included Nazarene businessmen, the general secretary, two pastors, and two district superintendents. Thane Minor, vice president for international marketing of Rileys Datashare International, and a former military officer, chaired the commission. The commission identified key problems. Lines of accountability for headquarters executives were vague and undefined. No structure or procedure for evaluating existing programs or prioritizing budgets was in place. The relationship between the General Board and the Board of General Superintendents was unclear and there was no regular communication between General Board meetings. Procedures for the selection and termination of headquarters personnel were not clearly defined.[6]

The general superintendents began implementing the commission's recommendations while the study was in process. A newly designated Headquarters Planning and Budget Council coordinated, facilitated, and formulated an annual budget and monitored expenditures. The General Board Executive Committee expanded its role. Headquarters operations were realigned into five divisions, headed by a director, who reported directly to a general superintendent. Each of the former departments was redesignated a "ministry" or "service" and assigned to a division. The "ministry" function of the former Department of Education and Ministry was renamed Pastoral Ministries and assigned to the Division of Church Growth. The Department of Education became Education Services. The changes added another tier or level in organization and procedures. The new structure emphasized rank, authority, and adherence to chain of command communications. Following the changes, the general secretary recorded that the church's "management environment" had experienced its "most radical revisions" since the General Board was first organized in 1923. The persons heading up now mid-level departments had no direct access to general superintendents. They worked within strict lines of accountability. The implementation of this reorganization lowered morale. NTS professor Paul Bassett observed, "The theological presuppositions implicit in the form of administration recently established in the general offices clearly contradict most Christian theological anthropologies and ecclesiologies, including the Wesleyan/Arminian."[7]

To guard against such contradictions, it became important to emphasize the denomination's doctrine of the Church. Functional, ethical, and missional statements overshadowed theological reflections about the church. Nazarenes found themselves, in practice, having to choose between two popularly held views of the church. The first one, typical of evangelical Baptist culture, was that the church was the local autonomous congregation. The second view, typical of institutional Christianity over the centuries, was that "the Church is embodied in the bishop" or "the Church is the hierarchy." Nazarenes familiar with their history recognized the role of representative government in the Church of the Nazarene mediating between these polarities. The principles of voluntary association coupled with the accountability of Christian discipleship embodied a "believers church" model.[8]

A formulation of the doctrine of the Church in an article of faith emerged late in the church's history. At the first meeting of the "Doctrine of the Church Commission," Henry Spaulding, its chair, asked "Why a commission—now?" and concluded that there had been a "studied ambiguity" about various models of church organization. The Commission presented its report to the 1989 General Assembly, which voted to add an article of faith on the church. Subsequently, two-thirds of the church's district assemblies ratified the delegates' action. The four paragraphs of the new article set forth the nature of the church, the marks of the church, the mission of the church, and the historical reality of the church. The Protestant marks or identity of the church were articulated in the second paragraph: living faith, biblical preaching, the sacraments, and discipline. The mission or task of the church was twofold, to "continue the redemptive work of Christ in the world" and to do so "in the power of the Spirit." The historical reality of the church was both universal and local.[9]

Further restructuring came in 1994. Upon the retirement of Norman Miller as general treasurer and the resignation of Moody Gunter as Finance Division director, the General Board established the position of a chief financial officer responsible to the general superintendents. At the same time, the position of general secretary was strengthened. The general secretary became responsible for the day-to-day operations of headquarters.[10]

Meanwhile, the church became more intentional about both its stewardship of funds and care for retired pastors, but few others outside North America had viable recourses.[11]

The church placed new emphasis on planned giving. The church moved the fund-raising responsibilities of Nazarene Compassionate Ministries from the Church Growth and World Mission divisions to the Stewardship/Planned Giving office. In 1995 Steve Weber, who had directed NCM, was elected Stewardship/Planned Giving director.[12]

ETHICS AND SOCIETY

Nazarenes tested and redrew the boundaries between themselves and the world in the years 1976-2000. Abortion, AIDS-HIV, church/state relations, drugs and substance abuse, euthanasia, homosexuality, marriage and divorce, nuclear warfare and weapons, race and racial prejudice, and challenges to the traditional family begged relevant response. But it became increasingly difficult to detect which responses were born in the mission of the church and which were carried along by societal currents. What were the nonnegotiable principles of a twenty-first-century Holiness church?[13]

In the aftermath of the Vietnam War the Church of the Nazarene shared the dilemma with other Christians of how Christianity related to society. The church must be careful, Don Kraybill warned, of "civil religion," which was "an informal marriage between church and state." South Africa was one context in which the tacit endorsement by the Church of the Nazarene of the civil religion of the ruling party created serious tensions in the church.[14]

Throughout these years the General Assemblies reaffirmed the 1972 General Assembly's position on the church and state that reminded Nazarenes "that our great Protestant heritage be understood and safeguarded" and "that both our political and religious freedom rest upon biblical concepts of the dignity of man as God's creation and the sanctity of his individual conscience." The church encouraged "our people to participate in political activity in support of these historic concepts and to be ever vigilant against threats to our precious freedom."[15] James McGraw, who taught preaching at NTS, concurred that "the social and moral issues of our day cannot be ignored" and argued that "the pulpit is the place where God's Word should be proclaimed as it relates to these needs." The public preaching of the Word and the private exercise of individual conscience, coupled with vigorous evangelism and mission in the world, were typical Nazarene responses to the issues of church and society in the last quarter of the twentieth century.[16]

Rules remained a part of the church's stance in the world. The Church of the Nazarene was unapologetic about prohibitions but increasingly stressed these in the context of equally important affirmatives. The General Rules commended the positive: "doing that which is enjoined in the Word of God" and "abiding in hearty fellowship with the church" while at the same time "avoiding evil of every kind." In 1975 *Herald of Holiness* editor W. T. Purkiser wrote, "Affirmatives are ideals, and ideals always have more dynamic power than prohibitions."[17]

Nazarenes realized the complexity of the abortion issue, particularly as it related to adolescent girls who became pregnant. The 1972 General Assembly passed a statement on abortion that was included in the Appendix of the *Manual*. The statement, placed among the Special Rules in the 1976 *Manual*, admonished that induced abortion was "permissible only on the basis of sound medical reasons affecting the life of the fetus and that of the mother." It was not to be used as a "convenience" or method of population control. James McGraw, writing on abortion in 1977, used the analogy of a device placed in a victim's automobile "designed to explode somewhere en route" and prevent the arrival of a person "on the way" somewhere. Should the unborn fetus not yet be a person (for the sake of argument) but "on the way to becoming a person," then "abortion is a violent interdiction, by choice, against the arrival of that potential person at his or her intended destination." McGraw respected modern scientific findings and even the use of genetic engineering, but the intentional ending of life even for the purpose of stopping suffering was not acceptable. Sanctity of life extended to the yet unborn child; so McGraw (and the church as a whole) opposed abortion on demand.[18]

The 1980 *Manual* added scripture references, but the statement on abortion remained the same. The 1985 *Manual* added the note that any responsible opposition to abortion required commitment to programs providing care for mothers and children. The 1989 *Manual* further enlarged the statement on abortion. It advised believers to provide love, prayer, and counsel for women with unwanted pregnancies. The statement placed abortion within a larger ethical issue, noting that unwanted pregnancies often resulted from a breakdown of Christian standards.

Protesting entertainment trends, in 1977 the church endorsed a nationwide, week-long television boycott. "We appeal to Nazarenes to join with a broad coalition of national groups," in order to "resist the rising tide of television sex, perversion, and violence, wherever it exists." Contradictory standards with respect to TV and the movies incensed one *Herald of Holiness* reader. Editor William McCumber responded, "Inconsistency is the price the church pays for being made up of human beings and for living through cultural and social changes." But on another occasion McCumber lamented, "Our culture is dominated by a household appliance."[19]

"Tobacco never found a friend in the Church of the Nazarene," McCumber wrote in 1978. "A church that stands opposed to [smoking] need not be apologetic. Smoking deserves every enemy it has. For it betrays every friend it makes." The church had taken a stand against the use of tobacco long before the popular vendettas against the tobacco industry of the 1990s.[20]

Sharp words revealed strong convictions regarding homosexuality. The 1972 General Assembly passed a statement on homosexuality, which was included in the Appendix. In 1976 this statement was placed in the Special Rules. The church recognized "the depth of the perversion that leads to homosexual acts" but affirmed "the biblical position that such acts are sinful and subject to the wrath of God." The church expressed its confidence that the grace of God was "sufficient to overcome the practice of homosexuality" and deplored "any action or statement that would seem to imply compatibility between Christian morality and the practice of homosexuality."

David Wright in 1980 wrote, "homosexuality is sin" and "an acquired degeneracy, never a genetic deformity which one is hopeless to change." Wright continued, "Homosexuality is a condition from which there is always a complete cure and total deliverance."[21] Not all Nazarenes were so sure. In 1981 the church, led by Michael Christensen, launched Golden Gate Ministries in San Francisco. It was patterned on the Lamb's Club ministry in New York City, where Christensen had served. Christensen envisioned compassionate ministry to the hungry and homeless, counseling services, an employment agency, and business ventures that would provide jobs. Soon Golden Gate Ministries was assisting persons with AIDS, many of whom were gay men. Christensen and his fellow ministers rejected the view that AIDS was a punishment for homosexuality. If it were, Christensen reasoned, AIDS would not affect heterosexuals or innocent children.[22]

General Superintendent Eugene Stowe worried that the Golden Gate ministry might misrepresent the church's stand. Though the church must show compassion, as it would to alcoholics or drug addicts, Stowe wrote to Christensen, it must clearly stand against "sinful practices." Stowe urged Christensen to consult with his district superintendent. He believed that neither individual Nazarenes nor the church as a whole would or should support a ministry that reflected any ambiguity about this.[23]

Christensen consulted his district superintendent, Clarence Kinzler. Together they attended a healing service at a Metropolitan Community Church, a gay and lesbian congregation. Unsure at first if he should be there, Kinzler thought he heard a "still small voice of Jesus" saying: "If I were in bodily form in San Francisco tonight, I would be exactly where you are." When Kinzler was introduced as a district superintendent of the Church of the Nazarene, the congregation "went crazy. They clapped and clapped until they clapped me to tears," Kinzler said. "They knew where the Church of the Nazarene stood on their practice of homosexuality, but that someone would value them as human beings and step across the separating walls, was hope to them in their addicted, frenetic lifestyle that was taking such a toll upon their very lives. My heart was broken," Kinzler continued, "as I saw young men, mere boys, jamming the middle aisle, waiting for someone to pray for them a prayer of healing."[24]

In 1984 the Church of the Nazarene held a Conference on AIDS. American Red Cross President Richard Schubert, a Nazarene, the keynote speaker, considered this the "first large-scale denominational forum for educating a group of church people about AIDS and offering some ideas for understanding the disease on both theological and practical levels."[25] While Harold Ivan Smith thought that "the hysteria and rhetoric of some Christians against AIDS is producing a daily round of applause in hell," another

Nazarene warned those with AIDS of "God's abiding wrath upon all those who practice unnatural vices. We fail them if we do not warn them of His severity as well."[26]

The 1989 *Manual* put the paragraph on homosexuality in a broader statement on human sexuality that began: "The Church of the Nazarene views human sexuality as one expression of the holiness and beauty that God the Creator intended for His creation." The church viewed "all forms of sexual intimacy that occur outside the covenant of heterosexual marriage as sinful distortions of the holiness and beauty God intended for it."[27]

Through its examination of abortion and homosexuality, issues unthought of in an earlier generation, the Bible remained the cornerstone of Nazarene decision making. "Because the New Testament ethic expresses the living Christ who is the author of a new humanity, it has a dynamic that allows it to address life redemptively anywhere and in every era."[28] Out of its faith in the Bible and its own leaders, the church's *Manual* affirmed the possibility of cultural adaptations to Nazarene rules. The church remained on a quest to find the balance "between being culturally relevant on the one hand and losing the core of our message on the other," as Paul Benefiel, retiring Los Angeles district superintendent, noted in 1992. The "Nazarene witness is culturally conditioned." Benefiel wanted the church to develop contextual awareness in order to reach a society that was characterized by many problems, including broken or dysfunctional families. The process of finding the balance, Benefiel reflected, was neither short nor quick.[29]

Marriage and divorce debates indicated that the church was overcoming its rigidity on the issue. The report of the Special Commission on "Marriage and Divorce in Our Society," presented to the 1993 General Assembly, indicated that there were, in fact, no biblical grounds for divorce, not even adultery. All marriage vows were permanent. The church urged strong premarital counseling that recognized this. The same report, however, indicated that due to the fallenness of human beings and the imperfection of the world, the permanence of marriage was an "ideal" rather than a prescriptive "law." Divorce was a forgivable sin. It did not exhaust the supply of God's grace. "Where a marriage has been dissolved and remarriage has followed," the report advised, "the marriage partners, upon genuine repentance for their sin, are enjoined to seek the forgiving grace of God and His redemptive help in their marriage." The report recommended that a person was not disqualified from either membership or ordination in the Church of the Nazarene due to marriage failure. Whether divorce occurred before or after conversion was irrelevant.[30]

At the same General Assembly the report of the Special Christian Action Committee dealt with life-support systems, genetic engineering and gene therapy, euthanasia, and abortion. The report affirmed the principles of "respect for the inviolable dignity of human life, human equality before God," and humility "before a graciously sovereign God."[31]

These moral concerns went far beyond the rules over which Nazarenes had once obsessed. Yet delegates vigorously debated the Special Rule banning movie attendance. Three choices were open to Nazarenes, reminded *Herald of Holiness* editor Wesley Tracy: to maintain the status quo with regard to movies, and live with the tension between selectivity and boycott; to harmonize the church's stance by boycotting all electronic entertainment media; or to harmonize the church's position by shifting to selectivity based on Christian principles in regard to all entertainment media. The 1993 assembly left the rule as it was.[32]

The 1997 General Assembly in effect lifted the ban on movies while admonishing Nazarenes to be careful of all forms of entertainment. The church acknowledged that "we are living in a day of great moral confusion in which we face the potential encroachment of the evils of the day into the sacred precincts of our homes through various avenues such as current literature, radio, television, personal computers, and the Internet," and warned that it was "essential that the most rigid safeguards be observed to keep our homes from becoming secularized and worldly." In their "obligation to witness against whatever trivializes or blasphemes God," and "to endeavor to bring about the demise of enterprises known to be the purveyors of this kind of entertainment," Nazarenes were to avoid "all types of entertainment ventures and media productions that produce, promote, or feature the violent, the sensual, the pornographic, the profane, or the occultic, or which feature or glamorize the world's philosophy of secularism, sensualism, and materialism and undermine God's standard of holiness of heart and life."[33]

Following this decision, one person wrote to the *Herald of Holiness*: "I really cheered when I heard that the General Assembly voted to make it OK for Nazarenes to attend movies," and asked: "Don't you agree that it was long overdue?" Tracy answered that Nazarenes sought to remain a "principled people" in an "age of high-tech sin," ones able to "resist and avoid sub-Christian and sinful entertainment in any medium in which it is delivered."[34]

In contrast to the boycott of the Walt Disney Company advocated by the Southern Baptist Convention in 1997, the Church of the Nazarene substituted a request to the Walt Disney Company chairman that it "seriously consider the return to the moral values on which the corporation first established its mission," and warned that the company would be monitored for its response.[35]

To another social issue, pornography, general church leaders called upon "Nazarenes in every society and community to stand in opposition to this rapidly growing pornography industry." How were they to do so? The church endorsed a "democratic" rather than "totalitarian" way of dealing with this as well as other issues and called for a recovery of "a sense of right and wrong rooted in an awareness of God."[36]

James Dobson

While the church responded to these issues, one of its members, James Dobson, rallied many Nazarenes and other evangelicals and moved them toward making their stands political. Dobson was the son of James Dobson Sr., a Nazarene evangelist and art professor who taught at Pasadena and MidAmerica. After attending Pasadena College, the younger Dobson earned a Ph.D. in child developmental psychology at the University of Southern California. Dobson served as associate clinical professor of pediatrics at USC for fourteen years and was on the staff of Children's Hospital in Los Angeles for seventeen years.[37]

Dobson first came to public attention in 1970 when he published *Dare to Discipline*. Coming as it did in the midst of the Vietnam War and its protests, hippies, drugs, and "free love," *Dare to Discipline* offered an alternative to permissive childcare. Dobson criticized the lack of discipline in schools as well as homes. He foretold a "sweeping sexual revolution."[38] Though advocating discipline and structure, Dobson understood and warned against child abuse. "When the child asks, 'Who's in charge?' tell him. When he mutters, 'Who loves me?' take him in your arms and surround him with affection. Treat him with respect and dignity, and expect the same from him."[39] The relationship between child and parent was to be modeled on the relationship between God and human beings, which was "a love unparalleled in tenderness and mercy. This same love," Dobson continued, "leads the benevolent father to guide, correct—and even bring some pain to the child when it is necessary for his eventual good."[40]

Following *Dare to Discipline*, *Hide and Seek* (1974) taught parents how to build self-esteem in children. Dobson invited parents to ask whether the home was a place where children were respected, admired, and granted human worth.[41] "While the spirit is brittle," Dobson wrote, "and must be treated gently, the will is made of steel." The parents' goal, Dobson believed, was "to shape the will of the child, but leave his spirit intact."[42]

Later books emphasized the importance of the family, which, Dobson stated, "was designed by God Almighty to have a specific purpose and function: when it operates as intended, the emotional and physical needs of husbands, wives, and children are met in a beautiful relationship of symbiotic love. But when that function is inhibited or destroyed, then every member of the family experiences the discomfort of unmet needs. That is my message."[43]

In order to be a good mother, Dobson advised women, who made up the majority of his constituency, that they needed self-esteem and a positive self-image. While Dobson believed that women should "submit" to their husbands, he recognized that there should be "a distinct element of dignity and self-respect throughout the husband-wife relationship."[44] Dobson advised wives not to be treated as "doormats" by their husbands. Love must be "tough" enough not to be taken advantage of. Wives must never feel guilty for causing their husbands' abuses and, if it came to that, they must separate from abusive husbands.[45] Dobson warned women against being so submissive to husbands that they failed to take spiritual leadership of the family, if their husbands did not.[46]

Mothers, in order for children to receive the full benefits of their love and concern, Dobson advised, should not work outside the home. Parents should not leave childrearing to others. Dobson ran into vocal opposition from women when he expressed these views in the 1970s.[47]

Largely because of the feminist movement, Dobson believed, men were suffering identity crises. Husbands were "obligated" by divine plan to lead their families. When a man fell "in love with a woman, dedicating himself to care for her and protect her and support her," he became "the mainstay of social order."[48]

In 1977 Dobson began Focus on the Family. Its purpose was to strengthen both marriages and parenting. Its need arose, in part, from the ways in which mass media such as television portrayed and ridiculed family relationships and, it seemed to Dobson, worked "relentlessly to shred the last vestiges of Christian tradition."[49] Dobson warned against extremists who wanted to take away parents' right and responsibility to discipline their children.[50]

In 1980 the Focus on the Family radio program was receiving three hundred letters a day.[51] By 1996, Focus on the Family's staff included twelve hundred persons who processed ten thousand letters and thirty-five hundred phone calls a day and published ten magazines and distributed 130,000 cassette tapes monthly. Four thousand radio stations in sixty countries carried

Dobson's program. His organization received as much as $100 million a year. By 1996, in addition to giving instruction on parenting and marriage, Focus on the Family effectively lobbied the United States Congress on such issues as abortion.[52]

Dobson firmly believed that unborn children had souls and personhood. "No social or financial considerations can counter-balance our collective guilt for destroying those lives which were being fashioned in the image of God Himself." "It is my deepest conviction," Dobson continued, "that He will not hold us blameless for our wanton infanticide."[53]

While not all Nazarenes followed Dobson, and some would have found places where he was out of step with the Holiness Movement's uplifting of women, he reflected the views of many. His Nazarene roots kept him apart from close cooperation with charismatics such as Pat Robertson. But like Robertson and Jerry Falwell, Dobson accentuated the divisions or "culture war" in American society over moral issues. Dobson's background in the Church of the Nazarene gave him a sense of moral rectitude and rightness that some associates judged to be arrogance.[54]

THE ETHICS OF RACE

During these years the Church of the Nazarene awakened to the issues of race. Such reflection came partly in relation to the church's return to urban ministries. Tom Nees, for instance, out of his work at the Community of Hope in Washington, D.C., came to see racism as America's "besetting sin." In 1982 the Community of Hope held a conference on race and reconciliation in which whites expressed their fears and confessed their guilt, while African-Americans voiced their anger at being ignored, insulted, and kept down.[55] Larry Lott, an African-American pastor in Kansas City, found other African-Americans to be "surprised when they find people of color in the Church of the Nazarene." Lott believed that "because of our doctrine of entire sanctification we have a mandate to preach against all forms of evil. Racism is sin." "Our ministers of all colors," Lott continued, "should preach our full doctrine if we want to find complete liberation from racism."[56]

Within several districts, superintendents and pastors made significant steps toward multiculturalism. In 1993 General Superintendent Hurn appointed Roger Bowman, an African-American,

Roger Bowman

superintendent of the Los Angeles District. The district assembly reelected him superintendent in 1995. Bowman had pastored in Mississippi, San Diego, and Los Angeles before moving to headquarters as assistant to Raymond Hurn in the Home Missions' urban/ethnic ministries. In 1990 he joined the faculty of Nazarene Bible College. Bowman appealed to Nazarenes to "color us Christian" rather than "black" and "white." He said that though "for the most part the overt racial strife of the sixties is behind us," the "problem of prejudice is still around."[57] In 1999 Bowman retired from his service as DS and was appointed a missionary to the USA/Canada field. He became responsible for training African-Americans on seven Southern districts.[58]

In the South, even if belatedly, Nazarenes saw some progress. Cheryl Albert noted that when she moved to South Carolina in 1970 the Church of the Nazarene was completely segregated, but that by the time of the 1994 South Carolina District Assembly, "there was a Black pastor singing in the elder's choir. Three black pastors [were] on the district, and one of the ordinands was a black woman. I am so proud to be part of a church that welcomes all people and allows everyone to answer the call of God. Integration didn't come in my time," she continued, it came in "God's time," when people were "willing to listen to God's quiet voice."[59] Other districts made similar progress.

Nazarenes in South Africa also reflected a "waiting on God's time" attitude. Amid the entrenched apartheid system, Nazarene leaders were ill equipped to act in ways that were socially responsible and effective. Racially segregated districts challenged institutional values. A group of South African Nazarene leaders attended the Conference on Mission and Evangelism in Durban in 1973. This event, along with other developments, began to spur Nazarenes toward a new recognition that Christians bore a great and growing responsibility to bring down the walls of apartheid. The 1976 Soweto Uprising took place while delegates were attending the General Assembly in Dallas, Texas. Many Nazarenes in South Africa experienced these events as political developments beyond the scope of their reach or immediate responsibility. District leaders exchanged letters with those most closely involved in the geographic neighborhood of Soweto. In 1979 more than two thousand delegates from all strata of South African society, including a representative but small number of Nazarene leaders, attended the South African Leaders Conference.[60] Strong feelings were implicit in the motion at the 1985 General Assembly: "Resolved that the General Assembly review the organizing of districts in the Republic of South Africa with a view to bring about a closer relationship between the various race groups in our church in the RSA environment." In 1986 General Superintendent Strickland preached in Capetown to a racially mixed group that included blacks, Indians, "Coloureds," and whites and, as a former missionary to South Africa, recognized the extraordinary significance of the event.[61]

Still, the church waited for political events to change the social situation. At the 1999 Africa Region gathering of one thousand people Rudie Booyens from South Africa welcomed the delegates by saying, "It is a joy and privilege to have you visit the Rainbow Nation of South Africa." Pastor Bessie Tshambe, pastor of the largest Nazarene church in Africa, in Maputo, Mozambique, led the congregation in prayer. Only a few years before, it would have been very difficult or even impossible to stage such an event in the polarized society of the old apartheid South Africa.[62] Friday Ganda, Kenya Southwest district superintendent, commented, "when I looked at the Gospel of Christ, the blood of Christ not only joins us to God, but ties us to one another as blood brothers and sisters. We should be knit together and look at one another as children of God the Father and live as a united family [with] no more divisions in language or colour."[63]

NAZARENES IN POLITICAL SPHERES

The social and political situation in Nicaragua in the 1970s and 1980s drew Nazarenes apart. The country was enmeshed in civil war. In the 1970s a coalition against the regime of Anastasio Somoza included many workers, businessmen, and Roman Catholic priests. Somoza had perpetuated, in their view, the rule of the elite while millions suffered in poverty. Somoza received support from the American government. Opposition forces to Somoza included the "Sandinistas." To avoid the conflict, some Protestants fled from the cities. Many could not see how they could support armed action against the government. They questioned how anyone could be a Sandinista and remain a Christian. Others (including some Nazarenes) saw in revolution the only hope for the nation. They enthusiastically joined the Sandinista rebels. Those who supported the Sandinistas saw similarities between its values and those of Christ's kingdom, and did not want to see Protestant churches sidelined, as they had been in the Cuban revolution. The revolution in Nicaragua divided the family of God.[64]

The Sandinistas succeeded in 1979 after the country experienced a major earthquake and U.S. President Jimmy Carter withdrew military and economic support from Somoza. Nazarene missionaries left Nicaragua in 1979. The church's two districts united under Superintendent Faustino Zepeda, but some Nazarene pastors and laypersons fled the country. Zepeda died in 1986 and was succeeded by Nicanor Mairena. Gradually, membership began to grow. In 1989 the ministerial training program restarted, and the church began to print literature. More than before the revolution, women assumed positions of leadership in the church. Membership in 2000 reached eight thousand four hundred.[65]

Nuclear disarmament elicited sharp responses among Nazarenes around the world. In the mid-1980s Morris Chalfant explained: "Every nuclear weapon in the world should be destroyed—not just limited!"[66] Timothy Smith proposed that the "actual task Christians face is to persuade one or other of the superpowers to take the initiative in nuclear disarmament—take the first step. No fight ever came to a halt by instantaneous bilateral agreement. One participant must step back first." But a *Herald of Holiness* reader thought that disarmament was appeasement and fatal capitulation. "Nowhere does the Bible justify pacifism and unilateral disarmament."[67]

In 1986 David Tarrant from the British Isles wrote to the Internationalization Commission, "Without making any judgment as to the rightness or wrongness of this stance regarding President Ronald Reagan's 'star wars' program from an American point of view, it seems clear that the strength of feeling in European countries regards this policy as tragically mistaken."[68] Antinuclear objections for many Christians were not "rooted in mere godless humanism" but in "Christian morality," Tarrant continued. He did not want the church to operate under the banner, "In Nukes We Trust." Nazarenes can "pray effectively only if we refuse to let the world squeeze us into its own mould—in this case, the mould of reliance for our defense on devilish instruments of mass destruction."[69] Similarly, Bryan Stone appealed for "Christian realism" based on the gospel rather than on "political realism" based on human resources. Christian realism claimed that grace and not sin has the "last word." Christian realism challenged the "world's definition of 'power.'" It affirmed "hope as a reality to be lived out of the present." The church, Stone wrote, needed to "recapture the power of that defenseless and yet very disarming child from Bethlehem."[70]

At the same time, the church regained contacts with the Church of the Nazarene in Cuba. H. T. Reza, a citizen of Mexico still, in spite of his many years in the United States, made several trips to Cuba. Regional Director James Hudson visited Cuba with him in 1987, and Robert Scott and Robert Prescott (again with Reza) visited the country the following year. They set up a district structure, with Aramis Galvez as superintendent. The church cooperated with the Cuba Council of Churches and because of that cooperation the Church of the Nazarene was able to send money into the country. By 2000, membership on the district had reached forty-three hundred with thirty-five churches.[71]

The church faced blatant persecution in Mozambique. The revolutionaries were Marxist. They secured independence from Portugal in 1975. Missionaries evacuated. The Bible school closed. Benjamin Langa wrote in August 1977 that "we were shamefully condemned" and "expelled" from the missionary compound. All Christians were "accused as reactionaries, thieves, anti-Revolutionaries." From 1975 to 1982 the government actively suppressed religion. The Marxist government banned Bible teaching. "Religion here was to be stamped out," Langa wrote, "by every possible means carried out by the local educational authorities."[72] Christians in Mozambique suffered greatly. Nazarene pastors and laypersons were targets of attack and many lost their lives. Leaders such as Mario Matsinhe, Benjamin Langa, Simeao Mathe, and Simeao Mandlate led the church in their country through years of political and social turmoil such that when a missionary visited the country in 1981, he found that the great majority of the church had remained firm and steadfast. In 1986, when it became possible, Nazarene Compassionate Ministries began sending food and clothing. Because of the denomination's scattered churches throughout Mozambique, it became one of the country's primary relief agencies. In spite of these hardships, the Mozambique Central District reached regular or self-supporting status in 1992. The oppression lasted until 1994. By 2000, there were 55,730 Nazarene members in Mozambique.[73]

Hutu and Tutsi Nazarenes in Rwanda-Burundi were among those trapped in a crisis of dual loyalties between those owed to Christ and those owed to tribe and nation. Not only Methodists and Anglicans but also Nazarenes were confronted with deadly tribal conflicts within their churches. A cover of *Time* magazine portraying this horror included a photograph inside a local Church of the Nazarene. Nonetheless, Nazarene pastors in Rwanda organized relief efforts for refugees. By 2000, there were twenty-seven thousand Nazarene members in Rwanda.[74]

The Church of the Nazarene in Japan lamented that it had not done more toward peace during the Second World War. On March 15, 1993, the Church of the Nazarene in Japan issued a "Confession" in which it stated its "regret" that it "did not resist the aggression, but rather cooperated with it." At the 1995 regional conference in Manila, before a vast Sunday crowd, Yoshiaki Aoki, Japan district superintendent at the time, made an official apology to the people of the nations of the Asia-Pacific Region that had suffered at the hands of the Japanese troops prior to and during World War II. Presiding General Superintendent Donald Owens responded to this apology, accepting it on behalf of the entire region and the denomination.[75]

The separation of church and state was the guideline for practical action globally. The World Mission Division kept Nazarene missionaries from taking political stands, even though this in itself sometimes implied support for the status quo. In a few places around the world Nazarenes as individuals became involved in political affairs. In the Asia-Pacific Region, Liuga Faumui, a Nazarene layperson from Western Samoa, served with the United Nations in several locations. Later he was elected to Parliament in Western Samoa. Dr. Ansito Walter, who had become a Nazarene while doing graduate studies in California, served as governor of the Micronesian island of Chuuk and persuaded the Church of the Nazarene to send missionaries to his country. More typically, Nazarenes demonstrated their interest in transforming society through compassionate ministries. Nazarenes became well known for their educational, health, and feeding programs in Haiti. The Community Based Health Care system established by Carolyn Myatt first in India and then in

---

CONFESSION OF JAPANESE CHURCH OF THE NAZARENE

We the Church of the Nazarene in Japan, as a faith community called and gathered by our only Lord Jesus Christ, confess the following with aspiration to peace.

We recognize that our country caused great sorrow and pain among Asian and other countries and people living in those countries and regions including our own during the War of aggression.

The churches who belong to the Church of the Nazarene regret and repent the fact that we did not resist the aggression, but rather cooperated with it.

In addition, we of the Church of the Nazarene are sorry for the fact that we did not express our repentance officially for 48 years after the War, and we ask forgiveness for this also.

We promise that we will always remember the fact that our country invaded our neighboring countries, and that we will do our best not to repeat the same sins.

We seek for reconciliation with people in Asian and other countries, and with resident foreigners in Japan, in whatever circumstance, on the basis of this repentance.

Fifteenth of March 1993
Higuchi Shigeru, District Superintendent
Church of the Nazarene in Japan

Papua New Guinea provided a model for others and, in the case of PNG, the nation as a whole. In Thailand, missionary Ceny Hirahara and a small band of Nazarenes ministered to AIDS victims in that country.

In Swaziland, Nazarenes had a long history of compassionate ministries. They also held a variety of high positions. In 1996 Sibusiso Barnabus Dlamini, the son of a Nazarene pastor, became prime minister of Swaziland. Prior to this, Dlamini had served as a minister of finance and, when appointed prime minister by the king, was deputy director of the World Bank.

In America, Nazarenes were represented in both major political parties. Northwest Nazarene University Professor Helen Wilson headed the Canyon County Democratic Party for several years. In 1989, after several years on the Quincy, Massachusetts, City Council, James Sheets, a Nazarene and graduate of ENC, and Democrat, was elected mayor.[76] In 1996, Vincent Snowbarger of Kansas was elected to the United States Congress (the first time a Nazarene had been elected) as a Republican. Snowbarger attended the Olathe, Kansas, Church of the Nazarene. Previously, Snowbarger, a lawyer, had served in the Kansas legislature.[77]

In 1998, when faced with moral scandal in their own country during the presidency of Bill Clinton, the general superintendents issued a political statement imploring Clinton to "give serious and prayerful consideration to resigning from the office of the president."[78] But the general superintendents were reluctant to speak out on ethical issues facing other nations.

NAZARENE EDUCATION AND SOCIETY

Traditionally Nazarenes considered education and evangelism to be appropriate means of engagement with the world. Mission and education were not separated. The educational institutions of the church intended to influence public life. Those who served in the colleges were on the frontlines of the church's advance. Yet Nazarene colleges, even from their origins, were caught between denominational purpose and social redemption. Persons wanted to be both loyal and faithful members of the church and credible and authentic witnesses in the world.[79]

The first Faith and Learning Conference was held in 1978 on the campus of MidAmerica. "You have seen an historic Christian first tonight," remarked Asbury Theological Seminary President Dennis Kinlaw. "You Nazarenes with your educational institutions possess a great sleeping giant."[80] Kinlaw asked the question, based on the fact that there were many Methodist degree-granting institutions in the United States and eight Nazarene colleges, "Is this one reason why the Church of the Nazarene is able to move toward the center of

American life while Methodism in the land of John Wesley still maintains a status little better politically than that of a sect?" Yet the upward mobility of graduates from Nazarene colleges and universities had the attendant price to pay of the church's becoming, Kinlaw lamented, "less distinguishable from the surrounding culture."[81]

In distinctive ways, each Nazarene college responded to the challenges of society. From the beginning of MidAmerica Nazarene College, President Curtis Smith had sustained fund-raising campaigns. Smith's "Seed-Faith Campaign" raised $2 million between 1970 and 1985. Three periods of growth at MANC distinguished these years: 1973-82 was a period of steady and sometimes spectacular growth; 1983-88 was a period of sharp decline and leveling off; and 1988-97 was a time of renewed growth and vigor. Major buildings added in these years included Dobson Hall, a Fine Arts Building completed in 1976; Smith Religion Building, 1977; Gilliland Physical Plant Building, 1977; Field House, 1978; Metz Career Education Building, 1981; Uphaus Hall, a residence hall for women, 1981; Weatherby Chapel, 1982; and Mabee Library, 1985. At the end of twenty-five years, 1968-93, the college plant had an estimated value of over $28.7 million. Traditions included the close college-church relationship; the American Heritage theme; an open admissions policy that welcomed students "of all ages, races, religions, and economic backgrounds"; personalized study; and four interdisciplinary courses. The mix was conservative and innovative.[82]

In 1985 Donald Owens succeeded Curtis Smith to become the second president of MANC. Following Owens's election as general superintendent, MANC trustees elected Richard Spindle president. Spindle had earned graduate degrees, including a doctor of education in 1976, from Southwestern Baptist Theological Seminary. Spindle had served pastorates in Texas from 1965 to 1973, then had taught at Nazarene Bible College in Colorado Springs from 1973 to 1978. He then became executive coordinator for the Christian Life and Sunday School Division at headquarters for two years before joining the MANC faculty in the field of Christian education. If Smith had been a "pastor-evangelist with a knack for public relations and a genius for raising money," Donald Metz recorded, and Owens a "missionary-teacher with a passion for global service and a rare capacity as a peacemaker and healer," Spindle was "an educator-administrator with a scholar's love of learning and an executive's organizing skills."[83] MidAmerica became a university in 1997.[84]

Mount Vernon's first baccalaureate graduation was held in 1976. William Stroud, president of First Knox National Bank, cochaired major fund-raising drives from the Mount Vernon community. A radio station that began operations in 1980 gave added recognition of MVNC in the local community and eventually all of Knox County. By 1986 the MVNC Weather Station served the community as well as the college.

E. LeBron Fairbanks became president of Mount Vernon in 1989. Both William Prince, one of his predecessors, and Fairbanks had served the church outside the United States. Fairbanks had been academic dean of European Nazarene Bible College from 1978 to 1982, then had taught at Bethany, and had followed Donald Owens as president of Asia-Pacific Nazarene Theological Seminary in the Philippines. Fairbanks stated his intent "to lead the [MVNC] campus to think more globally, live more simply, give more generously, love more deeply."[85] In 1990 the Templeton Foundation honored MVNC as one of the schools that promoted the "development of character and values in education." A Free Enterprise Business Center opened in 1994. The school instituted EXCELL (Executive Center for Lifelong Learning), a degree completion program for adults. In 1994 MVNC began a master of ministry program, and the following year a master of arts in education. In 1997 the school dedicated the Thorne Library/Learning Resource Center. While developing a strong infrastructure, faculty, students, and graduates participated in various urban and global ministries.[86]

In early 1981, Stephen Nease, who had been the founding president of Mount Vernon and then president of Bethany (1972-76) and Nazarene Theological Seminary (1976-81), became president of ENC. Nease had served in the administration of Edward Mann and revived the ministers' and laymen's retreats that Mann had used successfully. Nease refocused attention on the alumni and the traditional base of the college's support. Finances remained a concern. Sharp increases in housing costs in the Boston area compounded the financial pressures and problems. Nonetheless, Nease oversaw several construction projects, including the completion of the Edith F. Cove Fine Arts Center and an expanded library.[87]

Upon Nease's resignation from the presidency of ENC in 1989 in order to become the denomination's first commissioner of education, ENC's Board of Trustees elected Cecil Paul as president. Paul had taught psychology at ENC for many years, had developed the school's M.A. program in pastoral counseling, and had served as director of graduate studies from 1979 to 1987. In 1987 he became director of the Communications Division at headquarters in Kansas City. As president of ENC Paul brought gender issues to the foreground and appointed two women as vice presidents of the school, Maxine Walker, vice president of academic affairs, and Jan Lanham, vice president of student affairs. But after three strenuous years, Paul suffered a brain hemorrhage and died.[88]

Kent Hill served as ENC president from 1992 to 2000. Hill had earned a Ph.D. in Russian history and had served as director of the Institute on Religion and Democracy in Washington, D.C., for seven years prior to going to ENC. Historian James Cameron remarked that Hill "brought to his assignment a fresh perspective, an openness, honesty, and sense of realism." Hill crafted a Culture of Quality to define and chart his own course. In 1996 the mission statement was revised to read: "The mission of Eastern Nazarene College is to serve God, the church and the world, by providing a quality liberal arts education in a distinctly Christian and Wesleyan environment." Hill hired only clearly committed Christians to teach in the adult education program, which generated income for the school. His announcement of this elicited "charges of intolerance, bigotry, and mean-spiritedness." But Hill won public support by defending both pluralism and religious freedom. He held that "the right to maintain and nurture distinctive religious communities (Catholic, Protestant, Jewish, Muslim, Buddhist, or New Age) is not just legal, it lies at the heart of a vibrant, diverse, pluralistic society."[89] But finances pressured the college. Hill resigned to take a government position in Europe.[90]

Ponder Gilliland was elected to the presidency of Bethany Nazarene College in 1985, succeeding John Knight, who had been elected to the general superintendency. Gilliland had served as senior pastor at Bethany First Church since 1970. The relationship between Bethany First Church and the college had been an example to the rest of the church. One of Gilliland's first actions was to change the name of the school to Southern Nazarene University, the first Nazarene school since the early years to designate itself a "university." Actually the idea of Nazarene universities had persisted in the Church of the Nazarene. But when Olivet's Harold Reed proposed building a great Nazarene "university" in 1958, the idea was regarded more as "impractical" than "inappropriate."[91]

Athletic prowess (particularly at men's and women's intercollegiate basketball) secured a national reputation for Bethany. In 1981 the men's team was national champion of the NAIA, and from 1989 the women's team won the championship for four consecutive years.[92]

When Gilliland retired as president of SNU in 1989, trustees elected Loren A. Gresham, who had taught political science at the school since 1967 and had served as university provost from 1985 to 1989.[93]

During the 1990s Northwest Nazarene College ranked among the top ten liberal arts colleges in the West according to the *US News and World Report*. Gordon Wetmore served as president from 1983 to 1991. He was followed by Leon Doane, an alumnus who had been vice president for West

One Bank in Boise, Idaho. Doane died in 1993. Richard Hagood succeeded him. Under his leadership, in 1997 NNC (which became NNU in 1999) launched a master of business administration program.[94]

The primary advances at Olivet in the years 1976-97 were the major buildings added and the shift from college to university status as well as the commitment to graduate education. John Bowling became president of Olivet upon Leslie Parrott's retirement in 1991. Traditional Nazarene philosophies of education endured. In 1995 Bowling claimed that "fulfilling the Great Commission through the twin thrusts of evangelism and education" was still the hallmark of the Church of the Nazarene. "Two of the sterling characteristics of the work of the early Nazarenes were a commitment to world evangelism and a commitment to higher education."[95]

Millard Reed, pastor of Nashville First Church since 1974, succeeded Homer Adams as president of Trevecca in 1992. At his inauguration Reed asked, "What of the call to holiness at the close of the millennium?" TNC could not be satisfied to "simply provide a Christian atmosphere," Reed answered, but "must take on the times. It must engage this upside-down, inside-out, mixed-up time with the look-back, look-forward, look-inward, look-outward message of full salvation."[96] Trevecca offered doctoral degrees in education.

For a short time, beginning in 1976, Point Loma offered a doctoral program in education based on a cooperative arrangement with Northern Arizona University. In 1978 the trustees approved the restructuring of Point Loma's administration proposed by President W. Shelburne Brown to give him more time to be involved in constituency relations. He appointed two vice presidents, Keith Pagan and Robert Foster.[97] When Brown died of cancer in 1978, trustees chose Bill Draper, pastor of College Church of the Nazarene in Bourbonnais, Illinois, to succeed him. Draper had served as assistant to the president at Mid-America from 1967 to 1973. Draper, too, succumbed to cancer in 1983.[98] Jim Bond served as Point Loma's president from 1983 to 1997. In this position Bond strongly defended the historic commitments of Nazarene education to liberal arts and scientific inquiry. To emphasize the Nazarene connection, in 1983 the name of the institution was changed from Point Loma College ("An Institution of the Church of the Nazarene") to Point Loma Nazarene College. In 1998, it became Point Loma Nazarene University.[99]

Point Loma opened the Wesleyan Center for Twenty-First Century Studies. Maxine Walker became the director in 1993. The center sponsored interdisciplinary conferences and oversaw the publication of various studies.[100]

EDUCATION FOR THE CHURCH IN THE WORLD

Nazarene commitment to education expanded in areas outside North America. Once again, ministerial education held the priority.

The founding of regional schools continued with Asia-Pacific Nazarene Theological Seminary. In 1977 the General Board approved plans for the establishment of a graduate school to "serve districts and mission fields in the Far East." Donald Owens was elected to head the new seminary at this meeting. In 1979, the church purchased a site in Taytay, Rizal, Philippines. The proximity of the location to Manila was a deciding factor, as leaders hoped that the cosmopolitan setting would provide models for evangelism for the other cities of Asia and the Pacific. The Church of the Nazarene had directed its attentions to Metro Manila only a few years earlier. Extension classes from NTS began in 1980. Meanwhile, Owens became director of the Asia Region and moved to Manila. Owens searched for residential faculty members and initiated construction of an administration and classroom building. Regular classes began in November 1983. The school offered a master of divinity program and master's degrees in both religious education and, later, Christian communication.

E. LeBron Fairbanks, formerly academic dean of European Nazarene Bible College and at the time teaching at Bethany, became president of the seminary in 1984. In 1988, the school received full recognition from the Philippine government's Department of Education. In 1989, when Fairbanks was elected president of Mount Vernon Nazarene College, trustees chose John Nielson, vice president of Eastern Nazarene College, and formerly a missionary to Denmark, as president. By 2000 APNTS graduates were ministering in Australia, Bangladesh, Canada, Ethiopia, Hong Kong, India, Indonesia, Japan, Kenya, Korea, Myanmar, New Zealand, Papua New Guinea, the Philippines, Samoa, Thailand, and the United States.[101] Hitoshi (Paul) Fukue, a Japanese scholar and pastor, served as president of APNTS from 2003 to 2007.

The school in Korea grew tremendously. Donald Owens, when he arrived in Korea in 1954, had founded a Bible school to train ministers. For decades the school had no standing with the Korean government and could not offer degrees. Graduates were unable to proceed further in their studies. The government (attempting to decongest Seoul) made it clear that it would not accredit the school unless it moved out of Seoul. In 1978 the mission and districts decided to sell the compound on which the school and missionary residences were located. Most of the proceeds went toward the school's relocation and the remainder to the district and to the mission. The church purchased thirty-two acres in Chonan, south of Seoul, on which to build, and the school moved there in 1981. Korean government recognition began in 1982 when the school gained the standing of a trade or vocational school. In 1991, after further accreditation, the school offered bachelor's degrees. It achieved university status in 1996. Under the leadership of long-serving missionary William Patch, Korea Nazarene University, as it was now called, offered several majors that focused on rehabilitation. Campus facilities were constructed to meet the needs of the physically disadvantaged. The school became a recognized leader in South Korea in these fields and received substantial government funding. Through well-educated Korean scholars, the school expanded its religion department to include graduate degrees. Eventually enrollment surpassed five thousand.[102]

The Seminario Nazareno Mexicano was established in 1981 under the leadership of H. T. Reza. The church sold the property of the Bible college in San Antonio to purchase ten acres in the southern section of Mexico City. Reza served as president until 1986. Upon his retirement, Alberto Guang became president. Guang had earned a Ph.D. at Fuller Theological Seminary's School of Missions and had served as a professor and administrator at the Nazarene seminary in Costa Rica. The school in Mexico offered the Licenciatura of Theology and bachelor of theology.[103]

In 1993 the establishment of Africa Nazarene University marked a significant advance not only for Africa but for the church. As late as 1980 there was only one African pastor with a bachelor's degree. Many who studied abroad never returned to Africa or lost touch with the Church of the Nazarene. The original proposal included four divisions: a graduate level offering master of divinity, master of arts and master of religious education degrees; a degree level offering bachelor's programs primarily for students from East Africa; a Bible college at the diploma and certificate level; and a technical training school (as a means of reducing subsidy). This proposal won the support of the general superintendents and General Board in 1987. The church purchased an eighty-acre campus in Nairobi, Kenya.[104]

Mark Moore provided pioneer leadership in the school's formative stage from 1988 to 1991, serving as provost. Leaders soon found, however, that Kenya required that schools operate liberal arts undergraduate programs in order to grant graduate degrees. Plans shifted and ANU became the first institution of the church outside of the United States specifically established as a liberal arts college. Moore secured dozens of Work and Witness teams and brought hundreds of Nazarenes to Nairobi to help in the construction of university facilities. The Kenyan government granted a Letter of Authority for the university to open in August 1994, and classes began with sixty-five students from seventeen African countries.[105]

At the first graduation ceremony in May 1998, twenty-six degrees were conferred by the chancellor, Ted Esselstyn, and Leah T. Marangu, the vice-chancellor. Marangu, a native of Kenya, had received a Ph.D. from Iowa State University in 1975. Marangu and her husband, also a native of Kenya, taught at Olivet before returning to Kenya, and then she chaired the home economics department of Kenyatta University in Nairobi. She also served on Kenya's Commission of Higher Education. Marangu believed that graduates needed to be "tenaciously committed to the mission of salvation and compassion as the people of God."[106] The Kenyan government granted a full charter to the university in October 2002.[107]

A similar school, intending to serve both South America and Portuguese-speaking Nazarenes from throughout the globe, opened in Campinas, Brazil, in 2008.

CHURCH CONNECTIONS

Nazarene Publishing House remained the largest Holiness literature publisher in the world and, by 1980, ranked as the fifth largest religious publisher in North America. For decades, the Nazarene hymnal and Sunday School literature, both published by Nazarene Publishing House, were important commonalities among English-speaking Nazarenes around the world. One could walk into any English-speaking church around the world and find a connecting link. However, by the 1970s some large congregations were using Sunday School literature and hymnals published by other evangelical publishing houses.

As manager of NPH, "Bud" Lunn, like his father, took a "hands-on" approach. He guarded against any careless expense. By 1994 book sales at NPH exceeded $2 million, an all-time high. In 1995, 613,611 books were printed or reprinted at NPH, including more than 250,000 copies of the new hymnal *Sing to the Lord*.[108]

Robert Brower served as president of Nazarene Publishing House from 1995 to 1998. Bower had served on the faculty and administration of Trevecca and MidAmerica. He found that while for many years NPH had been competing with publishers to serve the church, now it was "competing with new national and global organizations with a broad array of religious publishing materials and products." Brower prepared the church for the new "Age of Communication."[109]

Brower brought the editorial and production functions of Beacon Hill Press of Kansas City under one manager, first Hardy Weathers, and later Kelly Gallagher. Publishing and production on a somewhat "haphazard, unsolicited manuscript" basis was replaced by "publishing by design" where solicited, planned publications were projected, more effectively connecting "mission"-driven and "market"-driven products. The publishing house produced Stan Toler's Stewardship materials in this way. Brower became president at Point Loma when Jim Bond was elected general superintendent.[110]

The *Herald of Holiness* and the *Preacher's Magazine* were streamlined for survival. William McCumber edited the *Herald of Holiness* until his retirement in 1989 and was followed by Wesley Tracy, who served until 1997. The 1997 General Assembly decided to combine the *World Mission* magazine with the *Herald of Holiness*. Franklin Cook became the editor of the newly designed publication, *Holiness Today*. Whereas in its early years, the *Preacher's Magazine* had provided a forum for preachers on a wide variety of subjects, the magazine became more focused on preaching itself. More and more was being published online at the clergy development Web site.[111]

The denomination became more aware of its responsibilities and accountability within a broader evangelical culture. On local levels, often Nazarenes were leaders of evangelical associations. The church had decided, finally, to become partners in the Christian Holiness Association (CHA) in 1969 and, after many years of hesitation, the National Evangelical Association (NAE) in 1984. General Secretary B. Edgar Johnson became president of the NAE in 1990. Nazarenes cooperated as well with the Lausanne Committee for Word Evangelism. In 1986 Roger Parrott, who had served on the administration of MidAmerica Nazarene College, became director of United States Operations for the Lausanne Committee for World Evangelization.[112]

The Church of the Nazarene remained unknown to many Christians. In 1994 Nazarene Theological College in Manchester, England, hosted a worldwide broadcast to a potential audience of 100 million persons. "It grieves me that our church is so little known in Britain, but it doesn't have to stay that way," said Gordon Thomas, dean of students. A world away, Jose Pacheco, administrative coordinator for Spanish publications for the Church of the Nazarene, was named to the international editorial board of the Wesley Heritage Project. The Church of the Nazarene was the most influential Wesleyan denomination in the Spanish-speaking world, according to Pacheco.[113]

In 1999 the Church of the Nazarene joined the World Methodist Council. This council had been organized in 1881, and at the time of joining Nazarenes became one of nearly one hundred denominations around the world that traced their spiritual and theological lineage to the eighteenth-century Wesleyan Revival. To the council, Nazarenes brought "a passion for world evangelization" and an eagerness to "experience and share the evangelization ethos of this great association," according to General Secretary Jack Stone. But there was some consternation in Nazarene ranks over this move. A century earlier people made the conscious choice to leave churches that had shown clear signs of diluting the strength of their doctrines and becoming indistinguishable from complacent, comfortable Christianity.[114]

CONCLUSION

The Church of the Nazarene's growth rate, it often seemed, was maximal when its position in society was the most marginal. Another way of stating this is to construe the story as a move to the center, away from a "sectarian shield" mentality toward a "permeable filter" relationship with the surrounding culture. Increasingly the church saw itself as a recognized denomination with presence and influence. The church provided a clear voice, speaking out against many kinds of evil and demonstrating compassion. The church saw itself as being unequivocally committed to Christ's gospel and the cause of the Kingdom.

Nazarenes tried to organize so as to be more effective in their work in the world. The church by its very nature existed between gospel and culture. Its task was to "hear the gospel that calls Christian believers to know, value and intend things in a very different way" than other persons in surrounding cultures.[115] They faced the most serious issues that existed in global societies, such as substance abuse, abortion and the right to life, divorce and dying, violence and nuclear disarmament, racism and gender discrimination, entertainment and media misuse, and bioethics. Nazarenes realized that the pull to either conservative or liberal stances in society needed to be countered by centering upon the church's mission. What did it mean to be Christian in the world?

Sociologists suggested that when there was too little identification with the culture, churches became subcultural ghettos, and that when churches assumed too much of the culture's perspectives and values, they became domesticated and their message nullified. While third generation Nazarene young people found their forebears too peculiar and countercultural, new Nazarenes in the 1990s rediscovered the biblical notion of the people of God as a "contrast-society." This required reimagining the church as one both "catholic" and "local" but resolutely missional and connectional.[116]

TWENTY-SIX

Outreach:
Evangelism and Compassion

Like many denominations, the Church of the Nazarene had spent decades separating evangelism and compassionate ministry. "The Great Reversal," a term that historian Timothy Smith used, described the "danger of coming apart on the question of whether the gospel is personal or social."[1] Smith's own historical investigations established links between holiness and social reform in the nineteenth century and influenced a generation of evangelical scholars.[2]

In reacting against the "social gospel," many evangelicals equated biblical themes with sociopolitical conservatism. Conformity with cultural economic values moved Nazarenes away from close engagement with disadvantaged persons. While Nazarenes maintained hospitals and clinics abroad, they were less involved in meeting physical needs in their own neighborhoods. After World War II Nazarene imagination had been captured by the impassioned appeals of J. B. Chapman in 1948, "All Out for Souls" and "Evangelism First!" Compassionate ministry was a secondary mission, never to compete with the first. Evangelism and end-time urgency were dominant characteristics of mission. General Secretary B. Edgar Johnson commented, "My concept of the Church of the Nazarene has always been that it is an 'evangelistic movement'—revivals, outreach, growth, its trademark at home; and evangelism through missions its extension around the world."[3] In the late 1960s and 1970s a strong denominational emphasis on church growth developed. Evangelism was primary chronologically, theologically, and strategically. "Why feed people who are going to hell?" asked a visitor to the Community of Hope in Washington, D.C.[4]

Meanwhile, world crises prompted urgent attention to humanitarian concerns and called for the full depth and range of denominational resources. Nazarene Compassionate Ministry became integral to the denomination's mission and identity. This led to the emergence of a fully orbed mission—the whole gospel for the whole world. By the turn of the century the church had returned to nineteenth-centuries models that wedded revivalism and social involvement.[5]

EVANGELISM AND CHURCH GROWTH

During the years 1976 to 1997, general leaders spurred a new focus on church planting and church growth. Donald McGavran and the Church Growth Movement coming from Fuller Theological Seminary in Pasadena, California, made a deep impression on Paul Orjala, missions professor at NTS; Raymond Hurn, Home Missions department director; Bill Sullivan, Evangelism and Church Growth director; and key district superintendents. McGavran taught that "people like to get converted with their own kind of people." This meant concentrating on one socioeconomic or ethnic group in planting churches. The church identified "target groups" in "target communities" so that, for instance, a narrow band of "15- to 40-year-olds" within a fairly affluent city suburb were "prospects for the gospel."[6]

Raymond Hurn

Raymond Hurn (1921-2007) brought the denomination into the forefront of the Church Growth Movement. Hurn was born in Oregon and attended Bethany Nazarene College, graduating in 1943. Later he studied at Oklahoma University and Fuller Theological Seminary. He pastored churches in Hays, Kansas; Tulsa; Atlanta; Medford, Oregon; and Norman, Oklahoma. In 1968, after nine years as superintendent of the West Texas District, Hurn became secretary of the Department of Home Missions. In this capacity, Hurn spearheaded the denominational thrust in church growth. Hurn's publications included *Mission Possible* (1973); *Black Evangelism* (1973); *Which Way from Here?* (1974); *The Rising Tide: New Churches for the New Millennium* (1997); *Spiritual Gifts Workshop* (1978); and *Finding Your Ministry* (1979). He also edited the *Mission Action Handbook*.

In 1985, after seventeen years as director of Home Missions, Hurn resigned. He intended to begin a new career teaching at Nazarene Bible College in Colorado Springs. Unexpectedly, the 1985 General Assembly elected him general superintendent. Even after his election as general superintendent, Hurn gathered and developed materials helpful to the leadership of districts and published the *District Superintendents' Sourcebook*.

Fuller itself rated Hurn among top church executives in his understanding of church growth principles and his ability to implement them on a denominational level. Hurn stressed that the "very lifeblood of the denomination is to divide and multiply." "Renewing the characteristics of a religious movement is paramount for both large and small churches as the new century arrives," he wrote in 1997.[7]

To Hurn, church planting was a matter of institutional life and death. Under Hurn's guidance district superintendents emerged, once more, as the promoters, and developers of new churches. "Whereas early-day district superintendents had risen to prominence as church planting evangelists," Hurn pointed out, their successors "had their energies drained away in maintenance of denominational machinery."[8] Hurn aimed to make district superintendents specialists in church growth. The first comprehensive seminar on church development exclusively for Nazarene district superintendents was held March 21-25, 1977, in Kansas City, with Peter C. Wagner and John Wimber of Fuller Theological Seminary and Paul Orjala of NTS as primary speakers. Local churches used Paul Orjala's *Get Ready to Grow: A Strategy for Local Church Growth* in a denomination-wide study in February and March 1978.[9] Later that year seventy-six superintendents in Britain, Canada, and the United States completed Phase I of the denomination-wide church growth study. Home Missions began basic church growth training and teaching about spiritual gifts.[10]

The Oregon Pacific District, under the leadership of Superintendent Carl Clendenen, was one of the areas that saw fast growth in the late 1970s by planting as "many churches as possible as quickly as possible." The Oregon Plan for Church Planting resulted in new work in fifty-six communities within a three-year period, and twenty-five newly organized Churches of the Nazarene.[11] Beaverton, Oregon, lay leaders, for instance, responded eagerly to the challenge to partner with pastoral and district leaders in starting fifteen new Nazarene congregations in 1980. Taking his cue from the rapid expansion of the church in Oregon, Hurn encouraged superintendents to set specific goals for new churches to begin on their districts. In recruiting pastors, the district superintendent looked for those who they believed could begin new churches.[12]

Nazarene scholars, who believed their task was to provide theological insight, felt themselves sidelined as the church moved in this direction. To address this concern, in June 1978 Hurn brought together a symposium of church leaders and scholars, including Paul Orjala, Mildred Wynkoop, Morris Weigelt, Frank Carver, Rob Staples, Irving Laird, Paul Bassett, Donald Owens, Bill Sullivan, and Alex Deasley, to discuss church growth. C. Peter Wagner lectured and then applied his lectures to the Nazarene context. But critics questioned using programs rooted in other traditions and linking a sociological method to the denominational mission. To some such criticisms, Bill Sullivan responded, "As prayer is essential to building God's kingdom, so is research to the human side of the Kingdom enterprise. It is imperative that we know the most effective means for spreading the gospel."[13]

From church planting strategies targeting specific groups, Nazarenes sensed the need to reengage in ministries in cities. In 1979 the office of Urban Missions was established, and the Reaching the Cities thrust was initiated. Leaders set a goal to plant one thousand churches during the Diamond Jubilee Year (1983). On the anniversary date, October 13, 1983, Nazarenes organized one hundred eighty new churches, ninety-five of which were in the United States and Canada. The church exceeded the goal of one thousand new churches by five hundred sixty. Local churches were primarily responsible for birthing these new congregations. The ten-year Thrust to the Cities began in 1985 at the Anaheim General Assembly under Michael Estep. The Church Growth Division selected key world city areas for 1986, alternating each year with a key city in the United States.[14]

From 1985 until his retirement in 2003 Sullivan served as executive director of the newly created Division of Evangelism and Church Growth. Prior to coming to Kansas City in 1980, Sullivan had served as a pastor in Colorado and as district superintendent in North Carolina. Sullivan pursued a doctor of ministry at Fuller Theological Seminary in the area of church growth. Sullivan saw the work of the church as broadly classified in two major categories: evangelism and education. The responsibilities of the Church Growth Division fell within the evangelizing category. Donald McGavran provided the authority for distinguishing evangelism even further from "discipling." But Sullivan backed away from implementing altogether McGavran's homogenous unit principle in the United States, where he saw it as misplaced. Sullivan was pragmatic, nonetheless, wanting the most effective, ethical, and biblical methods of evangelism. His responsibility was for "the growth of the number of churches and the growth of the size of the churches. There are other kinds of growth but they are not final measures."[15] In 1989 Sullivan launched *Grow: A Journal of Church Growth, Evangelism, and Discipleship* "to contribute to the advancement of God's kingdom by fostering growth in the Church of the Nazarene." It offered practical strategies for local churches. *Grow* introduced Nazarenes to many lively and innovative congregations. Under Sullivan the NewStart program shifted the initiative to local churches and pastors rather than headquarters. The premier issue of *NewStart* appeared in the winter of 1996-97 with the understanding that the most effective means of winning lost people to Jesus Christ was through planting new churches.[16]

RESEARCH AND CHURCH GROWTH

General Superintendent Eugene Stowe declared that "the systematic and scientific study of Nazarene church growth is an idea whose time has come." While leaders became convinced that God willed "the growth and the multiplication of the church," diagnostic and procedural tools gave leaders handles for their task.[17] The Church Growth Resource Center began under the Home Missions department. It provided adequate data and accurate interpretation for making informed, strategic decisions. Dale Jones served as the division's statistician. He gathered and analyzed information, such as income and educational levels, for areas chosen for new church plants. The center proved an effective resource.[18]

The Association of Nazarene Sociologists of Religion (ANSR) began in 1982 to provide the denomination with assistance by suggesting what outreach techniques were most effective in given contexts. Finding such scholarship useful, Bill Sullivan quickly authorized and funded ANSR meetings. Annual topics included Assimilation, Urban Ministry, Internationalization, "Dropouts," and Changing Worship Styles. ANSR sponsored "Listening Post," a semiannual survey centering on how Nazarenes responded to the circumstances and challenges of society. ANSR offered a range of leadership resource seminars and strategies to build bigger churches. Partly as a result of these initiatives, the number of churches of one thousand members or more doubled between 1988 and 1998.[19]

A similar organization, the Association of Nazarenes in Social Work, began in 1983. The mission of ANSW was "to provide opportunities through which Christians in social work may enrich their understanding of the dynamic relationship between life in Jesus Christ and the philosophy and practice of the social work profession. ANSW encourages awareness of contemporary human need in the community and of the social work profession as a means of ministering to this need."[20]

In another initiative, in 1989 the General Superintendents and the General Board authorized the Hiram F. Reynolds Institute. Robert Scott, after concluding his service as director of World Mission, became the institute's director. The institute's purpose was to "develop strategies and structures for mission implementation into the twenty-first century, for the global effectiveness of the Church of the Nazarene." It explored crucial issues that affected the future of the Church of the Nazarene, and proposed spiritual and organizational strategies that would enable the church to be a "vision-driven, Great Commission movement in our world." In practical terms this meant prodding the General Board to think both "globally and locally," since the interrelatedness of people globally and locally lay at the heart of the church. The institute concluded that "a fundamental key to a positive future for the Church of the Nazarene in the new millennium is only possible through an authentic spiritual awakening and a Holy Spirit directed revival throughout our global church family." The institute, which concluded its work in 1997, recommended that the church's distinctive theology be "encased in language of as much brevity and preciseness as possible to be grasped by our various constituencies around the world," especially new Nazarenes.[21]

ETHNIC MINISTRIES

A global vision included seeing North America itself as a mission field and planting new churches among unreached ethnic groups in various cities. Hurn's first assignment in the Home Missions department was overseeing the merger of black churches into districts of their geographic area. Hurn drew together a Negro Advisory Committee, later renamed the Interracial Committee. Warren Rogers and Roger Bowman worked with Hurn to develop new approaches to evangelize African-Americans.[22] "Evangelism is so much more than verbalization of the gospel," Bowman wrote in 1975. "It is building bridges to people so that we can help them. There is no greater witness than a sermon in shoes."[23]

In 1976 the Home Missions department convened the first conference on urban/ethnic ministries. In that year there were 216 North American Nazarene congregations in which an ethnic minority predominated. Other conferences drew African-American Nazarenes together. "The Dream Becomes a Reality" was the title of a Church Extension Ministries report on the first National Black Churchman's Conference, held in Orlando, Florida, in June 1984. "Everyone who was there, both Black and White, stood in awe and praises at the moving of God's Spirit," wrote Charles Johnson.[24]

The New York District under the leadership of District Superintendent Dallas Mucci from 1980 took on an intentionally multicultural approach. The district planted fifty churches between 1982 and 1992. Thirty-six of these were a direct result of the 1988 Thrust to the City campaign. It began churches among Koreans, Haitians, Hispanics, and Caribbeans, and African-Americans.[25]

By 1992 there were 650 multicultural churches or missions with a total of 33,198 members in the United States and Canada. In 1995 and 1996 minorities, including immigrant groups, started more churches than the

English-speaking white majority. Tom Nees, director of Multicultural Ministries, attributed the rapid growth of the immigrant churches in the United States and Canada to the church's world mission enterprise. By 1996 there were 530 active Churches of the Nazarene that reported a primary cultural group other than white, English-speaking. "My interest," said Nees, "is not to simply identify minority groups but to provide a process where the church becomes inclusive, working together to reach all cultural groups in the U.S.A. and Canada."[26]

The 1998 Multicultural Ministries Conference focused on reconciliation. "The Church of Jesus Christ is not a church that is separate or exclusive. It is a church for all people, regardless of color, language, or race. It is a church of all peoples," said Jerry Porter in opening the plenary session. Cheryl Sanders, a Church of God (Anderson) pastor and scholar, appealed for an inclusive church. "Let there be no mistake. Pentecost was a multicultural, multinational, multiracial witness to God's work." Christianity's recent interest in developing an inclusive, multicultural church was not new, she said, but "an emphasis that has been central to its self-understanding from the beginning."[27]

COMPASSIONATE EVANGELISM

Before the 1970s, compassion among Nazarenes, except in such places as Papua New Guinea, Swaziland, and India, had been privatized and localized. But increasingly Nazarenes applied the doctrine of perfect love to the social distress of humanity. "We do not exact vows of poverty from those who join us," but, Wesley Tracy asked, "are we truly His if we fail to remember the poor?"[28]

In 1974 a group of Nazarene leaders, including John L. Knight, who then headed the Evangelism department, Paul Orjala, Raymond Hurn, H. T. Reza, Mendell Taylor, John A. Knight, then president of Mount Vernon Nazarene College, and William Prince, rector of European Nazarene Bible College, attended the International Congress on World Evangelization at Lausanne, Switzerland. They heard German theologian Peter Beyerhaus and Latin American theologian Samuel Escobar call for the Church to embody a gospel that both identified with the oppressed and transformed society. The *Lausanne Covenant* expressed clearly "penitence both for our neglect and for sometimes having regarded evangelism and social concern as mutually exclusive." It went on to say that the "salvation we claim should be transforming us in the totality of our personal and social responsibilities." The document stated that "there is no biblical dichotomy between the word spoken and the word made visible in the lives of God's people." Lausanne affirmed, empowered, and impelled Nazarenes to overcome any polarity between the gospel as word proclaimed and the gospel as word embodied in Christlike compassionate ministry. It related the preaching of the gospel to the transformation of society and not just to the conversion of individuals. Calls for a recovery of social justice and compassion in a world conference on evangelization made an impact, as did a confession of failure: "We confess with shame that we have often denied our calling and failed in our mission."[29]

By the 1970s Haiti contained more Nazarenes than any other country outside of the United States. It set an example, followed in America and elsewhere, of compassionate evangelism. Nazarenes sponsored mobile medical clinics and community-based health care. The church ran nutrition and health education centers and an immunization program. It began agricultural projects such as pig raising and sponsored vocational courses in typing, sewing, woodworking, and welding. As the per-capita income and giving of Haitian Nazarenes rose, the church established a credit union. Such ministries, Howard Culbertson observed, "mark the Church of the Nazarene as an organization that cares about people. They are signs of the Kingdom."[30] Finding public education inadequate, Nazarene missionaries began literacy programs and primary schools. By 1980, the church was maintaining one hundred day schools that taught fourteen thousand students; by 1990 there were two hundred fifty schools teaching twenty-five thousand students. Nazarene membership in Haiti reached over eighty-three thousand in 2000.[31]

Two weeks after an earthquake shook Guatemala in 1975, the *Herald of Holiness* announced that it would accept contributions to provide food, shelter, and medical care for those suffering. The Guatemala Earthquake Reconstruction Fund was officially set up as a 10 Percent Credit Offering Fund. (Local churches received an award from the NWMS if they contributed 10 percent of their budget to Nazarene World Missions.) An astonishing response followed. The Nazarene Medical Action Fellowship flew in medical supplies, three doctors, and a nurse. By the completion of the project, within a year and a half, Nazarenes had given over $300,000 for the crisis in Guatemala.[32]

Nazarenes in Nicaragua responded with compassion to the needs of their own country. The denomination's Compassionate Ministries sent food and clothing, and local Nazarenes formed "viveres por trabajo" (food for work) programs. This project aimed to "put tools in the hands of the people so that instead of dependency they can rise to the challenge of self-sufficiency."[33] The Nazarenes also became active in CEPAD, the "Comite Evangelico Pro-Ayuda a los Damnificados," to which almost all Protestant groups in Nicaragua belonged. It cooperated with the government on social programs. Nicanor Mairena, the Nazarene district superintendent, served on CEPAD's Executive Board. Its activities included setting up a rehabilitation program for released prisoners, establishing sewing shops for women, providing psychiatric care, building elementary schools, evangelizing, championing human rights, and providing mortuary services (as it was "very expensive to die in Nicaragua!").[34] Juan Romero, a Nazarene pastor, ran a home for children.[35]

At the same time several social-ministry oriented congregations emerged in the United States. These included the Lamb's Center in New York under the leadership of Paul Moore; the Community of Hope in Washington, D.C., under Tom Nees; Golden Gate Ministries in San Francisco under Michael Christensen; Bresee Institute at Los Angeles First Church under Ron Benefiel; Shepherd Community in Indianapolis under John Hay; and Liberation Community in Fort Worth under Brian Stone.[36]

The Lamb's Club ministry in Manhattan provided the model for other work. In June 1974 Paul Moore, pastor of the Lamb's Club, and Gordon Cosby, pastor of the Washington, D.C., Church of the Savior (non-Nazarene) spoke to Nazarenes in Kansas City about the hope that Jesus brought to the inner city. "The need at the heart of the major cities is so tremendous as to be crushing." There were critical shortages of space, food, and resources. Each person living in such situations discovered the enemy within—an inner oppression. Christians needed to be in these places and learn how "to infect the situation with hope." They can do so because they are rooted in Jesus Christ.[37] Later pastors Orville Jenkins Jr., David Best, and John Calhoun maintained the various ministries of Lamb's. By 1990 the church included a support group for persons with HIV/AIDS. Pastors paid much of their attention to fund-raising for various ministries.[38]

Tom Nees

In 1976 Tom Nees was the young pastor of Washington, D.C., First Church, "struggling," he reflected, "to find a way to minister to the poor of my city." The son of L. Guy Nees, Tom Nees had studied at NNC and NTS and had pastored in Washington state, California, and Ohio before being called to Washington First Church. The youth movement of the 1960s, coupled with the Wesleyan renaissance and, in particular, the book *John Wesley: Christian Revolutionary*, by Mildred Wynkoop, reinforced in Nees the desire to see the Church of the Nazarene actively involved in society.[39]

Along with some members of Washington First, Nees participated for fifteen months in a local organization known as

Jubilee Community, which acquired apartment buildings that it then renovated for housing for poor people. Nees did the same, securing $75,000 from various sources, including the Washington District, for the purchase of a rundown apartment building. Nees also received a $100,000 grant from the city's Department of Housing and Community Development. Laypersons and youth from the Washington District and elsewhere renovated the building. The Community of Hope opened its doors to the poor in 1976. "To evangelize in an area surrounded by people in need of food, clothing, shelter, health care, jobs, legal aid, and education," Nees realized, required that the church "equip its members for compassionate ministry to the whole person."[40]

Nees saw the Community of Hope as bridging the separation between social ministry and gospel proclamation. The Community of Hope, said an early statement of its general definition, "Seeks to become a cross-cultural community, welcoming into its membership people of all racial, ethnic and social backgrounds, reflecting the pluralism of the city and the bond which unites people together in Christ. The particular focus of service is to the poor within the city who are denied the critical minimums of decent housing and adequate opportunities for education and vocational development." Nees believed that those with diverging views of what evangelism and Christian compassion meant could connect in that "all of them wanted the needy people they see every day in their compassionate ministry programs [to] become followers of Jesus." Compassion should not be "bait to engage in manipulative evangelism," nor could it be bypassed by people who had dedicated their lives to the reality that "Jesus is the Way." Evangelism without compassion was "evangelism without the gospel." Equally, "compassion without proclamation of the kingdom of God" was but "humanitarianism, something short of life-changing good news." "Compassion is how the gospel of the kingdom is made known. The Word becomes flesh again and again in deeds of kindness and the struggle for justice," Nees claimed. Jesus was the one who called His followers to "be compassionate as your Father is compassionate" (Luke 6:36, NEB).[41]

In 1978 Nees, speaking at NTS, alerted students to the connections between the inner spiritual life and a holistic ministry in society: "Inner-city ministry is tough work which requires a commitment within. At the heart of inner-city missions is the New Testament word of salvation for both individuals and our society."[42] Violence and, eventually, AIDS challenged ministry at the Community of Hope. Nees quoted Jack Nelson: "The poverty so enraged me that I wanted to scream at God. Then I came to a painful realization. In the suffering of the poor, God was screaming at me."[43]

Ministries at the Community of Hope included health care, legal aid, housing assistance, and programs in child development. It received referrals from the city's welfare system, and provided ninety days shelter for homeless families. While staying at the Community of Hope, these families received health care and legal aid and, before leaving, a grant for the deposit necessary for renting an apartment. By 1985 the Community of Hope had a staff of thirty-five and a budget of $900,000, about a third of which came from individual donors and the remainder from various government and private grants. By 1988 the annual budget had climbed to $1.37 million.[44]

While Nees was ministering to the poor in Washington, the same city's First Church, under the leadership of Samuel Smith, opened its own doors wide to minorities and drew members from the diplomatic community.[45]

In 1977, soon after graduating from the Nazarene Bible College in Institute, West Virginia, JoeAnn Ballard started Neighborhood Christian Center in Memphis in cooperation with Young Life and Youth for Christ. In seventeen years the Neighborhood Christian Center expanded to eighteen centers. Ballard explained that though the work concentrated on compassionate ministries, "I don't think you can get to the heart of the problems of the urban poor without addressing their spiritual needs, and that's where Christianity becomes a big part of our work."[46] In 2005, when Ballard opened another Neighborhood Christian Center, the centers were serving about one hundred thousand people per year.

These centers birthed churches. In 1994 the Memphis Fellowship Church was the only black Church of the Nazarene on the Tennessee District. In 2008 there were fourteen Black churches on the district, with such names as the Look at God Church of the Nazarene, Restoration Tabernacle, Emmanuel Church, and the Holiness Tabernacle. The number of Black members on the Tennessee District rose in the same period of time from 85 to 1,193.[47]

Mother Teresa's work in Calcutta, India, inspired Michael Christensen's ministry in San Francisco. "Sometimes you must be confronted with poverty in another culture before you can recognize it in your own,"[48] Christensen noted. Mother Teresa's view of compassion was not that all Christians should become social workers but that all should embody that mourning for the world that truly reflected Christ's being present with the poor as His own brothers and sisters.[49]

The general superintendents supported such ministries. "Where Christian holiness is truly alive, compassion is its beautiful fruit," read a "Proclamation" of the Board of General Superintendents in December 1981. The Christmas season should be an occasion of remembering the poor and neglected, but

Nazarenes, the general superintendents admonished, should be always "seeking to do good to the bodies and souls of men; feeding the hungry, clothing the naked, visiting the sick and the imprisoned, and ministering to the needy, as opportunity and ability are given."[50] Similarly, in a "Pastoral Letter," the Board of General Superintendents in 1983 noted that "a new social consciousness has moved across our church." The "sense of 'holy compassion' was an authentic expression," the superintendents recognized, "of the American Holiness Movement's roots in the Wesleyan Revival." In fact, the general superintendents affirmed, "the ministry of compassion was emphasized in such a manner as to place it very near to the center of the fundamental reason for the church's existence." The leaders urged this moral response to the poor in "light of the biblical perspective as well as our distinctive mission." Such social ministries should be "incorporated in the total program of evangelism," and ministry should be "to the entire community" without exclusion of people from lower socioeconomic levels. In 1984 the Board of General Superintendents formed the Hunger and Disaster Relief Fund Committee.[51] Once more, the general superintendents recognized that such ministries recovered the original mission and practice of the church. William Greathouse quoted Bresee: "This is the test which we desire all men to apply to the Church of the Nazarene. First, it entered an open door. It did not seek the rich," and "to these people [the poor] they went."[52]

Adding to the rationale, in a paper he presented to a Caribbean Nazarene Regional Conference, Timothy L. Smith insisted that Christianity offered solutions to the social problems of the contemporary world, beginning with "a *scriptural analysis* of the condition of the poor." Wesleyan theology enabled Nazarenes to make ethical judgments about the exploitation of the poor and forbade any "deferral of doing right." A Christ-centered gospel was "set to deliver us from all sin, now, including any willing participation in social or economic evil." Nazarenes could recover "the biblical promises to the poor," Smith said. "Those promises are both individual and social, temporal and eternal." He called for Nazarenes to resist "millenarianism" but to join efforts "to prepare a Kingdom for the King," and to stand against contemporary equivalents of slavery. "The promise of salvation we preach to the poor," Smith continued, "is both social and spiritual." The church "must recognize and challenge social and structural injustice wherever it appears." Both deliverance from the terrible consequences of violence and the need to react violently were a part of Wesleyan liberation thought, and it was part of "our joy and duty" to imitate the "peaceableness of Jesus."[53]

Steve Weber

Nazarene Compassionate Ministries began formally in early 1984 with Steve Weber as director. Weber's task was to coordinate and evaluate requests for aid, monitor disbursements, and enlist support and finances. Weber's experience while serving as a missionary in Haiti from 1975 to 1984 significantly shaped the developing Nazarene consciousness of holistic mission. Weber observed that while some Nazarenes visiting Haiti felt that the "church had gone liberal," most were impressed by the integration of evangelistic mission with compassionate ministry.[54]

The first Nazarene Compassionate Ministries Conference was held at NTS in 1985. One who attended, Linda Wilcox, had been disappointed at the very few opportunities for women and ethnic minorities in leadership. But she "felt tremendous hope for the Church of the Nazarene" through attending the conference. "There was a new imperative to meet the human needs around us—individually and collectively."[55] At subsequent general and regional conferences NCM representatives interfaced with NWMS district and local leaders, Nazarene Health Care Fellowship members, prison chaplains, and teachers and students. In many of the new countries that the church entered in the 1980s and 1990s compassionate ministries preceded or accompanied the church.

In 1985 Bryan Stone, then a Ph.D. student at Southern Methodist University, founded Liberation Community in Fort Worth, Texas. Its particular ministry provided housing for the poor. Corporations donated homes that they had acquired in failed savings and loans. Many of these homes were in the inner city. Liberation Community renovated the homes and sold them to low-income families. The proceeds were placed in a revolving loan fund, which, in turn, enabled other low-income families to afford housing. Liberation Community provided a home ownership course for new and potential buyers. It provided legal aid and advocacy as well. In 1988 the work expanded from its base to include a community in Riverside. By the time Stone left the work in 1993, the yearly budget for Liberation Community was about $200,000.[56]

Shepherd Community in Indianapolis began in 1986 under the leadership of Dean Cowles. It started as a partnership between the large Westside Church, pastored by J. K. Warrick, and Central Church, in a deteriorating part of the city. Serving the homeless and very poor, initial ministries included a food pantry, clothing room, after-school educational program, furniture

> The purpose of the Liberation Community in Fort Worth, Texas, was to help provide an opportunity for individuals to become empowered and to serve in cooperative ministry in the inner city; to become a visible part of the body of Christ in the city of Fort Worth in worship and study of God's Word, in compassionate ministry for the needy, in Liberation for the oppressed, in renewal for the city, in emphasizing the full dignity and worth of all persons while seeking to break the barriers of prejudice to race, class, sex, and reputation; to announce the path of peace and non-violence as the Christian means for redeeming the world.[57]

assistance, a Bible club, counseling, and day care. Later, it opened a "justice" department. Mark Lingle, who coordinated this aspect of the ministry wrote: "God brings justice to our own lives by breaking down the barriers and prejudices that exist in our own hearts and minds. He then opens us up to a new love, a love of his Spirit, that allows us not to be service providers, but involved partners in the lives of the people we serve."[58] Shepherd Community received the full support of District Superintendent John F. Hay Sr. His son, John F. Hay Jr., became pastor of Shepherd Community in 1987. Cowles served as director until 1992, when he began a two-year stint as a missionary to Kenya, and then returned. In 1996 Cowles began a similar ministry in Denver.[59]

Compared to the new models provided by these churches, the Kansas City Rescue Mission remained more traditional. It was a project of the Kansas City District, begun under Superintendent Jarrette Aycock in 1950. In 1991 the city government forced it to relocate because of a development project. Under Joe Colaizzi, the center offered basic literacy training as well as shelter for homeless men.[60]

Nazarene Compassionate Ministries found a place among the church's structures. While Nees remained actively involved in the Community of Hope until 1994, in 1988 he became administrative director of Nazarene Compassionate Ministries Canada/USA. In 1991 he became president of NCM, a foundation incorporated to raise funds. NCM's Board of Directors was nominated by the Board of General Superintendents and elected by the General Board. By 1992 there were fifty-one local churches in the United States and Canada with nonprofit compassionate ministries centers. These gained recognition as "Good Samaritan" churches.[61]

Outside North America, the historic Raleigh Fitkin Hospital in Swaziland was nationalized in 1992. This followed a policy shift in World Mission away from medical institutions and toward "community based health care." At the time of nationalization the Raleigh Fitkin Hospital was receiving about $500,000 from the general Church of the Nazarene, which made up less than 20 percent of its operating costs, the rest coming from the Swazi government and various humanitarian foundations. The hospital was placed under the administration of the Swaziland Church of the Nazarene.[62]

In 1992 Nazarene physician Gary Morsch founded Heart to Heart International. Reflected Morsch, "Heart to Heart did not begin with a grand strategy. We did not set out to build a world-class relief organization." Though this was not under the denomination, Heart to Heart was operated by Nazarenes. The organization worked with companies such as Hallmark and found funds to minister to children in devastated areas. In 1995 Heart to Heart organized the largest private humanitarian shipment to Vietnam in twenty years with $7 million worth of medical equipment and supplies provided by NCM. "Though old wounds often heal slowly, this airlift will be a significant part of the healing so many of us long for," Morsch summarized.[63]

Meanwhile, the Nazarene Health Care Fellowship, made up of various Nazarene health professionals, took upon themselves various projects such as supplying equipment for the surgical room in the hospital in Papua New Guinea. NHCF opened chapters in other countries as well.[64]

In 1995 Steve Weber shifted to the Stewardship/Planned Giving office as its director, but he continued to oversee the production of NCM promotional and educational materials. Gustavo Crocker took charge of NCM operations outside of North America, while Tom Nees oversaw NCM services in the United States and Canada and, at the same time, served as Multicultural Ministries director.

Nees developed an "Introduction to Compassionate Ministries: A Seminar for Churches."[65] It emphasized neighborhoods as spaces to be transformed by ministry that transcended class, gender, and race barriers. In 1998 reports indicated that 107 Compassionate Ministry Centers and nearly seven hundred Good Samaritan churches existed. Their combined budgets exceeded $30 million. The spread of these churches revealed a "grassroots movement initiated entirely without general church orchestration from Kansas City," Tom Nees believed. Some of these Good Samaritan centers were established in neighborhoods near a local Church of the Nazarene, but not necessarily identified by name as connected.[66]

The response to crises in various countries continued time after time. In 1997, for instance, Nazarenes gave over $380,000 in a ten-week period in response to drought in Haiti and proved to be an efficient "delivery system" as it responded to devastating floods in Mozambique and to famine in Ethiopia.[67]

Theological discussions sustained the church's commitment to compassionate ministries. John A. Knight affirmed in his 1997 message to the Annual Leadership Conference: "Compassionate ministry seeks to deal with the *whole* person—body, mind, soul, and spirit. It endeavors to alleviate the result of negative conditions—including hurt, pain, suffering, and, where possible, tries to alter the conditions themselves." In defining "compassionate ministry," Knight distinguished it from the "social gospel." "Compassionate ministry," Knight declared, "is part of the genius of the Church of the Nazarene." Jesus' compassion was inclusive, worldwide, universal, practical, and forgiving.[68] Christian compassion, said Bryan Stone at the 1998 NCM conference, merged "charity with justice, worship with activism, protest with pastoral care, preaching with advocacy, and empowerment with evangelism."[69]

CONCLUSION

The church witnessed a remarkable recovery of ministry in inner cities and a simultaneous surge of compassionate ministries. The church worldwide perceived itself to possess a holistic missional identity. These developments made it possible to speak of a great reversal of the "Great Reversal." A new partnership between evangelism and compassionate ministries in holistic mission emerged. The wedding ceremony may have come in 2003, with the election of Tom Nees as director of the church's USA/Canada Mission Evangelism Division.[70]

TWENTY-SEVEN

Local Churches and Congregations

The denomination's Article of Faith on the church described both its local and universal characteristics, but the balance was not always struck. In 1976 the church reaffirmed that "the primary church is the local church,"[1] yet over the next three decades leaders centralized authority not only in Kansas City but also in regional offices.[2]

NEIGHBORHOODS NEAR AND FAR

In an age when a new global spirit permeated religion and society, "glocalization" captured the interconnection between the local and the global. "Interrelatedness" was the new key word and concept.[3] A Nazarene leader responsible for denominational children's ministries in these years recalled that "one could go anywhere in America in the early 1970s and visit a local congregation and know immediately that one was in a Nazarene church." By 2000 the statement was less valid. Nazarene styles of worship varied tremendously, and a fascinating variety of congregational models had emerged. Beneath these, there remained still some identifiable unity of mission and a distinguishing spirit or ethos among Nazarenes.[4]

Nazarene congregations were challenged to act responsibly in mission in their local contexts but with a global consciousness. Between "local" and "global" what connections were necessary or viable? The Work and Witness program of the World Mission Department and such agencies as Heart to Heart International typified the "glocalization" phenomenon in Nazarene circles. Thousands of Work and Witness teams provided ordinary people with the vision and the connections to do "extraordinary things." Heart to Heart represented the same spirit of volunteerism and compassion.[5]

James McGraw warned that "Bigger Is Better" and "Money Can Buy It" sentiments tempted pastors to focus on statistics rather than on "the persons these numbers represented."[6] Likewise, Ray Hurn wrote that "we should avoid the 'edifice complex,' being sure that our buildings are contributions to our mission, not monuments to our pride." M. A. Lunn concurred. "The church has prospered," Lunn wrote. "We have graduated from a 'sect' to a recognized, respectable denomination. Our churches are no longer situated on the wrong side of the tracks. Our 'store front' places of worship are almost a rarity. We are constructing churches that are a credit to the best neighborhoods." "There is not a thing wrong with that," said Lunn, "SO LONG AS the poor are welcome and the ill clad made to feel at home. There is no virtue in a plain, weather-beaten, run-down-at-the-heels, eyesore place of worship. But if our progress is marked by conformity to the ways of the world and the easygoing practices of thousands of church members, our improved status is subject to question."[7] Richard Thompson, a small church pastor, remarked: "The tiny church is a significant part of the universal Church of our Lord Jesus Christ, and its value and potential cannot be ignored." Indeed, two-thirds of all Nazarene churches had less than one hundred members.[8]

The Division of Evangelism and Church Growth categorized congregations by size. It held Small Church Institutes for churches with less than 100 members, Intermediate Church Initiatives for churches of 100 to 249 members, and the "K-Church" Projects for churches of 250 members or more. The aim was to establish "fellowship with peers in a focused process of training that will result in personal growth, numerical growth, and the strengthening of their churches."[9] The desire for maximum impact and visibility took shape in the 1960s and 1970s in, for example, the building of new sanctuaries and complexes at Bethany First Church, Denver First Church, and Pasadena First Church in California. These became examples of Nazarene "superchurch" congregations. In 1997 there were forty Churches of the Nazarene that reported at least one thousand in membership or average attendance. Twenty-eight of these were in the United States, three in Brazil, two each in Haiti and Korea, and one each in Cambodia, Guatemala, India, Mexico, and Mozambique.[10]

In addition to denominational conferences, Nazarene pastors and leaders of all sized churches attended seminars conducted by the new breed of evangelical superchurch pastors. General Superintendent Eugene Stowe recommended the large, "seeker friendly" Willow Creek Community Church as a model to pastors in North America. The Yoido Full Gospel Church in Seoul, pastored by Yongi Cho, stimulated the growth of cell groups and house churches around the world as well as Korea. John Maxwell, a successful Wesleyan Church pastor, became a best-selling author among Nazarenes. By the 1990s even old Sharpe Memorial Church in Glasgow, Scotland, planned intentionally "seeker sensitive" worship services. About one hundred "neutral name" churches across the United States existed in 1997. District superintendents and church planting supervisors asked, "Should we or should we not mention our denominational affiliation in our church name?"[11] With the phenomenal success of independent congregations around the world, some questioned whether denominationalism was necessary or viable.[12]

NAZARENE CONGREGATIONS

Nazarene congregations remained places where the Word was preached, where members' understanding of the world and salvation were Wesleyan, and where the central issue was holiness of heart and life. The local church was a place to feel at home. Members were on a journey. Pastor Kenn Coil of the Gateway Church of the Nazarene in Temecula, California, put it this way, "We seek to welcome everyone with love and acceptance. We hear every week from first time visitors in our worship service, 'We feel at home here; we sense the presence of the Lord in this place. There is grace in this place.'" Not only should the local church be open to all in the community, but it should be wholly open to God in worship as well, Nazarenes contended. That is, the whole church in worship meant welcoming everyone into the fullness of Christian identity, through the worship of Word, Sacrament, and Spirit. "We intentionally seek a blended form of worship," Pastor Coil said, one that combines the contemporary with the traditional, the preaching of the Word with singing in the Spirit, and the regular celebration of the death and resurrection of Christ at the communion table together."[13]

Pastor Ron Benefiel similarly desired Los Angeles First to center its attention on the needs of the surrounding community. He recovered a sense of "parish" or commitment to the land and neighborhood. Through the efforts of Benefiel and Fletcher Tink, Los Angeles First began the Bresee Institute for Urban Training. It drew Nazarenes and others to the city for specific theological education in context to meet urban challenges. Benefiel wanted Los Angeles First Church to "be the kind of church where everyone is welcome—a church for all people." The "multicongregational" church flourished "with three different languages, three different skin colors, and three different national origins." Worship provided a "natural bridge of language and culture" between Korean, English, and Spanish-speaking believers.[14] "They were genuinely and earnestly optimistic about the transforming power of the grace of God," Benefiel said to his people. The congregation resisted moving out of the neighborhood even when its cultural makeup changed. Twenty-nine cultural groups participated among the five thousand gathered to celebrate the one hundredth anniversary of the church in 1995.[15]

Pastor Miguel Armoa wanted to wrap the arms of the Moreno Church of the Nazarene, Buenos Aires, around its entire community by visualizing "a church without walls." Similarly members of Ed Meenderink's Kerk van de Nasarener in Vlaardingen, Netherlands, asked themselves: "How would Jesus conduct a church gathering in our situation so that all kinds of people would feel at home?" Meenderink himself had been raised totally outside of any church. Soon after becoming a Christian, he attended the Haarlem Church of the Nazarene and felt called to preach. He sensed that people needed "balance between a formal and a charismatic service. Freedom and spontaneity are important to us. We believe and experience the way a Nazarene church can have Spirit-filled, enthusiastic services with spontaneity while avoiding the extremes of the Pentecostal movement."[16] The church bridged generations and patterns of worship. About eight hundred persons, including children and youth, attended. Meenderink's preaching used contemporary, "normal" language. Fifty-five percent of the people had no "Christian memory" or church background.[17]

Nazarene churches in Korea planted congregations and sent missionaries. Nazareth Church, the denomination's oldest church in South Korea, established five daughter churches and contributed funds for buying land in China and for building other churches in Thailand and the Philippines. The role of the church, said Pastor Ryu Doo-hyun, was "evangelism—education—service" taken from Acts 5:42.[18] The Living Stone Church of the Nazarene was one of six new churches started during the Seoul Thrust to the Cities in 1992. In the beginning days, Pastor Park Yu-sok, a new graduate of Korean Nazarene Theological College, "fasted and prayed for three weeks, taking only water." "My heart was sick but I kept praying and knocking on doors," he said. "We grow through prayerful evangelism and careful presentations of God's word." A Korean Air Force major, a new convert, became the key layperson in this new church.[19] More than five hundred persons attended the Nam Seoul (South Seoul) Church, pastored by General Board member Kim Young-baek. The theme of the church was "Give Me This Mountain," from Josh. 14:12 (a Korean gospel song used the same lyrics). The church used laypersons in key leadership roles. Thirty percent of the congregations were new believers. Outreach came through teaching persons to play music instruments, Chinese and English language study, and ministry to preschool children. The large Anjung Church included rural farmers mixed with factory workers and some small-business owners. Members built the first building with bricks they themselves had made. Oh Jong-hwan, the pastor, also planted other churches in the area and inspired several to become pastors. The Anjung Church ministered to the elder folk of the area with compassionate ministries. The church's motto was "A Church Overflowing with Blessing and Grace."[20]

Meanwhile local congregations in such places as Rwanda-Burundi found themselves caught in wars and violence. Part of their task was to interpret life in situations of grim suffering and death and to make sense of this.[21]

Creative spaces were sought for holy places in cities where economic costs skyrocketed. For decades the church owned the twentieth floor of a commercial building in Hong Kong, which it used as its central church. Such circumstances around the world spurred the multiple use of facilities. Local congregations saw "multiple use" of resources as both good stewardship and an outreach ministry.[22]

Remaining downtown, Nashville First Church and neighborhood churches networked with agencies such as The Salvation Army, Union Rescue Mission, Traveler's Aid, Big Brothers, and Christian Counseling Services to form the East Nashville Cooperative Ministry. It provided food, clothing, gasoline, medicine, and transportation to the needy.[23]

Members of the Fairview Village Church of the Nazarene in a suburb of Philadelphia stated that their purpose was "to be a biblically shaped community of grace where Jesus is Lord in worship, education, service and witness." The Fairview congregation consisted of 50 percent former Roman Catholics and 40 percent with a variety of church and nonchurch backgrounds. Only 10 percent of the members were Nazarenes of long standing.[24]

The College Church in Bourbonnais, Illinois, also formed its mission statement, "to produce fully devoted followers of Jesus Christ." The pastor, Dan Boone, broke this down into four categories of ministry: "worship, disciple-making, service, and evangelism." Typically Nazarenes focused church ministry on evangelism followed by discipleship and service.[25]

PASTORAL LEADERSHIP AND PREACHING

Communicators and motivators dominated the era of the 1970s to the 1990s. Some Nazarene pastors felt that they had to "perform like superstars" each time they were in front of their congregations. James McGraw identified this as an "affliction of our times" rooted in "false ideas about 'success' in ministry." Pastors, McGraw admonished, needed instead to measure success by faithfulness, watchfulness, and biblical patterns of ministry.[26] McGraw, who taught a generation of preachers at NTS, wanted pastors to become "bifocal" in their preaching, gazing equally upon the Word of God and the world of human needs. He wanted preachers to remember that congregations preferred to "see a sermon than to hear one any day."[27]

Nazarenes placed high value upon sermons. J. Kenneth Grider asked preachers, "When your people come into God's house," and "sit erect to

Almighty God," "what do you, as God's spokesperson, say to them?" "If the expository type of sermon is used," the preacher is "more likely to present a truly biblical, doctrinally sound, hearer-related, and hearer-accepted message."[28] Successful preaching, Wesley Tracy observed, blended *kerygma* and *didache*—"the teaching and discipling ministry." Preaching needed to provide doctrinal clarity and substance. "When confusion and uncertain trumpets clutter the doctrinal stage," said Tracy, it was time to step "back to simple Bible basics." Preachers and teachers needed to probe "behind the abstract creedal statements to the real experiences of God's people, which gave birth to the doctrines in the first place."[29]

But the priority of preaching underwent reappraisal. Members called for shorter sermons. Others questioned a pulpit-centered ministry. To a few, preaching seemed "nonproductive, ineffective, [and] only marginally relevant." Laypersons called upon Nazarene pastors to be successful managers and therapists as well as faithful shepherds and preachers, noted C. S. Cowles.[30]

Many Nazarenes still resonated strongly with revivalism. General Superintendent Prince called preachers to make their "proclamation clearly evangelistic" because their business was "to confront a sinning world with a speaking and a saving God."[31] Nazarenes were children of revival to whom joyful expression of heartfelt worship was natural. To dismiss or diminish the expectancy of revival was to live "beneath our privileges." More than two hundred thirty persons testified to spiritual victories in a fifty-day spontaneous revival in Lexington, Kentucky, in the summer of 1994, for instance.[32]

While still vitally interested in evangelism, Nazarene pastors became more aware of the need for discipleship training following conversion. Sermons were less crisis-oriented and more related to the day-to-day needs of living the Christian life. Sunday School material as well as sermons reflected this reorientation. But some Nazarenes were uncomfortable with this search for relevance, with Sunday School lessons that talked about "sex and the like," and teachers felt uncomfortable talking about such issues, which, said one, would be better left to pastors, James Dobson, or others. Discipleship training aimed, nonetheless, to produce laypersons competent and spiritually fired enough to witness to family members, neighbors, friends, and coworkers regarding their faith.[33]

MINISTRY OF SERVICE

Among Protestants in general there was a growing sense of the importance of laity, and many denominations sought to maximize the talents and abilities of laypersons. The postwar years had witnessed the pull toward the advanced education and training of clergy. Pastors came to consider themselves as "professionals." As churches grew beyond the five hundred mark they hired full-time staff members to minister in particular areas such as Christian education and youth ministries. This obscured the role of laypersons in the church. But the years after 1976 witnessed "a period of the reassertion of interdependence" between laity and clergy, noted Paul Bassett, in which each was saying to the other: "We're your partners here; you're our partners here."[34] C. J. Adams reflected that "in the process of institutionalization, the boundaries between clergy and laity have sometimes been overemphasized." "The New Testament," Adams continued, did "not reflect such a sharp distinction between clergy and laity as the church in later times has drawn."[35] Similarly, Pastor H. B. London saw the partnership between clergy and laity to be one of "professionals among professionals."[36]

Laypersons, stressed Jim Garlow, were *Partners in Ministry,* the title of his denomination-wide study book in 1980. At the time, Garlow was serving as minister of lay development at Bethany First Church. Garlow believed that all believers were ministers and "priests." Laypersons were called and gifted, and they were to be trained and sent. "Specialized ministry" consisted of preaching or teaching the Word of God, administering the sacraments of the Lord's Supper and baptism, administering the church for the sake of order, and enabling others. "Specialized" or "ordained" ministers equipped laypersons for ministry. The ordained minister was called upon to "be the equipper of many ministers—lay ministers," but "the term ministry should never be reserved for those who are ordained. It belongs," wrote Garlow, "to the *laos,* the people of God. The terms ministry and laity cannot be separated, if we desire to use them biblically."[37] Garlow himself implemented these ideas as pastor of the Metroplex Church in Fort Worth, Texas, which he started in 1983 with 11 members, and which, when he resigned in 1995, had 651 members. Garlow then took John Maxwell's place as pastor of the Skyline Wesleyan Church in San Diego, California.

The church designated the first year of the 1980-85 quinquennial "Celebration of Christian Holiness" as the "Year of the Minister" and the second as the "Year of the Layman." The Nazarene form of government, said Jerald Johnson, "paved the way for the Church of the Nazarene to share not only responsibility but authority as well with the laity."[38]

"Empower the laity!" was the watchword of the "Year of Increased Lay Involvement" in 1994-95. The emphasis was on cooperation and delegation of responsibility so that laypersons would not be robbed of "wonderful opportunities to be involved in ministry."[39] Among the presenters at an International

Congress on Lay Ministry held in Kansas City in 1995, NTS professor Roger Hahn dealt with the New Testament background for understanding lay and clergy relationships in ministry. "The church as a whole," Hahn believed, is like Israel "as a whole, a holy and royal priesthood," where "every believer is gifted for ministry." The Anglican and Methodist tradition may have blinded Nazarenes, Hahn said, "to the fact that the New Testament makes no distinction between ordained and unordained ministry." He proposed that talk should not be of "clergy" and "lay" ministry, but "the ministry of Christ that belongs to us all." Hahn continued, "Perhaps it's our marriage to secular contemporary culture that has seduced us into believing that we can call it 'church' when we have a staff of paid clergy performing in front of spectator lay people."[40] In 1997 General Superintendent Knight reaffirmed that "the responsible participation of the laity in the discharge of the Church's divine calling is not primarily a matter of idealism, enthusiasm, or organizational efficiency. It is fundamentally and foremost a new grasp of the meaning of the gospel."[41]

WORSHIP

Holiness people steered a middle path between highly liturgical and highly emotional forms of worship. Simplicity appealed to them. They adopted worship styles that reflected their tastes, and without thinking much about it integrated Word, Spirit, and sacraments. Traditionalists wanted old ways, with a few objecting to the substitution of the *New International Version* for the King James Version. To various degrees, Pentecostalism on one side, and liturgical traditions on the other, influenced Nazarene worship.[42]

Music was central to worship. Church music, C. Dale German wrote in 1976, "can have variety, versatility, and flexibility." A people's involvement through their latent musical ability had a lot to do with a growing church, in his opinion.[43] At the same time, noted James McGraw, excessive amplification, contrived choreography, and lack of substance deterred worship.[44]

A study by the Association of Nazarene Sociologists of Religion in the mid-1990s classified Nazarene congregations by worship style. The "traditional" Nazarene congregations, which defined themselves closely by *Manual* language and order, made up 85 percent of all churches. A "charismatic" worship style distinguished 10 percent of other congregations. Neo-Wesleyan "liturgical" congregations that stressed sacramental worship made up 5 percent of Nazarene churches. Eighty-seven percent of the Nazarenes polled said they liked worship services that made them think, while 67 percent said they wanted "worship to stir my emotions."[45]

Increasingly the term "re-traditioning worship" proved helpful in calling the contemporary church to reconsider the riches of the church's traditions and its balanced worship of Word-Table-Spirit. Part of the re-Wesleyanization of the denomination took the form of a reappraisal of the importance of the sacraments. The way the church worshipped was the truest indicator of its life. The sacraments were critical resources for the Christian journey. "Liturgy was part of the very path to salvation"[46] Paul Bassett taught NTS students. William Greathouse warned of a "market mentality" seeping into Nazarene worship. He mourned the crowding out of congregational singing and its substitution with entertainment. It represented, to Greathouse, "an invasion of the church by the spirit of the age. A narcissistic culture demands entertainment, and we can be religiously entertained and left untouched by the Spirit of Christ."[47]

Rediscovered Methodist and Anglican liturgy created, in a few places, a Nazarene "high church." Wesley Tracy commented in his introduction to Jesse Middendorf's *The Church Rituals Handbook*, published in 1997, that when evangelicals avoided the depth of liturgy, they were robbing themselves of the "meaning and beauty" of sacraments and ceremonies. Through ceremonies, the congregation participated in worship. In the baptism of a child, for instance, ritual called upon the whole "family of faith" to participate. Middendorf himself defended and explained on the principle of prevenient grace the practice of infant baptism. Middendorf's "Rite Two" for Communion included identifiably Anglican elements such as the prayer that begins "Almighty God, unto whom all hearts are open, all desires known," and the Nicene Creed. He included Advent and Easter season rituals as well as an "Order for Anointing and Prayer for Healing," and John Wesley's Covenant Service.[48] *The Preacher's Magazine* introduced Nazarene pastors to the Lectionary, based on the Christian calendar.[49]

Most churches found a middle way. In 1983, when Lillenas Publishing issued supplementary indexes to the church's *Worship in Song*, the editors plaintively argued, in "these days of glorifying the amateur and the commonplace," only through hymns were "the highest possible literary standards" maintained. When churches overused "popular ditties in vogue as a major part of worship," and avoided hymns with proven depth, they were in danger of elevating the spirit at the expense of the mind.[50]

"Our pastors will need to have clear vision, steady hands, and patient hearts," wrote Doug Samples, to develop worship with both "deep roots" and "great shade" for a new day. He urged blending the old and new and merging the "great hymns of the past with the contemporary sounds of today."[51]

But Roland Feltmate, a Nazarene pastor in Canada, was convinced that a "blended" worship would only guarantee "that every worshiper would be offended at least once each Sunday." He wanted worship to be faithful to the Bible, attentive to the Protestant tradition, and effective in the local context. The church needed a pragmatic traditionalism, he said. Music was a "cultural language" and made sense "only in the language of the culture for which it is intended."[52]

In whatever language, Nazarenes had an affinity for "songs of spiritual experience." "This is the pattern that is repeated over and over—a person has as encounter with Almighty God and seeks to express the wonder and glory of that experience in a song of testimony and praise."[53] Nazarenes appreciated the subjective side of worship. "Contemporary worship," Wesley Tracy observed, all but dismissed the three objective parts of worship (reading, preaching, and sacrament) in favor of the two subjective parts (singing and praying). This was a far greater issue to Tracy than music style preferences.[54]

Throughout the world, Nazarenes compared their churches to large independent and Pentecostal churches. Regional Director Richard Zanner faced the influence and impact of such trends in Africa. He recommended that Nazarenes neither "superficially condemn or ridicule these movements" nor be "too quick in assessing and judging" their own churches by comparison. "Do consider such charismatic super churches to be a challenge to yourself," Zanner continued, "your own congregation, and even your denomination." He admonished, "There is something beautiful about an enthusiastic, joyful, and victorious forward march, as long as biblical ethics are upheld, the unbeliever is being reached, and cheap sensationalism remains excluded."[55]

Such music and worship styles lessened the church's hostility toward Pentecostalism. Unthinkable in earlier years, Pentecostals preached in Nazarene pulpits. Jack Hayford, for instance, preached at Pasadena First Church in 1995 at the invitation of Pastor Steve Green.[56]

Yet the church still stood firmly against the actual speaking in tongues in Nazarene worship. In fact Green's invitation came less than a year after Nazarenes had expelled Al Woods, the pastor of the Totem Park Church of the Nazarene in Fairbanks, Alaska, which had grown to twelve hundred members, for being "charismatic." Woods proceeded to organize his own independent Door of Hope Church in the same city, and only thirty members remained in the Nazarene church.[57] At the 1997 General Assembly the general superintendents reported, "We will not allow the surface winds of fanaticism or the under-surface tides of theological uncertainty to change our course." They reaffirmed the judgment that "neo-pentecostal ecstatic prayer

Regarding the steady growth of tongues-speaking churches, and the interest of Nazarenes in Pentecostalism, the Board of General Superintendents issued this Statement on February 12, 2000:

> From time to time the Board of General Superintendents has been asked the question, "Do Nazarenes believe in the acceptability of neo-Pentecostal manifestations such as being slain in the Spirit, shaking, incessant laughter, and other similar phenomenon? Are these acceptable forms of worship in the Church of the Nazarene?"
>
> As you know, the Church of the Nazarene made a decision many years ago to disassociate itself from classical Pentecostalism by removing the name "Pentecostal" from the Church of the Nazarene. This was not done lightly. The early Holiness Movement in the United States soon became divided over the issue of tongues-speaking and other Pentecostal manifestations. The Church of the Nazarene felt led by the Spirit to place its emphasis on a changed life as being evidence of the baptism with the Holy Spirit. We did not then, nor do we now, accept tongues-speaking or prayer language as being evidence of the baptism with the Holy Spirit. Nor are these practices accepted in our churches.
>
> We make no condemnation of those who practice such things. In fact, we are always grateful for all good men and women everywhere who are accomplishing objectives that advance the work of Christ. However, these phenomena are not a part of our accepted worship experience. This is not who we are. This is not what we do. Where such arises, it is the responsibility of the pastor to explain gently our identity and worship practices and to suggest that those who insist on involvement with neo-Pentecostal manifestations relate to those churches that support such practices.
>
> It is also the responsibility of our district superintendents and general superintendents to support our pastors as they deal with these delicate issues. Obviously, it is easy to be misunderstood when informing our people that such is not acceptable. Therefore, we want to be cautious and Christlike in providing our people with the information that indicates a lack of support for such practices. Again, this is not part of our identity; this is

> not who we are. It is strongly felt that by ignoring such practices or even supporting them, we are sowing seeds for the divisiveness that has historically accompanied such activities. Let us be strong and clear in this matter and not fail in our responsibility to clearly declare what we are and what we are not.
>
> At this point, we would not suggest long debates or endless discussions but rather a clear, gentle, and simple declaration that this is not a part of the Church of the Nazarene. We would rather keep it in the form of a helpful conversation as opposed to a declaration, General Assembly resolution, or even a Board of General Superintendents' ruling, which might draw more attention to the situation than is necessary or helpful. If, however, there proves to be a need for more concrete action, further consideration will be given to the possibility of specific action.

language shall be interpreted as inveighing against the doctrines and usages of the Church of the Nazarene."[58] Trips outside the United States as well as within it caused the general superintendents to be alarmed over the possibility of tongues-speaking in the Church of the Nazarene. Though, unlike 1976, the general superintendents did not publish a warning to the entire church, they did circulate a cautionary statement.

CONCLUSION

Nazarenes witnessed a recovery of the long cherished assertion that the vital life and heart of the Church of the Nazarene rested in its local congregations and laypeople. This rediscovery came in the context of global consciousness. "Glocalization," the term for this new reality, accompanied growing diversity in the Church of the Nazarene. Local churches faced questions about their connections with the denomination. But throughout Nazarenes remained consistent about winning people to Christ, bringing them together for fellowship in local churches, drawing them to Christlikeness, and developing realistic and strong global connections. Through a variety of congregational models, Nazarenes preserved distinctives in the midst of great and growing cultural diversity.

Local churches took responsibility for their own growth and for starting new churches in their communities. While programs for growth swayed them, they found a variety of means for remaining true to their heritage and roots. What Nazarenes shared was the desire to be a "believers' church" that discipled converts in the life of holiness. While a survey in 1999 found that "secularization" (a former generation might have said "worldliness") within the denomination troubled many Nazarenes, local congregations remained "contrast societies" rather than "conformist societies."[59]

TWENTY-EIGHT

THE NAZARENE MIND

The Pilot Point union evidenced the impulse to gather together. Under one tent were social differences and compromise on nonessentials. The overarching canopy provided a new dwelling for God's people among the denominations, new hope, and new resolve. A certain ethos and way of being the church in the world emerged. The "Nazarene mind" was a way of obedience to Christ in the service of the Church. Nazarenes surrendered sovereignty of both self and society to the kingdom of God. Entire sanctification as doctrine and experience unified those gathered.

One hundred years later circumstances had dramatically changed, both inside and outside the church. Through ethnic conflicts, hunger, earthquakes, and the collapse of old structures and systems, more and more people were uprooted and spiritually homeless. The Church of the Nazarene was successful and secure as a denomination. As the church became more global, how did Nazarenes express and embody holiness? A visitor to the Nazarene world would have found unity and diversity in both thought and practice pulsating within the church. The church's "particular identity" was still defined by its "calling to exemplify, teach, and preach a particular facet of that redemptive history—holiness of heart and life,"[1] as historian Paul Bassett said. But how that identifying core was preached and taught varied. The church gave more attention to energetic engagement in mission than to extended debates about the meaning of entire sanctification.[2]

"Global communion" was a significant concept. The church was *eschatological*, looking toward fulfillment in the reign of God, and it was *eucharistic*, focused on the breaking of bread together and the drinking of the one cup of Christian memory and hope. These were essential characteristics of the Nazarene mind.

LANGUAGE

Traditional language was not always understood. Nazarene theologian J. Kenneth Grider called entire sanctification the "distinctive doctrine of Wesleyanism,"[3] but the church could not expect unhesitating loyalty to positions that people could not understand. Nazarenes struggled and stretched to find new language. MidAmerica theologian Frank Moore explained that entire sanctification was "the gift that replaces our self-centeredness with Christ-centeredness."[4] Similarly, a Nazarene catechism from Africa centered upon both the community of faith and Christlikeness: "The Church of the Nazarene is a family of believers in Jesus Christ who have joined together to worship and serve God and to become more like Him."[5]

Wesley's concept of the "second blessing" or "entire sanctification" was by no means his major preoccupation but rather the *"means* through which the *goal* of the Christian life could be realized here and now," Mildred Bangs Wynkoop observed. This continuity of grace stood against the "apocalyptic interpretation of Christian experience." Wynkoop stressed that, "Wesley understood God's grace as operating in the context of human experience—in history." Crisis experiences that occurred in the fog of emotion and that did not flow outward to "the social connections of which everyone is a part" were suspect.[6]

Wynkoop observed three streams of "contradictory Wesleyanisms" in contemporary life in the late 1970s. One represented the central "return to Wesley." Another was a "Puritanical, legalistic, moralistic concern laced tightly with scholastic rigidity and stereotyped terminology." It focused rather unyieldingly on rational doctrine. A third, on the other side, was a stream with "strong emotional emphasis" and a "mystical flavor prevailing." It stressed the experiential (or, baptism of Pentecost) aspect of holiness. In fact, most Nazarenes embraced some intertwining of all three. However, when Nazarenes failed to stress the continuity of grace between conversion and entire sanctification, she said, they lost "the whole Wesley" and undermined the church's distinguishing doctrine.[7]

Like Wynkoop, those most influenced by the theology of John Wesley himself often used the language of *transformation* and *transforming grace* and spoke of a *transforming moment* and a *transforming journey.* PALCON 1995 sounded the note of "transformation" strongly in the church's understanding of entire sanctification. Here the key theme was "Transforming Ministry: The Optimism of Grace." John A. Knight echoed this theme in his address delivered to the Christian Holiness Association in 1996, titled "The Radical Optimism of Grace," which he claimed was "inherent in our heritage." God's grace, William Greathouse concurred, was "transforming and renewing," and the human response was to place *"all* of life in the stream of transforming grace." The "transforming moments of conversion and sanctification" should be placed in the context of a "transforming journey." Transformation was "the renewal of the soul in the image of God."

Some changes were generational, others social. "Generation Xers" offered creative and insightful ways of integrating *vulnerability* and *authenticity* into the doctrine. Tim Crutcher and his wife, Rhonda, serving in Belgium, looked for something more real than the timeworn testimony. "My generation is interested in people, not in facades and performances," wrote Tim Crutcher. "Godliness is only appealing in the context of humanity. They are far more interested in people whose testimony says, 'God has forgiven me in spite of my past failures and sins,' than people who proudly state, 'I'm saved, and sanctified and haven't sinned since.'"[8]

William Greathouse

CONFERENCE THEOLOGY

At their own conferences, Nazarene theologians sought ways to integrate the church's doctrine of entire sanctification into the larger scope of Christian theology. Paul Bassett explained, "What really distinguishes the holiness movement is its understanding of entry into the experience of Christian perfection and its way of relating the doctrine of perfection to the rest of Christian theology."[9] Though trying in measured ways to speak to the wider church, Nazarenes still talked mostly to themselves and like-minded Wesleyans. Nazarene Theology Conferences, initiated in 1958, served the purpose of dialogue. The first was sponsored by NPH. The second in 1967 had the theme "A Wesleyan Critique of Contemporary Theology." The third, held in 1969, dealt with "Holiness in Learning and Life." The fourth, in 1972, highlighted "Current Issues and Trends in the Theology of the Church." The fifth focused on "The Nature of Biblical Authority." The sixth, in 1982, looked at "Higher Education and Our Holiness Mission." The seventh theology conference, in 1987, was cosponsored by the Board of General Superintendents, the Council of Education, and NPH, indicating greater participation and direction by the general church. Under the cochairmanship of John A. Knight, general superintendent, and Mark Moore, secretary for Education Services, the program featured theology, biblical studies, ethics, anthropology and sociology, the sacraments and Nazarene higher education, worship and debate, seminars and discussion. Gen-

John A. Knight

eral superintendents and administrators found none of the scholars to be detached from vital involvement in the church's worship and mission. For the first time there were representatives from Nazarene schools outside North America. However, unofficial reports from those who attended the 1987 conference suggested that there was an attempt to resist the appearance of any diversity or debate on issues of fundamental Nazarene doctrines.[10]

Other conferences were held in 1989 at Olivet, in 1992 in Kansas City, and in 1996 at Bethany. The Consultation on Religion and Science for Professors of Science and Religion in the Colleges and Universities of the Church of the Nazarene was held in Kansas City in 1998, sponsored by the Resource Institute for International Education.

Scholars during this period stressed that diversity was inherent in the heritage and was occasioned by the cultures in which the church flourished. Transmission necessitated diversity. Entire sanctification could not be understood or defined apart from historical change and culture. Stephen Gunter, for instance, noted that Wesleyan doctrine was modified in North America to suit the New World. The experiences of conversion and entire sanctification, so central to Methodism in England, were "re-ified" or made "real and concrete" in North America. The pragmatic temper of Americans wanted to make things happen in the everyday world but also to make faith work in the realm of the spirit and religious life. Gunter saw this happening in the Holiness Movement. "Revivalism has adopted the psychology of conversion experience from Jonathan Edwards, and from [Phoebe] Palmer we inherit the psychology of the experience of entire sanctification." One clear change was in the identification of entire sanctification with the "baptism of the Holy Spirit," which could be identified as a "pentecostal shift." The second tendency was toward pragmatism, a "method that worked." The side-effect made "experience an idol."[11]

In the context of conferences such discussion was fine. But there were limits to diversity. In 1976 NTS hired Rob Staples in theology and Charles Isbell in Old Testament. While Staples weathered theological storms, Isbell and other scholars left the Church of the Nazarene during these years over various issues.[12]

Formal statements of intent such as the "Core Values Document" released toward the end of the century remained specific and clear: "The mission of the Church of the Nazarene is to respond to the Great Commission to 'go and make disciples of all nations' with a distinctive emphasis upon entire sanctification and Christian holiness."[13]

THEOLOGY IN SERVICE OF THE CHURCH

To early Nazarenes such as E. F. Walker, James B. Chapman, and H. Orton Wiley there would have been no separation between "church" and "academy" or between "scholars" and "administrators," for they were in fact "scholar-administrators." The same pattern returned upon the election as general superintendent of William Greathouse in 1976 and John A. Knight in 1985. Nonetheless, young theologians had become somewhat separated from the "practical" business of the church. The 1982 Nazarene Theology Conference began with words of caution and control from an administrator, and words of dissent and debate from a theologian, signaling tension and the separation between the "church" and the "academy." But the conference initiated debate more than argument. To some the tension lay between the supposed rift between Wesley's "Christological" and the Holiness Movement's "pneumatological" emphases. Church administrators dealt with the impact of pentecostal worship and "tongues-speaking" as threats to the denomination rather than as matters of theological debate, while laypersons' search for personal spirituality depended little on creeds and doctrines. Pastors felt pressure to promote charismatic corporate worship. Some wished for more independency and less denominational identity and found thoughtful conformity to wider evangelical impulses the path of least resistance. Theologians rarely reached people in daily life. Henry Spaulding expressed concern over this, the "growing gap between pastors and theologians." He reminded that "Wesleyan theology, properly conceived, always seeks a union between these two publics."[14]

THE THEOLOGICAL CONTINUUM

Nazarenes had little debate with classical Christian beliefs. They pressed, however, for *experienced* doctrine. They wanted to know whether entire sanctification remained a beautiful *teaching* about the completion of faith in love or whether in fact Christlikeness might become the norm for life this side of the end (the *eschaton*). Nazarenes claimed that Jesus promised the gift of the Spirit to be with them to cleanse and to empower them to fulfill the Great Command to love God and neighbor in this life, even if in a very qualified and provisional sense. God had promised to write his covenant on their hearts, to strip aside sin, and to put sin to death by being crucified with Christ.

They were to present their bodies as living sacrifices here and now so as to experience the liberating freedom of the Spirit. The love of God, Nazarenes believed, was poured out in their hearts through the Holy Spirit. Nazarenes believed that entire sanctification was the *beginning* completed. It opened one's inmost heart to God and to one's brother and sister. It represented the moment of completing initiation into a life of pardon and Christian sanctity. Entire sanctification was the celebration of this "end of the beginning moment," renewed again in every "present moment" of the journey.[15]

Nazarene doctrine represented more than a commitment to holiness, theologians taught the church. "The aim of any Arminian/Wesleyan perspective," said Paul Bassett, involved worshipping and glorifying God, and loving and serving neighbors. Bassett warned: "Institutional self-preservation and self-serving would constitute the ultimate blasphemies."[16]

Henry Spaulding proposed centering Nazarene theology upon a pastoral and interdisciplinary perspective. He appealed for an "openness to dialogue" and the recognition that theology was "not so much a catalog of answers but a way of construing the world." He predicted that "Nazarene theology will be less systematic and more diverse than in the past." Spaulding's "Nazarene mind" was unafraid to engage the world.[17]

One controversial attempt to engage modern thought was H. Ray Dunning's *Grace, Faith, and Holiness*, published in 1988. There had been rivalry between those who supported traditional language and those who favored a more "relational" than "substantival" understanding. Dunning wanted the "dynamic character of history, the fluid nature of language, and the shifting cultural scene" to be taken seriously so as to enable the dialogue of theology to take place, not only between generations, but between different traditions. Dunning went so far as to say, "the fact is that probably every denomination reflects several different traditions that agree on certain central commitments, but there is usually also diversity at several significant points."[18]

This "diversity" ignited a painful controversy. MidAmerica Academic Dean Metz noted that Dunning's work represented a "transition theology" that stood between "classical" Wesleyan thought and the "liberal humanistic thought of Paul Tillich and that movement, or theology, which for want of a better term, is called Neo-Orthodoxy." "Neo-orthodoxy is not Wesleyan— nor Biblical," claimed Metz. He attempted to "sound the alert" within the denomination to these aberrant doctrinal matters.[19]

Dunning in subsequent defenses of his work made clear his stance on a number of issues raised by J. Kenneth Grider, Metz, and others. "[E]very part of it [a systematic theology], every doctrine, every formulation is filtered through and informed by a controlling perspective." "If ever there was a time, and I'm not certain there was, when Nazarenes were of one mind in this regard it is not now." Therefore no one systematic theology should be defined as an "official one." His own work involved an important "paradigm shift," he admitted, with respect to the image of God (*imago dei*) in humanity, with the result that theological anthropology was interpreted in a *relational* rather than a *substantive* way.[20]

"What then should be the norm?" Dunning asked. His answer was "it must be Wesleyan in the classical sense." He proceeded to sketch the "specific contours" of such a "Wesleyan norm." The reconciliation between God and humanity, rather than simply "justification by faith," was central. Grace as both healing and forgiving came into focus. The Incarnation as well as the Atonement played significant roles. If with Wesley, sanctification is put "in the context of a *transformation* of being" [emphasis added] and interpreted in terms of love (or the "faith that works by love," as Wesley said) then it is a scintillating possibility rather than a legal requirement. "I must conclude that sanctification is a Christological doctrine and all references to the Spirit's work in us must be informed by this transforming element."[21]

Dunning and other scholars also noted affinities between John Wesley and Eastern Orthodoxy. Though Wesleyans, like other western Christians, studied the Bible seriously, with Eastern Orthodox Christians they also took seriously the "vision" of God and "incorporated the best emphases of both Western and Eastern thought in [their] preaching and teaching." Dunning noted, "Justification is at home in the legal-minded (Latin) West and sanctification is more at home in the mystical East."[22]

If so, Wesleyan theology might have broad appeal. Japanese leader Hitoshi (Paul) Fukue said, "There are not a few Asian Christians who assert that theology developed in the Western countries during the past two thousand years is too rationalistic and abstract for Asian minds, which are more relational and concrete." The question became, "Should Asian Christians attempt a direct flight from Israel to Asia without all the stop-overs and delays in the West?" Fukue's response was, "No, Asian and Western Christians need to listen together to the Word of God directly and sensitively." As they "interpenetrate each other with their own unique understandings of faith" they will listen to and learn from each other. Like Pastor Kamegaya, a converted Buddhist priest, who restrained an eager Japanese youth from plucking a small branch of cherry blossoms from a tree, saying, "Please, let them be. They are the gift of my heavenly Father. He has given me all things in Christ, they are mine. I prefer to keep my blossoms right there on the tree." This was way "beyond the West and beyond the East. It was biblical Christianity."[23]

Korean theology intersected with holiness at the points of religious disciplines and power. Kim In-Gyeong Lundell, who worked among Korean Nazarene churches in southern California, encountered a district superintendent who was aghast that the Koreans were allowing members to smoke and drink. The position of the Korean pastors was that they should be allowed, so long as they were making progress. What constituted "holiness" in the mind of the district superintendent had little to do with "holiness" in the mind of the Koreans. They associated holiness with going to church and believing in Christ, which, in itself, for Koreans was a radical commitment. Koreans attended early morning and midnight prayer meetings. They respected elders more than democratic procedures. Finally, holiness rested in power over evil, not rules; holiness was the deliverance of the Holy Spirit.[24]

Hispanic American scholars and others found a theology of liberation in Wesleyanism. Jonathan Salgado appealed for "an effort to re-discover the social ethics of sanctification." He appealed for a much expanded understanding of the nature of entire sanctification, encompassing far more than the merely private and personal domain. He spoke from experience in Mexico and Guatemala where the preaching of holiness had to contend with specific forms of political oppression, social injustice, and religious domination. He wanted the church to reexamine its "concept of the nature of the separation between the Church and the world." A "Culture Christianity" would equate sociopolitical conservatism with the gospel and held the danger of "reducing the Gospel to a formula for success and equating the triumph of Christ with obtaining the highest number of 'conversions.'" Correct intellectual belief needed to become a vigorous Christian concern with "transformation." Conversion, he claimed, would be a "scandal to accepted wisdoms, status quos, and oppressive arrangements."[25] Similarly, Enrique Guang, from the Seminario Nazareno De Las Americas in San Jose, Costa Rica, wondered about what "should be done to revive that Wesleyan-Nazarene praxis" of seeing humanity whole, and of being present through "a real commitment to the poor" impelled by the gospel as Phineas Bresee was in Los Angeles in the late nineteenth century. "What happened to the church?" in the intervening period, Guang asked.[26]

Nazarene theology was not only a matter of church doctrine and orthodoxy, nor of personal holiness or spirituality, but an issue of believing communities covenanted together and formed together by obedience in mission. Angelito Agbuya of the Philippines asked the question, "How should the denomination's interest in internationalization affect the way it understands the church more generally and the Church of the Nazarene more specifically?" "Any discussion on the subject of internationalization must begin in the nature of God Himself," he claimed. "The Church can be said to be truly international when she is able to welcome outsiders" and when she is "not defending the privileges of a select group." He added, "Although the Christian community is now worldwide, it is not truly world-encompassing."[27] Clear indications emerged of a broader and deeper understanding of the church's cardinal teaching. Vern Hannah reflected that for a long time the perception had been that entire sanctification dealt with original sin in individuals and that "cleansing from sin" referred to this as an inward, personal problem. The Canadian claimed that such a preoccupation could tend to introspectiveness and preoccupation with sin in personal terms. "We believe," said Hannah, "that coming into this fallen world humanity both shapes and is shaped by its culture: a syndrome of exploitative systems which are self-serving and independent from God. Evil as systemic thus becomes entrenched, perpetuated and enforced by each succeeding generation." His point was that sin had social consequences and dimensions. Nazarenes did not escape complicity with social and systemic evil, wherever they lived.[28]

Entire sanctification may not always have been mentioned or even understood, but life was being formed in a family and believing community whose habits and practices yearned toward Christlikeness. "The term *sanctification* communicates a point of departure as well as a destination. It means placing *all* of life in the stream of God's transforming grace," explained Frank Moore. "It is like stepping through a door into a room of growth, which continues for the rest of our lives."[29]

The theology conferences reflected an attempt to show that entire sanctification was not a "theological provincialism" but should be articulated in the language of doctrine and life in a manner that revealed its complex connection with the whole range of Christian truth. "Our people reflect upon their faith as it touches all of life," Paul Bassett noted. This meant that they reflected "far beyond the ranges of the doctrine of entire sanctification." They needed "whole systems of doctrine."[30]

In biblical studies Nazarenes wrestled for hermeneutical integrity—interpreting the Scriptures faithfully.[31] Alex Deasley proposed that the question was, "Is the church open to a relationship with biblical exegesis that is genuinely dialogic?" Deasley claimed that "the church is quickened and renovated, and saved from the petrification of holding to positions that have no other claim to cogency than repetition, or holding positions which have a better claim, but holding to them lifelessly."[32] Kent Brower posed the same question in different terms, "Can one maintain scholarly integrity as a biblical scholar in a Nazarene context?" His answer was a "yes" qualified by crucial conditions. There should be a clear understanding of the nature of the hermeneutical enterprise (the task of reading and interpreting Scripture) by both scholar and church. There should be an environment of mutual trust and accountability that fostered two-way listening and talking and reaped the fruits of scholarship. Scholars should challenge the church "not hostilely but by way of invitation."[33] In response, by 2008 NPH had launched an ambitious project to produce a new commentary series written from a Wesleyan perspective and based on sound scholarship.

CREATION

As they had during the 1920s, Nazarenes again found themselves in the middle of a battle over whether creation or evolution accurately explained the origin of life. The issue in the late-twentieth-century culture wars resurged as a major dividing line between fundamentalists and other Christians.[34]

ENC professor of physics Karl Giberson warned against diverting energies from Kingdom tasks to distracting controversies "irrelevant" to spiritual matters. In 1993 Giberson published *Worlds Apart: The Unholy War Between Religion and Science*. Max Reams of Olivet Nazarene University evaluated it as one of "the best books I have seen which relates science and theology," but another *Herald of Holiness* reader proposed a balanced presentation of these two sides—those who hail the book "with joy" and those who condemn it "with fervor"![35]

On the other side, Thomas Lorimer, pastor of the Fort Madison, Iowa, Church of the Nazarene, saw in science no evidence for evolution. Creation and evolution were incompatible, he argued. Among other pastors who took a similar position, Dennis Swift, pastor of the Beaverton, Oregon, church, broadcast a half-hour radio program, "Creation—The Bible Was Right After All." Alvin Jolley, pastor of the Hallwood Community Church of the Nazarene in Marysville, California, believed that evolution represented "antibiblical, relativistic, humanistic, anti-traditional liberal subjectivism."[36] Those who defended such positions started Nazarenes in Creation, chaired by James Woolbright, with a publication by the same title. "Nazarenes in Creation" was "dedicated to reestablishing biblical creationism within our church." Those in Nazarenes in Creation appealed to A. M. Hills rather than H. Orton Wiley, and such 1920s publications as Basil Miller and U. E. Harding's *Cunningly Devised Fables*. There must be no ambiguity on the infallibility of the Bible.

"If you write off Genesis as a metaphor, you lose the basis upon which to proclaim the Gospel."[37]

The colleges became frontline targets for Nazarene creationists. "It is a known fact that many of the teachers in our Nazarene schools don't believe in the Bible creation theory. When are we going to invite those teachers to go elsewhere?" wrote one reader to the *Herald*'s "Question Box." Editor Wesley Tracy replied that he had never found any Nazarene professor disavowing Genesis but appealed to his questioner not to insist that Genesis taught that God had created the universe in six days: Nazarene educators long had disagreed on how and when, the time and method, of creation.[38]

> In March 2000 Robert Brower, PLNU president, issued a "University Position Statement" on Creation and Evolution:[39]
>
> PLNU's commitments regarding the issue of creation and evolution coincide with our Christian heritage as a University in the Wesleyan and evangelical traditions of the Christian faith and as an institution of learning within the Church of the Nazarene. We affirm Genesis 1:1 that God is Creator and Colossians 1:19-20 that through Christ God is reconciling all things to himself. We do not support approaches or theories that purport that humankind and the universe occurred from entirely naturalistic forces, for we believe that God acted as creator.
>
> PLNU rests its position and teaching regarding creation and evolution upon the position expressed in the *Manual/1997-2001* (the official governing document of our sponsoring denomination, the Church of the Nazarene) and its statements regarding the church's view of scripture and the acts of creation.
>
> In our position regarding creation and evolution the University affirms the position of the church, Genesis 1:1, that God is Creator and that scientifically verifiable discoveries contribute to our understanding of the natural world. We believe that the attempt to draw the Christian community into debates regarding specific time frames or conditions of creation distracts from the core belief that God acted as Creator. Beyond this, we do not support or promote any position that attempts to polarize the Christian community by insisting upon adherence to a particular interpretation of the time frame or the mechanism of God's creation.

Point Loma faced challenges from the Christian Heritage College, in nearby El Cajon, which championed a "six-day creation" theory. In 1999 David Noebel, president of Summit Ministries, pointedly asked why any Christian parent would send their son or daughter to PLNU and risk the chance that the child would return "home a socialist or an evolutionist."[40] But Point Loma refused to permit polarization on the question of method and time in relation to the created order.

LAST THINGS LAST

At the 1993 meeting of the Wesleyan Theological Society, held at Southern Nazarene University, the topic was "Wesleyan Theology and Eschatology." The conference concluded that "John Wesley's view of last things cannot be harmonized with Scofield dispensationalism which sees the Church merely as a hyphen in God's ongoing relation to Israel." William Greathouse commented after the conference that the "modern holiness movement has not laid great stress on eschatology and generally has treated the various millennial theories as nonessential to salvation." "This was the first time WTS has attempted to grapple seriously with eschatology as an attempt to formulate a doctrine of last things that is consistent with Wesley's plan of salvation."[41]

The Wesleyan doctrine of last things was different from both Roman Catholic and traditional Protestant views, while remaining totally committed to the classic Christian faith, according to H. Ray Dunning. Nazarenes had a *dynamic* interpretation of history and time and a *synergistic* understanding of the divine-human relation and salvation. Divine initiative and human response were inseparably connected. The word of God reached human beings in particular times and places and was not "dropped into a cultural or historical vacuum," said Dunning. Jesus was God's incarnate Word, and so Jesus became for human beings the "new hermeneutic" or way of understanding revelation and prophecy, time and history. Dunning emphasized that "the Wesleyan commitment to synergism rejected the idea that God enters into unconditional covenants with humankind." Nazarenes might have agreed with Michael Lodahl, that their main purpose was "to seek to *serve* the present age, and indeed to *preserve* it, rather than to flee it or hope for its soon demise."[42]

The popular search for personal spirituality placed less emphasis on creeds and doctrine. Laypersons were influenced by literal and apocalyptic readings of the Christian Scriptures just as surely as they were influenced toward creationism and charismatic corporate worship.

CONCLUSION

The Church of the Nazarene was self-consciously conservative in its theological integrity and mission. The first challenge to be faced by theologians was the church's reluctance, according to William Greathouse, to combine biblical faithfulness with theological reflection and to move from an evangelistic to a reflective mode in theology and education.[43] For Greathouse, theology was the primary enterprise of the church. "Theology is life, and, rightly understood, the task of the Church is theological," he said. Such a theology would be embodied in congregations of believers whose integrity in diversity would match the integrity in diversity of the biblical record itself.[44]

During the years 1925-76 increasing separation occurred between institutionalized compassion (in hospitals and clinics "overseas") and "evangelism first" (at "home"). After 1976 this gap narrowed. The sacramental sensibility of the *catholic* or universal Christian mind, the rational order of the *Puritan*, or logical mind, and the experiential naïveté of the *Pentecostal*, or interactive and "participatory" mind, were all strands in the "Nazarene mind." Ultimately captive to none of these, nevertheless it was enriched by all.

What, if anything, now tied Nazarene theology together? What provided the unifying orientation or disposition in very diverse global congregations? Regardless of the theological methods used by different thinkers, Nazarene theology continued to find its unity in the Wesleyan conviction, still universally shared, that divine grace imparted to human life exerted a transforming effect on individuals and on social contexts. Entire sanctification on a personal level was a crucial moment in this transforming journey.

Entire sanctification was neither an embattled creed nor an imposed lifestyle but the energizing center of a cross-shaped life and witness. This cardinal center forged the Nazarenes' response to a changing postmodern world. Love poured out in compassion became apparent in the global and neighborhood ministries of the church. Nazarene theology remained not a matter of church doctrine and orthodoxy, nor of personal holiness or spirituality. It guided believing communities formed by obedience to Christ's mission. Entire sanctification required the costly price of love poured out in life. While the Nazarene mind drew upon Catholic, Reformed, and Holiness traditions, it remained unique. Entire sanctification lay at the center of a way of life as the moment of complete commitment to that journey.

"Called unto Holiness" has been the "watchword and song" of Nazarenes as they sought to embody their calling in the world. And the prayer continued. "May the God of peace himself sanctify you wholly; and may your spirit and soul and body be kept sound and blameless at the coming of our Lord Jesus Christ. He who calls you is faithful, and he will do it."[45]

CONCLUSION

Nazarenes at the turn of both the twentieth and twenty-first centuries wanted to institutionalize the living biblical faith taught by Methodism's John Wesley and apply to their contexts his understanding of Christian life. None advocated giving up this heritage. Latter-day Nazarenes took advantage of every rising tide of opportunity for the gospel to be spread and remained committed to assuring holiness's contemporary vitality.

Pilot Point provided a reference marker for the unifying and distinguishing direction of the church. After one hundred years, Nazarene thought and life exhibited a growing diversity of rich variety and depth with respect to geographic region, culture, and education. It gently resisted the formulation or imposition of any singular or uniform mind-set or worldview or institutional set of rules. It did, however, reveal a disposition that was distinctive in all the various contexts where the Nazarene global family was found: an intuition that God imparted grace to ordinary people of all walks of life and that this grace exerted a transforming effect on individuals and societies through communities attempting to embody Christlikeness in their habits and practices.

One might be tempted to compare succeeding generations to the pioneers who gathered at Pilot Point. Had the church lost something valuable of its original purpose? Had it declined away from its past? The first Nazarenes, and their successors, faced challenging difficulties from inner as well as outer forces. Holiness coexisted with humanity from the beginning. If one were looking for the perfect past by which to compare the present, where would one look? The Church of the Nazarene is part of a longer history than simply the one hundred years of its formal existence. One could look to the nineteenth-century Holiness Movement or to the eighteenth-century Wesleyan revival or to the various influences that gave rise to Methodism, Puritanism, and Pietism, traceable to the Reformation, or to the Early Church itself for a rule of life and doctrine from which the church descended. Perhaps something historians can say is this, that the Church of the Nazarene—from the time of the passing of the first generation in the 1910s, through the dark 1940s, and shadowing the 1958 and 1983 Pilot Point celebrations—*always* has been fearful of departing from its original message. Nazarenes nervously wondered whether the next generation would embrace and internalize the church's message to the world. Leaders called upon Nazarenes themselves to be revived in order to fulfill the church's mission. The church moved forward.

Nazarenes have been concerned about right doctrine, the Word spoken to humankind. They have had as Articles of Faith not ones that either John Wesley or Phineas Bresee composed or called councils to decide. The doctrines were given to Nazarenes, as if a gift, from the centuries. What Nazarenes were as concerned with as much as doctrine was experience. There must be, Nazarenes declared, an encounter and a hallowing relationship with God in Christ through His Spirit. To possess doctrines that they had not experienced, and yet passed on, would not do. This was *not* Nazarenes' passion or calling, to pass on theology divorced from experience. The consuming desire along Nazarenes' walk for one hundred years was not to transmit doctrine; it was, rather, to draw many into the transforming presence of God through Christ's sanctifying Spirit.

In this mission the Church of the Nazarene remained a Wesleyan and basically Methodist denomination. If Methodism, in its early days, could be called "Arminianism on fire," the holiness churches could be called "Wesleyanism on fire." By the twenty-first century the Church of the Nazarene could not be mistaken for a Methodist church. Both had changed a great deal over the previous century. They had traveled different paths, possessed different visions, were pulled by very different susceptibilities. The Church of the Nazarene, like every denomination, had developed its own ethos and identity. Still, consciously, it considered itself Wesleyan to the core.

The initial call of the Holiness Movement, taken up by Phineas Bresee, was to "Christianize Christianity." As a movement one could envision how that could be done. John Wesley's Methodist Societies, as long as they remained within the Church of England, could be revitalizing agencies within the established church. Similarly, as long as committed Holiness people remained within their denominations, they could be the "yeast" or the "leaven" working toward revival and renewal. But once the Holiness people were pushed out of or left the older denominations, how could they retain such an influence to rejuvenate religion? As a denomination, the Church of the Nazarene faced perennially its own need for renewal. Almost inadvertently, Nazarene education proved to be one way of influencing the wider Church. Young women and men, Nazarene or not, who came through Nazarene colleges, left with some greater knowledge—and hopefully experience—of Christian holiness. Another way that Nazarenes possessed wider influence was through their deeds. Though never to the extent to which other groups might be identified with benevolent works, Nazarenes demonstrated love through compassion. The church's bid to remain international was radically optimistic and required every fiber of perfect love. By being a community motivated by Jesus' Sermon on the Mount and by remaining brash enough to believe that Jesus expected people to live by these standards here and now, Nazarenes hoped to set an example for other Christians.

Nazarenes never come together as a whole. Physically, they are scattered in various nations. In that sense, like other denominations, the Nazarene church is constructed or imagined. As Nazarenes grew to greater maturity, they walked along a path together in increasingly diverse company. As Nazarenes expanded globally, North American perspectives, though still strong, admitted their own parochialism. At the same time, being Nazarene was for many a primary means of self-identity, and the church provided an integrative mental and spiritual structure for interpreting and experiencing life, wherever it might be lived.

The Nazarene story is not of a glorified church "without spot or wrinkle." The Church of the Nazarene is a denomination that always has been in the process of formation. Not a denomination that has arrived, the church yearned and learned to know what it meant to be a holy community in various contexts. Any church that might have "arrived" would have lost its mission and sense of movement. Nazarene history is of a movement aiming to do the seemingly impossible: to organize Holiness experience, practice, and doctrine. Nazarenes were still a pilgrimage people, a church on a journey, not yet finished, not yet arrived, but still finding out in very different contexts what it meant here and now to be both a corporate body and holy.

APPENDIXES

APPENDIX A

GENERAL SUPERINTENDENTS

Name	Lived	Served	Position at Time of Election
Phineas F. Bresee	1838-1915	1907-15	Pastor, Los Angeles, California, First Church of the Nazarene
Hiram F. Reynolds	1854-1938	1907-32	Foreign Missions Secretary, Association of Pentecostal Churches of America
Edgar P. Ellyson	1869-1954	1908-11	President, Peniel University
Edward F. Walker	1852-1918	1911-18	Evangelist
W. C. Wilson	1866-1915	1915	District Superintendent, Southern California
John W. Goodwin	1869-1945	1916-40	Pastor, San Diego, California, First
Roy T. Williams	1883-1946	1916-46	Evangelist
James B. Chapman	1884-1947	1928-47	Editor, Herald of Holiness
Joseph G. Morrison	1871-1939	1936-39	Foreign Missions Secretary
Orval Nease	1891-1950	1940-44	Church Schools Editor
		1948-50	Vice President and Graduate School Dean, Pasadena College
Howard V. Miller	1894-1948	1940-48	Dean of Theology, Northwest Nazarene College
Hardy C. Powers	1900-1972	1944-68	Superintendent, Iowa District
Gideon B. Williamson	1898-1981	1946-68	Pastor, Kansas City First
Samuel Young	1901-1990	1948-72	President, Eastern Nazarene College
Daniel I. Vanderpool	1891-1988	1949-64	Superintendent, Northwest District
Hugh C. Benner	1899-1975	1952-68	President, Nazarene Theological Seminary
V. H. Lewis	1912-2000	1960-85	Evangelism Secretary
George Coulter	1911-1995	1964-80	World Missions Secretary
Edward Lawlor	1907-87	1968-76	Evangelism Secretary
Eugene Stowe	1922-	1968-93	President, Nazarene Theological Seminary
Orville Jenkins	1913-2007	1968-85	Home Missions Secretary
Charles Strickland	1916-88	1972-88	President, Nazarene Bible College
William Greathouse	1919-	1976-89	President, Nazarene Theological Seminary
Jerald Johnson	1927-	1980-97	World Mission Director
Raymond Hurn	1921-2007	1985-93	Church Growth Director
John A. Knight	1931-2009	1985-2001	President, Bethany Nazarene College
William Prince	1930-	1989-2001	President, Mount Vernon Nazarene College
Donald Owens	1927-	1989-97	President, MidAmerica Nazarene College
James Diehl	1937-	1993-2009	Pastor, Denver First Church
Paul Cunningham	1937-	1993-2009	Pastor, Olathe, Kansas, College Church
Jerry Porter	1949-	1997-	Superintendent, Washington, D.C., District
Jim Bond	1935-	1997-2005	President, Point Loma Nazarene College
W. Talmadge Johnson	1937-	2001-2005	Sunday School Director
Jesse C. Middendorf	1943-	2001-	Pastor, Kansas City, Missouri, First
Nina Gunter	1940-	2005-2009	General Director, Nazarene Missions International
J. K. Warrick	1945-	2005-	Pastor, Olathe, Kansas, College Church

Appendix B

OTHER GENERAL OFFICERS

General Secretaries

Robert Pierce	1907, 1908
F. C. Epperson	1911
F. M. Mendell	1915
E. J. Fleming	1919-40
C. Warren Jones	1940-44
S. T. Ludwig	1944-64
B. Edgar Johnson	1964-90
Jack K. Stone	1990-2007
David P. Wilson	2007-

General Treasurers

E. G. Anderson	1919-26
M. Lunn	1926-32
J. G. Morrison	1932-33
M. Lunn	1934-45
John Stockton	1945-70
Norman O. Miller	1970-94
Robert L. Foster	1994-2002
Marilyn McCool	2002-

Editors, *Herald of Holiness/Holiness Today*

Benjamin F. Haynes	1912-22
James B. Chapman	1922-28
H. Orton Wiley	1928-36
D. Shelby Corlett	1936-48
Stephen S. White	1948-60
W. T. Purkiser	1960-75
John A. Knight	1975-76
William E. McCumber	1976-89
Wesley Tracy	1989-97
R. Franklin Cook	1997-2004
Dave Felter	2004-

Editors, *Preacher's Magazine*

J. B. Chapman	1926-47
D. Shelby Corlett	1947-48
L. A. Reed	1948-52
D. Shelby Corlett	1953-54
Lauriston J. Dubois	1954-61
Norman R. Oke	1961-63

Richard S. Taylor	1964-72	
James McGraw	1972-78	
Neil B. Wiseman	1978-80	
Wesley Tracy	1980-89	
Randall Denny	1989-99	
Neil B. Wiseman	1999-2000	
David Busic	2000-2008	
Jeren Rowell	2000-2008	

World Mission Department Executives

H. F. Reynolds	1908-15	General Missionary Secretary
H. F. Reynolds	1915-22	General Superintendent of World Missions
E. G. Anderson	1922-25	World Missions Secretary
H. F. Reynolds	1925-27	World Missions Secretary
J. G. Morrison	1927-36	World Missions Secretary
C. Warren Jones	1936-48	World Missions Secretary
Remiss Rehfeldt	1948-60	Executive Secretary
George Coulter	1960-64	Executive Secretary
E. S. Phillips	1964-73	Executive Secretary
Jerald Johnson	1973-80	Executive Secretary
L. Guy Nees	1980-86	Director of World Missions
Robert Scott	1986-94	Director of World Missions
Louie Bustle	1994-	Director of World Missions

World Missionary Society Presidents

Susan N. Fitkin	1919-48
Louise Robinson Chapman	1949-64
Mrs. L. S. Oliver	1973-80
Mrs. Gordon Olsen	1965-72
Lela Jackson	1981-89
Barbara Flemming	1990-96
Beverlee Borbe	1998-2001
Eunice Brubaker	2002-

World Missionary Society Executives

Mary L. Scott	1950-75
Wanda Knox	1975-80
Phyllis Hartley Brown Perkins	1981-84
Nina Gunter	1986-2005
Daniel D. Ketchum	2006-

Other Sheep/World Mission Editors

C. A. McConnell	1913-16
E. G. Anderson	1916-26
H. F. Reynolds	1926-28
J. G. Morrison	1928-36
C. Warren Jones	1936-48
Remiss Rehfeldt	1948-60
George Coulter	1960-64

E. S. Phillips	1964-73
Jerald Johnson	1974
[Name is changed to World Mission in September 1974]	
Helen Temple	1974-84
R. Franklin Cook	1985-92
D. LeRoy Stults	1992-97
R. Franklin Cook	1997-98

General Nazarene Young People's Society Presidents

Donnell J. Smith	1923-32
G. B. Williamson	1932-40
M. Kimber Moulton	1940-48
Mendell Taylor	1948-52
Ponder Gilliland	1952-56
Eugene Stowe	1956-60
James Snow	1961-64
John Hancock	1964-69
James Bond	1969-72
Talmadge Johnson	1972-77
Holland Lewis	1977-80
Daniel Ketchum	1980-85
W. J. (Woodie) Stevens	1985-89
Rick Power	1989-93
Jim Williams	1994-96
Bruce Oldham	1996-2001
Deirdre Brower	2001-2005
Monte Syr	2005-

Nazarene Young People's Society Executives

D. Shelby Corlett	1923-36
S. T. Ludwig	1936-42
John Peters	1942-43
S. T. Ludwig	1943-44
Lauriston J. DuBois	1944-56
Ponder Gilliland	1956-60
Paul Skiles	1961-74
Melvin McCullough	1974-77
Gary Henecke	1978-82
Larry Leonard	1982-86
Gary Sivewright	1986-91
Fred Fullerton	1991-2000
Gary Hartke	2000-

NOTES

Introduction

1. See Nazarene *Manual* (Kansas City: Nazarene Publishing House, 2005), 16.
2. Paul M. Bassett and William M. Greathouse, *Exploring Christian Holiness*, vol. 2: *The Historical Development* (Kansas City: Beacon Hill Press of Kansas City, 1985) carefully examines the Church of the Nazarene's roots with respect to the doctrine of Christian perfection. See also the six-volume *Great Holiness Classics* (Kansas City: Beacon Hill Press of Kansas City, 1984-97); Harold E. Raser, "Trunk and Branches: the Nazarene Family Tree," *Holiness Today* (April 1999), 2-4; and Wesley Tracy and Stan Ingersol, *Here We Stand: Where Nazarenes Fit in the Religious Marketplace* (Kansas City: Beacon Hill Press of Kansas City, 1999).
3. Steven Ozment, *Protestants: The Birth of a Revolution* (New York: Doubleday, 1993); Paul M. Bassett, "The Holiness Movement and the Protestant Principle," *Wesleyan Theological Journal* 18 (Spring 1983): 7-29.
4. Kathryn T. Long, "Consecrated Respectability: Phoebe Palmer and the Refinement of American Methodism," in *Methodism and the Shaping of American Culture*, eds. Nathan O. Hatch and John H. Wigger (Nashville: Abingdon, 2001), 281-307.
5. H. Richard Niebuhr, *Christ and Culture* (New York: Harper and Row, 1951).
6. Timothy L. Smith, *Called unto Holiness: The Story of the Nazarenes: The Formative Years* (Kansas City: Nazarene Publishing House, 1962), 266-71, 288-97.
7. Arthur M. Schlesinger Jr., "History and National Stupidity," *New York Review of Books* (April 27, 2006), 14, 16. Schlesinger cites his own neglect, in his *Age of Jackson*, of Americans' treatment of Indians.
8. Eric Foner, *Who Owns History? Rethinking the Past in a Changing World* (New York: Hill and Wang, 2002), 77, 109, 165.
9. Albert C. Outler, "Theodosius' Horse: Reflections on the Predicament of the Church Historian," *Church History* 34 (September 1965), 253.

Chapter 1

1. See *Journal of the Sixth General Assembly, 1923*, 148-49.
2. See the Nazarene *Manual* for 1923, 1928, and 1932.
3. *Journal of the Sixth General Assembly, 1923*, 295. See also J. B. Chapman, *A History of the Church of the Nazarene* (Kansas City: Nazarene Publishing House, 1926), 33, 64-67.
4. See John Kent, "Methodism and Social Change," in *Sanctification and Liberation*, ed. Theodore Runyon (Nashville: Abingdon, 1981), 83-101; John Kent, *Wesley and the Wesleyans: Religion in Eighteenth Century Britain* (Cambridge: Cambridge U. Press, 2002).
5. See John R. H. Moorman, *A History of the Church in England* (New York: Morehouse-Barlow, 1959), 161-79.
6. See Marion Hatchett, "The Traditional Anglican Liturgy," in *The Complete Library of Christian Worship*, vol. 2: *Twenty Centuries of Christian Worship*, ed. Robert Webber (Nashville: Star Song, 1994), 204.
7. John Foxe's oft-read *Book of Martyrs* presented a Protestant version of persecution under the Roman Catholic monarch Mary. See William Haller, *The Elect Nation: The Meaning and Relevance of Foxe's Book of Martyrs* (New York: Harper and Row, 1963); A. G. Dickens, *The English Reformation* (New York: Schocken, 1964).
8. See Herbert McGonigle, *Sufficient Saving Grace: John Wesley's Evangelical Arminianism* (Carlisle, Cumbria: Paternoster, 2001).
9. Overviews of Puritanism include William Haller, *The Rise of Puritanism* (New York: Columbia U. Press, 1938), and Alan Simpson, *Puritanism in Old and New England* (Chicago: U. of Chicago Press, 1955).

10. See Peter Gay, *The Enlightenment: The Rise of Modern Paganism* (New York: W. W. Norton, 1995); Peter Gay, *The Enlightenment: The Science of Freedom* (New York: W. W. Norton, 1996); Frederick Dreyer, "Faith and Experience in the Thought of John Wesley," *The American Historical Review* 88 (February 1983): 12-30.

11. See Philip Jacob Spener, *Pia Desideria*, trans. and ed. Theodore Tappert (Philadelphia: Fortress, 1964); Dale Brown, *Understanding Pietism* (Grand Rapids: Eerdmans, 1978); Ted Campbell, *The Religion of the Heart: A Study of European Religious Life in the Seventeenth and Eighteenth Centuries* (Columbia: U. of South Carolina Press, 1991); J. Steven O'Malley, "Pietistic Influence on John Wesley: Wesley and Gerhard Tersteegen," *Wesleyan Theological Journal* 31 (Fall 1996): 48-70.

12. On this aspect of Anglicanism in Wesley's day see Leslie W. Barnard, "The Use of the Patristic Tradition in the Late Seventeenth and Early Eighteenth Century," in *Scripture, Tradition and Reason*, eds. R. Bauckham and B. Drewery (Edinburgh: T & T Clark, 1988), 174-203; Robert D. Cornwall, "The Search for the Primitive Church: The Use of Early Church Fathers in the High Church Anglican Tradition, 1680-1745," *Anglican and Episcopal History* 59 (1990), 303-29.

13. Recommended studies of John Wesley's life and thought are Henry D. Rack, *Reasonable Enthusiast: John Wesley and the Rise of Methodism*, 3rd ed. (London: Epworth, 2002); Richard P. Hietzenrater, *Wesley and the People Called Methodists* (Nashville: Abingdon, 1995); and Randy Maddox, *Responsible Grace: John Wesley's Practical Theology* (Nashville: Kingswood, 1994). Bernard Semmel, *The Methodist Revolution* (New York: Basic Books, 1973), analyzes the interplay between Methodism and its social environment. David Hempton, *Methodism: Empire of the Spirit* (New Haven, CT: Yale U. Press, 2005), compares early British and American Methodism. A solid biography of Charles Wesley is G. M. Best, *Charles Wesley: A Biography* (London: Epworth, 2007).

14. See Albert C. Outler, "The Wesleyan Quadrilateral in John Wesley," *Wesleyan Theological Journal* 20 (1985), 7-18; Donald Thorsen, *The Wesleyan Quadrilateral: Scripture, Tradition, Reason and Experience as a Model of Evangelical Theology* (Grand Rapids: Zondervan, 1990); Ted Campbell, "The 'Wesleyan Quadrilateral': The Story of a Modern Methodist Myth," in *Doctrine and Theology in the United Methodist Church*, ed. Thomas Langford (Nashville: Kingswood, 1991), 154-61; W. Stephen Gunter, ed., *Wesley and the Quadrilateral: Renewing the Conversation* (Nashville: Abingdon, 1997).

15. Helpful in defining and describing evangelicalism in a comparative and cross-cultural way are *Evangelicalism: Comparative Studies of Popular Protestantism in North America, the British Isles, and Beyond, 1700-1990*, eds. Mark A. Noll, David W. Bebbington, and George A. Rawlyk (New York: Oxford U. Press, 1994); *Amazing Grace: Evangelicalism in Australia, Britain, Canada, and the United States*, eds. George A. Rawlyk and Mark Noll (Grand Rapids: Baker, 1993); and Mark A. Noll, *The Rise of Evangelicalism: The Age of Edwards, Whitefield and the Wesleys* (Downers Grove, IL: InterVarsity, 2003).

16. Scholarship focusing on the relationship between the American and British revivals include Leigh Eric Schmidt, *Holy Fairs: Scottish Communions and American Revivals in the Early Modern Period* (Princeton, NJ: Princeton U. Press, 1989); Marilyn J. Westerkamp, *Triumph of the Laity: Scots-Irish Piety and the Great Awakening, 1625-1760* (New York: Oxford U. Press, 1988); Michael J. Crawford, *Seasons of Grace: Colonial New England's Revival Tradition in Its British Context* (New York: Oxford U. Press, 1991); and Harry S. Stout, *The Divine Dramatist: George Whitefield and the Rise of Modern Evangelicalism* (Grand Rapids: Eerdmans, 1991).

17. See *The Writings of James Arminius*, 3 vols. (repr., Grand Rapids: Baker, 1956); Carl Bangs, *Arminius: A Study in the Dutch Reformation* (New York: Abingdon Press, 1971), especially 332-55; Richard A. Muller, *God, Creation, and Providence in the Thought of Jacob Arminius* (Grand Rapids: Baker, 1991); McGonigle, *Sufficient Saving Grace*, chap. 2.

18. McGonigle, *Sufficient Saving Grace*, 71, 95; Frank Baker, *John Wesley and the Church of England*, 2nd ed. (London: Epworth, 2000), 16, 70; Albert C. Outler, "Methodism's Theological Heritage: A Study in Perspective," in *The Wesleyan Theological Heritage: Essays of Albert C. Outler*, eds. Thomas C. Oden and Leicester R. Longden (Grand Rapids: Zondervan, 1991), 196-200. See also Jaroslav Pelikan, *The Growth of Medieval Theology, 600-1300* (Chicago: U. of Chicago Press, 1978), 80-95, 271-77.

19. Rack, *Reasonable Enthusiast*, 24-33. See also Robert Tuttle, *Mysticism in the Wesleyan Tradition* (Grand Rapids: Zondervan, 1989), 51-52.

20. McGonigle, *Sufficient Grace*, 177.

21. See especially Wesley's anti-Calvinist sermon "Free Grace," in *The Works of John Wesley*, vol. 3: *Sermons III, 71-114*, ed. Albert C. Outler (Nashville: Abingdon, 1986), 544-63.

22. See James Arminius, "On the Free Will of Man and Its Powers," in *The Works of James Arminius*, vol. 2, trans. James Nichols and William Nichols (Grand Rapids: Baker, 1986), 489-96; John Wesley's letter to John Mason, in *The Letters of the Rev. John Wesley*, vol. 6: *December 11, 1772-March 12, 1780*, ed. John Telford (London: Epworth, 1931), 239; Wesley, "On Working Out Your Own Salvation," *The Works of John Wesley*, vol. 3, 207; "The Principles of a Methodist," *The Works of John Wesley*, vol. 9: *The Methodist Societies: History, Nature, and Design*, ed. Rupert E. Davies (Nashville: Abingdon, 1989), 64.

23. John Wesley, "The Witness of the Spirit, Discourse I and II," 267-98, and "The Witness of Our Own Spirit," 299-313, and "The Great Privilege of Those That Are Born of God," 431-43, in *The Works of John Wesley*, vol. 1: *Sermons I, 1-33*, ed. Albert C. Outler (Nashville: Abingdon, 1984).

24. See Harald Lindström, *Wesley and Sanctification* (1946; repr., Grand Rapids: Zondervan, n.d.), and Leo George Cox, *John Wesley's Concept of Perfection* (Kansas City: Beacon Hill Press, 1964).

25. Wesley, "A Farther Appeal to Men of Reason and Religion," in *The Works of John Wesley*, vol. 11: *The Appeals to Men of Reason and Religion and Certain Related Open Letters*, ed. Gerald R. Cragg (Oxford: Clarendon, 1975), 106.

26. John Wesley, "The General Deliverance," 436-50, "The General Spread of the Gospel," 485-99, and "The New Creation," 500-510, in *The Works of John Wesley*, vol. 2: *Sermons II, 34-70*, ed. Albert C. Outler (Nashville: Abingdon, 1985). On the Eastern currents in Anglicanism that influenced Wesley, see Steve McCormick, "John Wesley's Use of John Chrysostom on the Christian Life: Faith Filled with the Energy of Love," Ph.D. diss., Drew U., 1983, and McCormick, "Theosis in Chrysostom and Wesley: An Eastern Paradigm on Faith and Love," *Wesleyan Theological Journal* 26 (Spring 1991): 38-103; Ted Campbell, *John Wesley and Christian Antiquity: Religious Vision and Cultural Change* (Nashville: Kingswood, 1991); and Michael J. Christensen, "Theosis and Sanctification: John Wesley's Reformulation of a Patristic Doctrine," *Wesleyan Theological Journal* 31 (Fall 1996): 71-92.

27. John Wesley, "A Plain Account of Christian Perfection," in *The Works of John Wesley*, vol. 11: *Thoughts, Addresses, Prayers, Letters*, 3rd ed. (Kansas City: Beacon Hill Press of Kansas City, 1979), 366-446, and widely reprinted.

28. John Wesley, *The Works of John Wesley*, vol. 20: *Journal and Diaries*, ed. Reginald Ward and Richard P. Heitzenrater (Nashville: Abingdon, 1991): 327-28; and "The More Excellent Way," in *The Works of John Wesley*, vol. 3, 263-77. See Theodore Jennings, *Good News to the Poor: John Wesley's Evangelical Economics* (Nashville: Abingdon, 1990), 97-117.

29. *The Letters of the Rev. John Wesley*, ed. John Telford (London: Epworth, 1931), 8:238.

30. John Wesley, "A Short Account of the Life and Death of the Reverend John Fletcher," in *The Works of John Wesley*, vol. 11: *Thoughts, Addresses, Prayers, Letters*, 3rd ed. (Kansas City: Beacon Hill Press of Kansas City, 1979), 273-365.

31. On Fletcher's views on sanctification see *The Works of the Rev. John Fletcher*, 4 vols. (New York: Carlton and Phillips, 1854), 2: 627-57; Joseph Benson, *The Life of the Rev. John W. De La Flechere* (New York: Methodist Book Concern, n.d.), 203; John Knight, "John Fletcher's Influence on the Development of Wesleyan Theology in America," *Wesleyan Theological Journal* 13 (1978), 13-33. On the Fletcher-Wesley disagreement, M. Robert Fraser, "Strains in the Understanding of Christian Perfection in Early British Methodism," Ph.D. diss., Vanderbilt U., 1988, and Randy L. Maddox, "Wesley's Understanding of Christian Perfection: In What Sense Pentecostal?" *Wesleyan Theological Journal* 34 (Fall 1999): 78-110.

32. John Wesley, *A Plain Account of Christian Perfection* (Repr., Kansas City: Beacon Hill Press of Kansas City, 1966), 34.

33. See Harold R. Raser, *Phoebe Palmer, Her Life and Thought* (Lewiston, NY: Edwin Mellen, 1987), 231-41.

34. See John L. Peters, *Christian Perfection and American Methodism* (New York: Abingdon, 1956), 201-16.

35. John Fletcher, *The Works of the Reverend John Fletcher*, vol. 2 (Salem, OH: Schmul, 1974), 261-67. See John A. Knight, *The Holiness Pilgrimage: Reflections on the Life of Holiness* (Kansas City: Beacon Hill Press of Kansas City, 1973), 63-81.

Chapter 2

1. See *World Religions in America: An Introduction*, ed. Jacob Neusner (Louisville, KY: Westminster/John Knox, 1994).

2. J. Hector St. John Crevecoeur, quoted in Sidney E. Mead, *The Lively Experiment: The Shaping of Christianity in America* (New York: Harper and Row, 1963), 14.

3. Sources include Sydney E. Ahlstrom, *A Religious History of the American People* (New Haven, CT: Yale U. Press, 1972); Richard E. Wentz, *Religion in the New World: The Shaping of Religious Traditions in the United States* (Minneapolis: Fortress, 1990); Peter W. Williams, *America's Religions: Traditions and Cultures* (Urbana: U. of Illinois Press, 1998).

4. Jack Greene, *Pursuits of Happiness: The Social Development of Early British Colonies and the Formation of American Culture* (Chapel Hill: U. of North Carolina Press, 1988).

5. See Mead, *Lively Experiment*, 55-71. See also William R. Estep, *Revolution Within the Revolution: The First Amendment in Historical Context, 1612-1789* (Grand Rapids: Eerdmans, 1990).

6. See R. Laurence Moore, *Selling God: American Religion in the Marketplace of Culture* (New York: Oxford U. Press, 1994); James R. Rohrer, *Keepers of the Covenant: Frontier Missions and the Decline of Congregationalism, 1774-1818* (New York: Oxford U. Press, 1995), 3-4, 115-16, 134-35, 152.

7. See Mead, *Lively Experiment*, 103-33.

8. Nathan O. Hatch, *The Democratization of American Christianity* (New Haven, CT: Yale U. Press, 1989), studies the many ramifications of the democratic impulse in American religion.

9. See C. C. Goen, *Revivalism and Separatism in New England, 1740-1800: Strict Congregationalists and Separate Baptists in the Great Awakening* (New Haven, CT: Yale U. Press, 1962), 269, 277-79; Jay P. Dolan, *The American Catholic Experience: A History from Colonial Times to the Present* (Notre Dame: U. of Notre Dame Press, 1985), 158-94; Timothy L. Smith, "Congregation, State and Denomination: The Forging of the American Religious Structure," *William and Mary Quarterly*, 3rd series, 25 (1968), 155-76.

10. Frank Baker, *From Wesley to Asbury: Studies in Early American Methodism* (Durham, NC: Duke U. Press, 1976); Dee E. Andrews, *The Methodists and Revolutionary America, 1760-1800: The Shaping of an Evangelical Culture* (Princeton, NJ: Princeton U. Press, 2000), 39-41.

11. Rhys Isaac, *The Transformation of Virginia, 1740-1790* (Chapel Hill: U. of North Carolina Press, 1982), 68-69, 120, 189-92; Andrews, *Methodists*, 31-47.

12. John Wesley, "To Our Brethren in America, September 10, 1784," in *The Letters of the Rev. John Wesley*, vol. 7, ed. John Telford (London: Epworth, 1931), 238-39. See Frank Baker, *John Wesley and the Church of England* (London: Epworth, 1970), 256-82; Rack, *Reasonable Enthusiast*, 506-26.

13. See L. C. Rudolph, *Francis Asbury* (Nashville: Abingdon, 1966), and Darius Salter, *America's Bishop: The Life of Francis Asbury* (Nappanee, IN: Francis Asbury Press of Evangel Publishing House, 2003).

14. Salter, *America's Bishop*, 91-95.

15. Andrews, *Methodists*, 66-72.

16. Frederick Norwood, *The Story of American Methodism: A History of the United Methodists and Their Relations* (Nashville: Abingdon, 1974), 154.

17. Edwin Gaustad, *Historical Atlas of Religion in America* (New York: Harper and Row, 1962), 80.

18. John H. Wigger, *Taking Heaven by Storm: Methodism and the Rise of Popular Christianity in America* (New York: Oxford U. Press, 1998), 48-79; Christine Leigh Heyrman, *Southern Cross: The Beginnings of the Bible Belt* (New York: Alfred A. Knopf, 1997), 87-89.

19. Valuable studies include Timothy L. Smith, *Revivalism and Social Reform in Mid-Nineteenth Century America* (Nashville: Abingdon, 1957); William G. McLoughlin, *Modern Revivalism: Charles Grandison Finney to Billy Graham* (New York: Ronald Press, 1959); William G. McLoughlin, *Revivals, Awakenings, and Reform* (Chicago: U. of Chicago Press, 1978).

20. See Schmidt, *Holy Fairs*. See also Charles A. Johnson, *The Frontier Camp Meeting: Religion's Harvest Time* (Dallas: Southern Methodist U. Press, 1955); Dickson Bruce Jr., *And They All Sang Hallelujah: Plainfolk Camp Meeting Religion, 1800-1845* (Knoxville: U. of Tennessee Press, 1975); Paul K. Conkin, *Cane Ridge: America's Pentecost* (Madison: U. of Wisconsin Press, 1990); Kenneth O. Brown, *Holy Ground, Too: The Camp Meeting Family Tree* (Hazleton, PA: Holiness Archives, 1997).

21. Horace Bushnell, *Views of Christian Nurture, and of Subjects Adjacent Thereto* (Hartford, CT: Edwin Hunt, 1847). See also John Williamson Nevin, *The Anxious Bench* (Chambersburg, PA: Publication Office of the German Reformed Church, 1843). Mormonism was the largest of the many new religious movements that began in connection with revivals and awakenings in nineteenth-century America. See Jan Shipps, *Mormonism: The Story of a New Religious Tradition* (Urbana: U. of Illinois Press, 1985); Richard L. Bushman, *Joseph Smith: Rough Stone Rolling* (New York: Alfred A. Knopf, 2005). See also Keith J. Hardman, *Charles Grandison Finney, 1792-1876: Revivalist and Reformer* (Syracuse, NY: Syracuse U. Press, 1987; repr., Grand Rapids: Baker, 1990), 237-39, 391-94.

22. *Lectures on Revivals of Religion*, ed. William G. McLoughlin (Cambridge, MA: Harvard U. Press, 1960), 13. See Charles E. Hambrick-Stowe, *Charles G. Finney and the Spirit of American Evangelicalism* (Grand Rapids: Eerdmans, 1996).

23. Norwood, *Story of American Methodism*, 154; Gaustad, *Historical Atlas of Religion in America*, 79-80. See also Wigger, *Taking Heaven by Storm*.

24. See Peters, *Christian Perfection*, but compare Allan Coppedge, "Entire Sanctification in Early Methodism: 1812-1845," *Wesleyan Theological Journal* 13 (Spring 1978): 34-50.

25. Peters, *Christian Perfection*, 121-23.

26. Ibid., 101-19.

27. Rohrer, *Keepers of the Covenant*; Ahlstrom, *Religious History*, 455-71. On nineteenth-century American Calvinism see E. Brooks Holifield, *Theology in America: Christian Thought from the Age of the Puritans to the Civil War* (New Haven, CT: Yale U. Press, 2003), 341-70, and Mark A. Noll, *America's God: From Jonathan Edwards to Abraham Lincoln* (New York: Oxford U. Press, 2002), 293-330. See also Sidney E. Mead, *Nathaniel William Taylor, 1786-1858: A Connecticut Liberal* (Chicago: U. of Chicago Press, 1942), and Bruce Kuklick, *Churchmen to Philosophers: From Jonathan Edwards to John Wesley* (New Haven, CT: Yale U. Press, 1985), 94-111, which emphasizes Taylor's closeness theologically to Jonathan Edwards.

28. The classic study is Smith, *Revivalism and Social Reform*. See also Donald W. Dayton, *Discovering an Evangelical Heritage* (New York: Harper and Row, 1976), and Robert Abzug, *Cosmos Crumbling: American Reform and the Religious Imagination* (New York: Oxford U. Press, 1994).

29. Charles G. Finney, *Reflections on Revival*, comp. Donald W. Dayton (Minneapolis: Bethany Fellowship Press, 1979), 113-14. Hatch, *Democratization of American Christianity*, chap. 1, sets the stage. George Thomas speaks of the "isomorphism" or congruence of revivalism with the various impulses of American society in *Revivalism and Cultural Change: Christianity, Nation Building, and the Market in Nineteenth-Century United States* (Chicago: U. of Chicago Press, 1989). See especially pp. 2, 5, 8, 18, 49-50, 82-93, 88, 97, 115, 174-75. See also Timothy L. Smith, "Righteousness and Hope: Christian Holiness and the Millennial Vision in America, 1800-1900," *The American Quarterly* 31 (Spring 1979): 21-45.

30. Harold E. Raser, "Views on Last Things in the American Holiness Movement," in Dunning, *Second Coming*, 161-85. See also Timothy L. Smith, "Social Reform: Some Reflections on Causation and Consequence," in *Rise of Adventism*, ed. Edwin S. Gaustad (New York: Harper and Row, 1974), and Smith, "Righteousness and Hope," 21-45.

31. Smith, *Revivalism and Social Reform*, documents the spread of perfectionist teaching well beyond the boundaries of Methodism. On Methodism's growth see Roger Finke and Rodney Stark, *The Churching of America 1776-1990: Winners and Losers in Our Religious Economy* (New Brunswick, NJ: Rutgers U. Press, 1997), 54-108; and Wigger, *Taking Heaven by Storm*.

32. For Finney see the biographies by Hambrick-Stowe and Hardman cited above.

33. Garth M. Rosell and Richard A. G. Dupuis, eds., *The Memoirs of Charles G. Finney: The Complete Restored Text, Annotated Critical Edition* (Grand Rapids: Zondervan, 1989), 391-92, 393. See Charles G. Finney, *The Promise of the Holy Spirit*, ed. Timothy L. Smith (Minneapolis: Bethany, 1980), and Charles G. Finney, *Views on Sanctification* (Oberlin: James Steele, 1840). For Mahan see his *Scripture Doctrine of Christian Perfection: With Other Kindred Subjects, Illustrated and Confirmed in*

a Series of Discourses Designed to Throw Light on the Way of Holiness (Boston: D. S. King, 1839), and Edward H. Madden and James E. Hamilton, *Freedom and Grace: the Life of Asa Mahan* (Metuchen, NJ: Scarecrow, 1982).

34. Rosell and Dupuis, eds., *Memoirs*, 391. See also Hambrick-Stowe, *Finney*, 181-82.

35. Rosell and Dupuis, eds., *Memoirs*, 383-410; *Finney*, 159.

36. See Smith, *Revivalism and Social Reform*. Connecting Christian perfection and abolitionism is Douglas M. Strong, *Perfectionist Politics: Abolitionism and the Religious Tensions of American Democracy* (Syracuse, NY: Syracuse U. Press, 1999). See also Richard J. Carwardine, *Evangelicals and Politics in Antebellum America* (1993; repr., Knoxville: U. of Tennessee Press, 1997), 134, 231, 242, 268, 302. Casting doubt on the connection between the mid-century revival and social reform is Kathryn Long, *The Revival of 1857-58: Interpreting an American Awakening* (New York: Oxford U. Press, 1998), 95.

37. See Richard Wheatley, *The Life and Letters of Mrs. Phoebe Palmer* (New York: Palmer and Hughes, 1876), and Thomas F. Oden, *Phoebe Palmer: Selected Writings* (New York: Paulist Press, 1988). Biographies of Phoebe Palmer include Charles E. White, *The Beauty of Holiness: Phoebe Palmer as Theologian, Revivalist, Feminist, and Humanitarian* (Grand Rapids: Francis Asbury Press, 1986), and Raser, *Phoebe Palmer*.

38. Quoted in Peters, *Christian Perfection*, 99-100.

39. Wheatley, *Life and Letters*, 25-26.

40. See Raser, *Phoebe Palmer*, 34-61. See also Kendra Weddle Irons, "Phoebe Palmer: Chosen, Tried, Triumphant—An Examination of Her Calling in Light of Current Research," *Methodist History* 37 (October 1998): 28-36; Diane Leclerc, *Singleness of Heart: Gender, Sin and Holiness in Historical Perspective* (Lanham, MD: Scarecrow, 2001), chap. 4, "'Dignified Daughters': Entire Devotion and the Emancipated Praxis of Phoebe Palmer," 105-40.

41. Wheatley, *Life and Letters*, 488.

42. Phoebe Palmer, *The Promise of the Father; or, A Neglected Specialty of the Last Days* (Boston: Henry V. Degen, 1859). See Raser, *Phoebe Palmer*, 199-210.

43. See George Hughes, *Fragrant Memories of the Tuesday Meeting and the Guide to Holiness* (New York: Palmer and Hughes, 1886).

44. Wheatley, *Life and Letters*, 220-23. See Raser, *Phoebe Palmer*, 211-18. On the Five Points Mission and House of Industry see Ladies of the Mission, *The Old Brewery and the New Mission House at the Five Points* (New York: Stringer and Townsend, 1854); Carroll Smith-Rosenberg, *Religion and the Rise of the American City: The New York City Mission Movement, 1812-1870* (Ithaca, NY: Cornell U. Press, 1984), chap. 8; Tyler Anbinder, *Five Points: The 19th-Century New York City Neighborhood That Invented Tap Dance, Stole Elections, and Became the World's Most Notorious Slum* (New York: Plume Books, 2001), chap. 8.

45. Smith, *Revivalism and Social Reform*, 124-25.

46. See Harold Raser, "'I Commend unto You Phoebe'—With Some Reservations: The Legacy of Phoebe Palmer and the Future of the Holiness Movement," *The Tower: The Journal of Nazarene Theological Seminary* (1998), 17-32.

47. See *An Account of the Experiences of Hester Ann Rogers* (New York: Lane and Scott, 1850), 137-38; Raser, *Phoebe Palmer*, 164, 245-49.

48. William Erastus Arnold, *Pentecostal Herald* (February 1899), 1.

49. Wesley, *A Plain Account*, emphasis added.

50. See Morton White, *Pragmatism and the American Mind: Essays and Reviews in Philosophy and Intellectual History* (New York: Oxford U. Press, 1973), and Ann Taves, *Fits, Trances, and Visions: Experiencing Religion and Explaining Experience from Wesley to James* (Princeton, NJ: Princeton U. Press, 1999).

51. Phoebe Palmer, *The Way of Holiness, with Notes by the Way* (New York: Piercy and Reed, 1843), 1.

52. Phoebe Palmer, *Faith and Its Effects: Fragments from My Portfolio* (New York: the author, 1845), 104.

53. Donald A. Thorsen, *The Wesleyan Quadrilateral: Scripture, Tradition, Reason and Experience as a Model of Evangelical Theology* (Grand Rapids: Zondervan, 1990).

54. F. H. Newhall, "Religion Not Theology," *Christian Advocate* (October 21, 1880), 675.

55. See Taves, *Fits, Trances, and Visions*, 266-69; Grant Wacker, *Heaven Below: Early Pentecostals and American Culture* (Cambridge, MA: Harvard U. Press, 2001), 84-86.

56. See Carol V. R. George, *Segregated Sabbaths: Richard Allen and the Rise of Independent Black Churches, 1760-1840* (New York: Oxford U. Press, 1973); C. C. Goen, *Broken Churches, Broken Nation: Denominational Schisms and the Coming of the Civil War* (Macon, GA: Mercer U. Press, 1985); Howard A. Snyder, *Populist Saints: B. T. and Ellen Roberts and the First Free Methodists* (Grand Rapids: Eerdmans, 2006).

57. See *Guide to Holiness* (July 1873), 26. Also Hughes, *Fragrant Memories*, 176-77; Raser, *Phoebe Palmer*, 126-41, 222-26; Melvin Dieter, *The Holiness Revival of the Nineteenth Century*, 2nd ed. (Lanham, MD: Scarecrow, 1996), 79-81; Snyder, *Populist Saints*, 572-82.

58. Cited in Delbert Rose, *A Theology of Christian Experience: Interpreting the Historic Wesleyan Message* (Minneapolis: Bethany, 1965), 36. See Dieter, *Holiness Revival*, 79-116, and Charles Edwin Jones, *Perfectionist Persuasion: The Holiness Movement and American Methodism, 1867-1936* (Metuchen, NJ: Scarecrow, 1974), 16-78.

59. From an insert with the heading "General Camp-Meeting" carried in *Guide to Holiness* (July 1867) (emphasis added). Eyewitness accounts are Alexander McLean and J. W. Eaton, eds., *Penuel, or Face to Face with God* (New York: W. C. Palmer Jr., Publisher, 1870), and George Hughes, *Days of Power in the Forest Temple: A Review of the Wonderful Work of God at Fourteen National Camp Meetings, from 1867-1872* (Boston: John Bent and Company, 1873).

60. See Kenneth O. Brown, *Inskip, McDonald, Fowler: "Wholly and Forever Thine": Early Leadership in the National Camp Meeting Association for the Promotion of Holiness* (Hazleton, PA: Holiness Archives, 1999).

61. Quoted in Dieter, *Holiness Revival*, 97. Not so different, Randall Balmer's description of a holiness camp meeting in *Mine Eyes Have Seen the Glory: A Journey into the Evangelical Subculture in America* (New York: Oxford U. Press, 1989), 188-207. See McLean and Eaton, *Penuel*, and Hughes, *Days of Power*. Also see William McDonald and John E. Searles, *The Life of Rev. John S. Inskip* (Boston: McDonald and Gill, 1885), 146-84. See Jones, *Perfectionist Persuasion*, 25-46.

62. McLean and Eaton, *Penuel*, 381.

63. See Rose, *Theology of Christian Experience*, 43-47; Jones, *Perfectionist Persuasion*, 22-23.

64. See McDonald and Searles, *Life of Rev. John S. Inskip*, esp. 224 ff.; Rose, *A Theology of Christian Experience*, 43-44.

65. McDonald and Searles, *Life of Rev. John S. Inskip*, 333. See William Carey, *Story of the National Holiness Missionary Society* (Chicago: National Holiness Missionary Society, 1940). For Taylor see David Bundy, "Bishop William Taylor and Methodist Mission: A Study in Nineteenth Century Social History, Part I: From Campmeeting Convert to International Evangelist," *Methodist History* 27 (July 1989): 198-212, and "Bishop William Taylor and Methodist Mission: A Study in Nineteenth Century Social History, Part II: Social Structures in Collision," *Methodist History* 28 (October 1989): 3-21.

66. Floyd Cunningham, *Holiness Abroad: Nazarene Missions in Asia* (Lanham, MD: Scarecrow, 2003), 73-74.

67. "Answers to Inquiries," *Christian Advocate* (June 19, 1884), 401.

68. M. S. Terry, "Chiliasm and Universalism," *Christian Advocate* (March 8, 1888), 151.

69. In Brown, *Inskip, McDonald, Fowler*, 251; see 225, 250-51.

70. See also Isaiah Reid's comments in *Echoes of the General Holiness Assembly Held in Chicago, May 3-13, 1901*, ed. S. B. Shaw (Chicago: S. B. Shaw), 325-26, and Smith, *Called unto Holiness*, 126-28.

71. *A History of the Revival of Holiness in St. Paul M.E. Church, Providence, R.I., 1880-1887: For a Statement of the Circumstances Which Led to the Formation of the South Providence Holiness Association and the People's Evangelical Church* (Providence, RI: E. L. Freeman and Son, 1887). See also Bertha Carton and Ira Durham Vennard, eds., *The Stalwart of the Old Guard: The Life and Labors of Lyman Blackmarr Kent* (N.p.: Christian Witness, 1912); C. B. Jernigan, *Pioneer Days of the Holiness Movement in the Southwest* (Kansas City: Nazarene Publishing House, 1919); John T. Benson Jr., *A History 1898-1915 of the Pentecostal Mission, Inc., Nashville, Tennessee* (Nashville: Trevecca, 1977); Jones, *Perfectionist Persuasion*, 47-77.

72. For a firsthand account of Holiness urban social work see Rees, *Miracles in the Slums; or, Thrilling Stories of Those Rescued from the Cesspools of Iniquity, and Touching Incidents in the Lives of the Unfortunate* (Chicago: Seth C. Rees, 1905). See also Timothy L. Smith, "Holiness Social Work in America, 1850-1910," paper presented before the Nazarene Theological Seminary Breakfast Club, January 4, 1956; Norris Magnuson, *Salvation in the Slums: Evangelical Social Work, 1865-1920* (Repr., Grand Rapids: Baker, 1990).

73. The destabilizing challenges facing urban Protestants are discussed in Paul Boyer, *Urban Masses and Moral Order in America, 1820-1920* (Cambridge, MA: Harvard U. Press, 1978), especially chaps. 8 and 11; and Kevin J. Christiano, *Religious Diversity and Social Change: American Cities, 1890-1906* (Cambridge: Cambridge U. Press, 1987), chaps. 7-8.

74. *Christian Advocate and Journal* (November 27, 1875), 380. Emphasis added.

75. Quoted in Peters, *Christian Perfection*, 139.

76. Ibid.

77. On the Plymouth Brethren, Clarence B. Bass, *Backgrounds to Dispensationalism: Its Historical Genesis and Ecclesiastical Implications* (Grand Rapids: Baker, 1960; repr., Grand Rapids: Baker, 1977), and F. R. Coad, *A History of the Brethren Movement* (Vancouver: Regent College Publishing, 1968). For restorationism see David Harrell, *Quest for a Christian America: The Disciples of Christ and American Society to 1866* (Nashville: Disciples of Christ Historical Society, 1966), and Richard Hughes, ed., *The American Quest for the Primitive Church* (Urbana: U. of Illinois Press, 1988).

78. Asbury Lowrey, in *Advocate of Christian Holiness* (June 1873), 265.

79. George Hughes, ed., *Holiness Yearbook, 1893* (New York: Palmer and Hughes, 1893), 31.

80. See Timothy L. Smith, "The Holiness Crusade," in *The History of Methodism*, vol. 2, ed. Emory S. Bucke (New York: Abingdon, 1964), 608-27.

81. See Daniel Sidney Warner, *Bible Proofs of the Second Work of Grace: Or Entire Sanctification as a Distinct Experience Subsequent to Justification, Established by the United Testimony of Several Hundred Texts—Including a Description of the Great Holiness Crisis of the Present Age, by the Prophets* (Goshen, IN: Evangelical United Mennonite Publishing Society, 1880), and *The Church of God: or What Is the Church and What Is Not?* (Moundsville, WV: Gospel Trumpet, 1902). See John W. V. Smith, *Quest for Holiness and Unity: A Centennial History of the Church of God (Anderson, Indiana)* (Anderson, IN: Warner, 1980); Barry Callen, *It's God's Church!: The Life and Legacy of Daniel Warner* (Anderson, IN: Warner, 1995).

82. Quoted in Peters, *Christian Perfection*, 142.

83. Wheatley, *Life and Letters*, 450.

84. Henry C. Sheldon, "Changes in Theology Among American Methodists," *American Journal of Theology* 10 (1906), 45-50. See Harold Paul Sloan, *The Child and the Church* (Red Bank, NJ: Standard Publishing, 1916). See also Smith, *Called unto Holiness*, 42, 45-46, and Peters, *Christian Perfection*, 133-80.

85. Quoted in Peters, *Christian Perfection*, 148.

86. Smith, *Called unto Holiness*, 27-53.

87. *Proceedings of Holiness Conferences Held at Cincinnati, November 26th, 1877, and at New York, December 17th, 1877* (Philadelphia: National Publishing Association for the Promotion of Holiness, 1878 [repr., Garland, 1985]), 80-81, 87, 138-39, 223; S. B. Shaw, ed., *Proceedings of the General Holiness Assembly Held in the Park Ave. M.E. Church in Chicago, May 20-26, 1885* (Grand Rapids: S. B. Shaw, 1885); S. B. Shaw, ed., *Echoes of the General Holiness Assembly Held in Chicago, May 3-13, 1901* (Chicago: S. B. Shaw, 1901), 9, 32-33, 113, 275, 325. See Dieter, *Holiness Revival*, 247-65; Smith, *Called unto Holiness*, 28-47.

88. Peters, *Christian Perfection*, 148-49, lists ten groups, but does not, for example, list Warner's Church of God, or other similar restoration groups that claimed not to be churches or denominations at all. See Jones, *Perfectionist Persuasion*, 90-105; and Charles E. Jones, *A Guide to the Study of the Holiness Movement* (Metuchen, NJ: Scarecrow, 1974).

89. Smith, *Called unto Holiness*, 12.

Chapter 3

1. Jones, *Perfectionist Persuasion*, 122-23.

2. The full story of events at St. Paul, as told by founders of the People's Evangelical Church, is *A History of the Revival of Holiness in St. Paul's M.E. Church, Providence, R.I., 1880-1887,* 9. For anti-Roman Catholic feeling in Providence in the 1850s see Ray Billington, *The Protestant Crusade, 1800-1860: A Study of the Origins of American Nativism* (1938; repr., Chicago: Quadrangle, 1964), 311.

3. See *History of the Revival of Holiness,* 11-12, 21-22, 29.

4. Ibid., 56.

5. Ibid., 4-6, 70, 74, 78, 85-86.

6. Stan Ingersol, "Our New England Roots: 100 Years of Organized Witness," *Herald of Holiness* (May 1990), 18.

7. *Report of the Central Evangelical Holiness Association* (Providence, RI: Office of Beulah Christian, 1894), 20.

8. *Manual of the People's Evangelical Church of Providence, R.I.* (Providence, RI: Beulah Christian, 1895), 7.

9. *Manual of the First Pentecostal Church of Lynn, Mass.* (Providence, RI: Pentecostal Printing, 1898), 7-8.

10. *Records of the Annual Meetings of the Central Evangelical Holiness Association* (Providence, RI: Press of George A. Wilson, 1896), 8, 20-21.

11. Smith, *Called unto Holiness,* 58-60.

12. For Reynolds see Chapman, *History of the Church of the Nazarene,* 138-44; Amy N. Hinshaw, *In Labors Abundant: A Biography of H. F. Reynolds* (Kansas City: Nazarene Publishing House, n.d.), and the "Autobiographical Memoirs" in the Nazarene Archives, on which her book is based; J. Timothy White, "Hiram F. Reynolds: Prime Mover of the Nazarene Mission Education System," Ph.D. diss., U. of Kansas, 1996, 38-88, especially pp. 53-56. See also Smith, *Called unto Holiness,* 60-61; James McGraw, "The Preaching of Hiram F. Reynolds," *Preacher's Magazine* (April 1954), 3-5. On Copeland's role see Steve Cooley, "My Dear Brother Copeland," *Herald of Holiness* (September 15, 1984), 9.

13. For BeVier, see *Association of Pentecostal Churches of America Minutes of the Eleventh Annual Meeting* (Providence, RI: Pentecostal Printing, 1906), 20.

14. Mendell Taylor, *Fifty Years of Nazarene Missions,* vol. 1: *Administration and Promotion* (Kansas City: Beacon Hill Press, 1952), 11. For the Northeastern context see Clifton J. Philips, *Protestant America and the Pagan World: The First Half-Century of the American Board of Commissioners for Foreign Missions, 1810-1860* (Cambridge, MA: East Asian Research Center, Harvard U. Press, 1969), 22-23.

15. Samuel Capen, president of the American Board of Commissioners for Foreign Missions, quoted in Valentin H. Rabe, *The Home Base of American China Missions, 1880-1920* (Cambridge, MA: Harvard U. Press, 1978), 154. See also Robert Wiebe, *The Search for Order, 1877-1920* (New York: Hill and Wang, 1967).

16. *History of the Foreign Missionary Work of the Church of the Nazarene* (Kansas City: General Board of Foreign Missions, Church of the Nazarene, 1921), 7-8. See also Hiram Reynolds, "The Missionary Work," May 23, 1907, Nazarene Archives.

17. Reynolds, "Missionary Work."

18. Smith, *Called unto Holiness,* 70; Cunningham, *Holiness Abroad,* 5.

19. Cited in Smith, *Called unto Holiness,* 72.

20. *Association of Pentecostal Churches of America Minutes of the Fourth Annual Meeting* (Providence, RI: Pentecostal Printing, 1899), 35.

21. *Manual of the First Pentecostal Church of Lynn, Mass.,* 7-8; "Minutes of the Missionary Committee of the Association of Pentecostal Churches of America" (December 15, 1899); Association of Pentecostal Churches of America, *Minutes of the Tenth Annual Meeting* (Providence, RI: Pentecostal Printing, 1905), 49; *Association of Pentecostal Churches of America Minutes of the Ninth Annual Meeting* (Providence, RI: Pentecostal Printing, 1904), 21; Stan Ingersol, "The Association of Pentecostal Churches of America: A Centennial Sketch," *Herald of Holiness* (July 1996), 30-31.

22. See "Minutes of the Missionary Committee of the Association of Pentecostal Churches of America" (July 6, 1897; September 10, 1897; and December 9, 1897); Reynolds, "Missionary Work";

Constitution of the Association of Pentecostal Churches of America (Providence, RI: Beulah Christian, 1897), 7-9; Cunningham, *Holiness Abroad*, chaps. 1—2.

23. *Association of Pentecostal Churches of America Minutes of the Seventh Annual Meeting* (Providence, RI: Pentecostal Printing, 1902), 56-58; "Minutes of the Missionary Committee of the Association of Pentecostal Churches of America" (April 12, 1906). See Susan N. Fitkin, *Grace More Abounding: A Story of the Triumphs of Redeeming Grace Through Two Score Years in the Master's Service* (Kansas City: Nazarene Publishing House, n.d.); Basil Miller, *Susan N. Fitkin: For God and Missions* (Kansas City: Nazarene Publishing House, n.d.), 57-67, 70; Rebecca Laird, *Ordained Women in the Church of the Nazarene: The First Generation* (Kansas City: Nazarene Publishing House, 1993), 83-91. Compare Dana L. Robert, "Holiness and the Missionary Vision of the Woman's Foreign Missionary Society of the Methodist Episcopal Church, 1869-1894," *Methodist History* 39 (October 2000), 15-27.

24. "Fitkin Sells Again," *Time* (June 15, 1931). See Miller, *Susan N. Fitkin*, and Stan Ingersol, "Mother of Missions: The Evangelistic Vision of Susan Norris Fitkin," *Herald of Holiness* (January 1991), 44. Fitkin's autobiography is *Grace Much More Abounding*.

25. Taylor, *Fifty Years of Nazarene Missions*, 1:85-136.

26. Cunningham, *Holiness Abroad*, 7.

27. Ibid., 9.

28. "Minutes of the Missionary Council of the Association of Pentecostal Churches of America" (April 18, 1903, and April 15, 1905); Roy Swim, *A History of Missions of the Church of the Nazarene* (Kansas City: Nazarene Publishing House, 1936), 30-31.

29. Stan Ingersol, "A Model Pastor: John Short and the Cambridge Church," *Herald of Holiness* (October 1998), 10.

30. *The Doctrines and Discipline of the Evangelical Association* (Cleveland: Thomas and Mattill, 1898), 23.

31. Ingersol, "Model Pastor," 10. See Smith, *Called unto Holiness*, 61-66, 80-81.

32. *Manual of the People's Evangelical Church*, 6; *Articles of Faith and Government of the Lincoln Place Pentecostal Church, Lincoln Place, Pa.* (Providence, RI: Pentecostal Printing, 1904), 6. For the broader issue, Paul M. Bassett, "The Theological Identity of the North American Holiness Movement," in *The Variety of Evangelicalism*, eds. Donald Dayton and Robert K. Johnston (Knoxville: U. of Tennessee Press, 1991), 72-108.

33. *Manual of the People's Evangelical Church*, 9, 22; *Manual of the Beulah Pentecostal Church of Hopewell Junction, New York* (Providence, RI: Pentecostal Printing, 1901), 9-10, 23.

34. Ernest E. Angell, "Memorial Sermon," 1900 (file 651-29).

35. *Association of Pentecostal Churches of America Minutes of the Sixth Annual Meeting* (Providence, RI: Pentecostal Printing, 1901), 45-46. The issue also caught the attention of the WCTU. See Ian Tyrrell, *Woman's World, Woman's Empire: The Woman's Christian Temperance Union in International Perspective, 1880-1930* (Chapel Hill: U. of North Carolina Press, 1991), 214-15.

36. "Minutes of the Association of Pentecostal Churches of America 1903" (Providence, RI: Pentecostal Printing, 1903), 51-52.

37. J. Fred Parker, *From East to Western Sea: A Brief History of the Church of the Nazarene in Canada* (Kansas City: Nazarene Publishing House, 1971), 15-18.

38. Ross Cribbis, "A Brief History of the Holiness Movement in the Maritime Provinces of Canada," submitted to Canada Atlantic District Preachers' Meeting, November 1962 (file 736-40); Ira F. McLeister and Roy S. Nicholson, *Conscience and Commitments: The History of the Wesleyan Church of America*, fourth ed., eds. Lee M. Haines Jr. and Melvin E. Dieter (Marion, IN: Wesley Press, 1976), 301-4.

39. Fred MacMillan, *Profiles of Faith: History of the Canada Atlantic District of the Church of the Nazarene* (Kankakee, IL: Adcraft Printers, 1976), 6-7. See also William Stewart, "Love Does That: The Beginning of the Church of the Nazarene in Canada," *Holiness Today* (July/August 2005), 32.

40. Parker, *From East to Western Sea*, 18-19; MacMillan, *Profiles of Faith*, 4-12; Neil E. Hightower, ed., *Love Does That: The Story of the Nazarenes in Canada* (Brampton, ON: Church of the Nazarene Canada, 2002), 13-22; Smith, *Called unto Holiness*, 75-76.

41. Smith, *Called unto Holiness*, 76.

42. *Association of Pentecostal Churches of America Minutes of the Fourth Annual Meeting* (Providence, RI: Pentecostal Printing, 1899); Smith, *Called unto Holiness*, 77.

43. See E. G. Anderson, *Annual Report and Survey of the Fields Occupied by Missionaries of the Pentecostal Church of the Nazarene, 1917-1918* (Kansas City: General Foreign Missionary Board, [1918]), 7-8.

44. "Minutes of the Missionary Committee of the Association of Pentecostal Churches of America" (December 15, 1899).

45. *Association of Pentecostal Churches of America Minutes of the Tenth Annual Meeting* (Providence, RI: Pentecostal Printing, 1905), 14. See "Minutes of the Missionary Committee of the Association of Pentecostal Churches of America" (April 12, 1906); *Association of Pentecostal Churches of America Minutes of the Ninth Annual Meeting* (Providence, RI: Pentecostal Printing, 1904), 21.

46. James R. Cameron, *Eastern Nazarene College: The First Fifty Years* (Kansas City: Nazarene Publishing House, 1968), 17-18.

47. "Report of Educational Committee," in *Association of Pentecostal Churches of America: Minutes of the Sixth Annual Meeting, April 9-14, 1901;* Cameron, *Eastern Nazarene College*, 22-27; Virginia L. Brereton, *Training God's Army: The American Bible School, 1880-1940* (Bloomington: Indiana U. Press, 1990), 62.

48. Quoted from Cameron, *Eastern Nazarene College*, 21-22.

49. "First Day, Tuesday, April 14," in *Association of Pentecostal Churches of America: Minutes of the Eighth Annual Meeting, April 14-19, 1903;* and "Fifth Day, Saturday, April 18," in *Association of Pentecostal Churches of America: Minutes of the Eighth Annual Meeting, April 14-19, 1903;* Cameron, *Eastern Nazarene College,* 29.

50. The sources give slightly different accounts and interpretations of the events. Compare Cameron, *Eastern Nazarene College*, 18-34, and Smith, *Called unto Holiness,* 81-84.

51. Cameron, *Eastern Nazarene College,* 51-71, 130-39. See also Stan Ingersol, "Native Son: The Life and Work of Ernest E. Angell," *Herald of Holiness* (August 15, 1988), 11.

52. Cunningham, *Holiness Abroad,* 50. (The following section is taken from this source, 50-57, which see for further documentation.) See M. D. Wood, *Fruit from the Jungle* (Mountain View, CA: Pacific Publishing, 1919).

53. See *Pentecostal Mission and Missionaries* (Providence, RI: Pentecostal Printing, [1905]).

54. "Minutes of the Missionary Committee of the Association of Pentecostal Churches of America" (December 11, 1897 [Article 12], and April 15, 1898).

55. For example, *Beulah Christian* (January 1898), 5. See Wade C. Barclay, *History of Methodist Missions,* part two, *The Methodist Episcopal Church, 1845-1939*, vol. 3, *Widening Horizons, 1845-1895* (New York: Board of Missions of the Methodist Church, 1957), 553, 595, 645-46, 650.

56. Missionary Committee to Wood, May 2, 1898; Reynolds to F[red] Hillery, September 12, [1898]; H. B. Hosley to Wood, December 22, 1898; Wood, *Fruit from the Jungle,* 276-86.

57. Cunningham, *Holiness Abroad,* 52-53. See Wood to Reynolds, March 24, 1898. On ordination see *Constitution of the Association of Pentecostal Churches of America* (Providence, RI: Beulah Christian, 1897), 8-9.

58. Cunningham, *Holiness Abroad,* 53.

59. Wood to Reynolds (September 18, 1905). See Cunningham, *Holiness Abroad,* 53. See also Cameron, *Eastern Nazarene College,* 45-46; Gary B. McGee, "'Latter Rain' Falling in the East: Early-Twentieth-Century Pentecostalism in India and the Debate over Speaking in Tongues," *Church History* 68 (September 1999), 652-56; Stanley Burgess, "Pentecostalism in India: An Overview," *Asian Journal of Pentecostal Studies* 4 (January 2001), 88-89.

60. See M. D. Wood, *A Life Saving Station* (Igatpuri, India: Watchman Press, n.d.), 6 pp.

61. November 8, 1905, letter. See Cunningham, *Holiness Abroad,* 55.

62. Cunningham, *Holiness Abroad,* 55. See Smith, *Called unto Holiness,* 74-90, and, regarding Pettit, Cameron, *Eastern Nazarene College,* 27-29.

63. Cunningham, *Holiness Abroad,* 55.

64. Ibid., 56.

65. Tracy to Reynolds (November 9, 1905), Reynolds papers.

66. Julia Gibson, *A Cry from India's Night* (Kansas City: Nazarene Publishing House, 1914), 8; see also 109-15 on child widows and 155-65 on child wives.

67. "Minutes of the Missionary Committee of the Association of Pentecostal Churches of America" (December 19, 1900).

68. See also Paul S. Dayhoff, in *Dictionary of African Christian Biography*, available on-line at www.dacb.org.

69. *Records of the Annual Meetings of the Central Evangelical Holiness Association* (Providence, RI: Press of George A. Wilson, 1896), 8, 21; L. S. Tracy to Reynolds, November 9, 1905; Russell V. DeLong and Mendell Taylor, *Fifty Years of Nazarene Missions*, vol. 2: *History of the Fields* (Kansas City: Beacon Hill Press, 1955), 284-85; Smith, *Called unto Holiness*, 82-87; J. Fred Parker, *Mission to the World: A History of Missions in the Church of the Nazarene Through 1985* (Kansas City: Nazarene Publishing House, 1988), 191-97; Jose Delgado, "The Providence Connection: To Cape Verde and Back," *Holiness Today* (March 2001), 8-11.

70. Smith, *Called unto Holiness*, 77-78.

71. Christiano, *Religious Diversity and Social Change*, 144, and see 87-88, 151-55. See Wiebe, *Search for Order;* Ben Primer, *Protestants and American Business Methods* (Ann Arbor, MI: UMI Research Press, 1979), chaps. 4—5; Smith, *Called unto Holiness*, 65-66. An influential study is Arthur M. Schlesinger Sr., "A Critical Period in American Religion, 1875-1900," reprinted in *Religion in American History: Interpretive Essays*, eds. John M. Mulder and John F. Wilson (Englewood Cliffs, NJ: Prentice-Hall, 1978), 302-17.

72. *Association of Pentecostal Churches of America Minutes of the Tenth Annual Meeting* (Providence, RI: Pentecostal Printing, 1905), 14, 49; "Minutes of the Missionary Committee of the Association of Pentecostal Churches of America" (June 27, 1907, and December 12, 1906).

73. Smith, *Called unto Holiness*, 72-73. See also Stan Ingersol, "The Ties That Bind, Part I," *Herald of Holiness* (October 15, 1988), 11.

Chapter 4

1. Catherine Albanese, "Religion and the American Experience: A Century After," *Church History* 57 (September 1988), 337-51, uses California as a "metaphor" for reflecting upon American religion in the twentieth century. Similarly, Sandra Sizer Frankiel, *California's Spiritual Frontiers: Religious Alternatives in Anglo-Protestantism, 1850-1910* (Berkeley: U. of California Press, 1988), which contains a chapter on Phineas Bresee, 103-19.

2. The three major biographies of Bresee are E. A. Girvin, *Phineas F. Bresee: A Prince in Israel* (Kansas City: Nazarene Publishing House, 1916), written by a close personal associate of Bresee and based on conversations with and letters from Bresee stretching over a period of nearly 20 years; Donald P. Brickley, *Man of the Morning: The Life and Work of Phineas F. Bresee* (Kansas City: Nazarene Publishing House, 1960), based on its author's doctoral dissertation; and Carl Bangs, *Phineas F. Bresee: His Life in Methodism, the Holiness Movement, and the Church of the Nazarene* (Kansas City: Beacon Hill Press of Kansas City, 1995), the product of many years of research by a Methodist historian whose parents were among the first generation of Nazarenes in the Pacific Northwest.

3. See Bangs, *Phineas F. Bresee*, 19-20; and Strong, *Perfectionist Politics*.

4. Girvin, *Phineas F. Bresee*, 28.

5. Bangs, *Phineas F. Bresee*, 21-22, 24-27.

6. Girvin, *Phineas F. Bresee*, 27-28.

7. Ibid., 28.

8. Girvin, *Phineas F. Bresee*, 29, has an account of Bresee's first sermon.

9. Girvin, *Phineas F. Bresee*, 34.

10. Bangs, *Phineas F. Bresee*, 57-60.

11. Girvin, *Phineas F. Bresee*, 35-36.

12. Ibid., 36; Bangs, *Phineas F. Bresee*, 60-61.

13. Girvin, *Phineas F. Bresee*, 37-38.

14. Bangs, *Phineas F. Bresee*, 62-64.

15. Girvin, *Phineas F. Bresee*, 39-40; Bangs, *Phineas F. Bresee*, 66. For the broader issues see Donald Matthews, *Slavery and Methodism: A Chapter in American Morality, 1780-1845* (Princeton, NJ: Princeton U. Press, 1965); and William Gravely, *Gilbert Haven: Methodist Abolitionist: A Study in Race, Religion, and Reform, 1850-1880* (Nashville: Abingdon, 1973), chap. 2.

16. Girvin, *Phineas F. Bresee*, 39-40.

17. Ibid., 16. Bresee apparently did not confine the practice of displaying the American flag in church to the Civil War years. The flag was also prominently present in the front of the the first permanent structure occupied by the Church of the Nazarene in Los Angeles, according to one photograph of the interior (although it is not clear what the occasion of the photo may have been). See photo in Bangs, *Phineas F. Bresee*, 224.

18. Girvin, *Phineas F. Bresee*, 40-44.

19. Bresee, "Righteousness in Politics," in his *Sermons on Isaiah* (Kansas City: Nazarene Publishing House, 1926), 61-69. See Brickley, *Man of the Morning*, 100-102; Bangs, *Phineas F. Bresee*, 62.

20. See William Chazanoff, *Welch's Grape Juice* (Syracuse, NY: Syracuse U. Press, 1977). From this time until 1984 the American Methodist *Discipline* forbade the use of fermented wine at Communion.

21. See John J. Rumbarger, *Profits, Power, and Prohibition: Alcohol Reform and the Industrializing of America, 1800-1930* (Albany: State U. of New York Press, 1989). An older study linking prohibition to social reform is James Timberlake, *Prohibition and the Progressive Movement, 1900-1920* (1963; repr., New York: Atheneum, 1970), a view accepted and further elaborated in Norman Clark, *Deliver Us from Evil: An Interpretation of American Prohibition* (New York: W. W. Norton, 1976), 5, 70, 93-94, 113. However, Gaines M. Foster, *Moral Reconstruction: Christian Lobbyists and the Federal Legislation of Morality, 1865-1920* (Chapel Hill: U. of North Carolina Press, 2002), 193-220, sees little linkage between the Progressives and those who were pressing Congress for a prohibition amendment.

22. Girvin, *Phineas F. Bresee*, 45-47.

23. Ibid., 47; Bangs, *Phineas F. Bresee*, 68.

24. Girvin, *Phineas F. Bresee*, 50, 61.

25. Girvin (ibid., 50-71) provides details of Bresee's ministry in these various churches. Also see Bangs, *Phineas F. Bresee*, 70-121, for analysis. See Gravely, *Gilbert Haven*, 195-98, dealing with Haven's election as bishop.

26. Girvin, *Phineas F. Bresee*, 50.

27. Ibid., 51 (emphasis added).

28. Ibid., 52.

29. Ibid., 81. See Bangs, *Phineas F. Bresee*, 71-80, for analysis of Bresee's "crisis experience" at Chariton.

30. See Bangs, *Phineas F. Bresee*, 81-82, 110-12, on Bresee's work with Simpson College.

31. Ibid., 112-13.

32. See ibid., 102-4.

33. Girvin, *Phineas F. Bresee*, 76.

34. Ibid., 76. See Bangs, *Phineas F. Bresee*, 99. For somewhat different accounts see Brickley, *Man of the Morning*, 82-84, and Smith, *Called unto Holiness*, 94-95, which follow the account provided in Girvin, *Phineas F. Bresee*, 72-76. However, Bangs, *Phineas F. Bresee*, 97-104, shows that the events were more complex than this.

35. Girvin, *Phineas F. Bresee*, 77-78.

36. Ibid., 78. On migration to California from persons born in such states as New York and Iowa see John H. M. Laslett, "Historical Perspective: Immigration and the Rise of a Distinctive Urban Region, 1900-1970," in *Ethnic Los Angeles*, eds. Roger Waldinger and Mehdi Bozongmehr (New York: Russell Sage Foundation, 1996), 48-49. Also see the September 2004 issue of the *American Quarterly*, devoted to "Los Angeles and the Future of Urban Cultures."

37. Kevin Starr, *Inventing the Dream: California Through the Progressive Era* (New York: Oxford U. Press, 1985), 40-41. Chapter 2 of this book, "Early Sojourners and Formulations," 31-63, provides an overview of the character of Southern California, and especially Los Angeles, at the time the Bresees arrived.

38. Ibid., 49.

39. See Frankiel, *California's Spiritual Frontiers*.

40. Girvin, *Phineas F. Bresee*, 80; Bangs, *Phineas F. Bresee*, 128-31.

41. Girvin, *Phineas F. Bresee*, 80-81; Smith, *Called unto Holiness*, 96.

42. Kevin Starr, *Americans and the California Dream, 1850-1915* (New York: Oxford U. Press, 1973), 201. See also Gregory Singleton, *Religion in the City of Angels: American Protestant Culture and Urbanization: Los Angeles, 1850-1930* (Ann Arbor, MI: UMI Research Press, 1979), 138.

43. See Bangs, *Phineas F. Bresee*, 147-67, for an analysis of his Pasadena tenure. See also Girvin, *Phineas F. Bresee*, 86-87, and Jeanne Halgren Kilde, *When the Church Became Theatre: The Transformation of Evangelical Architecture and Worship in Nineteenth-Century America* (New York: Oxford U. Press, 2002), especially 84-145.

44. Ervin S. Chapman, superintendent of State Anti-Saloon League of Southern California, "A Prince Among Men: Phineas F. Bresee," *New Voice* (February 26, 1903), 3. See Brickley, *Man of the Morning*, 161-62; Bangs, *Phineas F. Bresee*, 163-66, and also see Gilman Ostrander, *The Prohibition Movement in California, 1848-1933* (Berkeley: U. of California Press, 1957).

45. See Girvin, *Phineas F. Bresee*, 80-96.

46. Ibid., 81.

47. Ibid., 82.

48. Ibid., 82-83. Also see Brickley, *Man of the Morning*, 89-94; Bangs, *Phineas F. Bresee*, 142-44; Bangs, *Phineas F. Bresee*, 42-144; Frankiel, *California's Spiritual Frontiers*, 110-14.

49. See Article X, *Manual, 2001-2005, Church of the Nazarene*, 31, for the "baptism" phraseology. Also, see Girvin, *Phineas F. Bresee*, 51-52.

50. Girvin, *Phineas F. Bresee*, 85. See A. M. Hills, *Phineas F. Bresee: A Life Sketch* (Kansas City: Nazarene Publishing House, 1930), 29-30; Brickley, *Man of the Morning*, 89-94.

51. For accounts of this movement see B. A. Washburn, *Holiness Links* (Los Angeles: Pentecostal Office, 1887); Josephine F. Washburn, *History and Reminiscences of Holiness Church Work in Southern California and Arizona* (South Pasadena, CA: Record Press, 1912); L. A. Clark, ed., *Truths of Interest: Origin and Distinctive Teachings of the "Holiness Church"* (El Monte, CA: Standard Bearer Publishing House, 1939); and Dennis Rogers, *Holiness Pioneering in the Southland* (Hemet, CA: n.p., 1944). See also Dieter, *Holiness Revival*, 224-30. Some of these congregations later embraced tongues-speaking and left the organization, while other congregations retained their distinctive Holiness identity and in 1946 merged with the Pilgrim Holiness Church (now the Wesleyan Church). See Paul Westphal Thomas and Paul William Thomas, *The Days of Our Pilgrimage: The History of the Pilgrim Holiness Church* (Marion, IN: Wesley, 1976), 229-30.

52. Quoted in Bangs, *Phineas F. Bresee*, 130.

53. See Timothy D. Hall, *Contested Boundaries: Itinerancy and the Reshaping of the Colonial American Religious World* (Durham, NC: Duke U. Press, 1994), especially chap. 2.

54. Bangs, *Phineas F. Bresee*, 130.

55. An edited transcript of the sermon is in *The Southern California Methodist Quarterly* 1 (January 1884), 5-9.

56. *California Christian Advocate* (December 26, 1883).

57. Girvin, *Phineas F. Bresee*, 84-85.

58. Ibid., 88.

59. Ibid., 88-89. On Bresee's street meetings and special Holiness revivals see ibid., 86-87. See J. A. Wood, *Perfect Love: Plain Things for Those Who Need Them Concerning the Doctrine, Experience, Profession, and Practice of Christian Holiness*, rev. ed. (South Pasadena, CA: the author, 1887). On Wood see also Delbert R. Rose, *Vital Holiness: A Theology of Christian Experience; Interpreting the Historic Wesleyan Message*, third ed. (Minneapolis: Bethany Fellowship, 1975), 48-53.

60. Girvin, *Phineas F. Bresee*, 90-91.

61. Ibid., 90-96. See Bangs, *Phineas F. Bresee*, 170-76, for analysis of these events.

62. Bangs, *Phineas F. Bresee*, 174-76. For Vincent also see Anne Boylan, *Sunday School: The Formation of an American Institution, 1790-1880* (New Haven, CT: Yale U. Press, 1988), 90-92, 130, 149.

63. Girvin, *Phineas F. Bresee*, 98, see 97-98; Bangs, *Phineas F. Bresee*, 177, 180-82.

64. See Bangs, *Phineas F. Bresee*, 183-85.

65. See Manie Payne Ferguson, *T. P. Ferguson, the Love Slave of Jesus Christ and His People and Founder of Peniel Missions* (Los Angeles: Published for the author, n.d.).

66. Quoted in Jones, *Perfectionist Persuasion*, 73.

67. Girvin, *Phineas F. Bresee*, 76.

68. Ibid., 99.

69. "The New Mission," *Los Angeles Times* (July 10, 1894), 3; Manie Payne Ferguson, *T. P. Ferguson*; Jones, *Perfectionist Persuasion*, 71-78. See George Grubb, "Christ Is All, and in All," in *Some Addresses on Holiness*, third series, *Delivered at the Star Hall Convention, Manchester, October 9th to 16th, 1892* (London: S. W. Partridge, n.d.), 13-30. On Keswick see David Bebbington, *Holiness in Nineteenth-Century England* (Carlisle, England: Paternoster, 2000), 73-90.

70. See Edward Lawrence Potter, *The Widney Family*, M.A. thesis, U. of Southern California, 1966, and Carl R. Rand, *Joseph Pomeroy Widney: Physician and Mystic*, ed. Doris Sanders (Los Angeles: Salerni Collegium and U. of Southern California School of Medicine, 1970). Also see Frankiel, *California's Spiritual Frontiers*, 95-102.

71. Girvin, *Phineas F. Bresee*, 101. Girvin, 99-100, gives Bresee's account of the events; Bangs, *Phineas F. Bresee*, 188-89, provides analysis.

72. Girvin, *Phineas F. Bresee*, 101.

73. See the *Los Angeles Times* (October 7, 1895), 6.

74. Girvin, *Phineas F. Bresee*, 103.

75. Jernigan, *Pioneer Days*, 156; Donald W. Dayton, *Theological Roots of Pentecostalism* (Grand Rapids: Francis Asbury Press, 1987), 115-41.

76. See Smith, *Called unto Holiness*, 49-52, 107-9.

77. For the larger discussion, see Taves, *Fits, Trances, and Visions*, 47-65.

78. For discussion of some of these issues see Brickley, *Man of the Morning*, 121-31; Smith, *Called unto Holiness*, 106-10; Bangs, *Phineas F. Bresee*, 189-92; Jones, *Perfectionist Persuasion*, 107-8. Thirty-seven years later Nazarene "Bud" Robinson held evangelistic meetings at Peniel Hall. See *Herald of Holiness* (September 2, 1931), 17.

79. Girvin, *Phineas F. Bresee*, 103. The spot where the rented hall stood is now occupied by the Ronald Reagan State of California Office Building, on Main Street between 3rd and 4th Streets.

80. Ibid., 120.

81. Regarding the exact numbers see Bangs, *Phineas F. Bresee*, 198.

82. See Local Church Minutes, "Meeting of the Congregation," Los Angeles (October 30, 1895), 3-4.

83. In Richard W. Fox, *Jesus in America: Personal Savior, Cultural Hero, National Obsession* (San Francisco: HarperCollins, 2004), 292.

84. See Paul A. Carter, *The Spiritual Crisis of the Gilded Age* (DeKalb: Northern Illinois U. Press, 1971), 138-40; Susan Curtis, *A Consuming Faith: The Social Gospel and Modern American Culture* (repr., Columbia: U. of Missouri Press, 2001), 36-48. Gladden was born a year earlier and grew up just a few miles west of Bresee in New York state.

85. Summary of the sermon in the *Los Angeles Times* (October 21, 1895), 6.

86. See discussion of the name in Smith, *Called unto Holiness*, 110-11, and Bangs, *Phineas F. Bresee*, 196-97. Bangs's interpretation of the name "Church of the Nazarene" and Widney's motivation overstates its unorthodox connotations. See Potter, *Widney Family*, 99-100, 112-23, and Rand, *Joseph Pomeroy Widney*, 74-78, on some of Widney's controversial but much later ideas.

87. Quoted in Smith, *Called unto Holiness*, 111-12.

88. Girvin, *Phineas F. Bresee*, 107.

89. Ibid., 107-9.

90. *The Manual of the Church of the Nazarene Promulgated by the Assembly of 1898* (Los Angeles: Committee of Publication, 1898), 4.

91. Ibid., 14-18, 25-27.

92. See, for example, W. K. Brown, "Woman Was in the Christian Ministry and Invested with Authority in Paul's Day," 623-24; J. N. Brown, "That Scriptural Argument," 624; and Harvey Williams, "Conclusions of a Rustic on the Woman Question," 625, all in *Christian Advocate*, Supplement (September 18, 1890). Opposing seating women at General Conferences, James M. Buckley, "Making Void the Law of God—Once More," *Christian Advocate* (November 6, 1890), 731-32. See also "The General Conference: Proceedings from Day to Day," *Christian Advocate* (May 14, 1896), 321-25.

93. Girvin, *Phineas F. Bresee*, 152-53; Bangs, *Phineas F. Bresee*, 207-15. See Potter, *Widney Family*, 98-123; Frankiel, *California's Spiritual Frontiers*, 95-100.

94. Girvin, *Phineas F. Bresee*, 153.
95. Ibid., 132. On Company E and the Brotherhood of Saint Stephen see pp. 130-33.
96. *Nazarene Messenger*, quoted in Smith, *Called unto Holiness*, 135.
97. Mendell Taylor, *Nazarene Youth in Conquest for Christ* (Kansas City: Nazarene Publishing House, 1948), 13-16.
98. Brickley, *Man of the Morning*, 222-41.
99. Smith, *Called unto Holiness*, 112-21.
100. Ibid., 116.
101. Ibid., 117.
102. On Wallace, see Laird, *Ordained Women*, 62-68.
103. Girvin, *Phineas F. Bresee*, 207. Thomas D. Hamm, *The Transformation of American Quakerism: Orthodox Friends, 1800-1907* (Bloomington: Indiana U. Press, 1992), chaps. 4 and 5, shows that many Quakers already had joined the Holiness Movement.
104. See Girvin, *Phineas F. Bresee*, 199-208, 242-62; Smith, *Called unto Holiness*, 140-44.
105. Girvin, *Phineas F. Bresee*, 242-46.
106. See ibid., 220-33, 263-73, 335-36; Smith, *Called unto Holiness*, 144-50.
107. Girvin, *Phineas F. Bresee*, 340-41. See Cunningham, *Holiness Abroad*, 11-14.
108. See *Manual of the Church of the Nazarene, 1898*, 23 (emphasis added).
109. From Mae McReynolds' profile file, Nazarene Archives: *Nazarene Messenger* (May 10, 1906); *Proceedings of the Third General Assembly of the Church of the Nazarene, October 7, 1911*; *Other Sheep* (December 1917), 1-3, 5; Martha Curry, "The Women of the Fifth General Assembly," *Herald of Holiness* (October 8, 1919), 8-9; obituary in the *Herald of Holiness* (March 30, 1932), 16.
110. Cunningham, *Holiness Abroad*, 57-58.
111. Ibid., 58.
112. Ibid.
113. See Ronald B. Kirkemo, *For Zion's Sake: A History of Pasadena/Point Loma College* (San Diego, CA: Point Loma Press, 1992), 7-8.
114. Brickley, *Man of the Morning*, 191-220, provides a general account of Bresee's role in education.
115. See Kirkemo, *For Zion's Sake*, 6-11.
116. Ibid., 10-26.
117. Bresee, *Sermons from Matthew's Gospel* (Kansas City: Nazarene Publishing House, n.d.), 131.
118. Timothy L. Smith, "Introduction," to *The Certainties of Faith: Ten Sermons by the Founder of the Church of the Nazarene* (Kansas City: Nazarene Publishing House, 1958), 11. See also Girvin, *Phineas F. Bresee*, 108, 133-42.

Chapter 5

1. Long, *Revival of 1857-58*, 8. See also Smith, *Revivalism and Social Reform;* and John Corrigan, *Business of the Heart: Religion and Emotion in the Nineteenth Century* (Berkeley: U. of California Press, 2002), which concerns Boston in particular.
2. See J. Lawrence Brasher, *The Sanctified South: John Lakin Brasher and the Holiness Movement* (Urbana: U. of Illinois Press, 1994), 1-40; Joe Richardson, *Christian Reconstruction: The American Missionary Association and Southern Blacks, 1861-1890* (Athens: U. of Georgia Press, 1986); Reginald F. Hilderbrand, *The Times Were Strange and Stirring: Methodist Preachers and the Crisis of Emancipation* (Durham, NC: Duke U. Press, 1995); and Briane Turley, *A Wheel Within a Wheel: Southern Methodism and the Georgia Holiness Association* (Macon, GA: Mercer U. Press, 1999).
3. See Brasher, *Sanctified South*, 32-40, and Dieter, *Holiness Revival*, 103-4. See also Smith, "The Holiness Crusade"; Hunter D. Farish, *The Circuit Rider Dismounts: A Social History of Southern Methodism, 1865-1900* (Richmond, VA: Dietz Press, 1938), 72-76.
4. Among Robert Harris's published works are *America and Africa* (Chicago: J. L. Regan Publishing Co., 1887), *Experiences of the Cowboy Preacher* (Nashville: the author, 1893), and *Why We Left the M.E. Church, South* (Milan, TN: Milan Exchange Office, 1894). Among Mary Harris's published works is *Life and Work of Mary Lee Cagle: An Autobiography* (Kansas City: Nazarene Publishing House, 1928). The substantial manuscript collection in the Nazarene Archives has been examined

and interpreted by Robert Stanley Ingersol, "Burden of Dissent: Mary Lee Cagle and the Southern Holiness Movement," PhD diss., Duke U., 1989, which informs this chapter throughout. See also Smith, *Called unto Holiness*, 153-59. For Free Methodism see Benjamin Titus Roberts, *Why Another Sect?* (Rochester, NY: Earnest Christian Publishing House, 1879); Wilson T. Hogue, *History of the Free Methodist Church of North America* (Winona Lake, IN: Free Methodist Publishing House, 1915); Leslie Ray Marston, *From Age to Age a Living Witness: A Historical Interpretation of Free Methodism's First Century* (Winona Lake, IN: Light and Life Press, 1960). For an account of the Free Methodist Church in Texas see Jernigan, *Pioneer Days*, 86-90.

5. Harris, *America and Africa*, chap. 7, 2-3. On faith work and the various Holiness groups that espoused it, see Jones, *Perfectionist Persuasion*, 62-78; and for the broader context see Klaus Fiedler, *The Story of Faith Missions* (Oxford: Regnum, 1994).

6. See Ingersol, "Burden of Dissent," 77-94, for description and analysis of Harris's mission work in Africa.

7. Cagle, *Life and Work of Mary Lee Cagle*, 17, 20. See Susie C. Stanley, *Holy Boldness: Women Preachers' Autobiographies and the Sanctified Self* (Knoxville: U. of Tennessee Press, 2002), especially chap. 5. See also Anne F. Scott, *The Southern Lady: From Pedestal to Politics, 1830-1930* (Chicago: U. of Chicago Press, 1970).

8. Cagle, *Life and Work of Mary Lee Cagle*, 17.

9. Ibid., 18.

10. Ibid., 20.

11. Robert Lee Harris was apparently previously married and had two children from that marriage. Details of the marriage and how and when it ended are unknown. See Ingersol, "Burden of Dissent," 99.

12. Cagle, *Life and Work of Mary Lee Cagle*, 22.

13. On the Holiness critique of post-Civil War Methodism see Harold E. Raser, "'Christianizing Christianity': The Holiness Movement as a Church, *The* Church, or No Church at All?" *Wesleyan Theological Journal* 41 (Spring 2006), 116-47.

14. See Ingersol, "Burden of Dissent," 115-17, for analysis of this incident and its fallout.

15. Ingersol, "Burden of Dissent," 108-10.

16. On the Vanguard Mission and related groups see Jones, *Perfectionist Persuasion*, 64-70.

17. Cagle, *Life and Work of Mary Lee Cagle*, 22. See Harris, *Why We Left the M.E. Church, South*.

18. See Ingersol, "Burden of Dissent," 133-34. See also Ingersol, "Christian Baptism and the Early Nazarenes: The Sources That Shaped a Pluralistic Baptismal Tradition," *Wesleyan Theological Journal* 27 (Spring-Fall, 1992): 161-80.

19. Cagle, *Life and Work of Mary Lee Cagle*, 23.

20. Ibid., 24.

21. Ibid., 28.

22. Ibid., 29.

23. See ibid., 29-39. See also Fannie McDowell Hunter's sermon in *Women Preachers* (Dallas: Berachah Press, 1905), 48-61.

24. See John Wesley, *Advice to the People Called Methodists with Regard to Dress* (London: John Parmore, 1780), in *The Works of John Wesley*, vol. 9: *The Methodist Societies: History, Nature, and Design*, ed. Rupert E. Davies (Nashville: Abingdon, 1989), 123-31.

25. *Guide to Holiness* (February 1875), 49-50, a statement that challenges Kathryn Long's thesis that Palmer represented an embourgeised Methodism in contrast to B. T. Roberts. See Long, "Consecrated Respectability: Phoebe Palmer and the Refinement of American Methodism," in Hatch and Wigger, ed., *Methodism and the Shaping of American Culture*, 281-307.

26. Wallace Thornton, *Radical Righteousness: Personal Ethics: The Development of the Holiness Movement* (Salem, OH: Schmul, 1998); Rodney L. Reed, "Worship, Relevance, and the Preferential Option for the Poor in the Holiness Movement, 1880-1920," *Wesleyan Theological Journal* 32 (Fall 1997): 80-104.

27. Ted Ownby, *Subduing Satan: Religion, Recreation, and Manhood in the Rural South, 1865-1920* (Chapel Hill: U. of North Carolina Press, 1990), 121, 132, 171, 197-99; Paul Harvey,

Redeeming the South: Religious Cultures and Racial Identities Among Southern Baptists, 1865-1925 (Chapel Hill: U. of North Carolina Press, 1997), 84-86, 93-95, 133.

28. Snyder, *Populist Saint*. Putting the Free Methodist position in the broader stream of Wesleyan theology is Mary A. Tenney, *Blueprint for a Christian World* (Winona Lake, IN: Light and Life, 1953).

29. Cagle, *Life and Work of Mary Lee Cagle*, 20.

30. Ibid., 32.

31. Ibid., 32-33.

32. See Smith, *Called unto Holiness*, 153-59.

33. Cagle, *Life and Work of Mary Lee Cagle*, 45.

34. Ibid., 47-53.

35. See Ingersol, "Burden of Dissent," 157-88, for detailed description and analysis of these developments.

36. See Dennis Rogers, *Holiness Pioneering in the Southland* (N.p.: 1944); Jernigan, *Pioneer Days*, 86-93, 110.

37. Henry C. Morrison, *Life Sketches and Sermons* (Louisville, KY: Pentecostal Publishing Company, 1903), 33; Jernigan, *Pioneer Days*, 100; Smith, *Called unto Holiness*, 160-61. See also Farish, *Circuit Rider Dismounts*, 163-208. On Northern Methodist inroads into the South following the Civil War, also see Gravely, *Gilbert Haven*, and Hilderbrand, *Times Were Strange and Stirring*, 4-6.

38. Jernigan, *Pioneer Days*, 19-23.

39. On several of the better-known Holiness bands and their activities see Jernigan, *Pioneer Days*, 37-60. See also Oscar Hudson, *This I Remember: True Incidents of Pioneer Days* (Kansas City: Beacon Hill Press of Kansas City, 1965).

40. Jernigan, *Pioneer Days*, 91. For a similar account see Robert K. Gilmore, *Ozark Baptizings, Hangings, and Other Diversions: Theatrical Folkways of Rural Missouri, 1885-1910* (Norman: U. of Oklahoma Press, 1984), 173-75, 212-15.

41. Walter N. Vernon et al., *The Methodist Excitement in Texas: A History* (Dallas: Texas United Methodist Historical Society, 1984), 202-9.

42. Jernigan, *Pioneer Days*, 97-108; Bud Robinson, *Sunshine and Smiles: Life Story, Flash Lights, Sayings and Sermons* (Chicago: Christian Witness, 1903), 73-75. See also Charles Franklin Wimberly, *A Biographical Sketch of Henry Clay Morrison: The Man and His Ministry* (New York: Revell, 1922); Smith, *Called unto Holiness*, 159-71.

43. Jernigan, *Pioneer Days*, 101.

44. For Jernigan's participation at the 1901 General Holiness Assembly see *Echoes of the General Holiness Assembly, Held in Chicago, May 3-13, 1901*, ed. S. B. Shaw (Chicago: S. B. Shaw, 1901), 318.

45. Jernigan, *Pioneer Days*, 105-6.

46. *Holiness Association of Texas Year Book 1906-07* (N.p., n.d.), in the "Merging Religious Bodies" microfilm. This evidence seems contrary to the idea that Southern Holiness groups stressed purity and individual rather than social ethics. See also statement from A. M. Hills, who had left Peniel for England but who considered racism "one of the saddest evidences of the depravity of the race," in A. M. Hills, *The Cleansing Baptism* (Manchester: Star Hall, [1908]), 9-10. Contrast Leonard Sweet, "A Nation Born Again: The Union Prayer Meeting Revival and Cultural Relativism," in *In the Great Tradition: Essays on Pluralism, Voluntarism, and Revivalism*, eds. Joseph D. Bon and Paul R. Deckar (Valley Forge, PA: Judson, 1982), 207-8.

47. See Lula Schmelzenbach, *The Missionary Prospector: A Life Story of Harmon Schmelzenbach, Missionary to South Africa* (Kansas City: Nazarene Publishing House, 1937); Harmon F. Schmelzenbach III, *Schmelzenbach of Africa: The Story of Harmon F. Schmelzenbach, Missionary Pioneer to Swaziland, South Africa* (Kansas City: Nazarene Publishing House, 1971).

48. L. Paul Gresham, Waves Against Gibraltar: A Memoir of Dr. A. M. Hills, 1848-1935 (Bethany, OK: Southern Nazarene U. Press, 1992), 118-19.

49. Smith, *Called unto Holiness*, 165. See also Paul Rees, *Seth Cook Rees: The Warrior Saint* (1934; repr., Salem, OH: Schmul, 1987), 71.

50. Gresham, *Waves Against Gibraltar*, 117-28.

51. Loren P. Gresham and L. Paul Gresham, *From Many Came One, in Jesus' Name: Southern Nazarene University Looks Back on a Century: A Pictorial and Synoptic History of SNU* (Virginia Brooks, VA: Donning, 1998).

52. Bud Robinson, *My Life Story* (Kansas City: Nazarene Publishing House, 1928), 73. Also see Basil Miller, *Bud Robinson: A Miracle of Grace* (Kansas City: Beacon Hill Press, 1947).

53. W. G. Airhart, "Why You Should Move to Peniel," *Texas Holiness Advocate* (July 12, 1906), 4; Smith, *Called unto Holiness*, 165-66.

54. Jernigan, *Pioneer Days*, 155-57.

55. See ibid., 109, 114; Rees, *Warrior Saint*, 54-55. On the Apostolic Holiness Church as the league came to be known, see Jones, *Perfectionist Persuasion*, 99-105.

56. Jernigan, *Pioneer Days*, 111.

57. Jernigan himself printed Morrison's remarks in *Pioneer Days*, 111-12. Also see Smith, *Called unto Holiness*, 167.

58. Quoted in Smith, *Called unto Holiness*, 167.

59. Jernigan, *Pioneer Days*, 113-14; Chapman, *My Wife* (Kansas City: Nazarene Publishing House, 1940), 5-6. Also see Chapman, *A History of the Church of the Nazarene*, 29-30; D. Shelby Corlett, *Spirit-Filled: The Life of James Blaine Chapman* (Kansas City: Beacon Hill Press, 1948), 59-61.

60. Jernigan, *Pioneer Days*, 113-15, 123; Ingersol, "Christian Baptism and the Early Nazarenes," 161-67.

61. Jernigan, *Pioneer Days*, 56-57; Rees, *Miracles in the Slums;* Rest Cottage Association, *The White Slaves of America: A Book on Rescue Work* (Pilot Point, TX: Evangel Publishing, 1907). See J. P. Roberts, *The White Slaves of America: A Book of Rescue Work by Rest Cottage Association* (Pilot Point, TX: Evangel Publishing Company, 1907), 14-16, and "White Slaves," *Highways and Hedges* (September 1, 1909), 3-4, in *To Rescue the Perishing, to Care for the Dying: Historical Sources and Documents on Compassionate Ministries Drawn from the Inventories of the Nazarene Archives*, ed. Stan Ingersol (Kansas City: Nazarene Archives, 1985). See also Rees, *Warrior Saint*, 64-68.

62. Jernigan, *Pioneer Days*, 114-15.

63. Cagle, *Life and Work of Mary Lee Cagle*, 63.

64. Ibid., 72.

65. Jernigan, *Pioneer Days*, 119-21; J. Fred Parker, "Those Early Nazarenes Cared," *Preacher's Magazine* (September/October/November 1983), 32P-32T.

66. Ingersol, "Burden of Dissent," 184-88; Smith, *Called unto Holiness*, 156-58.

67. Cagle, *Life and Work of Mary Lee Cagle*, 85, 89-176.

68. See Ingersol, "Burden of Dissent," 203-7.

69. *Holiness Church of Christ Manual, Made by a Committee That Met at Rising Star, Texas, in November 22, 1904.*

70. *Manual [of the] Holiness Church of Christ*, Pilot Point, Texas, November 7-12, 1905 (Greenville, TX: Holiness Advocate Publishing Company, 1905), 24 f.

71. Jernigan, *Pioneer* Days, 123; Ingersol, "Burden of Dissent," 216-18; Smith, *Called unto Holiness*, 168-71.

72. Cunningham, *Holiness Abroad*, 9-10.

73. Ibid., 10.

Chapter 6

1. *Christian Witness* (February 21, 1895), 3.

2. *Nazarene Messenger* (August 18, 1904), 6.

3. Ibid. (July 30, 1903), 6.

4. Smith, *Called unto Holiness*, 205.

5. Dieter, *Holiness Revival*, 208-19.

6. *Nazarene Messenger* (October 17, 1901), 1.

7. Ibid. (September 27, 1906), 6.

8. *Herald of Holiness* (November 12, 1913), 13.

9. Cameron, *Eastern Nazarene College*, 58-60; Cunningham, *Holiness Abroad*, 4-9.

10. C. W. Ruth, *Entire Sanctification: A Second Blessing, Together with Life Sketch, Bible Readings, and Sermon Outlines* (Chicago: Christian Witness, 1903), 11. Pages 9-14 contain a "Life Sketch."

11. Brickley, *Man of the Morning*, 210, 245; Kirkemo, *For Zion's Sake*, 6-7.

12. See Smith, *Called unto Holiness*, 129-30; Dieter, *Holiness Revival*, 264. See also C. W. Ruth, *The Pentecostal Experience* (Chicago: Christian Witness, 1909), and C. W. Ruth, *The Second Crisis in Christian Experience* (Chicago: Christian Witness, 1912).

13. *Nazarene Messenger* (December 14, 1905), 4. On Goodwin see A. E. Sanner, *John W. Goodwin: A Biography* (Kansas City: Nazarene Publishing House, 1945), especially pp. 81-160.

14. *Minutes of the Missionary Committee* (June 27, 1906), 104-5.

15. Ibid., 105.

16. *Nazarene Messenger* (September 27, 1906), 6.

17. "Report of the Special Committee on Church Union at the General Assembly of the Church of the Nazarene, 1906," as quoted in *Beulah Christian* (November 10, 1906), 8.

18. Ibid., 9.

19. *Nazarene Messenger* (February 14, 1907), 6.

20. Ibid. (March 7, 1907), 6.

21. *Beulah Christian* (February 23, 1907), 8.

22. For the "basis of union" see *Manual of the Pentecostal Church of the Nazarene, 1907*, 16-17; for the Nazarene policy on church property see *Manual of the Church of the Nazarene, 1905*, 64-65.

23. See *Beulah Christian* (April 20, 1907), 5; *Nazarene Messenger* (April 25, 1907), 7.

24. Girvin, *Phineas F. Bresee*, 323, see 318-26.

25. *Nazarene Messenger* (May 2, 1907), 4.

26. Ibid. (October 17, 1907), 1-2.

27. *Beulah Christian* (October 19, 1907), 3-4.

28. *Nazarene Messenger* (October 24, 1907), 3.

29. See citation of handwritten record of the balloting kept by H. G. Trumbauer, in Thomas A. Miles, "C. W. Ruth and the Church of the Nazarene: The Story of His Vision of a National Holiness Denomination," M.Div. thesis, Nazarene Theological Seminary, 2000, 180-82.

30. *Proceedings of the First General Assembly of the Pentecostal Church of the Nazarene, 1907*, ed. Robert Pierce (Los Angeles: Nazarene, [1907]), 58.

31. Girvin, *Phineas F. Bresee*, 350.

32. This is evident in the per capita giving that can be computed based on merger statistics. Compared to the members of the Holiness Church of Christ, who gave $6.50 per person per year for all purposes, the Nazarenes gave $14.11 per person per year, and the members of the Association of Pentecostal Churches of America $21.51 per member per year at the time of the 1907 merger. Based on notes from Mendell Taylor's Nazarene History and Polity class at Nazarene Theological Seminary. See also Smith, *Called unto Holiness*, 200-201, and Bangs, *Phineas F. Bresee*, 187, 188, 200, for the middle-class orientation of Bresee's congregation in Los Angeles. But compare Randall J. Stephens, *The Fire Spreads: Holiness and Pentecostalism in the American South* (Cambridge, MA: Harvard U. Press, 2008), 58-65, which casts doubt on class origins and argues that Holiness people were the same "upcountry" Southerners who had preferred union to civil war.

33. *Proceedings of the First General Assembly*, 15. See also Jernigan, *Pioneer Days*, 123-24; Smith, *Called unto Holiness*, 216.

34. *Holiness Evangel* (November 1, 1907), 4.

35. Cunningham, *Holiness Abroad*, 9-11.

36. *Holiness Evangel* (January 15, 1907), 4.

37. See W. B. Godbey, *Autobiography* (Cincinnati, OH: God's Revivalist Office, 1909); and H. C. Morrison, *The Second Coming of Christ* (Louisville, KY: Pentecostal Publishing Company, 1914). For premillennialism among Southerners in the Holiness Movement see Stephens, *Fire Spreads*, 161-85, and Harold E. Raser, "Views on Last Things in the American Holiness Movement," in H. Ray Dunning, ed., *The Second Coming: A Wesleyan Approach to the Doctrine of Last Things* (Kansas City: Beacon Hill Press of Kansas City, 1995), 161-85. See also Dayton, *Theological Roots of Pentecostalism*, 143-71. On premillennialism, Timothy Weber, *Living in the Shadow of the Second Coming: American Premillennialism 1875-1982* (Grand Rapids: Zondervan, 1983); and Paul Boyer, *When Time Shall Be No More: Prophecy Belief in Modern American Culture* (Cambridge, MA: Harvard U.

Press, 1992). See also Charles R. Wilson, *Baptized in Blood: The Religion of the Lost Cause, 1865-1920* (Athens: U. of Georgia Press, 1980), 58-78.

38. *Manual of the Church of the Nazarene, 1905, with Changes Adopted at the Assembly of 1906,* 23.

39. *Nazarene* (July 13, 1899), 2.

40. Jernigan, *Pioneer Days,* 155-57; Charles Cullis, *Faith Cures: Or, Answers to Prayer for the Healing of the Sick* (N.p.: Willard Track Repository, 1890). See Dayton, *Theological Roots of Pentecostalism,* 115-41; Nancy A. Hardesty, *Faith Cure: Divine Healing in the Holiness and Pentecostal Movements* (Peabody, MA: Hendrickson, 2003); Wacker, *Heaven Below,* 1-3, 26-28, 191-92; and Stephens, *Fire Spreads,* 174-76.

41. A. M. Hills, *The Tobacco Vice* (Cincinnati: Revivalist Office, 1904), 86; see 26-28, 65, 67, 75.

42. *Manual of the Pentecostal Church of the Nazarene, 1907,* 22.

43. Ibid., 26-27.

44. Ibid., 28-29.

45. Compare the *Manual of the Church of the Nazarene, 1905 With Changes Adopted at the Assembly of 1906,* 33, with the *Manual of the Pentecostal Church of the Nazarene, 1907,* 34.

46. *Holiness Evangel* (November 1, 1907), 6. On the issue of secret societies also see Charles Mosher, *The Secret Is Out! A Study of the Oath-Bound Secret Societies* (Kansas City: Beacon Hill Press, 1960).

47. Smith, *Called unto Holiness,* 215.

48. Ibid., 171-79, 216.

49. *Nazarene Messenger* (October 31, 1907), 1.

50. Ibid. (October 1, 1908), 1.

51. Smith, *Called unto Holiness,* 217-18. For Ellyson see Chapman, *History of the Church of the Nazarene,* 144-47; Kirkemo, *For Zion's Sake;* and Hamm, *Transformation of American Quakerism,* 74-97, 160-68, 226, note 61.

52. Smith, *Called unto Holiness,* 248.

53. *Nazarene Messenger* (April 16, 1908), 6.

54. Ibid. (April 23, 1908), 6.

55. See Miles, "C. W. Ruth and the Church of the Nazarene," 8-18, 40-108.

56. Ibid., 52-57; Smith, *Called unto Holiness,* 77.

57. Miles, "C. W. Ruth and the Church of the Nazarene," 69-108.

58. See the *Nazarene Messenger* (November 19, 1908), 7-10. See also Smith, *Called unto Holiness,* 230; Thomas and Thomas, *Days of Our Pilgrimage,* 86-90.

59. Schmelzenbach, *Missionary Prospector,* 43.

60. *Holiness Evangel* (September 30, 1908), 2.

61. *Beulah Christian* (October 24, 1908), 6.

62. See C. A. McConnell, *The Potter's Vessel* (Kansas City: Beacon Hill Press, 1946), 54-55.

63. Compare the statements in the *Manual of the Pentecostal Church of the Nazarene, 1907,* 26-29, 32-33, and the *Manual of the Pentecostal Church of the Nazarene, 1908,* 32, 35-37.

64. *Beulah Christian* (October 24, 1908), 3.

65. Jonnie Jernigan, *Memories of Pilot Point by One Who Was There* (Kansas City: Nazarene Publishing House, 1983), 28.

66. *Proceedings of the Second General Assembly of the Pentecostal Church of the Nazarene* (Los Angeles: Nazarene Publishing Company, [1908]), 31; Girvin, *Phineas F. Bresee,* 408-15.

67. *Proceedings of the Second General Assembly,* 39, 54.

68. Edward J. Blum, *Reforging the White Republic: Race, Religion, and American Nationalism, 1865-1898* (Baton Rouge: Louisiana State U. Press, 2005), 7-9, and throughout.

69. For the rural to urban migration see Christiano, *Religious Diversity,* 70-74.

70. Helpful is H. Ray Dunning, "Nazarene Ethics as Seen in a Theological, Historical, and Sociological Context," Ph.D. diss., Vanderbilt U., 1969. Also see Smith, *Called unto Holiness,* 220-23, and Long, "Consecrated Respectability," 281-308.

71. *Holiness Evangel* (September 30, 1908), 2.

Chapter 7

1. *Proceedings of the Third General Assembly of the Pentecostal Church of the Nazarene*, ed. Fred Epperson (Los Angeles: Nazarene Publishing House, [1911]), 14, 24-25; Gaar, "Pentecost, and the Route to It," in *The Nazarene Pulpit: A Collection of Sermons from Well Known Preachers* (Kansas City: Nazarene Publishing House, 1925), 116-24; Smith, *Called unto Holiness*, 229-34.

2. See Farish, *The Circuit Rider Dismounts*, chap. 8; and Don H. Doyle, *Nashville in the New South, 1880-1930* (Knoxville: U. of Tennessee Press, 1985), 124-28, and throughout, for the social and political context of Nashville during these times.

3. See Foster, *Moral Reconstruction*, 27-46, 193-220.

4. See Benjamin Franklin Haynes, *Tempest-Tossed on Methodist Seas; or, A Sketch of My Life* (Kansas City: Nazarene Publishing House, 1914; repr., Louisville, KY: Pentecostal Publishing, 1921), esp. 98-158. See also Paul Isaac, *Prohibition and Politics: Turbulent Decades in Tennessee, 1885-1920* (Knoxville: U. of Tennessee Press, 1965), 75; Ivan A. Beals, *Seventy-Five Years of Heralding Scriptural Holiness by the Editors of the Herald of Holiness* (Kansas City: Nazarene Publishing House, 1987), 17-32; Stan Ingersol, "Man of Zeal and Courage: The Methodist Roots of B. F. Haynes," *Herald of Holiness* (June 15, 1987), 11.

5. Studies include Merle McClurkan Heath, *A Man Sent of God: The Life of J. O. McClurkan* (Kansas City: Beacon Hill Press, 1947); Smith, *Called unto Holiness*, 180-204; Mildred Bangs Wynkoop, *The Trevecca Story* (Nashville: Trevecca, 1976); Benson, *Pentecostal Mission*; and William J. Strickland (with H. Ray Dunning), *J. O. McClurkan: His Life, His Theology, and Selections from His Writings* (Nashville: Trevecca, 1998). On the Cumberland Presbyterians, see E. B. Crisman, *Origin and Doctrines of the Cumberland Presbyterian Church, in Two* Parts (Memphis: Cumberland Presbyterian Publishing House, 1856); and Ewell K. Reagin, *What Cumberland Presbyterians Believe* (Memphis: Frontier Press, 1968).

6. Heath, *Man Sent of God*, 28-31.
7. Ibid., 31-39.
8. Ibid., 45.
9. Ibid., 56.
10. See Benson, *Pentecostal Mission*, 21.
11. The Tulip Street building (long since demolished) occupied a spot less than a hundred yards from the present site of First Church of the Nazarene. See Benson, *Pentecostal Mission*, 20-21. See also Heath, *Man Sent of God*, 56-60.
12. Benson, *Pentecostal Mission*, 21-23; Wynkoop, *Trevecca Story*, 46-48.
13. Benson, *Pentecostal Mission*, 24.
14. Ibid., 24-26.
15. For Pentecostal themes in the Holiness Movement, see Dayton, *Theological Roots of Pentecostalism*, 68-113. See also Robert M. Anderson, *Vision of the Disinherited: The Making of American Pentecostalism* (New York: Oxford U. Press, 1979); Edith L. Blumhofer, *Restoring the Faith: The Assemblies of God, Pentecostalism, and American Culture* (Urbana: U. of Illinois Press, 1993); Wacker, *Heaven Below*; and Cecil M. Robeck Jr., *Azusa Street Mission and Revival: The Birth of the Global Pentecostal Movement* (Nashville: Thomas Nelson Publishers, 2006).
16. Joseph E. Campbell, *The Pentecostal Holiness Church, 1898-1948* (Franklin Springs, GA: Pentecostal Holiness Church Publishing House, 1951), 345, 423-39; Benson, *Pentecostal Mission*, 93.
17. See Albert E. Thompson, *The Life of A. B. Simpson* (New York: Christian Alliance, 1920); David Hartzfeld and Charles Nienkirchen, *The Birth of a Vision* (Camp Hill, PA: Christian Publications, 1986); Robert L. Niklaus, John S. Swain, and Samuel J. Stoesz, *All for Jesus: God at Work in the Christian and Missionary Alliance over One Hundred Years* (Camp Hill, PA: Christian Publications, 1996); William Boyd Bedford, "'A Larger Christian Life': A. B. Simpson and the Early Years of the Christian and Missionary Alliance," Ph.D. diss., U. of Virginia, 1992.
18. See books by A. B. Simpson: *The Four-Fold Gospel* (New York: Alliance, 1890); *The Apostolic Church* (New York: Christian Alliance, 1898); *The Coming One* (New York: Christian Alliance, 1912); *The Gospel of Healing* (New York: Christian Alliance, 1915); *Wholly Sanctified* (New York: Christian Alliance, 1925); *The Christ Life* (New York: Christian Alliance, 1925). See also Gerald E. McGraw, "The Doctrine of Sanctification in the Published Writings of Albert Benjamin Simpson,"

Ph.D. diss., New York U., 1986, and Charles Nienkirchen, *A. B. Simpson and the Pentecostal Movement: A Study in Continuity, Crisis, and Change* (Peabody, MA: Hendrickson Publishers, 1992).

19. So argues Wynkoop, *Trevecca Story*, 32; 29-36. See Smith, *Called unto Holiness*, 183-84; Strickland, *J. O. McClurkan*, 87-93.

20. Benson, *Pentecostal Mission*, 27-28; Wynkoop, *Trevecca Story*, 51-52.

21. *Zion's Outlook* (February 7, 1901), 8, quoted in Smith, *Called unto Holiness*, 183. See Doyle, *Nashville*, 107-20, 135-42.

22. Benson, *Pentecostal Mission*, 30; Wynkoop, *Trevecca Story*, 55-56; Strickland, *J. O. McClurkan*, 37-38.

23. Heath, *Man Sent of God*, 61. Wynkoop, *Trevecca Story*, 53-54, details the transfer to the Pentecostal Alliance.

24. Wynkoop, *Trevecca Story*, 56-59.

25. Benson, *Pentecostal Mission*, 30-33.

26. Smith, *Called unto Holiness*, 185-86; Wynkoop, *Trevecca Story*, 59-62; Strickland, *J. O. McClurkan*, 36-41.

27. *The Manual of the Church of the Nazarene* (Los Angeles: Nazarene Publishing House, 1898), 13-14.

28. George Marsden, *Fundamentalism in American Culture: The Shaping of Twentieth–Century Evangelicalism, 1870-1925* (New York: Oxford U. Press, 1980), 94-95; Dieter, *Holiness Revival*, 254, 264; Paul M. Bassett, "The Fundamentalist Leavening of the Holiness Movement: 1914-1940," *Wesleyan Theological Journal* 13 (Spring 1978): 65-91.

29. Wynkoop, *Trevecca Story*, 60.

30. See Raser, "Views on Last Things," 161-85. For McClurkan's views see "Second Coming of Christ" in Strickland, *J. O. McClurkan*, 123-34. For other Southern thought see L. L. Pickett, *The Blessed Hope of His Glorious Appearing* (Louisville, KY: Picket Publishing, 1901), and Andrew Johnson and L. L. Pickett, *Post-Millennialism and the Higher Critics* (Chicago: Glad Tidings, 1923). For the Southern context see Stephens, *Fire Spreads*, 161-85. Also see Weber, *Living in the Shadow*, 78-80; Ernest R. Sandeen, *The Roots of Fundamentalism: British and American Millenarianism 1800-1930* (Chicago: U. of Chicago Press, 1970); and James H. Moorhead, "The Erosion of Postmillennialism in American Religious Thought, 1865-1925," *Church History* 53 (March 1984): 61-77.

31. Heath, *Man Sent of God*, 65.

32. Ibid., 64.

33. On the founding of the school and its early development, including the name change, see Heath, *Man Sent of God*, 64-72; Wynkoop, *Trevecca Story*, 61-91; Strickland, *J. O. McClurkan*, 46-60. For the eighteenth-century Trevecca see Heitzenrater, *Wesley and the People Called Methodists*, 240. Compare Brereton, *Training God's Army*, 41-49.

34. See Benson, *Pentecostal Mission*, 79; Strickland, *J. O. McClurkan*, 44-45; Smith, *Revivalism and Social Reform*, 220-22, 233.

35. Benson, *Pentecostal Mission*, 44.

36. Smith, *Called unto Holiness*, 186; Strickland, *J. O. McClurkan*, 42.

37. Benson, *Pentecostal Mission*, 206-7.

38. McClurkan to Bresee (January 1, 1907), in Strickland, *J. O. McClurkan*, 147-49.

39. Bresee to McClurkan (August 1, 1907), in Strickland, *J. O. McClurkan*, 150-51.

40. Benson, *Pentecostal Mission*, 118, 181-82, 192-93, 214.

41. "State of Tennessee Charter of Incorporation," April 21, 1902. Compare Robert, *American Women in Mission*, 204-5.

42. *Zion's Outlook* (November 7, 1901), 9.

43. Cunningham, *Holiness Abroad*, 17-18.

44. Benson, *Pentecostal Mission*, 113. See also Gary A. Henecke et al., *A Century in Christ, 1898-1998* (Nashville: First Church of the Nazarene, 1998), 16-17.

45. Benson, *Pentecostal Mission*, 30-31, 40, 45, 63-65, 81, 85, 101, 113, 118, 120, 129, 151, 156, 161, 181, 192, 194.

46. R. S. Anderson to E. G. Anderson, April 19, 1915, and June 1, 1915 (file 218-22); R. S. Anderson, "A Brief History of the Church of the Nazarene and Its Activities in Guatemala and

British Honduras (before and after its union with the Pentecostal Mission)," 17 pp. (file 861-34); DeLong and Taylor, *Fifty Years of Nazarene Missions,* 2:145-50, 313-15.

47. See J. O. McClurkan, *How to Keep Sanctified* (Repr., Kansas City: Nazarene Publishing House, n.d.). See also John B. Boles, *Religion in Antebellum Kentucky* (Lexington: U. Press of Kentucky), 47-51; Conkin, *Cane Ridge,* 151-63. Bradley Longfield minimizes the theological differences between the Cumberland Presbyterians and other Presbyterians in *The Presbyterian Controversy: Fundamentalists, Modernists, and Moderates* (New York: Oxford U. Press, 1991), 9-27. McClurkan's contemporary William Jennings Bryan also grew up in the Cumberland Presbyterian church (see Longfield, *Presbyterian Controversy,* 209-30), and, like McClurkan, Bryan felt comfortable among Methodists. See Michael Kazin, *A Godly Hero: The Life of William Jennings Bryan* (New York: Alfred A. Knopf, 2006), 111, 125, 276.

48. Smith, *Called unto Holiness,* 191-92.

49. Ibid., 182. See Robert R. Chiles, *Theological Transition in American Methodism: 1790-1935* (Nashville: Abingdon, 1965), 114-83.

50. Emphasizing the continuities between the Holiness Movement in America and the British Isles is Jack Ford, *What the Holiness People Believe: A Mid-Century Review of Holiness Teaching Among the Holiness Groups of Britain* (Birkenhead, Cheshire: Emmanuel Bible College and Missions, n.d.). See also Dieter, *Holiness Revival,* 129-41, 146-59.

51. Alex Deasley, *Doctrines Are Different* (Kansas City: Beacon Hill Press, 1961), 51. Also see T. A. Noble, *Called to Be Saints: A Centenary History of the Church of the Nazarene in the British Isles, 1906-2006* (Manchester: Didsbury, 2006).

52. "The Late Mr. F. W. Crossley, J.P.," *Manchester Faces and Places* (June 1897), 130.

53. See also J. Rendel Harris, ed., *The Life of Francis William Crossley* (London: N.p., 1899); *Oxford Dictionary of National Biography,* eds. H. C. G. Matthew and Brian Harrison (Oxford: Oxford U. Press, 2004). Also compare Bebbington, *Holiness in Nineteenth-Century England.*

54. In *F. W. Crossley: In Memorium* (Manchester: N.p., [1897]), 36.

55. Ibid., 45. E[lla] K. Crossley and M. A. Hatch wrote the foreword to Hills's *Scriptural Holiness and Keswick Teaching Compared* (1912; repr., Salem, OH: Schmul, n.d.).

56. Grubb, "Christ Is All, and in All," 15; *Way of Holiness* (April 1909), 8. See, for example, 1915 issues of the *Way of Holiness.*

57. Mrs. Rendel Harris, "Address," in *Addresses on Holiness* (second series) *Delivered at the Star Hall Convention,* 177. See Rendel Harris's addresses on pages 1-46 and 195-207 in the same.

58. [Mary R.] Hooker, comp., *Reader Harris, K.C, 1847-1909: Thanksgiving and Remembrance After Twenty-Five Years* (London: Westminster City Publishing, 1934); Jack Ford, "Adventures of an Agnostic," *Flame* (July-August 1960), 28, 30; Ian M. Randall, "The Pentecostal League of Prayer: A British Holiness Movement," *Wesleyan Theological Journal* 33 (Spring 1998), 185-200; Noble, *Called to Be Saints,* 142-46.

59. *David Thomas: Founder of the International Holiness Mission* (London: International Holiness Mission, n.d.), 5-6, 78-91. See also *Addresses on Holiness* (second series) *Delivered at the Star Hall Convention, Manchester, October 18th to 25th, 1891,* ed. Isabella Leonard (London: S. W. Partredge, [1891]), which contains the addresses of Rendel Harris, William McDonald, and others. On John Thomas in Korea, see, e.g., W. S. Milbank, "Holiness for Korea," *Holiness Mission Journal* (July 1910), 80-81; C. E. Cowman, "Oriental Missionary Society: Korea's Crisis Hour," *Holiness Mission Journal* (August 1910), 94-95; E. A. Kilburne, "The Work in Korea," *Holiness Mission Journal* (December 1911); and *Way of Holiness* (February 1916).

60. George Sharpe, *This Is My Story* (Glasgow: Messenger Publishing, n.d.), 31.

61. Ibid., 53-66, 125-28. See also Jack Ford, *In the Steps of John Wesley: The Church of the Nazarene in Britain* (Kansas City: Nazarene Publishing House, 1968), 35-41.

62. See the summary in Stan Ingersol, "George Sharpe and the Pentecostal Church of Scotland," *Holiness Today* (December 1999), 32-33.

63. Sharpe, "The Holiness Movement in Scotland," *Way of Holiness* (May 1909), 33.

64. "Committees—Assembly, 1912" and "Report of the Executive Committee to the Assembly 1912," Box 76, Nazarene Theological College, Manchester; Sharpe, *This Is My Story,* 39; Olive M. Winchester and Ross E. Price, eds., *Crisis Experience in the Greek New Testament* (Kansas City: Beacon Hill Press, 1953); Ford, *In the Steps of John Wesley,* 55-57.

65. "Call for the First Assembly of the Holiness Churches and Missions of Great Britain," May 7-9, 1909, Box 76, Nazarene Theological College, Manchester.

66. Ella K. Crossley, *Holiness Teaching* (Manchester: Bookroom, Star Hall, n.d.), 9.

67. Ibid., 7, 17, 25-26, 44-45, 63-64.

68. "Church Extension and Evangelism" [1909], Box 76, Nazarene Theological College, Manchester.

69. Ibid.

70. "Minutes of the Seventh Annual Assembly," The Pentecostal Church of Scotland (April 1-5, 1915), Box 76, Nazarene Theological College, Manchester.

71. Reynolds, "Around the World Trip, to the General Missionary Board of the Pentecostal Church of the Nazarene," n.d., 13.

72. Ibid., 11; Olive Winchester to H. F. Reynolds (March 27, 1913), copy in Box 39, Nazarene Theological College, Manchester; Reynolds to George Sharpe (October 30, 1914; December 22, [1914]; and March 1, 1915), Box 76, Nazarene Theological College, Manchester.

73. "A Meeting of the Special Committee Appointed by the Assembly to Consider the Question of Church Affiliation" (April 10, 1914); "The Pentecostal Church of Scotland. Union of British and American Churches"; "Report of the Special Committee of the Proposed Union of the Pentecostal Churches of Scotland and the Pentecostal Church of the Nazarene, n.d., adopted by the General Assembly of the Church of the Nazarene [1915]—all in Box 76, Nazarene Theological College, Manchester. See *Proceedings of the Fourth General Assembly of the Pentecostal Church of the Nazarene*, ed. Fred H. Mendell (Kansas City: Nazarene Publishing House, [1915]), 25-26.

74. See the 1912 through 1916 issues of *The Way of Holiness*, Nazarene Theological College, Manchester; M. Winterburn, comp., *The Manchester Tabernacle of the International Holiness Mission* (N.p., 1944).

75. George Frame, "The Preaching of George Sharpe," *Preacher's Magazine* (July 1958), 10.

76. Smith, *Called unto Holiness*, 307. See, for example, Morrison, "Can a Modernist Be a Christian?" *Herald of Holiness* (May 14, 1924), 3.

77. J. G. Morrison, *Interesting Incidents* (Kansas City: Nazarene Publishing House, n.d.), 66. Also see J. G. Morrison, *Other Days: Boyhood Reminiscences of Frontier Hardships* (Kansas City: Nazarene Publishing House, n.d.).

78. Quoted in C. T. Corbett, *Soldier of the Cross: The Life Story of J. G. Morrison, 1871-1939* (Kansas City: Beacon Hill Press, 1956), 38.

79. C. A. Armstrong, "The Great Division," in E. O. Grunstead et al., *History of the Methodist Church in North Dakota and Dakota Territory* (Nashville: Methodist Publishing House, 1960), 54.

80. Ibid.

81. Ibid., 60; see 52-60.

82. See J. G. Morrison, *Our Lost Estate* (Kansas City: Nazarene Publishing House, 1929), particularly 31, 46-52, 55, 63, 65, 99-106, 115-17, 136, 150. Compare Corbett, *Soldier of the Cross*, 94.

83. See Corbett, *Soldier of the Cross*.

84. Dieter, *Holiness Revival*, 3.

Part II Introduction

1. Smith, *Called unto Holiness*, chap. 11.

Chapter 8

1. Methodist Protestants broke from the Methodist Episcopal Church in 1828. By 1939 the bishop in Episcopal Methodism was part of a more democratic system than in 1828 or even in Bresee's time, and a three-way reunion that year brought back together the M.E. Church, the M.E. Church, South, and the Methodist Protestant Church to form the Methodist Church.

2. See J. B. McBride, *Herald of Holiness* (September 29, 1915), 5. The Wesleyan Methodist Church did not adopt the office of general superintendent until 1959.

3. Bresee, "The General Superintendency," *Herald of Holiness* (August 4, 1915), 6.

4. McGraw, "Preaching of Hiram F. Reynolds," 4.

5. Stan Ingersol, "Nazarene Odyssey and the Hinges of Internationalization," *Wesleyan Theological Journal* (Spring 2003): 66-82.

6. James McGraw, "The Preaching of Edward F. Walker," *Preacher's Magazine* (September 1954), 3-5.

7. Walker, Diary, MS, Edward F. Walker Collection, Nazarene Archives (416-11). See *Pentecostal Herald* (September 28, 1898), 16; J. B. Chapman, "A Peerless Preacher—E. F. Walker," *Preacher's Magazine* (August 1939), 2-3; C. J. Kinne, "Biographic Sketch," *Herald of Holiness* (May 22, 1918), 3; James Proctor Knott, "Early Nazarene Leaders—Rev. E. F. Walker," *Young People's Journal* (April 1931), 5-6; *Christian Witness and Advocate of Bible Holiness* (July 4, 1918), 8; Smith, *Called unto Holiness*, 224. See Edward F. Walker, *"Sanctify Them": A Study of Our Lord's Prayer for His Disciples*, first published in 1899, reprinted several times by Nazarene Publishing House, and revised by J. Kenneth Grider in a 1968 edition.

8. John T. Jones to E. F. Walker (May 28, 1912); H. B. Hosley to Walker (May 25, 1912); Phineas Bresee to Hosley (July 2, 1912); and see other letters and documents on the matter in file 173-49, Reynolds papers.

9. *Proceedings of the Fourth General Assembly*, 1915, 31-33; Mallalieu A. Wilson, *William C. Wilson: The Fifth General Superintendent* (Kansas City: Nazarene Publishing House, 1995), 88. According to folklore, Bresee stated that one general superintendent was "nearly dead" and another was "non compo mentis." In another version, Bresee said that Reynolds was the church's only "real" general superintendent.

10. It is unclear whether Ellyson intended to accept the election when he arrived at the General Assembly, but strong evidence connects his conversation with Walker to his announcement not to accept it. Concerning Ellyson's termination as president of Nazarene University in 1913, see Kirkemo, *For Zion's Sake*, 34-35. Also see Wilson, *William C. Wilson*, 87-90, and the manuscript on which the book is based, "Well, Glory," 192-93, Nazarene Archives; and *Proceedings of the Fourth Annual General Assembly of the Pentecostal Church of the Nazarene*, ed. Fred H. Mendell (Kansas City: Nazarene Publishing House, [1915]), 34, 36, 42.

11. Wilson, *William C. Wilson*, 92-93.

12. Compare Sanner, *John W. Goodwin*, to Goodwin's autobiographical remarks in Lecture 19, Pasadena College, n.d. (file 2101-18). Goodwin taught at Pasadena College after retiring from the general superintendency in 1940.

13. *Proceedings of the Fourth General Assembly of the Pentecostal Church of the Nazarene*, ed. Fred H. Mendell (Kansas City: Nazarene Publishing House, [1915]), 41.

14. On healing see John W. Goodwin, *The Secret Place of Prayer* (Kansas City: Nazarene Publishing House, 1928), 154-75.

15. Sanner, *John W. Goodwin*. See John W. Goodwin, *Living Signs and Wonders* (Kansas City: Nazarene Publishing House, 1923), and Goodwin, *Secret Place of Prayer*. See also Cameron, *Eastern Nazarene College*, 122-25.

16. Mathis to Williams (March 7, 1939). G. B. Williamson, *Roy T. Williams: Servant of God* (Kansas City: Nazarene Publishing House, 1947); J. B. Chapman, "General Superintendent Williams as a Preacher," *Preacher's Magazine* (September-October 1947), 3-4; Henecke et al., *Century in Christ*, 29. See A. E. Sanner to Williams (September 17, 1941); Joseph Sanning, U.S. Department of Agriculture, to Williams, June 12, 1942; Williams to Lloyd Sullivan, Denton, Texas (October 3, 1941) (file 534-7); and see file 497-7.

17. James McGraw, "The Preaching of Roy T. Williams, *Preacher's Magazine* (June 1954), 5-8, which seems to be based on James R. Emmel, "Speaking and Speeches of Roy Tilman Williams," M.A. thesis, U. of Oklahoma, 1950. See 121, 123, 125, 126, 145.

18. McGraw, "Preaching of Roy T. Williams," 5-8.

19. See Corlett, *Spirit-Filled*.

20. See Rees, *Miracles in the Slums*, and Rees, *Seth Cook Rees*. The plan to unite the Independent Holiness Church with the International Holiness Union and Prayer League failed after C. A. McConnell, editor of the *Texas Holiness Advocate*, opposed the proposal. See Jones, *Perfectionist Persuasion*, 113-25, and Thomas and Thomas, *Days of Our Pilgrimage*, 10-16, 45-46, 56, 92-95. For Friends' involvement in the Holiness Movement see Hamm, *Transformation of American Quakerism*, 102-11.

21. Rees, *Seth Cook Rees*, 86-97; Smith, *Called Unto Holiness*, 273-81. See Seth C. Rees, *The Ideal Pentecostal Church* (Cincinnati: Revivalist Office, 1897), chap. 9, "A Demonstrative Church." On Rees's theology of the church, see Melvin Dieter, "Primitivism in the American Holiness Tradition," *Wesleyan Theological Journal* 30 (Spring 1995), 88-91.

22. "Pastor Wins Fight for Seat" and "Rev. Matthews Accepted as Delegate," undated clippings [1915] from Los Angeles area newspapers, Anonymous Scrapbook No. 2, Nazarene Archives, 123. See also Wilson, "Well, Glory," 180.

23. Glennell P. Young to Brother Cornell [April 1915].

24. Pentecostal Church of the Nazarene, *Manual*, 1911, 60-63. See Bangs, *Phineas F. Bresee*, 260-67; Kirkemo, *For Zion's Sake*, 12-13.

25. Rees to "Dear Brother" (June 17, 1915) (marked "Exhibit A").

26. Wilson, "Well, Glory," 181. See also "Closes Home for Fallen Women" and "Nazarenes to Discontinue Work," undated clippings, Anonymous Scrapbook No. 2, 124-25; "Deplores Anything That Cools Religious Fervor," in the same, 129.

27. Smith, *Called unto Holiness*, 119-20.

28. Wilson, "Well, Glory," 181-82.

29. Rees, Open Letter (February 26, 1917); J. P. Coleman, *That Our People May Know* (Pasadena, CA: N.p., 1924), 6-10. See also Smith, *Called unto Holiness*, 275; Kirkemo, *For Zion's Sake*, 38-39. See also Walter C. Brand and C. N. Welts, Letter to the District Advisory Board et al. (June 22, 1915); Fred C. Epperson to Bresee (June 22, 1915).

30. *Minutes Ninth Annual Assembly Pentecostal Church of the Nazarene of the Southern California District* (June 23-27, 1915), 16, 39.

31. Wilson, "Well, Glory," 180, 185. See also Coleman, *That Our People May Know*, 14-15; Kirkemo, *For Zion's Sake*, 40-47; Smith, *Called unto Holiness*, 275-76.

32. See Herbert S. Johnson and Earl Hinchman to Howard Eckel (April 6, 1916); "Elders Accuse Noted Divine" and "To Defense of Their Pastor," undated newspaper clippings, Reynolds Collection (425-1); "Wild Scenes at Church Trial," "Crowd Sings and Prays at Trial of Pastor," and "200 of Flock Fight to Face Charges with Pasadena Preacher," undated clippings, Anonymous Scrapbook No. 2, Scrapbook Collection, Nazarene Archives, 115-16. See also Kirkemo, *For Zion's Sake*, 50.

33. Kirkemo, *For Zion's Sake*, 51; Rees to Goodwin (February 23, 1917); "Row Splits Nazarene College," clipping dated March 3, [1916], Church History Commission papers (367-13).

34. Coleman, *That Our People Might Know*, 19; Kirkemo, *For Zion's Sake*, 51.

35. Rees to Goodwin (February 23, 1917); Howard Eckel, *A Plain Statement of Why the University Pentecostal Church of the Nazarene Was Disorganized* (N.p.: n.p., 1917).

36. *Manual*, 1911, 46; Walker to Rees and others (March 1, 1917).

37. Rees, Open Letter (February 26, 1917); E. G. Anderson to Reynolds, telegram (March 6, 1917); Wiley to Reynolds, telegram (March 7, 1917); W. H. Hoople to Reynolds (April 4, 1917).

38. *Proceedings of the Tenth Annual Assembly of the Southern California District Pentecostal Church of the Nazarene* (June 21-25, 1916); A. O. Hendricks to Reynolds (March 10, 1917); Rees to Goodwin (March 14, 1917); Eckel to Reynolds (March 19, 1917).

39. Bud Robinson to Reynolds (March 28, 1917); Reynolds to Robinson (March 31, 1917).

40. C. Howard Davis to Reynolds (April 3, 1917); R. B. Mitchum to Reynolds (April 4, 1917); J. C. Henson to Reynolds (April 4, 1917); Z. B. Whitehurst to Reynolds (April 4, 1917); W. H. Hoople to Reynolds (April 4, 1917); DeLance Wallace to Reynolds (April 4, 1917); U. E. Harding to Reynolds (April 5, 1917); William E. Fisher to Reynolds (April 5, 1917).

41. C. E. Cornell to Reynolds (April 1, 1917); Walker to Reynolds (April 2, 1917); W. S. Knott to Reynolds (April 2, 1917); J. H. McIntyre to Reynolds (April 2, 1917); Wiley to Reynolds (April 2, 1917).

42. "Minutes of the General Superintendents' Meeting, Kansas City" (April 4 and 5, 1917); "To whom it may concern," *Herald of Holiness* (April 18, 1917), 9.

43. Eckel, *Plain Statement*; Smith, *Called unto Holiness*, 281; Thomas and Thomas, *Days of Our Pilgrimage*, 92-94. Nettie Soltero was the sister of Nazarene missionary Roger Winans. McConnell only stayed with Rees a short time, then returned to Texas and was associated thereafter with Nazarene colleges at Peniel and Bethany.

44. Wiley to C. Howard Davis (September 1, 1917); Wiley to R. E. Dunham (December 11, 1917). See Smith, *Called unto Holiness,* 281-86.

45. Charles E. Howard, "Reminiscence," 4; Wiley to Brother and Sister Nease (N.d.); Wiley to Ada Bresee (March 20, 1918); Wiley to Mr. and Mrs. DeLance Wallace (February 5, 1918).

46. Thomas and Thomas, *Days of Our Pilgrimage,* 92-95. Wiley described a meaningful reunion at the 1930 Pilgrim Holiness Church's General Conference, where he brought greetings from the Church of the Nazarene. Rees was the general superintendent, W. C. Stone the general secretary, and Harry Hays the general treasurer. Wiley met former Pasadena College students and had a reunion with G. Arnold Hodgin, who had returned from visiting the "foreign fields." See "The General Conference of the Pilgrim Holiness Church," *Herald of Holiness* (October 1, 1930), 3.

47. Southern California District, *Proceedings of the Twelfth Annual Assembly,* 1918, 24; "Funeral Thursday for Dr. E. S. [sic] Walker," undated clipping, Anonymous Scrapbook No. 2, 118; *Manual,* 1919, 48; John Matthews, "Open Letter," *Herald of Holiness* (December 22, 1920), 9. J. P. Coleman records an irony: when Matthews left the Pilgrims, he told them that he did so because "the Holy Ghost had departed from the place." See Coleman, *That Our People May Know,* 29.

48. E. F. Walker, "What Ought to Be Done with the General Superintendency?" *Herald of Holiness* (July 4, 1917), 8; James B. Chapman, "Our Connectional Officers," *Herald of Holiness* (August 8, 1917), 6.

49. See H. F. Reynolds, *World-Wide Missions* (Kansas City: Nazarene Publishing House, 1915); White, "Hiram F. Reynolds," 89-179; and Cunningham, *Holiness Abroad,* 59, 98-109, 147-50. The H. F. Reynolds Collection in the Nazarene Archives contains over 2,000 photographs, many of which Reynolds received from others, but many others of which he took.

50. "Proceedings of the First Annual Mission Council of the Church of the Nazarene in Peru" (October 13-19, 1924) (file 241-32).

51. Note letterhead of V. G. Santin to E. G. Anderson, April 20, 1923 (file 390-19); [Peru missionaries] to E. G. Anderson, July 28, 1923 (file 241-31); Anderson, "Closing Our Mission Stations," *Other Sheep* (December 1925), 2-3; Anderson, "Victory," *Other Sheep* (January 1926), 1; Reynolds to J. D. Scott, October 16, 1925 (file 178-19).

52. Williams, "Notes on the Missionary Trip Around the World" (file 544-1).

53. 1928 *Proceedings of the General Board,* 57; Chapman, *History of the Church of the Nazarene,* 142-43. In a classic understatement, Chapman noted that "it would be difficult to give any adequate account of the many and varied activities of Dr. Reynolds since he entered the General Superintendency." The Reynolds Collection in the Nazarene Archives contains over 25,000 pieces of correspondence, very little of it addressed to Reynolds' home or office. His correspondents had to follow his published itinerary in the church paper and send mail to him in transit. He banged out his replies on a portable typewriter, which he carried on his travels. For his colleagues' opposition to Reynolds' proposed trip, see John W. Goodwin to H. F. Reynolds, February 10, 1927 (file 915-10).

54. J. B. Chapman, "Report to the Board of General Superintendents, the Missionary Department, and the General Board" (October 22, 1931) (453-6). Chapman's *30,000 Miles of Missionary Travel* (Kansas City: Nazarene Publishing House, n.d.) recounts his trip to Central and South America, the British West Indies, Africa, and Great Britain.

55. Wiley to H. G. Cowan (November 1, 1917), Northwest Nazarene University Archives.

56. Rev. Hunt to R. T. Williams (March 24, 1917), R. T. Williams Collection (503-16); H. V. Miller to J. W. Goodwin (N.d.), and Miller to Goodwin (January 26, 1925), both in the Goodwin Collection (540-23).

57. *Litany for Ordination and Consecration,* booklet (N.d.), but from the 1916-28 time period, file 2226-19.

58. This section draws upon Cunningham, *Holiness Abroad,* 101-18, which see for further documentation.

59. Cunningham, *Holiness Abroad,* 101.

60. Ibid., 102.

61. Ibid.

62. Ibid., 103.

63. Ibid., 104.

64. Ibid., 104-5.

65. Ibid., 105.
66. Ibid., 106.
67. Ibid.
68. Ibid., 106-7.
69. Nagamatsu to Anderson (August 13, 1923). See Cunningham, *Holiness Abroad,* 107-8.
70. Cunningham, *Holiness Abroad,* 108.
71. Ibid., 108-9.
72. Reynolds, "Missionary Service" (June 10, 1917).
73. Cunningham, *Holiness Abroad,* 110. Compare Robert, *American Women,* 231-40.
74. Cunningham, *Holiness Abroad,* 110.
75. Ibid.
76. J. G. Morrison, "Minutes, 1931, Department of Foreign Missions," 14 (file 451-35); *Journal of the Seventh General Assembly,* 179-80; *Proceedings of the General Board of the Church of the Nazarene,* Special Sessions (Kansas City: General Board of the Church of the Nazarene, [1929]), 11.

77. The statistics are from Chapman, *History of the Church of the Nazarene,* 70, and Swim, *History of Missions,* 33-34. See also E. G. Anderson, *Annual Report and Survey of the Fields Occupied by Missionaries of the Pentecostal Church of the Nazarene, 1917-1918* (Kansas City: General Foreign Missionary Board, Pentecostal Church of the Nazarene, [1918]), 3 (file 230-15a); E. G. Anderson, "Farewell," *Other Sheep* (November 1920), 1.

78. File 239-21. Reynolds remained as chairman of the General Board of Foreign Missions from the time of his resignation as general secretary in 1915 until the time of the reorganization of the board system in 1923. See Taylor, *Fifty Years of Nazarene Missions,* 1:34-35.

79. B. F. Haynes, "Our General Superintendents," *Herald of Holiness* (August 15, 1923), 4; Wilson, *William C. Wilson,* 87.

80. *Minutes of the General Board* (1923), 22; Allie Irick to Reynolds and Goodwin (July 14, 1922).

81. E. G. Anderson, "What Shall We Do?" *Other Sheep* (June 1921), 1; Anderson, "We Must Not Fail," *Other Sheep* (August 1921), 1-2; B. F. Hayes, "Misconceptions That Hurt," *Herald of Holiness* (October 19, 1921), reprinted in *Other Sheep* (November 1921), 1-2; *Other Sheep* (December 1921), 12; Anderson, "Victory," *Other Sheep* (March 1922), 1.

82. Anderson, "Report of the General Board of Foreign Missions, Church of the Nazarene to the Sixth General Assembly, Kansas City, September 20, 1923," printed in *Other Sheep* (October 1923), 2-7; Anderson, "What Shall We Do?" *Other Sheep* (November 1923), 5; *Proceedings of the Church of the Nazarene: First to Eighth Sessions, October 1 to 4, 1923; Ninth to Thirty-third Sessions, December 4 to 14, 1923,* 10, 22-23, 33, 39.

83. Girvin to Goodwin (February 3, 1922) and Girvin to Goodwin (June 20, 1922), Goodwin Collection (530-35); J. B. Chapman, "The Greatest Work of the General Assembly," *Herald of Holiness* (October 24, 1923), 2.

84. Carlos Miller to E. G. Anderson (February 24, 1924); Anderson to Miller (October 6, 1925); Anderson to Miller (December 28, 1925); Swim, *History of Missions of the Church of the Nazarene,* 167-68. Anderson, "Twenty Missionaries to Go," *Other Sheep* (September 1924), 3; Anderson, "Twenty Missionaries Sailing Soon," *Other Sheep* (September 1924), 8-9; Anderson, "Will You Help Send Them?" *Other Sheep* (November 1924), 15; Anderson, "Will We Maintain Them?" *Other Sheep* (December 1924), 2-3.

85. L. Milton Williams to J. W. Goodwin, H. F. Reynolds, and R. T. Williams (May 15, 1925) (file 472-28); E. G. Anderson to Executive Committee of the General Board, "Exhibit VI" (N.d.) (file 211-43).

86. J. I. Hill, Mrs. Paul Bresee, C. B. Widmeyer, P. G. Linaweaver, C. H. Babcock, E. A. Girvin, and C. E. Cornell, to general superintendents and members of the General Board (October 23, 1924), and E. J. Fleming to [each of the above named] (November 13, 1924) (file 221-42); E. J. Fleming to M. L. Staples (October 1, 1925) (file 646-9); "Minutes of the Special Committee" (file 221-41); Smith, *Called unto Holiness,* 339-40.

87. Outline of Investigation (file 239-21); E. G. Anderson letter to the General Board, in *Proceedings of the General Board of the Church of the Nazarene: Annual Session, February 10-15, 1927 and Supplement Special Session, September 23-25, 1926,* 31-32.

88. After resigning, Anderson briefly engaged in the manufacture of candy in Chicago, then joined Abraham Fitkin supervising an orphanage in North Carolina. See Lunn to Anderson (January 7, 1927); Anderson to Lunn (August 29, 1927, and September 9, 1927); Anderson to Goodwin (October 20, 1927); Mrs. Z. A. Walton to publishers of the *Herald of Holiness* (December 20, 1927); Lunn to Mrs. Z. A. Walton (December 22, 1927) (all in file 239-22). From 1932 to 1936 Anderson served as executive field secretary at Eastern Nazarene College. In 1949 Anderson joined the International Gospel League headed by Nazarene Basil Miller. *Herald of Holiness* (February 10, 1926, and April 6, 1927). See Anderson to the Board of General Superintendents (February 19, 1925); Reynolds to Goodwin (February 2, 1926). On Lunn see John C. Oster, *Serving Those Who Serve: 75 Years of Pensions and Benefits* (Kansas City: Board of Pensions and Benefits USA, Church of the Nazarene, 1993), 27-33.

89. Reynolds, "Important Notice," *Other Sheep* (June 1926), 4; *Proceedings of the General Board of the Church of the Nazarene: Annual Session, February 10-15, 1927 and Supplement Special Session, September 23-25, 1926,* 86-95.

90. *Journal of the Seventh General Assembly* (Kansas City: Nazarene Publishing House, 1928), 61, 103; 1928 *Manual,* 32-33. See also "Report of the Special Committee on Men and Methods," *Proceedings of the General Board of the Church of the Nazarene: February 11 to 16, 1926,* 25; J. G. Morrison, "A Great General Board Session," *Other Sheep* (October 1927), 2-3; "Quadrennial Report of the Committee on Finance and Investments of the General Board," *Proceedings of the General Board of the Church of the Nazarene: Special Sessions, June 12-22, 26, 1928 at Columbus, Ohio, and January 15-18, 1928, at Kansas City, Missouri,* 13-16.

91. J. G. Morrison, "To Our Guatemalan Church Members and Converts" (June 28, 1930) (file 218-42), and almost identical letters to other churches, as, for example, Morrison, "To Our Chinese Church Members and Converts" (June 28, 1930) (file 412-26). See Reynolds to Richard S. Anderson (May 7, 1926) and Emma Word to Richard S. Anderson (July 10, 1926) (file 218-35); Morrison, "The Tide Is Turned," *Other Sheep* (June 1928), 5; "Extracts from the Quadrennial Missionary Report," *Other Sheep* (August 1928), 7-10; Taylor, *Fifty Years of Nazarene Missions,* 1:35-38; Smith, *Called unto Holiness,* 339-41.

92. J. G. Morrison, "Items of Missionary Interest in General Board Proceedings," *Other Sheep* (February 1931), 16; and "The January Session of the General Board," *Other Sheep* (March 1931), 4; Morrison, "A Self-Denial Month," *Other Sheep* (November 1931), 2; Morrison, "The Self-Denial Offering," *Other Sheep* (January 1932), 2.

93. 1932 *Manual,* 150 (par. 280.9). A corresponding paragraph was added to the duties of the general superintendents (see p. 139, par. 263.3): "The Board of General Superintendents, with the General Board, is authorized and empowered to apportion the general budget to the several Assembly Districts in harmony with 280.9" (see pp. 186-87); *Journal of the Eighth General Assembly* (Kansas City: Nazarene Publishing House, 1932), 132-33; 1932 *Manual* (1932), 57 (par. 62.14); 1956 *Manual,* 318 (par. 592).

94. For example, a memorial was rejected by the 1952 and 1960 General Assemblies that proposed General Budget financing of the church's colleges. Another memorial proposed creating a separate budget for home and foreign missions. See *Journal of the Thirteenth General Assembly* (1952), 130-31 (Report No. 1), and *Journal of the Fifteenth General Assembly* (1960), 140.

95. Chapman, Induction Service for General Superintendent Williamson (file 1233-31).

Chapter 9

1. For example, see Isaac, *Prohibition and Politics,* 263-66.

2. Brickley, *Man of the Morning,* 161, 164.

3. *Proceedings of the General Assembly of the Pentecostal Church of the Nazarene* (Los Angeles: Nazarene Publishing Company, 1907), 47, 57-58.

4. *Proceedings of the Third General Assembly of the Pentecostal Church of the Nazarene,* ed. Fred Epperson (Los Angeles: Nazarene, [1911]), 35.

5. Cited in Isaac, *Prohibition and Politics,* 75. See Haynes, *Tempest-Tossed on Methodist Seas;* Beals, *Heralding Scriptural Holiness,* 17-32; Stan Ingersol, "Nazarene Roots," *Herald of Holiness* (June 15, 1987), 11; Stan Ingersol, "Nazarene Roots," *Herald of Holiness* (July 15, 1987), 9.

6. *Herald of Holiness* (April 23, 1913).

7. *Proceedings of the Southern California District, 1939*, 84-85.

8. Profile file, Nazarene Archives; Stan Ingersol, in *Herald of Holiness* (November 15, 1986).

9. *Proceedings of the Fifth General Assembly of the Pentecostal Church of the Nazarene* (Kansas City: Nazarene Publishing House, 1919), 115-18.

10. Richard S. Anderson, "Revival in Churches of the Nazarene, at Tactic, Guatemala" [1926] (file 218-35).

11. Chapman, editorial, *Herald of Holiness*, November 23, 1921.

12. *Proceedings of the Fifth General Assembly of the Pentecostal Church of the Nazarene* (Kansas City: Nazarene Publishing House, [1919]), 115-16. On the Christian Amendment see Foster, *Moral Reconstruction*, 107-10.

13. S. D. Athans to General Foreign Missionary Board (October 2, 1916) and S. D. Athans to E. G. Anderson (November 16, 1916) (both in file 389-22); Carlos Miller to Reynolds (December 25, 1918) (file 210-54).

14. C. E. Cornell, "Will Red Blooded American Men and Women Turn Anarchists?" *Herald of Holiness* (December 14, 1921), 3; *Manual* (1928), 243; W. T. Purkiser, *Called unto Holiness*, vol. 2: *The Second Twenty-Five Years, 1933-58* (Kansas City: Nazarene Publishing House, 1983), 76-77.

15. R. E. Gilmore to Arthur B. Cook (February 22, 1935), Gilmore papers, Northwest Nazarene U.; R. V. DeLong to William Borah (September 24, 1936) and Borah to DeLong (September 27, 1936), DeLong papers, NNU.

16. *Pentecostal Messenger* (February 1913), 4; A. J. Vallery, "Bethany Training Home," *Herald of Holiness* (April 21, 1920), 12; Oscar Hudson, "Orphanage Campaign Opens," *Herald of Holiness* (September 15, 1920), 9; various articles in the "Orphanage" issue of the *Herald of Holiness* (November 10, 1920). For an account of Hudson's earlier role in establishing an orphanage in Pilot Point that was later moved to Peniel, see his autobiography, *This I Remember*, 39-45. See also Elizabeth Woolsey Spruce, "The Story of My Family," an edited transcript of oral history interviews, 71; *Other Sheep* (May 1941), 5; Parker, "Those Early Nazarenes Cared," 32P-32T.

17. *Herald of Holiness* (March 19, 1913).

18. John W. Goodwin, "Holiness Children," *Herald of Holiness* (November 10, 1920).

19. E. J. Fleming, ed., *Yearbook—Church of the Nazarene—1923* (Kansas City: Nazarene Publishing House, 1923), 18-22, 27; Fleming, ed., *Yearbook—Church of the Nazarene—1924* (Kansas City: Nazarene Publishing House, 1924), 41; Fleming, ed., *Yearbook—Church of the Nazarene—1925* (Kansas City: Nazarene Publishing House, 1925), 37-41.

20. "What Is the Future of the Church of the Nazarene?" *Herald of Holiness* (September 12, 1923), 1.

21. Basil Miller and U. E. Harding, *"Cunningly Devised Fables": Modernism Exposed and Refuted* (N.p., n.d.), 86. See "Address of the General Superintendents," *Herald of Holiness* (October 3, 1928), 9; Chapman, "The Church and Nonspiritual Agencies," *Herald of Holiness* (September 13, 1922), 1; Chapman, "Individual and Social Christianity," *Herald of Holiness* (January 26, 1927), 1. See also Smith, *Called unto Holiness*, 305-21, 337-41; Dunning, "Nazarene Ethics," 186-91.

22. *Herald of Holiness* (October 25, 1933), 1, quoted in Purkiser, *Called unto Holiness,* 68.

23. *Herald of Holiness* (March 23, 1935), 4, quoted in Purkiser, *Called unto Holiness,* 74.

24. Parker, *Mission to the World,* 90-92. See L. Alline Swann, *Song in the Night: The Story of Dr. and Mrs. Thomas E. Mangum* (Kansas City: Beacon Hill Press, 1957).

25. F. C. Sutherland, *China Crisis* (Kansas City: Nazarene Publishing House, 1948), 86-87 (and the remainder of the chapter, which is titled "Healing the Sick"); Lillian Cole, "Pigg's Peak, Africa," *Other Sheep* (December 1916), 3.

26. Miller, *Susan N. Fitkin,* 162.

27. Parker, *Mission to the World,* 123-28.

28. Ibid., 130; William C. Esselstyn, *Nazarene Missions in South Africa* (Kansas City: Nazarene Publishing House, 1952), 60-61.

29. Chapman, report to the general superintendents; "Minutes of the China Council" [1935]; Wiese to Jones (July 16, 1946); Susan N. Fitkin and Emma B. Word, *Nazarene Missions in the Orient* (Kansas City: Nazarene Publishing House, n.d.), 87. On Wesche see "Minutes of the Council Meeting," 1934.

30. Amy Hinshaw, *Messengers of the Cross in China* (Kansas City: Women's Foreign Missionary Society, Church of the Nazarene, n.d.), 86-91; Peter Kiehn, "Rev. Clarence J. Kinne, a Missionary," *Other Sheep* (August 1933), 11; "Mrs. C. J. Kinne Joins Heavenly Host," *Herald of Holiness* (February 10, 1926), 20; *Herald of Holiness* (November 16, 1932), 17; L. C. Osborn, *The China Story* (Kansas City: Nazarene Publishing House, 1969), 42-45. See also *Herald of Holiness* (November 16, 1932), 17; *Yearbook, 1925*, 25; L. A. Reed and H. A. Wiese, *The Challenge of China* (Kansas City: Nazarene Publishing House, 1937), 85.

31. Anderson, "Brief History of the Church of the Nazarene" (file 861-34); Swim, *History of Missions*, 143.

32. India Mission Council, *New India and the Gospel* (Kansas City: Nazarene Publishing House, 1954), 115-18; *Other Sheep* (October 1938), 22; Orpha Speicher, "In India Again," *Other Sheep* (May 1945), 4-5; "Workers Together," *Other Sheep* (February 1948), 6.

33. Parker, *Mission to the World*, 608-9.

34. *Proceedings of the Sixteenth Annual Assembly of the Kansas District Church of the Nazarene, Hutchinson, Kansas, September 2-6, 1925*, 44. See Ownby, *Subduing Satan*, 21-37; on general trends see Paula Fass, *The Beautiful and the Damned: American Youths in the 1920s* (New York: Oxford U. Press, 1977). Italian families in Harlem, New York, had the same proscriptions against promiscuous dating, movies, and bobbed hair through the 1930s. See Robert Orsi, *The Madonna of 115th Street: Faith and Community in Italian Harlem, 1880-1950* (New Haven, CT: Yale U. Press, 1985), 122-23, 126.

35. On the link between jewelry and missions see, for example, A. J. Smith to J. G. Morrison (January 29, 1931), enclosing two rings to be sold; Mrs. J. W. Cavender to the General Board (March 17, 1941) and M. Lunn to Mrs. J. W. Cavender (April 1, 1941) (file 1002-13). See Purkiser, *Called unto Holiness*, 61-66.

36. J. E. Cook, *W. M. Tidwell (A Life That Counted): The Life of William Moses Tidwell* (Ann Arbor: Malloy, n.d.), 13. See Clifford Keys to Goodwin (April 15, 1929) and Goodwin to Keys (April 27, 1929) (file 540-8); *Manual*, e.g., 1932 edition, 44, 361. See also Thornton, *Radical Righteousness*, 136.

37. Roger Morris, pastor, Paris, Kentucky, to Chapman (N.d.), with Chapman's handwritten note to [J. G.] Morrison on the reverse side (file 472-22); Roy Pegram to R. T. Williams (May 22, 1939) (file 534-4).

38. File 2101-10.

39. Smith, *Called unto Holiness*, 289-97. See R. Laurence Moore, *Religious Outsiders and the Making of Americans* (New York: Oxford U. Press, 1986), esp. chap. 6.

40. J. Elwin Wright, "An Historical Statement of Events Leading Up to the National Conference at St. Louis," in *Evangelical Action! A Report of the Organization of the National Association of Evangelicals for United Action*, ed. Executive Committee (Boston: United Action Press, 1942), 14.

41. Paine, "The Possibility of United Action," in *Evangelical Action*, 53.

42. E. H. Edwards, Seattle, Washington, to C. W. Jones (October 20, 1942).

43. Corlett to General Superintendents (May 12, 1943) (file 790-1); *United We Stand: A Report of the Constitutional Convention of the National Association of Evangelicals, May 3-6, 1943*, printed in *A New Evangelical Coalition: Early Documents of the National Association of Evangelicals*, ed. Joel Carpenter (New York: Garland, 1988). See also Bruce Shelley, *Evangelicalism in America* (Grand Rapids: Eerdmans, 1967), 71-72; Purkiser, *Called unto Holiness*, 71.

44. Reynolds to E. J. Fleming (April 1, 1925) and "Report of Staples Committee" (file 453-11); C. E. and Mae T. Roberts to Chapman (September 10, 1938).

Chapter 10

1. Cunningham, *Holiness Abroad*, 99-100.
2. Ibid., 100.
3. Ibid., 147.
4. Ibid., 148-49.
5. Ibid., 149.
6. Ibid., 149-50.
7. Ibid., 59.

8. Ibid., 63-64.
9. Ibid., 64-65.
10. On India and China see Cunningham, *Holiness Abroad*. On Peru, "Proceedings of the Second Annual Assembly of the Missionary District of Peru," Monsefu, November 13-21, 1922," containing "Proposed Division of Territory Between the Church of the Nazarene and the Free Church of Scotland" (file 241-30); [Peru missionaries] to E. G. Anderson (November 18, 1922), and a pamphlet in file 241-30; Guy H. McHenry, "The Nazarene Responsibility in Peru," *Other Sheep* (November 1927), 14. See also R. Pierce Beaver, *Ecumenical Beginnings in Protestant World Mission: A History of Comity* (New York: Thomas Nelson, 1962), 81-101, 153-54.
11. Carlos Miller to E. G. Anderson (October 28, 1919) (file 210-54).
12. Reynolds, "The Meaning of Present Conditions" (N.d.) (file 262-56). See likewise [Reynolds], *History of the Foreign Missionary Work* (Kansas City: General Board of Foreign Missions, Church of the Nazarene, 1921), 58-59.
13. Undated policy, about 1921, very much like the previous policies issued for Japan and India in 1914, Reynolds papers (files 183-9 and 282-44).
14. For example, see Reynolds, "Around the World Trip," to the General Missionary Board of the Pentecostal Church of the Nazarene [1914]; Hinshaw, *In Labors Abundant*, 262.
15. Fitkin, *Holiness and Mission*, 72.
16. *Proceedings of the General Board of the Church of the Nazarene*, Annual Session, February 9 to 11, 1928 (Kansas City: General Board, [1928]), 56.
17. Williams, "Notes on the Missionary Trip Round the World" (file 544-1).
18. *Journal of the Seventh General Assembly of the Church of the Nazarene*, eds. E. J. Fleming and M. A. Wilson (Kansas City: Nazarene Publishing House, 1928), 178. See 1928 *Proceedings of the General Board*, 20; *Journal of Seventh General Assembly*, 174.
19. Morrison to [R. T.] Williams (June 11, 1938); Paul A. Williams, "A History of the Church of the Nazarene in Continental Europe," M.A. thesis, Emporia State U., 1982, 93-96.
20. Rebecca Krikorian, *Jerusalem: The Life Sketch of Miss Rebecca Krikorian and Her Nephew Rev. Samuel Krikorian Together with Their Divine Call to Open a Field of Work in Jerusalem* (Kansas City: General Foreign Missionary Board, Pentecostal Church of the Nazarene, 1919); Amy Hinshaw, *Messengers of the Cross in Palestine, Japan and Other Islands* (Kansas City: Woman's Foreign Missionary Society, Church of the Nazarene, n.d.), 7-16, 21-23; Helen Temple, *Of Whom the World Was Not Worthy: The Story of Samuel Krikorian, First Nazarene Missionary to Palestine* (Kansas City: Nazarene Publishing House, 1972), 53-63. For a broader context see Joseph L. Grabill, *Protestant Diplomacy and the Near East: Missionary Influence on American Policy, 1810-1927* (Minneapolis: U. of Minnesota Press, 1971), 46-53, 247-68; and on the WCTU connection to Rebecca Krikorian see Ian Tyrell, *Woman's World/Woman's Empire: The Woman's Christian Temperance Union in International Perspective, 1880-1930* (Chapel Hill: U. of North Carolina Press, 1991), 143.
21. Temple, *Of Whom the World Was Not Worthy*, 64-68.
22. See Hinshaw, *Messengers of the Cross in Palestine*, 32-38.
23. Santin to Missionary Board (August 15, 1918) (file 390-19). See DeLong and Taylor, *Fifty Years of Nazarene Missions*, 2:107-9; Smith, *Called unto Holiness*, 250-57. See also Debra J. Baldwin, *Protestants and the Mexican Revolution: Missionaries, Ministers, and Social Change* (Urbana: U. of Illinois Press, 1990).
24. H. T. Reza, *Washed by the Blood: Stories of Native Workers Connected with the Ministry of the Church of the Nazarene in the Mexican Field* (Kansas City: Beacon Hill Press, 1953), 17. Reza was Santin's son-in-law.
25. V. G. Santin to E. G. Anderson (April 30, 1925) (file 390-19); Santin to M. Lunn (May 2, 1930) and Santin to J. G. Morrison (October 2, 1930) (file 390-21); V. G. Santin to C. Warren Jones (June 28, 1937) and Santin to Jones (September 28, 1938), Jones to Santin (August 5, 1940) (file 390-24); Alfredo Santin to Jones, December 24, 1939 (file 390-15); Reza, *Washed by the Blood*, 13-18.
26. Amy N. Hinshaw, *Native Torch Bearers*, 3rd ed. (Kansas City: Nazarene Publishing House, 1934), 136-38; see 134-50.
27. Ibid., 108, 110.
28. Ibid., 106-10.

29. Ibid., 110-17, 119-21.
30. Ibid., 123-32.
31. "The Start of Our Work in Brava," Folios for History of the Foreign Missionary Work of the Church of the Nazarene," [1921], 262-56; Hinshaw, *Messengers of the Cross in Palestine*, 85-90.
32. Swim, *History of Missions*, 184-91; Earl Mosteller, "As Others See Cape Verde Nazarenes," *Other Sheep* (September 1958), 5, 12; "A Proposito da Nossa Capa," and Daniel Barros, "Um Marco Historico," both in *O Arauto da Santidade* (Agosto 1989), 3, 26.
33. "Missionary Questionairre" (file 679-17).
34. "Policy of the General Board to Govern Its Work in Foreign Fields," *Proceedings of the Church of the Nazarene: First to Eighth Sessions, October 1 to 4, 1923; Ninth to Thirty-third Sessions, December 4 to 14, 1923*, 63-64; also see file 305-15, Nazarene Archives.
35. Cunningham, *Holiness Abroad*, 22.
36. "Policy of the General Board of the Church of the Nazarene to Govern Its Work in Foreign Fields," undated (copy in file 305-15 was that of Reynolds), and the nearly identical "Policy" dated June 11, 1932 (file 764-27).
37. Cunningham, *Holiness Abroad*, 116-17.
38. Ibid., 23.
39. J. Glenn Gould, *Missionary Pioneers and Our Debt to Them* (Kansas City: Nazarene Publishing House, [1935]), 39.
40. Cunningham, *Holiness Abroad*, 24.

Chapter 11

1. *Proceedings of the Third General Assembly of the Pentecostal Church of the Nazarene*, ed. Fred Epperson (Los Angeles: Nazarene, [1911]), 16, 20; *Proceedings of the Tenth Annual Assembly of the Southern California District Pentecostal Church of the Nazarene*, June 21-25, 1916; DeLong and Taylor, *Fifty Years of Nazarene Missions*, 2:123-26.
2. E. Y. Davis to J. G. Morrison (October 8, 1928) (file 389-29); E. Y. Davis profile file, Nazarene Archives.
3. *Journal of the Seventh General Assembly*, 91-93; Elizondo to Emma Word (February 19, 1931), and various letters in file 390-9.
4. *Proceedings of the Seventeenth Annual New York District Assembly*, 12, 22; *Proceedings of the Eighteenth Annual New York District Assembly*, 24-25; *Proceedings of the Nineteenth Annual New York District Assembly*, 23-24.
5. Nona Moore Floyd, *"Holiness unto the Lord": A History of the Batesville Church of the Nazarene* (N.p.: n.p., 2000), 11-15; *Herald of Holiness* (July 20, 1932), 26; *Stillwater NewsPress* (March 7, 1989), 4C.
6. *Herald of Holiness* (January 5, 1935).
7. Weekly Bulletin of Los Angeles First Church (March 26, 1916), 4; John A. Tice, *First Church of the Nazarene, Elmira, New York*, bound typescript, 1999, 9.
8. Anne Firor Scott, "The 'New Woman' in the New South," in *Making the Invisible Woman Visible* (Urbana: U. of Illinois Press, 1984), 198. See also John Patrick McDowell, *The Social Gospel in the South: The Woman's Home Mission Movement in the Methodist Episcopal Church, South, 1886-1939* (Baton Rouge: Louisiana State U. Press, 1982).
9. *Proceedings of the Seventeenth Annual New York District Assembly*, 42-43; *Proceedings of the Nineteenth Annual New York District Assembly*, 40-41; *Proceedings of the Twentieth Annual New York District Assembly*, 43.
10. These percentages were calculated from statistical tables IX and X in the General Secretary's Report to the Twenty-third General Assembly. See *Journal of the Twenty-third General Assembly* (Kansas City: Nazarene Publishing House, 1993), 274-79.
11. *Herald of Holiness* (March 9, 1935), 15-16; *Herald of Holiness* (March 30, 1935), 118-19; *Herald of Holiness* (April 27, 1935), 21.
12. Margaret Stewart, "A Day in Our Girls' School at Chikhli, India," in *Distinctive Days on Mission Fields*, comp. Edith P. Goodnow (Kansas City: Nazarene Publishing House, 1943), 15. See also, for example, Susan N. Fitkin, *A Trip to Africa* (New York: [privately printed], n.d.), 33-36. See Robert, *American Women*, 160-62.

13. *Arkansas District Church of the Nazarene Forty-First Annual Assembly Journal* (1948); *Arkansas Democrat* (September 24, 1949), 7; *Pine Bluff Commercial* (October 11, 1958); *Arkansas Democrat* (October 1, 1960), 4; *Herald of Holiness* (January 21, 1970), 17; Agnes Diffee profile file; see file 654-36 for membership figures.

14. Mary Cooper Diary (February 22, 1927; March 7, 1927; April 18, 1928; June 29, 1927; July 18, 1927; and throughout), and various undated letters to "dear ones at home" or "dear ones in the Lord" (in file 1312-3), Nazarene Archives. Also see Mary Cooper profile file, Nazarene Archives, and Betty L. Emslie, *With Both Hands: The Story of Mary Cooper of Gazaland* (Kansas City: Nazarene Publishing House, 1970), 61-63, and throughout.

15. See, for instance, "Policy for Home Missions," in *Proceedings of the Church of the Nazarene: First to Eighth Sessions, October 1 to 4, 1923; Ninth to Thirty-third Sessions, December 4 to 14, 1923,* 42-43; "Report of the Department of Home Missions," *Proceedings of the General Board of the Church of the Nazarene: February 12-21, 1925,* 48-49.

16. Bud Robinson, *Sunshine and Smiles: Life Story, Flash Lights, Sayings, and Sermons* (Chicago: Christian Witness, 1903), 50.

17. Ibid., 55-56.

18. Cited in Miller, *Bud Robinson,* 76.

19. Robinson, *Sunshine and Smiles,* 78.

20. [Sallie] Robinson, *Buddie and I* (Kansas City: Nazarene Publishing House, 1913), 29, 34-37. See also Robinson, *Sunshine and Smiles,* 71-75.

21. Robinson, *Sunshine and Smiles,* 104. See James McGraw, "The Preaching of Bud Robinson," *Preacher's Magazine* (January 1954), 9-12.

22. J. B. Chapman, *Bud Robinson: A Brother Beloved* (Kansas City: Beacon Hill Press, 1943), 166.

23. P. H. Lunn in Chapman, *Bud Robinson,* 148.

24. Chapman, *Bud Robinson,* 91. See also Miller, *Bud Robinson.*

25. Lewis T. Corlett to J. B. Chapman (November 28, 1942), copy in Corlett papers, Northwest Nazarene U. Archives, printed in Chapman, *Bud Robinson,* 164. See various stories from district superintendents, pastors, and others in the same book.

26. *First Church of the Nazarene Henryetta, Oklahoma: Centennial Celebration,* 19; *Herald of Holiness* (February 25, 1925), 14.

27. R. S. Anderson to E. G. Anderson (October 28, 1916; December 16, 1916; and January 30, 1917), and R. S. Anderson to "Dear Friends" (December 30, 1916) (file 219-13); Anderson, "They That Sow in Tears Shall Reap in Joy" (file 218-48). See also Richard Anderson to E. G. Anderson (April 4, 1921) (file 218-27), Nazarene Archives.

28. V. G. Santin to H. F. Reynolds (April 25, 1916) (file 390-18).

29. S. D. Athans to E. G. Anderson (November 16, 1916) (file 389-22).

30. Fitkin, *Trip to Africa,* 25, 36-37, 40.

31. Louise Robinson Chapman, *Footprints in Africa* (Kansas City: Nazarene Publishing House, 1959), 39.

32. Cooper, "Three Tent Meetings" (file 1312-3), Nazarene Archives.

33. Kitagawa to C. Warren Jones (October 15, 1935); "Brother and Sister Staples Return from Japan," *Other Sheep* 25 (February 1938), 12. See Eckel to Word (August 6, 1935); Kitagawa to Word (May 3, 1940); Fitkin and Word, *Nazarene Missions in the Orient,* 30, 39-40, 46. See Cunningham, *Holiness Abroad,* 111-17.

34. Jernigan to Reynolds (December 11, 1908) (file 169-39). See Smith, *Called unto Holiness,* 255-56.

35. *Proceedings of the Third General Assembly,* 1911, 22-23. See also Charles Jones, "Disinherited or Rural? A Historical Case Study in Urban Holiness Religion," *Missouri Historical Review* 66 (April 1972), 395-412.

36. *Herald of Holiness* (November 16, 1932), 8, and *Herald of Holiness* (April 17, 1937), 10.

37. "Report of Executive Field Secretary to the Annual Session of the General Board," *Proceedings of the General Board of the Church of the Nazarene: Annual Session, February 9 to 11, 1928,* 14.

38. *Methodist Review* (January 1890); Memphis *Daily Commercial* (May 20, 1894); and Haynes, *Tempest-Tossed on Methodist Seas.* See also Chapman, "A Man of Zeal and Courage," *Herald of Holi-*

ness (October 23, 1923), 1; Stan Ingersol, "Man of Zeal and Courage"; and Ingersol, "B. F. Haynes and the *Herald of Holiness*," *Herald of Holiness* (July 15, 1987), 9.

39. Cornell, "Godly People Ought to Know About President Taft," *Herald of Holiness* (June 12, 1912), 6.

40. See, for example, Haynes: *Herald of Holiness* (October 2, 1912), 1-6; "Come unto Me," *Herald of Holiness* (April 14, 1920), 1; "The Kingdom of God," *Herald of Holiness* (May 19, 1920), 3; "The Need of the Hour," *Herald of Holiness* (August 11, 1920), 1; "Right to Strike," *Herald of Holiness* (September 22, 1920), 2; "Are We Drifting Back to Savagery?" *Herald of Holiness* (January 5, 1921), 2; "Our Country Becoming Militaristic," *Herald of Holiness* (April 13, 1921), 2; "A Labor Dictatorship," *Herald of Holiness* (June 1, 1921), 2; "On the Brink of Anarchy," *Herald of Holiness* (February 22, 1922), 1. Other articles published during the time reflect the topics of the era: W. E. Shepard, "Fads, Fakes, Freaks, Frauds, and Fools," *Herald of Holiness* (January 26, 1921), 7 (April 5, 1922), 1, and (February 4, 1923), 4l; C. E. Cornell, "The Paramount Need of a World in Peril," *Herald of Holiness* (September 29, 1926), 5. See Smith, *Called unto Holiness*, 264-65; Beals, *Heralding Scriptural Holiness*, 12-13, 17-32.

41. Reynolds, open letter to the Pentecostal Church of the Nazarene (October 18, 1916); H. Orton Wiley, "In Memory of J. F. Sanders," *College Clarion* (March-April 1928): 1-2; DeLance Wallace resignation letter to the General Superintendents (February 24, 1922) (file 530-46); Goodwin to R. T. Williams (March 2, 1922) (file 540-31); *Herald of Holiness* (February 10, 1926), 7; M. Lunn, "Growth and Development of the Publishing House" *Herald of Holiness* (October 16, 1929), 10-11; Roger Swanson, "The Story of a Nazarene Layman," typescript, Mervel S. Lunn profile folder, Nazarene Archives.

42. See James B. Chapman, *The Terminology of Holiness* (Kansas City: Beacon Hill Press, 1947).

43. "Twin Enemies of the Home," *Herald of Holiness* (July 12, 1922), 1. See also Chapman, "The Power of Separateness," *Herald of Holiness* (May 20, 1925), 1; Beals, *Heralding Scriptural Holiness*, 33-46.

44. Beals, *Heralding Scriptural Holiness*, 47-60. See also Carl Bangs, *Our Roots of Belief: A Biblical and Faithful Theology* (Kansas City: Beacon Hill Press of Kansas City, 1981).

45. Beals, *Heralding Scriptural Holiness*, 50-58, 61-63. See also Lewis T. Corlett, *Thank God and Take Courage: How the Holy Spirit Worked in My Life* (San Diego: Point Loma Press, 1992), 30-31.

46. *Nazarene Messenger* (November 19, 1908), 15.

47. Ibid. (May 25, 1905), 9; (November 7, 1907) 6-7; (October 31, 1907) 5; (November 19, 1908) 15.

48. *The Pentecostal Bible Teacher*, 1911-16.

49. See Edgar P. Ellyson, *The Pastor and His Sunday School Responsibility* (Kansas City: Department of Church Schools, n.d.); Edgar P. Ellyson and H. Orton Wiley, *Leadership Training Course: A Study of the Pupil* (Kansas City: Nazarene Publishing House, 1930).

50. Chapman, *History of the Church of the Nazarene*, 23; Wilson, "Well, Glory," 131.

51. Tice, *First Church of the Nazarene, Elmira, New York*, 9; Bulletin, Pasadena First Church, Sunday, July 6, 1924, in Anonymous Scrapbook II, 105, Nazarene Archives.

52. Wilson, "Well, Glory," 124.

53. William E. Fisher Collection, Nazarene Archives.

54. Keith E. Smith, *A History of the First Church of the Nazarene, Hartford, Connecticut, 1914-2007*, bound typescript, 2007, 23.

55. Ibid., 27.

56. Weekly Bulletins of Los Angeles First Church, March 26, 1916, 2-3, March 11, 1928, and January 5, 1930.

57. *Herald of Holiness* (February 25, 1925), 14.

58. Ibid.; *First Church of the Nazarene Henryetta, Oklahoma: Centennial Celebration*, 33.

59. Tice, *First Church of the Nazarene, Elmira, New York*, 12.

60. *Herald of Holiness* (January 5, 1935), 25; *Herald of Holiness* (January 19, 1935), 29-30.

61. Bangs, *Phineas F. Bresee*, 239.

62. Ellen Weiss, *City in the Woods: The Life and Design of an American Camp Meeting on Martha's Vineyard* (New York: Oxford U. Press, 1987); Jones, *Perfectionist Persuasion*, 25-46; Bangs, *Phineas*

F. Bresee, 105-6, 239; Edith Blumhoffer, *Her Heart Can See: The Life and Hymns of Fanny J. Crosby* (Grand Rapids: Eerdmans, 2005).

63. Wilson, *William C. Wilson*, 71.

64. See Haldor Lillenas, *Down Melody Lane: An Autobiography* (Kansas City: Beacon Hill Press, 1953).

65. Chapman, "The Pioneers Are Passing," *Herald of Holiness* (June 16, 1930), 5-6; clipping from an unidentified Nashville newspaper (June 26, 1930), in the John T. Benson profile folder, Nazarene Archives; John Lakin Brasher, *Glimpses* (Cincinnati: Revivalist Press, 1954), 45-46.

66. James R. Goff Jr., *Close Harmony: A History of Southern Gospel* (Chapel Hill: U. North Carolina Press, 2002), 67; see 66-79, 163.

Chapter 12

1. See A. M. Hills, "A Creedless Christianity Impossible," *Herald of Holiness* (October 17, 1923), 3.

2. John C. Greene, *The Death of Adam* (Ames: Iowa State U. Press, 1959), 1-10. See David Livingstone, *Darwin's Forgotten Defenders: The Encounter Between Evangelical Theology and Evolutionary Thought* (Grand Rapids: Eerdmans, 1987). On Christians' involvement in shaping social sciences, see Henry F. May, *Protestant Churches and Industrial America* (New York: Harper and Row, 1967), 170-81.

3. See James R. Moore, *The Post-Darwinian Controversies* (Cambridge: Cambridge U. Press, 1979), which shows that evangelicals did not respond uniformly but ranged from rejection to acceptance. The differences between evangelical liberals and modernists are explored in H. Shelton Smith, Robert Handy, and Lefferts Loetscher, *American Christianity: An Historical Interpretation with Representative Documents* (New York: Scribner's, 1963), 2:215-308.

4. Widney's belief in the Aryan race's superiority are found in a series of books written, published, and sent to colleges and universities at his own expense in the 1930s. These include *The Faith That Has Come to Me* (1932), *The Three Americas: Their Racial Past and the Dominant Racial Factors of Their Future* (1935), *Race Life and Race Religions* (1936), *Civilizations and Their Diseases* (1937), and *The Song of the Engle Men* (1937), among others. Clues to his later beliefs were signaled earlier in *Race Life of the Aryan Peoples* (1907).

5. "Church of the Nazarene, Resignation of Rev. J. H. Hynd," clipping from English newspaper, David Hynd Collection, copy in John Hutton Hynd folder, Nazarene Archives. See St. Louis Ethical Society website, http://www.ethicalstl.org/history.html#J.HUTTON). See also http://www.umsl.edu/~whmc/whmrelig/whm0361.htm. Edward Boyd profiled Templeton's evangelistic career in "Religion's Super-Salesman," *American Magazine* (August 1953), 40-41, 78-82. A notable expression of Templeton's skepticism is found in his *Farewell to God: My Reasons for Rejecting the Christian Faith* (1999).

6. Sandeen, *Roots of Fundamentalism*, 103-31. The Princeton teaching on inerrancy is set in its broader context by Holifield, *Theology in America*, 379, see 377-89. See D. G. Hart, *Defending the Faith: J. Gresham Machen and the Crisis of Conservative Protestantism in Modern America* (Grand Rapids: Baker, 1994), chap. 4, "Science and Salvation."

7. See Bass, *Backgrounds to Dispensationalism*. On Scofield see George M. Marsden, *Fundamentalism and American Culture: The Shaping of Twentieth-Century Evangelicalism, 1870-1925* (New York: Oxford, 1980), esp. chap. 6, "Dispensationalism and the Baconian Ideal."

8. See Sandeen, *Roots of Fundamentalism*, and Weber, *Living in the Shadow*.

9. Hills, "The Silver Jubilee Anniversary," *Herald of Holiness* (November 22, 1933), 10-11. Donald W. Durnbaugh, *The Believers' Church: The History and Character of Radical Protestantism* (New York: Macmillan, 1968), 32-33, describes leading characteristics of the believers' church style of Protestantism.

10. See H. Richard Niebuhr, *The Social Sources of Denominationalism* (New York: Henry Holt, 1929), 17-21, and throughout; Smith, *Called unto Holiness*, 266-71; and Carl Bangs's review of *Called unto Holiness* in *Christian Century* (November 7, 1962), 1356. The believers' church concept influenced Dieter's *Holiness Revival* and has shaped more recent interpretations of the Holiness Movement.

11. See Mark R. Quanstrom, *A Century of Holiness Theology: The Doctrine of Entire Sanctification in the Church of the Nazarene 1905 to 2004* (Kansas City: Beacon Hill Press of Kansas City, 2004), Appendix 2, 203-8, for a convenient list of these books.

12. See *Wesley's Sermons: Ten Select Sermons* (Kansas City: Nazarene Publishing House, 1915). Wesley's *A Plain Account of Christian Perfection* was required beginning with the 1952 *Manual*.

13. *Preacher's Magazine* (January-February 1946), 4.

14. Church of the Nazarene, *Manuals*, 1911-44. For discussions of Ralston and Miley and other developments in Methodist theology, see Chiles, *Theological Transition*; Thomas A. Langford, *Practical Divinity: Theology in the Wesleyan Tradition* (Nashville: Abingdon, 1983). Also see Holifield, *Theology in America*, chap. 12, "Methodist Perfection," 256-72.

15. Edgar P. Ellyson, *Theological Compend* (Chicago: Christian Witness, 1908), and Edgar P. Ellyson, *Doctrinal Studies* (Kansas City: Nazarene Publishing House, 1936). See Chapman, *History of the Church of the Nazarene*, 144-47.

16. Gresham, *Waves Against Gibraltar*, 62-63. See Louise L. Stevenson, *Scholarly Means to Evangelical Ends: The New Haven Scholars and the Transformation of Higher Learning in America, 1830-1890* (Baltimore: Johns Hopkins U. Press, 1986), 97-101.

17. Gresham, *Waves Against Gibraltar*, 33-77. Gresham includes a useful list of Hills's books and summarizes their contents. Composition drafts of *Fundamental Christian Theology*, showing Hills's literal "cut" and "paste" from previous works, some going back decades, are in the Nazarene Archives.

18. Paul M. Bassett, "A Study in the Theology of the Early Holiness Movement," *Methodist History* (April 1975): 61-84, especially 66. A. M. Hills, *Fundamental Christian Theology* (Pasadena: C. J. Kinne, 1931), 1:370-74, and *Fundamental Christian Theology: Abridged Edition* (Pasadena: C. J. Kinne, 1932), 230-34. But see Hills's criticisms of Finney's understanding of both free will and entire sanctification in Hills, *The Life of Charles G. Finney* (1902; repr., Salem, OH: Schmul, 1991), 221-29, 234-35. Also see Quanstrom, *Century of Holiness Theology*, 64-70, and Chiles, *Theological Transition*, 144-83.

19. Bangs, *Our Roots of Belief*, 73.

20. "Dr. H. Orton Wiley," *Herald of Holiness* (October 4, 1961), 11; Ross E. Price, *H. Orton Wiley: Servant and Savant of the Sagebrush College* (Kansas City: Printed for Northwest Nazarene College by Nazarene Publishing House, 1968), 12-13; Price, "The Wiley Lectures for 1984 Given at Point Loma Nazarene College," January 31—February 3, 1984.

21. Langford, *Practical Divinity*, 137. See Buckham's positive assessment of both Olive Winchester and Wiley in his letter to R. V. DeLong, March 25, 1930, accreditation files, Northwest Nazarene U. archives. On Wiley's view of Buckham see Wiley's lectures at Nazarene Theological Seminary, *A Study of the Philosophy of John Wright Buckham in Its Application to the Problems of Modern Theology* (Kansas City: N.p., 1959). See also Mildred Bangs Wynkoop, "Personalism vs. Non-Personalism or Theology vs. Mechanism," philosophy paper, Pasadena College, April 1929, and Wynkoop, "The Philosophy of Idealism and Its Influence on Religion in America," term paper, Northern Baptist Theological seminary, November 17, 1953, Nazarene Archives. See also Frankiel, *California's Spiritual Frontiers*, 114-16, and James Matthew Price, "The Influence of Personalism on the Theology and Education of H. Orton Wiley," *Wesleyan Theological Journal* 41 (Fall 2006): 142-60.

22. Bangs, *Our Roots of Belief*, 73.

23. H. Orton Wiley, *Christian Theology*, vol. 2 (Kansas City: Beacon Hill Press, 1952), 356-57. Compare Hills, *Fundamental Christian Theology*, 1:370-75, 400-405. See Bangs, *Our Roots of Belief*, 71-78, and Chiles, *Theological Transition*, 144-83.

24. Bangs, *Our Roots of Belief*, 79. See also Ross Price, "Dr. Wiley—Eminent Theologian," *Clarion* (November 1961), 3; Kirkemo, *For Zion's Sake*, 35-37, 78-79, 90-91; Quanstrom, *Century of Holiness Theology*, 75-89.

25. Ross E. Price, "Some Data About Miss Olive M. Winchester, Th.D.," 8 pp. typescript, 1986, Olive Winchester profile folder, Nazarene Archives.

26. *Herald of Holiness* (April 31, 1935), 5; *Herald of Holiness* (September 14, 1935), 7; *Herald of Holiness* (September 21, 1935), 6; *Herald of Holiness* (December 7, 1935), 8. See also Price, "Some Data About Miss Olive M. Winchester," and records of her career in the various schools in which

she taught: Cameron, *Eastern Nazarene College*, 35, 108, 115; John E. Riley, *From Sagebrush to Ivy: The Story of Northwest Nazarene College, 1913-1988* (Nampa, ID: Northwest Nazarene College, 1988), 72; Kirkemo, *For Zion's Sake*, 142-43. Critical of Winchester's approach to the aorist tense's defense of the second blessing is Randy Maddox, "The Use of the Aorist Tense in Holiness Exegesis," *Wesleyan Theological Journal* 16 (Fall 1981), 106-18.

27. Cagle, *Life and Work of Mary Lee Cagle*, 119. See also Mary King Snowbarger, oral history, edited by Willis Snowbarger, Nazarene Archives, 11. See Ingersol, "Christian Baptism and the Early Nazarenes," 24-38.

28. *Journal* of the Eastern Oklahoma District, 1924: 16-17, and the San Antonio District *Journal*, 1927: 36. Also see the Eastern Oklahoma District *Journal*, 1928: 22. Infant baptisms conducted by General Superintendent Williams are found in the *Journal* of the San Antonio District, 1921: 30, and, in the same, 1926: 26; also the *Journal* of the Western Oklahoma District, 1931: 31, and, in the same, 1934: 37. On an infant baptism conducted by Chapman, see the Western Oklahoma District *Journal*, 1929: 28. On Goodwin, see, in the same, 1932: 36; 1935: 45; and the San Antonio District *Journal*, 1936: 31.

29. Church of the Nazarene, *Manual*, 1936, 213-14.

30. *Herald of Holiness* (December 13,1922), 2; *Herald of Holiness* (August 2, 1922), 2; *Herald of Holiness* (January 10, 1923), 3; *Herald of Holiness* (February 7, 1923), 3; *Herald of Holiness* (November 5, 1945), 8.

31. S. S. White, "Jesus' Baptism," *Herald of Holiness* (May 6, 1959), 12-13. See also Martin E. Marty, "Baptistification Takes Over," *Christianity Today* (September 2, 1983), 33-36; Finke and Stark, *Churching of America*, 145-98; Rob L. Staples, *Outward Sign and Inward Grace: The Place of Sacraments in Wesleyan Spirituality* (Kansas City: Beacon Hill Press of Kansas City, 1991), 162; J. Kenneth Grider, "Holiness Baptistificaton," *Preacher's Magazine* (September/October/November 1996), 28.

32. Sandeen, *Roots of Fundamentalism*, 172-87. On Southern premillennialism see Stephens, *Fire Spreads*, 161-85. See Melvin E. Dieter, "The Post Civil War Holiness Revival: The Rise of the Camp Meeting Churches," in Wayne E. Caldwell, ed., *Reformers and Revivalists: The History of the Wesleyan Church* (Indianapolis: Wesley Press, 1992), 177-78; *Manual of the International Apostolic Holiness Church* (Cincinnati: God's Revivalist Press, 1916-19), 14, 17-18; Pilgrim Holiness Church, *Manual* (Indianapolis: Pilgrim Holiness Advocate, 1930), 20-21; Thomas and Thomas, *Days of Our Pilgrimage*, 16-17.

33. William B. Godbey, *Signs of His Coming* (Nashville: Pentecostal Mission Publishing Company, n.d.), is one of several books by Godbey setting forth his millennial views. Also see his obituary, *Pentecostal Herald* (September 29, 1920), 8. J. O. McClurkan adopted the "Eleventh Hour" terminology popularized by F. L. Chappell in *Chosen Vessels* (Repr., Salem, OH: Allegheny Wesleyan Methodist Connection, 1978), 191-99. See Haynes, *Tempest-Tossed on Methodist Seas*, 71-92.

34. C. B. Jernigan, *The World War in Prophecy* (N.p., n.d.) and *The Great Red Dragon and the Time of the End* (Bethany, OK: N.p., 1919). See the E. E. Angell Collection, "Sermons: 'S'" files, especially file 653-3, and prophecy clippings file, 701-10, and compare his sermon "The Day of the Lord (II Peter 3:10-14)" (file 651-19); B[asil] W. Miller and G[eorge] F. Owen, *Behold He Cometh: Inspirational Messages on the Second Coming* (Kansas City: Nazarene Publishing House, 1924); and Miller and Harding, *"Cunningly Devised Fables."*

35. See Hills, *Fundamental Christian Theology*, 2:339-60; Price, "Some Data on Miss Olive Winchester," 7-8; Price, "Dr. Wiley—Eminent Theologian," 3; Bangs, *Our Roots of Belief*, 72; Kirkemo, *For Zion's Sake*, 93; Raser, "Views on Last Things," 185. Nazarene theologian J. Kenneth Grider proposed a "realized millennialism" close to the amillenialist point of view, in *A Wesleyan-Holiness Theology* (Kansas City: Nazarene Publishing House, 1994), 535-40.

36. J. B. Chapman, "Nazarene Schools and Darwinism," *Herald of Holiness* (July 20, 1921), 3. See also J. B. Chapman, "The Atheism and Immorality of Evolution," *Herald of Holiness* (September 13, 1922), 1; J. B. Chapman and Basil W. Miller, *Evolution Has Failed* (Kansas City: Nazarene Publishing House, n.d.).

37. *Young People's Journal* (January 1931), 3-4; *Young People's Journal* (May 1931), 3-4; *Young People's Journal* (June 1931), 4; and other issues. The James Orr quote appeared in *Young People's Journal* (December 1931), 3.

38. See Hills, *Fundamental Christian Theology*, 1:263-79; Goodwin, "Lecture 14-15" (file 2101-14), Nazarene Archives; Wiley, *Christian Theology*, 1:454-58, 462-66. Likewise, Chapman, "The Question Box," *Herald of Holiness* (July 28, 1947).

39. A. M. Hills, "Who Was It That Was Progressing Backwards?" *Herald of Holiness* (February 22, 1922), 4-5.

40. A. M. Hills, "The Scofield Reference Bible Examined for the Nazarenes," *Herald of Holiness* (September 10, 1932), 3.

41. See J. B. Chapman: "Victories," *Herald of Holiness* (February 7, 1923); "We Cannot Hook Men for God with Question Marks," *Herald of Holiness* (September 30, 1925), 1; "The True Safe Guard Against the Inroads of Heresy," *Herald of Holiness* (October 7, 1925), 1; "Heresy and Apostasy," *Herald of Holiness* (September 28, 1927), 1; and, on the Scofield Bible, J. B. Chapman to Belle Simpson (January 23, 1941) (file 472-22).

42. See, for example, J. B. Chapman: "The Victories of the Fundamentalists," *Herald of Holiness* (February 7, 1923), 2; "Laying the Ax at the Root of the Tree," *Herald of Holiness* (February 27, 1924), 1; "Revivals, Spurious and Genuine," *Herald of Holiness* (January 14, 1925), 1; "Where Shall We Place the Emphasis?" *Herald of Holiness* (August 11, 1926), 1; "Heresy and Apostasy," *Herald of Holiness* (September 28, 1927), 1; *Journal of the Seventh General Assembly of the Church of the Nazarene* (Kansas City: Nazarene Publishing House, 1928), 45; J. B. Chapman, "What Is Fundamentalism?" *Herald of Holiness* (October 6, 1926), 1. On Machen see Hart, *Defending the Faith*.

43. W. R. Cain, "Fundamentalists," *Herald of Holiness* (November 21, 1923), 5.

44. S. S. White, "The Holiness School and Modernism," *Herald of Holiness* (January 16, 1924), 9; Cornell, "The Paramount Need of a World in Peril," *Herald of Holiness* (September 29, 1926); S. S. White, "The Holiness School and Fundamentalism," *Herald of Holiness* (August 22, 1928), 8-9. On essentialism see Floyd Cunningham, "Harold Sloan and Methodist Essentialism," *Asbury Theological Journal* (Spring 1987), 65-76.

45. See Goodwin, "Lecture Five," n.d. (file 2101-14), Nazarene Archives. "Articles of Religion," in the *Encyclopedia of World Methodism* (Nashville: United Methodist Publishing House, 1974) provides the Anglican and Methodist creeds laid out in parallel fashion. See 147-48 for the articles on Scripture. Also see Thomas Oden, *Doctrinal Standards in the Wesleyan Tradition* (Grand Rapids: Francis Asbury Press of Zondervan, 1988); Bassett, "Theological Identity of the North American Holiness Movement," 72-108.

46. Wiley, *Christian Theology*, 1:140-43. See Bassett, "Fundamentalist Leavening," 65-67. Wiley's master's thesis was a study of the prologue to John's Gospel, and "Logos" doctrine remained an important element in his thinking. On Wiley's influence on this matter, see Paul T. Culbertson, "A History of Nazarene Doctrinal Positions on Biblical Authority," 1975 Nazarene Theology Conference (file 729-37), 3-4. Culbertson was a close Wiley associate and states that all evidence indicates that "Wiley himself wrote Article IV."

47. See documents related to this case in file 887-6, Nazarene Archives.

48. Gilmore to Williams (November 20, 1935), file 503-15.

49. Gilmore to R. V. DeLong (November 24, 1935), DeLong papers, Northwest Nazarene U. Archives.

50. Douglas R. Chandler, *Pilgrimage of Faith: A Centennial History of Wesley Theological Seminary, 1882-1982*, ed. C. C. Goen (Cabin John, MD: Seven Locks Press, 1984), 130-31. See Gilmore to Guy McShane, Chairman, Board of Directors, NNC (June 5, 1935), Gilmore papers, Northwest Nazarene U. Archives; Gilmore to DeLong (September 10, 1935); DeLong to Gilmore (September 21, 1935); J. G. Morrison to R. V. DeLong (November 11, 1935), all in DeLong papers, Northwest Nazarene U.; Gilmore to R. V. DeLong (October 6, 1935) and Gilmore to Williams (November 4, 1935) (both in file 503-15), Nazarene Archives; Riley, *From Sagebrush to Ivy*, 97-105.

Chapter 13

1. See, for instance, A. M. Hills, "The Religious Influences of the Big College," *Herald of Holiness* (August 21, 1929). Good histories include Cameron, *Eastern Nazarene College*; Riley, *From Sagebrush to Ivy*; Kirkemo, *For Zion's Sake*; Gresham and Gresham, *From Many Came One*.

2. J. B. Chapman, "Educational Standards," *Herald of Holiness* (October 6, 1920), 5.

3. Smith, *Called unto Holiness*, 172, 257-58; Gresham and Gresham, *From Many Came One*, 35-38.

4. See Leona Bellew McConnell, "A History of the Town and College of Bethany, Oklahoma," M.A. thesis, U. of Oklahoma, 1935; Gresham and Gresham, *From Many Came One*.

5. Cameron, *Eastern Nazarene College*, 135-42; Smith, *Called unto Holiness*, chap. 11.

6. Cameron, *Eastern Nazarene College*, 118, 145.

7. Ibid., 152.

8. Bertha Munro, *The Years Teach: Remembrances to Bless: An Autobiography* (Kansas City: Beacon Hill Press of Kansas City, 1970).

9. Cameron, *Eastern Nazarene College*, 163.

10. Ibid., 194-96, 316, 319, 331-37.

11. Ibid., 227-40.

12. James P. Knott, *History of Pasadena College* (Pasadena: Pasadena College, 1960), 17-24; Kirkemo, *For Zion's Sake*.

13. Knott, *History of Pasadena College*, 26-34. See A. O. Hendricks to business manager, Pasadena College (May 1, 1954) (file 367-12).

14. Knott, *History of Pasadena College*, 35-62, 86-87; Kirkemo, *For Zion's Sake*, especially chaps. 8—9.

15. *Oasis* (1932), 104; [Bertha Dooley], *Northwest Nazarene College: Twenty-Five Years of Progress* (N.p., [1938]), 78.

16. *Oasis* (1931), 93; *Oasis* (1935), 94; *Oasis* (1936), 70; *Oasis* (1938), 98.

17. "Minutes of the Board of Regents, March 13, 1935," Gilmore papers, Northwest Nazarene U. Archives; Morrison to DeLong, Haverhill, Massachusetts (July 26, 1935), DeLong papers, Northwest Nazarene U. Archives.

18. *Oasis* (1930), 14, and, on bobbed hair, see the pictures in the same.

19. [Dooley], *Northwest Nazarene College*, 55; Purkiser, *Called unto Holiness*, 128-29.

20. Riley, *From Sagebrush to Ivy*, 83.

21. Ibid., 96.

22. Ibid., 93, 106.

23. *Oasis* (1932), 75-76.

24. [Dooley], *Northwest Nazarene College*, 53-55.

25. Ibid., 61; Riley, *From Sagebrush to Ivy*, 106.

26. Purkiser, *Called unto Holiness*, 125-27.

27. Wynkoop, *Trevecca Story*, 108-11.

28. The complex story is told in Wynkoop, *Trevecca Story*, 136-65.

29. Quadrennial Report of the Department of Foreign Missions, *Journal of the Tenth General Assembly*, 1940, 339-45.

30. Bessie Beals, "Annual Council Meeting, India, 1940," *Other Sheep* (September 1941), 17-18.

31. Orpha Cook, "A Visit at the Boy's School," *Other Sheep* (May 1940), 23-24.

32. Anderson, "Brief History of the Church of the Nazarene" (file 861-34); Parker, *Mission to the World*.

33. "Annual Station Report: Daming," 1923; Hinshaw, *Messengers of the Cross in China*, 75-81; Sutherland, *China Crisis*, 77-78. See also Robert Sutherland and John Sutherland, *Behind the Silence: The Story of Frank and Ann Sutherland* (Kansas City: Nazarene Publishing House, 1999).

34. A. J. Smith, *Jesus Lifting Chinese: Marvelous Spiritual Awakenings in China* (Cincinnati: God's Bible School and Revivalist, n.d.), 27-33, 55, 107; Smith to Reynolds (December 16, 1926, and January 10, [1927]). See Cunningham, *Holiness Abroad*, 159.

35. John Pattee, *Hazardous Days in China* (Pasadena, CA: the author), 39-43; Lillian Pattee, "Three Hour Testimony Meeting," *Other Sheep* (February 1941), 24; Osborn to Remiss Rehfeldt (February 5, 1955). See also C. Ellen Watts, *John Pattee of China and the Philippines* (Kansas City: Beacon Hill Press of Kansas City, 1984), 51-66; "Report of Committee on Memorials" (N.d. [received at headquarters December 16, 1938]); Wiese, "The Bible School Our Life Line," *Other Sheep* (April 1939), 24-25; Wiese, "Bible School Evangelistic Bands," *Other Sheep* (June 1939), 16-17; Sutherland, *China Crisis*, 77-81.

Chapter 14

1. Purkiser, *Called unto Holiness*, 98.
2. Esselstyn to J. G. Morrison (August 11, 1933) (file 634-15); Morrison, "Deals Remain," *Other Sheep* (February 1932), 3.
3. General leaders to Board of General Superintendents (January 19, 1932) and M. Lunn and J. G. Morrison to Board of General Superintendents (January 19, 1932) (both in file 453-40).
4. J. G. Morrison, "The Ax Begins to Cut" and "We Can and We Will," *Other Sheep* (October 1931), 2; Morrison, "The General Superintendents Call for Sacrifice," *Other Sheep* (November 1932), 2; Purkiser, *Called unto Holiness*, 86-89.
5. The story is told in G. B. Williamson, *Roy T. Williams: Servant of God* (Kansas City: Nazarene Publishing House, 1947), 80-82.
6. J. G. Morrison, "Shall the Clock Chime Victory? Or Toll Despair?" *Other Sheep* (March 1933), 2-3; Morrison, "Success in Spite of Depression," *Other Sheep* (March 1933), 6; Morrison, "A Threatening Situation," *Other Sheep* (September 1933), 4-5; Morrison, "The Precarious Condition of Mission Fields," *Other Sheep* (June 1934), 3.
7. *Herald of Holiness* (January 19, 1935), 6, 32, cited in Purkiser, *Called unto Holiness*, 105.
8. J. G. Morrison, "Special Thanksgiving Offering in November," *Other Sheep* (September 1934), 3; Morrison, "A Crusade for Souls," *Other Sheep* (March 1935), 2-3; Morrison, "The Crusade for Souls Sacrifice Offering Easter Sunday," *Other Sheep* (March 1935), 6-7; Purkiser, *Called unto Holiness*, 93, 105-7.
9. J. G. Morrison, "Our Task for 1936," *Other Sheep* (February 1936), 1; *Journal of the Tenth General Assembly* (N.p., [1940]), 313. Between 1920 and 1940 the Methodist Episcopal Church, the Methodist Episcopal Church, South, and the Protestant Methodist Church, which united in 1939 to form the Methodist Church, rose, collectively, from 6.14 to 7.36 million members, an increase of about 20 percent. For the Methodist figures see *Historical Statistics of the United States*, Part 1 (Washington, DC: Bureau of the Census, 1975), 389-92.
10. *Herald of Holiness* (October 20, 1920), 10, cited in Oster, *Serving Those Who Serve*, 19.
11. Purkiser, *Called unto Holiness*, 120-22.
12. Ibid., 120-22; Oster, *Serving Those Who Serve*, chaps. 1—4.
13. *Journal of the Fourth General Assembly* (1915), 58.
14. Oscar Hudson, "Thoughts on the European War," *Pentecostal Messenger* (October 1, 1914), 1-2, cited in Stan Ingersol, *Herald of Holiness* (October 15, 1986), 11; J. W. Goodwin, *Signs and Wonders*, 150; "Minutes of the Eleventh Annual Assembly of the New York District" (April 17-21, 1918), 15-16; Smith, *Called unto Holiness*, 279.
15. *Journal of the Tenth General Assembly* (1940), 179-80; C. W. Jones to E. E. Grosse (April 9, 1941) (file 920-62).
16. J. B. Chapman, "A Message to President Harding," *Herald of Holiness* (December 14, 1921), 2; Chapman, "Shall America Enter the World Court?" *Herald of Holiness* (November 7, 1923), 2; *Journal of the Tenth General Assembly* (1940), 176. For the broader issues see Joel A. Carpenter, *Revive Us Again: The Reawakening of American Fundamentalism* (New York: Oxford U. Press, 1997), 97-100, 104-5.
17. General Superintendents' Quadrennial Address, *Journal of the Tenth General Assembly*, 214.
18. *Journal of the Tenth General Assembly*, 205.
19. Ibid., 214.
20. Ibid., 217, see 203-24.
21. Frame to C. Warren Jones (September 18, 1941) (file 920-62); Orval Nease to C. Warren Jones (November 11, 1941); Sharpe to Williams (April 18, 1941). See Ford, *In the Steps of John Wesley*, 152-53, 209-10.
22. M. L. Sison, Gainsville, Texas, to Williams (April 19, 1942). No response is on file (534-7).
23. C. W. Jones to Paul C. French, National Service Board (April 9, 1941); S. T. Ludwig to Board of General Superintendents (January 5, 1942); Ludwig to O. J. Nease (January 5, 1942); H. C. Overmyer [National Service Board] to Jones (August 12, 1943); Jones to E. LeRoy Dakin [National Service Board for Religious Objectors] (February 9, 1944, and March 31, 1944); Dakin to Jones (March 23, 1944, and May 9, 1944); Dakin to Ludwig (October 12, 1945). The National

Service Board asked the Church of the Nazarene to contribute $12,712 for these men's stay in conscientious objector camps.

24. DeLong, "Colleges and National Defense," *Herald of Holiness* (July 26, 1941); letters in L. T. Corlett papers, Northwest Nazarene U. Archives.

25. *Ask Doctor Chapman* (Kansas City: Nazarene Publishing House, 1943), 191-92.

26. [D. Shelby Corlett], Editorial, *Herald of Holiness* (August 2, 1943); C. W. Jones to E. LeRoy Daken (March 31, 1944); *Nazarene Chaplain* (February 27, 1945).

27. *Twenty-Ninth Annual Assembly Journal of the San Antonio District Church of the Nazarene* (Kansas City: Nazarene Publishing House, 1942), 26.

28. Ishida Manabu, "Live Peace! A Commentary on the Confession of Responsibility of the Church of the Nazarene in Japan During the Second World War," English version published by the Department of Social Affairs of the Church of the Nazarene in Japan (Oyama-shi, July 1994), 55.

29. Quoted in Manabu, "Live Peace!" 47-48.

30. Fitkin, *Holiness and Mission*, 25.

31. Quoted in Manabu, "Live Peace!" 49. See also 13.

32. See Cunningham, *Holiness Abroad*, 118-24, for this and following section.

33. Kitagawa to Jones (October 25, 1939). See also Manabu, "Live Peace!" 51.

34. Eckel to Jones (March 22, 1938).

35. Cunningham, *Holiness Abroad*, 206-8.

36. Ibid., 208-9. See also Kang Sam Young, *A History of the Church of the Nazarene in Korea* (N.p., n.d.), translated by Lee So Young, Asia-Pacific Nazarene Theological Seminary, 1997.

37. Eckel to Jones (December 5, 1939). See Eckel to Jones (March 21, 1938) and the long letter of Eckel to Jones (March 11, 1939).

38. Eckel to Jones (March 11, 1939). But note Alice Spangenberg, *Oriental Pilgrim: Story of Shiro Kano* (Kansas City: Beacon Hill Press, 1948), 41-43.

39. See Manabu, "Live Peace!" 7.

40. Cunningham, *Holiness Abroad*, 121-22.

41. Isayama to Jones, August 24, 1941.

42. Cunningham, *Holiness Abroad*, 122-23.

43. Ibid., 124-25.

44. Spangenberg, *Oriental Pilgrim*; Cunningham, *Holiness Abroad*, 123-24.

45. Cunningham, *Holiness Abroad*, 125.

46. Ibid., 160.

47. Ibid., 161.

48. Translations of the Chinese letters (undated) are in file 453-29, Nazarene Archives; Cunningham, *Holiness Abroad*, 161.

49. Chapman, "To the China Mission Council," in a report to the general superintendents, Department of Foreign Mission and General Board, Church of the Nazarene, with a cover letter to [Emma] Word (December 31 [1935]); Cunningham, *Holiness Abroad*, 163.

50. Cunningham, *Holiness Abroad*, 166.

51. Katherine Wiese to Jones (November 28, 1946), World Mission office (reel 49); Cunningham, *Holiness Abroad*, 168.

52. Cunningham, *Holiness Abroad*, 169.

53. Orval Nease, "Foreign Visitation: 1948," 9.

54. Osborn to Swiss Consul General (June 25, 1942), which details the property holdings, assessed to be about $600,000 (file 453-29); Pattee, *Hazardous Days in China*, 72-82; Mary L. Scott, *Kept in Safeguard* (Kansas City: Nazarene Publishing House, 1977), 30-47; Cunningham, *Holiness Abroad*, 169.

55. John Pattee, "Effect of the War on the Churches of Chengan County," *Other Sheep* (October 1942), 11-12.

56. Cunningham, *Holiness Abroad*, 170-71.

57. Quoted in Holland B. London, *Wake Up, America* (Kansas City: Beacon Hill Press, 1946), 26.

58. *United Stewardship Council Statistics*, issued for 1942 (file 534-7).

59. *Quadrennial Reports to the Eleventh General Assembly,* 61, 66, 75; Jones to Miller (May 28, 1943); Miller to Jones (June 4, 1943) (file 920-62).

60. *Quadrennial Reports to the Eleventh General Assembly of the Church of the Nazarene* (N.p., [1944]), 102.

61. File 920-62.

62. "A Nazarene Manifesto" (file 1233-38).

63. Nease to Williams, March 18, 1942 (file 534-38).

64. D. S. C. [D. Shelby Corlett] to Nease (March 20, 1942).

65. See Purkiser, *Called unto Holiness,* 151-55.

66. Nease to "Dear Brother" (Board of General Superintendents) (May 15, 1944) (file 920-62).

67. General Superintendents' Address, *Quadrennial Reports to the Eleventh General Assembly of the Church of the Nazarene* (N.p., [1944]).

68. Quoted in Purkiser, *Called unto Holiness,* 155.

69. Ibid., 152.

70. Purkiser, *Called unto Holiness,* 155. See also H. V. Miller to R. T. Williams, March 29, 1944.

71. Purkiser, *Called unto Holiness,* 155.

72. Williams to Chapman (January 21, 1944, and February 3, 1944). See also H. V. Miller to Williams (March 29, 1944).

73. Williams to Board of General Superintendents (December 25, 1945).

74. See Corlett, *Spirit-Filled.*

Part III Introduction

1. David Fromkin, *In the Time of the Americans: The Generation That Changed America's Role in the World* (New York: Alfred A. Knopf, 1995), 427-28, 457-63.

2. Richard Pierard, "Pax Americana and the Evangelical Missionary Advance," in *Earthen Vessels: American Evangelicals and Foreign Missions, 1880-1980,* eds. Joel A. Carpenter and Wilbert R. Shenk (Grand Rapids: Eerdmans, 1990), 155-79.

3. William R. Hutchison, *Errand to the World: American Protestant Thought and Foreign Missions* (Chicago: U. of Chicago Press, 1987), 176-202.

4. Charles Forman, "A History of Foreign Mission Theory in America," in *American Missions in Bicentennial Perspective,* ed. R. Pierce Beaver (Pasadena, CA: Wiliam Carey, 1977), 103-6; Andrew Walls, "The American Dimension in the History of the Missionary Movement," in *Earthen Vessels,* 1-25.

5. Robert Wuthnow, *The Restructuring of American Religion: Society and Faith Since World War II* (Princeton, NJ: Princeton U. Press, 1988), 145-49, 182-83.

6. On demographics see Ken Armstrong, *Face to Face with the Church of the Nazarene* (Boulder, CO: Johnson, 1958), 7-17, and Robert L. Ingle, "The Changing Spatial Distribution of the Church of the Nazarene," MS thesis, Oklahoma State U., 1973.

7. Thornton, *Radical Righteousness,* 126-44.

Chapter 15

1. *Journal of the Twelfth General Assembly of the Church of the Nazarene,* eds. S. T. Ludwig and Greta Hamsher (N.p., [1948]), 162. See 154-56, 164.

2. *Herald of Holiness* (February 7, 1949), 5-6.

3. Jerald Johnson, *Hardy C. Powers: Bridge Builder* (Kansas City: Nazarene Publishing House, 1985), 31-58.

4. Samuel Young, "Hardy C. Powers," n.d., in Powers profile file.

5. Eugene Stowe to Williamson, n.d. (file 1234-11); Audrey J. Williamson, *Gideon: An Intimate Portrait* (Kansas City: Beacon Hill Press of Kansas City, 1983), 31-32.

6. C. T. Corbett, *Pioneer Builders: Men Who Helped Shaped the Church of the Nazarene in Its Formative Years* (Kansas City: Beacon Hill Press of Kansas City, 1976), 36-40.

7. *Herald of Holiness* (January 31, 1949); Vanderpool, "D. I. Vanderpool," written for Frank Watkin, n.d., in Vanderpool profile file; Emmalyn Vanderpool to S. T. Ludwig (April 30, 1958); *D. I. Vanderpool: His Stories and Anecdotes*, comp. Wilfred N. Vanderpool (Kansas City: Nazarene Publishing House, 1985).

8. Powers to Board of General Superintendents (November 29, 1950); Williamson to Board of General Superintendents (December 7, 1950).

9. Hugh C. Benner, "The Young Preacher and Home Missions," *Herald of Holiness* (February 11, 1953), 4; Corbett, *Pioneer Builders*, 13-18.

10. "Things GSs Do" (file 2304-21); Johnson, *Hardy C. Powers*, 51-58.

11. S. W. Strickland, "A Limited Episcopacy," *Preacher's Magazine* (January 1961), 13-15. Similarly, R. V. DeLong to W. E. Snowbarger (May 12, 1970) (file 492-27).

12. See also Joe Olson, "Meet Our Leaders," *Herald of Holiness* (March 12, 1952), 4-6; Johnson, *Hardy C. Powers*, 52, see 52-58, 74; Jerald Johnson to Audrey Williamson (May 10, 1985); David Whitelaw interview with Tommie Parrish (June 3, 2000).

13. Edward Lawlor, *The Covenant Supreme* (Kansas City: Beacon Hill Press, 1952), 21.

14. C. William Fisher, *Our Heritage and Our Hope* (Kansas City: Beacon Hill Press, 1958), 17, 19.

15. Purkiser, *Called unto Holiness*, 51-52; E. O. Chalfant, *Forty Years on the Firing Line* (Kansas City: Beacon Hill Press, 1951), 51-52, and throughout.

16. C. T. Corbett, *Our Pioneer Nazarenes* (Kansas City: Nazarene Publishing House, 1958), 91-96; Purkiser, *Called unto Holiness*, 52-53.

17. A. E. Sanner, *The Key Works: Story of the Nazarene Memorial Auditorium* (N.p., n.d.); Corbett, *Our Pioneer Nazarenes*, 103-8; Harold Sanner, "Church Planter Par Excellence," manuscript, 1988.

18. Some of these are described in Corbett, *Pioneer Builders*, 141-59.

19. Corbett, *Pioneer Builders*, 141-45.

20. *Getting the Glory Down: The Best Works of E. O. Chalfant and Selected Messages by Morris Chalfant*, comp. Morris Chalfant (N.p., n.d.).

21. *Herald of Holiness* (April 2, 1945), 12; *Louisiana District Bulletin* (August 1960); *Herald of Holiness* (January 28, 1970), 9. John Stockton, *Investments: Here and Hereafter* (Kansas City: Nazarene Publishing House, 1964), contains autobiographical information.

22. *Journal of the 19th General Assembly of the Church of the Nazarene*, ed. B. Edgar Johnson (1976), 468; Lunn, "Personal Forty-Year Report to the General Board" (February 1986).

23. *Herald of Holiness* (July 6, 1960), 14-15; Weekly Summary, Nazarene News Service (May 12, 1995).

24. *Herald of Holiness* News Supplement (June 1968), 1-2. See Edward Lawlor, "Yes, I Became a Protestant," tract (N.d.); "Eugene Stowe Accepts Seminary Presidency," *Herald of Holiness* (May 4, 1966), 18; Corbett, *Pioneer Builders*, 18-23.

25. "Guidelines for General Superintendents" (N.d.) (file 1233-38).

26. *Journal of the Eighteenth General Assembly of the Church of the Nazarene*, ed. B. Edgar Johnson ([Kansas City: Nazarene Publishing House, 1972]), 171-74; Jerald Johnson and Carol Zurcher, *Strickland Safari: A Legacy of Commitment and Service* (Kansas City: Nazarene Publishing House, 1993).

27. Edward Lawlor, "Our Traditional Concepts and Our Tomorrows" (October 7, 1975).

Chapter 16

1. General Superintendents, *Journal of the Twelfth General Assembly of the Church of the Nazarene* (N.p., [1948]), 163.

2. E.g., L. J. DuBois, "Democracy—Battleground of the Century," *Conquest* (July 1947), 4-7.

3. W. C. Esselstyn to Herbert A. Lord (May 17, 1954, and July 1, 1954) (file 699-5). For British Holiness Movement sentiment see Maynard James, "Antichrist," *Flame* (March-April 1949), 14-16.

4. Cunningham, *Holiness Abroad*, 172-74, which see for documentation for the above paragraphs.

5. Hugh C. Benner, "The 'Go' in the Gospel," in *For the Healing of the Nations: Ten Missionary Sermons*, comp. C. Warren Jones (Kansas City: Beacon Hill Press, 1954), 50; Rehfeldt, "The Verdict Is Yours" (file 1382-9); Eleuterio Pitong, "From Communism to Christ," *Other Sheep* (July 1952), 11; E. S. Phillips to whom it may concern, August 21, 1967 (file 567-8). See also London, *Wake Up, America*, 26; Shelby Corlett, "Christianity and Communism," *Herald of Holiness* (June 16, 1947); Stephen S. White, "Communism with a Capital 'C,'" *Herald of Holiness* (January 2, 1952), 12; C. Warren Jones, "Our Foreign Policy," *Other Sheep* (January 1955), 3; Darold Wilson and Gerdonna Wilson, *Questions of a Nazarene Layman* (N.p., n.d.), 34-35.

6. Report of the Commission on Communism (file 1007-13), Nazarene Archives.

7. H. T. Reza, *Through a Long Tunnel: A Story of Survival in Cuba* (Kansas City: Nazarene Publishing House, 1976), 60; H. T. Reza, *After the Storm, the Rainbow: The Church of the Nazarene in Cuba* (Kansas City: Nazarene Publishing House, 1993), 36, 50-51.

8. DeLong, *What We Can Do About Communism* (N.p., 1963), 89, see 74, 75-78, 81. Similarly, Mendell Taylor, *America at the Crossroads: A Religious Heritage to Be Preserved* (Kansas City: Beacon Hill Press of Kansas City, 1965).

9. Notebook of H. A. Wiese (file 2069-25). See also Mary Li, "Autobiographical Statement" (November 4, 1990) (file 1269-27).

10. Carl Bangs, *The Communist Encounter* (Kansas City: Beacon Hill Press, 1963), 67, 75-79, 83, 91-93; Wilson and Wilson, *Questions of a Nazarene Layman*, 6-12, 52-54. See also Timothy L. Smith, "The Case for Compassion," *Seminary Tower* (Fall 1963), 5-6.

11. George Coulter to H. C. Powers [1962] (file 2131-44).

12. James Kratz, [Annual Report] (October 16, 1961) (file 409-1a).

13. Hynd, "Holiness and Race Relations" (N.p., n.d.) (file 457-17); George Frame, *Blood Brother of the Swazis: The Life Story of David Hynd* (Kansas City: Beacon Hill Press, 1952), 16; "A Pioneer Steps Aside," *Other Sheep* (January 1962), 3-6; Hilda Kuper, *Sobhuza II: Ngwenyama and King of Swaziland* (London: Duckworth, 1978), 210, 217, 220, 305.

14. Jerald Johnson to D. H. Spencer (December 13, 1974). See Ephraim Dlamini profile file; Johnson to Spencer, March 7, 1975; Eastern Nazarene College, *Christian Scholar* (March 1978).

15. George Coulter to E. S. Phillips (December 22, 1965); E. S. Phillips to Enrique Rosales (May 20, 1966); David Sol to E. S. Phillips (September 20, 1966); H. T. Reza and others, *Missions: Both Sides of the Coin: Mexico, American Indian, Home Missions Fields* (Kansas City: Nazarene Publishing House, 1973), 26-27; Moises Esperilla, *South of the Border*, trans. Susan Hayes (Kansas City: Nazarene Publishing House, 1981), 88-90.

16. File 777-14; Esperilla, *South of the Border*, 88-90.

17. "Welcome Home, Hugh Friberg," *World Mission* (October 1976), 13; "The Mission World," *World Mission* (December 1976), 22.

18. Alex B. Patterson profile file; Trevecca Nazarene College *Messenger* (Winter 1972).

19. Elizardo Urizar Leal profile file.

20. *Herald of Holiness* (April 16, 1952), 20; "Orange Juice as White House Beverage Urged on 'Ike,'" *Herald of Holiness* (February 4, 1953), 14; S. S. White, "President Eisenhower," *Herald of Holiness* (October 26, 1955), 12.

21. Jenkins, "Contending for the Faith" (October 23, 1960) (file 646-50).

22. S. T. Ludwig to T. E. Martin (October 25, 1960). For other pro-Nixon sentiment see Norman Oke, "Books in Review," *Herald of Holiness* (August 31, 1960), 11; Wilson Lanpher, "Symbol of Protestant Amiability," *Herald of Holiness* (August 31, 1960), 17-18.

23. Samuel Young to Roger Mann (May 17, 1961), in response to Mann to Young (May 8, 1961); Mann to Dean Wessels (April 21, 1961, and May 6, 1961) (file 1384-23).

24. *Oasis* (Nampa, Idaho: Northwest Nazarene College, 1968), 166; *Oasis* (1969), 178; Bev Snowden, "America, My America," *Conquest* (August 1969), 1; *Miami News* (June 16, 1972); Kirkemo, *For Zion's Sake*, 290-92. For example, Martha Ludwig Keys, see Esther Stineman, *American Political Women: Contemporary and Historical Profiles* (Littleton, CO: Libraries Unlimited, 1980), 91-93.

25. Richard Schubert profile file; John Kenyon, "Gentle Man of Steel," *Christian Herald* (October 1981), 48, 52-54.

26. Purkiser, "The Answer Corner," *Herald of Holiness* (October 28, 1964).

27. Cited in *Hallelujah March: 75 Years of the Church of the Nazarene in West Texas (1908-1983)* (Lubbock, TX: Duncan Press, 1982), 66.

28. Charles Yell, "Viet Nam Victory," *Conquest* (February 1967), 38; "At Ease: Viet Nam—A Soldier's Point of View," *Conquest* (January 1968), 32-33, 41.

29. C. William Fisher, *Our Goal Is Excellence: A Compilation of Radio Messages* (Kansas City: Beacon Hill Press of Kansas City, 1971), 25.

30. Susan Hagman to Willis Snowbarger, May 6, 1969 (file 499-1). See also, e.g., Paul M. Bassett, "Proper Principles and Social Action: Strange Bedfellows," *Herald of Holiness* (January 2, 1968), 3-4; Mary Augsbury, "On Narrowing the Generation Gap," *Herald of Holiness* (August 7, 1968), 4; Jim Bond, "Ask Jim," *Conquest* (December 1970), 20-21.

31. Ford, *In the Steps of John Wesley,* 152-53, 209-10. See also Donald Dayton and Lucille Dayton, "An Historical Survey of Attitudes Toward War and Peace Within the American Holiness Movement," paper presented at a seminar on Christian Holiness and the Issues of War and Peace, June 7-9, 1973, 24-25; Timothy L. Smith, "The Holy Spirit and Peace," in *Perspectives on Peacemaking: Biblical Options in the Nuclear Age,* ed. John A. Bernbaum (Ventura, CA: Regal, 1984), 103-5.

32. Mildred Bangs Wynkoop, *John Wesley: Christian Revolutionary* (Kansas City: Beacon Hill Press of Kansas City, 1970), 14, 47-48. Cf. Timothy L. Smith, "On Secular Aspirations to Perfection and Wesleyan Christianity's Response," *Centrifuge* (August 1969), 4 (file 499-7).

33. "Serving the Colored Within Our Gates," *Herald of Holiness* (June 1, 1960), 9. For much of what follows see Roger Bowman, *Color Us Christian: The Story of the Church of the Nazarene Among America's Blacks* (Kansas City: Nazarene Publishing House, 1975). Also compare Cheryl J. Sanders, *Saints in Exile: The Holiness-Pentecostal Experience in African American Religion and Culture* (New York: Oxford U. Press, 1996); James E. Massey, "Race Relations and the American Holiness Movement," *Wesleyan Theological Journal* 31 (1996): 40-50. See Paul Pitts, Alabama district superintendent, to C. Warren Jones, January 8, 1941, on the possibility of several Churches of God in Christ led by S. H. Smith joining the Church of the Nazarene.

34. "Policy Covering the Setup and Organization for the Colored Work as Authorized by the General Assembly" (file 195-50); John W. Oliver, "Reaching the Colored People," address delivered at Ministerial Convention, Jonesboro, Arkansas, April 13-15, 1949 (file 199-43). For earlier evidence of concern toward African-Americans see A. S. London, "The Christian Religion and the Negro," *Other Sheep* (May 1940), 9.

35. "By-Laws" (file 602-29); "Nazarene Bible Institute," June 23, 1949, and Hale to District Superintendent (June 9, 1949) (file 195-50); Benner papers (file 2304-21); Hale to R. W. Hurn (July 24, 1972, and August 13, 1972) (file 199-41); Hale to Mr. and Mrs. Philip Juergens (December 1, 1973), and "Autobiographical Notes" (file 1071-17).

36. Hale to S. T. Ludwig (July 21, 1948) (file 195-49); Hale to Ludwig (October 3, 1949) (file 195-50); Third Annual Board Meeting of the Trustees of Nazarene Bible Institute (January 9, 1951) (file 906-11); Nazarene Training College Board of Trustee Minutes (January 8, 1952), and Annual Report of R. W. Cunningham (January 13, 1959) (file 602-29); "United States Negro" (file 199-49); Willis Snowbarger, "Report on Visit to Nazarene Bible Institute, October 17-20, 1965" (file 492-25).

37. Roy F. Smee, S. T. Ludwig, and Alpin P. Bowes, *Enlarge Thy Borders: The Story of Home Missions in the Church of the Nazarene* (Kansas City: Nazarene Publishing House, 1952), 59; Alpin Bowes, "Evangelizing the Negro," *Herald of Holiness* (February 11, 1953), 9; "Gulf Central District Assembly," *Herald of Holiness* (May 27, 1959), 14.

38. S. T. Ludwig to C. C. Johnson (March 23, 1949); "United States Negro" (file 199-49); E. E. Hale to R. W. Hurn (July 24, 1972); Warren Rogers, "Bishop C. P. Jones" [1972] (file 199-42).

39. Elbert Dodd to D. I. Vanderpool (November 6, 1950). See Elbert Dodd to S. T. Ludwig (December 7, 1944); D. A. Murray to Paul Pitts (October 22, 1950); M. M. Snyder to H. C. Powers (December 29, 1950); M. M. Snyder to D. I. Vanderpool (January 29, 1951).

40. C. S. Goodwill to J. D. Saxon (file 906-11); J. D. Saxon to D. I. Vanderpool (November 30, 1950); C. S. Goodwill to J. D. Saxon (December 2, 1950); J. D. Saxon to Roy Smee (February 17, 1951); Alpin Bowes to D. I. Vanderpool (February 21, 1951).

41. Alpin Bowes, "Colored Work Conference," *Herald of Holiness* (April 1, 1953), 15; "Gulf Central District Assembly," *Herald of Holiness* (May 27, 1959), 14.

42. "United States Negro" (file 199-49); file 199-50; Warren Rogers and Kenneth Vogt, *From Sharecropper to Goodwill Ambassador* (Kansas City: Beacon Hill Press of Kansas City, 1979), 33-39, 45-46.

43. Warren Rogers to Alpin Bowes (March 4, 1964); Rogers to Fred Hawk (August 21, 1964) (file 199-3); file 199-51; Rogers, *Sharecropper*, 35.

44. *Herald of Holiness* (July 10, 1968), 17; Rogers, *Sharecropper*, 45-46, 50, 54-55, 63-65.

45. E. E. Hale, Report of the President (January 13, 1953, and January 1954); Special Meeting of Board of Trustees (February 24, 1954); Report of R. W. Cunningham (January 10, 1956, and January 13, 1959) (all in file 602-29).

46. Report of R. W. Cunningham (1965 and March 21, 1966) (file 602-29); *1965-66 Catalogue* (file 492-25); Willis Snowbarger, "Report on Visit to Nazarene Bible Institute, October 17-20, 1965" (file 492-25); Annual Meeting, Board of Trustees (April 10, 1967) (file 602-29); Cunningham, Report (November 26, 1968); *Christian Scholar* (February 1969), 1.

47. Meeting of the Home Missions Department, September 16, 1968, in *Proceedings of the General Board* (Kansas City: N.p., 1969), 33; Special Meeting of the Board of Trustees of Nazarene Training College (January 16, 1969) (file 602-29); file 199-44.

48. Bowman, *Color Us Christian*, 59-63; *Home Missions Alert!* (1977).

49. Harper L. Cole, "A Study of the Governance Style of A. B. Mackey, President of Trevecca Nazarene College, 1936-1963," Ed.D. diss., Oklahoma State U., 1978, 176.

50. "United States Negro" (file 199-49); Census of Non-White Students in Nazarene Colleges (December 1, 1970) (file 199-41); "Rogers Chapel" (file 199-51).

51. Alpin Bowes to Warren Rogers (September 8, 1964) (file 199-3); Wynkoop, *Trevecca Story*, 210, 220.

52. *Darda* (Nashville: Trevecca, 1972), 98.

53. *Darda* (1973), 205, 261; *Darda* (1974), 107.

54. Darrell Garwood, *Crossroads of America: The Story of Kansas City* (New York: Norton, 1948), 304-5.

55. *Journal of the Twelfth General Assembly*, 61.

56. Purkiser, *Called unto Holiness*, 241-43.

57. M. A. Lunn to V. H. Lewis (September 3, 1964); Memo to Board of Publication (September 11, 1964); and "Nazarene" (N.d.) (file 971-35).

58. Purkiser, *Called unto Holiness*, 274-75.

59. 1956 Nazarene *Manual*, 325-26; Rogers, *Sharecropper*, 38.

60. Michael S. Lenrow and others, *Fair Housing: An Overview with Special Reference to Kansas City, Missouri* (Kansas City: Institute for Community Studies, 1968), 11-16; A. Theodore Brown and Lyle W. Dorsett, *K.C.: A History of Kansas City, Missouri*, 256-58, 266-67; Sherry L. Schirmer and Richard McKinzie, *At the River's Bend: An Illustrated History of Kansas City* (Marceline, MO: Walsworth, 1982), 215-19. See Albert Harper, "Toward Christian Understanding," *Herald of Holiness* (February 3, 1965), 5-6.

61. "Kansas City Park Avenue" (file 199-51).

62. "30th Anniversary: First Church of the Nazarene, Kansas City, Missouri: 1911-1941" (file 755-2); *Journal of the Twelfth General Assembly*, 64; *Kansas City Times* (July 25, 1955, and August 25, 1955) (file 775-44); Charles Jones, "Holiness Worship" (1976), 15 (file 1016-2).

63. Kansas City First Church Board Meeting Minutes (February 8, 1971, and June 29, 1971) (file 1255-21); Howard Hamlin, notes (file 693-52); *Kansas City Star* (January 2, 1977) (file 775-44).

64. O. J. Finch, Kansas District Superintendent, to Louise R. Chapman (November 11, 1943); "Biracial Program Begun at Kankakee Church," *Herald of Holiness* (January 22, 1969), 15 (file 199-51).

65. "Lift Up Thy Prayer for Our United States Negro Work," n.d. (file 199-39); D. I. Vanderpool to R. T. Williams Jr. (November 8, 1956); R. T. Williams Jr. to D. I. Vanderpool (January 8, 1957); "United States Negro" (N.d.) (file 199-49); John Eppler, "Nazarene Minister Defends Role in City Sanitation Controversy," *Reveille Echo* 41 (November 13, 1969), 1-2; Hugh E. Cosby, "One of the Church Leaders in the Oklahoma City Area," *Reveille Echo* (n.d.); obituary, *Daily Oklahoman* (May 21, 1995).

66. *Herald of Holiness* (June 25, 1958), 14; "Building for Eternity: 1908 to 1958; Our Golden Anniversary: First Church of the Nazarene, Saint Louis, Missouri, 1958" (file 775-52); "Five New Negro Churches," *Herald of Holiness* (October 15, 1969), 13-14 (file 199-51).

67. "United States Negro" (files 199-3, 199-49, 199-51 and 199-52); *Herald of Holiness* (August 13, 1969), 13.

68. *South Arkansas District Twenty-First Annual Assembly Journal* (1973), 39; Paul Holderfield and Kathy Tharp, *Brother Paul: The Paul Holderfield Story* (Kansas City: Beacon Hill Press of Kansas City, 1981), 9-10, 21-23, 29.

69. Polly Appleby, *What Color Is God's Skin? Stories of Ethnic Leaders in America* (Kansas City: Beacon Hill Press of Kansas City, 1984), 28-42; Neil B. Wiseman, "Charles Johnson's Legacy of Leadership," *Grow* (Fall 2005), 42-45; Ida Brown, "Pioneers Remember Struggle for King's Dream," *Meridian Star* (January 14, 2007).

70. Vernon Thomas to S. T. Ludwig (December 29, 1945) (file 195-48); [Cora] Mann to R. W. Hurn (October 10, 1972); "50th Anniversary: The Beulah Church of the Nazarene, 1974," brochure (file 775-71); Dallas Mucci, "Anatomy of a Congregation," *World Mission* (November 1987), 2-3; "Taking Their Mission Seriously: Brooklyn Beulah Celebrated 80 Years," *Grow* (Summer 2004): 47-49.

71. Robert Goslaw to Alpin Bowes (May 6, 1964) (file 199-7); Clarence Jacobs, "Personal Evangelism in the City," in *Black Evangelism—Which Way from Here?* comp. R. W. Hurn (Kansas City: Nazarene Publishing House, 1974), 37-45; Clarence Jacobs and Alpin Bowes, *From Jamaica to New York City* (Kansas City: Nazarene Publishing House, 1989); files 199-50 and 199-51.

72. "United States Negro" (file 199-49); files 199-3, 199-51, and 199-52. "Five New Negro Churches," *Herald of Holiness* (October 15, 1969), 13-14; James F. Kay, "New Hope in Watts," *Herald of Holiness* (June 26, 1968), 12-13. See also file 199-50.

73. For Bresee, see file 367-12, Nazarene Archives; for Fitkin, *Trip to Africa*, 12, 42. See also Ronley Bedart, "What Holiness Means to Race Relations," *Nazarene Preacher* (November 1971), 5-7, 45.

74. Clarence Barrows to D. I. Vanderpool (February 6, 1953); Milton Bunker to D. I. Vanderpool (February 9, 1953).

75. F. O. Parr, *Perfect Love and Race Hatred* (privately printed, [1964]), 90.

76. Ibid., 83.

77. Ibid., 81. See Harper, "Toward Christian Understanding," 6.

78. Parr, *Perfect Love,* 84-85.

79. Ibid., 23, 86.

80. Wendell Wellman, "A Sick Society: Condition, Cause and Cure," *Herald of Holiness* (October 9, 1968), 7; Guy Nees, "The Role of the Church in Today's Social Revolution," *Herald of Holiness* (February 12, 1964), 5-6. See also Timothy L. Smith, "Christians and the Crisis of Race," *Christianity Today* (September 29, 1958), 6-8; Ross W. Hayslip, "What Is the Social Gospel?" *Herald of Holiness* (March 12, 1969), 7.

81. *Herald of Holiness* (February 12, 1964), 5-6.

82. "Strong Race Relations Stand Considered," *Herald of Holiness* Supplement (June 1968), 6.

83. See *Herald of Holiness* (July 16, 1969), 14.

84. "Black Outreach Report" (January 12, 1973) (file 199-41); see file 199-7.

85. Michael Haynes, "Three Minutes to Midnight: The Evangelical and Racism," *Evangelical Missions Quarterly* (Fall 1968), 5; Sanders, *Saints in Exile,* 103.

86. "Memorandum to Missionaries" [about 1968] (file 770-12).

87. W. C. Esselstyn to Herbert A. Lord (May 17, 1954, and July 1, 1954) (file 699-5). Cf. Betty L. Emslie, *Continent in a Hurry: A Study of Nazarene Missions in Southern Africa* (Kansas City: Nazarene Publishing House, 1966), 15.

88. Hynd to Powers (August 27, 1949) (file 2304-21). See Hynd, "Holiness and Race Relations" (N.p., n.d.) (file 457-17).

89. David Hynd, *Africa Emerging* (Kansas City: Nazarene Publishing House, 1959), 88-89, 110, 126. See Charles Strickland's explanation of the social situation in his *African Adventure* (Kansas City: Nazarene Publishing House, 1959), 25-33.

90. [James], "My Meeting with Dr. Banda," *Flame* (May-June 1960), 26-28. See Noble, *Called to Be Saints*, 235.

91. Tarrant, "Answer," *Flame* (September-October), 1960, 20. See "Segregation or Integration—Which?" *Flame* (May-June 1961), 28-29 and (November-December 1961) 14-15; and see Box 218, Nazarene Theological College, Manchester.

92. *Miami News* (June 22, 1972).

93. Johnson and Zurcher, *Strickland Safari*, 66-67.

94. Cf. Al Truesdale, "Christian Holiness and the Problem of Systemic Evil," *Wesleyan Theological Journal* 19 (Spring 1984), 47-54.

Chapter 17

1. *Quadrennial Reports to the Eleventh General Assembly of the Church of the Nazarene* (N.p., [1944]), 75, 102; Jones, "A Plain Statement of Facts," *Other Sheep* (March 1947), 1; "The Woman's Foreign Missionary Society of the Church of the Nazarene," 12 [1948] (file 423-7); *Other Sheep* (July 1949), 17; *Other Shee*, (July 1950), 17. See Russell V. DeLong, *We Can If We Will: The Challenge of World Evangelism* (Kansas City: Nazarene Publishing House, 1947); *Herald of Holiness* (February 11, 1959), 3-4; Parker, *Mission to the World*, 635.

2. C. Warren Jones, *Look on the Fields* (Kansas City: Nazarene Publishing House, 1950), 91. See likewise "The Woman's Foreign Missionary Society of the Church of the Nazarene," 12 [1948] (file 423-7); Hardy C. Powers, "The Church at Home and Abroad," *Herald of Holiness* (March 12, 1952), 3.

3. *Missionary Policy: Department of Foreign Missions, General Board, Church of the Nazarene* (Kansas City: N.p., 1951), 5-6, 46-48; Benner, "The 'Go' in the Gospel," 50.

4. Hardy C. Powers, *"Pilot Points" of the Church of the Nazarene* (Kansas City: Nazarene Publishing House, [1958]), 18.

5. Hugh C. Benner, *Rendezvous with Abundance* (Kansas City: Beacon Hill Press, 1958), 116-17.

6. "Pilot Point Revisited," *Herald of Holiness* (November 26, 1958), 4-7.

7. Jones, "Our Foreign Policy," *Other Sheep* (January 1955), 3. Compare Harold Lindsell, *Missionary Principles and Practice* (Westwood, NJ: Fleming H. Revell, 1955), 163-64, 205-76.

8. Evelyn M. Witthoff, *Oh Doctor! The Story of Nazarene Missions in India* (Kansas City: Nazarene Publishing House, 1962), 43, 83-88, and D. Kharat, "Hospital Evangelism," *Other Sheep* (May 1965), inside back cover.

9. Bronell Greer, "Nazarene Troika," mimeographed [1969], Part Three, "Evangelism and the Evangelist," 31-32. See Greer, "Nazarene Troika," Part One, "Manual," 47; Part Two, "Missionary Policy," 51, 53, 60, 63-65, 69, 73, 75-76; Part Three, 20-21, 23-24, 25-26, 31-34.

10. Ernesto Bello, "Nuestra Iglesia Ante La Condicion Politica y Social de Nuestro Tiempo" (December 1-5, 1969) (file 553-9).

11. In DeLong, *We Can If We Will*, 191, 197-98. See likewise Esselstyn, *Nazarene Missions in South Africa*, 78-90.

12. G. B. and Audrey Williamson, *Yesu Masiki Jay: A First Hand Survey of Nazarene Missionary Progress in India* (Kansas City: Beacon Hill Press, 1952), 65-66.

13. G. B. Williamson, *Preaching Scriptural Holiness* (Kansas City: Beacon Hill Press, 1953), 49.

14. G. B. Williamson, "Will Democracy Live?" sermon (file 1234-1). See also G. B. Williamson, "Christian Education in Foreign Fields," in C. Warren Jones, ed., *Missions for Millions* (Kansas City: Nazarene Publishing House, 1948), 14-15; G. B. Williamson, "The Mission of the Church," *Preacher's Magazine* (January 1954), 7-8; G. B. Williamson, *The Labor of Love: Evangelism in the Local Church* (Kansas City: Beacon Hill Press, 1955), 5. Compare Hutchison, *Errand to the World*, 97-111.

15. David Hynd, "The Healing Urge of the Church," in *For the Healing of the Nations*, 72-73. See David Hynd, "The Holy Spirit and Healing," *Herald of Holiness* (March 10, 1954), 21; Hynd, *Africa Emerging*, 66-70, 75, 118-23. See also "Special Medical Study Committee" (May 4-5, 1973) (file 1357-22).

16. Smee, Ludwig, and Bowes, *Enlarge Thy Borders,* 66-67. See also Purkiser, *Called unto Holiness,* 197-200, 300.
17. Smee, Ludwig, and Bowes, *Enlarge Thy Borders,* 20.
18. File 568-4.
19. *Journal of the Twelfth General Assembly* (Kansas City: N.p., [1948]), 253; Purkiser, *Called unto Holiness,* 228-33; Chapman, "The Revival I Need," reprinted in *Grow* (Summer 1996), 12; Floyd Cunningham interview with Alpin Bowes (June 9, 1999) (transcripts in Nazarene Archives).
20. See *All Out for Souls,* ed. Russell V. DeLong (Kansas City: Nazarene Publishing House, [1947]); "The Meeting on Personal Evangelism" (September 16, 1947) (file 920-62); Harvey S. Galloway, "Sixth Quadrennial WFMS Convention," *Other Sheep* (September 1948), 14-16; Mendell Taylor, *Exploring Evangelism: History, Methods, Theology* (Kansas City: Nazarene Publishing House, 1964), 636.
21. Albert Harper and Elmer Kauffman, *First Steps in Visitation Evangelism* (Kansas City: Nazarene Publishing House, 1948), 14, 18, 54-57, 60, 67, 82-90. See also D. Shelby Corlett, *Soul Winning Through Visitation Evangelism* (Kansas City: Nazarene Publishing House, 1948); Stephen S. White, "Home Missions and Evangelism," *Herald of Holiness* (February 11, 1953), 13; Roy F. Smee, "Evangelism in Pastoral Calling," *Preacher's Magazine* (March 1954), 9-11. For Kauffman, see *This Life: The Whole Family's Magazine,* ed. Arvin A. Scharer, vol. 1, 3 (1940), 73 (file 628-8).
22. Harold Reed, *You and Your Church* (Kansas City: Beacon Hill Press, n.d.), 17. See Thomas A. Ainscough, "Seeking the Lost," *Other Sheep* (May 1949), 4; Alpin P. Bowes, ed., *He That Winneth Souls: Illustrations of Personal Evangelism in the Mid-Century Crusade for Souls* (Kansas City: Nazarene Publishing House, 1950); Remiss Rehfeldt, "Crusade Now," *Other Sheep* (April 1953), 1-2; J. W. Ellis, *We Are Witnesses* (Kansas City: Beacon Hill Press, 1956); Harriette Kelly, "How I Became a Nazarene," *Herald of Holiness* (November 27, 1957), 11; D. I. Vanderpool, "World Invasion," *Herald of Holiness* (December 2, 1959), 1.
23. *Herald of Holiness* (March 5, 1958), 31.
24. George Coulter, *The Crusade for Souls and the Standards of the Church* (Kansas City: Nazarene Publishing House, 1953), 15 pp. See also Lawlor, *Covenant Supreme.* Dean Kelley came to similar conclusions about the relation between strict boundaries and growth in *Why Conservative Churches Grow: A Study in Sociology of Religion* (New York: Harper and Row, 1972), 119-29.
25. V. H. Lewis, "Evangelism," *Preacher's Magazine* (April 1958), 26; Jimmy Dobson, "A Plea for and a Defense of the Traditional Nazarene Revival," *Preacher's Magazine* (May 1961), 26-29. See also Fletcher Spruce, *Revive Us Again* (Kansas City: Nazarene Publishing House, 1953).
26. Paula Greer, *Herald of Holiness* (April 14, 1947), 14; Andres Valenzuela, *Other Sheep* (January 1969), 6-8.
27. *Herald of Holiness* (February 15, 1977), 32.
28. C. William Fisher, "Why the Double Standard?" *Herald of Holiness* (November 12, 1958), 4-5; Mendell Taylor, "A Tribute to Dr. James McGraw," September 20, 1977, in James McGraw profile file; Paul Martin, *Get Up and Go: Devotions for Teens* (Kansas City: Beacon Hill Press of Kansas City, 1966), and Paul Martin, *The Holy Spirit Today* (Kansas City: Beacon Hill Press of Kansas City, 1970), and also see Paul Martin's profile file; C. Hastings Smith profile file; "Weekly Summary," Nazarene News Service (November 20, 1992).
29. Nettie Miller, "I Am a Preacher," *Conquest* (June 1947), 42-43; Nettie Miller, *Trumpets in the Camp* (Kansas City: Beacon Hill Press, 1949); *Flame* (March-April 1949), 31; Chapman, *Footprints in Africa,* 54-56; Emslie, *With Both Hands;* "Tribute to C. Helen Mooshian," *Convention Herald* (May/June 2003), 8-9, 11; C. Helen Mooshian, *His Ambassador* (N.p., n.d.); Estelle Crutcher profile file; Doris McDowell profile file; Kirkemo, *For Zion's Sake,* 183-84, 193; Eleanor Cunningham, "Remarkable Lady: Doris M. McDowell," *New Horizens* (Summer 1993), 5.
30. Juliet Ndzimandze, "All I Am I Give to God," *Other Sheep* (September 1971); Chuck Gailey, *Daughter of Africa: The Story of Juliet Ndzimandze* (Kansas City: Nazarene Publishing House, 1998), 32, 37, 43-44, 53, 55; Paul S. Dayhoff, comp., *Living Stones in Africa: Pioneers of the Church of the Nazarene,* rev. ed. (N.p., 1999), 13-16.
31. John Oster, "History of Home Missions: A Research Document," May 1979. On Smee also see Mendell Taylor, *Fifty Years of Nazarene Missions,* vol. 3: *World Outreach Through Home Missions* (Kansas City: Beacon Hill Press, 1958), 29-30.

32. H. C. Powers to David Hynd (September 16, 1949); Johnson, *Hardy C. Powers,* 59-72. See Taylor, *Fifty Years of Nazarene Missions,* vol. 3.

33. *Herald of Holiness* (July 6, 1960), 21; Roy Smee to "Pastor" (December 2, 1960); Samuel Young to Alpin Bowes (July 26, 1961); Alpin Bowes to Samuel Young (December 18, 1962); Oster, "History of Home Missions," 82-94.

34. "Powers Cites Primacy of Call to Evangelize," *Herald of Holiness* (July 6, 1960), 20; Roy Smee to All Superintendents (February 23, 1961); "Study of Churches Organized per Quadrennia" (N.d.) (file 1384-13); Taylor, *Exploring Evangelism,* 640.

35. "Review First Four Years in Area of Evangelism," *Herald of Holiness* (July 6, 1960), 20; V. H. Lewis, *The Church—Winning Souls* (Kansas City: Nazarene Publishing House, 1960), 57, 68; Oster, "History of Home Missions," 72 ff.; Cunningham interview with Alpin Bowes.

36. Raymond W. Hurn, *Mission Possible: A Study of the Mission of the Church of the Nazarene* (Kansas City: Nazarene Publishing House, 1973), 82.

37. Paul Orjala, *Get Ready to Grow: Principles of Church Growth* (Kansas City: Beacon Hill Press of Kansas City, 1978), 63-70. See Raymond W. Hurn, *The Rising Tide: New Churches for the New Millennium* (Kansas City: Beacon Hill Press of Kansas City, 1997), 48, 52-53.

38. "The Institutionalization of Home Missions," from a manuscript prepared by the Department of Home Missions; Johnson, *Hardy C. Powers,* 62; Noble, *Called to Be Saints,* 275-76.

39. *Arkansas Democrat* (September 24, 1949), 7; *Pine Bluff Commercial* (October 11, 1958); *Arkansas Democrat* (October 1, 1960), 4 (in Agnes Diffee profile file).

40. Various articles in the June 1, 1960, issue of *Herald of Holiness;* Purkiser, *Called unto Holiness,* 214-16; Dean Nelson, *Small Medium, Large Impact: The Miracle of World Mission Radio* (Kansas City: Nazarene Publishing House, 1993), 21-25. For Fisher's sermon brochures see file 457-32.

41. Nelson, *Small Medium,* 30, 35. See *Other Sheep* (June 1959), inside back cover; "Spanish Radio Ministry Expands," *Herald of Holiness* (June 1, 1960), 11; Reza and others, *Missions: Both Sides of the Coin,* 31-33; Stan Ingersol, "H. T. Reza: The Gospel of Grace in the Spanish Tongue," *Holiness Today* (June 2000), 31.

42. Phyllis Helm, "Nazarenes on the Air in India," *Other Sheep* (May 1962), 8-10; Nelson, *Small Medium,* 81-86.

43. *Herald of Holiness,* Special Issue (1959), 12; Nelson, *Small Medium,* 31-32.

44. Adrian Jones, *Shade-Tree Evangelism* (Kansas City: Beacon Hill Press of Kansas City, 1973), 30, and throughout. See also ideas presented in *The Whole Church Evangelizing,* comp. John L. Knight (Kansas City: Nazarene Publishing House, 1970), and Wesley Tracy, *New Testament Evangelism Today* (Kansas City: Beacon Hill Press of Kansas City, 1972), chap. 3, "Whatever It Takes," 47-74; E. G. Theus, "Possibilities of Television," *Herald of Holiness* (February 11, 1953), 10-11; "Television Can Serve the Church," *Herald of Holiness* (September 17, 1969), 13.

45. H. C. Thomas, "The University Avenue Story," *Herald of Holiness* (November 13, 1968), 12; Bennett Dudney, "Church Growth Study for the Period 1959-1968" (December 1969) (file 230-20); "Teens Serve in Bus Ministry," *Conquest* (November 1973), 19; file 1255-21. Compare Elmer Towns, *World's Largest Sunday School* (Nashville: Thomas Nelson, 1974), 15-26, 54-57, 75-83.

46. Leslie Wright, comp., "Outreach Ministries of Long Beach First Church of the Nazarene," *Director's Digest* (Spring 1973).

47. Franklin Cook and Al Truesdale, *The New Milford Story* (Kansas City: Nazarene Publishing House, 1983), 27.

48. Paul Moore and Joe Musser, *Shepherd of Times Square* (Nashville: Thomas Nelson, 1979), 15-59.

49. C. Neil Strait, "A Night with the Jesus People," *Conquest* (October 1972), 8.

50. "Coffee House Experiment," *Conquest* (January 1970), 1-3; Howard Culbertson, "If Just a Cup of Coffee," *Conquest* (March 1971), 17-18; Paul Moore to Dallas Baggett (January 7, 1972) (file 1387-32); Paul Moore, "The Maranatha Story," *Good News of Jesus,* Special General Assembly Edition [1972] (file 775-65); Strait, "A Night with the Jesus People," 6-11; Cook and Truesdale, *New Milford Story,* 27. See also John Oster, "The Second Manhattan Project," *Herald of Holiness* (June 6, 1973); Moore and Musser, *Shepherd of Times Square;* file 192-18A, Nazarene Archives.

51. John Henderson, *Conquest* (August 1970), 34.

52. Mabel Murphree with Harry Wiese, "Historical Sketch of the First Chinese Church of the Nazarene of Los Angeles," March 1973 (file 2069-31); Notebook of Harry A. Weise (file 2069-25); Harry Wiese, "History of the First Chinese Nazarene Church," March 27, 1973 (file 2069-31).

53. Wiese to Board of Foreign Missions (December 1, 1951); Wiese to Remiss Rehfeldt (December 18, 1951); Wiese to D. I. Vanderpool (December 17, 1951; May 23, 1952; September 1952) and "Chinese Budget," Vanderpool papers; *Herald of Holiness* (November 12, 1952), 14; Smee, Ludwig, and Bowes, *Enlarge Thy Borders,* 60; "San Francisco Chinese Mission," *Herald of Holiness* (January 14, 1953), 16; Taylor, *Fifty Years of Nazarene Missions,* 3:146-47; Jerald Johnson, "'Great Things' in China," *World Mission* (April 1980); Mary Li, "Autobiographical Statement" (file 1269-27); "Mary Li," *World Mission* (July 1991), 19.

54. C. Warren Jones, "The Red Men's Eighth Annual Assembly," *Other Sheep* (October 1952), 3; D. Swarth, "Progress on the North American Indian District," *Other Sheep* (October 1955), 11; DeLong and Taylor, *Fifty Years of Nazarene Missions,* 2:134-41; C. Warren Jones, "Educating Indian Youth," *Other Sheep* (February 1955), 3; "North American Indian District," *Other Sheep* (January 1962), 12; Clara Verner, *Our Original Citizens: The Story of Nazarene Work Among the North American Indians* (Kansas City: Nazarene Publishing House, 1971); F. Charles Scrivner, "History of the Church of the Nazarene North American Indian District, 1905-1987" [1987].

55. Reza and others, *Missions: Both Sides of the Coin,* 64-65.

56. Ira True, "Arizona, a Great Challenge," *Other Sheep* (December 1945), 5; Reza and others, *Missions: The Other Side of the Coin,* 67-69; *Herald of Holiness* (December 18, 1957), 17; "Cuban Work in Miami," *Other Sheep* (January 1962), 7; file 568-4.

57. Report of W. S. Purinton, superintendent, Hawaii, to Home Missions department (N.d.) (file 1385-22); *Other Sheep* (July 1968), 20-21.

58. See, e.g., William A. Eckel to Emma Word (August 6, 1935); Hiroshi Kitagawa to Word (May 3, 1940); Fitkin and Word, *Nazarene Missions in the Orient;* file 423-7.

59. J. B. Chapman, "The Nazarene Missionary Society," [1947], 6 pp. (file 389-19); Taylor, *Fifty Years of Nazarene Missions,* 1:116-19; Louise R. Chapman, "The N.F.M.S.," *Herald of Holiness* (February 18, 1953), 6; Parker, *Mission to the World,* 72-73.

60. Helen Temple, *Louise Robinson Chapman: On Assignment from God* (Kansas City: Nazarene Publishing House, 1993), 42-46 and throughout.

61. See, for example, *N.F.M.S. Ideas: Helps for Leaders of Local N.F.M.S. Groups* (Kansas City: Nazarene Publishing House, 1953).

62. "Minutes of the Women's General Foreign Missionary Council" (January 2-9, 1950) (file 353-14); file 835-25.

63. Helen Temple profile file; Mary Scott to Rhoda Olsen (August 19, 1972) (file 423-19); *World Mission* (March 1985); Phyllis Perkins, *Women in Nazarene Missions: Embracing the Legacy* (Kansas City: Nazarene Publishing House, 1994), 18-25.

64. Parker, *Mission to the World,* 73.

65. "The Opportunity of a Lifetime: A Salute to *World Mission* Magazine," *World Mission* (December 1998), 11.

66. James Hudson, *Work and Witness: One of the Great Success Stories of Nazarene Missions* (Kansas City: Nazarene Publishing House, 1983).

67. Robert D. Wood, *In These Mortal Hands: The Story of the Oriental Missionary Society: The First Fifty Years* (Greenwood, IN: OMS International, 1983).

68. See "Heart of India Mission Band" pamphlet [1920]; J. G. Morrison, "Supported by Nazarene Money," *Other Sheep* (May 1933), 4; Leighton Tracy to Morrison (June 5, 1933); and Basil Miller, *Mother Eaton of India* (Los Angeles: Bedrock), 32-34, 37, 41-42, 49-52, and throughout.

69. R. R. Miller to Foreign Missionary Committee (December 22, 1956); Michael Varro to George Coulter (December 1, 1966; July 16, 1967; and March 20, 1979); Helen Hammond and Robert Bruce Hammond, *Bondservants (Prisoner of War Book),* tenth ed. (Pasadena, CA: VOCA Missionary Society, 1978); Jones, *Guide to the Study of the Holiness Movement,* 412.

70. Basil Miller, *Dreams Fulfilled: My Mission Career* (Pasadena: World-Wide Missions, 1971), 47.

71. See *Herald of Holiness* (June 15, 1978), 29; Jones, *Guide to the Study of the Holiness Movement,* 416; E. S. Phillips to George Coulter (July 25, 1966) and Samuel Young to E. S. Phillips

(February 18, 1969). E. G. Anderson, the former Nazarene missions secretary, worked with both Eaton and Miller during the late 1940s and 1950s.

72. Coulter file 1269-14; E. S. Phillips, *Man of Missions: Messages from the Pulpit of E. S. Phillips* (Kansas City: Beacon Hill Press of Kansas City, 1974), 59.

73. Federico Guillermo, "El Superintendente Nacional en el Desarrollo de la Iglesia del Nazareno en Centroamerica," Conferencia Centroamericana Pastores, December 1-5, 1969 (file 553-9).

74. *General Board Proceedings*, 1972, 187-89.

75. "Quadrennial Plan 1968-1972" (in, e.g., file 1359-9); R. Franklin Cook, *The International Dimension: Six Expressions of the Great Commission* (Kansas City: Nazarene Publishing House, 1984), 15-19, 37, 52-54.

76. Mission Council of the Guatemalan Mission District, n.d. (file 2131-44); "Progress of the Indigenous Church Plan in the Guatemala Field," [1942] (file 1269-14); G. B. Williamson, *Sent Forth by the Holy Ghost: The Life of R. C. Ingram* (Kansas City: Nazarene Publishing House, 1960), 69; Cook, *International Dimension*, 33-34.

77. Compare 1968, 1972, and 1976 editions, *Church of the Nazarene Manual*, pars. 301.1 and 301.4; transcription of conversation between Powers and Guillermo (October 27, 1963), George Coulter to H. C. Powers (N.d.), and Powers to William Sedat (October 31, 1963) (all in file 2131-44); Parker, *Mission to the World*, 45-46.

78. R. Franklin Cook, *A Cup of Warm Ink: The Story of the First 25 Years of the Spanish Department* (Kansas City: Nazarene Publishing House, 1971), 19-21, and throughout.

79. See Reza, *Washed by the Blood*; H. T. Reza, *Our Task for Today* (Kansas City: Nazarene Publishing House, 1963), 83.

80. Paul Orjala, *Publishing the Word* (Kansas City: Nazarene Publishing House, 1965), 56.

81. R. Franklin Cook, *Reza: His Life and Times* (Kansas City: Beacon Hill Press of Kansas City, 1988).

82. *Herald of Holiness* (July 5, 1961); Jerald Johnson, Foreword to Cook, *Reza*, 7-8; Reza, *After the Storm*, 63-65; Ray Hendrix, "Will You Help Us Celebrate Our Golden Anniversary?" *Herald of Holiness* (September 1996), 42-43; Stan Ingersol, "H. T. Reza," 30-31. For Reza's influence see Reza to George Coulter (March 9, 1966) and Reza to E. S. Phillips (June 3, 1966) (both in file 777-14); Reza to Phillips, October 2, 1969 (file 567-8).

83. Harold Raser, *More Preachers and Better Preachers: The First Fifty Years of Nazarene Theological Seminary* (Kansas City: Nazarene Publishing House, 1995), 87-88.

84. Ted Hollingsworth, "Advance in Australia," *Conquest* (February 1947), 25-26; Ted Hollingsworth, "Albert Berg: Our First Australian Nazarene," *Conquest* (March 1947), 34-40; Ted Hollingsworth, "Alfred Chesson—Man of Prayer," *Conquest* (April 1947), 37-40; Ted Hollingsworth, "Douglas Pinch: Missionary to the Aborigines," *Conquest* (May 1947), 39-45; Ted Hollingsworth, "Arthur Clarke—Soldier," *Conquest* (June 1947), 28-31.

85. Sidney Knox to Remiss Rehfeldt (February 16, 1958); Wallace White to Samuel Young (July 27, 1962).

86. "Henceforth . . . a Crown of Righteousness," *Other Sheep* (December 1958), 6, 10; Dudley Powers to Samuel Young (October 25, 1962) and to Wallace White (November 13, 1963); Carol Anne Eby, *Wanda* (Kansas City: Nazarene Publishing House, 1991), 15-47.

87. Samuel Young, "In the Jimmi Valley" (file 1385-13).

88. See Sidney Knox to Remiss Rehfeldt (September 5, 1956, and June 29, 1957); Sidney Knox, "School Has Begin in New Guinea," *Other Sheep* (January 1958), 7, 10; Wallace White to Samuel Young (December 11, 1961; February 8, 1962; March 3, 1962; June 14, 1962; and July 28, 1962); March 22-25, 1967, Council Meeting, including various reports (file 412-3); "Quadrennial Plan 1968-1972" (file 1359-9).

89. Lee Eby, "Bible School Report," March 22-25, 1967, Council Meeting.

90. Bruce Blowers, *The New Guinean Frontier* (Kansas City: Nazarene Publishing House, 1969), 16, 26, 59. See "Our Medical Work in New Guinea," *Other Sheep* (August 1961), 8-9; Samuel Young to Wallace White (March 19, 1962); White to Samuel Young (March 3, 1962; July 27, 1962; July 28, 1962; and May 23, 1963); White to George Coulter (September 16, 1963); "Joint Session with National Church," *Other Sheep* (February 1967), 11; Wallace White, "Red-Letter Day at Kudjip," *Other Sheep* (August 1967), 8-11.

91. White to Young (July 23, 1966). See also Wallace White to E. S. Phillips (June 26, 1967), H. C. Powers to Phillips (October 16, 1967), and Glenn M. Irwin to George Coulter and E. S. Phillips (December 13, 1968).

92. "Executive Committee Report," March 22-25, 1967, Council Meeting.

93. Everette Howard and Jorge de Barros, *The Seed and the Wind* (Kansas City: Nazarene Publishing House, 1982), 63-84.

94. Remiss Rehfeldt, "Eyes on Brazil," *Herald of Holiness* (March 5, 1958), 15-16; Earl Mosteller, "As Others See Cape Verde Nazarenes," *Other Sheep* (September 1958), 5, 12; Acacio Pereira, *Confessions of a Confessor*, trans. Margaret Wood (Kansas City: Nazarene Publishing House, 1984); "A Proposito da Nossa Capa," and Daniel Barros, "Um Marco Historico," both in *O Arauto da Santidade* (Agosto 1989), 3, 26; Dayhoff, comp., *Living Stones*, 76-78; Maria Guerreiro, *Portugal: A Place of Refuge* (Kansas City: Nazarene Publishing House, 1999), 18, 26-27, 46-47, 55, 59.

95. Parker, *Mission to the World*, 576-81; Tim Crutcher, *By Grace Transformed: God at Work in Brazil* (Kansas City: Nazarene Publishing House, 1996). A congregation in Porto Alegre calling itself the Church of the Nazarene began in the 1910s. See Eugene Owen, U.S. Department of Labor, to C. W. Jones (March 18, 1942).

96. Vanderpool to fellow general superintendents (April 27, 1959) (file 906-7); Manuma to Samuel Young (March 25, 1961, and May 26, 1961) (file 1384-23); Young to Garsee (May 11, 1961) (file 1385-28); Manuma to "my fellowmen of the Church of the Nazarene" (January 27, 1962) (file 1384-23); Parker, *Mission to the World*, 616-19.

97. Paul Young Pyo Hong, "Spreading the Holiness Fire: A History of the O.M.S. Korea Holiness Church, 1904-1957," D.Miss. thesis, Fuller Theological Seminary, 1996, 212-13.

98. Remiss Rehfeldt to G. B. Williamson (July 31, 1953); Chung to Rehfeldt (December 4, 1953, and April 5, 1954).

99. Cunningham, *Holiness Abroad*, 205-30.

100. Owens, "Church Growth in Korea," in *Ministering to the Millions*, comp. Department of World Missions (Kansas City: Nazarene Publishing House, 1971), 102-8.

101. Elizabeth Cole, *Give Me This Mountain* (Kansas City: Nazarene Publishing House, 1959); J. Kenneth Grider, "A Nazarene Mother Teresa [Ruth Matchett]," *Herald of Holiness* (May 15, 1989), 16; Perkins, *Women in Nazarene Missions*, 66-69.

102. Hamlin, "Address to the Staff and Friends of Raleigh Fitkin Memorial Hospital," May 30, 1964.

103. Hamlin to Dave and Geneva Barton (April 10, 1973).

104. See Hamlin, "Annual Report of the Medical Superintendent RFMH to the Swazi-Zulu Regional Missionary Council" (August 25, 1966) (file 770-6); Hamlin to Ken Bedwell (December 15, 1967); W. C. Esselstyn to Members of the Swazi-Zulu Region (December 15, 1967); Hamlin to Ron and Shelva Calhoun (November 1969) (file 690-34); Dallas Mucci, *"This Pair of Hands": Howard Hamlin, M.D., Man with a Mission* (Kansas City: Beacon Hill Press of Kansas City, 1988), 95-96, 103-4.

105. H. Kenneth Bedwell to "Friend" (1972) (file 686-45); Jerald Johnson to Minister of Health, Republic of South Africa (November 19, 1975).

106. Oscar Stockwell, "Rev. Benjamin Langa: District Superintendent in Mozambique," *Other Sheep* (August 1969), 2. See C. S. Jenkins, "A Faithful Church," *Other Sheep* (January 1959), 2; *Other Sheep* (March 1959), 8; Frank Howie, *The Mozambique Story* (Kansas City: Nazarene Publishing House, 1993); Lorraine Schultz with C. Ellen Watts, *Only One Life: The Autobiography of Lorraine O. Schultz* (Kansas City: Nazarene Publishing House, 1997), 43-63.

107. See India Mission Council Journals for 1954, 1955, 1956, 1957, 1960; D. I. Vanderpool to Powers (April 21, 1959), Vanderpool papers; M. V. Ingle, "Radio Marathi," *World Mission* (May 1985), 6; Padu Meshramkar, "The Indian Source," *World Mission* (March 1986), 17; Parker, *Mission to the World*, 235-38, 242.

108. Parker, *Mission to the World*, 548-52.

109. Ira Taylor, "Aguaruna Trip," *Other Sheep* (February 1956), 5-7; Ethel K. Dickerman, *The Call of the Aguaruna* (Kansas City: Nazarene Publishing House, 1967); Barbara W. Jones with Pauline Spray, *In the Footsteps of Pioneers* (Kansas City: Nazarene Publishing House, 1983); Parker, *Mission to the World*, 552-53.

110. J. Fred Parker, "Translator for the Kekchis," *Conquest* (January 1949), 32-38; Olive G. Tracy, *We Have Seen the Sun* (Kansas City: Nazarene Publishing House, 1961); "New Day for the Kekchi Indians," *Other Sheep* (February 1962), 6-9; Lorraine O. Schultz, *Bringing God's Word to Guatemala: The Life and Work of William and Betty Sedat* (Kansas City: Nazarene Publishing House, 1995), 51-84.

111. See, for example, R. Franklin Cook, *Nazarenes in Mexico* (Kansas City: Nazarene Publishing House, 1973), 49.

112. C. Warren Jones, "Puerto Rico" (file 195-48); file 654-34; Parker, *Mission to the World*, 453-62.

113. Kathleen Spell, ed., *Haiti Diary: The Intimate Story of a Modern Young Missionary Couple's First Few Years in a Foreign Country; Completed from the Letters of Paul Orjala* (Kansas City: Beacon Hill Press, 1953), 95; see 13, 19, 66, 94-95.

114. Linda Crow, *Haiti, I Love You* (Kansas City: Nazarene Publishing House, 1970), 25-27, 61; Paul Orjala, *Christ in the Caribbean* (Kansas City: Nazarene Publishing House, 1970), 100-109.

115. Paul Orjala, "Church Growth in Haiti," in *Ministering to the Millions*, 73-82; statistics from the Office of the General Secretary.

116. Parker, *Mission to the World*, 478-80. See Culbertson, *Kingdom Strikes Back*, 64-74.

117. Alfredo del Rosso, "How I Came in Touch with the Second Blessing Holiness and the Church of the Nazarene" (June 16, 1953) (file 1646-28); Parker, *Mission to the World*, 349.

118. Paul W. Worcester, *The Master Key: The Story of the Hephzibah Faith Missionary Association* (Kansas City: Nazarene Publishing House, 1966), 32, 47, and throughout.

119. Worcester, *Master Key*, throughout. However, six Hephzibah churches in Nebraska joined the Wesleyan Methodist Church, as did the Hephzibah mission field in Haiti and the Brainerd Indian Training School in Hot Springs, South Dakota. See Wayne E. Caldwell, "A Merger Envisioned: Formation of the Wesleyan Church," in Caldwell, ed., *Reformers and Revivalists: The History of the Wesleyan Church* (Indianapolis: Wesley Press, 1992), 630.

120. Parker, *Mission to the World*, 561.

121. D. W. Dixon, "Centenary Celebration 5th-6th October 1985: Church of the Nazarene Clapham Junction" (file 736-67); Ford, *In the Steps of John Wesley*, 91-92.

122. Ford, *In the Steps of John Wesley*, 94.

123. Ibid., 104-5, 126; Mrs. D. B. Jones, Reginald Jones, and Harold Jones, *David Jones: Ambassador to the Africans* (Kansas City: Beacon Hill Press, 1955).

124. "Report of Joint Investigation Committee" of the IHM and Advisory Board of the Church of the Nazarene, Leeds, December 4-5, 1951, Box 223, Nazarene Theological College, Manchester.

125. Ford, *In the Steps of John Wesley*, 129. See also David Hynd, "In Unity Is Strength," *Herald of Holiness* (February 25, 1953), 4-5; H. Kenneth Bedwell, *Black Gold*, rev. ed. (Kansas City: Beacon Hill Press, 1953).

126. David Hynd, C. S. Jenkins, and H. K. Bedwell, "Minutes of the I.H.M. Exploratory Committee with the Executive Committee of the Church of the Nazarene," Johannesburg (March 1, 1952) (file 1312-33).

127. See "Minutes of the Meeting of the IHM Exploratory Committee," Johannesburg (March 1, 1952); W. Henson, general secretary, IHM, to deacons and members, friends and fellow-workers (May 1952); E. M. Jones, "Our Spoke in the Wheel: A Stirring History of IHM Missionary Work in South Africa," all in Box 23, Nazarene Theological College, Manchester.

128. "Special Announcement," *Africa Calling* (July-September 1952) (file 1312-33); "Union of the International Holiness Movement," *Other Sheep* (January 1953), 1; Ford, *In the Steps of John Wesley*, 126-29; *Other Sheep* (June 1968), 22; H. Kenneth Bedwell to "Friend" (1972) (file 686-45); Jerald Johnson to Minister of Health, Republic of South Africa (November 19, 1975); Reginald E. Jones, *The ELM That Grew at Acornhoek: The Story of the Beginning Years of the Ethel Lucas Memorial Hospital* (Kansas City: Nazarene Publishing House, 1975). On problems at the hospital, see, e.g., Samuel Hynd to Samuel Young (March 17, 1961); "Special Medical Study Committee" (May 4-5, 1973) (file 1357-22).

129. E.g., Maynard James, "The Coming Antichrist," *Flame* (March-April 1939), 6-7; Maynard James, "The Battle of Giants: Further Reflections on the Common Market," *Flame* (September-

October 1962), 12-14. See Ford, *In the Steps of John Wesley,* 120; Noble, *Called to Be Saints,* 111-15, 142, 145-47, 235.

130. Maynard James, "Speaking in Tongues: Divine—Demonic—Psychic," *Flame* (September-October 1939), 14-15.

131. *The Calvary Holiness Church: What It Is and What It Stands For* (N.p., n.d.), 20 pp., Box 162, Nazarene Theological College, Manchester; Ford, *In the Steps of John Wesley,* 139-52, 166-72.

132. Ford, *In the Steps of John Wesley,* 173, see 169-74.

133. "Minutes of Calvary Holiness Church Executive Council and the Church of the Nazarene British Isles Advisory Council" (February 9, 1955), and Samuel Young to W. T. Purkiser (March 22, 1972) (both in file 642-14). See Ford, *In the Steps of John Wesley,* 171-74; Purkiser, *Called unto Holiness,* 262-65. See also Paul James, *A Man on Fire: The Story of Maynard James* (Ilkeston, England: Moorley's Print and Publishing, 1993), 144-51.

134. Jack Ford, "Statement Re. Nazarene Doctrine in the Old Cross Mission, Ashton-under-Lyne," c. 1963, Box 218, Nazarene Theological College, Manchester.

135. File 654-27; Parker, *From East to Western Sea,* 66, 70-71.

136. "Minutes of Commission on Relations with National Holiness Association" (January 10, 1956) (file 487-20). See "Bishop Urges Unity," *Herald of Holiness* (July 10, 1968), 13; Kenneth Geiger to G. B. Williamson (July 15, 1968) (file 1234-11).

137. Caldwell, "A Merger Envisioned," 649-50; "National Holiness Association Study Conference on Federation of Churches, November 30-December 2, 1966" (file 371-19); T. E. Martin, "The Holiness Churches and Ecumenism," *Herald of Holiness* (December 15, 1965).

138. "Holiness Bodies Seek Bond of Understanding," *Herald of Holiness* (July 6, 1960), 18; "Holiness Leaders Wrestle with Problems of Unity" (file 1180-36). See G. B. Williamson, "Much Land Ahead in Peru," *Herald of Holiness* (August 11, 1947), 8; "Holiness Bodies Seek Bond of Understanding," *Herald of Holiness* (July 6, 1960), 18; Peter Burkhart, "The Days of History for the Establishing of the Church of the Nazarene in Guyana, South America" (February 1997).

139. Jun Vencer, "The Evangelicals in the Philippines: A Brief History of the Philippine Council of Evangelical Churches (PCEC)," *Evangelicals Today* (October 1994), 26. See also Samuel Young to Jarrell Garsee (November 19, 1962) (file 1385-28).

140. J. Kenneth Grider, "Amsterdam and Evanston: An Evaluation," *Preacher's Magazine* (December 1954), 22. See also, against ecumenism, Darold Wilson and Gerdonna Wilson, *Questions of a Nazarene Layman* (N.p., n.d.); and C. William Fisher, "Unfinished Business on the Church's Agenda," undated sermon brochure in file 457-32.

141. Wilson and Wilson, *Questions of a Nazarene Layman,* 22, 27.

142. Warren W. Ost to Edward Lawlor (April 27, 1962); W. E. Snowbarger to B. Edgar Johnson (February 24, 1969); H. Dale Mitchell to B. Edgar Johnson (February 25, 1969); M. A. Lunn to B. Edgar Johnson (February 27, 1969); Kenneth Rice to B. Edgar Johnson (March 4, 1969) (all in file 403-8).

143. Board of General Superintendents, "Concerning the National Council of Churches," *Herald of Holiness* (May 9, 1962), 11.

144. Harper, "Department of Church Schools Affiliation with the National Council of Churches" (6 pp.) (file 403-8). See also George Coulter to B. Edgar Johnson (December 26, 1968) (file 403-8).

145. Wilson and Wilson, *Questions of a Nazarene Layman,* 6-12, 52-54; "Summary of Minutes," Commission to Study Relationships of Departments of the Church of the Nazarene to Program Units of the NCC (May 13-14, 1969) (file 403-8). See Howard Keene to W. T. Purkiser (November 22, 1962) (file 890-19); *The East Tennessee Nazarene* (July 1968), and E. E. Zachery to B. Edgar Johnson (February 18, 1969) (both in file 403-8). See also James DeF. Murch, "America's Churches at the Crossroads," *Moody Monthly* (February 1969), 30-33, 61-62.

146. Reza, "The National Council of Churches and the Spanish Nazarene Work in the Western Hemisphere" (7 pp.) (file 403-8). See E. S. Phillips to B. Edgar Johnson (February 18, 1969) (file 403-8).

147. Report of the Commission to Study Existing Relationships of the Church of the Nazarene with Divisions and Subsidiary Groups Related to the National Council of Churches, and B.

Edgar Johnson to R. H. Edwin Espy, general secretary, National Council of Churches (both in file 403-8); *Proceedings of the General Board of the Church of the Nazarene* (N.p., 1970), 19-20.

Chapter 18

1. See, e.g., Harold Reed, *You and Your Church* (Kansas City: Beacon Hill Press, n.d.), 60-78; Harold Frodge, *Turning Point: The Conversion of Harold C. Frodge* (N.p., [1957]), 20.

2. D. Shelby Corlett, "Our Church Standards," *Herald of Holiness* (June 9, 1947), 2-3. See also, in the same issue of the *Herald,* Mary White, "Should We Have Church Rules of Conduct?" 6. Similarly, L[eo] C. D[avis], "Use of Cosmetics," Southwest Indiana District *Crusader* (January 1959) (file 423-7).

3. Corlett, "Our Church Standards," 2-3; *Journal of the Twelfth General Assembly* (Kansas City: N.p., [1948]), 168-69.

4. "Tobacco Is Harmful," *Herald of Holiness* (March 24, 1947), 3; "You Can't Laugh Off the Cigarette," *Herald of Holiness* (June 9, 1947), 4; Thomas J. Parent, "Reasons I Don't Smoke," *Herald of Holiness* (June 4, 1952), 11; A. S. London, "The Curse of the Cigarette," *Herald of Holiness* (January 28, 1953), 10-11; A. S. London, "The Liquor Habit: No Respecter of Persons," *Herald of Holiness* (May 22, 1957), 8; "The Question Box," *Herald of Holiness* (May 22, 1957), 17; E. S. Phillips in *Bethany Church of the Nazarene Weekly News* (January 17, 1964).

5. Philip Cole, "This Is No Time for Compromise!" *Herald of Holiness* (July 6, 1960), 6. See Eva V. Beets, "Why I Quit Going to the Picture Show," *Herald of Holiness* (November 19, 1952), 6; Edward Nagel, "What Is Wrong with the Movies?" *Herald of Holiness* (November 9, 1955), 9-10.

6. See, e.g., J. Grant Swank, "Movies and You," *Conquest* (September 1965), 10-11; Robert Hollings, "Movies—Pro and Con," *Conquest* (February 1966), 37; Dallas Mucci, "Dancing Witness," 8-12, and "Dancing Point of View," 12-13, *Conquest* (February 1967).

7. Albert Harper, *Christian Simplicity: An Honest Look at the Dress Question* (Kansas City: Nazarene Publishing House, 1960), 10-12 (from *Herald of Holiness* articles published in 1959). See E. E. Martin, "Question and Answer" [on skating rinks], *Conquest* (March 1947), 50-51; E. E. Martin, "What Has the Church Against Bowling?" *Conquest* (November 1950), 44; Glenn Griffith, "Nineteen Reasons Why I Am Leaving the Church of the Nazarene" (N.d.) (file 850-38); "The Question Box," *Herald of Holiness* (July 31, 1957), 17; "The Question Box," *Herald of Holiness* (January 21, 1959), 17; Purkiser, *Called unto Holiness,* 266-73.

8. For example, Lora Lee Parrott, *Christian Etiquette* (Grand Rapids: Zondervan, 1953), 52, and throughout. See Eric Jorden, "A Word to the Wise . . . by a Fellow Pastor," *Preacher's Magazine* (May 1954), 29, which is a reflection on *Blueprint for a Christian World* (1953), written by Alice Tenney.

9. Griffith, "Nineteen Reasons Why."

10. Jim Bond to Elden Rawlings (December 1, 1966); "All-America Athletes Can Be Christian," *Herald of Holiness* (September 6, 1967), 10-11. See also Harley Duncan, "Playing Ball with the Boys," *Preacher's Magazine* (January 1961), 28; Henry Hill, "Beginnings of the Church Athletic Program," in Henecke et al., *Century in Christ,* 62.

11. Harold Reed, "All to the Glory of God," Olivet Chapel Message (September 4, 1957) (file 1158-17); "Minutes of the Meeting of General Superintendents and College Presidents" (December 13-14, 1965) (file 662-22); *Herald of Holiness* (March 7, 1968); Riley, *From Sagebrush to Ivy,* 104; *The Olivet Story: An Anecdotal History of Olivet Nazarene University, 1907-1990,* as told by Leslie Parrott ([Bourbonnais, IL]: Olivet Nazarene U., 1993), 120.

12. William Tidwell, "The Two Programs or the Bible Program and the Program of Apostate Christendom," tract (file 1558-37). See also William Tidwell, *Dressed-Up Sin and Other Sermons* (Kansas City: Beacon Hill Press, 1951); Griffith, "Nineteen Reasons Why."

13. Cole, "This Is No Time for Compromise!" 6.

14. Harper, *Christian Simplicity,* 10-12. See also Tidwell, *Dressed-Up Sin,* 12-14; Griffith, "Nineteen Reasons Why"; D[avis], "Use of Cosmetics."

15. Miller to Mrs. Rosco Bechtel (October 11, 1948) (file 920-62).

16. Williamson, "Christian Simplicity and Modesty," *Herald of Holiness* (April 23, 1952), 3; Spencer Johnson, "A Defense of Womanhood," tract, n.d. (file 1068-8); Norman R. Oke, "What's Happened to Modesty?" *Herald of Holiness* (July 16, 1958), 5; Special Meeting of the Brazil Naza-

rene Mission Council (November 16, 1971) (file 409-1a); Leon Chambers to Samuel Young (April 15, 1970) and Samuel Young to Leon Chambers (April 27, 1970) (file 1387-30); Johnson, *Hardy C. Powers*, 28.

17. V. D. Perryman to D. I. Vanderpool (April 30, 1952); Vanderpool to Perryman (May 20, 1952); *Herald of Holiness* (September 30, 1953) and *Herald of Holiness* (November 4, 1953), cited in Purkiser, *Called unto Holiness*, 271. See Williamson, *Gideon*, 87-90.

18. Pitts to Rehfeldt (November 2, 1957), World Mission Office; Pitts, *Voices* (1958), 4-7, 8-9, 11-12, 17-18; *Echoes from the Philippines* (May 1961); Thornton, *Radical Righteousness*, 140-42.

19. Tidwell, "Television a Satanic Miracle," tract (file 1558-37).

20. See "An Exposure of Satan's Propaganda Agency, the Television," tract published by the Moline, Illinois, Church of the Nazarene (N.d.) (file 1068-8); 1952 *Manual*, 320; James T. Patterson, *Grand Expectations: The United States, 1945-1974* (New York: Oxford U. Press, 1996), 348.

21. Griffith, "Nineteen Reasons Why."

22. Cook, *W. M. Tidwell*, 51-55, 58-63, 66-67, 129. See also Wynkoop, *Trevecca Story*, 50, 196-98, 272, 286.

23. On the Louisiana dissidents see Elbert Dodd, "Report," 43, and Paul Pitts and Spencer Johnson, "State of the Church," 52-53, in *Louisiana District Church of the Nazarene Forty-Fifth Annual Assembly Journal* (1955); *Louisiana District Assembly Journal* (1956), 41; *Louisiana District Assembly Journal* (1957), 36; Spencer Johnson, "Twenty-One Reasons Why I Am Leaving the Church of the Nazarene"; Spencer Johnson, "Preaching the Standards of God's Word," n.d. (file 586-48); and Johnson, *Evangelism* (Nampa, ID: N.p., n.d.).

24. Griffith, "Nineteen Reasons Why." See also Griffith, "The Challenge of This Tragic Hour," presented to the Idaho-Oregon-Utah District, about 1945 (file 1314-35); Griffith, *A Voice in the Midnight Hour*, comp. Donald Hughes (Denver: N.p., n.d.), especially the sermon on "True Holiness," 66-82; H. E. Schmul and E. Fruin, comps., *Profile of the I.H. Convention: A 25 Year Historical Scan of the Inter Church Holiness Convention* (Salem, OH: I.H. Convention, [1987]), 38-42; Thornton, *Radical Righteousness*, 132-38; Mark Sidwell, "Glenn Griffith and the Conservative Holiness Movement," *Biblical Viewpoint*, 79-87.

25. Hendricks to Griffith, March 20, 1956, reprinted in Thornton, *Radical Righteousness*, 316-19.

26. *Manual of the Bible Missionary Church, 1956* (Independence, KS: Religious Press, [1956]); Oscar Finch (Superintendent of the Colorado District) to Vanderpool (September 29, 1956); Jones, *Guide to the Study of the Holiness Movement;* Arthur C. Piepkorn, *Profiles in Belief: The Religious Bodies of the United States and Canada*, vol. 3: *Holiness and Pentecostal* (New York: Harper and Row, 1979); J. Gordon Melton, *Encyclopedia of American Religions*, 4th ed. (Detroit: Gale Research, 1993), 396-97. The story of three BMC leaders who left the Church of the Nazarene is told in *To Shine in Use: The Life Story of Rev. Henry A. Erdmann, John H. Abrahams, Albert Crane*, ed. Hal Joiner (Natchitoches, LA: Anchor Publications, [1975]). See also Elbert Dodd, *Old Time Gospel Messages* (Rock Island, IL: Holiness Press, 1963).

27. *Wesleyan Holiness Association of Churches Declaration of Principles, 1962* (N.p., [1962]), 1-2; *Wesleyan Holiness Association of Churches Declaration of Principles, 1981* (N.p., [1981]), 1-3, 16-22; Melton, *Encyclopedia of American Religions*, 399. On King, *Time* (August 22, 1960); Noble Shirkey to Richard Sutcliffe (October 27, 1960); S. T. Ludwig to Richard T. Sutcliffe (November 4, 1960).

28. Pitts, "Report," *Journal* (1957), 35-36 (see also Roy Copelin's "Report," 49).

29. Cunningham, *Holiness Abroad*, 245-46.

30. Pitts, *Voices* (1958), 23-24.

31. Cunningham, *Holiness Abroad*, 248-50, which see for documentation.

32. Earl Hunter, "Robbed," mimeographed [n.d.] (file 1026-21); Earl and Mabel Hunter to Christian Friends, June 25, 1966 (file 1384-11); Miller, *Dreams Fulfilled*, 65-70.

33. Williamson, "Enlarge the Outer Court," *Herald of Holiness* (September 18, 1957), 1. See also Williamson, "Holy Living," undated sermon ms. (file 1232-15).

34. Benner, *Rendezvous with Abundance*, 88-90. See also Hardy Powers, *Manual, Church of the Nazarene 1908-1958: Then—Now* (Kansas City: Nazarene Publishing House, 1958), 66.

35. W. Shelburne Brown, *Let's Look at Our Rules: A Study of Our General Rules* (Kansas City: Beacon Hill Press, 1956), 3, 14; Lyle Prescott, "How Shall We Deal with Standards?" *Herald of*

Holiness (September 30, 1959), 5. See also C. William Fisher, "A Meaningful Religion Has Ethical Demands," sermon tract (file 457-32).

36. Finch to Vanderpool (September 29, 1956). See "The Question Box," *Herald of Holiness* (August 26, 1959), 17; Prescott, "How Shall We Deal with Standards?" 5-6.

37. A. J. Smith, *Bible Holiness and the Modern, Popular, Spurious* (N.p., [1953]), 114-15.

38. Wynkoop, "Religious Existentialism; IV. Life Spiritualized by Love," *Preacher's Magazine* (October 1958), 12.

39. Ponder Gilliland, *Believe and Behave* (Kansas City: Beacon Hill Press, 1960), 16, 39-40, 54-55, 57. See William D. Brooks, *Bethany: A History of the World's Largest Nazarene Church* (Monticello, AK: Village Printing, 1985), 156.

40. John May, "Holiness in Our Day," *Herald of Holiness* (August 31, 1960), 3-4.

41. Taylor, *Fifty Years of Nazarene Missions,* 1:47-51; Parker, *Mission to the World,* 38-40; Thornton, *Radical Righteousness,* 138-43.

42. Pamphlet, "Historic Enon Covenant," Vanderpool papers; Rehfeldt to D. I. Vanderpool (April 2, 1959); file 1026-21. See Rehfeldt, "Survival at Stake," tract [n.d.] (file 645-26); Vanderpool to Powers, Williamson, Young, and Benner (April 31, 1959). See Rehfeldt, *Survival at Stake* (N.p.: H.E.H. Printing, n.d.), a 24-page pamphlet (file 645-26).

43. Vanderpool to Benner (March 29, 1960); *Other Sheep* (August 1960), 4; Vanderpool to Young (September 27, 1960); Vanderpool to Young (August 9, 1961). See also *Herald of Holiness* (July 6, 1960), 14.

44. Remiss Rehfeldt to District Advisory Board, Indianapolis District (July 25, 1967); Duane Landreth to R. Rehfeldt (July 26, 1967).

45. Nazarene Information Services, August 15, 1967; Information Services, Church of the Nazarene, "Dr. Remiss Rehfeldt Resigns as District Superintendent—Dr. Leo C. Davis Named Acting District Superintendent" (August 24, 1967); John and Lillian Pattee to George Coulter and V. H. Lewis (October 19, 1963); Charles Tryon to E. S. Phillips (September 29, 1967); Robert McCroskey to Coulter [1968] (file 1357-23); Pattee to Coulter (June 8, 1968).

46. "Church of Bible Covenant: Proposed Articles," First General Convention, August 10-13, 1967, Cleveland, Indiana; *Articles of the Church of the Bible Covenant, 1970* (N.p., [1979]), 4, 7-8, 9-14, 16-20, 73-75; Chris Howlett, "Through the Blood of the Everlasting Covenant: The Story of the Church of the Bible Covenant," unpublished paper (1994), 7-8.

47. Nazarene News, March 1992; Marvin Powers profile file.

48. "After a Record Year, Nazarenes Set New Standards," *National Observer* (June 24, 1968) (file 1233-38). See Ronald Paul Benefiel, "The Church of the Nazarene: A Religious Organization in Change and Conflict," Ph.D. diss., U. of Southern California, 1986, 28-31.

49. Jerry McCant, *The Meaning of Church Membership* (Kansas City: Beacon Hill Press, 1973), 44.

50. Albert Gamble, "Legalism Versus Love," *Herald of Holiness* (August 7, 1968), 6.

51. McCant, *Meaning of Church Membership,* 43-44, 109-12.

52. *Darda* (Nasville: Trevecca, 1966), 127; various other editions of *Darda;* Wynkoop, *Trevecca Story,* 222.

53. Dunning, "The Theological Basis of the Wesleyan Ethic," ms. (1969), 12-15. See Dunning, "Nazarene Ethics." Regarding Southern mores see Ownby, *Subduing Satan.* See also Russell V. DeLong, "Thirtieth Anniversary Address," Nazarene Theological Seminary, October 22, 1974 (file 2054-3).

54. Richard Taylor, *Preaching Holiness Today* (Kansas City: Beacon Hill Press, 1968), 117-18. See also Arnold Airhart, "Conduct and the Bible," *Herald of Holiness* (February 5, 1969), 6.

55. Ross Price, "How Ought a Christian Family to Keep the Lord's Day," *Herald of Holiness* (February 5, 1969), 5. D. Shelby Corlett's *The Christian Sabbath,* rev. ed. (Kansas City: Beacon Hill Press, 1964), was simply an affirmation of worship on Sunday, as opposed to "seventh-day" teachings.

56. Elbert Dodd, *Gospel Messages for Today* (N.p., n.d.), 48.

57. *Conquest* (May 1970), 37; Southern District Assembly Coloured and Indian Region, 4th District Assembly Minutes (January 3-5, 1968), 18 (file 636-18); Special Meeting of the Brazil Nazarene Mission Council (November 16, 1971) (file 409-1a).

58. Edward Lawlor, *Strengthen the Things That Remain* (Kansas City: Nazarene Publishing House, 1972), 7-8. See also Dallas Mucci, "Your TV May Be a Cyclops," *Conquest* (March 1967), 16-19.

59. V. H. Lewis, "Promoting and Preserving Our Holiness Heritage in the Holiness Ethic of the Church of the Nazarene," address to the Commission on Holiness Ethics [1976].

60. David Riesman, quoted in Patterson, *Grand Expectations*, 338.

61. 1972 Nazarene *Manual*, 400.

62. *Manual/1972, Church of the Nazarene*, eds. B. Edgar Johnson et al. (Kansas City: Nazarene Publishing House, 1972), 51.

63. Umf. Mazibila, "The Place of Plural Wives," in Minutes of Swaziland Native Ministers and Missionaries, October 10-13, 1960 (file 671-6).

64. Herman Spencer to Jerald Johnson (March 6, 1975) (file 1586-11).

65. Neville Bartle, "The Nazarene Church's Stand on Polygamy in PNG," [1974] (file 1586-11).

66. Bruce Blowers to V. H. Lewis (January 13, 1975), enclosing "Mission Council of Papua New Guinea to the Board of General Superintendents" (file 1586-11).

67. Board of General Superintendents, "Statement on Polygamy" (December 9, 1975) (file 1586-11).

68. *Journal of the Nineteenth General Assembly* (1976), 174-83; 1976 *Manual*, 29-30. See J. Weldon McClung Jr., "Nazarenes and the Movies: A Question of Ethics," *Herald of Holiness* (August 1, 1986), 15.

69. Compare Church of the Nazarene *Manual* 1944, 1948, 1952, 1956, 1960, 1964, 1968, 1972, and 1976 editions—especially the first and last mentioned. See *Journal of the Eighteenth General Assembly of the Church of the Nazarene*, ed. B. Edgar Johnson ([Kansas City: Nazarene Publishing House, 1972]), 159-63. See also Wallace Thornton Jr., "Embourgeoisement and the Formation of the Conservative Holiness Movement," *Wesleyan Theological Journal* 33 (Fall 1998), 172-97; Robert W. Wall, "The Embourgeoisement of the Free Methodist Ethos," *Wesleyan Theological Journal* 25 (Spring 1990), 117-29.

70. *Miami News* (June 22, 1972).

Chapter 19

1. Louise Robinson Chapman, *Footprints in Africa* (Kansas City: Nazarene Publishing House, 1959), 39; Gustavo R. Luna, "Un Estudio Sobre el sistema de Membresia en la Iglesia del Nazareno en Centro America," Conferencia Centroamericana de Pastores, December 1-5, 1969 (file 553-9).

2. Milo L. Arnold, *Excuses Answered: How to Answer the Excuses People Give When Invited to Attend Church* (Kansas City: Beacon Hill Press, 1964), 14.

3. J. B. Chapman, "The Question Box," *Herald of Holiness* (March 31, 1947), 11; S. S. White, "The Question Box," *Herald of Holiness* (April 9, 1958), 17, and (September 16, 1959), 17.

4. Fisher, *Our Heritage and Our Hope*, 12.

5. Rachel Jackson to G. B. Williamson (May 25, 1957), and Charlotte Longman to Williamson (May 27, 1957) (file 908-11).

6. Jackson W. Carroll, Douglas W. Johnson, and Martin E. Marty, *Religion in America: 1950 to the Present* (San Francisco: Harper and Row, 1979), 23-24.

7. Fletcher Spruce, *Storehouse Tithing Enlistment Program* (Kansas City: Nazarene Publishing House, 1966), 25.

8. Ibid., throughout. See also N. B. Herrell, *The Way to Christian Prosperity* (Kansas City: Beacon Hill Press, 1951); M. Lunn, *Treasures in Heaven: The Abundant Life of Stewardship* (Kansas City: Nazarene Publishing House, 1963), 71-81; Samuel Young, *Giving and Living: Foundations for Christian Stewardship* (Kansas City: Beacon Hill Press, 1974), 58-59.

9. Oster, *Serving Those Who Serve*, 51-53.

10. Louis A. Reed, "The Counselor's Corner," *Preacher's Magazine* (May-June 1950), 5-6.

11. Lewis T. Corlett, *Holiness, the Harmonizing Experience* (Kansas City: Beacon Hill Press, 1952), 61-76. See also L. A. Reed, *Holiness and the Christian Life* (Kansas City: Beacon Hill Press, 1947), 16-17; A. S. London, "Christ and the Problem of Despondency," *Herald of Holiness* (August 31, 1960), 8-9; Lewis Corlett, "Holiness and Nervous Reactions," in *Further Insights into Holiness:*

Nineteen Leading Wesleyan Scholars Present Various Phases of Holiness Thinking, comp. Kenneth Geiger (Kansas City: Beacon Hill Press, 1963), 333-49; and Lewis T. Corlett, *Thank God and Take Courage: How the Holy Spirit Worked in My Life*, ed. Frank Carver (San Diego: Point Loma Press, 1992), 34-37.

12. Corlett, *Holiness, the Harmonizing Experience*, 68. On D. Shelby Corlett, see Purkiser, *Called unto Holiness*, 223-24.

13. Cecil Paul, "The Care of Souls: Pastoral and Psychological," in *The Church in a Changing World: Selected Papers from the Nazarene Theology Conference*, ed. W. T. Purkiser (Kansas City: Beacon Hill Press of Kansas City, 1972), 35.

14. James Hamilton, *The Ministry of Pastoral Counseling* (Kansas City: Beacon Hill Press of Kansas City, 1972), 46. See also James Hamilton, *Harmony in the Home: A Study of Christian Family Relationships* (Kansas City: Beacon Hill Press of Kansas City, 1976); Cecil Paul and Jan Lanham, *Choices: In Pursuit of Wholeness* (Kansas City: Beacon Hill Press of Kansas City, 1982).

15. James Hamilton, *The Faces of God: How Our Images of God Affect Us* (Kansas City: Beacon Hill Press of Kansas City, 1984).

16. See, for example, Leslie Parrott, *The Power of Your Attitudes* (Kansas City: Beacon Hill Press of Kansas City, 1967); Parrott, *Easy to Live With* (Kansas City: Beacon Hill, 1970); Laurel E. Yoder, *Nobody Loves Me—and I Can't Say I Blame Them* (Kansas City: Beacon Hill Press of Kansas City, 1980).

17. Jarrell Garsee, James Hamilton, and Cecil Paul, *What You Always Wanted to Know About Your Pastor-Husband* (Kansas City: Beacon Hill Press of Kansas City, 1978); Cecil Paul, *Passages of a Pastor* (Grand Rapids: Zondervan, 1981), 51; James Hamilton, *The Pair in Your Parsonage: A Guide for Understanding Clergy Couples* (Kansas City: Beacon Hill Press of Kansas City, 1982).

18. See "The Question Box," *Herald of Holiness* (May 22, 1957), 17; "The Question Box," *Herald of Holiness* (November 27, 1957), 17; S. S. White, "Beware of a Divided Rulership in the Home!" *Herald of Holiness* (June 4, 1958), 12.

19. See, e.g., Basil Miller, *Missionaries in Action*, vol. 2: *On the Central American and Argentinean Fronts* (Kansas City: Nazarene Publishing House, 1942), 20-24, 56-62; Carol Gish, *Touched by the Divine: The Story of Fairy Chism* (Kansas City: Beacon Hill Press, 1952); Eugenia P. Coats, *Beloved of Guatemala: The Life of Neva Lane* (Kansas City: Beacon Hill Press, 1957); Elizabeth Cole, *Give Me This Mountain* (Kansas City: Nazarene Publishing House, 1959); L. David Duff, *The Ramsey Covenant: A Story About Evelyn Ramsey, M.D.* (Kansas City: Nazarene Publishing House, 1985); Eby, *Wanda*; Carolyn Myatt, *A Tapestry Called Orpha* (Kansas City: Nazarene Publishing House, 1991); Perkins, *Women in Nazarene Missions*; Eunice Bryant, *Run with the Torch: The Church of the Nazarene in El Salvador* (Kansas City: Nazarene Publishing House, 1995); Valerie Friesen, *Journeys of Faith: From Canada to the World* (Kansas City: Nazarene Publishing House, 2001); Helen Temple, *Adventure with God: The Jeanine van Beek Story* (Kansas City: Nazarene Publishing House, 2002).

20. The July 2, 1945, issue of the *Herald* was devoted to women. See Harrison Davis, "Silver Anniversary at Hiroshima," *Other Sheep* (February 1960), 4; DeLong and Taylor, *Fifty Years of Nazarene Missions*, 2:241, 243, 245, 249; Ruth Saxon, *Flares in the Night: The Story of Nazarene Missions in Trinidad and Tobago* (Kansas City: Nazarene Publishing House, 1970), 23-35.

21. Based on notes of Dorothy Ahleman (file 2027-19). See Dorotea M. Ahleman, *Iglesia Del Nazareno Bodas De Oro 1919-1969 Distrito Argentino* (Argentina, 1970), 8, 10, 19, 24-30, 35, 43, 96, 181; Ahleman, *English Guide for Fiftieth Anniversary Book* (N.p., n.d.), 42; Helen Temple, "She Dared to Give God Her Dreams," *World Mission* (August 1986), 2-3; Stan Ingersol, "Knowledge and Vital Piety: Lucia de Costa's Enduring Witness," *Herald of Holiness* (April 1996), 13.

22. Richard Houseal, "Women Clergy in the Church of the Nazarene: An Analysis of Change from 1908 to 1995," M.A. thesis, U. of Missouri-Kansas City, 1996, 22, 72.

23. Emma Irick, *The King's Daughter* (Kansas City: Pedestal, 1973), 55-60, 64; George W. Rice, *A Preacher Named Emma* (Kansas City: Beacon Hill Press of Kansas City, 1995). Also see Stanley, *Holy Boldness*.

24. *Herald of Holiness* (April 30, 1958), 2; *Herald of Holiness* (August 31, 1960), 21.

25. *Herald of Holiness* (June 23, 1965), 15.

26. See Audrey J. Williamson, *Your Teen-Ager and You* (Kansas City: Beacon Hill Press, 1952), and *Love Is the Greatest: Devotional Messages on 1 Corinthians 13* (Kansas City: Beacon Hill Press of Kansas City, 1975); Nazarene News Service, Weekly Summary (December 16, 1994).

27. Lora Lee Parrott, *How to Be a Preacher's Wife and Like It* (Grand Rapids: Zondervan, 1956), 80 and throughout. See also Esther Lewis, *We Also Build: The Role of the Minister's Wife* (Kansas City: Beacon Hill Press of Kansas City, 1969).

28. Houseal, "Women Clergy," 22, 54, 72. See, for example, Lora Lee Parrott, *Christian Etiquette*, 111-12. Compare Margaret L. Bendroth, *Fundamentalism and Gender: 1875 to the Present* (New Haven, CT: Yale U. Press, 1993), 89-96, 98-100, 105-17; Michael S. Hamilton, "Women, Public Ministry, and American Fundamentalism, 1920-1950," *Religion and American Culture* 3 (Summer 1993), 180-88. See also Laird, *Ordained Women*, 13-19, 143-51; Kirkemo, *For Zion's Sake*, 103-4, 193-94, 348, 384-85; Paul Bassett, "The Ordination of Women to Ministry in the Church of the Nazarene," *Tower* 4 (2000), 59-65.

29. *Fifty Years and Beyond: A History of the Chicago Central District Church of the Nazarene* (N.p., 1954), 26-27, 52, 64, 66; Alpin Bowes, "Little Things Make a Big Difference," *Herald of Holiness* (February 6, 1952), 7-8.

30. Oster, "History of Home Missions"; *Bethany First Church of the Nazarene, Bethany, Oklahoma* (N.p., 1969).

31. Norman R. Oke, *We Have an Altar: A Manual on Altar Work* (Kansas City: Nazarene Publishing House, 1954), 17, 20-29, 43.

32. *Herald of Holiness* (December 15, 1977), 31; Brooks, *Bethany*.

33. Erwin G. Benson, "Sunday Schools Must Have Room," and Bowes, "Little Things Make a Big Difference," both in *Herald of Holiness* (February 6, 1952), 7-8; Alpin Bowes, "Changes in Church Building," *Herald of Holiness* (February 18, 1954), 15.

34. Files 654-38, 654-40 and 654-41; Bennett Dudney, "Church Growth Study for the Period 1959-1968" (December 1969) (file 230-20). Compare Emslie, *Continent in a Hurry*, 46-47.

35. Files 654-39, 654-41, and 794-19; *Bethany First Church of the Nazarene, Bethany, Oklahoma* (N.p., 1969); *Herald of Holiness* (July 16, 1969), 13; *Herald of Holiness* (July 23, 1969), 17.

36. Ponder Gilliland profile file.

37. Leslie Parrott, "Sanctified Promotion," *Preacher's Magazine* (May 1954), 30-32. These ideas were expanded upon in Leslie Parrott, *Building Today's Church: How Pastors and Laymen Work Together* (Kansas City: Beacon Hill Press of Kansas City, 1971).

38. "After a Record Year, Nazarenes Set New Goals," *National Observer* (June 24, 1968); Earl Lee, *The Cycle of Victorious Living* (Kansas City: Beacon Hill Press of Kansas City, 1971).

39. Files 654-41 and 1531-27. See Patterson, *Grand Expectations*, 333-37.

40. *Fifty Years and Beyond*, 22-23; files 714-64 and 714-65; Neil Wiseman, "Chicago First Gains 300 in Worship," *Grow* (Summer 2003), 12-16; Kevin Ulmet, "Back into the City: Historic Church Returns to Inner-City Chicago," *Grow* (Spring 2008), 20-22.

41. File 714-34; Baltimore "First Church of the Nazarene Dedication Booklet" (file 755-2).

42. *Century in Christ*, 92, 99.

43. Roy Fralin to B. Edgar Johnson, October 25, 1973 (file 775-10); "Church Planter Serves One Church for 50 Years," *Grow* (Fall 1999), 2-7.

44. Don Hughes, "Some Thoughts on the Future of the DCE in the Church of the Nazarene," *Directors' Digest* (Winter 1969); Bennett Dudney profile file.

45. *Newsletter* (October 1960); file 527-1.

46. Fletcher Spruce, "The Roots of the Problem," paper presented at Conference of Superintendents, Kansas City, Missouri, January 11, 1966 (file 654-59); "Ministry, 1950-70" (file 654-46).

47. Byron LeJeune, "Preaching as the Center of Worship," in *Preaching and Church Music: Papers Presented at Conference Held at Trevecca Nazarene College, October 29—November 2, 1962*, ed. Amy Person (mimeographed). See Stephen S. White, "Too Bad We Can't Have Any Emotion," *Herald of Holiness* (January 27, 1960), 13.

48. *Alabama District Church of the Nazarene Sixtieth Annual Assembly Journal* (1968), 68.

49. Richard Taylor, "Holiness Preaching That Communicates," in *Further Insights into Holiness*, comp. Kenneth Geiger (Kansas City: Beacon Hill Press, 1963), 277; Andrew Cone, "Special Music," *Preacher's Magazine* (October 1959), 35-36.

50. Parrott, *Building Today's Church*, 124.

51. J. C. Dobson, "Clichés and Sacred Concepts," *Nazarene Preacher* (October 1970), 6-9. See, for example, James McGraw, comp., *The Holiness Pulpit* (Kansas City: Beacon Hill Press, 1957); Fletcher Spruce, *Fighting the Stars and Other Sermons* (Kansas City: Beacon Hill Press, 1957); Ross Price and Oscar Reed, eds., *Faith in These Times: Sermons by Pasadena College Ministers* (Kansas City: Beacon Hill Press, 1961); and McGraw, comp., *The Holiness Pulpit*, No. 2: *Sermons by Contemporary Leaders of the Holiness Movement* (Kansas City: Beacon Hill Press of Kansas City, 1974).

52. McCumber, "Scriptural Elements in Holiness Preaching," in *Preaching and Church Music*. See also C. W. Perry, "The Present Need—A Holiness Emphasis," *Preacher's Magazine* (November-December 1946), 30-31; Taylor, *Preaching Holiness Today*, 118-19 and throughout.

53. Harrell Lucky, "Religious Jazz," *Herald of Holiness* (July 9, 1969), 13; Gary L. Hubartt, "A Study of the Hymnody of the Church of the Nazarene," master of music thesis, U. of Southern California, 1977, 72, 80. See R. W. Stringfield, "Ministering Through Music," *Preacher's Magazine* (May 1954), 10-12; various church bulletins (files 775-38, 775-41, 775-52, 794-1, 794-19); Brooks, *Bethany*, 180.

54. "The Question Box," *Herald of Holiness* (November 27, 1957), 17; Don Moore and Tom Tinker, "Children's Church," *Directors' Digest* (Spring 1971); Esther Nielson, "Children's Church and Worship," *Directors' Digest* (Winter 1972).

55. David Whitelaw's conversation with Milton Parrish (March 10, 2002).

56. Jerry Johnson, *Let's Go Dutch: The Church of the Nazarene in Europe* (Kansas City: Nazarene Publishing House, 1971), 63.

57. David Tarrant, "Answer," *Flame* (September-October 1961), 22-23.

58. George Coulter, "Report of Trip to Korea" [1967]; R. Franklin Cook, *Water from Deep Wells* (Kansas City: Nazarene Publishing House, 1977), 76.

59. Crow, *Haiti, I Love You*, 39-42.

60. Emslie, *Continent in a Hurry*, 46-47.

61. Roy Fuller to V. H. Lewis (October 26, 1976); E. S. Phillips to Samuel Young (N.d.) (file 1387-62). Note that the *Manual* separated infant baptism and infant dedication until 1972, when the ceremonies were combined. They were also combined in the 1976 *Manual* but separated again in 1980 and after.

62. Orville W. Jenkins, *The Church—Winning Sunday Nights* (Kansas City: Nazarene Publishing House, 1961), 42 and throughout; Parrott, *Building Today's Church*, 92-100.

63. Hugh C. Benner, *Singing Disciples: Toward Better Church Music* (Kansas City: Nazarene Publishing House, 1959), 54. See *Rejoice and Sing: A Hymnal for All Services with Accent on Youth*, comp. R. W. Stringfield and others (Kansas City: Lillenas, 1958), 188-232; Eugene Stowe, "Youth and Music," *Herald of Holiness* (Special Issue, 1959), 14-15; various church bulletins (files 775-38, 775-41, 775-52, 794-19); Parrott, "What Is Nazarene Music?" Hubartt, "Study of the Hymnody," 83, 88; Henecke et al., *Century in Christ*, 46.

64. Ray H. Moore, "Singing in the Evangelistic Service," *Preacher's Magazine* (May 1954), 13-15; Raymond C. Kratzer, "A Look at the Facts," *Preacher's Magazine* (January 1961), 26-27; Milo Arnold, "Eleven O'clock Evangelism," *Preacher's Magazine* (July 1961), 26-27; Leslie Parrott, "What Is Nazarene Music?" 1961 Church Music Conference (mimeographed); Hubartt, "Study of the Hymnody," 81; Murray L. Pallett, "Sunday Evening Evangelism," in *The Whole Church Evangelizing*, comp. John L. Knight (Kansas City: Nazarene Publishing House, 1970), 53-64.

65. Lowel W. Coey, "The Midweek Prayer Meeting," *Preacher's Magazine* (March 1958), 31-32.

66. Jantz, "Evangelism Through Music, from the Evangelists' Points of View," *Directors Digest* (Summer 1974). See File 794-67; Ron Lush file.

67. Lester Dunn, Panel Discussion, 1961 Church Music Conference. See Benner, *Singing Disciples*, 21; Parrott, "What Is Nazarene Music?" L. Alline Swann, "The Goals of Nazarene Church Music," 1961 Church Music Conference.

68. "Dr. Haldor Lillenas," *Herald of Holiness* (September 30, 1959), 14; Fred A. Mund, *Keep the Music Ringing: A Short History of the Hymnody of the Church of the Nazarene* (N.p., 1979), 14, 18-19; Steven W. Bradley, "Hymnic Trends in the Church of the Nazarene," master of music thesis, Baylor U., 1983, 13-14, 40. See also Lillenas, *Down Melody Lane*.

69. Mund, *Keep the Music Ringing,* 25. See "Minutes of Meeting No. 3," October 2, 1970 (Box 728); Eleanor Whitsett, "A History of the Lillenas Publishing Company and its Relationship to the Music of the Church of the Nazarene," U. of Missouri–Kansas City, 1972, 7; Hubartt, "Study of the Hymnody," 130, 171-72; Bradley, "Hymnic Trends," 47.

70. Hubartt, "Study of the Hymnody," 193-211; Mund, *Keep the Music Ringing,* 35-36. For the context see Edith Blumhofer and Mark A Noll, eds., *Singing the Lord's Song in a Strange Land: Hymnody in the History of North American Protestantism* (Tuscaloosa: U. of Alabama Press, 2004).

71. *Preacher's Magazine* (September 1958), 49; Mund, *Keep the Music Ringing,* 16, 20, 21.

72. Whitsett, "A History of the Lillenas Publishing Company," 9, 10-13; Floyd Hawkins, *The Way of Gladness* (Gladstone, MO: Floyd W. Hawkins, 1996).

73. Ron Lush, *Use Them or Lose Them: The Participating Music Program* (Kansas City: Nazarene Publishing House, 1968), throughout.

74. Hubartt, "Study of the Hymnody," 105.

75. Leslie Parrott [secretary of the commission and director of its research project], "What Is Nazarene Music?" *Journal of the Sixteenth General Assembly,* 195-200; Benner, *Singing Disciples,* 56. See also *Herald of Holiness* (Special Issue, 1959), 15.

76. Benner, *Singing Disciples,* 20; Benner, "Keynote Address," and James R. Bell, "What Are the Goals of Nazarene Church Music?" 1961 Church Music Conference. Similarly, Edward Lawlor, "Music and Evangelism," at the same conference.

77. Paul Willwerth, Panel Discussion, 1961 Church Music Conference; Hugh C. Benner, "Closing Observations," at the same conference.

78. James E. Miller, "A Survey of Current Musical Practices in Selected Churches of the Nazarene," master of church music thesis, Southern Baptist Theological Seminary, 1974, 176; 194-98.

79. *Nazarene Messenger* (December 13, 1906). See Robert Owens, "The Azusa Street Revival: The Pentecostal Movement Begins in America," in *The Century of the Holy Spirit: 100 Years of Pentecostal and Charismatic Renewal, 1901-2001,* ed. Vinson Synan (Nashville: Thomas Nelson, 2001), 39-68.

80. Edith Blumhofer and Grant Wacker, "Who Edited the Azusa Mission's Apostolic Faith?" *Assemblies of God Heritage* (Summer 2001), 15-21. In other work as well, both Blumhofer and Wacker have minimized the Holiness roots of the Pentecostal movement. See Grant Wacker, "The Travail of a Broken Family: The Wesleyan Holiness Responses to Early Pentecostalism, 1906-1926," *Journal of Ecclesiastical History* 47 (July 1996), 505-28; Wacker, *Heaven Below;* Edith Blumhofer, *Restoring the Faith: The Assemblies of God, Pentecostalism, and American Culture* (Urbana: U. of Illinois Press, 1993).

81. "Questions Answered," *Herald of Holiness* (January 3, 1923).

82. B. F. Neely, *The Bible Versus the Tongues Theory* (Kansas City: Nazarene Publishing House, n.d.), 7, 56 (the book was based on a series of articles that had appeared in the *Herald of Holiness* in 1923); Pascal Belew, *Light on the Tongues Question* (Kansas City: Nazarene Publishing House, 1926).

83. C. W. Ruth, "Tongues," reprinted in *Herald of Holiness* (February 12, 1964), 10-11; Timothy L. Smith, *Speaking the Truth in Love: Some Honest Questions for Pentecostals* (Kansas City: Beacon Hill Press of Kansas City, 1977), 12, 24, 30-31, 37, 40.

84. John W. May, "Mysteries at Pentecost," *Herald of Holiness* (February 6, 1952), 14. Similarly, D. Edwin Doyle, "Paul and the Tongues Theory," *Preacher's Magazine* (October 1959), 17-20.

85. W. T. Purkiser, *Spiritual Gifts: Healing and Tongues: An Analysis of the Charismatic Revival* (Kansas City: Nazarene Publishing House, 1964). See *Herald of Holiness* (August 13, 1969), 18; Richard S. Taylor, *Tongues: Their Purpose and Meaning* (Kansas City: Beacon Hill Press of Kansas City, 1973), 9-11, 15, 17, 20-21, 25; W. T. Purkiser, *God's Spirit in Today's World,* rev. ed. (Kansas City: Beacon Hill Press of Kansas City, 1976), 64, 67; Smith, *Speaking the Truth in Love.* Another defense of this accepted position is Gary Goodell, *Heavenly Tongues or Earthly Languages? What the Bible Says About Speaking in Tongues* (Kansas City: Beacon Hill Press of Kansas City, 1989), 21, 26, 35, 38. In a variation on the point that the gift of tongues was a known language, C. L. Newbert attempted to show that the gift of tongues in both the Book of Acts and in the Letter to the Corinthians was the Hebrew language. See C. L. Newbert, *New Testament Tongues and the Keepers of the Dead Sea Scrolls* (Kansas City: Pedestal, 1985), which was based on a Boston U. Ph.D. dissertation.

86. Ralph Earle, "The Holy Spirit and the Gift of Tongues," lecture delivered at Olivet Nazarene College, February 25, 1972 (file 1279-27); Norman Oke, *Facing the Tongues Issue* (Kansas City: Beacon Hill Press of Kansas City, 1973), 30, 37; Albert Harper to Board of General Superintendents (December 12, 1963) (file 1233-38).

87. Metz, *Speaking in Tongues* (Kansas City: Nazarene Publishing House, 1964), 54, 57-58, 64-68, 72, 76, 88. This book was abridged and reprinted by Beacon Hill Press of Kansas City in 1971 under the title *Speaking in Tongues: A Biblical Analysis*. See also Metz, "The Gifts of the Spirit in Perspective," in *The Word and the Doctrine: Studies in Contemporary Wesleyan-Arminian Theology* (Kansas City: Beacon Hill Press of Kansas City, 1965), 317-33, and his commentary on 1 Corinthians in the Beacon Bible Commentary series.

88. Harvey Blaney, *Speaking in Unknown Tongues: The Pauline Position* (Kansas City: Beacon Hill Press of Kansas City, 1973), 24; see 19-20. See also Harvey Blaney, "St. Paul's Posture on Speaking in Unknown Tongues," *Wesleyan Theological Journal* 8 (Spring 1973), 52-60. See likewise Charles Isbell, "Glossolalia and Propeteialalia: A Study of I Corinthians 14," *Wesleyan Theological Journal* 10 (Spring 1975), 15-23.

89. T. W. Willingham, "I Believe in the Gift of Tongues," August 29, 1965, circulated in Ben Lemaster to Bud Camfield, April 21, 1995; Dick Howard, *Tongues Speaking in the New Testament* (N.p: [privately published], 1980), 20-23, 83-85. Note that Howard's book was not published by Nazarene Publishing House.

90. Roger Kerr, "It Was Good for Paul and Silas," *Reveille Echo* (December 3, 1971) (file 642-14).

91. Wilbur Jackson, "A More Fruitful Ministry," in *The Acts of the Holy Spirit Among the Nazarenes Today* (Los Angeles: Full Gospel Business Men's Fellowship International, 1973), 9-13. See also Garreth L. Clair, "The Holy Spirit—Facts and Heresy," *Preceptor* (June 1976), 13-20 (file 660-2); Kelly Davis to B. Edgar Johnson (December 6, 1976) (file 736-95).

92. Brazil Mission Council Minutes (quoting the April 15, 1971, letter from Lewis to Mosteller) (file 409-1a). See especially Bob Burke, with David A. Womack, *Push Back the Darkness: The Story of Don Stamps and the Full Life Study Bible* (Springfield, MO: Lumina Press, 1995), 133, which quotes from primary sources.

93. Burke, *Push Back the Darkness*, 137-39.

94. *Other Sheep* (September 1971), 25; "Minutes of the Thirteenth Annual Mission Council Meeting" (September 22-25, 1971), and "Special Meeting of the Brazil Nazarene Mission Council" (November 16, 1971) (with V. H. Lewis) (both in file 409-1a); Amphilophio de Mello Filho, Jose Ulisses Peruch, and Joachim Lima (Brazil District Advisory Board) to George Coulter (February 15, 1973) (file 567-8); Burke, *Push Back the Darkness*, 123-40.

95. Warren Black, "A Nazarene Finds a New Dimension," *Voice* (June 1972), 3-7, 26-28; Warren Black, "A New Dimension," in "The Acts of the Holy Spirit Among the Nazarenes Today," 23-29. See *Miami Herald* (June 17, 1972).

96. Hugh C. Benner, transcript of message to the 1972 General Assembly. See "To the Delegates of the 18th General Assembly Meeting in Miami, Florida, June 15-23, 1972" (file 736-95); *Journal of the Eighteenth General Assembly of the Church of the Nazarene*, ed. B. Edgar Johnson (Kansas City: Nazarene Publishing House, 1972), 58; see 73-74.

97. *Journal of the Eighteenth General Assembly*, 142.

98. See Stan Pulliam, "The Divisiveness of Tongues: Myth vs. Fact," tract printed by the Wesleyan Holiness Charismatic Fellowship (file 1269-31).

99. *Journal of the Nineteenth General Assembly of the Church of the Nazarene*, ed. B. Edgar Johnson (Kansas City: Nazarene Publishing House, 1976), 240; "The Position of the Church of the Nazarene on Speaking in Tongues," *Herald of Holiness* (October 15, 1976), 4-5, signed by all six general superintendents. Note the similar sentiments of Wesleyan Church leaders in *No Uncertain Sound: An Exegetical Study of I Corinthians 12, 13, 14* (Marion, IN: Wesley Press, 1975), 69.

100. Randy Maddox, "Nazarenes and Tongues," *Nazarene Seminarian* (October 22, 1976); Mary Allison, "Speaking in Tongues Issue Sharply Divides Church of the Nazarene," *Kansas City Star* (November 13, 1976), front page; Mrs. Lloyd Mitchell to Eugene Stowe (November 18, 1976) (file 1354-16). For a defense of the general superintendents' position by a later general superin-

tendent, see John L. Knight, *What the Bible Says About Tongues-Speaking* (Kansas City: Nazarene Publishing House, 1988), 24, 28-31.

101. Maynard James, *I Believe in the Holy Ghost* (Minneapolis: Bethany Fellowship, 1965), 113-21; James, "Light on the 'Tongues' Problem," *Flame* (March/April 1985), 9-10; Paul James, *A Man on Fire*, 144-51.

Chapter 20

1. John Riley, *This Holy Estate (Guidance in Christian Homemaking)* (Kansas City: Beacon Hill Press, 1957), 109-11.

2. John L. Knight, "I Believe in Child Conversion," *Herald of Holiness* (April 1, 1953), 8; Knight, "I Believe Children Should Join the Church," *Herald of Holiness* (April 8, 1953), 4; Melza Brown, "Child Evangelism by the Pastor," *Preacher's Magazine* (August 1954), 15-16; *Preacher's Magazine* (September 1954), 11; Earl Wolf, "How to Lead Our Children to Christ," *Preacher's Magazine* (May 1958), 13-14; Mary E. Latham, *Teacher: You Are an Evangelist* (Kansas City: Beacon Hill Press, 1963); "Summary of the Chicago Central District Workshop on the Day Nursery and Kindergarten Program," September 12, 1964, *Directors' Digest* (Spring 1967).

3. *Herald of Holiness* (January 28, 1953), 5; Betty Bowes, *The Ministry of the Cradle Roll* (Kansas City: Beacon Hill Press of Kansas City, 1970), 7-10, 14-16, 19-22, 33-35, 49, 58, 63.

4. Melza Brown, "Child Evangelism by the Pastor," *Preacher's Magazine* (September 1954), 11; *Herald of Holiness* (September 14, 1955), 5; *Herald of Holiness* (December 31, 1958), 11; Church Growth Statistics, Church of the Nazarene (October 17, 1995); Patterson, *Grand Expectations*, 314.

5. *Here's How: Practical Plans for Building the Sunday School* (Kansas City: Nazarene Publishing House, 1960), 46 and throughout.

6. Bennett Dudney, "Church Growth Study for the Period 1959-1968" (December 1969) (file 230-20); Dick Edwards, "And Now We Are Two" (February 5, 1967), First Nazarene Church of Long Beach, *Directors' Digest* (Spring 1967); Paul Miller in *Miami Herald* (June 18, 1972); Kenneth Rice, "The Challenge of Contemporary Trends," *Multiple Staff Digest* (Winter 1975).

7. A. Milton Smith, "Am I a Loyal Church Member?" *Conquest* (June 1947), 14-15, and entire issue; Audrey Williamson, *Your Teen-Ager and You*, 47, 80-86.

8. Vickie Wonders, "A Case of Mistaken Identity," *Conquest* (June 1969), 10-11.

9. "Let's Go to Institute," *Conquest* (August 1947), 31-36. See Mont Hurst, "Are You a Resourceful Faithful Witness?" *Conquest* (January 1947), 23-24; Carl Bangs, "Personal Evangelism," *Conquest* (October 1948), 28-31; Bangs, "Personal Evangelism," *Conquest* (November 1948), 34-37; Bangs, "Personal Evangelism," *Conquest* (December 1948), 48-51; Ponder Gilliland, "We Have Found a Challenge," *Conquest* (February 1949), 8-11; R. T. Kendall, "The Teenager and His Relationships in Life," *Conquest* (February 1953), 58-60; Eugene Stowe, *Christian Courtship* (Kansas City: Beacon Hill Press, 1964), 12-13, 16, 19, 21, 23-26, 31-32; Francisco Martinez, "El Problema Moral y Social," Conferencia Centroamerican de Pastores (December 1-5, 1969) (file 553-9).

10. Paul Miller, "Nazarene Young People's Society International," *Conquest* (November 1967), 2-6; "Something New in India," *Conquest* (November 1967), 8-9.

11. "Quadrennial Goals Again," *Herald of Holiness* (September 3, 1952), 12; Lauriston DuBois file.

12. *The Nazarene Voice* (July 1960), 4 (file 2131-25); David Whitelaw and Floyd Cunningham conversation with Paul Skiles, June 1, 2000.

13. General Nazarene Young People's Society, *Teen Guide to Witnessing and Soul Winning*, rev. ed. (Kansas City: Nazarene Publishing House, 1967), 89; *Conquest* (November 1968), 12, 18, and various other *Conquest* issues.

14. Jan Decker to Paul Skiles (February 7, 1971) (Box 942). See also Shoemaker, *Leader's Guide to WOW*.

15. *The Link* (November 1, 1963) (file 2131-25); *Conquest* (December 1965), 13; John Smee, "Nazarene Evangelistic Ambassadors Changed My Life," *Conquest* (April 1966), 7-11; Sharon Hoecker, "Confession of a Quizzer," *Conquest* (November 1966), 39; *Conquest* (January 1967), throughout; Gary Sivewright, "Student Mission Corps," *Conquest* (April 1969), 5-7, 41; *Conquest* (July 1969), throughout; Jim Copple, "True Revolution," in *Crucible of Concern: The Student Mission*

Corps in Action, comp. Franklin Cook (Kansas City: Nazarene Publishing House, 1974), 30-37 and throughout; David Whitelaw and Floyd Cunningham, conversation with Paul Skiles (June 1, 2000).

16. "Jim Bond, General NYPS President and Now Missionary to Brazil," *Conquest* (September 1970), 25-27.

17. Paul Skiles to All North American District Presidents, January 23, 1973 (Box 953). See Paul Skiles, "Innsbruck Incident—An NYPS First," *Conquest* (December 1965), 1-7; Gene Van Note, "International Institute 1966," *Conquest* (September 1966), 24-30; Norm Shoemaker, *Leader's Guide to WOW: A Workshop on Witnessing* (Kansas City: Department of Youth, 1970); Howard Culbertson, "An Out-of-Sight Week," *Conquest* (January 1971), 1-7.

18. Don Hughes, "Tested Teen Techniques," *Directors' Digest* (December 1961).

19. "A Handbook for the Bresee Fellowship," prepared by S. T. Ludwig (file 1220-54); "The Campus and the Christian Dimension" tract (file 499-7); William E. Saunders Jr. to Willis Snowbarger (May 6, 1968); Angel R. Hernandez to Snowbarger (June 24, 1968); fine 499-1; Danny Steele, "Why a Campus Christian Center?" (22 pp.), delivered at Campus Ministry Conference (July 10-11, 1969) (file 499-5).

20. Don Posterski to Paul Miller (December 1, 1971). See copies of *Campus Ministry Bulletin* in file 499-24; see also file 499-1.

21. Ann Kiemel, "Depending on the Holy Spirit," and Ann Kiemel, "Reaching the Teens on the High School Campus," *Director's Digest* (Winter 1971), section IV.

22. Willis Snowbarger, "Commencement," *Herald of Holiness* (December 24, 1969), 6-7; Ann Kiemel, *I'm Out to Change My World* (Nashville: Image, 1974), 72; Ann Kiemel, *I Love the Word Impossible* (Wheaton, IL: Tyndale House, 1976), 53-54. See James R. Cameron, *The Spirit Makes the Difference: The History of Eastern Nazarene College, Part II, 1950—2000* (Quincy, MA: ENC Press, 2000), 262-63.

23. Kiemel, "Reaching the Teens," 6-7.

24. David Whitelaw and Floyd Cunningham, conversation with Paul Skiles (June 1, 2000). A few exceptions are Phyllis Naylor, "Song of Uninvolvement," *Conquest* (August 1969), 17-19, and "Four Vignettes from an African Family Tree," *Conquest* (April 1970), 1-3, 37-39; Sue Briquette, "A Short Story About Why Blacks Revolt," *Conquest* (February 1973), 21-23. See also William Goodman, *Only Dopes Use Drugs* (Kansas City: Beacon Hill Press of Kansas City, 1978).

25. R. R. Hodges, "Christian Service Training" report to the 1948 General Assembly (file 486-20); A. F. Harper and Norman Oke, "Annual Report of the Christian Service Training Commission," 1955 (file 486-21); Norman Oke personnel file; "Minutes of the Christian Service Training Commission" (September 8, 1960), D. I. Vanderpool to Bennett Dudney (May 12, 1964), and CST Commission Minutes (November 10, 1964 and December 1, 1964), all in file 230-34; "Brief Statement of the History of CST" [1968] (file 285-2); Bennett Dudney file.

26. *Christian Service Training: Your Nazarene Blue Book* (Kansas City: Commission on Christian Service Training, 1952), 6-9, 11, 18, 27; "Brief Statement of the History of CST" [1968] (file 285-2); file 230-39.

27. Sam Stearman, *Senior Adult Ministries with Brother Sam* (Kansas City: Beacon Hill Press of Kansas City, 1974), passim; Donald W. Welch, "American Adult Sunday School Leadership in the Church of the Nazarene, 1907-1994," Ph.D. diss., U. of Kansas, 1994, 72-75.

28. "Curriculum Growth, 1945-1975" (Box 258); Donald W. Welch, "American Adult Sunday School Leadership," 76.

29. Paul Bassett, "Albert F. Harper: A Man for His Time," *Seminary Tower* (Spring 1987), 6. See Albert F. Harper, *The Story of Ourselves: A Study in the Growth of Personality for Teachers and Parents* (Kansas City: Beacon Hill Press, 1944), 149-50 (pp. 162-63 in later printings), which recounts his conversion; "Have You Met Albert F. Harper?" *Conquest* (January 1951), 24-28; Riley, *From Sagebrush to Ivy*, 106; Welch, "American Adult Sunday Leadership," 41.

30. "Curriculum Growth, 1945-1975" (Box 258). See Lillian Peck, *Better Primary Teaching* (Kansas City: Nazarene Publishing House, 1957).

31. Stephen S. White, "Some Outstanding Events," *Herald of Holiness* (February 1, 1956), 5.

32. Harper, "Aldersgate Curriculum Materials," *Church School Builder* (July 1964), 31. See also Wayne E. Caldwell, ed., *Reformers and Revivalists: The History of the Wesleyan Church* (Indianapolis: Wesley Press, 1992), 331-32, 366-68, 649-51.

33. Kenneth Rice file; Welch, "American Adult Sunday School Leadership," 55-57.

34. D. I. Vanderpool to Elbert Dodd (November 18, 1954) (file 906-29); Harper, "Church Schools," Report to the 18th [1972] General Assembly (Box 258); Darold Wilson and Gerdonna Wilson, *Questions of a Nazarene Layman* (N.p., n.d.), 1-4, 22, 27; S. T. Ludwig to General Superintendents and Executive Secretaries (June 29, 1955) (Harper file); Harper, "Department of Church Schools Affiliation with the National Council of Churches" (6 pp.) (file 403-8); Welch, "American Adult Sunday School Leadership," 59-67.

35. Harper, "Department of Church Schools Report to Task Force '70," August 11, 1970 (Box 258); Tracy, *New Testament Evangelism Today.*

36. Christian Education Committee (May 12, 1975) (file 777-9).

37. A. F. Harper's "Church Schools Report" to the 18th [1972] General Assembly (Box 258). Also Harper, "Workers Together with Him" [1974] (Box 258); Donald Metz to the Board of General Superintendents, "Report of the Pastor's Curriculum Seminar" [1974], Box 258; written comments of Wesley Tracy to Floyd Cunningham (March 30, 2000).

38. A. F. Harper, "Church Schools," Report to the 18th [1972] General Assembly (Box 258). See "Curriculum Growth, 1945-1975" (Box 258); Welch, "American Adult Sunday School Leadership," 76; written comments of Wesley Tracy to Floyd Cunningham (March 30, 2000).

39. Donald Metz to the Board of General Superintendents, "Report of the Pastor's Curriculum Seminar" [1974] and other committee minutes and reports in Box 258; Metz, "Toward a Philosophy for Adult Christian Education," in *How to Teach Adults Without Really Suffering*, comp. Wesley Tracy (Kansas City: Beacon Hill Press of Kansas City, 1976), 24-36.

40. Welch, "American Adult Sunday School Leadership," 77, 80, 82, 84.

Chapter 21

1. For statements of her philosophy of education, see Munro, *Years Teach*, 270; Munro, "My Philosophy of Education," January 1972, Mount Vernon Nazarene College Archives. See also Cameron, *Eastern Nazarene College*, 371.

2. "A Philosophy of Education for the Church of the Nazarene," June 20, 1952 (file 1220-54)

3. Munro, "Our Philosophy in Action," Education Conference, October 17-19, 1951 (file 879-51).

4. On the role of teachers, see also Paul T. Culbertson, "The Effective Nazarene College Teacher" (June 16, 1956) (file 1220-54), and Spruce, "Roots of the Problem," 24. See also Ralph E. Perry, "A Study of the Objectives in Higher Education of the Six Liberal Arts Colleges of the Church of the Nazarene," Ph.D. diss., Bradley U., 1952, 25-32, 65, 193. For background into the relation between religion and science in American culture in the postwar years, depicting the optimism among evangelicals that the two could be reconciled, see James Gilbert, *Redeeming Culture: American Religion in an Age of Science* (Chicago: U. of Chicago Press, 1997), chap. 7.

5. G. B. Williamson, "Inauguration of Dr. John Riley," file 1234-1. See also G. B. Williamson, "The Interdependence of Christian Education and Evangelism," delivered at Olivet Nazarene College (N.d.) (file 1234-1).

6. Hugh C. Benner, "Nazarene Beginnings," *Herald of Holiness* (March 11, 1953), 7. Likewise, Samuel Young, "A Plea for Perspective and Commitment," address delivered at inauguration of Stephen W. Nease, June 14, 1969, Mount Vernon Nazarene College Archives.

7. H. C. Benner, "Keynote Address," Seventh Educational Conference, October 12, 1959 (file 879-54) (and see "Report of Workshops at the Seventh Educational Conference," October 12-15, 1959, in the same file); Lewis, "Promoting and Preserving Our Holiness Heritage," 5.

8. Perry, "Study of the Objectives in Higher Education," 9; Cameron, *Eastern Nazarene College*, 349-50, 373-74; "Education Commission Minutes" (April 29-30, 1963) (file 619-12); *Oasis* (1972), 36; Kenneth B. Slifer, "Relative Importance of Selected Factors Influencing Choice of College Among College Freshmen Affiliated with the Church of the Nazarene," Ed.D. diss., Auburn U., 1973, 78-82; Wynkoop, *Trevecca Story*, 206; Kirkemo, *For Zion's Sake*, 183, 199; file 874-48; Cameron, *Spirit Makes the Difference*, 14-15.

9. Joseph M. Hopkins, "Good News for Church Colleges!" *Christian Century* (August 21, 1954), 490-91.

10. E. S. Mann, "Founder's Day Address," Northwest Nazarene College, September 29, 1972; 1973 Statistics, Department of Education and Ministry (file 568-4); E. S. Mann, *Linked to a Cause: A Personal History of Eastern Nazarene College* (Kansas City: Pedestal Press, 1986), 114-15; Oren Randall Spindle, "An Analysis of Higher Education in the Church of the Nazarene, 1945-1978," Ed.D. diss., Oklahoma State U., 1981, 204-5.

11. Williamson, "Inauguration of Dr. John Riley" [1952] (file 1234-1). See also Donald S. Metz, *MidAmerica Nazarene College: The Pioneer Years, 1966-1971* (Kansas City: Nazarene Publishing House, 1991), 55-72.

12. Leslie Parrott, research director, "A Study of the Educational Structure in the Church of the Nazarene," summary report to Lilly Endowments, Indianapolis, Indiana [1964]; Spindle, "Analysis of Higher Education," 218-20, 224-26. See also Alvin R. Atwood, "A Study of Student Personnel Services Available in Colleges of the Church of the Nazarene in the United States with Certain Recommendations for Improvement," Ph.D. diss., East Texas State U., 1970.

13. *Herald of Holiness* (April 1970), 16; Kirkemo, *For Zion's Sake*, 325.

14. Theodore Mickle Jr. to Edward S. Mann [1973] (file 229-5); *Conquest* (October 1965), 41-42; Al Truesdale to Mike Neely (August 6, 1969, and April 20, 1970), Curtis Smith to Mike Neely (February 13, 1970), and Willis Snowbarger to Mike Neely (February 21, 1970), all in file 227-22; Spindle, "An Analysis of Higher Education," 233, 274-77.

15. Wynkoop, *Trevecca Story*, 206; Harper L. Cole, "A Study of the Governance Style of A. B. Mackey, President of Trevecca Nazarene College, 1936-1963," Ed.D. diss., Oklahoma State U., 1978, 64, 123, 150, 175, 203-7; Homer J. Adams, *Reminiscences of Dr. A. B. Mackey* (Nashville: Trevecca Press, 1997), 39-45.

16. *Trevecca Nazarene College Bulletin General Catalogue, 1950-1951*; Cole, "A Study of the Governance Style of A. B. Mackey," 73-82, 86-87; Adams, *Reminiscences*, 49-66.

17. Wynkoop, *Trevecca Story*, 217.

18. *Trevecca Messenger* (October 1967), 1; Wynkoop, *Trevecca Story*, 218-31; Greathouse, "Reflections and Concerns" (April 1990), and Paul Bassett, "W. M. Greathouse from One Historian's Point of View" (April 12, 1990) (file 1219-7).

19. *Trevecca Nazarene College Messenger* (Winter 1974), 1; Wynkoop, *Trevecca Story*, 235-40; Spindle, "Analysis of Higher Education," 197-98.

20. *Bethany Nazarene College Bulletin, 1961-1962; Arrow* (1968), 18-19; Roy Cantrell profile file.

21. Gresham and Gresham, *From Many Came One*, 97.

22. Spindle, "Analysis of Higher Education," 252, 261-62; Thornton, *Radical Righteousness*, 225-26.

23. Ruth Vaughn, *Fools Have No Miracles: The Story of the Bethany Nazarene College "Miracle Offering"* (Kansas City: Nazarene Publishing House, 1971); C. Paul Gray, *Journey into Faith: The Story of a Nazarene Pilgrim* (Bethany, OK: Southern Nazarene U., 1995), 272-73; Gresham and Gresham, *From Many Came One*, 92-106.

24. Interview in *Arrow* (1973), 18-19.

25. Mann, *Linked to a Cause*, 106-13.

26. Munro, *Years Teach*, 27-28, 49, 87, 112, 132, 134, 155, 232, 332. See *Herald of Holiness* (August 15, 1952), 35; Cameron, *Eastern Nazarene College*, 88, 130; Hazel Lee, *One in the Bond of Love* (Kansas City: Beacon Hill Press of Kansas City, 1984).

27. Mann, *Linked to a Cause*, 58; Cameron, *Spirit Makes the Difference*, 71-75, 98; *Christian Scholar* (December 1964), 1.

28. D. I. Vanderpool to Samuel Young (July 11, 1955) (file 9066-4); Mann, "The Responsibilities of a Faculty Member," at the Seventh Educational Conference (October 14-17, 1957) (file 879-54); Cameron, *Spirit Makes the Difference*, 63-64.

29. "Prexy Comes to Chat," *Campus Camera* (September 18, 1968), 1, 6; various articles in *Campus Camera Special Edition: Student-Faculty Retreat* [Fall 1968]; "Named Dean of Students," *Christian Scholar* (July 1969), 1; Cameron, *Spirit Makes the Difference*, 213-18, 245-47.

30. "Minutes of the Meeting of General Superintendents and College Presidents" (December 9, 1968) (file 662-22); Ed Mann to Edward Lawlor (October 16, 1969) and Edward Lawlor, memo (March 2, 1970) (both in file 621-22); Cameron, *Spirit Makes the Difference*, 242, 246-47, 255, 260.

31. Spindle, "Analysis of Higher Education," 198-99; Cameron, *Spirit Makes the Difference*, 261, 278, 283-88.

32. Corbett, *Pioneer Builders*, 66-70; Mervyn Goins, "Harold W. Reed: Contributions to Christian Higher Education," Ph.D. diss., U. of Oklahoma, 1991, 8, 52-59, 109-10, 122-25; NCN News (August 5, 2008).

33. Harold Reed, "The President's Annual Report: The State of the College 1949-1974," Olivet Nazarene College, February 13, 1974 (file 757-47); Carl S. McClain, *I Remember: My Fifty-Seven Years at Olivet Nazarene College* (Kansas City: Pedestal Press, 1983), 197-211; *Olivet Story*, 99.

34. McClain, *I Remember*, 164, 189; Goins, "Harold W. Reed," 11; Harold W. Reed, *The Dynamics of Leadership* (Kankakee, IL: Reed International Institute, 1982), 192-94, 215-17.

35. E. W. Martin to E. S. Mann (April 20, 1973) (file 229-5); Reed, "The President's Annual Report: The State of the College 1949-1974"; David J. Spittal, "The Image of Olivet Nazarene College as Perceived by Selected Institutional Reference Groups," Ed.D. diss., Ball State U., 1975, 312-14; McClain, *I Remember*, 182-85; Willis Snowbarger, in *The Olivet Story*, 109-10.

36. Vanderpool to Riley (June 7, 1957) (file 908-7).

37. Vanderpool to Riley (December 9, 1957; April 28, 1958; and October 12, 1961) (all in file 908-7).

38. Riley, "Are the Problems on Campus Regarding the 'Spiritual Atmosphere' That School Men Face a Reflection of the Church in General?" (file 619-2).

39. "Minutes of the Meeting of General Superintendents and College Presidents" (December 9, 1968) (file 662-22); Riley, *From Sagebrush to Ivy*, 172-75; *Oasis* (1965), 235; *Oasis* (1968), 70; *Oasis* (1969), 81; *Oasis* (1970), 57, 73.

40. *Oasis* (1965), 42-43; *Messenger* (February 1966); *Messenger* (May 1969), 3; *Oasis* (1973), 147.

41. Purkiser, "Opening Address of President to Faculty," Pasadena College (September 5, 1956) (file 1589-13).

42. Kirkemo, *For Zion's Sake*, 202, 206-9, 357.

43. DeLong, *Education, Character, Religion* (Pasadena, CA: Pasadena College, 1957); Kirkemo, *For Zion's Sake*, 233-34.

44. Kirkemo, *For Zion's Sake*, 220-58, 358.

45. "A Statement by Russell V. DeLong to the General Superintendents Concerning His Resignation as President of Pasadena College" (N.d.), and DeLong to Howard Hamlin (June 4, 1969) (both in file 688-3). On DeLong see Corbett, *Pioneer Builders*, 54-58; *Herald of Holiness* (March 1, 1981), 20-21; Riley, *From Sagebrush to Ivy*, 83-84, 96, 105-6, 113-15; Kirkemo, *For Zion's Sake*, 228-45; Raser, *More Preachers*, 35-36, 46.

46. Kirkemo, *For Zion's Sake*, 240-44, 247.

47. Ibid., 253-57.

48. Ibid., 264, 276; see 261-76, 279.

49. J. C. Dobson, "Cliches and Sacred Concepts," *Nazarene Preacher* (October 1970), 9; Kirkemo, *For Zion's Sake*, 248-49, 292-97, 307-9, 330-32. See Reuben Welch, *When You Run Out of Fantastic, Persevere* ([Nashville]: Impact, 1976); Reuben Welch, *To Timothy and All Other Disciples: Probing Thoughts from Second Timothy* (Kansas City: Beacon Hill Press of Kansas City, 1979).

50. "A Day of Reflection," November 14, 1969, and David Rodes to Mike Neely (N.d.) (file 227-22); Kirkemo, *For Zion's Sake*, 287-92.

51. Kirkemo, *For Zion's Sake*, 310-28, 350-52; Spindle, "Analysis of Higher Education," 201, 247.

52. *Herald of Holiness* (April 22, 1946), 14-15; Merne A. Harris, *The Torch Goeth Onward: Tested but Triumphant* (University Park, IA: Vennard College, n.d.), 65-67. Later Kletzing was taken over by the Chicago Evangelistic Institute and was called Vennard College until it closed in 1995.

53. "Minutes of the General Board" (January 1950), 128, cited in Spindle, "Analysis of Higher Education," 193.

54. Spindle, "Analysis of Higher Education," 187-88.

55. "Report of Workshops at the Seventh Educational Conference" (October 12-15, 1959); H. C. Benner, "Keynote Address," Seventh Educational Conference (October 12, 1959) (file 879-54).

56. *Journal of the Twelfth General Assembly of the Church of the Nazarene*, eds. S. T. Ludwig and Greta Hamsher (Kansas City: N.p., 1948), 115-16; W. E. Snowbarger to S. T. Ludwig (March 9, 1959) (file 879-54).

57. Leslie Parrott, research director, "A Study of the Educational Structure in the Church of the Nazarene," summary report to Lilly Endowments, Indianapolis, Indiana [1964]. See file 654-61.

58. Williamson, "Plea for Nazarene Bible College" [1964] (file 1234-1); Otto Stucki, "Amendment to Report of the Education Commission" (file 492-6); Williamson to Darrell Johnson (October 19, 1971) (file 1233-38); Williamson, *Gideon,* 109-20; Johnson, *Hardy C. Powers,* 56-57.

59. *Journal of the Sixteenth General Assembly of the Church of the Nazarene,* 71-73, 186-91; Minutes, Nazarene Bible College Board of Control (September 3, 1965), and Strickland to Willis Snowbarger (September 13, 1965) (both in file 492-6); Johnson and Zurcher, *Strickland Safari,* 71-72.

60. Question and Answer with Kenneth Armstrong, *Blueprint for Living* (May 4, 1968) (file 519-22); "'College' Brings Pastor Nazarene Censure," *Detroit Free Press* (October 13, 1969) (file 519-22); and see John Wesley Colleges brochure, and other promotional materials in file 519-22.

61. Leonard Yourist, "Foundation Has Holdings," *Weekly Eccentric* (file 492-27); R. V. DeLong to Board of Trustees (May 21, 1970) and other documents in file 492-27, including the "Articles of Incorporation of John Wesley Educational and Development Foundation"; *Blueprint for Living* (June 1970) (file 519-22); *Owosso Argus-Press* (December 1, 1971) (file 686-36); *Journal of Miracles: The Exciting Story of John Wesley College* (N.p., n.d.) (file 519-22).

62. Lawlor to Armstrong (January 21, 1969) (file 492-27); "'College' Brings Pastor Nazarene Censure"; Loyal Boulton to Kenneth Armstrong (November 9, 1970) and E. W. Martin to Samuel Young (February 16, 1972, and October 21, 1970) (all in file 1387-27); *Owosso Argus-Press* 118 (August 11, 1972).

63. *Herald of Holiness* (June 15, 1966); *Herald of Holiness* (October 26, 1966); *Kansas City Times* (February 8, 1967); *Kansas City Times* (February 10, 1967); *Olathe Daily News* (October 11, 1968); Elmer Towns, "The College That Faith Built," *Christian Life* (June 1974) (file 404-42); Metz, *MidAmerica,* 94-100, 142-44, 324.

64. Metz, *MidAmerica,* 111.

65. Gray, *Journey into Faith,* 272. See R. Curtis Smith to Samuel Young (September 1, 1967) (file 1387-30); *Olathe Daily News* (May 18, 1989); R. Curtis Smith profile folder; Metz, *MidAmerica,* 87-94, 106-11.

66. Metz, *MidAmerica,* 11, 19, 138, 166, 416.

67. "Flavoring Theme Added by Metz," *Olathe Daily News* (October 11, 1968) (file 404-42); "Faith, Patriotism Guide Nazarene College," *Kansas City Times* (March 15, 1969), C1; John T. Davis, "Nazarene College Thrives on Strictness," *Kansas City Times* (October 13, 1975), 12A; Metz, *MidAmerica,* 138-40, 161, 167.

68. Metz, *MidAmerica,* 125, 166-68, 174, 221-25; Gary Kisner, "Structured Life at Nazarene School," *Kansas City Times* (March 15, 1969), 2C; Curtis's President's Report, cited in Spindle, "Analysis of Higher Education," 212.

69. Davis, "Nazarene College Thrives on Strictness," 12A; Spindle, "Analysis of Higher Education," 192; Metz, *MidAmerica,* 87-97, 99-101, 106-11, 162-65; Donald S. Metz, *Some Crucial Issues in the Church of the Nazarene* (Olathe, KS: Wesleyan Heritage Press, 1994), 87-104; "MNU Mourns Death of Dr. Donald Metz," NCN News (September 20, 2008).

70. "'A' College Board Meeting" (May 24, 1966), and "Site Selection Committee," Zone A Nazarene College (September 12-13, 1966), Mount Vernon Nazarene College Archives; *Mount Vernon News* (February 10, 1967), 1; Betty Taylor, "New College Pioneers at Lakeholm," *Conquest* (October 1969), 4-12; *Herald of Holiness* (October 9, 1968), 18; Spindle, "Analysis of Higher Education," 191-92; Stephen Nease, "The Early Days of Mount Vernon Nazarene College" (October 12, 1993) (file 1315-42); Adams, *Reminiscences,* 65.

71. *Mount Vernon Nazarene College Admissions Bulletin* 1968-1969, 4; John Knight to Edward Mann (December 22, 1972) (file 229-5).

72. Nease, "Inaugural Response" (June 14, 1969), Mount Vernon Nazarene College Archives. See Charles McCall, Novice Morris, Juanita Ferguson, and Jan Hendrickx, *Coming of Age: Mount*

Vernon Nazarene College, 1968-1993 (Mount Vernon, OH: Mount Vernon Nazarene College, 1994), 5-19.

73. Nease, "The Early Days of Mount Vernon Nazarene College." On qualifications for a dean, see Nease to Thurman Coburn (January 17, 1967), Nease papers, Mount Vernon Nazarene U. Archives.

74. Robert Lawrence, "Developing Academic Responsibility" [1966] (file 873-37); 1973 Statistics, Department of Education and Ministry (file 568-4). See *Coming of Age*, 5-25.

75. See J. B. Chapman to M. O. Osborn (October 15, 1946), cited in Stan Ingersol, "The Advocate of Graduate Theological Education," *Herald of Holiness* (January 15, 1986), 9; S. T. Ludwig to M. Lunn (September 6, 1944), and J. B. Chapman, "What We Expect of Our Seminary," Convocation Address (September 28, 1945), cited in Ingersol, "The Nazarene Seminary and Aspiring Love," *Herald of Holiness* (January 15, 1987), 9.

76. Quoted in Raser, *More Preachers*, 28.

77. See R. V. DeLong, "Thirtieth Anniversary Address," Nazarene Theological Seminary (October 22, 1974) (file 2054-3); Spindle, "Analysis of Higher Education," 194; Raser, *More Preachers*, 3, 17, 20-31.

78. Corbett, *Pioneer Builders*, 130-33; Raser, *More Preachers*, 34-49; Nazarene News Service, Weekly Summary (May 26, 1995).

79. DeLong to Corlett (June 23, 1953; July 27, 1953; August 6, 1953; August 10, 1953; and August 15, 1953), Corlett to DeLong (July 1, 1953, and July 17, 1953) (all in file 2054-3); E. E. Grosse, in *Herald of Holiness* (May 12, 1954), 19, on DeLong's resignation; Raser, *More Preachers*, 83.

80. William C. Miller, "The Governance of Theological Education: A Case Study of Nazarene Theological Seminary 1945-1976," Ph.D. diss., Kent State U., 1983.

81. Lewis T. Corlett, "Nazarene Theological Seminary and 'Crusade for Souls Now,'" *Herald of Holiness* (February 4, 1953), 5. See also Griffith, "Nineteen Reasons Why" (N.d.) (file 850-38); Spruce, "The Roots of the Problem."

82. Greathouse, "Reflections and Concerns" (April 1990), and Bassett, "W. M. Greathouse from One Historian's Point of View" (April 12, 1990) (file 1219-7).

83. Spindle, "Analysis of Higher Education," 194-95.

84. *Journal of the Sixteenth General Assembly of the Church of the Nazarene*, eds. B. Edgar Johnson and J. H. Mayfield (Kansas City: Nazarene Publishing House, 1964), 71-73; Minutes, Nazarene Bible College Board of Control (September 3, 1965), and Strickland to Willis Snowbarger (September 13, 1965) (both in file 492-6); Johnson and Zurcher, *Strickland Safari*, 71-72.

85. Snowbarger to Strickland (October 31, 1968 [file 492-6], and November 17, 1969), Strickland to Board of Trustees (November 2, 1970) (both in file 492-6); Strickland, "Presenting the Proposed ThB Program at NBC" [December 1969] (file 492-6); "Nazarene Bible College Initial Evaluation" (April 27-29, 1974) (file 571-6); memorandum dated January 15, 1973, and Edward S. Mann to College Presidents (April 19, 1973) (both in file 492-6).

86. Inaugural of L. S. Oliver as president (file 492-6).

87. H. T. Reza, *Prescription for Permanence: The Story of Our Schools for Training Ministers in Latin America* (Kansas City: Nazarene Publishing House, 1968), 16, 70. See, e.g., G. B. Williamson, "Christian Education in Foreign Fields," in *Missions for Millions*, ed. C. Warren Jones (Kansas City: Nazarene Publishing House, 1948), 14-15; "Overseas Bible Colleges," *Other Sheep* (April 1958), 13; Williamson, "The Interdependence of Christian Education and Evangelism," speech delivered at Olivet, n.d. (file 1234-1); C. Warren Jones, "A Teaching Ministry," *Other Sheep* (March 1956), 3; Donald Owens, "Commencement Day in Korea," *Other Sheep* (May 1959), 6; Roy E. Coplin, *Life in a Nazarene Bible College: The Story of Missionary Education in the Philippines* (Kansas City: Nazarene Publishing House, 1962).

88. Marjorie Burne, "Bremersdorp Nazarene Mission Nurses' and Teachers' Graduation," *Herald of Holiness* (February 6, 1952), 15; David Hynd, "A Tribute to Miss Margaret Latta, M.B.E." *Other Sheep* (October 1962), 6, 12.

89. Harrison Davis and Doris Davis to "Dear Ones at Home" (July 20, 1960), Davis papers. See Cunningham, *Holiness Abroad*, 127.

90. Wynkoop, "Educational Problems in Japan" (April 1963), 22 pp. (file 1387-74).

91. Wynkoop, "Educational Problems in Japan"; see Cunningham, *Holiness Abroad,* 127-28.

92. Dorothy J. Thomson, *Vine of His Planting: History of Canadian Nazarene College* (Edmonton: Commercial Printers, 1961), esp. pp. 31-32.

93. A. E. Airhart, "Report of the President" (March 6-7, 1962), and "Report of the Dean of the College—March 1970" (both in file 492-12); Parker, *From East to Western Sea,* 97-107.

94. Minutes, Nazarene Training College Area Board Meeting, Trinidad (May 30, 1961); Wesley Harmon, "To the Members of the Board of Control of the Nazarene Training College 1966 Annual Meeting"; "Recommendations from the Principal and Administration Council," 1967; Annual Meeting of the Area Board of Caribbean Nazarene Theological College (September 17-18, 1974) (file 416-14); Saxon, *Flares in the Night,* 48-60.

95. Oscar J. Finch to G. B. Williamson, n.d. (file 492-23); *Nazarene Bible School Newsletter* (Autumn 1966); R. L. Lunsford, "Director's Annual Report," February 17, 1967; Parker, *Mission to the World,* 394; Donald Reed, "The Birth of a Bible School," *Holiness Today* (April 2000), 8-10.

96. Finch to G. B. Williamson (N.d.) (file 492-23); R. J. Cerrato to George Coulter (August 9, 1962) (file 2131-25); "Nazarenes to Open European Bible School," *Herald of Holiness* (July 14, 1965), 18.

97. Nielson, "A Pilot Program in Education" (June 28, 1967) (file 492-24). See also Nielson, "First Annual Report of the Rector to the College Board of European Nazarene Bible College" (January 18, 1967), and Nielson, "European Nazarene Bible College—1965-1969" (both in file 492-23). See also "Seventeen Enroll in European Bible College," *Herald of Holiness* (February 15, 1966), 14; Nielson, "A Pilot Program in Education," *Herald of Holiness* (January 24, 1968), 4-5; Bennett Dudney, *ENBC: Miracle in Busingen* (Kansas City: Nazarene Publishing House, 1980).

98. *Herald of Holiness* (May 21, 1969), 17; Willis Snowbarger to Bill Prince (February 6, 1970) (file 492-23); *Herald of Holiness* (July 15, 1970), 13. See also Connie G. Patrick, *The Miracle Goes On: European Nazarene Bible College* (Kansas City: Nazarene Publishing House, 2000).

99. Hilario Pena, "Spanish Bible and Missionary Training Institute," *Other Sheep* (August 1947), 5; *Seminario Nazareno Hispano-Americano Catalogo General* (N.d.) (file 565-6); Reza, *Washed by the Blood,* 31-32; Helen Temple, *Like a Tree by the River: The Story of C. E. Morales* (Kansas City: Nazarene Publishing House, 1973), 76-78.

100. Samuel Young and H. T. Reza, "A Condensed Report on the All Central American Bible Institute" (1966) (file 565-6).

101. Committee Meeting Minutes on Central America Nazarene Seminary (file 565-6).

102. *Prospecto Instituto Biblico Nazareno, 1966-67* (file 565-6).

103. "Report of Trip to Central America Regarding the Nazarene Central American Seminary" (file 565-6); Young and Reza, "A Condensed Report"; Consejo De Admistracion del Seminario Nazarene Centroamericano (November 30, 1970); W. Howard Conrad to Helen Temple (June 17, 1972) (file 1850-16); *El Seminarista* (Marzo-Mayo 1974); *El Seminarista* (Junio-Agosto 1974); *El Seminarista* (Junio-Agosto 1975) (file 451-16). On Conrad see also Students, Nazarene Bible School in Peru, to General Superintendents (March 18, 1968) (file 567-8).

104. Minutes of a Swaziland Nazarene Education Committee Meeting Held at Bremersdorp (March 29, 1961); Ted Esselstyn, Lula Schmelzenbach Memorial Nazarene Bible College Report to the Ninth Annual Council (August 1970); L.S.M. Nazarene Bible College Tenth Annual Report, 1973; Lula Schmelzenbach Memorial Nazarene Bible College Prospectus, Acornhoek (N.d.) (file 635-16).

105. *Catalogue of the Nazarene Bible College* [1956]; Richard S. Taylor, *Our Pacific Outposts* (Kansas City: Beacon Hill Press, 1956), 109-10; Nelson G. Mink, *Southern Cross Salute: The Church of the Nazarene in Australia and New Zealand* (Kansas City: Nazarene Publishing House, 1969), 66-72; Cook, *Water from Deep Wells,* 145-58.

106. Berg to Samuel Young (November 29, 1962); H. S. Palmquist to Samuel Young (September 27, 1966); Nelson Mink to George Coulter (July 22, 1968); Josephine Spratt to Coulter (October 15, 1969); Coulter to Berg (September 4, 1970); Berg to Coulter (August 11, 1970); Berg to Raymond Hurn (February 15, 1971); Chester Mulder to Coulter and Hurn (July 3, 1971); "The Annual Meeting of the Nazarene Bible College Board" (September 15, 1972).

Chapter 22

1. D. I. Vanderpool to Mrs. Carl Collett (September 19, 1951); C. W. Butler, "A Dangerous Heresy," *Herald of Holiness* (April 20, 1955), 3; Edward Lawlor, "The Conservative Theological Position and the Spirit of Evangelism," *Preacher's Magazine* (September 1958), 27; L. J. DuBois, "The Theology Workshop," *Herald of Holiness* (August 5, 1958), 7; John G. Merritt, "Fellowship in Ferment: A History of the Wesleyan Theological Society, 1965-1984," *Wesleyan Theological Journal* 21 (Spring-Fall 1986), 186-203.

2. Carl Bangs, *Our Roots of Belief,* 71; 70-79. On Wiley see also Ross Price, *H. Orton Wiley: Servant and Savant of the Sagebrush* (Kansas City: Nazarene Publishing House, 1968), 42-43, 49-52; Bassett, "Fundamentalist Leavening," 65-67, 74, 79-80, 82-85; Kirkemo, *For Zion's Sake,* 77-79, 87-94, 202-26; Thomas Langford, *Practical Divinity,* vol. 1: *Theology in the Wesleyan Tradition* (Nashville: Abingdon, 1998), 121-24; Quanstrom, *A Century of Holiness Theology,* 75-89.

3. Al Truesdale to Floyd Cunningham (July 27, 2005); Max Otto cited in John Higham, *Hanging Together: Unity and Diversity in American Culture,* ed. Carl J. Guarneri (New Haven, CT: Yale U. Press, 2001), 56.

4. James McGraw, "The Preaching of Stephen S. White," *Preacher's Magazine* (August 1960), 5-8; Corbett, *Pioneer Builders,* 50-54; Quanstrom, *Century of Holiness Theology,* 108-15.

5. White, "What We Believe," *Herald of Holiness* (April 3, 1957), 12. See Lindström, *Wesley and Sanctification,* and White, "John Wesley *a la* Harold [sic] Lindström," *Herald of Holiness* (April 9, 1958), 12-14, and editorials in *Herald of Holiness* (April 16, 1958), 12-13.

6. White, "Two Major Trends in My Theological Thinking," *Preacher's Magazine* (October 1963), 6-9, 37. See Wynkoop, "Personalism versus Non-Personalism or Theology versus Mechanism," paper, Pasadena College (April 1929), and Wynkoop, "The Philosophy of Idealism and Its Influence on Religion in America," term paper, Northern Baptist Theological Seminary (November 17, 1953). See also Sam Powell, "A Critical Analysis of Relational Theology," in Festschrift written for Rob Staples. On Personalism see Langford, *Practical Divinity,* 164-70; Paul Deats, "Introduction to Boston Personalism," in *The Boston Personalist Tradition in Philosophy, Social Ethics, and Theology,* eds. Paul Deats and Carol Robb (Macon, GA: Mercer U. Press, 1986), 1-14; and Thomas Jay Oord, "Wesleyan Theology, Boston Personalism, and Process Theology," in *Thy Nature and Thy Name Is Love: Wesleyan and Process Theology in Dialogue,* eds. Bryan Stone and Thomas Joy Oord (Nashville: Abingdon, 2001), 379-92.

7. On Brightman see Rufus Burrow Jr., *Personalism: A Critical Introduction* (St. Louis: Chalice, 1999), 157-69, 182-83.

8. Charles R. McCall, "Undergraduate Teaching in Bible and Doctrine," Nazarene Theology Conference (November 27-29, 1972).

9. See Robert Griffin, "Accountability and Undergraduate Teaching in Bible and Doctrine," Nazarene Theology Conference (November 27-29, 1972).

10. Kirkemo, *For Zion's Sake,* 209, 218-19, 222-24.

11. Prescott Johnson, "The Odyssey of Spirit," Manuscript in the Nazarene Archives, 81, and throughout. Similarly, see, e.g., Thomas Starnes, "The Lost Childhood of Gary Hart: Growing Up Nazarene Marks You Forever," *Washington Post* (May 24, 1987), D2, in Thomas Starnes profile file; and, regarding Tom Boyd, *Oklahoma Daily* (June 26, 1990), and *Oklahoma Observer* (July 10/25, 1991), Tom Boyd profile file.

12. Gary Hart, *The Good Fight: The Education of an American Reformer* (New York: Random House, 1993), 24. See also E. J. Dionne, "The Elusive Front-Runner," *New York Times Magazine* (May 3, 1987), 31, 36; Garry Wills, *Under God: Religion and American Politics* (New York: Simon and Schuster, 1990), 41-50; Richard B. Cramer, *What It Takes: The Way to the White House* (New York: Random House, 1992), 331-32, 335, 342.

13. Bangs to Friend (April 10, 1961) (mimeographed form letter); Bangs to S. T. Ludwig (April 11, 1961, and July 12, 1961). See Carl Bangs, *Arminius: A Study in the Dutch Reformation,* 2nd ed. (Grand Rapids: Zondervan, 1985). See also R. V. DeLong to Willis Snowbarger (November 28, 1969; May 12, 1970; and April 9, 1970) (all in file 492-27).

14. E.g., John Riley, "Holiness—Crisis and Progress," in *Insights into Holiness: Discussions of Holiness by Fifteen Leading Scholars of the Wesleyan Persuasion* (Kansas City: Beacon Hill Press, 1962), 91-106.

15. S. S. White, "Eradication Versus Suppression," *Preacher's Magazine* (January-February 1949), 25-28; White, "Wesley's Beliefs," *Herald of Holiness* (January 15, 1958), 12; White, "The Question Box," *Herald of Holiness* (April 27, 1960), 17.

16. H. Orton Wiley, "Eradication," *Preacher's Magazine* (January-February 1948), 18-19.

17. S. S. White, "Let's Grow in Grace!" *Herald of Holiness* (February 28, 1958), 13. See White, "Wesley and Eradication," *Preacher's Magazine* (July-August 1948), 11-13. Out of a series of articles in *The Preacher's Magazine* White produced *Eradication: Defined, Explained, Authenticated* (Kansas City: Nazarene Publishing House, 1954). White published only two other small books: *Essential Christian Beliefs* (Kansas City: Nazarene Publishing House, 1942) and *Five Cardinal Elements in the Doctrine of Entire Sanctification* (Kansas City: Nazarene Publishing House, 1948). See also S. S. White, "The Question Box," *Herald of Holiness* (December 16, 1959), 17-18.

18. Paul Bassett, "In Honor of J. Kenneth Grider," *Wesleyan Theological Journal* 34 (Fall 1999), 281-86.

19. J. Kenneth Grider, "Carnality and Humanity: Exploratory Observations," *Wesleyan Theological Journal* (Spring 1976), 81-91; J. Kenneth Grider, *Entire Sanctification: The Distinctive Doctrine of Wesleyanism* (Kansas City: Beacon Hill Press of Kansas City, 1980), 105-13. Similarly, Delbert Gish, *Practical Problems of the Christian Life* (Kansas City: Beacon Hill Press, 1964), 83-87, and Donald Metz, *Studies in Biblical Holiness* (Kansas City: Beacon Hill Press of Kansas City, 1971), chap. 12, "Imperfect Perfection," 221-43. Other books written along the same lines on a more popular level, distinguishing between the carnal and the human, include J. E. Williams, *You're Human Too!* (Kansas City: Beacon Hill Press, 1963), and Leon Chambers and Mildred Chambers, *Human Nature and Perfecting Holiness* (Fairfax, AL: Leon Chambers, 1972).

20. J. Kenneth Grider, *Repentance unto Life: What It Means to Repent* (Kansas City: Beacon Hill Press of Kansas City, 1965), 39-44; J. Kenneth Grider, *A Wesleyan-Holiness Theology* (Kansas City: Beacon Hill Press of Kansas City, 1994), 42-62, 111, 243-45, 275-77. Compare George Croft Cell, *The Rediscovery of John Wesley* (New York: Henry Holt, 1935), 242-72; Chiles, *Theological Transition*, 144-83. See J. Kenneth Grider, *What It Means to Repent* (Kansas City: Beacon Hill Press of Kansas City, 1965), 43-44; and J. Kenneth Grider, "Arminianism," in *Evangelical Dictionary of Theology*, ed. Walter A. Elwell (Grand Rapids: Baker, 1984), 81.

21. Richard S. Taylor, "J. Kenneth Grider—The People's Theologian" (November 14, 1991) (file 1561-32).

22. Richard Howard, *Newness of Life: A Study in the Thought of Paul* (Kansas City: Beacon Hill Press of Kansas City, 1975), 10-13, 17-19, 33, 102-3, 134-48. See Grider, *Entire Sanctification*, 131-34.

23. Richard S. Taylor, "The Balance in Christian Holiness Between Likeness and Unlikeness to God," *Wesleyan Theological Journal* 8 (Spring 1973), 33-37.

24. Richard S. Taylor, "Sanctification and the Sin Problem," *Herald of Holiness* (April 28, 1947), 5.

25. Richard S. Taylor, *The Disciplined Life* (Kansas City: Beacon Hill Press, 1962), 92-93; Richard S. Taylor, *Life in the Spirit: Christian Holiness in Doctrine, Experience, and Life* (Kansas City: Beacon Hill Press of Kansas City, 1966), 195-96; Richard S. Taylor, *Exploring Christian Holiness*, vol. 3: *The Theological Formulation* (Kansas City: Beacon Hill Press of Kansas City, 1985), 213-36.

26. Richard S. Taylor, "Some Recent Trends in Wesleyan-Arminian Thought," *Wesleyan Theological Journal* (1971), 5-12.

27. Purkiser, "The Answer Corner," *Herald of Holiness* (September 17, 1969), 18.

28. E.g., Cell, *Rediscovery of John Wesley*; Maximin Piette, *John Wesley in the Evolution of Protestantism* (London: Sheed and Ward, 1937).

29. See, for example, Basil Miller, *John Wesley* (Grand Rapids: Zondervan, 1943), 82, 99-102; Robert Mortensen, "The Life and Significance of John Wesley," *Preacher's Magazine* (May-June 1950), 13-17; Lauriston DuBois, "Wesley's Contribution to Protestant Worship," *Preacher's Magazine* (August 1960), 1-4; T. Crichton Mitchell, *Mr. Wesley: An Intimate Sketch of John Wesley* (Kansas City: Beacon Hill Press, 1957). Compare Randy Maddox, "Respected Founder/Neglected Guide: The Role of Wesley in American Methodist Theology," *Methodist History* 37 (1998), 71-88.

30. Lindström, *Wesley and Sanctification*, 44-49, 117-18; Cox, *John Wesley's Concept of Perfection*. See White, "John Wesley *a la* Harold [sic] Lindström," 12-14, and editorials in *Herald of Holiness* (April 16, 1958), 12-13.

31. William M. Greathouse, "The Dynamics of Sanctification: Biblical Terminology," Nazarene Theology Conference (December 4-6, 1969) (file 729-33). See William M. Greathouse, "Sanctification and the Christus Victor Motif in Wesleyan Theology," *Wesleyan Theological Journal* (Spring 1972), 47-59. See also Rob L. Staples, "Tribute to William M. Greathouse," *Wesleyan Theological Journal* 33 (Spring 1998), 224-30.

32. See Wynkoop interview with Stan Ingersol (March 25, 1991); William Greathouse to Donald Metz (January 31, 1994), 5; Rob L. Staples, "Tribute to William M. Greathouse," *Wesleyan Theological Journal* 33 (Spring 1998), 224-30.

33. William M. Greathouse, *Nazarene Theology in Perspective* (Kansas City: Nazarene Theological Seminary, 1969), 12-13, 15, 16, 21, 24, 34-35. See also William M. Greathouse, "The Church of the Nazarene," *Ecumenical Review* (July 1971), 303-16.

34. Wynkoop interview with Janet Smith Williams (March 1981), Nazarene Archives; Wynkoop, "Satisfactions; Regrets; Concerns," paper presented February 27, 1992 (file 1561-32); Carl Bangs, "Mildred Olive Bangs Wynkoop," and other material in Wynkoop profile file, and in files 1427-2 and 1427-3.

35. Mildred Bangs Wynkoop, *A Theology of Love: The Dynamic of Wesleyanism* (Kansas City: Beacon Hill Press of Kansas City, 1972), 53-75, 85-86, 91-92, 95, 97, 105-7, 163, 198, 252. See Mildred Bangs Wynkoop, "Existentialism in Theology," *Asbury Seminarian* (Fall 1956); "The Communion of the Holy Spirit," *Wesleyan Theological Journal* (Spring 1968), 57-66; "A Hermeneutical Approach to John Wesley," *Wesleyan Theological Journal* (Spring 1971), 13-22; "John Wesley—Mentor or Guru?" *Wesleyan Theological Journal* (Spring 1975), 7-8.

36. Wynkoop, "Re—Relational Theology—What?" class handout, Nazarene Theological Seminary (March 10, 1977); Wynkoop, *Theology of Love*, 24, 150-151, 164, 303.

37. Wynkoop, *Theology of Love*, 308-9, 337-62.

38. Ibid., 11, 42, 47, 49, 73, 321. See as well Wynkoop's articles on "Religious Existentialism" in *Preacher's Magazine*: "I. Sanctification Is Existential" (July 1958), 2; "II. Love Is Existential" (August 1958), 16-20; "III. Practical Norm of Love" (September 1958), 29-31; "IV. Problem of Theological Words" (April 1961), 16-18. See also Mildred Bangs Wynkoop, "The Word Became Flesh: Closing the Holiness Credibility Gap" (file 729-33); Mildred Bangs Wynkoop, "Theological Roots of Wesleyanism's Understanding of the Holy Spirit," *Wesleyan Theological Journal* 14 (Spring 1979), 78.

39. *Seminary Tower* (Summer 1973), 9-10.

40. Metz, *Some Crucial Issues*, 169-79; Taylor, *Exploring Christian Holiness*, 98-100, and "Why the Holiness Movement Died," *God's Revivalist and Bible Advocate* (March 1999), 25-26; Grider, *Wesleyan-Holiness Theology*, 276, 285-86. See Leo Lawrence to M. A. Lunn (October 9, 1973); W. T. Purkiser to M. A. Lunn (October 31, 1973) (Box 728). See Quanstrom, *Century of Holiness Theology*, 141-50.

41. Knight, *Holiness Pilgrimage*, 11.

42. Ibid., 81.

43. Ibid., 17. See John A. Knight, *In His Likeness: God's Plan for a Holy People* (Kansas City: Beacon Hill Press of Kansas City, 1976).

44. Rob Staples, "The Present Frontiers of Wesleyan Theology," *Wesleyan Theological Journal* 12 (Spring 1977), 5-15.

45. Rob Staples, "Sanctification and Selfhood," *Wesleyan Theological Journal* 7 (Spring 1972), 1-9, 14, 19.

46. Reuben Welch, *We Really Do Need Each Other* (Nashville: Impact Books, n.d.), 68. See Ponder Gilliland, "Problems of Failure in the Sanctified Life" (file 729-33). See also James F. Ballew, *Growth in Holiness* (Kansas City: Beacon Hill Press of Kansas City, 1967), 38-39; Wynkoop, "A Wesleyan View on Preaching Holiness," *Wesleyan Theological Journal* 4 (Spring 1969), 16-26; J. Glenn Gould, *Healing the Hurt of Man: A Study of John Wesley's "Cure of Souls"* (Kansas City: Beacon Hill Press of Kansas City, 1971).

47. See Articles V and X in various editions of the *Manual*.

48. Wiley, *Christian Theology*, 2:444, 468-73. See Rob L. Staples, "The Current Debate on the Baptism with the Holy Spirit" (privately circulated, 1979), 39.

49. An early dissenting view to the association of Pentecost with entire sanctification was A. J. Smith, *Bible Holiness and the Modern, Popular, Spurious* (N.p., [1953]), 92-95. Two influential books representing Calvinist exegesis, yet widely read by Nazarene theologians, were James Dunn, *The Baptism of the Holy Spirit: A Re-examination of the New Testament Teaching on the Gift of the Spirit in Relation to Pentecostalism Today* (Naperville, IL: Alec R. Allenson, 1970), and Frederick Dale Bruner, *A Theology of the Holy Spirit: The Pentecostal Experience and the New Testament Witness* (Grand Rapids: Eerdmans, 1970). See Staples, "Current Debate on the Baptism with the Holy Spirit"; Alex Deasley, "Entire Sanctification and the Baptism with the Holy Spirit: Perspectives on the Biblical View of the Relationship," *Wesleyan Theological Journal* 14 (Spring 1979), 27-44; H. Ray Dunning, *Grace, Faith, and Holiness: A Wesleyan Systematic Theology* (Kansas City: Beacon Hill Press of Kansas City, 1988), 408, 420, 422, 467-71. See also Wynkoop, "Theological Roots," 77-98; Donald W. Dayton, "The Doctrine of the Baptism of the Holy Spirit: Its Emergence and Significance," *Wesleyan Theological Journal* 13 (Spring 1978), 114-25; Donald W. Dayton, *Theological Roots of Pentecostalism*, chap. 4, "The Triumph of the Doctrine of Pentecostal Spirit Baptism."

50. J. Kenneth Grider, "Spirit-Baptism the Means of Entire Sanctification," *Wesleyan Theological Journal* 14 (Fall 1979), 31-50; Grider, *Entire Sanctification*, 44-90. See also, e.g., D. Shelby Corlett, *The Baptism with the Holy Spirit* (Kansas City: Beacon Hill Press, 1947), 17-40, 49-51; D. Shelby Corlett, *Lord of All: A Discussion of Some Important Aspects of the Wesleyan Doctrine of Entire Sanctification* (Kansas City: Beacon Hill Press, 1962), 28, 85; D. Shelby Corlett, *God in the Present Tense: The Person and Work of the Holy Spirit* (Kansas City: Beacon Hill Press of Kansas City, 1974), 54-55; W. T. Purkiser, *Conflicting Concepts of Holiness*, rev. ed. (Kansas City: Beacon Hill Press of Kansas City, 1972), 15-16, 27-33, 55-60; Richard Taylor, *Exploring Christian Holiness*, 158-66.

51. S. S. White, "The Question Box," *Herald of Holiness* (December 4, 1957), 17.

52. "The Revised Standard Version," *Herald of Holiness* (December 19, 1951), 13-14. Likewise, *Herald of Holiness* (September 3, 1952), 15. See, by Holiness scholar Jasper Huffman, *The Revised Standard Version: An Appraisal* (Winona Lake, IN: Standard Press, 1953), 57-59, 68-69. See also Stephen Paine, "Twentieth Century Evangelicals Look at Bible Translation," *Wesleyan Theological Journal* 4 (Spring 1969), 79-90; Robert Branson, *God's Word in Man's Language* (Kansas City: Beacon Hill Press of Kansas City, 1980), 34-37; Jack Lewis, *The English Bible from KJV to NIV: A History and Evaluation* (Grand Rapids: Baker, 1981), 118-19.

53. *Herald of Holiness* (February 4, 1953), 3. See also Vanderpool to Young (July 30, 1953) (file 906-4).

54. For the entire RSV controversy in the Church of the Nazarene see Larry M. Baucom, "The Reaction of the Church of the Nazarene to the Historical Critical Method of Biblical Study," Ph.D. diss., Florida State U., 1995, 50-84, and, for the general picture, see Peter Thuesen, *In Discordance with the Scriptures: American Protestant Battles over Translating the Bible* (New York: Oxford U. Press, 1999). Thuesen mentions the change regarding "consecration" and "sanctification" on 86-87.

55. Harper to Samuel Young (July 15, 1953) (file 906-4); Harper, "From Which Bible Shall I Memorize?" (N.d.); "Suggestions for Guidelines in Choosing Memory Verses"; Harper to Board of General Superintendents (August 11, 1970); George Coulter to Harper (September 17, 1970), Box 258. See also W. T. Purkiser to Howard Keene (November 29, 1962); H. Blair Ward to J. Fred Parker (December 15, 1978) (Box 728), and tracts by Leo Davis published in the 1980s (file 637-18).

56. Ralph Earle, *How We Got Our Bible* (Kansas City: Beacon Hill Press of Kansas City, 1971), 113.

57. See Earle, *How We Got Our Bible*, 74-78, 102-3; and the "Preface" to Ralph Earle, Harvey J. S. Blaney, and Carl Hanson, *Exploring the New Testament* (Kansas City: Beacon Hill Press, 1955). Earle published these as *Word Meanings in the New Testament*, 6 vols. (Kansas City: Beacon Hill Press of Kansas City, 1974-82). See also Erwin G. Benson, "The Reception of the RSV" (November 3, 1955), file 727-14.

58. Earle to V. H Lewis and other General Superintendents (February 10, 1975) (file 621-39). See also Branson, *God's Word*, 62-69; Baucom, "The Reaction of the Church of the Nazarene," 84-101.

59. Purkiser, "Keynote Address," 1958 Theology Workshop, 10 (file 729-31).

60. See, e.g., John Riley, *The Golden Stairs* (Kansas City: Beacon Hill Press, 1947), 23-35; Earle, "Verbal Differences in Parallel Passages in the Synoptics and Their Implications for a Doctrine of Divine Inspiration," *Asbury Seminarian* (Spring-Summer 1954); Earle, "Wesley and the Methodists," *Preacher's Magazine* (July 1959), 20-23; Purkiser, in *Exploring Our Christian Faith* (Kansas City: Beacon Hill Press, 1960), 60-80; Wynkoop, "Some Positive Aspects of Biblical Preaching," *Preacher's Magazine* (February 1961), 16; John Cotner, "Report of the Study Group on the Holy Scriptures" (file 729-31); Frank Carver, "The Bearing of Hermeneutical Issues on the Question of Biblical Authority" (December 1-3, 1975) (file 729-37); Staples, "Present Frontiers," 12-13.

61. Harold Lindsell, *The Bible in the Balance* (Grand Rapids: Zondervan, 1979), 107; see 106-9. See the response of Paul Bassett, "The Theological Identity of the North American Holiness Movement," in *The Variety of American Evangelicalism*, ed. Donald Dayton and Robert K. Johnston (Knoxville: U. of Tennessee Press, 1991), 72, 94. See also Timothy Smith to B. Edgar Johnson (January 30, 1978), and J. Kenneth Grider, "Wesleyanism and the Inerrancy Issue," *Wesleyan Theological Journal* 19 (Fall 1984), 52-61.

62. Harold W. Reed to H. C. Benner (December 4, 1957) (legal file). See Reed's less strident stand in his book *You and Your Church* (Kansas City: Beacon Hill Press, n.d.), 51, and his understanding of Wesleyanism as a mediating theology in Reed, "Relationships in Theology: Liberalism, Wesleyan-Arminianism, Fundamentalism" (N.d.) (file 727-14). See also Carl Bangs to Nazarene Archives (April 29, 1991) (file 1297-38).

63. Earl Barrett, *A Christian Perspective of Knowing* (Kansas City: Beacon Hill Press of Kansas City, 1965), 16, 48, 113.

64. Ralph Earle, *What the Bible Says About the Second Coming* (Repr., Grand Rapids: Baker, 1973), 9 and throughout. See also Ralph Earle, "Revelation," in *Beacon Bible Commentary*, vol. 10, 461-62.

65. Roland E. Griffith, *The Gospel of the Second Coming* (Kansas City: Beacon Hill Press, 1946), 73, 85; C. T. Corbett, *Ready for the Rapture* (Kansas City: Beacon Hill Press, 1962), 20, and see 6, 16.

66. J. Grant Swank, *Moments to Go: A Study of the Second Coming* (Kansas City: Beacon Hill Press of Kansas City, 1974), 49-61, 68-93; Ivan A. Beals, *Come Soon, Lord Jesus: A Study of the Second Advent* (Kansas City: Beacon Hill Press of Kansas City, 1977), 35-36, 107, 116-18. See also Maynard James, *Daniel's Forecast* (Kansas City: Beacon Hill Press, 1964); Leon Chambers and Mildred Chambers, *Interpreting Satan—Antichrist: His World Empire* (N.p., 1973); Harold Raser, "Views on Last Things in the American Holiness Movement," in *Second Coming: A Wesleyan Approach to the Doctrine of the Last Things*, ed. H. Ray Dunning, 184-85. For the broader evangelical context see Paul Boyer, *Time Shall Be No More: Prophecy Belief in Modern American Culture* (Cambridge, MA: Harvard U. Press, 1992).

67. W. T. Purkiser, Richard Taylor, and Willard Taylor, *God, Man, and Salvation* (Kansas City: Beacon Hill Press of Kansas City, 1977), 9, 42-43. Compare Brevard Chiles, *Biblical Theology in Crisis* (Philadelphia: Westminster, 1970), 44-47.

68. Wiley, *Christian Theology*, 1:454-56.

69. Wilbur Mullen in *Exploring Our Christian Faith*, 146. See likewise W. T. Purkiser, *Our Wonderful World* (Kansas City: Beacon Hill Press of Kansas City, 1974), 62-65; W. T. Purkiser, C. E. Demaray, Donald Metz, and Maude Stuneck, *Exploring the Old Testament* (Kansas City: Beacon Hill Press, 1955), 70-72; S. S. White, "The Question Box," *Herald of Holiness* (March 9, 1960), 17; Russell V. DeLong, *So You Don't Believe in God?* (Kansas City: Beacon Hill Press of Kansas City, 1976), 52-61; Purkiser, Taylor, and Taylor, *God, Man, and Salvation*, 52-59. Also see Kirkemo, *For Zion's Sake*, 297-98, 332-33; Ronald Numbers, *The Creationists* (New York: Alfred A. Knopf, 1992), 305-7.

70. Mel-Thomas Rothwell, "Evolution and Christian Thought Today as a Theologian Sees It," Eleventh Education Conference (1967) (file 547-4). See also Stephen Nease's notes on the conference in Mount Vernon Nazarene University Archives.

71. Robert Lawrence, "Problems Confronting the Scientist and Theologian in the Church of the Nazarene" (December 9, 1967) (file 547-5); Karl Giberson, *Worlds Apart: The Unholy War Between Religion and Science* (Kansas City: Beacon Hill Press of Kansas City, 1993), 106-10, 173-75; Karl Giberson and Donald A. Yerxa, *Specie of Origins: America's Search for a Creation Story* (Lanham:

Rowman and Littlefield, 2002); Kirkemo, *For Zion's Sake,* 210, 297-300; Gilbert Ford, conversation with Floyd Cunningham (June 13, 2000). Compare Bernard Ramm, *The Christian View of Science and Scripture* (Grand Rapids: Eerdmans, 1954), esp. 262-63; Gilbert, *Redeeming Culture,* 154-63; Ronald L. Numbers, "Creation, Evolution, and Holy Ghost Religion: Holiness and Pentecostal Responses to Darwinism," *Religion and American Culture* 2 (Summer 1992), 145-50; Numbers, *Creationists,* 299-300, 306. See also Cameron, *Spirit Makes the Difference,* 110-15; Gilbert Ford, conversation with Floyd Cunningham (June 13, 2000).

72. Church History Commission, "Introduction," to Smith, *Called unto Holiness,* 9-10; Church History Commission file, Nazarene Archives; Smith, *Called unto Holiness,* 350-51. See also Timothy L. Smith, *Nazarenes and the Wesleyan Mission: Can We Learn from Our History?* (Kansas City: Beacon Hill Press of Kansas City, 1979); Stan Ingersol, "Timothy Smith and the Recovery of the Nazarene Vision," *Holiness Today* (March 1999), 30-31.

73. Smith, *Called unto Holiness,* 216-17, 203-4, 220-23, 266-71, 289-97, 348.

Part III Analysis

1. H. Richard Niebuhr, *Christ and Culture* (New York: Harper and Row, 1951), 47-66, 194; see 190-218.

2. J. Ray Shadowens, "The Fiftieth Anniversary of 'All Out for Souls,'" *Grow* (Summer 1996), 15.

3. Wilfred L. Winget, "The Holy Spirit and the Holiness of the Church: A Study in the Theology of the Church of the Nazarene," Ph.D. diss., Vanderbilt U., 1966, 250.

4. Benner, *Rendezvous with Abundance,* 116-17. Hear also his sermon at the 1960 General Assembly, "Pattern for Survival," *Minister's Tape Club* (Kansas City: Beacon Hill Press of Kansas City, 1981).

5. Morris Chalfant, "Son, Be True, Son, Be True," *Herald of Holiness* (December 23, 1959), 11.

6. See Winget, "Holy Spirit and the Holiness of the Church," 359, 369-70.

Chapter 23

1. Tracy and Ingersol, *Here We Stand,* 23-24.

2. *Journal of the Nineteenth General Assembly* (1976), 245-331, 471.

3. *Herald of Holiness* (December 15, 1976), 35; *Nazarene News Service Weekly Summary* (November 1, 1991); *Quadrennial Report to the Twenty-Fourth General Assembly* (1997), 5, 490-497. See also "The Church at Work: General Statistics," *Herald of Holiness* (April 1998), 32-33; General Secretary, "Annual Church Statistical Reports" (December 4, 2000); "Called unto Holiness—A New Century: 2008 Annual Report of the Board of General Superintendents," *Holiness Today* (May/June 2008), 18-23.

4. Dwight Swanson, "Re-minting Christian Holiness," Part 21: "Holiness in Time and Space," *Flame* (October-December 2001), 9-10.

5. Stan Ingersol, "When Christians Gather: Conferences That Shaped Nazarene Life," *Holiness Today* (May 2001), 10-13. See H. Ray Dunning, "Reactions to WTS Conference on Eschatology," presented at the conclusion of the annual meeting of the Wesleyan Theological Society, Southern Nazarene U., Bethany, Oklahoma, in November 1993.

6. See Stan Ingersol, "Nazarene Odyssey and the Hinges of Internationalization," *Wesleyan Theological Journal* 38 (Spring 2003), 66-92.

7. Compare Carl Dudley and Earle Hilgert, *New Testament Tensions and the Contemporary Church* (Philadelphia, PA: Fortress, 1987), 9-37.

8. Culbertson, "Come Share the Dream" *Herald of Holiness* (General Assembly Issue, June 1997), 27-29.

9. Lawlor, "Valedictory Address," *Journal of the Nineteenth General Assembly* (1976), 27-33.

10. See "Directory" and "Proceedings," *Journal of the Nineteenth General Assembly* (1976), 5-40.

11. Gary Henecke, "Heirs of Holy Intensity," *Herald of Holiness* (July 1998), 10-13.

12. "Revival Breaks Put at Philadelphia Assembly," *Herald of Holiness* (July 1995), 14. Philip K. Clemens, "What Do You Mean You Want Exciting Worship?" *Herald of Holiness* (December 1996), 40-41. "If It Truly Is Worship, Then It Is Exciting!" *Herald of Holiness* (November 1995), 16-21.

13. "I Have the Nazarene Enthusiasm," *Herald of Holiness* (June 1997), 4-5. See Stan Ingersol, "They Shared a Dream," *Herald of Holiness* (June 1997), 14-19.

14. "A Moment or a Journey?" *Holiness Today* (April 2002), 35. See Steven Cooley, "Applying the Vagueness of Language: Poetic Strategies and Camp Meeting Piety in the Mid-Nineteenth Century," *Church History* 63 (1984), 584. See also Cooley, "The Possibilities of Grace: Poetic Discourse and Reflection in Methodist/Holiness Revivalism," Ph.D. diss., U. of Chicago, 1991.

15. Dean Nelson, "Paul Orjala: Living the Language of God," *Holiness Today* (October 2000), 10-12.

16. Ken Hendrick, April 1992 (David Whitelaw notes).

17. See Richard Zanner, *Night Hunt in Kisumu and Other Unforgettable Stories from Africa* (Kansas City: Beacon Hill Press, 2001), 10.

18. *Journal of the Twenty-Fourth General Assembly* (1997), 474-78.

19. *Herald of Holiness* (August 1997), 4-5.

20. Daniel R. Gangler, reporting on Thomas Boomershine's work at the United Theological Seminary, Dayton, Ohio, in *United Methodist Reporter* (September 6, 1996), 4. See also John G. Stackhouse, "The True, the Good, and the Beautiful Christian," *Christianity Today* (January 7, 2002), 58-61.

21. Russell D. Bredholt Jr., Samuel L. Dunn, Joseph F. Nielson, G. Ray Reglin, *A Great Commission Movement: The Church of the Nazarene in the Twenty-First Century* (Kansas City: Beacon Hill Press of Kansas City, 1993), 33. See also Bassett, "Holiness Movement and the Protestant Principle," 7-29.

22. Gordon Thomas, "Who Cares About Holiness Anyhow?" *Holiness Today* (January 2002), 26.

23. Jerald Johnson, "Treasures and Promises" and "Mileposts in a Life of Service," *Herald of Holiness* (June 1997), 8-9. See Nazarene Archives File 302-124; *Journal of the Twenty-Fourth General Assembly* (1997), 49-50; *Proceedings of the General Board* (1974), 160; Jerald Johnson, "The Challenge of the Middle," *Herald of Holiness* (March 1994), 7.

24. *Proceedings of the General Board* (1974), 160. See also Johnson, "The Challenge of the Middle," *Herald of Holiness* (March 1994), 7.

25. *World Mission* (March 1986), 2-3. See Nees, *Winds of Change 1980-85: The Church in Transition* (Kansas City: Nazarene Publishing House, 1991).

26. *World Mission* (April 1986), 11; Robert Scott, *All Over the World . . . Our Family* (Kansas City: Nazarene Publishing House, 1994).

27. *NNS Weekly Summary* (February 25, 1994).

28. David Whitelaw, conversations with various district superintendents and pastors.

29. *Journal of the Twentieth General Assembly* (1980), 40; *Journal of the Nineteenth General Assembly* (1976), 27, 58; "One World, Fewer and Fewer Languages," *Holiness Today* (January 2000), 4-5. See also, James McGraw, "The Use and Abuse of Language," *Preacher's Magazine* (1976), 51.

30. "Greathouse Calls for Return to Movement" in *Herald of Holiness* (April 1989), 25. See Summary CV in William Greathouse files in Nazarene Archives (302-123); William M. Greathouse, "The Secret of Holy Living," *Herald of Holiness* (June 1997), 34-36; William M. Greathouse, *Wholeness in Christ: Toward a Biblical Theology of Holiness* (Kansas City: Beacon Hill Press of Kansas City, 1998), 7-8.

31. See file 302-125, Nazarene Archives, including Summary CV. See also, Bonnie Perry, "John A. Knight: A Nazarene," *Holiness Today* (May 2001), 22-23.

32. *Proceedings of the General Board of the Church of the Nazarene and Its Departments* (1990), 193. See *Journal of the Nineteenth General Assembly of the Church of the Nazarene* (1976), 11-19, and *Journal of the Twenty-Fourth General Assembly* (1997), roll of delegates; "One World, Fewer and Fewer Languages," *Holiness Today* (January 2000), 4-5.

33. "Meet Donald D. Owens," *Herald of Holiness* (November 1989), 16-17, 38; Nazarene Archives file 302-128; "Owens Becomes Second President of MANC," *Herald of Holiness* (September 1, 1985), 35. See also "Nazarenes Live in Privileged Times" and "Mileposts in a Life of Service," *Herald of Holiness* (June 1997), 10-12.

34. Owens, "The Commission on Internationalization," *World Mission* (May 1989), 4-5.

35. "Meet William J. Prince," *Herald of Holiness* (January 1990), 14-15; Nazarene Archives file 302-127; Mark Graham, "William J. Prince: The Man from Altus," *Holiness Today* (May 2001), 26-27.

36. "Pastors Elected to Board of General Superintendents," *Herald of Holiness* (September 1993), 3 (file 302-130).

37. *Journal of the Twenty-Fourth General Assembly* (1997), 67; "Porter Elected General Superintendent," *NCN Daily Summary* (June 26, 1997); *Herald of Holiness* (August 1997), 4.

38. "Porter and Bond Elected as General Superintendents," *Herald of Holiness* (August 1997), 4; see also Nazarene Archives, File 302-132, Jim Bond.

39. Likewise see L. Guy Nees, "A Struggle for Identity," a paper delivered at the annual Nazarene College Presidents' Conference, Phoenix, Arizona (November 30, 1977); Ron Benefiel, "The Church of the Nazarene: Undercurrents of a Changing Identity," in David P. Whitelaw, ed., *Maps and Models for Ministry* (San Diego: Point Loma Press, 1996), 77-92; G. L. Forward, "Servant or CEO?: A Metaphor Analysis of Leadership as a Dichotomous Variable and What Should Be Done About It," presented at the Religious Communication Association Convention, Chicago (November 1999). Compare David Martin, "The People's Church: The Global Evangelical Upsurge and Its Political Consequences," in *The Desecularization of the World: Resurgent Religion and World Politics*, ed. Peter L. Berger (Grand Rapids: Eerdmans, 1999).

40. "Mother Church Celebrates Centennial," *Herald of Holiness* (January 1996), 24. Similarly, see *Journal of the Twenty-Third General Assembly* (1993), 250; Donald Owens, "Nazarenes Live in Privileged Times," *Herald of Holiness* (June 1997), 10-12.

41. See Talmadge Johnson and Stan Toler, *Rediscovering the Sunday School* (Kansas City: Beacon Hill Press of Kansas City, 2000).

42. Helen Temple, *Preacher with a Mission: The Story of Nina Griggs Gunter* (Kansas City: Nazarene Publishing House, 1998).

43. NCN News, July 1, 2005.

44. See "General Superintendents Move to Clarify Nazarene Mission," and "Background Information," Board of General Superintendents (February 15, 2007).

45. On Radi see *World Mission* (August 1994), 10.

Chapter 24

1. Compare Rodney Clapp, *Border Crossings: Trespasses on Popular Culture and Public Affairs* (Grand Rapids: Brazos, 2001).

2. Compare David Martin, *Tongues of Fire: The Explosion of Protestantism in Latin America* (Oxford: Basil Blackwell, 1990), 3-46 and 275-95.

3. See W. E. McCumber, "Answer Corner," *Herald of Holiness* (September 1985), 31; Jamie Gates, "The Strength of Diversity," in *Generation X-ers Talk About the Church of the Nazarene*, ed. Thomas J. Oord (Kansas City: Nazarene Publishing House, 1999), 127-35; R. Franklin Cook, "Challenge: The Connected Church," *Holiness Today* (April 2000), 22-28. See also papers generated for the 2002 Theology Conference in Guatemala. Compare Enrique Dussel, *The Invention of the Americas: Eclipse of "the Other" and the Myth of Modernity*, trans. Michael D. Barber (New York: Continuum, 1995), 10-11; Wilbert Shenk, "Under the Mustard Tree," *International Bulletin of Missionary Research* 20 (April 1996), 50-57; "Now That We're Global," *Christianity Today* 16 (November 1998), 45-76.

4. *Journal of the Eighteenth General Assembly* (1972), 405-11.

5. Paul Orjala, "Are We an International Church?" *World Mission* (January 29, 1975), 14-15.

6. *Journal of the Twentieth General Assembly* (1980), 232-54; *Herald of Holiness* (February 15, 1976), 22; Personal notes of David Whitelaw (January 31, 1978).

7. *Journal of the Eighteenth General Assembly* (1972), 415. "Nazarene World Youth Conference Attracts Crowd," *Herald of Holiness* (July 1, 1978), 35; "Highlights of the 1996 General Board," *Herald of Holiness* (May 1996), 16; "Equipping Youth to Be Global Christians," *World Mission* (August 1998), 14-16; Paul Skiles, interview with Cunningham and Whitelaw (June 1, 2000).

8. *Journal of the Twentieth General Assembly* (1980), 295.

9. *Journal of the Twentieth General Assembly* (1980), 237, 249. These "Bases of Internationalization" were restated in the *Journal of the Twenty-Third General Assembly* (1993), 214.

10. Jerald Johnson, *The International Experience* (Kansas City: Nazarene Publishing House, 1982), 7-10. See Helen Temple, "Let's Go International," *World Mission* (January 1976), inside front and back covers.

11. "The Church of the Nazarene International," *Herald of Holiness* (April 1980), 12-14.

12. Tarrant to Donald Owens (October 23, 1986), copied to commission members for the meeting in 1987. See also "Giving to Others: Another Perspective," *Holiness Today* (April 2000), 25.

13. "1999 Regional Conference" (November 24-28, 1999), Johannesburg.

14. Stephen Heap to Whitelaw (July 25, 2000). See Richard Zanner, "The Church of the Nazarene International," *Herald of Holiness* (April 1980), 12-14.

15. *Journal of the Twenty-First General Assembly* (1985), 350-53, 355, 357, 647; *Journal of the Twenty-Third General Assembly* (1993), 211-27. See also various articles in the June 1985 issue of *World Mission*.

16. *Journal of the Twenty-First General Assembly* (1985), 349.

17. Donald Owens, "The Commission on Internationalization," *World Mission* (May 1989), 4-5.

18. *Journal of the Twenty-First General Assembly* (1985), 160; see 125-63.

19. *Journal of the Twenty-Second General Assembly* (1989), 293-300.

20. As background see *The Church in a Changing World: Selected Papers from the Nazarene Theology Conference*, ed. W. T. Purkiser (Kansas City: Beacon Hill Press of Kansas City, 1972).

21. "Survey of the Church of the Nazarene: Executive Summary," prepared by the Gallup Organization (December 1, 1989), 7; Russell Bredholt to writer (July 18, 2000).

22. *Weekly Summary* (March 5, 1993); *Journal of the Twenty-Third General Assembly* (1993), 211-27.

23. 1993 *Manual*, 154.

24. Johnson, "Untied or United? Some Thoughts on Internationalization of the Church of the Nazarene," *Herald of Holiness* (April 1994), 18-21.

25. "Superintendents Call for Focus on Mission," in *Herald of Holiness* (May 1995), 22. Johnson also enumerated the goals of the denomination for the next six years: 1.5 million members; fifteen thousand churches; twenty new countries entered. See also Bredholt et al., *A Great Commission Movement*.

26. *Proceedings of the General Board* (1976), 125-26; *Proceedings* (1998), 128; Russell Bredholt to writer (Tuesday, July 18, 2000, and Tuesday, July 25, 2000). The elephant comment originated with Pierre Trudeau.

27. See Ron Benefiel, review of *The Wolf Shall Dwell with the Lamb*, by H. F. Law, Guatemala Global Theological Conference (April 2002). See also John A. Knight, "One," *Herald of Holiness* (May 1997), 7; Wilbert Shenk, "Marks of a Global Church History," *International Bulletin of Missionary Research* (April 1996), 56. Also see Andrew Walls, *The Missionary Movement in Christian History: Studies in the Transmission of Faith* (Maryknoll, NY: Orbis, 2000), 3.

28. Mario Zani, "Globalization Through the Cross," induction message, Nazarene Theological Seminary, 1999.

29. Mario Zani, "Globalization," quoting Wesley Brown, "The Globalization of Theological Education," 1987 address to seminary presidents, Scottsdale, Arizona.

30. Mario Zani, "Globalization," 6. Compare Charles Gailey, "When Did the Church of the Nazarene Become International?" *Herald of Holiness* (June 1989), 10-11.

31. Richard Houseal, "Women Clergy in the Church of the Nazarene," 22. See W. E. McCumber, "The Answer Corner," *Herald of Holiness* (August 15, 1978), 31. See Ingersol and Tracy, *Here We Stand*, 63, 172; Janine T. Metcalf, "Partners in Ministry: Women and Men Serving/Leading Together," in *Maps and Models*, 101-7.

32. William Greathouse, "Women in Ministry," *Herald of Holiness* (June 15, 1982), 2.

33. Melvin Shrout, "The Return of the Deaconness," *Herald of Holiness* (March 1983), 11-12; Steve Cooley, director of Archives, "The Nazarene Deaconess," *Herald of Holiness* (July 15, 1984), 9; Ross E. Price, "Mother Was a Deaconess," *Herald of Holiness* (July 15, 1984), 10.

34. Eby, *Wanda*; Perkins, *Women in Nazarene Missions*; Temple, *Preacher with a Mission*.

35. Jane Brewington, in flyers handed out at the 1993 General Assembly.

36. Floyd E. Disney, "Embracing Change: The Shape of Ministry in the 21st Century," *Herald of Holiness* (February 1992), 16-19.

37. Laird, *Ordained Women*, 151-52.

38. Gordon Wetmore, "Perspective" on "God-Called Women," *Seminary Tower* 49 (Fall 1993), 1-2.

39. Robert Edge, "Come to the Water," *Herald of Holiness* (July 1994), 30-33. See also Stan Ingersol, "Holiness Women," *Christian Century* (June 29-July 6, 1994), 632; *New Horizons: A Newsletter for Clergywomen in the Church of the Nazarene* (Fall 1995, Spring 1997, and Summer 1997).

40. *Multicultural Newsletter* (September 1998), 2.

41. Janine Tartaglia Metcalf, *Ablaze with Love*, video, produced in partial fulfillment for the doctor of ministry at Asbury Theological Seminary, 2002. In the same year, Janine Metcalf began pastoring the El Cajon Church of the Nazarene.

42. See also Leclerc, *Singleness of Heart*; and Laird, *Ordained Women*.

43. *World Mission* (August 1994), 10. See *I Am Not Ashamed: Sermons by Wesleyan-Holiness Women*, ed. Diane Leclerc (San Diego: Point Loma, 2005).

44. *Nazarene News* (July 6, 1990); Jeanette Gardner Littleton, "The District Superintendent's Name Is Rosa," *Herald of Holiness* (August 1997), 24-27.

45. Marilyn Willis, "The People's Church," *Herald of Holiness* (November 1998), 2-3; A. Brent Cobb, *Hands for the Harvest: Laborers for the Lord in the Far East* (Kansas City: Nazarene Publishing House, 2002), 17-31.

46. Cobb, *Hands for the Harvest*, 55-62; Helen Temple, *Adventure with God: The Jeanine van Beek Story* (Kansas City: Nazarene Publishing House, 2002).

47. *Grow* (Summer 2004), 36-37; *Holiness Today* (July/August 2005), 6.

48. NCN News (March 17, 2007); NCN News (May 24, 2007).

49. Zanner to coworkers (December 1999); *Trans African* (2002), 3:20. See Ella Finkbeiner, *They Stand Tall: Stories of Leaders in the European Church* (Kansas City: Nazarene Publishing House, 1972), 22-30; *Journal of the Twentieth General Assembly* (1980), 205-6; Michael Estep in "A Legacy of Communications," *Holiness Today* (April 2000), 48.

50. On the beginnings in Kenya see Harmon Schmelzenbach, *The Edge of Africa's Eden* (Kansas City: Nazarene Publishing House, 1991), in Côte d'Ivoire see Ron Farris, *God Loves Yopougon* (Kansas City: Nazarene Publishing House, 1992).

51. Dennis Schmelzenbach, "Our First Missionary," *World Mission* (July 1976), 8; and Carol Zurcher, "Farewell to Their First Nazarene Missionary," *World Mission* (August 1976), 10-13. See also Richard Zanner, "Committed," *Trans African* (July-Aug 1994), 8-9; "Nazarene Mission-Air," *Trans African* (January-February 1995), 1-7.

52. *Herald of Holiness* (February 15, 1989). See Miller's magazine *World-Wide Missions* (May 1961, September 1961, February 1964, April 1965, November 1968, October 1970, and May 1973). On different Nigerian groups less successfully assimilated into the Church of the Nazarene, see David Hynd to H. C. Powers (December 22, 1949), Powers to Hynd (December 19, 1950), and Powers to E. I. E. Hinshaw (September 10, 1951) (all in file 2304-21); Parker, *Mission to the World*, 199-200.

53. "Church in Africa Moving Toward Maturity," *Herald of Holiness* (January 1993), 12. See also John Cunningham and Elaine Cunningham, *Madagascar: Island at the End of the World* (Kansas City: Nazarene Publishing House, 1994); Zanner, "Breathe a Prayer . . . and Let Us Have Some Salt!" *Trans African* (March-April 1995), 8-9; "The Nazarene World," *Trans African* (November-December 1995); *Herald of Holiness*, General Assembly Issue (June 1997), "Regions Summary Report."

54. "Mission Statement for the Church of the Nazarene—Africa Region," *Trans African* (May-June 1993), 17.

55. Ted Esselstyn, "Remembering Issues in Africa," Global Theological Conference, Guatemala (April 2002), 1-3.

56. *NNS Weekly Summary* (February 25, 1994). See also *World Mission* (March 1997).

57. *World Mission* (May 1988), 10; *World Mission* (January 1990) (entire issues); *Thailand: Land of the White Elephant*, eds. Jean Knox and Michael McCarty (Kansas City: Nazarene Publishing

House, 1997); *Proceedings of the General Board* (1997), 206-7; Brent Cobb, "Asian Missionary to Asians," *World Mission* (May 1997), 10-11, 16.

58. *Herald of Holiness* (August 15, 1981), 34; "Rench Elected Director of Asia Region," *Herald of Holiness* (November 1985), 35; *Herald of Holiness* (April 1986), 35; *World Mission* (October 1994), 6.

59. "Nazarenes Make Historic Visit to North Korea," *Herald of Holiness* (November 1996), 8.

60. Hightower, ed., *Love Does That*. See also Ruth Hightower, *His Mandate in the Land of the Maple Leaf* (Kansas City: Nazarene Publishing House, 1981).

61. Neil Hightower, "Report," 2, 5.

62. Hightower, ed., *Love Does That*; "Report," 5.

63. Neil Hightower in a letter and document of response (March 22, 2002).

64. *NNS Weekly Summary* (April 22, 1994).

65. "Regional Directors for Revamped Regions," *Herald of Holiness* (April 1986), 35; *World Mission* (July 1993), unnumbered pages; "Smee Appointed to Caribbean Region," *Herald of Holiness* (May 1994), 48. See John Smee, *The Rising Caribbean Tide* (Kansas City: Nazarene Publishing House, 1978), 9.

66. *Herald of Holiness*, General Assembly Issue (June 1997), "Regions Summary Report."

67. "Two New Regional Directors Named," *Herald of Holiness* (June 15, 1983), 24; *World Mission* (April 1985), 10; "First Eurasia Regional Conference," *Herald of Holiness* (August 15, 1987), 24-25; Nees, *Winds of Change*, 29-39; *World Mission* (July 1993); R. Franklin Cook to David Whitelaw (January 26, 2001).

68. *Rom-Aid News* (Winter 1993); Tim Crutcher, *Romania: Out of the Gray* (Kansas City: Nazarene Publishing House, 1996); Cameron, *Spirit Makes the Difference*, 544-45.

69. Sharon Martin, *Treasures in the Darkness: Stories from Behind Broken Walls* (Kansas City: Nazarene Publishing House, 1995); Carla Sundberg with Gene Van Note, *Faxes from Russia* (Kansas City: Nazarene Publishing House, 1996).

70. Paul Greer, "Karnataka-Andhra Pradesh: Another New District in South India," *World Mission* (November 1982), 5.

71. Vijai Singh, "A Spreading Vine," *World Mission* (September 1989); *Nazarene News* (February 9, 1990).

72. John Haines, "I Knew You'd Come," *World Mission* (February 1993), 2-3; Michael Estep, "Bangladesh," *Herald of Holiness* (May 1997), 16.

73. "Church of the Nazarene Enters Pakistan, the 113th World Area," *Herald of Holiness* (February 1997), 12; *Global Glimpses* (April/May/June 1997).

74. *Holiness Today* (March 2003), 8-9.

75. Hugh Rae, *Scholarship on Fire: A Personal Account of Fifty Years of the Nazarene College in Britain* (Manchester, UK: Agape Press, 1994). In Appendix I, see Kent Brower, "The Quest for British Degree Validation," 167-80; Hugh Rae to David Whitelaw (January 22, 2001).

76. R. Franklin Cook, "Eurasia Region Institutions," e-mail to David Whitelaw (January 26, 2001); *Herald of Holiness*, General Assembly Issue (June 1997), "Regions" Summary Report; *Journal of the Twenty-Fourth General Assembly* (1997), 512-13.

77. *Holiness Today* (March 1999), 14.

78. *NNS Weekly Summary* (June 16, 1995).

79. J. Fred Parker, *Continental Mission: The Church of the Nazarene from Mexico to Argentina* (Kansas City: Nazarene Publishing House, 1984); "NTS Profile [Mario J. Zani]," *Herald of Holiness* (July 1993), 35; "Tenor of Revival Highlights MAC Regional Conference," *Herald of Holiness* (August 1995), 6; *World Mission* (July 1993); *Herald of Holiness*, General Assembly Issue (June 1997), "Regions" Summary Report.

80. See *Herald of Holiness* (January 15, 1978), 35, and "Highlights of the First Regional Council of South America," *Herald of Holiness* (August 15, 1987), 22-23.

81. William and Juanita Porter, *Walk About the Land: God's Time for Venezuela* (Kansas City: Nazarene Publishing House, 1986).

82. See *NNS Weekly Summary* (April 15, 1994); *World Mission* (July 1993); also "SAM Region Evangelizing," *Herald of Holiness* (November 1995), 12; "Radi Replaces Bustle," *Herald of Holiness*

(June 1994), 11; *Herald of Holiness,* General Assembly Issue (June 1997), "Regions" Summary Report; interview with David Whitelaw and Louie Bustle (June 4, 2000).

83. *Journal of the Nineteenth General Assembly* (1976), 449-54; information from files of Beryl Dillman, Point Loma Nazarene U.

84. Charles Gates, "WOMEC and Its Function," Commission on Education, 1986; *Handbook for Accreditation, Curriculum, and Degree Granting Processes for Nazarene World Area Theological Education Institutions,* published by WOMEC in 1987.

85. *Journal of the Twenty-Second General Assembly* (1989), 260-80.

86. Ibid.

87. "A Summary Report of the Education Commission," *Journal of the Twenty-Second General Assembly* (1989), 32-33. See letters and documents sent from the general secretary's office (August 27, 1986), cosigned by Gordon Wetmore (chair) and Willis Snowbarger (research director); and "Recommendations" in Report of the Nazarene Education Commission.

88. *Journal of the Twenty-Third General Assembly* (1993), 146-47, 664.

89. "Lambert Elected Education Commissioner," *Herald of Holiness* (July 1994, 48).

90. *Journal of the Twenty-Fourth General Assembly,* 510-22. See also *Journal of the Twenty-Second General Assembly* (1989), 137; *Proceedings of the General Board* (1998), 111. Also, interview with Louis Bustle by David Whitelaw (June 2, 2000); Lambert, "Resource Institute for International Education," *Proceedings of the General Board* (1997), 215; "Introducing the Resource Institute for International Education" (pamphlet, undated).

91. See *Proceedings of the General Board* (1998), 104-12.

92. Jerry Lambert, "A Philosophy of Education: Church of the Nazarene," unpublished address; Jerry Lambert, "Great Commission Pastors for the Twenty-First Century" (Revised March 4, 1999); *Herald of Holiness* (June 1997).

93. Cook, "Challenge: The Connected Church," 23; see 22-28.

Chapter 25

1. Ron Benefiel, "A Church for All the People," *Herald of Holiness* (October 1995), 12-16. See "The Church of the Nazarene: Undercurrents of a Changing Identity," in *Maps and Models,* 78; see 77-92. Compare Smith, *Called unto Holiness,* 50, 111, 266, 270-71; George Hunsberger and Craig van Gelder, eds., *The Church Between Gospel and Culture: The Emerging Mission in North America* (Grand Rapids: Eerdmans, 1996); Wacker, *Heaven Below,* chap. 11, "Boundaries."

2. See, for example, "Transforming Ministry: Vision and Hope for a New Century" Theme for PALCON, 1995, sponsored by Pastoral Ministries, Division of Church Growth; John A. Knight, *Bridge for Our Tomorrows: A Millennial Address to the Church of the Nazarene* (Kansas City: Beacon Hill Press of Kansas City, 2000). Compare David Lyon, *Jesus in Disneyland: Religion in Postmodern Times* (Cambridge: Polity Press, 2000), 98-101, citing Roland Robertson's concept of "glocalization"—the adaptation of a global outlook to local conditions.

3. Compare Rodney Clapp, *A Peculiar People: The Church as Culture in a Post-Christian Society* (Downers Grove, IL: InterVarsity Press, 1996); Ron Benefiel, "The Church of the Nazarene: Undercurrents of a Changing Identity," in *Maps and Models,* 78.

4. *Journal of the Nineteenth General Assembly* (1976), 185. Also, Millard Reed to David Whitelaw (December 18, 2000).

5. *Journal of the Nineteenth General Assembly* (1976), 185; see 184-203; Bill Young, interview with David Whitelaw (January 24, 2001).

6. *Proceedings of the General Board* (1980), 197; *Journal of the Twenty-First General Assembly* (1984), 287-346, 417.

7. "Toward an Agenda for Nazarene Theology," paper presented at the Seventh Nazarene Theology Conference (1987), 2. See *Proceedings of the General Board* (1980), 193-204; *Proceedings of the General Board* (1982), 15-16; General Superintendents' Report to the General Board, 1982; Report of the General Board Organization Commission, *Journal of the Twenty-First General Assembly* (1984), 289-91; *Journal of the Twenty-First General Assembly* (1984), 417; 287-346; Paul Skiles interview (June 6, 2000); Millard Reed to David Whitelaw (December 18, 2000); Floyd Perkins, conversation with David Whitelaw (August 9, 2000).

8. Stan Ingersol, *Herald of Holiness* (June 1997), 16. Compare W. R. McNutt, *Polity and Practice in Baptist Churches* (Philadelphia: Judson Press, 1935), 21-24, in Winthrop S. Hudson, ed., *Baptist Concepts of the Church* (Philadelphia: Judson, 1959), 216.

9. "Report of the Doctrine of the Church Commission," in *Journal of the Twenty-Second General Assembly,* 255-59; Henry Spaulding to David Whitelaw (November 20, 2000). See *Journal of the Twenty-First General Assembly* (1984), 213, 219; "Minutes of the Church Commission Meeting," copy from files of George Lyons, member of the commission (September 19-20, 1986). See also Stephen Gunter, "The Church: A Biblical-Theological Definition," *Preacher's Magazine* (1981), 38-40.

10. *NNS Weekly Summary* (February 25, 1994).

11. Oster, *Serving Those Who Serve*; *Proceedings of the General Board* (1995), 44-45, 63-67; "Single Pension Plan Proposed," *Herald of Holiness* (May 1995), 22; "Go-Ahead Given to 'Single' Pension Plan," *Herald of Holiness* (August 1995), 7; John Stockton, interview (June 4, 2000); interview with Tommie Parrish (June 4, 2000). See *Proceedings of the General Board* (1995), 38-39; Neil Hightower to David Whitelaw (April 2002).

12. "Weber Changes Posts," *Herald of Holiness* (December 1995), 14.

13. See *Journal of the Nineteenth General Assembly* (1976), 142; "Discrimination," *Journal of the Twenty-Third General Assembly* (1993), 160.

14. Don Kraybill, "Civil Religion vs. New Testament Christianity," *Herald of Holiness* (November 15, 1976), 10-11. See also Tom Sine, "Back to the Gospel: Depoliticizing the Church in '96," *Herald of Holiness* (August 1996), 8-13; and Ralph Lentz, "Letters: Disappointed, Extremely," *Herald of Holiness* (December 1996), 15.

15. 1972 *Manual,* Appendix, par. 704.5, "Separation of Church and State." Compare 1993-97 *Manual,* Appendix, par. 904.7, "The Church and Human Freedom."

16. James McGraw, "Among Ourselves," *Preacher's Magazine* (February 1977), 33.

17. W. T. Purkiser, "Nazarene Affirmatives," *Herald of Holiness* (July 30, 1975), 18.

18. James McGraw, "Abortion and the Bible," *Preacher's Magazine* (February 1977), 1-2. See also James Dobson, *Family Under Fire: A Conference Book* (Kansas City: Beacon Hill Press of Kansas City, 1976), 102-14, which includes a discussion on the abortion issue among Dobson, Paul Cunningham, David Hernandez, James Dobson Sr., Aarlie Hull, Jim Davis, and Neil Wiseman.

19. *Herald of Holiness* (April 1, 1977), 20; "Church Joins Coalition in TV Program Protest," *Herald of Holiness* (September 1, 1977), 39; McCumber, "Movies and Television," *Herald of Holiness* (August 1, 1977), 19; Paul Skiles, "What's This I Hear About Nazarene Television and 20/20 Vision?" *Herald of Holiness* (July 1, 1979), 8-11. Also see *Herald of Holiness* (October 1989), 2-3, 16-28.

20. *Herald of Holiness* (September 1, 1978), 16-17.

21. David C. Wright, "Holiness: Hope for the Homosexual," *Herald of Holiness* (December 1, 1980), 14-15.

22. Michael Christensen, *City Streets, City People: A Call for Compassion* (Nashville: Abingdon, 1988), 60, 197-211; Michael Christensen, *The Story of the Bridge,* 19 pp. (N.d.) (file 500-68); Michael Christensen, "Nothing Can Separate Us from the Love of God," *Herald of Holiness* (March 15, 1988), 8-9.

23. Stowe to Christensen (August 8, 1989) and Christensen to Stowe (September 7, 1989). See also Stowe to Christensen (October 3, 1989) and Christensen to Stowe (November 16, 1989) (all in file 1041-60).

24. Clarence Kinzler, "Articulating and Living Christian Holiness in a Pluralistic World," paper presented to the Eighth Theology Conference, 1992. See Christensen to Stowe (November 16, 1989). See also Bettie C. Emberton, "Multifaceted Problem," *Herald of Holiness* (March 15, 1981), 4; "AIDS Conference Challenges Church to Reach Out in the Name of Christ," *Herald of Holiness* (March 15, 1988), 35; J. Grant Swank, "Evangelicals and the 'Homosexual Problem,'" *Preacher's Magazine* (September/October/November 1997), 17.

25. "Nazarenes Sponsor First Denominational Conference on AIDS," *Herald of Holiness* (July 1, 1984), 4, 20.

26. Harold Ivan Smith, "AIDS: The Spiritual Fallout," *Herald of Holiness* (April 1, 1984), 14-15. See also Letters, "Finds Smith Confused," *Herald of Holiness* (July 1, 1984), 4, 20; *Christianity To-*

day (October 7, 1988); Rick L. Williamson, "My Friends Are Dying: My Friends Have AIDS," *Preacher's Magazine* (September/October/November 1996), 38.

27. 1989 *Manual*, 53. See also Wesley Tracy, "Editor's Choice: Wise Up on the Gay Issue," *Herald of Holiness* (September 1991), 10-11; *Herald of Holiness* (February 1992), 4; Grider, *Wesleyan-Holiness Theology*, 415.

28. *Journal of the Twenty-First General Assembly* (1985), 67, 69-70; *Journal of the Twenty-Second General Assembly* (1989), 217-19; see 214-34.

29. Paul Benefiel, "Relevant to the Times, True to the Gospel," *Herald of Holiness* (September 1992), 2-5.

30. "Special Report," *Herald of Holiness* (July 1993), 5-9; *Weekly Summary* (August 13, 1993). See Alex Deasley, *Marriage and Divorce in the Bible and the Church* (Kansas City: Beacon Hill Press of Kansas City, 2000).

31. *Journal of the Twenty-Third General Assembly* (1993), 153-56. See Al Truesdale, *A Matter of Life and Death: Bioethics and the Christian* (Kansas City: Beacon Hill Press of Kansas City, 1990); Al Truesdale, *God in the Laboratory: Equipping Christians to Deal with Issues in Bioethics* (Kansas City: Beacon Hill Press of Kansas City, 2000).

32. Wesley Tracy, "The Question Box," *Herald of Holiness* (November 1993), 30.

33. 2001-5 *Manual*, 45-46.

34. Wes Tracy, "The Question Box," *Herald of Holiness* (October 1997), 34-5.

35. *Journal of the Twenty-Fourth General Assembly* (1997), 94-95; "Christian Action Committee Responds to Disney Entertainment," *Herald of Holiness* (July 1997), 14.

36. "A Nazarene Statement," *Herald of Holiness* (November 1, 1982), 34. See also *Journal of the Twenty-First General Assembly* (1985), 223; *Herald of Holiness* (July 1, 1976), 12-15; Al Truesdale, "The Enemy Within," *Herald of Holiness* (June 1, 1985), 12-13; William Goodman, "Defensive Action Against Pornography," *Herald of Holiness* (February 15, 1989), 7.

37. James Dobson, *Straight Talk to Men and Their Wives* (Waco, TX: Word, 1980), 11-23, describes James Dobson Sr. See Tim Stafford, "His Father's Son," *Christianity Today* (April 22, 1988), 16-22; Gil Alexander-Moegerle, *James Dobson's War on America* (Amherst, NY: Prometheus, 1997), 29.

38. James Dobson, *Dare to Discipline* (Wheaton, IL: Tyndale, 1970; repr., 1986), 146; see 81-112, 146-65.

39. Ibid., 36.

40. Ibid., 196. See also James Dobson, *The Strong-Willed Child: Birth Through Adolescence* (Wheaton, IL: Tyndale, 1978), 74-76, 118-21.

41. James Dobson, *Hide and Seek* (Old Tappan, NJ: Fleming Revell, 1974), 58.

42. Ibid., 85.

43. James Dobson, *What Wives Wish Their Husbands Knew About Women* (Wheaton, IL: Tyndale, 1975), 185.

44. Dobson, *Hide and Seek*, 137-38; Dobson, *What Wives Wish Their Husbands Knew*, 22-41, 56-57.

45. James Dobson, *Love Must Be Tough: New Hope for Families in Crisis* (Waco, TX: Word, 1983; repr., 1996), 19.

46. Dobson, *Strong-Willed Child*, 220-21; *Straight Talk*, 73, 103. A positive assessment of Dobson's affect upon women is Colleen McDannell, "Beyond Dr. Dobson: Women, Girls, and Focus on the Family," in *Women and Twentieth-Century Protestantism*, eds. Margaret L. Bendroth and Virginia L. Brereton (Urbana: U. of Illinois Press, 2002), 113-31. In the same book, page 41, Gaston Espinosa, in "Women in the Latino Pentecostal Movement," mentions the impact of Dobson upon Latina women.

47. Dobson, *What Wives Wish Their Husbands Knew*, 78.

48. Dobson, *Straight Talk*, 157; see 57-69; *What Wives Wish Their Husbands Knew*, 162; *Love Must Be Tough*, 19, 73-74, 132-33.

49. Dobson, *Straight Talk*, 102.

50. Dobson, *What Wives Wish Their Husbands Knew*, 134-39; *Straight Talk*, 59-64.

51. Dobson, *Straight Talk*, 85.

52. Publisher's Preface to Dobson, *Love Must Be Tough* (1996 repr. ed.); Alexander-Moegerle, *James Dobson's War*, 32-33, citing an ABC television news profile.

53. Dobson, *Strong-Willed Child*, 230.

54. Alexander-Moegerle, *James Dobson's War*, 74, 76. Also see Timothy Simpson, "Focus on Dobson," *Christian Century* (September 24-October 1, 1997), 843, 845. In comparison to Dobson, one might look at the work of former Nazarene Grace Ketterman. See Grace Ketterman and Bonnie Perry, "I Hate It When She Screams," *Herald of Holiness* (August 1989), 16-18; Grace Ketterman, "Positive Parenting," *Herald of Holiness* (October 1993), 12-13, 40-41; Grace Ketterman, *The Complete Book of Baby and Child Care*, rev. ed. (Grand Rapids: Fleming H. Revell, 1985); Grace Ketterman, *Surviving the Darkness* (Nashville: Thomas Nelson, 1988); Grace Ketterman, *Understanding Your Child's Problems* (Grand Rapids: Fleming H. Revell, 1983); Ketterman, *Mothering: The Complete Guide for Mothers of All Ages* (Nashville: Thomas Nelson, 1991); Grace Ketterman, *Verbal Abuse* (Ann Arbor, MI: Servant, 1992).

55. *Community of Hope Journal* (Spring 1982); Tom Nees, "Free at Last," *Soujourners* (June 1982), 18-19.

56. "Toward Reconciliation: A Dialogue on Race Relations and the Church of the Nazarene," *Herald of Holiness* (March 1994), 19-28.

57. Bowman, *Color Us Christian*, 9-10.

58. See *NNS Weekly Summary* (August 14, 1992); Thomas G. Nees, *The Changing Face of the Church: From American to Global* (Kansas City: Beacon Hill Press of Kansas City, 1997), 50; Carmen Ringhiser, "A New Start for the Bowmans," *Holiness Today* (August 1999), 37.

59. Cheryl Albert, "Readers Write, 'Grace and Integration,'" *Herald of Holiness* (January 1995), 6.

60. *Journal of the Twenty-First General Assembly* (1985), 618; personal account of David Whitelaw.

61. *Journal of the Twenty-First General Assembly* (1985), 221-24; *Nazarene News* (November 21, 1986); *Nazarene News* (January 16, 1987); observations of the writer.

62. See "The Quiet Revolution," *Holiness Today* (January 2000).

63. Friday Ganda, "Is It Tribalism or Holiness?" *Trans African* (October 1996-March 1997), 27-28.

64. Sergio Franco, *Wounded, but Transformed: A Story of Christians in Nicaragua Today: A Story of Good News* (Kansas City: Nazarene Publishing House, 1990), 75; see 24-75.

65. Franco, *Wounded*, 80-92, 107-10. See also *World Mission* (October 1988) (entire issue); Roger Lancaster, *Thanks to God and the Revolution: Popular Religion and Class Consciousness in the New Nicaragua* (New York: Columbia U. Press, 1988), 100-121.

66. "Who Really Is for Peace?" *Herald of Holiness* (March 15, 1984), 12-13. See Ivan Beals, "Though Fear Shakes, the Foundation Is Firm," *Herald of Holiness* (March 15, 1984), 16-17; Leslie Wooten, "Deploy More Nukes?" *Herald of Holiness* (March 15, 1984), 10-11. See also *Journal of the General Assembly* (1985), 210; "Letters: No Simple Answers," *Herald of Holiness* (August 1, 1983), 20; "Letters: Thoughts on Peace," *Herald of Holiness* (February 1, 1984), 4, 20.

67. Timothy Smith, "Giving Life to the Future," *Herald of Holiness* (November 15, 1983), 10-11; Paul Kellogg, "Letters: Muddle-headed Thinking Charged," *Herald of Holiness* (April 15, 1984), 20. See also Timothy Smith, "The Holy Spirit and Peace," in *Perspectives on Peacemaking: Biblical Options in the Nuclear Age*, ed. John Bernbaum (Ventura, CA: Regal, 1984).

68. "Letters: Thoughts on Peace," *Herald of Holiness* (February 1, 1984), 4,20; David J. Tarrant letter to Donald Owens (October 23, 1986). See War and Military Service, *Manual*, par. 904.8; *Herald of Holiness* (August 1, 1983), 20.

69. David J. Tarrant, "In Nukes We Trust," *Herald of Holiness* (August 1, 1984), 6-7.

70. Bryan Stone, "Christian Realism, *Herald of Holiness* (November 1, 1984), 6-7. See Stone, "In the World but Not of It," *Herald of Holiness* (August 1, 1986), 8-9. See also Al Truesdale, "Letters: Protest Registered," *Herald of Holiness* (September 1, 1984), 20.

71. *Inter-Mission* (February 1987); Robert Scott, "I Left Some of My Heart in Cuba," and Robert Prescott, "Wait and Witness in Cuba," *World Mission* (February 1989), 8-9; General Secretary, "Annual Church Statistical Reports" (December 4, 2000).

72. Benjamin Langa to "My dear Bros and Sis's in Jesus," Manjacaze (August 3, 1977) (file 1312-3).

73. Jerald Johnson to George Coulter (October 20, 1975); *Herald of Holiness* (October 22, 1975), 35; *Herald of Holiness* (March 1, 1976), 35; *Herald of Holiness* (June 1, 1976), 39; *Herald of Holiness* (September 1, 1976), 35; *Herald of Holiness* (October 15, 1976); Mozambique Field Council, Sixth Annual Council Journal, 1976 (file 636-16); Armond Doll, *The Toothpaste Express: Letters from Prison* (Kansas City: Beacon Hill Press of Kansas City, 1976), 62; *Nazarene News* (November 21, 1986); *Nazarene News* (January 6, 1989); *World Mission* (February 1989) (entire issue); *Weekly Summary* (November 20, 1992); Frank Howie, *The Mozambique Story* (Kansas City: Nazarene Publishing House, 1993), 13-22; Lorraine Schultz, "Where Are They?" *World Mission* (October 1995), 14-15; Dayhoff, *Living Stones in Africa*, 58-59, 71-73.

74. *Herald of Holiness* (July 1996), 48; information from Ted Esselstyn.

75. See *Asia Pacific Ambassador* (October 1995), 5; and John P. Bowen, "Japanese Church Seeks Reconciliation with Nazarenes in Korea," *World Mission* (February 1996), 2; Cobb, correspondence to David Whitelaw (January 29, 2001).

76. Obituary, *Idaho Statesman* (August 19, 2005); Cameron, *Spirit Makes the Difference*, 472.

77. *Weekly Summary* (August 2, 1996); *Weekly Summary Special Bulletin* (November 7, 1996).

78. *NCN News* (September 18, 1998).

79. Stan Ingersol, "Nazarene Roots: The Inherent Tension in Nazarene Education," *Herald of Holiness* (April 15, 1989), 9. See Ed Robinson, "For Such a Time as This," *Herald of Holiness* (February 1994), 36-39. See also "Sociologists Explore Ministerial Preparation," *Herald of Holiness* (May 1994), 25.

80. *Herald of Holiness* (May 15, 1978), 35. See also Neil Wiseman, "Faith and Learning Conference—An Historic Christian First," *Herald of Holiness* (November 1, 1978), 12-13.

81. "You Own the Waterhole—Guard It!" *Herald of Holiness* (April 15, 1978), 18A-D.

82. Metz, *MidAmerica*, 181-94, 239, 254-58, 271, 330-40.

83. "Owens Becomes Second President of MANC," *Herald of Holiness* September 1, 1985, 35; "Spindle Accepts Presidency at MANC," *Herald of Holiness* (November 1989); Metz, *MidAmerica*, 380.

84. Metz, *MidAmerica*, 18; "MidAmerica Nazarene College Becomes a University," *Herald of Holiness* (May 1997), 12.

85. "Fairbanks Elected at MVNC," *Herald of Holiness* (October 1989), 48; "LeBron Fairbanks," *Communicator* (1993), 4-5; *Coming of Age: Mount Vernon Nazarene College, 1968-1993* (Mount Vernon, OH: Mount Vernon Nazarene College, 1994); "Fairbanks Inaugurated at MVNC," *Herald of Holiness* (May 1990), 32.

86. Genevieve Cubie, "Nazarene Centennial History Project Document" (February 12, 2001); Laura Bowman, office of the president, letter and accompanying documents and data, from MVNC (February 12, 2001). See also Scott Jarrett, "Town 'n Gown," and Fairbanks, "Growth Spurts Bring Challenges," *The Communicator* (1994); Fairbanks, "The Dog Barks, but the Caravan Moves On," *Communicator* (1996), 4.

87. Cameron, *Spirit Makes the Difference*, 385-411.

88. "Paul Is New ENC President," *Herald of Holiness* (October 1989), 48; Cameron, *Spirit Makes the Difference*, 467-96; "Eastern Nazarene President Dies," *Herald of Holiness* (September 1992), 48; Maxine E. Walker, ed., *Grace in the Academic Community: A Collection of Essays to Honor the Life of Cecil R. Paul* (San Diego: Point Loma Press, 1996).

89. Hill, President's Report to the Board of Trustees, October 19, 1993, 10. See "Eastern Nazarene College Fights Charges of Intolerance," *Herald of Holiness* (July 1993), 11.

90. Cameron, *Spirit Makes the Difference*, 497-523. See *Herald of Holiness* (December 1992), 48; *Christian Scholar* (Summer 1996).

91. Metz, *MidAmerica*, 60.

92. C. Paul Gray, correspondence to David Whitelaw (December 11, 2000).

93. "Gilliland Accepts Presidency of BNC," *Herald of Holiness* (September 1, 1985), 35; *Herald of Holiness* (December, 1989), 36.

94. Richard Hagood to David Whitelaw (March 18, 2002). See Metz, *MidAmerica*, 68; "Doane Elected President at NNC," *Herald of Holiness* (September 1992), 48; *Weekly Summary* (March 5, 1993); "Partnership Agreement Joins NNC and NTC," *Herald of Holiness* (November 1996), 9.

95. John C. Bowling, "A Century of Service," *Herald of Holiness* (October 1995), 46; John Bowling to David Whitelaw (February 6, 2002). See *Herald of Holiness* (March 1, 1976), 32; "ONU Inaugurates Twelfth President," *Herald of Holiness* (January 1992), 17.

96. Metz, *MidAmerica*, 72; "Reed Inaugurated as TNC President," *Herald of Holiness* (January 1992), 16.

97. *Herald of Holiness* (February 1, 1976), 22; *Herald of Holiness* (May 15, 1978), 20.

98. *Herald of Holiness* (December 15, 1978), 35; *Herald of Holiness* (June 15, 1978), 26; "Bill Draper Succumbs to Cancer," *Herald of Holiness* (June 1, 1983), 35.

99. Kirkemo, *For Zion's Sake*. See also *Promise and Destiny: Grace in the History of Point Loma Nazarene University* (San Diego, CA: Point Loma Press, 2001); "Point Loma Board of Trustees Changes College Name," *Herald of Holiness* (April 15, 1983), 35.

100. Robert Brower, *Signatures of the Past, Present, and Future* (1998); Herb Prince, *A Wesleyan Way* (1999); Karl Martin, *The Evangelical Church and American Popular Culture* (2000); Frank Carver and Margaret Stevenson, *Pursuing the Call* (2001); Maxine Walker, ed., *Grace in the Academic Community*; David Whitelaw, ed., *Maps and Models*.

101. *Journal of the Twenty-Fourth General Assembly*, 50. See also *Herald of Holiness* (February 15, 1977), 35; *Journal of the Twenty-First General Assembly* (1985), 648. See also "Fairbanks Inaugurated as New President of APNTS," *Herald of Holiness* (April 1, 1985), 35.

102. Mary Mercer, "The College That Miracles Built," *World Mission* (February 1982), 12-14; Shin Min-gyoo, "An Analysis of the Variable[s] That Affect the Financial Support of Korea Nazarene Theological College by the Korean Church," in [*The Gospel and Theology*] (Chonan, Korea: Nazarene Theological College, n.d.), 110-13; *Together* (February 1992), 1; *Proceedings of the General Board* (1997), 218; Sun-Won Kim, "A Critical Reflection on the History of the Church of the Nazarene in Korea," Guatemala Global Theology Conference, 2002; *Korea Nazarene University Bulletin 2003-2004*.

103. *Nazarene News* (December 19, 1986); Cook, *Reza*, 118-24; Nees, *Winds of Change*, 44-45.

104. "Minutes of the Working Committee on the Development of the Proposed Africa Nazarene University College" (January 25-30, 1988); "Historical Statement Regarding the Proposed Africa Nazarene University College" [1988]; Zanner, "Come and See What God Has Done!" *Trans African* (2002), 3:1. See also Theodore Essylstyn, *Dreams, Doors, and Degrees: The Story of Africa Nazarene University* (Kansas City: Nazarene Publishing House, 2000).

105. "Vision into Reality (Proposed) Africa Nazarene University–Kenya," *Trans African* (July-August 1992), 4-5. See also *Journal of the Twenty-Third General Assembly* (1993), 147-48, 260-80; "Africa University to Open in August," *Herald of Holiness* (February 1994), 20.

106. *Trans African* (1998), 5.

107. Leah Marangu, "A Long Journey Begins with One Step," *ANU Trumpet* (March 1999), 1; "Marangu Installed as Vice-Chancellor at Africa Nazarene University," *Herald of Holiness* (February 1997), 6; "Leah T. Marangu Installed as Vice-Chancellor of Africa Nazarene University," *World Mission* (May 1997), 2. See also *ANU Trumpet* (July 1997 and October 1997); *Nairobi Daily* (May 30, 1998); Ted Esselstyn, "From Dream to Reality," *Trans African* (1998), 2; *Trans African* (2002).

108. See *Herald of Holiness* (November 1, 1976), 35; *Herald of Holiness* (October 15, 1978), 23; *Journal of the Twentieth General Assembly* (1980), 284.

109. Robert Brower, interview (November 3, 2000). See also "Brower Elected President of Nazarene Publishing House," *Herald of Holiness* (February 1995), 48.

110. "Highlights of 1996 General Board," *Herald of Holiness* (May 1995), 23.

111. David Busic and Jeren Rowell, "The Preaching Life," *Preacher's Magazine* (Advent/Christmas 2007-8), 48.

112. "Johnson Becomes First Nazarene President of NAE," *Herald of Holiness* (May 1990), 32. Compare *Herald of Holiness* (July 30, 1975), 22. See Quadrennial Address of the Board of General Superintendents, *Journal of the Eighteenth General Assembly* (1972), 200; William Greathouse to B. Edgar Johnson, January 25, 1983 and February 24, 1984; *Proceedings of the General Board of the*

Church of the Nazarene and Its Departments, Sixty-First Annual Session, Kansas City, Missouri (February 27-28, 1984), 21; B. Edgar Johnson to Billy Melvin, executive director, NAE (March 1, 1984); General Secretary's Report, *Journal of the Twenty-First General Assembly* (1985), 418; "Evangelicalism to Continue Growth," *Herald of Holiness* (November 1995), 42; "Roger Parrott Accepts Position with Lausanne Committee," *Herald of Holiness* (December 15, 1986), 2.

113. "NTC Hosts World Service," *Herald of Holiness* (September 1994), 12; "Wesley Heritage Project Recruits Pacheco," *Herald of Holiness* (September 1994), 13.

114. News Release, General Secretary's Office (September 30, 1999). See also "Merger of Holiness Churches," *Journal of the Twenty-Second General Assembly* (1989), 131.

115. Hunsberger and van Gelder, *The Church Between Gospel and Culture,* xvii.

116. See for example, Ron Benefiel, "The Church of the Nazarene: Undercurrents of a Changing Identity," in *Maps and Models,* 77-92; Wesley Tracy, "The Question Box," *Herald of Holiness* (December 1997), 37.

Chapter 26

1. David O. Moberg, *The Great Reversal: Evangelism and Social Concern,* rev. ed. (Philadelphia: Holman, 1977), 11.

2. Many of Smith's themes were popularized by Dayton in *Discovering an Evangelical Heritage.* See also Timothy L. Smith, "History of Compassionate Ministries," presented at Nazarene Compassionate Ministries Conference, 1985, 37-38; Timothy Smith, "Internationalization and Ethnicity: Nazarene Accomplishments and Problems," in *Evangelism and Social Redemption,* eds. Albert L. Truesdale Jr. and Steve Weber (Kansas City: Beacon Hill Press of Kansas City, 1987).

3. *Journal of the Eighteenth General Assembly* (1972), 214.

4. See Tom Nees, "Why We Do What We Do," Nazarene Compassionate Ministries Conference, October 29—November 1, 1998, available on-line, http://didache.nts.edu.

5. See Tom Nees, "The Holiness Social Ethic and Nazarene Urban Ministry," D.Min. diss., Wesley Theological Seminary, 1976; L. Guy Nees, "Ministering to the Whole Person," *Herald of Holiness* (November 1, 1983), 9-11; Nees, *Winds of Change.*

6. *Journal of the Eighteenth General Assembly* (1972), 206; *Proceedings of the General Board* (1977), 121; Raymond Hurn to Whitelaw (June 24, 1999). See also Hurn, *Mission Possible.* Compare Donald A. McGavran, *Effective Evangelism: A Theological Mandate* (Phillipsburg, NJ: Presbyterian and Reformed Publishing Company, 1988); Jim Dorsey's oral interviews with Bill Sullivan (January to May 2000); and David Whitelaw's conversations with Ray Hurn (June 2, 2000). See also Dean Nelson, "Paul Orjala: Living the Language of God."

7. See Nazarene Archives File 302-126; tribute of Bill Sullivan on his completion of service in the Division of Church Growth, 1985; *Journal of the Twenty-First General Assembly* (1985), 629. "Passing the Torch," and "Superintendents Recognized for Years of Service," *Herald of Holiness* (May 1993).

8. Glen Van Dyne, "Raymond W. Hurn to New Career," *News Release* from Church Extension Ministries (December 13, 1984); "Raymond Hurn to New Career," *Herald of Holiness* (January 1, 1985), 33-34; *Home Missions ALERT!* Nazarene Archives, 715-8; Hurn, "It's Back to Church Planting for the Nazarenes," *Global Church Growth* (January 1982), 160-63.

9. See *Journal of the Nineteenth General Assembly* (1976), 137; *Herald of Holiness* (January 15, 1977), 26; *Herald of Holiness* (November 1, 1977), 4-5; "Nazarene District Leaders Study Church Growth," *Herald of Holiness* (December 15, 1977), 32-33; *Proceedings of the General Board* (1981), 125; Hurn to Whitelaw (June 24, 1999).

10. See *Journal of the Eighteenth General Assembly* (1972), 27; Hurn, *Rising Tide,* 53. See also *District Superintendent's Handbook* (Kansas City: Nazarene Publishing House, 1990).

11. Church Extension Ministries, comp., *Total Mobilization* (Kansas City: Church Extension Ministries, 1982), 65.

12. Raymond W. Hurn, "Beaverton Church Will Start 15 New Nazarene Congregations in 1980," *Herald of Holiness* (February 15, 1980), 18-19. See Church Extension Ministries, comp., *Total Mobilization.*

13. *Journal of the Twenty-Second General Assembly* (1989), 579. *See Herald of Holiness* (May 1, 1976), 24; *Proceedings of the General Board* (1977), 121-25; "Nazarene Denomination Takes Church

Growth Leadership," *Herald of Holiness* (February 15, 1978), 19; *Herald of Holiness* (September 15, 1978), 20-21; *Finding Your Ministry: A Study of the Fruit and Gifts of the Spirit* (Kansas City: Beacon Hill Press of Kansas City, 1979), 9; *Proceedings of the General Board* (1980), 135-36; Hurn to Whitelaw (December 27, 2001). Also, for criticism of the church growth movement from a Holiness perspective, see Richard S. Taylor, *Dimensions of Church Growth: The Upward, Downward, Inward Factors* (Grand Rapids: Zondervan, 1989), 19-28, 54-56.

14. *Herald of Holiness* (January 15, 1984), 26-27; *Journal of the Twenty-First General Assembly* (1985), 412; *Herald of Holiness* (May 15, 1978), 21; *Proceedings of the General Board* (1979), 146-54.

15. *Proceedings of the General Board* (1982), 90; Bill Sullivan, "Nazarene Evangelism: More Future than Past," interview by Wesley Tracy; *Herald of Holiness* (May 15, 1980), 20-21; "Minutes of the Special Session of the General Board," following General Assembly (1980); *Proceedings of the General Board*, 53, 149; "Division of Church Growth," *Herald of Holiness* (June 15, 1985), 11; "Sullivan Honored," *Herald of Holiness* (February 1995), 10. See Nees, *Changing Face of the Church*, 61-62. See *Proceedings of the General Board* (February 25-29, 1980), 21-22, 25-29, 43, 135. See also *Proceedings of the General Board* (February 23-27, 1981), 125; Report of the Church Growth Division, *Journal of the Twenty-First General Assembly*, 622; *Proceedings of the General Board* (February 25-29, 1980), 20; *Grow* (Winter 2002-3). See also Mark Metcalf, "Electronic Evangelism," *Herald of Holiness* (May 1995), 12-13; "Tribute to Bill M. Sullivan," *Grow* (Summer 2007), 17.

16. See *Grow* (Winter 1992), inside cover; "Church Growth Principles from Scripture," *Grow* (Spring 1994), 32-36; *Quadrennial Reports to the Twenty-Fourth General Assembly* (1997), 462-63; *Proceedings of the General Board* (1998), 150. See also Bill Sullivan, *Starting Strong New Churches: Discover the Most Effective Strategy to Reach People for Christ* (Kansas City: NewStart, 1997); Jim Dorsey, *Starter Kit for Starting Strong New Churches: Ideas for Church Start Leaders* (Kansas City: NewStart, 1997); Lyle Pointer and Jim Dorsey, *Evangelism in Everyday Life: Sharing and Shaping Your Faith* (Kansas City: Beacon Hill Press of Kansas City, 1998).

17. Richard Smith, "The Theology of Church Growth," *Herald of Holiness* (May 15, 1976), 12-14. See also *Herald of Holiness* (May 1, 1977), 24-25.

18. *Herald of Holiness* (November 1, 1983), 13; "General Superintendents Remember Past—Look to Future," *Herald of Holiness* (May 1996), 14.

19. See "Nazarene Sociologists of Religion Meet," *Herald of Holiness* (May 15, 1986), 24; Jon Johnston and Bill Sullivan, eds., *The Smaller Church in a Super Church Era* (Kansas City: Nazarene Publishing House, 1986); *Journal of the Twenty-Second General Assembly* (1989), 579; "Creed: A Conference on Changing Worship Styles," *Herald of Holiness* (January 1995), 16; insert between pages 24-25, *Herald of Holiness* (October 1997).

20. "The Association of Nazarenes in Social Work (ANSW)," *Herald of Holiness* (January 1, 1983), 28. See also, *Herald of Holiness* (October 15, 1983), 16-18.

21. Reynolds Think Tank Materials, Files, Documents, Reports in Ron Benefiel's personal library; Hiram F. Reynolds Institute, Meeting with Board of General Superintendents (December 8, 1994); *Proceedings of the General Board* (1994), 27, 30; *Journal of the Twenty-Fourth General Assembly* (1997), 291; Robert Scott, director, and members, "Final Report to the Board of General Superintendents," Reynolds Research Institute (March 26, 1997). See Scott to members of the institute (February 26, 1997), accompanying the "AD 2025: A Picture: The Global Family/Church of the Nazarene—Two Scenarios Developed by Reynolds Research Institute."

22. Hurn to Whitelaw (December 27, 2001). See Rogers, *Sharecropper*, 8, foreword by Raymond Hurn.

23. Bowman, *Color Us Christian*. See also *Home Missions ALERT!* (1977); Hurn, *Mission Possible*; Hurn, *Rising Tide*, 52-53.

24. *Home Missions ALERT!* (1977); *Herald of Holiness* (August 15, 1984); Glen L. Van Dyne, "The Dream Becomes a Reality," *Home Missions ALERT!* (1984).

25. *Thrust to the Cities New York* (April 1988) (brochure); *Weekly Summary* (November 20, 1992); "Metro New York District Leads USA Districts in Growth: Interview with District Superintendent Dallas D. Mucci," *Grow* (Winter 1993-94), 1-4.

26. *Journal of the Twenty-Third General Assembly* (1993), 624; "Nees Elected to New Post," *Herald of Holiness* (July 1995), 17. See Steve Weber, "Nazarene Compassionate Ministries Restructured," *Bridge* (Fall 1995), 2; Tom Nees, "Report on Multicultural Ministries in Church Growth

Division Report to the General Assembly," *Quadrennial Reports to the Twenty-Fourth General Assembly* (1997), 465-68. See also Nees, *Changing Face of the Church.*

27. *Multicultural Newsletter* (September 1998), 2.

28. Wesley Tracy, "The Author's Standpoint: 'Remember the Poor,'" *Herald of Holiness* (June 1, 1978), 18. See also R. Franklin Cook and Steve Weber, *The Greening: The Story of Nazarene Compassionate Ministries* (Kansas City: Nazarene Publishing House, 1986).

29. *The Lausanne Covenant* and "A Response to Lausanne," reprinted in Missiology Study Guide of the University of South Africa, 1983. See "Nazarene Leaders Attend World Evangelization Conference" and "Church Mission Discussed at International Congress on World Evangelization," *Herald of Holiness* (August 28, 1974), 22, 30. See also Hurn, "Changing Assumptions," in *Rising Tide,* 52-55.

30. Howard Culbertson, *The Kingdom Strikes Back: Signs of the Messiah at Work in Haiti* (Kansas City: Nazarene Publishing House, 1990), 40.

31. Spell, ed., *Haiti Diary,* 38; Orjala, *Christ in the Caribbean,* 49-50; Parker, *Mission to the World,* 477; Culbertson, *Kingdom Strikes Back,* 23, 57-58.

32. Editorial, *Herald of Holiness* (February 26, 1975), 28; See *Herald of Holiness* (March 15, 1976); *Herald of Holiness* (July 1, 1976), 35; *Herald of Holiness* (November 1, 1976), 35; *Herald of Holiness* (February 1, 1978), 27; *Journal of the Twentieth General Assembly* (1980), 515.

33. Franco, *Wounded,* 130.

34. Ibid., 137-38.

35. Ibid., 137-38, 143-44.

36. Neil B. Wiseman, comp., *To the City, with Love: A Sourcebook of Nazarene Urban Ministries* (Kansas City: Beacon Hill Press of Kansas City, 1976). See, for example, Doug McConnell, "The Bresee Institute for Urban Training: A Study in the Analysis of Urban Training," M.A. thesis, Fuller Theological Seminary, 1985; and Christensen, *City Streets.*

37. Transcription of Cassettes 14 and 19, Department of Home Mission Files, Nazarene Archives, Kansas City (June 26, 1974). See also *Herald of Holiness* (June 6, 1973); John C. Oster, "A Church in Mid-Miracle," *Herald of Holiness* (October 22, 1975), 14-15; *Herald of Holiness* (February 15, 1977), 35; Paul Moore and Joe Musser, *Shepherd of Times Square* (Nashville: Thomas Nelson, 1979); William Greathouse, "The Neglected Quarters," *Herald of Holiness* (December 1, 1982), 2.

38. *Herald of Holiness* (February 1, 1985); David Best, newsletter (February 11, 1990).

39. Tom Nees, "Taking Holiness to the Streets," *Holiness Today* (January 2004), 30-31. See Wynkoop, *John Wesley: Christian Revolutionary.*

40. Tom Nees, "Hope for the City," *Herald of Holiness* (December 1, 1982), 6-7; *Washington Post* (July 20, 1983). See Elizabeth O'Connor, *The New Community* (New York: Harper and Row, 1976), 45-48; Tom Nees, "Low Income Housing—Too Costly for the Poor," *Mission Journal* (March 1977).

41. Nees, "Why We Do What We Do," 3-5. See also *Herald of Holiness* (October 13, 1971); "Washington, D.C., Ministry Grows," *Herald of Holiness* (July 1, 1978), 35; Nees, *Compassion-Evangelism* (Kansas City: Beacon Hill Press of Kansas City, 1996), 1-11, 13.

42. *Herald of Holiness* (October 15, 1978), 39; Nazarene Archives, 473-25; letter from Tom Nees and family (April 4, 1979), Nazarene Archives, 473-26.

43. Tom Nees, "Compassion Fatigue," *Herald of Holiness* (February 1994), 40-41.

44. *Community of Hope Journal* (Spring 1983 and Winter 1985); *Community of Hope Annual Report 1988* (brochure); Nazarene Archives 869-5. See also NCN (September 12, 2003).

45. Nees, *Changing Face of the Church,* 13.

46. "Nazarene Lay Woman Takes Christ to the Poor for 17 Years," *Grow* (Spring 1994), 38-39.

47. Neil Wiseman, "Neighborhood Christian Center Opens Impressive New Facilities in Memphis," *Grow* (Fall 2005), 25-29; "The Mission in Memphis: New Leaders for Black Churches," *Grow* (Summer 2008), 15-17.

48. Christiansen, *Call for Compassion,* 35-52.

49. In 1993 Calcutta itself, which had not been touched by Nazarenes for a generation, became the target of Nazarenes' Thrust to the Cities campaign. See *Nazarene News* (February 9, 1990) for

John Knight's visit, and "Prince Visits India," *Herald of Holiness* (April 1995), 20. See also John and Doris Anderson, "A Return to Calcutta," *World Mission* (February 1995), 7.

50. Board of General Superintendents, "Proclamation," *Herald of Holiness* (December 1, 1981), 5, repeated in a similar "Proclamation," *Herald of Holiness* (November 15, 1984), 5.

51. "Hunger and Disaster Fund Statement," Nazarene Archives 867-15, which also includes related pamphlets.

52. Pastoral Letter from the Board of General Superintendents, "The Gospel to the Poor," *Herald of Holiness* (December 1, 1983), 5. See also William Greathouse, "The Neglected Quarters," *Herald of Holiness* (December 1, 1982), 2; Jerald Johnson, "The Church and Its Social Concern," *Herald of Holiness* (March 1, 1983), 2.

53. Timothy L. Smith, "A Wesleyan Theology of Salvation and Social Liberation," paper presented to the Caribbean Nazarene Regional Conference, *Preacher's Magazine* (June-July-August 1989), 40-41, 57. See also Smith, "Holiness and Radicalism in Nineteenth-Century America," in *Sanctification and Liberation*.

54. "Weber Appointed Coordinator of Nazarene Compassionate ministries," *Herald of Holiness* (April 15, 1984), 35. See Culbertson, *Kingdom Strikes Back*.

55. Nazarene Archives (799B-151); "First Nazarene Compassionate Ministries Conference Attracts Huge Crowd," *Herald of Holiness* (January 15, 1986), 26-27. See Truesdale and Weber, eds., *Evangelism and Social Redemption*; Linda Patterson Wilcox, "The Readers Write: 'Compassionate Ministries,'" *Herald of Holiness* (June 1990), 10.

56. *Liberation Community, Fort Worth, Texas* (brochure); *NNS Weekly Summary* (July 26, 1991); *Grow* (Fall 1991). See also Bryan Stone, *Compassionate Ministry: Theological Foundations* (Maryknoll, NY: Orbis, 1996).

57. Ibid.

58. "Personalizing Community Justice," *Shepherd Community* [newsletter] (December 1991/January 1992).

59. *Indianapolis News* (December 12, 1987), A-11; *Shepherd Community* [newsletter] (Summer 1992; Spring 1995; and Fall 1996), Nazarene Archives.

60. Bert Hotchkiss to Friend (October 10, 1962); *Herald of Holiness* (November 10, 1965); Joe Colaizzi to Friends (Summer 1990); Kansas City RM: A Progress Report (Summer 1991).

61. Steve Weber and Bob Prescott, "Nazarene Compassionate Ministries," *Herald of Holiness* (December 1, 1985), 8-9; "Nazarene Compassionate Ministries, Inc Established," *Herald of Holiness* (June 1990), 32; *NNS Weekly Summary* (March 13, 1992); Nees, *Compassion-Evangelism*, 4; *Quadrennial Reports to the Twenty-Fourth General Assembly* (1997), 468.

62. Richard Zanner, "RFM Changes Hands... Continues Service," *Trans African* (May-June 1992), 8-9. *World Mission* (February 1992), 7-8. See Parker, *Mission to the World*, 89-96, for an overview of the early years of Nazarene Compassionate Ministries.

63. "NCM Joins Heart to Heart in Historic Airlift to Vietnam," *Herald of Holiness* (July 1995), 15. See "Heart to Heart Targets Balkans with Aid/Bears," *Herald of Holiness* (January 1995), 16; *Herald of Holiness* (July 1995), 15. See Gary Morsch and Dean Nelson, *Heart and Soul: Awakening Your Passion to Serve* (Kansas City: Beacon Hill Press of Kansas City, 1997), including Richard Schubert's "Foreword."

64. *Nazarene Health Care Fellowship* (November 1994).

65. Nazarene Archives (1170B-1 to 10; 1220-63). Nazarene Archives (130Y-11); Nazarene Archives (357-28); "Doing the Lord's Work in the 'Me Decade,'" *Herald of Holiness* (March 15, 1980), 12-13; Tom Nees, "On the Book *Compassion Evangelism*," interview by Bryan McLaughlin (July 1996); Nees, *Compassion Evangelism: Meeting Human Needs* (Kansas City: Beacon Hill Press of Kansas City, 1996).

66. *Quadrennial Reports to the Twentieth General Assembly* (1980), 468; *Proceedings of the General Board* (1998), 161. See also "Europe Hosts Second NCM Conference," *Herald of Holiness* (January 1995), 15.

67. "Nazarenes Respond to Haitian Drought," *Herald of Holiness* (October 1997), 48. See also Steve Weber, "Delivery System for Mercy," *Herald of Holiness* (February 15, 1985), 3.

68. See also John A. Knight, interview by Nazarene Compassionate Ministry, *Compassionate Samaritan* (1998).

69. Stone, "Subversive Compassion," paper presented at the Nazarene Compassionate Ministries Conference, 1998. See also *Christians at Work in a Hurting World*, ed. Stephen M. Miller (Kansas City: Beacon Hill Press of Kansas City, 1990); Stone, *Compassionate Ministry*.

70. *Grow* (Spring 2003), 3.

Chapter 27

1. *Journal of the Nineteenth General Assembly* (1976), 185; see 184-203.

2. Bill M. Sullivan, *Starting Strong New Churches* (Kansas City: NewStart, 1997), 42-43; "The Win Arn Church Growth Report: Pastoral Tenure and Church Growth," *Grow* (Fall 1992), 61; *World Mission* (August 1998), 5; General Secretary, "Annual Church Statistical Report" (December 4, 2000).

3. Roland Robertson, "Glocalization: Time-space and Homogeneity-Heterogeneity," in *Global Modernities*, eds. Mike Featherstone and others (London: Sage, 1995). See also John Urry, *Consuming Places* (London: Routledge, 1994).

4. David Whitelaw, interview with Bill Young (January 24, 2001); R. Franklin Cook to Whitelaw (January 26, 2001).

5. See Richard Schubert, "Foreword," to Morsch and Nelson, *Heart and Soul*, 9-10, 13-15.

6. James McGraw, "Forgive Us Our Syndromes," *Preacher's Magazine* (July 1977), 1-2.

7. "Planting New Churches: Our Home Mission Heritage," *Herald of Holiness* (October 1, 1983), 6-9.

8. Richard Thompson, *The Tiny Church in a Big Church World* (Kansas City: Nazarene Publishing House, 1991), 63, 67. See also Bill Sullivan, *Ten Steps to Breaking the 200 Barrier* (Kansas City: Beacon Hill Press of Kansas City, 1988); "Smaller Church Resource Launched by Church Growth Division," *Grow* (1992), 1 and inside front cover.

9. *Grow* (Fall 1992), 13.

10. "Where Are the Mega-Churches?" *World Mission* (November 1998), 7.

11. "Sharpe Memorial Church of the Nazarene: 90 Years 1906-1996," Ninetieth Anniversary Celebration Booklet, published by the church at Burgher Street, Parkhead, Glasgow, Scotland (September 1996); Doug Samples, "Deep Roots-Great Shade," *Herald of Holiness* (January 1998), 5-7; Ted Esselstyn to David Whitelaw (January 1, 2000); Larry McKain to David Whitelaw (April 26, 2002). See G. A. Pritchard, *Willow Creek Seeker Services: Evaluating a New Way of Doing Church* (Grand Rapids: Baker, 1996).

12. See Russell Bredholt, "Challenge: A Denominational Church," *Holiness Today* (December 2000), 24-27.

13. Ken Coil, interview by David Whitelaw, Temecula, California (April 23, 2002). Compare Robert Webber, *Worship, Old and New* (Grand Rapids: Eerdmans, 1982); Robert Webber, *The Worship Phenomenon: A Dynamic New Awakening* (Nashville: Abbott Martin 1994), and Robert Webber, *Evangelicals on the Canterbury Trail: Why Evangelicals Are Attracted to the Liturgical Church* (Waco, TX: Word, 1985).

14. Neil Wiseman, "To the City with Love: Three Congregations Flourish at the Mother Church," *Herald of Holiness* (February 15, 1976), 12-13.

15. See Ron Benefiel, "A Church for All People," 12-15; Roger Bowman, "Antioch, Los Angeles, and Tomorrow," 16-19; Glen Van Dyne, "Sunday Morning at Los Angeles First Church," 20-21; and "The Faces of Los Angeles First Church," 22-25 (all in *Herald of Holiness* [October 1995]). See also Neil Wiseman, comp., *To the City with Love: A Source Book of Nazarene Urban Ministries* (Kansas City: Beacon Hill Press of Kansas City, 1976), 52-54; McConnell, "The Bresee Institute for Urban Training"; *Journal of the Twenty-Third General Assembly* (1993), 250; "Mother Church Celebrates Centennial," *Herald of Holiness* (January 1996), 24; Benefiel, "Transitional Communities: Multi-Congregational Ministry," *Urban Mission* (June 1995), 38-47.

16. Linda Crow, *Profiles of Change: A Witness from Four European Christians Who Have Been "Through the Fire"* (Kansas City: Nazarene Publishing House, 1987), 43-57; Debbie Salter Goodwin, "A Church Without Walls," *World Mission* (September 1998), 14-15.

17. Neil Wiseman, "Grace for Secular Society," *World Mission* (November 1998), 16-17.

18. In-soon Yoon, "Celebrating Half a Century," *World Mission* (November 1998), 8-9.

19. "Pastor's Three-Week Fast Helps Plant Seoul Church," 54-55, and "Korean Air Force Major Finds Christ in Thrust Church," *Grow* (Spring 1993), 8-9.

20. Information to David Whitelaw from Tim Mercer.

21. Report by Theodore Esselstyn.

22. "Creative Spaces for Holy Places," report on New England conference for multicongregational church leaders held at First Church, Malden, Massachusetts, in 1992, *Grow* (Fall 1992), 48-49; Jack Holstead, *On This Rock: The Church of the Nazarene in Hongkong* (Kansas City: Nazarene Publishing House, 1996), 36-41.

23. Thelma Gomer, "A Caring Church," *Herald of Holiness* (December 1, 1982), 12-13.

24. Randall Davey to the writer (August 25, 2000).

25. Dan Boone to Keith Bottles, Chicago Central District Church of the Nazarene, Bourbonnais (August 6, 1991); *College Church Communique* (September 10, 1992 and January 28, 1993).

26. James McGraw, "The Motivators" and "Among Ourselves," *Preacher's Magazine* (September 1977), 1-2, 33 (inside back page); "Saw Wood and Say Nothing," *Preacher's Magazine* (October 1977), 1-2.

27. James McGraw, "From the Editor–Bifocal Preaching," *Preacher's Magazine* (May 1976), 1. See James McGraw, "A Message in the Shape of a Man," *Preacher's Magazine* (June 1976), 1, and "Among Ourselves," *Preacher's Magazine* (March 1977), 33.

28. J. Kenneth Grider, "A Plea for Expository Preaching," *Preacher's Magazine* (October 1977), 3-5.

29. Wesley Tracy, "Introduction" to *Go, Preach: The Preaching Event in the 90s* (Kansas City: Nazarene Publishing House, 1992).

30. C. S. Cowles, "Emergence of the 'Postpreaching' Era," *Preacher's Magazine* (March 1977), 3-6.

31. In Tracy, *Go, Preach*.

32. "Special Outpouring in Kentucky," *Herald of Holiness* (March 1995), 40. See *Herald of Holiness* (January 1, 1977), 4-5.

33. See "Petition" from various churches in Florida to Wesley Tracy (April 1992) (file 1292-15). For example, see Win Arn and Charles Arn, *The Master's Plan for Making Disciples*, Nazarene version edited by Bill M. Sullivan (Kansas City: Nazarene Publishing House, 1984).

34. Paul M. Bassett, "The Role of the Nazarene Layperson in Light of Church History," presented at the International Congress on Lay Ministry, Kansas City (January 1995). See Tom Barnard, "A Survey of Churches of the Nazarene with Paid Staffs," Bethany Nazarene College, 1971; W. E. McCumber, "The Answer Corner," *Herald of Holiness* (June 1, 1985), 31. For an early dissent to the emphasis upon lay ministries see Richard S. Taylor, "The Spirit and the Church's Mission in the World," in *The Church in a Changing World: Selected Papers from the Nazarene Theology Conference*, ed. W. T. Purkiser (Kansas City: Beacon Hill Press of Kansas City, 1972), 62-63. Compare John Collins, *Are All Christians Ministers?* (Collegeville, MN: Liturgical Press, 1992); David Wells, *No Place for Truth, or, Whatever Happened to Evangelical Theology?* (Grand Rapids: Eerdmans, 1993), 113-14.

35. C. J. Adams, "Leadership in the Church," *Preacher's Magazine* (April 1976), 19-21.

36. H. B. London, "The Minister as a Professional," *Preacher's Magazine* (September 1976), 12-15.

37. James Garlow, *Partners in Ministry: Laity and Pastors Working Together* (Kansas City: Beacon Hill Press of Kansas City, 1981), 46; 41. See also James Garlow, *LITE: Lay Institute to Equip* (Kansas City: Beacon Hill Press of Kansas City, 1980).

38. Jerald Johnson, "The Transition," *Herald of Holiness* (September 1, 1981), 5.

39. Hazel Bailey, "Empower the Laity!" *Herald of Holiness* (September 1994), 28; "Lay Congress Held," *Herald of Holiness* (March 1995), 10. See also Gary Morsch and Eddy Hall, *Ministry: It's Not Just for Ministers* (Kansas City: Beacon Hill Press of Kansas City, 1994).

40. Roger L. Hahn, "The Role of the Nazarene Layperson in Light of Scripture," presented at the International Congress on Lay Ministry, Kansas City (January 1995).

41. John Knight, "The Lay Revolution," *Herald of Holiness* (August 1997), 1.

42. "Petition" to Wesley Tracy from various churches in Florida (April 1992) (file 1292-15).

43. C. Dale German, "There's Music in Your Church," *Preacher's Magazine* (October 1976), 12-13. See also C. Dale German, "My Objections to 'Christian' Rock," *Herald of Holiness* (August 15, 1983).

44. James McGraw, "Whatever Happened to Church Music?" *Preacher's Magazine* (August 1977), 1-2.

45. "ANSR Studies Nazarene Worship Styles," *Herald of Holiness* (June 1995), 16.

46. Paul M. Bassett, "Full Salvation and the Liturgy of the Early Church," *Preacher's Magazine* (September/October/November 1981), 24-27.

47. Greathouse, "The Present Crisis in Our Worship," lecture at Nazarene Theological Seminary, quoted in Rob L. Staples, "Tribute to William M. Greathouse," *Wesleyan Theological Journal* 33 (Spring 1998), 224-30.

48. Jesse Middendorf, *The Church Rituals Handbook* (Kansas City: Beacon Hill Press of Kansas City, 1997), 9, 20-22, 149-50.

49. Randall Davey to Davie Whitelaw (August 25, 2000). See, for example, *Preacher's Magazine* (Advent/Christmas 2000-2001), 2, 38.

50. *Worship in Song Supplementary Indexes* (Kansas City: Lillenas, 1983), 12-13.

51. "Cyberfacts," *World Mission* (November 1998), 6.

52. Roland Feltmate, "What We Learned About Worship," *Herald of Holiness* (November 1995), 18-20. See Victor Parachin, "Hymns: The Speech of Angels," *Herald of Holiness* (January 1994), 32-33.

53. Keith Schwanz, "Songs of Spiritual Experience," *Herald of Holiness* (November 1997), 28-31.

54. Wesley Tracy, "The Question Box," *Herald of Holiness* (November 1998).

55. Richard Zanner, "The Challenge from the Charismatic SuperChurches," *Herald of Holiness* (December 1, 1982), 6-7 (reprinted from the *Trans-African,* 1982). See also Zanner, "Largest Congregation Outside US Dedicates Building," *Herald of Holiness* (January 15, 1980), 47; and "Church of the Nazarene Strong in Africa," *Herald of Holiness* (January 1, 1987), 1-2.

56. "Nazarenes, Pentecostals Bridge Differences at Pasadena Service," *Los Angeles Times* (March 4, 1995), B4-B5.

57. Al Woods to E. R. "Bud" Camfield (October 5, 1994). Camfield circulated the letter widely.

58. *Journal of the Twenty-Fourth General Assembly* (1997), 71-72, 158. See also *Journal of the Twenty-First General Assembly* (1985), 408; Wesley Tracy, "The Question Box," *Herald of Holiness* (October 1997), 34; *Trans-African* (January 1998), 19.

59. Richard Houseal and Kenneth Crow, "Secularization within the Church of the Nazarene," paper delivered at the Association of Nazarene Sociologists of Religion (March 1999). Compare Philip D. Kenneson, *Beyond Sectarianism: Re-imagining Church and World* (Harrisburg, PA: Trinity Press International, 1999).

Chapter 28

1. Paul M. Bassett, "Our History and His Story," Global Theology Conference, 2002.

2. See Samuel Powell and Michael Lodahl, eds., *Embodied Holiness: Toward a Corporate Theology of Spiritual Growth* (Downers Grove, IL: InterVarsity, 1999).

3. Grider, *Entire Sanctification,* 7. See also Bebbington, *Holiness in Nineteenth-Century England,* 65.

4. Frank Moore, *Coffee Shop Theology: Translating Doctrinal Jargon into Everyday Life* (Kansas City: Beacon Hill Press of Kansas City, 1998), 11, 70.

5. Theodore Esselstyn, *Following Jesus Together: An Orientation to the Church of the Nazarene in Africa* (Florida, RSA: Africa Nazarene Publications, n.d.), 1. See also Michael Lodahl, *The Story of God: Wesleyan Theology and Biblical Narrative* (Kansas City: Beacon Hill Press of Kansas City, 1994), 9-11.

6. Wynkoop, "Theological Roots of the Wesleyan Understanding of the Holy Spirit," *Wesleyan Theological Journal* 14 (Spring 1979): 77-98.

7. Ibid., 79-80.

8. Tim Crutcher, "Labels, Assumptions, and a Generation Called 'X'," in *Generation Xers Talk About the Church of the Nazarene,* ed. Thomas Jay Oord (Kansas City: Nazarene Publishing House, 1999), 18-19.

9. Bassett, "Full Salvation and the Liturgy," 24-26.

10. Program, Seventh Theology Conference, 1987. See announcement "Nazarene Theology Conference Planned for 1987" with details of planning and participants, *Herald of Holiness* (August 15, 1986), 35.

11. W. Stephen Gunter, "The Reification of Experience in Revivalist Theology," Seventh Theology Conference, 1987, 1-7. See David Whitelaw, "Tapestries and Trajectories in the New South Africa: Contrasts and Comparisons with Patterns of Church Historiography on the North American Continent," *Studia Historiae Ecclesiasticae* 22 (1996), 166; see 149-81. See also editor, *Herald of Holiness* (May 1, 1979), 18; Bebbington, *Holiness in Nineteenth-Century England,* 61-71.

12. "Isbell Concludes Teaching Assignment at Nazarene Theological Seminary," *Herald of Holiness* (May 15, 1980); Bruce McCormack to the author (April 16, 2002).

13. *Manual/Church of the Nazarene 1997-2001,* 252.

14. See Eugene L. Stowe, "Higher Education and Our Holiness Heritage" and William M. Greathouse, "The Wesleyan Hermeneutic of Entire Sanctification," Sixth Theology Conference, 1982; Paul M. Bassett, "Toward an Agenda for Nazarene Theology," Seventh Nazarene Theology Conference, 1987, 8, 10; Henry Spaulding, "Centering Our Theology: An Agenda for Nazarene Theology," Seventh Nazarene Theology Conference, 1987, 1-8. See Karl Martin, *The Evangelical Church and American Popular Culture* (San Diego: Point Loma Press, 2000). Examples of the "preached form" would include the sermons of Albert J. Lown, published in the *Herald of Holiness;* for example, "Heart Holiness" (July 30, 1975), 16-17.

15. David Whitelaw, "Fitness for Life's Journey: Entire Sanctification," *Holiness Today* (April 1999), 20-22.

16. Paul M. Bassett, "Toward an Agenda for Nazarene Theology," paper, Seventh Nazarene Theology Conference, 1987, 15-16; "The Position of the Church of the Nazarene on Speaking in Tongues," Statement by the Board of General Superintendents, *Herald of Holiness* (October 15, 1976), 4-5; J. Kenneth Grider, "Holiness Doctrine at Anaheim," *Herald of Holiness* (May 1, 1986), 16-17.

17. Henry Spaulding, "Centering Our Theology: An Agenda for Nazarene Theology," Seventh Nazarene Theology Conference, 1987, 1-8.

18. H. Ray Dunning, "Grace, Faith, and Holiness," paper presented to the Seventh Nazarene Theology Conference, 1987, 1-20. See also Dunning, *Grace, Faith, and Holiness,* 10-11.

19. Donald Metz to William Greathouse and H. Ray Dunning, with copies to several dozen leaders including the entire Board of General Superintendents, the presidents of educational Institutions USA/International, the Nazarene archivist, and a number of other pastors and leaders, dated March 3, 1994. See also Metz, *Some Crucial Issues.*

20. "Systematic Theology Presented at Theology Conference," *Herald of Holiness* (May 1, 1987), 23.

21. Dunning, "Grace, Faith and Holiness," 1-20.

22. Ibid., 14. See also K. Steve McCormick, "Theosis in Chrysostom and Wesley: An Eastern Paradigm on Faith and Love," and Troy W. Martin, "John Wesley's Exegetical Orientation: East or West?" both in *Wesleyan Theological Journal* 26 (1991).

23. Hitoshi (Paul) Fukue, "Beyond Christ and Culture," Global Theology Conference, Guatemala (April 2002), 1-3.

24. In-Gyeong Kim Lundell, *Bridging the Gaps: Contextualization Among Korean Nazarene Churches in America* (New York: Peter Lang, 1995), 5-6, 105-7, 132.

25. Jonathan Salgado, "An Important Item for the Theological Agenda," Seventh Nazarene Theology Conference, 1987, 1-8.

26. Enrique Guang, "Reflections on the Theology of Liberation in Light of Wesleyan Theology and the Church of the Nazarene," paper presented to Seventh Nazarene Theology Conference, 1987, 1-15.

27. Angelito Agbuya, "Internationalization," Seventh Nazarene Theology Conference, 1987, 1-9.

28. Al Truesdale, "Christian Holiness and the Problem of Systemic Evil," *Wesleyan Theological Journal* 19 (Spring 1984), 39-59. See also Vern Hannah, "Toward a Re-Evaluation of Our Concept of Original Sin," Seventh Nazarene Theology Conference, 1987, 1-24.

29. Frank Moore, *More Coffee Shop Theology: Translating Doctrinal Jargon into Everyday Life* (Kansas City: Beacon Hill Press of Kansas City, 1998), 68. Also see Moore, *Breaking Free from Sin's Grip: Holiness Defined for a New Generation* (Kansas City: Beacon Hill Press of Kansas City, 2001), 55-63.

30. Bassett, "Toward an Agenda for Nazarene Theology," 14-15.

31. Alex Deasley, "Hermeneutical Integrity and the Nazarene Biblical Scholar," and Kent Brower, "The Church and the Biblical Scholar," Seventh Nazarene Theology Conference, 1987.

32. Deasley, "Hermeneutical Integrity," 10.

33. Brower, "Church and the Biblical Scholar," 1, 10, 12.

34. James D. Hunter, *Culture Wars: The Struggle to Define America* (New York: Basic Books, 1991).

35. Karl Giberson, "Trustees of the Truth," *Herald of Holiness* (November 15, 1988), 12-13; Karl Giberson, *Worlds Apart: The Unholy War Between Religion and Science* (Kansas City: Beacon Hill Press of Kansas City, 1993); "Preview," *Herald of Holiness* (September 1993), 16; Garry M. Wright, "Readers Write: 'Creation Science,'" *Herald of Holiness* (December 1993), 5. See also Timothy Cassity, "The Evolutionary Effect," *Herald of Holiness* (April 1, 1988), 15.

36. Alvin Jolley, "Selling Our Birthright for a Mess," *Nazarenes in Creation* (March 1995) (file 1312-21).

37. *Nazarenes in Creation* (March 1995). See Thomas Lorimer, "Why I Don't Believe in Evolution," *Preacher's Magazine* (June/July/August 1997), 25-27.

38. Wesley Tracy, "The Question Box," *Herald of Holiness* (December 1994), 41.

39. Robert Brower to Colleagues (March 30, 2000), with the attached statement, which had been received by the Board of Trustees meeting March 10 of that year.

40. David Noebel, "From the President's Desk," *Summit Ministries* (1999).

41. Dunning, "Reactions to WTS Conference on Eschatology" (unpublished response at the conference). See *Wesleyan Theological Journal* 29 (1994).

42. Dunning, "Presuppositions of a Wesleyan Eschatology," in Dunning, ed., *Second Coming: A Wesleyan Approach to the Doctrine of Last Things*, 189-202; Michael Lodahl, quoted in "Editorial Notes," *Wesleyan Theological Journal* 29 (1994): 6.

43. Greathouse, "Preserving Our Nazarene Heritage," *Herald of Holiness* (May 1, 1980), 2.

44. Greathouse, "Preserving Our Nazarene Heritage," 2; Greathouse, *Nazarene Theology in Perspective;* Greathouse, *Wholeness in Christ.*

45. *Worship in Song* (Kansas City: Lillenas, 1972); and 2 Thess. 5:23-24, RSV.

BIBLIOGRAPHY

The richest resources for the study of the Church of the Nazarene are in the Nazarene Archives located at the church's headquarters in Lenexa, Kansas. It contains rich repositories of the church's departments and leaders. The church's periodicals, beginning with the *Herald of Holiness* and *Other Sheep* magazines, are valuable sources of information. The *Wesleyan Theological Journal* and *Methodist History* contain numerous helpful articles. Below are some other important secondary sources, many of which discuss the Wesleyan setting out of which the Church of the Nazarene emerged.

Selected Secondary Sources

Andrews, Dee. *The Methodists and Revolutionary America, 1760-1800: The Shaping of an Evangelical Culture*. Princeton, NJ: Princeton U. Press, 2000.

Armstrong, Ken S. *Face to Face with the Church of the Nazarene*. Boulder, CO: Johnson, 1958.

Bangs, Carl. *Our Roots of Belief: Biblical Faith and Faithful Theology*. Kansas City: Beacon Hill Press of Kansas City, 1981.

_____. *Phineas F. Bresee: His Life in Methodism, the Holiness Movement, and the Church of the Nazarene*. Kansas City: Beacon Hill Press of Kansas City, 1995.

Bassett, Paul M. "Culture and Concupiscence: The Changing Definition of Sanctity in the Wesleyan/Holiness Movement, 1867-1920." *Wesleyan Theological Journal* 28 (Spring-Fall 1993): 176-98.

_____. "The Fundamentalist Leavening of the Holiness Movement: 1914-1940." *Wesleyan Theological Journal* 13 (Spring 1978): 65-91.

_____. "The Theological Identity of the North American Holiness Movement." In *The Variety of Evangelicalism*, ed. Donald Dayton and Robert K. Johnston, 72-108. Knoxville: U. of Tennessee Press, 1991.

Beals, Ivan A. *Heralding Scriptural Holiness*. Kansas City: Nazarene Publishing House, 1987.

Bebbington, David. *Holiness in Nineteenth-Century England*. Carlisle, England: Paternoster, 2000.

Benson, John T., Jr. *Pentecostal Mission, 1898-1915: A History*. Nashville: Trevecca Press, 1977.

Brickley, Donald P. *Man of the Morning: The Life and Work of Phineas F. Bresee*. Kansas City: Nazarene Publishing House, 1968.

Cell, George C. *The Rediscovery of John Wesley*. New York: Henry Holt, 1935.

Chapman, J. B. *A History of the Church of the Nazarene*. Kansas City: Nazarene Publishing House, 1926.

Chiles, Robert E. *Theological Transition in American Methodism: 1790-1935*. New York: Abingdon, 1965.

Coppedge, Allan. "Entire Sanctification in Early American Methodism: 1812-1835." *Wesleyan Theological Journal* 13 (Spring 1978): 34-50.

Cox, Leo G. *John Wesley's Concept of Perfection*. Kansas City: Beacon Hill Press, 1964.

Cunningham, Floyd T. *Holiness Abroad: Nazarene Missions in Asia*. Lanham, MD: Scarecrow, 2003.

_____. "Telling the Story of the Church of the Nazarene: A Wesleyan Reflection on Church History." *Mediator* 4 (2002): 1-14.

Dayton, Donald W. *Discovering an Evangelical Heritage*. New York: Harper and Row, 1976.

_____. *Theological Roots of Pentecostalism*. Grand Rapids: Zondervan, 1987.

DeLong, Russell, and Mendell Taylor. *Fifty Years of Nazarene Missions*. 3 vols. Kansas City: Beacon Hill Press, 1952-58.

Dieter, Melvin E. *The Holiness Revival of the Nineteenth Century*. Second ed. Lanham, MD: Scarecrow, 1996.

Ford, Jack. *In the Steps of John Wesley: The Church of the Nazarene in Britain*. Kansas City: Nazarene Publishing House, 1968.

_____. *What the Holiness People Believe: A Mid-Century Review of Holiness Teaching Among the Holiness Groups of Britain*. Berkenhead, Cheshire, England: Emmanuel Bible College and Missions, n.d.

Frankiel, Sandra Sizer. *California's Spiritual Frontiers: Religious Alternatives in Anglo-Protestantism, 1850-1910*. Berkeley: U. of California Press, 1988.

Girvin, E. A. *Phineas F. Bresee: A Prince in Israel: A Biography*. Kansas City: Nazarene Publishing House, 1916.

Gravely, William B. *Gilbert Haven, Methodist Abolitionist: A Study in Race, Religion, and Reform, 1850-1880*. Nashville: Abingdon, 1973.

Gresham, L. Paul. *Waves Against Gibraltar: A Memoir of Dr. A. M. Hills, 1848-1935*. Bethany, OK: Southern Nazarene U. Press, 1992.

Hambrick-Stowe, Charles E. *Charles G. Finney and the Spirit of American Evangelicalism*. Grand Rapids: Eerdmans, 1996.

Hamm, Thomas D. *The Transformation of American Quakerism: Orthodox Friends, 1800-1907*. Bloomington: U. of Indiana Press, 1988.

Hardman, Keith J. *Charles Grandison Finney, 1792-1875: Revivalist and Reformer*. Syracuse, NY: Syracuse U. Press, 1987.

Hatch, Nathan O., and John H. Wigger, eds. *Methodism and the Shaping of American Culture*. Nashville: Abingdon, 2001.

Heitzenrater, Richard P. *Wesley and People Called Methodists*. Nashville: Abingdon, 1995.

Hempton, David. *Methodism: Empire of the Spirit*. New Haven, CT: Yale U. Press, 2005.

Henecke, Gary A., et al. *A Century in Christ*. Nashville: First Church of the Nazarene, 1998.

Hills, A. M. *P. F. Bresee, D.D.: A Life Sketch*. Kansas City: Nazarene Publishing House, n.d.

Hinshaw, Amy N. *In Labors Abundant: A Biography of H. F. Reynolds*. Kansas City: Nazarene Publishing House, n.d.

_____. *Messengers of the Cross in Palestine, Japan, and Other Islands*. Kansas City: Nazarene Publishing House, n.d.

_____. *Native Torch Bearers*. Kansas City: Nazarene, 1934.

Ingersol, Stan. "Christian Baptism and the Early Nazarenes: The Sources That Shaped a Pluralistic Baptismal Tradition." *Wesleyan Theological Journal* 25 (Fall 1990): 14-38.

_____. "The Ministry of Mary Lee Cagle: A Study in Women's History and Religion," *Wesleyan Theological Journal* 28 (Spring-Fall 1993): 176-98.

_____, ed. *To Rescue the Perishing, To Care for the Dying: Historical Sources and Documents on Compassionate Ministries Drawn from the Inventories of the Nazarene Archives*. Second ed. Kansas City: Nazarene Archives, 1998.

Jernigan, C. B. *Pioneer Days of the Holiness Movement in the South West*. Kansas City: Nazarene Publishing House, 1919.

Johnson, Curtis. *Islands of Holiness: Rural Religion in Upstate New York, 1790-1865*. Ithaca, NY: Cornell U. Press, 1989.

Jones, Charles E. "Beulah Land and the Upper Room: Reclaiming the Text in Turn-of-the-Century Holiness and Pentecostal Spirituality." *Methodist History* 32 (July 1994): 250-59.

_____. *A Guide to the Study of the Holiness Movement*. Metuchen, NJ: Scarecrow, 1974.

_____. *Perfectionist Persuasion: The Holiness Movement and American Methodism, 1867-1936*. Metuchen, NJ: Scarecrow, 1974.

Kent, John. *Wesley and the Wesleyans: Religion in Eighteenth-Century Britain.* Cambridge: Cambridge U. Press, 2002.
Kirkemo, Ronald B. *For Zion's Sake: A History of Pasadena/Point Loma College.* San Diego: Point Loma Press, 1992.
Laird, Rebecca. *Ordained Women in the Church of the Nazarene: The First Generation.* Kansas City: Nazarene Publishing House, 1993.
Langford, Thomas. *Practical Divinity: Theology in the Wesleyan Tradition.* Nashville: Abingdon, 1983.
Leclerc, Diane. *Singleness of Heart: Gender, Sin, and Holiness in Historical Perspective.* Lanham, MD: Scarecrow, 2001.
Lindström, Harald. *Wesley and Sanctification: A Study in the Doctrine of Salvation.* Repr., Wilmore, KY: Francis Asbury, 1980.
Long, Kathryn T. *The Revival of 1857-58: Interpreting an American Religious Awakening.* New York: Oxford U. Press, 1998.
Madden, Edward H., and James E. Hamilton. *Freedom and Grace: The Life of Asa Mahan.* Metuchen, NJ: Scarecrow, 1982.
Maddox, Randy L. *Responsible Grace: John Wesley's Practical Theology.* Nashville: Abingdon, 1994.
Magnuson, Norris. *Salvation in the Slums: Evangelical Social Work, 1865-1920.* Metuchen, NJ: Scarecrow, 1977.
Marsden, George M. *Fundamentalism and American Culture: The Shaping of Twentieth-Century Evangelicalism, 1870-1925.* New York: Oxford, 1980.
Matthews, Donald G. *Slavery and Methodism: A Chapter in American Morality 1780-1845.* Princeton, NJ: Princeton U. Press, 1965.
McGonigle, Herbert B. *Sufficient Saving Grace: John Wesley's Evangelical Arminianism.* Carlisle, Cumbria: Paternoster, 2001.
Metz, Donald S. *Mid America Nazarene College: The Pioneer Years, 1966-1991.* Kansas City: Nazarene Publishing House, 1991.
_____. *Some Crucial Issues in the Church of the Nazarene.* Olathe, KS: Wesleyan Heritage, 1994.
Noble, T. A. *Called to Be Saints: A Centenary History of the Church of the Nazarene in the British Isles, 1906-2006.* Manchester: Didsbury Press, 2006.
Oden, Thomas C. *Doctrinal Standards in the Wesleyan Tradition.* Grand Rapids: Francis Asbury, 1988.
Outler, Albert C. *The Wesleyan Theological Heritage.* Eds. Thomas C. Oden and Leicester R. Longden. Grand Rapids: Zondervan, 1991.
Parker, J. Fred. *From East to Western Sea: A Brief History of the Church of the Nazarene in Canada.* Kansas City: Nazarene Publishing House, 1971.
_____. *Mission to the World: A History of Missions in the Church of the Nazarene Through 1985.* Kansas City: Nazarene Publishing House, 1988.
_____. "Those Early Nazarenes Cared: Compassionate Ministries of the Nazarenes." *Preacher's Magazine* 59 (September/October/November 1983): 32P-32T.
Peters, John. *Christian Perfection and American Methodism.* Nashville: Abingdon, 1956.
Piette, Maximin. *John Wesley in the Evolution of Protestantism.* London: Sheed and Wood, 1937.
Purkiser, W. T. *Called unto Holiness. Vol. 2: The Second Twenty-Five Years, 1933-58.* Kansas City: Nazarene Publishing House, 1983.
Quanstrom, Mark. *A Century of Holiness Theology: The Doctrine of Entire Sanctification in the Church of the Nazarene, 1905 to 2004.* Kansas City: Beacon Hill Press of Kansas City, 2004.
Raser, Harold. *More Preachers and Better Preachers: The First Fifty Years of Nazarene Theological Seminary.* Kansas City: Nazarene Publishing House, 1995.
_____. *Phoebe Palmer: Her Life and Thought.* Lewiston, NY: Edwin Mellen, 1987.

Richey, Russell E. *Early American Methodism*. Bloomington: Indiana U. Press, 1991.

Riley, John E. *From Sagebrush to Ivy: The Story of Northwest Nazarene College, 1913-1988*. Nampa, ID: Northwest Nazarene College, 1988.

Rudolph, L. C. *Francis Asbury*. Nashville: Abingdon, 1966.

Salter, Darius. *America's Bishop: The Life of Francis Asbury*. Nappanee, IN: Francis Asbury Press, 2003.

Sanders, Cheryl J. *Saints in Exile: The Holiness-Pentecostal Experience in African American Religion and Culture*. New York: Oxford U. Press, 1996.

Schneider, A. Gregory. "A Conflict of Associations: The National Camp-Meeting Association for the Promotion of Holiness Versus the Methodist Episcopal Church." *Church History* 66 (June 1997): 268-83.

_____. "Objective Selves Versus Empowered Selves: The Conflict over Holiness in the Post-Civil War Methodist Episcopal Church." *Methodist History* 32 (July 1994): 237-49.

_____. *The Way of the Cross Leads Home: The Domestication of American Methodism*. Bloomington: Indiana U. Press, 1993.

Semmel, Bernard. *The Methodist Revolution*. New York: Basic Books, 1973.

Smith, Timothy L. *Called unto Holiness: The Story of the Nazarenes: The Formative Years*. Kansas City: Nazarene Publishing House, 1962.

_____. *Nazarenes and the Wesleyan Mission: Can We Learn from Our History?* Kansas City: Beacon Hill Press of Kansas City, 1979.

_____. *Revivalism and Social Reform in Mid-Nineteenth Century America*. New York: Abingdon, 1957.

Snyder, Howard A. *Populist Saints: B. T. Roberts and the First Free Methodists*. Grand Rapids: Eerdmans, 2006.

_____. *The Radical Wesley and Patterns for Church Renewal*. Downers Grove, IL: InterVarsity, 1980.

Stanley, Susie C. *Holy Boldness: Women Preachers' Autobiographies and the Sanctified Self*. Knoxville: U. of Tennessee Press, 2002.

Stephens, Randall J. *The Fire Spreads: Holiness and Pentecostalism in the American South*. Cambridge, MA: Harvard U. Press, 2008.

Stout, Harry. *The Divine Dramatist: George Whitefield and the Rise of Modern Evangelicalism*. Grand Rapids: Eerdmans, 1991.

Strickland, William J., with H. Ray Dunning. *J. O. McClurkan: His Life, His Theology, and Selections from His Writings*. Nashville: Trevecca U., 1998.

Strong, Douglas M. *Perfectionist Politics: Abolitionism and the Religious Tensions of American Democracy*. Syracuse: Syracuse U. Press, 1999.

Swim, Roy. *A History of Missions of the Church of the Nazarene*. Kansas City: Nazarene, [1936].

Taves, Ann. *Fits, Trances, and Visions: Experiencing Religion and Explaining Experience from Wesley to James*. Princeton, NJ: Princeton U. Press, 1999.

Taylor, Mendell. *Nazarene Youth in Conquest for Christ*. Kansas City: Nazarene Publishing House, 1948.

Thornton, Wallace. *Radical Righteousness: Personal Ethics and the Development of the Holiness Movement*. Salem, OH: Schmul, 1998.

Tracy, Wesley, and Stan Ingersol. *Here We Stand: Where Nazarenes Fit in the Religious Marketplace*. Kansas City: Beacon Hill Press of Kansas City, 1999.

Turley, Briane K. *A Wheel within a Wheel: Southern Methodism and the Georgia Holiness Association*. Macon, GA: Mercer U. Press, 1999.

Wacker, Grant. *Heaven Below: Early Pentecostals and American Culture*. Cambridge, MA: Harvard U. Press, 2001.

_____. "The Holy Spirit and the Spirit of the Age in American Protestantism, 1880-1910." *Journal of American History* 72 (June 1985): 45-62.
Watson, David. *The Early Methodist Class Meeting: Its Origins and Significance.* Nashville: Discipleship Resources, 1985.
White, Charles E. *The Beauty of Holiness: Phoebe Palmer as Theologian, Revivalist, Feminist, and Humanitarian.* Grand Rapids: Zondervan, 1986.
Wigger, John. *Taking Heaven by Storm: Methodism and the Rise of Popular Christianity in America.* New York: Oxford U. Press, 1998.
Wynkoop, Mildred Bangs. *The Trevecca Story, 1901-1976.* Nashville: Trevecca, 1976.
Yrogoyen, Charles, Jr., ed. *The Global Impact of the Wesleyan Traditions and Their Related Movements.* Lanham, MD: Scarecrow, 2002.

www.ingramcontent.com/pod-product-compliance
Lightning Source LLC
Chambersburg PA
CBHW052107010526
44111CB00036B/1539